ERRATA

Due to printing errors, code lines on
the following pages are missing some
of the necessary quotation marks.
Please refer to the companion disk in
the back of this book— it includes a
correct version of all code in this book.

pages xxiii, 40, 50, 170, 171, 313, 319,
370, 371, 372, 493, 760, 764, 777, 779,
799, 801, 802, 804, 805, 830, 831, 920,
923, 931, 936, 937, 938, 940, 942, 943,
944, 945, 946, 955, 1108, 1123, 1143,
1176, 1177, 1178, 1240, 1242, 1255,
1266, 1267, 1268, 1269, 1270, 1271,
1279, 1280, 1282, 1283, 1286, 1289,
1290, 1326, 1328, 1329, 1330, 1338,
1341, 1342, 1359, 1360

THE VISUAL
GUIDE TO

VISUAL
BASIC™ 4.0
FOR WINDOWS™

· · · · · · · · · · · · · · · · ·

The Illustrated,
Plain-English
Encyclopedia to
the Windows™
Programming
Language

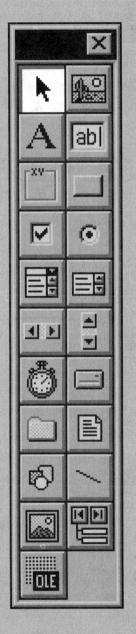

Richard Mansfield

VENTANA

The Visual Guide to Visual Basic 4.0 for Windows: The Illustrated, Plain-English Encyclopedia to the Windows Programming Language
Copyright © 1995 by Richard Mansfield

Library of Congress Cataloging-in-Publication Data
Mansfield, Richard.
    The visual guide to Visual Basic 4.0 for Windows : the illustrated, plain-English encyclopedia to the Windows programming language,
/ Richard Mansfield. — 1st ed.
        p. cm.
    Includes index.
    ISBN 1-56604-192-9
    1. Windows (Computer programs) 2. Microsoft Visual Basic for Windows. 3. BASIC (Computer program language) I. Title.
QA76.76.W56M46 1995
005.265—dc20   95-2588
                                                              CIP

Book design: Marcia Webb
Cover illustration: Jeff Brice

Acquisitions Editor: Sherri Morningstar
Art Director: Marcia Webb
Copy editor: Marion Laird
Design staff: Bradley King, Charles Overbeck, Dawne Sherman
Developmental Editor: Tim C. Mattson
Editorial Manager: Pam Richardson
Editorial staff: Angela Anderson, Amy Moyers, Beth Snowberger
Print Department: Kristen De Quattro, Dan Koeller
Production Manager: John Cotterman
Production staff: Patrick Berry, Scott Hosa, Lance Kozlowski, Jaimie Livingston
Technical Director: Dan Brown

 Index service: Stephen Bach
Proofreader: Marion Laird
Technical review: David Fullerton

First Edition 9 8 7 6 5 4 3 2 1
Printed in the United States of America

Ventana Communications Group, Inc.
P.O. Box 13964
Research Triangle Park, NC 27709-3964
919/544-9404
FAX 919/544-9472

Trademarks

About the author

Richard Mansfield's books have sold more than 300,000 copies worldwide. He was editor-in-chief of *Compute* magazine for seven years. His published work includes columns on computer topics, magazine articles and several short stories. He is author of *Machine Language for Beginners* (Compute Press), *Visual Basic Power Toolkit* (Ventana), and twelve other computer books. He is currently a full-time author.

Acknowledgments

This book grew and grew. Visual Basic is so rich and powerful that endeavoring to provide an encyclopedic reference to this language exceeded all our predictions about how much time it would take and how large the book would eventually be.

I have spent over a year writing this book and the good people at Ventana have worked with me on this—by far the largest book they've published—with patience, forbearance, and grace under pressure.

For their important contributions to bringing this book to print I thank Marion Laird, Pam Richardson and Fran Phillips Quigg.

Special thanks to John Cotterman for his coordination of the difficult production process and to Karen Wysocki for her thoughtful, inventive design. Thanks also to Scott Hosa, Patrick Berry, Lance Kozlowski and Jaimie Livingston, the desktop publishers, who both tolerated considerable revisions and several iterations of the text and figures.

Thanks also to Matt Wagner, agent extraordinaire, for recommending me to Ventana and vice versa. For their assistance from the source, I thank Steve Podradchik and Troy Strain of Microsoft. For his many contributions I thank Robert Lock. For their enduring understanding, friendship and good cheer, I thank Jim Coward and Larry O'Connor.

Above all, for her constant support and good council during this work, I gratefully acknowledge Elizabeth Woodman. And for his suggestions which shaped the nature and thrust of this book (not to mention having thought up the title), I thank Joe Woodman.

DEDICATION
· · · · · · · · · · · · · · · · · · ·
FOR JIM

CONTENTS

SECTION III Appendices

INTRODUCTION

Above all, I wanted this book to be readable and clear. So much writing about computer languages and programming gets bogged down in extreme precision, at the expense of clarity. The second main goal was that the book be practical—the examples should be *useful.* For the most part, the examples have been chosen because they demonstrate a command or feature of the language, but also because they accomplish something you might actually want to do in real-world programming.

Visual Basic offers a radically new, radically easier way to create programs for the Windows operating system. Now that Windows 95 will become the standard operating system for personal computers, Visual Basic must respond to the new structures and techniques involved in writing programs for Windows 95 instead of Windows 3.1: 32-bit vs. 16-bit, Object-oriented programming versus "procedural" programming, the increasing use of Object Linking & Embedding technology, and so on. To expand itself to include these new capabilities, Visual Basic Version 4 is in some ways quite different from VB3 and earlier versions. It's not a new language, but it has grown to embrace some very new methods and commands. Because of the massive changes to Visual Basic (VB) that occurred in VB Version 4, this introduction concludes with a list of these changes and points you to locations within the book where you can find extensive descriptions and examples of the new commands and new styles of programming.

The book begins and ends with tutorials. Section I is for those new to Visual Basic. It covers the primary features of Visual Basic 4.0—all the menu options; programming and debugging strategies; and a step-by-step construction of a useful graphics viewer utility. At the end of the book, Appendix A explains how to use the Windows API (Application Programmers Interface) to add new capabilities to Visual Basic.

The bulk of *The Visual Guide to Visual Basic,* Section II, is a reference book, organized like an encyclopedia. Here are in-depth explanations of every element of Visual Basic. It's an alphabetic collection of descriptions of the nature and behavior of commands and features of the language. Section II, "Reference A–Z," then, is a compendium that can be referred to regularly, to clarify Visual Basic and spark the programmer's imagination.

There are seven categories in each entry:

• **Description**–a general overview of the utility of the entry, and its place in the general scheme of Visual Basic.

• **Used with**–the other Visual Basic elements with which the entry interacts.

• **Variables**–the syntax and punctuation required by the entry, and any exceptions, alternatives or variations. This section shows you how to write a line of programming that will invoke the entry and make it work in a program.

• **Uses**–sensible, real-world answers to the question "What is this good for?" Most elements of the language have one or more uses. In some cases, however, the only comment under Uses is "None." (See "Let.") VB does have a few inexplicable remnants from earlier versions of Basic.

• **Cautions**–things to watch out for. Why it might not work as expected. Exceptions to the rule, conflicts, and workarounds.

• **Example**–in many computer books, many of the examples are unreal. They just show the syntax and punctuation, but nothing really happens. This book tries to avoid that by providing tested, practical examples that do something meaningful and demonstrate the real utility and behavior of the command or feature.

• **See also**–related entries, alternatives, or suggested further reading.

Who Needs This Book?

Anyone interested in programming Visual Basic, whether they've been programming for 15 years or only one day. Just as a dictionary is useful to both a sixth grader and John Updike, this book can assist anyone from the beginner to the accomplished professional programmer.

Although probably helpful to beginners, *six pages* on the uses of For...Next may be considered by veterans to be an unnecessary amount of detail. However, Visual Basic is rapidly evolving and even old pros will likely be interested in the new Property procedures, Objects, Collections, Class Modules, the 18 pages on Form design in the entry on "Line," and the 39 pages describing the Link commands. And most of us, even if we write in Visual Basic every day for years, sometimes need a clear, illustrated quick refresher on things like the subtle interactions between ClipControls, AutoRedraw, and Paint. I hope this is one book that you'll want to keep close to your computer whenever you're programming in Visual Basic.

What s New in Visual Basic Version 4

Here is a list of the new features in VB4. Words or concepts which can be found elsewhere in the book are italicized boldface.

1. Passing data between Forms. In VB3 and earlier, you could declare Public Variables as a way of communicating between your Forms. However, now in VB4 you can declare a Public Sub or Public Function and pass data to this now-Public procedure from outside the Form in which the procedure resides.

2. You can now create VB *Objects* that outside applications like Excel can directly employ via OLE Automation. These Objects, built with the new VB4 *Class Modules*, can have their own Methods and Properties. You can also create Objects for use with your VB programs themselves. Finally, Class Modules permit you to practice elements of Object Oriented Programming, such as encapsulation. There is also a new, built-in *Object Browser*.

3. Three new *procedures* join the traditional two (Subs and Functions). *Property Get*, *Property Let* or *Property Set* are now used to add Properties to Objects created by a Class Module.

4. The VB editor is now directly extensible—you can write project managers or other programmer aids (or buy them), then use the *Add-Ins* feature to merge them into your programming environment.

5. The Grid Control is now "data-bound" meaning that it can be linked to a Data Control and serve as an entrance into a database. Also now data-bound are the OLE, ListBox and ComboBox Controls. What's more, a Control can now be bound to a Data Control that's not on the same Form, and you can also share Recordsets among Controls located on different Forms. The database language is richer, and there are many new techniques. For one example, you can use the BOFAction and EOFAction commands to tell the Data Control what to do if the user tries to scroll past the beginning or end of the file. See "*Data*."

6. In keeping with the attractive 3D sculpted, dimensional look of Windows 95 programs, VB now has an *Appearance* Property for Forms. It makes most Controls look better and reduces our reliance on the SSPanel and other Sheridan 3D Controls as a way of improving the way Text Boxes and other Controls look to the user.

7. Forms, PictureBoxes and the Printer now have a *PaintPicture* Method. This Method achieves the same thing as the API BitBlt call but may be easier for some VB programmers to use than calling on the API for special visual effects.

8. There are new *NegotiateMenus* and NegotiatePositions Properties with which you can control how OLE Objects behave during "in-place editing." This OLE phenomenon can occur (thanks to the operating system) when the user double-clicks on a linked or embedded Object.

9. Control over Controls. You can reposition or resize any Control, pixel by pixel, using the arrow keys, then, when you've perfected the look of a Form, click on the "Lock Controls" Button and they're frozen in place and can't be moved. These techniques are described in *Section I*.

10. New, simplified and enhanced techniques have been developed for use with the *Font*, *Error*, *Common Dialog* and *Printer* Objects.

11. *Multiple Document Interface* Forms have additional capabilities. Child Forms can now be hidden. MDI Forms have Picture and BackColor Properties now.

12. VB 4 now comes in two flavors: 16-bit for creating Windows 3.1 applications, and 32-bit for creating Windows 95 or NT applications. This shift to 32-bit applications has little impact on the VB programmer. The primary changes occur when calling the API–libraries that used to be named "USER" are now named "USER32," and parameters that used to be Integers are now Long, etc. These differences are described with examples in *Appendix A*. VB now also embraces Visual Basic for Applications (*VBA*)– the new language replacing previous macro languages in all Microsoft applications (Word hasn't yet made this transition).

13. You can now insert, into your finished .EXE code, auto-incrementing version numbers, copyright information, comments, trademarks, descriptions and so on. Select "Options" after choosing "Make EXE File" from the VB File Menu. This is described in *Section I*.

14. Conditional compilation is now available. It uses the new *#If...Then...#EndIf* structure to skip over and ignore any programming you put between the #If and #EndIf. It ignores programming if the condition is False. In other words, you can use this structure to create alternative versions of your program. Functions or Subs can be conditionally compiled and you can even bracket more than one procedure in the "conditional zone."

15. A new editor. In VB 4, you can choose between two ways of entering and editing your programming. First, there is the unique Visual Basic programming environment–you work within (and, indeed, *see*) only one Sub or Function at a time–moving between them with the PgUp and PgDn keys. This is the editor that's been in use since the first version of Visual Basic. Many people consider this "encapsulating" approach a considerable improvement over typical, classic program editors where all the programming is contiguous as if it were typed on a huge roll of paper towels and you scroll forward and backward to locate the various procedures. However, VB4 also permits this "continuous" approach–it's up to you to decide which style of editing suits you best. The "continuous" style does draw a helpful line between each Sub or Function–so you can see where one ends and the next begins. To switch between these editing styles, click on the Tools menu, then choose Options and Editor. Select or deselect "Full-Module view." Note that the separator lines between procedures are also optional.

Another nice new feature of the editor: the "line-continuation character." Now you can break a line of programming by ending it with a space followed by the _ underline character. VB will still think it's a continuous line (as it must be to be properly evaluated by VB), but you can now break (press ENTER) on long lines so the whole line is visible and doesn't run off the right side of the screen.

Before:

```
Declare Function BitBlt Lib gdi32 Alias BitBlt (ByVal hDestDC As Long, ByVal
X As Long, ByVal Y As Long, ByVal nWidth As Long, ByVal nHeight As Long,
ByVal hSrcDC As Long, ByVal XSrc As Long, ByVal YSrc As Long, ByVal dwRop
As Long) As Long
```

Now:

```
Declare Function BitBlt Lib gdi32 (ByVal hDestDC As Long, _
ByVal X As Long, ByVal Y As Long, ByVal nWidth As Long, _
ByVal nHeight As Long, ByVal hSrcDC As Long, ByVal XSrc As Long, _
ByVal YSrc As Long, ByVal dwRop As Long) As Long
```

To trick VB into thinking it's a single, continuous line, *you must use a space character* (press the Spacebar) followed by an underline character (SHIFT+hyphen). So this isn't a line-continuation *character;* it's a *pair* of line-continuation characters. Also, you can't use this technique to break up a text "string," like: Print "This line should be snapped."

16. The new *Collection* Object can be used as a substitute for traditional Arrays. Collections are more flexible than Arrays.

17. A new Boolean (two states only: True/False) *Variable* type and a new Byte data type (holds numbers from 0-255; useful for pulling in data one byte at a time from a disk file. See *"Open."*)

18. You can now name parameters (arguments) for Objects and a few Methods and, if you wish, any Sub or Function that you write. This has two advantages: (1) it's more descriptive so your programming is easier to read and (2) you can rearrange the order of the arguments. For more on this, see Sub, Function or *Named Parameters*.

19. Arguments in procedures (Subs or Functions) can now be optional. This permits you to make your procedures more general-purpose since they can manipulate various amounts of supplied data. (See "Sub" or "Function" or *"IsQueries."*) However, the ParamArray feature, described below, adds even more flexibility when passing arguments.

20. Using the new ParamArray command you can pass *any number of arguments to a Sub or Function, and they can be of any Variable type.* Talk about flexibility. See "Sub" or "Function."

21. Since VB Version 3, you could create an Array made up of Variants. But now, with VB4, you can assign an ordinary Array (or Arrays) *to a Variant.*

22. In VB4, many *Const*ant definitions are now built in. You don't have to load in a separate file of predefinitions, or define them yourself by hand. They're just *there.* Press F2 and look under "Constants."

23. There's a new Picture *Object* that you can program with. (Also see the entry for the new ImageList Control. Both of these new techniques are ways to store graphics instead of filling your Form with invisible Picture or Image Controls to hold graphics you'll later want to display.) Here's an example showing how to use the Picture Object. Each time you click on the Command Button, you are cycled between four .BMP pictures:

```
Dim Picobj(0 To 3) As Picture

Private Sub Command1_Click( )
Static c As Integer
Picture = Picobj(c)
c = c + 1
If c = 4 Then c = 0
End Sub

Private Sub Form_Load( )
Pics = Array("tempx", "hub5", "tempp", "t1")
For I = 0 To 3
    n$ = "C:\" & Pics(I) & ".BMP"
    Set Picobj(I) = LoadPicture(n$)
Next I
End Sub
```

Replace "tempx," "hub5," "tempp," "t1" with the filenames of .BMP files on your hard drive. And change "C:\" to their path. Note, too, the new Array *Function* (which see). If this doesn't work for you, click on the Tools Menu and choose References. Make sure that the "Standard OLE Types" library is selected.

24. The **With...End With** structure allows you to set multiple Properties in a more straightforward way.

25. The **For Each...Next** structure let's you loop through all the elements of an Array, or a Collection of Objects, without having to know, in advance, how many elements there are.

26. User-Defined **Types** can now include dynamic Arrays of strings.

27. In previous versions of VB, the file that contained information about an entire project (program) had the extension .MAK. Among other things, this "project file" listed the path and filename of every Form in the project. Now, this file has the extension .VBP (for "Visual Basic Project).

28. Windows 95 boasts a variety of new features such as tabbed dialog boxes (called "property sheets" because they are normally employed to allow users to adjust options and preferences); a slider (a discontinuous scroll bar); a progress bar (a discontinuous status indicator); and so on. These eight new Controls are covered in the entry **Windows 95 Controls**. There's also a new RichTextBox Control that expands the capabilities of the traditional VB TextBox—permitting various kinds of formatting, font variety, italics, color and other word-processor-like text-entry facilities. For more on this, see "TextBox."

The Three Editions

VB4 is sold in three versions. The Standard Edition contains all the essentials and appears to be primarily targeted at the programmer who doesn't require heavy-duty database programming facilities or a set of Windows 95 and other desirable, but not essential, Controls like the 3D Command Button and the Graph Control. This Edition of VB is good for those who want to give VB a try or are new to programming.

The Professional Edition includes the set of 28 extra Controls; a report designer; a "hotspot" editor with which you can define zones within a graphic that when clicked can trigger help information or macros; and additional database support including the SQL language. For many programmers, this Edition will do everything they want to do.

The Enterprise Edition is for those needing industrial-strength database tools—particularly for network support. It also includes tools for managing groups of programmers.

What s Next?

Whether this is the first day you've ever tried to program a computer or you've been at it for decades, Visual Basic will reward your efforts by multiplying and amplifying whatever you do. It's unlike any previous language, offering built-in prewritten functionality (the Controls), an extremely flexible programming instrument (the Editor), and all this in a highly visual environment. In addition to an attempt to cover VB's great breadth, this book also endeavors to go into considerable depth. One target for in-depth coverage is the visual element of contemporary programming (see the entry on "Line") which is still all too often neglected in books on programming. Among other things, programs that are visually rich offer a user interface that is more efficient and, ultimately, more fun to work with. Just as Windows is an improvement over DOS primarily because it is a *graphic* rather than *text-based* environment, Visual Basic is fundamentally visual and can produce graphically appealing results.

So go ahead—follow the step-by-step overview of VB in the first three tutorial sections of this book, or jump around, trying out examples throughout the book. Whatever approach you take and whatever your level of programming expertise, Visual Basic will likely seduce you. For most programmers, in the past few years VB has become the language of choice for Windows programming.

SECTION 1

A
STEP-BY-STEP
GUIDE
TO PROGRAMMING

VISUAL
BASIC

PART ONE

OPENING WINDOWS

Programmers have wrestled for years with computer languages—various ways of telling the computer what to do. Visual Basic has more power than most of the older languages. What's more, many elements of a Visual Basic program—particularly the tricky visual elements—are already written for you. Visual Basic is a breakthrough.

Visual Basic (VB) provides such a full set of built-in intelligent tools that creating programs for the Windows environment can be astonishingly easy. You can just drag and drop an entire Directory List Box onto a window in your program. All the directories and subdirectories are automatically visible. If you click on one of the directories in the box, the box reacts by changing to that directory and showing you any of its subdirectories. You don't have to write a single word of programming to create this fully functional Directory list.

Visual Basic is often fun to use, but it's also quite powerful. Over one million copies of VB have been sold, and it's widely used to create programs for business, shareware and other purposes. With VB, you can write efficient, polished programs every bit as professional as commercial applications. Yet, creating a Visual Basic program is much easier than writing in C or other computer languages.

Designing Instead of Writing

If you are new to programming, the first phase of writing a program in Visual Basic will seem more like designing a picture than writing out cryptic, half-mathematical instructions for a machine to follow. If you have struggled with more primitive languages, it will seem paradoxical that programming for a sophisticated environment like Windows should prove easier than programming for the more elementary world of DOS.

Visual Basic contains so many built-in features that creating the user-interface elements of a program is more like picking out a backyard deck from a catalog than building it yourself, plank by plank.

But Visual Basic's tools and custom Controls are more than simply nice-looking; they also know how to *do* things. Perhaps the quickest way to grasp what makes Visual Basic so special is to think of it as a collection of prebuilt robot parts. You just choose the parts you want on the visible surface of your program.

Visual Basic provides all the visual components necessary for computer interaction: List Boxes that automatically alphabetize and arrange items in columns; Scroll Bars; resizable windows; push buttons; and more.

These Tools Come With Built-In Capabilities: A Text Box automatically wraps words around to the next line and responds to the directional arrow keys, and the Backspace, DEL, ENTER, CAPS LOCK and SHIFT keys. It would take days to construct this in C; placing it into a window in Visual Basic takes seconds.

In addition, you can customize each tool by selecting qualities from the *Properties Window.* For example, some of the choices for a Text Box's Properties are BackColor, BorderStyle, DragIcon, Enabled, FontBold, FontSize, ForeColor, Height and Width, Index, LinkMode, MousePointer, Name, ScrollBars, TabStop, Text and Visible.

Want to change the background color of a Text Box? Just click your mouse on BackColor and select from a palette:

Figure 1-1: Changing colors is as easy as clicking.

You can also click on the View Menu and select Color Palette to create custom colors.

And You Can Edit Objects Globally: Want to change the color of five Labels? Drag the mouse around them to "select them as a group." This is just the way you would group visual objects in a graphics program. (Or you can also group them by holding down the SHIFT key and clicking on each Label you want to change.) VB is so intelligent that its Properties Window (where the qualities of objects, such as their size or color, are adjusted) will now display the Properties that the selected objects *have in common.* After selecting all the Labels whose colors you want to change, just double-click on the Properties Window BackColor item. The Color Palette will appear. Click on the color you want and, voilà, all the selected Labels change from white to magenta.

Want to copy a group of selected Objects within a given Form or from one Form to another, or cut and paste them? It's just as easy as copying and pasting text in a well-designed word processor—delete, cut, copy or paste them using the same Windows conventions that you would with words: click on an Object, or if you want to manipulate a group of Objects, drag the mouse around them to select them. (Remember, if you don't want to drag the mouse around them—perhaps they're not contiguous—hold down the SHIFT key and click the mouse. This adds an Object to a selected group.)

Then, as in a word processor:

• The DEL key *deletes* the Object or group.

• SHIFT+DEL *cuts* (deletes, but copies to the Clipboard for any later pasting you might want to do. This is the way you *move* Objects from one window to another).

• CTRL+INS *copies* the selected Object(s) to the Clipboard, from which they can be pasted as often as you want. *The Properties of the Object(s)* (qualities such as color, width, text fonts and so forth) *will also be copied*.

• SHIFT+INS *pastes* the Object(s).

If you are in the habit of using non-Windows conventions, you can also use a parallel set of keyboard-only commands that mimic the behavior of the Windows commands, such as CTRL+C, which copies, and CTRL+V, which pastes.

Drawing in the Design Phase

One very important Visual Basic breakthrough is a reversal of the normal approach to programming: Instead of spending weeks writing instructions that tell the computer how to make your program respond and how it should look, you simply *draw* the program. You drag the various items you want onto a window (called a *Form* in Visual Basic), select their qualities and then see how your program looks to the user.

This design stage takes very little time. You don't write a single instruction to the computer—you click, drag and drop. You can resize, reposition and delete things. And from each item's individual Properties Window, you can select its qualities, adjusting aspects of behavior and appearance. This way to organize a program and achieve an interface between computer and user is both quick and intuitive. You are, in effect, describing how the program should behave, but you're describing it *visually*. And recall that many of the tools you assemble on a window come from the factory already functional, equipped to react intelligently when the user types or clicks the mouse.

This approach also helps you build the rest of the program (when you write specific commands for the computer to follow) more efficiently. In Visual Basic, you draw the goal onscreen so that the final product is there for you to see. In Part Two, we'll focus on how to make the computer behave appropriately in ways that are not already built into the Objects and tools that Visual Basic supplies. In other words how to *program* in Visual Basic.

PART TWO

THE ELEMENTS OF VISUAL BASIC

This book describes each command and feature of Visual Basic in alphabetical order. The purpose and use of some of these commands are obvious: *End* shuts down a running program; *Caption* is the text in the bar at the top of a window or the words you want to display in a Label. However, commands such as *Dim* are computer-related, and the *Link* command is peculiar to the Windows environment. We have endeavored to provide clear, easily understandable descriptions of every command and tool in Visual Basic.

Programming, nevertheless, is a new way of thinking if you have not programmed before. Visual Basic itself is a novel language if you *have* programmed. So here's an overview of Visual Basic's features, menus and techniques.

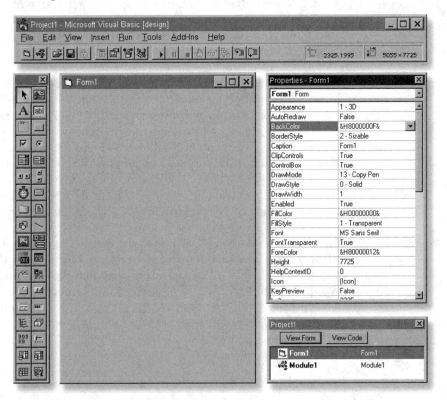

Figure 1-2: When you first start Visual Basic, you see the Properties Window, the Toolbox, the Project Window, the Toolbar and a blank Form.

The Form

What happens when you first start up Visual Basic? It looks something like Figure 1-2, although the positions and even the visibility of some of these elements may differ depending on the state Visual Basic was in when you last shut it down. Also, loading in a previously written program can shift the items onscreen. These items are the various windows and menus you use to program in Visual Basic.

You might want to run Visual Basic now so you can follow along with this tour of its features. If you don't see a Toolbox or a Project Window, click on them in the View Menu at the top of the screen.

The primary unit of organization in Visual Basic is the Form. A Form becomes a window when the program runs. However, if you wish, a Form need not be visible; it can merely be a way of gathering related items together, a method of organizing the program. Usually, though, a VB program consists of at least one visible Form. There's something powerful inside each Form: a whole set of *Events*. Double-click on the Form to get into the heart of a VB program, the Event structures.

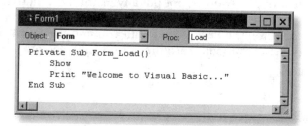

Figure 1-3: Beneath a Form are the Events, the places where the program reacts to changing conditions while it runs.

Now a new window appears, which looks and acts somewhat like a word processor. Here's where you write our instructions, telling VB how to behave while your program runs.

At the top of this window are two drop-down menus. The one labeled Object: contains a list of any items ("Controls" such as Text Boxes or Command Buttons) that you've put on this Form. The Form itself, or any Controls on it, can *react* while the program runs. Click on the Object: Menu and you'll see the following words:

```
(General)
Form
```

We haven't placed any Object—Text Box, Command Button, Picture Box, etc.—from the Toolbox onto this Form. The only Object at this point is the Form itself. The word *Form* is highlighted because that's where we currently "are"; the Form is the Object we can currently write instructions for, in one or more of its Events.

What Are Events?

Events are all the things that might happen to an Object when the user runs the program. Click on the Events Menu (it's labeled Proc: for *Procedure,* another name for an Event, Subroutine or Function). Scroll down and you'll see that there are 25 different possible Events for a Form. Because a Form turns into a window when a program runs, there are Click and DblClick Events. The user might click on the Form. You can write instructions inside the Click Event to tell the Form what to do if the user does that. If you don't want anything to happen when the user clicks on the form, don't put any instructions inside the Form's Click Event.

Note that Events are not *qualities,* such as size, color, appearance and so forth. VB refers to an Object's qualities as its *Properties.* We'll get to those in a minute.

Events are *actions.* Something happens to an Object—and that triggers the Event. VB is always watching what's going on while a program is running. If the user clicks on this Form, VB triggers the Form_Click Event. Then any instructions you might have put into this Form's Click Event would be carried out at once. If you've not put any instructions in that Event, nothing happens.

Let's try it. Scroll the Proc: Menu until you find the Event called "Click" and then type the following into the Form's Click Event:

```
Private Sub Form_Click ( )
Top = 0
Left = 0
End Sub
```

Now run the program by pressing the F5 key, and try clicking on the window. It moves smartly up against the top-left corner of the screen. We told the Form to react to a click by moving itself to zero from the top and zero from the left of the screen. Now stop the program by double-clicking on the box in the upper left corner of the Form, by clicking on End in the Run Menu, or by clicking on the black square in the group of icons on the Visual Basic Toolbar at the top of the screen. (As usual, Visual Basic gives you a variety of ways to accomplish something; use whatever approach you prefer.)

Now let's say we want to tell the program how to react to a *double* click, so we type our instructions into the DblClick Event:

```
Sub Form_DblClick ( )
WindowState = 2
End Sub
```

Press F5 again to run the program, and notice that a double click results in the Form expanding to fill the entire screen.

Most of the Action Takes Place in Events: *Top, Left* and *WindowState* are *Properties* of a Form. *Click* and *DblClick* are *Events* of a Form. Sometimes you want an Event to change a Property, and that's what we've been doing in these first two experiments. You don't always change Properties in your programming. In fact, it's more common to react to the triggering of an Event to print something the user want's printed, or to perform other tasks. But it is from within Events that the majority of the action takes place in Visual Basic. After all, the Events are how Visual Basic responds to what users do with their keyboard or mouse.

You would never write instructions into all the Events of a Form or other object like a Picture Box or a Text Box. Click is very common, but the Paint Event (which is triggered when Visual Basic redraws Forms and Controls on the screen because they had been covered up) is something you normally just let happen without instructing your program to react in any fashion. You just put into Events those instructions that are appropriate to the goals you have for your particular program. Normally, your program will have no reaction to the usual Windows activity of repainting a Form after that Form had been covered up by another window or something.

Nonetheless, for each Object there is a full, specialized selection of Events. Events are *specialized* because only Events that make sense for each Object are available for that Object. For instance, a Picture Box has a Paint Event, but a Text Box does not. (Similarly, the Properties available for each Object are tailored to its function. A Picture Box has a Picture Property, but no Text Property. Vice versa for a Text Box.)

Properties Are *Qualities*

Events are things that could happen to an Object. Each Object—each Form and each kind of *Control*—also has its own specialized list of *qualities* called *Properties*. A Form has a FontSize Property because you can print text on a Form, and the current setting of the Form's FontSize Property determines how large the letters will be. A Scroll Bar cannot be printed on, so it has no FontSize Property. For these same reasons, a refrigerator has a temperature control but no volume control.

You can adjust these qualities (these *Properties*) while you are designing the program, or you can make them change (most of them, anyway) while the program is running. In the example above, we made the Top and Left Properties of the Form change when the Click Event was triggered.

To change the qualities of an Object while you are designing your program, you use the Properties Window. To see how this works, select a Label from the Toolbox by clicking on the capital A icon:

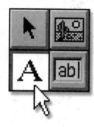

Figure 1-4: Selecting a Label.

Each time you click on the Label icon in the Toolbox, you can draw another Label onto the Form. When you drag your mouse on the Form, you're creating and sizing a new Label that will now become part of this Form. (An alternative approach is to double-click on the capital A icon in the Toolbox, which instantly puts the selected item in the middle of the Form. You can double-click repeatedly, piling items on top of each other in the center of the Form, and then drag them apart to position each one where you want it.)

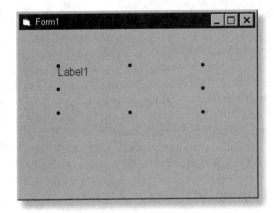

Figure 1-5: A Label placed on the Form.

After you've added a new Object, it will be highlighted with a special frame as shown in Figure 1-5. If your new Label isn't framed like that, click once on the Label and it will be framed. Then change its Caption Property by typing a new caption into the Properties Window:

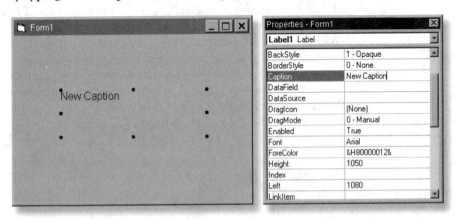

Figure 1-6: The new caption appears as you type it in.

Finally, to make the size of the Label precisely fit the size of its message, scroll the Properties Window and double-click on the AutoSize Property. Notice that there are three ways to adjust this Property. Once you've highlighted AutoSize in the Properties Window, you can press *t* or *f* from the keyboard to select between the options. You can click on the arrow to drop down a list of choices, then click on a choice. Or you can double-click on the word *AutoSize* to toggle between the two possible values, True or False. Whatever approach you prefer, after you change the AutoSize Property to *True,* the Label border is an exact snug fit.

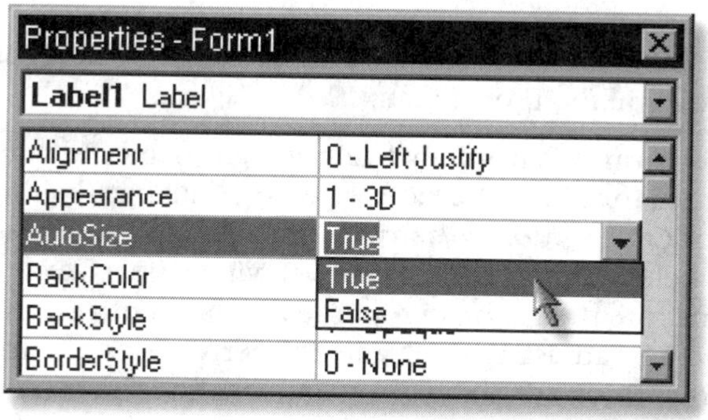

Figure 1-7: AutoSize takes care of the border for you.

So far, so good. But how would we make the program itself change Properties while the program is running? Events do it. Just as we earlier made the Form react to a click by changing its position and size, we can make the Label react to a change in conditions while the program runs. The Event that triggers a reaction need *not* be one of the Label's own Events, however. You can instruct an Event in one Object to affect other Objects as well.

Let's say we want to animate the *Label* to have it slide over to the side if the user clicks on the *Form.* Double-click on the Form and scroll in the Proc: Menu to get to the Form's Click Event and then type this:

```
Sub Form_Click ( )
    Label1.Move 0
End Sub
```

Here we are saying, "Go over to the far left, the 0 horizontal position, within this Form." You could also put this same instruction into the Label1_Click ( ) Event if you prefer, or the KeyPress Events of either Object, or the MouseMove Events, or anyplace else that makes sense to you. Try out the program by pressing F5; then click with the mouse to move the Label. Now stop the program by double-clicking on the button in the upper left corner of the window. Let's see what happened to the Object: Menu. Double-click on the Form and pull down the Object: Menu.

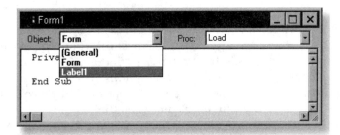

Figure 1-8: We now have a new item listed along with the Form and (General).

Click on Label1 in the Object: Menu and notice that it has its own full set of Events over in the Proc: Menu.

Automatic Names: VB automatically assigns names to your Objects when you add them to a Form. (What we've been calling "Objects" are called *Controls* or *Custom Controls* in VB.) If you add another Label, VB will name it Label2; add a Text Box, and VB will name it Text1, and so on. These names are themselves Properties of the Controls, and you can change them by adjusting the Name Property of any Control in the Properties Window. However, many programmers find the names that VB gives to things work just fine and are adequately descriptive.

Other Structures, Other Locations: What about the (General) that is listed as an Object of this Form in the Object: Menu? If you click on (General), you'll see that VB has placed your cursor at the top of the programming window, above any Events (in the programming window, Events are called "Subs").

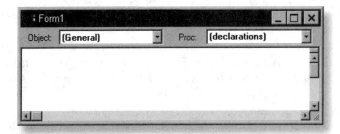

Figure 1-9: The General Declarations section of a Form is at the top.

You can put two kinds of things in General Declarations:

• Definitions of Variables, Constants or Arrays that you want available to all the Events in this Form. (See the entries on "Arrays" and "Variables" in the alphabetic section.) Unless you define (Declare) a Variable up here at the top—outside of any *Sub*—then the Variable can be used only inside the Event where it was declared. It is not usable by other Events.

• Custom Subs or Functions ("procedures"). Procedures are like Events but are not triggered automatically by VB. Instead, procedures are "called" from other locations within the Form (you just name the procedure and VB carries it out). All references to "Subs" in the following are meant to include Functions as well. A Function (which see under the "Function" entry in the alphabetical reference section) is a specialized kind of Sub.

Why Use Subroutines?

Here's how it works. Let's say that in our program we want to put "Visual Basic is effective" on both a Label and the Form that holds the Label, and perhaps other places as well. In other words, we want to take this action more than once. We *could* repeat the instructions to accomplish this in both the Label's and the Form's individual Click Events. But that would mean writing the instructions twice. When you are doing something complicated, there can be many instructions. So, rather than repeat yourself, put tasks that are used by more than one Event into a "Sub." (See the entry on "Sub" for more information.)

Type the following into the General Declarations and then press ENTER:

```
Sub PrintVB
```

Visual Basic creates a new Subroutine for you that, like an Event, is bracketed by *Sub* and *End Sub*, between which you put your commands, your instructions. Put the text as shown in Figure 1-10 into this new Subroutine:

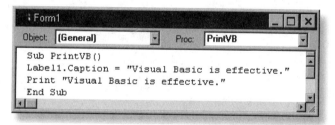

Figure 1-10: Creating a Subroutine.

Note that we put text inside a Label by changing its Caption Property, whereas text put inside a Form is *printed*. Printing is called a *Method* in VB—to distinguish it from changes made to Properties.

TIP ·

We didn't have to identify the Form, Form1.Print, since it's assumed. We're writing these instructions within Form1, so if you leave off an identifier—*Print* as opposed to *Picture1.Print* your command will be carried out on the Form instead of some other Object. By the way, there's another shortcut: each Object has a default Property. It's usually the most commonly used Property of that Control. For instance, the Text Property of a Text Box, the Caption Property of a Label, and so on. If you are changing the default Property of an Object, you don't need to type in the Property. To change our Label's Caption, we could write:

    Label1.Caption = "Visual Basic is effective."

OR

    Label1 = "Visual Basic is effective."

Now, to use this Subroutine and make it perform its task, we merely provide its name, just as if it were a new command we had added to VB's vocabulary:

    Sub Form_Click ( )
        PrintVB
    End Sub

And, since we want this action to take place even if the user clicks in the Label, mention the Sub's name in the Label1_Click Event, too:

    Sub Label1_Click ( )
        PrintVB
    End Sub

When the user clicks on either of these Objects, the Subroutine will do its work. (Notice that the Caption, once changed, remains the same no matter how often you click. However, printing keeps putting the same message on different lines. Printing on a Form is like printing to the printer.)

· ·

Going Farther Out: Modules

In older versions of Visual Basic, only the host Form could use Subs you put into the General Declarations section of that Form. Now, with Visual Basic Version 4, however, you can use a Form's Sub from another Form by merely adding the host Form's name to it, as if you were providing its "address": Form1.PrintVB. (This won't work, however, if you've used the

Private command in front of your Sub: Private Sub PrintVB. That word *Private* restricts the Sub's "scope" to the host Form. In this case, Form1.)

However, many programmers prefer to use a *Module* to hold any Subs they write (as opposed to Visual Basic's Event Subs which must remain in the host Form.) Some programmers also prefer to put into a Module any Variables or Constants that they intend to use globally from any Form in their program.

A Module is something like the General Declarations section of a Form, but Modules are never visible when the program runs. They are merely places that some programmers like to put general-purpose Subs or Variables that can be used from any location in your program. (One advantage of this approach is that when a Variable or Sub is in a Module, you don't have to *address* it with the host Form's name. You can just name the Sub. So it's simpler. PrintVB rather than Form1.PrintVB.)

In earlier versions of Visual Basic the second important use for Modules was that you could only "declare" *Global Variables* (see "Public") in Modules. Global Variables are accessible from anywhere in the entire program. With Visual Basic 4, however, you can access any Form's Public Variables from anywhere. But, again, you must address it: Form1.MyVar if you want to access it from outside Form1. So, perhaps it's best to put into a Module any Variables (or Constants) that you want to use program-wide. This way you can just use the Variable's name and not have to address it with the host Form's name.)

To create a Module, pull down the Insert Menu and select Module, or, more easily, click on the second icon on the Toolbar. Now look at the Project Window. (If it's not visible, click on the View menu on VB's Menu Bar, or press CTRL+R, or click on the icon ninth from the left on the Toolbar.) You'll see that *Module1* has been added to Form1. Click on Module1 to highlight it; then click on View Code at the top of the Project Window.

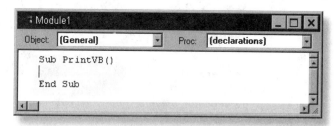

Figure 1-11: A Module ready for you to enter programwide Subroutines or Variables.

The Module looks familiar, doesn't it, like the General Declarations section of a Form? But the difference is that Subroutines or Variables you put in here can be more conveniently used anywhere in your program. You don't have to provide the "address" of a Form. Plus, you'll find them all together in one convenient container instead of having to look in the code windows of various Forms. This *globalization*—making Subroutines (and Functions) and Variables (and Arrays and Constants) conveniently available everywhere—is the essential virtue of Modules.

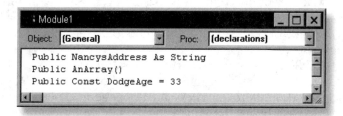

Figure 1-12: Announce any programwide Variables in a Module.

Note that, like Forms, Modules have Object: and Proc: pull-down menus. (Subroutines and Functions, like Events, are sometimes referred to as *Procedures*; hence, *Proc:*.) Also note that any Variables (or Constants or Arrays) that you want to make global and programwide in scope must have that word *Public* in front of its declaration—*even in a Module*. This requirement, however, isn't true of Subs or Functions. They default to Public.

The Toolbox

The Toolbox contains Visual Basic's objects ("Controls"). You can find a general description, suggested applications, techniques, examples and cautions for each of these tools in the alphabetical reference section of this book. Or just click on one of the tools in the Toolbox, drag it onto a Form and try out the object. Or press F1 to get a description of the Control's basic purpose and features. Except for the Timer and OLEClient, they will all be familiar to anyone who has used Windows.

Figure 1-13: Here s where you get the various objects to put on your program s windows.

TIP ·

Custom Startup: If you find that you always want the Sheridan 3D Controls to appear on your Toolbar, or some other startup condition, some other configuration of VB whenever you first run it—you can create a special project that will become your preferred "blank VB template." Whenever you start VB running, or select New from the File menu, this template will be loaded automatically. You might want Form1 to have a different BackColor, or you might have a favorite set of Custom Controls or Add-Ins that you want available for any new project. Here's how to create your own default setup.

To establish your preferred startup conditions for the VB editing/programming environment, start VB running and use the Tools menu "Custom Controls" to add any of your favorites to the Toolbar. Make any other adjustments you prefer—repositioning or resizing the Properties window, etc. Don't forget to adjust any preferences you want to change in the Tools menu, Options. Now click on Form1 in the Project Window and in the File menu select "Remove File." (Otherwise, VB will create Form1 and Form2 when it starts running.)

Finally, in the File menu select "Save Project As" and name it AUTO32LD.VBP (if you're using the 32-bit version of VB4) or AUTO16LD.VBP (for the 16-bit version of VB4) or AUTOLOAD.MAK (for VB3 or earlier versions of VB). Now shut down VB and restart it. You should see the template conditions that you established. (There's nothing much you can do, however, about the location of the Project Window. It has a mind of its own.)

• •

THE MENUS

To complete our tour of Visual Basic's program-writing environment, let's look at the items on the pull-down menus at the top.

Figure 1-14: A Picture Box with an image of escaping cows.

Look at the frame around the Picture Box in Figure 1-14. It has small black tabs that you can use to adjust its size. This frame also indicates that the Picture Box is the currently "active" Object, the Object that has the "focus." (In other words, the Object you can do things to.)

The Properties Window lists the qualities of the Object that has the current focus (the Object that is highlighted by that frame). If no frame is visible or no Control exists on the Form, then the Form itself has the focus. When you look at the Properties Window, you'll see the Properties of the Object with the focus frame or, lacking that, the empty Form's Properties. To move the focus to something, just click on it. To move the focus to the Form in Figure 1-14, you could click on the white space surrounding the Picture Box.

The two sets of numbers on the far right of the Menu Bar show the current position and size of whatever Object is framed. These size and position numbers are visible only if you use, as most do, the Toolbar. Turn it on in the View Menu. In this example, the numbers tell us about the Picture Box. If no Object is framed, the numbers report the position and size of the Form itself, relative to the computer's monitor screen. To give a Control the focus, click on it. The Menu Bar then reports on the Control's position and size, and lists its Properties in the Properties Window.

In some situations—particularly when you are designing a window—this position and size information can be helpful. Drag a Control around its Form and notice how the Top/Left position numbers change. When you resize a Control by dragging one of the black tabs of its focus frame, the Height/Width figures change in the Menu Bar. All these positional data also change in the Properties Window.

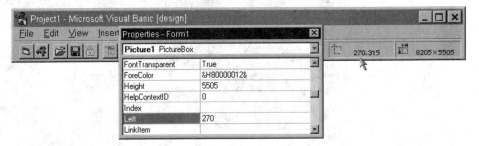

Figure 1-15: The Properties Window. Note the size and position information at the far right of the Menu Bar.

The Picture Box position information on the Menu Bar says 270,315 which means that the Picture is 270 "twips" over from the left and 315 twips down from the top of its Form. Twips are VB units of measurement. There are 1,440 of them per inch, so you can be highly specific about adjusting the size and position of objects and Forms.

The Picture's current size is 8,205 twips wide by 5,505 twips high. (Notice that these coordinates are always given in the format: horizontal, vertical or X,Y. It's width,height and left,top. You'll use this same coordinate system to describe the size and location of such things as geometric shapes if you use the Circle command, for example.)

If you look at the Properties Window, at the Picture's Height Property, you'll see that VB has conveniently adjusted it to 5,505. You are free to readjust the height, either by typing a new number into the Properties Window or by dragging one of the tabs (the "handles" on the frame around the Picture). (Or indeed, you could do it dynamically while your program is running: Picture1.Height = 3000 or perhaps Picture1.Height = Picture1.Height / 2.)

By the way, creating animation in VB is surprisingly easy. Manipulating the Move, Visible and size and position commands (Height, Width, Top and Left) can make things come alive and move about the screen. For more on the meaning of twips and how to control the position and size of Objects, see "ScaleMode."

The File Menu

Now pull down the File Menu on the Menu Bar.

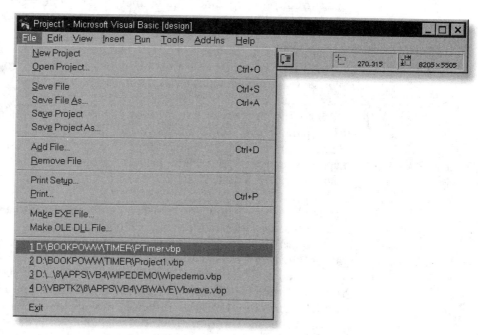

Figure 1-16: The drop-down File Menu. Notice the four most recent projects are listed at the bottom. Click to retrieve one of them.

On this menu most of these file-management options operate the same way that they would in a word processor or a graphics program. The first one cleans out whatever you might have done and presents you with a blank Visual Basic project (VB refers to programs as *Projects,* for some reason.) New provides you with the same virgin VB design environment you would get if you shut VB down and restarted it. "Open Project" loads in a previously saved project from disk.

"Save File" will save an individual Form or Module to disk. If its not a new Form or Module, it will just replace the previous version of itself. "Save File As" allows you to change the name of the Form or Module, or make a copy of it that's saved to a new location on the disk. "Save Project" and "Save Project As" do the same thing, but save all the Forms and Modules, along with a special .MAK file which describes to VB all the components of a VB project.

"Add File" lets you import and merge an existing Form or Module into your current project. Some programmers like to collect prewritten, pre-tested Subs and Functions and store them in a Module for importation and reuse their various projects.

"Remove File" removes the currently active Form or Module from the project. (The one removed is the one highlighted in the Project Window.) If you've made any changes to the Form or Module, VB will ask if you want to save it before removing it from the project.

"Print Setup" is the standard Windows facility for changing printers or printer parameters. "Print" allows you to print (or print to a file) the selected section of your programming, an entire Form or Module, a visual image of your Forms, the whole project, or just the "code" (the lines of programming). It's quite flexible for those who like hard-copy records of their work.

"Make EXE File" is how you transform your project into a normal, runable .EXE file like any other Windows "executable" program. After you've tested it and you're satisfied with it, the "Make EXE File" option is where you turn your project into a regular Windows program. You can also select various options such as which icon to use (from those you've selected in the Icon Property of your Forms). VB comes with an excellent set of professional icons. (If there's no ICONS subdirectory in your VB directory, rerun VB setup and choose "Custom." Then deselect all options except "Icons" and setup will install them for you.) You can also change the name of your project here, insert comments, legal descriptions, version information and so on. However, before creating an .EXE file, you might always want to modify some of the Project Options found under the Tools menu.

"Make OLE DLL File" allows you to create objects that can be used by other programs. A .DLL object can run faster than an .EXE object (see "Class Module").

The Edit Menu
The names and behaviors of most of the first nine items on the Edit Menu are the same as those you would find in any editing environment, such as a word processor.

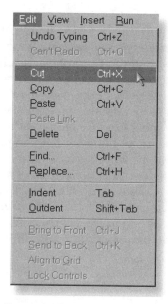

Figure 1-17: In VB, the Edit Menu is similar to a word processing menu.

The Undo option reverses your previous edit: if you've deleted some text in your program, click on Undo to get it back. (Click Redo to undo the Undo—in this case, Redo would again delete the text you had just restored with the Undo.) Cut, Copy, and Paste operate as you would expect, and they work with either the text in your code window or the objects (Controls) on your Form. Delete is the same as Cut, but no copy is saved in the Clipboard for a possible future Paste. To find out more about the specialized Paste Link item, see "LinkMode."

The Find and Replace options search (or search with replace) through all the code windows in your project, through only the current module, through only the current procedure, or through only the currently selected text. (*Current* here means where your insert cursor is.) However, remember that searching or replacing defaults to *Module* (meaning the current Form or Module) rather than the entire project as you might expect.

Indent and Outdent are somewhat curious. They merely move your insert cursor right by one Tab or back by one Tab (much more easily accomplished with the Tab and Delete keys).

BringToFront and SendToBack are handy if you have overlapping Controls on a Form. They give you a quick way of reordering which Control is on "top" or on the "bottom." There are situations when you might want to pile, say, Picture Boxes one on top of the other, like a spread of cards or cascading windows.

Use the Align to Grid item to move the currently highlighted Control (the Control with the "focus") to a grid—a set of imaginary horizontal and vertical lines. Both the position and size of the Control can be changed this way. This enables you to align your Controls precisely while designing the program, resulting in a more polished-looking Form when the program runs. This Align to Grid option on the Edit Menu interacts with the Align to Grid option in the Tools/Environment Options Menu. If the Align to Grid item is turned on in the Tools Menu, all Controls that you place on Forms will automatically snap to the grid. However, many people leave that option turned off, giving themselves finer control over an object's position and size. Also, you can make the grid visible or invisible, and as tight or as coarse as you want. However, remember that the *only thing* that the Align to Grid item in the *Edit* menu does is simply snap the active Control to the grid if the automatic Align to Grid option in the *Tools/Environment Options* Menu is turned off.

TIP
. . . .

Create Attractive Forms: Few elements of program design are more important (and more often overlooked by programmers) than the *visual* impact of an application. Just as a piece of Kleenex hanging out of your ear would make an interviewer uneasy when you're applying for a job, sloppy or generic-looking Forms (unaligned Controls, a plain white background, etc.) disconcert users of your programs.

Microsoft has a whole team of designers exploring how to make the most out of the visuals on a computer monitor. The quality of their work is reflected in the sleek, polished and professional look of Microsoft applications and Windows 95. To get an idea of amateur vs. professional Windows design, compare the icons on the Compuserve Wincim.Exe button bar with the icons on the button bar of any Microsoft application, like Word for Windows.

There are several suggestions about professional Window design in the entries on "Appearance" and "Line," including ways to add subtly textured backgrounds; creating brushed aluminum Forms and Control Buttons; framing zones within a Form; and so on. However, the most fundamental design rule of all is to align your Controls.

Figure 1-18: Before: The eye is highly sensitive to even slight misalignments of your Controls.

Figure 1-19: After: gradient backgrounds, aligned Controls and framing make your applications look more professional.

. . . .

Alignment means that in a row of Command Buttons, all the Buttons should be precisely the same size (Height and Width Properties should be identical) and that either their Top or Left Properties should also be identical for positional alignment. A quick way to do this is to select all of them (hold down Shift while clicking on each one). Then in the Properties Window type in a Height and Width. That will force them all to share these measurements. Likewise, if the Command Buttons are stacked vertically, they should share the same Left Property. If stacked horizontally, they should share the same Top Property.

The eye is sensitive to misalignment even as small as a single *pixel*. In the same spirit, if a Picture Box, for example, is 100 twips from the left side of your Form, it shouldn't be 120 twips down from the top–thereby creating a lopsided frame around the Box.

One thing which irritated programmers prior to Visual Basic 4 was that after you'd carefully arranged and sized your Controls so they looked great on the Form, they could so easily be dislodged and misaligned when clicked on. (Double-clicking on a Control is the best and quickest way to get to that Control's Events in the Code Window. So, while you were programming, you'd be double-clicking and accidentally nudging Controls all the time.)

Lock Controls is a welcome addition, new in Visual Basic 4. After you've got your Controls arranged on a Form just precisely the way you want them to look, select Lock Controls. When clicked, the black "focus" squares will now be displayed as hollow–indicating that the Controls have been locked and can't be moved or resized (unless you toggle off the Lock Controls feature).

Nudge & Other Tricks

A few tips on formatting Controls visually. VB4 has added another useful feature, the *nudge*. It can be quite frustrating trying to drag a Control just one pixel to the left, right, up or down, to make it line up perfectly. Now, fortunately, you can select a Control, then, holding down the CTRL key, click on any of the arrow keys to move the Control one pixel at a time in any direction. Holding down the SHIFT key resizes the Control one pixel at a time. Likewise, if you have grouped several Controls (by dragging around the outside of them, or by holding SHIFT and clicking on each one), they will move as a group. Also, when you want a set of Controls to be lined up so their left or top positions are all identical, group them, then click in the Properties Window and double-click on the Left or Top Property. (Or type in a precise location). They will align perfectly. The same trick can be used to make them all the same Height or Width.

Finally, if you're planning to create several Controls that you want to look essentially identical, here's another shortcut. Let's assume you want to create three Command Buttons each of which is the same size, has Arial as its Font and is set to 12 as the FontSize. Double-click on the Command Button on the Toolbox to put one onto the Form. Then adjust its Properties as you wish. When finished, click on the Button on the Form to "select" it. Then press CTRL+C to copy the button to the Clipboard. Now press CTRL+V to create a new copy of that Button. VB will prompt you, "You already have a control named Command1. Do you want to create a control array?" Answer "No." Then press CTRL+V repeatedly until you have all the clone buttons that you want—each sharing the font, size, etc. Properties of the original. Remember, too, that if you want to reproduce a group of Controls on a different Form, you can use this same technique. Group the Controls, then press CTRL+C. Now click on the other Form and press CTRL+V. (No programming you've written for these Controls will be copied, just the Controls themselves.)

The View Menu

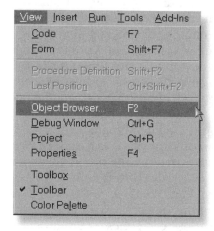

Figure 1-20: The View Menu governs what you see in the VB editor.

You can use the Code option on the View Menu to switch from viewing a Form's surface to viewing its interior, the place where you can write your programming into the Form's Events or its General Declarations section. However, most programmers use the shortcut of double-clicking on the Form, or one of the Controls on it, to get into the Event level.

The name of this area of a Form, *Code,* may be confusing if you are new to programming. In the early days, a decade or so ago, the word *code* was an apt description of the digits or three-letter acronyms like ROR and STA (for Rotate Right and Store in Accumulator) that made up the language with which humans spoke to computers. It's misleading, but many computer programmers still refer to computer language instructions and commands—programming—as code. This usage creates the incorrect impression that communicating with a computer, telling it what you want to do, is mystifying, deliberately obscure. In the Basic language, to its great credit, many of the commands and much of the "sentence structure" is in English. For example, the Basic command *Stop* is still sometimes referred to as "code," but we all understand it. There's nothing cryptic about *stop.*

The Procedure Definition option and the Last Position option are both related to the Search option in the Edit menu. Recall that when you create a Sub or Function (a procedure), it can be called (invoked) from anywhere in your program if you've made it Public (in a Form) or placed it in a Module. In other words, there might be many places throughout your program where you just name the procedure to trigger it. If you are reading your programming and have forgotten exactly what that procedure does, or want to edit it, you can just place your cursor on the procedure's name and then select Procedure Definition. You will be instantly taken to the location of the procedure where you can read or edit it. The Last Position option will cycle you through the most recent locations of your cursor (where you've been reading or editing your programming). This is the equivalent of the SHIFT+F5 (Previous Edit) feature in Word for Windows.

The Object Browser is new in VB4 and also appears in other recent Microsoft applications such as the latest version of Excel. Objects are the rage these days, involving OLE (Object Linking and Embedding), OLE Automation (one program utilizing features of another) and a style of programming (OOP, Object Oriented Programming) well suited to the Event-driven environment of Visual Basic and, indeed, Windows itself. Event-driven means that the user, not the programmer, is essentially in charge of what happens when. By clicking and via the keyboard, the user determines which Controls and Windows are activated and in what order.

The primary function of the Object Browser is to show you which Objects are available in various categories (your particular project; VB in general; specialized subsections of VB such as the Common Dialog Control and Database Control; any other Objects you might have made available to your program via the Tools/References or Tools/Custom Controls menu options; and predefined Constants). In addition to showing you the Objects, the Object Browser also displays Objects' syntax, or allows you to paste that syntax into your programming. In other words, it's a kind of viewer and help file so you can keep the ever-proliferating Objects straight and know which ones are currently available to you. (You can make new Objects available by using the References option on the Tools menu, which we'll get to shortly.)

Objects—the word evokes the vision of a frozen river breaking up in the spring: there's lots of noise, and things are fracturing and floating free. Objects represent a significant change in the way programmers approach the job of building an application. (During the next few years, users, too, will feel the real impact of this new computing paradigm.) In any case, VB and C are leading the way into OOP programming. For more on OOP, see "Objects."

The "Debug Window" is where you can fix problems or track down errors in your programs. (For a complete overview of debugging in VB, see Appendix B.)

Locating Elusive Errors: Programmers call errors *bugs*. Legend has it that in the 1950s, an early vacuum-tube monster computer attracted moths to its glowing glass tubes. There are several versions of this now-mythical story, but here briefly is the one we prefer: the insects dived toward the lights within the room-sized computing engine. Like salmon cutting themselves on the rocks of a waterfall in their frenzy to mate, moths mindlessly immolated themselves in the innards of this early computer.

It seems that moths are so attracted to light that they're willing to ignore dangerous heat. Science has not yet been able to fully explain this apparently pointless, bizarre self-sacrifice, although there are theories that moths get their sense of direction from the safe cool light of the moon, and make a mistake. This behavior was sometimes of interest to humans because of the effect moth debris had on the wires and connections within the computer. The dead bugs had to be tracked down and physically removed so a program would run properly. Hence, we still say, "Getting the bugs out of the program."

The Project, Properties, and Toolbox can all be brought to the front (if they get covered up or have been closed by, in Windows 95, clicking on the X button in the top right of the window). You can restore one of these windows by clicking on those respective options in the View Menu.

The VB design environment—where you write your programs—can display seven windows in addition to the Forms or Modules you are working on. Usually you'll probably want to have two of them kept visible at all times— the Properties Window and the Toolbox Window. The Toolbox contains the Objects (the "Controls," as they are called) that you can put onto a Form: Command Buttons, Pictures, Labels, Text Boxes (mini-word processors) and so on.

The Toolbar just under the menus can be toggled visible or invisible. The Toolbar is an optional set of icons beneath VB's menus, but most people use it and leave it visible. The icons represent, in order from left to right: Add a new Form to your program, Add a new Module, Open Project (load in a previously written VB program), Save Project (save the current project so that in case of a power failure you won't lose the work you've been doing), Lock Controls (prevent them from being moved or resized), Menu Editor (create menus for a Form), Properties (show the Properties Window), Object Browser (show it), Project (show the Project Window which lists all Forms and Modules in your program), Start (or ReStart) your program running so you can see how it behaves, Break (pause the running program and show the location in your programming "code" where you broke; you can restart it following this pause), End (stop a running program), Toggle (Set or Clear) a Breakpoint (see Appendix B), Instant Watch (see Appendix B), Calls (go to a particular Event, Sub or Function), Step Into (Single Step, line by line, through the program while you watch what happens; this way you can see where things go wrong. This is a very useful debugging technique), Step Over (move past the current procedure, then resume Single-Stepping. This one is used when you come to a line that calls a Sub or Function which you know to be bug-free and don't want to step through).

The Color Palette is the standard Windows feature which allows you to define custom colors in addition to those available on the standard palette.

The Insert Menu

Figure 1-21: The Insert Menu.

This menu is relatively straightforward. The Insert Procedure option adds a new Sub or Function to the current Form or Module. You can do the same thing by moving to the General Declarations section of a Form and typing Sub MySub (where *MySub* is whatever name you want to give to this new Sub) and then pressing ENTER. VB will handle the details of adding the ( ) and the End Sub.

Insert Form creates a new Form. If you've got the default Form1 that VB provides when you start VB running (or select New Project from the File menu), the inserted Form will be named Form2. Of course, you can change the Name Property of this Form if you want to in the Properties Window. Most people add a new Form by clicking on the leftmost button on the Toolbar.

Insert MDI Form puts a windows-within-window Form into your program (see "Multiple Document Interface (MDI)"). Insert Module creates a new Module. Most people add a new Module by clicking on the button second to the left on the Toolbar. Insert Class Module puts a specialized kind of Module into your program—it's the way you create objects or OLE servers (see "Objects") and is new with VB4.

Insert File is quite like the Add File option in the File Menu, but Add File brings an entire .FRM (Form), .BAS (Module), or .CLS (Class Module) into your program. Insert File inserts whatever .TXT file or other file you want to merge into the currently active Module or Form, at the insertion point, the location of your insertion cursor (the vertical line that shows where things will appear when you type something on the keyboard). Insert File, then, is like pasting that file's contents into the current Module or Form. (Since VB programming is written and saved as simple ASCII text, however, you could also just cut and paste from a .TXT file or word processor to import prewritten procedures or programming fragments.)

The Run Menu

Press the F5 key to start your programs running so you can test them; it's easier than pulling down the Run Menu. Unhappily, there is no shortcut key for stopping a program; you must either resort to this Run Menu (the "End" option), double-click on the button in the upper left of the active window in your program, or click on the End button on the Toolbar (or use the ALT+F4 Windows shortcut).

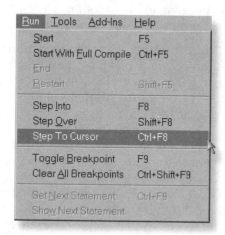

Figure 1-22: The Run Menu

You should choose the " Start With Full Compile" option if you're testing an OLE Server (see "Class Module"). Your program will be completely "compiled" (the entire thing will be translated into runnable computer codes—and various kinds of errors will be checked for) prior to actually running. This temporarily overrides whatever settings you've chosen for the Compile on Demand option on the Advanced Options page of the Tools|Options menu (described below). If you *don't* use this "Full Compile" approach, your program might "hang" due to an error that normally would have been caught during the compilation process (and thereby halt execution until you've fixed the error).

There are two ways to resume if program testing was stopped by VB because an error was detected, or if you halted execution by clicking on the Break button (or pressing CTRL+Break). Restart starts your program again from scratch (resetting all Variables and other conditions. The other approach is to *resume* ("Continue") where you left off. In other words, if you were looping: For I = 1 To 500, and broke into the program when I was 356, selecting the Continue option will start the program with I being 356 (Restart would reset I to 0). During a program break in execution, the Run option on the Run menu, as well as the Run button on the Toolbar, change to "Continue." Unlike many other computer languages, VB permits you to make changes—correct an error by typing in new commands or edit the existing commands—and then resume execution from where you left off.

This is a tight, efficient feedback loop (you don't have to make a change then wait until your program recompiles then start execution from scratch).

The remaining options on the Run Menu are useful for debugging (see "Appendix B"). Step Into (previously known as Single-Step) is most easily invoked by repeatedly pressing the F8 key. Each press of F8 moves execution of your program forward by a single line through your programming. The Debug Window pops up and you can keep an eye on your Variables while going through the program in slow motion. The current line to be executed is highlighted in both your Code Window and the Debug Window.

Stepping Through a Program: Single Step and Procedure Step are quite valuable when you are trying to track down the more elusive errors that can bedevil a programmer. VB automatically flags typos and other things it doesn't understand, but some errors are problems of logic rather than syntax. In other words, a logic bug occurs when VB understands and carries out instructions, but it doesn't produce the results you had in mind.

This distinction between syntax and logic errors is similar to telling someone who has just entered the Metropolitan Museum of Art to "keep going bevik to get to the Greek statues." Of course, *bevik* has no meaning; it's a syntax error. VB would report this kind of error and halt program execution until you'd fixed it. But if you say, "Keep going left and you'll get to the Greek statues," you've committed a logic error: there are many rooms in the museum, and you would continually enter and then exit the Persian Art rooms if you always turned left.

Use Single Step to see the effects of each line of instructions you have put into your program. The instructions are carried out in order; therefore, single-stepping can often help you see where things go awry. If single-stepping stops working (e.g., pressing F8 causes nothing to happen), you need to pretend you are the user and click on something, or otherwise interact with the program. You have, in other words, moved out of a procedure and your program is waiting for the user to trigger a new Event. So click on a Command Button or something to get the action going again, and the single-stepping will resume through the instructions in that new Event.

You'll probably want to use the Debug Window's "Immediate" option while single stepping. Clicking on the Immediate button permits you to ask to see the current state of a Variable by typing **? Form1.Top** or **? M$**. VB will then answer your questions, telling you the coordinate for the top of Form1 or the current value in the Variable *M$*. You could also cut and paste a Variable's name or a whole "expression" (a combination of Variables or Constants, such as Form1.Top + Form2.Top). Even more helpful, *you can change the contents of a variable within the Immediate Window*. Say you wonder what would happen if your variable *MyVar* was changed from its current 23 to 25000. In the Immediate Window, type

```
MyVar = 25000
```

and press ENTER. Now MyVar holds 25000.

The "Watch" button on the Immediate Window won't do anything unless you've already specified a Variable or expression that you want to Watch (see the Tools Menu, Add Watch option).

The Step Over option lets you move past a Sub or Function that you think isn't the source of your problems. In other words, if you have written a Function that runs a For Next loop 30,000, you probably don't want to single-step through all that. VB *will* execute that procedure, then halt again when it finishes so you can continue single stepping.

Choosing Step to Cursor is a way to have VB automatically execute all your programming between the current location in the program lines (wherever the program was halted) and the new location of the cursor (you click somewhere within your programming to establish a new cursor location). This is similar to Step Over but allows you to avoid tedious and unnecessary single stepping through some lines of programming (while still having VB execute those lines so you can see their effect on the program).

All of the above (Step Into, Step Over, Step to Cursor) cause the programming to be *executed,* to happen as if a user were running the program. Each intervening instruction is carried out, even if you select Step Over or Step to Cursor. The only difference is you don't have to watch each line being executed step by step. So it speeds things up. But what if you want to *avoid* having a procedure or some lines of programming executed? This is one way to debug: if you suspect a zone of programming is causing your problem, you could refuse to execute it and if the problem then disappears, you can suspect those skipped lines. To do this, select the Set Next Statement option.

Set Next Statement allows you to move your cursor anywhere in your program while program execution is paused (Break), and click on a line. Then, selecting Set Next Statement will cause the program to start running *from that statement* instead of where the program was when it paused. Remember that the intervening programming is not executed.

Show Next Statement reveals the instruction that comes after the current one if perhaps it is located somewhere outside the current Event or Subroutine.

Among the most useful debugging tools are breakpoints. If you know your program works fine up to a certain point, put a breakpoint at that location. VB will halt execution at the breakpoint line and you can then start single-stepping from there. As an example, let's say that everything is working splendidly when you click, so you know that the Click Event instructions are solid. But something is terribly wrong when you double-click. Put a breakpoint at the top of the DblClick Event (right after Sub Command1_Click, for example). Your program will run normally (and swiftly) until it encounters the breakpoint. Then it will stop, and you can press F8 to go into the single-step mode.

You set a breakpoint by locating the place in your program where you want the program to halt. In the word processor mode (the "Code" Window), find the suspect area of your program. Then move the cursor to a line that precedes the area you think might be causing trouble. Press F9 while your cursor is on that line, which will make the line go bold. You can remove that breakpoint by pressing F9 again. You can remove all breakpoints by clicking on Clear All Breakpoints.

The Tools Menu

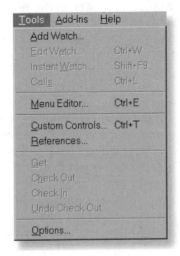

Figure 1-23: The Tools Menu

The first four items on the Tools Menu are also for debugging. With the Add Watch option you can specify a particular Variable or condition (and "expression" such as F = 22 or F > 22) and then see the action of the Variable *F* or the expression F = 22 while the program is running. In other words, VB can react (by showing changes in the Variable or "expression," or by halting the program) when a specified condition occurs. Note that you should usually highlight the Variable or expression you're interested in, then click on Add Watch. This way the *scope* (or context) will be correct. For instance, if you add a watch for a Variable that you haven't yet typed into your program, then type it in after adding the watch, VB will report "Expression not defined in context."

TIP •

Also be aware that a Watch in VB defaults to highly local scope: to the current Form or Module and, worse, to the current *procedure* (the Sub or Function). One of the most common debugging tactics is to notice that, for some reason, the variable *MyTaxes* is surging somewhere in your program and growing from the expected $10,000 or so to $100,000, which is more than your income. Clearly this variable goes haywire somewhere, but you don't know where. If you add a Watch (Break on: MyTaxes > 20000), VB will halt the program when this expression becomes true, when your taxes Variable grows larger than 20,000. This should trap the error. But if you leave the "context" local to the particular procedure which was current (had the cursor in the code window)—or even the particular Form—you could well miss the real location of this error. It might be in a different procedure or Form or Module. To avoid this, set the Context in the Watch window to All Procedures and All Modules (VB confusingly refers to Forms and Modules collectively as *Modules*).

• •

The Edit Watch option brings up a window where you can delete or change the current Watch. The *current* Watch is the one that's highlighted in the Watch "Pane" in the Debug Window.

Instant Watch is similar to requesting information in the Immediate "Pane" of the Debug Window (as described above). You highlight a Variable or expression in your code window while a running program is in Break (pause) mode, then select Instant Watch (or press SHIFT+F9). A window appears and you can see the current status of that selected Variable or expression.

The Calls option is rarely needed unless you are in the habit of having one procedure call another (which calls another, etc.). In other words, you "nest" Subroutine or Function calls. Calls will show you where, in nested Subroutines, the program was halted. This reveals the flow of the program, the path by which the program got to its current location. You'll see a list of Subroutines, starting from the current one and going down through any still-active Subroutines in the nest.

VB makes it quite easy to add menus to your Forms and you do it by selecting the Menu Editor option. For more on this, see "Menu." The Custom Controls option brings up a list of ancillary Controls and other optional items. Here's where you can add any of these Objects to your Toolbox so you can conveniently place them on your Forms. (If you want to make a Control or Object a permanent part of your Toolbox, do it when VB first starts running and Autoload.Mak is the active project. Then save Autoload.Mak.)

VB ships with a set of core Controls, like the Text Box and Label Control. However, VB also includes add-on optional Controls like the Grid and Common Dialog Controls. In addition, you can purchase sets of third-party Custom Controls from such companies as Sheridan and Crescent.

Along with Custom Controls, this window will also display any Objects that OLE-capable applications have registered in Windows as available to be embedded or linked into other applications. These Objects are called "insertable Objects" in this Custom Controls window. For instance, Microsoft Word permits a "Document" to be inserted; Windows permits a "Sound"; CorelDRAW a "Graphic"; and so on. Just what insertable Objects you'll see listed depend on what applications you've got installed in Windows on your computer. Be warned that some of these Objects aren't very stable and (unlike Custom Controls) might cause you problems if you try to insert them and use them. For more on this topic, see "OLE" and "Link-Mode."

The References Window displays a list of Objects (or collections of Objects) that are known to exist (are registered) in your Windows system. Selecting one of these Objects doesn't add it to your ToolBox (though you might see some of the same Objects listed here as you see listed as insertable Objects in the Custom Controls window. When you select an item from the References Window, that Object is added to your program. It becomes usable by your program and you can manipulate any Properties or Methods that it offers. The Object will be added to those listed in your Object Browser (press F2) along with VB's Objects and all the rest of the tools available to you while programming. In the Object Browser you can see the Object's Properties and Methods, and the syntax necessary to access them.

This new Object reference will remain with your program, even when you shut VB down and start it back up again and reload the program. If you use a Class Module to write an Object application, it, too, will appear in the References Window and can be added in this way to your program's available Objects. For more on this, see "Objects."

Version Control
The "Get," "Check In," "Check Out," and "Undo Check Out" options are for version control, an administrative tactic used to maintain the latest, best version of a project when several programmers are working together, or when a project is large and complex. The Enterprise Edition of VB4 includes Microsoft SourceSafe, an add-in that controls who gets to read, or change, programming (source code) in a project. Acting like a librarian, it preserves the most recent several versions of each Form or Module, and grants or refuses permission for various programmers to read or edit these Forms or Modules. All this clerical overhead is sometimes necessary to keep things straight when more than one person is working on the same project (which is the latest version?). The Get option allows you to read (but not

edit) a copy (not the original) of the most recent version of a file, a group of files, or an entire project. It can also give you read-only copies for compiling and testing purposes (but you still can't *change* this programming). The Check In option allows you to save changes to the "Master" (the latest, best) copy of the project. The Check Out option gives you a *writeable* (editable) copy of the Master. Undo Check Out removes the copy and cancels any editing you've done to it.

Options

Clicking on the Options selection in the Tools menu brings up a tabbed dialog box (or what in Windows 95 they call a "Property Sheet"). Within these various "Tabs" or pages, you can decide how VB will look and act in a variety of respects. The Environment options govern VB's design environment in general and are remembered from session to session by a VB.INI file in your Windows directory. You can turn the grid on and off and make it finer or coarser. You can force any of the ToolBox, Properties, Project or Debug windows to always push to the top of any other visible windows.

   You can choose to have VB automatically save your project before you run (test) it, in case your program freezes the machine. You can turn off "ToolTips" those brief descriptions of buttons on Toolbars or Toolboxes that show up when you hold your mouse pointer over a button for a second.

   The Require Variable Declaration option forces you to *explicitly* define the *type* of each Variable you use in your programs. Some languages (Cobol, Pascal, etc.) *require* explicit declarations; VB, fortunately, makes Variable declaration your choice. Some argue that the benefit of requiring Variable declaration is that VB will catch some typos. If you say If Nervf = 5 and you've never defined a Variable called Nervf (you meant to type Nerve), VB will bring the typo to your attention.

   Without required declaration, VB would just think you were creating a new *implicit* Variable (one that you've just used but didn't formally declare). The command If Nervf = 5 would never execute because Nerve might equal 5 at some point while the program runs, but Nervf never can because it's just a misspelling. The drawback to explicit declarations is that you have more work to do: a program can have many Variables, and you'll have to define the nature of each one. It's possible that the time spent fixing the occasional bug resulting from mistyped Variable names is less than the time spent declaring every Variable.

   The next option on the Environment page is Auto Syntax Check. If you set it on, VB will display an error dialog box and tell you of any typos or errors *every time* you press ENTER after writing a line of instructions (or use the arrow keys to move off that line). Many programmers leave it off, preferring to separate the inspired creation phase of their programming from the rather clerical job of checking for proper syntax and spelling. If you were writing a letter in a word processor, you would probably want the flow of your ideas to remain uninterrupted by niggling details. It's easy enough to turn on a spelling checker after you have finished. In the same way, when you test your program by running it with the F5 key or attempt to make an .EXE file out of it, Visual Basic will inform you of any errors it detects in your spelling, punctuation and grammar. At that point, you can either retype the offending item or press F1 to get advice about the probable cause of the error.

As a generalization on the issue of requiring Variable declarations, people who write programs by themselves often prefer to leave "Require Variable Declarations" turned off; people who program in teams tend to leave it on. Your co-programmers might be execrable typists. (You can also use the Option Explicit command to create the same effect as changing "Require Variable Declarations" to "Yes" in the Environment options page.)

The options on the Project page specify various qualities for your current program.

The Startup Form

Though the user generally determines the order in which events happen when your VB program runs, there is "a starting place," where the first things happen when the user first runs the program. One Form (called the *Startup Form*) will always be the first Form VB looks at when the program starts to run. Here you'll want to do the housekeeping: perhaps setting up Variables, making things visible or invisible, filling List Boxes with their lists, creating Control Arrays (which see) and otherwise preparing the program for the user.

The instructions in any Form's Form_Initialize Event will take place before the user can see the Form (the window). You therefore put any preliminary housekeeping instructions for your entire program in the Form_Initialize (or Form_Load) Event of the "Startup Form." (If you want, you can use an alternative startup location, called Sub Main, which allows a Module to start things off when your program runs. See "Startup Form" for more information on these options.)

Most Properties—colors, sizes, etc., of the objects you're putting into your windows—can be defined while you are designing your program. However, a few Properties cannot be known, nor can they be adjusted, until the program actually starts to run. For example, you cannot fill a List Box with the user's available printer font names until the program is running on the user's computer. Each user's printer can offer different fonts, different typefaces. If you want to let the user select a printer font, you can't create such a list until the program runs and takes control of the user's computer. When it does have control, your program can then check out the Printer.Fonts list (see "Printer"). It can then fill the List Box with the names of the fonts available on the user's printer.

Which Form is the Startup Form? Unless you change it using this "Startup Form" item in the Options Menu, the Startup Form will be the first Form that appears when you start programming. And its name (the Form's Name Property) will be Form1, unless you have changed that Property. Your program can have more than one Form, but only one can be the Startup.

Sometimes you will want to designate an alternative Form as the Startup, the one that specifies the first things to happen when your program runs. Perhaps after you've finished programming, you decide to display a logo or a title window to give the user something to look at while your housekeeping initialization takes place. Use the Startup Form option to make this adjustment and change the Startup Form to this new title window Form.

The *Project Name* option is confusing; it isn't the *filename* with which you save your project. Nor is it the name that identifies your program in the VB design environment Title Bar (by default this is always Project1, but you can change it to a more meaningful name with the File/Save File As option). Instead, Project Name should probably be called Object Name, since it only works with an Object you create in a Class Module that you later save as an .EXE file (so it can be a Server). The Project Name is how an outside Client application identifies your object. See "Objects."

The *Help File* option is where you specify the filename of a Help file, if you want to create one for your program. For more on this option, see "HelpContextID, HelpFile."

Application Description is whatever text you want displayed when your object is selected for viewing in the Object Browser.

StartMode for normal, traditional .EXE files is left with the default "Stand-alone" option selected. However, when you use a Class Module to create a Server object that can be used by outside applications, select "Object Application." (See "Class Module.")

The Compatible OLE Server list is where you can optionally type in the name of the .EXE file that you created of your current program (from "Make .EXE File in the File Menu). This applies only when you use a Class Module to create a Server object that can be used by outside applications. When you list an .EXE file, VB watches any future changes you make to the program to see if incompatibilities or problems will occur (that didn't occur when you tested earlier versions of your object server).

Editor

The Editor page governs how you want the text in your code window to appear, while you're writing programs. It might well have been called the *Format* page. You can choose the Font and FontSize, the colors indicating various special conditions like comments or breakpoints, and also whether or not "auto-indent" is active. *Auto-indent* is useful because it simplifies the job of indenting in loops (VB retains the current tab location after you've hit the ENTER key on a line). For example, most programmers like to visually indicate a loop structure by indenting its contents:

```
For i = 1 To 10
    N = i
    V = i + 5
Next i
```

With auto-indent on, once you've pressed the Tab to move over and type N = I, you can then press ENTER and VB will move you over right under the N so you can type the next line without having to hit TAB again to indent it. The Tab Width defines how many spaces over VB moves when you press the TAB key.

Foreground and Background colors can be adjusted or left "Automatic" (Windows default settings). *Full Module View* displays all the Subs and Functions (the "procedures") in your current Form or Module, one after the other, like a traditional programmer's editor. However, you can choose to have the Subs and Functions (and any General Declarations at the top) separated visually by a line that VB inserts between each procedure. Alternatively, you can deselect Full Module View and use the Visual Basic-style editor that many programmers have come to regard as superior. It displays only a single procedure at a time, and you can quickly move to other procedures by using the PgUp or PgDn key.

Advanced

The Advanced page of the Tools|Options menu collects some sophisticated options, and a few that didn't fit elsewhere on the other pages. *Upgrade Custom Controls* determines whether VB should use the latest version of a Custom Control referenced in your program. With all the DLL's, OCX's and VBX's and other objects now floating around in Windows, there can be more than one version of the same Custom Control on your hard drive (I've got three versions of THREED.VBX.) Whenever you add newer versions of Custom Controls, they are registered in your VB.INI file. But the older registrations remain there as well. Upgrade Custom Controls can insure that you're using the latest version.

The *Background Project Load* option should probably be left on. It doesn't freeze the computer until an entire project (VB program) is loaded into the VB design environment. Instead, it allows you to keep working, continuing to complete the load during those eternities (by the computer's sense of time) between your keystrokes or mouse moves.

Compile On Demand is also a way to work more efficiently within the VB environment. Leave it on if you want to test your projects more rapidly (especially big projects). Without Compile On Demand, when you press F5 or select Run to test your program, it won't start running until every last line has been translated into runable (computer-understandable) code.

The Background Compile option is similar. It decides whether, while the program is running, any idle time is used to finish compiling the project in the background. This can make the program run faster during your testing.

Break on All Errors forces VB to halt execution if any error occurs. (If you put On Error Resume Next commands into your programs, and you should, VB would normally continue right on past the error and you, while testing your program, would perhaps be unaware that the error had occurred. See "On Error.") *Break in Class Module* permits VB to halt execution when a problem arises inside a Class Module (otherwise, VB will halt in the "Controlling" client application, which, during testing, is some VB programming that you've written to test your Class Module's behavior. See "Objects." *Break on Unhandled Errors* halts your program during testing if there is no active error handler (On Error Resume Next, for example) and an error occurs.

The Use OLE DLL Restrictions option forces VB to treat an object that you're testing with the same strict rules that apply if the object were being run by an ordinary application. (See "Class Module.") Unfortunately, you can't test an object that you intend to make into a .DLL file in a real-world situation ("in-process" as it's called) within the VB programming environment. Instead, you have to test "out-of-process" and use a second running instance of VB—start VB twice—to "call" and test your .DLL. However, you can at least simulate the restrictions imposed on an in-process server (.DLL) by turning on this Use OLE DLL Restrictions option.

Command-Line Arguments

Ralph is the Command-line argument in C:\WP\WP.EXE, Ralph. In other words, *Ralph* is the optional text or graphics file to load into a program when it starts running. Or sometimes a Command-line argument is a "switch" or series of switches, usually separated by the "/" (forward slash) symbol. To allow the user to run your program and have it run full-screen when it starts up, you could allow this kind of syntax:

```
MYPROGRAM.EXE /Fullscreen
```

The Command-line argument feeds VB a Variable called *Command$*, which, in this instance, contains the text "/Fullscreen," and you could react to this in the Form_Load or Form_Initialize Event of the Startup Form, as follows:

```
Sub Form1_Load ( )
If Command$ = /Fullscreen  Then
    WindowState = 2
End If
End Sub
```

A Command-line argument is a way for the user to set preconditions and preferences for your program's initial startup behavior. Specifying the Command-line argument enables you to test a Command$ in your program to make sure your program reacts to it correctly. To do this, you must select Start from the Run Menu. (For more information, see "Command$.")

Conditional Compilation Arguments

New in VB4 is the ability to write sections of a program that won't become part of the final .EXE application when you "Make .EXE File" from the File menu. Why would you write part of a program that never gets into the final version? Maybe you need two different versions for two different kinds of users. For example, say that you write a great utility and decide to put it out as shareware. You could have a function that's called every 15 minutes and that displays a "nag-screen" asking the user to register the product. However, this function is only conditionally compiled because you also want to create a registered version of the application which bypasses this nag-screen. This way, you put a Constant in your program and only have to change that Constant to cause or avoid compilation of the conditional sections. Conditional zones in the program are marked off by the new #If...Then #EndIf commands (which see) and the Constant is like any other except it's preceded by a #. The following would compile the nag screen version because the #Const is defined as true:

```
#Const Unregistered = True
Sub ShowNagScreen( )
    MsgBox  Please Register
End Sub
Private Sub Form_Load( )
#If Unregistered = True Then
    ShowNagScreen
#End If
End Sub
```

However, if you prefer, you can omit the #Const line above and leave it out of your programming. Instead, you can put it into the Project Options Window in a different way. Leave out the #Const = and don't use True or False. Instead, you must use –1 for True and 0 for False:

```
Unregistered = -1
```

OR

```
Unregistered = 0
```

The Add-Ins Menu

Figure 1-24: The Add-Ins Menu.

If you want to expand the Visual Basic design environment, here's where you do it. If you have elected to install it during setup (and you have the Professional or Enterprise Edition of VB), you should see Report Designer. You should also see Data Manager.

What's listed when you click on the Add-In Manager will depend on which add-ins available from Microsoft and other sources you've installed on your computer. Add-ins can include special report designers, database creators, project-management librarians like Microsoft SourceSafe for group-programming, and so on. In fact, if you have the Professional or Enterprise editions of VB, you can write your own add-ins to customize or extend the environment within which you write your VB programs. Several sample add-ins, written in VB, are included in the Professional edition to get you started. Also look for the file Samples.Txt in your VB directory which describes the sample Add-ins.

The Help Menu
Press the F1 key anytime to get help. Alternatively, you can use this Help Menu, but most people find it easier to summon help by pressing F1.

We've now finished our introductory tour of Visual Basic's programming features. Let's put theory into practice by creating a short program.

CREATING A PROGRAM

A Disk View Program in 10 Minutes

Let's see how surprisingly easy it can be, via Visual Basic, to go from idea to reality. Here we'll create a program that can move around all the disk drives attached to the computer, showing every file, like an "elementary file manager." The figures in this section will be in Windows 3.1 style, which is still supported by VB4—a generally flat, two-dimensional look. We don't want to appear to be a Windows 95 chauvinist (though, truth be told, we are), so we're abandoning the Windows 95 look that's been used in all figures up to this point and now giving equal time to the less attractive Windows 3.1-style Controls. Note that the programming here is the same in either VB4 32-bit (Windows 95) or VB4 16-bit (Windows 3.1)—it's just that the quality of the *appearance* of the final product suffers somewhat.

1. Start Visual Basic; if it's already running, click on New Project in Visual Basic's File Menu. Now you have a clean slate to work on. The Toolbox, containing objects that make up a Windows program, is shown in Figure 1-25. We want to focus on the file-management Controls.

Figure 1-25: The Toolbox with the Drive List Box highlighted.

2. Click on the Drive List Box. Then hold down your left mouse button and *draw* the box on the blank form.

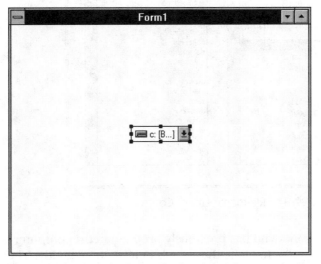

Figure 1-26: Now the Drive List Box is in place on the Form.

3. Now select and draw a Directory List Box and a File List Box onto the Form, shown in Figures 1-27 and 1-28.

Figure 1-27: The Directory List Box.

Figure 1-28: The File List Box.

Now your Form should look something like Figure 1-29, although you can position and resize these file-management boxes however you want to.

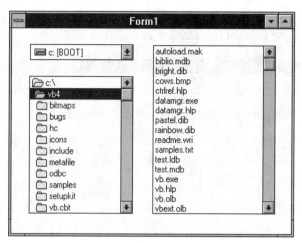

Figure 1-29: The file-management Controls.

4. Anyone who has previously programmed a computer will be startled at how easy it is to make these tools behave intelligently. They already react to mouse clicks on their arrow buttons, and the Directory Box reacts to double-clicks on directory names as well. Start the program running to see what you can do by clicking. When you press F5, your program behaves exactly as if it were running in Windows itself.

5. Now we'll make the program fully functional. Stop the program from running by double-clicking the button on the top left of the Form, by selecting End from the Run Menu or by clicking on the black square "Stop" icon on the Toolbar. Now you're back where you were, ready to finish designing the program.

Each of these three Controls has a Property, a quality, that identifies the contents of the Box. For the Directory and File Boxes, this quality is called the "Path." For the Drive Box, it is simply called the "Drive." When you double-click on a drive name, the Drive Property of the Drive Box automatically adjusts to contain the name of the new drive. Likewise, the Path Properties of the Directory and File Boxes change as appropriate when they are double-clicked. So, your program can always query the Drive or Path Properties. This will tell you if the user has moved to a different location on the disk drive (by clicking on your Directory and File Boxes).

Each Control Also Has Events: In addition to its list of qualities (the Properties), each Control has a list of "Events." Recall that Events are things that might happen to the Control while the program is running. The user might click it, so there is a Click Event. The user might double-click it, so there is a DblClick Event. To see the possible Events that can happen to the Drive List Box, double-click on it. This opens up a window, the place where you tell Visual Basic what to do if an Event occurs.

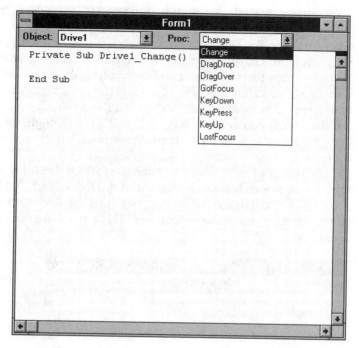

Figure 1-30: Possible Events for a Drive Box (Proc means Procedure, another word for Event).

The pull-down menu in Figure 1-30 shows all the Events that could happen to a Drive List Box. Depending on what kind of program you are writing, you'll use none or a few of the Events for any particular Control. Rarely, if ever, would you need to write instructions in all the Events of a Control.

For our purposes, we need to react to only one of these Events; we want our program to respond if the user ever clicks on the list of disk drives in the Drive Box, thereby *changing* the selected disk drive. We want our program to react to this by adjusting the Path of the *Directory* List Box. Remember that clicking on its list will automatically adjust the Drive Property of the Drive List Box but will not automatically affect the other Boxes. If the user switches drives, we want that change reflected in the Directory Box as well. In other words, *we want an Event in one Box to cause a change in another Box.*

Visual Basic's Vocabulary: We now come to another efficiency of Visual Basic: its vocabulary often sounds like English rather than computer language. All versions of Basic have this advantage over most other computer languages, and that's one reason for the enduring popularity of Basic. Instead of calling this OBJ3X4.22, we are calling it a Drive List Box—which is pretty much what it is.

If you are new to programming, don't worry if you don't immediately understand the meaning of every word in Visual Basic or the "sentence structure." You'll soon catch on to foreign words and structures. And, what's more, no harm can come from typing something wrong. Visual Basic just stops the program and shows you that you've made an error and, to the best of its ability, *where* you made the error and *how* to fix it. If you do mistype or misstate something, Visual Basic provides a message that describes what you've done wrong. If that's not enough, press F1 for further help, or look up the offending command in the reference section of this book.

In any case, our goal here is to have the Path of the Directory Box change if the user changes (clicks on) the list in the Drive Box, thereby switching to another drive. On a separate line, between the line that says "Sub Drive1_Change" and the line that says "End Sub," type the line as shown in Figure 1-31.

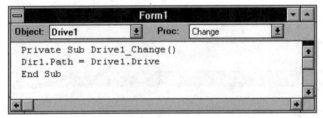

Figure 1-31: Changing the Directory Box s Path from within an Event of the Drive Box.

Now press F5 and click on some other disk drive, to trigger a change in the Drive Box; then notice how the Directory List changes as well.

6. All that's left to do is to make the File Box change when the Directory Box changes. In the code window, click on the arrow next to the word Object, and then click on Dir1 (that's the Directory List Box's default Name that VB gave it when you placed it on the Form). Don't forget that you can change the names of Controls, if you want, by selecting *Name* in the Properties Window and typing over the old name. But Visual Basic provides good usable names for you; many programmers rarely change the Names.

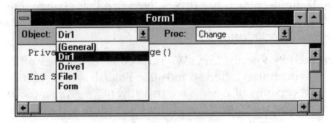

Figure 1-32: The list of Controls (Objects) that are active in our program.

Click on Dir1 in the Object: Menu (see Figure 1-32); then type the text into the Change Event of the Directory Box, as shown in Figure 1-33.

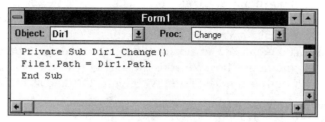

Figure 1-33: Causing the File List to update itself when the Directory List changes.

What happens to the list of files if the user changes the *Drive* instead of the Directory? In other words, we didn't tell the File Box how to react to a change in the Drive Box.

We didn't need to. Recall that we told the Drive Box to update the Directory Box's Path as necessary if the user clicks on the Drive Box. However, the change to the Directory Box triggers its Change Event. Therefore, the instructions we put into the Directory Box's Change Event (to update the File Box) are also carried out. In this way, the behavior of one Event can indirectly affect one or more other Events. As this example demonstrates, although the user often triggers Events via the keyboard or mouse, the *program* can also trigger Events.

But Visual Basic is even more efficient than this. What would happen if there were too many files to list them all visibly in the File Box?

Two Simple Lines of Programming: Try out the program. Press F5 and double-click in the various Boxes. You'll notice that Visual Basic does a lot of the housekeeping. We had to tell it only two things: (1) Change the list of directories when the user changes the drive; and (2) Change the list of files when the user (or the program itself) changes the directory. Try switching to your Windows directory, so you'll get a list of files too long to display in the File Box. There it is: Visual Basic automatically supplies a Scroll Bar.

No other computer language currently available enables you to create a program nearly this quickly. Nor will any other language allow you to accomplish all this with only two simple lines of programming.

How hard would it be to make this program display any graphic image in a .BMP file, like the wallpaper files that come with Windows? Not hard at all. In fact, we're going to do that next. You may want to save the program at this point by selecting Save Project from the File Menu.

Expanding the Program

To expand the Disk View program we just wrote and saved, let's make it into a graphics viewer. Following that, we'll discover how Visual Basic's design tools are used when creating a program.

If you need to, reload the Filename Viewer now by selecting Open Project from Visual Basic's File Menu. Click on View Form in the Project Window. You should see your Form with a Drive Box, a Directory and a File List Box, just as it was when you saved it. Take a minute to click on Auto-3D (to make it True) in the Properties Window for a more professional look. (You won't see any change in design mode, but press F5 to run the program, and notice how VB adds metallic gray to the background and sinks the Controls into the Form with highlights and shadows.)

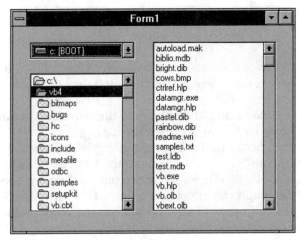

Figure 1-34: The Filename Viewer Form.

We want to add three qualities to our program:

1. It should expand a Picture Box to fit the size of any .BMP graphic loaded into it.

2. The Picture Box should move itself, so it covers up the File Boxes until the user clicks on the Picture.

3. The File List Box should display only the names of files with the .BMP extension, not *all* filenames, as it currently does.

Let's do it. Add a Picture Box to the Form. It doesn't matter where you put it or what size it is; just click on the Picture Box Icon.

Figure 1-35: The Picture Box Icon.

Then press and hold the left mouse button anywhere on the Form. Drag the mouse to create the Picture Box on the Form.

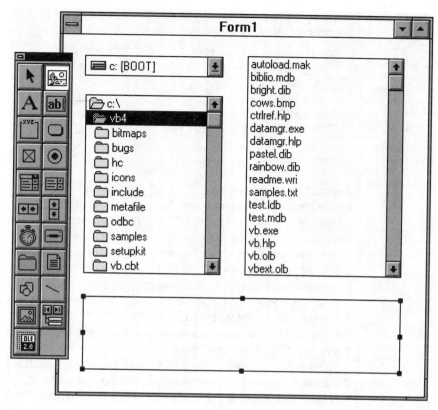

Figure 1-36: A Picture Box on the program s Form.

Now click on the Form and select Caption from the Properties Menu. Type in "GRAPHICS VIEWER." Then double-click on the Form to reveal the "Code Window" (the place where you put instructions that are to be carried out when the program runs). Remember that the Code Window contains all the Events for each Form and each Control.

Put in Housekeeping Details

Form_Load is the second Event that happens when a program runs (Form_Initialize is first, but both happen before the user sees your Form). This Load Event is automatically triggered when the user starts up your program. (If there is more than one Form in your program, only one of them will be designated to be the Startup Form. For more details, see "Startup Form.")

Pull down the Proc: Menu (the list of various Events that a Form can react to) and click on the Load Event. (VB defaults to the Load Event, so if you double-click on the Form itself, you'll automatically land inside the Load Event in the Code Window.) The Form_Load Event (or Form_Initialize Event) is where you put preliminary housekeeping tasks you want carried out before the program becomes visible to the user and before any other Events take place (except Initialize).

Into the Form_Load Event, type the following:

```
Sub Form_Load ( )
Picture1.Top = 0
Picture1.Left = 0
Picture1.AutoSize = True
Picture1.Visible = False
File1.Pattern = *.BMP
End Sub
```

Format to Suit Yourself: When typing in these commands, you can capitalize or not, as you want. You can also skip lines, use tabs or format in whatever fashion you prefer. Visual Basic ignores these things. By convention, the names of Controls such as Picture1 are usually given initial caps. Many programmers, though, avoid this convention because it means extra work, and Visual Basic doesn't care—such conventions are strictly to make programs more readable for those programmers who think they do.

First, we cause the Picture Box to move to the upper left corner of the Form so that the Picture's top and left sides are against the top and left of the Form. The 0 in these cases refers to coordinates—locations within the Form (see "Top" or "Left" entries).

Picture Boxes have a Property called *AutoSize,* which means that the Boxes will expand or contract to fit the graphics they contain. This quality can be either True or False, either on or off. It *defaults* to off, so Visual Basic doesn't resize Picture Boxes unless you specifically tell it to. That's what we're doing here. By saying Picture1.AutoSize = True, we are saying, "Turn on the automatic resizing for this Picture Box."

How Our Program Should Respond

When the program starts running, we want the user to see and use the three File Boxes, not the Picture Box, so we turn the Picture's Visible Property off. Then we create a "filter" for the File List Box. Its Pattern Property is usually *.* (show everything), as in the DOS DIR command. But we can change it to show just the files that end in .BMP and are therefore Bit-Mapped Picture files—the kind we want to view.

When the user double-clicks on the File List Box, the program should respond by copying the selected picture from the disk to the Picture Box. Then the File Boxes should become invisible, and the Picture Box should become visible. What Event do we want to trigger these actions? The File1 DblClick Event. Select the Object: Menu and click on File1. Then, from the Proc: Menu, select DblClick and type the following into the Event:

```
Sub File1_DblClick ( )
If Right$(File1.Path, 1) <> \ Then
    Graphic$ = File1.Path + \ + File1.FileName
```

```
      Else
          Graphic$ = File1.Path + File1.FileName
      End If
      Picture1.Picture = LoadPicture(Graphic$)
      Drive1.Visible = False
      Dir1.Visible = False
      File1.Visible = False
      Picture1.Visible = True
      End Sub
```

If...Then Is Fundamental

The only part of this program that's not immediately obvious is the first five lines, which load the picture in from the disk.

If...Then is a fundamental aspect of every entity—computer or otherwise. If it rains, then the ground gets wet. If you are hungry, then you eat. If...Then responds to current conditions; it's a way to describe cause and effect when teaching the computer how to respond. We use If...Then in a program to make it react intelligently to the immediate environment, to changing circumstances. We explicitly list the actions the computer should take if something happens.

We need an If...Then structure at this location in this program because when you're in the root directory (such as C:\), there is a "\" symbol on the end of a Path Property, and otherwise there is no "\" symbol. The Path varies depending on where you are on the disk drive. But we cannot simply always add the "\" or we would get C:\\MYPICTURE.BMP, and that would cause the program to come to a halt. So the If...Then structure says, "If there *isn't* a "\", add one between the Path and the filename. Or Else if there *is* a "\", just put the two pieces of text—the Path plus the filename—together."

If the Path says "C:\WINDOWS," then attach a backslash (\) to the end of this text so it becomes C:\WINDOWS\—and we can add the filename C:\WINDOWS\MARILYN.BMP. Or, Else, if the Path is C:\, we do not need to add the "\" symbol.

But where does *Graphic$* come from? We made up the name *Graphics$*; it's not part of Visual Basic's vocabulary. Graphic$ is a *Variable*. Simply put, a Variable is a name you make up that can "hold" information; it's like writing "OUR VACATION TO EUROPE" on a manila envelope and putting money, maps or whatever into the envelope.

You can replace information in a Variable (Graphic$ = "something" replaces whatever text was in Graphic$ with the text *something*); add to the existing information (Graphic$ = Graphic$ + "more" adds the text *more* to whatever text already resides in Graphic$); or take all information out (Graphic$ = "" says that Graphic$ equals nothing; it's an "empty text Variable"). Variables, too, are a major aspect of computer languages, just as nicknames and proper nouns are a major aspect of human language. (See "Variables.")

We are using Graphic$ to hold the precise location of the filename the user has selected. The File Box's Path Property has the Drive and Directory names. The Path might be something like this: C:\WINDOWS\BMPS\—or whatever directory the user has selected when he or she double-clicked. However, the particular filename must be specified as well and added to this Path.

List Is a Built-In Array

All the filenames currently visible in a File Box are held in a list called the File Box's List Property. The specific filename the user has selected is identified by a number, known as the *ListIndex* Property. We get the actual location by using both the number and the name, just as you add the number 545 to the name Main Street to identify Wilson's Qwik Kleen laundromat. The number, 545, isn't enough, nor is Main Street. Together, though, they identify a particular thing. Combining names with index numbers is another powerful and important tool in computer programming; it's a way to organize Variables, to group them into a larger structure called an *Array* (See "Arrays").

When we have the address of the .BMP file the user wants, we use VB's LoadPicture command to put the selected picture into the Picture Box. Then we just reverse the Visible Properties, hiding the File Boxes and revealing the Picture. For now, the Picture is the only thing visible on our Form, our window.

One thing remains to be done: the user should be able to look at more pictures. This is accomplished by merely returning the program to its original state. We want the Picture Box to become *invisible* and the File Boxes to become *visible* when the user clicks on the Picture.

Select Picture1 from the Objects: Menu and select its Click Event from the Proc: Menu. Then type in the commands that make the File Boxes visible and the Picture invisible:

```
Sub Picture1_Click ( )
Drive1.Visible = True
Dir1.Visible = True
File1.Visible = True
Picture1.Visible = False
End Sub
```

Press the F5 key and try the program. You can now view any .BMP file on any disk.

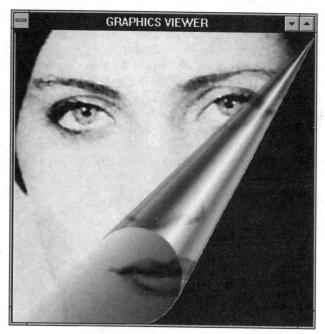

Figure 1-37: A complete .BMP viewer created with only 17 lines of programming

Beyond Visual Basic

Relatively speaking, Visual Basic has a large vocabulary for a computer language. Where more primitive languages have as few as 50 words, VB has more than 400, (more than 1,000 if you include the database language). With that many separate commands, there is little VB cannot accomplish. For many people, Visual Basic's tools and facilities are all that will ever be needed to build sophisticated Windows programs. Visual Basic is a powerful language.

Yet for the adventurous, there is more. From within Visual Basic you can tap into more than 600 commands that Windows itself uses to run things. Many of these commands are highly specialized. For example, do you want to instantly expand an icon to a full-size picture? How about complete control over the duration, timbre and volume of several channels of sound? These and many more capabilities are available to the Visual Basic programmer via the API (the Application Program Interface), a collection of Subroutines built into Windows.

Actually, when using the API, we don't go *beyond* VB as much as *beneath* it. We'll learn to access this engine room under Windows. It can be surprisingly simple once you know how, and you'll be able to add many new special features to VB and take complete control over the way your Windows environment works.

Throughout this book are occasional examples of API Functions (see "Declare" for some examples of fancy graphics manipulations). Sometimes, one of these API Functions is preferable to a VB command because the API is faster or does something VB cannot do. For instance, in the entry on "Beep," we describe the feeble VB Beep sound command but suggest you use the more powerful API alternative. Many of the API's Functions are both lightning-fast and extraordinarily flexible. Appendix A includes numerous API examples and will prepare you to add the API to your VB set of tools. However, the great bulk of this book, Section II, is devoted to the many and powerful words in the vocabulary of Visual Basic itself.

SECTION II

REFERENCE

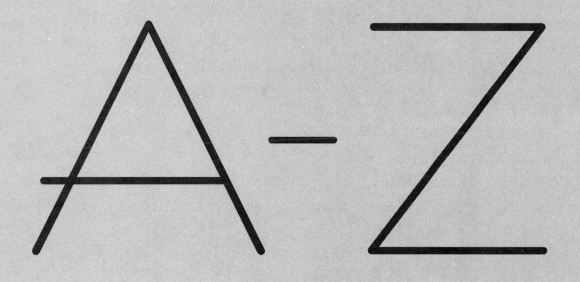

BS

Description   Abs is a rarely used function that gives you back a Variable of the same type. If the Variable was negative (such as –51), Abs changes it to positive (51). If it was positive, it stays positive. In effect, Abs removes any minus sign (–) from any number. You can use any numeric Variable of any type with Abs. (See "Variables" for more on numeric Variable types.)

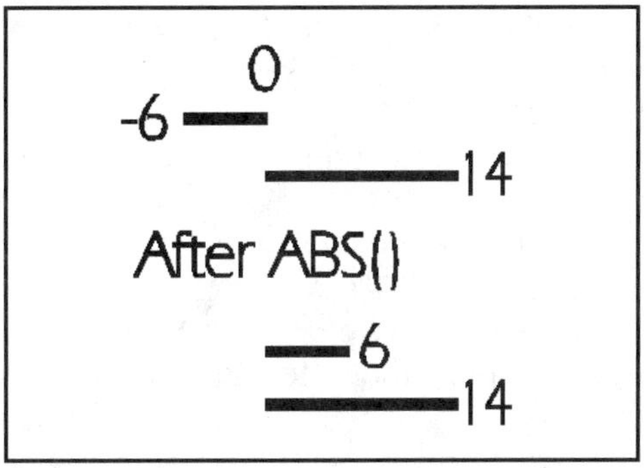

$$-6 \xrightarrow{\quad 0 \quad} \underline{\qquad\qquad} 14$$

After ABS()

$$\underline{\qquad} 6 \underline{\qquad} 14$$

Figure A-1: Abs changes any negative number into a positive number, but leaves positive numbers unchanged.

Variables   **Variable type:** Numeric expression

    x = –12
    Abs (x)

Uses   • The only time you'll need to use Abs is when you want to find out the difference between two numbers but don't know which is the smaller number (in other words, which to subtract from the other). For example, your program is running and you don't know the current numbers in the Variables Payment and Cost. To find out the difference between them, you would program the following:

    Difference = Abs(Payment – Cost)

   If Payment = 17 and Cost = 14, then Difference = Abs(Cost – Payment) would result in Difference having a value of 3. (Without the Abs, the results wouldn't be the same in both versions because subtracting the larger from the smaller number would give you a negative number.)

Example   X = –12: Y = 14
    ?Abs(X), Abs(Y)

Results in   12   14

A . . . **57**

$\bigwedge$CTIVATE, $\bigcap$EACTIVATE  EVENT

Description   The Activate Event is triggered when a Form (window) in your program gets the *focus* (becomes the "active window"). The Deactivate Event occurs when an active window loses the focus to another Form (this other Form's Activate Event is then triggered). Activate and Deactivate only work among the Forms in a VB program, not between the VB program and other Windows programs.

     The window with the focus is the one that will respond to keypresses. The Title Bar of the active window is also a different color from the Title Bars of all inactive windows.

     In Windows, only one window at a time is active, meaning it is the window that can accept information from the user's keyboard or movements of the mouse. The user can change the focus to a different window by clicking on it or by pressing ALT+ESC, ALT+F4, ALT+TAB, CTRL+F4 or CTRL+TAB (shortcut keys for maneuvering between active Windows applications or between child windows within a multiple-window application [MDI]).

     Your program can also shift the focus—making a new window the active one—by invoking the Load, Show or SetFocus command. The Deactivate Event is designed to allow you to react when a Form becomes inactive. This paired set of Events—Activate and Deactivate—is similar to other pairs in VB such as GotFocus/LostFocus and Load/UnLoad. The GotFocus/LostFocus commands of a Form do not trigger when another Form gets the focus unless there are no Controls on the Forms. This is the reason for the existence of the Activate/Deactivate Events. GotFocus/LostFocus perform the same job for Controls that Activate/Deactivate do for Forms.

Used with   Forms and Multiple Document Interface (MDI) Forms

Variables

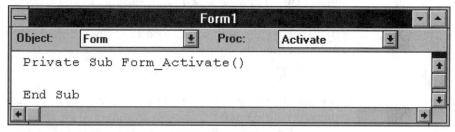

Figure A-2: You put your commands inside the Event, describing how the program should react if the Form is Activated or Deactivated.

Uses
• Use the Activate Event to react when a window gets the focus. For example, several documents can be open in Word for Windows (making it an MDI, Multiple Document Interface, style of window). When you give one of these "child windows" the focus, Word reacts by putting the child window's file name on the main Word Title Bar.

• Use the Deactivate Event to signal the user that the Form has lost focus by disabling (Enabled = 0) all the Controls or otherwise making the Form pale or visually "inactive." Or perform other tasks, such as saving data, in response to the Form's loss of focus.

Cautions
• Activate/Deactivate do not trigger if the focus is moved to or from your VB application and other Windows applications. The Events respond only to shifts in focus between the Forms (windows) of your VB program.

• When used with an MDI Form (see "Multiple Document Interface [MDI]"), the child Forms can trigger only each other's Activate/Deactivate Events. In other words, the parent Form gets triggered if the focus shifts among it and other VB Forms.

Example
Create two Forms, and in each Form's Activate Event, type:

```
Sub Form_Activate ()
    Caption = "ACTIVATED!"
End Sub
```

And in each Form's Deactivate Event, type:

```
Sub Form_Deactivate ()
    Caption = ""
End Sub
```

In Form1's Load Event, type this:

```
Sub Form_Load ()
    Form2.Show
End Sub
```

See also
ActiveControl; Initialize; LostFocus; Multiple Document Interface (MDI) Form; QueryUnload; Screen.ActiveForm; SetFocus; Terminate

ACTIVECONTROL
PROPERTY

Description
ActiveControl is the way to find out (while your program is running) which Control Button, List Box or whatever has the *focus*—in other words, which Control was used last or was most recently tabbed to or clicked on with the mouse.

The Control with the focus is the one affected by certain actions, particularly typing on the keyboard. If you've got two Text Boxes, the one with the focus will display any characters the user types in.

You can also use ActiveControl to find out about or change the Properties of the Control with the focus.

Used with   The Screen Object along with the currently active (focused) Control

Variables   To find out the Caption of the currently active Control:

    X$ = Screen.ActiveControl.Caption

OR (to change the Caption of the currently active Control):

    Screen.ActiveControl.Caption = "New Name"

But this can be risky. See "Cautions."

Uses   There are two ways to know what the user is doing with the mouse (or TAB key) while your program is running: ActiveControl or the more commonly used GotFocus Event (which see).

ActiveControl or GotFocus lets you give programs some degree of artificial intelligence. If there are several Controls on one of your windows (Forms in VB), ActiveControl lets you know which one the user most recently accessed (or which one is active when the program starts or a window is opened).

A More Intelligent Response: Sometimes you might want to make a shortcut for the user. For example, you could make a database program respond more intelligently if you knew which button a user had most recently pressed (Add, Search, Replace, whatever). Your program could react by adding new Command Buttons or Menus, or by displaying appropriate information and options.

Cautions   • An error occurs if you request information that's unavailable. For instance, asking for the Caption Property of a Text Box generates an error, since a Text Box has no Caption Property.

• You cannot access the Name Property of any Control, because that Property is unavailable while a program is running. However, you can use the If TypeOf command to find out which *kind* of Control is active.

To solve the problem raised in the first bullet item:

    If TypeOf Screen.ActiveControl Is CommandButton Then

• You must always use the Screen Object with this:

    Screen.ActiveControl, **not** ActiveControl

Example   Here is a brief example that produces the results in Figure A-3. Into the Form_Click procedure, put this:

```
Sub Form_Click ()
    x$ = screen.activecontrol.text
    Print x$
End Sub
```

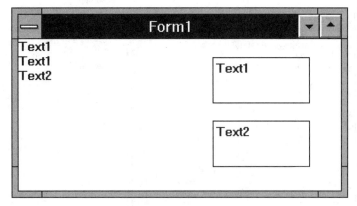

Figure A-3: Find out which Control is active.

Whenever you click on the Form, VB reports to you which of the two Text Boxes has the focus. By clicking on one or the other of the Text Boxes, you change the focus and thus change what x$ reports to you.

Here's an example of finding out the Properties of the active Control. Type this into the Text1_GotFocus Event:

```
Sub Text1GotFocus ()
text2.fontname = "roman"
x$ = screen.activecontrol.fontname
If LCase$(x$) = "helv" Then
    Print "This is Box #1"
Else
    Print "This is Box #2"
End If
Print "The name of its Font is: ";
Print x$
End Sub
```

Note that we put this example into the GotFocus Event of Text1. This creates what seems to be a paradox: if its GotFocus Event is triggered, doesn't that mean that Text1, by definition, has the focus and must be the active Control? Isn't ActiveControl then redundant?

No. Sometimes you'll use the commands in one Event by simply calling that Event (by naming it) from within another Control. Here, our goal is to allow the user to click on either Text Box and get an accurate report. So, rather than repeat all the commands, we simply "call" from the GotFocus Event of Text2. In other words, a click on Text Box #2 will trigger the commands within Text1_GotFocus. (See "Sub" for more on this technique.)

When you click on one of the Text Boxes, you'll get a report of the font used by the (now-active) Control. Clicking *makes* a Control "active." Click on the other Control, and the report changes:

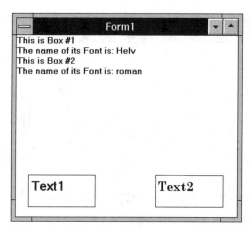

Figure A-4: ActiveControl can report that Control s Properties.

Only One Text Box Can Have the Focus: If you've got several Text Boxes on your screen, the program's user could type into any of them. But, as mentioned earlier, only one of them can be active (have the focus) at one time, and the text will appear in that Text Box. To shift the focus, the user can click on something else with the mouse or use the TAB key (which cycles through all the Controls on the window). The programmer, too, can set the focus, using the SetFocus Method.

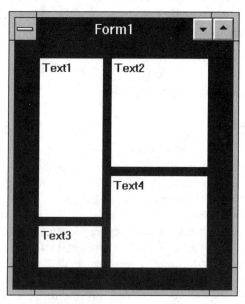

Figure A-5: Only one of these Text Boxes can accept typing   from the user at any given time.

See also   ActiveForm; Index; LostFocus; Me; Objects; Screen; SetFocus

ACTIVEFORM

PROPERTY

Description ActiveForm tells you (while your program is running) which window has the *focus* (that is, which window is currently being used, is currently active). You may never need this command unless you frequently use Modules. (See "Uses.")

In Windows, although several windows might be doing something at once (multitasking), only one window can accept user commands (typing, mouse movements) at a time—the active window, the window that has the focus.

And because in VB nothing will usually be happening in your program unless a window is active, you generally know which is the active window. When you're writing your program, you're writing instructions to be carried out for the window (Form) you're currently programming. So, you wouldn't need to use Screen.ActiveForm to find out which window is active. Also, a VB window won't have the focus unless it has nothing on it— no Controls (or unless all the Controls are disabled).

Used with The Screen Object

Variables To find out which window (which Form) has the focus:

    x$ = Screen.ActiveForm.Caption

OR (to change the caption of the active window):

    Screen.ActiveForm.Caption = "I AM ACTIVE"

Uses • ActiveForm may come in handy if you make frequent use of *Modules.* Modules are similar to Forms, but they never become visible and they have no Events because they have no Controls. Instead, Modules are used as containers for Subroutines or Functions (see "Sub").

A Subroutine in a Module may need to respond differently depending on which Form is "calling" the Subroutine. You might have written a Subroutine that can increase the size of a window. You might want to increase one window more than another, so you'll want to know which window is active when the Subroutine is called. To find out how this works, see "Example" below. (You could also use the Me command, which see.)

Caution You must use the word *Screen* with ActiveForm: Screen.ActiveForm (not just ActiveForm).

Example Create two Forms and a Module (by selecting New Form and New Module from the VB File Menu). Put a Timer on Form1. Then, in Form1's Load Event, type this:

```
Sub Form_Load ()
    form2.Show
    timer1.interval = 5000
End Sub
```

Only Form1 will be visible when the program starts running, so we force Form2 to be visible as well. Then we set the Timer to do its thing every five seconds. All the Timer is going to do is "call" on the Subroutine we called Bigger in Module1:

```
Sub Timer1_Timer ()
    Bigger
End Sub
```

The Subroutine Bigger has the job of widening a window, but it will discriminate between the windows. It will widen Form1 more than Form2—so the Subroutine has to know which of the two windows is currently active when it is "called" by the Timer. Type this into Module1:

```
Sub Bigger ()
If LCase$(screen.activeform.caption) = "form1" Then
    form1.width = 4000
Else
    form2.width = 3000
End If
End Sub
```

We use LCase$ to force the caption we're testing to all lowercase letters. If you aren't sure about the case of a text Variable, it's common practice to force it into lowercase so that capitalization can be ignored when two text items are being compared. (For an alternative approach, see "StrComp.")

When this program is run, the Sub learns which Form to widen based on the ActiveForm.Caption.

See also   ActiveControl; Me; Objects; Screen

ADD, REMOVE .... METHOD

Description   Add puts a new "member" into a Collection "object." Remove takes a member out of a Collection.

Consider using Collections (which see) instead of the traditional arrays. Collections behave like mini-databases. You can add and remove items from them rather easily, and there are several parameters you can use with Add— a Collection is more flexible than an Array. What's more, you can mix different data types (see "Variables") within a Collection. Arrays require some rather cumbersome programming if you need to change or edit any of the elements (members) of the Array.

To a Collection, you can *Add* or *Remove* Objects or Forms—almost anything (except Controls). Or you can just create a Collection of pieces of data, as you would have done with an Array.

Used with   Almost any kind of Object or data. Technically, you use Add to make a new member of a "Collection Object."

Variables   **For Add:**

```
Object.Add Item, [Key], [Before], [After]
```

Key, Before and After are all optional arguments. *Object* here is the name of your Collection.

Key: You can provide an associated key when you add a member to a collection. This key (a text "string" variable) could be used instead of the numeric index to identify a particular member:

```
Dim MyNames As New Collection
Private Sub Form   Load( )
Show
For I = 1 To 20
    MyNames.Add "Name" & I, "Key#" & I
Next I
Print MyNames(3)
Print MyNames("Key#12")
End Sub
```

OR you can use *named arguments* (which see) instead of separating the arguments by commas:

```
Dim MyNames As New Collection
Private Sub Form   Load( )
Show
For I = 1 To 20
    MyNames.Add Item:="Name" & I, Key:="Key#" & I
Next I
Print MyNames(3)
Print MyNames("Key#12")
End Sub
```

The virtue of named arguments (aside from the clarity they lend to your programs when you try to read them) is that you can mix and match parameters, moving the arguments around any way you want. Because the arguments are named (identified), VB can accept them in any order. And you don't have to do the old comma repetition technique to place a parameter in its proper location if you want to use the default parameters for the rest of the arguments: Circle (10,12),1222, , , 144. This switching of parameters would work equally well as the above example:

```
MyNames Add Key:="Key#" & I, item:A$
```

Before: This allows you to specify *where* within the Collection you want to Add or Remove a member. The member just before the Before identifier is added or removed. It can be a number or numeric expression (which must be between 1 and the total members—the Collection's Count Property acts like an Array's Ubound Function). Alternatively, you can use a text "string" variable here, to match the *key* of the member.

```
Dim Mynames As New Collection
Private Sub Form   Load( )
Show
For I = 1 To 20
    Mynames.Add "Name" & I, "Key#" & I
Next I
Mynames.Add Item:="THIS IS A NEW ONE INSERTED", Before:=12
For Each whatever In Mynames
    Print whatever
Next
End Sub
```

After: Same as Before, but the member immediately following the After identifier is added or removed.

For Remove:

```
Object.Remove index
```

The index can be a number (like the index number for a traditional Array) or an expression that evaluates to a number. Alternatively, it can be a text "string" variable (or literal, like "This Item"). However, if you use a text expression, it must correspond to a Key created via the Add command. Note that you cannot supply a piece of actual text that appears within the Collection itself as a member (element).

```
Dim Mynames As New Collection
Sub Form Load( )
Show
For I = 1 To 10
    Mynames.Add "Name" & I, "Key#" & I
Next I
Mynames.Remove (3)
For Each whatever In Mynames
    Print   whatever
Next
End Sub
```

To remove *all* the elements of a Collection, you can do this:

```
For X = 1 To Mynames.Count
    Mynames.Remove 1
Next
```

OR

```
For Each Thing In Mynames
    Mynames.Remove 1
Next
```

The reason for removing element #1 each time through this loop is that when you Remove an element, the indexes of other elements in the Collection are adjusted to maintain the accurate count from 1 to the Count Property (the highest index in the Collection). Therefore, to Remove 1 over and over is like repeatedly pulling out the bottom card of a deck until the entire deck is gone.

Uses   Where you might have previously used an Array, consider using a Collection object, to which you can conveniently add or remove one of the members of that collection.

Cautions   • You cannot (at this time) make a Collection out of Controls. This differs from VBA in Excel. Once you place a Control (such as a Picture Box) onto a worksheet (Excel's equivalent of VB's Form)–an *implicit* Collection of Picture Boxes is created. You don't have to define this collection (Dim MyCol As New Collection). It already exists, and you can Add to it or Remove from it freely.

In VB, the only way to dynamically add a Control, or to group Controls and treat them as an Array, is to use the Load command (which see) to create a Control Array (which see). A Control can be removed from a Control Array by changing its Name Property, but this cannot be done while a program is running (only in the Properties Window during program design). In this and other ways, a Control Array is less flexible than a Control Collection would be, but as yet, this facility isn't available in VB. A Control Array resembles a traditional Array more than it does a Collection.

• Every Collection has a Count Property which you can use to determine the total number of items (elements) in the Collection. This is the same as the ListCount Property of a ListBox. However, you can use the For Each...Next structure (which see) and let VB worry about the number of elements in your Collection.

• Note that the index used to identify an element for the Remove command doesn't use parentheses, as would an Array's index number.

Example   In VB4, each Control has a default Property (its "Value" is the technical term). It's the most commonly used Property with that particular Control (and the one that's highlighted in the Properties Window when you click on the Control). For instance, the default for a Text Box is the Text Property; for a Command Button, it's the Caption; for a Shape, the Shape Property. The use of this in programming is that when you're working with a Control's default Property; you don't have to specify the Property in your programming.

A ... **67**

```
Text1.Text = "David"
```

is the equivalent of:

```
Text1 = "David"
```

A Collection "object" has three Methods: Add, Remove and *Item*. Interestingly, it also has a default Method, the Item. So, you need never specifically type in the word *Item*, though you can. Here's an example using both Things.Item and Things:

```
Dim Things As New Collection
Private Sub Form_Load( )
Show

For I = 1 To 5
    Things.Add "Thing#" & I
Next I

Print Things.Item(3)
Print Things(3)
End Sub
```

See Also: Array; Collections; Control Array; Index; Load

ADDITEM   METHOD

Description   Allows you to add a word or words (a text "string" Variable) to a List Box, Grid or Combo Box while your program is running. For Box Controls, AddItem is extremely useful.

Used with   List or Combo Boxes and Grid Controls

Variables   To add the text in the Variable something$ at the position in the Box specified by the number in the numeric Variable index%:

```
List1.AddItem something$, index%
```

OR (to add the literal text "something" at the end of the list if the Sorted Property of the Box is False, or in the correct alphabetical position within the list if the Box's Sorted Property is True): List1.AddItem something

OR (to add an item to a Combo Box): Combo1.AddItem something$, index%

Uses   Provide the user with selections to choose from; add new items to selection Boxes; or allow the user to add or remove items (see "RemoveItem").

Cautions   • An Index% is optional. If you specify an Index%, then your something$ is placed at the Index% you specify (overriding the Sorted Property that keeps the items in alphabetical order). The first item in a list is Index% 0. So, if you want to place your Something$ as the second item in the box:

```
List1.AddItem Something$, 1
```

OR (to use a numeric Variable instead of a literal number):

```
ind% = 1
List1.AddItem Something$,ind%
```

• The text you provide to AddItem will be inserted into the correct alphabetic order if the Sorted Property of the box is True. The text will be placed at the end of the list if the Sorted Property is False.

Example This example demonstrates how to allow the user to add items to a List Box by typing them into a Text Box. Put a List Box and a Text Box on a Form. Use the Properties Window to set the List Box's Sorted Property to "True." (Sorted cannot be adjusted while a program is running.)

In the Text Box's KeyPress Event, we'll react when the user presses the ENTER key (code 13, see "Chr$"):

```
Sub Text1_KeyPress (keyascii As Integer)
If keyascii = 13 Then
    list1.AddItem  text1.text
    text1.text = ""
End If
End Sub
```

We add the item to the List Box, then empty the Text Property of the Text Box, readying it for any additional items the user may wish to type in.

See also RemoveItem

 LIGN

PROPERTY

Description Use Align to create a Toolbar (a row of icons across the top of a window) or a Status Bar (a thin band of information across the bottom of a window). A normal Picture Box (Align = 0) can be placed by the programmer anywhere on a Form; it can be any size desired. A Picture Box with its Align Property set to 1 or 2 will be automatically stretched to the exact ScaleWidth of the host Form and will be moved to the top (1) or bottom (2) of the Form.

Used with Picture Boxes or Data Controls

A . . . **69**

Variables **Variable type:** Integer

You can set Align in the Properties Window.

OR (to set Align while a program is running):

```
Picture2.Align = 2
```

There are three possible states for the Align Property:

0 The default for a normal (non-MDI) Form. You can make the Picture's position on the Form and its size whatever you want.

1 The default for an MDI Form (see "Multiple Document Interface (MDI)"). The Picture Box or Data Control appears against the top of the Form (like a Toolbar) and automatically becomes the same width as the ScaleWidth of the Form.

2 The Picture Box or Data Control appears against the bottom of the Form (like a Status Bar) and automatically becomes the same width as the ScaleWidth of the Form.

Uses   • Create a Toolbar (a set of icons lined up across the top of a window like those in the VB design environment).

• Create a Status Bar, with information about the currently opened file, the current page number in a word processing application, etc.

• If you set more than one Picture Box's Align Property to the same option (for instance, Picture1.Align = 2:Picture2.Align = 2), they will stack themselves against the top or bottom of the Form. In this way you can create multiple Toolbars (as there are in Word for Windows).

Cautions   • Put a Data Control's Scroll Bar beyond the reach of any maximized child window (the Data Control won't be covered up).

   In effect, Picture Boxes or Data Controls placed on MDI Forms extend the virtual border of the MDI Form. In practical terms, this means that even if the user maximizes or moves child windows within the MDI Form, the windows can never cover the Picture Boxes or Data Controls.

Example

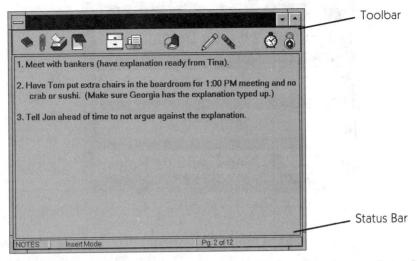

Toolbar

Status Bar

Figure A-6: Two Picture Boxes one serving as a Toolbar, the other as a Status Bar.

To create a Toolbar, using the Image Control is the best choice. Place as many Images on the Picture Box as you wish, then fill each with an .ICO by adjusting the Image's Picture Property. We gave the Form a more professional look by creating shaded lines between the Text Box and the Status Bar, as well as two small vertical lines within the Status Bar itself to divide the fields (see "Line Control" for more on this technique).

See also   Data Control; Line Control; Multiple Document Interface (MDI) Form; NegotiateToolbars; Picture Box

ALIGNMENT

PROPERTY

Description   The Alignment Property governs whether the text in a Label, DBGrid or Text Box is flush left (the default), flush right or centered within the Box. For Option Buttons and Check Boxes, it governs whether the button and box symbols align on the left or the right in the Box.

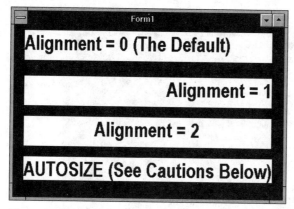

Figure A-7: Left-justify, right-justify and center Alignment Property options.

The Alignment Property allows you to control the placement of text in some Controls to achieve the look you want. If you don't adjust the Alignment, Visual Basic sets this Property to 0.

The Alignment Property also can tell you how the text is aligned while your program is running.

Used with   Check Boxes, DBGrids, Labels, Option Buttons and Text Boxes

Variables   **Variable type:** Integer (Enumerated)

You can set the alignment of a Label by adjusting the Properties Window while you're designing your program.

OR (to make the text buttons or boxes in Option Buttons or Check Boxes left-justified): alignment = 0

OR (to make the text buttons or boxes in Option Buttons or Check Boxes right-justified): alignment = 1

OR (to center the text in a Label while the program is running):
alignment = 2

OR (to find out the alignment of a Label while the program is running):
x = label1.alignment

Uses   • Reformat the text in a Label (only a Label's alignment can be changed while a program is running).

• Create a more pleasing display.

• Control precisely where your text will appear on a window, no matter what typeface or type size is used.

For example, set Alignment to center the text within a Label Box you create. Make that Label Box the same size as a Picture Box. Then any text of any size that's entered in the Label will be perfectly centered relative to the picture. If the text changes while the program runs, the new text will be centered as well.

Cautions • Caption text in a Label may be chopped off or appear asymmetrical and ragged. To solve the problems of truncated or unsightly Label text, you can adjust the size of the Label and the Caption text while designing your program. But what if text will be assigned to the Caption while the program is running? You may not know the amount of text that might be assigned, or the text lengths that should be accommodated, since the Label will change as circumstances warrant.

One solution is to use the AutoSize Property. If you set AutoSize to True (−1), the text in a Label will be on a single line and the Label will stretch to accommodate the amount of text (the Caption Property). (If you want two lines of text, you can create a second Label and place it under the first.) However, with AutoSize set to False (0), a Label Box's text may not fit the size of the Box, in which case it will wrap down to the next line and be cut off *vertically*. (See Figure A-8.) Using the AutoSize Property can solve this problem, but then the Alignment Property's effect will be nullified.

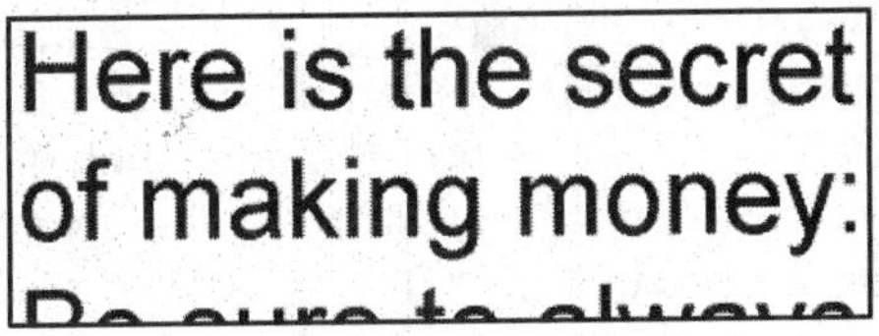

Here is the secret of making money:

Figure A-8: AutoSize prevents sheared-off text like this.

If you want Labels that will preserve the integrity of varying amounts of text while a program runs, the best solution is to make your Label Box large enough to hold the largest message you're likely to need. Then leave AutoSize off (set at 0) and Alignment set to center the text.

• A Label can contain a maximum of 255 characters per line.

Example   label1.alignment = label2.alignment

Results in   Both labels will be aligned the same way.

See also   AutoSize

PP

OBJECT

Description   App, short for *application*, refers to the program itself—the currently running application. It is used to identify qualities about the program, much the way the word *screen* (for Screen "Object") is used by a program to find out qualities of the user's monitor.

   You attach App to one of its Properties with a period (.), the way you attach a Form's name to a Control to identify it (Form1.Command1).

Used with   App is used with its Properties: EXEName, HelpFile, Path, PrevInstance, StartMode, Title.

Variables   App returns a text ("string") Variable describing an aspect of a running program. You must use App while the program is running, and you can only query it; you cannot use App to change the Path, Name, etc., of the program.

   To find out where the user has saved your program on disk:

        X$ = App.Path

Uses   • **App.EXEName** tells you the name of the running program (in case the user renamed it). EXEName provides information required by some API Routines (see Appendix A). Also, some programmers include a self-modifying section within a program for security, password or shareware-registration purposes (see the Example under "MkDir").

   • **App.Path** tells you the disk path of the program. This is useful if you want to store data in the same directory as the program, or you want to have your program self-modify and therefore need to save the .EXE program while it's running (thereby replacing the original version).

   • **App.HelpFile** identifies the filename of a Help file if you have created one to go with your program. The VB Professional Edition includes a Help file construction program to build Help files. If you have a file and identify it with App.HelpFile = C:\MYDIR\MYFILNM, then whenever the user presses F1, your Help file will become visible. (Also see "HelpContextID.")

   • **App.PrevInstance** tells your program if the user has other "instances" of the same program currently running. Some programs permit you to run several copies of the program at the same time. For example, a graphics file viewer might allow you to click repeatedly on its icon in Program Manager— launching it over and over so you could view and compare different images in each "instance" of the program. Word for Windows, however, refuses to share its resources with a second "instance" of itself. If you want your program to refuse to have more than one copy running at a time, put the following in the Startup Form's Load Event:

        If App.PrevInstance Then MsgBox ("This program is already running"):End

• **App.StartMode** tells your running program whether it was started as a normal, self-sufficient Windows program, or as the object ("server") of OLE Automation (which see):

```
If App.StartMode = 0 Then Print "StandAlone"
If App.StartMode = 1 Then Print "OLE Server"
```

You can also *change* (set) this Property, for debugging purposes, but it doesn't appear in the Properties Window and can't be adjusted while the program is running. You must change it in the Tools Menu, Project Options window. When you do set the Property to "Object Application," you can debug it as if it had been started by an OLE Automation *controller* program.

• **App.Title** identifies the program's "title," the name that appears in Windows's Task Manager to refer to your program. You can change this Property while your program is running, but it will not remain a permanent change once the program is exited. You can also assign the Title in the Make EXE File dialog box in VB's File Menu.

Cautions   All App Properties use text ("string") Variables except PrevInstance and StartMode, which are Boolean (True/False –1 or 0) integers.

Example   Create a New Project in the Files Menu. In the Form_Click Event, type:

```
Sub Form_Click ()
    Print    "Exename: "; App.EXEName
    Print    "Path: "; App.Path
    Print    "HelpFile: "; App.HelpFile
    Print    "PrevInstance: "; App.PrevInstance
    Print    "Title: "; App.Title
End Sub
```

Results in   Exename: Project1
Path: C:\VB
HelpFile:
PrevInstance: 0
Title: Project1

See also   EXEName; HelpFile; OLE Automation; Path; PrevInstance; Title

STATEMENT

Description AppActivate sets the focus to another application—not to another window within your Visual Basic program. You provide the name of the target application (the name that appears in the Title Bar of the application you want). You must spell the name exactly as it appears in the Title Bar, but you can use either uppercase or lowercase letters; AppActivate is not "case-sensitive."

Variables To use a text Variable to activate a program:

    AppActivate Formcaption$

OR (to use literal text to activate a program):

    AppActivate "Notepad"

Uses • AppActivate is useful for moving between applications. For example, you could design a Form that allows a user to choose applications from a menu or set of icons—something like Task Manager or Program Manager but much more customizable. In general, though, the Shell command is probably more useful than AppActivate since it doesn't require, as AppActivate does, that an application already be loaded and running.

The SendKeys command (which see) fools Windows into thinking something is being typed on the keyboard. It can be used to feed some initial commands to an application that was AppActivated or Shelled.

Cautions • AppActivate does not change the application's state (minimized or maximized). Use SendKeys (which see) to accomplish that.

OR (to wait until your program has the focus before activating):

    Appactivate "Notepad" True

• Nor does AppActivate load an application not already active in Windows (use Shell instead).

• If an application isn't available when you try to AppActivate it, you'll get an "Illegal Function Call" error message. Use error trapping (see "On Error").

• If you've got more than one application running with the same title (such as two Notepads), Windows selects the one to give focus to.

• The name you provide AppActivate must exactly match the title (the "caption" on top of the application's main window):

Right: visual basic help v b.hlp

Wrong: visual basic help

Example   Sub Form Click ()
                   AppActivate "norton desktop"
                 End Sub

Results in   Norton Desktop comes out from behind anything that was hiding it, lights
                 up with the "active window" color on its Title Bar, and is available for input
                 from the user. It "gets the focus" and becomes the application that re-
                 sponds to anything the user types in on the keyboard.

See also   Load; SendKeys; SetFocus; Shell; Show; Title

 PPEARANCE

PROPERTY

Description In VB4 there is a new Property for Forms, and all the core Controls in VB
                 (Command Button, List Box, TextBox, PictureBox—the first 16 Controls on
                 your Toolbox with the exception, for some reason, of ScrollBars). Hap-
                 pily, this new feature, Appearance, defaults to True. It adds *dimension* to
                 your VB program.

                 If Windows was a leap forward from DOS because Windows was visually
                 rich, then Windows 95 among other things improves on Windows 3.1 by
                 adding many subtle improvements to the graphic surface. Primary among
                 these improvements is the 3D *sculpted* quality of Forms, Controls and other
                 elements of the user interface. Now, VB4 (32-bit version only) adds all this
                 by default. You can, of course, set the Appearance Property to False—but
                 why would you?

                 Some of the effects will not be visible unless the Form's BackColor is light
                 gray, (HC0C0C0&). It changes Picture Box BackColor to light gray, too. You
                 can change these BackColors, but you'll loose the effect of 3D bordering.

                 For years VB programmers have been using SSPanels and other tricks to
                 create this sculpted look (see "Line" for a whole slew of tricks). Now,
                 though, you can achieve many subtle but important visual effects merely by
                 leaving the Appearance Property set to its default True.

                 Appearance does several desirable things. Since VB version 1, the Com-
                 mand Button has been the handsomest of all the Controls. The reason is
                 that it always looked *sculpted;* it was always realistic-looking (3D) compared
                 to the other Controls. Soon after VB 1.0 was launched, Sheridan Software
                 Systems started selling an aftermarket product called THREED.VBX which
                 provided several great-looking three-dimensional Controls: Check Box,
                 Option Button, Frame, enhanced Command Button (it could also be loaded
                 with a .BMP image), Panel (great for framing other Controls), and a "Group
                 Push Button." Microsoft since absorbed THREED into VB itself and you'll

find it in the Professional Edition of VB as the set of "SS" (Sheridan Software) Controls. However, most VB Controls remained flat and crude looking.

A dimensional Control significantly improves the appearance of your Forms. It adds highlights and shadows to a Control, giving it visual depth. It makes some Controls (like the Command Button) seem to rise out of the background, and others (like a Text or Picture Box) seem to sink into it.

Used with   Forms, MDI Forms, the core VB Controls

Variables   The Appearance Property can only be changed while you're designing your program; it cannot be changed while the program is running. Click on the Property in the Properties Window.

Uses   Make your Forms look more professional and visually appealing.

Cautions   • There is a new Windows 95 shape for the Option Button—it changes from the older-style diamond to a new circular shape. Also, the Check Box's inner symbol changes from a ✖ to a ✔. You can expect all new Windows applications to follow these new conventions. This is another reason to always leave Auto3D to True for all your Forms as you and your programs' users migrate rapidly to Windows 95.

• Although it has this Property, the Image Control is unaffected by it.

Examples

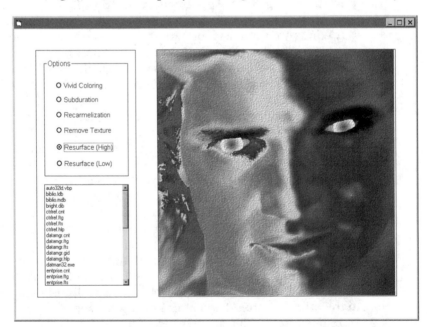

Figure A-9: BEFORE: Without Auto3D, notice the flat appearance of the various Controls.

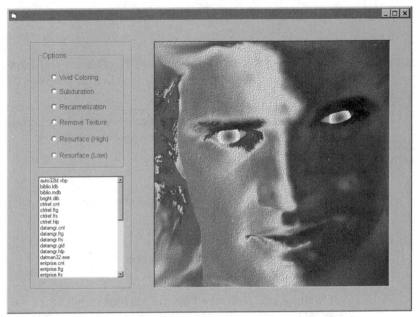

Figure A-10: AFTER: Turn Auto3D on and the Controls gain depth.

See also　Line

RCHIVE

PROPERTY

Hidden, Normal, ReadOnly, System

Description　This is a switch that is normally set to –1 (on) by Visual Basic unless you deliberately change it. This Property permits or forbids the user to see the names of archived files within a File List Box. ("Archive" here means that a file has been changed since it was last backed up.)

The Archive Property is one of a group of file "attributes" that also includes Hidden, Normal, ReadOnly and System. Any or all of these file types can be permitted to be listed or concealed—either while you are designing a program or while the program is running.

Used with　File List Boxes

Variables　**Variable type:** Boolean

To permit archive files to be listed in a File List Box—this is the VB default:

```
File1.archive = True
```

OR (to exclude listing of archive files in a File List Box):

```
File1.archive = False
```

Cautions There is also a ReadOnly Property of Text Boxes and Data Controls. In those Controls, ReadOnly determines whether the user can edit the Control's contents.

Uses • If you want to see a list of files that need to be backed up (because they've been modified), try the example that follows.

Example Put a File List Box on a Form.

```
Sub Form_Click ()
file1.hidden = 0      'refuse to show any of these file types
file1.normal = 0
file1.readonly = 0
file1.system = 0
file1.archive = —1 'allow archive files to show
End Sub
```

Assuming you've backed up the current directory (a backup program will reset all backed-up files' archive attributes to show they've been backed up), then only files altered since the backup will appear in your File List Box when you test this example.

See also File List Box; FileAttr; GetAttr; Path; Pattern; SetAttr

ARRANGE

See Multiple Document Interface (MDI) form

 RRAY

FUNCTION

Description The Array command creates a strange (at least in terms of traditional programming) kind of Variable—a Variant that contains an interior "list" of separate, indexed items of data. It's sort of like a quick, crypto Array. This new Array Function behaves like the DATA...READ commands found in traditional versions of Basic (like QuickBasic) but never allowed into VB.

Used with   Real Arrays or Collections (which see), to fill them with some reasonably small quantity of items of data.

Variables   The Array command can be used to establish an initial set of data items within an Array.

The Array function is similar to this traditional Array:

```
Dim ThisArray (1 to 5) As Variant
    ThisArray(3) = "Susan"
Debug.Print ThisArray(3)
```

Results in   Susan

However, when you use the Array command, you can *change* the elements in the Array, like this:

```
Sub DoChange( )
    Dim vArray As Variant
    vArray = Array(5,10,15, 20,25,30)
    MsgBox vArray(0)
    vArray(0) = 6
    MsgBox vArray(0)
End Sub
```

And you can access the individual items, or "read them," for display, for information that your program needs or for other purposes.

The abandoned DATA...READ commands were less flexible than the new Array Function (Array can change individual items while the program is running, but DATA couldn't). However, the most likely use for the Array Function is the same as DATA...READ was used for in early (pre-VB) versions of Basic. In earlier versions of Basic, you could insert a (usually brief) list of information into your program this way (remember, they used line numbers in those days):

```
10 DATA ones, tens, hundreds, thousands, millions
20 DIM NUMBERS(4)
30 FOR I = 0 to 4
40 READ NUMBERS(I)
50 NEXT I
60 PRINT  NUMBERS(2)
```

Results in   hundreds

You typed in some pieces of data into your program following the DATA command. Then you used the READ command to fill an Array with that data when the program ran. This was useful for such things as the days of the week, months of the year and other small lists of data.

When DATA and READ were jerked out of Basic with the arrival in 1991 of Visual Basic 1.0, some people complained. The answer was that you should individually assign Variables (the program would run marginally faster, it was said):

```
Numbers(0) = "ones"
Numbers(1) = "tens"
Numbers(2) = "hundreds"
Numbers(3) = "thousands"
Numbers(4) = "millions"
```

As you can see, DATA...READ was easier on the programmer–there was less typing.

Now with VB4, DATA...READ is back, in disguise, and in an improved, high-efficiency format: The Array Function. Now you can do the same kind of thing with the Array Function:

```
Private Sub Form  Load( )
Show
Numbers = Array("ones", "tens", "hundreds", "thousands", "millions")
Print Numbers(3)
End Sub
```

Results in thousands

(If you thought this result should be *hundreds*, see "Cautions" below.)

Uses When you want to fill an array with a reasonably small amount of data, use the Array Method. This way, you don't have to bother opening a disk file and bringing in the data from there (as you would with an .INI file, for example). Nor do you have to repeatedly and explicitly assign values to each element in your Array (as you did in VB, pre-VB4).

Cautions • Remember that Arrays, including, alas, the Array Function, default to a zeroth item. This zeroth curiosity means that "ones" is Numbers(0) and "tens" is Numbers(1), and so on, in our example.

In the above example, you'll find that printing Numbers(3) results in "thousands." To avoid this absurd arrangement in your programs, you can force all arrays to start with element #1 by inserting this command at the "module level" (not inside any Sub or Function):

```
Option Base 1
```

Example
```
Option Base 1
Sub Testit( )
Numbers = Array("ones", "tens", "hundreds", "thousands", "millions")
Print Numbers(3)
End Sub
```

Results in hundreds

See also Arrays; Collections; Option Base

ARRAYS

Description

Arrays are Variables that have been clustered together. Once inside an Array structure, the Variables share the same text name and are identified by an *index number*. Since numbers can be manipulated mathematically (and text names cannot), putting a group of Variables into an Array allows you to easily and efficiently work with the entire group. You can manipulate the elements (the items) in the Array by using Loops such as For...Next and Do...Loop structures.

Arrays are used in computer programming for the same reason ZIP Codes are used by the U.S. Postal Service. Picture hundreds of postal boxes with only unalphabetized, unorganized text labels. Imagine the nightmare of sorting thousands of letters each day into boxes that are not in some way indexed and numerically ordered.

However, in VB4 there is a new, interesting alternative to traditional Arrays—see "Collections."

Numbers vs. Names: Arrays are extremely useful. For example, if we want to manipulate the names of people coming to dinner this weekend, we can create an Array of their names: Dim Guest (1 To 5) As String. This creates five "empty boxes" in the computer's memory, which serve as spaces for text ("string") Variables. However, instead of five unique individual labels for the five Variables, the Variables in this cluster share the label Guest$, and each box is identified by a unique index number from 1 to 5.

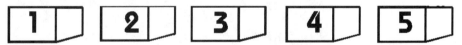

Figure A-11: An empty Array.

To fill this Array with the names of the guests, we assign the names just as we would to normal Variables but use the index number. (You can tell an Array from a regular Variable because Arrays always have parentheses following the Array name.) We'll put the names into the Array:

```
Guest$(1) = "Lois"
Guest$(2)= "Sandy"
Guest$(3)= "Rick"
Guest$(4)= "Jim"
Guest$(5) = "Mom"
```

Now the "boxes" somewhere in the computer's memory have been filled with information:

Figure A-12: The Array now has data.

The process of filling an Array can be accomplished in several ways: by having the user type in the Array items, by reading the data in from a disk file or, as we did, by directly filling the Array with pieces of information.

Now that we have the Array filled, we can manipulate it in many ways, much more efficiently than if we were using ordinary Variables. What if we wanted to know if a particular name existed in the Array?

```
For I = 1 To 5
    If      Guest$(I) = "Rick" Then Print "Rick has been invited."
Next I
```

The key to the utility of Arrays is that you can search them, sort them, delete or add to them *using numbers* instead of text to identify each item. Index numbers are much easier to access and manipulate than text labels.

Why Arrays Are Efficient: As an example, how would you figure your average electric bill for the year? You could go the cumbersome route, using an individual Variable for each month:

```
JanElect   = 90
FebElect   = 122
MarElect   = 125
AprElect   = 78
MayElect   = 144
JneElect   = 89
JulyElect  = 90
AugElect = 140
SeptElect = 167
OctElect = 123
NovElect = 133
DecElect = 125

YearElectBill = JanElect+FebElect+MarElect+AprElect+MayElect+
JneElect+JulyElect+AugElect+SeptElect+OctElect+ NovElect+DecElect
```

OR you could use an Array to simplify the process:

```
Dim MonthElectBill(1 To 12)

MonthElectBill(1) = 90
MonthElectBill(2) = 122
MonthElectBill(3) = 125
MonthElectBill(4) = 78
MonthElectBill(5) = 144
MonthElectBill(6) = 89
```

```
MonthElectBill(7) = 90
MonthElectBill(8) = 140
MonthElectBill(9) = 167
MonthElectBill(10) = 123
MonthElectBill(11) = 133
MonthElectBill(12) = 125

For I = 1 to 12
Total = Total + MonthElectBill(I)
Next I
```

By grouping all the Variables under the same name, you can manipulate the Variables by individual index number. This might look like a small saving of effort, but remember that your program will probably have to use these Variables in many situations. And you'll have to save them to disk. If they're in an Array, you can save them like this:

```
For I = 1 to 12
Print #1, MonthElectBill(I)
Next I
```

If they're not in an Array, you need to do this:

```
Print #1, JanElect
Print #1, FebElect
Print #1, MarElect
Print #1, AprElect
Print #1, MayElect
Print #1, JneElect
Print #1, JulyElect
Print #1, AugElect
Print #1, SeptElect
Print #1, OctElect
Print #1, NovElect
Print #1, DecElect
```

Unless you have put these variables into an Array, you'll have to access each by its text name every time you deal with this group.

Variables
Arrays can be created by using one of four Array-making commands: Global, Dim, ReDim or Static. (See "Uses" and "Cautions" for more about using these commands.) Each command defines a *range of influence* or *scope* (which sections of your program can access the Array).

However, all four of these commands create Arrays in the same way: by "dimensioning" the new Array. This means that the computer is told how much space to set aside for the new Array. We'll use the Global command in the examples below, but the Dim, ReDim and Static commands would follow the same rules.

To create space for 51 text Variables that share the label Name$ and are uniquely identified by an index number ranging from 0–50, type the following in a Module: Global Names$(50)

OR (to create a *multidimensional Array*):

Multidimensional Arrays: The following example will be an Array with twelve "rows" and three "columns." This is a way to associate related information, such as names—each with an address and phone number Variable associated with it. VB allows you to create as many as 60 dimensions for a single Array! But few people can visualize, or effectively work with, more than two or three dimensions. That makes sense. We live in a four-dimensional world, but even the fourth dimension, time, is hard to integrate mentally with the other three.

A two-dimensional Array is like a graph, a crossword puzzle or a spreadsheet—cells of information related in an X,Y coordinate system. A three-dimensional Array is like a honeycomb—it has not only height and width; it also has *depth*.

Most of us check out at this point. A four-dimensional Array cannot be physically constructed, so there is no example of one to study. Go beyond four dimensions and you've gone past physics into an abstract domain that would challenge Leonardo.

To make a two-dimensional Array: Global Names$ (1 To 12, 1 To 3). You would read a two-dimensional Array like this: X$ = Names (6,2) to, for example, find out the address of the sixth person, whose name would be in Names (6,1) and whose address, you decided, would be in Names (6,2).

OR (to define a *dynamic Array*):

Dynamic Arrays: These are handy because they conserve memory. Dynamic Arrays come into existence in your program when they're needed but then go away as soon as you leave the Event, Sub or Function in which they reside. The ReDim Statement is used within an Event, Sub or Function to bring a dynamic Array to life, but you can optionally declare them using Global with empty parentheses: Global Ages ( ) As Integer

(Then, within an Event, you would use ReDim to bring the dynamic Array into existence and to provide its actual size):

```
Sub Form_Click()

ReDim Ages (1 To 100) As Integer

End Sub
```

OR (combine several declarations on one line following a Global, Dim, ReDim or Static command by separating the different Arrays or Variables with commas):

```
Global A, B( ), Counter(22) as Integer, X$, L (–12 To –4)
```

New in VB4
Array Default: Arrays default now to the Variant type unless you specify otherwise. You can therefore mix text, numbers and date/time data within the same Array.

Arrays of Arrays: You can create Arrays of other Arrays. In VB4, you can now assign regular Arrays to a Variant Array. Not only are you thereby creating an *Array of Arrays* but, again, you can mix and match the data types of the various Arrays you assign to the Variant Array:

```
Private Sub Form   Load()
Show

Dim MyFirstArray(4) As String

For I = 1 To 4
    MyFirstArray(I) = Chr$(I + 64) 'put a few letters into the array
Next I
Dim MySecondArray(4) As Integer
For I = 1 To 4
    MySecondArray(I) = I 'put a few numbers into the array
Next I

Dim MyArrayOfArrays(2) As Variant
MyArrayOfArrays(1) = MyFirstArray()
MyArrayOfArrays(2) = MySecondArray()

For I = 1 To 4
    Print MyArrayOfArrays(1)(I);
    Print MyArrayOfArrays(2)(I)
Next I
End Sub
```

Notice the unique double set of parentheses used when accessing an Array of Arrays.

Uses
• When you have a collection of related information—such as the names, telephone numbers, addresses and birthdays of all your friends and relatives—use an Array.

Arrays group Variables under a common name so that they can be identified within a Loop or other structure by accessing their index numbers.

Cautions
• When you first dimension an Array, all the elements of a numeric Array are set to 0, and all elements of a text Array (string Array) are set to empty strings (""). If you want to return an Array to this virgin state (after having used it to hold Variables you no longer need), use the Erase command (which see).

• When you dimension an Array, you must pay attention to the scope (the range of influence) you want the Array to have. If you want an Array to be accessible to the entire program—so it can be looked at or changed from any location—you must use Global instead of Dim. The Global command can be used only in a Module.

If you want the Array to be accessible only from within an individual Form or Module, use the Dim command in the Declarations section of the Form or Module. This makes the Array available to all the Events (Subroutines or Functions) within *that* Form but unavailable to other Forms or Modules.

Use the Static command to declare an Array when you want the Array to retain its Variables but be accessible only within the Event (or Sub or Function) within which the Array is declared. In practice, Static is useful with individual Variables but is less often used with Arrays. (See "Static.")

Use the ReDim command to declare an Array when you want the Array to lose its Variables and be accessible only within the Event (or Sub or Function) within which the Array is declared. (Such an Array is called *local* as opposed to *global*.) This tactic saves space in the computer's memory because the Array is created but then extinguished after the program moves out of the Event. By contrast, the Static command preserves the contents of a local Array—taking up room in the computer's memory while the program runs.

You can't *imply* an Array. Some earlier versions of Basic allow you to imply an Array by just using it, like this:

```
Sub Form_Click
For I = 1 to 8
    A(I) = I
Next I
End Sub
```

This "implicit" use of Arrays is not permitted in VB. VB requires that you formally declare all Arrays using Global (in a Module); or Dim (in Forms' or Modules' General Declarations sections); or ReDim (in Event Procedures, Subs or Functions). However, VB *does* allow implicit Variables.

• You can use Global with the special Type Variable structure. A Type Variable has several features in common with an Array, and you will find Type Variables useful if you work with random-access files. (See "Type.")

• Unless you specify otherwise, an Array will provide index numbers that start from zero rather than 1. You can use the Option Base command (which see) to avoid this, or you can specify that 1 is the first index when you create the Array: Dim X(1 To 35).

The Zeroth Oddity: To a computer, the lowest entity in a group is the *zeroth* entity. Most humans prefer to think of the floors of a building starting at floor one and going up. Except in England, the first floor is the ground floor. But computers have at least this much in common with the British—the first element of a group is the zeroth.

This Array will have 26 elements (26 index numbers) ranging from 0 to 25: That's just the way computers operate: Dim X (25).

To create an Array of 25 elements in which the first element has an index of 1, use Dim X (1 To 25) or use Option Base, which see.

• The ReDim command is somewhat different from Global, Dim and Static (the other commands that create Arrays). ReDim sets aside space in the computer's memory to *temporarily* hold an Array that will have a brief life and then go away. Arrays created with ReDim expand and then collapse, like a mud bubble in the hot pits at Yosemite Park.

ReDim works only within an Event Procedure of a Form, or within a Subroutine or Function of a Module. A ReDimmed Array comes into existence between the Sub...End Sub or the Function...End Function. It cordons off some of the computer's memory to hold an Array, but when that particular Subroutine or Function is finished doing its work, the set-aside memory is released back to the computer for general use.

Arrays that bloom and fade like this within a single procedure are called *dynamic* rather than *static*. Static Arrays, created by using the Global, Dim or Static command, offer permanent storage.

ReDim can create Arrays with a maximum of 60 dimensions. ReDim can be employed to redeclare an Array that has previously been declared using Global or Dim with empty parentheses ( ). Such a Global or Dim command alerts VB that this will be an Array, but doesn't declare the size of the Array (how many elements it should be sized to hold). When you use this approach, *you can ReDim no more than eight dimensions.*

If there is no previous Global or Dim referring to this same Variable (by using the same name to declare it), you can use ReDim to create an Array with as many as 60 dimensions—but who would?

• How often can you ReDim a temporary (dynamic) Array? The number of elements in a ReDimmed Array can be changed at any time:

```
ReDim This$(4)
This$(3) = "Nadia C."
Print This$(3)
ReDim This$(5)
This$(4) = "Thomas R."
```

This is perfectly legal. However, while you can change the number of elements, you *cannot* change the number of dimensions in the Array.

Wrong:
```
ReDim This$(4)
This$(3) = "Nadia C."
Print This$(3)
ReDim This$(5, 2)
This$(3,1) = "Thomas R."
```

That second ReDim attempted to create a two-dimensional Array. The Array had already been declared one-dimensional.

Likewise, you cannot change the Variable type of an Array by ReDimming:

Wrong:
```
ReDim This$(4)
This$(3) = "Nadia C."
Print This$(3)
ReDim This (5) As Integer
```

This$ started out as a text Variable, and you attempted to redeclare it as a numeric "Integer" Variable Type. See "Variables."

See also   Collections; Control Array; Dim; Erase; Global; LBound; Option Base; ReDim; Static; UBound; Variables

 SC

FUNCTION

Description   In computers, the letters of the alphabet are coded into numbers ranging from 0 to 255. Universal standards–the ASCII and ANSI codes–have been adopted. (See "Chr$.") The Asc function tells you which numeric value has been assigned to a particular letter, according to the ANSI character code that's used in Windows.

Asc is no longer of much use to the programmer. It used to be more important before Visual Basic came along to handle the input and output for you.

Used with   Text characters

Variables   To find out the code of a literal text letter:
```
x = Asc("F")
```

OR (lowercase):
```
x = Asc("f")
```

OR (to use a text Variable. If b$ is longer than a single letter, you get the ANSI code of the first letter): x = Asc(b$)

Uses   • One use for the Asc command is as a simple encryption option. The user could save text files that are unreadable unless the password is known. (This isn't a very tough code to crack, but it's more trouble than most people would go to.)

First you decide on the code value; here we used 22, but you could allow the user to enter a password and, for example, use the Asc value of the third letter in the password as your secretcode Variable.

The first Loop in this example picks off each character in a$, the text Variable we're going to encode. Each character is put into x$. Then, we build a new text Variable called encrypt$ by adding each new character after we've distorted it by subtracting our secretcode from the Asc value of the original character.

The second Loop just reverses the process to decode the encrypted text—in this case we *add* the secret code value to each character and build a text Variable called final$.

```
secretcode = 22
a$ = "This is the message."
For i = 1 To Len(a$)
    x$ = Mid$(a$, i, 1)
    encrypt$ = encrypt$ + Chr$(Asc(x$) —secretcode)
Next i
For i = 1 To Len(encrypt$)
    x$ = Mid$(encrypt$, i, 1)
    final$ = final$ + Chr$(Asc(x$) + secretcode)
Next i
Print a$
Print encrypt$
Print final$
```

Results in   This is the message.
>RS]
S]
^RO
WO]]KQo|
This is the message.

Cautions   • x = Asc(b$) If b$ here is longer than a single letter, you get the numeric value of the first letter only.

• c$ =   This creates a text Variable called a "string Variable" (a letter or series of letters). In this example, we are providing an empty set of quotation marks and the result is called a "null string." That means it has no characters in it. If you feed a null string to Asc

```
x = Asc(c$)
```

you'll generate an error when the program is run.

Example   Print Asc("x")

Results in   120

See also   Chr$ (this is the opposite of Asc; Chr$ returns the printable character equivalent of an ASCII code number). Unlike Asc, Chr$ has several uses, particularly to allow you to access and show (or print) characters that are not available from the standard keyboard. Chr$ can also be used to send special configuration codes to the screen or printer.

TN

FUNCTION

Description   Atn gives you the arctangent (the inverse tangent) of a number, a numeric Variable or a numeric Constant. The result is an angle, expressed in radians, of the numeric expression you provided to the Atn command. You can get the arctangent of any type of Variable (Integer, Floating Point, etc.).

Used with   Numeric expressions (see Variables)

Variables
```
Print Atn(x)
F = Atn(.5)
```

Uses   • Advanced mathematics

   If you're working with trigonometry, you'll sometimes need to use the value of pi stored in a Constant or Variable. Here's how to stuff pi into a Variable:
```
p# = 4 * Atn(1)
```

Example
```
z = Atn(3.3)
Print z
```

Results in   1.276562

See also   Cos; Sin; Tan (other trigonometric functions)

UTOREDRAW

PROPERTY

Description   Sometimes a Form or Picture Box will be moved, resized or completely or partially covered onscreen by something else. When this happens, any graphics you've created with VB's Line, Circle or PSet drawing methods can be partially or entirely erased. Text printed (using the Print command) on a Picture Box or Form is affected the same way.

   There are two ways to retain graphics that have been altered by window activity–AutoRedraw and Paint. If you set the AutoRedraw Property on True (-1), Visual Basic will save the graphic in memory and repaint it as necessary. Or you, the programmer, can use the Paint Event to recreate graphics by putting the graphic drawing instructions into the Paint Event.
Conserving Memory: As an alternative to AutoRedraw, if your graphic is very large, you might want to save memory by recreating the graphic or

printed text each time it's needed. You would put your Line, Circle, etc., instructions in the Form or Picture Box Paint Event. A Paint Event automatically happens whenever a Form or Picture Box is moved, resized or uncovered, or the Refresh command is used. Therefore, the graphics instructions you've placed in a Paint Event will happen automatically at the right times. If you take this approach, be sure that the AutoRedraw Property is off (0 or False).

Used with   Forms and Picture Boxes (not available for Image Controls)

Variables   **Variable type:** Integer (Boolean)

You can set the AutoRedraw Property in the Properties Window while designing your program.

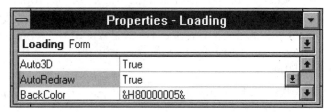

Figure A-13: Any drawn image on this Form will persist.

OR (while the program is running, to cause automatic repainting of a Picture Box): Picture1.AutoRedraw = True

OR (to turn off a Form's automatic redrawing while the program is running): Form1.AutoRedraw = False

OR (to find out the status of the AutoRedraw switch while the program is running): x = AutoRedraw

If x = 0, the Form is not set to do automatic redrawing.
If x = –1, the Form is set to do automatic redrawing.

Uses   • AutoRedraw makes your graphics *persistent* by saving an image of the Picture Box or Form in memory while your program runs. This makes a program start up more slowly; it also uses up memory in the computer while the program runs. The trade-off is that you don't have to worry about other windows erasing part or all of your graphics or printed text (or resizing the window in question).

• AutoRedraw can be made to interact with the Cls command. Review the example under "Cls."

• With AutoRedraw set to True, you can copy drawn or printed graphics between Picture Boxes using the Image Property:

Picture2.Picture=Picture1.Image

Cautions
• Large graphics can use large amounts of memory. A full screen of graphics at high resolution can use one-half to three-quarters of a million bytes! Using AutoRedraw on several Forms can eat up memory quickly.

• If you don't turn on AutoRedraw, put all your programmed graphics (Circle, Line or PSet) and printing (using the Print command) into the Paint Event of a Form or Picture Box.

• Unless you set it, AutoRedraw is not used by VB–the default is no Auto-Redraw.

• AutoRedraw does not need to be used with icons, bitmap pictures (.BMP pictures like those created with paint programs), or .WMF (Windows Meta-file images); bitmap pictures and icons are redrawn by VB automatically and automatically persist. Only graphics created by programming with Line, Circle or PSet and printed text need the AutoRedraw Property.

• When you iconize a Form, if a Form's AutoRedraw is off, ScaleHeight and ScaleWidth are changed to reflect the real size of the icon. However, if AutoRedraw is on, those two Properties stay the size of the window at its "normal" larger size.

Example
Create a solid box by putting the following into the Form_Click Event:

```
Sub Form_Click ()
    Line (400, 400) —(2000, 2000), QBColor(0), BF
End Sub
```

Leave AutoRedraw off. It should look something like this:

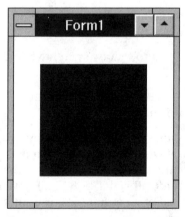

Figure A-14: A newly drawn box.

If you move another window in front of this Form, partly covering the drawn box, it will look like this:

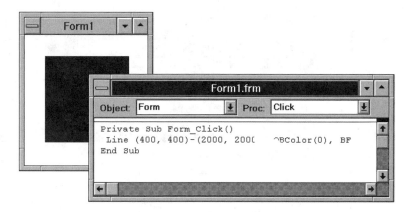

Figure A-15: If the box is partly covered, then the drawing is erased.

When the box is again uncovered, you get this:

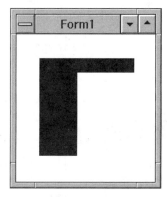

Figure A-16: AutoRedraw prevents this kind of erasure.

A similar problem afflicts text that is printed on a Form or Picture Box:

Figure A-17: Printed text, which is also vulnerable to being covered, can benefit from AutoRedraw.

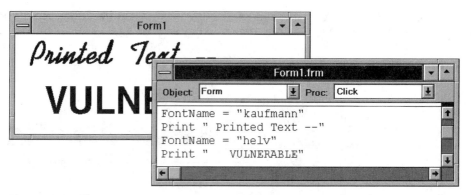

Figure A-18: After being covered . . .

Figure A-19: . . . the text is erased.

Figure A-20: Clipping also happens when a user resizes a window. This text will be clipped if the window is dragged larger.

See also   ClipControls; Image Control and Property; Paint; ReSize

AUTOSHOWCHILDREN
PROPERTY

See   Multiple Document Interface (MDI)

AUTOSIZE
PROPERTY

Description   AutoSize looks at the contents of a Label or Picture Box and makes the border of the item fit the contents. AutoSize defaults to Off.

Used with   Labels, Picture Boxes

Variables   **Variable type:** Integer (Boolean)

To use the Properties Window to set AutoSize while designing your program, do this:

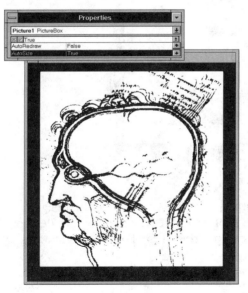

Figure A-21: The Picture Box makes itself only as large as the drawing it contains.

OR (while the program is running, to make the size of a Label fit snug against its text [its Caption]):

    Label1.AutoSize = −1

OR (to make a Picture Box no longer automatically size while the program is running): Picture1.AutoSize = 0

Uses
- Use AutoSize to create neatly formatted borders around pictures and labels.
- When you change pictures or labels dynamically (while your program is running), AutoSize prevents the graphics or text from being partially clipped off. Also, it makes the frames around them look right and doesn't waste space on a window.

Cautions
- When AutoSize is on, the Alignment Property of a Label has no effect.
- If you turn on AutoSize while a program is running, the upper left corner won't move, but everything else around the frame will snap to the size of the contents.

Example
With its AutoSize Property Off (set to 0, the default), this Picture Box is larger than the photo it contains:

Figure A-22: The Picture Box is too large.

To make the Picture Box exactly embrace the image it contains, turn AutoSize On in the Properties Menu while you are designing the program. Alternatively, you can put this in the Form_Load Event:

    Picture1.AutoSize = −1

Figure A-23: Now, with AutoSize on, the Picture Box embraces the photo inside it.

See also   Alignment; Image Control; Stretch (makes an image expand to fill the size of an Image Control)

 ACKCOLOR

PROPERTY

Description BackColor is the background color for an object or Form; it's like colored paper on which text or graphics appear. For a Form, it's the color between the outer border of any Controls and the inner border of the Form (the space on the Form not covered by objects). The printed text or graphics (drawn with the Line, Circle or PSet command) are in the *ForeColor*.

Used with Forms, Check Boxes, Combo Boxes, Command Buttons, Directory, Drive and File List Boxes, Frames, Grids, Labels, List Boxes, OLE Controls, Option Buttons, Picture Boxes, Shapes and Text Boxes

Variables **Variable type:** Long

To adjust the BackColor while designing your program, you can use the Properties Window and the Color Palette:

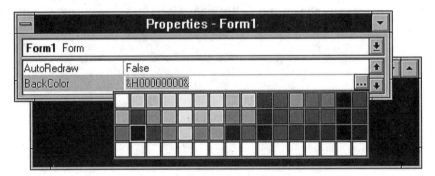

Figure B-1: Use the Color Palette to select the BackColor and to design new colors.

OR (to change the color while your program is running, using the full available range of colors—see "RGB"): BackColor = 8 (This can be a number between 0 and 16,777,215.)

OR (to use the QBColor Function while the program is running, provide a number between 0 and 15): BackColor = QBColor (4)

OR (to find out what color is currently being used):

    X& = [form.][control.]BackColor

(The & means this number can be as large as 16,777,215. See "Variables" for the meaning of numeric Variable symbols.)

Uses   Create pleasing relationships between Forms and Controls; create the color in the background of the window.

Cautions   • If you change the BackColor on a Form or Picture Box *while your program is running*, all text and graphics are erased–even icons or bitmap pictures.

• If you make no changes to BackColor, the colors that have been selected in the Windows Control Panel will be used.

• The range of possible colors in Visual Basic is large. All the colors and hues are there, but it's not a continuum like a rainbow or a color wheel; they're not sequentially arranged from 0 to 17 million. VB and Windows use a scheme that puts *some* shades of orange around 75,000 and other oranges around 33,000. For example, 33,023 is a pumpkin orange and 75,050 is an "olive drab."

• The BackColor Property of *Command Buttons* can seem to have no effect, but it does. Four pixels, in the four corners of the Button, display the Button's BackColor. On many computer monitors, this can result in an odd, unpleasant effect unless you set the Button's BackColor to match the Form or Picture Box on which the Button resides.

Example   When this Form is loaded, we set its BackColor to orange. Then we add 3 to that number to set the BackColor of a Picture Box within the Form to a different shade of orange. However, if we added 20, we'd shift the Picture Box color into green. See "Cautions."

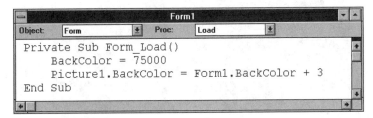

```
Object:  Form              Proc:   Load
Private Sub Form_Load()
    BackColor = 75000
    Picture1.BackColor = Form1.BackColor + 3
End Sub
```

Figure B-2: RGB colors are not numbered in a continuum like a rainbow.

See also   ForeColor; QBColor; RGB

 ACKSTYLE

PROPERTY

Description   The BackStyle determines whether the background area of a Label or Shape Control covers what's behind it (the Form or Picture Box or whatever) or allows whatever is behind to show through.

Used with   Labels, OLE Controls and Shape Controls

B . . . **101**

Variables   You can set the BackStyle Property in the Properties Window.

OR (to set the BackStyle while the program is running, to make the background show through the Label): Label1.BackStyle = 0

OR (to make the Label cover the background): Label1.BackStyle = 1

Uses   In most applications, it looks better to set a Label to transparent, thereby superimposing the Label's text on the background.

Cautions   • Unless BackStyle is set to Opaque (1), the BackColor Property will have no effect.

• It is harder for Windows to redraw transparent Labels or shapes than opaque ones. If you use too many transparent Controls, your program's visuals might become unacceptably sluggish (when another window is moved on top of, then off, your Form, etc.).

Example   Put an Image Box on a Form, make it about as large as the Form and set the Image's Stretch Property to True. Then double-click on the Picture Property of the Image (in the Properties Window) and pull in a .BMP file. Now place two Labels on top of the Image. Adjust their FontSize Properties and turn the BackStyle of one Label to "Transparent."

Figure B-3: Most of the time, "Transparent" Labels are more attractive.

See also   BackColor; FillStyle; FontTransparent; Label; Shape

BEEP

STATEMENT

Description Beep is an extremely primitive command. It has one sound—of one pitch, with one duration. Visual Basic's audio capabilities are rather embarrassing. While VB shines in visual effects, it can emit only this one offensive noise.

Variables Beep uses no Variables.

Uses You can alert someone with Beep.

Cautions • You'd probably annoy people with this noise; it's an unpleasant and monotonous intrusion. Until future VB versions incorporate audio that at least marginally compares to its video capabilities, avoiding Beep is best.

Example

```
Beep
```

OR we can use some of the full-featured sound capabilities built into Windows. This is an API call—a request from your Visual Basic program to utilize some of Windows's built-in power. You don't need to understand *how* this works to put the technique to use in your programs. But if you're interested in the many other things the API (Application Programming Interface) can do, see Appendix A.

Put the statements below into a Module. Each line must be continuous. You must not separate a line with a Carriage Return by pressing the ENTER key. For example:

Right:

```
Declare Function StartSound Lib "sound.drv" () As Integer
```

Wrong:

```
Declare Function StartSound
Lib "sound.drv" () As Integer
```

Now, enter the following into the Module:

```
Declare Function OpenSound% Lib "sound.drv" ()
Declare Function SetVoiceSound% Lib "sound.drv" (ByVal nSource%, →
    ByVal Freq&, ByVal nDuration%)
Declare Function StartSound% Lib "sound.drv" ()
Declare Function CloseSound% Lib "sound.drv" ()
Declare Function WaitSoundState% Lib "sound.drv" (ByVal State%)
```

These declarations open a door into Windows itself, a door through which Visual Basic can access all that Windows is able to do.

Visual Basic offers a profusion of commands, which can manipulate Windows in very powerful ways, but there are some things that are not yet included in the VB set of commands. Control over sound is one of them. Beep, I ask you?

Don't Hesitate to Employ the Monkey-See, Monkey-Do Approach: Adding internal Windows commands to VB is not terribly difficult, but it *can* sometimes seem to be until you know a few ground rules. To find out how to access the 600-plus Windows Routines you can add to your VB repertoire of tricks, take a look at Appendix A. If you want, you can explore a whole new world of control over the Windows environment. Also, you can just follow a monkey-see, monkey-do approach and get perfect results (if you don't have any typos).

In any event, putting the preceding declarations into a VB program gives you lots of possible sounds. To play around with these sound commands, just change the frequency and duration to make different sounds. Here's an example of how to make a few different sounds.

```
Sub Form_Click ()

t = OpenSound()

'Change the following duration and frequency numbers as desired

duration% = 500: frequency& = 400

frequency& = frequency& * 65536
t = SetVoiceSound(1, frequency&, duration%)
t = StartSound()
While (WaitSoundState(0) <> 0): Wend
t = CloseSound()

End Sub
```

You can put the above lines within a For...Next Loop to get special effects such as sirens, etc. Likewise, you can play tunes by adjusting the SetVoiceSound line then using the line over and over to make the different tones in your song.

Note: This may seem perplexing if you're not a professional programmer. However, you can make use of it without understanding it—just the way you do a few things to get from your home to Los Angeles without understanding how airplanes fly. Here's how:

1. Type in the declarations.

2. Put the declarations into a file from within VB by saving a text file called SOUND.TXT. (Press CTRL+A.)

3. Then, to make sounds in other programs, just import the text file by loading it into your program via the Insert File option in VB's Insert Menu. Put it into a Module so that you can call up these functions from anywhere in your program.

See also   Appendix A (for more information on using the API)

 ORDERCOLOR

PROPERTY

Description BorderColor determines the color of the Line Control or the outline of a Shape Control.

Used with Line and Shape Controls only

Variables You can adjust the BorderColor in the Properties Window. (You can also set colors using RGB numbers, which see.)

OR (to set the BorderColor while a program is running):

```
Shape1.BorderColor = QBColor(5)
```

OR (to find out the BorderColor): X = Shape1.BorderColor

Uses • Add variety to your graphics by adjusting BorderColor, BorderStyle, BorderWidth and other Properties of Shapes and Lines.

Example

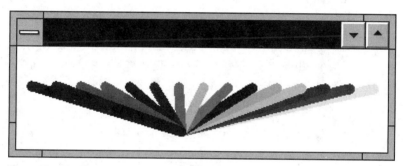

Figure B-4: A fan of the 16 BorderColors.

```
Sub Form_Load ()
line1(0).BorderWidth = 10
For i = 1 To 15
    Load line1(i)
    line1(i).BorderColor = QBColor(i)
    line1(i).X1 = line1(i — 1).X1 + 300
    line1(i).Visible = —1
Next i

End Sub
```

See also BackColor; BorderStyle

BORDERSTYLE

PROPERTY

Description   Determines which of the several built-in frames will appear around a window (a Form) in your VB program. Or whether or not a Label, Image, Grid, OLEClient, Picture Box or Text Box will have a frame. Or which of seven styles (dots, dashes) will be used with a Shape or Line Control.

For a Form or Picture Box, you cannot adjust the BorderStyle Property while the program is running. You must decide on a style while designing your Forms and set the BorderStyle Property using the Properties Window.

• Labels, Images, OLEClients, Picture Boxes and Text Boxes have only two possible border style settings:

0 = No border (the default for Labels, OLEClients and Images)

1 = Single thin line (the default for Picture Boxes, Grids and Text Boxes)

• Forms have four possible border variations:

0 = None

1 = Fixed Single

2 = Sizable (the default; a user can change the size of the window, iconize it, close it and move it around the screen)

3 = Fixed Double (cannot be resized, iconized or moved except with an [optional] Control-menu box)

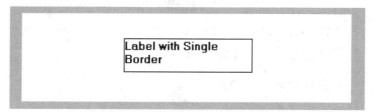

Figure B-5: A borderless Form.

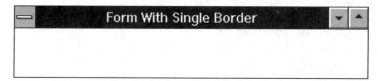

Figure B-6: Form with Fixed Single option.

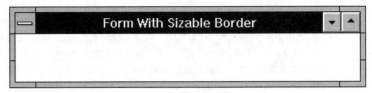

Figure B-7: Form with Sizable option (the default).

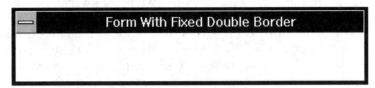

Figure B-8: Form with Fixed Double option.

- Shapes and Lines have seven possible variations:

    0 = Transparent (no border)

    1 = Solid (the default; the line is *centered* on the outer border)

    2 = Dash

    3 = Dot

    4 = Dash-Dot

    5 = Dash-Dot-Dot

    6 = Inside solid (the border builds *inward* from the outer edge
        of the Control)

Used with   Forms (and MDI Forms—see "Multiple Document Interface"); Grids; Images; Labels; Lines; OLEClients; Picture Boxes; Shapes; Text Boxes

Variables   **Variable type**: Integer (Enumerated)

For a Form or Picture Box, set the BorderStyle while designing your program. (See "Description.")

OR (to add a border to a Text Box while your program is running):

    Text1.BorderStyle = 1

OR (to remove a border from a Label while the program is running):

    Label1.BorderStyle = 0

OR (to find out the BorderStyle of a Label while the program is running):

    x = Label1.BorderStyle

B ... **107**

Uses • A Form with a Fixed Single BorderStyle is useful as an alternative to the MsgBox Function. MsgBox always requires the user to click on it. You might want to send a message to your program's user and then have the program remove the message automatically. To do this, you can show a Fixed Single Bordered Form (turn off the Form's ControlBox Property from the Properties Window, then make it disappear by using a Timer).

This method gives you far more flexibility than the Print command. It's often best to use a separate Form (window) for messages that you will Show then Hide.

In the Example below, we've added one of the icons from VB's icon library, put it into a Picture Box (with no border), then created a Text Box with no border and put our message into the Caption Property. Why not just use the Print command? Because using a Text Box along with its Top and Left Properties simplifies formatting. You can float the Box anywhere easily, and you'll know you won't be interfering with anything on the window proper. And, as with any Form, you can create a pleasing appearance with all the other formatting, font and color capabilities in VB. To control the length of time the message appears on the screen, use a Timer (see "Timer" for information on delays).

• Use the various options and Properties of a Form (Min and Max buttons, Control-menu box, etc.) to govern how much control the user has over a particular window. You can permit the user to move or shrink a window, or refuse access to aspects of the size and position of window control.

• You could turn a Label's border off and on to draw attention to it.

Cautions • Though it's not often useful, you *can* turn on and off the border styles of Labels, Picture Boxes, Grids, OLEClients, Images, Shapes and Lines *while the program is running*. You cannot change the borders of Forms and Text Boxes, however, during the run. That can be assigned only via the Properties Window while you're creating a program.

Alternating between some of the dotted or dashed BorderStyles of a Shape or Line could create an interesting animated marquee effect to draw attention to something (use a Timer and the Static command).

• A Text Box has a border by default; a Label has no border by default.

• Almost every element of VB programming uses –1 to mean True or On, and 0 to mean False or Off. However, BorderStyle uses 1, not –1, for On.

• If a Form has a menu, you can use only Sizable (style 2) and Fixed Single (style 1) BorderStyles. If you select None or Fixed Double, the fact that the menu exists causes VB to change the BorderStyle to Fixed Single.

Example   Creating your own Message Boxes gives you control over icons, text position and many other design elements. In addition, you can determine how long the message is displayed (and what causes it to go away).

Figure B-9: Using custom Message Boxes is often better than using the built-in MsgBox Function.

See "Uses" for details about this example.

See also   BorderColor; BorderWidth

BorderWidth

PROPERTY

Description   BorderWidth determines how thick a line is drawn for a Line or Shape Control.

Used with   Shape and Line Controls only

Variables   You can set the BorderWidth in the Properties Window while designing your program.

OR (to set the BorderWidth while a program is running):

    Shape1.BorderWidth = 4

OR (to find out the BorderWidth): X = Shape1.BorderWidth

Uses   • Add variety to your graphics by adjusting BorderWidth, BorderStyle, BorderColor and other Properties of Shapes and Lines.

Example

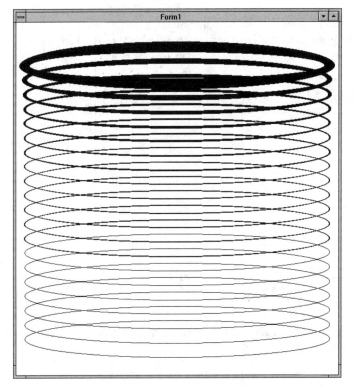

Figure B-10: A cascade of BorderWidths on an oval Shape Control.

```
Sub Form_Load ()
shape1(0).Visible = False

For i = 1 To 20
    Load shape1(i)
    shape1(i).BorderWidth = 20 / i
    shape1(i).Top = shape1(i − 1).Top + 400
    shape1(i).Visible = True
Next i
End Sub
```

We'll create a Control Array (which see) so that 20 clone shapes will grow out of Shape1 and inherit Shape1's Properties. First, put a Shape near the top of a Form; then set its Shape Property to "Oval" and its Index to 0.

Now, because we are only using Shape1(0) as a template, we make it invisible and then use the Load command to create 20 replicas. We move each new clone Shape up 400 twips from the previous one and also decrease the BorderWidth Property of each clone starting with a BorderWidth of 20 and dividing by the index *i* each time. Then, because clone Controls are never visible when first created, we set each one Visible.

See also   BorderColor; BorderStyle; DrawWidth

CALL

Description This Statement is somewhat unusual in that it's never really needed. As far as VB is concerned, the following two lines will accomplish exactly the same thing:

```
BEEPER
CALL BEEPER
```

Like other holdovers from early versions of the Basic computer language (such as the Let command), Call is included to permit compatibility with programs written some time ago, or to allow people to use it for personal reasons. It *can* make your programs more readable because it immediately identifies the situation as a *Subroutine call*, not some other command within VB itself.

Subroutines are quite important in programming. They allow you to write little self-contained "black boxes" that can be plugged into any other section of your program to perform a specific function. They're plugged in by simply using the name of the Subroutine. It's as if you're adding a new command to VB that you can use whenever you wish, merely by naming it.

"Calling" a Subroutine: VB comes with many built-in Subroutines. All the Events are Subroutines, and you can use them anytime by simply "calling" on them from anywhere within the Form they reside in. The simplest way is to just name the Event. This will carry out whatever commands are inside the Label1_Click Event, even though you're invoking it from within the Form_Click Event:

```
Sub Form_Click ()

Label1_Click
End Sub
```

But you can also use this: Call Label1_Click

Even though in this example the user didn't click on Label1, you're making your program act as if that had happened. The user clicked on the Form, but the Label1_Click Event (a Subroutine) was "called."

Also, most of the commands in VB are in a sense prewritten Subroutines. When you use the Cls command, you're "calling" a routine in VB that clears the current Form or other object of its graphics and text. Without Cls, you would have to devise your own way to accomplish this—perhaps printing blank lines all the way down the window or loading in a blank Picture Box.

There *are*, of course, things that VB doesn't supply. That's why you have to write parts of your program—for things peculiar to your program.

If you write some useful Subroutines, you can save them in a Module or as a text file and use them in other programs by simply loading them in (from the VB Insert Menu).

Used with Subroutines (see "Sub")

Variables Call Sort

OR (to provide Variables to the called Subroutine, list them after the name of the Sub, enclosed in parentheses): Call Sort (WhatToSort)

Uses Subroutines (and their close relatives, Functions) are valuable when you are going to need to do something repeatedly in different parts of your program. See the Example below or see "Sub."

Cautions • If you *do* use Call, you must put any *arguments* in parentheses. Arguments are Variables you want to send to the Subroutine you are calling (see the Example). If you don't use Call (merely name the Subroutine when you want to use it), you must *not* use parentheses.

• Sometimes you don't want a Subroutine to change a Variable you pass to it—you're merely giving the Sub information but don't want the Variable changed when the Sub is finished. To do this, enclose the passed Variable in parentheses. This means you would have to use *two sets* of parentheses if you also use Call:

```
Sort (WhatToSort)
Call Sort ((WhatToSort))
```

Example Let's say that for some reason you need to Beep a different number of times depending on the place in your program. You could, of course, simply type in Beep:Beep or Beep:Beep:Beep to show the number of times it's needed; but doing this each time would make your program unnecessarily larger.

Make a Subroutine and name it whatever you want:

```
Sub DoBeeps (NumberOfTimes)

for i = 1 to numberoftimes
    beep
next i
End Sub
```

Put this Subroutine in a Module. Now any time you want a Variable number of beeps, you can simply do this:

```
DoBeeps 5
```

OR

```
DoBeeps 7
```

OR

```
number = 3
DoBeeps number
```

OR

    Call DoBeeps (3)

See also   Function; Sub

 ANCEL

PROPERTY

Description   The Cancel Property can be used to make one of the Command Buttons on a Form double as the ESC key. In other words, pressing the ESC key on the keyboard will trigger the Command Button's Click Event, just as if the user had mouse-clicked on the Button. Cancel can also be used with an OLE Control.

In many programs the ESC key is used to move back a level, to the previous state. For instance, say that the user has selected a Button labeled Save, so your program shows a file-saving window with various options. One of those options would be Cancel. You could set the Cancel Property of the Command Button that you've labeled "Cancel." Then the user can either click on your Cancel Button or press the ESC key to achieve the same result—return to the previous window, thus aborting the file-saving.

Used with   Command Buttons and OLE Controls

Variables   **Variable type:** Boolean

While designing your program, you can turn on the Cancel Property of a Command Button in the Properties Window.

OR (to make Command1 the Command Button with the Cancel feature, while the program is running): Command1.Cancel = −1

OR (to make this Button stop being the Cancel Button: all Command Buttons are set to 0 unless you change one. If you do change one, all other Command Buttons have their Cancel Properties automatically set to "Off"):

    Command1.Cancel = 0

Uses   Over the years, people have gotten used to using the ESC key to go back one level in a series of menus, undo the previous action, or even exit a program. It may be a good idea to allow them that alternative.

Cautions   • Only one button on a given form can be the Cancel Button, but VB handles this for you. Whenever you set one of the buttons to Cancel, any other button that has that Property loses it.

• If you have other Controls on a Form that contain a Cancel Button, pressing the ESC key does not trigger their KeyPress, KeyDown or KeyUp Events, as it normally would. This has the effect of reserving the ESC key for special actions governed only by whatever commands you have put within your designated Cancel Button's Click Event.

• There is a similar Property of Command Buttons called Default. This Property causes the ENTER key to trigger a Command Button if its Default Property is set to On (–1).

Example   If a window has a Command Button called Undo, you could make it the Cancel Button. Then, if the user is typing something (and Undo is a way to erase and start over), it would be more convenient to press ESC from the keyboard than to reach over for the mouse and locate the Undo Button. At least, you offer that option.

Here we've got a small Text Box that is used to enter phone numbers. To quickly erase an entry, the user can press Undo, or hit the ESC key, either one. Turn on the Cancel Property in the Properties Window.

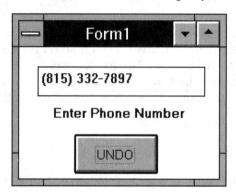

Figure C-1: Pressing either the Undo Button or the ESC key will clear the Text Box of the phone number.

The Command1 Button has this in its Click Event:

```
Sub Command1_Click()
    text1.text = ""
End Sub
```

See also   Default

CAPTION

PROPERTY

Description
Caption determines the text that will appear on a Form's title bar or within or near a Control. If a Form is iconized, the Caption will appear beneath the icon as an identifier. Captions are not required; you can delete them in the Properties Window, or delete or change them while a program is running.

Used with
Forms, Check Boxes, Command Buttons, Data Control, Frames, Labels, Menus and Option Buttons

Variables
Variable type: Text (string)

You usually set a Caption while designing a program, using the Properties Window.

OR (to change a Caption while a program is running): Label1.Caption = "ON"

OR (to find out the Caption of a Command Button while a program is running): X$ = Command1.Caption

OR (to assign a "quick access key" to a Caption, so the user can press ALT(+ a key) to trigger the Control. See the fourth item in Uses.):

    Command1.Caption = "&Quit"

The Q will be underlined in the Caption, and the Command Button will be triggered if the user presses ALT+Q.

Uses
• Provide the user with information about how to use a Control; the general purpose of a window (Form); or the name of the entire application (the "Startup" Form's Caption, the main window Caption).

• A very useful feature of the Caption Property of a Form is that it is still displayed when the Form is shrunk by the user into an icon. This means that you can not only identify the icon with a text description, but you can also change an icon's description while the program is running. We take advantage of this in the Example for the entry on "Timer" to continually update and display the elapsed time for an iconized timer program.

• If conditions change while a program is running, you might want to change a Caption to reflect the new situation.

• Keyboard-bound users might appreciate being able to avoid reaching for the mouse to select a Control. Many users prefer to avoid using the mouse to make selections during typing-intensive jobs, such as word processing or text entry, so they can keep their hands on the keyboard. Here's how to let the user press an ALT+S key combination to select a button that sorts something in your program. Type **&Sort** as its Caption and you'll see the special effect illustrated in Figure C-2.

The letter following the & in your Caption will be underlined. Then, like the ALT+key convention used for selecting menu items, pressing the ALT key along with the letter following the & will have the same effect as if the user had mouse-clicked on the Control. (The commands you have put into that Control's Click Event will take place.)

Figure C-2: The underline indicates that ALT+S will activate this Command Button.

If you want to actually use an ampersand (&) as part of the Caption, insert two of them:

```
Command1.Caption = "This&&That"
```

Cautions • It's easy enough, especially when you are first working with VB, to get Captions mixed up with the Text Property of a Text Box. Here's the difference: the term "Caption" applies to text at the top of Forms and Frames—like captions that accompany pictures in books and other publications.

On the other hand, a Text Box doesn't have a Label (a Caption) on it; it's prepared to receive large amounts of, for example, word processed text. So, VB refers to the text inside a Text Box as the Text Property.

• Also, don't confuse the Caption Property with a Control's Name Property. Name is an internal VB label for the Control—you use it in programming to refer to that Control. But a Name is never seen by the user. Likewise, a Form has a Name Property also used as an internal housekeeping label by VB and the programmer.

• Captions that are too large will be clipped off by VB.

• Unless you change them in the Properties Window or while the program is running, all Captions will default to the Names of Controls and the Names of Forms. Remember that you can delete Captions in the Properties Window while creating your program. Or you can delete them while a program is running by giving them an empty text Variable:

```
Label1.Caption = ""
```

Example Figure C-3 shows where Captions are displayed on Controls that can have them:

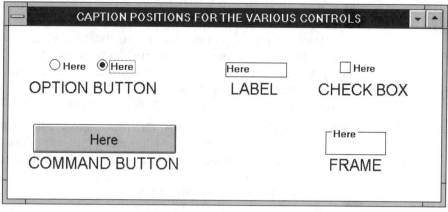

Figure C-3: "Here" is the Caption.

See also   Name; Text

See   CCur

Description   Uses for CCur are very limited, but it could come in handy for some applications. Essentially, CCur transforms a number into a Currency type number (one that can only have four digits past the decimal point: 1.7778).

Numeric Variable Types: There are several types, or classes, of numbers in Visual Basic, each having different strengths and weaknesses. Some, such as the Integer type, can hold only a limited range of numbers and are less precise than others. But Integers are the easiest for computer calculations, so your program will run the fastest when you use Integers. Other types are more precise (many decimal places) or have larger ranges; but these take up more room in the computer's memory and take longer to compute.

Unless you specify otherwise, numeric Variables in VB default to a type called "Variant" (which see).

When you use a numeric Variable and don't attach any of the special symbols described below, it is by default a Variant data type for VB 2.0 and 3.0. It looks at what you are doing here and *knows* that you need some precision (some numbers beyond the decimal point): X = 15/40 will result in .375 as the answer. The result of any math will be correct up to five digits to the right of the decimal point. (See "Variant.")

There are, however, several other types of numbers in VB.

X% Integer: No decimal points. Can only include numbers between –32,768 and 32,767. Can make mathematical parts of your programs run up to 25 times faster. Attaching the % symbol to a Variable forces it to include no digits to the right of the decimal point. In effect, there is no decimal point, and any fraction is stripped off.

> X% = 1 / 20 results in X% becoming 0
>
> X = 1 / 20 is .05
>
> X% = 15 / 4 results in X% being 4 (it gets rounded off)
>
> X = 15 / 4 makes X 3.75

X& Long Integer: No decimal points. Can range from –2,147,483,648 to 2,147,483,647. Strips off any fractional part, but is capable of calculating with large numbers.

X! Single-Precision Floating-Point: Huge range.

X# Double-Precision Floating-Point: Extremely huge range.

X@ Currency: Ranges from –922,337,203,685,477.5808 to the number 922,337,203,685,477.5807. This is the special type we'll use with the CCur example below. It has a *fixed* point rather than a *floating* point (although it does have a fractional component of four decimal points). The Currency numeric Variable type is superior in its accuracy, since it stores its number internally as decimal, not binary, digits. This prevents rounding errors that are anathema to financial calculations—even a misplaced penny here or there can ruin an accounting. (For more on the types and uses of numeric Variables, see "Variables.")

Variant: The VB 2.0 and 3.0 default (see "Variant"). Variants attach *no* symbol to the Variable's name.

• New in VB4 are the Boolean and Byte types (see "Variables").

Used with   Variables, to change a number into a Currency type number

Variables   To change a Variable into a Currency type: money = CCur (somenumber)

OR (to change a "literal number" into a Currency type):

> dollarscents = CCur (15.88888)

OR (to change a numeric expression [see "Variables"] into a Currency type): money = CCur (somenumber + 15.88888)

Uses   There aren't many practical uses for CCur. Use it if you ever need to force a result to high precision (accuracy) involving calculations with currency.

Cautions   • Some numbers, such as 1 divided by 3, can generate endless digits to the right of the decimal point. There must be a limit to the physical size of numbers that the computer can work with; or you could fill the computer's memory with infinite digits by this simple instruction: X = 1/3

The computer would go on generating a series of .33333333s until it filled up with them or burned down, whichever came first. But try this:

    X = 1/3
    Print X

Results in   .3333333

But, if you add the # symbol to X, you can get more digits—15 instead of 7—because the # symbol makes a Variable into a Double-Precision Floating-Point number, and it can carry a fraction out further than a Single-Precision Floating-Point numeric Variable type. In other words, different types of Variables have different ranges and different degrees of precision. *Ranges* used here means the span of numbers that a Variable can contain (the Integer type has a small range from –32,768 to 32,767). *Precision* means how many digits can be used to express the fractional portion to the right of the decimal. The greater the range or precision, the longer it takes the computer to calculate the result. And the more memory the Variables take up. That's why you're allowed the option of specifying a great range or precision by adding a symbol and transforming a Variable into a different type.

Here's the effect of giving the Variable X a double-precision specificity:

    X# = 1/3
    Print X#

Results in   3333333333333333

Unless you're involved in scientific work—astronomy or atomic physics, for example—where you're dealing with extremely large or small numbers, you can probably ignore these issues surrounding numeric Variable types. You want to know that they exist as a resource and how to use them if necessary, but most of your everyday applications would never need such precision or range. Most computing involves real-world number ranges. Therefore, you normally won't need to add type symbols to your numeric Variables. Just use *X* or *Y* or *BowlingScores*. And, the new Variant default number type will make intelligent adjustments to the "type" for you.

Integers: Since VB 2.0 and 3.0 default to Variants, it's generally sufficient to remember only one other type, the Integer type. Attaching the Integer %

symbol to a Variable prevents it from ever having a fractional part (no decimal point ever appears). You can also create Integers by stating:

```
Dim X as Integer
```

OR: DefInt X (This makes Integers of all Variables whose names begin with an X. See "DefType.")

The value of Integers is in counting and other purposes where you don't want to worry about rounding errors should fractions appear. Integers are easier for the computer to calculate with, too, so your program will run as much as 25 times faster if you use Integers when you can. Because of this, many programmers put DefInt A-Z in their programs in the General Declarations section of each Form. (You cannot use DefInt in a Module to make the effect programwide. DefInt A-Z must be put into each Form or Module where you want it to have effect.)

Adding DefInt means that instead of Variants, VB will default to Integers unless you specify otherwise for individual Variables (by adding the type symbols) where you need fractions or other special effects. See "DefType" for more on this.

Example   Here's how to take a Variant value (representing the retail price of a hat) and get a markdown expressed as a Currency type Variable:

```
retail = 54
markdown! = .33

deduct@ = Ccur(retail * markdown!)

print deduct@
```

Results in   17.82

See also   CDbl; CInt; CLng; CSng; DefType; Variables; Variant

CDBL

FUNCTION

Description   CDbl is a command you can safely ignore unless you're deeply into arcane numeric manipulations.

CDbl changes a numeric expression—a literal number, a Variable or a combination of them—into a Double-Precision Floating-Point number. (See "Variables.")

You might assume that if you're, say, dividing one Integer by another, forcing double-precision would result in greater accuracy. However, the results of a calculation with or without CDbl are the same. The type of

Variable that gets the answer of a calculation (RESULT% in RESULT% = 5 /2) determines the precision and range of the calculation. (See "Variables" for more information on numeric types.)

Used with   Numbers

Variables   result = CDbl (somenumber)

OR (to use a more complex "numeric expression"): result = CDbl (x / y)

Example   Dividing 33% by 12% (both Integers) results in

```
x% = 33
y% = 12

result# = x% / y%
Print result#
```

Results in   2.53846153846154

Using CDbl to "force double-precision arithmetic" gives the same result. However, what if you divide two floating-point numbers such as 3.141592649 and 2.1323456221? Multiplying or dividing two single-precision numbers can give a result that can be properly expressed only in double-precision numbers. Or even if the result of a calculation requires only single-precision numbers, the intermediate value of a calculation (the temporary value at a given point) can require double-precision numbers to avoid losing significant digits. Putting the calculation in CDbl( ) forces the whole calculation to be performed in double-precision numbers. For most of us, this is unnecessary most of the time. The difference between the precision of 355/113 and pi is so small that if you used it to calculate the circumference of the solar system using the distance between Pluto and the sun, the discrepancy would be about the size of an atom.

```
x% = 33
y% = 12
result# = CDbl(x% / y%)
Print result#
```

Results in   2.53846153846154

The Variable type that gets the result determines the precision of the calculation. 33% divided by 13% (start out as before with Integers):

```
x% = 33: y% = 12
result% = x% / y%
Print result%
```

Results in   3

Because the result Variable was an Integer type, there is no activity to the right of the decimal point in the answer.

See also CCur; CInt; CLng; CSng; DefType; Variables; Variant

CHANGE

EVENT

Description The Change Event detects when the user (or, in some cases, your program) does something to a Control. Precisely what triggers its Change Event varies from Control to Control:

• Combo and Text Boxes—when the user types something in (or when your program changes the Text property while running).

• Directory and Drive List Boxes—when the user selects a new directory or drive (or when your program changes the Path or Drive Property while running).

• Scroll Bars—when the Control Bar is adjusted by the user (or when your program changes the Value Property while running).

• Label—when your program changes the Caption Property while running.

• Picture Box—when your program changes the graphics via the Picture Property while running. (Interestingly, the *drawing* commands—PSet, Circle, Line and Print—do *not* trigger a Change Event.)

Used with Combo Boxes, Directory & Drive List Boxes, Horizontal & Vertical Scroll Bars, Labels, Picture Boxes & Text Boxes

Variables

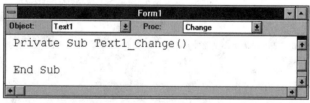

```
Private Sub Text1_Change()

End Sub
```

Figure C-4: Part of your program can be put into a Change Event.

Uses • Various special visual effects

• Updating information based on the user's interaction with a Control. For instance, before the user tries to shut down your program, you might want to first provide a reminder that a change was made to a Text Box and ask if the change should be saved to disk.

Cautions • Change can cause a domino effect if you create a self-changing Control. For example, you can't allow your program to insert new text into a Text Box by using that Box's Change Event. *The new text you printed would itself represent a change.* Therefore, it would trigger Change continually. Avoid writing commands within a Control's Change Event Procedure that themselves cause changes to that Control.

• Change does not work for a Combo Box when its Style Property is set to DropDown List.

Example One intriguing, and often useful, effect is to create two or more pictures that will move, or switch on and off (via their Visible Properties), in response to the user's adjustments. This is not only attractive; it informs the user in a very dramatic way of the effects he or she is having on the program.

Say you were writing a program where the user could flip through the months of a calendar by sliding a Horizontal Scroll Bar. You could create four icons, one for each season, then set the Scroll Bar's Min Property to 0 and Max Property to 12. By using an If...Then or Select Case structure, you would always know which season's picture to display, based on the location of the Scroll Bar Button.

Here's a simple example that demonstrates the idea. We'll create two icons, one with a dull ruby-colored light and one with a bright green light. We'll also give the green light more shadow. (If you're using two similar icons, it's a good idea to give them different amounts of shadow; the one with more shadow seems to "pop up" toward the viewer with a 3D effect.)

Housekeeping Details Are Handled in Form_Load: We start off, as is often the case in VB, with some initial housekeeping details. (You'll usually put startup tasks in the Startup Form's Form_Load section for these things, since that Form's Event is automatically triggered when a VB program starts running.) One Form in every program is designated the "Startup Form" (which see). It's usually the first Form that was created when you began designing your program, but you can choose a different Form as the Startup Form in VB's Options Menu.

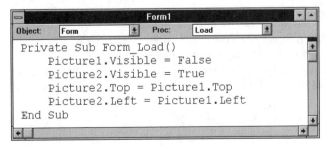

Figure C-5: Put preliminary startup tasks into the Form_Load Event.

Here we simply turn on one light and turn off the other, then position them so they will appear in the same spot on the screen. (We've already turned off their Border Property and turned on their AutoSize Property.) Here's what the Form looks like while you're designing the program:

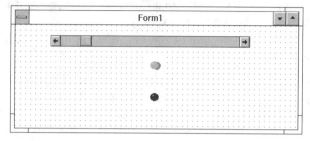

Figure C-6: The Form with its two graphics and a Horizontal Scroll Bar.

Then we enter the following to turn the lights on and off depending on where the Scroll Bar's Button is located. (In this example, we set the HScroll1.Min Property to 0 and its Max Property to 100.)

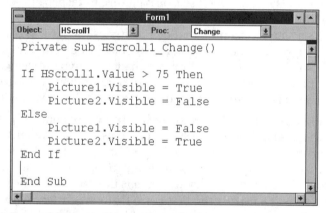

```
Private Sub HScroll1_Change()

If HScroll1.Value > 75 Then
    Picture1.Visible = True
    Picture2.Visible = False
Else
    Picture1.Visible = False
    Picture2.Visible = True
End If

End Sub
```

Figure C-7: Use a Change Event for instant response any change to the button in a Scroll Bar will trigger the effects.

Since we want immediate effects, we put this animation into the Scroll Bar's Change Event. This way, in any situation when the Scroll Bar is disturbed—whether the user clicks on one of the end arrows, drags the button, or clicks within the bar—we react at once and make the light indicate the position within whatever we are scrolling. Any disturbance triggers Change.

Here's what the window looks like when it runs:

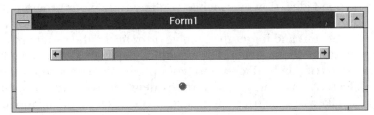

Figure C-8: The light before hitting the trigger point in the Scroll Bar.

And when we get above our trigger point . . .

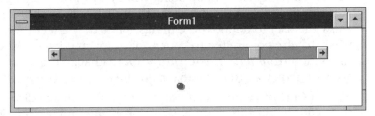

Figure C-9: Triggering the green light by moving the button inside the Scroll Bar.

See also   Click; DblClick; KeyDown; KeyPress; LostFocus; PatternChange

 HDIR

STATEMENT

Description   ChDir changes the default directory. A computer is "in" a particular disk drive directory at any given time. Unless otherwise instructed, the computer will save disk files into the default directory. Likewise the computer searches first the default directory to load files, then goes through the directories listed in the PATH statement in your AUTOEXEC.BAT file.

Used with   The disk drives

Variables   To use a text Variable to describe the new directory:

ChDir NameOfNewDirectory$

OR (to explicitly describe a literal directory): ChDir "C:\DOS"

Uses   Let the user change the default directory from within your program.

Cautions • Using ChDir to make your application's directory the default might seem a good idea. However, while you're writing your program, this could cause mysterious errors if you create a new directory (for a later version of the program) and forget that you've *hard-wired* the program to look for things in the older directory. For example, you'll get a confusing mixture of old icons (if you load icons into your program while it runs) and new program features that you've added to the new version of the program.

Likewise, the user might have problems if he or she moves your application to a different location on the disk or changes the directory name.

Normally, it's best to let the *user* pick the names and control the organization of the directory (and drive). And many users prefer to control the default directory as well, deciding whether or not to change the default to your application's directory at the time they launch your application. Try to allow the user to define these things, since they affect the computer in ways that are not limited to your application and its needs. Give the user the option *from within your program* to change the default directory if it seems a good idea to make that adjustment. (See "Drive List Box.")

• Don't ChDir to a nonexistent directory. As with any disk file manipulation, you should anticipate possible problems and use the On Error command (which see).

Example
```
d$ = "C:\MYAPP"
ChDir d$
```

See also CurDir$; ChDrive; Dir$; EXEName; MkDir; On Error; Path; RmDir

ChDrive

STATEMENT

Description ChDrive changes to a different disk drive. The computer is "on" a particular drive at any given time. For most people, most of the time, it's drive C:, the hard drive designation for the average IBM computer. Unless otherwise instructed, it's on the current drive (and into the current directory) that the computer saves files. Likewise it's the current drive through which the computer searches when looking for a file to load.

Used with The disk drives

Variables To use a text Variable to describe the new directory:
```
ChDrive NameOfNewDrive$
```

OR (to explicitly describe a literal drive): `ChDrive "C:"`

Uses   If your application involves disk access, you may want to offer the user the option of switching between disk drives. Allow the user to make this decision (and supply the drive name) from within your application. (See "Drive List Box.")

Cautions   • Try to avoid hard-wiring disk file access and let the user decide on drive (and directory) names and organization, since these things affect the computer in ways that are not limited to your application and its needs.

• Don't ChDrive to a nonexistent drive. As with any disk file manipulation, you should anticipate possible problems and use the On Error command.

Example
```
d$ = "E:"
ChDrive d$
```

ChDir; **See also** ; Dir$; EXEName; MkDir; On Error; Path; RmDir

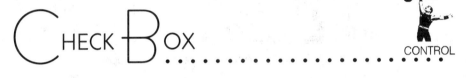

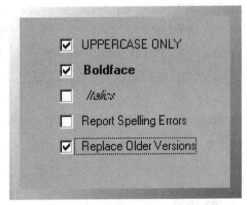

Figure C-10: A typical group of Check Boxes.

Description   Check Boxes allow the user to select from among options and always see the status of the Boxes on the screen. The Value property of Check Boxes determines whether a given Box is unchecked, checked or "grayed." Grayed means it cannot be selected by the user at this particular time; it is inactive and unavailable as an option.

The user can trigger a Check Box by clicking anywhere within the frame of a Check Box (on the Box image, on the Caption or even outside the Caption if the frame is larger). The Box that has the focus is indicated visually, while the program runs, by a dotted-line box around the Caption:

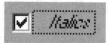

Figure C-11: This Check Box "has the focus" it's framed by a light line.

In other words, if a particular Check Box—among all the Controls on a window—has the focus, it will have that faint gray line around it. (See "ActiveControl" for more about focus.)

Variables   A Check Box is a Control, so you can adjust its Properties by using VB's Properties Window while designing your program:

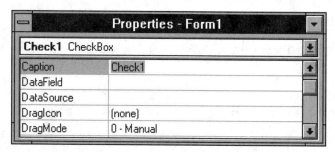

Figure C-12: Setting one of a Check Box's Properties during program design.

OR (to change a Check Box's Caption while the program is running):
Check1.Caption = "Disk Directory"

OR (to change the type size of a Check Box's Caption): Check1.FontSize = 12

OR (to make one Box the same size vertically as another):
Check1.Height = Check2.Height

OR (to find out the status of a Box): Selected = Check1.Value

The possible Values are:

0   Unchecked

1   Checked

2   Grayed (temporarily unavailable, disabled)

Uses   • Use Check Boxes when you want the user to be able to customize or otherwise control the way your program operates.

• Check Boxes are not the most visually attractive Controls. If you need them, you might want to make them visible in a special window of their own (selected, say, when the user clicks on a Command Button with the Caption "OPTIONS"). Then Hide that window when it's no longer needed.

Alternatively, you can fiddle with the way these Controls appear: make them overlap to bring the text lines closer together; offset the lines, staggering them; put them on top of a 3D frame or a picture; or use icons to cover the Check Boxes themselves with more dramatic visual symbols. (See the Example that follows.)

Cautions
• Check Boxes should not be confused with Option Buttons. Check Boxes allow the user to select all, any or none of the available Boxes. On the other hand, Option Buttons are mutually exclusive. In other words, when you press an Option Button, the other Option Buttons pop out and are deselected, just like the buttons on a car radio (provided the Option Buttons have been grouped on a Form or within a Frame or Picture Box Control). (See "Option Button.")

Use Check Boxes when you want the user to be able to simultaneously activate more than one option from a list. Use Option Buttons where only one option can be selected at a time.

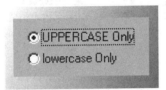

Figure C-13: Option Buttons are the usual alternative to Check Boxes.

Example
Here's a dramatic variation on the rather tired-looking VB Check Boxes—using Picture Boxes instead. This approach gives you much more control over the look of your project. You can put the Caption *on* the icon or .BMP file you design, or add Labels to your window.

Here we use Picture Boxes with Captions drawn right on the .BMP picture. These were designed in PBRUSH.EXE, the paint program that comes with Windows. We'll use the Picture Box Click Event instead of the Check Box Click Event to trigger whatever the program needs to do. There's no real penalty for using Picture Boxes instead of Check Boxes, except the time it takes to design the drawings.

Imagine how these images look *superimposed*; that is, only one of these is visible at any one time (switching places each time the user clicks on one of them). Notice the shadowing effects under the check mark and around the frame that make it seem that a button is being pushed and released. (See the Example for the Change Event to learn a simple way to animate superimposed images.) Here's what it looks like when the user has clicked on this option to select it:

Figure C-14: An attractive alternative to a plain Check Box.

And, when deselected:

Figure C-15: Nothing compels you to use VB's built-in Controls when something else would look, or operate, better.

Check Box Properties
Alignment • BackColor • Caption • DataField • DataSource
DragIcon • DragMode • Enabled • FontBold • FontItalic • FontName
FontSize • FontStrikethru • FontUnderline • ForeColor • Height
HelpContextID • hWnd • Index • Left • MousePointer • Name
Parent • TabIndex • TabStop • Tag • Top • Value • Visible • Width

Check Box Events
Click • DragDrop • DragOver • GotFocus • KeyDown • KeyPress
KeyUp • LostFocus • MouseDown • MouseMove • MouseUp

Check Box Methods
Drag • Move • Refresh • SetFocus • ZOrder

See also Option Button

CHECKED

PROPERTY

Description The Checked Property does for menus what a Check Box Control does for Forms; when a menu item is selected, a check mark displays that choice:

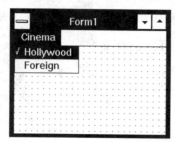

Figure C-16: Menus can include checked items to indicate the active selection.

Figure C-17: A check mark can show which item is selected in a mutually exclusive group.

Used with Menus

Variables **Variable type:** Integer (Boolean)

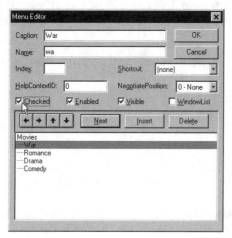

Figure C-18: You can set default check marks within the Menu Design Window.

OR (to display a check mark next to the menu item named "Drama" while a program is running): Drama.Checked = –1

OR (to display no check mark next to the menu item named "Drama" while a program is running): Drama.Checked = 0

OR (to find out if an item in a menu is checked while a program is running): IsOn = Drama.Checked.

(IsOn will be –1 (yes) or 0 (no), depending on whether or not there is a check mark next to the menu item named "Drama" while a program is running.)

Uses • Let the user see which options in a menu have been selected or are currently in effect.

• Let your program add or remove check marks while running, to reflect current conditions.

Cautions • When you create items in menus, you give each a Name. The menu items then appear in the list of objects on your Form, just as if they were Text Boxes or Command Buttons or some other Control:

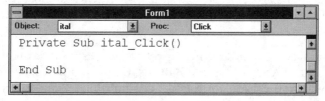

Figure C-19: Each of these new menu objects also has an Event the Click Event.

OR (to toggle Ital.Checked on and off each time the menu item is clicked): Ital.Checked = Not Ital.Checked.

(With this, the Ital menu item acts like a light switch: when clicked it goes on, when next clicked it goes off, when clicked again it goes on, and so forth.)

Example   If Ital.Checked = −1 Then Ital.Checked = 0

See also   Menu

CHOOSE

FUNCTION

Description   The Choose Function is of limited use. It's like the On GoTo command or a severely atrophied version of Select Case. Choose selects an item from a list of items, based on an expression (which then serves as an index into the list). The theoretical advantage of Choose, I guess, is that you can put the list all on one line.

Used with   Lists from which you want to select one item

Variables   Print Choose(2 + 1, "First", "Second", "Third")

Results in   Third (because 2 + 1 = 3)

Uses   You can use Choose with Control Arrays, providing a custom response based on the user's behavior (see the Example below). However, it is difficult to think of situations where the Select Case command wouldn't provide an easier, clearer structure for this sort of multiple-choice situation.

Cautions   • Choose looks at each item in the list that follows the index expression. Therefore, you could trigger undesired behavior if you try to perform some action (such as displaying a MsgBox) within the list. (A MsgBox would appear for *each* item in the list, regardless of which item was finally selected.)

If the result of evaluating the index expression is less than one or greater than the number of items in the list, Choose returns a Null.

The items in the list are *Variant* Variables (or expressions). The list can contain up to 13 items. Note that unlike Arrays and most lists (such as List1.List) in VB, the items in a Choose list start with an index of *1* (not the usual 0).

Example   The primary value of Choose is probably to respond to the user's clicking on a Control Array of Option Buttons, Command Buttons, etc. Choose is a somewhat more compact way of accomplishing some of what the Select Case command can also do.

Create an Array of Command Buttons by putting four of them on a Form and changing each of their names to *Command1*. Then, in their Click Event, you can respond as follows:

```
Sub Command1_Click (index As Integer)
Print Choose(index + 1, "First", "Second", "Third", "Fourth")
Print " Button"
End Sub
```

Notice that you have to add 1 to the index because the first member of our Control Array has an index of 0.

See also   IIF; On GoSub; Select Case; Switch

 HR$

FUNCTION

Description   In computer language, all characters (which include the uppercase and lowercase letters of the alphabet, punctuation marks, numbers and special symbols) have a numeric code—from 0 to 255 (though this is changing in VB4. See "New in VB4" later in this section.) The computer works exclusively with numbers. The only purpose of text, from the computer's point of view, is to facilitate communication with humans.

When you type in the letter *a*, the computer "remembers" it as the number 97. When that character is to be printed on the screen or on paper, the computer translates 97 back into *a*. Although we think of text in terms of information, to the computer the text characters are merely graphic images that, when strung together, have meaning to humans. It will be an important step toward artificial intelligence when text has as much meaning to the computer as mathematical and numeric data already does.

Some text code numbers are not directly visible—for example, a Carriage Return code that moves the text down one line when the user presses the ENTER key. There are times when you'll want to create a text (string) Variable that can be printed directly to your screen or your printer. If you're working with a Control that has no provision for Carriage Returns built into it (such as VB's MsgBox and InputBox$), you can simulate it by creating a Carriage Return text Variable:

```
CR$ = Chr$(13) + Chr$(10)
```

The 10 in the code is for "Line Feed" and is sometimes required. (Also, some printers won't respond to a Carriage Return code, Chr$(13), alone but need a Line Feed code added to it.)

There is more than one set of character codes, but VB and Windows use the ANSI code. You can find the ANSI Character Code table by pressing F1 to access VB's Help. However, you might find the ASCII Code, which is similar, more informative. The ASCII code, a part of which is shown in the following Figure C-20, was used by previous versions of Basic.

New in VB4

This entry, Chr$, describes character codes used since programming began. But with the 32-bit version of VB4, things have changed. It was long assumed that since a single byte can express 256 different numbers, a single byte was plenty big enough to hold the alphabet (26 lowercase, 26 uppercase), 10 digits and miscellaneous punctuation, with room left over for some dingbats like the smiley face.

But what about other alphabets, non-English alphabets? Some of them are rather large, too. OLE and the NT operating system have abandoned the familiar single-byte ASCII and ANSI codes in favor of a new two-byte code, UniCode. Two-byte units can express over 65,000 numbers, so UniCode has lots of room to provide code numbers for many alphabets of the world, including Chinese.

In the past, some programmers have relied on text (string) variables being one-byte large. They could store, retrieve and manipulate information efficiently in strings or string Arrays. For example, there is a whole set of string manipulation commands—like Left$, Mid$, Right$, InStr$, Chr$, Space$ and others which were heavily relied on by some for low-level database management programming. In other words, they stored any kind of data, not just text, in string Variables and Arrays. Programs written using these techniques will no longer work correctly in 32-bit Visual Basic.

There is a new *byte* variable data type (a single byte) in VB4 which can be used instead of the text string Variable data type. However, existing programs relying on the single-byte text data type will have to be rewritten to use the byte type. What's more, all the string manipulation commands commonly used in this kind of programming don't work with the byte data type. String manipulation commands in VB4/32-bit work as they always did with text, but in 2-byte chunks. The byte data type does have a few commands dedicated to it: InputB$, RightB$, MidB$ and LeftB$, which work the same way as their namesakes but on single bytes (instead of the new 2-byte units).

However, if you are planning to work with database programming, you might be better off using the VB4 Data Control or database language commands (see "Data Control").

Used with   Text Variables

Variables   CR$ = Chr$(13)

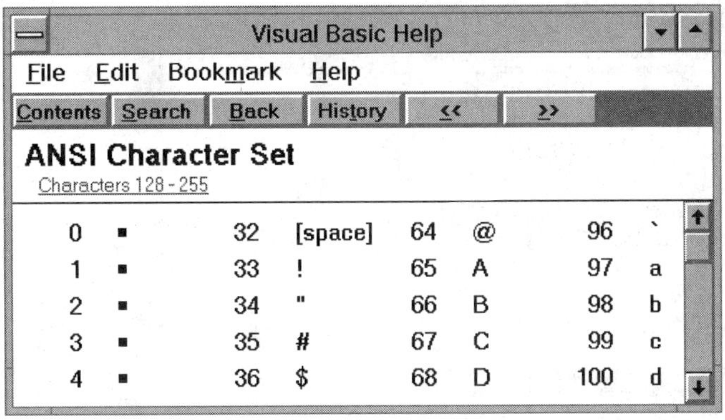

```
┌─────────────────────────────────────────┐
│ ▬           Visual Basic Help        ▼ ▲ │
│ File  Edit  Bookmark  Help               │
│ Contents Search  Back  History  «   »    │
│ ANSI Character Set                       │
│ Characters 128 - 255                     │
│                                          │
│   0  ▪    32  [space]  64  @   96  `  ▲  │
│   1  ▪    33  !        65  A   97  a     │
│   2  ▪    34  "        66  B   98  b     │
│   3  ▪    35  #        67  C   99  c     │
│   4  ▪    36  $        68  D  100  d  ▼  │
└─────────────────────────────────────────┘
```

Figure C-20: To view the ANSI or ASCII codes, press F1 and search VB's Help Menu.

Uses   • Create special string Variables that can accomplish what the screen and/or printer can't express directly. (You'll see how to simulate a double quote for MsgBoxes in the Example.)

• Communicate directly with your printer via its special codes. The HP LaserJet, for example, can perform a great variety of formatting and graphic tricks through codes. You create a Variable by combining literal characters (ones you can see onscreen) with the invisible formatting character codes (the ones that require Chr$).

Since Windows uses printer "drivers," this will not work:

```
Down$ = Chr$(27) + "&a4R"
Print "Here we are"; Down$; "and now we are here, four lines lower."
```

To send codes directly to your printer, you will have to use the API. See Appendix A for more about accessing the API. If direct printer control is an important issue to you, you'll need to work with the *Microsoft Windows Programmer's Reference*. There are some API provisions for sending codes. One, for instance, can control the number of copies printed.

• Print special symbols that you cannot enter from the keyboard because there aren't enough keys for these symbols.

The program shown in Figure C-21 shows some of the symbols. You can see the full set by looking under ANSI in VB's Help or by running the following program, substituting For I = 0 To 255 and removing the semi-colons so that each character prints on its own line on the paper.

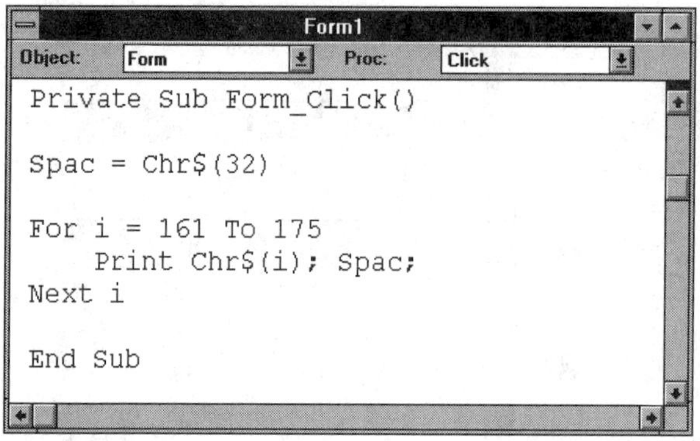

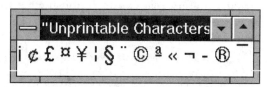

Form1
Object: Form
Proc: Click
Private Sub Form_Click()
Spac = Chr$(32)
For i = 161 To 175
Print Chr$(i); Spac;
Next i
End Sub

Figure C-21: This program produces a partial list of special symbols.

And you'll get this result:

"Unprintable Characters
¡ ¢ £ ¤ ¥ ¦ § ¨ © ª « ¬ - ® ¯

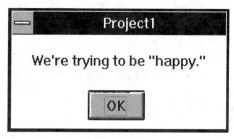

Figure C-22: Some of the special symbols.

Note that we defined Chr$(32), which is a "space" character. Since space can be typed, however, we could also have simply done this: space$ = " "

Example You cannot put quotes around words in MsgBoxes because the " (the quote mark) represents the end of the message. However, there is a way:

```
quot$ = Chr$(34)
MsgBox ("We're trying to be " + quot$ + "happy." + quot$)
```

This is the result:

Project1
We're trying to be "happy."
OK

Figure C-23: Printing quotation marks requires a little extra programming.

This accomplishes the same thing:

```
MsgBox ("We're trying to be " + chr$(34) + "happy." + chr$(34))
```

However, if you're going to need the special character often, it's more efficient, and more easily understood, if you create a Variable like quot$.

See also Asc

 INT

FUNCTION

Description CInt is hardly used. CInt "forces" a number to become an integer (see "Variables"). Assigning a number to an Integer Variable does the same thing as CInt, and is preferable.

```
y = 77.22
result = Cint (y)
Print result
```

Results in 77

The following produces exactly the same result:

```
y = 77.22
r% = y
Print  r%
```

Results in 77

The type of Variable that gets the answer of a calculation (RESULT% in RESULT% = 5 / 2) determines the precision and range of the calculation. There are several "types" of numeric Variables in VB (see "Variables").

Used with Numbers

Variables result = Cint (somenumber)

OR: result = Cint (x / y)

(You can use any calculation inside the parentheses—using any mixture of numeric Variable types, literal numbers, Constants and operators. For more on these numeric expressions and types, see "Variables.")

Example
```
r = Cint (12.55)
Print r
```

Results in 13

See also CCur; CDbl; CLng; CSng; DefType; Fix; Int; Variables

CIRCLE

METHOD

Description   The Circle command draws circles, arcs or ellipses on a Form, a Picture Box or the paper in the printer. Computers and printers can approach graphics in two ways: by using an actual copy of the picture or by describing the picture mathematically: Circle (Horizontal location, Vertical location) Size

VB can work with both kinds of graphics. On the one hand you can import a .BMP, .ICO or .WMF file (via the Picture Property) and VB embeds it in your program like a photocopy of the original. On the other hand, you can use Circle, Line, PSet, FillStyle, QBColor, RGB (and the other graphics Properties and commands) to create a drawing on the fly while the program is running. What's inside your program in this case is a mathematical description of the position, size, shape, color and texture of your drawing, not a point-by-point copy of the drawing. These two different approaches apply to all computer graphic activity (bitmapped fonts—each in a single type size—versus scalable font languages such as TrueType; and painting programs such as PBRUSH.EXE, which come with Windows, versus drawing programs like CorelDRAW).

More about Bitmaps: An icon is a bitmapped picture, as is a .BMP file (BMP stands for bitmapped picture). You create an icon by controlling *every dot (pixel) that will appear in the picture.* You may not need to work on that level; you can instead paint with a broad brush, fill whole areas or use a "spray paint" tool. But if you want to work on each bit, you can. And every dot will be stored on disk or within a program or sent to the printer. Although this may seem wasteful of computer memory (a high-resolution full-screen image can take up nearly one million bytes, 1mb), it does make it somewhat easier for you to "paint" the images. It's also more intuitive because the screen becomes your canvas and you can use various tools (pens and brushes and so forth).

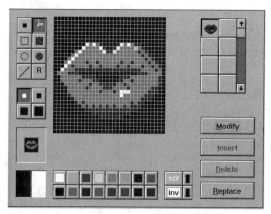

Figure C-24: A bitmap icon being created in Norton's Icon Editor.

As shown in Figure C-24, you can see each "bit" of the picture and, in the small version to the left, the final result as your eyes blend the bits into what appears to be a solid, continuous image.

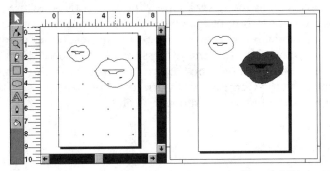

Figure C-25: A picture similar to the one in Figure C-24, but here created with outlines and color fills in CorelDRAW.

You work with a drawing program like CorelDRAW in a fundamentally different way. First the shapes are drawn by joining lines into enclosed areas, then colors are "described" for those shapes. The result can be translated into a bitmapped image and saved that way, or saved as a *vector image* (a mathematical description of the shapes and their locations, colors and textures).

Used with   Forms, Picture Boxes and the printer

Variables   The simplest use of the Circle command requires numbers only for X, Y and Radius: Circle (X,Y), Radius.

X and Y are the horizontal and vertical locations, respectively, of the center of the circle. Radius is the distance out from the center where the circle should be drawn. X is the number of twips (there are 1,440 of them per inch) over from the left of the window. Y is the number of twips down from the top of the window. In the case of a Picture Box, the measurements are from the left side and top of the Box. The printer measures over and down from the side and top of the paper. (For more about twips and alternative methods of locating and sizing objects, see "ScaleMode.")

Radius describes the size of the circle; it's the distance between the outer edge and the center. Radius * 2 is the *diameter*, the measurement derived from placing a ruler directly through the center point of the circle.

So, a simple circle can be drawn on a window in the following way:

Circle (600, 600), 300

The Circle Method has several optional Variables beyond the required (X,Y),Radius. The full list of options for the Circle command goes like this, and we'll look at each in turn:

Circle STEP (X,Y), Radius, Color, Start, End, Aspect

STEP positions the circle on the Form or Picture Box, just as (X,Y) does. The difference is that (X,Y) refers to a particular location on a Form or Picture Box, while STEP refers to the location of the previous circle you drew. Every time you draw a circle, the CurrentX and CurrentY Properties are set to the position of the center of that new circle. So you can use STEP to create new circles relative to previous circles, rather than changing (X,Y) directly. That way, there's less for you to worry about when drawing a series of circles. When the Step command is used, the values of X and Y are added to the CurrentX and CurrentY Properties.

This illustration was created using STEP:

Figure C-26: Use the Step command to position relative to the previously drawn object.

In this fashion:

```
CurrentX = 100: CurrentY = 200    ' Set initial location for first shape

For I = 1 To 7
    Circle STEP(300,200), 300, , , , 1 / i
Next I
```

Note: Some Events, such as MouseDown, reset the CurrentX and CurrentY Properties. So you could allow the user to click on various places in a Form, and circles would appear (using STEP as the location where the click happened).

COLOR determines the color of the line used by the circle (see "QBColor" and "RGB"):

```
For I = 1 To 7
    Circle (500 * I, 1000), 300,QBColor(3), , , 1 / i
Next I
```

If you omit the color Variable, the outer Line around the CIRCLE will be set to the ForeColor Property of the Form or Picture Box. But the color of any *fill* for a circle is decided by the FillColor Property of the Form or Picture Box on which the circle is drawn.

This would seem to mean that all circles on a given Form or within a given Picture Box must have the same fill color, rather restricting your design options. However, Visual Basic is almost always wonderfully flexible—often if you can check on the condition of something, you can also *change* its condition and modify things to suit yourself. In this case, if you want circles of various colors, simply assign FillColors as you go. Each time you want to change the color of a circle, just change the FillColor right before you draw the circle.

QBColors: In the next few years, computers will achieve CD-quality sound and high-quality color (millions of colors). Today, the average IBM computer video card produces 16 colors. The QBColor Function does 16 colors, so you can easily define FillColor. (The RGB function allows you to specify 16.777216 million different colors, but only the more fortunate among us have graphics cards today that can make all these distinctions.)

Here's how to set the colors prior to each Circle draw (this also shows the 16 QBColors):

```
'
fillstyle = 0
currentx = 200: currenty = 500
fontsize = 12
For i = 0 To 7
    fillcolor = QBColor(i)
    Circle Step(900, 0), 400
    x = currentx: y = currenty
    currentx = currentx - 200: currenty = currenty + 400
    Print i: currentx = x: currenty = y
Next i

currentx = 200: currenty = 1800

For i = 8 To 15
    fillcolor = QBColor(i)
    Circle Step(900, 0), 400
    x = currentx: y = currenty
    currentx = currentx - 200: currenty = currenty + 400
    Print i: currentx = x: currenty = y
Next i
```

Figure C-27: Programming that dynamically changes colors as you draw

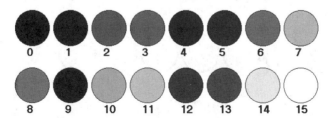

Figure C-28: And here's what you see.

You could put other colors inside circles by fiddling with the PSet command or by adjusting the DrawMode Property (although some of the colors cause odd dithering effects). But these approaches are often more trouble than they are worth.

Other elements of your drawing are also governed by the host Form or Picture Box and will be the same for all images drawn on that host unless you change them just before you invoke your Circle command.

Figure C-29: The DrawWidth Property sets the size of the line, shown here from 1 to 7.

DrawMode determines in what fashion your drawing is superimposed on the Form. Figure C-30 illustrates the interaction with the background for each of the 16 possible DrawModes (which see):

Figure C-30: DrawMode can cause strange, unpredictable effects.

Figure C-31: The Form's or Picture Box's FillStyle Property determines the texture of the fill.

START and END allow you to interrupt the completion of a circle to draw partial circles (arcs) and pie shapes. START is where, on your circle, the outline should become visible; END specifies where it should stop.

Figure C-32: Various partial circles.

```
Sub Form_Click ()
Print : Print : Print
Print
Print "                                          1                    2

currentx = 200: currenty = 500
For i = 1 To 7
Circle Step(900, 0), 400, , 0, 3 / i
Next i

currentx = 500: currenty = 1600
For i = 1 To 7
Circle Step(900, 0), 400, , 3 / i, 0
Next i

End Sub
```

Figure C-33: The programming that created the effects shown in Figure C-32.

Ellipse—A Distorted Circle: ASPECT allows you to make ellipses (stretched-out circles). ASPECT is the general shape of an object, expressed as a ratio between its width and height. The default is 1 (a perfect circle). You can use whole numbers or fractions to distort a circle into an ellipse.

This program shows the effect of ASPECT, changing it five times from 1 up to 5, and from 1 down to .2.

```
For I = 1 to 5

Circle (500 * I, 500), 300, , , , i

Circle (500 * I, 1000), 300, , , , 1 / i

Next I
```

Results in

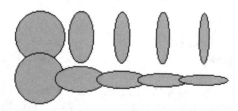

Figure C-34: Ellipses created by distorting circles.

Uses
• Save memory by creating graphic effects by describing them mathematically rather than by holding full copies within the program.

• Create more interesting backgrounds and frames for your windows.

Cautions
• See "AutoRedraw" for information about dealing with images that can be erased when temporarily covered by other windows, or resized.

• You need not include all possible Variables for the Circle Method; but if you leave any out, you must still use commas as spacers:

```
Circle (X,Y),Radius, , , , Aspect
```

Example　This creates a pattern by repeatedly adding 100 to the X position and to the radius. That has the effect of enlarging the circle and moving its center point to the right.

```
For I = 100 to 600 Step 100
Circle (800 + I, 1100), 300 + I
Next I
```

Results in

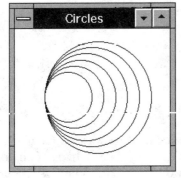

Figure C-35: A design created with the Circle command by repeatedly shifting the center point.

See also　AutoRedraw; BackColor; CurrentX, CurrentY; DrawMode; DrawWidth; FillColor; FillStyle; ForeColor; Line Control; Line Method; Point; PSet; QBColor; RGB; ScaleMode; Shape

OBJECT

Description　With VB Version 4 there is a new kind of Module. With a Class Module you can create a new *class* (a template for Objects) by defining Properties and Methods of your class.

　A *class* is rather like a genetic code—it's a detailed description of the appearance (Properties) and capabilities (Methods) of an Object. For example, when you add a Form to a VB project, VB brings a *particular* Form (an Object) into being based on the generic Form description (the "class"). This particular Form is an *Object*. So you use the class to bring into being ("instantiate") an Object (an instance of the class) based on the general qualities and behaviors described by the class.

　After an Object exists, the user or the programmer can be permitted to activate its Methods or change its Properties. Which Properties and Methods (if any) are user- or programmer-accessible depends on the person who designed the class. Properties and Methods in a class can be made Public or Private.

The Class Module is where VB allows you to define the Methods and Properties of a new class and to create the programming that makes those Methods and Properties do their job.

You define the nature—the qualities and behaviors—of your new Object by writing procedures. Properties are written in the new Property Let, Property Set and Property Get procedures. (Or you can merely use Module-level Variables, Variables you declare in the General Declarations section of the Class Module, above any Subs or Functions. However, when you create a Property for an Object, you usually have to write some programming to make that property have an effect. For instance, one of your Property's jobs could be setting the color of a Form that you're displaying. Since Properties sometimes *do something*, you can put the programming that does the job within the Property Let procedure.)

Methods are written with ordinary Subs or Functions. You cannot define any *Events*. There is no facility for that.

If you want to create more than one class, you must use a separate Class Module for each. A given VB program, however, can contain multiple Class Modules (therefore, multiple classes) if you wish.

Like an ordinary Module, a Class Module never becomes visible while a VB program is running. You can however make Forms visible and interact with the user that way from the programming within your Class Module.

Used with

Objects, as the place in VB where you design your own, original Objects

Variables

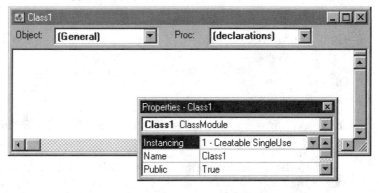

Figure C-36: The code window for a Class Module looks pretty much like a Form or regular Module.

A Class Module has three built-in Properties:

Instancing: This Property, when Creatable is set to 1 or 2, permits other applications (outside your VB program) to create new instances of your class (to make Objects based on the class). Note that Instancing defaults to 0-False.

Public: When Public is True, other applications can (via programming in them) utilize, adjust, trigger or otherwise make use of the Properties and

Methods in Objects created out of your class. However, you can still seal off individual procedures by declaring them as Private:

```
Private Function MyFunct( )
```

Note also that when Public is False, your object can still do things when it's created by an outside application. But the things it does are whatever programming you put in the Class Module. You can, for example, put some programming inside the Class Module's Initialize Event which will be carried out as soon as an Object is created (instantiated).

Name: The Name property is whatever name you want to give to your class. This will be used when creating this Object from the outside, to test it or to use it.

Uses A Class Module allows you to design your own, original Objects. These Objects can then be used by your VB Program, by other VB programs, or by outside applications like Excel.

Cautions • You can't just call Subs or Functions in a Class Module directly, either from an outside application or from within the same VB project where the Class Module resides. You must first create an Object (the Module itself is merely a *class,* a template out of which concrete, usable Objects are created). Objects are created by establishing (Dim) a new Object Variable of the "classname" type. In other words, if your Class Module's name is Class1, you create an Object of that kind like this:

```
Dim ThatOne As New Class1
```

Then you can read or write to a Property within the Class Module like this:

```
X = ThatOne.FSize
```

OR:

```
ThatOne.FSize = 16
```

OR you can invoke a procedure in the Class Module like this:

```
X = ThatOne.showit("This one")
```

The above works for contacting the Object from within the same project where the Class Module resides. To create an Object from within an outside application, there is an additional step. See "Outside Application Access" later in this section.

• You can't create a Class Module while a VB program is running (that is, you cannot write some programming that, when run, creates a Class Module). You must add a Class Module to your VB program from the Insert Menu. Of course you can create an *Object* of an existing Class Module while a program is running. See the "Caution" item above.

• A Class Module has only two Events: Intialize and Terminate (which see).

• Two Properties of a Class Module interact: Public and Creatable. If the Public Property is false, then your VB program ("project") can create an Object out of it, but no other outside application can create an Object of it. If the Public Property is True, then outside applications cannot *create* an Object out of it—instantiate it with programming like this:

```
Dim myObj As Object: Set Obj = CreateObject("Display.Class1")
```

However, if your VB program itself creates an Object out of it (Dim myclassobj As New Class1), then the Object exists and can be accessed by outside applications.

Finally, if both the Public and Createable Properties are True, then either your VB program or outside applications can create (instantiate) an Object from it, and of course both can access it as well.

• Each Object requires a separate Class Module, but you can have as many Class Modules in a given project as you require.

Examples   These examples are all intended to be tried in Windows 95 using the VB4 32-bit version.

For the first example, we'll create an Object Application (or "Server," as it's called). It's a special kind of VB .EXE file that can be accessed by outside applications (other VB applications, or OLE-capable applications like Microsoft Excel).

It will display a Form with which the user selects a disk path then clicks on a Command Button to display up to sixteen .BMP files. However, first we'll make it work as a stand-alone VB program—calling on the Class Module Object from within the VB application itself. That's one way to test it.

Start a new project from the File Menu. Then in the Insert Menu, click on Form to create Form1 (if one doesn't already exist). From the same menu, click on Form again to create Form2. Finally, click on Class Module to create a new Class Module with the default name Class1. In the Properties Window for this Class Module, change the Public Property to True and the Instancing Property to 1 or 2.

On Form1, put a Drive List Box, a Directory List Box, a File List Box and a Command Button. Type ***.BMP** into the File List Box's Pattern Property to *.BMP.

Figure C-37: To find out how to create these metallic effects on Forms and Buttons, see Line.

Into the various Events of these Controls, type this:

```
Private Sub Dir1_Change( )
    File1.Path = Dir1.Path
End Sub

Private Sub Drive1_Change( )
    Dir1.Path = Drive1.Drive
End Sub

Private Sub Command1_Click( )
    Dim classobj As New Class1
    p$ = Dir1.Path
    If Right$(p$, 1) <> "\" Then p$ = p$ & "\"
    p$ = p$ & File1.FileName
    cnt = File1.ListCount
    classobj.showbmps p$, cnt
End Sub
```

The significant line above is Dim classobj As New Class1. This creates an Object Variable that we've named classobj and tells VB that the Object pointed to by *classobj* is of the Class1 type. (In fact, this line creates both the Variable you use to refer to the Object and an actual instance (Object) based on the Class Module named Class1.

Stretch Form2 until its Height Property says 7500 and its Width Property says 7000. Put an Image Control on Form2. Set its Stretch Property to True and both its Height and Width Properties to 1750. Set the Image Control's Index Property to 0, thus making it part of a Control Array.

Now in the Class Module, type this:

```
Public Sub ShowBmps(pathname As String, cnt)
Form1.Hide
Form2.Show
Form2.image1(0).Visible = False
For i = 0 To 3
    For j = 0 To 3
    x = x + 1: If x > cnt Then Exit Sub
    If x > 16 Then Exit Sub
    Load Form2.image1(x)
    n$ = Form1.File1.List(x - 1)
    n$ = pathname & n$
    Form2.image1(x).Picture = LoadPicture(n$)
    Form2.image1(x).Top = 1750 * i
    Form2.image1(x).Left = 1750 * j
    Form2.image1(x).Visible = True
    Form2.Refresh
Next j
Next i
End Sub
```

This ShowBmps procedure is a Method of the Object defined by this Class Module. It hides Form1 (after the Command Button is clicked) and shows Form2 where the images will be displayed. We use the algorithm explained in "Control Array" to tile the various .BMP files. We also Exit the Sub if the number of displayed images is about to exceed the total (cnt) number of .BMP images available in the disk path indicated by the user. Likewise, we exit if the total exceeds 16, the amount permitted by the size of Form2.

We use the Refresh command to force Form2 to display each image as it's loaded into the new Image Control.

At this point you can test it. Press F5, then move around your hard drive until the File List Box displays some .BMP files. Then click on the Command Button.

Outside Application Access

Our Object has a visible user interface (Form1 and Form2). Objects don't necessarily have to make themselves visible to the user—they can simply supply data, do a complex calculation, or perform some other service that doesn't require input from the user or any display to the user. They can pop up invisibly in the lower regions of the OS, bubble around a bit doing their job, then go back into nothingness.

However, our .BMP display Object does show a couple of Forms to the user. In this situation, we can leave the StartUp Form (in the Tools menu, Project Options) set to Form1. That's what we want to show the user when our Object first starts.

Now, to put this new Object of ours on disk and register it with Windows 95 (so that any OLE-capable application can use it), click on the Tools Menu and select Options, then select Project. Leave the Startup Form as

Form1. Change the Project Name to Display. Click on the Startmode Ole Server Option Button. In the Application Description write something like "Shows BMPS."

Note that *Project Name* is a very bad label for this concept. Confusing is putting it mildly. Even though Project Name defaults to the program name (Project1, in this case), this Project Name is *not* the project in the sense of the VB program (which is the way the word *project* is normally used in VB). Instead, Project Name is one half of the two-part description used by an outside program to create an Object out of our Class Module. An outside application will activate our Object with this:

```
Dim Obj As Object
Set Obj = CreateObject("Display.Class1")
```

Letting the OS Know

For an outside application to be able to contact and instantiate (bring to life) our Object, we have to *register* it with the Windows 95 operating system. This enters the Object into the Windows 95 Registry (the new replacement for WIN.INI/SYSTEM.INI, though those files also exist for backward compatibility with Windows 3.x applications that expect to use them).

The easy way to register is to just create the .EXE file (from the File Menu). Then run the program. Documentation differs on this issue at the time of this writing. Some say merely creating an .EXE file registers it; others say running it the first time registers it. To be safe, run it. From the File Menu select Make EXE File. Now shut down your VB program (save the Forms and Project if you wish). Then run the "Object" .EXE file that you created from within Windows 95 as if it were a normal .EXE program. Now shut the EXE down.

Notice after you shut this program down that *it still exists as an Object*. That is, it's there within Windows 95 waiting to be reactivated if necessary. It's an Object on the loose. Press CTRL+ALT+DEL and you'll see it listed there as "Project 1" even though you thought you closed it down. Objects float around unless you specifically shut them down by destroying them with the Nothing command from within the testing, or "calling," outside application (as we'll do shortly). For now, though, you can destroy this one by selecting Project 1 and clicking on End Task.

How Does It Get Registered for a User?

Fine for you, but when you distribute your Object to others, how will it manage to be registered on *their* machine? If you have them install it via the Setup Toolkit method, that will do it. Or they could be asked to run it. It only takes one time running the .EXE Object to register it. Or your program could detect an error when you're trying to create this Object (the OS reports the Object doesn't exist) and you could then run it via the VB Shell command.

Now Restart VB4. Click on the Tools Menu, then select References. You should see a list of possible "things" that can be accessed, including one called Show BMPs. (Or, if you didn't fill in the Application Description text box, you'll see one called Display.) In any case, click on the check box to make it "referenced." Finally, in the VB design environment, press F2 to bring up the Object Browser to see if it's now really there as an Object that can be utilized.

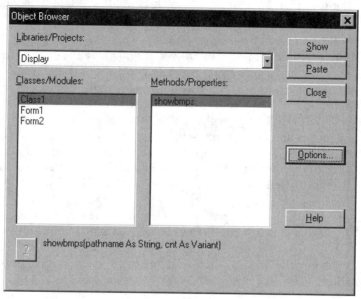

Figure C-38: Our Display Object Application is now registered as a legitimate Object.

Testing

With VB4 you can now run more than one instance of VB. This means two different VB4 environments can be running at the same time. One way to test a new Object is to activate it in a second, "controller" instance of VB. In the controller instance of VB you can write a little program that will activate the server Object, then put it through its paces to see if there are bugs. However, you can also just shut down VB, restart it with a clean, empty VB program and contact the Object. We'll do it that way here, for simplicity.

Be sure you're starting with a clean, new Project. Either shut down and restart VB, or select New from the File Menu. Click on the Tools Menu, then References and be sure that Show BMPs is selected. Now, in Form1 of our new test "controller" program, type this:

```
Dim ob As Object
Private Sub Form_Click( )
```

```
        Set ob = Nothing
    End Sub
    Private Sub Form_Load( )
        Set ob = CreateObject("Display.Class1")
    End Sub
```

Now run this controller test program by pressing F5 and your Object should pop into being and display its Form1 with the File Access Boxes and the Command Button, ready to show .BMPs. When finished, click on the controlling Form1 to kill the Object (Set ob = Nothing).

What if They Move It?

The user might move our Object, might copy the .EXE to another directory. Fortunately, Windows 95 is pretty good about tracking things like this (as long as the move occurs within the same hard drive). If they move it with Windows 95's Explorer, the registry will be updated and will contain the correct path. Things will work as they should. However, if the user deletes or moves an Object from within DOS, there's not much Windows 95 can do about it. The registry entry becomes invalid and you get an error message to the effect that the Object can't be created. It also doesn't appear in the Tools|References list as an active, available Object. However, if the .EXE itself is run again (Objects aren't intended to be explicity activated by users; rather, other applications are supposed to make use of them), the registry will be updated with the correct path, even if the Object was moved to a different disk drive. The best place to store your Objects is probably the Windows\System directory—users rarely tamper with things in there.

A Custom MessageBox

Let's try another example, and this time we'll add a Property as well as a Method to an Object.

The InputBoxes and MessageBoxes provided by applications' macro languages, and even those built into VB, are visually uninteresting. Essentially monochromatic, flat with few 3D Effects. Let's create an Object, a custom MessageBox. It will have sculpted visual effects and etched lettering. The controlling application can access this Object's one Method, Showit(capt), which centers the box and displays the Caption, *capt*, provided by the outside application. The Object will also have a Property (FSize) with which the outside application can determine the font size of the message.

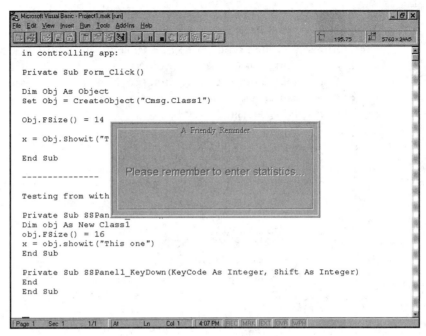

Figure C-39: Our substitute MessageBox.

Start a new project and put an SSPanel, one of the custom Controls from the set of Sheridan 3D Controls (look in the Tools|Custom Controls Menu), on Form1. Size it to the exact dimensions of the Form, so you don't see the Form at all. (The new positioning and sizing, pixel-by-pixel, techniques help here: press CTRL+arrow keys or SHIFT+arrow keys.)

Set the SSPanel's BevelInner Property to 1, its BevelOuter Property to 2. Change its Font3D Property to 3, Inset. Then stretch an SSFrame as large as possible without covering the borders of the SSPanel. Set the SSFrame's ForeColor Property to dark gray, not black–to lighten the Caption. Type **A Friendly Reminder** into its Caption Property and change the font to Times New Roman.

Finally, put another SSPanel on top of the Frame, setting the SSPanel's BevelInner and BevelOuter Properties to 0 (None) so there will be no frame. Set the ForeColor Property to medium gray and the font to Arial.

From the Insert Menu, select Class Module. In the Property Window, change the Public Property to True. In the Tools Menu select "Project Options" and then type **Cmsg** into Project Name and click on the OLE Server button. If you type in a Project Description, this will be what you will see listed under the Tools|References menu when you create a refer-ence to this Object (as described below). Otherwise the name of the Object will be "Cmsg."

In the Class Module, type this:

```
Public Property Let FSize(which)
    Form1.FontSize = which
End Property

Public Function showit(capt)
    X = Screen.Width / 2
    Y = Screen.Height / 2
    Form1.Left = X - (Form1.Width / 2)
    Form1.Top = Y - (Form1.Height / 2)
    Form1.Print capt
    Form1.Show
End Function
```

The Property of our Object, FSize, accepts a Variant, *which.* This Prop-erty merely adjusts the FontSize of the SSPanel where we'll display our messages. The Function (a Method of our Object) centers the message Form, puts a Caption on the SSPanel, then Shows the Form.

We can test our Object by simply adjusting its Fsize Property and supply-ing its showit Method with a caption. Type this into Form1:

```
Private Sub Form_Click()
    Dim obj As New Class1
    obj.FSize() = 16
    X = obj.showit("This one")
End Sub
```

We define an Object (named "obj") as an instance of the Class1 type. (Class1, by itself, is a *class,* a prototype or template, describing the qualities and behaviors of Objects that can be created—instantiated—out of it. Note also that Class1 is merely the default name that VB gave this Class Module. You can change this name if you wish.) **Note:** *You can't just call Subs or Functions in a Class Module.* You must create an Object out of the class, then refer to that Object and the procedure together: obj.showit, for example.

Next we set the font size Property. Notice that accessing an Object's Properties is virtually identical to accessing an ordinary VB Property except that you must include the parentheses following the Property name. Finally, we invoke the Method; this syntax is indistinguishable from calling an ordinary Function, except the Object's name is prepended to the Function name. (Recall that you can also write Methods in your Class Modules as Subs if you wish.)

Then press F5 to run the program and click on the SSPanel.

To finish the job, to make this an Object usable by outside applications, we'll replace the programming that tests the Object. The outside application will be responsible for adjusting the FSize Property, supplying the caption and triggering the showit Method:

```
Private Sub SSPanel2_Click( )
    End
End Sub
```

This way, the user can shut down the Object by clicking on the message box.

Now, to register this Object with the operating system, select Make Exe File from the File Menu, then save it to disk. From Window's Run option, run the .EXE file. This registers it, making it available to other applications that can control and manipulate Objects.

To test the Object from an outside application, close down VB, then start it running again. You'll have a new, clean, blank Form1—an empty program. You'll now need to establish a "Reference" in VB4 to this object. So click on the Tools menu, then select References. You should see your Object in the list. Click on the check box so it's checked. Now VB4 can test it.

Now type this into the Form_Click Event:

```
Private Sub Form_Click()
Dim obj As Object
Set obj = CreateObject("Cmsg.Class1")
obj.FSize() = 14

x = obj.showit("This Message")
Set obj = Nothing
End
End Sub
```

From an outside application, we must use the CreateObject command to summon our Object. The Object being created is named in two parts. First the "Project Name," Cmsg, that we gave it in the Tools Menu, "Project Options" window, then the Name Property of the Class Module, Class1.

As always, you should destroy an Object when finished with it: Set Obj = Nothing. You don't want loose Objects floating around, clogging up the operating system.

See also: Objects; Property Let,Get,Set

LEAR

METHOD

Description Clear cleans out the contents of a List Box, Combo Box or the Windows Clipboard.

Used with Combo Boxes, the Clipboard and List Boxes

Variables List1.Clear

OR: Clipboard.Clear

Uses • For an Undo feature in your application. Save current information for backup purposes. You can allow the user to have a safety net by saving his or her work periodically to a file or to the Clipboard. However, if you use the Clipboard and use the Clear Method, you might want to alert the user the first time you're planning to purge the Clipboard to avoid accidentally losing valuable material. (See "Cautions.")

Your Undo feature could be a Command Button that replaced text in a Text Box when the user decided that the previous version was preferable. (You would have saved that text when the user selected your Clear command or your Save command. The idea is that whenever the user moves forward in your application, you save his or her most recent work to the Clipboard with the SetText or SetData command, which see.)

• Remove all items in a List or Combo Box before entering a new list of items. Unless you use Combo1.Clear, any new items you put into the Combo (or List) Box will be *added* to the existing items (see "AddItem").

• The Clipboard can use up part of the valuable, and limited, 128k memory segment used by all Windows applications. After importing a large item via the Clipboard, you would want to use Clear to free up that memory.

Cautions • Clear for the Clipboard should probably be invoked only with permission from the user. Windows can have only one Clipboard open at a time, so you'll be flushing it when you use the Clear command. There may be another application currently storing something for the user; or the user might have put something there for safekeeping.

• Windows won't notify you that there's something already *in* the Clipboard and that you're now flushing it out.

• Windows is rather cavalier about the Clipboard. In many situations, all you have to do is press CTRL+INS to blow out whatever is in the Clipboard and replace it with the current data. You can save a copy of the current screen to the Clipboard by pressing Print Screen twice; or save an image of the currently active window by pressing ALT+Print Screen. Windows never warns the user that the Clipboard is about to be erased with new data, but you can be more considerate by alerting your users of an impending Clear.

Example   We save the picture to the Clipboard by clicking anywhere on the graphic:

```
Sub Graphic1_Click()
    Clipboard.SetData Picture1.Picture
End Sub
```

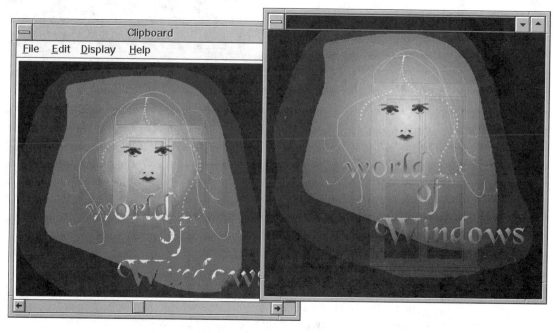

Figure C-40: Copying a graphic from a VB program to the Windows Clipboard.

Clicking anywhere on the Form's frame will purge the Clipboard:

```
Sub Form_Click()
    Clipboard.Clear
End Sub
```

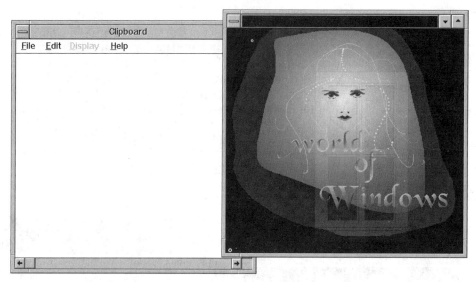

Figure C-41: Clear has emptied the Clipboard.

See also   Clipboard; GetData; GetFormat; GetText; SetData; SetText

CLICK

EVENT

Description   Click reacts when the left mouse button is pressed while your Visual Basic program is running. Click is, as you might expect, one of the most important events in a mouse milieu. It's always happening in Windows—it's often the primary way that a user communicates with a program. The *left* button always means that something on the screen has been selected. The *right* (and *middle*, in some cases) button can mean various things to various programs. But the left button nearly always means: *do this, this thing that I've moved to and am now choosing by clicking it.*

```
Sub Picture1_Click
End Sub
```

In many VB programs, you'll put a considerable percentage of the program's instructions between the Sub_Click and End Sub commands of various Controls and Forms. The Click Event is the area where you'll locate many of the things you want to happen while a VB program runs.

"Events" are described in detail in "A Step-by-Step Guide to Programming" at the beginning of this book.

A Click Event is also triggered in the following special circumstances:

• Pressing the arrow keys to select something in a Combo or List Box.

• Pressing the Spacebar if a Command or Option Button or a Check Box has the focus (see "ActiveControl" for more about *focus*).

• Pressing the ENTER key when a Command Button on the Form has its Default Property set to –1 (True).

• Pressing the ESC key when a Command Button on the Form has its Cancel Property set to –1 (True).

Used with   Forms, Check Boxes, Combo Boxes, Command Buttons, Directory & File List Boxes, Frames, Grids, Images, Labels, List Boxes, Menus, OLE, Option Buttons, Picture Boxes and Text Boxes

Uses   • Allow the user to control how a program responds or is configured.

• The Click Event is used more frequently than any other Event in VB.

Cautions   • MouseDown, MouseUp, Click—this is the order in which these Events are detected and acted upon (for File List Boxes, List and Picture Boxes and Labels).

This makes it possible for you to fine-tune response to the mouse in these Controls. For example, you might create a Picture Box icon that behaves two different ways: one way when the user simply clicks, another way when the user holds down the mouse button.

The MouseUp Event, in particular, will allow you to know (when used in conjunction with the Timer Function) precisely how long the mouse button was held down. Your program can respond in different ways depending on how the user applies the mouse to your Picture Box.

Example
```
Sub Command1_Click
    ShoePicture.Visible = 0
End Sub
```

Figure C-42: When the user clicks the mouse on this Command Button...

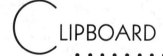

Figure C-43: ...the shoe promptly disappears.

See also   DblClick; MouseDown; MouseMove; MouseUp

CLIPBOARD

OBJECT

Description   This is the command you use to access the Windows Clipboard.

Variables   To erase the Clipboard:

```
Clipboard.Clear
```

OR (to get some text from the Clipboard): T$ = Clipboard.GetText()

OR (to get a graphic image from the Clipboard):

```
Picture1.picture = clipboard.GetData()
```

OR (to save a graphic image from the Form to the Clipboard):

```
Clipboard.SetData Picture
```

OR (to save a graphic image from a Picture Box to the Clipboard):

```
Clipboard.SetData Picture1.Picture
```

OR (to save text to the Clipboard): Clipboard.SetText Text1.Text

Uses   • Allow users to export and import pictures or text between your application and other applications.

• Permit cutting, copying and pasting pictures or text, like the typical Windows application does through an Edit Menu.

Cautions • There can be only one Clipboard at a time, and only one item in the Clipboard at a time. You may want to notify the user if something is being overwritten (at least the first time the Clipboard is accessed from within your application) in case there's something in the Clipboard the user wishes to keep.

• The Clipboard gives no warning that it is being overwritten.

Example To copy a selected area of text to the Clipboard, use the SelText command with a Text Box. Here, when the user clicks on the Form, the selected text is copied. Presumably in an application you'd use a menu or Command Buttons for cutting, pasting and copying.

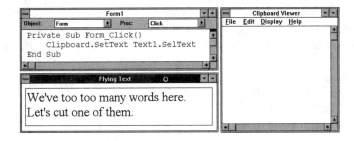

Figure C-44: Dragging to highlight the offending item prior to moving it into the Clipboard.

Results in

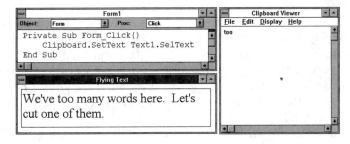

Figure C-45: The data moves to the Clipboard.

Clipboard Methods
Clear • GetData • GetFormat • GetText • SetData • SetText

See also Clear; GetData; GetFormat; GetText; SelText; SetData; SetText

CLIPCONTROLS

PROPERTY

Description   ClipControls determines whether VB defines a zone within a Form (or Picture Box or Frame) that should be repainted if a Form is resized or covered then uncovered by another Form. This is essentially an issue involving how VB should handle *drawn* graphics (with the PSet, Line or Circle command, or with the Print command for text).

If your Form has no drawn or printed elements, for example, but many non-overlapping Command Buttons, you can speed up the repainting of that Form by setting ClipControls to False. If your Form has drawn or printed elements, the safest way to ensure that they display correctly each time the Form is repainted is to put the drawing or printing commands within the Form's Paint Event—and leave ClipControls set to True. Even if you set ClipControls to False, the improvement in the speed of repainting is often not noticeable.

ClipControls, which defaults to True, is a Property of the "container" Objects in VB—Picture Boxes, Frames and Forms. If other Controls are placed on these Objects, they will also be moved around the screen if the Objects are moved.

Graphics Methods: Visual Basic and Windows follow a complex set of rules and protocols for the display of graphics onscreen. For one thing, in VB there are three "layers," three zones that determine what covers what when images overlap. The lowest layer, the one that gets covered by any other layer, includes graphics that are drawn (using the PSet, Circle or Line command) or Printed using the Print command. Also on this background layer are images imported into the Form via its Picture Property.

The middle layer—which covers drawn graphics but is covered by most Controls (like Command Buttons)—is composed of the Image Control, the Picture Box and Labels.

On top of everything are most of the rest of the Controls—File Boxes, Scroll Bars and so on.

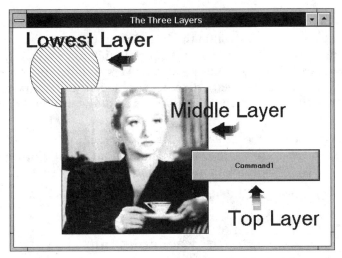

Figure C-46: The three "layers" the zones in VB that determine what covers what when two or more things overlap.

Experimentation is your best approach with this overlap issue. The ClipControls and AutoRedraw Properties, along with whether or not you put draw commands (PSet, Circle or Line) and Print within the Paint Event of the Form, determine the behavior of overlapping visuals. Microsoft suggests that you put draw commands within the Paint Event, but you can get some interesting effects by putting them elsewhere.

Used with   Forms, Frames and Picture Boxes

Variables   You must adjust ClipControls within the Properties Window while designing your program; you cannot change it while a program is running.

Uses   Turn ClipControls off to speed up repainting, but this can cause odd, unintended graphics effects (when drawing commands are not within the Paint Event or when the AutoRedraw Property is set to False). And the speed increase is often unnoticeable.

Cautions   • When AutoRedraw (which see) is True, you can speed things up by turning ClipControls to False. No graphics foul-ups will occur with Auto-Redraw on. And with ClipControls off, VB can re-Paint faster.

• If AutoRedraw is False (the default), you should put any drawing or printing commands within the Paint Event; otherwise, a new drawing or printing will overprint existing Controls and other visuals (shown in the Example). Also, if another window covers and then uncovers your Form (or the Form is enlarged), drawn or printed visuals can be erased. See "AutoRedraw" for a complete discussion of the pros and cons of this Property.

• Don't "nest" a Control with ClipControls set to True inside a Control with it set to False. For example, don't put a Frame (with ClipControls set to True) inside a Form with its ClipControls Property set to False.

Example

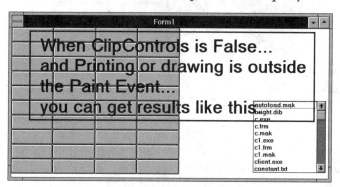

Figure C-47: With ClipControls off, printing or drawing can *overprint* Controls.

To try out the effects of drawing and printing with ClipControls off, start a New Project and set Form1's ClipControls Property to False. Then put a Command Button on the Form and set its Index Property to 0. This will let us create a Control Array (which see). Then put a File List Box on the Form. Now, in the Form_Load Event, create the Control Array:

```
Sub Form_Load ()

Show
Rows = 10
Columns = 4
Movedown = command1(0).Height
Moveacross = command1(0).Width
command1(0).Visible = 0

For I = 0 To Rows — 1
    For J = 0 To Columns — 1
        x = x + 1
        Load command1(x)
        command1(x).Top = Movedown * I
        command1(x).Left = Moveacross * J
        command1(x).Visible = —1
    Next J
Next I

End Sub
```

Finally, we'll draw a square and print some text:

```
Sub Form_Click ()

drawwidth = 3
Line (500, 100) – (8500, 2500), , B
currentx = 800: currenty = 200
fontsize = 24
Print "When ClipControls is False..."
currentx = 800
Print "and Printing or drawing is outside"
currentx = 800
Print "the Paint Event..."
currentx = 800
Print "you can get results like this."
End Sub
```

Also try moving this drawing-printing activity out of the Click Event and into the Form's Paint Event to see the difference in VB's behavior.

See also   AutoRedraw; Paint

FUNCTION

Description   CLng is one of a group of commands whose inclusion in VB may be mystifying (others in this family are listed under "See also"). The reason these commands are included in Visual Basic is that they're carryovers from Microsoft's DOS-based Basic language. Including them in VB can make it easier to convert programs written in earlier Basic into VB programs.

CLng accomplishes the same thing that assigning a number to a Long Integer Variable type accomplishes, but assigning is a preferable approach. For more information on numeric Variable types, see "Variables."

```
y = 44.12
r = CLng (y)
Print r
```

Results in   44

The same result can be achieved in this preferred fashion:

```
y = 44.12
r& = y
Print r&
```

Results in   44

The type of Variable that gets the answer of a calculation (the Variable "RESULT&" in RESULT& = 5 / 2) determines the precision and range of the calculation.

Used with Numeric expressions (see "Variables")

Variables result& = CLng (somenumber)

OR: result& = CLng (x / y)

(You can use any calculation inside the parentheses—using any mixture of numeric Variable Types, literal numbers, Constants and operators. For more on these numeric expressions, see "Variables.")

Example
```
x% = 777
result& = CLng (x%)
```

See also CCur; CDbl; CInt; CSng; DefType; Fix; Int; Variables

 LOSE

STATEMENT

Description Close shuts a previously opened disk file (or several). While a file is open, the computer can keep some information from that file in a "buffer" in the computer's memory. This is because the computer operates much more quickly within its memory than it does going to and from the disk. If you're writing a letter or painting a picture, it's more efficient for the computer to maintain the information in memory—and make changes to it in memory—than to keep reading and writing to the relatively slow disk. However, it's important that the final version of that information be stored on disk. Close causes the file to be sent to the disk.

Note: Both the Data and OLE Controls have a Close *Method* command. See those entries for more.

Used with Disk Files

Variables To close all opened files:
```
Close
```

OR (to close a specific file): Close #1

OR (to close several specific files): Close #1, #8, #3

Uses Whenever you Open a file, be sure to use Close before your program is shut down. Often, Close is one of the commands you'll put in the Click Event of the Command Button or Menu Item you label *Quit*. When the user wants to exit your program, you need to make sure that any changes to data are saved safely to the disk. Other times you'll open a file, read or write to it, then close it again—all within the same Event or Subroutine.

Cautions   There are several types of files you can open: Binary, Sequential and Random. They serve different purposes, but any type of file is *closed* via the Close command. For more information on file management, see "Open."

Example   Close   (by itself closes *all* open files)

Close #1   (Closes only the file that was Opened as #1. Each file you open is given an individual digit to identify it for use by Write #, Print #, Close and other file-manipulation commands to identify each file.)

See also   End; Get; Input #; Input$; Line Input #; Open; Print #; Put; Reset; Seek; Stop; Write #

Cls

METHOD

Description   Cls removes any graphics drawn (with the Circle, Line or PSet commands) or any text printed (with the Print command).
Cls gives you a clean Form background or Picture Box.

Used with   Forms, Images and Picture Boxes

Variables   Used by itself, Cls clears the current Form:

Cls

OR (to clear a Picture Box): Picture1.Cls

OR (to clear a Form other than the one within which the Cls command is located): Form5.Cls

Uses   • Cls can contribute to animation by replacing graphics on the fly while your program is running. (As an alternative, you can turn on and off the Visible Property.)

• Cls can remove messages or graphics when they're no longer needed on a Form or Picture Box.

Cautions   • After a Cls statement, the CurrentX and CurrentY Properties are reset to 0,0 (the upper left corner).

• Cls does *not* clear Picture Boxes, Images (or the backgrounds of Forms) when they hold bitmap images you imported with the Picture Property or the LoadPicture command. The only way to clear these is to load in a blank bitmap with the LoadPicture command. Picture1.LoadPicture( ) contains no information between the parentheses about which picture to load, so the Picture Box will be blanked. Or you could turn a Picture Box's Visible Property off (False).

• Cls works only on graphics drawn while your program is running using the Circle, Line, PSet or Print command.

• The AutoRedraw Property can be made to interact with Cls, resulting in additional special effects. (See the Example.)

Example   We'll draw a patterned background, then print a message on top of it. Because of the way we manipulate the AutoRedraw Property, the message will be susceptible to Cls but the background will not be affected.

```
Sub Form_Load ()

autoredraw = −1
Show
BackColor = &HFF8080

howmany = 20

For i = 1 To howmany
Line (i * scalewidth / howmany, 0)-(i * scalewidth / howmany, →
    scaleheight), QBColor(1)
Next i

autoredraw = 0

forecolor = QBColor(0)
fontsize = 12
message$ = "OUR DISAPPEARING MESSAGE"
currentX = scalewidth / 2 - TextWidth(message$) / 2
currentY = scaleheight / 2 -TextHeight(message$) / 2

Print message$

End Sub
```

First we turn on the AutoRedraw Property. This prevents Cls from operating if AutoRedraw is turned off just before a Cls takes place. The Show command is necessary when you're drawing graphics on a Form (if the Form is not currently visible). You must first Show the Form, or nothing will be drawn within a Form_Load Event.

We picked out the BackColor, a navy blue, from VB's Color Palette Window. You can find out which RGB number will produce the color you want by using the Properties Window to set a Form's BackColor; VB puts the number into the Properties Window. The Variable Howmany will determine how many pinstripes we'll draw in the For...Next Loop just following. (See "Line" for an explanation of the Line command Variables.)

Persistent Graphics: Now we turn AutoRedraw off. This will have the effect of making the pinstripe graphics *persistent*–they were drawn while

AutoRedraw was *on*. Now that we've turned AutoRedraw off, anything printed or drawn from here on will be vulnerable to a Cls. Finally we print our vulnerable message on the screen. The manipulations of ScaleWidth and Height and TextWidth and Height will center any text for you. We're moving the current location (where the printing will start) to one half of the width and height of the current object—in this case, our Form. Then we adjust for the size of the text itself.

Here's what we see when the Form loads:

Figure C-48: This text has been left vulnerable to a Cls command.

Now, by changing the AutoRedraw Property to False *just before using the Cls*, we preserve anything we drew while AutoRedraw was True but *remove* anything drawn while AutoRedraw was False:

```
Sub Form_Click ()
    autoredraw = False
    Cls
End Sub
```

Clicking on the Form removes the message, since it was drawn while AutoRedraw was False:

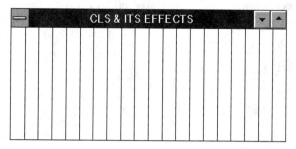

Figure C-49: The drawn background cannot be erased by the Cls command, but the text disappears.

See also   AutoRedraw; CurrentX, CurrentY; LoadPicture; Visible

COLLECTIONS

OBJECT

Description When you think of an "object," the idea suggests something singular and self-contained: a handfull of cancelled stamps thrown across the floor wouldn't be an object, though each individual stamp would be an object. However, it's possible to consider a container to be an object, and it in turn contains other objects. For example, a stamp collector's album is an object, and it contains stamp objects. A *collection*, therefore, can be an object.

In VB4 you can gang items together into a kind of "Array" called a *Collection Object*. This is very handy because VB4 allows you to manipulate the items (the "elements") in a Collection more freely and efficiently than you can manipulate the items in a traditional Array. In fact, when you are tempted to use an Array, consider instead the virtues of putting your data into a Collection.

A Collection is a meta-Object, or cluster. (Think of it as an Array of related Objects. Just what their relationship is depends on you. They're related because you decided to add them to this particular Collection.)

You can use Collections to manipulate an individual Object (element) within the Collection. Or since a Collection is itself an Object, you can manipulate Properties of the entire Collection at once. In other words, Collections have their own Properties (Count) and Methods (Add, Remove an item).

Used with Ordinary data, or Objects

Variables You create a Collection like this:

```
Dim MyThings As New Collection
```

Then you access and manipulate that Collection with the Add and Remove Methods, or the Count Property: MyThings.Add This

OR, to use a Variable:

```
A$ = This
MyThings.Add A$
```

OR, to add a numeric and a text element:

```
MyThings.Add 124.3
MyThings.Add  Sandhausen
```

OR, to add Objects:

```
Dim SomeBoxes As New Collection
Dim T1 As Object
Dim T2 As Object
Private Sub Form_Load( )
Set T1 = text1
Set T2 = Text2
```

```
SomeBoxes.Add T1
SomeBoxes.Add T2
For I = 1 To SomeBoxes.Count
    SomeBoxes(I).Text = They re all the same
Next I
End Sub
```

Uses • A Collection can contain data of various types, mixed together into the Collection. For instance, you could put text and numeric data in the same collection:

```
Dim MixedBag As New Collection

Private Sub Form_Load( )
Show

MixedBag.Add  Delores
MixedBag.Add  Murphy
MixedBag.Add 55

For i = 1 To 3
  Print MixedBag(i)
Next i

End Sub
```

(You could also do this, however, with an Array of the Variant type.)

• When you declare a Collection, you don't provide it with the number of items you expect it to contain (an Array must specify the quantity of items it will hold).

• You can manipulate a Collection more easily than an Array. The Add Method allows you to put new data into the Collection as often as you want; to provide a separate text "index" to each element; to insert an element "Before" or "After" another element. The Remove Method allows you to get rid of an element. The Count Property tells you how many items are currently stored in the Collection.

• A Collection Object can contain other Objects.

Cautions • Most Objects can be part of a Collection. However, you can't, at the time of this writing, use Add to add Controls to a Collection (though Controls *are* Objects). This differs from VBA in Excel. Once you place a Control (such as a Picture Box) onto a worksheet (Excel's equivalent of VB's Form)—an *implicit* Collection of Picture Boxes is created. You don't have to define this collection (Dim MyCol As New Collection). It already exists and you can Add to it or Remove from it freely.

In VB, the only way to dynamically add a Control, or to group Controls and treat them as an Array, is the Load command (which see) to create a Control Array (which see). A Control can be removed from a Control Array by changing its Name Property, but this cannot be done while a program is running (only in the Properties Window during program design). In this and other ways, a Control Array is less flexible than a Control Collection would be, but as yet this facility isn't available in VB. A Control Array resembles a traditional Array more than it resembles a Collection.

Remember to always evaporate an Object when it is no longer needed:

```
Set SomeShapes = Nothing
```

Example

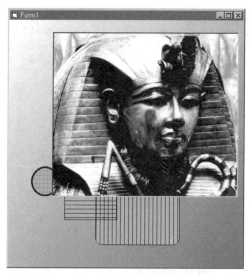

Figure C-50: Here we ll simulate a Collection of three Shape Controls and one Picture Box Control.

Figure C-51: After we change their Left Properties in the Collection, they line up on the left.

You *can* simulate a Control Array with a Collection. This example confers one special advantage over just using a Control Array. You can mix *various kinds of Controls* into the Collection, then easily manipulate any Properties they might have in common. Here we'll move three Shapes and a Picture Box to line them up to one horizontal location by setting all their Left Properties. First, we create the collection, then use the Set command to create four *Object Variables* (S1 through S4) which point to the four Control Objects. Then we *can* use the Add Method to put these Object Variables into our Collection. Now we go ahead and move them all over to line up horizontally by changing a Property they have in common—Left:

```
Dim SomeShapes As New Collection
Sub Form_Click( )
Set S1 = Shape1
Set S2 = Shape2
Set S3 = Picture1
Set S4 = Shape3

SomeShapes.Add S1
SomeShapes.Add S2
SomeShapes.Add S3
SomeShapes.Add S4

For I = 1 To SomeShapes.Count
   SomeShapes(I).Left = 700
Next I

End Sub
```

See also   Add, Arrays, Objects

 OLUMNS

PROPERTY

Description   The Columns Property allows you to change the style of a List Box from its default (a single column of items) to a newspaper-style "snaking," multiple-column list of items. When Columns is set to the default 0, if there are more items than can be displayed within the Box, a Vertical Scroll Bar is automatically attached to the Box, and the user can scroll through the list.

If Columns is set to a number other than the default 0, the items in the list appear in the number of columns specified, moving to the next column when the list fills to the bottom of each column. A Horizontal Scroll Bar is attached to the Box, allowing the user to scroll horizontally through the columns.

Used with   List Boxes and DBGrids

Variables   **Variable type:** Integer

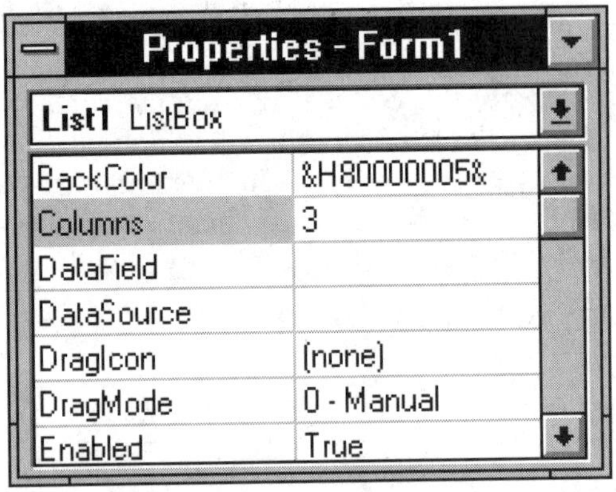

Figure C-52: You can set the Columns Property in the Properties Window.

OR (to change the number of Columns while the program is running):

    List1.Columns = 5

OR (to find out how many Columns are currently active): X = List1.Columns

Uses
• If you have many items to display in a List Box, then use Columns to make more of the items visible at a glance to the user. Also, using Columns instead of simply stretching a long vertical list gives you more ways to design good-looking Forms.

• Because you can change Columns while the program is running, you could measure the longest item of data (see "TextWidth") and then, by dividing List1.Width by Columns, determine if you should make the Width larger or smaller to fit the data. Alternatively, you could allow the user to specify the size of the List Box or the number of visible columns.

Cautions
• The number you give to the Columns Property divides the List Box into that many visual columns. In other words, if you set Columns to 4, the cur-rent width of the List Box will be divided into four columns. VB will print the items on top of each other unless your data fits in the space you provide. Be sure when designing your program that your Form width is sufficient to hold the largest item of data that will be placed into the Box.

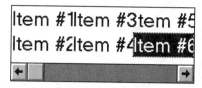

Figure C-53: The data will be clipped if there are too many columns to fit into the List Box's width.

Example

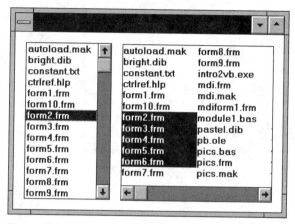

Figure C-54: The List Box is more flexible than other boxes: it offers multiple columns, horizontal scrolling and multiple selections.

Put a File List Box and a List Box on a Form. Set the List Box's Columns Property to 2 and its MultiSelect Property to 1 (Simple). Then, in the Form_Load Event, type the following to fill the List Box with all the filenames in the File List Box:

```
For i = 0 To file1.ListCount — 1
    list1.AddItem file1.List(i)
    Next i
End Sub
```

Now you can allow the user to select several files simultaneously (for copying, moving or deleting). In addition, the List Box uses space on your window more efficiently—more information can be visible to the user before scrolling becomes necessary.

See also List Box; MultiSelect

CONTROL

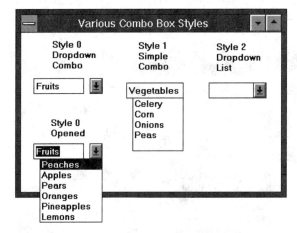

Figure C-55: Combo Boxes come in three styles.

Description   Combo Boxes are similar to List Boxes: a List Box simply provides a list of options the user can choose from, but a Combo Box offers its list and also allows the user to type in additional items. (In one style of Combo Box, the user is not allowed to type in additional items. See "Cautions.")

Your program detects the user's selections—they trigger the Box's Click Event. Your program also knows when the user starts typing—that act triggers the Box's Change Event.

Used with   Lists that you want the user to be able to modify

Variables   Your program can add or remove items from a Combo Box:

Combo1.AddItem "New York"

OR (to add a Variable): Combo1.AddItem N$

OR (to remove the fourth item from a Combo Box): Combo1.RemoveItem 3

The items in a List or Combo Box start with a zeroth item, so the fourth item is removed by requesting number 3.

Uses   • Offer the user choices but accept alternatives. For example, if your program dialed the telephone and was an electronic substitute for a Rolodex, you could keep track of the six most frequently dialed people. Then when the program was started, you would show a List Box with these people already there so the user could just click on one of them.

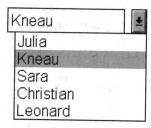

Figure C-56: The highlighted item is the currently "selected" option in the list.

Pressing ENTER would select the one that's highlighted. Pressing arrow keys moves the user up and down the list. The Sorted Property was set to –1, so the items in the list are alphabetized. And—the main feature—there's a place for the user to simply type in a person who is not listed in the top six.

Cautions
• **Generally Avoid This One:** You may want to avoid the default Drop-down Combo style (the 0 setting). The Box's arrow button is separated from the Text Box portion. When it first appears, only the Text Box appears. To select from the options, the user must click on the arrow. You will probably want to use the second style, which shows the whole list of options right from the start. Some programmers, however, use Dropdown Combo when they're pretty certain that the single piece of text that shows within the (undropped) box will be the text the user wants to select and that the user will rarely need the other options that remain invisible. Concealing the unneeded text can make for a clean, uncluttered layout, and therefore a more attractive window. Note that a Combo Box's list can drop below the host window.

• **The Zeroth Problem:** Because computer language designers still cling to the confusing habit of starting a count from zero, the first style of Combo Box is 0, the second is 1 and the third is 2. This can be a source of error; it also makes memorizing things difficult. (See "Arrays" for a cure.)

• **Use This One:** When you set its Style Property to 1, a Combo Box becomes a "simple" box—the box's list is always displayed so there's no arrow button. This is your best choice unless your Form is so crowded that you need to conserve space by using the arrow instead of the list.

• **Avoid This One at All Costs:** With its Style Property set to 2, the Combo Box becomes a Dropdown List Box and combines the weaknesses of a List Box (the user cannot type in alternatives to the listed items) with the drawbacks of the Dropdown Combo Box (no information on the options until the user clicks on the arrow button).

Style 2 does not trigger a Change Event, since nothing can be typed into it. The Click (not DblClick) and the DropDown Events are the only Events that Style 2 will trigger. The DropDown Event allows you to fix the list if you want to update it before the user sees it. DropDown is triggered when the user tries to see the list.

Unlike the other Combo Box styles, you cannot modify the Text Property of Style 2. Its one *raison d'être* is, as the manual says, that it "conserves screen space"—but often at the expense of user comfort and convenience.

Example

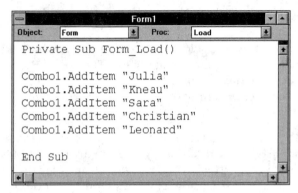

Figure C-57: You generally put items into a Combo or List Box in the Form_Load Event.

Combo Box Properties
BackColor • DataField • DataSource • DragIcon • DragMode • Enabled
FontBold • FontItalic • FontName • FontSize • FontStrikethru
FontUnderline • ForeColor • Height • HelpContextID • hWnd • Index
ItemData • Left • List • ListCount • ListIndex • MousePointer • Name
NewIndex • Parent • SelLength • SelStart • SelText • Sorted • Style
TabIndex • TabStop • Tag • Text • Top • Visible • Width

Combo Box Events
Change • Click • DblClick • DragDrop • DragOver • DropDown
GotFocus • KeyDown • KeyPress • KeyUp • LostFocus

Combo Box Methods
AddItem • Clear • Drag • Move • Refresh • RemoveItem • SetFocus
ZOrder

See also   AddItem; Clear; List Box (the user cannot type in any alternative to what's in the list); ListCount; ListIndex; Refresh; RemoveItem; Text Box

Command Button

Description   The Command Button is perhaps the most popular Control in Visual Basic. It provides visually intuitive, direct access—the user sees the Caption and simply clicks the mouse on it to get something done. The animation offers good, strong feedback; there's a real sense that something has happened, unlike some other VB selection methods. Put a group of buttons into a window and it can look like a control panel on the Starship *Enterprise*.

Figure C-58: Command Buttons are "activators." Here the Buttons display new windows in the program.

Used with   Virtually everything. This is Visual Basic's "make something happen" button.

Variables   You can adjust a Command Button's various Properties from the Properties Window while designing your program:

Properties - Form1	
Command1 CommandButton	
Name	Command1
TabIndex	1
TabStop	True
Tag	
Top	4695
Visible	True

Figure C-59: Using the Properties Window to change the qualities of a Command Button.

OR (to adjust the FontSize of the Command Button's Caption while the program is running): Command1.FontSize = 14

OR (to find out the Command Button's FontName while the program is running): X$ = Command1.FontName

Uses   Use Command Buttons any time the user needs to make something happen in the program. Accompany them with Picture Boxes, Labels and animated Events (such as icons rearranged onscreen by the Move command) and you'll be tapping into the real power of Visual Basic.

Cautions   • Be sure to set the BackColor Property of a Command Button to match the BackColor of the Form or other object surrounding the Button. Otherwise, four pixels in the corners of the Button can be the wrong color and look funny onscreen.

   • The SSCommand Button offers several advantages over the ordinary Command Button (3-D Fonts, Picture Property). In the Tools menu, click Custom Controls. Then select Sheridan 3-D Controls.

Example   This program is essentially a database, disguised as an "electronic cookbook." All the usual database and word processing options are available by clicking on Command Buttons. Some of the Buttons reveal currently hidden (their Visible Property = 0) additional groups of Command Buttons.

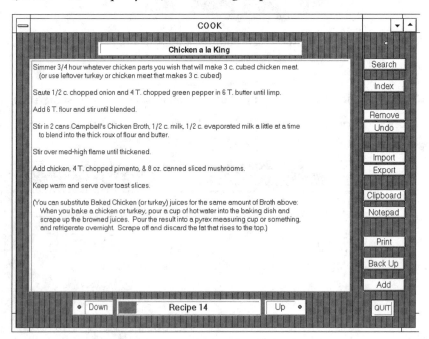

Figure C-60: A window filled with Command Buttons.

Command Button Properties

BackColor • Cancel • Caption • Default • DragIcon • DragMode
Enabled • FontBold • FontItalic • FontName • FontSize
FontStrikethru • FontUnderline • Height • HelpContextID • hWnd
Index • Left • MousePointer • Name • Parent • TabIndex • TabStop
Tag • Top • Value • Visible • Width

Command Button Events

Click • DragDrop • DragOver • GotFocus • KeyDown • KeyPress
KeyUp • LostFocus • MouseDown • MouseMove • MouseUp

Command Button Methods

Drag • Move • Refresh • SetFocus • ZOrder

See also   Cancel; Default

COMMAND, COMMAND$ FUNCTION

Description   When your program starts, Command$ can pass some information—from the user to the program—about what should happen first.

Command$ mimics the user's typed command or instruction when the program first opens up and needs guidance from the user. Command$ can be a way to load in a file to a word processor or establish conditions or options in the program that the user routinely prefers.

Command does the same thing as Command$, but Command provides a *Variant* Variable instead of a text (string) Variable type. (See "Variables.")

Used with   Any program

Variables   From within File Manager or other program launcher, you name the program you want to run, followed by a Command$:

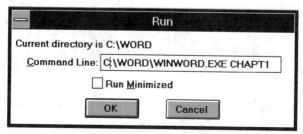

Figure C-61: How Windows's File Manager accepts command strings.

In this case, we're starting Word for Windows (from within File Manager's Run Window). We've added the name of a file, CHAPT1, that gets fed to Word as the document we want opened when Word starts. Many programs allow you to give them a Command$, and you might want to offer this feature in your Visual Basic programs.

Uses
• Allow the user to customize program startup.

• Allow the user to select (when launching your program from the general Windows environment) the data your program will first operate upon, or the options that will be operative at startup.

Many of the Windows shells, the RUN command from Program Manager and PIFs allow users to configure program startup in a certain way–to specify what they want to feed the program when it starts. Command$ is the thing fed to it from the outside that a Visual Basic program absorbs into itself. You can have your program look at Command$ and decide what to do before the user even gets control.

Cautions
While you're designing a VB program, you can test Command$ by using the Command Line Argument feature in the VB Tools Menu "Project Options." This will pass the Command$ to the VB program when you want to test the effects by pressing F5 to start your program.

Example
You can allow the user to start your program with several instructions. Conventionally, multiple startup instructions are separated either by spaces or by slashes (/). Here, we might be telling our VB program to run as an icon, to use full menus and to load in all data beginning with the letter S.

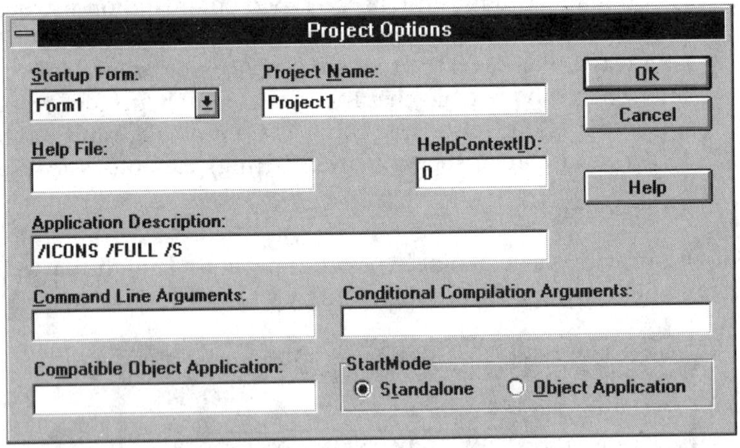

Figure C-62: Command strings can include several instructions to the program.

What happens first when a VB program is run by the user? There's always one Form that's designated the *Startup Form* (which see). By default, this will be the first Form you work with when designing your program. However, you can change the Startup Form in the Options Menu.

So, when a VB program runs, it first looks for instructions in the Startup Form's Form_Load Event. It's there, in that Event, that you would examine any Command$.

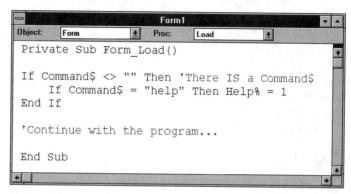

```
                          Form1
Object:   Form          ▼    Proc:    Load              ▼
Private Sub Form_Load()

If Command$ <> "" Then 'There IS a Command$
    If Command$ = "help" Then Help% = 1
End If

'Continue with the program...

End Sub
```

Figure C-63: If your program accepts command strings, you will want to examine them in the Form_Load Event.

Here we've previously defined a Variable in a Module:

```
Global Help As Integer
```

so that it can be accessed *anywhere* in our entire program. Now, in the Startup Form_Load Event, we decide whether to set HELP% to 1 or leave it at the default of 0. If the user has supplied a Command$ consisting of the text "help," then we set HELP% to 1. We've decided that this will mean that our VB program will provide automatic Help message boxes from time to time, to guide the user through the features of the program. If, for example, the user selects a Command Button labeled INDEX, we might put this in the Click Event of that Button:

```
If HELP = 1 Then
    MsgBox ("Index gives you a list of all the entries.")
End If
```

Once the user learned how to use our program, these Help messages would become tiresome, so by then the user would not provide any Command$ requesting them.

Of course, you could have a Menu or Command Button *within* your VB program that turned Help messages on or off. But some people like to start programs with custom features or data set up at the launch of the program. Command$ is particularly useful to load in data—to let the user specify, for example, which text file should be loaded into a word processor.

See also   Startup Form

COMMON DIALOG

CONTROL

Figure C-64: The Common Dialog Control icon in the Toolbox.

Description   To prevent each programmer from designing, for example, unique file-management windows, Microsoft has established a standard window with which the user can access disk files. The Common Dialog Control also includes standardized windows for accessing the printer, displaying a Help file, choosing colors, and choosing typefaces (fonts). When you use the Common Dialog Boxes, the user will already know how to work them, where the buttons are, etc. The goal is that for disk access, printer control, and color and font changes, every Windows program will present the user with the same Dialog Boxes. Plus, you can avoid a lot of programming by simply using this handy Control.

Depending on which of the Common Dialog Method commands you use, a different dialog window is displayed, waiting for user input:

CommonDialog1.ShowOpen   Open Disk File
CommonDialog1.ShowSave   Save As (to disk file)
CommonDialog1.ShowColor   Select a color
CommonDialog1.ShowFont   Select a font (and fontsize)
CommonDialog1.ShowPrinter   Print (and Printer Setup)
CommonDialog1.ShowHelp   Run the Windows Help program WINHELP.EXE

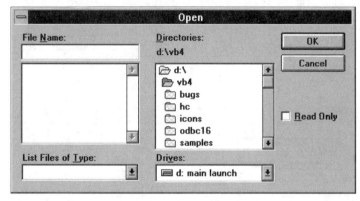

Figure C-65: The Open Disk File Dialog Box.

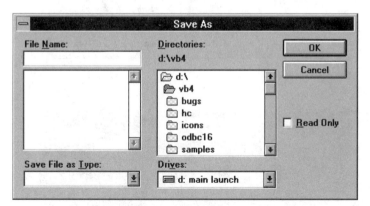

Figure C-66: The Save File As Dialog Box.

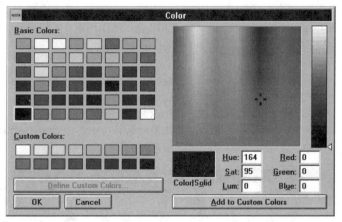

Figure C-67: The Color Dialog Box.

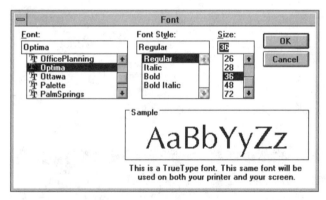

Figure C-68: The Font Dialog Box.

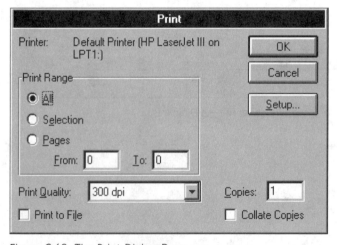

Figure C-69: The Print Dialog Box.

Used with   Forms, to provide a standardized user interface

Variables   To title a Dialog Box:

CommonDialog1.DialogTitle = "FILE"

OR to trigger an "error" if the user selects the Cancel Button on a Dialog Box:

CommonDialog1.CancelError = True   (the default is false)

Each of the Dialog Boxes has a CancelError, DialogTitle, HelpCommand, HelpContext, HelpFile and HelpKey Property. But they differ in which other Properties they have. For instance, the Font Dialog Box has a Font-Size Property, which tells your VB program what size the user selected. The Font Dialog Box also has Max and Min Properties to allow you to set upper and lower fontsize limits beyond which the user cannot choose. On the other hand, the two file-access Dialog Boxes have no font Properties but do have an InitDir Property, which allows you to specify which disk directory will be displayed as the default.

Each Box has a Flags Property, but the meaning of the flags differs for each Box. For more on the various Properties, see "Common Dialog Box Properties" later in this section.

Uses   To allow the user to customize the BackColor Property of Forms or Controls; to control the printer; to change screen or printer fonts; to load or save disk files; and to display online help.

Cautions   • If your program uses Common Dialog Controls, the program's user must have the files COMMDLG.DLL and CMDIALOG.VBX in his or her Windows\System directory. You can use the VB Setup facility to ensure that these files are stored in Windows\System. For VB4, the required files are COMDLG16.OCX and COMDLG32.OCX.

• You have no control over where onscreen a Common Dialog Window will appear.

• Like the MsgBox and InputBox Functions, the Common Dialog puts up rather two-dimensional displays. You might want to design your own custom Dialog Boxes. To retain compatibility with other Windows applications, you can follow the layout—the position of Labels, Text Boxes and so on—of the Common Dialog Control. But design your own backgrounds and add 3D framing (see "Line").

• You'll get a "No Fonts Exist" error message if you try to display the Font Dialog Box without first setting the Flags Property to either 1 (show screen fonts), 2 (show printer fonts), or 3 (show both): CommonDialog1.Flags = 2

• The Common Dialog is an invisible Control when a program runs, only being displayed when you activate it. When, in your program, you include the command CommonDialog1.ShowColor, the color selection Box will appear. The word you use in place of ShowColor determines which of the six Dialog Boxes appears when the Action Property is specified within the program.

Example

```
Sub Form_Load ()
    CommonDialog1.Flags = 3
    CommonDialog1.Color = QBColor(14)
    CommonDialog1.ShowColor
End Sub
```

This program displays the Color Dialog Box. Before activating the Box with the ShowColor Method, we first set two flags and a default color. "Flags" can be added together. In other words, you can set more than a single Flag at a time. If you set the Color Box Flag Property to 1, whatever is specified in the Color Property will be shown as the default color when the Box first appears to the user. If you set the Color Box Flag Property to 2, the "Define Custom Colors" window will be displayed along with the smaller Colors Box. Because we want to do both of these things, we add 1 + 2 and set the Flags Property to 3.

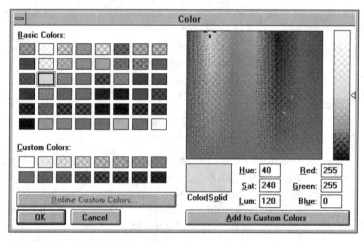

Figure C-70: The full Color Dialog Box is displayed, along with a default bright yellow color selection.

After setting the Flags, we define the default color as QBColor(14), a bright yellow. (Even if you define the Color Property, the user still won't see that color displayed as the default color unless the Flags Property is also set to 1, or 1 plus some other flag number.) Finally, we show the Box onscreen with the ShowColor Method. The Method determines which of the Common Dialog Boxes will be displayed—in this case it will be the Color Dialog Box.

Common Dialog Box Properties

• Each type of Box has several unique Properties. However, they all have a CancelError, DialogTitle, HelpCommand, HelpContext, HelpFile and HelpKey Property. First we'll define the Properties they have in common and then describe the unique Properties.

• When a Property (such as Flags) can be set to several different numbers, we've provided the actual numbers here. Some programmers prefer to use Constants rather than actual numbers in these cases:

Flags = vbCCShowHelp instead of Flags = 8.

If you prefer to use the predefined Constants that Microsoft provides, look in VB Help under the name of the Property (such as Flags), then look for Constants.

• When a Property (such as Flags) can be set to several different numbers, you can trigger more than one of those options by simply adding the numbers together. For example, when you display the Color Dialog Box, setting Flags = 4 prevents the user from selecting the Define Custom Colors Button. Another option, setting Flags = 8, displays a Help Button. If you want to do both, allow no Custom Colors Button and display a Help Button, add the two Flag values, like this:

CommonDialog1.Flags = 12

OR: = vbCCPreventFullOpen + vbCCShowHelp

CancelError: If the user closes a Box by selecting the Cancel button, VB will generate an error if you have set the CancelError Property to True (default is False). An error 32755 is triggered and you can trap it and react to it if you wish, just as if it were a normal VB error (see "On Error").

DialogTitle: You assign a text (string) Variable to the DialogTitle Property and that word or phrase will be displayed as the title of the Box.

HelpCommand, HelpContext, HelpFile and HelpKey Properties: The HelpContextID and HelpFile Properties (which see) work as they do with other VB Controls. However, the HelpCommand and HelpKey Properties are unique to the Common Dialog Boxes.

HelpCommand allows you to specify what will be displayed to the user when the user requests help. (HelpCommand is used in conjunction with the HelpFile and, potentially, the HelpContext Properties.) For HelpCommand the possible settings are:

CommonDialog1.HelpCommand = 1	Shows the Help screen for a particular context. The context must first be defined in the Help-Context Property of the Common Dialog Control.
CommonDialog1.HelpCommand = 2	Tells the Help application that this particular Help file is no longer needed.
CommonDialog1.HelpCommand = 3	Shows the index screen for a help file.
CommonDialog1.HelpCommand = 4	Shows the standard "How to use Help" screen.

CommonDialog1.HelpCommand = 5   If your Help file has more than a single index, this setting makes the index defined by the HelpContext Property the current index.

CommonDialog1.HelpCommand = 257   Shows the screen for a particular keyword. The keyword must first be defined in the HelpKey Property.

The HelpContext Property works for Common Dialog Boxes the way that the HelpContextID Property works for most other Controls. See "HelpContextID."

Specific Properties

Color Dialog Box

Color: Color allows your program to define which color will be initially displayed in the Color Dialog Box when it appears onscreen or returns to your VB program the user's chosen color. The Property is a Long Integer and conforms to the behavior of the RGB Function (which see). Note that you cannot get the results of the user's choice from this Property unless your program first sets the CC_RGBINIT flag. (See Flags.)

Flags:

CommonDialog1.Flags = 1   Causes the color defined by the Color Property to be displayed when the Box is first displayed to the user.

CommonDialog1.Flags = 2   Opens the full Color Dialog Box (including the "Define Custom Colors" window).

CommonDialog1.Flags = 4   Prevents the user from selecting the "Define Custom Colors" button.

CommonDialog1.Flags = 8   Displays a Help button.

File Access Dialog Box

DefaultExt: This three-letter text (string) Variable is displayed to the user. If the user doesn't add a filename extension of his or her own, the DefaultExt is added to the user's filename and the file is saved. Typical extensions are .DOC, .TMP and .TXT. Used only with Open File Box.

FileName: Used with both Open and Save File Boxes, this text Variable specifies the full path (C:\WINDOWS\FILENAME.EXT, for example) of a file. A list of filenames is displayed in the File Boxes, and if the user selects one and clicks on the OK button (or double-clicks on the filename), the FileName Property then contains the full path for that file. The file can then be loaded from, or saved to, disk. You can also establish a default filename to be displayed in the Box's Text Box by setting the FileName Property prior to displaying the File Dialog Box.

FileTitle: This Property contains the filename (not the full path) of the file selected in an Open or Save File Box. The FileTitle Property cannot be changed by your VB program; you can only read the information from the Property. If the Flags Property is set to 256, however, nothing will be returned if your program attempts to read this information.

Filter: Similar to the DefaultExt Property defined above, but can be used with both Save and Open File Dialog Boxes. The Filter is a text Variable that your program can assign to display only certain files in a Box's list of files. If you want to show only those files with a .DOC extension, you would program this: CommonDialog1.Filter = "WORD Files|*.DOC"

Notice that the description of the filter comes first, separated by a pipe symbol, then the actual filter. You can also concatenate several filters and they will be displayed for the user to select among:

CommonDialog1.Filter = "WORD Files|*.DOC|Text Files|*.TXT|Letters to Karen|K*.*"

FilterIndex: If you have more than one Filter, you use the FilterIndex Property to specify which of the Filters will be displayed as the default.

Flags: The Flags Property is a collection of several "switches" that control how the Box looks, which options are checked, etc.

Flags =		
	1	When the Box is displayed, the Read Only Check Box is displayed with a check mark. You can also check the Flags Property to see the status of this Check Box when the user closes the Dialog Box.
	2	If the user saves with a filename that already exists on the disk, a message box will appear, asking the user to confirm that he or she wants to overwrite the existing file.
	4	Eliminates the Read Only Check Box.
	8	Causes the current directory to be retained. (In other words, even if the Dialog Box displays a different directory, the directory that was current when the Box was displayed will remain the current directory.)
	16	A Help button is displayed.
	256	Invalid characters will be permitted in the filename the user selects or types.
	512	Allows the user to select a group of files rather than a single file (by holding down the SHIFT key and using thE arrow keys to expand the selection). You can detect which files the user selected by looking at the FileName Property. All the selected files are listed in a text (string) Variable, separated by spaces.
	1024	You can check the Flags Property when the user closes the Box. If this flag is set, it means that the user specified a file extension (like .TXT) that differs from the default file extension used in the Box.
	2048	The user is permitted to type in valid file paths only. If the user enters an invalid path, the Box displays a warning message.

4096 Prevents the user from typing in a filename that is not listed in the Dialog Box. Setting this Flag automatically also sets the 2048 Flag.

8192 The user will be asked if he or she wants to create a new file. Setting Flags to this also sets the Flags Property to include the values 4096 and 2048, described above.

16384 The Dialog Box will ignore network-sharing violations.

32768 The selected file will not be read-only and will not be in a write-protected directory.

InitDir: Determines the initial directory that is displayed when the Box is shown to the user. If InitDir isn't specified, the current directory is displayed.

MaxFileSize: Defines how large the FileName Property can be in bytes. The default is 256 bytes, but the permissible range is 1 byte to 2,048 bytes. Obviously this property is for uses beyond Windows 3.1, resting, as it does, on top of DOS, which allows a maximum of 11 characters in a filename—8 for the name, 3 for the extension.

Font Dialog Box

Flags:

1 Displays only screen fonts.

2 Lists only printer fonts.

3 Lists both printer and screen fonts.

4 Displays a Help button.

256 Strikethrough, underline, and colors are permitted.

512 The Apply Button is enabled.

1024 Only those fonts that use the Windows Character Set are allowed (no symbols fonts).

2048 No Vector Fonts are permitted.

4096 No Graphic Device Interface font simulations are permitted.

8192 Displays only those font sizes between the range specified in the Min and Max Properties.

16384 Displays only fixed-pitch (not scalable) fonts.

32768 Allows the user to choose only fonts that can work on the screen and the printer. If you set this flag, you should also set the 131072 and 3 flags.

65536 If the user tries to select a font or style that doesn't exist, an error message is displayed.

131072 Displays only scalable fonts.

262144 Displays only TrueType fonts.

FontBold, FontItalic, FontName, FontSize, FontStrikeThru, and Font-Underline: These Properties can be either assigned by your program or selected in the Dialog Box by the user. They behave the same way as they do when they are Properties of other Controls. For more, see the entries under FontItalic, etc.

Max, Min: Although font sizes can be as small as 1 point (a character will be 1/72 of an inch tall) up to 2048 points—you can set the Max and Min Properties of the Font Dialog Box to specify a limited range of permitted font sizes that the user can select. For example, if you allow the user to customize the FontSize for a Label Control, you want to limit the size so the text isn't clipped off when displayed within the Label. You specify the limits with an integer that describes the largest or smallest permitted point size you will allow. Before you can specify this range, however, you must set the Flags Property to 8192 (see "Flags" in preceding entry).

Printer Dialog Box

Copies: Your VB program or the user can specify the number of copies of a document that will be printed. The Copies Property will always be 1 if the Flags Property is set to 262144.

Flags:

0	Allows you to establish (or query) the "All Pages" Option Button.
1	Allows you to establish (or query) the Selection Option Button.
2	Allows you to establish (or query) the Pages Option Button.
4	Disables the Selection Option Button.
8	Disables the Pages Option Button.
16	Allows you to establish (or query) the Collate Check Box.
32	Allows you to establish (or query) the Print To File Check Box.
64	The Print Setup Dialog Box is displayed (instead of the normal Print Dialog Box).
128	Even if there is no default printer, no warning message is displayed.
256	Causes a device context to be returned in the Box's hDC Property, which points to the printer selection made by the user.
512	Causes an "Information Context" message to be returned in the Box's hDC Property, which points to the printer selection made by the user.
2048	Displays a Help button.
262144	With this flag set, the Copies Control is disabled if the selected printer doesn't allow multiple copies of documents. If the printer *does* allow multiples, with this flag set the requested number of copies is listed in the Copies Property.
524288	Hides the Print To File Check Box.

FromPage, ToPage: Your VB program or the user can specify a range of pages to be printed within a document. For these Properties to have any effect, you must first set the Flags Property to 2.

hDC: See "hDC."

Max, Min: Your VB program can limit the range of the FromPage and ToPage boundaries. Set Min to specify the earliest permitted starting page number, and set Max to specify the last page number permitted.

PrinterDefault: This Property is normally True (–1) and in that state VB will make appropriate changes to the WIN.INI file if the user selects a different printer setup (a different page orientation, switching to a FAX device as the default printer, etc.). If you set this Property to False, the user's changes will not be saved in WIN.INI and will not become the current default setup for the printer.

See Also   InputBox, MsgBox

CONDITIONAL COMPILATION

See   #If...Then...#Else

#CONST

See   #If...Then...#Else

CONST

STATEMENT

Description   A *Constant* is something that will not change while your program runs. In fact, the essence of a Constant is that it can never change. It's immutable. It's a fact. For instance, the distance between New York City and Boston, the name of the president of the University of Chicago in 1936, the MVP of Super Bowl VII are Constants. Your spouse is (probably) a Constant. The clothes he or she wears are a Variable.

Many programmers never use Constants. A Variable can perform the same job if you don't change the Variable–if you only get information from it and never adjust its value. Although a Variable could change while your program runs, in practice you can use a Variable just as you would a Constant if you give it a value (such as PrezChic$ = "Robert Hutchins") and never change that value.

In the following example, we use Variables for Cost and Total since we'll be calculating the totals of many items in our program. However, the sales tax is made a Constant, since it will not change. If the tax is raised, you go back into your program and change the Constant.

```
Public Const Tax = 1.06

Cost = 12.59
Total = Tax * Cost
```

You can omit the Public declaration and just use Const Tax = 1.06, but if you *do* use Constants, you may want to put them in a Module so they'll be available to use everywhere in your program.

In fact, you can omit the Const and just say Tax = 1.06. In this case, Tax is a *Variable* since you didn't explicitly call it a Constant. Nonetheless, if you don't reassign a new number to it anywhere in your program, then for all practical purposes it acts like a Constant.

New in VB4

VB's Constants

VB also recognizes a large group of Constants that are "built into" the VB language itself for things like colors, shapes, virtually every Property of every Control. For instance, you can specify a dotted BorderStyle for a Shape Control without using a Constant, if you wish, like this:

```
Shape1.BorderStyle = 3
```

OR, you can use the Constant that VB will automatically recognize for the dotted BorderStyle (you don't have to even load in CONSTANT.TXT in VB4—see "Uses"):

```
Shape1.BorderStyle = vbBSDot
```

If you're using VB4, you can quickly locate, and even paste right into your program, any of the built-in Constants. Just press F2, then select VB, VBA, or the name of the Custom Control in the Libraries list you're working with. Then look in the Classes/Modules list for the name of the Object, or look for an entry named "Constants."

Used with   Information that will not change

Uses   • If you're afraid you might accidentally change a Variable you don't want to change, use Const.

You can use Constant strings (text Variables), too: Language$ = Norwegian

You can add Variable type symbols to Const declarations:

```
Const HugeNumber! = 23425290
```

(Also see "Variables.")

• Many programmers feel that Constants add clarity to their programming—making the code easier to read.

• Prior to VB4, VB came with a file of prewritten Constants that you could add to your programs. To put it into a Module, you would choose File from the Insert Menu (select Load Text from the VB File Menu prior to VB4) and load in "CONSTANT.TXT." However, now with VB4 this memory-inefficient approach (your .exe files got very large) is no longer necessary. VB4 has a huge set of built-in Constants, so you don't need to include CONTANT.TXT.

• Some programmers find that Constants come in handy when utilizing the features of the Windows API. (If the following comments are Greek to you, see Appendix A, where the powerful API is defined and explained with examples.) You would define the values "passed" to the API, such as WM_MSG or other Windows Constants. Many programmers feel that it is good programming practice to use Constants throughout a program where a particular number will not change. In other words, to refer to a particular address, such as the White House, put it into a Constant rather than inserting the actual, literal text: Const WH$ = "White House, Wash. DC" would create this new Constant. Then use the Constant wherever in the program you need to refer to this address. The reason is that if you later need to change the address—in the event of a coup, for example—you could just change the definition of the Constant (Const WH$ = "White House, New Orleans, LA"), and all references to the address would automatically be corrected throughout the program. This is a simpler way to update a program than having to search through the program for each literal address. (Variables can be used in place of Constants for this same purpose.)

• In VB 2.0 and 3.0, the words TRUE and FALSE have been built into the language and now supply –1 and 0 when used: Visible = TRUE is the same as Visible = –1.

Cautions

• Using Constants can be potentially confusing if you do try to change (to vary) one of them: TAX = TAX + 1. This will produce the "Duplicate Definition" error message, which means you have used the same name for two different things. In this case, the original Constant and, VB assumes, a new Variable also called *TAX*.

Professional programmers follow the convention of using all capitals to signify that something is a Constant: TAX. For Variables, conventionally only the first letter is capitalized. In Visual Basic, the convention is that Properties and Events use initial caps to illustrate the words compressed into a single name—FontSize, KeyPress, etc. However, many programmers simply leave everything in lowercase. Typing is easier that way.

Example

```
Public Const HOURSINADAY = 24
```

Some VB programmers put special Constants into a Module and use the Public command to access them throughout their program. Some programmers include the 16 QBColors—Public Const Gray=8, for instance.

See also   Variables

CONTROL ARRAY

Description

When you have several Controls of the same type performing similar functions, this valuable feature allows you to manipulate them efficiently. Also, a Control Array is the only way to create a new Control (such as a brand-new Text Box) while a program is running.

Arrays are like a bank of Post Office boxes. Once they are grouped together, you can manipulate the entire collection quickly, as a unit, without having to provide the name of each box. This can be done because each item in an Array has the same name, but each is distinguished from the others by a unique *index number*.

For example, when boxes are identified by index numbers, you can say, "Empty all the boxes from #4 to #15." That's much easier than saying, "Empty Mr. Johnson's Box. Empty Ms. Philips's Box. Empty Dr. Jordan's Box," and so on.

Arrays work with the For...Next Statement. You can quickly Loop through an Array, empty it, search for a particular item, put something new into each item, etc. If we created a Control Array of Text Boxes, we could "empty" all of them easily with a For...Next Statement:

```
For I = 4 to 15
    Text(I).Text = ""
Next I
```

(The "" symbol means *no text*.)

Control Arrays Are Efficient: Grouping Controls in this way lets you manipulate their Properties *mathematically*. Because they're now labeled with numbers, not text names, you can use them in Loops and other structures (such as Select Case) as a unit, easily changing the same Property in each Control by using a single Loop.

One way to create a Control Array is by giving more than one Control *the same Name Property*, thereby collapsing two or more Controls into one. This "Metacontrol" can be affected as a unit by referring to the index number of each item within the group. There will also be a single set of Events for the entire Array. (The other way of creating a Control Array is to set the Index Property of a Control while designing the program.)

Before creating the following Control Array out of three Command Buttons, you would find six items listed in the "Object:" Menu of Form1:

```
(General)
Form
Picture1
Command1
Command2
Command3
```

Now we'll change all the Command Button Names to the same Name, *Selection*. They then collapse into a single entity, a Control Array with the name Selection( ), the parentheses indicating they are part of a group and are differentiated only by an index number within parentheses ( ):

(General)
Form
Picture1
Selection( )

For this Control Array that we named Selection( ), we can write a general-purpose GotFocus_Event, by simply accessing Selection( ) from the Object Menu and choosing its GotFocus_Event. Notice that there is now only one GotFocus Event for all three Command Buttons. The original three Got-
Focus Events of the Command Buttons that we collapsed into this Array have themselves collapsed into a single Event. In fact, each Event in a Control Array is shared by all of the members of that Array.

This GotFocus_Event will now be triggered when any of the three Command Buttons in Figure C-65 gets the focus. Yet we can still react differently to each of the Buttons by using their individual index numbers within a Select Case structure like this:

```
Sub Selection_Click (Index as Integer)

    Select Case Index

        Case 0
            x% = Shell("C:\WINDOWS\NOTEPAD.EXE", 3)
        Case 1
            y% = Shell("C:\WW\WPWIN.EXE", 3)
        Case 2
            z% = Shell("C:\WORD\WINWORD.EXE", 3)

    End Select
End Sub
```

Figure C-71: These three large Command Buttons are members of a Control Array.

We could make all of the Buttons in Figure C-71 invisible, change their shape, shuffle their positions, make them tiny or whatever else we wanted to do—all by putting them within a Loop. (See the Example that follows.)

Used with   Controls

Variables   To make one item in a Control Array visible: Picture(3).Visible = True

OR (to position one Label in a Control Array of Labels higher on the window than another member of the Array): Label(11).Top = Label(5).Top −1000

Uses   • Handle many Controls as a single entity. The members of a Control Array share the same Events. In other words, clicking on Command1(0), Command1(1) or Command1(2)—three members of the Control Array called Command1( )—triggers the same Click Event. You can tell which Button was clicked by its index number. A triggered Event provides the index number of the Control that triggered the Event:

```
Sub Command1_Click (Index as Integer)
     If index = 1 Then...
End Sub
```

Note how the Event above differs from a normal Click Event, one that is not a member of a Control Array. A normal Click Event does not have "Index as Integer":

```
Sub Command2_Click ()
End Sub
```

• Create controls while your program is running. (Control Arrays are the only way to do this. See the Examples that follow.) To create new members of a Control Array, you use the Load command. To remove members, you use Un-Load.

• Make groups of Controls. You could create menus of choices—using for example a bank of Command Buttons—that can change while the program runs (disappear, reposition, change captions, become Enabled, etc.) in response to user actions.

A Responsive, Intuitive Program: In this example, the Controls disappear when the user is typing into the database and reappear when the user needs them. A Timer creates a slight delay; movement of the mouse triggers the return of the Controls. This not only makes the Form more attractive; it's also one more way that Visual Basic can easily create more responsive and intuitive programs than can other programming languages.

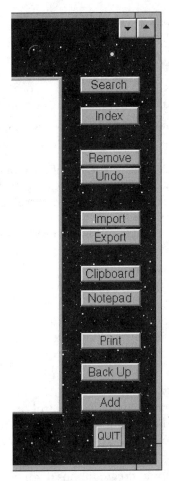

Figure C-72: Consider using a Control Array if you have a group of related Controls.

Figure C-73: All the Controls can be quickly hidden by using a Loop.

Making this entire set of Command Buttons disappear or reappear is as simple as this:

```
For I = 1 to 11
    Command(I).Visible = False
Next I
```

• Control Arrays are useful when you are creating a Menu (which see).

• Use Control Arrays for various kinds of animation.

Cautions   • The index numbers of the items in a Control Array do not need to be sequential, though there's no good reason you should want them not to be.

- Control Arrays differ from ordinary Arrays in several other ways as well:

   ▪ You do not declare a Control Array (with Global, Dim, ReDim or Static commands) as you must for an ordinary Array in VB.

   ▪ A Control Array can have only one dimension. (See "Arrays.")

   ▪ You can have up to 255 Controls in a Control Array. (A single Form is limited to a total of 255 Controls.)

   ▪ You create a Control Array by giving Controls (of the same type) the same Name while designing your program. You can also create a Control Array by setting the Index Property of a Control.

   ▪ You cannot "pass" an entire Control Array. Ordinary Arrays can be passed as a single entity. (See "Sub" for more on "passing.")

- If you use the Load command to create new members of a Control Array while a program is running, the new ones will be invisible unless you set the Visible Property to –1 as they come in. (See the Example.)

When new members of a Control Array are created (either while you're designing your program or while the program is running), each new member initially shares all the Properties of the original member of the Array. The only Properties that are not "inherited" from the parent Control are Visible, Index and TabIndex.

After a member of a Control Array has been created, you can adjust its Properties individually. It need not retain the same Properties as the other members of its Array, although it does inherit them.

If you use the Load command with the index number of an existing member of a Control Array, VB will generate an error message. Each newly created member of a Control Array must have a unique index number.

The UnLoad command can remove members of a Control Array while a program is running. However, it can be used only with members created while the program was running (with the Load command). It cannot remove members if you created them while designing the program (by giving them the same Name Property).

- If you are working on your program and write some commands within a Control, you cannot then use that particular Control to create a Control Array. Visual Basic allows you to set such a Control's Index Property (or give another Control the same Name), so it will seem as if you have successfully created a Control Array. But, when you try to run this program, you'll get an error message, "Incorrect number of event procedure arguments." (It doesn't matter if you've put programming commands within a Control that you intend to *add* to an existing Control Array. This problem occurs only when you're trying to create a new Control Array.)

Solution: Remove any programming from within a Control that you intend to use to create a Control Array. Or create a Control Array from a brand-new (empty) Control.

Example   There are two ways to create a Control Array:

• While designing your program, you can explicitly set the Index Property of a Control (or simply give more than one Control the same Name). Visual Basic will automatically add the next index number in sequence if you keep adding Controls with the same Name. Also, you can change the Index Properties and VB will make any necessary adjustments to all the rest of the index numbers in that Array.

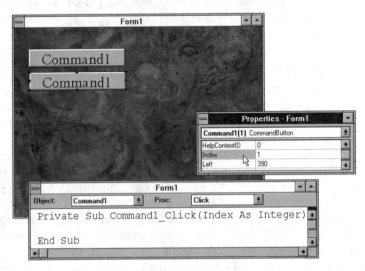

Figure C-74: Create a Control Array by changing the Index Property of any Control.

There are several things to notice in Figure C-68. Both Labels have the same Name (although they can certainly have different Captions and other Properties). The "Object" name includes parentheses ( ) to indicate that it's part of a Control Array. And the Sub includes (Index as Integer). In other words, the unique Name for each Control is the Array Name Label1 *plus* the index number in parentheses.

There is only one Click Event for this entire Array.

This, and the fact that they also inherit Properties when they're created, is why these Control Arrays are so efficient. To italicize all their Labels, we only have to use this simple Loop:

```
Sub label1_Click (Index as Integer)

For I = 1 to 2
    Label1(I).FontItalic = True
Next I
End Sub
```

And this can be extended to as many as 255 Labels (the maximum number of Controls permitted on a single Form).

All Properties can be the same among the Controls in a Control Array (except their index numbers and TabIndexes). Or their Properties can differ; it's up to you.

• The second major feature of Control Arrays is that you can use them to create new Controls while your program runs. In this example, our program will make tiled wallpaper out of a single Picture Box.

Create a Picture Box by double-clicking on the Toolbox Picture Icon:

Figure C-75: Double-click on the Picture Box icon.

Now you have your seed. Set its Index Property to 0. Giving a Control an index number (usually 0, since it's the first member of the Array) creates a Control Array. Then move down to the Picture Property and pull something into the seed:

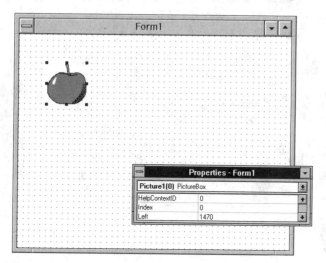

Figure C-76: The seed cherry.

We could clone this cherry 255 times using the Load command! But we only need 35 replications to fill our Form with a tiled background.

One of the magic things about using the Load command to clone Controls is that each clone will share most of the qualities of the original. (Individual indices, however, are necessary so you can tell each of them apart and tell each one what to do and how to appear.) The clones also do not inherit the TabIndex or Visible Properties of the parent. But they inherit everything else, including a graphic.

We decide what qualities we want this whole host of copies to have by setting the Properties of the first one, the one we draw on the Form and give Index 0.

In this example, we're setting the Pictures' BorderStyle to 0 (because we decided that we don't want a tic-tac-toe look), and we're setting AutoSize to –1 so the fit can be tight without overlapping. That's it. You could, of course, define everything from AutoRedraw, to Font, to the way the mouse looks when it comes on top of these items (using the MousePointer Property), to the Width. Adjust any Property you want to adjust. You can govern the appearance and qualities of these parthenogenetic babies just as you would with normal Controls.

Now there remains only the "simple" matter of filling our Form with this cherry in the manner of Warhol. Placing things into a structured pattern in a computer can be confusing. It would be easy if you could drag them around with a mouse, or if there were a command in VB that filled a Form with a Picture (like the Tile option in the Windows Desktop's Wallpaper window). But that isn't yet available.

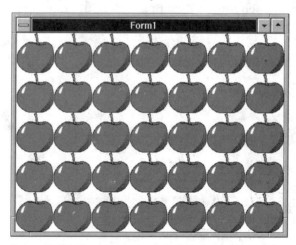

Figure C-77: The clones in their full glory fill the window.

To Fill a Form With Repeating Graphics: It's a mind-bender (an afternoon's worth). Here's the solution. You can use this method for any visual Array of any size with any number of elements to make tiled wallpaper.

```
Sub Form_Load ()

Rows = 7
Columns = 8

Movedown = Picture1(0).Height
Moveacross = Picture1(0).Width
Picture1(0).Visible = False
```

```
        For I = 0 to Rows —1
           For J = 0 to Columns —1
               x = x + 1
               Load Picture1(x)
               Picture1(x).Top = Movedown * i
               Picture1(x).Left = Moveacross * j
               Picture1(x).Visible = True
           Next J
        Next I
        End Sub
```

Set the rows and columns to the number you want (they can be larger than the current window size). Put a Picture1(0) on the Form (it doesn't matter where). Set its Index Property to 0, its BorderStyle to None, and AutoSize to True.

There is one drawback to this approach: if your computer's graphics are slow, the redraw of the tiles will be slow whenever a window is moved or resized. To speed things up, use larger original images for Picture1(0) (and fewer rows and columns). Or make the graphics persistent by setting the Form's AutoRedraw Property to On.

See also   Array; Index; Load; Multiple Document Interface; Objects; UnLoad

 ONTROLBOX

PROPERTY

Description   In the Windows interface, a ControlBox appears on many windows to allow the user to manage the window—close, size, move, iconize, restore or switch to something else. Clicking on the box drops a menu down. (A ControlBox is sometimes called a *Control-menu box*.)

ControlBox

Figure C-78: You'll find a ControlBox in the upper left corner of most windows.

Figure C-79: A conventional Windows ControlBox.

In practice, few people actually use the menu that drops down under a ControlBox. Instead, they use the mouse to directly resize, minimize, maximize or close a window.

Used with   Forms only

Variables   **Variable type:** Integer (Boolean)

A ControlBox will appear on each window (Form) in your program unless you deliberately remove it while designing the program. ControlBoxes cannot be added or removed while a program is running. To eliminate a Form's ControlBox, you must use VB's Properties Window.

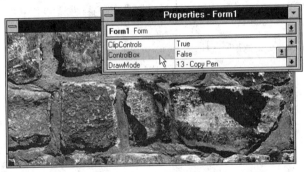

Figure C-80: Adjust the ControlBox within the Properties Window.

Uses   • If you turn the ControlBox Property off, you can use a Form as a large Picture Box, not as a normal window. The user cannot then access the ControlBox menu; there's no ControlBox. The resizing arrows in the upper right corner of a window still permit maximizing and iconizing.

See "BorderStyle" for information about your options. You can choose to offer the user the ability to resize, minimize, maximize or otherwise manipulate a Form. In VB, you can decide which facilities and menus will be available to the user when a program runs. Whether or not you want to remove the ControlBox, and its menu, is one of those decisions.

Cautions   • If you've set the Form's BorderStyle Property to 0 ("no border"), then ControlBox has no effect and the Box will not appear.

• If you've set the MaxButton and MinButton Properties to 0, these options will not appear on the ControlBox menu.

• You cannot change the ControlBox Property while your program is running.

• If you turn off the ControlBox, it will still be visible while you're designing your program. It will not appear, however, when your program runs.

Example See Variables above.

See also BorderStyle; MaxButton; MinButton

Cos

FUNCTION

Description Cos gives you the cosine of an angle, expressed in radians. You provide a *numeric expression*: a literal number, a numeric Variable, a numeric Constant or a combination of these. You can get the cosine of any type of Variable (Integer, Floating-Point, etc.). (See "Variables" for a definition of *expression* and numeric Variable *types*.)

Variables
```
Print Cos(x)
```
OR
```
F = Cos(.3)
```

Uses Advanced mathematics; Trigonometry

Example
```
z = Cos(.3)
Print z
```

Results in .9553365

See also Atn; Sin; Tan

CreateObject

FUNCTION

See OLE Automation

CSng

FUNCTION

Description CSng has no particular uses. The results of a calculation with or without CSng are the same. The type of Variable that gets the answer of a calculation (RESULT% in RESULT% = 5 / 2) determines the precision and range of the calculation. CSng's purpose is to force "Single-Precision Floating-Point" arithmetic. This is one of the several types of numeric Variables that VB can work with. See "Variables" for more on the types.

Used with　Numbers, to force single-precision arithmetic

Variables　To change a Variable into a Single-Precision Floating-Point numeric type:

r = CSng (somenumber)

OR (to change a "literal number"): d = CSng (15.88888)

OR (to change a "numeric expression"—see "Variables"):

m = CSng (somenumber + 15.88888)

See also　CCur; CDbl; CInt; CLng; DefType; Variables

FUNCTION

Description　CurDir$ tells you which is the "current" directory, but it also includes the drive name as well. CurDir$ collapses two functions into one: "Tell me which drive I am on now and which directory I am in."

The computer is always "on" a particular drive (usually C:, the hard drive in most computers) and "in" a particular directory within that drive. To find out which drive and directory are the current ones, use CurDir$.

Used with　File and disk manipulations

Variables　Print CurDir$ "C"

(The "C" drive identification is optional.)

Uses　• If you're trying to find a file or save a file, you may need to see if the current directory is the one you intend to use.

CurDir$ can tell you whether your program, or the user, should change drives or directories before saving or looking for a disk file.

Cautions　• You get something like this when you use CurDir$:

X$ = CurDir$
Print X$

Results in　C:\VBASIC

You'll sometimes want to extract the actual directory name. Here's how to extract the two pieces of information that CurDir$ gives you:

```
Sub Form_Click ()

lngth% = Len(CurDir$)
x% = InStr(CurDir$, "\") - 1
drivename$ = Left$(CurDir$, x%)
directoryname$ = Right$(CurDir$, lngth% - x%)
Print drivename$
Print directoryname$

End Sub
```

Results in (Now we've separated the drive and directory names):
C:
\VBASIC

Any existing subdirectory names will be included within directoryname$ and can be, if necessary, similarly extracted via the InStr Function.

• CurDir$ (and the optional drive identification string) are not case-sensitive. "MYDir" is the same as "mydir." And, you can use a Variable–CurDir$(Drive$)–or directly supply the literal text–CurDir$("C").

• If you do add an optional drive identification such as "C" or "D," these must be legal drives on that computer, or you'll get an error message when the program runs. Each disk drive has a "current" directory at any given time. If you switch from C: to D:, the computer will be "in" the current directory on D:. This is why you're permitted to supply CurDir$ with a drive identifier. That way, you can find out "current" directories on drives other than the one you're "on"–CurDir$(X$).

Example Here we switch to a directory named DATA, if we're not in it already. Use Error Trapping (see "On Error" or Appendix B) when dealing with the disk drives. In this example, there might be no existing directory called "DATA," yet we're trying to change to that directory.

```
If CurDir$ <> "c:\data" then ChDir "data"
```

See also ChDir; ChDrive; EXEName; MkDir; On Error; Path; RmDir

PROPERTY

Description The CurrentX and CurrentY Properties are quite useful when drawing graphics or when printing.

To remember which is X and which is Y: Y looks something like an arrow pointed downward. Y governs vertical (up-and-down) location. X is the horizontal orientation. When you know the X and Y "coordinates" of an object, you know exactly where you are on the surface of a Form, within the borders of a Picture Box, or on a sheet of paper in the printer.

You can think of CurrentX combined with CurrentY as a kind of invisible cursor for graphics. It's the place where Line, Circle and PSet—the graphics Methods—will draw something. Likewise, the Print command puts text at the CurrentX and CurrentY position.

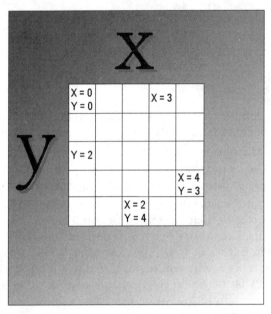

Figure C-81: Any coordinate can be identified by X,Y.

Used with   Forms, Picture Boxes and the printer

Variables   **Variable type:** Single

To change the current position: CurrentX = 1500

OR (to find out what the current position is): Location = CurrentX

OR (to use a Variable to adjust the current vertical position):
```
Z = 500
CurrentX = Z
```

The above examples default to the current Form as the place that CurrentX and CurrentY are located.

There are several optional identifiers you may want to use:

To find out where you are located within a Picture Box:
```
Location = Picture1.CurrentX
```

To move down on the paper in the printer:

```
printer.Print "HERE";
printer.currenty = printer.currenty + 1200
printer.Print "HERE"
```

Results in   HERE

HERE

Uses   • Use graphics to create attractive backgrounds for Forms.

• Center text on a window, or otherwise arrange it symmetrically. (See the Example.)

• Animation

Cautions   • When you first load a Form or Picture Box, both the CurrentX and the CurrentY will be 0. This means that the location is in the upper left corner of the space. Similarly, when a new page is about to be printed in the printer, its CurrentX and CurrentY are 0 as well.

• Various commands change the CurrentX and CurrentY:

▪ Circle: Locates X & Y to the center of the drawn circle.
▪ Cls: Clears the graphics and text and resets X & Y to 0,0 (upper left corner).
▪ Line: X & Y become the end point of the line. In this example, CurrentX gets set to 300 and CurrentY becomes 500. A line is drawn (from)–(to), in this manner:

```
(StartingX, StartingY)–(EndingX, EndingY)
Line (0,0) – (300,500)
Print "CurrentX is"; CurrentX; " CurrentY is"; CurrentY
```

Results in

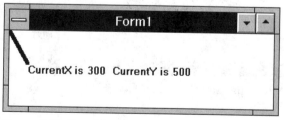

Figure C-82: The CurrentX and CurrentY are located at the end of the most recently drawn line.

▪ Print: Prints at CurrentX & CurrentY, then acts as Print normally would (no punctuation at the end of the text and Print moves down to the next line; a semicolon moves to the next space on the same line; and a comma moves to the next Tab location).

■ PSet: Moves X & Y to the location of the dot you're drawing (to the coordinates you specified for the PSet).

■ NewPage: Ejects the current piece of paper from the printer, and resets X & Y to 0,0–the top left of the next page.

• Unless you adjust a Form's or Picture Box's ScaleMode Property, VB assumes that you want CurrentX and CurrentY to operate in twips (as opposed to inches or pixels or some other way of measuring distance). For more information, see "ScaleMode."

Example 1   Here's a way to create different backgrounds every time this Window is loaded. Note that you always need to specify Show before drawing on a Form in its Load Event.

```
Private Sub Form_Load()
Show
Randomize Timer

DrawWidth = 2

For t = 1 To 5
    x% = Int(ScaleWidth * Rnd)
    y% = Int(ScaleHeight * Rnd)
    Circle (x%, y%), x%
Next t

For t = 1 To 40
    x% = Int(ScaleWidth * Rnd)
    y% = Int(ScaleHeight * Rnd)
    DrawWidth = t
    PSet (x%, y%), QBColor(4)
Next t

End Sub
```

Figure C-83: Never the same wallpaper twice with this program.

Results in

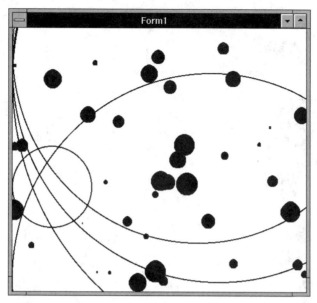

Figure C-84: One of the millions of results possible with the program shown in Figure C-83.

Example 2   **Centering Text:** To print something dead-center on a window:

```
Sub Form_Click()

T$ = "CENTERED"
tx = textwidth (T$) /2
ty = textheight (T$) /2

fx = scalewidth / 2
fy = scaleheight / 2

currentX = fx - tx
currentY = fy - ty

print T$

End Sub
```

TextWidth tells you the width of some text (in its current FontSize and FontName). ScaleWidth tells you the width of the Form, excluding its borders. Dividing these items in half and subtracting half of the text's width from half of the window's width positions you to print the text in the horizontal center of the window. The Height Properties work exactly the same way for the vertical position. If we set CurrentX and CurrentY to the calculated position, the text will be printed right in the middle.

See also   Circle; Cls; Left; Line; Move; PSet; ScaleHeight, ScaleWidth; ScaleLeft, ScaleTop; ScaleMode; Top

Data

CONTROL

Figure D-1: The Data Control Icon on the Toolbar.

Description   This Control is like a periscope at sea—there's a large machine beneath it. With the Data Control, you get an entree to databases and also to a whole specialized language built into VB with which you can control those databases.

Databases are orderly collections of information. Orderly because you can edit, add and delete from the information and quickly search or sort that information. The information isn't just in a flat, one-dimensional list; it's more like a table or spreadsheet. And with the hundreds of database-related commands in VB, you can query and organize database tables, fields and indexes in a sophisticated, fully professional fashion. VB includes the engine that runs Microsoft's Access Database Management System.

By themselves, the Data Control's Properties, Events and Methods allow you to manage an existing database in various ways. Beyond the Data

Control's facilities, however, VB provides a complete, advanced database language. With these commands, your program can do things directly to a database (as opposed to the user typing in changes, moving through the records via the arrows on the Data Control and so on). In fact, you can completely ignore the Data Control and construct a sophisticated database management system of your own.

The Data Control is not the only way to access and manage databases with VB. With VB Version 4, you can also use data access objects—a whole set of "classes" that in effect permit efficient, thorough data manipulation. VB4 includes so many robust and full-featured data management tools that a full description of the new VB "DDL" (Data Definition Language) is quite beyond the scope of this book. It would require an entire book to explore this rich language. However, in this section we'll cover the Data Control and select aspects of the DDL as well.

Uses   Open, access and manipulate existing databases. To create a new database, you can use the DDL or use the VB Data Manager, as shown in the Example below.

Cautions   • If you have worked with databases before, there is one major mindset to get rid of or you won't be comfortable programming the Data Control (or using the DDL language commands built into VB). *There is no fixed order to the records. There is, technically speaking, no "first" record nor is there a "record #5."*

Field and record order is arbitrary. There is no significance in any one record being first, or any field coming before another. After all, several users could be manipulating the same data simultaneously, but in different ways; there could be more than one way of ordering (indexing) the same set of data (alphabetically within one field isn't the only possibility); and anyway the sorting is done by the language, not the programmer. The idea is that data is in flux, at least potentially—it's relativistic; data can be rearranged freely, with different Recordsets displaying different subsets of the data though SQL queries and so on.

When records are added or deleted, VB's commands and the built-in database engine will sort the table according to whatever index you defined as primary. If you try to show a user the "record number" of the current record, you'll find that task especially difficult to program in VB—this is not the way "relational" databases are supposed to be approached. Objects are "relative" in a relational database. Trying to visualize or display absolute, fixed orientations between data in a relational database is as pointless as trying to describe the "first" or "closest" skater in a roller rink. The data in a relational database is "in motion," like skaters circling around a rink—position and order are continually subject to change.

Beyond that, you, the programmer, are not responsible for the physical organization or storage of the data on disk. You are insulated from the tedium of manipulating the actual data. Instead, you use the Data Control's Properties, Methods and Events (as well as the complete Data Definition

Language, if you have the Professional Version of VB). These high-level commands permit you to manage the data in a more abstract fashion than was common even a few years ago.

New Position Information

There are, in VB4, two new Properties of a Recordset that do, in fact, allow you to pinpoint the "location" of a record within the Recordset. You are encouraged to avoid using these Properties as a way of moving records around within the Recordset, or attempting to use them as a way of making a particular record current (use Bookmarks instead). However, for dynaset- or snapshot-type Recordsets, you can use the AbsolutePosition or Percent-Position Properties to report to the user his or her "position" within a set of records. Here's how:

VB comes with a sample database called BIBLIO.MDB. Put a Text Box, three Labels and a Data Control on a Form. Set the Data Control's Database-Name Property to c:\VB\biblio.mdb or whatever path is appropriate on your disk. Set the Data Control's RecordSource Property to Authors. Set the DataSource Property of the Text Box to Data1 and its DataField to Author. Then, in the Data Control's Reposition Event, type this:

```
Private Sub Data1_Reposition( )
    label1.Caption = Data1.Recordset.AbsolutePosition + 1
    label2.Caption = Data1.Recordset.PercentPosition
    label3.Caption = Data1.Recordset.RecordCount
End Sub
```

We have to add one to the AbsolutePosition because this Property starts counting the first record as the zeroth record. In any case, you can use these two Properties to display a gauge to your user, or otherwise visually indicate their current location within a recordset.

Example When using the Standard Edition of VB, you can access and manipulate existing databases (Microsoft Access; dBASE III and IV; Paradox 3.X; Btrieve; FoxPro 2.0 and 2.5; or ODBC). When using the Professional Edition, you or the user can build and define new databases while the VB program is running. You can also utilize the object-oriented DDL language. You can't do all that with the Standard Edition, but you can use the Data Manager to create and define a new, empty database and then add some data. In effect, the Standard Edition allows you to give the user a defined database, and to manage and manipulate it in somewhat limited ways, but you can't create a VB program that allows the *user* to build a new database *structure*, to define its tables, fields and indexes.

In this example, we'll create a new database to hold information about a videotape collection. Using the facilities of VB's Standard Edition, we'll build a database from scratch. In the process, you'll learn to use the Data Control, the Data Manager and several of the database commands built into VB, in support of the Data Control.

But first we should briefly define Microsoft database terminology.

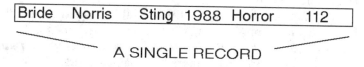

DATABASE
TABLE

FIELDS

Title   Director   Stars   Year   Category   Length

Bride   Norris   Sting   1988   Horror   112

A SINGLE RECORD

Figure D-2: Databases are organized into tables, then fields and then records.

What Are Tables, Fields, Records and Indices?

A table is the largest unit of organization within any given database. If you're organizing a complicated mass of information, like the data about a company, you might want to create several tables—a separate table for each broad category of information: inventory, payroll, invoices due, bank loans, personnel and suppliers. But because we're only doing one main category—videotapes—we'll just create one table.

Within each table are fields (see Figure D-2). Fields are subcategories (fields are to tables what tables are to databases). Under the Personnel Table, a company might have several fields: Employee ID Number, Name, Address, Phone, Date Hired, Sick Days, Attitude, etc. Each field must have a Variable type assigned to it, and usually a length as well—such as Employee ID Number (Long) Name (text,30 characters) Address (text,60 characters) Phone (text,11 characters) Date hired (date) and so on. We'll see how to define these types shortly.

Think of fields as the various qualities that you might want to know about each person or thing in a table. For our Video database, we'll create fields for Title, Director, Stars, Year, Category (like Westerns) and running length. These are the qualities of each video that we want to file away in our database. Some or all of these fields will be filled with the actual, specific *data* about each video.

So, underneath a table is a series of categories called fields. Microsoft sometimes calls fields *columns* because the data in any given field can be read vertically down a page. In other words, if you list the video titles down the left side of a page, you'll see that each field creates a separate column. The *horizontal* information—the title of a particular video, and all the descriptions of its qualities in the various fields—is called a *row*, or *record*. Thus, the smallest complete container of information (the various data about a single videotape) is a *record*.

How do fields differ from records? A *field* is a general category of information, a quality like "the title," for all records. A *record* is specific information, data entered into the database, about a single finite entity—in our example, about a single videotape. A record lists the qualities that, taken together, fully describe a particular object. In our videotape database, a particular record might contain the following data: "Some Like It Hot, Billy Wilder, Marilyn Monroe, Tony Curtis, Jack Lemmon, 1960, Comedy, 130 minutes long." A particular field might contain Comedy, Western, Historical, Comedy, War, etc.

A database can have many tables. A table can have many fields. A record is a particular item (or "row") in a database—*a record is the actual information that has been filled into the fields of a table in a database*. Fields and tables are empty containers with names like TABLE:VIDEOS, FIELD: TITLE, FIELD: DIRECTOR, FIELD: STARS, etc. A record is the specific information about an entity: Some Like It Hot, Billy Wilder, Marilyn Monroe, etc.

Creating a Database

Let's make a functioning database. Let's show all the categories (fields) for each record, all the record titles, the number of records, a List Box with the titles. We'll also allow the user to move to a record by clicking on its title in the List Box; or to move through the data to the next or previous record, or to the first or last record; to search for any title by giving only a partial description; or to edit, add or delete any record.

In other words, let's build a simple database management program. If you've not worked with VB much, you'll probably be startled at how easy this process is. If you have worked with VB, you'll be reassured that you're using the right language to program in Windows; nothing comes close to the simplicity and efficiency of Visual Basic.

Start a New Project from the File Menu. Now we'll use VB's Data Manager to define our tables, fields and index—our empty shell database. Select Data Manager from the VB Add-Ins Menu. (Answer "No" if you're asked about adding a security file.) Now click on the Data Manager's File Menu and select New Database. Name the database "Video" and save it as the default type (Access). Now you can add tables, fields and indexes to your database. You can design the interior, describing the "filing cabinets," "folders" and methods of organization. After you have defined this shell, you can then use the Data Manager to enter actual *data*, the records.

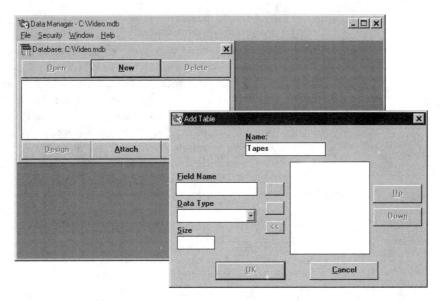

Figure D-3: Here s where you define the fields and indexes in your new database.

While you're still in the Data Manager, click on New and create a Table called "Tapes." In the Field Name box, type Title. This will be our first field for each videotape. For Field Type, select Text. For Size, type 100. Click on the little button next to Field Type to move this field into the large list box. Our database now has a text type field named Title that can have as many as 100 characters in it (that is, each record can describe a title in 100 characters or less). Field types vary in the amount of characters (or size of the numbers) that can be entered and saved in that type of field. Text fields can be anywhere from 1 to 255 characters large. (If you want a field that can hold large amounts of text, select the Memo type. The only disadvantage of the Memo type field is that, unlike other fields, it cannot be used as an index to a table. However, ordering the data by memos wouldn't make too much sense anyway. More about indexes shortly.)

Now continue adding fields in the following order: Director (Text), Stars (Text), Year (Integer), Category (Text) and Length (Integer). Define the size of the text fields as large as you think you might need: perhaps 50 (bytes or "characters") for Director, 150 for Stars, etc.

If you make any mistakes, use the second button to delete, or use the Up and Down buttons to rearrange the order of the fields. You can also edit the Type and Size of any highlighted field. (In VB 3, you had to be careful because once a field was added, it could not be removed. You had to redefine the entire table from the start if you goofed.)

At this point, click on OK to save the Table. Now we'll make the Title field our index into this Table. In effect, this means that the records will be arranged alphabetically based on the title of each movie in our tape collection. Recall, though, that by "arranged" we mean displayed to the user in this order. This doesn't mean that they are necessarily stored on disk in this order. The database system built into VB handles this issue about the physical storage arrangement. You the programmer don't know the order in which the data are stored, nor do you need to.

To make the Title field our index, click on the word Tapes to select our table (in the data manager). Then click on Design so we can get down into the Table Editor. Click on the Indexes button then click on Add. For the Index Name, type in the word **Pointer**. (This is like a variable name assignment—you can use whatever name for this index that you wish.) Then click on Primary Index and select the word Title in the Fields in Table list. Click on the Add button. Then click OK followed by Close, followed by Close again. Then close the Data Manager.

You have just made the Title field the main index (and the only one we'll use) to this table. The records will be sorted by title, in ascending order (A-Z, chosen when we clicked on Add and this Title field was recognized as text—Asc, for the ASCII code, a collection of printable symbols including the alphabet). By the way, your VB program can request that the sort order be instantly changed—you can specify that the records be sorted based on some criteria other than the primary index (for an example, see Record-Source later in this section).

What Is an Index?
An *index* in a database is a way of ordering the records. We made the title field the index. VB *automatically* sorts records for you, automatically keeps them in order. Therefore, the first record will always be the one with a title that's lowest in the alphabet. You could make a different field the index or even have more than one index. But there will always be a primary index. Indexes speed up searches and sorts. A primary unique index will give the fastest results on its specified column during a search or sort of the records in that column. An index on a numeric field will sort in numeric order.

Now we have our database shell. We've defined its containers, its shape, its organization. But there's no *data* in our database yet, just a table, an index, and some fields. It's like a new filing system with labels on all the folders, stickers on all the filing cabinets—but no papers have yet been placed into these folders and cabinets. It's an empty database.

The Data Control cannot access an empty database. To be specific, you can't use a MoveLast or FindFirst command on an empty database because you'll get the error message "no current record."

In other words, you can't use a command or allow anything else to happen that requires a record to be present (such as the user clicking on one of the arrows in the Data Control). But you can check the BOF (Beginning Of File) and EOF (End Of File) Properties when the application first loads, to see if they are both simultaneously "True." This means that you are located at the start and the end of this database. The only way you can be simultaneously at the start and the end is if the database has no records at all. If this is the case, you can use the AddNew command at this point to put a record into the database before allowing the user to, for example, click on the Data Control. However, we'll use the Data Manager to seed our database with a record, thus avoiding the problem of an empty database.

You must have at least one record, *some actual data*, before the Data Control can get a grip on a database. (In the Professional Edition of VB 3.0, you can use several commands that allow you (or your user) to create, define and fill a new database while the program is running. But in the Standard Edition of VB, the database must already exist.)

So we'll make a record; we'll put some data into our Video database. Open the Database Manager again from VB's Add-Ins menu. Click on File, then open the VIDEO.MDB database.

We have only one table in our database—Tapes. Click on Tapes to select it, then click on Open. Now click on the Add button to prepare the Database Manager to put a new record into the database (in this case, the first and only record). Now you can fill in the fields with data as shown in Figure D-4. When you're finished, click on Update. You must click on Update: if a record is edited, the changes are held in a temporary buffer rather than immediately saved to the database on the disk. Likewise, when a new record is added to the database, it too is held in a buffer.

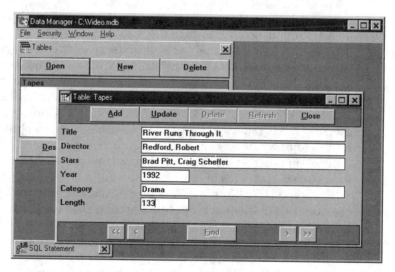

Figure D-4: Entering data using the Data Manager

In a program, to actually store a new or edited record in the database disk file, your program must include the Update command. (Alternatively, a record is also automatically stored if the user moves to a different record by clicking on one of the Data Control's arrows, or if your program moves to a different record with one of the Move or Find commands.) As you can see, there are several ways that a record is committed to permanent storage in the disk file; but just typing something into a Text Box or the Data Manager doesn't automatically make that change part of the database. This might seem strange, but among other things, it makes programming an Undo feature much easier.

In any case, close the Data Manager now and we'll prepare a VB Form to access our Video database. Click on the Toolbox to place a Data Control on your Form. In the Properties Window, type the following into the Data Control's DatabaseName Property: **C:\VB\VIDEO.MDB** (or type whatever path is the correct location on disk of your VIDEO.MDB file). Then into the RecordSource Property, type **tapes**.

Tip: As a shortcut, you can double-click on the DatabaseName and RecordSource Properties in the Properties Window and VB will fill in the values for you or at least show you a list of options or let you browse the disk. Or click on the down arrow on the Properties List Box to get a list of fields to choose from.

Or, if you prefer to put all this into your program, so it happens when the program starts running, you can type this into your Form's Form_Load Event:

```
Data1.recordsource = "Tapes"
Data1.DataBaseName = "C:\VB\VIDEO.MDB"
```

Your Data Control will now be able to talk to the database. You can now use the AddNew, Delete, FindFirst, MoveLast and other VB commands to manage and maneuver through the database.

To start working with our new database, we'll need to first add a Text Box so we can see some of the data in the database and modify it. Click on the Text Box icon in the ToolBox to add a Text Box to the Form. To make the Text Box react to the Data Control, we have to "bind" it to the Data Control. To bind our Text Box, in the Properties Window type **Title** into the Text Box's DataField Property. As a result, the Text Box will display the Title field of whatever record is currently being accessed by the Data Control (in other words, the name of one of our videotapes). Remember, there are several fields in our database's table.

Next, type **Data1** into the Text Box's DataSource Property (or double-click on the DataSource Property). Entering Data1 tells the Text Box that it is now "bound" to the Data1 Control. When the Form is Loaded, the Text Box will automatically show the first record in the database. And whenever the user clicks on an arrow in the Data Control, moving elsewhere in the database, the Text Box will show the title for the new "current" record.

Now run your program. You should see "River Runs Through It" in the Text Box when the Form appears. A database accessed by a Data Control is automatically opened when its Form becomes visible.

Fleshing Out the Program

We now have a database with a single record stored in it. Let's add some functionality to our program so the user can add, update and view as many records as desired. First, we'll want to bind some additional Text Boxes to Data1 so the other fields can be displayed and modified. Add five more

Text Boxes, one for each of the other fields: Director, Stars, Date, Category and Length. In each Box's DataSource Property, type Data1 (or just double-click on it and VB will fill in the only possibility). In each Box's DataField Property, type in the respective field's name. Alternatively, you can really speed things up by holding down the SHIFT key, clicking on each Text Box (to group them), then double-clicking on the DataSource Property in the Properties List Box. VB will fill in "DATA1" for you in each of the grouped Text Boxes' DataSource Properties in one swift stroke.

Then add a Label next to each Text Box to identify the contents of that field (see Figure D-5). Now run the program again and see the data automatically displayed in each Box.

Put a Command Button on the Form and caption it "Add New Record." In the Button's Click Event, type the following:

```
data1.Recordset.AddNew
```

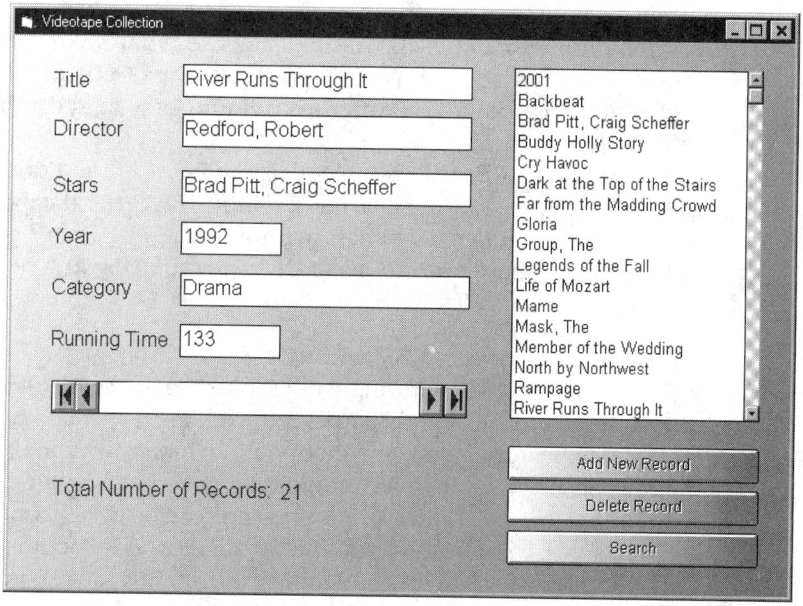

Figure D-5: Our functioning database manager.

Now, whenever the user clicks this Button, all the Text Boxes go blank and the user can type in a new entry, a new record into the database. Try adding several videos to the database. You can leave some of the fields blank if you want, but at least fill in the Title field—that's our index and VB alphabetizes the list based on the title.

Note: Remember that simply typing in new data doesn't automatically *add* that data to the database on disk. When the user adds a new record or edits an existing record, the changes are kept in a buffer until the user moves to a different record or adds a new record. Likewise, your program can force data to be saved if you use the Update command or one of the

Move commands. But if the user just clicks on the Add New Record Button, types in some data and then stops the program, the current record will not be saved to the database.

Programmatic Database Management

You can, of course, bypass the Data Control entirely. VB gives you the commands necessary to manage databases directly via programming alone. A Data Control does automate some kinds of database access. For example, after you've set the Data Control's DatabaseName and RecordSource Properties, simply running your program automatically creates a Recordset. Nonetheless, for the greatest flexibility and control, programming your database is the way to go. Let's take a look at some of the more important concepts in VB database management.

The Meaning of Recordset

When a database is opened, a phantom *Recordset object* is automatically created. In our example above, the database is automatically opened when Form1 is Loaded because Form1 contains a Data Control with its Database-Name and RecordSource Properties pointing at a valid database file and a valid table within that file.

In a sense, the Recordset "object" is the heart of the Data Control. The Data Control uses its Recordset as a window into the database. Likewise, when you manipulate a database without using the Data Control (using only database commands to make things happen), you'll be working with Recordsets too.

Differences Between VB3 and VB4

In VB3 there were three primary objects used to access a database: the Table object, Dynaset object and ShapShot object. Each specialized in a different kind of data manipulation, so you opened whichever type of object suited your purposes. A Table object could read or write to a particular, single table within a database. A Dynaset object could read or write to all or parts of various tables, even from various databases—it was sometimes the result of a query across several tables, providing, for example, all records prior to October, 1993. A Snapshot object was like a dynaset, but could only read and display the data—nothing could be edited, added or deleted.

Now, with VB4, you are asked to ignore these three VB3-style objects. Just use Recordsets only. For compatibility with existing programs, the three older VB3 objects are still recognized and acted on in VB4—but they are less efficient and offer fewer options than the new, expanded VB4 Recordset object. Note that the three techniques—table, dynaset, snapshot—still exist, but as flavors of a Recordset object, rather than as separate objects. In other words, you use a parameter in VB4 to define which kind of Recordset you want to use.

Here's a brief list of the different syntaxes between VB3 and VB4:

```
OpenDatabase
```

Before you can open any of the three kinds of Recordset objects, you must first open the database itself. This syntax is identical in VB3 and VB4:

```
Dim MyDatabase as Database
Set MyDatabase = OpenDatabase("Video.mdb")
```

Then you can open one of the three flavors of Recordset:

To open a table-type Recordset:
VB3

```
Dim MyTable As Table
Set MyTable = MyDatabase.OpenTable("Tapes")
```

VB4

```
Dim MyTable As Recordset
Set MyTable = MyDatabase.OpenRecordset("Tapes", dbOpenTable)
```

(Note the dbOpenTable parameter. This Constant can be found in the Objects Browser, and it creates a Table-style Recordset. This Recordset type is similar to the earlier VB3 Table object but has additional functionality and efficiency. To find the rest of the database-related constants, press F2, select "DAO" from the Libraries/Projects list. Select Constants from the Classes/Modules list. Along with dbOpenTable you'll find dbOpenDynaset and dbOpenSnapshot.)

To open a dynaset-type Recordset:
VB3

```
Dim MyDynaset As Dynaset
Set MyDynaset = MyDatabase.CreateDynaset("Tapes")
```

VB4

```
Dim MyDynaset As Recordset
Set MyDynaset = MyDatabase.OpenRecordset("Tapes", dbOpenDynaset)
```

To open a snapshot-type Recordset:
VB3

```
Dim MySnapshot As Snapshot
Set MySnapshot = MyDatabase.CreateSnapshot("Tapes")
```

VB4

```
Dim MySnapshot As Recordset
Set MySnapshot = MyDatabawe.OpenRecordset("Tapes", dbOpenSnapshot)
```

Note that in VB4 you can also use the following alternative syntax:

```
Set MySnapshot = MyDatabase!Titles.OpenRecordset(dbOpenSnapshot)
```

After you've programmatically brought a Recordset object into existence (or the Data Control creates one) you can use the Recordset to move around within the data. A Recordset is a symbolic representation—a ghostly

Array—that has structure and data, like a database. But when you query or edit a Recordset, the changes are not saved to disk.

Recordsets can be complex; they can point to more than one table at a time, for example. And, too, more than one database can be open at a time (via multiple Data Controls), so more than one Recordset object can be floating around. But in our example, we have a single database, and the Recordset is the collection of data that we're manipulating. You always refer to this Recordset when accessing, editing or saving data to the data-base pointed to this way: data1.Recordset.

A Recordset is a copy of an opened database, not the actual database file itself. Therefore, in a multiuser environment (networking, or more than one copy of a VB program running at the same time), other users could update information in the database by editing, adding or deleting records—but your program would not notice these changes. Whenever you want to be sure that your program is working with a current, accurate representation of the database, use the Refresh command: Data1.Refresh. This rebuilds the Recordset (as if you had opened the database for the first time) and gives you the current status of the database and its record.

A List Box to Show All Records

If you are using VB4, there is a new "Data-aware" List Box (along with several other newly "aware" Controls described below). If you're using VB4, ignore the discussion immediately below. Just add a DBList Control to your Toolbox. From the VB Tools menu, select "Custom Controls." Then click on "Microsoft Data Bound List Controls." (If you don't see this item, select it in the Tools menu under "References" then select it in "Custom Controls" as well.)

In the DBList's Property Window, in the DataSource and RowSource Properties type "DATA1" and in the DataField and ListField Properties type "Title." With the DBList Box, you can skip the programming we'll now describe to make an ordinary List Box display all the titles and switch to the correct record when the user clicks in the list.

To make a DBList Control switch to the record the user clicks on, put this in the DBList_Click Event:

```
Private Sub DBList1_Click( )
    Dim x As Variant
    x = DBList1.SelectedItem
    Data1.Recordset.Bookmark = x
End Sub
```

Note that the DBList Control is a one-dimensional list (has no Columns Property, thus cannot have multiple columns). This might make you ask why it has a RowSource Property (the Name of the Data Control (such asData1) to which the DBList is bound). The DBList and DBCombo controls have DataSource and RowSource properties because you can display a list of values from one table but save it to another table.

Ordinary List Boxes are not "data-aware"; unlike the VB4 DBList Control, a regular List Box cannot be bound to a Data Control and automatically display information from a database. But by using some of VB's database language commands, we can fill a regular List Box with all the titles in our videotape database.

A List Box will provide an alternative way for the user to select a particular record. Instead of clicking on the arrows in the Data Control to move through the records, the user can click on any title in the List Box and that record instantly becomes the current, visible record. We'll also add a Label that will display the total number of records, so put a List Box and a Label on the Form. Change the Label's Name Property to Label7. In the Form's Paint Event, type the following:

```
Dim d As Variant
data1.Recordset.MoveLast
totalrecords = data1.Recordset.RecordCount
label7.Caption = Str$(totalrecords)
data1.Recordset.MoveFirst
list1.Clear
For i = 0 To totalrecords - 1
    d = data1.Recordset.Fields(0).Value
    If IsNull(d) Then d = ""
    data1.Recordset.MoveNext
    list1.AddItem d
Next i
data1.Recordset.MoveFirst
```

First, we want to calculate the total number of records in our database table. To calculate, we must move to the last record with the MoveLast command. Then we can query the RecordCount Variable. (It is possible, through deletions or other activity, that a RecordCount will not be accurate. Moving to the last record forces VB to check the actual current number of records. After that, the RecordCount will be accurate.) We put that number into our Variable called *totalrecords* and display it to the user in Label7.

Then we use the MoveFirst command to make the first record the current record. The current record is the one that can be edited and that will be displayed in any bound Controls like our Text Boxes.

Now we fill the List Box by looping from 0 (the first record) to *totalrecords-1* (the last record). Notice the Fields command (Method). This command specifies which of the fields in our table is being accessed. The first field (our "Title" field) is Field(0). The "Value" of that field is its data: *A River Runs Through It* or *The Godfather*. Or you can use an alternative method of identifying the field; you can name the field instead of providing its index number: d = data1.Recordset.Fields("Title").Value

In any case, a field may be empty (Null), so we use the IsNull command to check for that possibility. If so, we make our Variable *d* hold a null text (string) Variable. If you don't use a null Variable, a null will cause an error message. Then we move to the next record with the MoveNext command and add the contents of our Variable *d* to our List Box.

Note: If you're using the DBList Control (thereby avoiding the programming necessary to fill an ordinary List Box), you should nonetheless put the following into the Form's Paint Event. This provides the user with a record count at the bottom of our Form:

```
Private Sub Form_Paint
    data1.Recordset.MoveLast
    totalrecords = data1.Recordset.RecordCount
    label7.Caption = Str$(totalrecords)
End Sub
```

Queries

A programmer must do two main things when managing a database: search and sort. VB handles the sorting for you, maintaining a Recordset in alphabetical or numeric order based on whatever index you've selected as primary. For searching, much of the work is also done for you because VB includes a complex, complete searching language called SQL (Structured Query Language). With it, you can ask almost any kind of question (show me a list of all movies between 1970 and 1980 starring either Kneau Reeves or Sondra Locke).

There are several excellent books on SQL–it's beyond the scope of this book to cover the language. If you intend to use VB to manipulate databases, you might want to study a book on SQL to take full advantage of its capabilities. But here's one example: we'll allow users to get a list of titles that match their query. The query can be partial, the same way that DOS allows you to see all filenames starting with S if you add an * (asterisk): DIR S*.* for example.

We'll also use a query to allow the user to click on our List Box and cause the selected record to be displayed in our Text Boxes (the record is made the "current" record).

Put another Command Button on the Form and caption it "SEARCH." In that Button's Click Event, type the following:

```
Sub Command2_Click ( )
list1.Clear
x$ = InputBox("Which Title?")
quer = "[Title] Like '*" + x$ + "*'"
data1.Recordset.FindFirst quer
Do Until data1.Recordset.NoMatch
    list1.AddItem text1.Text
    c = c + 1
    data1.Recordset.FindNext quer
Loop
label7.Caption = Str$(c)
End Sub
```

First, we clear out the titles in the List Box and ask the user to enter the search criterion. Then we combine the user's query with the name of the Field to search. (This is an SQL query.) The Like command can match partial words and ignores capitalization. We also surround the query with asterisks, so anything before or after the query will trigger a match. Notice that the actual query data, X$, is surrounded by single quotation marks. Now the user can enter *ve* and trigger *Fever*, *To Have or Have Not* and any other title with the characters *ve* inside somewhere.

Then we use the FindFirst command to locate the first match in the table. Within a Loop, we continue to find each match in the table, via the FindNext command. The Variable *c* keeps track of how many matches occur (which we later put into our "Number of Records" Label). The NoMatch Property is either True or False; it is changed to True when no match is found.

Locating a Particular Record

We'll use a modified version of our search query technique to move to a record when the user clicks on its title in the List Box. In the List Box's Click Event, type the following:

```
Sub List1_Click ( )
x$ = list1.List(list1.ListIndex)
quer = "[Title] = '" + x$ + "'"
Data1.Recordset.FindFirst quer
End Sub
```

First, we put the title the user clicked on into the Variable X$. Then we define the Variable *quer* as a title that equals X$. Remember that here, and in the previous search example, you must surround the target text Variable with single quotation marks. Finally, we request that the current record be the first one that matches our query.

Deleting Records

All that remains is to add a facility for the user to remove records. Add another Command Button to the Form. Change its Caption to "Delete Record." Then, within the Button's Click Event, type the following:

```
Data1.Recordset.Delete
```

Our semifunctional database manager is nearly complete. We can still make some improvements before it is a first-class application. As with all disk-access programs, you should insert On Error commands into your programming to react to problems. If an untrapped error occurs, VB will shut down your program. (Some data access errors, however, don't crash the VB program. They merely present the user with a disconcerting message.)

Also, when the user adds or deletes a record, the List Box should RemoveItem and the Total Records Label should be changed to report the new total. More complex searches should be allowed, including combinations of criteria and expansion of the search beyond the Title field. We should add an Undo feature. The user should be able to send data to his or her printer. The user also should be allowed to choose the printer and screen fonts. We should use the Clipboard as a way of importing data files from disk and add a Command Button captioned "Quit." Finally, we should employ Visual Basic's impressive visual facilities to make the Form look gorgeous (to find out how to get the metallic look of Figure D-5, see the entry for "Line").

Our example illustrates all the main techniques for managing an elementary, single-table, straightforward database. However, there is much more database facility in VB than we have space to explore here. SQL and DDL are entire languages in themselves.

Data Control Properties

Several of the Data Control's Properties operate as they do for other Controls (these Properties are not unique to the Data Control). See the entries elsewhere in this book for more on Align, BackColor, Caption, DragIcon, DragMode, Enabled, FontBold, FontItalic, FontName, FontSize, FontStrikethru, FontUnderline, Forecolor, Height, Index, Left, MousePointer, Name, Tag, Top, Visible and Width.

The following Properties are unique to the Data Control: BOFAction, EOFAction: These Properties tell the Data Control what action it should take if the current record becomes impossible—lower or higher than the beginning or ending of the file. In other words, if the BOF or EOF Properties become True.

When BOF is True, this means that we're at the start of the data, therefore such behaviors as MovePrevious are impossible—there is no previous record. BOFAction can be in two states:

Data1.BOFAction = 0 (the default) triggers MoveFirst (causes the current record to be the first record).

Data1.BOFAction = 1 triggers a Validation Event on the "impossible" before-the-start record, followed by a Reposition Event. The button on the Data Control that allows you to move one record "down" is disabled.

The EOFAction Properties behave the same way for 0 and 1, but there is a third possible setting for EOFAction:

Data1.EOFAction = 2   Triggers an AddNew

BOF and EOF Properties

EOF, End Of File, is not unique to the Data Control; it is also used with ordinary disk file management (see "Open"). However, BOF, Beginning Of File, is unique. You don't need to worry about BOF when the user is merely clicking on the arrows within the Data Control—the Control makes sure the user can't click past the start of a list of records.

However, if you decide to make the Data Control invisible and substitute your own Command Buttons or provide other methods of moving to previous records, the BOF Property can prevent confusion. You can test the BOF when your program uses the MovePrevious command to move back down one record in a database (toward the first record). It is possible that your current record is the first record, in which case a MovePrevious would put you before the beginning of the file–which would be an impossibility. However, the BOFAction Property will trap this error. You might, though, want to disable your "move down" Control in this situation so the user inderstands that there's nothing more in that direction.

Similarly, you might want to test for an EOF before using the MoveNext command. Technically, BOF and EOF are Properties of the Recordset of the Data Control, not of the Control itself.

Connect: You can assign a text (string) Variable or literal text to this Property either while you're designing or while your program is running. Assigning to this Property is necessary only if you are managing a non-Microsoft (not an Access-type) database. The Data Control can manipulate data from a variety of different databases–Paradox, Access, dBASE, etc. If you want to open a Microsoft Access database (or one created in that style with VB–see the Example), leave this Property blank. Then set the DatabaseName Property to the full path of the database file, for example:

```
Data1.DatabaseName = "C:\TESTS\MYBASE.MDB"
```

If you don't intend for your program to be used on a network (and don't want the user to have SHARE.EXE running in the AUTOEXEC.BAT file), set the Exclusive Property to True, as follows: Data1.Exclusive = True. Finally, set the ReadOnly Property, as follows: Data1.ReadOnly = False. Now, any bound Controls (like a Text Box that you've "bound" to the Data1 Data Control) will display data from the MYBASE.MDB database.

However, some other database formats require that the Connect Property be defined prior to opening a database: for example, Data1.Connect = "Paradox 3.X" (That 3.X is necessary. Technically speaking, if you are trying to access one of these non-Access, non-Microsoft databases, the Connect Property's text ("string") Variable must match what is in the installable ISAM section of the VB.INI disk file. If you were to change the Connect text Variable in the VB.INI file, you would also have to change it in your program. Furthermore, if you make a runnable .EXE program out of your VB program (see the VB File Menu), you need to create an .INI file with the same name as your .EXE program. This .INI file must have the installable ISAM section in it for the Connect text Variable to still work.)

Database: This Property can only be "read" while a VB program is running. That is, you cannot redefine this Property while a VB program is running. In fact, you define it only indirectly while designing. It refers to the Database Object; the Database Property is a way of naming the Database Object. This Property gives you a way to get information about the database being accessed and to manipulate the data within it.

When you define some of the Properties of a Data Control in the Properties Window and then run the program, VB automatically opens that particular specified database. In the process, a "Database Object" is created. (You can also create an object while a VB program is running by defining those same Properties—DatabaseName, Exclusive, ReadOnly and, optionally, Connect.) In any event, the Database Object is then your avenue to controlling and accessing the open database. The Database Property of a Data Control is the name of that Database Object. You can use the Database Property in the following way to, for example, force a database to close:

```
Data1.Database.Close
```

OR (to print the names of all the fields in a particular table):

```
Dim MyTable As Recordset
Set MyTable = Data1.Recordset
Dim Fld as Field
For Each Fld in MyTable.Fields
    d = Fld.Name
    list1.AddItem d
Next Fld
```

OR, more simply:

```
Dim Fld As Field
For Each Fld In Data1.Recordset.Fields
    d = Fld.Name
    List1.AddItem d
Next Fld
```

Notice that there are several objects in this example. MyTable is a Recordset object. Fields is a built-in collection of field objects within the Recordset object. A collection is very much like an Array. When we created our Video database using the Data Manager, we defined the "shell," the structure of that database.

You can, in fact, programmatically find out everything about the structure and qualities of a database. This example shows how to find out the wealth of details about the first field in our Video database. (The first field is Fields(0) because the Fields collection starts counting with a zeroth item.):

```
Private Sub Form_Load( )
Show
Dim MyDatabase As Database
Set MyDatabase = OpenDatabase("C:\Video.mdb")
Dim MyTable As Recordset
Set MyTable = MyDatabase.OpenRecordset("Tapes", dbOpenTable)
Dim n As Field
Set n = MyTable.Fields(0)
Print "Field Name: "; n.Name
Print "AllowZeroLength: "; n.AllowZeroLength
Print "Attributes: "; n.Attributes
Print "CollatingOrder: "; n.CollatingOrder
Print "DefaultValue: "; n.DefaultValue
Print "OrdinalPosition: "; n.OrdinalPosition
Print "Required: "; n.Required
```

```
        Print "Size: "; n.Size
        Print "SourceField: "; n.SourceField
        Print "SourceTable: "; n.SourceTable
        Print "Type: "; n.Type
        Print "ValidateOnSet: "; n.ValidateOnSet
        Print "ValidationRule: "; n.ValidationRule
        Print "ValidationText: "; n.ValidationText
        Set MyDatabase = Nothing
        Set MyTable = Nothing
        Set n = Nothing
        End Sub
```

Results in

```
Field Name: Year
AllowZeroLength: False
Attributes: 33
CollatingOrder: 1024
DefaultValue:
OrdinalPosition: 3
Required: False
Size: 2
SourceField: Year
SourceTable: Tapes
Type: 3
ValidateOnSet: False
ValidationRule:
ValidationText:
```

TableDefs

The TableDefs collection (of TableDef objects) holds the details about a database. Your VB program can query the TableDefs structure for those details. If the user, for instance, is permitted by your VB program to define new tables, fields, indices etc. while the program is running, your program can then find out about these new structures, their qualities, their names and so on. You could also use TableDefs or TableDef to determine the structure of unknown databases. The TableDef object contains the structure of a particular table—its fields and indices.

You can also manipulate the structure of a table by using a TableDef object. For example, you could read (or change) the fields, indices, Table-Name Properties. You could also adjust or get information about a table via the OpenRecordset Method to create a table-, dynaset-, or snapshot-type Recordset object based on the table definition. If you only want to read (query) a table, it's often more direct, though, to use the Recordset Property rather than the Database Property to get this same information.

DatabaseName: This Property is one of four that tell a Data Control which database to open and how to open it. DatabaseName is the full path and filename for Microsoft Access or Btrieve files (C:\FILES\MYFILE.MDB). The Connect Property is not used.

For all other types of databases, the DatabaseName Property is the disk path, but not the filename ("C:\MYFILES"). That, along with the Connect and

RecordSource Properties, identifies the particular database file. Note that you can change the DatabaseName Property during design or running of a VB program. But to open a new database, you must use the Refresh command (Data1.Refresh) to complete opening that new database. And don't forget to close an already opened database before changing to a new one.

EditMode: The behavior of the Data Control is fairly automatic. When the user changes some text in a bound Text Box, VB handles the busywork necessary to prepare the database to be changed. When a new record is moved into the Text Box (via MoveNext or MoveFirst or some other command, or simply by the user clicking on the Data Control's Scroll Bar), an edited record is automatically saved to the database. VB handles much of the underlying database management for you. EditMode is useful, though, if you want to get in there and do some of this manipulation yourself.

EditMode can only provide information while a program is running. It tells you if the current record has not been changed (EditMode = 0); if the Edit command has been used, putting the current record into the copy buffer and making it available for editing (1); and if the AddNew command has announced that the current record resides in the copy buffer and is now ready to be saved. For more information, see "Validate" under "Data Control Events" later in this section.

Exclusive: Exclusive is one of the four Properties (along with Database-Name, ReadOnly and Connect) that define which database is opened under a Data Control and how it is to be accessed. Exclusive, when True, means that only a single user on a network will be allowed to access this database at any one time or that only one running VB program can access the database at a time. (A user may be running more than one "instance" of your VB program.) One benefit of setting Exclusive to True is that the user of your program need not be running the SHARE.EXE DOS program in order to run your VB program. However, Exclusive is, by default, set to False—and Microsoft strongly discourages avoiding the use of SHARE.EXE. (These rules are not applicable to Windows 95 or NT. And with Exclusive set to True, things go faster.)

Options: In VB3, there were three distinct types of database objects—Table, DynaSet and SnapShot. Now, in VB4, there is only the Recordset object, with three flavors parallel to the Table, DynaSet and SnapShot. (See "Differences Between VB3 and VB4" above.)

Options describes the qualities of a Recordset. When a Data Control's RecordSource Property is set to a valid table and its DatabaseName Property is set to the path of a valid database file (and, optionally, its Read-Only, Exclusive and Connect Properties are also set), running the VB program and Showing or Loading the Form on which the Data Control resides actually opens that database. This automatically creates a Recordset.

If a bound Control's DataField Property also names that same table, data will automatically appear in the Text Box or other bound Control. But you want to search, sort and otherwise manipulate that data. Using VB commands to access the Recordset is one way.

A Recordset is an object: It is a view or window into a database. A Recordset contains the information in a database (or selected information, based on a query) at a particular time. It is not the same, necessarily, as the database itself. The database may be changed and the Recordset discarded (not used to update the database). Likewise, a Recordset might contain only records starting with the letter M. You can create a Recordset Variable as follows:

```
Dim MyRec As Recordset
Set MyRec = Data1.Recordset
```

These two lines create a new Recordset object Variable called MyRec and fill it with the Recordset that VB automatically created via the Data Control. This Recordset is derived from the database you defined in the Control's DatabaseName Property.

Alternatively, you can bypass the Data Control and contact a database Recordset via programming alone:

```
Dim MyDatabase as Database
Set MyDatabase = OpenDatabase("Video.mdb")
Dim MyTable As Recordset
Set MyTable = MyDatabase.OpenRecordset("Tapes", dbOpenTable)
```

You can find out the qualities of the original Data Control Recordset (or change those qualities) by querying or changing the Options Property of the Data Control.

Data1.Options =

dbDenyWrite	1	Even if the Data Control's Exclusive Property is set to False, other users cannot change anything in this Recordset.
dbDenyRead*	2	Other users cannot even read this Recordset.
dbReadOnly	4	Nobody can make any changes to this Recordset (it's ReadOnly).
dbAppendOnly	8	Append Only; you can add records but not read existing records
dbInconsistent	16	Any fields can be updated.
dbConsistent	32	(Default) Only fields that don't affect other records in the Recordset can be updated.
dbSQLPassThrough	64	When using an SQL statement as the Record Source Property, the statement is sent to an ODBC database.
dbForwardOnly*	256	The records can only be accessed in a "forward" direction. The only Move Method is MoveNext. (This has no effect if you're using a Data Control, only with programmatic data access.)

| dbSeeChanges* | 512 | Causes an error if another user in a networked environment is making changes to data that you are also editing. |

*New in VB4.

To use more than one of these options, add the values. Setting Options=9 would prevent other users from changing the Dynaset and also make it Append Only. You could, for instance:

```
Data1.Options = dbDenyRead + dbReadOnly
```

To find out if a cluster of Options are active:

```
If Data1.Options And dbDenyRead + dbReadOnly Then...
```

Note: If you adjust the Options Property while the VB program is running, you must then invoke the Refresh Method or no change will take place.

ReadOnly: If ReadOnly is set to True, the data can be displayed but not changed. This setting prevents people without passwords, for example, from modifying a database but allows them to view the data. If ReadOnly is set to False (the default), the database can be viewed and changed. If you do set it to True and then decide to permit modification of the data by changing it to False while a program is running, you must first close (Data1.Database.Close) and refresh (Data1.Database.Refresh) the database. You can then reopen the database by adding the following:

```
Data1.ReadOnly = False and Data1.DatabaseName = "C:\VIDEO.MDB"
Data1.Refresh
```

Recordset: Allows you to access the Data Control Recordset, or create new Recordset objects out of existing ones. You might, for example, want to manipulate the Data Control's Recordset with database programming commands (DDL). Or you might want to open one Recordset to merely look at, and another one to edit. You can generate lots of these Recordset objects, if you want to.

```
Data1.Recordset.AddNew
```

OR

```
Dim MyTable As Recordset

Set MyTable = Data1.Recordset
```

RecordsetType: This is the flavor of the Recordset that is created automatically when VB opens a database file according to the specifications in a Data Control's DatabaseName and RecordSource Properties. See the example above for some sample uses. In VB4, the RecordsetType is, by default, a DynaSet. (See "Differences Between VB3 and VB4" earlier.) Here are the possible values:

Data1.RecordsetType =

vbTableType   0 A table-type Recordset.
vbDynasetType   1 (Default) A dynaset-type Recordset.
vbSnapshotType   2 A snapshot-type Recordset.

Note: The values you can assign to the RecordsetType Property value are not the same as the values used to identify Recordset object types. When you use the OpenRecordSet command (another way to create a new Recordset), these are the possible values:

```
dbOpenTable    1       (Default)
dbOpenDynaset  2
dbOpenSnapshot 4
```

So, if you're trying to define or find out the type of a Recordset object, you must use the DB, not the VB, Constants' values:

```
Dim MyDatabase as Database
Set MyDatabase = OpenDatabase("Video.mdb")
Dim MyTable As Recordset
Set MyTable = MyDatabase.OpenRecordset("Tapes", dbOpenTable)
If MyTable.Type = dbOpenTable Then
    Print "It's a Table-type Recordset"
End If
```

RecordSource: This Property tells you the name of a table, the current table within the currently open database. This table is the source of the records displayed in bound Controls like a Text Box, the table whose fields and indices are used by the various database manipulation commands. In other words, the DatabaseName Property defines which database file is open and the RecordSource Property defines which table (if there are more than one) should be used to access data. (Further down this hierarchy, there's the DataField Property of a bound Control.)

You can freely change the RecordSource while designing or running a VB program. However, if you do change it during runtime, be sure to also change any bound Controls' DataField Properties to match a field within this new table. After changing RecordSource, you must use the Refresh Method.

Changing the Sort Order

A RecordSource need not be a table; it can also be an SQL statement (or a QueryDef, which is a kind of "compiled" SQL query). Let's try an SQL example here as a demonstration of the flexibility of the Data Control and VB's database commands. Here's an alternative way to change the displayed order of a database, using an SQL (Structured Query Language) statement:

```
Data1.RecordSource = "Select * from Tapes Order By [Director]"
Data1.Refresh
```

Try this with our Video example above and notice that, suddenly and automatically, the database is sorted by the Director field instead of the Title field.

Data Control Events

Like many other Controls, the Data Control has DragDrop, DragOver, MouseDown, MouseMove and MouseUp Events. See these entries elsewhere in this book. Three Events are unique to the Data Control, however.

Error:

```
Sub Data1_Error([Index As Integer,] DataErr As Integer, Response As Integer)
```

Index refers to the index number of the Data Control, if it's a member of a Control Array (which see).

DataErr is an error number, and Response can be either 0 (continue) or 1 (the default, "Display the error message").

As with most VB programming that involves disk or printer access, you put error-handling commands within your programming (see "On Error"). However, the Data Control includes this Error Event to handle errors that cannot be trapped by any programming (because the program isn't actively running within any Sub or Event when this kind of error occurs).

Nonprogrammatic errors can happen if the user clicks on one of the Data Control arrows to move to a different record; when a database is automatically opened because a Form containing a Data Control is Loaded; or when a custom Control uses a database language command like MoveNext. You can use the Error Event to trap such errors and respond appropriately.

Reposition: When a Form on which a Data Control resides is first Loaded, the database is opened and the first record is made the current record. Also, when a user clicks on an arrow in a Data Control, or your program uses one of the Move or Find commands (such as FindLast), a new record becomes the current record. In both of these situations, the Reposition Event is triggered. If you want your program to respond whenever a new record is displayed, you can put your response within the Reposition Event.

Validate: Validate, like Reposition, is triggered when a new record is about to become the current record, but Validate *triggers just before a new record becomes current*. As soon as the user or some command causes a Move or some other repositioning within the database, the Validate Event triggers and gives you the opportunity to do something before your current record is no longer current. It's triggered by the Update, Delete, Bookmark, UnLoad, Move and Find commands; user-clicking on the Data Control; and Close commands. It's triggered often, as you can see by running our example program and putting a breakpoint within the Data Control's Validate Event (press F9). Run the program and you'll see Validate triggering like a monkey in a hot cage.

```
Sub Data1_Validate ([ index As Integer,] Action As Integer, Save As Integer)
```

The Validate's "Action" Variable tells you what command or behavior triggered the Validate Event. You can also set the Action Variable, thereby changing one behavior into another, according to the following list:

vbDataActionCancel	0	Prevent the Move behavior (or whatever triggered the Validate Event)
vbDataActionMoveFirst	1	The MoveFirst command
vbDataActionMovePrevious	2	The MovePrevious command
vbDataActionMoveNext	3	The MoveNext command
vbDataActionMoveLast	4	The MoveLast command
vbDataActionAddNew	5	The AddNew command
vbDataActionUpdate	6	Update
vbDataActionDelete	7	The Delete command
vbDataActionFind	8	A Find command
vbDataActionBookmark	9	The Bookmark Property was set
vbDataActionClose	10	The Close command
vbDataActionUnload	11	The Form is being UnLoaded

The Validate's Save Variable is True or False, based on whether or not data in a bound Control has been changed.

Validate, as its name implies, is most useful if you want to check the data that the user is trying to enter into the database. Is the text the user entered too long? In the wrong format? Into the Validate Event, you can insert programming that will test all bound Controls for changes (by checking their individual DataChanged Properties). If you want to disallow a change, set that Control's DataChanged Property to False, and the data will not be saved to the database. Likewise, you can look at what the user has done and, if necessary, set the Action Variable to cause a different command to be carried out (Data1.Action = 7 causes a deletion; Action = 0 prevents anything from happening). In other words, although Validate might have been triggered by a MoveLast command, you can "intercept" that command and refuse to permit the move by using Action = 0, or "translate" to a different command by using Action = 1, for example.

Data Control Methods
Drag, Move, Refresh and ZOrder (which see) behave as they do for other Controls. However, the Data Control has two unique Methods: UpdateControls and UpdateRecord.

UpdateControls: When you use this command (Data1.UpdateControls), you cause the current record from the Recordset to be displayed in any bound Controls. But doesn't this happen automatically anyway? Yes, usually, but not always. Let's assume that a user of our videotape database entered 1858 for the date of a movie. In the Validate Event you want to check for, and reject, numbers lower than 1900, for this particular field. Because changed data hasn't yet become part of the database when Validate is triggered, you can reject the erroneous editing by restoring whatever was in the Text Box before the user made the mistake: Data1.UpdateControls will replace the bad entry with whatever is already in the database. You also can use UpdateControls as your program's response to the user clicking an Undo Button.

UpdateRecord: When you use this command (usually in the Validate Event), you cause the current contents of all bound Controls to be saved to the database. Any changes the user has made, for example, will now be saved. The command Data1.UpdateRecord *does not trigger any Events.* By contrast, the Update command triggers the Validate Event. (Putting an *Update* command within a Validate Event will retrigger the Event over and over causing an "endless Loop." This, in fact, is why Microsoft created the UpdateRecord command—to use in the Validate Event.)

Recall that many other activities (the Move and Find commands, clicking on the Data Control, etc.) also cause the current contents of bound Controls to be saved to the database. The Update command is used primarily when you are not relying on the Data Control and other Controls bound to it to make changes to a database. You are, in other words, programming changes. Here's an example that doesn't even involve the user (or a bound Control) in making a direct change to the database:

```
Data1.Recordset.Edit
Data1.Recordset.Fields("Title") = "Earthquake"
Data1.Recordset.Update
```

This example would be useful if you are bypassing bound Controls, using, say, an InputBox to get data from the user, rather than a bound Control.

Bound Control Properties

In VB3 there were eight Controls that could be *bound* to a Data Control: Text Boxes, Images, Picture Boxes, Labels, Check Boxes, Masked Edit, 3D Panels, and 3D Check Boxes. To this list, VB4 adds Combo Boxes, List Boxes and Grid Controls.

When a Control is bound it means that you've put a Data Control on a Form, then added one of these "data-aware" Controls and set two of the Control's Properties. The DataSource Property must be the name of the Data Control (such as "Data1"). The DataField Property names one of the fields in the database. (To complete the link to the database, the Data Control's DatabaseName Property contains the path to the database, such as "C\VIDEO.MDB." And the Data Control's RecordSource Property names the Table within the database that is to be displayed, such as "Tapes.")

Note that with VB4 there are two kinds of data-aware List Boxes and two kinds of Combo Boxes. The ordinary VB List Box and Combo Box are now data-aware (they have DataField and DataSource Properties). However, to fill them with, say, the Title field for each record in our Video Tapes Table, you have to program it using the AddItem command. For a programming example, see "A List Box to Show All Records" earlier in this section.

The other data-aware List Box and Combo Box Controls are called DBList and DBCombo. These Controls will automatically fill with data, but you don't have to write any programming—just set three Properties. To bind a DBList, in the DBList's Property Window, in the DataSource and Row-

Source Properties type "DATA1" and in the DataField and ListField Properties type "Title."

Note that the DBList and DBCombo Controls are missing some useful Methods that are available to ordinary List and Combo Controls, such as Clear, RemoveItem and AddItem. Likewise, Properties such as ListCount are missing.

To add one of these DB Controls to your Toolbox, click on the VB Tools menu, then select Custom Controls. If you don't see "Microsoft Data Bound List Controls" listed, look in the Tools Menu and click on References. Select "Microsoft Data Bound List Controls" in References, then go back to Custom Controls and select them there as well.

Microsoft expects to add additional "data-aware" Controls in the future. There are also third-party data-aware Controls available.

Most data-aware Controls have three data-related Properties, which follow:

DataSource: DataSource is the name of a Data Control to which you want the Control bound. If a Text Box's DataSource Property is "Data1," then the Box is said to be "bound" to the Data Control Named "Data1" and will therefore display information from any database opened by the Data Control.

DataField: This Property determines which field in the database will be displayed by the bound Control.

DataChanged: This Property shows whether the contents (the data) displayed by a bound Control have been changed (the user edited something, or it was changed programmatically, not merely read). DataChanged will be True if the data changed, False if it didn't.

The DBList and DBCombo Controls, however, have a slew of data-related Properties. They have DataSource and DataField (but no DataChanged). In addition, they have the following nine Properties:

RowSource: This names the Data Control (like Data1) that the DBList Control is bound to.

ListField: The Field's Name, the active Field in the current Recordset.

BoundColumn: This is the Field object's Name. After a selection is made, this is the Field in the Recordset (identified by the RowSource Property) that is passed back to the DataField.

BoundText: Whatever text is in the BoundColumn field. After a selection is made, this is passed back to the DataSource. It updates the field identified by the DataField Property.

Text: The text in the selected element in the list.

MatchEntry: Determines how the list is searched when the user types in something to search for. If MatchEntry = 0 (the default), then the list is searched using the first letter of the items in the list. If the user keeps on typing the same letter, the entire list is cycled through. If MatchEntry = 1 then all characters typed by the user are used as the basis of the search.

SelectedItem: This gives you the Bookmark (which see) of the selected item (in the Recordset pointed to by the RowSource Property).

VisibleCount: How many items in the list that the user can currently see on the screen.

VisibleItems: This is an array of "Bookmarks." There's one for each item in the list. You can use these Bookmarks to get items from the active Recordset (the one that filled the list in the first place).

General Database Manipulation Commands

In addition to the Methods contained within the Data Control, there are several general database commands that are particularly valuable. These commands actually work with the Recordset (of the Data Control, or any other Recordset). Technically, these commands are Methods of a Recordset object. (Don't become lost in the object-oriented-programming house of mirrors. A Recordset, for example, can be a Property of a Data Control. Yet that same Recordset can have its own set of Properties and Methods.) In any case, the following Recordset Methods are worth knowing about, even if you only intend to use the Data Control. With these commands, you considerably expand your ability to manipulate and govern a database through programming.

Edit:

```
Data1.Recordset.Edit
```

This command permits your program to make a change to the current record. The Edit command is unnecessary when the user makes a change to the data in a bound Control (the user can simply type in changes to a bound Text Box, for example). But if you want your program, not the user, to make a change to a record directly, you must first use the Edit command. If you don't, an error is generated. The Edit command, in effect, "opens" a record for editing via programming rather than user interaction with a Data Control or a Control bound to the Data Control.

Edit is generally coupled with two other commands, Fields = and Update, to make a change to a particular entry within a database. Do the following:

```
Data1.Recordset.Edit
Data1.Recordset.Fields("Title") = "Danger Mouse"
Data1.Recordset.Update
```

No matter what was in the Title field of the current record, it's now Danger Mouse.

Note that you must follow Edit with an Update command, if you intend to actually store the programmatic changes to this record in the database.

AddNew:

```
Data1.Recordset.AddNew
```

This command clears any bound Controls, removes anything that's in a Text Box, for example, allowing the user to enter an entirely new record to the database.

Technically, the AddNew command creates a copy of the current record and stores the copy in a "copy buffer." That record is finally stored in the actual database file when the Update command is executed (or the user moves through the database by clicking on the Data Control).

Likewise, you can use AddNew to have your program add a new record directly into a database, without intervention by the user, like this:

```
Data1.Recordset.AddNew
Data1.Recordset.Fields("Title") = "Song of Serene"
Data1.Recordset.Fields("Director") = "Foxy Jones"
Data1.Recordset.Fields("Year") = 1956
Data1.Recordset.Update
```

Note that you must follow AddNew with an Update command, if you intend to actually store this programmatic new record in the database.

Update: The Update command is used both with user, or direct, programming and for editing existing records or adding new records. Update *saves* changes to the database. However, many other activities (the Move and Find commands, clicking on the Data Control, etc.) also cause the current contents of bound Controls to be saved. Therefore, the Update command is used primarily when you are not relying on the Data Control and other Controls bound to it to make changes to a database. The user isn't involved; you are, in other words, *programming* changes to the database when you write your program.

Delete:

```
Data1.Recordset.Delete
```

This command deletes the current record from the database. However, any bound Controls will still display the data for this record. Therefore, the Delete command is usually followed by the MoveNext command, to display the next record in the database table and make it the current record. You might also want to check the EOF Property of the Recordset to see if you're deleting the last record. If so, you can invoke MovePrevious. However, the EOFAction Property defaults to an automatic MoveLast, which should keep things tidy and display what is, after your Delete of the last record, your new last record. Just using Delete by itself is likely to confuse the user— who sees the now-nonexistent record still sitting there onscreen in a bound Control.

Move Commands

Several commands make a different record the current record (a current record is the one that shows up in bound Controls and that can be edited, deleted, etc.).

MoveFirst, MoveLast, MoveNext and MovePrevious are self-explanatory.

```
Data1.Recordset.MoveFirst
Data1.Recordset.MoveLast
Data1.Recordset.MoveNext
Data1.Recordset.MovePrevious
```

Note that each of these commands can be within your program or automatically carried out when the user clicks on one of the four arrows on the Data Control.

You must use MoveLast when you want to get an accurate count of the number of records in a Table, as follows:

```
data1.Recordset.MoveLast
totalrecords = data1.Recordset.RecordCount
```

Find Commands

The FindFirst, FindLast, FindNext and FindPrevious commands are similar to the four Move commands, but you provide the Find commands with a *specification*, like *greater than* or *equals* or some other search criteria. If a record matches the criteria, that record is made the *current* record. Therefore, if you use MoveFirst, you will be sent to the first record in the current table. But if you use FindFirst, you will be moved to the first record in the current table *that matches the criteria* you've specified.

```
Data1.Recordset.FindFirst search criteria
Data1.Recordset.FindLast search criteria
Data1.Recordset.FindNext search criteria
Data1.Recordset.FindPrevious search criteria
```

The search criteria can be virtually any kind of expression. If no record satisfies the criteria, the Data Control's NoMatch Property is made True. Here's a typical use of the FindFirst command. This example locates and makes current the first record in the table whose title starts with the letter M:

```
quer = "[Title] Like 'M*'"
data1.Recordset.FindFirst quer
```

There's a little kink when you use the Find commands: If there isn't a match, the first record becomes the current record, if you're using Find-First. Or the last record becomes current, if you're using FindLast. This could easily confuse and upset the user. To prevent this, mark your current record with a Bookmark, then return to that place if the search fails:

```
Curr = data1.Recordset.Bookmark
data1.Recordset.FindFirst "Title = 'Glorix' "
If data1.Recordset.NoMatch Then
  data1.Recordset.Bookmark = Curr
End If
CancelUpdate
Data1.Recordset.CancelUpdate
```

This code is useful to put in the Click Event of a button labeled "Undo." It restores a record to its original state if the user types in some changes then decides to undo those changes. (However, once the user clicks on a Data Control button, making some other record the current record, CancelUpdate cannot do anything about the previously edited record.) It also works to remove an AddNew.

Clone

```
Dim Rse as Recordset
Set Rse = Data1.Recordset.Clone( )
```

At this point, the Recordset named Rse contains a copy of the Data1.Recordset, an exact copy. Now that there are two Recordsets, each can have a different current record, but Bookmarks can be used interchangeably between them. When first created, the clone doesn't have a current record—so employ one of the Find or Move Methods to establish which record is current.

Close

```
Data1.Recordset.Close
```

This command shuts down the Recordset (the Recordset object is, in effect, set to "Nothing.") You can also use Close with the Database object (Data1.Database.Close). Close can also be used with QueryDefs and Workspaces. Note that if you close the current Recordset or Database, then the user clicks on the Data Control, an "Object is invalid or not set" error message is triggered.

Closing a Recordset saves any changes to the current record; closing a Database does not. Use the Update Method before Close, to save editing to the database.

Building Databases Programmatically

The Professional Edition of VB provides a set of commands with which you can create new databases, including defining tables, relationships, indices, fields and so on. In other words, via programming alone a database can be built from scratch, or an existing database can be modified.

The primary value of these commands—CreateDatabase, Createfield, etc.— is that they permit the user to define the structure of a new database or modify an existing one. Clearly, if you, the programmer, want to create or modify a database, you can do it while designing your program—you don't have to do it while the program is running. (Or you could use VB's Database Manager, found in the Add-Ins Menu.)

However, if you want to extend to the user the ability to get in there and really describe and control the structure of a database, this is the way to do it.

Creating a Database, Table & Fields

We created an example database above, VIDEO.MDB, using the Data Manager. For those who have the Professional Edition of VB4, here's how to create the same database, but this time without using the Data Manager. The whole thing is built, its structure defined, and some actual data plugged into it by the following programming. You don't put a Data Control or anything else on the Form, just type this in:

```
Sub Form_Click( )
Dim MyTable As TableDef, MyField As Field
Set MyDatabase = CreateDatabase("VIDAUTO.MDB", dbLangGeneral)
Set MyTable = MyDatabase.CreateTableDef("Tapes")
Set MyField = MyTable.CreateField("Title", dbText, 100)
MyTable.Fields.Append MyField
Set MyField = MyTable.CreateField("Director", dbText, 50)
MyTable.Fields.Append MyField
Set MyField = MyTable.CreateField("Stars", dbText, 150)
MyTable.Fields.Append MyField
Set MyField = MyTable.CreateField("Year", dbInteger)
MyTable.Fields.Append MyField
Set MyField = MyTable.CreateField("Category", dbText, 50)
MyTable.Fields.Append MyField
Set MyField = MyTable.CreateField("Length", dbInteger)
MyTable.Fields.Append MyField
MyDatabase.TableDefs.Append MyTable
Set MyRec = MyTable.OpenRecordset
MyRec.AddNew
MyRec("Title") = "A River Runs Through It"
MyRec("Director") = "Redford, Robert"
MyRec![Stars] = "Brad Pitt, Craig Scheffer"
MyRec(3) = 1992
MyRec(4) = "Drama"
MyRec(5) = 133
MyRec.Update
MyRec.Close
MyDatabase.Close
End Sub
```

Run this, then in the Add-Ins Menu, select "Data Manager." Open your new database and double-click on the "Tapes" Table to open it. You should see all the fields defined, along with data in each field.

In the first line of our program, we establish TableDef and Field objects. Then we create the actual database, naming it "VIDAUTO.MDB" and create a table within the database named "Tapes." Then we create our six fields, Appending each one in turn to the database. Finally, to the TableDefs (a collection of Table objects) we Append this new table. (The collection was empty, now it has one member.)

At this point we have defined our database and could use the Close command. But we want to also add some data, creating the first actual record. So we open a Recordset, naming it MyRec. In effect, this Recordset object permits us to edit, create or move within records in this Table.

The AddNew command creates a new, empty record (it's the only record, but that doesn't matter to the AddNew command). Then we fill each of the six fields in our new record, in turn, with data. (You don't have to fill them all, or in turn.) Finally, we make the record an actual part of the database with the Update command then close the Recordset and database.

Notice that there are three possible syntaxes you can use when putting data into a field—we've used all three in the example:

```
MyRec("Director") = "Redford, Robert"
MyRec![Stars] = "Brad Pitt, Craig Scheffer"
MyRec(3) = 1992
```

In the first two styles, you state the Recordset object's Name, followed by the name of the field, an equals sign, then the data itself. The third style merely uses the position of the field in the record, like an array. In this case, it's field (3) which is actually the fourth field, "Year," but remember that the fields start with "field zero."

This third "indexed" style permits you to fill a record using a loop. If you want, you could fill it like this:

```
MyData = Array("A River Runs Through It", "Redford", "Brad Pitt, Craig
     Scheffer", 1993, "Drama", 133)
MyRec.AddNew
For i = 0 To 5
     MyRec(i) = MyData(i)
Next i
```

Or just bring in the pieces of data from a disk file, stuffing them into the loop. The Array Function creates an array of Variants. (For more on this new "Array" Function, see "Array.")

Seeding

When the user (or you) programatically create a database from scratch, it's empty. There's no actual data in it, just the names of table(s) and field(s) and potentially other things like indices. The database is designed but vacant.

To populate the database with actual data, you must open a Recordset then use the AddNew command. You can't use MoveFirst, Edit or other commands—there is no First record, the EOF and BOF Properties are identical. The database is a void.

However, by using AddNew, you create space for the first record; you open the group of fields within that record, making it ready to receive the data.

DataSource, DataChanged

PROPERTY

See   Data Control

Date

FUNCTION

Description   Several functions in VB give you information about your computer (such as CurDir, which tells you the currently active drive and directory, and Time$ which tells you the current time). Date tells you what day the computer thinks it is. Date is similar to typing DATE in DOS: C:> DATE

Uses   • Stamp the date on Printed documents.

• Use it with features such as calendars or datebooks within databases, word processors or other applications.

Cautions   • Since the DATE contains three pieces of information, you may want to extract just the month, day or year. To do this, use the InStr Function (which see). Alternatively, use the Day, Month and Year commands. This used to be called Date$.

Example   PRINT DATE

Results in   11–10–1995

See also   Date (Statement); Day; Format; Month; Now; Time; Year

Date

STATEMENT

Description   Changes the computer's current date stamp. Not useful; see "Cautions" below. (Also see "Date" used as a Function, which *is* useful.)

Variables	Date = "12–14–1999"

OR (to use a Variable):

    d = "12–14–99"

    Date = d

Cautions • The date will not be reset to the real date when you turn off your computer (if your computer has a battery). This could cause problems because disk files saved after you use Date will have that false date stamped on them in the Directory.

Example   Date = "12–12–1999"

See also   Date (Function); Format; Now; Time

FUNCTION

Description   DateSerial transforms dates (such as 1995) into numbers in a series so you can manipulate the dates mathematically.

Suppose you arbitrarily decide that January 1, 100 A.D., will be day 1 of a huge list that includes every day thereafter (through the year 9999). Then you give a date such as November 14, 1992, to your assistant, and ask her to find a serial number for that date. She discovers that November 14, 1992, is day 33922 on the list; so the serial number for that date is 33922. Now, give her another date. With a serial number for each of the two dates, you can perform math on the dates. For example, you can get the number of days between the two dates.

Astonishing as it seems, Visual Basic can provide and manipulate individual serial numbers for every second of every day between January 1, 100, and December 31, 9999. These serial numbers also include coded representations of all the hours, days, months and years between 100 and 9999.

Variables   X# = DateSerial(1992, 6, 2)

Variable type: Double-Precision Floating-Point (Variant)

OR (to use Variables or even calculations): X# = DateSerial(yr,mnth - 2,dy)

Uses • Create calendars and other applications involving manipulation of dates as if they were numbers in a series.

• Using Date$, automatically generate a "registration number" the first time your customer uses the program. That number could be put into your program's .INI file and displayed on the startup screen (the way VB does). This sort of thing is thought to have a mild deterrent effect on people who might be tempted to copy programs. Of course, it's easy to copy an .INI file. A better way would be to create a dummy Variable *within your program,* like this:

```
Global Const Place = "NEVERUSED"
```

in a Module. Find out the location of the Variable in the finished .EXE program (using the Norton Utilities Disk Editor to search for "NEVER-USED"). Then, in place of that text, stuff the registration number when the program first runs (by Opening as Binary your .EXE file and using the Put command to store the registration number).

Cautions
• Dates prior to Dec. 30, 1899, give negative serial numbers.

• Use the Abs function to find days-between-dates.

• You must supply DateSerial with the date in this peculiar order: year, month, day.

• You can include arithmetic when you provide the date to be serialized: (x# = DateSerial(1993, 12 − 2, 8)

• The number of seconds in a span of 9899 years is obviously quite large. There are 31,536,000 seconds in a single year. That is why you may want to add a # symbol to the X that will hold the serial number returned by DateSerial. The # symbol makes a Variable a Double-Precision Floating-Point Variable (see "Variables"). This type of Variable is capable of holding an extremely large range of numbers. VB date/time serial numbers contain the day, month and year to the left of the decimal point, and the hour, minute and second numbers to the right of the decimal point. However, the meaning of the serial number is encoded. There is no direct way to examine the serial number and extract the various information contained therein. That is why VB provides various functions—Second, Minute, Hour, Day, Month, Year—to decode that information for you.

Example
Here we'll show the number of days in the first six months of 1992. This reveals, via month #2, that it is a leap year.

```
Sub Form_Click()

Print "In 1992..."

x = DateSerial(1992, 1, 1)  'Get January 1st serial number

For I = 2 to 7
n = DateSerial(1992, I, 1)
    ? "Month Number "; I - 1; "has "; Abs(x -n); "days."
  x = n
Next I

End Sub
```

See also
Date; DateValue; Day; FileDateTime; Format; Month; Now; TimeValue; Weekday; Year

DATEVALUE

Description   DateValue translates a *text* representation of a date (such as Jan 1, 1992) into a VB date/time serial number that can be computed with, and manipulated, mathematically. DateValue's job is similar to DateSerial's job. (DateSerial translates a *numeric* expression into a date/time serial number. See "DateSerial" for more.)

Variables   **Variable type:** Text ("string")

DateValue (Date$)

OR DateValue (dat$), where you can create dat$ in any of the following formats: Dat$ = "1–1–1992"

OR 1–1–92

OR Jan 1, 1992

OR January 1, 1992

OR 1–Jan–1992

OR 1 January 92

Uses   • The uses for DateValue are the same as DateSerial (which see); however, DateValue is more flexible in the variety of Variables it can translate. While DateSerial gives you the same results, DateValue accepts *text* as a Variable rather than numbers. Therefore, for situations where the user is typing in a date, DateValue is somewhat easier to work with.

• DateValue can translate a wide variety of text representations (review "Variables" above).

• If you know the date—June 24, 1982, for instance—you know the month and year, but not the day of the week. DateValue offers a way to find that out (although there is a Weekday command for that purpose built into VB).

Cautions   • If numbers are used (instead of words like January), the order of the month, day, year will depend on the date setting as defined in the International part of the Windows WIN.INI file.

• DateValue can handle dates between 1-1-100 and 12-31-9999.

• Dates prior to Dec. 30, 1899, give negative serial numbers.

• If you leave out the year, DateValue will assume the current year.

```
Sub Form_Click ()

X# = DateValue("Mar 23")
Print Format(X#, "m-d-yyyy")

End Sub
```

Results in   3-23-1995

Example   Using DateValue along with the powerful Format$ Function, we can easily provide the day of the week for any date between the mid-18th century and the late 21st. (You can also use the Weekday function to do this.)

On October 22, 1962, President Kennedy appeared on television at 7 PM EST to make an announcement "of the greatest urgency."

He began, "Good Evening, my fellow citizens. The government, as promised, has maintained the closest surveillance of the Soviet military buildup on the island of Cuba. Within the past week, unmistakable evidence has established the fact that a series of offensive missile sites is now in preparation on that imprisoned island . . . ."

```
Dateinhistory$ = "Oct 22, 1962"
x = DateValue(Datinhistory$)
Theday$ = Format(x, "dddd")
Print Theday$
```

Results in   Monday

See also   Date; DateSerial; Day; FileDateTime; Format; Month; Now; TimeSerial; TimeValue; Weekday; Year

AY

FUNCTION

Description   Day extracts the day of the month from the serial number created by the DateValue, DateSerial or Now Function.

(See "DateSerial" for more on VB's date/time serial numbers.)

Variables   `Print Day(Now)`

Results in   5

(if it's the fifth of the month)

Uses   Calendar applications and calculations involving dates

Cautions   • Day can handle dates between 1-1-100 and 12-31-9999
• Dates prior to Dec. 30, 1899, use negative serial numbers.

Example
```
X# = DateValue("December 22, 1914")
D = Day(X#)
Print D
```

Results in   22

See also   DateSerial; DateValue; Day; FileDateTime; Hour; Minute; Month; Second; TimeSerial; TimeValue; Weekday; Year

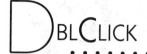

EVENT

Description   DblClick is the Event that happens when you click the mouse twice rapidly. The interval between clicks can be adjusted in Windows's Control Panel in the Mouse Double Click Speed box.

Any commands you have placed within a Control's DblClick Event—a Command Button Control, for instance—will be carried out if the user double-clicks on that Command Button.

Used with   Forms, Combo Boxes, File List Boxes, Frames, Grids, Images, Labels, List Boxes, OLE, Option Buttons, Picture Boxes and Text Boxes.

Uses   • Do several things at once. There is something of a convention in Windows applications whereby a *Click Event* simply selects something for highlighting, yet a *DblClick Event* both selects and causes what was selected to happen.

For instance, from within a File List Box that allows the user to open a new file, a single click would only highlight the selected filename (or perhaps move the filename into a default filename box at the top of the list). This allows the user to type in additional information, or ponder his or her choice. A double-click on a file name, however, could cause several things to happen: the File List Box closes and the filename double-clicked upon is summarily loaded into the application.

Cautions   A double-click has special effects on two Controls:

• The drive name you double-click on in a Drive List Box is automatically inserted into the Drive List Box's Path Property. Also, double-clicks will move around the disk drive through various directories (without your having to write any instructions, such as ChDir, in a Drive List Box Event, or having to update the visible list). Drive and Directory List Boxes have no DblClick Event.

• The filename you double-click on in a File List Box is automatically inserted into the File List Box's FileName Property.

Example

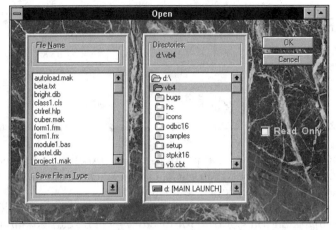

Figure D-6: A custom-designed disk access system (see "Line" for the Subroutine called DrawFrameOn, which creates various framing effects).

Double-clicking on a Drive List Box or Directory List Box maneuvers you around the disk drive. VB handles all the details when you use those Controls.

See also   Click; MouseDown; MouseMove; MouseUp

Debug

OBJECT

Description   Debug can help you track down errors in your programs. When things aren't working as they should, you can use this technique to get a report of the current state of Variables. Debug.Print will print the value of Variables in the Debug Windows. In practice, though, there are better ways to "debug" your programs. See Appendix B for a complete discussion of debugging.

Used with   The "Debug Window"

Variables   Debug.Print A$

OR (to see several Variables, and to find out which Event was active when the Variables were printed by Debug.Print in the Debug Window):

```
Sub Command1_Click ()

Debug.Print "We're in Command1 now, and..."
Debug.Print "X = "; x, b, c, d, b * d

End Sub
```

Uses Debug.Print can be useful within For...Next, Do...Until, and other Loops where your Variables are changing rapidly, something is going awry and you cannot put your finger on the problem.

Cautions • Some people prefer a printed list of Variables and their values. It's easy to put that command within a suspect Loop or other area in your program:

    Printer.Print A, B, C

This would be a substitute for Debug.Print A, B, C.

Example
```
For I = 100 To 1000 Step 100
Picture1.Move I
Debug.Print I
Next I
```

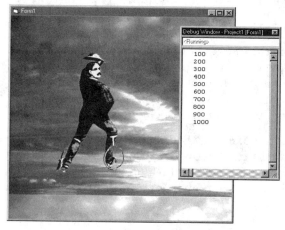

Figure D-7: You can watch the Variables in your program change in the Debug Window.

See also Appendix B

DECLARE

STATEMENT

Description Declare is a remarkably powerful tool; it allows you to add more than 600 capabilities to Visual Basic—all the commands built into Windows itself. Using Declare, you can open a door and walk down into the Windows "engine room." There you can take control directly and entirely of each Windows feature.

Do you need more than the primitive Visual Basic Beep command? You can specify the frequency, channel, duration and other aspects of a sound (see "Beep"). Do you want to instantly blow up an icon to full screen size? How about shrinking, stretching, reversing images—instantly?

These and many other features are available to you by using the Declare Statement to contact Windows's internal services. Although this is a sophisticated feature, you need not understand the technique to make good use of it. See Appendix A for a full exploration of the ways you can use Declare to open up a whole new toolbox of commands and features.

Used with   Windows's Internal Facilities

Variables   Declare Sub *Name* Lib *"Name"* ()

OR: Declare Function *Name* Lib *"Name"* () [as Variable type]

Uses   When there's something you need done that VB does not offer

Cautions   You'll get an error message—or things simply won't happen as you expect—if you fail to type in the Declare and its Variables precisely as required. Typos are not allowed; if you're having a problem, the first thing you must do is proof your typing. VB does not provide you with very meaningful error messages when you use Declare.

Example   Put two Picture Boxes on a Form. Load a .BMP graphic into one of them by using the Properties Window to specify the Picture Property. Then, using Windows's powerful StretchBlt feature, we'll instantly copy the picture to the second box and see how it's automatically resized to the dimensions of the second box.

From this...

Figure D-8: We can instantly copy and shrink this graphic...

to this.

Figure D-9: Reduced version of the original displayed in Figure D-8.

We aren't going to explain here how all this works—you can just type in the example and fiddle with the Variables to get different effects. (See Appendix A for a detailed discussion of these matters.)

To set up this trick, type the following into a Module. Each Declare must be on a single line. Do not press ENTER where you see an arrow.

```
Declare Function SetStretchBltMode% Lib "Gdi" (ByVal destinationHdc%, →
    ByVal StretchMode%)

Declare Function StretchBlt% Lib "GDI" (ByVal hDC%, ByVal X%, ByVal Y%, →
    ByVal nWidth%, ByVal nHeight%, ByVal hsourceDC%, ByVal Xsource%, →
    ByVal Ysource%, ByVal nsourceWidth%, ByVal nsourceHeight%, ByVal →
    dwRop&)
```

(*You need to make sure that each Declare is all on one line*. Keep typing the list of Variables in parentheses, don't hit the ENTER key, and the window will scroll horizontally until you're finished.)

The easiest way to access Windows's internal features is to save sets of Declares. You can then load them into your programs as needed (with Add File from VB's File Menu or Load Text from VB's Code Menu). That way, you don't have to type them each time you need them. You might want to use VB's Save File or Save Text feature to make these StretchBlt Declares permanently available to you for other programs you write. Declares are a headache to type in when they're long like the preceding examples. And you do need to proof them to make sure you haven't got any typos.

Now we make sure the Variables are of the type that the Declare Statements want: (See "Variables" for a discussion of Variable "types.")

You Have to Do this Only Once: Type the following into the Form's General Declarations section:

```
Dim copymode As Long, i As Integer
Dim sourceWidth As Integer, sourceHeight As Integer
Dim destinationWidth As Integer, destinationHeight As Integer
```

Remember, you need to do this only once; thereafter you can load this chunk of typing into any of your programs' Forms' General Declarations sections when you want to transform pictures.

Now that we've Declared our Functions and dimensioned our Variables, here's how to use Windows's StretchBlt tool. Change the Name Property of the Picture Box that has the .BMP graphic in it to "Source," and change the Name of the empty Picture Box to "Destination," so we can refer to them by these names. The Name is up to you, of course, but we're using these names in this example.

```
Sub Form_Load ()

Show

Copymode = &HCC0020

Sourcewidth = source.ScaleWidth
Sourceheight = source.ScaleHeight
Destinationwidth = destination.ScaleWidth
Destinationheight = destination.ScaleHeight
Source.ScaleMode = 3
Destination.ScaleMode = 3

X% = StretchBlt(destination.hDC, 0, 0, destinationWidth, destination- →
    Height, source.hDC, 0, 0, sourceWidth, sourceHeight, copymode)
End Sub
```

That's it. Press F5 to run the program.

Now for a Couple of Variations: Use the mouse to change the shape of the Picture Box called "Destination" and run the program again.

Figure D-10: Strange transformations take place when you change the shape of a box.

The .BMP graphic will make itself fit into whatever shape you make the Destination Picture Box. Also, you can create as many Destination Boxes as you wish, filling them by merely repeating three key lines. Create a new Picture Box and give it the Name "SecondBox." Then insert these three lines just above the End Sub:

```
destinationWidth = Secondbox.ScaleWidth
destinationHeight = Secondbox.ScaleHeight
X% = StretchBlt(Secondbox.hDC, 0, 0, destinationWidth, destination- →
     Height, source.hDC, 0, 0, sourceWidth, sourceHeight, copymode)
```

Now we get another copy:

Figure D-11: You can create as many copies as you wish another way to make wallpaper designs.

Here's another trick: Change the Variable Copymode to this, and you'll negativize the image:

```
Copymode = &H330008
X% = StretchBlt(destination.hDC, 0, 0, destinationWidth, destination- →
     Height, source.hDC, 0, 0, sourceWidth, sourceHeight, copymode)
```

Figure D-12: You can even create negative X-ray images.

We've hardly scratched the surface of what you can do with Declare. The full complement of the 600 available Windows features is beyond the scope of this book. However, you will find a thorough explanation on using Declares in Appendix A. If you're interested in exploring this rich area further, locate a copy of *Microsoft Windows Programmer's Reference* (Microsoft Press), a huge, complex, sometimes even abstruse, book written for C programmers. Also, the Professional Visual Basic has an online Help file that includes all the API features defined in a format that VB will understand.

Nevertheless, you can use the API information, just as you can cook in a microwave oven without knowing the laws of thermodynamics. Merely slavishly copy a Declare; make sure you keep your Variable types straight when you Dim them (make them identical to the types in the Declare); and keep the Declare Statement on one line.

Now, one final stunt before we leave our StretchBlt program. You can copy *part* of a picture by defining the source Variables differently. Here we say that we want to copy less than the full height of the source picture:

Sourceheight = source.ScaleHeight —170

Figure D-13: Select only part of an image, and blow it up or shrink it.

Or we can blow it up, crop it and flip it—all at once:

Sourceheight = source.ScaleHeight - 300

Figure D-14: You can manipulate it almost any way you want to.

Clearly, by exploiting this one Declare we've got the beginnings of a photo-retouching or image-manipulation application. And you'll find much more in Appendix A.

See also   Appendix A; Dim; Function; Sub

EFAULT

PROPERTY

Description   Default allows you to temporarily make one of the Command Buttons on a Form double as the ENTER key. In other words, if the user presses the ENTER key on the keyboard, that triggers the Default Command Button's Click Event, just as if the user had mouse-clicked on the Button. The OLE Control also has a Default Property.

The Default command determines which Command Button of several on a Form will respond to the ENTER key (as well as to a mouse click). Only one Command Button at a time can be the "Default" Button. However, the "Default" condition only applies if the user doesn't shift the focus to another Control by clicking on a second Command Button.

In many programs, pressing the ENTER key tells the computer that the user has finished typing in some text, a number (in a calculator application) or some other data. Just as the Carriage Return key on an old-fashioned typewriter signified the end of a line, the ENTER key on a computer often represents the completion of some task. Say that you label one of your Command Buttons DONE or CALCULATE or something like that, so that it will respond the same way your program responds when the user presses the ENTER key. In this hypothetical example, the response might be to accept a number in a "calculator." Then you make that Command Button the "Default" Button. Now the user can either click on your Default "Enter" Command Button or alternatively press the ENTER key to achieve the same result—accept the user's number.

Used with   Command Buttons and OLE Controls

Figure D-15: The Default Property can only be used with Command Buttons.

Variables   **Variable type:** Boolean

You can set the Default Property from the Properties Window while designing your program:

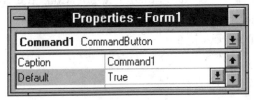

Figure D-16: Optionally set Default in the Properties Window while designing your program.

OR (to change which Button is the Default while a program is running:)
    Button1.Default = True

Cautions   • It's risky to assign a *delete* or *quit* or some other drastic action to the Default Command Button. The user might accidentally hit the ENTER key while typing.

• Default is normally inactive (False) for all Command Buttons you create. To make one of the Buttons the Default, you must explicitly set its Default Property to True in the Properties Window (or set it within your program by Command5.Default = True).

• If one Button is made the Default, VB sets all other Command Buttons' Default Properties to "False," (0). In other words, only one Button on a given Form can be the Default Button, but VB handles this for you. Whenever you set one of the Buttons to be the Default, any other Button that had that Property loses it.

• If you have a Default Command Button on a Form, then all other Controls on that Form *cannot detect it if the user presses the ENTER key*. Normally, the KeyPress, KeyDown or KeyUp Events of various Controls can detect that the user pressed ENTER on the keyboard. However, when a Command Button has its Default Property on, all the other Controls are paralyzed with respect to the ENTER key–they just cannot respond to it. The only exception to this is if the focus is set *to another Command Button on that Form, a Button which doesn't have its Default Property on.* (See "Active-Control" for a definition of *focus*.)

• If you use Default, the user can't insert lines into a multiline Text Box without using CTRL+ENTER.

Example This program manages images, allowing you to move through a directory full of pictures, adding or deleting the images.

Notice two things about the Next Command Button: There is a faint line around its caption, and its border is darker than the others. Its Default Property has been set to True, so when the Form is first loaded, it's the key that would respond to the ENTER key (in addition to responding to a mouse click like any of the others).

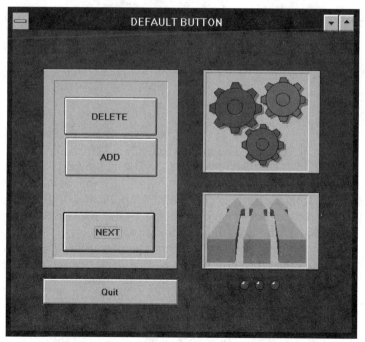

Figure D-17: The Command Button labeled NEXT is special here.

Now, if the user clicks on the Add Button, then Add gets the focus and would respond to the ENTER key.

Figure D-18: The Add Button gets the focus.

However, when the program first runs or the Form reappears, the Default Property determines which of the Buttons, at least initially, is set to respond to the ENTER key.

See also   Activate, Deactivate; ActiveControl; Cancel; GotFocus; LostFocus; Screen Object; SetFocus; TabIndex; QueryUnLoad

DefType

STATEMENT

(DefInt, DefBool, DefByte, DefDate, DefObj, DefLng, DefSng, DefDbl, DefCur, DefStr, DefVar)

Description   This Statement has one very valuable application: it can make some programs run 25 times faster (or more). DefInt A-Z makes *any* program faster—how much faster depends on how much arithmetic the program does. (See the Example below.) Many programmers consider DefInt A-Z valuable enough to insert it into the General Declarations section of each Form and Module they create in Visual Basic. Other than for this purpose, these eleven Def*type* commands aren't used often.

In essence, the eleven Def*type* commands force Variables to become a certain Variable *type* (Integer, Long, string, whatever) if they start with the letters following the Def*type* command. DefInt a-c means that all Variables in the Form that have names such as "Average," "Cartons" and "bubbles" will be Integers. For more information on Variable types, see "Variables."

When you use DefInt A-Z, it means that all your Variables will be Integers unless you specify otherwise by attaching a special symbol or by using a

Global, Dim, ReDim or Static command to define them as something other than Integers (see "Variables"). A computer can perform integer arithmetic much quicker than it can calculate with other kinds of Variables.

Used with   Integer, Boolean, Byte, Date, Object, Long, Single, Double, Currency, Variant and string Variables

Variables   To make all Variables Integer types:

    DefInt A-Z

OR (to make any Variable starting with the letters *a* through *f* a text ["string"] Variable): DefStr a - f

OR (to make Variable *B* a Double-Precision Floating-Point numeric Variable type): DefDbl B

Uses   To speed up a program (see the Example)

Cautions   • Put Def*type* in the General Declarations section of each Form or Module that you want them to affect. Def*type* can have impact only on the Form or Module within which it resides.

• Dim Statements negate the effect of the Def*type* in any particular instance (see the Example). This way you can define a general range but create individual exceptions. And attaching a Variable type symbol (see "Variables") will also negate the general rules established by a Def*type* command. If you've put DefInt A-Z into the General Declarations section of a Form, then do this:

    Birthday$ = "September 30, 1945"

The $ symbol makes an exception of the Variable, *Birthday$*. This Variable will now violate the general rule and be a text "string" Variable, not a numeric Variable of the Integer type.

• It doesn't matter if you use capital or lowercase letters: DefInt A-Z and DefInt a-z have the same effect.

• Once you have defined a type, you don't need to use the Variable-type symbols (%, !, $, & and $) unless you want to create a different type of Variable.

(Before DefInt is used):

X% = X% + 1 (You must use the % if you want X to be an Integer Variable type in your program. Without the % symbol attached, Variables will default to the Variant type. That's the VB default type. All Variables in VB will default to this type unless you set up a different default with Def*type*. See the Example.)

(Now, by using DefInt): DefInt X - Z

X = X + 1 (After using DefInt, the Variable *X* is an Integer type of Variable, so you need not attach the % symbol to force it to be an Integer type.)

The Global, Dim, ReDim and Static commands also make a Variable the type they define it as. Many programmers, however, prefer to use the type *symbols* each time they use a Variable's name, since these symbols make it easier to see what's happening when you read over the lines in your program. A symbol attached to a Variable's name immediately shows you what type that Variable is.

Special Note: Even though we've been dwelling on Variable types here, please be aware that in most of your programming you need not concern yourself with the types of Variables you're working with. All you have to do is distinguish between numeric and text types, and even this isn't usually necessary if you use the Variant Variable type. Variant is VB's default type (see "Variables").

Example   Unless you specify otherwise with Global, Dim, Static or Def*type* Statements (or by adding a type symbol like # to a Variable's name), all your numeric Variables will default to the Variant type.

A Single-Precision Floating-Point Variable can hold the number .34592, as well as 14,000,231.72274; but there is a cost when you use a Variable type with an immense range. Doing arithmetic (especially dividing Floating-Point numbers) puts a strain on the computer. The computer has to follow more complicated rules when fractions are involved. It even takes longer to add 2 + 2 in Floating-Point mode than it would if you were using the Integer Variable type for the same calculation.

Integer types use no fractions (no decimal point) and have a relatively small range—they can handle only slightly more than 60,000 numbers (from –32,768 to 32,767). However, that range is all most of us need for many real-world situations (the majority of For...Next Loops, the number of students in a school, a checking account balance, our salaries, etc.).

In fact, you'll need a greater range rarely. As for precision (using fractions), many applications don't need them either. And, if you *do* need extra range or precision, simply Dim those particular Variables into the type you want and let most of your Variables remain Integer types. (If you need range but no fractions, use the Long Integer type, which can manipulate numbers between –2,147,483,648 and 2,147,483,647. This couldn't handle Bill Gates's checking account, but it would suffice for most of us.)

For all these reasons, many programmers routinely put the following statement in the General Declarations section of every Form they use when writing a Visual Basic program: DefInt A-Z

This forces all Variables into Integer types, unless you specify otherwise using Global, Dim or Static commands, or add a Variable type symbol to a Variable's name. Don't be concerned about needing to figure out what type each Variable should be. Just make them all Integers unless you like the convenience of Variants. (Variants are a bit slower than Integers and they use up more memory. See "Variables.") It'll be obvious when you need more range or precision, or when a Variable name should have a $ symbol added to show that it's text, not a number.

Let's see how much faster things run with DefInt. We'll count from one to three million using a Floating-Point Variable, then use DefInt to force Integer arithmetic and count again.

Here's the program:

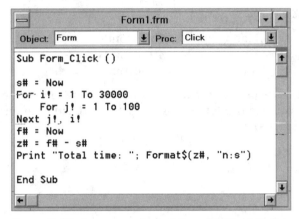

Figure D-19: A program to test the effects of DefInt

It takes five minutes and 42 seconds for this program to finish counting (on a 386 machine running at 33 MHz).

Now, the same program but remove the exclamation points and with a DefInt turbocharger inserted:

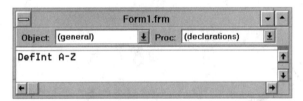

Figure D-20: Putting DefInt into the General Declarations greatly speeds things up.

We can now get this job done in 14 seconds—25 times faster when DefInt A-Z is added to the Declarations!

Many current Windows applications work within a 16-bit world, and many businesses still use 386 computers. However, when Windows, in its NT and Win 95 versions, moves us to 32 bits, the speed of integers will be greater yet. Interestingly, there will be no improvement in floating-point arithmetic at all when computers have 32-bit-wide pathways (fractions are always hard to deal with).

However, if you move from a 386 to a 486 or Pentium machine, the speed improvements aren't nearly as impressive (there's a built-in math coprocessor). In this example, we compared the elapsed time between Single-Precision-Floating-Point (the ! symbol) Variables as opposed to Integer

Variables (removing the ! and typing in DefInt A-Z to change the VB default from Variant to Integer, so the I and J Variables are Integers).

What are the results on a 486/66? To get more precision, we changed the second loop to the following:

```
For j! = 1 To 1000
```

and got the following results:

Single-precision-floating-point: 53 seconds
Variant   49 seconds
Integer   32 seconds

Nonetheless, DefInt A-Z can be worth including in your programs (or at least see if you can use Integers instead of the default Variants, in time-critical situations).

See also   Appendix C; Dim; Variables; Variant

STATEMENT

See   DefType

STATEMENT

Description   The Dim command can accomplish four things:

- Designate a Variable's *type* (String, Integer, Form, etc.—see "Variables")
- Create a fixed Array
- Create a dynamic Array
- Create a fixed-length string

Dim is one of four VB commands used to announce that a Variable is of a certain type or that an Array is being created. The other three commands are ReDim, Static and Public. (See "Variables" for types; also see "Arrays.")

Used with   Variables

Variables   To tell VB that *Customers* is a text "string" Variable, not a numeric Variable:

```
Dim Customers As String
```

OR (to create space in the computer's memory for 500 numbers, each with an index so you can use Loops to conveniently access them—For I = 1 to 30: Print Accounts(I): Next I. This creates, in other words, an *Array*):

    Dim Accounts(1 to 500)

OR (to create space for two Arrays, each with *double* indexes):

    Dim X (1 to 50, 1 to 400), Y (1 to 50, 1 to 500)

Each of these Arrays—X( ) and Y( )—has been defined (dimensioned) as a two-dimensional Array. A two-dimensional Array can be accessed in this fashion:

    For I = 1 to 50
      For J = 1 to 500
              Print (I,J)
      Next J
    Next I

This will print all the elements in the Y( ) Array

OR (used with ReDim, to create a *dynamic* Array, one that appears when an Event, Subroutine or Function is triggered, does its thing, and goes out of existence when the Event is finished): Dim Tempwords$ ( )

OR you can use an alternative syntax here: Dim Tempword ( ) As String

The important thing is the empty parentheses that indicate the creation of a dynamic Array. However, using Dim in this fashion is optional. ReDim can be used by itself with no preceding Dim:

(Then, within the Event):

    Sub Form_Click()

    ReDim Tempwords (30)
    End Sub

OR (to create a fixed-length text string Variable. In this case, the Variable *Phoneno$* is 10 bytes long and can contain 10 text characters):

    Dim Phoneno As String * 10

OR (to create an *object* Variable of the "Form type" [see "Objects"]):

    Dim MyFrm As Form

Uses
- To specify a type of Variable (Dim Names As String).
- To set aside some space in the computer's memory to hold a collection of related pieces of information (called an *Array*).
- To set aside space for a fixed-length string. There are two types of string (text) Variables, *dynamic* and *fixed-length* (see "Variables"). Fixed-length strings are often used with random-mode files and the associated Type command (see "Type").

- Dim with empty parentheses ( ) announces a dynamic Array. A dynamic Array saves space because the Array, later redimensioned (ReDim) within an Event Procedure (a Sub or Function procedure), can be freely resized to use up only the amount of space needed. A dynamic Array can be resized more than once, to reflect current needs as the program runs. And dynamic Arrays can create a big temporary Array, then let go of the memory when it is no longer needed. However, you can use ReDim by itself; the original Dim isn't required by VB. (See "Arrays.")

- Create object Variables—Arrays and Variables of the "Control" or "Form" types (see "Objects").

Cautions
- When you first use Dim, all the elements of a numeric Array are set to 0, and all elements of a text Array (string Array) are set to empty strings ("").

- Like many other VB commands, Dim is sensitive to the context in which it's used. A Variable declared with the Public command can be accessed *anywhere* in the program. The Dim command is always used at the Module or Form level, in the General Declarations section. A Variable declared with the Dim command applies to all the procedures (any Event, Subroutine or Function) within that Module or Form. Use Static or ReDim (both commands can substitute for Dim, but they have other special qualities) at the lowest level (*within* procedures) for Variables that apply only within that procedure. See "Variables" for more about the different "ranges of influence" that Variables and Arrays can have (it's called *scope* in VB).

Example
(See "Arrays" for further information about how to use this essential programming tool.)

Here we want to use big fractions, so we've chosen the "Double" type of numeric Variable (see "Variables"). In the General Declarations section of a Form, type the following:

```
Dim Fractions (1 to 3, 1 to 3) As Double
```

Then in a Click Event, load things into this Array:

```
For I = 1 to 3
For J = 1 to 3
Fractions (I,J) = I + J / 9
Next J, I
```

This is what the Array we just created and loaded with fractions might look like if we could see inside the computer's brain:

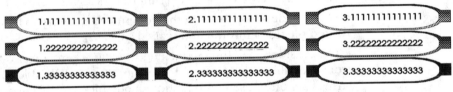

Figure D-21: A somewhat fanciful representation of an Array.

See also   Arrays; DefType; Erase; LBound; Objects; Option Base; Public; ReDim;
UBound; Variables; Variant

 IR

Description   Dir provides you with the name of a file or files that match the *file specification* that you give Dir. The file specification can include any of the approaches you use when asking for a DIR in DOS. You can use * and ? wildcards, and you can specify drives, directories, subdirectories, etc. You can use Dir for, among other things, finding out if a particular file exists on the disk drive.

Dir allows your *program* to search for and manipulate files with no intervention from the user. (The Directory, Drive and File List Boxes are Controls that allow the *user* to interact with files on disks, although your program can make use of them, too.)

However, Dir is less flexible and less efficient than using Drive, Directory and File List Box Controls, which have many built-in features (such as their List Property) that can be used to manage files across the user's entire system. If you don't want any input from the user, simply set the Visible Property of these Controls to 0. When invisible, your program can make full use of their facilities, but the user won't even be aware that they exist.

Used with   Disk files

Variables   To find the first filename that matches the specification *.* (in other words, any file) in the C:\TEMP directory. F$ will contain the first filename in that directory.

```
F$ = Dir("C:\TEMP\*.*")
```

OR (to use a text Variable instead of literal text):

```
D$ = "C:\TEMP\*.*"
F$ = Dir(D$)
```

OR (the first time you use it, you must provide Dir with a file specification. But after that, you can use it with no specification to get the next file that matches the specification you've established): F$ = Dir

The Dir Function always needs the path argument: (C:\TEMP*.*), for example. But there's an optional "attributes" argument, too:

```
Dir(pathname[, attributes])
```

Here are the Constants (or equivalent values) you can supply to limit the items displayed when using Dir:

vbNormal	0	Normal. vbHidden	2
Hidden. vbSystem	4	System file vbVolume	8
Volume label vbDirectory	16	Directory or folder	

Uses
• Determine if a particular file exists.
• Automate housekeeping tasks, such as finding and deleting .TMP files (using the Kill Statement).
• Write a "FindFile" Subroutine so you can locate a given file in any directory on any hard drive. This way, your program could look all through the user's hard drive(s) and the user wouldn't even have to specify a path to locate a file.

Cautions
• The first time you use Dir, it's necessary to provide a path or filename: Dir("C:\TEMP*.*"). Thereafter, you can use Dir by itself and the path or file specification you provided earlier will be assumed. The file specification is the same you would give when using the DIR command from DOS, and can include the ? and * wildcards.

• You can change the path or file specification as often as desired.

• When Dir does not find any files that match, it returns an empty string to let you know that it's finished looking. Test for the empty string like this:

```
F$ = Dir ("D:\*.tmp")
If F$ = "" Then Exit For
```

Note that when searching, repeated use of Dir will continue giving you additional filenames that match the specification. Eventually, of course, Dir will turn up empty; at that point, you'll be given an empty text Variable ("") instead of a filename.

• Files are not given to you sorted by size, date or name.

• Just as with DOS's DIR command, it doesn't matter whether the file specification you give to Dir is in capital or lowercase letters.

Example
This Subroutine locates and displays any files with a .TMP extension in the drive C: root directory:

```
Sub Form_Click ()

D$ = Dir("c:\*.exe")
Print D$

Do Until D$ = ""
i = i + 1
D$ = Dir
Print D$
Loop

Print i; "Files Matched"
End Sub
```

Note that we had to first set up the file specification C:*.EXE before we could use a Loop structure to repeatedly ask Dir for additional matching files. Within the Loop, though, we need not provide anything to Dir. All we have to do is keep Looping until Dir gives us back an empty text Variable.

See also   CurDir; Drive, Directory & File List Boxes; EXEName; Path

DIRECTORY LIST BOX .... CONTROL

Figure D-22: The Directory List Box symbol in the Toolbox.

Description   A Directory List Box displays an ordered list of the user's disk directories and subdirectories, and automatically reacts to mouse clicks to allow the user to move among them. It is like lists found in many Windows programs and is in standard Windows format. A Directory List Box works in conjunction with the Drive and File List Boxes to allow the user complete access to all the files on all disk drives and CD–ROM units attached to his or her computer.

    See Drive List Box for an example of using the Directory List Box along with Drive and File List Boxes to create a complete file access system for the user.

Variables   As with any Control, you can adjust the available Properties with the Properties Window while you're designing your program:

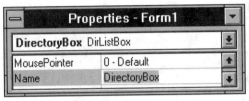

Figure D-23: Changing Properties while designing your program

OR (to change a Property while the program is running): Dir1.FontSize = 12

OR (to find out the current path while a program is running):

    Currentdirectory$ = Dir1.Path

Uses   • Permit the user to see a list of directories and subdirectories, and move among or access files within them.

    • Combined with Drive and File List Boxes, the user can access files anywhere on his or her system.

Cautions   • The most important Property of a Directory List Box is its Path Property. This Property maintains the pathname (C:\VB\ICONS, for example) of the choice the user has made when clicking on the Directory List Box to move around a disk drive. To build a full file-access system, use the Directory List Box's Path in conjunction with the ChDir command; the Path and Pattern Properties of a File List Box; and the Drive Property of a Drive List Box. For an example of such a system, see "Drive List Box."

    • The List Property tells you the names of the subdirectories below the current directory.

    • The ListCount Property tells you the number of subdirectories below the current directory.

    • The ListIndex Property points to the position of the current directory within the ListCount.

Example   This example prints a list of all the subdirectories under the current directory. Note that you can use the Directory List Box (and the Drive and File List Boxes) for useful information needed by your program. In other words, you don't need to use these boxes for user access only; they have several useful automatic features you can use within your program to check on or change the status of the disk drives. Just create the boxes while designing the program, but make them invisible so the user will not be able to access them. Then you can use them in ways similar to what we've done in this example, but, instead of printing the subdirectories, your program might, for example, report to the user: "You do not have a C:\TEMP directory. Would you like one created at this time to hold backup files?"

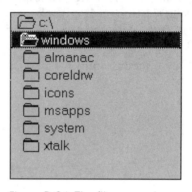

c:\windows\almanac
c:\windows\coreldrw
c:\windows\icons
c:\windows\msapps
c:\windows\system
c:\windows\xtalk

Figure D-24: The file-access boxes can also be used while remaining invisible to the user.

```
Sub Form_Click ()
Print : Print : Print
For i = 0 To Dir1.ListCount − 1
  Print Dir1.List(i)
Next i
End Sub
```

Notice that the ListCount Property, working with the List Property, gives you access to all the information you need about the user's drive. Adding Drive and File List Boxes, along with their Path, Drive and Pattern Properties, allows your program or the user to completely manage all files.

Directory List Box Properties
BackColor • DragIcon • DragMode • Enabled • FontBold • FontItalic FontName • FontSize • FontStrikethru • FontUnderline • ForeColor Height • HelpContextID • hWnd • Index • Left • List • ListCount ListIndex • MousePointer • Name • Parent • Path • TabIndex TabStop • Tag • Top • Visible • Width

Directory List Box Events

Change • Click • DragDrop • DragOver • GotFocus • KeyDown
KeyPress • KeyUp • LostFocus • MouseDown • MouseMove • MouseUp

Directory List Box Methods

Drag • Move • Refresh • SetFocus • ZOrder

See also Visual Basic provides a wealth of ways to access and manage disk drives
and the files therein. Here is a complete alphabetical list of the VB commands related to file management:

AppActivate; Archive; Change; ChDir; ChDrive; Close; CurDir; Dir; Drive;
EOF; EXEName; FileAttr; FileName; FreeFile; Get; Hidden; Input; Input #;
Kill; Line Input #; List; ListCount; ListIndex; Loc; Lock; LOF; MkDir; Name;
Normal; On Error; Open; Path; PathChange; Pattern; PatternChange; Print
#; Put; ReadOnly; Reset; RmDir; Seek; Shell; System; Unlock; Write #

(See "Drive List Box" for an extended example of a file-access window.)

Do...Loop

STATEMENT

Description This is the most powerful of the commands generally called *Loops*. A Loop
structure halts the program's forward progress until something happens to
fulfill the requirements of the Loop. It's as if some repetitive task interrupts
your stroll in the woods–remove burrs before continuing on.

An alternative to the Do...Loop structure is For...Next. It's the most
commonly used Loop structure. If you know how many times a Loop
should repeat the commands within it, use For...Next. For...Next uses a
counter to determine how long to continue repeating. The counter is the I
Variable in For I = 1 to 300. "I" will keep increasing by 1 each time the Loop
repeats. When the Loop has repeated 300 times, the program will continue
on past the For...Next Loop.

The reason that For...Next is used so often is that when you're writing
your program, you often know how many times you want something done:
Print the total number of names in an Array; put 12 Picture Boxes on the
screen; and so forth. For I = 1 to 100 makes the program repeat a Loop 100
times, doing whatever is within the Loop 100 times:

```
For I = 1 to 100
  Print I,
Next I
```

This produces a list of the digits from 1 to 100.

Another alternative is the new For Each...Next structure for use with Collection "Arrays." See "For Each."

Do...Loop. You use a Do...Loop structure when you can't know while you're writing your program how often the Loop should repeat. Perhaps your program asks the user to specify the number of times something should appear onscreen; or perhaps you're listing the number of files on the user's disk. The number of times a Loop should execute these things will be different for each user of your program and perhaps each time a particular user runs the program.

The Do...Loop structure keeps going through its Loop until some condition happens, rather than counting up to a number like For...Next. Exactly what the condition is will vary. So you don't know, when creating the program, the literal number to provide.

Sometimes you use For...Next even if you don't know how many times it will Loop until the program actually runs. For that, you'd Loop a variable number of times. For example, you'd use For I=1 to *Items* to start a Loop that reads in a number of items in a file, where the count was stored as the first line in the file itself. Sometimes the essential difference between For and Do Loops is not how many times the Loop runs, but that For runs a Loop a certain number of times and Do runs it while a certain condition remains true.

Nevertheless, Do...Loop is used when you can't know while designing your program the number of Loop repetitions you'll need: "Get enough bags of potato chips for the number of people coming over tonight for the party." Another way to state the difference is that you use a Do...Loop based on current conditions while the program is running.

Do...Loop is also quite flexible in that you can set up interior tests and quit the Loop with the Exit Do command. And you can place a quit condition at the beginning or end of the Loop. Putting the quit condition test at the end ensures that the Loop *will always happen at least once*. If you put the test at the start of the Loop and the test fails, the Loop will never happen. VB will skip over the commands within the Loop. If you want the Loop to always execute at least once, put the condition test at the bottom of the Loop.

```
Do Until Eof(1)
Line Input #1,Text$
If Text$<>"" Then
   Text1.Text = Text1.Text + Text$
End If
Loop
```

In the example above, you don't know whether you've arrived at the EOF (End Of File) until you read in the file off the disk drive. However, if this file was just opened and the Loop exits on the first pass, then this tells you that the file is empty.

Do...Loop also permits two kinds of conditional tests: *While* and *Until*. This distinction is only a matter of how you want to express things, like the difference between "Sweep *until* the porch is clean" vs. "Sweep *while* the porch is dirty." The computer doesn't care about such things. However, expressing the condition in a particular way can sometimes make your meaning clearer to you and other humans who read your program.

The third available Loop structure is While...Wend, a less powerful version of Do...Loop that merely continues Looping while a condition remains true. To Loop as long as X is less than 100:

```
While X < 100: X = X + 1: Print X: Wend
```

While...Wend has no exit command, and this structure is limited to testing the condition at the start of its Loop. You may want to use the Do...Loop structure, and forget that While...Wend exists at all—it's limited and unnecessarily crude in a language that includes Do...Loop.

Accomplish the above with:

```
Do While X < 100
    X = X + 1
    Print X
Loop
```

Variables   To test the exit condition within the Loop:

```
Do
  Print Y
  Y = Y + 1
    If Y > 11 Then Exit Do
Loop
```

OR (to test the exit condition at the start of the Loop using Until):

```
Do Until Y > 10
    Print Y
    Y = Y + 1
Loop
```

OR (to test the exit condition at the start of the Loop using While):

```
Do While Y < 11
    Y = Y + 1
Loop
```

OR (to test the exit condition at the end of the Loop using Until):

```
Do
    y = y + 1
Loop Until Y = 10
```

OR (to test the exit condition at the end of the Loop using While):

```
Do
    y = y + 1
Loop While Y < 10
```

There are times when you need to put the exit condition test at the end. See the Example below.

Uses   • As a generalization, when you want something done repeatedly but don't know the number of times you want it repeated, use a Do...Loop instead of a For...Next Loop. For...Next is for when you do know the number of times something should be done.

Use Do...Loop when you know a condition that must be satisfied rather than the precise number of times a task should be performed.

For...Next is: "Brush my hair 150 times."

Do...Loop is: "Brush my hair until it shines."

Cautions   • You can inadvertently create the dreaded infinite Loop when using a Do...Loop in one of your programs. Like many of life's cul-de-sacs—and we all know most of them—when your program gets into an infinite Loop, it will keep going round and round with no way out. An infinite Loop ties up the computer, freezes it, and the user must press the BREAK key to regain control. The computer is attempting to finish an unfinishable job. You've accidentally given the Loop an exit condition that will never be satisfied, and therefore the Loop will never be exited. Unlike For...Next, which at least has been given an upper limit, a specified number of times it will Loop, a clumsily constructed Do...Loop could go on forever. Here's one:

```
X = 55

Do Until X < 0
Print "HELLO OUT THERE!"
Loop
```

Results in   HELLO OUT THERE!
HELLO OUT THERE!
HELLO OUT THERE!
HELLO OUT THERE!
... *ad infinitum*.

The exit condition we've given this Loop—that the Variable X becomes less than zero—could never come true. There is no command within the Loop that could cause X to go below zero. The user can stop this runaway state only by turning off the computer or pressing the BREAK key.

Other examples of infinite Loops:

```
Do Until 5 = 10
Loop

Do While Marilyn Monroe Is Remembered
Loop
```

• If you want to get complicated, nest one Do...Loop inside another:

```
Sub Form_Click ()

F = 0
```

D... **279**

```
        Do Until F = 5
            Do Until G = 6
                Print G;
                G = G + 1
            Loop
        Print
        F = F + 1
        Print F
    Loop

    End Sub
```

Results in

```
0 1 2 3 4 5
1
2
3
4
5
```

You might want to avoid putting one Do...Loop inside another because things can get too complex quickly. Be aware that nested Do...Loops are strange, counterintuitive things. Nesting For...Next Loops can also be fairly confusing, but at least they're usually understandable—ultimately.

Many professional programmers nonetheless accept the challenge of nested Do...Loops. Such Loops are commonly used when you want to read some information then take action on the data. Here's an example:

```
Open ListFile$ For Input As #1
Do Until File$=""
    Line Input #1, File$
    Open File$ For Input As #2
    Do Until Eof(2)
            Line Input #2, Text$
            Print Text$
    Loop
Loop
```

This will open a file that contains a list of other files' filenames and then open each of these other files and print their contents to the screen.

Example

Say the user types in a sentence. You cannot know while you're writing your program what kind of sentence the user will type; but your program has to count the number of words in that sentence for some reason.

The InStr command can count the spaces in the sentence, thereby telling you the number of words. InStr will give back a 0 when it cannot find any more spaces. In this situation you want to place the "exit condition" at the end of the Loop. This way, the Loop happens at least one time, no matter what the user types. In other words, we want to do the following:

Do "find the next space"

Until we get a 0

(We get a 0 when InStr returns 0 to us, saying that it cannot find any more spaces inside the user's message.)

```
Sub Form_Click

A$ = "I cannot be at the office tomorrow."

    ' (Let's say that this is what the user typed in)

Lastposition = 1    'start off with the first letter in the sentence.

Do
    Pointer = InStr(Lastposition, A$, " ")
    X = X + 1
    Lastposition = Pointer + 1
Loop Until Pointer = 0

Print "The number of words in the sentence is: "; X

End Sub
```

Results in   The number of words in the sentence is: 7

(We put the conditional test at the *end* of the Loop this time because our pointer, when we enter the Loop, is zero and that would have bounced us right off the Loop before we had even gotten started if the test were at the start of the Loop.)

See also   For...Next; For Each; While...Wend

FUNCTION AND STATEMENT

Description   DoEvents lets other things happen in Windows while your program is running. It releases the computer to see if things outside your program are waiting to happen. This is *multitasking*. The computer keeps switching, rotating between running programs, giving each of them a little slice of time to do something, then going on to the next active program.

Perhaps the user has started calculating a spreadsheet or downloading something with the modem. Then he or she starts your VB program. You want the user to be able to access, or start, other applications while your VB program is running. This isn't usually an issue. Windows will automatically interrupt your running VB program between each command, between each line. But there are some commands, some structures, that can take over the computer entirely and prevent the computer from multitasking until they have finished their job. The If...Then and Do...Loop structures are the common offenders: as long as one of the Loop Structures is actively Looping, multitasking cannot take place *unless you include a DoEvents within the Loop*.

D...**281**

```
For I = 1 to 30000
X = DoEvents()
Next I
```

Technical Note: To be precise, the DoEvents command allows other Windows programs to read the messages from their own queues and do something with them. (Windows 3.1 programs are always communicating via messages, and storing them if they can't act on them right away.) Windows uses what is called *cooperative multitasking*, which means another application can run only if the one running relinquishes the computer's brain (the *CPU*). VB temporarily stands aside to allow other programs to access the CPU when it comes upon the DoEvents Function. Cooperative multitasking is distinguished from an alternative that's called *pre-emptive multitasking* in which the CPU itself can force a program to pause. With this approach, the CPU acts as traffic cop and switches to another program because the first program's allotted "time slice" has been used up.

Variables

```
X = DoEvents ()
```

The *X* is necessary because a Function must always give something back, even if you don't want or need it. The parentheses ( ) are necessary because all Functions must have them, even if they're not used. It doesn't matter to Visual Basic what the Variable X ends up with when the DoEvents command is executed. Nor does it matter to Visual Basic that the parentheses ( ) sit there; they merely signify that we're using a Function. They are required punctuation but used with DoEvents are utterly pointless. These kinds of peculiar syntaxes, punctuations and phantom reports are beginning to disappear from computer languages, but you still need to know them. (Someday soon, you'll be able to say "DoEvents" and the computer will know exactly what you mean.)

   X will tell you, should you want to know, how many VB Forms are currently loaded, how many of your Visual Basic windows have been brought into being after your program started running. This information, almost completely useless, is not the purpose of the DoEvents command.

Uses

If you're going to do something time-consuming in a VB program, such as sort a large Array or perform a lengthy calculation, insert a DoEvents inside a Loop that would otherwise tie up the computer for a long time. This allows other programs to share the computer's time and lets the user contact the computer through the keyboard or mouse.

Cautions

• If in some critical section of your program you *want* to lock things up (preventing your VB program from being interrupted by keyboard, mouse or other programs), don't use DoEvents in that section. You might need to do this if your program is receiving information from a modem.

• DoEvents extracts a penalty—it slows down execution of your Loop or whatever structure it is within.

Example

```
For I& = 1 to 2000000000
   For J = 1 to 1000
   Next J
   CLS
   Print I&
Next I&
```

This would count one thousand times two billion, and would take a while. To prevent the computer from freezing up and refusing to allow the user to do other things while your program counts, insert DoEvents:

```
For I& = 1 to 2000000000
   X = DoEvents ()
   For J = 1 to 1000
   Next J
   CLS
   Print I&
Next I&
```

If you run this program, you will notice that the version with the Do-Events( ) allows its window to be resized, iconized and even placed behind other windows. Also, you can type into a word processor, or access any other program. All the while, VB is continuing its job of counting but not locking up the computer.

RAG

METHOD

Description The Drag Method is a peculiar, intriguing facility, although you won't find uses for it in every program. It does two things. First, it allows you to *force* a drag to take place: the cursor will fly directly to a Control and pick it up! The user does not even hold down the mouse button to start this dragging. It's as if a picture or button were a powerful magnet that just got turned on, caused the mouse cursor to fly onto it, then attached itself to the cursor ready to be lifted anywhere.

The second strange effect is that it *inverts* the normal dragging technique. In Windows, dragging is normally accomplished when a user moves the mouse cursor on top of an object, presses and holds the mouse button, then moves the mouse, pulling the object around the screen. However, when you invoke the Drag Method (Picture1.Drag 1), the user can move the picture without holding down a mouse button. As you might expect, pressing a mouse button "drops" the picture.

The easy way to manage dragging pictures, buttons, icons, etc., is to set the Control's DragMode Property (which see) to Automatic (1). This allows the user to drag the Control, and VB handles the situation. You don't need to worry about the Drag Method at all. However, you can create some special effects by leaving the DragMode Property at default (0 "Manual") and controlling things more directly yourself with the Drag Method.

Drag gives you three options. Set it to 1 and you then permit the Control to be dragged (it was undraggable prior to this). If you set Drag to 2 then the dragged Control is forcibly dropped, even though the user may keep trying to drag it further. (This generates a DragDrop Event for the Control or Form the dragged item was over when you forced the dragged Control to drop.) Set Drag to 0 and any dragging action is terminated (*not* generating a DragDrop Event).

Used with Any Control (except Data, CommonDialog, Lines, Menus, Shapes and Timers). Not applicable to Forms.

Variables Picture1.Drag 0 (terminate dragging)
Picture1.Drag 1 (start a dragging activity)
Picture1.Drag 2 (terminate dragging and cause a DragDrop Event in whichever Control, or Form, the picture was located at the time)

Uses • The Drag Method is the only way in VB to summarily cancel a drag operation in progress (see the first item in "Cautions"). The Drag Method also adds a strange inverted drag style, along with *compelling* a drag Event to begin (without the user's starting to drag anything).

The Drag Method provides an approach for the indolent among us; by combining the Drag Method with the DragOver Event, the user can move items around on a screen without holding the mouse button down. This technique is more like pointing at something with a sticky wand and effortlessly sliding it elsewhere onscreen. (See the Example for more on this approach.)

Another possible use for Drag: you may write a game where accidentally dragging over a monster immediately causes a DragDrop, even though the user is still trying to escape by pressing the button on the mouse.

Cautions • You don't need to use the Drag Method simply to govern whether a Control can be dragged or not while your program is running. Just turn on or off the Control's DragMode (automatic vs. manual) Property.

• Dragging and then dropping, by themselves, do not *move* the dragged item to a new location. To accomplish that, you must work with the DragDrop Event.

• You cannot utilize the Drag Method in combination with Control Arrays. You must use individual Controls (where each Control has a different Name). (See "Control Array.")

Example We're going to make it as easy as possible for the user to spend money. Here's a Budget program where the user moves an amount of money from each budget category to a wastebasket to pay monthly bills. Depending on the category, the wastebasket may flare up in flames and smoke—a graphic reminder of priorities—for instance, entertainment vs. health care.

However, the true novelty of this program is that the user doesn't drag but merely moves the mouse cursor on top of the chosen pile. The pile of money rises onto the cursor with no mouse buttons pressed. The user then glides the money onto the wastebasket, where, again with no mouse buttons pressed, the money goes up in flames.

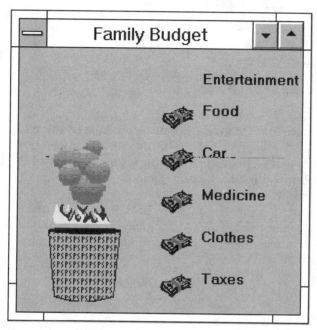

Figure D-25: Pulling money from Entertainment to the wastebasket results in combustion.

As is so often the case in Visual Basic, the technique for "sticky dragging" is remarkably simple. So much functionality is already written into VB that writing impressive programs—particularly creating a clever user interface—often takes only minutes.

In the Entertainment Money MouseMove Event, put this:

```
Sub Picture1_MouseMove (Button As Integer, Shift As Integer, X As Single,→
    Y As Single)

picture1.Drag 1
picture1.visible = False
End Sub
```

MouseMove detects that the mouse cursor has entered this Picture Box's space onscreen. We merely instruct that the Picture snap onto the cursor like a fly to flypaper, and that the Picture itself go invisible. Precisely *what* the Picture we're now dragging looks like is determined by that Picture's

DragIcon Property (which see). In this case, we provided a stack of bills that has started to catch fire.

The only other thing to do is cause the flaming money to drop into the wastebasket and the fire and smoke to appear. In this case, we're using the DragOver Event instead of MouseMove because we don't want flames every time the cursor passes over the wastebasket.

```
Sub Picture2_DragOver (source As Control, X As Single, Y As Single, State →
    As Integer)

source.Drag 0
picture4.visible = True
picture5.visible = True
picture4.visible = False
picture5.visible = False

End Sub
```

The Source for DragOver Events is the dragged thing's name, so it's a way of forcing the dragging to stop (again without any mouse button action on the user's part). The DragIcon disappears into the wastebasket, then we briefly turn on the fire (Picture4) and the smoke (Picture5), then make them invisible again.

These are two separate pictures because in the actual program we used a Timer to slightly delay the appearance and disappearance of the smoke. It's pretty effective, however, even without controlling the timing of the animation to that extent.

See also   DragDrop; DragIcon; DragMode; DragOver

DRAGDROP
EVENT

Description   Dragging, in Windows, means relocating something on the screen by moving the cursor (the mouse arrow) on top of it, pressing and holding the mouse button, then moving the mouse to slide the object around the screen. When the user releases the mouse button, that is a DragDrop.

The drop triggers the DragDrop within the borders of the Control where the dragged item was when the mouse button was released. If the item is not over a Control when dropped, the item falls onto the Form itself.

Used with   Forms, and every Control except Data, Lines, Menus, Shapes and Timers.

Uses   • Allow the user to customize the way the program looks, the location of items onscreen.

• Allow copying between files or records, deleting, appending, and so forth, by "physically" lifting one thing onto another. For example, deletion can be handled within the DragDrop Event of a picture of a trash can. Or Notepad can be loaded in (with the Shell Function), allowing the user to read the text represented by a file icon dropped onto a Notepad icon.

Cautions

• *You must memorize this*: The DragDrop Event *of the thing that's being dragged* does not determine whether the thing moves when dragged and dropped. The DragDrop Event *of the target, usually the underlying Form,* must contain the instructions about what to do when something is dropped on it. DragDrop really means DragDroppedOn.

If an item is dropped onto a Control (or the Form) and you've put no instructions into the DragDrop Event of the object that was dropped onto, then nothing will happen. The "dropped" item will still appear in its original place on the Form, and nothing else will happen. This is desirable because you don't want to have to return things to their original state by writing something explicit within every Control's DragDrop Event Procedure. So, if the user makes a mistake and tries to drop something in the wrong place, the Form just doesn't respond.

But remember that, counterintuitively, the DragDrop Event of the thing that's dragged is not where you put instructions about what's to happen when it's dropped. Instead, you put those instructions into the DragDrop Event of the background (the Form) or a target Control upon which the dragged item may be dropped.

• Dropping an item somewhere new onscreen does not move it to that location. You need to specify the new location using the new X,Y coordinates (see the Example).

Example

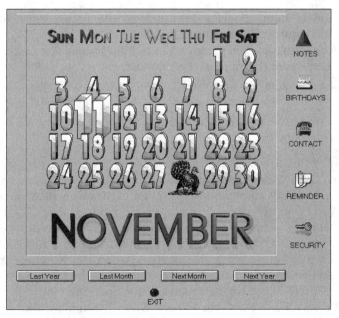

Figure D-26: A calendar application with icons you can drag and drop.

The first thing you do in preparing a Drag Event is decide on the Drag-Icon, the image that will appear while the user drags the object. Double-click on DragIcon in the Properties Window and select one.

You Can't Overlap Controls: The calendar program we're going to create allows us to, among other things, drag icons onto various dates. It would be best if we could *move* icons (and any other Controls) around, anywhere, within a VB Form–the way we can move windows around within Windows.

Unfortunately, the current version of VB doesn't provide for reliable movement of one Control over another. Overlapping, or placing Controls one on top of another, can make them unstable. Sometimes they land an inch away from where they were dropped; or one Control may completely cover another.

In this application, we use a workaround, involving the PSet Method and the target's DrawWidth Property, that allows the user to stamp dates with a symbol instead of using an icon. Here, the circle, in a color from the icon, gets stamped onto the calendar when we drop the icon. (It's on November 14, but because it's red it shows up very well.)

A DragDrop Event provides you with three pieces of information– DragDrop (Source As Control, X As Single, Y As Single).

Source, in the information offered to you in a DragDrop Event, is the picture or icon or Control that has been dropped. Sometimes you'll want to use the Select Case Statement here to make different things happen, depending on which icon or Control the user has dragged and dropped. In any event, *Source* allows you to easily do something to the thing the user moved, make Source.Visible = 0, or whatever else you want to happen to the moved item. You can also use the word "Source" instead of naming the item to adjust its Properties.

Here's what we did to cause the red dot to land in exactly the right place on the picture (bitmap) of the calendar:

```
Sub Picture2_DragDrop (Source As Control, x As Single, y As Single)

picture2.DrawWidth = 8
picture2.PSet (x, y), QBColor(12)
End Sub
```

By setting the DrawWidth Property to 8, we make a big dot. You can make DrawWidth *really* big and create balloon-sized dots with PSet if you wish. The PSet command isn't limited to pixels, as its name would suggest.

In addition to *Source* information, we're given X and Y–the horizontal and vertical locations *within the target object* where the drop occurred. We take that X,Y location from the DragDrop Event and PSet a blob onto the calendar in precisely the location we want–just where the user released the icon. So, by setting the X and Y of the PSet, we thereby neatly place it where the user dragged and dropped the icon.

We decided to leave our original Notes pyramid symbol where it is, so it can spawn new blobs if the user wants to attach more notes to the calendar.

See also   Drag; DragIcon; DragMode; DragOver

PROPERTY

Description   The DragIcon Property determines how the cursor looks while an item is being dragged. The "cursor" in Windows is the mouse pointer. It normally looks like an arrow; when an item is dragged, a faint gray box appears to be dragged by the cursor:

Figure D-27: The default DragIcon is a gray box.

However, you can cause the cursor to change into some other icon while the user is dragging.

Used with   Any Control except CommonDialog, Data, Lines, Menus, Shapes and Timers. Not used with Forms.

Variables   You can select a DragIcon image directly from the Properties Window, just as you would select a Picture Property.

OR (to assign one Control's DragIcon to another Control):

    Picture1.DragIcon = Picture5.DragIcon

OR (to load in an image while the program runs):

    Picture1.DragIcon = LoadPicture("C:\WINDOWS\ICONS\LIPS.ICO")

OR (for esoteric situations, you can ask for the identifying number of an item's DragIcon):

    X = Picture1.DragIcon
    Print X

(You'll get a unique number, such as 15446, for each Control that has a DragIcon. If a Control has no DragIcon, you'll get 0.)

Uses   • Help the user understand the implications of an action. Change a Drag-Icon while the program runs, to allow the user to see that, for instance, if he or she drops the icon in the trash can, the item the icon represents will

D . . . **289**

be deleted. Perhaps you would create a special version of an icon with a large black X through it. When the user drags the original icon in the vicinity of a TrashCan Picture Box, the new X'ed icon would appear. In the TrashCan's DragOver Event, you would dynamically change the DragIcon by the following: Picture1.DragIcon = XIcon.DragIcon

The XIcon.DragIcon could be on the Form but have its Visible Property set to False. Or you could use the LoadPicture Function.

• Improve the visual experience by avoiding the default gray box during dragging.

Example   Command1.DragIcon = InvertedButton.Icon

See also   Drag; DragDrop; DragMode; DragOver

PROPERTY

Description   DragMode makes a Control draggable.

DragMode can be set to Automatic (1) to permit something to be dragged around the window while a program is running. The default (0) is called Manual and the item will not be draggable unless you intervene with additional instructions involving the "Drag Method" (which see).

Used with   Every Control except CommonDialog, Data, Lines, Menus, Shapes and Timers. Not used with Forms.

Variables   **Variable type:** Integer (enumerated)

DragMode can be set directly in the Properties Window while you are designing a program.
OR (it can be set while the program is running):

        Picture1.DragMode = 1

Uses   Allow an item to be moved (to be dragged) around the screen.

Cautions   • When set to Automatic, the picture or icon or whatever will not respond to mouse clicks. If you want a Control to be able to respond to more than simply being dragged somewhere, you must leave the DragMode set to Manual (the default), and work with the Drag Method (which see).

Example
```
Sub Form_Show ()
If Setup = 0 Then
  Doubleicon.DragMode = 0
Else
  Doubleicon.DragMode = 1
End If
End Sub
```

In this program, we *sometimes* allow the icons to be moved to places the user prefers. However, this is permitted only when the user has selected Setup mode, wherein the Global Variable *Setup* is set to 1 (Setup = 1), and automatic dragging is thereby permitted. Otherwise, dragging is prohibited, and a mouse click on DoubleIcon causes other effects in the program.

See also Drag; DragDrop; DragIcon; DragOver

DRAGOVER

EVENT

Description When one Control is dragged over another (or over a Form), a DragOver Event occurs, alerting the invaded Control or Form that dragging is happening within its space. When triggered, a DragOver Event provides you with four pieces of information—the Variables inside the parentheses:

```
Sub Label1_DragOver (Source As Control, X As Single, Y As Single, State → As
    Integer)
End Sub
```

The invader is identified (with the name "Source"). The current position of the invader within the invaded Control or Form is reported with X,Y. The status of the invader—whether it's just entering, within or just leaving—is reported with the State Variable.

Used with All Controls except CommonDialog, Data, Lines, Menus, Shapes and Timers. Used with Forms.

Uses • Cause some special effect when a dragged item enters the space of a Control or Form. A dragged icon could disappear in flames when dropped into a trash can. (See the Example under "Drag Method.") Or a message could be printed to the user explaining what would happen if the item were dropped into this space (see Example below).

• Change the DragIcon Property in some way (invert it, turn it into a different image) as another way of indicating what dropping would do in the current location.

• Allow the user to drag a pointer around the screen, causing things to happen by touching various areas in your window (but without having to actually drop the icon). This way, a user could pick up, say, a brush-shaped cursor and choose a color, a pen shape, a texture and other selections from various palettes—without doing more than simply guiding the brush cursor around the window.

Example One popular programming technique involves a Text Box, the contents of which vary depending on the current situation while a program is running. Many programs include a Status Bar, usually along the bottom of the main window, which contains information about the current state of things. Here's what this bar looks like in WordPerfect for Windows:

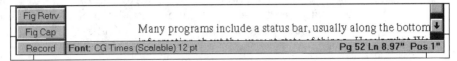

Figure D-28: WordPerfect's Status Bar

The Status Bar changes in response to what happens while the program runs. It reports the current position of the cursor, the state of such Variables as Font, etc. It can be a short help feature that's always on duty. And it's often an aid when you're learning to use new software. (Since this sort of thing can be annoying after you know how to run a program, the user should have the option of turning off a Status Bar—for the same reason that bicycle training wheels are detachable.) For an alternative way to create Status Bars (and Toolbars), see "Multiple Document Interface" or "Align."

A similar effect is achieved by allowing the user to move an icon around the screen, touching various objects for further information. Here we have a program that illustrates the history of bicycles. When the user drags the INFO icon on top of a picture, the bicycle's name and a brief explanation of that model appears, each in a Text Box.

Figure D-29: An alternative to clicking, you can display information in response to dragging.

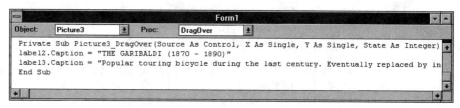

```
                                    Form1
Object:    Picture3          Proc:      DragOver
Private Sub Picture3_DragOver(Source As Control, X As Single, Y As Single, State As Integer)
label2.Caption = "THE GARIBALDI (1870 - 1890)"
label13.Caption = "Popular touring bicycle during the last century. Eventually replaced by in
End Sub
```

Figure D-30: Within the DragOver Event of each picture we put the text we want displayed.

See also   Drag; DragDrop; DragIcon; DragMode

 RAWMODE

PROPERTY

Description   DrawMode can create special visual effects. It governs the interaction between the background color and the color of a line, circle, other drawn graphic or printed text. If you wish, the computer can take a look at the background color and line color, and then, based on a mathematical relationship between the two colors, create a new color for the line.

In practice, you'll usually leave DrawMode set to its default, which means that VB simply uses the color you've selected as the ForeColor (for your line, graphic or whatnot), and does not try to blend the BackColor into it. However, for the adventurous, there are 15 other possible DrawModes.

Used with   Forms, Lines, Picture Boxes, the printer and Shapes.

Variables   **Variable type:** Integer (enumerated)

You can select a DrawMode from the Properties Window while designing your program.

OR (to set the DrawMode while the program is running): DrawMode = 12

OR (to find out what DrawMode is in effect while a program is running):

X = DrawMode

The DrawMode options are:

1   Blackness (just the color black)
2   Not Merge Pen (the inverse of 15)
3   Mask Not Pen (combines the inverse of the foreground color with the background color)
4   Not Copy Pen (inverse of foreground color)

5   Mask Pen Not (combines the inverse of the background with the foreground color)

6   Invert

7   Xor Pen (foreground and background colors that are present in one, but not both)

8   Not Mask Pen (inverse of mask pen)

9   Mask Pen (colors present in both foreground and background, combined)

10   Not Xor Pen (inverse of Xor Pen)

11   Nop (nothing happens, no drawing)

12   Merge Not Pen (background combined with inverted foreground color)

13   Copy Pen, the default (draw with ForeColor unchanged)

14   Merge Pen Not (combines foreground with inverted background color)

15   Merge Pen (combines foreground and background colors)

16   Whiteness (pure white fills the drawn space)

Uses   • Specialized drawing applications, such as "erasing" colors

• Of the 16 DrawModes, perhaps 6 and 7 are the most useful (aside from 13, the default). They "invert" the background color and, used with backgrounds that have pictures in them, can create an X-ray or "ghosting" effect. (See the Example.)

• DrawMode 13, the default, creates no special effects—it merely superimposes the ForeColor on top of the BackColor, as if you had used a crayon on paper. The background is covered over by the drawn lines or text.

Cautions   • Many of the DrawModes will produce unpredictable effects, varying for each color combination.

Figure D-31: To create an X-ray effect, set DrawMode to 6.

```
Sub Form_Click ()

picture2.DrawMode = 6
picture2.picture = picture1.picture
x = picture2.left + picture2.width
y = picture2.top + picture2.height

picture2.Line (0, 0)-(x, y), QBColor(8), BF

End Sub
```

Here we created two Picture Boxes and set their AutoSize Properties to 1 so their frames will be the same size as the images they contain. Then we loaded a drawing into Picture1 by setting its Picture Property in the Properties Window while designing our program.

We made Picture2 show the same drawing as Picture1. Finally we created a box exactly the size and location of Picture2 by adding Picture2's Left to its Width, and its Height to its Top. With these coordinates, we use the Line Method to draw a box, set its color to medium gray (QBColor 8), and then instruct the computer to fill in the box (BF).

Figure D-32: To create a ghosting effect, set DrawMode to 7.

Figure D-33 shows the results of printing a dot (PSet, with DrawWidth set to 30) with the ForeColor set to red and the BackColor set to blue in the top row, white in the bottom row. All 16 possible DrawModes are illustrated. Notice that number 13, the default, is the normal, expected result of putting a crayon to paper; but some of the modes draw nothing visible against the background. There is less variety in the second row because white interacts less noticeably with a foreground color. On a black-and-white screen, of course, there is very little variety among the 16 modes.

Figure D-33: All 16 possible DrawModes.

See also   Circle; DrawStyle; DrawWidth; Line; PSet

PROPERTY

Description   The DrawStyle Property determines whether a drawn line will be solid (the default); a combination of dots and dashes; or invisible. DrawStyle affects the results of Line and Circle "graphics" commands. It does not affect PSet or text printed with the Print command.

Used with   Forms, Picture Boxes and the printer

Variables   **Variable type:** Integer (enumerated)

You can select the DrawStyle from the Properties Window while designing your program:

0	The Default (a solid line)
1	Dash
2	Dot
3	Dash-dot
4	Dash-dot-dot
5	Invisible
6	Inside Solid

OR (to set the DrawStyle while the program is running): DrawStyle = 1

OR (to find out what DrawStyle is in effect while the program is running):

X = DrawStyle

Uses   Create special effects in drawings, on borders, etc.

Cautions   • If the DrawWidth Property is set larger than 1, you will get a solid line, not dots and dashes.

Example

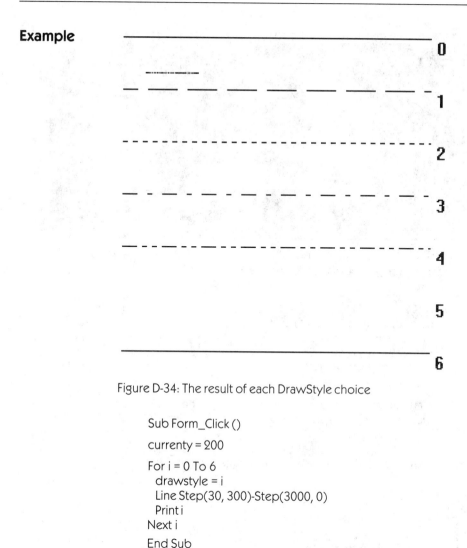

Figure D-34: The result of each DrawStyle choice

```
Sub Form_Click ()
currenty = 200
For i = 0 To 6
  drawstyle = i
  Line Step(30, 300)-Step(3000, 0)
  Print i
Next i
End Sub
```

DrawStyle 6 applies only to boxes drawn using a wide DrawWidth. It's a solid line, like the default DrawStyle 0. However, DrawStyle can cover up part of the picture it frames. The default 0 setting causes a line to be drawn *centered* on the dimensions of the box (and part of the line may be cropped depending on the arguments you give the Line Method). On the other hand, DrawStyle 6 is more like matting a picture: a thick line is drawn completely *within* the dimensions of the box, forming a border and covering more of the picture. This means that the *entire* width of your line will cover the picture (With DrawStyle 0, only 50 percent of your line would cover your picture.)

In Figure D-35, the picture on the left is bordered by DrawStyle 0, the default. The one on the right is the "entirely within" style 6.

Figure D-35: DrawStyle 6, on the right, creates a line entirely *inside* the picture's border, covering more of the picture.

```
Sub Form_Click ()

picture2.picture = picture1.picture
picture1.drawwidth = 25
picture2.drawwidth = 25
picture1.drawstyle = 0
picture2.drawstyle = 6

picture1.Line (0, 0)-(picture1.width, picture1.height), QBColor(7), B
picture2.Line (0, 0)-(picture2.width, picture2.height), QBColor(7), B

End Sub
```

See also   BorderStyle; Circle; DrawMode; DrawWidth; FillStyle; Line; PSet

PROPERTY

Description   The DrawWidth Property offers you considerable variety when you're drawing frames or other graphic objects. It determines the thickness of drawn lines, circles and dots.

Used with   Forms, OLE Controls, Picture Boxes and the printer

Variables   **Variable type:** Integer

OR (to change the DrawWidth while the program is running):

```
DrawWidth = 25
```

OR (to determine the current DrawWidth while a program is running):

```
X = Picture1.DrawWidth
```

Uses
• Adjust the size of lines you draw while the program runs. You can change the DrawWidth in between drawing commands, which means that a DrawWidth isn't fixed for all the graphics that you draw on a single Form or Picture Box or send to the printer. You can draw several objects in several line thicknesses by adjusting the DrawWidth Property on the fly.

• When using PSet, DrawWidth controls the "brush size" of the line. (PSet, which prints a dot, causes a rounded line to appear when PSet's location is moved or dragged by the user.)

Cautions
• If you change DrawWidth to greater than the default, which is 1, you turn off the dot and dash modes of the DrawStyle Property; consequently, you can only get a solid line.

• DrawWidth interacts with the ScaleMode Property of a Form, Picture Box or the printer. The default ScaleMode in VB is a *twip*, which means 1/20th of a *point*. (A point is a printers' typesetting measurement equal to 1/72nd of an inch.) So a twip is very tiny indeed—about .0007 inch—allowing you to be very precise and use thousands of them to size or position things on the screen. (For more on the various scales in VB, see "ScaleMode.")

Example
Here are 15 DrawWidths ranging from 1 to 30 (with twips as the Scale-Mode):

```
Sub Form_Click ()

For i = 1 To 30 Step 2
  drawwidth = i
  Line (i * 200, 300) – (i * 200, 1900)
Next i

End Sub
```

Figure D-36: You can choose how "fat" your lines will be.

See also
Circle; DrawMode; DrawStyle; FillStyle; Line; PSet; ScaleMode

RIVE

PROPERTY

Description
The Drive Property tells you which disk drive is currently "selected" by the user while a program is running. The only Control that has a Drive Property is a Drive List Box.

The Drive Property cannot be changed while you are designing your program, but it can be changed while the program is running if the user clicks on a Drive List Box.

Your program itself can also change the Drive Property to change the selected drive. *The "selected" drive is not identical to the "current" drive,* although the Drive Property defaults to the "current" drive (unless the user or your program changes the Drive Property).

Selected merely means that the user has clicked on a drive name in a Drive List Box. The only things that happen are that the selected drive name reverses (white on black) to show which drive is selected; and the Drive List Box's ListIndex Property also adjusts to point to the selected drive. To actually make that selected drive the "current" drive (from which files can be accessed with no additional path information), you have to use the ChDrive Statement.

Used with
Drive List Boxes only

Variables
Variable type: Text (string)

To change the selected drive while the program is running:
    Drive1.Drive = "c:"

OR (to find out which drive is "selected" while the program is running):
    x$ = Drive1.Drive

Uses
• When combined with Drive, Directory and File List Boxes and other file-manipulation commands such as Open, ChDir, MkDir, Kill and ChDrive, you can allow the user complete control over the files on his or her drives. This means: files can be created and sent to the directory of the user's choice; files can be replaced or deleted; and all the other file-system Control Events (such as creating new directories) can be accessed by the user from within your program. Also, your program itself can directly change, or get information from, the Drive Property.

See the Example under "Drive List Box" for a demonstration of a complete file-access system.

Cautions
• When your program is setting the selected drive (Drive1.Drive = "c"), only the first character is used by VB; and it must be the identifier of an existing drive, or else there will be an error.

• Changing the selected drive triggers a Change Event in the Drive List Box.

• If your program sets the Drive Property, the Drive List Box's List Property will be updated, which helps your program keep track of any changes on a network while your program runs.

• When your program asks information of the Drive Property (x$ = Drive1.Drive. Result: PRINT X$ yields: C: Fixed), the information includes a: or b: or c: [volume name] (for hard drives), or G:\\Server\Share (for networks).

• If the user or your program changes the Drive Property, this is merely an informational change—it switches the highlight in the Drive List Box to a different drive name, and updates the List Property. To actually *change* the current drive, you must also use the ChDrive Statement.

Example   The file-management Properties demonstrated below are related but provide different information in different forms. See each Property for more specific information.

```
A$ = Drive1.Drive
B$ = CurDir$
C$ = Dir1.Path
D$ = Drive1.List(ListIndex)

Print A$
```

Results in   c: [HARD DRIVE]

```
Print B$
```

Results in   C:\WINDOWS

```
Print C$
```

Results in   c:\windows

```
Print D$
```

Results in   a:

(For an example of how Drive, Directory and File List Boxes interact, see the Example in "Drive List Box.")

See also   Visual Basic provides a wealth of ways to access and manage disk drives and the files therein. Here is a complete alphabetical list of the VB commands related to file management:

AppActivate; Archive; Change; ChDir; ChDrive; Close; CurDir$; Dir$; EOF; EXEName; FileAttr; FileName; FreeFile; Get; Hidden; Input$; Input #; Kill; Line Input #; List; ListCount; ListIndex; Loc; Lock; LOF; MkDir; Name; Normal; On Error; Open; Path; PathChange; Pattern; PatternChange; Print #; Put; ReadOnly; Reset; RmDir; Seek; Shell; System; Unlock; Write #

DRIVE LIST BOX

CONTROL

Figure D-37: The Drive List Box symbol in the Toolbox.

Description
A Drive List Box displays an ordered list of the user's disk drives, and automatically reacts to mouse clicks to allow the user to move among them. It is like such lists found in many Windows programs and is in standard Windows format.

A Drive List Box can work in conjunction with the Directory and File List Boxes to allow the user complete access to all the files on all disk drives attached to his or her computer. See the following example to find out about using a Drive List Box along with Directory and File List Boxes to create a complete file-access system for the user.

Variables   As with any Control, you can adjust the available Properties with the Properties Window while you are designing your program.

OR (to change a Property while the program is running):

```
Drive1.FontSize = 12
```

OR (to find out the current disk drive while a program is running):

```
Currentdrive$ = Drive1.Drive
```

OR (to make a Directory List Box display the directories of the drive selected by a Drive List Box while a program is running):

```
Dir1.Path = Drive1.Drive
```

Uses   • Permit the user to see a list of disk drives and move among them.

• Combined with Directory and File List Boxes, the user can access files anywhere on his or her system.

Cautions   • Beware of changing a Property like FontBold (while your program is running)—it will cause a Drive Box to freeze up and refuse to respond to mouse clicks. The only font Properties that can be changed safely while a program is running are FontSize and FontName.

• The most important Property of a Drive List Box is its Drive Property. This Property always knows the name of the current drive or the choice the user has made when clicking on the Drive List Box to move among a computer's drives. Note that the drive name provided by the Drive Property will be whatever "volume label" was assigned to the disk when it was formatted. Instead of "C:" or "C:\" you might get "C: [HARD DRIVE]"

To build a full file-access system, use the Directory List Box's Path in conjunction with the ChDir command; the Path and Pattern Properties of a File List Box; and the Drive Property of a Drive List Box. (See the Example.)

• The ListCount Property gives you the number of disk drives active on the user's computer.

• The List Property shows the *names* of the drives on the user's computer.

• The ListIndex Property points to the position, within the List, of the current drive. (Note that the first drive is 0, the second 1, and so on.)

Example   This example demonstrates how to set up a complete file-access system so the user can move anywhere across all files, directories and drives available on his or her computer system. It is usually best to allow the user to manage files rather than to hard-wire file access into your program.

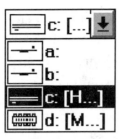

Figure D-38: The drive list showing symbols for the various disk drives and a ram drive on the bottom.

And here's ours:

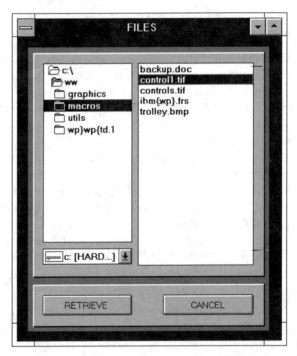

Figure D-39: The disk-access window we'll create in this example.

(Currently the most popular "look" in professional Windows applications is a brushed metallic effect. The VB Command Button is an example. This look is also variously referred to as "machined," "embossed" or "the Next look" [after Steve Job's Next computer]. To learn how to easily draw the brushed metallic frames seen in Figure D-39 and many other examples in this book, see "Line.")

The Drive, Directory and File List Boxes can work together to allow the user to move across all the filenames stored on the disk drives throughout his or her computer system. Similarly, if your program needs information about files stored on the user's system, you can create these Boxes, make them invisible by setting their Visible Properties to False, then access the information they provide while your program runs. With this technique, the user doesn't see the Boxes, but the Boxes provide your program with everything it needs to completely access all files.

Double-Click Conventions: By convention, a DblClick Event selects a new drive or a new directory from within those Boxes. Double-clicking also triggers the Change Event. A double-click within the File List Box opens (or otherwise targets) the double-clicked file.

To create a file-access system, we will need to respond to Change Events. The most general change is when the user selects a new drive; and we'll pass along that information to the Directory List Box in this fashion:

```
Sub Drive1_Change ()
  dir1.path = drive1.drive
End Sub
```

This changes the Directory List Box to show the directories within the newly selected drive.

In a cascading fashion, like falling dominos, our adjustment to the Path Property of the Directory Box triggers a Change Event in the Directory Box. So we'll use that to pass the information along to the File List Box:

```
Sub Dir1_Change ()
  file1.path = dir1.path
End Sub
```

Should the user merely select a new directory, that would itself trigger a Dir1_Change Event; so we need not make any additional provisions to let the user see the entire system and all the files available on any drive.

The default directory (the "current" directory) is not changed by these various maneuvers; however, the list of drives, directories and files the user sees on the screen *does* change. To change the "current" directory, add the ChDir Statement.

To show the filesizes, add this:

```
Sub File1_Click ()

n$ = dir1.path
If Right$(N$,1) <> "\" Then N$ = N$ & "\"

Open n$ For Binary As #1
s = LOF(1)
Close #1

size$ = Str$(s)
n$ = UCase$(n$)

text1.text = n$ + " is" + size$ + " bytes."
End Sub
```

And you'll see this:

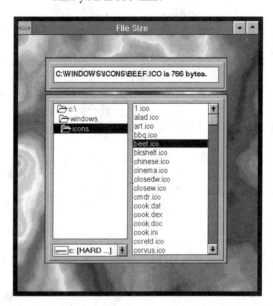

Figure D-40: You can display customized information such as file size, by using the various file-access Boxes.

Drive List Box Properties
BackColor • DragIcon • DragMode • Drive • Enabled • FontBold
FontItalic • FontName • FontSize • FontStrikethru • FontUnderline
ForeColor • Height • HelpContextID • hWnd • Index • Left • List
ListCount • ListIndex • MousePointer • Name • Parent • TabIndex
TabStop • Tag • Top • Visible • Width

Drive Box List Events
Change • DragDrop • DragOver • GotFocus • KeyDown • KeyPress
KeyUp • LostFocus

Drive List Box Methods
Drag • Move • Refresh • SetFocus • ZOrder

See also   Visual Basic provides many ways to access and manage disk drives and the files they contain. Here's a complete alphabetical list of the VB commands related to file management:

AppActivate; Archive; Change; ChDir; ChDrive; Close; CurDir$; Dir$; Drive; EOF; EXEName; FileAttr; FileName; FreeFile; Get; Hidden; Input$; Input #; Kill; Line Input #; List; ListCount; ListIndex; Loc; Lock; LOF; MkDir; Name; Normal; On Error; Open; Path; PathChange; Pattern; PatternChange; Print #; Put; ReadOnly; Reset; RmDir; Seek; Shell; System; Unlock; Write #

DROPDOWN

EVENT

Description

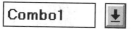

Figure D-41: A Combo Box before it's been clicked on

When the user clicks on the arrow to the right of a Combo Box (or presses the ALT+down arrow key), if the Box has the "focus," the Combo Box drops down, revealing a list of choices from which the user can select.

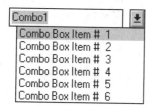

Figure D-42: After clicking on the Box, an options list drops down.

Clicking on the arrow icon causes a DropDown Event within the Combo Box. Your program can therefore respond to the fact that the list of choices is about to be revealed *before it is revealed*.

Used with

Combo Boxes only

Uses

If you're using a Combo Box to offer choices to the user, and if the list changes depending on program events, you might want to save some time by using the DropDown Event to update the list within the Combo Box. This way, you don't have to update the Box every time the list changes—only when the user tries to access the Box.

Cautions

• If the Combo Box's Style Property is set to 1 (Simple), the DropDown Event does not occur (the Event is never triggered).

Example

```
Sub Combo1_DropDown ()

If Startover = 1 Then
   For i = 0 To Combo1.ListCount — 1
            Combo1.RemoveItem 0
   Next i

   Startover = 0
End If
End Sub
```

This example assumes that another Control or Event in the program has requested that this Combo Box be cleared out. We know about this request because we created a Global Variable (accessible everywhere in the entire program) called *Startover* in a Module. Then, Startover was set to 1 (Startover = 1) in some other Event in the program.

Now, if the user should select the Combo Box, the ListCount Property (which always knows how many items are in a Box) is used with the RemoveItem command to remove each of the items in turn. Owing to a peculiarity in the way computers count, there is always a zeroth item in lists like this—i.e., items are counted starting at 0. There is no command that directly empties out a Box-type Control; you must Loop from 0 to ListCount, removing each item. By the way, notice that we also reset Startover to 0, so other places in the program can check the Startover Variable to see if the Box was cleared out. We want Startover to hold a 1 only if the program intends to clear out the Box's contents.

See Also   Change; Click; Style

ENABLED

PROPERTY

Description
The Enabled Property allows you to *freeze* a Control, Menu or Form while your program is running. While it is frozen (disabled), the user cannot click on it or otherwise interact with it. The Control is *visible*, in pale gray (just enough to show that it's asleep), but not accessible to the user. Disabled Controls are described as *grayed*. (Timers are a special case; see Uses.)

Used with
All Controls, Forms, Menus and Timers

Variables
Variable type: Integer (Boolean)

To change this Property while designing your program, use the Properties Window.

OR (to disable and freeze an object while the program is running. The user cannot click on it or do anything else to it. Also, it turns gray):

    Command1.Enabled = False

OR (This is the default. The object is accessible and reacts normally. The user can type into this Text Box and access it in other ways, depending on how its other Properties are set. For instance, the Box can be dragged if its DragMode has been set to 1): TextBox1.Enabled = True

Uses
• Show Controls and features that are part of your program but which, for one reason or another, are currently unavailable. For example, if the user has not typed anything into your program yet, there is no reason to have a Command Button labeled "Print" working; therefore, it can be disabled, grayed out. When the user starts typing (detected by a Text Box's Change Event), turn the Button back on (Command1.Enabled = True).

• Some Controls, like Text Boxes, can be altered by the user. However, sometimes you want to use these Controls in other ways, and you don't want them altered. A Text Box may simply be used like a Label, showing the user information that's not to be tampered with. If its MultiLine Property is set on (True), you can freeze the text inside the Text Box by setting its Enabled Property off (False). (If the MultiLine Property is off [False], the text will freeze but turn pale gray.)

• Timers are always invisible and are never directly accessed by the user. The Enabled Property of a Timer is used to reset it or start the Timer running. If a Timer is running when you disable it (Timer1.Enabled = False), it will stop running at that point in its countdown. If you Enable a Timer, you turn it on and it starts counting from zero up to the amount of its Interval Property. (It's important to be able to turn Timers on and off, as well as to reset them while your program is running. See "Timer" for more.)

Cautions
• All Controls, Forms and Menus start out with a default of Enabled. So if you do disable one, remember to turn it back on if you want the user ever to be able to access it.

• Even Timers are Enabled when the program first starts running—unless you use the Properties Window to initially disable the Timer. This is an important consideration because in many cases you'll want a Timer to start counting *only after something in the program triggers the Timer*. To prevent such a Timer from running free right from the start, set its Enabled Property off (False) using the Properties Window, or within the Form_Load Event: (Timer1.Enabled = False). Timers will not, however, start with their Interval Property at zero, so they won't automatically go off even with Enabled defaulting to On.

Example
Take a look at Figure E-1. Nothing can be printed now, nor can the printer setup be accessed. In the Form_Load Event we see:

```
Command1.Enabled = False
Command2.Enabled = False
```

This turns off the two top buttons. We didn't do anything to the "Activate" button, Command3, so it defaulted to Enabled.

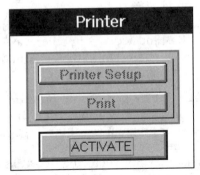

Figure E-1: The two printer-related buttons are disabled, but the ACTIVATE button is enabled.

The Printer buttons are pale gray. The only Command Button on this window that's alive at this point is the ACTIVATE button. In this program, the user must deliberately activate the printer-access features by clicking Command3, the button labeled ACTIVATE.

Clicking ACTIVATE triggers its Click Event, which contains:

```
Command1.Enabled = True
Command2.Enabled = True
```

Then the two printer-related Command Buttons return to life (their Captions take on a normal dark appearance), and their Events can be triggered.

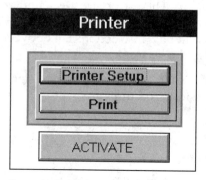

Figure E-2: All three buttons are Enabled. The user can access them.

ND   STATEMENT

Description   The End Statement is used in two unrelated ways.

• It shuts down a running program, notifying Visual Basic that a program should collapse and disappear from the user's screen.

• It brackets structures that can vary in length, such as Select Case...End Select. The End Statement notifies VB that some programming structure is completed. It's as if you handed someone a list that contained a *grouped list of instructions* (a *block* in programming lingo):

```
Sub Shopping()

    If Grocery Store Then
            1. Buy bread.
            2. Buy onions.
            3. Return that rancid roast beef.
    End If

    Drive the car

End Sub
```

Without the phrase "End If," the instructions to drive the car would be attempted in the store as part of the group of instructions we wanted carried out if we were located in the store. That, however, is not our intention. Programs are full of instructions. We need to let the computer know the difference between instructions that are enclosed within a *conditional* zone and instructions that are to be carried out regardless. The three instructions inside the If...Then structure are "conditional" on being in the store. Visual Basic knows which instructions are conditional and which are not, because conditional instructions fall between the If...Then and the End If commands in this example.

Used with   There are several *structures* in VB. End can be used to signify the conclusion of a structure. The possible structures are

    Function
    End Function

    If...Then
    End If

    Property Let (Get or Set)
    End Property

    Select Case
    End Select

    Sub
    End Sub

    Type
    End Type

    With
    End With

End Function, End Property and End Sub are always required; they show that a Function or Subroutine is complete. Visual Basic normally supplies these automatically. You click on a Procedure ("Proc") Menu within the VB Code Window (press F7) to select some Event that you want the program to react to. VB supplies the shell of the Event structure—the name of the Subroutine, any Variables available to the Subroutine and the End Sub.

    Sub Option1_DragOver (Source As Control, X As Single, Y As Single, →
        State As Integer)

    End Sub

In between the Sub... and End Sub Statements, you write your instructions describing how the program should react if this Event is triggered while the program runs.

Also, the *Select Case, Type, With* and *If* Statements (when If is used in its "block" style, not when it's all on a single line) all require that you use End Select, End Type, End With and End If Statements to let VB know they've ended.

Uses
• When the user wants to leave your program—often signified by clicking on a button marked "QUIT" or "EXIT"—you put the End Statement in that Event Procedure:

```
Sub Quitbutton_Click ()
    End
End Sub
```

Your program will then follow a set pattern to safely shut itself down and clean up any ambiguities or loose ends. The End command stops your program from running, closes any files that the program may have opened on a disk and shuts down any windows that may be visible.

• If...Then has two modes: single-line and multiple-line. An If...Then structure on one line does not use an End If Statement. Single-line If...Then Statements don't end with the word *Then*. The computer can tell that when some instructions follow the Then command on the same line, they complete the necessary action; in other words, the computer has all the information it needs to make the if/then decision:

```
If Numbercount = 15 Then Print "We re up to 15."
```

However, when the If...Then line ends with Then, some actions must follow, depending on the conditions between If and Then. In this mode the computer needs an End Statement. We must let the computer know that things are no longer *conditional*, no longer dependent on the item following If. In other words, when should VB resume carrying out the instructions you have written, regardless of that If?

```
If Numbercount = 15 Then

Print "We re to 15 that s it."

End If

Print "Now continue on with no conditions (always print this text)"
Print "It s outside of the If...Then...End If structure, so it always gets printed."
```

• Type, Sub, Function and Select Case are all Statements that require End. None of them can be made to fit onto a single line, and you can have as many lines between their beginning and end as you need. However, VB must be told when they do in fact End.

Cautions
• In a stand-alone program (one that doesn't require VB to run; i.e., that has been translated into an .EXE program by choosing Make EXE File from the VB File Menu), the Stop Statement acts like an End Statement, but first displays an error message.

- If you are counting on carrying out some cleanup or other essential tasks when your program ends, don't put them in the Form_UnLoad Event. The End command *does not trigger a Form_UnLoad Event.*

Example

```
Function square (X)
    X = X * X
End Function
```

See also   QueryUnLoad; Stop; UnLoad

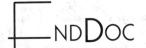 ND DOC METHOD

Description   EndDoc sends a message to Windows that closes a document being sent to the printer. This also allows Windows to clear the document out of the print spooler (Print Manager). The spooler can then start another document if one was waiting to be printed. (See more on print spoolers below.)

EndDoc signifies that a complete document has been sent from your program to the printer:

```
Printer.Print "First line of my document."
Printer.Print "Last line of my document."
Printer.EndDoc
```

This permits you to begin sending a second document. A *print spooler* is an area of memory (or space on a hard drive, or sometimes a separate dedicated peripheral). The print spooler is designed to accept and hold text or graphics on their way to the printer, and feed them to the printer without freezing your program. Since printers are relatively slow, it's often useful to "dump" a print job into a spooler in order to free up your program and let the user begin doing other things. The Windows Print Manager is, among other things, a spooler.

Used with   The printer only

Variables   Printer.EndDoc

Uses   • Abort a current printing job (see the Example)

- Start printing a second document

- Dump a document to a spooler

- If you use the EndDoc Method immediately following a NewPage Method,

```
Printer.NewPage
Printer.EndDoc
```

you can avoid that annoying problem of printing a blank page at the end of a document.

Example   If your program is capable of feeding long documents to the printer, you may want to add an abort feature so the user can step in to cancel printing.

In the General Declarations section of a Form, use the Dim command to create a Variable that will be accessible to all the Events in the Form:

```
Dim stopit As Integer
```

Then create a Command Button whose Caption reads "CANCEL PRINT-ING" and, within that button's Click Event, put the following:

```
Sub Command1_Click ()
    stopit = 1
End Sub
```

This is an artificial test; we'll print bogus data, but it illustrates the abort-print technique. Create a second Command Button and change its Name to *Printbutton*. This Button will trigger a simulation of printing a five-page document:

```
Sub PrintButton_Click ()

For z = 65 To 125
    c$ = c$ + Chr$(z)
Next z

For I = 1 To 5
    printer.Print printer.page
        For j = 1 To 40
                printer.Print c$
                x = DoEvents()
                    If stopit = 1 Then
                            printer.EndDoc
                            Exit Sub
                    End If
        Next j
    printer.NewPage
    Print "THIS PAGE"; I
Next I

End Sub
```

When you start this printing job, VB will start feeding the printer 40 of the fake lines of characters we created and put them into the Variable c$. The DoEvents command will check to see if anything else is happening at the time in Windows (namely that we clicked on the Button labeled CANCEL PRINTING). If we do click on that Abort Button, the Variable *stopit* will be changed to 1, and our For...Next Loop here will send an EndDoc command, and get out of both the Loop and the whole Event.

Note that the Priority setting in the Print Manager's Option Menu will have an effect on the speed with which you can abort a print job.

See also   KillDoc; NewPage; Page; Print; PrintForm

 NVIRON$

FUNCTION

Description   Environ$ gives you information about the user's system, in particular such definitions as the PATH, PROMPT and SET instructions (usually found in the AUTOEXEC.BAT file).

Variables   There are two ways to provide Variables to Environ$:

A request for a particular environment item (the item must be in capital letters): X$ = Environ$("TEMP")

OR a request for one of the items by its position in the list of items:

X$ = Environ$(2)

X$ will contain the second item in the environment list.

Uses   • To VB users, probably the most helpful information in the environment string is the user's path and the location, if any, of a TEMP space. Many people identify a place on the system where data can be stored temporarily. This is usually a RAM drive because it's far faster than a disk drive; and because when the computer is turned off, the RAM drive contents go away by themselves so they don't unnecessarily fill up the hard drive. Some commercial programs also use this information to speed up their programs. Candidates for TEMP storage space are multiple backup copies of a document, backups of the most recently deleted items (so there can be an Undo feature), etc. However, be aware that it's dangerous to save the *only* backup in a RAM drive–if the power goes off, there goes all the data in the RAM drive.

Putting the following statements in the computer's AUTOEXEC.BAT file tells any interested application to store temporary things in drive D:. If your program needs to store large amounts of data temporarily, store it in the place on the user's system that has been identified in this way:

```
SET TEMP=D:\
SET TEM=D:\
```

• Of less, but still practical, value is the PATH information (see "Cautions").

Cautions   • The first environment Variable will identify the location of the active COMMAND.COM file, one of DOS's important support files.

• You will likely find a PATH statement, showing the user's defined preferred path. There are two meanings to the word *path* in PC jargon. *The path* is a list of directories that the user has supplied in the AUTOEXEC.BAT file. It tells the computer that if a filename (and only the filename) is typed in at the DOS command (or requested from within a Windows program), the computer should look for that file in one of the disk directories specified in the path:

PATH=C:\NDW;C:\N;C:\DOS;C:\;C:\WINDOWS;C:\BATCH;C:\UTILS

A path, however, is the specific drive and directory that are appended to a filename during a disk access from DOS or Windows:

C:\WINDOWS\PROGMAN.EXE

• Sometimes commercial programs also utilize the environment Variable to hold a Variable or two of their own.

• If you request an item by name, you must use all uppercase letters ("PATH").

• If you request an item from Environ$ by position in the list, note that there is no 0 item. Start with item 1.

• If the environment item name (or item position) you request does not exist, the Environ$ Function will give you back an empty text ("string") Variable. (X$ = "")

• Important: If you use a RAM drive as your TEMP drive, Windows will probably crash if this temporary buffer (the RAM drive) overflows because too much is put into it. This is known to occur in programs such as AmiPro or CorelDRAW that can store up to 16 megabytes in their TEMP storage locations when they are working with particularly complex objects.

Microsoft does not recommend the use of a RAM drive as a TEMP drive unless you can allocate at least four megabytes of RAM. At this time, setting aside this much computer memory is difficult to do. You would need to have well over 8mb of extended memory to afford giving up that much space inside the machine.

Example 1

```
Sub Form_Click ()
Do

    c = c + 1
    x$ = Environ$(c)
            If x$ = "" Then Exit Do
    Print c; "."; x$
Loop

End Sub
```

Results in   (The exact result, of course, will depend on the environment settings of your particular computer.)

1. COMSPEC=C:\NDOS.COM
2. CMDLINE=win:
3. PATH=C:\NDW;C:\N;C:\DOS;C:\;C:\WINDOWS;C:\BATCH;
   C:\UTILS;C:\VBASIC\VBTOOLS;D:\;C:\BOOK\REFERENC
4. NU=C:\N
5. PROMPT=$p $s
6. TEMP=D:\
7. TEM=D:\
8. NBACKUP=C:\NBACKUP
9. windir=C:\WINDOWS

Any of the words to the left of the = sign (COMSPEC, NU, NBACKUP, etc.) are usable in the next example as Variables for the Environ$. Of course, there are other possible Variables on other computers.

Example 2   To find out the location of a TEM or TEMP area that you can use for your own purposes:

```
Sub Form_Click ()
X$ = Environ$("TEMP")
End Sub
```

Results in   The result, on my computer, is a RAM drive D:\

Now you can use X$ to save data to the disk location designated as a temporary zone:

```
AFileName$ = X$ + AFileName$
Open AFileName$ For Output As #1 ...etc.
```

See also   CurDir$; EXEName; Path

FUNCTION

Description   When you're pulling information into your program from within an opened file, EOF lets you know when you've reached the end of the file. That way, you don't keep on trying to get nonexistent information, or cause an error. EOF (and EOFAction) are also Properties of the Data Control, which see.

Used with   Opened disk files

Variables   To know when we've reached the end of the file Opened "As #1":

```
If EOF(1) = True Then
```

(This can also be shortened to:)

```
If EOF(1) Then
```

Uses • When used with sequential files, EOF tells you that the last character or item of data has been reached. (See "Input$" for more on sequential file access.)

• When used with random-access or binary files, EOF tells you that the most recent GET Statement failed to find another complete item. (See "Open" for more on random and binary file access.)

Cautions Programmers frequently use this statement structure with EOF:

```
Do While Not EOF(4)
```

(Here you would insert commands that read from, or write to, the file that was previously Opened As #4.)

```
Loop
```

This is equivalent to:

```
Do While EOF(4) <> 0   (as long as EOF(4) doesn t equal zero)
```

Example This example reads the CONFIG.SYS file and prints the user's FILES and BUFFERS settings on the window (the Form):

```
Sub Form_Click ()

PATHNAME$ = "C:\CONFIG.SYS"

If Dir$(PATHNAME$) <> "" Then
        Open PATHNAME$ For Input As #1
    Do While Not EOF(1)
        Line Input #1, X$
        If InStr(x$, "files") Then Print X$
        If InStr(x$, "buffers") Then Print X$
    Loop
Else
    Print PATHNAME$; "doesn t exist."
    Print "Please change PATHNAME$ and try again."
End If

Close
End Sub
```

Notes • Dir$, if empty (""), means that the file cannot be found, so we do what's in the Else section.

• Line Input # is a quick way to pull complete lines of text in from a file. A *line* is all the characters between the start of a line of text and the *Carriage Return* (the user pressed the ENTER key). Every time you hit the ENTER key, an invisible but highly useful *Carriage Return* character is inserted into a text string. These carriage returns are saved along with your text in most kinds of files.

• The InStr (in-string) command looks through a text ("string") Variable for a particular word or other specified series of characters or digits.

• The CTRL+Z character (ASCII 26) and the null character (ASCII 0) will trigger an EOF, even if there are characters or data in the file beyond that point. To avoid this, open the file AS BINARY (see "Open").

See also   Close; FileDateTime; Get; Input #; Input$; Line Input #; Loc; LOF; Open; Path; Seek

See "Open" for a complete discussion of file access.

See "Data" for a discussion of database management and the EOFAction and BOF commands.

ERASE

STATEMENT

Description   The Erase command works two ways, depending on whether it's applied to a *Static* or a *Dynamic* Array.

• With Static Arrays, Erase resets all the Array elements to zero (if they're numeric Variables), to "Empty" (if they're Variants), to "Nothing" (if they're Objects) or to "" (blank text Variables).

• With Dynamic Arrays, Erase collapses the entire Array structure and gives the computer back the use of the memory that the Array had occupied.

Even after Erase, a Static Array still exists like an empty honeycomb. A Dynamic Array after Erase, however, no longer exists.

• In an Array of Variants (which see), each element is reset to "Empty." In an Array of Objects (which see), each item is reset to "Nothing." In a programmer-defined Array (see "Type"), each element is reset according to its Variable type.

Used with   Arrays (which see)

Variables   Erase Letter$

Uses   • Free up computer memory for other uses when a Dynamic Array is no longer needed by your program.

• Make sure that a Static Array is completely clean, completely free of items.

Cautions
• Note that we declared the entire Subroutine in the example below as Static. Without being declared Static, all the Variables (including Arrays) within this Event (this Subroutine) would be temporary—dynamic when the Event is triggered but discarded when the program moves on to another Event. (The exceptions would be Arrays or Variables declared outside the Event with the Global or Dim commands, or Arrays or Variables declared inside the Event with the Static command: Static ThisVariable As Integer.)

With Static applied to the entire Event, however, all the Variables within it are permanent, persistent and stable as long as the program is running. That is, you can vary in the numbers (or text) they hold, but the Variable names, the memory space they reserve *and the data they hold* will not be destroyed when the program moves on to other Events.

Using Static is the only way to use a Dim Statement to build an Array within a Subroutine. Without Static, you have to use Redim (which creates dynamic, temporary Arrays).

Aside from using the Static command, you can also create permanent Arrays by putting a Dim Statement in the General Declarations section of a Form (or Module), thereby making the Array available for use by all procedures (Events, Subroutines or Functions) within that Form. Or, to make Variables or Arrays available to *all* areas, all Forms and Modules, in your program, declare an Array using the Global command within a Module.

For more information, see "Arrays."

Example
```
Static Sub Form_Click ()

Dim Test(1 To 20) As Integer

For i = 1 To 20
    Test(i) = i
    Print Test(i);
Next i

Erase Test
    Print "Erase Test ()"
    Print "Now the Test Array is Filled with Zeros..."

For i = 1 To 20
    Print Test(i);
Next i
End Sub
```

Results in
```
1 2 3 4 5 6 7 8 9 10 11 12 13 14 15 16 17 18 19 20
Erase Test ()
Now the Test Array is Filled with Zeros...
0 0 0 0 0 0 0 0 0 0 0 0 0 0 0 0 0 0 0 0
```

Figure E-3: An entire Array can be reset with the Erase command.

See also
Arrays; Dim; Public; Redim; Static

ERR

FUNCTION

Description: Err tells you what error occurred, if any, while a program is running. Err uses VB's error code system (to look up an error number, search Help for "Trappable Errors"). However, Err can now report an outside OLE entity as the source of an error, and accomplish other tasks. It has changed in VB4, expanded, and become an object.

Used with The On Error Statement and the Error Statement

Variables In VB4, Err has become an object, like the Screen object—a built-in object with its own Properties and Methods. Fortunately, Err is still compatible with the VB3 and previous uses, which we'll now describe. At the end of this entry, we'll list the new VB4 techniques so you can exploit the new Err object.

The following is the most frequent use of Err in VB3 and earlier. If an error has occurred while the program is running, this example provides the error code, which is held in Err, to the VB Error$ command. Error$ then translates that code into a brief text explanation of the code. This explanation is then presented to the user in a Message Box:

```
If Err Then MsgBox (Error$(Err))
```

OR (to find out what error code exists, if any):

```
X = Err
```

OR (to test your program's response to errors): If you want to simulate errors to test your program's response, you can set numbers into these Variables. You can deliberately put an error code into Err, allowing you to simulate errors while testing your program. In this way, you can see how your program responds and endeavor to make it handle errors effectively and gracefully. However, the Error Statement (which see) is easier to use than this technique and accomplishes the same thing:

```
Err = X
```

OR (to reset Err so that it no longer reports or triggers an error):

```
Err = 0
```

Uses:

• For a complete discussion of error handling, see "On Error."

• Error handling or trapping means making provisions in your program should something untoward happen while it is running that could cause problems. Disk access is a frequent source of errors because you generally do not know the configuration or contents of the user's disk drives while your program runs. (Various VB commands—such as Path, Environ$, EXEName—can let you explore the user's disk drives, however.) There are other sources of errors as well–generally when you try to access a peripheral or another application.

What you want to avoid is generating an error that shuts down your program or, worse, causes the computer to freeze up and become unresponsive, requiring the power to the computer to be turned off. To a programmer, this is a catastrophic collapse of craft.

• Error$ (Err) is sometimes used within error-handling sections of a program as a way to deal with errors not specifically addressed by that error-handling section. See "On Error" for more information.

Cautions   • Err starts out with a zero in it when the program starts running. And Err is reset to zero if your program moves on to a different Event (or Subroutine or Function), or if it runs past the following Statements: Resume Next, On Error GoTo or On Error Resume Next. The On Error GoTo commands must be in the same Event (or Subroutine or Function) that generated the error you're trying to trap.

Likewise, if a new error occurs, Err is reset to that new error code. So, if you use Err, use a separate, preferably Public, Variable to maintain the number code held in Err—unless you're going to handle the error within the same Event where the error occurred and before any other errors might occur. In a Module, type this: **Public E as Integer**. Then use E as a place to save any error codes (E = Err) if you aren't (as you should) handling them within the Event, Sub or Function where the error occurs.

Example   This procedure attempts to open Disk Drive Q:, which will fail, causing an error. We store the error number from Err into our Global Variable E, so that we can access it from anywhere in the program in case you want to test or report on it elsewhere in the program. We also use the Error$ Function to provide a printed message about the nature of the error: Sub Form_Click ( ) On Error Resume Next Open "q:\test" For Input As #1 E = Err Print E X$ = Error$(E) Print X$ End Sub

Results in   68 Device Unavailable

VB4 s New Err Object

Although for compatibility with programs written in VB3 or earlier, Err still works as described above, VB4 expands its capabilities. Necessitated by the additional new OLE error codes and the trend in Visual Basic toward descriptive programming, the Err Object surpasses the older Err Function in several ways.

With OLE, interactions and side effects are multiplied. For example, which of two applications locked in an OLE conversation is responsible for a particular error—or is the error a byproduct of their conversation itself, something that happened in the tunnel that connects them through the operating system? Also, with the new descriptive style, what used to be written as CommonDlg1.Action = 3 has become CommonDialog1.ShowColor. And what used to be Print Err becomes Print Err.Number.

Now the most common use of Err can be written two ways. The old way:

```
If Err Then MsgBox Error$(Err)
```

The VB4 way:

```
If Err Then MsgBox Err.Description
```

VB4 also features default Properties. For instance, the default Property of the Text Box is the Text Property. Therefore, you can omit the default (Text1 = "This" vs. Text1.Text = "This"). The default Property of the Err object is Number, which works out well. This makes it behave as it used to in VB3 and earlier.

Beyond the Description and Number Properties, the Err Object also has HelpFile and HelpContext Properties which can be used together to display to the user an entry in a Help file.

Finally, there is the Source Property, that provides a text "string" identifying the application (or object) that generated the error. When you use OLE, more than one application or Object can be active at the same time. It's obviously helpful to know which application or Object is the source of the error. The Err.Number is provided by the container application, according to its own internal error-handling scheme. But the server application, if that's where the error took place, is identified by the Source Property. (For more information, see "Object.")

This information permits your program to attempt to cope with the error, knowing that it came from outside your program. At the very least, you could provide a message to the user, naming the offending outside application or Object.

The Source Property will report an application's OLE identifier. When you create an Object by putting some programming into a Class Module (a stand-alone, special kind of .EXE file that can be used as an OLE server) in VB, you identify the class of that object by typing a name into the Module's Class Property in the Property window (the Name defaults to Class1). You also provide a "Project Name" by clicking on the Tools menu, then selecting "Project Options." Note that this is not necessarily the same as the .MAK file name with which you save your file. Both the .MAK filename and the OLE "Project Name" default to "Project1," but you can change either without affecting the other. In any case, if an error occurs while your server object is running, the Err.Source will be "Project1.Class1" unless you've changed the default "Project Name" or the Class Module's Name Property from their defaults.

If there's an error in your VB application (as opposed to an outside application or Object) during an OLE activity, the Err.Source will be a simple "Project1" (unless you've changed this in the Tools|Project Options window).

Clear: The new Clear Method of the Err object resets Err so that it no longer reports on or triggers one of your error handlers. It's the equivalent of the Err = 0 mentioned above.

Raise: The Raise Method expands on the capabilities of the (VB3 and earlier) Error command. It can be used to fake an error—to make VB react, to test how the program responds. For suggested tactics and uses, see "Error."

> Err.Raise(Number, Source, Description, HelpFile, HelpContext)

Number is required; all the other parameters are optional, and the purpose of each is described above. Number is a long integer. VB error codes are numbered between 0 and 65535 (even error numbers that you make up for your own error-trapping purposes). However, if you want to make up an error number for an OLE object you're testing, add your error number to the built-in Constant vbObjectError. For example, if you want to generate error number 155: Err.Raise (vbObjectError + 155).

If you only include the Number parameter with Raise, any active Properties of the Err object (Err isn't 0; it contains an error) will be used as the Source and other parameters.

The primary value of Raise (when compared to the older Error command) is in testing OLE server objects that you write (Class Modules). This is because the Err object has the Source Property to identify which object or application triggered the error.

See also Appendix B; Error; Error$, Class Module, OLE Automation. See "On Error" for a discussion of error handling and error codes.

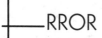

ERROR
STATEMENT

Description   Error deliberately mimics a Visual Basic error condition. VB behaves thereafter just as if the error you induced had really occurred. This allows you to test the ways your program responds to various errors and also to detect unanticipated errors. However the new Raise Method is more flexible than Error, especially for OLE programming. (See "Err.")

Used with   On Error GoTo

Variables   Error 58

Uses   • While testing your program, place an Error Statement in a potential danger spot (such as accessing the disk drive). Then run the program to see how effectively your program responds to the problem. For example, if the program tries to access drive A: but there's no disk in it, an error message will be generated. In the VB programming environment, the error will stop normal program execution and wait for you, the programmer, to fix the problem. However, in a finished .EXE program that runs by itself outside of the VB design environment, such an error would shut down your program.

The user would be returned to Windows—unless you effectively trap the error and deal with it, allowing your program to recover and continue on.

• Putting an Error statement in error-handling sections of your program alerts you to unexpected errors while you're testing your program; it provides a possible effective rescue while your program is run by a user. This process at least makes sure that *some* message will be provided to a user should the program shut down.

• For a complete discussion of error handling, see the "On Error" Statement. *Error handling* or *trapping* means making provisions in your program in case something happens while it's running to cause problems. You want to avoid generating an error that shuts down your program or, worse, causes the computer to freeze up and become unresponsive.

Cautions Although Visual Basic error codes range from 3 through 32766, only several hundred of these code numbers are actually used. (For a complete list, see Trappable Errors in VB's Help Menu.) Should you provide an unused error code, VB responds with the message "Application-defined or object-defined error."

Example This is a typical error-handling structure. First, there's the notice about where to go—a place in the Event where we've put the label *Showit*—if an error occurs (On Error GoTo Showit). Next, we use the Error Statement to *induce* a fake error. Then we Exit Sub to prevent the program from reaching the section labeled *Showit*—unless an error sends us there. The *Showit* section prints the error message, in this case a rather Kafkaesque remark, PERMISSION DENIED. Finally, the VB command Resume Next is used to send VB back up to the line *following* the error. Then we exit the Subroutine and go on with whatever else the program might have to offer:

```
Sub Form_Click ()

On Error GoTo Showit

Error 70

Exit Sub
Showit:
    Print Error$(Err)
    Resume Next
End Sub
```

See also Appendix B; Err; Error$
See "On Error" for a complete discussion of error handling.

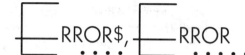 RROR$, RROR

FUNCTION

Description

While a VB program is running, an error (such as attempting to Open a file that does not exist on the disk drive) can occur. VB provides an error code (see "Err"). Error$ translates an error code into a brief descriptive phrase about the nature of the error. If you add any custom Controls to the Toolbox, they can also generate their own unique Err and Error$ messages. The codes and messages would vary from one add-on Control to another. Error$ is the equivalent of the New VB4 ERR.Description command. (See "Err.") Note that with VB4 you can use Error$ or Error interchangeably. Most commands that used to end up with a $ can now omit it (Format vs. Format$).

Used with Err

Variables

The following is the most frequent use of Error$. If an error has occurred while the program is running, this example provides the error code to the VB Error$ command. Error$ then translates that code into a brief text explanation of the code that is then presented to the user in a Message Box:

```
If Err Then MsgBox(Error$(Err))
If Err then Msgbox Err.Description
```

OR (to get a text description of the most recent error that occurred while the program is running): E$ = Error$

OR (to get a text description of the error represented by the error code in Err): E$ = Error$(Err)

Uses

• For a complete discussion of error handling, see the "On Error" Statement.

Error handling or *trapping* means making provisions in your program should something happen that could cause problems while it's running. You want to avoid generating an error that shuts down your program, or worse, causes the computer to freeze up and become unresponsive.

Cautions

• The Error$ function is often more useful to *you* while you're writing and testing a program than it is to the program's user. The user might not understand the message reported by Error$. Some kinds of errors will require rewriting a program; something a user is generally unprepared to do. However, other kinds of errors are caused by the user or because the program is, for instance, trying to access drive A: when the drive door has inadvertently been left open. When this happens, receiving a message from your program would at least allow the user to correct, or avoid, whatever behavior caused the problem. Furthermore, without such error trapping, Visual Basic would shut down your program in its tracks if an error like this should occur. With error trapping, the program can continue running and the user can close the drive door and again attempt to access drive A:.

• The exact wording of messages reported by Error$ may differ as Visual Basic evolves and new versions are distributed, but the *meaning* of the error codes will not vary. You can thus write error trapping into your programs without worrying that the traps and your built-in solutions will become obsolete.

Example

```
Sub Form_Click ()

On Error Resume Next
    Open "c:\test12.com" For Input As 1
Print Error$

End Sub
```

Results in   File Not Found (Since there is no file named "test12.com")

See also   Appendix B; Err; Error
See "On Error" for a complete discussion of error handling.

EXENAME

PROPERTY

Description   The EXEName Property applies only to the "App" Object (your entire program). EXEName reports the program's filename but leaves off the .EXE extension. Some API Routines need to know the name of your program; EXEName provides it.

You might wonder why you need to ask for a program's name since, having written the program, you already *know* the name. It is possible, however, that the user might rename the program; thus, EXEName.

Used with   App, the "application object"

Variables   You must use *App* with EXEName:

```
Print App.EXEName
```

OR

```
X$ = App.EXEName
```

Use   • To provide information required by some API Routines (see Appendix A).

• Some programmers include a self-modifying section within a program for security, password or shareware registration purposes (see the Example under "MkDir"). Using EXEName, you could be sure that you were saving the program on top of itself on the disk (in case the user had renamed the program). And using the "Path" Property would let you know where on the disk the user keeps your program.

Cautions
• If you test App.EXEName within the VB design environment, it will return the name of your project (without the .MAK extension). If you create an .EXE file and then test it, EXEName will give the name of the program, minus the .EXE extension.

• App is always required. You cannot say X$ = EXEName.

• App.EXEName can be accessed only for information; you cannot *change* the name of your program with App.EXEName = "Newname."

Example
```
Sub Form_Click ()
    Print App.EXEName
    x$ = App.EXEName
    Print x$
End Sub
```

Results in
Project1
Project1

See also
App; Appendix A; MkDir; Path

XIT .... STATEMENT

Description
Exit forces the program to leave early from a Function, Subroutine, Do...Loop or For...Next Loop.

Used with
Functions, Loops, Property Procedures and Subroutines

Variables
    Exit Do
OR
    Exit For
OR
    Exit Function
OR
    Exit Property
OR
    Exit Sub

Uses
Abort a running Loop or Procedure.

Cautions • If you nest Do...Loop or For...Next Loops:

```
For I = 1 To 50
    For J = 1 To 40
```

If *something happens, (perhaps the user presses a key)* Then Exit For
```
    Next J
Next I
```

By putting one Loop inside another, the interior Exit within the nested J Loop would only move your program back inside the I Loop. This means that more J's will again happen the next time through the I Loop. For this reason, you'll usually put an Exit Statement in the outermost nested Loop. You usually want to get out of the whole thing, not just inner Loops. However, a Loop seizes Control of the computer until it's finished Looping. For this reason, VB could not alert this Loop that the user had pressed a key—until the Loop was concluded. That would be too late. So, to permit interruptions of Loops, use the X = DoEvents( ) command:

```
For I = 1 To 50
    X = DoEvents()
        For J = 1 To 40
```

If *something happens, (perhaps the user presses a key)* Then Exit For
```
        Next J
    Next I
```

• The Exit command is perhaps most commonly used to provide several ways to get out of a Loop. Here's an example of a situation where you're searching through a piece of text. You want to quit if you come upon a special Control code (see "Chr$") or one of those Greek symbols (anything that's not a normal alphabetic character) embedded within the text.

```
Sub Form_Click ()

a$ = "This is the message."
a$ = a$ + Chr$(13) + "THIS FOLLOWS."
Print a$

L = Len(a$)
P = 1

Do
    x$ = Mid$(a$, P, 1)
            If Asc(x$) < 32 Then Exit Do
            If Asc(x$) > 126 Then Exit Do
    Print x$;
    P = P + 1
Loop Until P > L
```

First we create a Variable that includes an interior Control code: Chr$(13). While searching through each character in the Do...Loop, we check to see whether its ASC code value is less than 32 (which means it's a Control code) or above 126 (which makes it one of those symbols). In either case, we exit this Loop.

Example   In a Module, define a Public Variable—this makes the Variable available to be used by all areas of the program:

```
Public Kp As Integer
```

In the KeyPress Event, we'll have the program change Kp to 1 if the user presses a key. (All Variables start out with a default of 0 when your program first runs.):

```
Sub Form_KeyPress (KeyAscii As Integer)
    Kp = 1
End Sub
```

Then, in the Form_Load Procedure, put a couple of Loops and keep checking to see if the user pressed a key; to see if Kp changed to 1. If it does, we'll Exit the For...Next Loop:

```
Sub Form_Load ()

Show
For I = 1 To 5000
    For J = 1 To 20
        Print J;
    Next J
  Cls
  x% = DoEvents()
  If KP = 1 Then
    Print "Keypress"
    Exit For
  End If
Next I
End Sub
```

Recall that the DoEvents( ) Function prevents these Loops from taking control of the computer until they have finished. DoEvents( ) briefly lets events outside your program take place (so, for example, another program could run simultaneously, keypresses can be detected, printing can go on, the screen can be updated, etc.).

See also   End; Stop

Exp

FUNCTION

Description   Calculates e, the base of a natural log, to the power of x.

Used with   Scientific and advanced mathematical calculations

Variables   You can provide Exp with any numeric expression. (See "Variables" for a definition of "expression.")

To calculate using a Variable:

```
E = Exp(X)
```

OR (to use a literal number): E = Exp(2.5)

Uses
- Scientific calculators
- Calculating log values. This is used to calculate decibels, log charts and for many other scientific applications.

Cautions
- The exponent [the number inside the parentheses in Exp (X)] cannot be larger than 88.02969 if you're using Single-Precision Variables, or 709.782712893 with Double-Precision numbers.
- If you give Exp a Single-Precision or Integer Variable, it will calculate e with single-precision arithmetic. In all other cases, Exp is Double-Precision. See "Variables" for more information on precision.

Example
```
Sub Form_Click ()

E# = Exp(1)
Print E#
Singlep% = Exp(1)
Print Singlep%

End Sub
```

Results in   2.71828182845905
3

See also   Log; Sqr

FETCHVERBS

METHOD

See   OLE

FILE LIST BOX

CONTROL

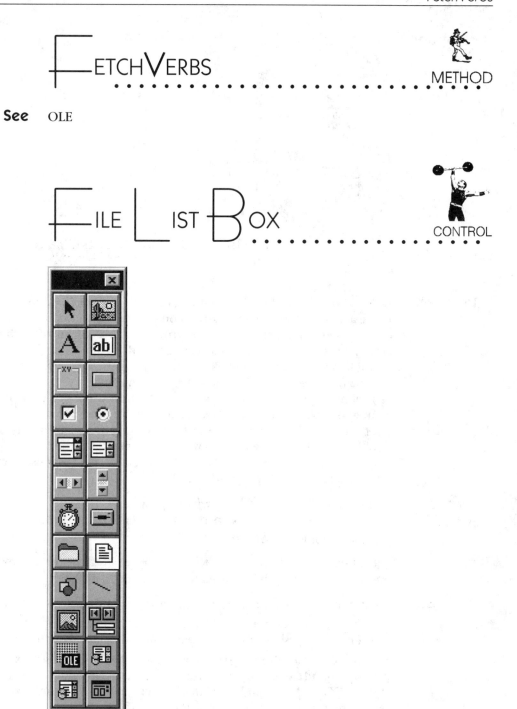

Figure F-1: The File List Box symbol in the Toolbox.

Description

Figure F-2: A File List Box displays an ordered list of the files in the "current" directory, in standard Windows format.

Used with   Drive, Directory and File List Boxes can work together to allow the user to move across all the filenames stored on disk drives throughout his or her computer system. Similarly, if your program needs information about files stored on the user's system, you can create these Boxes, make them invisible by setting their Visible Properties to False and accessing the information they provide while your program runs.

By convention, a DblClick Event selects a new drive or a new directory from within those Boxes. A double-click also triggers a Change Event. A double-click within the File List Box opens (or otherwise targets) the double-clicked file. However, your program must include instructions to respond in these ways to a DblClick Event, since that response is not built into Visual Basic For a File List Box.

Variables   To find out the current "path" while a program is running. For example: C:\WINDOWS is a complete path, including drive and directory:

    SelectedFile$ = File1.Path

OR (to switch the File List Box to the drive selected by the user by clicking on a Drive List Box while a program is running): File1.Path = Drive1.Drive

Uses   • Manipulate files—save, open and access files on the user's disk drives.

• Provide information—show the attributes of the files, or selectively display a list of only those files with particular attributes (see the Example).

• With the Pattern Property (which is unique to the File List Box Control), you can provide selective lists based on the familiar DIR DOS wildcards (*.* or *.TXT or *.EXE, and so forth). You can also use multiple patterns by separating them with a semicolon (*.*; *.TXT; *.EXE).

• See "Drive List Box" for a complete example of a VB file management system.

Cautions

• It is common practice in Windows applications to highlight an item in a File List Box when the user touches it with a single mouse click. The File List Box will do this for you automatically. You might want this highlighting to then cause a Text Box to show the size of the file or its "attributes" (hidden, read-only, etc.). A double-click, however, generally results in a more extensive response in Windows, some *action* rather than merely a display of information. For example, a double-click might open the selected file or save a file.

• Unhappily, the term "attribute" is used two ways in PC computerese. It generally refers to the five possible file states in DOS—Archive, Hidden, Normal (sometimes called User), ReadOnly and System. See "Archive" for more information. However, attribute is also used to refer to the five possible states of an opened file—Input, Output, Random Access, Append and Binary. See "FileAttr" for more information.

Example

Figure F-3: You can selectively display only files of a particular type   in this example, Hidden files.

The following combination of attribute Properties for the File1 File List Box causes only the Hidden files to be listed in the box. (See "Archive.")

```
Sub Form_Load ()

ChDir "c:\windows"

file1.archive = False
file1.normal = False
file1.hidden = True

End Sub
```

File List Box Properties

Archive • BackColor • DragIcon • DragMode • Enabled • FileName FontBold • FontItalic • FontName • FontSize • FontStrikethru FontUnderline • ForeColor • Height • HelpContextID • Hidden hWnd • Index • Left • List • ListCount • ListIndex • MousePointer MultiSelect • Name • Normal • Parent • Path • Pattern • ReadOnly Selected • System • TabIndex • TabStop • Tag • Top • TopIndex Visible • Width

File List Box Events

Click • DblClick • DragDrop • DragOver • GotFocus • KeyDown KeyPress • KeyUp • LostFocus • MouseDown • MouseMove MouseUp • PathChange • PatternChange

File List Box Methods

Drag • Move • Refresh • SetFocus • ZOrder

See also AppActivate; Archive; Change; ChDir; ChDrive; Close; CurDir$; Dir$; Drive; EOF; EXEName; FileAttr; FileName; FreeFile; Get; Hidden; Input$; Input #; Kill; Line Input #; List; ListCount; ListIndex; Loc; Lock; LOF; MkDir; Name; Normal; On Error; Open; Path; PathChange; Pattern; Pattern-Change; Print #; Put; ReadOnly; Reset; RmDir; Seek; Shell; System; Unlock; Write # (All are VB commands related to file management.)

See "Drive List Box" for a lengthy example of file management using all three file control tools—Drive, Directory and File List Boxes.

FILEATTR

FUNCTION

Description FileAttr is used with opened disk files in two ways:

• FileAttr tells you what *mode* an opened file is in (Input, Output, Random Access, Append or Binary).

OR

• FileAttr can give you the *handle* (a unique identification number) used by the operating system to identify this file. This is not the same as the VB filenumber (the *3* in Open "FILENAME" As #3), which is an identification used by VB and your program but not by the operating system.

Variables

Here, since we're using the number 1 in the parentheses, X will contain the mode of the file previously opened by the program as #12.

X = FileAttr(12, 1)

The meaning of the mode is described by the following list:

1	Input
2	Output
4	Random Access
8	Append
32	Binary

OR (now that we're using the number 2 in the parentheses, X will tell us the operating system handle): X = FileAttr(12, 2)

Uses

• See "Open" for a thorough discussion on manipulating the information stored in files.

Mode

If you need to know the mode of an opened file, FileAttr can tell you while your program runs, although, since you designed your program and the program itself must open a file in one of these modes, it's hard to imagine that you wouldn't know which mode you opened with.

Perhaps in a rare situation your program would open multiple files in different modes, and a common Subroutine would be used for data manipulation. In such a case, you could pass the file number to the Subroutine and use the FileAttr function to find out what mode the file was in and how to work with it.

Handle

There are some API "calls" (_lread, _lwrite, _lseek, etc.) that use this Handle; but it's unlikely that you would use these calls instead of the VB file commands. See Appendix A for information on the API.

Example

```
Sub Form_Click ()

Open "test" For Output As #14
    X = FileAttr(14, 1)
    Print X

    Y = FileAttr(14, 2)
```

```
        Print Y
        Close 14
        End Sub
```

Results in   2 (the Output mode)
             5 (the system handle)

See also   Archive
          See "Open" for a general discussion of file access and modes in VB.

STATEMENT

Description   FileCopy allows the user (or your program) to make copies of disk files.

Used with   Disk files

Variables   To copy a file from within the current directory to another filename in the same directory:

        FileCopy Source.Doc, Target.Doc

OR (to copy from one directory to another, you must include path information): FileCopy C:\Mydir\Source.Doc, C:\Utils\Target.Doc

OR (to use Variables): FileCopy S$, T$

Uses   Use FileCopy as part of a general disk-access and file-management option in your program. In combination with a List Box with its MultiSelect Property on, you can allow the user to copy or move groups of files as well.

Cautions   • Whenever your program accesses the user's disk drive, you must always take steps to prevent errors from shutting down your VB program. (See "On Error.")

• All the rules that apply to DOS file-copying apply to copying files in Windows: you cannot copy an Opened file (unless it was Opened for "read-only") (see "Open"); and you cannot use the same source and target filename to copy a file on top of itself within the same directory, etc.

• FileCopy requires that the Source and Target filenames used contain no "wild cards" (? or *).

• As in DOS, replacing a file by using a target filename that already exists generates no error. You might want to use a File List Box (see "List"), therefore, to see if the target filename the user has supplied already exists. If so, warn the user that an existing file is about to be destroyed.

Example

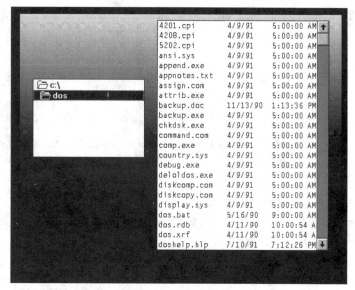

Figure F-4: Provide additional disk file information.

Put a File List Box on a Form; then type the following into the Form's Click Event:

```
Sub Form_Click ()
    ChDir "C:\"
    FileCopy "autoexec.bat", "autoexec.bk"
    File1.Path = "C:\"
    File1.Pattern = "a*.*"
End Sub
```

Press F5 to run this program and notice the new file, "autoexec.bk."

See also   Drive List Box (for a general discussion of file management in VB); Kill; Name (Statement)

 ILEDATETIME

FUNCTION

Description   FileDateTime tells you the date and time that a file was created or most recently modified.

Used with   Disk files

Variables   **Variable type:** Text ("string")

To get the date/time data on a particular file:

```
f$ = FileDateTime("c:\vb2\hc\bullet.bmp")
```

OR (to use a Variable):

```
X$ = "c:\vb2\hc\bullet.bmp"
f$ = FileDateTime(X$)
```

OR (to use in an expression): Print FileDateTime("c:\vb2\hc\bullet.bmp")

Uses   Use FileDateTime as part of a general disk-access and file-management option in your program. See "Drive List Box" for a general discussion of file management in VB.

Cautions   • You cannot use wild cards (* or ?) within the filename.

• The path is optional, but without it the filename must be in the current directory.

Example   We'll create a formatted file directory list (using a List Box instead of a File List Box to display date and time information for each file). First, we put a Shape on the Form and fill it with a color gradient .BMP picture as a background. Then put a File List Box, Directory List Box and List Box on the Form. Set the File Box's Visible property to False. We'll use the File Box because it's a quick way to get a list of the filenames in a directory. But we won't display it because we want to add date/time info to the filenames.

When the user double-clicks on the Directory Box, we want to display the new list of files. So, type the following into the Change Event of the Directory Box:

```
Sub Dir1_Change ()

list1.Clear
list1.FontName = "monospaced"
s$ = Space$(20)
file1.Path = dir1.Path

For i = 0 To file1.ListCount − 1
    x$ = file1.List(i)
    p$ = file1.Path
    If Right$(p$, 1) <> "\" Then p$ = p$ + "\"
    ss$ = Left$(s$, 15 − Len(x$))
    fd$ = FileDateTime(p$ + x$): l = Len(fd$)
    pr = InStr(fd$, " ")
If pr <> 0 Then
    d$ = Left$(fd$, pr − 1): t$ = Right$(fd$, l − pr)
Else
    d$ = fd$: t$ = ""
End If
    sss$ = Left$(s$, 10 − Len(d$))
    list1.AddItem x$ + ss$ + d$ + sss$ + t$
Next i
End Sub
```

First, we clear out any previous contents in the List Box and then set its FontName to monospaced so we can format the filename and the date and time information in neat columns. (You can set the FontName in the Properties Window instead.) Then we create a text Variable, s$, which will hold 20 space characters that we'll use to line up each entry in neat columns.

Now we get to the Loop that primarily deals with creating neat columns. We get each filename (List(i)) and the path. We make the usual adjustment to the path, adding "\" if necessary (see "Drive List Box"). Then we create ss$, which will hold the correct number of spaces to move the date 15 spaces from the left side of the List Box. (No filename can be larger than 12 characters, but some are shorter.) Next, we put the file's date/time information into Variable fd$ using the InStr command to find the space between the date information and the time information. If the Variable pr is 0, there was no time information (a current bug in VB refuses to report the time if it is 12 AM).

Finally, we create another TAB-like space in sss$ to go between the date and time data. We want the time to be 10 spaces from the start of the date data, so we subtract the length of the date information from 10. And then we add the entire filename+spacer+date+spacer+time to the List Box and loop back through to pick up the next filename and process it the same way.

To add file *size* information, you could open each file, use the LOF command to get its size and then close it.

See also   Drive List Box (for a general discussion on file handling in VB).

FILENAME
PROPERTY

Description   FileName causes a filename to be "selected" (highlighted) within a File List Box. The FileName Property also allows you or the user to provide a drive, directory or "pattern" (such as *.WRI)—and then the File List Box contents react to your new specification. This is very like the "DIR Filename" command in DOS.

Like many Visual Basic Properties, FileName is bi-directional: it can make a change to the associated Control, as described above, or it can tell you the current status of the Property. It's the difference between FileName = X$ and X$ = FileName. Sometimes the latter information is needed; more often, it's superfluous because it's already obvious. With FileName, it's likely that you'll never need to request the status, since the more useful List(ListIndex) Property offers the same information. Also, you'll want to detect changes the user makes to the File List Box within its Click and DblClick Events so you can respond at once.

Used with File List Boxes only

Variables **Variable type:** Text (string)

(The FileName Property cannot be adjusted via the Properties Window while you're designing your program.)

To change the filename pattern used by a File List Box. This pattern will show all files on the current directory: File1.FileName = "*.*"

OR (to change the Pattern, Path and Drive Properties. The File List Box now redraws to show all files whose names end in .EXE in the Windows directory): File1.FileName = "C:\WINDOWS*.EXE"

OR (to find out the FileName Property while the program is running. X$ now contains the FileName Property): X$ = File1.FileName

Uses • Allow the user or your program to specify, with the ? and * DOS DIR wildcards, what filenames will show in a File List Box.

• Allow the user or program to adjust the drive or directory being listed in a File List Box, without having to use Drive or Directory List Boxes.

• Use it in a File List Box's DblClick Event to read or otherwise access a particular file. When you use the DblClick Event in this way, the FileName Property will contain the highlighted filename. The List(ListIndex) command can also give you this same information.

Cautions • If in changing the FileName Property you change the path (C:\WINDOWS to C:\DOS), you trigger a PathChange Event in the File List Box. If you change the file specification pattern (*.TXT to *.DOC), you will trigger a PatternChange Event.

• If you set the FileName to a filename that is within the File List Box (even if the filename cannot be seen onscreen), you trigger a DblClick Event, and you highlight (select) that filename. The File List Box goes blank, removing all other filenames.

Example When the user hits the ENTER key, whatever was entered in the text box is sent to the File List Box's FileName Property, which immediately changes the contents of the File List Box. This is similar to the effect of typing DOS commands like DIR FILE *.*.

```
Sub Text1_KeyPress (keyascii As Integer)

If keyascii = 13 Then
    file1.filename = text1.text
End If
End Sub
```

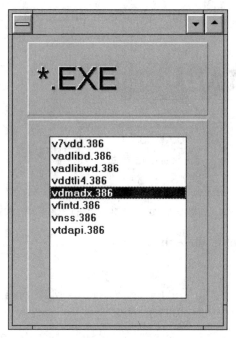

Figure F-5: The user can decide which file specification will be used to determine the displayed filenames.

See also   File List Box; Path; PathChange; Pattern; PatternChange

See "Drive List Box" for a lengthy example of file management using all three file control tools—Drive, Directory and File List Boxes.

Description   FillColor establishes the color that will be used to fill any circles or rectangles you create with the Circle and Line drawing commands or the interior of the Shape Control. However, when using FillColor *you must always first set FillStyle to 0* (adjust the FillStyle in the Properties Window or within your program: FillStyle = 0). Otherwise, FillStyle will default to 1 (Transparent), and you'll be puzzled when circles or rectangles or shapes are not filled with color, even though you've adjusted the FillColor Property. (Other FillStyles create colored patterns.)

Used with   Forms, Picture Boxes, the Printer and the Shape Control

Variables   **Variable type:** Long

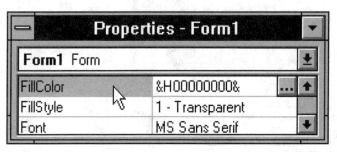

Figure F-6: Sometimes you'll set the color in the Properties Window of a Control.

OR (to change the color while the program runs):

```
Picture1.FillColor = QBColor (3)
```

You can change colors on the fly; each drawn object on a window (Form) can be filled with a different color. See the second item in Cautions.

Uses   Using FillColor you can create attractive background patterns on your windows without suffering the memory and speed penalties imposed when you use the Picture Property to provide graphics.

Cautions   • FillColor will not have a visible effect unless you first change the FillStyle Property from its default (1) to another setting (0 or 2–7). The default for FillStyle is 1 (Transparent).

• Since there is only one FillColor Property for a Picture Box or Form, it would seem that all objects would have to be filled with the same color. Fortunately, you can change the FillColor between each Circle or Line command, and each will be filled with the new color specified.

• There are several Properties that contribute to the look of a drawn box or circle. The Line and Circle commands themselves can include a color specification in the list of Variables you provide to them, but that specification determines only the color of the drawn object's *outline*. (If you don't provide this optional outline color Variable, the ForeColor Property determines the color of the outline.) FillColor, however, determines the color that fills the whole *interior* of the object.

The width of a drawn object's outline is determined by the DrawWidth Property. Whether the outline is solid, dashed, dotted, etc., is determined by the DrawStyle Property. How the drawn object interacts with the BackColor (inverting or combining colors, etc.) or a bitmap picture (icon, .BMP or .WMF that was imported using the Picture Property) is determined by the DrawMode Property. The FillStyle Property can create various interior textures—lines, diagonal lines, crosshatches, etc.

- If, for some reason, you want to duplicate the color selection that the user has selected as Windows default colors (the Control Panel Color settings), you'll need to load in the Constant.TXT file that comes with VB. Select the Code Menu, then Load Text. Within Constant.TXT is a list of Windows color Constants from which you can choose. Whatever the user has done to adjust these colors will be reflected in the FillColor.

- You can specify the color with QBColor, RGB or the new VB4 color constants. Press F2, select VB in the "Libraries" list, then select Constants in the "Classes" list. Look for names such as vbBlue and vbWhite.

Example

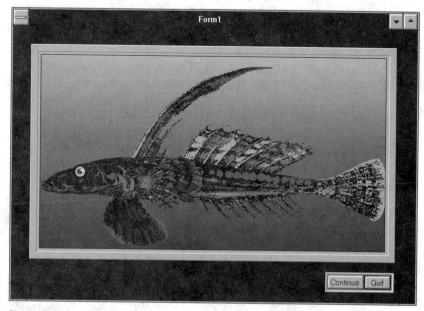

Figure F-7: Create various background designs by randomizing the qualities of a single shape. Here we use a randomized "fish scale" pattern as a background for the picture.

You can generate attractive backgrounds by randomizing a single element of the three RGB numbers. Here we're going to create the "Blue Marlin Fish Scale" texture—immensely popular as bathroom wallpaper during the early 1970s—by turning off red and green then randomly selecting the blues. We also cause the circles to overlap like scales by making the Circle command's radius Variable smaller than its X and Y positions.

```
Sub Form_Load ()

Show

Randomize

fillstyle = 0
```

```
For i = 0 To 42
        For j = 0 To 29
                randomblue% = Int(255 * Rnd + 1)
                FillColor = RGB(0, 0, randomblue%)
                Circle (200 * i, 200 * j), 150, , , , 1
    Next j, i
    drawframeon graphic1, graphic1, "outward", 200
    drawframeon graphic1, graphic1, "inward", 60
    drawframeon command1, command2, "outward", 45
    drawframeon command1, command2, "inward", 25
    graphic1.filename = "c:\book\bmps\fish.pcx"
    End Sub
```

(If the AutoRedraw Property is off (0), the circles will be lost if another window covers this one up.)

We used Deluxe Paint II to color a scanned black-and-white image of a fish. The DrawFrameOn Routine, which creates "machined" frames around Controls, is described in the entry on the Line command.

See also   BackColor; Circle; DrawMode; DrawStyle; DrawWidth; FillStyle; ForeColor; Line; QBColor; RGB; Shape

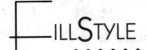

PROPERTY

Description   Creates patterns—horizontal, vertical, and diagonal lines and crosshatches—for the interior fill of drawn circles, boxes and Shape Controls. Also determines whether changing a Grid's Text Property changes only the active cell or all selected cells.

Used with   Forms, Grids, Picture Boxes, the printer and Shapes

Variables   **Variable type:** Integer (enumerated)

You can set the FillStyle in the Properties Window while designing your program.

OR (to set the FillStyle while the program is running): Form1.FillStyle = 3

OR (to find out a Picture Box's FillStyle while the program is running):

    X = Picture1.FillStyle

Here are the codes used by FillStyle for drawing:

0   Solid

1   Transparent (No fill—the Default)

2   Horizontal Line

3   Vertical Line

4   Upward Diagonal

5   Downward Diagonal

6   Cross

7   Diagonal Cross

Here are the codes used by the Grid Control:

0   A change to the Text Property affects only the active cell.

1   Affects all selected cells.

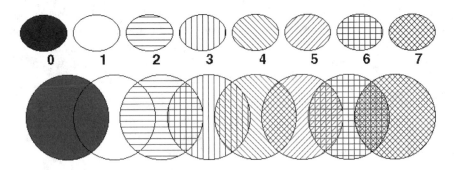

Figure F-8: You can draw more than once on the same space. By overlapping FillStyles you generate new textures.

Here is the program for the example above:

```
Sub Form_Load ()

Show

currenty = 600
fillcolor = QBColor(5)

For i = 0 To 7
        form1.fillstyle = i
        Circle Step(900, 0), 400, , , , , .75
        xx = currentx: yy = currenty
        currenty = currenty + 300
        Print i
        currentx = xx: currenty = yy + 600
Next i

currentx = 500
currenty = 2000
```

```
fillcolor = QBColor(13)

For i = 0 To 7
    form1.fillstyle = i
    Circle Step(800, 0), 700
Next i

End Sub
```

Uses   Create various patterns on the background of a Form, Picture Box or on the printer. Determine how the Text Property behaves in a Grid Control.

Cautions   • Changing the FillStyle is essential if you expect to see colors within boxes and circles drawn with the Line and Circle commands, or with Shape Controls. Oddly, FillStyle defaults to Transparent (style 1). You must set FillStyle = 0 (or adjust it in the Properties Window). The 0 changes the FillStyle to Solid so you can see it.

• If you're filling a box, use the B (Box) option with the Line command, *but do not use the BF (Box Fill) option*. Using BF fills the box solid with the *outline* color. (An outline of a box is the ForeColor Property of a Form or Picture Box, but it can also be adjusted in the optional color Variable that you can provide to the Line command.) If you want to use different colors and patterns within a box, leave off the F option when you use the Line command. See the Example.

Example 1   This herringbone pattern is created by alternating the two diagonal Fill-Styles in boxes drawn all over the screen. We didn't want the box outlines to show, just the fill; so we set the box outline colors to QBColor 15 (white) on a BackColor of white.

Figure F-9: Alternating diagonal fills create the herringbone background for this graphic viewer program.

```
Sub Form_Load ()
Show
fillstyle = 5: FillColor = RGB(0, 0, 0)

For x = 0 To 32
    If fillstyle = 5 Then
            fillstyle = 4
    Else
            fillstyle = 5
    End If

For y = 0 To 22
    Line (300 * x, 300 * y)—Step(350, 350), QBColor(15), B
Next y, x

End Sub
```

Example 2

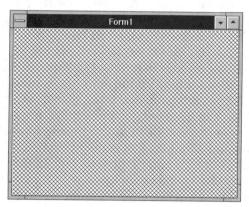

Figure F-10: The quickest way to create a background while a program is running is to fill a window with one FillStyle.

To fill an entire Form with a single FillStyle, use the ScaleHeight, Scale-Width, ScaleTop and ScaleLeft Properties. They define the dimensions of the whole Form (or Picture Box or Printed page). Create a single box based on these dimensions. This is the fastest way to texture a background.

```
Sub Form_Load ()
Show
fillstyle = 7
Line (scaleleft, scaletop)-(scaleleft + scalewidth, scaletop + scaleheight), →
    QBColor(15), B
End Sub
```

See also   Circle; FillColor; Grid; Line; Shape; Show

FINANCIAL FUNCTIONS

With Version 3.0, a set of Functions that provide some of the features of a financial calculator has been added to VB. Accountants and others involved in the mathematics of business can now use VB to build customizable financial calculating tools.

Variables

Because these are all Functions, you provide the data, and the Function "returns" an answer. For example, to figure out the total amount of interest you'll be paying for your home mortgage over the life of the loan, you must provide the following information: interestrate, paymentrange, totalperiods, presentvalue, futurevalue, whendue. Then the IPmt Function can give you the total interest that will be paid over the life of that loan.

Here's how: The *interestrate* is the interest rate of your loan and should be expressed as the *rate per month* because you pay monthly. Because you'll probably know the interest in terms of an annual rate, divide by 12. Our rate is 11%, so the *rate* figure should be .11 (the interest rate) / 12 (the months in a year). The resulting rate is .00917. (We'll use the name *irate* for interest rate Variable in this Function because VB has a command called *Rate*, which see later in this section. You can't name a Variable using a word that VB already uses for one of its built-in commands.)

The *paymentrange* is how much of the total time of the loan you want to figure the interest for. We'll use a For...Next Loop for this calculation, so the *paymentrange Variable* will change dynamically when we're calculating, moving us through the entire life of the loan.

The *totalperiods* is the number of times you pay the mortgage over the life of the loan. Ours is a 15-year mortgage, and we pay monthly. So the *totalperiods* is 15 * 12 (which results in 180).

The *presentvalue* means the total amount you're borrowing. Our house cost $50,000, but you should express this number as a negative, so it's −50000.

The *futurevalue* is the cash balance you want to have at the end of the mortgage. For loans, futurevalue is zero.

The *whendue* figure is either 1 or 0. It's 1 if payments are due at the beginning of each month; it's 0 if payments are due at the end of each month. We pay at the end, so whendue is 0.

Now that we've answered these questions, we can run the program to calculate the interest:

```
Sub Form_Click
irate = .00917
totalperiods = 180
presentvalue = -50000
futurevalue = 0
```

```
whendue = 0

For paymentrange = 1 to totalperiods
Tempinterest = IPmt(irate, paymentrange, totalperiods, presentvalue, →
    futurevalue, whendue)
Totalinterest = Totalinterest + Tempinterest
Next paymentrange
Print "The total that you'll pay for this loan is: $" + Format(Totalinterest +
ABS(presentvalue), "###,###,##0.00")
Print "Of that, the interest is: $" + Format(Totalinterest, "###,###,##0.00")
End Sub
```

Results in

The total that you'll pay for this loan is $102,316.33. Of that, the interest is $52,316.33.

For information about the Format and Abs commands, see their entries elsewhere in this book.

Cautions

• If you use any of these Functions in a VB program that you're going to give someone else to use, you need to make sure that he or she has the file MSAFINX.DLL in his or her Windows/System directory.

The Financial Functions

DDB: Calculates depreciation based on the double-declining balance method.

```
X = DDB(Cost, Salvage, Life, Period)
```

FV: Calculates the future value of an annuity (like a home mortgage). Payments and interest rate remain constant.

```
X = FV(irate, nperiods, payment, presentvalue, whendue)
```

IPmt: Calculates the interest payment for a given period of an annuity. Payments and interest rate remain constant.

```
X = IPmt(irate, paymentrange, totalperiods, presentvalue, futurevalue, →
    whendue)
```

IRR: Calculates the internal rate of return for a list of periodic payments and receipts.

```
X = IRR(Array(), guess)
```

(The Array must contain at least one payment [a negative value] and one receipt [a positive value]. The guess is what you expect IRR to calculate, and it's usually 10% [or .1].)

MIRR: Calculates the modified internal rate of return for a list of periodic payments and receipts.

```
X = MIRR(Array(), financeinterest, reinvestinterest)
```

(The Array must contain at least one payment [a negative value] and one receipt [a positive value]. The financeinterest is the interest payment rate on the loan; the reinvestinterest is the interest rate achieved via cash reinvestment.)

NPER: Calculates the number of periods in an annuity. Payments and interest rate remain constant.

> X = NPER(irate, payment, presentvalue, futurevalue, whendue)

NPV: Calculates the net present value of an investment when there is a discount rate. The Array of cash flow entries can be Variable.

> X = NPV(irate, Array())

(The rate is expressed as a decimal value. The Array must contain at least one payment [a negative value] and one receipt [a positive value].)

PMT: Calculates the payment of an annuity investment. The payments and interest rate are constant.

> X = PMT(irate, numberofpayments, presentvalue, futurevalue, whendue)

PPMT: Calculates the principal payment for a period in an annuity. The payments and interest rate are constant.

> X = PPMT(irate, paymentperiod, numberofpayments, presentvalue, →
> futurevalue, whendue)

PV: Calculates the present value of an annuity. The payments and interest rate are constant.

> X = PV(irate, numberofpayments, payment, futurevalue, whendue)

RATE: Calculates the interest rate of an annuity.

> X = RATE(numberofpayments, payment, presentvalue, futurevalue, →
> whendue, guess)

(The guess is what you expect Rate to calculate; it's usually 10% [or .1].)

SLN: Calculates a straight-line depreciation value.

> X = SLN(cost, salvagevalue, usefullife)

SYD: Calculates a sum-of-years depreciation value.

> X = SYD(cost, salvagevalue, usefullife, depreciationperiod)

Related Functions

The following Functions are also included in the MSAFINX.DLL library.

PARTITION: Shows where a particular item occurs within a series of ranges. Each of the Variables in the argument for the Partition Function is Long (see "Variables").

> X = Partition(number, start, stop, interval)

DATEADD: Allows you to add a time or date interval to a date. This way, you could find out what date it will be 200 days from now or what date it was 200 days ago, etc. This Function returns a Variant Variable.

X = DateAdd(whatinterval, numberofintervals, startdate)

Whatinterval is a text Variable or text literal, from one of the following options:

yyyy	year
q	quarter
m	month
y	day of the year (Jan. 1 is 1, Jan. 2 is 2, Dec. 31 is 365, etc.)
d	day
w	weekday (Calculates normal weeks. If today is Monday, one week from now is the next Monday. "Weekday" is 1 for Sunday, 2 for Monday, etc.)
ww	week (Calculates calendar weeks, the number of Sundays between the dates, on the theory that a week, *properly so called*, is from Sunday to Sunday.)
h	hour
n	minute
s	second

Numberofintervals is how many of the *whatinterval* you want to add or subtract. Make *Numberofintervals* negative to go backward in time.

Startdate is a Variant Variable (see "Variables") containing the starting date.

To find out the date 200 days from now, enter the following:

```
Sub Form_Click ()
    whatinterval = "d"
    numberofintervals = 200
    startdate = Date
    Print "Today is: "; startdate
    Print "200 days from now will be: ";
    Print DateAdd(whatinterval, numberofintervals, startdate)
End Sub
```

DATEDIFF: This Function is the opposite of DATEADD. DATEDIFF tells you how many days between two dates or how many hours between two years or how many weeks between now and the end of the year. In other words, it tells you how many of a particular time/date interval fall between two times or dates.

X = DateDiff(whatinterval, firstdate, secondate)

Whatinterval is a text Variable or text literal, from one of the options listed under DateAdd above. *Firstdate* and *Secondate* are the two separate times or dates. If *Firstdate* is later than *Secondate*, DateDiff will give you a negative number for an answer.

To find out how many weeks between now and the end of the year, enter the following:

```
Sub Form_Click ()
    whatinterval = "w"
    firstdate = Date
    secondate = "31-Dec-93"
    Print "Today is: "; startdate
    Print "The number of weeks left until the end of the year is: ";
    Print DateDiff(whatinterval, firstdate, secondate)
End Sub
```

DATEPART: Can tell you the day of the week, the quarter of a year, etc., of a particular date.

```
X = DatePart(whatinterval, whatdate)
```

Whatinterval is a text Variable or text literal, from one of the options listed under DateAdd above. It specifies what kind of answer you want: "the quarter" or "the day of the week" or whatever. *Whatdate* is the date you supply.

To find out what day Christmas falls on this year, enter the following:

```
Sub Form_Click ()
    whatinterval = "w"
    whatdate = "25-Dec-95"
    Print "This year, Christmas is on day ";
    Print DatePart(whatinterval, whatdate);
    Print " of the week."
End Sub
```

Fix

FUNCTION

Description   The Fix command strips off the decimal portion of any number—converting both positive and negative numbers. It doesn't really "round off" a number, but it does move negative fractional numbers *upward* toward zero. The Int Function also removes the fractional part of numbers; but with negative numbers, the Int command moves the number *downward*. For example, Int(-4.3) returns -5 and Fix(-4.3) returns -4.

The Mystery of Fix: It's something of a mystery why this bizarre command is included in Visual Basic. Like Abs, the Eqv operator and a few other commands, Fix is easily accomplished by combining a couple of other commands. It's unlikely that you'll ever need to do what Fix does; and if you should, it's even less likely you'll remember that Fix exists.

Used with   Numbers with fractions (floating-point numbers)

Variables $X = Fix(-7.488)$

Uses   Steve Cramp, this book's technical editor, thinks Fix would be useful if you were working on calculations involving money. Computing involving money invariably ends up with hundredths of cents. Dlrs=(Fix(Dlrs*100))/100 would clean it up. You would get amounts so that you don't add $8.053425 to your account and give the bank the .003425 cents.

Steve also observes that commands such as Fix, Abs and others are generally grandfathered from older versions of Basic. When you're writing a program and need one, though, it can be convenient to have it.

See also   Abs; CInt; Int; Sgn

Focus

See   GotFocus

Font

OBJECT

Description   In keeping with the new VB4 set of "Objects," the Font Object provides an alternative to the existing FontBold, FontItalic, FontName, FontStrikeThru, FontUnderline and FontSize Properties. (In fact, proper nomenclature now describes setting a Font Property as: "setting of a Font Object identified by the Font property of a TextBox Object." Before Object-oriented programming lingo became part of VB, we would just have said that we changed the TextBox's Font Property. Now—and in many other similar situations— we're to think of changing a Property as changing an *Object* that's merely "identified" by that Property.)

Whatever, you can still take the traditional approach:

```
TextBox1.FontBold = True
```

or you can be Object-oriented and do this:

```
Dim F As New StdFont
F.Bold = True
Set Text1.Font = F
```

Used with　Any Object on which you can print text–Forms, Check Boxes, printer, etc.

Variables　The Font Object has seven Properties: Bold, Italic, Name, Size, StrikeThrough, Underline, and Weight.

Technically, the Font *Object* is distinct from the new VB4 Font Property of Forms, Check Boxes, etc. For example, you can create a free-floating Font Object, describe its qualities (its Properties), then assign the Font Object to a particular object. See the Example.

The new VB4 Font *Property* can also be used, with the normal syntax:

```
Text1.Font.Bold = True
```

For the third possible way to change the qualities of text, see the entry on "FontBold."

Uses　Change the qualities of printed text.

Cautions　• There is no actual Font Object, so-called. You must use StdFont. See the Example below.

• There is no Transparent Property of the Font Object.

• The Weight Property is quite mysterious, since the same thing can be achieved by setting the Bold Property to True or False. The default Weight is 400 (nonbold text). Bold and Bold Italic have a Weight of 700. These are your only choices at this time, though in the future there may be additional Weights.

If you specify a Weight other than 400 or 700, it will be set to one of those numbers, whichever is closer. However, at this time the following accomplish the same thing:

```
Dim F as New StdFont
F.Bold = True

Dim F as New StdFont
F.Weight = 700
```

Example　Ordinarily you would change the qualities of the font in a Text Box or other Control by merely using the Font Property. However, if you wish, you can create a Font Object of the "StdFont" type. (Note how this differs from most Objects that you create. To create a printer Object, for example: Dim P As Printer. But for some reason this Font Object must be created as a *StdFont* Object.)

```
Dim F As New StdFont
F.Bold = True
Set Text1.Font = F
```

See also   FontBold, TextBox

ONTBOLD

PROPERTY

(Also FontItalic, FontStrikeThru, FondUnderline)

Description   These Properties govern many of the common variations of the appearance of printed text.

Figure F-11: All four font styles.

Used with   Forms, Check Boxes, Combo Boxes, Command Buttons, Directory, Drive & File List Boxes, Frames, Grids, Labels, List Boxes, Option Buttons, Picture Boxes, Text Boxes and the printer

Variables   **Variable type:** Boolean

Usually, you set these text styles in the Properties Window while you're designing your program.

OR (to change a text Property while a program is running):

    Label1.FontBold = False

Uses   • In applications where you want to use a variety of text styles.

• For Captions on Controls. It's often more attractive if you turn off Font-Bold; it's On by default.

Cautions   • FontSize, FontName, and font styles such as bold and italic are all global across a Control, so VB does not permit various sizes, faces or styles within, say, a given Text Box. This limits the extent to which a Text Box can substitute for a full-featured word processing program.

• FontBold and FontTransparent are normally on, the default. FontItalic, FontStrikethru, and FontUnderline default to Off.

• For most Controls, changing text appearance by adjusting these Properties while your program is running will immediately change what you see onscreen. However, changing text appearance within Forms and Picture Boxes or for the printer requires a repaint (see "Paint").

• In Version 3 of VB, the Drive List Box freezes up and stops responding to user mouse clicking if you try to change some Font Properties while the program is running. The only two that work are FontSize and FontName.

Example

Figure F-12: Adjusting font Properties while printing can lend variety to your windows.

Here we put a graphic of a lobster on a Form, using the Picture Property. Then we position the pieces of text with the CurrentX and CurrentY Properties and adjust several of the Font Properties:

```
Sub Form_Click ()

fontbold = 0
currentx = 350

fontsize = 36
fontname = screen.fonts(8)
Print "MENU"

currentx = 3700
currenty = 1250
fontsize = 22
fontunderline = —1
Print "  Lobster Vivre"
currentx = 3900
currenty = currenty — 100
Print "  Peche Bombe"
currentx = 4100
currenty = currenty — 100
Print "  Salade Demoge"

End Sub
```

See also   FontCount; FontName; Fonts; FontSize; FontTransparent; Printer; Screen

FONTCOUNT

PROPERTY

Description   The FontCount Property tells you how many text fonts (typefaces) are available for display on the video screen or how many are available to print on the printer.

FontCount is used with the Fonts Property. Fonts contains the names of the available fonts; FontCount tells you the number of fonts that exist.

Used with   The screen and the printer

Variables   **Variable type:** Integer

This Property cannot be adjusted while designing your program; you can only quiz it while a program is running. X tells you the number of available fonts that can be used with the printer:

    X = Printer.FontCount

Uses   • Since new fonts can be added and old fonts removed from a computer, you cannot know in advance what fonts (typeface styles) are available to use on the screen or printer. Exceptions are the basic Windows fonts— Courier (typewriter-like); Helvetica (sans-serif, for headlines and simple unadorned text); Modern (a type of Helvetica); Roman (the most popular font for most newspapers, magazines and books); Script (similar to hand-writing and used mostly for wedding announcements and greeting cards); and Symbol (graphic symbols, the Greek alphabet, math symbols, etc.).

• FontCount—in combination with the built-in Arrays Screen.Fonts( ) and Printer.Fonts( )—provides a way for your program to find out and access the available fonts.

• Provide a way for the user to change fonts while your program is running, by adjusting the FontName Property.

Cautions   • FontSize, FontName and font styles such as bold and italic are all global across a Control, so VB does not permit a variety of sizes, faces or styles within, say, a given Text Box. This limits the extent to which a Text Box can substitute for a full-featured word processing program.

• Be careful when making assumptions about available fonts. If you think your program would benefit from Times Roman rather than Helvetica, you could search the user's system by looking through the Screen.Fonts( ) or Printer.Fonts( ) Array. Then you could attempt to switch to a FontName with "Times" in it.

However, this can cause problems. Simply because a font is listed in Screen.Fonts( ) or Printer.Fonts( ) does not mean that it actually exists on the system. It is quite possible for a font that's been deleted from the disk drive to remain listed in the WIN.INI file—which is where Screen.Fonts( ) or Printer.Fonts( ) gets its information. The true FontCount might be 29, yet the Windows Control Panel tells you that you have 34. Adobe Type Manager might also add some fonts that are not reported by FontCount. The upshot of the downside? FontCount cannot be relied upon to provide an accurate font count.

Example   Print "You have "; Screen.FontCount; " fonts listed as available for the screen."

See also   FontBold; FontName; Fonts; FontSize; FontTransparent; Printer; Screen

ONTITALIC
PROPERTY

See   FontBold

ONTNAME
PROPERTY

Description   The FontName Property identifies, or allows you to change, the currently used font (text design) of a Control on a Form or on the printer.

Used with   Forms, Check Boxes, Combo Boxes, Command Buttons, Directory, Drive & File List Boxes, Frames, Grids, Labels, List Boxes, Option Buttons, Picture Boxes, the printer and Text Boxes

Variables   **Variable type:** Text (string)

Normally you'll adjust this Property while you're designing your program:

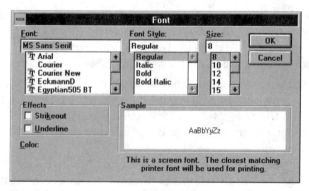

Figure F-13: Although available fonts vary from computer to computer, Windows always includes a version of Times Roman, Helvetica and Courier.

OR (to change it while the program is running):

Command1.FontName = "Roman"

OR (to find out which font is active while the program is running):

F$ = Combo1.FontName

Uses
- Allow the user to adjust the look of onscreen or printed text.
- Create more attractive windows by using various typefaces.
- Change typefaces dynamically in response to events in the program.

Cautions
- FontSize, FontName and font styles such as bold and italic are all global across a Control, so VB does not permit various sizes, faces or styles within, say, a given Text Box. This limits the extent to which a Text Box can substitute for a full-featured word processing program.

- Because FontNames returned by the Fonts( ) Property are drawn from a list in the WIN.INI file, the actual fonts might have been deleted from the computer's disk drive. It is best to allow the user to adjust this Property while your program is running, rather than to assume that a font will be available on a particular computer. And use On Error (which see).

Example
Form1.FontName = "Helv"

See also
FontBold; FontCount; Fonts; FontSize; FontTransparent; Printer; Screen

ONTS

PROPERTY

Description
Fonts( ) is an Array, a list of indexed information, maintained by Visual Basic. This list contains the names of all the fonts listed in Windows's WIN.INI file (in the Windows directory) as being available to use on the printer, and those listed as available for display on the screen.

Fonts are text character designs such as Helvetica or Times Roman or Courier. Fonts are primarily distinguished by whether or not they have *serifs* (small finishing strokes or flourishes). Times Roman has serifs. Helvetica does not; its letters are straight and unadorned. Serif fonts are usually used to set body text in books, magazines and newspapers. Fonts without serifs are often used for headlines and larger type.

The other primary distinction among fonts relates to letter spacing. Some fonts, such as Helvetica and Times Roman, produce *proportionally spaced* characters of varying widths. Type characters set in Courier are *monospaced*: when printed, each character in a line of type occupies the same amount of space.

Used with
The printer and the screen

Variables   **Variable type:** Text (string) Array

The Fonts Property cannot be adjusted while you are designing your program, nor can it be changed while the program is running. It is purely for information, so all you can do is find out what fonts are available on the user's computer.

To find out the *sixth* font listed as available on the user's computer (the index starts counting from 0): X$ = Printer.Fonts(5)

Uses   • Allow the user to select and change the fonts for the screen and printer.

• Test to see if a font exists, then change it (with the FontName Property) while your program is running. (But remember that the Fonts Property might list a font the user has erased from the disk drive. See Cautions.)

Cautions   • FontSize, FontName and font styles such as bold and italic are all global across a Control, so VB does not permit various sizes, faces or styles within, say, a given Text Box. This limits the extent to which a Text Box can substitute for a full-featured word processing program.

• All word processor programs allow the user to adjust various aspects of the text characters—size, style (italics, bold) and font—depending on the printer's capabilities. Although you cannot offer this flexibility in your programs, it is still sometimes worthwhile to provide the user with these options for various Controls. But avoid having your program unilaterally make font changes on the screen or printer. Lists of available screen and printer fonts are maintained in the user's WIN.INI file within the Windows directory; but these lists may not always be accurate since fonts may have been deleted from files on the user's hard drive yet still remain listed in WIN.INI. (See "Cautions" under "FontName.")

• **Duplicate Font Names:** When you Loop through the fonts using the FontCount command (see the Example below), you can get duplicate font names in the list. The FontCount and Fonts commands are not accurate when used by themselves. To get a true list of the available fonts, your program should *examine* the information provided by the Fonts command, then remove any duplicates it finds in the list. (To accomplish this, build an Array (which see) and then search through the Array for duplications.)

Example

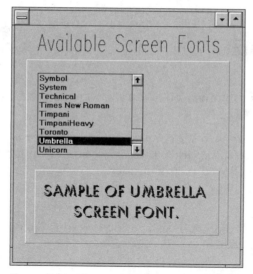

Figure F-14: Add a program option so users can select from their computers' available fonts. Also, show font samples as users browse.

Create a Form with a Label Captioned "Available Screen Fonts," a List Box and a Second Label. Type the following into two Events:

```
Sub Form_Load ()

For i = 0 To Screen.FontCount — 1
    list1.AddItem Screen.Fonts(i)
Next i

End Sub

Sub List1_Click ()

X$ = list1.list(list1.listindex)
label2.fontname = X$
label2.caption = "SAMPLE of " + label2.fontname + " Screen Font."

End Sub
```

See also   FontBold; FountCount; FontName; FontSize; FontTransparent; Printer; Screen

ONTSIZE

PROPERTY

Description   FontSize changes or informs you of the size of printed text (onscreen or on the printer).

Used with   Check Boxes, Combo Boxes, Command Buttons, Directory, Drive & File List Boxes, Forms, Frames, Grids, Labels, List Boxes, Option Buttons, Picture Boxes, Text Boxes and the printer

Variables   **Variable type:** Single

Often you'll set the FontSize by using the Properties Window while you're designing your program.

OR (to change the FontSize while the program is running):
    Picture1.FontSize = 14

OR (to find out what the FontSize is, while a program is running):
    X = Picture1.FontSize

Uses   • Adjust the sizes of various text elements on a Window. Allows you to create more attractive Forms.

• Allow the user to adjust the fonts of various Controls.

Cautions   • FontSize, FontName and font styles such as bold and italic are all global across a Control, so VB does not permit various sizes, faces or styles within, say, a given Text Box. This limits the extent to which a Text Box can substitute for a full-featured word processing program.

• Some screen or printer fonts will not print in all sizes (see the stair-step pattern that is created by trying to print a list of sizes from 5 to 24 in the Example below).

• The default FontSize is set by Windows.

• Font sizes may adjust themselves to slightly different values when you assign them. For instance, if you set a FontSize of 14, what you may actually get is 13.8.

Example

Figure F-15: There isn't a FontSize for every number you request.

```
Sub Form_Click ()
For i = 5 To 24
    fontsize = i
    x = fontsize
    Print " "; i; ". FONTSIZE Is Set to: "; x
Next i
End Sub
```

Notice that we're setting the FontSize to each number between 5 and 24. But what we get are at times fractional FontSizes, and at other times no change until we reach a threshold and VB can move up a size.

See also   FontBold; FountCount; FontName; Fonts; FontTransparent; Printer; Screen

 ONTSTRIKETHRU

PROPERTY

See   FontBold

FONTTRANSPARENT

PROPERTY

Description   FontTransparent provides a way for background graphics or colors to show through superimposed text.

Used with   Forms, Picture Boxes and the printer

Variables   **Variable type:** Integer (Boolean)

FontTransparent defaults to On, so you need to adjust it only if you want to turn it off. (See the second item in Uses.)

   FontTransparent can be set from the Properties Window while you're designing your program.

OR (while the program is running, to make the space around the letters opaque over the background): Picture1.FontTransparent = 0

OR (to find out, while the program is running, the status of the FontTransparent Property of this Form): X = Form1.FontTransparent

Uses   • Make your windows more attractive. Although it works only on Forms, Picture Boxes and the printer, allowing the background to show through the text is usually desirable and visually more appealing.

Figure F-16: Usually, a transparent font is more attractive. The background shows through the text.

Figure F-17: With FontTransparent turned off, the title covers the background and looks less professional.

• Selectively delete text from a window or Picture Box. Programmers who have written Basic programs in the DOS environment have sometimes used a technique of printing blank space characters over printed text to delete the text. This technique can come in handy sometimes. However, there are three things to remember if you use it in Visual Basic:

▪ FontTransparent must be turned off.

▪ You'll have to experiment with the number of spaces, since almost all Windows fonts are proportional, so the character widths vary. This means that you can't use four spaces to overprint four normal characters: that probably wouldn't amount to enough space to cover the text you want deleted.

▪ Any graphics in the background will also be deleted by the spaces.

Here's an example of the text-deletion technique. Put a Command Button on a Form:

```
Sub Form_Click ()
    Print "THIS"
End Sub

Sub Command1_Click ()
    FontTransparent = 0
    currentx = 0: currenty = 0
    Print   "        "
End Sub
```

We print the word THIS in the upper left corner of the Form. Then, when the Command Button is clicked, we move back up to the corner and superimpose some blank-space "characters" on the text.

Cautions • Unlike such text options as bold and italic, FontTransparent governs text in a more radical way than simply adjusting the appearance of characters displayed on the screen or printed. FontTransparent deals with an interaction between the background and the text. Most Controls cannot support this interaction; to make text appear attractive, you need to match the background and foreground color Properties (see the Example).

The way VB makes changes to Captions and Text Properties within most Controls differs fundamentally from the way VB prints to Forms, Picture Boxes and the printer. VB can effectively paste characters onto the backgrounds of these three targets.

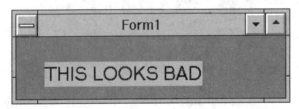

Figure F-18: Text that doesn't let the background show through looks pasted on.

The solution—if you can't get FontTransparent to work—is to try to match the BackColor to the background of the text itself.

Example FontTransparent applies only to Picture Boxes, Forms and the printer. If you try to create transparent text on top of most Controls, you'll probably end up with odd-colored boxes around some of your text. So what do you do when you want to place text over pictures or background colors without causing a box or outline of a different color around the text? How can you get clean, transparent backgrounds for text used with most Controls?

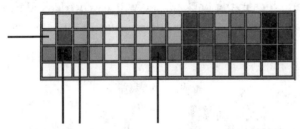

Figure F-19: Solid BackColors improve the look of your windows when FontTransparent isn't an option.

Match the Color: The solution is to choose background colors that match the forecolors. And you must use solid, not *dithered*, colors. (Dithered colors are the ones that come out with dots or crosshatches in them as the computer struggles to simulate them.) The computer can do primary colors with little trouble. But pastels are harder: you'll find that some text will cause a wrong-colored box on top of the background color (the BackColor Property). Use the Color Palette Window and mess around with ForeColor and BackColor until the text floats, as it should, invisibly on top of whatever Control you're designing.

See also   FontBold; FontCount; FontName; FontSize; Printer; Screen

FontUnderline

PROPERTY

See   FontBold

For Each...Next

STATEMENT

Description   This useful command is new to VB4. It's similar to the familiar For...Next command; both of them allow you to repeatedly carry out some task until completing a specific number of iterations. With For Each...Next, VB does something to each item in an Array or each item in a Collection of Objects. (See "Collection.")

But when you use For Each...Next, VB keeps track of the total number of items that must be manipulated. This saves you the trouble of finding out how many items or Objects are in the group (the Array or Collection). VB just steps through the group and does something for each item then automatically stops looping when the end of the collection is reached. VB thereupon moves on to the next command in your program.

Used with   An array or a "Collection" of Objects

Variables
```
For Each element In Array|Collection
    your programming goes here...
    [Exit For]
    your programming goes here...
Next [element]
```

Element is a variable (a Variant, or, in the case of a Collection, it can be a Variant or an Object type) that you supply and reuse within the For Each...Next structure. It's reused in this way:

```
Dim MyNames As New Collection

Private Sub Form_Load( )

Show
For I = 1 To 20
 MyNames.Add  Name  & I
Next I

For Each Thing In MyNames
 Print Thing
Next

End Sub
```

OR, to prematurely exit the loop:

```
For Each Thing In MyNames
 If Len(Thing) > 5 Then Exit For
 Print Thing
Next
```

Uses It's suggested that you use Collections now rather than Arrays (Collections, being mini-databases, are more flexible). Also, Collections are the way that you make Arrays of Objects. When you're programming with Objects, they can be cloned (new "instances" of them can be created). And this cloning might be done by the user or, indeed, by another Object running around manipulating your Object and instantiating it. The result of all this Robot-factory-gone-wild is that your program can lose track of the size of a Collection or Array. Collections have a Count Property which will give you this information (and Arrays have a UBound Function to tell you the number of elements to which they've been dimensioned), but it's much easier to let VB do it for you. For Each...Next allows you to forget about the total items in an Array or Collection and query or display or otherwise read through the items.

Cautions The Variable you use to access an array with For Each...Next must be a Variant type; with an Object collection the Variable must be either Variant or Object type. That is, you cannot use For Each...Next with a Variable that you have specifically declared (with the Dim, Private, Public or Global commands) to be a Text Variable or an Integer Variable or some other specific kind of Variable. (For more on Variable types, see "Variables.") For instance, this wouldn't work:

```
Dim fetchit as integer

For Each fetchit in MyArray
    Print fetchit
Next
```

But, of course, the elements stored *within* the Array or Collection that you manipulate with the For Each...Next command can be of any variable type; it's just that the *Variable* you use with the For Each...Next command must be a Variant. Recall that if you don't explicitly declare a Variable's type (if you don't use the DIM command in the above example and you just ignore the issue of explicitly describing your variable), the Variable will be, by default, a Variant type.

You cannot use For Each...Next to *affect* or change (write to) the items in an Array. You cannot do this:

```
For Each whateveritis In ourarray
    whateveritis = whateveritis + 1
Next whateveritis
```

because that would be making a change to the data in the Array (you *can* do this with the For...Next command). In other words, you can only get the items in the Array (read them) with For Each...Next; you cannot change them (write to them).

You cannot use For Each...Next with a user-defined Variable type. The Variant Variable type cannot handle a user-defined type.

Example   We'll create an Array (but we won't specify its Variable type, so it will be the default Variant type). Then we'll fill each element in the Array with a piece of text. Finally, we'll use For Each...Next to go through the Array and display each item.

```
Dim ourarray(1 To 3)

Sub testit( )

ourarray(1) =  Going
ourarray(2) =  around
ourarray(3) =  the bend.

For Each whateveritis In ourarray
 Print whateveritis
Next whateveritis

End Sub

Private Sub Form_Click( )
    testit
End Sub
```

Or to do the same thing in a Collection rather than an Array:

```
Dim Sentence As New Collection

Sub testit( )
```

```
Sentence.Add  Going
Sentence.Add  around
Sentence.Add  the bend.

For Each whateveritis In Sentence
 Print whateveritis;
Next whateveritis

End Sub

Private Sub Form_Click( )
 testit
End Sub
```

Note that we're using a Variant Variable, "whateveritis." It's a Variant because we didn't specifically declare that Variable to be of a type (Dim OurVariable as Integer, for example). Notice also that the For Each...Next command doesn't require that you specify when the loop should stop. VB does this job for you—that's the virtue of the For Each...Next structure. To do this same thing with For...Next, you would have to specify the limit of the loop—in this case, 3:

```
For whateveritis = 1 to 3
    Print ourarray(whateveritis)
Next whateveritis
```

See Also   Collections, Arrays, For...Next

FOR...NEXT
STATEMENT

Description   One of the most useful commands in any computer language, For creates a *Loop* that repeatedly carries out the instructions between it and its companion command, Next. The number of times the computer will Loop is defined by the two numbers listed right after the For:

```
For I = 1 To 100
    Print I
Next I
```

In this example, the value of the Loop counter Variable (in this case we used the Variable I) is incremented each time the program gets to the Next Statement. The Next Statement does three things: it adds one to the Variable I; it checks to see if I has reached the limit we set in the For Statement (100 in this example); and, if the limit has not been reached, Next sends the program back up to the For Statement to continue the repetitions. Any commands within the Loop are carried out each time the Loop cycles.

Variables The For Statement comes in three varieties:

• You can specify the number of Loops (see the Example).

• You can use other Variables to specify the number of Loops:

Say that you want to allow the user to specify how many copies of a document should be printed by the printer. In your program you put a Command Button labeled PRINT, which prints the contents of a Text Box to the printer. The PRINT Command Button's Click Event contains instructions to turn on a Text Box's Visible Property. The Text Box pops into view and its Text Property reads "HOW MANY COPIES?" The Text Box's Key-Press Event Procedure looks like this:

```
Sub Text2_KeyPress (keyascii As Integer)

If keyascii < 49 Or keyascii > 57 Then
    Exit Sub
Else
    Numberofcopies = keyascii – 48
End If
End Sub
```

Here we have to do a bit of manipulation because computers use the ANSI code for digits and alphabet letters. The digits are 49 to 58 (58 being 0). Notice that we ignore any keypresses beyond the 1 through 9 range. When the user presses a valid key, we get the *real* number by subtracting 48 from the code. (See "Chr$" for more on ANSI.)

Our Numberofcopies Variable now holds the number the user selected. We can use this Variable in our For...Next Loop:

```
For I = 1 To Numberofcopies
    Printer.Print Text1.Text
Next I
```

• There is an optional command that works with For...Next called *Step*. Step can be attached at the end of the For...Next structure to allow you to skip numbers, to *step* past them. When the Step command is used with For...Next, Step alters the way the Loop counts.

Normally, a Loop counts by one:

```
For I = 1 to 12
    Print I
Next I
```

Results in 1
2
3
4
5
6
7
8

9
10
11
12

However, when you use the Step command, you change the way a For...Next Loop counts.

It could count every other number (Step 2):

```
For I = 1 to 12 Step 2
    Print I
Next I
```

Results in   1
3
5
7
9
11

Or you could Step every seventy-third number (Step 73) or count down backwards (For I = 10 to 1 Step –1), and even count by fractions such as four steps for each number (Step .25).

```
For I = 15 to 90 Step 15
    Print I,
Next I
```

Results in   15   30   45   60   75   90

Additional Notes: For...Next Loops can be *nested*, one inside the other. At first, this sort of structure seems confusing, and it often is; but trying out various numbers for the counter Variables and moving commands around in the "inner" or "outer" Loop eventually produce the results you're after.

Nested Loops can be confusing because you've added a new dimension when you use an interior Loop. The inner Loop interacts with the exterior Loop in ways that are clear only to the mathematically gifted. Essentially, the inner Loop does its thing the number of times specified by its own counter Variable—multiplied by the counter Variable of the outer Loop.

Simply *hack* away, as computerists say, substituting counter numbers (and maybe moving commands from one Loop to the other) until things work the way they should. *Hacking* to a programmer means precisely the same thing as carving to a sculptor—chipping away until the desired shape emerges.

```
For I = 1 to 5
    For J = 1 to 10
            Print chr$(58 + I);
    Next J
Next I
```

Notice that you can start counting anywhere; you need not start the counter with 1. And the Step size can be whatever you wish, including negative numbers if you want to count *down* instead of up.

```
For I = 10 To 1 Step – 2
    Print I
Next I
```

Results in   10 8 6 4 2

The counter numbers and the Step number can be fractional:

```
For I = 12 To 13 Step 1/5   (you could also use .2 for the Step)
    Print I
Next I
```

Results in   12 12.2 12.4 12.6 12.8 13

You can even mix and match:

```
For I = 1 / 2 To 5.5 Step .7
    Print I
Next I
```

Results in   .5 1.2 1.9 2.6 3.3 4 4.7 5.4

Any *numeric expression* can be used with For...Next. (See "Variables" for a definition of "expression.") However, the range you're counting must be *possible*. The following is not possible:

```
For i = –10 To –20 Step 2
    Debug.Print "Loop"; i
Next
```

This Loop does nothing—it cannot. You're asking it to count downward, but your Step command is positive. As any intelligent entity would when confronted with a senseless request, Visual Basic does nothing with these instructions. You have to make the Step negative with -2:

```
For i = –10 To –20 Step –2
    Debug.Print "Loop"; i
Next
```

Additional Notes: It's common practice to indent the commands between For...Next, If...Then and other structures (Do...Loop, Select Case, etc.), which indicates that the indented items are subordinate, that they are controlled by a surrounding structure in some fashion.

If you *nest* a For...Next structure like a set of Russian dolls, you can condense the Next portion by using commas to separate the counter Variables after a single Next.

```
For I = 1 To 10
    For J = 4 To 755
        For K = 12.5 to 55
    Next K,  J,  I
```

This is exactly the same as:

```
For I = 1 To 10
    For J = 4 To 755
        For K = 12.5 to 55
        Next K
    Next J
Next I
```

Notice that you have to make this symmetrical, with the inner For counter (K, here) matched by an inner Next K.

Uses
• For...Next is useful when you want to repeat something a certain number of times, such as printing a particular number of copies of a letter, or drawing 75 circles on the background of a Form. The Do...Loop structure performs the same job as For...Next, but with For...Next you know how many iterations, how many repetitions, you want. With Do...Loop, you keep cycling through the Loop until some condition is satisfied (for example, until the user presses a key to stop the looping).

Also, you can vary events within the For...Next Loop by using the Counter to generate the variations:

To calculate 5 1/4 percent interest on savings for amounts between $1,000 and $10,000, in $1,000 increments:

```
For I = 1000 To 10000 Step 1000
    Print "The interest on $"; I; " is $"; I * .0525
Next I
```

The alternative structure is Do...Loop (and its less flexible cousin, While...Wend). You use a Do...Loop structure when you do not know how many times you want the instructions repeated—you therefore cannot supply the counter numbers you would give to a For...Next Loop. For...Next is used far more often, however. You usually *do* know the number of times you want something done.

Computer languages have evolved and become capable of giving you more specific information. For example, it used to be that when you opened a file on the disk drive, you had to worry about whether you might be pulling in characters past the end of the file. You had no way of knowing the size of the file, so you used a structure like this: Do Until EOF(1)...Loop, meaning, "Pull in characters until the End Of File marker appears."

Now, however, there is an LOF, Length Of File, command. You can know in advance how many characters are contained in any file, so you can use a For...Next structure if you wish. Besides, most of the time you'll know how many times you want something done when you write a program, and therefore you can set the counter in a For...Next Loop.

And, even if you can't know the precise number while creating your program, your program itself will usually know while running the number that should be used as the counter. If you allow the user to select the number of copies of the Text in a Text Box that will be sent to the printer, you won't know his or her choice when you design the program; but you can put the user's choice into a Variable that you give as the counter for a For...Next Loop:

```
Numberofcopies = Asc(InputBox$("How many copies do you want?")) – 48
For I = 1 to Numberofcopies
```

Do...Loop utilizes its associated commands—Until and While—to produce one of those readable lines of programming for which Basic is famous. Do Until Character$ = "M" is practically regular English.

```
Sub Form_Load ()

Show
On Error GoTo Problem

filename$ = InputBox$("Input Filename")
Open filename$ For Input As #1

Start:

Do Until character$ = "M" Or EOF(1)
character$ = Input$(1, #1)
    If currenty > scaleheight Or currentx > scalewidth Then Cls
    Print character$;

Loop

If EOF(1) Then Cls: Print "The word Microsoft Wasn't Found in "; filename$:
Close : Exit Sub

y$ = "M"
For i = 1 To 8
    x$ = Input$(1, #1)
    y$ = y$ + x$
Next i

If y$ = "Microsoft" Then
    Cls
    Print "Yes, we found the word "; y$; " in "; filename$: Close : Exit Sub
End If

GoTo Start

Problem:
    MsgBox (Error$(Err))
    Exit Sub
End Sub
```

Cautions • If you set up an impossible situation for the For...Next counter (such as For I = 5 To 2), nothing will happen. Such a Loop won't execute even once. (This is as opposed to ANSI standard Basic, where every For...Next Loop executes its contents at least once, even when your stated conditions are impossible.)

VB, by contrast, will understand that you can't count up from 5 to 2, since there is no negative *Step* command in your For...Next structure forcing the counting to go downward. VB will ignore such a Loop and just continue on past it.

• For...Next Loops can be as large as you wish, can contain as many instructions between the For and the Next as you want. On the other hand, you can put a small For...Next structure all on one line, too:

```
For J = 1 To 5: Print J: Next J
```

• The final J is optional, but omitting it makes your program slightly less easily understood, and the practice is frowned upon:

```
For J = 1 To 5: Print J: Next
```

• Also, avoid changing the counter Variable within the Loop:

```
For J = 1 To 5
    J = 3
Next J
```

• If you use Step 0, you will create a Loop that never ends. This is called an *infinite Loop* or an *endless Loop*, and such a structure has few uses. In effect, it causes the computer to go into a state of suspended animation. Unless you've made other provisions—for example, by putting an X = DoEvents( ) command within the infinite Loop, thereby allowing KeyPress or some other Event to intervene and take control of the program—the only way for the user to stop this endless thing is to press the BREAK key and halt the program in its tracks. Step 0 is not advised.

Example

```
For I = 1 To 50000
    If I = 34786 Then ? "Found It"
Next I
```

See also   Do...Loop; For Each...Next; While...Wend

ForeColor
PROPERTY

Description   ForeColor reports (or allows you to change) the color of Printed text; built-in text Properties (such as Captions); or graphics drawn with the Line, Circle or PSet command. It's as if you have a typewriter with a multi-colored ribbon for typing characters, or a set of colored pencils to draw shapes and lines.

Used with   Check Boxes, Column Object, Combo Boxes, Directory, Drive & File List Boxes, Forms, Frames, Grids, Labels, List Boxes, OLE, Option Buttons, Picture Boxes, Printer, Shapes and Text Boxes

Variables   **Variable type:** Long

To adjust ForeColor while designing your program, you can use the Properties Window and the Color Palette Window.

OR (to change the color while your program is running, using the full available range of colors–see "RGB"): [form.][control.]ForeColor = 8 (This can be a number between 0 and 16,777,215.)

OR (to use the QBColor Function while the program is running, provide a number between 0 and 15): ForeColor = QBColor (4)

OR (to find out what color is currently being used):
X& = [form.][control.]BackColor (The & means this number can be as large as 16,777,215. See "Variables" for the meaning of numeric variable symbols.)

Uses   • Create attractive Forms and Controls.

• Use different colors to highlight or subdue text messages.

Cautions   • ForeColor is nondestructive: it doesn't affect the colors of text or drawings that you've already placed on a Form or Picture Box. In this way, you can use as many different ForeColors as you wish on a single Form or Picture Box (see the Example).

• If you make no changes to ForeColor, it will use the colors that have been selected in the Windows Control Panel by the user.

• The range of possible colors in Visual Basic is very large, but it's not a continuum like a rainbow. For example, color 75,000 is orange, but 75,050 is an army green. All the colors are there, but they're not arranged sequentially from 0 to 17 million in a neat way like a color wheel. A total of nearly 17 million shades and hues are potentially available to you, but VB and Windows use a color scheme that puts some shades of orange around 75,000 and other oranges around 33,000, e.g., 33,023 is a pumpkin orange.

• ForeColor interacts with the optional color variable that you can add to the Line and Circle drawing commands. If a color variable is left out, Line and Circle default to the ForeColor Property of the Form or Picture Box on which they are drawn. For example, a filled box (the BF option with the Line command) will be filled with the ForeColor. However, a regular Box (the B without the F), will be filled with the current FillColor Property–and it will be invisible unless you also set the FillStyle Property to something other than its default 1 ("Transparent"). See "Line" and "Circle."

Example   This program draws a radiating series of lines, each in different ForeColors, to illustrate that every time you adjust the ForeColor Property, you don't cause all previously drawn graphics to change to that color. Try playing around with the DrawWidth and the Step size used with the For command.

```
Sub Form_Click ()
DrawWidth = 3
For i = 1 To 6000 Step 10
    forecolor = i * 20
    Line (i, 0)–Step(i + 400, 3200)
Next i
End Sub
```

See also   BackColor; Circle; FillColor; Line; QBColor; RGB

ORM   OBJECT

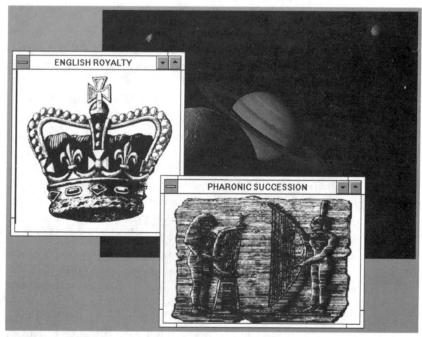

Figure F-20: Two Forms (two windows, in other words) against Windows wallpaper.

Description   A Form is the Visual Basic name for a window. But it's more than just a visual object; it is also a method of organization.

A Form is the primary programming unit in Visual Basic–within Forms you place Controls, such as Text Boxes or Picture Boxes. Within Controls are Events. And it's within Events that you write your instructions—the things you want the computer to do when your program runs.

VB is called an *event-driven language*: a VB program is made up of a collection of individual objects, such as Command Buttons, Pictures, Labels and other entities. VB is unlike traditional programming, where the programmer more completely controls events, and more thoroughly determines the order, interaction and duration of things that happen when a program runs.

In VB, by contrast, the programmer creates a set of tools (the Controls) each of which can perform some particular job, provide information or affect other Controls. Those tools are presented within windows (Forms), a type of organization not unlike the various drawers within your desk.

Traditional Programs Are Strict: A traditional program frequently starts out with a series of questions or behaviors to which the user *must* respond. Even lower in a traditional program, down a few menus, there is still a rigidity. A database, for instance, might require that you enter

1. Name

2. SS #

3. Address

4. Phone

and so forth, one piece of information at a time, for every entry. Furthermore, the entries must be made in a strict order. All this must happen before you can process some data relating to a new entry. What if you want to save only the name and phone number? Too bad.

With *event-driven* programs, it's becoming common to allow the user of a program to determine which tools to use and how and when to use them. The user also has more freedom to interact with, customize and control the overall organization, and determine the look and feel of the program and the objects therein. For example, dragging objects around (or even among) windows is far more intuitive and pleasant, since all of us have our different needs and preferences.

For programmers, too, Visual Basic heralds a new freedom. Much about programming has been simplified, and much of the tedium has been eliminated. The bulk of input/output (getting information from and to the user while the program runs) is already programmed for you in the various Controls. And arranging the Controls onscreen is as easy as using a painting program. In a reversal of tradition, you get to design and see what your program will look like *before you've written the program*. And in the act of creating Forms, you couple the logical part of your mind with the visual part—resulting in better, more holistically designed programs.

Variables   Since Visual Basic differs in some fundamental ways from traditional programming (it's both freer and, in some ways, more structured), it's worth learning the underlying structure of how you write programs in VB.

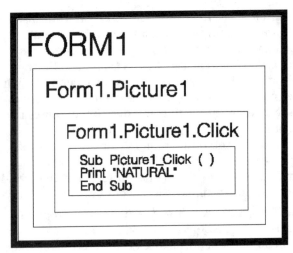

Figure F-21: Visual Basic is organized by objects within objects. A Form is the largest object.

The Form is a container for a series of smaller, nested entities: usually a Form holds several Controls, each Control holds several Events (Procedures), and some Events hold instructions (the commands you want the computer to follow to accomplish something).

This Form–Controls–Events–Commands structure affects the way you program in VB: you give things names that parallel this nesting sequence. VB supplies perfectly useful names whenever you create a new Form or Control, although you can change these names with the Name Property. The names can get rather long if they include the entire list of items within which they nest: Form1.List1.Drawmode, for example, describes Form/Control/Property. Notice that the identifying names are separated by periods.

The nesting also affects Variables according to *scope*. Essentially, scope is the zone of influence of a particular Variable. A Global Variable, for instance, has the greatest scope of all Variable types. A Variable can be accessed by everything in your program if it is placed in VB's outermost locale, a Module. You create a Public (Global) Variable with the Public (or Global) Statement: Public MyVariable. Now any Event within any Form or Control can get information about what is in MyVariable, and any of them can change MyVariable as well.

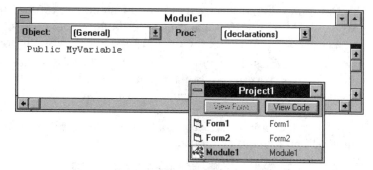

Figure F-22: The Module is Visual Basic's most generalized location; Variables declared here can speak to the entire program.

One step down from this are Variables that you declare in the General Declarations section of a Form. The General Declarations section is to an individual Form what a Module is to the entire program. These Variables will be available to all Controls and Events that are part of that Form. However, other Forms cannot access them. You use the Dim Statement to declare Variables in the General Declarations section of a Form.

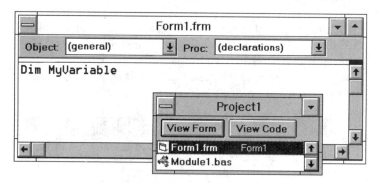

Figure F-23: Variables declared within General Declarations can speak to the entire Form (but not the entire program).

The Lowest Level—Events: At the lowest level, Variables within Events (Procedures) are like insects that live only briefly, do their duty, then die. Variables inside Events (unless otherwise declared within General Declarations or a Module) pop into existence when the program is running within that Event, and disappear again as soon as the program goes on to some other Event. (The Static command, which see, is an exception to this brief-life rule.)

When Variables live within a single Event, and their influence is limited to that Event, the following conditions apply:

• You can use the same Variable name in different Events, without risking untoward effects.

▪ Computer memory is used efficiently, since you can create even a large Array of information and manipulate it; then, when you're finished, the Array collapses, returning the memory space it occupied for other uses.

▪ Local Variables also eliminate one of the most frequent—and hardest-to-track-down—errors in traditional programming: two Variables with the same name that are interacting and messing each other up.

You need not declare Variables at the Event level; you can just use them. (This is called "implicit declaration.") If you wish to declare them, you use the ReDim statement (which see).

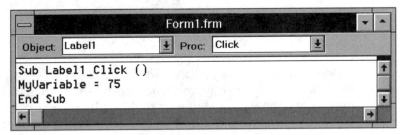

Figure F-24: When you simply assign a value to a Variable within an Event, the Variable can be used only within that Event.

Modules as Containers for Programwide Subroutines: Just as you use Modules to hold any Variables and Constants that you want to have influence throughout your program, you also use Modules to hold programming that will have global influence. Any part of your program can use a Subroutine or Function you've placed in a Module.

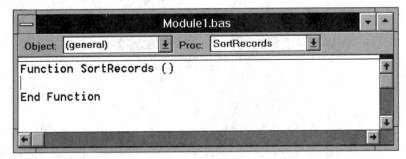

Figure F-25: A Module, a Form with no Events, is never visible when a program runs; it only contains Subroutines, Functions, Global Variables or Constants.

Using Modules is a convenient way to organize your work: any Subroutines, Functions or Variables placed within a Module are then available to be used from anywhere in your program.

Modules are the same as Forms, except that they have no visual component, Events, Properties or Controls. It's this lack of overhead that allows Modules to run slightly faster than Forms. When a program runs, the user can see your Forms as windows. Modules hide behind the scene. Modules are places to put lengthy Routines that may be needed in several places in your program—a sorting Subroutine, for example, that you feed the name of an Array you want sorted. Modules can also be reused in other programs.

There is one final division of labor in Visual Basic that also helps you keep things straight when you're programming: Events versus Properties.

Events "Happen": Events are triggered by things that happen while a program runs (such as mouse clicks or keypresses). Forms and Controls have Events, but the specific Events that can happen vary from Control to Control. For example, a click and a keypress can happen to a Command Button. A Text Box can respond to a keypress but not to a click, so a Text Box has a built-in KeyPress Event but no Click Event.

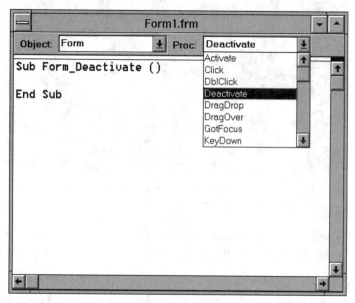

Figure F-26: The Events available to a given object (a Control or Form) are listed in the "Proc:" (for Procedure) drop-down menu.

It is within Events that you write most of your instructions that tell your program what to do (the only alternatives are to put the Subroutines or Functions you create in the General Declarations section of a Form, or within a Module). It works like this: you decide that a mouse click on the Command Button labeled "QUIT" should shut the program down:

Figure F-27: A Command Button is visible on a Form design window. Its Click Event is visible within the programming window. We changed its Name to "QuitButton."

In the above illustration, we've typed in the End command, which tells Visual Basic to shut this program down if the user clicks on the Button.

Properties Are Qualities: Each Property of a Form or Control (such as color or size) is like a built-in Variable; it can be adjusted by you or by the user of your program. You normally adjust Properties when you design the program, using the Properties Window that becomes visible when you are working with a Form.

However, you can also adjust most Properties while your program runs: Text1.Visible = 0 (makes a Text Box Control disappear. This particular Text Box is identified by the Name Property Text1.)

OR you can give the user access to Properties by presenting Menus or Controls, such as this:

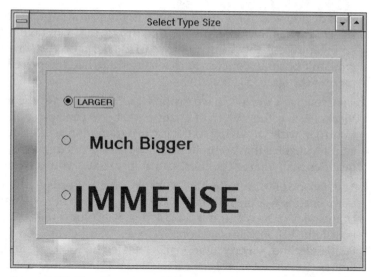

Figure F-28: It's often a good idea to let the user select Properties to suit his or her tastes.

The user can click on one of these three type-size options. This is a cluster of three Option Button Controls. Within each of their Click Events, you would put some instructions to adjust the FontSize Property. Lurking underneath the window in Figure F-29 are the Events for each Option Button the user sees and selects from:

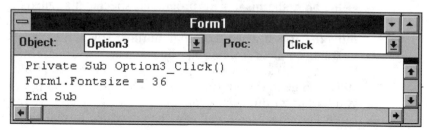

Figure F-29: Here, in the Events, is where you tell your program how to respond if the user clicks on a Button.

Uses

• Organize your programs by grouping related tools (Controls) onto a single Form. Create one Form that is the "mother of all Forms"–the Controls of the Mother Form invoke (Load or Show) other Forms in your program. (In VB, this Mother Form is called the *Startup Form*; see "Cautions" below.)

Note: A Startup Form is not required; it is not necessary to actually have a main Form. The startup section of a program could be placed into a section called Sub Main in a Module that, for instance, reads a data file from the disk and decides what mode to start the program in. This Sub could perhaps decide which Forms to show based on setup options the user had selected when the program was first installed. If you take this approach, you would probably want to show a Title Form on the screen, so the user wouldn't become concerned that something had happened to the computer if the startup is lengthy.

• Forms, like Controls, have Properties. In fact, one of the great strengths of Visual Basic is the wealth of qualities that you can adjust on Forms and Controls, without having to do any programming at all. You just select and adjust Variables that are built into these entities. For Forms, there are 47 qualities that you (or the user) can adjust to suit yourselves:

ActiveControl • AutoRedraw • BackColor • BorderStyle • Caption ClipControls • ControlBox • CurrentX • CurrentY • DrawMode DrawStyle • DrawWidth • Enabled • FillColor • FillStyle • FontBold FontItalic • FontName • FontSize • FontStrikeThru • FontTransparent FontUnderline • ForeColor • hDC • Height • HelpContextID • hWnd Icon • KeyPreview • Left • LinkMode • LinkTopic • MaxButton MDIChild • MinButton • MousePointer • Name • Picture • ScaleHeight ScaleLeft • ScaleMode • ScaleTop • ScaleWidth • Tag • Top • Visible Width • WindowState

Cautions

• You are limited to a total of 255 Controls per Form (but that will suffice, don't you think?).

• If you are drawing or printing to a Form in the Form_Load Event, first use the Show Statement, so the drawing will be visible.

• One of the Forms in your program is special: it's called the *Startup Form*, and any instructions you've put into its Form_Load Event will be the first thing to happen when the program runs. This is the place to put any instructions that set things up the way you want them, such as Loading or Showing additional Forms, specifying Properties, etc. Unless you deliberately change it, the Startup Form will be the first one you worked on when you started writing your program–the one that VB gave the Name *Form1*. In VB's Options Menu, you can change which form is the Startup Form if you wish. You can also start up a program from a Module. (See the first item in Uses.)

• You can force the user to respond to a Form. MsgBox is one such Form: when that Form Shows, everything else stops (the user cannot click on other windows, for example) until the Form is clicked OK. (See "Modal-State" under "Show.") This kind of Form is sometimes used to request the user to register a program before using it.

• If the user resizes or covers one of your Forms with another Form, this will cause anything drawn (using the Line, Circle or PSet command) or any text printed (with the Print command) to be erased. To prevent this, set the Form's AutoRedraw Property to –1 (True). The AutoRedraw Property defaults to 0 (False). (Also see "Paint" and "ReSize.")

• In Windows, Forms have three "states": Normal (partial screen), Minimized (icon) and Maximized (full screen). You can set these Properties prior to Loading a Form or change them while a program is running. The default is Normal. (See "WindowState" Property.)

• There are four possible BorderStyle Properties for Forms:

▪ **No Border**, as shown in Figure F-30.

Figure F-30: The simplest window entirely borderless.

▪ **Fixed Single** (as shown in Figure F-31), includes optional Maximize, Minimize and Control Box buttons. This border type cannot be resized other than via those buttons.

Figure F-31: This slightly more elaborate window cannot be stretched or shrunk by dragging on its frame, but can be moved around the screen.

▪ **Sizable** (the default), which has optional buttons and can be adjusted by dragging on the sides or corners. One drawback to a Sizable Form is that the user can change the size and destroy the look of your program. Controls could be covered, or the window could be expanded, leaving the Form visually out of balance.

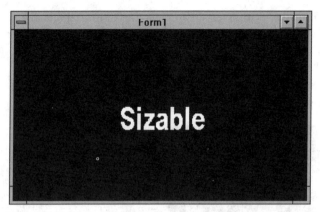

Figure F-32: The default and most common Windows style is the "Sizable" Form.

• **Fixed Double**, which is not sizable. Optional Control Box Button, but no Minimize or Maximize Buttons.

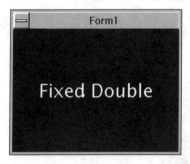

Figure F-33: The Fixed Double window is one step up from the Borderless window illustrated in Figure F-30.

Regarding Nomenclature
• Message Boxes (MsgBox and InputBox$, which see) are classified as Forms, but they have little in common with Forms, other than being windows. They are in a category of their own—they are Functions that generate windows when they do their (highly specialized) jobs.

• Events within Controls or Forms are sometimes referred to as *procedures*. In fact, when you look at an Event Menu within a Form's Code window, you'll see the abbreviation *Proc* right in front of the Event Menu. To avoid misunderstanding, think of procedures as Events (and Subroutines and Functions). This is not only less confusing but is also much more descriptive.

A similar unhappy confusion results from the fact that in VB Forms are described in two ways—as both *Forms* and *windows*. Let's call them Forms.

Form Events

Activate • Click • DblClick • Deactivate • DragDrop • DragOver GotFocus • Initialize • -KeyDown • KeyPress • KeyUp • LinkClose LinkError • LinkExecute • LinkOpen • Load • LostFocus MouseDown • MouseMove • MouseUp • Paint • QueryUnload Resize • Terminate • Unload

Form Methods

Circle • Cls • Hide • Line • Move • PaintPicture • Point • Print PrintForm • PSet • Refresh • Scale • SetFocus • Show • TextHeight TextWidth • ZOrder

See also   Hide; Load; Multiple Document Interface; Object; PrintForm; Show; UnLoad

FORMAT, FORMAT$ FUNCTION

Description   Format$ provides an extraordinarily flexible and powerful way to format numbers for displaying onscreen or printing. Format returns a Variant Variable type; Format$ returns a text Variable type. We'll just refer to it as Format$, but both commands work the same way.

Computers work only with numbers. Even images and text are coded into numbers before being manipulated inside the machine. However, to show onscreen or as printed text, the numbers must be translated back into symbols that we understand as letters of the alphabet, punctuation, digits 0 through 9 and symbols, such as @ and $.

Format$'s job is to format and display numbers as text characters according to your needs—as percentages, fractions and words. It can put the correct number of digits to the right of the decimal point. For dates, it can display the day's or month's full name, an abbreviation or only digits. For time, it can format with AM, PM and so forth.

Used with   Numbers

Variables   In most cases, you create a template that Format$ will imitate. In the following, we're saying, "Put in commas to separate large numbers into a more readable format."

```
X = 12000000
Print Format$(X, "##,###,###")
```

Results in   12,000,000 (Without Format$, this number would print as 12000000.)

OR (The Now command provides the current time and date according to the computer's internal clock. In the following example, we are asking to see the day of the week, the day of the month and the year):

```
Print Format$(Now, "dddd,mmmm dd, yyyy")
```

Results in   Thursday, December 12, 1992

Available Formats

X = 123456.78 (We'll use this Variable, X, in the following examples.)

? Format$(X)   No formatting. (There are no formatting instructions within the parentheses in this example—only the Variable X.)

123456.8

? Format$(X, "00000000000")   Displays leading or trailing zeros, if X contains fewer digits than the number of zeros you place in Format$.

00000123457

? Format$(X, "0.0000")   If you include a decimal point, either zeroes are added to the right of a decimal point (as many as you used in Format$), or the number is rounded to that many places.

123456.7813

? Format$(X, "###")   Follows the above rules for 0 but does not display leading or trailing zeros. These # symbols are merely spacers to show how you want the result to look—allowing you to place additional symbols, such as commas, where you want them to be located within the spacers.

123457

? Format$(X, "##.###")   Insert the decimal point where you want it. In this case, the decimal point's location will cause the number to be rounded to three places.

123456.781

?Format$(X, "000000%")   The number is multiplied by 100 and the percent sign (%) is placed wherever you've placed it in the template.

12345678%

?Format$(X, "###,###")   The comma is used to separate thousands.

123,457

Commas can also be used with no spacers (# or 0) to truncate numbers. For example, in financial reports of successful companies, the numbers are just too large, so all figures are expressed in millions. Then revenues would be listed in the format 100 (meaning $100,000,000). To adjust numbers in this fashion: use "##0,," which has the effect of removing the two sets of 000.

```
X = 100000000
Print Format$(X, "##0,,")
```

Results in   100

?Format$(X, "0000E+000") Scientific notation, meaning the digits listed, multiplied by the exponent listed after the E (you can also use e). An E+ puts a minus sign with negative exponents and a plus sign with positive ones. An E– just puts a minus sign in with negative exponents.

1235E+002

?Format$(Now, "hh:mm") Displays time. See below for the meaning of hh and mm. Other characters besides the colon are used if requested in the [International] settings in the WIN.INI file.

16:19

?Format$(Now, "dd/mmmm/yyyy") Displays a date. There are many formats for this; see d, m and y, below. Also, characters other than the slash are used if so requested in the [International] settings in the WIN.INI file.

?Format$(X, "$000") Adds a dollar sign to the number. You can also insert – + ( ) and a space character. All these characters can be stuffed right into your template wherever you need them, since Format$ knows what to do with them.

However, to add other characters, put a backslash (\) in front of each character you wish to add (the backslash itself won't be displayed):

```
X = 255
Print Format$(X, "\d\a\y #")
```

Results in   day 255

Or you can simulate double quotes to include longer text messages. You can enclose a group of characters within the Chr$(34) code for double quotes, and use the + operator to add this to the Format$ template. Here's an example:

```
q$ = Chr$(34) + "BUDGET:" + Chr$(34)
X = 400000
Print Format$(X, q$ + "$###,###")
```

Results in   BUDGET: $400,000

[See the "Chr$" Function for more on using Chr$( )]

Formatting Dates and Time: Many of VB's commands that manipulate dates and time produce a "serial number." This number contains a coded representation of date+time. Format$ can accept these serial numbers and format them in many ways according to your needs. For example, if you give the DateSerial command a year, month and day, it will give you back a serial number for that date. For the following examples of how to use Format$ with VB's date+time serial numbers, we'll use April 4, 1992.

```
X = DateSerial(1992, 12, 4)
Print Format$ (X, "ddddd")
```

Results in   12/4/92

You can also use the DateValue Function (which see) or the Now Function, which supplies today's date and time according to your computer's clock.

Days   **d**   Show the day with no leading zero.

      4

      dd   Show the day with a leading zero.

      04

      ddd   Show the day as a word, but abbreviated.

      Mon

      dddd Show the day as a complete word.

      Monday

      ddddd Show the day, month and year, as digits.

      4/4/1992

Months   **m**   Show the month with no leading zero (also used to display minutes, if preceded by an h, see "Time").

      4

      mm   Show the month with, if appropriate, a leading zero (also used to display minutes, if preceded by an h, see "Time").

      04

      mmm   Show the month as an abbreviated word.

      Apr

      mmmm Show the month as a complete word.

      April

Time   **h**   Show the hour with no leading zero.

      5

      hh   Show the hour with a leading zero, if necessary.

      05

      m   If used after an h or hh, show the minute with no leading zero (also used to display months, if it doesn't follow an h or hh).

      3

      mm   If used after an h or hh, show the minute with a leading zero if appropriate (also displays months, if it doesn't follow an h or hh).

      03

s   Show the second with no leading zeros.

6

ss   Show the second with leading zeros if necessary.

06

ttttt   Show the time as hour, minute, second. Also includes an "AM" or "PM." The format will conform to settings in the [International] section of the WIN.INI file. iTLZero= determines whether or not there will be a leading zero. sTime= determines which separator is used between h, m and s.

5:03:06

AM/PM   Show AM or PM, and use a 12-hour style clock. Use with the "h" symbols, but not ttttt; it adds its own AM and PM symbols.

```
Print  Format$(Now, "hhAM/PM")
```

Results in   05PM

am/pm   Same as AM/PM, but lowercase letters.

A/P   Same as above, but uses "A" instead of "AM," etc.

a/p   Same as above, but lowercase.

AMPM   This one is for fanatics. What should happen on the cusp between 11:59 and noon or midnight? It follows the definition in the WIN.INI file for s1159 and s2359. Defaults to AM/PM style.

Combining Formats: Format$, as you've doubtless concluded, is an almost morbidly compliant Function: you have almost total domination over its behavior. It also lets you include specifications that make it react differently depending on whether it's fed a positive number, a negative number or a zero.

If you extend the template (by creating up to three zones, separating them with semicolons), the following rules pertain:

• If you create two zones, the first zone works on positive numbers or zeros; the second, on negatives. Let's see just how this works, in case you ever want to be this particular about formatting numbers in the course of your endeavors.

```
Sub Form_Click ()
X = 55
Print Format$(X, "\P\l\u\s 00;\M\i\n\u\s 00")
X = −55
Print Format$(X, "\P\l\u\s 00;\M\i\n\u\s 00")
End Sub
```

Results in Plus 55
Minus 55

Format$ is selecting between the words *Plus* and *Minus* based on the number you give it. Feed Format$ a negative number and you trigger the second zone you've described; a positive number triggers the first zone.

• If you create *three* zones, the first formats positive numbers; the second, negative numbers; the third, zeros.

Uses • For accounting, scientific or other purposes where you need to present numbers in a particular format for readability, consistency, or conformity to accepted syntax and punctuation.

• For programs that must be adjusted to formats used in other parts of the world. For instance, many countries prefer 30-9-95, expressing the day before the month.

• When you need to put a number into a string Variable or in any other situation where a text Variable is required.

Cautions Format$'s simpler cousin, Str$, also transforms numbers into displayable text. But it formats in only one way: Str$ adds a space to the left of the number. This space is frequently annoying, although the idea is that it leaves room for a minus sign when you are trying to print in columns using tabs. It's annoying because when you print numbers converted by Str$, you'll often have to adjust for that leading blank space by using LTrim$.

• Use Format when you want a Variant variable as a result. Use Format$ to get a String (text) variable. See "Variables."

See also DateSerial; DateValue; Day; Now; Str$

RAME

CONTROL

Figure F-34: The Frame symbol in the Toolbox.

Description

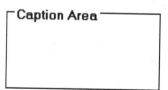

Figure F-35: A typical Frame showing the Caption location.

Frames have something in common with Forms: they are dual-purpose entities that help you organize your program both visually and structurally. However, Picture Boxes can do everything Frames can do, and much more. Often, you'll want to use Picture Boxes and forget about Frames.

Where Frames are sensitive to only 7 Events, Picture Boxes can respond to 19 Events.

Unlike a Picture Box, you cannot turn off the Border of a Frame (Frames have no BorderStyle Property), and a Frame cannot contain graphic images (Frames have no Picture Property either). Frames are hopelessly feeble compared to Picture Boxes.

A Frame or Picture Box can draw a visible line around a group of Controls. More importantly, a Frame or Picture Box can *group* Controls drawn on top of it. This "grouping" has two effects:

• While you design your program, you can drag the Frame around on the Window and the grouped Controls will follow as a unit. They have been contained within the Frame. This simplifies design and maintains the positional relationship between the grouped Controls. To group Controls, you must *first* create the Frame, then *single-click* on the Toolbox and *draw* each Control within the Frame. Alternatively, you can cut and paste Controls already on a Form. However, you cannot just drag existing Controls into a Frame to make them part of a group. Nonetheless, VB now allows you to surround a group of Controls by dragging the mouse around them (or by clicking on them while holding down the SHIFT key). Then they move in concert. So that the purpose for grouping within Frames is no longer of importance.

Variables   Normally set with the Properties Window while designing your program.

OR (to adjust a Property while your program is running):

    Frame1.Caption = "Select One..."

Uses   • There is only one instance where you might prefer to use the Frame Control instead of the more versatile Picture Box. A Frame sinks its Caption *into the Frame's border,* to the left side. If this appeals to you, then the Frame offers it.

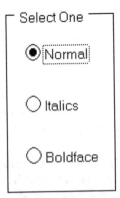

Figure F-36: The one thing a Frame can do that no other Control can is to embed a Caption within its border.

• VB offers a feature called *access keys*. If the user presses ALT+K (if K has been made an access key), a Control or Menu designated "K" will get the focus. (The Control "with the focus" will react to any keys typed on the keyboard. If there are two Text Boxes on a Form, the one with the focus will display the characters when the user types.) ALT+K in this instance will act as if the user had clicked on that Control or Menu.

Access keys offer the user an alternative to pressing the TAB key as a way of moving among the Controls on a Form. It is a Windows convention that pressing the ALT key with a designated access key automatically moves the focus directly to the Control thus designated. Any Control with a Caption Property can be assigned an access key. The Controls with Captions are Forms, Check Boxes, Command Buttons, Frames, Labels and Option Buttons. (Menus can also have access keys.)

You create an access key by placing an ampersand (&) in front of the letter you want to be the access key:

```
Command1.Caption = "&EXIT"
```

Or you can add the ampersand by using the Properties Window while designing your program.

Special Trick: Frames and Labels cannot get the focus, but they do have a TabIndex Property. They also have Caption Properties. You can use a Frame or Label to give an "access key" to a Text Box, Picture Box or other Control that normally couldn't have one (since those Controls don't have a Caption Property).

To attach a trick access key to a Text Box, for example, first make sure that the Frame or Label you're using for this trick has its TabIndex Property set to one number lower than the Text Box's TabIndex. Then, assign your access key to the Frame or Label. When the user presses the access key, the focus will not go to that Frame or Label (because they cannot get the focus). Instead, the focus will move to the next Control in the TabIndex order. So our Text Box will be accessed; it gets the focus and *that's* the trick.

Cautions
• When placing other Controls on top of a Frame, you must not double-click on the Toolbox. If you double-click, the Control can still be moved onto the Frame but will not be attached firmly to it. Instead, single-click in the Toolbox and *draw* the superimposed Control on top of the Frame.

Example

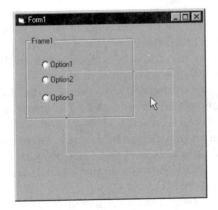

Figure F-37: Moving a Frame also stay
moves any Controls within it.

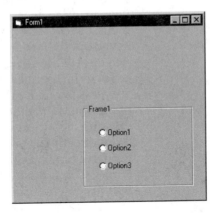

Figure F-38: Grouped Option Buttons
in position when a Frame is dragged.

While you're designing your Form, the three Option Buttons in Figure F-38 are grouped onto the Frame. Moving the Frame within the window while designing your program moves the Buttons along with the Frame. If you set the Frame's DragMode Property to Automatic, the *user* can also drag the Frame and the grouped Buttons while the program is running. Also, any Option Buttons that have been grouped can only be selected by the user in a mutually exclusive fashion. In other words, only one grouped Button at a time can be selected. By creating more than one Frame, however, you can make it possible to select more than one Option Button on a single Form (each Frame holds a separate group of Buttons).

Frame Properties
BackColor • Caption • ClipControls • DragIcon • DragMode • Enabled
FontBold • FontItalic • FontName • FontSize • FontStrikethru
FontUnderline • ForeColor • Height • HelpContextID • hWnd
Index • Left • MousePointer • Name • Parent • TabIndex • Tag
Top • Visible • Width

Form Events
Click • DblClick • DragDrop • DragOver • MouseDown
MouseMove • MouseUp

Form Methods
Drag • Move • Refresh • ZOrder

See also   Line (for a description of an easy, flexible way to draw a variety of attractive "metallic" frames around anything); Picture Box; Shape

REEFILE

FUNCTION

Description   FreeFile provides you with an unused file number, so you can open a file with a unique identifier.

When you Open a file on the disk drive (to read it, add to it, change it, whatever), you use a filenumber: Open "Test" For Input As 1. Then, in future references to the opened file, you use 1 (the filenumber) to identify this file: Input #1, for instance.

You cannot open two different files with the same number.

Used with   Disk files

Variables   X = FreeFile

Uses   • Normally, you would know when designing your program which files you had opened (and therefore which filenumbers you had used to open them). However, if your program allows the user to open files while the program runs, you may need FreeFile to provide you with unused filenumbers (you could not know in advance how many files the user had already opened and which filenumbers had been used). Note that you can't get a series of unique filenumbers by using FreeFile alone. FreeFile changes only when the Open command is used. X, Y and Z would all contain the same number in this example:

```
x=freefile
y=freefile
z=freefile
```

Moral: use the FreeFile command just prior to each time you use the Open command.

Example   X = FreeFile

Open Filename$ For Output As X

See also   Open

UNCTION

STATEMENT

Description   Functions are rather like super Variables. They act like Variables within other statements (within "expressions"), but they can also perform some action on the information they contain. Normal Variables cannot adjust the piece of text or number they hold. Normal Variables merely "contain" a piece of information–some outside agent must be used to change the contained data. A key distinction between a Function and a Subroutine is that a Function *can return* something to the location in the program that "called" the Function: X = Funct( ). The Variable X would be *given* something from the actions taken by the Function. Many times, though, you don't care what the Function returns and just ignore it.

```
X$ = "Hide the Secret."
```

X$ "holds" the phrase in this ordinary Variable, but cannot, by itself, have any effect on the phrase it holds. A Function is like an intelligent Variable: a Function can analyze, modify and report information, or take action based on the thing it holds.

Many Functions are built into Visual Basic, and you can create your own Functions too. InStr is an important built-in Function:

```
X$ = "WARNING!! The Martians Have Landed."

If InStr(X$, "Martians") <> 0 Then
     Print "Head for the ocean!"
Else
     Print "No Problem"
End If
```

The InStr Function returns (will be equal to) 0 if it doesn't find the word *Martians* inside X$. Otherwise, it returns the character position in X$ where the word *Martians* begins. Imagine how difficult getting this information would be using the Mid$ command or some other approach.

Notice that we used the Function as if it were a Variable. It's as if we said, If X <> 0 Then....; but instead the Function *did something*. It analyzed the X$ within the If...Then expression.

Functions are very similar to Subroutines. Both act as "containers" for an instruction or a series of instructions that you give to the computer so it can accomplish some task when the program runs.

Functions and Subroutines are the two basic units of organization when you're programming in Visual Basic (an Event is a Sub). Each Subroutine and Function has a name, so you can "call" (refer to) it to activate it.

Subroutines and Functions can accept Variables "passed" to them when you "call" them by name and put any Variable you want to pass following their names. Subroutines and Functions can also change the passed Variables.

Passing Variables: Here's an example of how to pass Variables. Create a Subroutine (in the General Declarations section of a Form or Module), and tell it that it will be getting a string Variable (some text) passed to it. This Sub (Subroutine) changes the ForeColor of Form1 to blue and prints the passed text; but it restores the original BackColor before it returns control to the calling instruction. In other words, you hand this Sub some text and it will print that text in blue, without permanently affecting the ForeColor:

```
Sub PrintsomethingInBlue (X$)
    Y& = Form1.ForeColor         'save the current ForeColor
    Form1.ForeColor = &HFF0000 'change the ForeColor to blue
    Print X$
    Form1.ForeColor = Y&          'restore the original ForeColor
End Sub
```

Now let's print something in black first and "call" the Sub, passing the literal text "This is Blue." (You can pass Variables or literals—see "Variables" for more on this distinction.) We could also pass a Variable like Y$. Note that if you do pass a Variable, the passed Variable name does not have to match the name of the received Variable in the Sub or Function (the name in the parentheses following the Sub's name).

The Sub receives an X$ in this example; we've said (X$), but you could pass it Y$ or any other Variable name. The X$ is for internal identification within the Sub and has no side effects on Variables outside of the Sub. The only restriction is that the passed and received Variables must be the same *type* (see "Variables"). In this case, we're passing and receiving a text ("string") Variable.

```
Sub Form_Click ()

    Form1.ForeColor = &H0
    Print "Black &..."
PrintsomethingInBlue "This is BLUE"
    Print "Now Back to Black...the Sub restored the original color"
End Sub
```

No commands in VB can appear outside Subroutines or Functions (or Events, which are a kind of Subroutine). Subroutines and Functions contain all your Instructions.

Right:

```
Function Printnumber ( )
    Print X
End Function
```

Wrong:

Visual Basic won't allow you to do the following; the instruction has no container. (The fact that you cannot use a free-floating command makes VB radically different from previous versions of the Basic Language.)

```
Print X
```

Writing an uncontained instruction will cause an error message to the effect that "End Sub or End Function must be last statement." In other words, no commands, no instructions to the computer can be free-floating without a Sub or Function to contain them and give them a name.

When you create them, you give Functions and Subroutines unique names. We called the example Function above "Printnumber." This way, other places within your program can refer to and use them. VB comes with over 500 separate commands, such as Print. When you write a Subroutine or Function, it's as if you are adding a new command to the language. And the program can then use this new command just as it would an existing command.

```
Function Printnumber (X)
    Print X
End Function
```

Note that you can pass one or more Variables to Functions. When you do that, you can decide elsewhere in the program which number will be printed. Here we *pass* the Variable Y to our PrintNumber Function. Recall that the Function manipulates X, but we're passing Y. That doesn't matter because as long as the Variables are the same type (in this case the default Variant type), the Function will accept whatever you pass it.

```
Sub Form_Click ( )
    Y = 45
    Result = Printnumber (Y)
End Sub
```

Also notice that before VB4 we could not simply name the Function to use it. The following would not work:

```
Printnumber (Y)
```

Before VB4, Functions had to be contained within "expressions." In other words, they must be part of a larger command, such as X = Functionname( ) or If Functionname( ) = 5 Then. This is the primary distinction between a Function and a Subroutine. Functions can "return" a value, and there must be somewhere (some Variable) to put this value, even if you don't use what is returned. A Subroutine, by contrast, returns nothing and can be simply "called" by giving its name:

X = Funct() (In VB3 and earlier, a Function must be part of an expression and must include parentheses—even if the parentheses are empty and you have no use for whatever is returned in the Variable X.)

Subrt (A Subroutine can simply be *named* to be used.)

Another way to think of this is that although both Subs and Functions can manipulate Variables, only a Function directly passes back Variables to the command that called the Function. We had to say Result = Printnumber(Y); we had to use the *Result* = even though the Variable *Result* is not used in this case. Nothing is passed back from our Printnumber Function, so nothing happens to *Result*. Nonetheless, you must always call upon a Function from within some kind of expression, or you'll get an error message. A lesser distinction between Functions and Subroutines is that prior to VB4, you enclosed the passed Variables within parentheses when using a Function. You omit the parentheses around passed Variables when calling a Subroutine:

Function ( )

```
X = PrintSomething (Z)
```

Subroutine

```
PrintSomething Z
```

Visual Basic has many built-in Functions:

```
X$ = UCase$("bombs away")
```

The UCase$ Function changes the characters involved to all uppercase:

```
Print X$
```

Results in   BOMBS AWAY

New in VB4

However, if you choose, you can now in VB Version 4 omit the parentheses and the return Variable when calling your Functions. This is then indistinguishable from calling Subs:

Prior to VB4:

```
X = MyFunction (PassedVar)
```

After VB4:

```
MyFunction PassedVar
```

OR

```
X = MyFunction (PassedVar)
```

Note, though, that if you do omit the parentheses, you must also omit the return Variable. You cannot simply omit one without the other.

VB's Events are built-in Subroutine structures. You provide the interior instructions that tell the computer how to behave when the Event is triggered:

```
Sub Form_Click ()
(Put your commands here.)
End Sub
```

Put Functions that are to be used by a single Form in the General Declarations section of the Form. Or, if you want them available to the entire program, put them in a Module. [If you want to restrict a Function to its home Module, use: Private Function Sort ().] You cannot construct Functions within Events, since a Subroutine or Function cannot be placed within an existing Subroutine or Function.

Used with   Create a Function when your program needs the same task performed from many different locations, *and* you also want the task to be used as part of an "expression." A Function doesn't require you to set up a Public Variable.

A Subroutine can perform its task by simply naming the Subroutine just like a Function. However a Sub cannot be used as part of an expression such as X = Functionname ( ) or If Functionname ( ) = 1 Then....

Why Subroutines and Functions Are Useful: Many programs, even some large ones, are written without creating any Functions. However, Subs and Functions are convenient when several of your Event Procedures have to do the same task, and you want to write the instructions for this task only one time.

Let's say that several of your Command Buttons need to clean off what has been printed on Form1 and change its BackColor Property to pink. You could do it this way:

```
Sub ResetButton_Click ()
    Form1.Cls
    Form1.BackColor = &HFF80FF
End Sub

Sub FinishSorting_Click ()
    Form1.Cls
    Form1.BackColor = &HFF80FF
End Sub

Sub InsertButton_Click ()
    Form1.Cls
    Form1.BackColor = &HFF80FF
End Sub
```

You can simply repeat the instructions in every Command Button's Click Event. However, it's easier in these situations to write a stand-alone Sub or Function, and just use it as you would any other word in VB's vocabulary. You've then created a custom feature to suit some frequent need peculiar to your program:

```
Sub CleanPink ( )
    Form1.Cls
    Form1.BackColor = &HFF80FF
End Sub
```

Now you simply write the name of this Subroutine in each of the Click Events:

```
Sub InsertButton_Click ()
    CleanPink
End Sub
```

You can see that this approach is more efficient, especially if the Clean-Pink task were quite lengthy and complex.

But when should you use a Function instead of a Subroutine? In the example above, a Function would be used exactly the same way, except you would be required to call the Function by putting it into an expression and using parentheses (even though they would be empty):

```
X = CleanPink ( )
```

Functions are less commonly used than Subroutines. A Function lends itself to cases where you want to use the Function within larger expressions such as:

```
If X = MyFunction (Z) Then...
```

You can always use a Subroutine instead of a Function, but this usually requires an extra step in programming:

```
MySubroutine Z
If X = Z Then...
```

Functions are also useful when you want to *return an error code*:

```
If SaveAllMyData("ThisFile.Dat") = FatalError Then End
```

Variables

No matter how many Variables you *pass* to a Function, it always returns only one Variable:

```
Function AddStrings$ (A$, B$)
    AddString$ = A$ + B$
End Function

X$ = AddStrings$ ("Hit", " The Deck")

Print X$
```

Results in

Hit The Deck

Here we passed two Variables; but, as always with a Function, we get only one back. In this case, X$.

Notice that the Variable you pass back is the name *of the Function*, AddStrings$. X$ equals AddString$, and AddStrings$ contains the result of the Function's actions. This is why we can think of Functions as super Variables. You can use them as if they were Variables, within all the kinds of "expressions" where Variables are used:

```
Print  AddStrings$ ("Hit", " The Deck")
```

Though you can only get one Variable back from a Function, you can still cause massive changes by using Subs or Functions. Variables that are passed to the Function, no matter how many you pass, can all be changed by the Function. When you return, you'll find that any Variables changed by the Function have indeed become different. The only exception to this is if you specifically protect a Variable using the ByVal keyword (see below).

• You can either pass Variables, or pass the literal thing you want changed. Above, we passed the literal "Hit" and "The Deck." Here we pass Variables:

```
d$ = "Hit"
y$ = " the Deck"
x$ = AddStrings$(d$, y$)
```

- Using the word Static preserves the contents of the Variables within the Function (or a Sub) for future use the next time you return to the Function. In other words, Static prevents the values of the Variables from being destroyed (though they can be changed). Normally, Variables local to a Function exist only while a Sub or Function is active.

    Static Function Runclose (one, two, three)

- A Function must follow the same rules that apply to any Variable. (You can't use words already used by VB itself, such as Print; you can't use words you used previously for Variables in the same Form; etc.)

    To make a Function available to all your Forms from anywhere in your program, put the Function (or Subroutine) into the General Declarations section of a Module.

- **Functions can have "Types" too:** Functions, like Variables, are types— string (text), Integer, long, etc. (for more about Variable types, see "Variables"). You can declare a Function type like this:

    Function Sort$ ()

OR

    Function Sort () As Long

    If you don't add a type symbol (like the $ which makes that a text-type Function) or the "As" command, the Function will be of the default data type. VB defaults to "Variant," but you can change it.

- The Variables passed to a Function are separated by commas.

- Any of the Variables passed to a Function can be changed by the Function. The only exception is if you use the ByVal keyword to protect a Variable. In that case, the passed Variable can be used for information and even changed temporarily while within the Function. But when you return to the place that called the Function, a Variable passed ByVal will not have been changed. In this example, X will not be changed, no matter what changes might occur to it inside the Function. Y, however, can be permanently changed by the Function:

    Function Newcost (X ByVal, Y)

    ByVal cannot be used with user-defined types (see "Type").

- If you're passing an Array (see "Arrays"), use the parentheses ( ), but do not include any dimensions that were declared. Fixed-length string Arrays are not permitted to be passed to a Function. Here's how to pass an Array:

    X = SortThem (MyArray())

- The "Variable type" of Variable(s) passed to a Function can be indicated by the As keyword, or by attaching a type symbol. Here are the two styles. Both passed Variables are text ("string") Variables; the $ is the type symbol for a text Variable:

    Function Square (X As String, Text$)

There are two special As types: As Form and As Control, which allow you to pass the identity of Forms or Controls.

This Function makes any Form the same size and color as another.

```
Function Equalize (FirstForm As Form, SecondForm As Form)
    SecondForm.Backcolor = FirstForm.BackColor
    SecondForm.Height = FirstForm.Height
    SecondForm.Width = FirstForm.Width
End Function
```

If the user changes the size of one of the Forms, the other could respond by mimicking the change. Then you would use this Function by passing the Forms' Names: X=Equalize(Form1,Form2)

• As usual, all Variables within a Function (except those passed to it) are local to that Function. They come into being when the Function runs; they die when the Function is finished with its job. The only exceptions are Variables declared in the General Declarations section of a Form or in a Module and therefore deliberately given wider scope. (See "Variables.")

• You must always call a Function by its name followed by parentheses ( ), even if the parentheses are empty because this particular Function does not receive Variables. The only exception is if you previously declared the Function's name with a Declare statement in a General Declarations section of a Form or in a Module. Or inVB4 you can omit the parentheses if you *also* omit the return Variable.

Uses • Use Functions when you need to accomplish the same task in several different places in one of your programs, and you also want to use the Function as part of an "expression."

A Function is exactly like a Subroutine, except that a Function can directly return a result to the place in your program that called the Function. In versions prior to VB4, a Function must be used within a larger structure (an expression) such as an If...Then Structure. For a definition of "expression," see "Variables."

OR (to restrict access to the function): Private Function Sort () As String

A special command, Private, is optional but can be used with Function. If you use Private, VB will "restrict access" to that Function to the Module within which the Function resides. The Function cannot then be called from within any other Module.

Cautions • Prior to VB4, you must use parentheses ( ) when calling a Function; you don't need to use them when calling a Subroutine. And prior to VB4, you must call a Function from within some kind of "expression":

```
Sub Formcolor ( )
    Form1.BackColor = Form1.BackColor + 10
End Sub
```

When calling this Subroutine, you can just use its name: Formcolor

Even when a Function doesn't have any Variables "passed" to it inside the parentheses:

```
Function Formcolor ( )
    Form1.BackColor = Form1.BackColor + 10
End Function
```

you still must use the parentheses when calling the Function in versions of VB3 and earlier: X = Formcolor ( )

And you must always call a Function as part of an expression. The X = expression is necessary prior to VB4, even if you don't care what happens to the X.

• You can use the Exit Function command to abruptly quit a Function prior to its normal conclusion (at the End Function command). Sometimes, based on things that happen while your Function does its tasks, you may want to quit early and not do everything that's listed to do within the Function.

You can use as many Exit Functions as you wish:

```
Function Newwidth (FormX As Form)

FormX.DrawWidth = FormX.DrawWidth + 1
If FormX.DrawWidth > 12 Then
    Exit Function
Else
    FormX.DrawMode = 7
End If

End Function
```

Example
```
Function Findcat (X As String)
    Findcat = InStr(X, "cat")
End Function
```

Here we created a specialized version of the built-in Visual Basic Function InStr. Our program often needs to check string Variables for the word *cat*. So, instead of writing InStr(X, "cat") every time we need to check, we wrote a Function in the General Declarations section of a Form. We could as easily have made this a Subroutine, but making it a Function gives us the added flexibility of being able to use it in expressions like this:

```
Sub Form_Click ( )
    N$ = "Hide the cat"
    M$ = "Feed the dog"
If Findcat (N$) Then
    Print "It was in N$"
End If
If Findcat (M$) Then
    ? "It was also in M$"
End If
End Sub
```

See also   Sub

GET

STATEMENT

Description The Get command reads characters from an Opened file. Get brings characters into your program from a disk file.

Used with Disk files opened in the binary or random-access modes. Files can be opened in a variety of ways (see "Open").

Binary mode allows you direct access to all characters (all bytes) in a file, even if they are not printable text characters. Some files, such as .EXE files, do not include exclusively text character information. Even some word processor files, like those saved in WordPerfect and Word formats, contain codes that are not text. And other files hold numerical data.

To examine or modify such files, the binary mode is the approach you'll want. Also, binary allows you to move to *any* point in the Opened file and read in any number of characters (or other Variable types) that you wish. How many characters are read in at one gulp depends on which Variable "type" you're using with the Get Statement (see "Variables" for a definition of "type"). You can move backward or forward or allow VB to pull in the data in sequence with repeated Gets (see the Example below).

Files opened in the random-access mode contain information stored in chunks of a specific, known length. This allows you to build database programs that can quickly locate any given record or, within each record, any particular zone (called a field). You create these files, so you know in advance how the records are organized–the number of bytes per record. Unlike binary, random-access cannot go to just any position within an Opened file; rather, it must pull data from the start of some record.

RECORD 1

NAME	ADDRESS	BIRTHDAY	AGE
Field #1	Field #2	Field #3	Field #4

RECORD 2

NAME	ADDRESS	BIRTHDAY	AGE

Figure G-1: Random-access files divide information into records, then fields. This is a way to store Arrays (which see).

Get (and its companion command, Put) cannot be used with *Sequential* files (see "Open").

Variables • Get is used to read disk information and put it into a Variable in your program. Get can pull in one character (one byte [see "Cautions"]) at a time, starting from the first character in the file. We'll store the data that we Get into a text ("string") Variable here, but you can work with any type of Variable:

Open the file as binary, then

```
A$ = String$(1, " ")
Get #1, , A$
```

First you define the length of the Variable using the String$ command (one character long in this case). Then you Get the first character in the file Opened as File #1. You would put this Get command into a Loop; each time you Get, VB moves you forward in the file, pulling off new characters, one at a time. (See the Example below.)

• To pull the fifteenth character into a Variable, by specifying the position (relative to the first character in the file):

Open the file as binary, then

```
A$ = String$(1, " ")
Get #1, 15, A$
```

• To pull in the first 15 characters, define 15 as the Variable's size:

Open the file as binary, then

```
A$ = String$(15, " ")
Get #1, , A$
```

• To pull in the first *record* from a file that you have organized as random-access (see "Open"): Get #1, , A$

You would put this Get into a Loop, and each time you Get, VB moves you forward in the file, pulling off each new record, one at a time.

• To pull in the twelfth record in a random-access file: Get #1, 12, A$

Uses   • To access information stored in binary or random-access files. You can Get the information into your program, look at it, and even modify it. If you modify it, you can save it back to the file with the Put Statement.

• Get is at a lower level than some of the other ways of pulling data into your program, such as Input$ and Line Input #. By lower level we mean that you can use any kind of Variable with Get, and you can go to any position within a file Opened as binary. That is, VB handles fewer of the details for you, and, as compensation, you have more freedom to determine exactly what, how much and where data will be pulled in from the file.

• For database programs, however, you'll find that the Data Control and the rich database programming language in VB is superior to the older Get/Put approach.

Cautions   • Files opened as binary can only use Get or Input$ to pull in information.

• Always use an error-handling Routine when you access files. (See "On Error.")

• You can use any Variable type with Get. (See "Variables" for types.)

• The Input$ command cannot be used with files Opened in the random mode.

• Text characters are stored as *two-byte* units in 32-bit VB4. This is for compatibility with OLE and NT which both use "UniCode" to represent many international alphabets. See "Chr$."

Example Put a Text Box and a Command Button on a Form. You must set the Text Box's MultiLine Property to True in the Properties Window before running this program. The MultiLine Property cannot be set while a program runs because if you turned it on and off, it would play havoc with the screen, among other things.

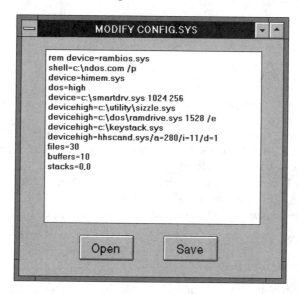

Figure G-2: This program allows the user to directly modify his or her CONFIG.SYS file.

```
Sub Command1_Click ()

A$ = String$(1, " ")

Open "C:\CONFIG.SYS" For Binary As #1

Do While Not EOF(1)
    Get #1, , A$
    b$ = b$ + A$
Loop

Text1.Text = b$

Close

End Sub
```

Notice that since Get (when used with a file Opened For Binary) always reads in as many characters as are in the Variable used in the Get Statement, you must specifically create a Variable of the length you need. Use the String$ Function for that. Here we asked that A$ be one character large, and we made it initially empty by specifying a single blank character, " ".

Then we created a Loop that keeps pulling in the next character in CONFIG.SYS, *While* we haven't reached the End Of File (of Opened file #1) EOF(1). Within this Loop, we keep lengthening the text Variable b$, building up b$ a character at a time, including any Carriage Returns and Line Feeds that, though not visible characters themselves, have the visible effect of moving us down one line.

See also   Open; Put; Seek

FUNCTION

Description   Using GetAttr, you can find the "attributes" of a disk file. SetAttr allows you to change the attributes. DOS permits you to give disk files special qualities via attributes—Archive, Hidden, Normal, ReadOnly and System. (GetAttr and SetAttr Functions are distinct from the Archive, Hidden, Normal, ReadOnly and System Properties of a File List Box. Those Properties merely filter which filenames will appear within the Box. See "Archive" for more.)

Used with   Disk files

Variables   **Variable type:** Integer

To get the attribute(s) of a file:

```
A = GetAttr ("C:\COMMAND.COM")
```

OR (to use a Variable):

```
F$ = "C:\COMMAND.COM"
A = GetAttr (F$)
```

Once you have the number representing the attribute(s) of a file, you use the And operator to test for the six possible attributes:

A filename can have more than a single attribute; attribute codes are "packed" into a byte.

To test for "Normal," for example, use the And command:

```
If A And 0 Then Print Normal
```

OR (to test for "Hidden"): If A And 2 Then Print "Hidden"

    0 = "Normal"

    2 = "Hidden"

    4 = "System"

    8 = "Volume Label"

    16 = "Directory"

    32 = "Archive"

Changing an Attribute

To add "Hidden" to the existing attribute(s), if any:

```
NewAttr = FileAttr XOR 2
SetAttr filename$, NewAttr
```

(See the Example for more on using XOR.)

Uses
- GetAttr can be part of a file-browsing aspect of a program to provide additional information to the user (beyond filesize, date and time). Also, you could create a backup program and check the Archive attribute to see if a file has changed since it was last backed up (and thus needs to be backed up again).
- SetAttr can be used in a backup program to reset the Archive attribute after a file has been backed up. You can also give the user the capability of hiding files, making them read-only, etc.

Cautions
- You cannot use wild cards (* or ?) within the filename.
- The path is optional, but without it, the filename must be in the current directory.
- You cannot use SetAttr with a currently Opened file (unless it is Open for "read-only"). See "Open" for more details.

Example

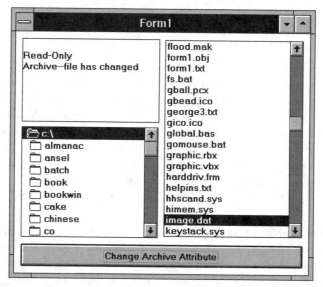

Figure G-3: GetAttr reveals the DOS file attributes of any file; SetAttr changes them.

We'll demonstrate how to query or change each file attribute. Put a Command Button, Directory List Box, File List Box and Label on a Form. We want to declare two Variables that can be accessed by any Event within our Form. FA will hold the file attribute, and FN will hold the filename. Type the following into the General Declarations section of the Form:

```
Dim fa As Integer
Dim fn As String
Dim f As String
```

Then type this into the Directory Box's Change Event to affect the File Box when the user changes directories:

```
Sub Dir1_Change ()
    file1.Path = dir1.Path
End Sub
```

Then, to report or change each file's attributes, type this into the File Box's Click Event:

```
Sub file1_click ()

cr$ = Chr$(13)
x$ = file1.List(file1.ListIndex)
p$ = file1.Path

If Right$(p$, 1) <> "\" Then p$ = p$ + "\"
fn$ = p$ + x$
fa = GetAttr(fn$)
If fa And 0 Then f$ = "Normal"
If fa And 1 Then f$ = = f$ + cr$ + "Read-Only"
If fa And 2 Then f$ = f$ + cr$ + "Hidden"
If fa And 4 Then f$ = f$ + cr$ + "System"
If fa And 8 Then f$ = f$ + cr$ + "Volume Label"
If fa And 16 Then f$ = f$ + cr$ + "Directory"
If fa And 32 Then f$ = f$ + cr$ + "Archive  file has changed"
label1.Caption = f$
End Sub
```

We use cr$ to force each attribute to go to a new line in the Label (see "Chr$"). Then we get the name of the file the user has selected by clicking, and put it into x$. We have to make an adjustment to the path by adding "\" for the root directory (see "Drive List Box"). Then we use GetAttr to get the attribute(s) of the file pointed to by the path+filename (p$ + x$).

Now a series of If...Then commands checks for each attribute, and, if True, the name of the attribute is added to f$ along with our Carriage Return character (cr$). Finally, we assign f$ to the Caption Property of the Label.

To Reset a File Attribute: The XOR command will "flip" an individual bit without disturbing the other bits in the number. More than one attribute can be "on," but they are all stored in a single integer—so you don't want to change more than the bit representing the attribute you are interested in.

In this example, we want to reset the archive attribute that is coded as the number 32. Here's how we flip it on and off each time the user presses the Command Button:

```
Sub Command1_Click ()
    fa = fa Xor 32
    SetAttr fn, fa
    file1_click
End Sub
```

See also   Drive List Box (for a general discussion on file handling in VB)

ETDATA

METHOD

Description   Transfers a picture from the Clipboard to your Visual Basic program.

Used with   The Clipboard "object." With GetData, you can send an image from the Clipboard to a Form, Image or Picture Box, the only three entities in Visual Basic that can contain graphics.

Variables   To retrieve a picture from the Clipboard that's a .BMP graphics file:

    Form1.Picture = Clipboard.GetData(2)

OR (to retrieve a picture from the Clipboard that is in Windows MetaFile format: use (8) to pull in a .DIB format image; use (2) for .BMP. .DIB means "Device-Independent Bitmap."): Form1.Picture = Clipboard.GetData(3)

The codes you can include in the parentheses are

2. BMP

3. WMF

8. DIB (Device-Independent Bitmap)

9. Palette (Color Palette)

Uses   • Allow the user to access pictures saved to the Clipboard from another program such as Paintbrush. This could be the basis for a painting program or a graphics database.

• Allow the user to change the backgrounds on your Forms, the way Windows allows you to adjust its "wallpaper."

• Ensure against unsatisfactory modifications of pictures. The Clipboard is a door through which you can get outside your program; it's a way to copy and retrieve data, or to interact with other programs that are operating at the same time. It's like the platform on which the crew of the *Enterprise* can beam up (or down). You can use it to import or export images.

But, in addition to this access to the outer worlds of Windows, the Clipboard can also be used as a faux disk—a place to temporarily put images (or text, using GetText and SetText). Thus, the Clipboard operates the same way as a RAM drive, a simulated disk drive that you set up in the CONFIG.SYS file to borrow computer memory for fast temporary storage.

If your program allows the user to modify or otherwise disturb a picture, you might want to first SetData and beam the unharmed original image down to the Clipboard, before the user gets a chance to change it. Should the user later decide that the improvements were after all a disgrace, you've got the original safely stashed away in the Clipboard. You've also thoughtfully provided a Command Button called "Undo" that, when pressed undoes the horror.

```
Sub UndoButton_Click ()
    Picture1.Picture = Clipboard.GetData(2)
End Sub
```

But beware that in a multitasking environment like Windows, other programs might use the Clipboard, thereby destroying your "saved" image. A safer approach is to save backup copies to a disk file.

Cautions   • In Windows, there can be only one Clipboard at a time. Unlike Notepad and most other Windows entities, Clipboard cannot co-exist with other active Clipboards.

• GetData can pull in four kinds of graphics from the Clipboard: .BMP Bitmap Picture; .WMF Windows Metafile; .DIB Device-Independent Bitmap; and Color Palettes. There are many other PC graphics file types such as .TIF, .GIF and .EPS. However, the Clipboard can accommodate only those four types.

You can use the GetFormat command to find out if the Clipboard contains the graphics type you're trying to import into VB.

Example   We stored a picture into the Clipboard, before the user could modify it:

```
Sub Form_Click ()
    clipboard.SetData form1.picture
End Sub
```

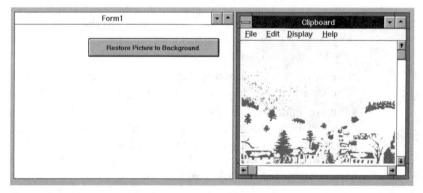

Figure G-4: Move graphics between the Clipboard and your VB programs.

Then, when the user presses the Command Button to which we've given the Name "Restore," the picture returns to the Form.

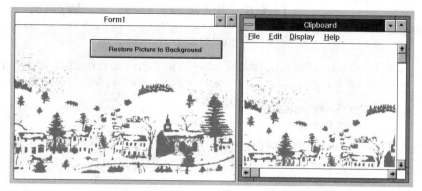

Figure G-5: The picture is copied back into our VB window.

```
Sub Restore_Click ()
    Picture = Clipboard.GetData(2)
End Sub
```

See also   Clear; Clipboard; GetFormat; GetText; SetData; SetText

ET FORMAT

METHOD

Description   GetFormat tells you what kind of thing is in the Clipboard. Is it in text format? Is it a .BMP graphic?

Used with   The Clipboard

Variables   X = Clipboard.GetFormat (1)

If $X = 0$, then you know that the Clipboard does not contain text. If X is –1, it does contain text data. The (1) tells GetFormat that we're asking if there is text in the Clipboard. After this command is carried out in VB while a program is running, the Variable X will contain either a –1 (for "yes") or a 0 (for "no").

Put these numbers in the parentheses following GetFormat( ) to get back a yes or no answer about the type of contents presently in the Clipboard:

1   Is it text?

2   Is it a Bitmap Picture (a .BMP file type) ?

3   Is it a Windows MetaFile picture (a .WMF file type)?

8	Is it a Device-Independent Bitmap picture (a .DIB file type)?
48896	Is it a Link (DDE, *Dynamic Data Exchange*)? As you may well suppose, based on the rather large leap from 8 to 48896, DDE is a whole strange category of its own. See "Link" for more.
9	Is it a Color Palette?

Uses   Verify that the type of data in the Clipboard is what you think it is before, say, trying to import a graphic image into your program (see "GetData").

Cautions   • GetFormat works like a Function: it returns some information. You must query GetFormat with a Variable: X = Clipboard.GetFormat(1)

• GetFormat answers only "yes" (–1) or "no" (0) to your query.

• Although the VB Reference book says the ( ) following GetFormat defaults to 1 and can be omitted, you'll get an error message if you try that.

Example

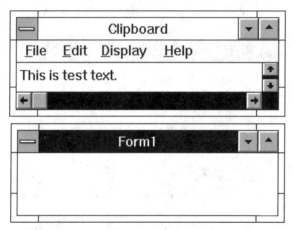

Figure G-6: This can form part of a cut, copy and paste feature. Move text between your programs and the Clipboard.

The Clipboard has some text in it, and our VB program contains these instructions:

```
Sub Form_Click ()

If Clipboard.GetFormat(1) Then
    X$ = Clipboard.GetText(1)
    Print X$
End If
End Sub
```

Recall that If...Then responds only to True/False situations—zero being False, and anything other than zero being True. When we say this: "If Clipboard.GetFormat(1)," we are actually saying this: "If anything other than zero." So, if there is text in the Clipboard, we get it into X$ and then Print it on the Form:

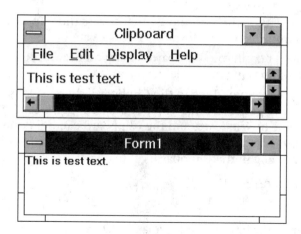

Figure G-7: The text is now copied into our program.

See also   Clear; Clipboard; GetData; GetText; SetData; SetText

GET**T**EXT

METHOD

Description   GetText can bring into your VB program any text that's in the Windows Clipboard.

Used with   The Clipboard "Object." Using GetText, you can copy all the text in the Clipboard into a text ("string") Variable in your VB program.

Variables   To get ordinary text:

```
X$ = Clipboard.GetText (1)
```

OR (to get linked text—see "Link"): X$ = Clipboard.GetText (48896)

Uses   • Import into your VB program text that was copied or cut from other programs, such as word processors.

• Provide an Undo feature. Before allowing the user to modify text in a Text Box, first temporarily store it in the Clipboard:

```
Clipboard.SetText Text1.Text, 1
```

Then, if the user presses a Command Button you've labeled Undo, the instructions in the Command Button restore the contents of the Clipboard to your Text Box:

```
Sub Command1_Click ()
    Text1.Text = Clipboard.GetText(1)
End Sub
```

G ... **421**

Cautions
• GetText, like the other "Methods" that access the Clipboard, works like a Function: it returns some information into a Variable.

• If there is no text in the Clipboard when you use GetText, you'll get back empty text (string) in your Variable: X$ = "".

• When you store something in the Clipboard, there is no guarantee that you'll be able to get back what you put in later. There can be only one Clipboard at a time in Windows, and the Clipboard can hold only one set of data at a time. Some other program could have replaced your data by storing something in the Clipboard.

Example
A$ = Clipboard.GetText(1)

Print A$

See also
Clear; Clipboard; GetData; GetFormat; SetData; SetText

GLOBAL

STATEMENT

See
Public

GoSub...Return

STATEMENT

Description
A Subroutine is like a little program within your larger program—performing some limited useful task (and usually available to be called upon to perform that task from anywhere in the program).

Creating a Subroutine is like teaching your dog to fetch the paper. After he learns the trick, you can sit in your rocking chair on the porch and just say *paper* and let him find it in your yard and bring it back.

A Subroutine is (1) available anytime; (2) part of a larger structure; (3) able to do something limited but useful; and (4) going to be needed by your program more than one time.

However, Visual Basic uses the Sub...End Sub structure for Subroutines. The GoSub...Return structure is strictly limited to tiny zones *within* a Sub...End Sub (or Function). As a result, GoSub...Return has little if any utility in Visual Basic.

Classic Subroutines: Visual Basic relies much less on classic Subroutines than do older computer languages. It used to be that a Basic program had many Subroutines, and you used the GoSub command often. The contributions of the abstract Subroutine structure are, of course, inherent to programming and will always exist as long as people need to communicate with computers. Subroutines are fundamentally efficient because they extend the language in much the same way that abbreviations and acronyms extend human language.

Just *how* the concept of the Subroutine is embraced by each computer language, though, can differ considerably. VB's design essentially eliminates the need for traditional Subroutines to which you would GoSub and then Return—everything in VB is a Subroutine, so in a way nothing is.

In place of GoSub...Return, VB coagulates all instructions, all commands into Sub...End Sub structures (or the similar Function structure). For more on how Visual Basic exploits the concept of Subroutines, see "Sub."

Used with　In Visual Basic, GoSub...Return is used *within* a given Event Procedure, Sub or Function structure. And GoSub...Return is available only to the structure within which it resides—thereby defeating one of the primary values of Subroutines—that they be available programwide. Also, GoSub...Return requires a Label and an Exit Sub or other command separating it from the body of the Event, Sub or Function. See the Example below.

In practice there is little use for GoSub...Return in Visual Basic. If you are tempted to use this structure, you might want to consider creating a separate Sub in a Module (see "Sub").

Variables　You cannot "pass" Variables to a GoSub...Return structure, but you don't need to. The GoSub...Return structure is within a Sub...End Sub or Function...End Function structure. The GoSub...Return structure therefore has access to all the local Variables within its host structure.

Uses　• None, in general

GoSub...Return is included in Visual Basic for compatibility with older versions of Basic. In Visual Basic there are better ways to achieve the effect of the traditional GoSub...Return.

Error trapping (see "Error") is perhaps the only common use of Subroutines nested within a Sub...End Sub structure. And even error trapping is usually done with On...GoTo, rather than GoSub...Return, in Visual Basic.

When you want to create a classic Subroutine, use Sub...End Sub.

One possible value of GoSub...Return is that it would likely execute more quickly than a Subroutine. It would not be necessary to "pass" Variables or do other housekeeping. If you wanted to do something repeatedly within a single Event (or Subroutine or Function), consider using On...GoSub.

Cautions　Be careful that your program doesn't "fall through" into a Subroutine. A Label identifies the start of a Subroutine within the Sub...End Sub structure, but the Label does not stop the computer from continuing into the Subroutine and carrying out the commands therein.

Just before the Label, you need to put an Exit Sub, Exit Function, End or GoTo command to prevent the computer from falling through into the Subroutine. You want the Subroutine to be used only when specifically called by the GoSub command. (See the Example below.)

Example   Since there is no common use for GoSub...Return in Visual Basic, this example is of necessity trivial. It merely serves to illustrate how GoSub...Return would be used if it ever were.

We created a Text Box. When you type in a character, the KeyPress Event (which is itself a VB Sub structure, as are all Events) detects which key was pressed. If it is the ENTER key (ASCII code 13), we are sent to the Subroutine down below. Notice that GoSub...Return *must be within a larger Sub...End Sub structure (or Function structure).*

Also, notice that you must use the Exit Sub just prior to the Subroutine's Label, "Beepit," or you would always "fall through" to the Subroutine and beep for every keypress. That you have to isolate interior Subroutines in this awkward fashion is another reason to avoid using GoSub...Return in Visual Basic.

```
Sub Text1_KeyPress (keyascii As Integer)

If keyascii = 13 Then GoSub Beepit

Exit Sub

Beepit:
    Beep
    form1.Print "Beep"
Return

End Sub
```

See also   Function; On GoSub, On GoTo; Sub

GotFocus

EVENT

Description   When a Control, such as a Text Box, *has the focus*, this means that any typing on the keyboard will cause characters to appear in that Text Box. Only one Control at a time can "have the focus," just as only one window in Windows can be *active* (able to receive user input) at any given time.

The user can change the focus either by clicking on a different Control or by using the TAB key to cycle among the Controls on the active Form.

The order in which the focus cycles is determined by how the Controls' individual TabIndex Properties are set. You can also adjust the focus while your program is running by using the SetFocus method—in this way, your *program*, rather than some action by the user, changes the focus.

Used with Check Boxes, Combo Boxes, Command Buttons, Directory, Drive & File List Boxes, Forms, Grids, Horizontal & Vertical Scroll Bars, List Boxes, OLE, Option Buttons, Picture Boxes and Text Boxes

Variables If you want your program to react when a Control gets the focus, put your instructions within that Control's GotFocus_Event:

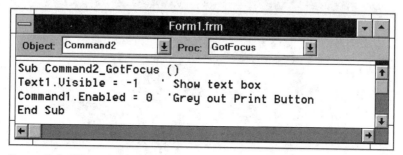

Figure G-8: When Command Button #2 gets the focus, Command Button #1 is disabled, grayed out and unavailable to the user.

Uses • Provide information or help specific to the Controls that the user is currently clicking (or tabbing). (See the Example below.)

• Disable (make a gray ghosted image with the Enabled Property set to 0); make invisible (Visible Property to 0); move; or otherwise adjust Controls that are not used with the Control that currently has the focus.

• GotFocus is primarily useful as a way to detect that the TAB key has shifted the focus. Some users don't use the mouse much, so a Click Event would not happen when they attempted to change focus with the TAB key.

Cautions • A Form itself can get the focus, but only under special conditions: either there must be no Controls on that Form or any extant Controls must be disabled (their Enabled Property set to 0).

• A Control's KeyDown, KeyPress or KeyUp Event cannot be triggered unless that Control has the focus.

• A Control cannot get the focus if its Enabled or Visible Properties are off (set to 0).

Example You can provide the user with information depending on which Control has the focus. Here in a database we offer the scientific name or a brief description of various fish:

```
Sub Command4_GotFocus ()
    Command1.Caption = "Thought extinct until, in 1923, found alive off →
        Zanzibar."
End Sub

Sub Command5_GotFocus ()
    Command1.Caption = "Irithicanthis Nominilus"
End Sub
```

Many programs provide a bar across the bottom of the screen, offering information about, for example, the current position of the cursor and the meaning of currently selected options. In Figure G-12 we've created such a bar by greatly distending a Command Button:

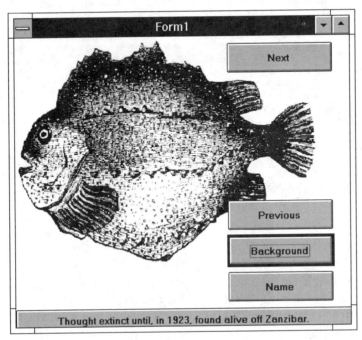

Figure G-9: The Command Button labeled "Background" has a darker border and a thin gray line around its Caption, showing that it has the focus.

Using MouseMove Instead: Another alternative—and an intriguing one—to GotFocus is the MouseMove Event. It detects when the mouse pointer is simply within the borders of a Control. No clicks are necessary: the user simply glides around, "touching" Controls—like Tinkerbell touches things with her wand. The touch causes something to happen, displays a brief explanatory message—for example, about the purpose of the touched Control. Unfortunately, only a few Controls, not including Command Buttons, respond to MouseMove. (However the Sheridan 3D Controls do respond.)

In any case, the above alternatives to GotFocus require a mouse, and that would exclude those still clinging to all-keyboard interaction with their computers. Some people still use TAB extensively to move around a window, changing focus as they go.

See also   Activate, Deactivate; ActiveControl; HideSelection; LostFocus; SetFocus; TabIndex

STATEMENT

Description GoTo is like the GoSub command, but without a matching Return Statement to send you back. GoTo sends your program to another location within a given Subroutine, Function or Event Procedure. The target of GoTo is generally a *label*; but it can also be a line number, if you are one who numbers your program lines. (This kind of label is not related to the Label *Control*. Rather, it is a name that you give to a location within your program by making it the first word on a line—and appending a colon):

    GOHERE:

Also, note that the GoTo command cannot jump to a target outside of the Sub, Function or Event within which it resides; it cannot jump to a label in another Sub, for instance.

Used with Labels. A Label must have an alphabetical first character and end with a colon: LABEL:

Variables To move to a different location: GoTo LABEL3

OR (to go to a different location based on some condition):

    If X = 12 Then GoTo CLOSEFILES

OR (if you number the lines in your programs): GoTo 500

Uses • GoTo has always been disparaged by professional programmers and by programming teachers because it can make programs difficult to understand. There have been instances, though, where a programmer has deliberately created wildly convoluted, obscure programs in the interest of job security. The GoTo command is certainly handy if you don't want anyone else to easily understand or maintain your programs.

A program has *flow*—the instructions within the program come one after another and the designated tasks are carried out in that order:

    Sub Form_Click

    Cls
    Print "Please Enter Your Name"
    X$ = InputBox$ ("")
    End Sub

After the user clicks on this Form:

1. The Form is cleared of any previous printing or drawing.

2. The message to enter a name is printed on the Form.

3. An InputBox appears, waiting for the user to respond.

It is not possible for the computer to first put up the InputBox, then clear the screen. The computer must follow these instructions in the order they are written by the programmer. The program is said to *flow* from 1 to 2 to 3 in a direct, sequential path down through the programmer's instructions.

However, flow can be interrupted by structures such as If...Then or by instructions such as Exit Sub:

```
If X$ <> "" Then Exit Sub
Cls
Print "Please Enter Your Name"
X$ = InputBox$ ("")
```

In the above example, the flow is interrupted if there is already something in the Variable X$ (If X$ does not equal empty text—"").

When this program runs, text in X$ would prevent the Cls, Print and InputBox$ instructions from ever being carried out. The program would jump right out of the Sub with the Exit Sub command.

It is often necessary to go back and "read" a program, to find the source of errors or to update the program and improve it. Sometimes you'll read a program months or years after you've written it. Sometimes, especially among professionals who program in groups, there's even a need to read other people's programming. For all these reasons, GoTo is discouraged. It causes an open-ended leap to another part of the program, interrupting the flow in a way that is hard to follow, particularly if there are many GoTos.

If your program needs to leap to a new location based on a current condition (as programs often do), there are many alternatives to GoTo. The most common of these are

```
Select Case...End Select
If...End If
```

Paired Instructions: Note that these alternatives are *paired* instructions; they create a structure, the purpose of which is easily understood. Instructions enclosed within a structure (sometimes called a "block") belong together and are governed by the purpose of the structure. No matter how many Elses and ElseIfs might be contained between an If and its End If, all the instructions between the boundaries of a structure are visibly related and all must react to the condition described by the If (here's an example: If X$ <> ""). Perhaps even more important to the readability of a program is the fact that paired instructions have a distinct, specific *end*.

By contrast, GoTo is not paired with anything except a target label, which means that GoTo creates no logical grouping of related instructions, no structure. That is why it can make a program harder to read.

The Death Dance: Programming was different just a few years ago. A large program could have page after page of instructions, and avoiding GoTo helped to clarify things. If you tried to draw a line that followed the flow of a program with dozens of GoTos, the line would resemble the death dance of a beheaded chicken—a virtually random pattern.

However, Visual Basic is by nature organized into small, self-contained Events whose purposes are generally obvious by their very names: Picture1_Click, Form2_GotFocus, Text1_Change and so forth. Readable structures emerge naturally from the sensible design of this language and the way it nudges you to encapsulate instructions within objects and Modules of limited size and purpose.

Because the dangerous power of GoTo is severely restricted in Visual Basic (GoTo cannot send your program leaping outside of the Event, Sub or Function within which it is located), there is little risk that the GoTo command could be abused as it sometimes was in the past. Nonetheless, given the available alternative commands, it is probably best to avoid GoTo. At some point, GoTo will disappear altogether from computer languages. No equivalent to GoTo exists in human language except perhaps when one loses the train of one's thought, is describing a dream or is interrupted during a conversation:

SHEILA: So, I said to Dave . . .

BARB: No, Sheila honey, go to the good part. What happened last night? Did he . . . you know?

Cautions
- The label to which GoTo leaps must follow the usual rules for names you make up (when naming Variables, for instance):
  - It must begin with an alphabetical character.
  - It cannot be longer than 40 characters.
  - Already used VB words such as Print cannot be chosen.
- You cannot use the same label name more than once within a Form.
- No distinction is made between uppercase and lowercase letters. You can GoTo "TARGET," and the label you're going to can be (lowercase) "target:"
- A label name must end with a colon (Target:) where it appears as the target, but the colon is omitted at the GoTo jump-off point that targets the label (GoTo Target).
- A label can be indented, as long as it is the first item on that line. It is common practice, however, to leave labels on a line by themselves, at the far left of a line, and to capitalize the first letter of the label's name.

Example
Put a Text Box on a Form. Then, in the Text Box's KeyPress Event, type this:

```
Sub Text1_KeyPress (KeyAscii As Integer)
```

```
If KeyAscii = Asc("a") Then GoTo LA
If KeyAscii = Asc("b") Then GoTo LB

Exit Sub

LA:
Print "The User pressed an a"
Exit Sub

LB:
Print "The User pressed a b"

End Sub
```

A better approach to the above job would be to use Select Case. This next example accomplishes the same thing as the previous example but is easier to program, read and understand:

```
Sub Text1_KeyPress (KeyAscii As Integer)

Select Case Chr$(KeyAscii)

    Case "a"
        Print "The User pressed an a"
    Case "b"
        Print "The User pressed a b"

End Select

End Sub
```

See also   GoSub; On GoSub, On GoTo

RID

CONTROL

Description   A Grid can be used to display tables or create a spreadsheet application. The Grid Control is unique among VB's Controls in that it includes dozens of Properties and is thus virtually a separate, functional program. Its closest relative on the Toolbox is the Text Box, with its built-in word processing features. However, a Grid has *51* Properties! Of these, 25 Properties are unique to the Grid Control and are highly specific, such as TopRow, ColWidth and CellSelected. Covering each of these Grid-specific Properties as a separate entry is beyond the scope of this book. The Properties are, however, simple, and you are referred to the VB manuals and online Help for specific details.

Figure G-10: The Grid Control on the Toolbox.

Used with Forms

Variables You can set some of the Grid Properties with the Properties Window while designing your program:

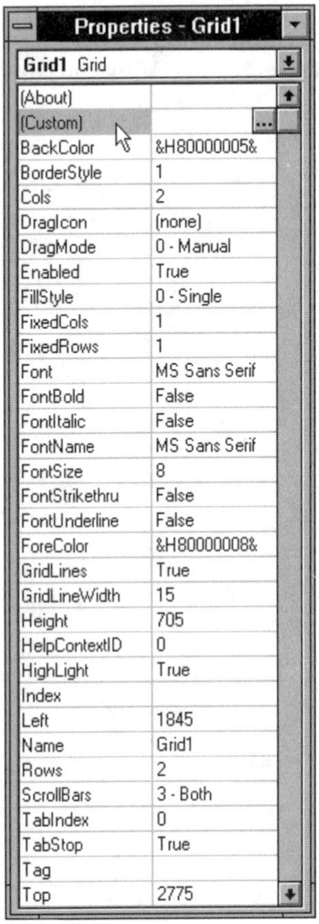

Properties - Grid1	
Grid1 Grid	
(About)	
(Custom)	...
BackColor	&H80000005&
BorderStyle	1
Cols	2
DragIcon	(none)
DragMode	0 - Manual
Enabled	True
FillStyle	0 - Single
FixedCols	1
FixedRows	1
Font	MS Sans Serif
FontBold	False
FontItalic	False
FontName	MS Sans Serif
FontSize	8
FontStrikethru	False
FontUnderline	False
ForeColor	&H80000008&
GridLines	True
GridLineWidth	15
Height	705
HelpContextID	0
HighLight	True
Index	
Left	1845
Name	Grid1
Rows	2
ScrollBars	3 - Both
TabIndex	0
TabStop	True
Tag	
Top	2775

Figure G-11: Thirty-one of a Grid's 51 Properties can be adjusted during program design. (Several of them are hidden under the Custom Property.)

However, a subset of Grid Properties can either be "read-only" (that is, they are merely for your program's information and cannot be changed, such as CellSelected), or they can be changed only while the program is running (such as ColWidth).

Uses
• Make traditional spreadsheet applications.

• Use the graphics capabilities of a Grid to show thumbnail sketches of .BMP or .ICO graphics (see the Example).

• Create tables.

Cautions
• The Grid (and OLE) Control, among others, may not appear in your toolbox. If it isn't there, use the Custom Controls item on the Tools Menu to add it. Also, if you give a finished .EXE program that contains a Grid to someone else to use, you must make sure that GRID16.OCX or GRID32.OCX is placed into his or her WINDOWS/SYSTEM directory; otherwise, your program won't run.

• There is a set of 15 Grid-specific error codes, numbered from 30,000 to 30,017 (see the VB *Programmer's Guide* for the meanings of these codes).

• The Picture Property, which allows you to display graphics within a Grid's cells, differs from the Picture Property of a Form, Image Box or Picture Box in two ways: (a) it cannot be a .WMF file (it must be .BMP or .ICO); and (b) it cannot be assigned while you are designing your program.

• The ScrollBars Property works as it does with a Text Box, except that it will not be visible unless there are more cells than can be viewed in the Grid.

• The Text Property of a Grid differs from the Text Property of a Text Box. For a Grid, Text tells your program the text ("string") in the currently selected cell (or allows your program to change the text in that cell). You cannot assign text while you're designing your program; if you want to fill cells with text, you must do it in the Form_Load Event the way you would fill a List Box (which see). The user cannot change the text in a cell by clicking on it to make it the current cell and then typing in something new. To allow the user to change the contents of a cell, you would have to do it indirectly—use a separate Text Box and have your program transfer its contents when the user clicks on a cell in the grid (Grid1.Text = Text1.Text). There can be no more than 255 characters in a given cell.

Example

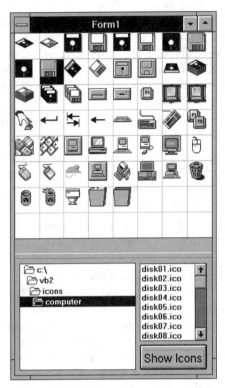

Figure G-12: We'll build an icon-viewer.

This icon-viewer application is another example of the extraordinary efficiency of VB as compared to previous programming languages. What used to take weeks of careful work can be put together in a matter of minutes.

Start a New Project from the File Menu; then add GRID, if necessary, by using the Tools|Custom Controls Menu.

Now add a Grid, a File List Box, a Directory List Box and a Command Button to the Form. Set the File List Box's Pattern Property to *.ICO.

In the Form_Load Event, we use the Grid Properties RowHeight and ColWidth to create cells slightly larger than icon images. Notice that the cells in a Grid are an Array (which see), so you access them with index numbers and can modify them in Loops. After establishing the size of our cells, we make the entire Grid slightly larger than the total number of cells:

```
Sub Form_Load ()
    For i = 0 To 7
        grid1.RowHeight(i) = 500
        grid1.ColWidth(i) = 500
    Next i
    grid1.Width = 8 * 550
    grid1.Height = 8 * 550
End Sub
```

Now, in the Directory List Box's Change Event, we'll cause the File List Box to react if the user switches directories (see "Drive List Box" for more on this):

```
Sub Dir1_Change ()
    file1.Path = dir1.Path
End Sub
```

All the action takes place when the user clicks on the Command Button:

```
Sub Command1_Click ()
If file1.ListCount = 0 Then Exit Sub
' Create the path
pa$ = dir1.Path
If Right$(pa$, 1) <> "\" Then pa$ = pa$ + "\"
' Clean out the cells
For r = 0 To 7
    For c = 0 To 7
        grid1.Col = c
        grid1.Row = r
    grid1.Picture = LoadPicture("")
    Next c
Next r
' Fill the cells
For r = 0 To 7
    For c = 0 To 7
        If x > file1.ListCount - 1 Then Exit For
        grid1.Col = c
        grid1.Row = r
        f$ = pa$ + file1.List(x)
        grid1.Picture = LoadPicture(f$)
        x = x + 1
    Next c
Next r
End Sub
```

We start off by checking to see if the ListCount is 0, which means that no files in the current directory match the .ICO Pattern. If there are .ICOs to look at, we create the appropriate path (see "Drive List Box").

Because the user might have already filled the cells by looking at another directory, we first want to have all the cells blank before showing the .ICOs in this new directory. Using the LoadPicture command with a blank, null "" argument erases the contents of the cell. Note that the Col and Row Properties have the effect of "selecting" which cell is "active." Assigning Col and Row is the way your program can imitate the effect of the user clicking on a particular cell. The "active" cell is the one that will receive text or graphics when you use the Grid1.Text = X$ or Grid1.Picture = LoadPicture command.

Having cleaned out the cells, we again use a Loop—this time keeping track of the number of .ICO files to be displayed by watching the ListCount Property. The line f$ = pa$ + file1.List(x) builds a complete path and filename by adding, for example, (pa$) C:\VBASIC\ICONS\FLAGS to (file1.List(x)), which will be each .ICO filename during the Looping.

Grid Properties
BackColor • BorderStyle • CellSelected • Clip • Col • ColAlignment Cols • ColWidth • DragIcon • DragMode • Enabled • FillStyle FixedAlignment • FixedCols • FixedRows • FontBold • FontItalic FontName • FontSize • FontStrikeThru • FontUnderline • ForeColor GridLines • GridLineWidth • Height • HelpContextID • HighLight hWnd • Index • Left • LeftCol • Name • Parent • Picture • Row RowHeight • Rows • ScrollBars • SelEndCol SelEndRow • SelStartCol SelStartRow • TabIndex • TabStop • Tag • Text • Top • TopRow Visible • Width

Grid Events
Click • DblClick • DragDrop • DragOver • GotFocus • KeyDown KeyPress • KeyUp • LostFocus • MouseDown • MouseMove MouseUp • RowColChange • SelChange

Grid Methods
AddItem • Drag • Move • ReFresh • RemoveItem SetFocus • ZOrder

hDC

PROPERTY

Description Briefly defined, hDC is the handle—a unique ID number assigned to the screen, printer or other "surface" on which the computer can create visual effects. Windows itself assigns these ID numbers, and Forms and Controls can be identified as part of an hDC. Handles are used when you access the Windows operating system directly (it's called the Application Programming Interface, the API). There are more than 600 Subroutines buried in the API, and learning to tap into them can greatly expand the power of Visual Basic. See Appendix A for a tutorial on the API.

Technically speaking, the hDC is not a handle assigned to a particular Form or Control *per se*. Rather, the hDC is a handle to what in Windows is called the "device context." A device context describes a drawing surface and its capabilities. hWnd (which see) is the actual handle to a particular Form or Control.

Used with Forms, Picture Boxes and the printer. (Unfortunately, the current version of VB does not provide a way to directly get the hDC handles of other Controls. There is a relatively simple way to do it, however. See Appendix A.)

Variables **Variable type:** Integer

Although called a Property, the hDC is actually a Windows Variable. You cannot change it; you can only "pass" it when you are calling an API Subroutine. Also, the hDC is assumed to be *dynamic* (it can change at any time while Windows is active), so you should not put the value of hDC into a Variable and try to use that Variable later. Always use the hDC itself, in case it has changed.

Uses hDC identifies the "device context" of an object (Form, Control or the printer) that you want affected by the actions of an API call. hDC is used mainly with API calls to GDI (Graphic Device Interface) routines such as BitBlt. For more on these features of Windows, see Appendix A.

Cautions • Do not store an hDC in a Variable. The hDC of an object can change while the program runs. Use hDC directly within the list of Variables you pass to an API Function. (See the Example below.)

• When you plan to use the API, you must first "declare" the API Function or Subroutine you want to access. These declarations are made in the General Declarations section of a Form or Module. It is necessary that a declaration be typed *entirely on a single line*, no matter how long the declaration might be. Do not hit the ENTER key when typing in an API declaration.

Example   To draw a pie shape, you can use the Pie Subroutine that's built into Windows API. While Pie is not a command in Visual Basic, you can access all the API Routines from VB.

First we put the following into a Module. Remember that although we can't print it that way in this book, the entire Declare statement must be on a single line when you type it into a Module. Just keep typing, and VB will scroll the page left as you create this huge line.

Notice that all this repetitive lingo is necessary but not complicated. See Appendix A to discover how easy it is to use many of the Windows API Routines. Some don't even require any Variables. This one, though, does:

```
Declare Sub Pie Lib "GDI" (ByVal hDC As Integer, ByVal x1 As Integer, →
    ByVal y1 As Integer, ByVal x2 As Integer, ByVal y2 As Integer, ByVal x3 →
    As Integer, ByVal y3 As Integer, ByVal x4 As Integer, ByVal y4 As Integer)
```

If you're using the 32-bit version of VB4, substitute "GDI32" for "GDI." Also, after the final parenthesis, add this: As Long

Then, after it's been declared, Pie can be used like any other Subroutine—just name it and feed it the Variables it wants. Pie, as you can see from its declaration, wants the hDC so that Pie can know where to draw the pie; then it wants six X,Y coordinates to tell it where on the Form to put the pie, how big to make it, its shape, and how big a slice to cut out of it. All drawing in Windows is done on a "device context," which can be thought of as similar to a sheet of paper. You can assume that a framed sheet of paper is a Form. The frame around the paper would be the hWnd and the sheet of paper itself would be the hDC. The result of this distinction is that when you want to *draw* something you have to do it on the paper (as is done with the API Routine called BitBlt; see "Declare"). To draw something, you use the hDC. By contrast, if you want to do something physical like move a window, you use the hWnd .

Figure H-1: Use built-in Windows features to create special geometric shapes.

Here's the place where we call upon Pie to do its work:

```
Sub Form_Load ()

Show
fillstyle = 0
Fillcolor = QBColor(13)

    Pie hdc, 50, 50, 475, 475, 300, 250, 400, 300
End Sub
```

The eight Variables describe the pie shape in the familiar X,Y (horizontal, vertical) system, requiring two Variables for each of the points:

Pie hDc, X1, Y1, X2, Y2, X3, Y3, X4, Y4

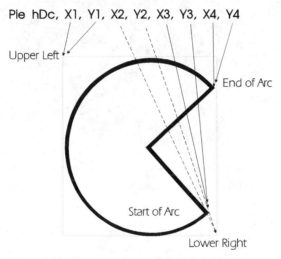

Figure H-2: The meanings of the Variables you provide to create a pie shape.

Here's another example:

Although Pie Variables that produce the series of shapes in Figure H-3 may look like part of the launch sequence for the Space Shuttle, it's not the result of any great grasp of geometry. It's the result of hacking (computer-ese for fiddling with parameters until you get what you're after). And how much of the screen the pie shapes take up will depend on the video driver you are using for Windows (VGA, Super-VGA, etc.). So, if the following makes a pie too large to view on your screen, fiddle with the numbers until it looks good. (Put all the Variables following Pie on a single line.)

```
Sub Form_Load ()

Show
fillstyle = 0

For i = 0 To 5
    fillcolor = QBColor(i + 8)
        If i = 5 Then fillstyle = 6: i = 7: z = 2
    Pie hdc, 50 - z * 20, (−5 * i + 50 * z) + 70, i * 40 + 600, 500, i * 50→
```

```
                     + 300, 400, 200, 400
              Next i
              End Sub
```

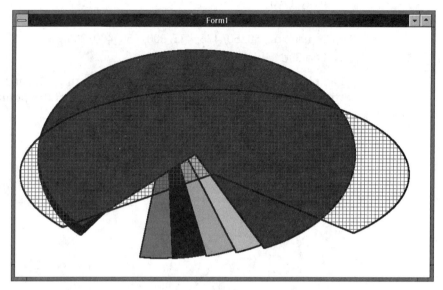

Figure H-3: Several overlapping pie shapes, with a change in FillStyle for variety.

See also   Appendix A; hWnd

HEIGHT

PROPERTY

Description   The Height Property allows you to find out the height of a Form or Control, or to change it. Height is also a property of the Printer "Object" and tells you the size of the paper the printer is currently using. Height is a property of the Screen "Object" and tells you the "logical" vertical dimension of the user's screen (for example, 480 or 600, etc.). (This is not the physical height of the screen; Windows doesn't know that, and doesn't care. The screen is drawn to relative specifications, not absolute sizes. In other words, given the same "logical" dimensions, your VB program would appear the same on a 13-inch and a 20-inch monitor: the Controls would appear larger, but they would be the same shape and the same relative distances from each other. They would not be "stretched apart" as if your program's window had been distended like a stretched sheet of rubber to fit the larger screen.)

Used with Forms, Check Boxes, Combo Boxes, Command Buttons, Directory, Drive & File List Boxes, Frames, Grids, Horizontal & Vertical Scroll Bars, Images, Labels, List Boxes, Multiple Document Interface (MDI) Forms, OLE, Option Buttons, Picture Boxes, Shapes, Text Boxes, the user's video screen and the printer

Variables **Variable type:** Single

Normally you would establish the height of a Form or Control while designing your program—by dragging the top of the object with the mouse.

OR (to make one Picture Box as tall as another):

    Picture2.Height = Picture1.Height

OR (to find out how high this Form is...the user might have stretched it):

    X = Form3.Height

OR (to specify a particular height, using the current ScaleMode, which see): Text1.Height = 400

OR (to use a Variable to set the height):

    X = 400
    Text1.Height = X

OR (to find out where on the screen you should place an object abutting the bottom of List1): Rightbelow = List1.Height + List1.Top

OR (to make a Control square): Picture2.Width = Picture2.Height

OR (to find out how tall this Form is...the user might have stretched it):

    X = Form3.Height

OR (to make a Control fill the entire window):

    Picture1.Width = ScaleWidth
    Picture1.Height = ScaleHeight

OR (to make a window fill the entire screen):

    Width = Screen.Width
    Height = Screen.Height
    Left = 0
    Top = 0

OR (to center the window within the screen):

    Left = (Screen.Width - Width) / 2
    Top = (Screen.Height - Height) / 2

OR (to make the window 80% the size of the screen, and centered):

    Width = .80 * Screen.Width
    Height = .80 * Screen. Height
    Left = (Screen.Width - Width) / 2
    Top = (Screen.Height - Height) / 2

OR (to find out where on the screen you should place an object that you want to be flush against the bottom of List1):

```
RightBeneath = List1.Top + List1.Height
```

Uses
• Restore related Controls to a uniform size (even if changed by the user).

• Draw objects on the Form for a background, using Line or Circle.

• Animate objects by enlarging them while the program is running. (Leave the Form and Picture Boxes' AutoRedraw Properties off [False], or you'll really slow things up with this technique.) See the Example below.

• Create pleasing or symmetrical arrangements of the items on a window.

• Adjust the height of a Form to uncover additional Controls based on a user action. For example, in a database program for customer info, if the user clicks on a box that says the customer has bought something, your program could uncover a suite of additional Controls that ask for further information.

Cautions
• If you're going to work in a visual environment, it's well worth memorizing how X,Y coordinates are used to describe the size and location of objects. X and Y together describe a particular point on the screen (or within a Form, or printed page).

X is always described first, then Y. One way to remember which is which is that Y looks like an arrow pointing downward (suggesting vertical orientation). X represents the *horizontal*; Y represents the *vertical* position.

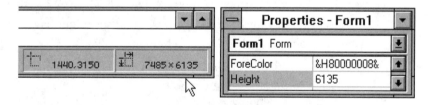

Figure H-4: The Height and Width are displayed on the far right in the Menu Bar.

Notice in Figure H-4 that the number 6135 is listed as the height of this Form, and that the same 6135 height also appears in the Y position in the box on the far right.

While you're designing a program, VB provides you with two continually updated X,Y descriptions of the currently selected object. The box on the far right always shows the X,Y *size* of an object, its width and height. The Box just to its left shows the X,Y *position* of the object within its container (a Control is contained by a Form; a Form is contained by the monitor screen). Nice as this feature is in theory, few people design with it. Dragging things around visually is so easy that the numbers seem superfluous.

• **Align To Grid:** You might find you have trouble getting just the precise height you want: VB will seem to prefer certain heights and snaps your objects to those num-bers. It's almost as if the heights are being rounded off by a secret method. In fact, this happens because the "Align To Grid" option is turned on by default in the Options Menu. If you want finer Control over height (or Top, Left and Width), turn off Align To Grid and you can slide things around very precisely. When you're designing your programs, you might find that it is best to turn off Align To Grid because that makes it easier to drag a Control to a certain size, to slide things around on a win-dow, etc. Then, after you've got the general look you're after, turn Align To Grid back on and, for instance, go back to adjust a row of Command But-tons to make all their heights the same or to line them up neatly in a row. Others might prefer the opposite approach—that is, leave Align To Grid on for the first sketch of the look of a window, then turn it off for fine-tuning later.

• **Scale Mode:** Height, like Top, Left and Width, can be measured in differ-ent ways. The ScaleMode Property of the current Form determines which "mode" is in effect for the objects on that Form. ScaleMode (which see) defaults to a measurement called *twips*—of which there are 1,440 per inch (as measured on paper, not necessarily on your screen). This is why you see numbers in the hundreds for objects whose heights don't seem all that big.

You can change the ScaleMode to:

Points (a printer's space-measuring unit: 72 points equal one inch)

Pixels (the tiny dots of light, virtually invisible on today's monitors)

Characters (120 twips wide, 240 twips high)

Inches

Millimeters

Centimeters

Or you can define your own coordinate system by directly changing the ScaleHeight + ScaleWidth or the ScaleLeft + ScaleTop Properties.

• **Granularity:** In the Windows Control Panel (Desktop item) there is an option you can adjust called *Granularity*, which decides how close objects on the screen can get to each other and by what degrees objects can be expanded or shrunk. This option isn't something you can directly adjust for your programs' users, but you might ask them to set it to zero. If it's any-thing other than zero, the positioning and sizing commands in your Visual Basic programs will be relatively crude. Objects will *jump* in increments of Granularity * 16 pixels when their Left, Top, Height or Width Properties are adjusted. This might not seem like much of a jerking (16 pixels is not much space), but things are smoother when Granularity is set to zero. That eliminates the bumpy motion (at a small cost in speed).

Example Show some Picture Boxes. Then let the user click on a picture to get information about it.

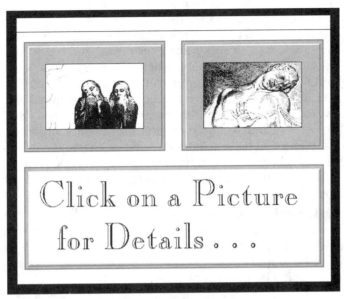

Figure H-5: One advantage of Visual Basic—the user can click on a picture.

Figure H-6: After clicking on a smaller version of this picture, the image expands and text is displayed to explain the image.

This effect is achieved by doing some business in the Form_Load Event and the Picture_Click Events:

```
Sub Form_Load ()
    Show
    Picture3.visible = 0
    drawframeon Picture1, Picture1, 400
    drawframeon Picture2, Picture2, 400
    drawframeon picture4, picture4, 10
    picture4.Print " Click on a Picture"
    picture4.Print " for Details . . ."
End Sub
```

If you want to see things drawn onto a Form when it loads, first use the Show command. Then turn off Picture3—the text description of a Clicked image—so it won't interfere with the frame drawn around Picture4.

We use Picture4 to display the "Click on a Picture for Details..." message. Why so many Picture Boxes, you ask? Why not use Text Boxes or Labels to provide instructions? The reason is that Printing to a Picture Box can allow the background color to show through. You set the Picture Boxes' Font-Transparent Properties to −1. Unhappily, only Forms, Picture Boxes and the printer are allowed the luxury of having the background color or graphic show through text. So, we Print to Picture Boxes and the result looks good.

(The DrawFrameOn Routine, which creates attractive "metallic" frames, is explained in the entry on the Line command.)

```
Sub Picture1_Click ()

Picture2.visible = 0
Picture3.visible = -1
Picture3.FontSize = 13.8
q$ = Chr$(34)
picture4.visible = 0

Picture1.Height = 4800
Picture1.Width = 2430
Form1.Refresh
drawframeon Picture1, Picture1, 100

currentX = 960
currentY = 2712
Picture3.Print "This detail from Blake's"
Picture3.Print "Dante's Inferno demonstrates"
Picture3.Print "the master's exquisite way"
Picture3.Print "with a line. The engraving"
Picture3.Print "is typical of Blake's " + q$ + "Cosmic" + q$
Picture3.Print "style. The legs are thought"
Picture3.Print "to have been copied from"
Picture3.Print "originals by Michelangelo."
Picture3.FontSize = 10
Picture3.Print
Picture3.Print "
    9 3/8 X 13 1/4" + q$
```

```
Picture3.Print
Picture3.Print "See it at the National Gallery of Art"

End Sub
```

Let's explain what's happening in this Sub. First we make Picture2 invisible (it's the one the user didn't select). Then we show Picture3, the text that gives the details about the selected picture. We set its FontSize. We define q$ as a quotation mark, using its "code." (You can't directly use quotation marks with a Print command inside the quotation marks proper— VB would think you were finished with the Print command because Print ends with a double-quote. See "Chr$" for more on this.)

We also make Picture4 invisible (that's the one that says "Click on a Picture..."). We don't need it anymore.

Now we expand Picture1's height and width. We Refresh the Form (without Refresh, fragments of the smaller frame around Picture1 would remain when we expanded it). And we call upon our own DrawFrameOn Subroutine (see "Line") to put a new frame around Picture1.

CurrentX and CurrentY is the position where the next Print action will take place (they're a description of the "cursor position"), so we reset them to where we want the following text to appear. Then we print information into Picture3. After a series of Prints, we use a "null Print"—the Print command with nothing to print—(Picture3.Print), which has the effect of moving us one line down in the Picture in order to add some space. Then, at last, we reduce the FontSize, because what we'll print at the bottom is less significant information.

If you are expanding one of a group of Controls, you might want to turn off the Enabled Property of all the other Controls in that group that aren't being expanded. This creates a dramatic visual effect. And in this application we're after dramatic effects, aren't we? (Picture Boxes, alas, don't yet respond to their Enabled Property in any visible way, except that you cannot tab to a disabled Picture Box. See "TabIndex.")

See also   CurrentX, CurrentY; Left; Scale; ScaleHeight, ScaleLeft, ScaleMode; Scale-Top; ScaleWidth; Top; Width

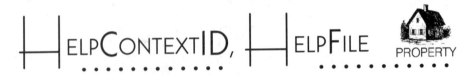

HelpContextID, HelpFile   PROPERTY

Description   Together, HelpContextID and HelpFile provide your VB program with the same kind of "Help" feature that comes with Visual Basic's design environment and other Windows applications.

The HelpFile is the name of a file you've created with the Windows Help Compiler. This compiler is available with the VB Professional package and with other language products as well. The HelpFile would contain whatever information you wanted to give the user about your program.

The HelpContextID is a number that identifies a location within your HelpFile. You can have as many screens of help as you want, and each can be identified by different HelpContextID Property settings for the various Controls and Forms in your program. If the user presses the F1 key, VB looks for a HelpContextID number in the currently active (with focus) Control. If no number is found in the Control's Property, then VB looks for a HelpContextID number in the Property of the Control's Form or container. If none is found, then VB displays the main, first screen of the HelpFile.

Used with   HelpFile is used with the App command (which see) to give the name of the Help file associated with your VB application.

HelpContextID is used with Check Boxes, Combo Boxes, Command Buttons, Directory, Drive & File List Boxes, Forms, Frames, Grids, Horizontal & Vertical Scroll Bars, List Boxes, Menus, OLE Controls, Option Buttons, Picture Boxes and Text Boxes.

Variables   **Variable types:** HelpFile (text "string" Variable); HelpContextID (long integer)

The word App refers to your VB application, and you use it in the following fashion to identify a HelpFile to be used with your program, probably in the Form_Load Event of your Startup Form.

Assuming that your HelpFile is named MyProgs.Hlp:

    App.HelpFile = "MyProgs.Hlp"

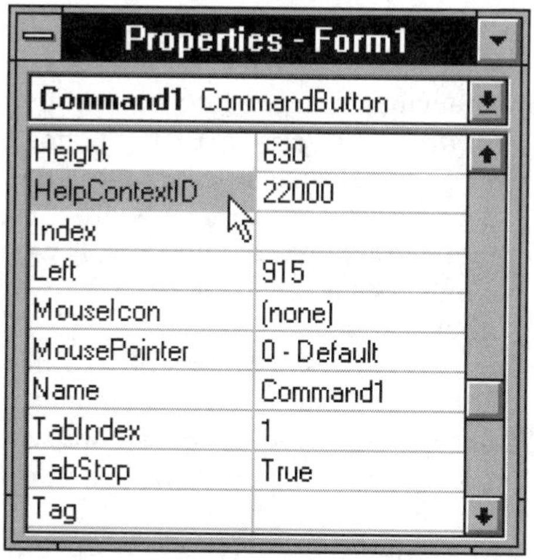

Properties - Form1	
Command1 CommandButton	
Height	630
HelpContextID	22000
Index	
Left	915
Mouselcon	(none)
MousePointer	0 - Default
Name	Command1
TabIndex	1
TabStop	True
Tag	

Figure H-7: You can set the HelpContextID in the Properties Window.

OR (to set the HelpContextID number for a Text Box while the program is running): Text1.HelpContextID = 2000

OR (to find out the HelpContextID number while the program is running):

X& = Text1.HelpContextID

Uses   Provide the user of your programs with context-sensitive help.

Cautions   If you don't want to create a complete Help feature for your program, see the Example under "Shell" for a simpler approach.

Example   We'll use VB's own HelpFile to illustrate how these two Properties work in a program. Start a New Project from the File Menu; then type this the Form_Load Event:

```
Sub Form_Load ()

app.HelpFile = "vb.hlp"
helpcontextid = 21003

End Sub
```

Now press F5 to run your program, and then press F1 to call up the Help screen within the VB.HLP file that is identified by 21003. In VB, the Help-ContextID refers to a screen that explains what a Form window is. If you create custom HelpFiles for your VB programs, the ID numbers and the information, of course, will differ.

EX$

FUNCTION

Description   Hex$ translates a normal decimal number into a computer-friendly hexadecimal number. Hex$ gives you a text Variable that contains the hex version of a decimal number. Now you can display this hex number or print it to the printer. Hexadecimal arithmetic is one of those weird compromises people have been making to facilitate talking to computers. It won't be around forever, but for now we must occasionally bend to the way the computer thinks rather than the other way around.

We're used to thinking of numbers in groups of 10, our decimal system. There's nothing magic about 10. Long ago it seemed like a natural grouping because that's the number of fingers we have to count with. There is nothing, though, in nature to suggest that ten is somehow special. We're just very, very used to it.

The computer bases its number system on 2–a *binary* system–because computers store and manipulate things in an on-off fashion, like a light switch. Consequently, numbers naturally cluster for the computer around the powers (multiples) of 2: 2 4 8 16 32 64 128 256 512 1,024. This is why computer memory is measured in kilobytes (1024 bytes), and why so many computer-based appliances offer, for example, 128 different sounds on a synthesizer or 256 storage places on a calculator. Visual Basic allows you 16 QBColor( )s, 16 DrawModes, 32,768 as a maximum range for a Scroll Bar, and so on. These are all powers of two.

Decimal Arithmetic Is Awkward for the Computer

An important byproduct of the number of digits you use is the way you count: we have 10 digits, 0–9, then we start over again with 10 and go forward. No matter how big the number, we express it with only 10 symbols, the 10 digits.

The arithmetic for this kind of counting is clumsy for the computer—it's not natural. The computer wants to work with things in groups of 8 or 16, but decidedly *not* 10. The number 10 has an awkward mathematical relationship to 2, and the computer wants things to work in relation to 2.

There arose two kinds of computer arithmetic, octal (based on groups of 8 digits) and hexadecimal (based on 16 digits). Hex, for short, is the more common one used to communicate with computers. Hex has 16 digits 0 1 2 3 4 5 6 7 8 9 A B C D E F. (We run out of traditional digits and have to start borrowing letters of the alphabet.)

Fortunately, VB has eliminated the need to use hex very often, although RGB colors can be set with hex. To indicate a hex number, you use the &H symbol before the number. By itself, 16 is 16 as we understand it—16 in hex (&H16) is 22 to us, in decimal.

Used with Variables

Decimal numbers to translate them into hex numbers

```
Hex$(15)
```

OR (to use a Variable instead of a literal number):

```
X = 15
Hex$(X)
```

Uses

• Use Hex$ if you ever need to display a number in the hexadecimal format. This is purely to allow the user to see what a hex equivalent would be. The resulting number is not a *numeric* Variable and so cannot be used in calculations. It is for display purposes only. If you want to do any mathematical things with it, use the number you gave to the Hex$ Function.

Today, hex numbers are most often used when communicating with something outside your computer. Some modem communications protocols use hex values encoded into text (string) Variables as their way of sending information over the phone lines.

Cautions

• Hex$ does not involve fractions, so it will round off any fractions.

• Hex$ does not turn a decimal number into another number; it gives you a text Variable that is not usable in mathematical calculations or as a Variable you could use for, say, an RGB color.

Example

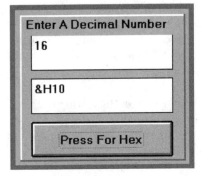

Figure H-8: This program translates decimal numbers into hexadecimal numbers.

```
Sub Command1_Click ()
Text2.Text = Hex$(Text1.Text)
End Sub
```

See also   Oct$; Val

IDDEN — PROPERTY

See   Archive

IDE — METHOD

Description   Hide makes a Form disappear from view but keeps it in the computer's memory. Any changes to the Form or the Controls on it that were made by the user or the program are retained.

If a Form will perhaps need to be displayed again while the program runs, then just Hide it, don't UnLoad it. If it will not need to be seen by the user any more, UnLoad it. Hiding keeps the visual elements of the Form available for quick redisplay with the Show method. (The Show command is the opposite of the Hide command.)

UnLoading frees up some of the computer's memory but destroys any changes to a Form's or its Controls' Properties that you or the user might have made. Also, using the Load Method to make a Form visible again will be slower than making it visible with the Show command. It takes longer to load something in from the disk than from the computer's memory.

The Repercussions of UnLoad: The UnLoad command not only makes a Form invisible, it also removes it from the computer's memory; therefore, all the Variables within this Form are lost. All Control Properties are reset to the values you assigned when designing the Form–any dragging or other changes to Control or Form Properties are lost.

Hide is precisely the same thing as setting a Form's Visible Property to Off (False). The Show command is the same as setting a Form's Visible Property to On (True). The approach you choose is a matter of personal preference–you might find that the words *Hide* and *Show* are more memorable than Visible's settings.

Used with   Forms only

Variables

Hide

OR

Form1.Hide

Uses   Use Hide instead of UnLoad if you need to make a Form invisible but you also want to:

• Retain any changes made to a Form or the Controls thereupon, changes made either by your program itself or by the user.

• Retain the Variables within the Form, but make it invisible to the user.

• Make the Form visible at a later time–it will pop onscreen more quickly if you Hide it than if you UnLoad it.

Cautions   • If things are still happening within the Event Subroutine that Hides the Form, the user cannot get control of the computer until those things have completed their tasks:

```
Sub Command1_Click
Hide
For I = 1 To 5000
    X = X + 1
Next I
End Sub
```

It would be preferable in the above example to put the Hide at the end of the Sub, rather than prior to some lengthy activity. You never want to mysteriously freeze the user out, preventing him or her from accessing the computer just because your program is finishing a job. A user may think the frozen screen means the program has gone haywire and simply turn off the computer and go away.

• If you use Hide with a Form that has not previously been Loaded into the computer's memory with the Load Statement, the Form will then be Loaded but remain invisible. Any reference to an UnLoaded Form causes it to be Loaded.

Example

```
Sub Form2_Load
        Form1.Hide
    End Sub
```

See also   Load; QueryUnLoad; Show; UnLoad; Visible

HIDESELECTION

PROPERTY

Description   Normally, if some text is selected (highlighted) in a Text Box, the text will revert to normal (unselected) if the user clicks on another Control or the Form. If you change the HideSelection Property to False, you can cause selected text to remain selected even when the Text Box loses the focus.

Used with   Text Boxes only

Variables

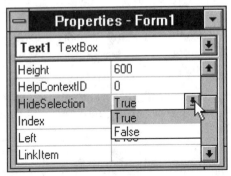

Figure H-9: You can adjust the HideSelection Property only in the Properties Window. It cannot be changed while the program is running.

Uses   If the user (or, rarely, your program) has selected some text in a Text Box, that text will be unselected if the *focus* shifts off the Text Box. The Control with the focus will react to any typing on the keyboard. The focus can shift if the user clicks on another Control, tabs to another Control or Window, or if your program uses the SetFocus command.

Cautions   If your program offers editing features such as Cut, Copy and Paste, you might annoy the user unless you change HideSelection to False. The user will expect to be able to highlight some text to be deleted and then temporarily click on a File List Box, for example. The user may not appreciate it if the simple act of utilizing another Control cancels the selection.

Example   We want to permit the user to select text in more than one Text Box at the same time. To reproduce this example, type the following into the Form_Load Event:

```
Sub Form_Load ()
    text1.Text = "Will selected text remain stable?"
    text2.Text = text1.Text
End Sub
```

Put two Text Boxes on the Form and, holding down the SHIFT key, click on the HideSelection Property in the Properties Window so it reads False.

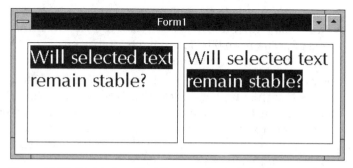

Figure H-10: Text in two Text Boxes selected simultaneously.

See also   GotFocus; SetFocus; SelLength, SelStart, SelText; Text Box

See   Scroll Bars

Description   Hour tells you the hour of the day, based on a special *serial* number that VB generates in response to such Functions as Now. Visual Basic has an

especially rich set of commands that deal with time and dates: you can manipulate time and dates *mathematically* based on this serial number to find out such things as whether or not 17 March 1784 was a Thursday; the number of days between 1 Feb. 1900 and 5 Jan. 2050; or how many Friday the 13ths occurred in 1950. VB gives you the powers of a calendar-oriented *idiot savant*.

For a complete description of these *serial* numbers, see "DateSerial."

Used with   A time or date *serial* number

Variables   X# = Hour(Now)

Uses   • Create "digital" clocks.

• Create Timers, using Hour with the Timer Control.

Cautions   • The Hour you get is in the military format: 0 is 12 AM, and 23 is 11 PM. However, this format does make it easier to perform arithmetic than having two sets of hours from 0 to 12, plus a text appendage of AM or PM to distinguish between day and night.

• A serial number you provide to Hour has a # attached to it. That symbol in VB means that the number is a *Double-Precision Floating-Point number* (it has an extremely large range and can include fractions and decimal points). See "Variables" for more information on the different available numeric "types" and their symbols. Alternatively, you can leave off the # and use VB's default variable type, Variant (which see).

• Serial numbers can range between 1 January 100 and 31 December 9999.

• The whole number portion of the serial number holds the date; the fractional part (to the right of the decimal point) holds the time.

Example
```
Sub Form_Click ()

x# = Now
Print "The serial number for Now is: "; x#
Print
Print "Which translates into..."
Hr = Hour(x#): Mn = Minute(x#): Sec = Second(x#)
D = Day(x#): Wkdy = Weekday(x#): Mnth = Month(x#): Yr = Year(x#)

Print
Print "Second: "; Sec
Print "Minute: "; Mn
Print "Hour: "; Hr
Print
   Select Case Wkdy
      Case 1
         dy$ = "Sunday"
      Case 2
         dy$ = "Monday"
      Case 3
         dy$ = "Tuesday"
```

```
        Case 4
           dy$ = "Wednesday"
        Case 5
           dy$ = "Thursday"
        Case 6
           dy$ = "Friday"
        Case 7
           dy$ = "Saturday"
    End Select

    Print "Name: "; dy$
    Print "Day: "; D
    Print "Month: "; Mnth
    Print "Year: "; Yr

    End Sub
```

Results in The serial number for Now is: 33581.7918055556

This translates into...

Second: 12
Minute: 0
Hour: 19

Name: Monday
Day: 9
Month: 12
Year: 1991

Note: In situations like this, the Select Case structure is somewhat cumbersome. Older versions of Basic had Data and Read Statements. This paired set of commands are worthwhile in some circumstances. They made things like naming the weekday a little simpler to deal with. But Data and Read have been eliminated in Visual Basic. (VB's elimination of the Data and Read commands is mystifying, given that some of the widely discredited and thoroughly dubious dinosaur commands, such as Let, have been retained.)

Here's how it used to be done: you put the information in a Data Statement, then pulled it into a temporary Array. All those repetitive Case and Variable assignments were unnecessary. From the Array, you could select what you wanted by just using the index number:

```
Data Sunday, Monday, Tuesday, Wednesday, Thursday, Friday, Saturday

For I = 1 To 7
    Read X$
    DayName$(I) = X$
Next I

Dy$ = DayName$(Wkdy)
```

But Visual Basic is wonderfully replete with commands for virtually everything you can think of. There is even a command that provides you with the name of the weekday so you can avoid all that Select Case business. Here's how to achieve the above result in a more direct fashion:

Replace this:

```
Select Case Wkdy
    Case 1
        dy$ = "Sunday"
    Case 2
        dy$ = "Monday"
    Case 3
        dy$ = "Tuesday"
    Case 4
        dy$ = "Wednesday"
    Case 5
        dy$ = "Thursday"
    Case 6
        dy$ = "Friday"
    Case 7
        dy$ = "Saturday"
End Select
```

With this:

```
dy$ = Format$(X#, "dddd")
```

See also   Date$; DateSerial; DateValue; Day; Format$; Minute; Month; Now; Second; Weekday; Year

PROPERTY

Description   hWnd gives you a *handle*–a Form's or Control's unique ID number assigned by Windows itself. Handles are used when you access the Windows operating system directly (it's called the Application Programming Interface, the API). There are more than 600 Subroutines buried in the API, and learning to tap into them can greatly expand the power of Visual Basic. See Appendix A for a tutorial on how to use the API.

The hWnd is similar to the hDC handle (which see), but VB includes an hWnd Property for most Controls, while the hDC Property is only available for Forms, Picture Boxes and the printer. hDC means *handle to device context*, and hWnd means *handle to window*. In any case, some API routines want the hWnd to tell them which window should be acted upon by the API subroutine, and other API routines want the hDC. You give them what they want.

Technically, every Control in VB is a window (a "child window" as it's called), and as such, each Control has an hWnd associated with it. Each Control also has an hDC. You might visualize the hDC as the town and the hWnd as a particular address in that town. Visual Basic doesn't provide direct access to the hDC handles of most Controls (as a Property), but you can obtain these handles if you need them. (The tutorial in Appendix A explains how.) The hWnd, however, is usually available directly in VB.

Used with　Check Boxes, Combo Boxes, Command Buttons, Directory, Drive & File List Boxes, Forms, Frames, Grids, Horizontal and Vertical Scroll Bars, List Boxes, OLE, Option Buttons, Picture Boxes and Text Boxes

Variables　**Variable type:** Integer

Although called a Property, hWnd is a Windows Variable. You cannot change it; you can only "pass" it when you are calling an API Subroutine. In a Module, type this:

```
Declare Function DestroyWindow% Lib "User" (ByVal hWnd As Integer)
```

Then, to use this Function somewhere in your program, type this:

```
X% = DestroyWindow (hWnd)
```

Uses　Use hWnd to identify the Form (the window) you want affected by the actions of an API call.

Cautions　• It is essential that an API declaration be typed entirely on a single line. No matter how long the declaration is—do not hit the ENTER key. See the Examples below.

• Do not store an hWnd in a Variable. The hWnd of a window can change while the program runs, so you should always use hWnd itself within the list of Variables you pass to an API Subroutine or Function.

• When you plan to use the API, you must first "declare" the Subroutine you want to access. These declarations are normally made in a Module so they will be available to any location in your program.

Example　One of the API calls in this example could be dangerous in the wrong hands. DestroyWindow, which is somewhat like UnLoad but more drastic, collapses and removes from memory the target window (and all its "child windows," the Controls on it).

The other API call we're going to illustrate is called FlashWindow, and it does just that. We'll create two Forms. When you click on the Second Form's plunger icon, it attacks the target window, causing the First Form to flash a few times then collapse.

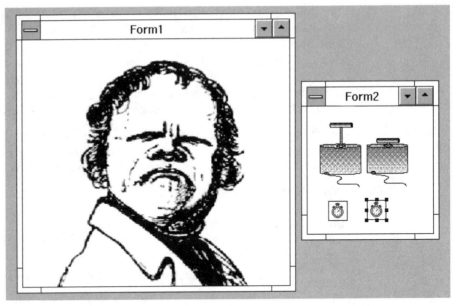

Figure H-11: The plungers and the Timers hint at the violence to come.

Form2 has two Timers on it, one to time the flashes and one to delay before doing the DestroyWindow. Set both Timers' Enabled Properties to 0 (False), so they won't start until we deliberately start them by clicking on the Picture Box of a plunger.

You must set the "Startup Form" (in the Options Menu) to Form2, so it is the one that Controls the program. After all, you're going to destroy Form1.

There are also two Picture Boxes, one with an image of the plunger up, the other with it down. Initially, only the up one is visible, so set the Visible Property of Picture2 to 0 (False).

In a Module, type these two API declarations. As always, when declaring for API Functions, make certain that each declaration is on a single line. Never use the ENTER key until you've written the entire declaration. These two are short, but some API declarations are very lengthy.

```
Declare Function FlashWindow% Lib "User" (ByVal hWnd As Integer, → ByVal
    bInvert As Integer)
Declare Function DestroyWindow% Lib "User" (ByVal hWnd As Integer)
```

Then, in the Form2_Load Event:

```
Sub Form_Load ()

    form1.Show
    picture2.left = picture1.left
    picture2.top = picture1.top
End Sub
```

We cause Form1 to be visible with Show. Then we set Picture2 into the same position as Picture1, although Picture2 remains invisible. This way, when the user clicks on Picture1, it disappears and is replaced by Picture 2 in the same spot. This makes it appear that the plunger goes down but nothing else about the picture changes.

Now, in the Picture1_Click Event, we'll conceal Picture1, reveal Picture2 and enable both Timers:

```
Sub Picture1_Click ()
    picture1.visible = False
    picture2.visible = True
    timer1.enabled = True
    timer2.enabled = True
End Sub
```

Finally, the real action—the flashing and the attack on Form1—takes place within Timers because both actions need to be delayed. We set the Interval Property of Timer1 to 300, and the Interval of Timer2 to 1500. Therefore, Form1 will flash five times, then be gone.

```
Sub Timer1_Timer ()
    x% = FlashWindow(Form1.hWnd, 1)
End Sub

Sub Timer2_Timer ()
    x% = DestroyWindow(Form1.hWnd)
End Sub
```

One Word of Warning: If you try to run this from within the VB design mode, it will cause an "UNRECOVERABLE APPLICATION ERROR" (UAE) or, with Windows 3.1, a "recoverable error" message which requires that you shut down VB (but Windows itself will continue to run). Win95 is much more forgiving in this respect. This reaction is caused by the fact that the VB design environment is not prepared to have one of its Forms suddenly cease to exist. So, to test this example you must first make an .EXE file (see the File Menu) and run it as a regular .EXE program that you start from within Windows. Windows can deal with disappearing windows. It's a good habit to always save your VB work (or the user's word processing or whatever) before calling the API. VB has no control over errors that might be generated by an API Function. And UAEs prevent you from saving any modifications or data entry that have taken place since the last disk save.

There are even more extreme API Subroutines, such as

```
Declare Function ExitWindows% Lib "User" (ByVal dwReserved As Long, →
    wReturnCode)
```

. . . then

```
x% = ExitWindows(0,0)
```

This Subroutine causes the entire Windows operating system to collapse, returning you to the DOS C:\ prompt.

See also   Appendix A; hDC

$\vdash$ . . . **459**

ICON

Description   The Icon Property allows you to select an icon to represent one of your Forms. It's like selecting a Picture Property for a Picture Box or Form, except that the icon image does not appear unless the user (or your program) causes the Form to be minimized while the program runs.

The icon image is embedded into the Form, so if the Form is minimized, the icon shows onscreen, symbolizing the Form and allowing the user to restore the entire Form to visibility by clicking on the icon. Also, a program's icon is used by the Windows Program Manager to launch the program in the first place. If you choose no icon, VB will give it a default icon (and one that is not very attractive at that). For your finished programs you may want to select from the excellent collection of icons provided with Visual Basic.

Used with   Forms and Multiple Document Interface (MDI) Forms only

Variables   **Variable type:** Integer

Normally you set this Property the same way you set a Picture Box's Picture Property—by pulling in the desired image using the Properties Window when you're designing the Form.

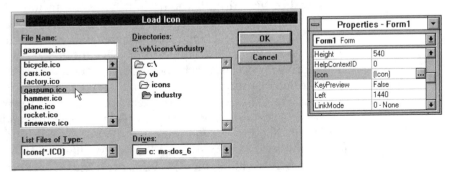

Figure I-1: Adding an icon to a window (Form)

But you can change a Form's icon while the program is running, by changing it to the icon of another Form in the program; to the icon of any Control's DragIcon Property; or by using the LoadPicture Function to pull an image in from the disk drive.

However, since icons are supposed to symbolize their Forms, they should usually remain stable and reliable cues to the purpose of a minimized Form.

Changing them while a program is running would be of value if the purpose of the Form itself were to change while the program is running, or if, for instance, you wanted to signal the user that a Timer had expired or some mail had come in over the modem. VB provides two identical mailboxes, but one has its red flag up. You could flip up that flag (by changing the icon) to alert the user that a letter is waiting to be read.

User Customization: Also, being able to change icons while a program is running lets the user customize this aspect of a program—always a desirable feature of any program. Such changes would not become a permanent part of your .EXE program, but you could set up an .INI file wherein the user would specify which icon(s) will be loaded in when the program starts. This approach—reading in user preferences from an .INI file—is widely used in Windows programming to permit the user to define his or her preferences. (See the Example below.)

```
Form1.Icon = Form3.Icon
```

Uses
- Utilize a symbol that demonstrates visually to the user the purpose or nature of the Form. For example, the icon for a word processing Form might be a pen or pencil.

    Since icons show up only when a window (Form) has been made invisible, it's the job of the tiny icon image to represent that window. Then, if the user needs to restore that window, he or she can identify the window by its icon, and double-click to restore the window to its previous size.

Cautions
- The VB *Language Reference* mistakenly says that the Icon Property cannot be changed while a program is running, but contradicts this advice in a special Note at the bottom of the page.

- Visual Basic comes with a large library of well-designed, graceful icons from which you can select what you need. Additional libraries are available on CompuServe and other telecommunication services. You can also design your own using the (somewhat slow) "Iconwrks" program supplied with VB or the effective "Iconedit" program supplied with Norton Desktop for Windows (from Symantec).

- You can even create an icon for your entire VB program. When you have finished testing your program and are satisfied with it, you create an .EXE version of the program that can be run from within Windows like any other application. Selecting the Make EXE File from the VB File Menu presents this window. It's here that you can assign an icon for the entire program, should the user minimize it:

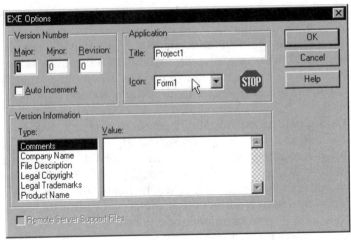

Figure I-2: You can select the icon for the entire program in the Make EXE File option from VB's File Menu.

Example   Here's how to use an .INI file to allow the user to customize your program with his or her own preferences. You would include a window (Form) captioned "Customize," or perhaps a menu item. Then, from within this window or menu you would allow the user to select such things as Font, Background Color, Icon, etc. The window or menu would then adjust one of the lines in the program's .INI file (by opening the .INI file, reading in the information, and changing the appropriate line). (See "Open.")

Now, assuming that you have an .INI file with a line that defines the user's choice for the program's icon:

```
ICON = C:\WINDOWS\ICONS\FRENCH.ICO
```

You could put the following .INI-checking Routine in the Startup Form's Load Event:

```
Sub Form_Load ()
On Error Resume Next

Open "C:\WINDOWS\MYPROG.INI" For Input As #1

ReDim a$(1 To 50)
x = 1

If Err Then MsgBox ("MYPROG.INI " + Error$(Err)): Exit Sub

Do While Not EOF(1)
   Line Input #1, a$(x)
   x = x + 1
Loop

Close

b$ = a$(1)
```

```
l = Len(b$)
p = InStr(b$, "=")
ic$ = Right$(b$, l − p − 1)

Icon = LoadPicture(ic$)

If Err Then MsgBox (ic$ + " " + Error$(Err))

End Sub
```

The first thing to do when accessing something on a disk is to use On Error Resume Next. It means: "If there's a problem, ignore it for now and keep going down the list of instructions and carrying them out. We'll deal with the error ourselves." Accessing the disk can cause errors if, for instance, the file you're trying to open doesn't exist, or is in a different location. (See "On Error" for more on disk error-trapping.)

Then we open the file, create an Array (which see) of text Variables called A$ and set our counter X to 1. Now we take care of a possible error when trying to open the .INI file. If Err Then MsgBox (Error$(Err)): Exit Sub means: "If the VB Variable Err is not 0, we know that the effort to Open failed." Show the user the problem by using VB's built-in Error$ Function. All we have to do is give Error$ the error code number (Err). Then we exit the Subroutine, aborting any further efforts to read the .INI file until the user does what's necessary to correct the problem on the disk.

The Loop reads in each line of the .INI file, putting each successively into A$(1), A$(2), etc., until EOF (End of File). Then we Close the .INI file. We know that the first line is supposed to be the icon definition, so we make B$ = the first line we pulled. This isn't necessary; we could continue to use A$(1), but B$ is simpler to type. Then we define L as the length, the number of characters in B$, because we have to remove the "ICON =" portion of B$. Therefore we need to know B$'s length.

We assign to Variable P the position within B$ where the "=" appears, using the InStr Function. Now we can extract the icon filename we're after by using the Right$ Function and assign the result to IC$:

```
ic$ = Right$(b$, l − p − 1)
```

This line means: "Make IC$ the text on the right side of B$, starting with the length of B$, less the character position of the "=", plus 1."

At last, we're ready to change the icon with the LoadPicture Function. We're accessing the disk drive one more time in this routine. So, again, just in case this .ICO file is missing or something else is amiss with the disk drive, we use our error reporting line.

See also   DragIcon; LoadPicture; MinButton

#IF...THEN...ELSE

STATEMENT

Description This special version of If...Then will skip over and ignore any programming you put between the #If and #EndIf. It ignores programming if the condition is false.

In other words, you can use this structure to create alternative versions of your program.

Used with "Conditional compilation": Making .EXE files of a program which differ from each other.

Variables You trigger the behavior of an #If...#EndIf structure by how you define a special kind of constant declaration–#Const. The value of this Constant is the condition which causes programming to either be, or not be, compiled when you make an .EXE file.

By typing the following at the top of a Module or Form, you establish that the special #Constant named "Registered" has a value of True:

```
#Const Registered = True
```

Then elsewhere in this Module or Form, you would test this #Constant's value to determine whether or not to display a nag screen to annoy users who had not paid for your shareware program:

```
#Const Registered = False
Private Sub Form_Click( )
#If Registered = False Then
    x = MsgBox("Please register this shareware...")
#End If
End Sub
```

This would result in the message box being displayed. If you then want to create a version of this program for registered users (that didn't display the message box), make this change:

```
#Const Registered = True
```

Note that the #Const declaration must be at the top of your editing window in the Form or Module–this way it can be seen by all your programming within that Form or Module.

However, a #Const declaration cannot be made programwide. You must put that #Const declaration in each Form or Module in your program where you intend to use the #If...#EndIf conditional compilation.

If you want to test various conditions or compile more than two versions of a program, use the #ElseIf or #Else commands. They work the same way as the ElseIf and Else commands within an If...Then structure (which see).

In fact, the only difference between #If...Then and If...Then syntax is that an If...Then statement can optionally be written on a single line (If x = 12 Then Beep), but #If...Then cannot.

Uses
• If you are creating two versions of a program, you can specify that some things are included or excluded—but most of the program remains the same for both versions. For instance, if you are writing for a 16-bit operating system like Windows 3.1 and a 32-bit OS such as NT or the new Windows 95—use conditional compilation. There isn't too much difference between 16- and 32-bit Microsoft operating systems (in terms of VB programming), but there are some differences. (See Chapter 27 in the VB4 Programmer's Guide manual that ships with VB4.)

Or perhaps you're Canadian and write for an English-speaking audience and a French-speaking audience.

Shareware authors might appreciate conditional compilation to make an .EXE file that displays reminder screens (for nonregistered users) and another .EXE for registered users that doesn't nag them.

Of course there are other ways to compile different versions of the same program. You could just cut and paste the lines that vary between the versions. You could alternatively comment out lines (put REM or ' in front of inappropriate lines). If the issue is merely runtime behavior (display a nag screen or don't), you could use an ordinary global (Public) Const or global Variable with an ordinary If...Then structure to determine behaviors. However, if the difference between your versions is in the syntax (32-bit vs. 16-bit API calls, for example), you'll either have to comment out some lines, or resort to conditional compilation.

Cautions
• It's unique, but #Const declarations are always Private. You can't make them programwide in scope by using the Public command. Therefore you must put any #Const declarations in each Form or Module in your program if you expect them to be effective within that Form or Module. For instance, if you declare a #Const in Form1, then in Form2 try to use it in Form2, the #Const will always be the default (False).

Even if you say in Form1:

```
#Const Register = True
```

Form2 will still think that Register is False. False is the default for anything, any variable or constant. So any #If...#EndIf structures in Form2 will ignore that True in Form1.

Example
Setting a #Constant named Quebec to True displays a message in French. Setting it to False displays the same message in English. At the top of the editing window in Form1, type:

```
#Const Quebec = True
```

Then, in the Form_Click Event type:

```
Private Sub Form_Click( )
#If Quebec = True Then
    MsgBox ("Gardez bien...")
```

```
    #Else
        MsgBox ("Take good care...")
    #End If
End Sub
```

See also   If...Then, Const

STATEMENT

Description   If...Then is one of the most important structures in any computer language, indeed in any kind of language.

If...Then is how decisions are made. Then, after the decision is made, actions are taken appropriate to the decision. A program is said to *branch* at this point, as if the path split into more than one trail. The path the program follows is decided here at the If...Then junction.

Many times a day we do our own personal branching using a similar structure: *If* it's cold outside, *then* we get the heavier jacket. *If* the car is locked, *then* we insert the key in the door. *If* we're too close to the edge of the driveway, *then* we adjust the steering wheel. This constant cycle of testing conditions and making decisions based on them is what makes our behavior intelligent.

But is there something sinister here? If...Then need not be what we call "*conscious*" decision-making; it can be hard-wired. Indeed the bulk of our brain activity is not on the conscious level. The part of the brain that gets messages about body temperature is always prepared: If your finger gets hotter than 150 degrees F, it immediately sends a message (via your brain) to your arm-retraction muscle unit. None of this If...Then behavior is consciously initiated by us. It can even happen during some stages of sleep if your hand should come in contact with something hot.

Worse than this, If...Then structures can also be hard-wired into inanimate objects. Microwave ovens refuse to respond to any effort to turn them on if the oven door is gaping open. This prevents a careless human from a local nuclear accident.

The microwave oven is not intelligent, but it acts intelligently because a rule is built into it. Interestingly, recent theories of consciousness suggest that if enough If...Then rules are collected together, interacting, then consciousness spontaneously arises—the way the right conditions can cause life to arise spontaneously out of sufficiently diverse chemicals.

When you write a program, you try to make it behave intelligently by giving it decision-making rules. If Err Then MsgBox (Error$(Err)). Put enough appropriate If...Then structures into your program so that you can anticipate whatever the user might do while the program runs. Your program will not become "conscious"—current computers don't have enough memory to hold the many instructions sufficient to reach the critical mass thought necessary for spontaneous consciousness (though current computers *do* have sufficient speed).

Nonetheless, when you write a program, you're teaching the computer to behave intelligently in whatever limited tasks your program is designed to accomplish. And a primary tool in this endeavor is If...Then.

Used with

Else. The Else command precedes any instructions that you want carried out if the original If...Then is not carried out.

```
X = InputBox$("How many calories did you take in today?")

If X > 3000 Then
        M$ = "Keep that up and you'll get huge."
    Else
        M$ = "Good self-control, on your part."
End If
Msgbox M$
```

ElseIf. This allows you to test more than one condition. In a way, it's like using two If...Thens in a row. However, an ElseIf doesn't get triggered unless a preceding If or ElseIf fails to trigger.

```
If X$ = "Bob" Then

    Print "Hello Bob"

ElseIf X$ = "Billy" Then

    Print "Hello Billy"

End If
```

Variables

If...Then tests to see if something is *true*. And if it is true, then the instructions within the If...Then structure are carried out. If it is not true, then your program ignores the instructions in the structure and goes on to the first instruction following the If...Then—the line following End If. (If you've included an Else or ElseIf, these are also checked to see if they are true.)

```
X$ = InputBox$ ("Please Enter The Password...")

If X$ <> Pass$ Then
    MsgBox ("Access Denied")
    End
End If
Print "Password verified. Thank you."
```

The <> symbol means "not equal." So the meaning of our If...Then test above is: If it is true that X$ doesn't equal the password (Pass$), then print a denied message and End the program. If the user *does* enter the word that matches Pass$, then nothing within the If...Then structure is carried out. Instead, the program goes past the structure and prints the thank-you message.

There are some optional variations to If...Then structures:

• You can put simple If...Thens on a single line, and in this case you do not use an End If (the If...Then structure is assumed to be completed by the end of the line). The computer knows that this is a single-line If...Then because some instructions follow the Then. In a multiline If...Then, the *Then* is the last word on the line, and the instructions are on following lines.

```
If X$ <>Pass$ Then MsgBox("Access Denied"): End
Print "Password Verified. Thank you."
```

• You can insert an *Else* between the If and the End If. Else means: If the test to see if something was true fails, do the following instructions, which in our example above would allow us to put the "Password Verified" message within the If...Then structure. This can make it easier to read and understand the intent of the structure. (It also creates a compact either/or structure. You can put a series of Else statements in an If...Then structure.)

```
If X$ <> Pass$ Then

    MsgBox ("Access Denied")

    End

Else

    Print "Password verified. Thank you."

End If
```

• You can nest several If...Thens within the same structure by using ElseIf. However, the Select Case structure is usually preferable in situations where you want to do multiple tests.

```
If X = 0
    Print "Zero"
ElseIf X = 1
    Print  "One"
ElseIf X = 2
    Print "Two"
End If
```

• There is a special kind of If...Then, peculiar to Visual Basic, which allows you to find out if a Name represents a certain kind of Control. Say we have an object on the Form to which we've given the Name *Showit:*

```
If TypeOf Showit Is TextBox Then
    Showit.Text = "Hi,  Johnny!"
ElseIf TypeOf Showit Is CommandButton Then
    Showit.Caption = "Hi, Johnny!"
End If
```

You'll want to remember the "TypeOf Is" instruction. There's no substitute for it in some (admittedly rare) situations. In the above example, we wanted to print a message. However, since a Command Button has no Text Property and a Text Box has no Caption Property, we had to find out which type of Control we were printing on. For more, see Objects.

• Your test condition for an If...Then need not be a single test; you can combine several tests using AND and OR:

(With AND, both of these conditions must be true for the instructions following Then to be carried out.)

```
If A$ = "Bob" AND B$ = "Ralph" Then
```

(With OR, if either one of these conditions is true, carry out the instructions following Then.)

```
If A$ = "Bob" OR B$ = "Ralph" Then
```

In short, If...Then can test "expressions," compound Variables, literals and Constants related to one another by "operators." (See Appendix C for a definition of "expression" and "operator.")

Uses
• Test a condition (a Variable, for instance) and, depending on the result, perform one set of commands instead of another.

• Test a condition, and depending on the result, then transfer the program to a different location using GoTo Label.

```
Sub Form_Load

Open "PROG.INI" For Input As 1

If Err <> 0 then
    GoTo Problem
End If

CLS
Exit Sub

Problem:
    Print "Error Occurred!"
End Sub
```

Cautions
Some programmers use this type of readable but dangerous abbreviation:

```
If X Then
```

or...

```
If NOT X Then
```

This kind of shortcut is possible, because just naming a Variable causes Basic to respond "True" if the Variable is –1 and "False" if it is 0. The NOT command reverses the test. NOT in the above example means: If X = 0.

Text Variables ("strings") respond "True" if they contain any text, and "False" if they are empty "" strings.

The danger in using this approach is that you can get erroneous reactions in special situations if you intend that any number other than zero in a Variable should cause a response of True. However, in Visual Basic, only –1 causes the IF NOT X to respond True.

It's safer to spell it out:

```
If X <> 0 Then
```

and...

```
If X = 0 Then
```

Example   In the General Declarations section of Form1, type in the following:

```
Sub Resize (x As Single, y As Single)

t = picture1.top
l = picture1.left

picture1.left = x

If l > x Then
    z = l − x
    picture1.width = picture1.width + z
Else
    z = x − l
        If x > l + picture1.width Then GoTo Ys
        picture1.width = picture1.width − z

End If

Ys:
picture1.top = y

If t > y Then
    z = t − y
    picture1.height = picture1.height + z

    Else
    z = y − t
        If y > picture1.height + t Then Exit Sub
        picture1.height = picture1.height − z
End If
End Sub
```

This Subroutine takes advantage of the fact that picture files saved in .WMF (Windows Metafile Format) will grow or shrink to fit the size of their container. In this example we created a Picture Box and filled it with a .WMF picture of the word RESIZE.

The Resize Subroutine above contains two main If...Then...Else structures, each with its own interior single-line If...Then to take care of the instances where the user clicks below or to the left of the Picture. We cannot shrink the Picture past its left or bottom borders. (The Picture cannot be smaller than "nothing" on one of its dimensions.)

From within the Form's MouseDown Event, we send the X,Y location of the user's click to the Resize Subroutine:

```
Sub Form_MouseDown (Button As Integer, Shift As Integer, x As Single, →
y As Single)
    Resize x, y
Cls
Drawframeon picture1, picture1, "inside", 100
End Sub
```

If they click *within* the Picture, we don't need the Resize Subroutine:

```
Sub Picture1_MouseDown (Button As Integer, Shift As Integer, x As →
Single, y As Single)

    picture1.width = x
    picture1.height = y
Cls
Drawframeon picture1, picture1, "inside", 100
End Sub
```

Finally, whenever the Picture is resized we want to use the DrawFrame-On Subroutine to create a metallic frame around the Picture. (See "Line" for information on DrawFrameOn.) We need that Cls to clear the background of the Form, or we'd leave remnants of Frames every time we resized.

Figure I-3: If...Then tells this program what to do. If the user clicks within the smaller graphic, there's a different effect than if the user clicks on the window itself.

See also   Select Case

IIF

Description Provides one of two answers, based on the truth or falsity of a tested expression. IIF is an abbreviated version of If...Then...Else. IIF stands for Immediate IF.

Variables
```
Z = 15
Print IIF(Z > 12, "Z is greater than 12", "Z is less than 12")
```

Format: IIF(expression to be tested, do this if true, do this if false)

Results in Z is greater than 12

Note that this format is precisely the same as the following:

```
Z = 15
Select Case Z
    Case > 12
        Print "Z is greater than 12"
    Case < 12
        Print "Z is less than 12"
End Select
```

OR

```
Z = 15
If Z > 12 Then
    Print "Z is greater than 12"
Else
    Print "Z is less than 12"
EndIF
```

Uses • Acts the same as If...Then or Select Case. It causes the computer to behave one way or another, based on the results of a test. In this case, the test is the truth or falsity of an expression.

Example The following example prints a warning to the user if the entered name is too long. Otherwise, it prints nothing, a "" null string.

```
N = InputBox("Please Enter Your Name")
Print IIf(Len(N) > 14, "There is only room for 14 letters, sorry.","")
```

See also Select Case; Choose; If...Then...Else; Switch

CONTROL

IMAGE

Description The Image Control is similar to the Picture Box Control except that an Image Control draws onscreen faster and uses fewer of the computer's resources (such as memory) because Images have far fewer Properties than Picture Boxes. Images are designed simply to display pictures imported from .BMP, .ICO, .WMF or .RLE (run-length-encoded, a compression technique) graphics files on disk.

Figure I-4: The Image Control's icon on the Toolbox.

One other important advantage is that graphics placed in an Image can be freely resized. You can stretch or shrink the graphics to suit your needs:

Figure I-5: With Image Controls, you can make photos or drawings any size you want.

Another difference between a Picture Box and an Image is that the latter is not designed to accept drawn graphics (using the Line, Circle or PSet command) or printed text (using the Print command). A Picture Box has 53 different Properties, many of them relating to the active drawing of graphics while a program is running (versus the importing of already created .BMP, .ICO, .WMF or .RLE graphics files). An Image Control has only 18 Properties. Among other things, an Image cannot engage in Dynamic Data Exchange (see "LinkMode").

The final primary difference is that other Controls can be "grouped" on top of a Picture Box (as they can on a frame). The value of this is that they then can act in concert; it is generally used to create a group of Option Buttons (which see), only one of which can be selected at a time. Image Controls cannot "host" other Controls in this way. But you're better off using the Frame Control for this purpose.

Used with   Forms

Variables   Because an Image Box is a Control, you will often adjust its Variables, its qualities, in the Properties Window while designing your program:

(to make changes to its Properties while the program is running):

    image2.Width = 4000

OR (to make changes by using a Variable while the program is running):

    image1.top = image4.top

OR

```
N = 800
Image1.Width = N
```

Uses
- Display .BMP or .RLE photographs or other images to make your programs more visually appealing. The primary reason for using an Image Control is to stretch or shrink a photo or graphic to suit your design objectives. Otherwise, you could use a Picture Box.

- The Image Control works with the LoadPicture command. This allows you to create a useful database of graphics. An Image not only allows you to stretch or shrink .BMP or .ICO files, it does the reverse—it forces all .BMP or .ICO images into a predefined size (if the Stretch Property is left False/Off). This creates a set of "thumbnail sketches" of large .BMP files and, while not as clear as the originals, gives the user a quick way to view and select from his or her graphics files. We'll illustrate this idea in the Example below.

- Change graphics dynamically while a program is running by using the LoadPicture command.

- Let the user view a close-up (blown-up) image by copying the image from a Picture Box (where it will be its real size) to a large Image Box:

```
Sub Form_Click ()
image2.Picture = picture1.Picture
End Sub
```

- In addition to stretching and shrinking, a number of exciting transformations can be achieved with graphics if you access the Windows API. (See Appendix A for examples of dynamic graphic manipulation using the StretchBlt Function. Also see "Declare.")

Cautions
- At the time of the writing of this book, attempting to import .WMF files into an Image Control has unpredictable results.

- If you import a graphics file while designing your program, the graphic *becomes part of the final runnable .EXE program.* This can make your .EXE quite large because graphics files are notoriously big.

- Both Picture Boxes and Image Controls have a Picture Property, so you can copy graphics between them: Image1.Picture = Picture1.Picture. However, you cannot copy *drawn* (Line, Circle or PSet) or Printed data from a Picture Box into an Image. (You *can* copy drawn or Printed data between Picture Boxes using the Image *Property* of Picture Boxes.)

Example
Before VB, this program could have taken weeks to program. We want to allow the user to peruse his or her disk drive and view a "sketch" of all .BMP files thereon. This would be an improvement over the Windows Desktop Menu—you can see and then click on your choice of Wallpaper.

We also want the user to be able to examine any .BMP full size by clicking on the picture. Here's how.

From the File Menu, select New Module and New Form and then type the following in the Module:

```
Global pa$
Global h, w
```

The Variable *pa$* will hold the name of the user's chosen filepath; *h* and *w* will hold the default height and width of Form1.

Then put an Image Box on Form1, make it about an inch square, and put it near the upper left corner of the Form. Put a second Image Box, of any size, anywhere on Form1. This second Box will hold the true-sized image if the user clicks on one of the sketches. On Form2, place a Directory List Box, a File List Box and a Command Button.

We'll start the program with Form1, so in Form1's Form_Load Event put the following to create an Image Box Control Array (see "Control Array"):

```
Sub Form_Load()

Rows = 7
Columns = 8

Movedown = image1(0).Height
Moveacross = image1(0).Width

w = image1(0).Width * Columns + 200
h = image1(0).Height * Rows + 200
Form1.Width = w
Form1.Height = h
Form2.File1.Pattern = "*.BMP"

image1(0).Visible = 0
image1(0).Stretch = −1
image2.Visible = 0
image2.Left = 0
image2.Top = 0

For I = 0 To Rows − 1
  For J = 0 To Columns − 1
    x = x + 1
    Load image1(x)
    image1(x).Top = Movedown * I
    image1(x).Left = Moveacross * J
    image1(x).Visible = −1
  Next J
Next I

Form2.Show

End Sub
```

We define the number of rows and columns we'll want on this Form (you can adjust these numbers). Then we define the size of each sketch-picture, based on whatever size you made Image1, and set Form1's size large enough to display the rows and columns. Also, we set File1's Pattern Property so it will list only .BMP files.

Next, we make both Image Boxes invisible and move Image2 to the top-left corner of the Form. Then we change Image1's Stretch Property from the default (Off) to On (–1), so when we Load in the various .BMP files—all different sizes—they will each be forced to fit inside the same space (about 1 inch if you wish). The size of the "seed" Image1 that you draw on Form1 is up to you; but after that, all the other Image Boxes that the program creates when it runs will be of that size. An explanation of how the Load command creates the entire collection of Image Boxes can be found in the Example under "Control Array."

The rest of the program is straightforward enough. When the user clicks on one of the "sketches," we want the small image in Image1 shown actual size in Image2.

```
Sub Image1_Click (index As Integer)
Caption = form2.File1.List(index – 1)
image2.Picture = image1(index).Picture
image2.Visible = –1
Form1.Width = image2.Width + 200
Form1.Height = image2.Height + 200
End Sub
```

First, we make the Form's caption display the name of the graphic the user clicked on; then we assign Image2's Picture to be the same as Image1's and make Image2 visible. We also make the Form resize itself to embrace only the new Image2.

When the user is through looking at the image in its actual size, we want to restore the Form so it shows all the sketches. Clicking on Image2 does this:

```
Sub Image2_Click ()
    Image2.Visible = 0
    Form1.Width = w
    Form1.Height = h
End Sub
```

In Form2, we have the usual small bit of programming that makes disk drive Controls work together by changing paths at the same time (see "Drive List Box"). We remember the name of the path in our Global Variable, *pa$*, and announce the number of .BMP files in the currently selected directory by making the File Box's ListCount the Caption of Form2:

```
Sub Dir1_Change ()
    file1.Path = dir1.Path
    pa$ = file1.Path
    form2.Caption = Str$(file1.ListCount) + " BMPS"
End Sub
```

Finally, here's how we respond if the user clicks on the Command Button captioned "Show Graphics":

```
Sub Command1_Click ()
form1.Image1(0).Picture = LoadPicture("")
tot = file1.ListCount
```

```
For i = 0 To 56
    form1.Image1(i).Picture = form1.Image1(0).Picture
Next i

For i = 1 To tot
    If Right$(pa$, 1) <> "\" Then pa$ = pa$ + "\"
    x$ = pa$ + file1.List(i − 1)
    form1.Image1(i).Picture = LoadPicture(x$)
    form1.Image1(i).Refresh
    form1.Caption = Str$(i) + " of" + Str$(tot)
Next i

End Sub
```

This last Event, where we trigger the loading in of all the sketches, truly takes advantage of the power of Control Arrays. First, we clean out any sketches left over from a previous viewing by putting empty "" pictures into each Image Box in the Array. Then we use LoadPicture again—this time supplying it with the name of each .BMP file in File1's List for the directory selected by the user. (For more about the need to check for a backslash (\) character, see "Drive List Box.") Then we Refresh each Image so the sketch will show up as soon as it's loaded, and show a running total of the importing images in the Form's Caption.

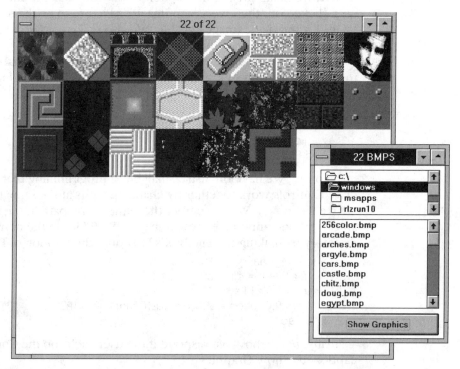

Figure I-6: With this program, you can see thumbnail images of all your .BMP files.

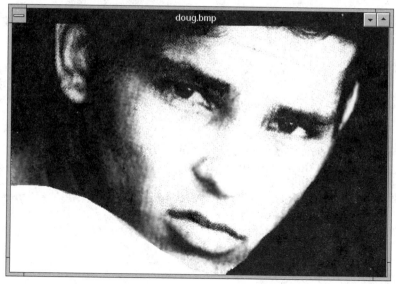

Figure I-7: When you click on a thumbnail, it blows up so you can see it full size.

It would take little extra work to make this program adjust the line in the WIN.INI file that describes the current .BMP file for Wallpaper. You could also expand this program to allow the user to move, delete and copy the sketches (and the .BMP files they represent). In this way, you would have a graphical file manager.

For an alternative approach to displaying collections of graphic images, see the Example under "Grid."

Image Properties
BorderStyle • DataField • DataSource • DragIcon • DragMode
Enabled • Height • Index • Left • MousePointer • Name • Parent
Picture • Stretch • Tag • Top • Visible • Width

Image Methods
Drag • Move • Refresh • ZOrder

Image Events
Click • DoubleClick • DragDrop • DragOver • MouseDown
MouseMove • MouseUp

See also   LoadPicture; Picture; Picture Box; Stretch

IMAGE

PROPERTY

Description Like hDC and hWnd (which see), the Image Property is a "handle"—a unique identification number provided by Windows itself. Image is a handle to a bitmap picture (such as a .BMP file). In particular, it is a handle to a *persistent* bitmap—a copy of the graphics in a Picture Box or Form that sits in the computer's memory because you've got the AutoRedraw Property set On (True).

The Image Property is the equivalent to the API's *hBitmap*. (For a complete tutorial on the API, see Appendix A.) The main use for Image is to copy *drawn* (Line, Circle or PSet) or *printed* (Print) data from one Picture Box to another: Picture2.Picture = Picture1.Image. (Also see "AutoRedraw.")

Used with Forms and Picture Boxes

Variables **Variable type**: Integer

The Image Property cannot be changed by your program. It is "read-only" and is used only to provide information to your program.

Uses Use Image with API features you access, as described in Appendix A. The Image Property is used with API calls involving BitBlt. You will see hBitmap (the Image Property is equivalent to hBitmap) referenced in such API calls as CreateDIBitmap. The Image Property can also be used with the other API calls that reference an hBitmap, such as SelectObject.

Cautions • As with any call to the API, you will want to first save to disk any changes or other data input that the user might have made while your program is running. API calls do not provide VB error messages.

Don't use Image with the DeleteObject API call. If Image is used in a SelectObject API call, be sure to select the previous object again before exiting the Event (or Subroutine or Function) that called the API. Otherwise, VB won't be able to delete the object if and when it needs to.

Example The Image Property is rarely used; but if you're interested in learning more about it, see the tutorial in Appendix A, which explains how to take advantage of the many valuable features of the Windows API.

The example below would copy the bits of Picture1 into a buffer pointed to by the Variable Y. The Variable X& tells how many bytes to copy. It would be easier in VB to just use the following:

```
Picture1.Picture = Picture2.Picture
```

In a Module or the General Declarations of a Form, you would type this (on a single line):

```
Declare Function GetBitmapBits Lib "GDI" (ByVal hBitmap As Integer, →
ByVal dwCount As Long, ByVal lpBits As Any) As Long
```

Then in an Event, you would "call" the API by substituting the Image Property for hBitmap:

```
Z& = GetBitmapBits (picture1.image, X&, Y)
```

See also   Appendix A; hDC; hWnd

IMAGELIST

CONTROL

See Windows 95 Controls

INDEX

PROPERTY

Description   You can create a group of Controls that, because you give them the same Name Property, become an *Array*. Then, you have two new techniques at your disposal: you can use the powerful Load Statement to create new Controls while the program runs, or you can manipulate the Array using Loops like For...Next.

• A Control Array can be manipulated *arithmetically*, because all the Controls in such an Array share the same text name; but each has a unique *Index*. An Index is a *number* and can therefore be controlled and adjusted by Loops. Ordinary Names with no Index are text, so you cannot manipulate them arithmetically within a Loop.

Creating a Control Array is a way to affect a whole group of Controls in the most efficient fashion. Here's the difference between using regular Names versus using a Control Array:

We want to make six Pictures invisible.

Without a Control Array:

```
Picture1.Visible = False
Picture2.Visible = False
Picture3.Visible = False
Picture4.Visible = False
Picture5.Visible = False
Picture6.Visible = False
```

With a Control Array:

```
For I = 1 to 6
Picture1(I).Visible = False
Next I
```

(See "Control Array" for examples and details about this unique and valuable feature of Visual Basic.)

• The Load Statement can generate new Controls while a program runs. (This is distinct from LoadPicture, which merely changes an image in an existing Picture Box.)

Load is an extremely powerful Statement; it dynamically *creates* Controls. They must be loaded as part of a Control Array, and they will, like all members of a Control Array, share the existing Event Procedures of the Array. Their Properties, however, will be copied from *the first member of the Array* (the member with the lowest Index number). You can, of course, change the Properties of these newborn Controls, but they arrive into your program as clones of the first member. The only exceptions to this shared-Properties rule are TabIndex and Index, which are necessarily unique numbers, and Visible, which is set to False (0) when a new Control is born.

For more about the Load Statement and the extraordinary effects it makes possible, see "Load."

Used with   Control Arrays created for any of the following Controls:

Check Boxes, Combo Boxes, Command Buttons, CommonDialogs, Data, Directory, Drive & File List Boxes, Frames, Grids, Horizontal & Vertical Scroll Bars, Images, Labels, Lines, List Boxes, Menus, OLEs, Option Buttons, Picture Boxes, Shapes, Text Boxes and Timers

Variables   **Variable type:** Integer

Normally you create a Control Array while designing a Form. You simply change the Name of a Control to the same Name as another Control of the same type.

We create two Command Buttons. VB names them for us: Command1 and Command2. To create a Control Array: From the Properties Window, give one of them the same Name as the other. In this case, we change Command2's Name to "Command1."

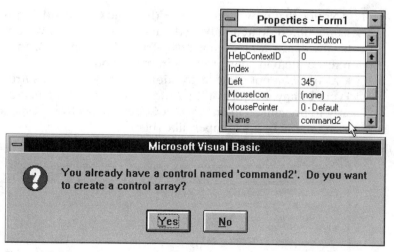

Figure I-8: Visual Basic's reaction if you give the same Name to more than one Control.

As soon as you change a Name to duplicate an existing one, VB brings up the message in Figure I-8, informing you that the name is already in use and asking if you want to create a Control Array. If you answer "yes," two things happen:

• Before the change, the Form's Object: Menu looked like this:

```
(General)
Command1
Command2
Form
```

And after you create the Control Array, it looks like this, the parentheses ( ) indicating an Array because it's between the parentheses that the Index numbers will go:

```
(General)
Command1()
Form
```

• The Event Subs for the new Command1() Control Array looked like this, before the change:

```
Sub Command1_Click
End Sub
```

After you create the Control Array, they change to this:

```
Sub Command1_Click (Index as Integer)
End Sub
```

Notice that now there is more than one Command Button with the same name, differentiated only by the Index number. Index numbers start with 0, so we now have Command1(0) and Command1(1); and that is how you refer to them in your program from now on.

Also, if you put some instructions in an Event of this Array, triggering this Event by any member of the Array will carry out the instructions. The only way to prevent all members of a Control Array from responding identically is to use the Index number, like this:

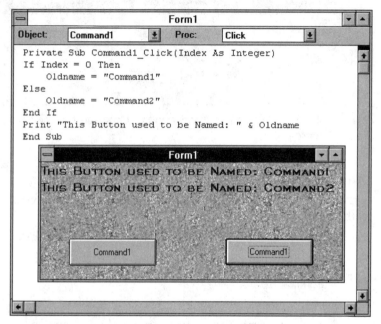

Figure I-9: You check the Variable Index to find out which of the members of a Control Array triggered an Event (all the members *share* Events in common).

Notice, too, that Captions are not automatically changed. They retain the names they were given when created as individual Controls. This is because although the members of a Control Array share *Events* in common, their *Properties* can be distinct (they can each be a different color, for instance).

OR

You can create an Array by merely setting the Index Property of a single existing Control. There is only one member of this Array when you do this, but you can use the Load command to create new members when the program is running. Alternatively, you can add new members while designing the program by changing Names to the Array's Name. To create a Control Array with the Properties Window, change the Index Property from blank to 0:

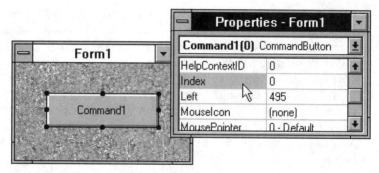

Figure I-10: You can create a Control Array by giving *any* index number to a Control (even 0, as used here).

OR

You refer to the members of a Control Array by using the Index number of the particular Control you are adjusting:

    Labelname(4).Left = 3000

Uses

• Group Controls into Arrays when you want them to share Event Procedures. In this way, you can write only one group of instructions in one Event Procedure but have that response available to all (or some) of the members of a Control Array.

For example, say that you want a group of Labels to sometimes lose their Enabled Property, becoming gray and dim onscreen, signifying to the user that they are temporarily unavailable for use in the current context. In the Example, you'll see how you can disable five Controls much more easily by grouping them into a Control Array. Control Arrays are especially useful if a group of Picture Boxes, Command Buttons or other Controls should sometimes act in concert while the program runs. You need describe the instructions for their common Event Procedures only once to have an effect on all of them (or, by using the Index Property, selectively on some of them).

Further, you can manipulate their Properties within For...Next or Do Loops or inside other structures such as Select Case, using the Index number instead of Names (which would force you to work with each Control individually instead of working with them inside a structure). This is a very efficient way to handle several Controls at once.

• Use the Load Statement to create groups of Controls while the program runs. See the Example that follows.

Cautions   • If VB creates Index numbers for you (during a Load Statement, or when you change a Control's Name to an existing Name), it will start with Index 0 and go up in order (1, 2, 3, etc.). However, you can change a Control's Index Property and are even allowed to use Index numbers that are *not sequential*: Button(4), Button(7), and so forth. You can use Index numbers from 0–32,767, although you are limited to no more than 255 Controls per Form. Except in very peculiar circumstances, though, you will want to leave Index numbers in sequence so you can utilize one of a Control Array's greatest features—manipulating the members of the Array within Loops.

• If you are working on your program and write some commands within a Control, you cannot then use that particular Control to create a Control Array. Visual Basic allows you to set such a Control's Index Property (or give another Control the same Name), so it will seem as if you have successfully created a Control Array. But, when you try to run this program, you'll get an error message, "Incorrect number of event procedure arguments." (It doesn't matter if you've put programming commands within a Control that you intend to *add* to an existing Control Array. This problem occurs only when you're trying to create a new Control Array.)

Solution: Remove any programming from within a Control that you intend to use to create a Control Array. Or create a Control Array from a brand new (empty) Control.

• If while the program runs you want to pull one of the Controls out of a Control Array and give it a separate identity, simply change its Name Property and it will go solo. (Note that this will create a discontinuous series of Index numbers. See the first Caution item.)

• If you are using the Load Statement and try to use an already existing Index number to create a new member of a Control Array, this will generate an error.

A Special Technique: You can create a Control Array of any Controls on a Form, even if the Controls are in separate frames. This is a handy technique to build a group of Option Buttons where more than one can be selected yet the Buttons can be treated as a group when providing instructions in their shared Events or adjusting the Properties of the Array. For example, Buttons for cheese, mushrooms, bacon and onions can be selected in any combination if each is in its own frame or Picture Box. However, their shared Event can Loop through the Buttons and figure the cost of the pizza just by adding the number of Option1(X) Value Properties of any Buttons that have been selected. (See "Control Array" for more on the applications and features of Control Arrays.)

Example   When we designed this Form, we only created the first Command Button and gave it a Caption of "Save." We then set its Index Property to 0 with the Properties Window, thereby creating a Control Array.

Figure I-11: This window was given only a single Command Button while the program was being designed. The other five Buttons are added automatically whenever the program runs.

Now we can use the Load Statement to create a group of Buttons while the program runs, and then use For...Next to adjust some of their Properties in a most efficient fashion:

```
Sub Form_Load ()

Show

ReDim Cap$(1 To 5)
Cap$(1) = "Open"
Cap$(2) = "Close"
Cap$(3) = "Import"
Cap$(4) = "Export"
Cap$(5) = "Cancel"

For I = 1 To 5
    Load Command1(I)
    Command1(I).Visible = True
    Command1(I).Top = Command1(I — 1).Top + 900
    Command1(I).Caption = Cap$(I)
Next I

End Sub
```

Notice that we adjust the Top position of each incoming Control by borrowing the Top from the previous Control in the Array (I–1) and then adding to it. This stacks them.

Now that we have an Array, we can quickly adjust Properties of some or all of the ganged Controls. It's always a good idea for your program to visually indicate current conditions. This helps the user know what's going on and makes the program easier and more pleasant to use.

Let's assume that it takes several seconds to save something to disk. We don't want the user to simply see an unchanged screen: how would that reassure the user that things were proceeding normally? So, when Save is selected, we instantly disable (gray out) all Controls that are inappropriate during the Save, leaving only Cancel still bold to signify that it is available:

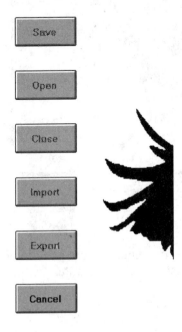

Figure I-12: Because they're all in a Control Array, we can quickly and efficiently disable five of these six Command Buttons.

```
Sub Command1_Click (Index As Integer)

If Index = 0 Then
    For I = 0 To 4
        Command1(I).Enabled = False
    Next I
End If

End Sub
```

See also   Arrays; Control Array; Load

INITIALIZE AND TERMINATE

EVENT

Description

These Events are most useful with Objects—in particular when you create a server object with a Class Module (see "Objects"). However, Initialize and Terminate can be used with ordinary Forms too.

Most Events are triggered by the *user* of a program and a few Events are programmed to be triggered by the running application. However a few Events are triggered by VB itself. When the user moves the mouse, the MouseMove Event is triggered and, therefore, any programming you've written within that Event will be carried out by VB. When the user presses a key, the KeyPress Event is triggered. However, some Events are triggered by behavior within the VB program rather than by a user.

When you start a VB program running, one Form (the "Startup Form," which see) is automatically copied from the disk into the computer's memory. In VB3 and earlier versions of the language, this Startup Form's Load Event was automatically triggered, merely by executing the VB program. Programmers often put any preliminary housekeeping programming into this Load Event (reading an .INI file, briefly displaying a title or copyright screen to the user, etc.)

If the VB program contained other Forms, they may or may not be Loaded, depending on program conditions. However, if they are Loaded, their Load Events too would be triggered. So, for any Form, the Load Event is automatically triggered when that Form comes into the computer's memory from the disk (and the UnLoad Event is triggered when the program is shut down or if the Form is deliberately unloaded with the UnLoad command (UnLoad Form4).

Now in VB4, however, Load and UnLoad are not the alpha and omega. Initialize is now the first Event triggered in any Form. Terminate is the last Event. In VB4, the Initialize Event is triggered, followed immediately (and automatically if a Form is being Loaded, as opposed to one of its procedures or Variables merely being accessed) by a triggering of the Load Event. Similarly, when a Form is removed from memory, Unload is triggered and *might* be followed by Terminate (it's quite possible to UnLoad *without* triggering Terminate, as we will see).

At first glance, Initialize and Terminate might seem redundant (and, indeed, in much VB programming they *are* redundant). "Loading" a Form means that it is brought into the computer's memory from the disk drive while a VB program is running. Usually, the purpose of Loading is to display to the user some new elements of your application's user interface (a new Text Box, a new group of Command Buttons, etc.) However, *any* *reference* to a Form's *visible* contents (its Controls, procedures or variables) will trigger an automatic Load of that Form. Once Loaded, the Form's visible contents become available and can be made visible by using the Show command.

Usually, VB programmers put generic shared procedures into a Module (not a Class Module) rather than a Form, but that's not compulsory. Perhaps you want to use a particular Function in Form2, but use it from Form1. When you call the Function in Form2, from Form1, if Form2 isn't already *instantiated* it will be–triggering its Form_Initialize Event. However, this form is *not* "Loaded" in the sense that its visible components are in memory. What's more, Form2's Load Event isn't triggered. If all you do is use Form2's Public procedures or Public Variables, Form2 will *never* "Load."

In any case, to understand the distinction between the Initialize and Load (or UnLoad and Terminate) Events, think of a Form Object as having two general kinds of data. First there is the potentially *visible* group of Objects (the Form and any of its Controls). Second there is an *invisible* kind of data that's located in the Form's General Declarations section (above the programming in any Events). General Declarations can contain Public Variable declarations (making these Variables available to all other Forms and Modules in the program). It can also contain Public procedures, Subs and Functions that you permit outside Forms or Modules to access by making them Public.

A reference to either Public data or procedures from outside the Form *implicitly* forces the Form to respond. However, accessing the first, "visible" kind of data (by, for instance: Form5.Text1.Text = "This") causes VB to automatically Load that Form. (In Object-oriented programming, this is called *instantiating* the Text Box.) Accessing the second "invisible" kind of data (by, for instance: Form5.Temperature = 22) doesn't cause VB to Load the Form, but will trigger the Initialize Event.

The Terminate Event is triggered when you *eliminate* a Form by using the Nothing command:

```
Form5 = Nothing
```

Unlike the UnLoad command (that triggers only the UnLoad Event), when you use the Nothing command, you trigger both UnLoad and Terminate.

Used with   A Form (or Forms Collection), MDI Form or a Class Module

Variables

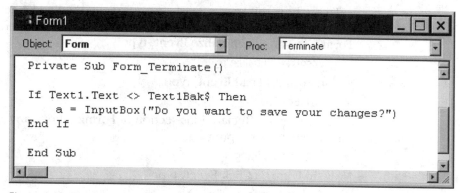

```
Form1                                              _ □ ×
Object:  Form              ▼    Proc:  Terminate        ▼

Private Sub Form_Terminate()

If Text1.Text <> Text1Bak$ Then
    a = InputBox("Do you want to save your changes?")
End If

End Sub
```

Figure I-13: To have your program respond when the entire Form *object* is removed from memory (not just its visible components), put programming into the Form s Terminate Event

Uses

For Initialize: A Class Module has no visible elements and, of course, there's no Load Event. In fact, a Class Module has only two Events—Initialize and Terminate. If you are creating a server object (requires the Professional version of VB4, see "Objects"), you might well want to set up some preliminary Constants or Variables, or do other housekeeping. Likewise, before a server object shuts down, things might need to be saved to disk or otherwise tidied up. The Initialize and Terminate are where you would do these things.

When you want to be sure that some programming executes if a Form's Public Variables or procedures are merely *accessed* without being "Loaded." You want VB to carry out some startup conditions (preliminary housekeeping or setting up some preconditions) for a Form that isn't, in the traditional sense, ever fully "loaded" into memory at all.

In other words, there may be situations in object oriented programming with VB (see "Objects") where you might want to access a Form's Public Variables or procedures. However you have no need for that Form's visible objects—such as setting a Text Box's Text Property—you can merely modify or query a Public Variable, or call a Public procedure. That would not trigger the Load Event in the Form, but would trigger its Initialize Event.

To see how this works, start a new Project, then add a new Form by clicking on the Insert Menu, then selecting "Form." You'll have Form1 and Form2. In Form2's Initialize Event, type

```
MsgBox "Initialize"
```

and in Form2's Load Event, type

```
MsgBox "Load"
```

In the General Declarations section of Form2 (above any Subs) create a Public variable by typing

```
Public X as Integer
```

Now, in Form1's Click Event, type

```
Private Sub Form_Click( )
    Form2.x = 33
    Print Form2.x
End Sub
```

and press F5 to run the program.

Result   Initialize (but no Load) is triggered.
Now change the programming in Form1's Click Event to

```
Private Sub Form_Click( )
    Form2.BackColor = vbRed
    Form2.Show
End Sub
```

Result   Intitialize, followed by Load, are triggered. And both occur before Form2 is Shown to the user.

For Terminate: When you want to program some shutdown behavior (saving the contents of a Public Variable to disk, for example) in a Form that was never actually Loaded (but where Public Variables, as described above, were used). In such a Form, VB can shut down a program without ever triggering the Form's UnLoad Event.

Cautions   • Some situations seem to violate the order in which these Events are supposed to take place. For example, the command

```
UnLoad Form2
```

should, you might think, trigger a Terminate Event in Form2 (along with the UnLoad and QueryUnLoad Events). It doesn't. The reason is that Form2 remains an accessible *object* (its Public Variables or Public procedures can still be used by other Forms) even after its "visible" potential has been removed from memory by the UnLoad command.

To trigger its Terminate Event, you would destroy Form2 as an object:

```
Form2 = Nothing
```

However, if no visible elements of Form2 had ever been Loaded (via Form_Load), the UnLoad Event would not be triggered—only the Terminate Event.

• Terminate isn't triggered if you end the program with the End command (without using the Nothing command to destroy the Form).

Here are some examples of the Events in Form2 that are triggered by various activities in Form1:

```
In Form1:
Form2.N = 1544  set a Form2 Public variable
Set Form2 = Nothing
```

Results in

Form2:

Form2_Initialize
Form2_Terminate

In Form1:

```
Form2.Show
Unload Form2
```

Results in

Form2:

Form2 Initialize
Form2 Load
Form2 QueryUnLoad
Form2 UnLoad

In Form1:

```
Form2.N = 1433  set a Form2 Public variable
Load Form2
Unload Form2
Set Form2 = Nothing
```

Results in

Form2:

Form2 Initialize
Form2 Load
Form2 QueryUnLoad
Form2 UnLoad
Form2 Terminate

Example   This program first displays the Initialize MessageBox, followed by the one in the Load Event:

```
Private Sub Form_Initialize( )
    MsgBox "This is the Initialize Event"
End Sub
Private Sub Form_Load( )
    MsgBox "This is the Load Event"
End Sub
```

Interestingly, however, if you place a Show command in the Form_Load Event, *it* will be triggered before the Initialize Event.

See also   Load, Objects, QueryUnLoad, UnLoad

INPUT

Description   Input # gets information from a disk file. The items of information in this file were previously saved using the sister command Write #, thereby creating a *sequential* file. Input #, however, is rarely used. The Line Input # and Input$ commands are usually preferable. Nonetheless, if the file in question was created by your program and is used for setup information or data storage, Input # can be easier to use than the Line Input # command for separating the individual pieces of data in the file (see parsing under "InStr"). Some of these decisions about which of two similar commands to use basically come down to programmer preference.

Note: Sequential files can also be created using the paired commands Line Input # and Print #. These are generally preferred over Input # and Write # because Line Input # is more efficient.

Line Input # reads in all characters until it finds a Carriage Return character (meaning the user pressed the ENTER key). Input # pulls in characters up to a Carriage Return, too, but it will also stop reading when it finds a comma. This is often an inconvenience, since commas are used frequently in text and should not be treated as a signal to stop reading a sentence or paragraph.

It's easier to get information in sentence or paragraph units rather than the smaller phrase units between commas. And there's another problem with Input # too: it strips off any spaces at the start of a line, potentially destroying some of the user's formatting that was originally typed in along with the text. (See "Cautions.")

Both Input # and Line Input # operate otherwise in identical fashion, throwing away the Carriage Return character and providing you with a clean text ("string") Variable for use in your program. It's just that Input # tries to do too much, and ends up failing to provide a stable, accurate representation of what is in a file.

Input$ Is a Good Alternative: Another retrieval command that you might want to consider for pulling in data from a sequential file is Input$ (which see), which preserves even the Carriage Return. Bringing in an exact image of whatever the user typed in Input$ is especially useful for word processing because the user's format can be exactly reproduced.

Input # is included in VB for compatibility with programs written in earlier versions of Basic. You'll likely want to use Line Input # or Input$ instead of Input #. And there's another choice you'll need to make as well—whether you want to create *sequential* files or *random* files. (See "Open.") As computing evolves, the sequential style is often preferred since it usually allows the user greater freedom. Random, however, is sometimes more efficient for the computer. The Input$ command cannot be used with files opened in the random mode.

Input # can also be used as a substitute for a pair of commands—Data and Read—that were part of earlier versions of Basic but are not included in Visual Basic. Here is an approach that lets you read information in a disk file and store it in your program during initialization:

```
Input #1,CustNo(X),CustName$(X),Address$(X)
```

(The preceding would be reading from a file with the data stored in this fashion:)

```
123,"Jones","123 Anywhere St., Mytown"
224,"Smith","45 New Rd., Mytown"
```

Sequential Versus Random Files: There are two primary ways to save and retrieve information to and from a disk: sequential files and random files. You choose between them based on the kind of information you will be saving. Use sequential files if the information is primarily text, or if the "records" (the individual items of information) can be of varying lengths. A collection of recipes would vary in length from two lines for boiling eggs to three pages for *Shock de la Maison Flambé*, the famous veal dish.

By contrast, some programs will accept information from the user only via records whose lengths are rigidly controlled: "Please Enter Your Telephone Number, 12 characters maximum, in the following format: ***_***_****." This kind of program will reject input that is, in this instance, more or less than 12 characters in length. Since names vary in length, this program would "pad" shorter names with spaces, creating Name records of equal length. In sum, all records of the same information must have the same size. This approach creates a *random-access* file (and as you can see, there's nothing random about the way it stores information). A random file is written to with the Put Statement and read from with the Get Statement.

Each Has Advantages: With ever-increasing disk sizes, computer memory and speed, more people are coming to prefer the greater freedom sequential files often give the user. All too frequently, in its effort to create records of fixed sizes, random access imposes an unseemly rigidity.

The advantage of random access is that the computer knows the precise length of each record, and can therefore locate record #412 rather quickly and bring it in from the disk to the computer's memory, or replace an edited version of it on the disk. It is called *random* because the computer can randomly access the records when they are of a known size, like shoe boxes in the stock room of a shoe store. However, in sequential files, there is a long string of data of different lengths (distinguished only by Carriage Returns or other "delimiters"). To get to a particular record, the computer has to feel its way along the string, looking at each delimiter to count up until it reaches the record it's after. Or it has to use a searching technique like the InStr command.

Used with   Sequential files

Variables To read in a text ("string") from a disk file:

```
Open "Myfile" For Input As #1
Input #1, Info$
```
OR
```
Input #1, Info$, A
```

(Here you are reading in a piece of text, then a number. You can request multiple Variables following the Input # Statement and mix different types of Variables. However, this is a risky business and is rarely done. See "Cautions.")

Uses Instead of Input #, use the more effective Line Input #, or Input$.

Cautions • Although you can use Input # to read numbers and put them into *numeric* Variables, sequential files are generally not used this way. This does not mean that you can't allow the user to save numbers; it's just that the numbers will be saved as text characters, indistinguishable from the letters of the alphabet. It is easy enough to translate the digits of a number in text back into a true, computable number. Just use the Val Statement:

```
X$ = "15"
Y = Val(X$)
Print 2 * Y
```

Results in 30

• Input # automatically strips off any leading spaces when it pulls in information from a file. That can destroy formatting your user might have found desirable when typing in the information. This is another reason to avoid using Input # and to use Line Input # or Input$ instead. If you are concerned about removing leading (or trailing) spaces, use LTrim$ or RTrim$.

• Blank lines are pulled in as empty text.

(If A$ = "" Then Print) would insert a blank line into text you were reading and then Printing to a Form. The "" means empty text ("string") Variable—A$ contains no text.

Example Let's take a look at the difference between Input # and Line Input # to see why the latter is often preferable.

Create a short test file using the Notepad, and save it as C:\TEST.TXT.

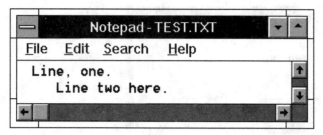

Figure I-14: For this example, create this text in Notepad, then save it as C:\TEST.TXT.

```
Sub Command1_Click ()

Open "C:\TEST.TXT" For Input As #1

Do While Not EOF(1)
      Input #1, D$
      Print D$
Loop

End Sub
```

Results in

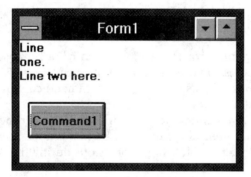

Figure I-15: Avoiding this kind of formatting oddity caused by the Input # command requires extra programming effort.

Notice that Input # has caused the comma to trigger a new line, and has removed the leading spaces that we put in front of the second line. Now try reading from the same file substituting Line Input #1, D$:

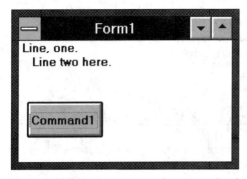

Figure I-16: Line Input # produces results that match the original formatting.

See also   Close; Input$; Line Input #; Open; Print # (use this one); Write # (avoid this one)

INPUT($), INPUTB   FUNCTION

Description   Input($) is used to get information from sequential or binary files. (See "Open" for a full discussion on creating and manipulating disk files, and the three types, or *modes*, of files.) The Input$ command cannot be used with files opened in random mode.

The Input$ Function is similar to Line Input #. However, because Line Input # is a *Statement*, it cannot be used in an *expression* like this: X$ = Input$(1,1) + "A" (although using expressions during file access is hardly ever done).

A more significant distinction is that Line Input # pulls in a line of text the ending of which is defined by a Carriage Return character (the user pressed the ENTER key while typing in the line).

Input$, on the other hand, does not automatically determine the number of characters that should be pulled in at one gulp from a file. Instead, *you* specify for Input$ the number of characters you want.

The InputB variation pulls in bytes rather than characters. (A text character *can* be a two-byte unit.)

Used with   Sequential and binary files. (See "Open.")

Variables   This will put 15 characters from the file Opened As #1 into X$

    X$ = Input$(15, 1)

OR this will put a single character into X$, the number of characters defined by a Variable in this instance:

```
n = 1
X$ = (Input$(n,1))
```

Uses
• Database management, or any programming where you want to save information to a file and later manipulate that information.

Specifically used with sequential or binary files (see "Open"), where you want a fine degree of control over how many characters are being pulled in at a time. Input$ gives you precise control as well over what you may want to do with special characters (such as Carriage Return characters) because Input$ can pull in characters one at a time from the file. *You can get an exact image of the entire file with Input$.*

If you were searching through a file looking for a particular word, you might want to use Input$(1,1) inside a Loop to search for the first character of the word you're after. Then, finding the first letter, you would try for a complete match.

However, it is more common to pull the whole file into the computer's memory and search through memory (this approach is much faster than searching through a disk file while it's still on the disk). You can then very quickly search through huge text Variables (up to 32,767 characters) using the InStr Function.

```
Sub Form_Click ()
Q$ = InputBox$("What text are you looking for?")
Open "C:\AUTOEXEC.BAT" For Input As #1
X$ = Input$(LOF(1), 1)
Close
Y = InStr(1, X$, Q$)
If Y <> 0 Then
    Print Q$; " Found"
Else
    Print Q$; " Not Found"
End If
End Sub
```

The LOF(1) means the entire Length Of the File, so we stuff the whole AUTOEXEC.BAT file into X$.

Then we search: Starting at character 1 using the InStr command, we look through X$, for Q$. If our word is found within X$, then Y will contain the character's position within X$ (starting from 1 and counting up). If our word isn't in X$, Y will equal 0.

Cautions • The InputB command reads *bytes*.

```
InputB (Numberofbytes, FileNumber)
```

The Input command reads *characters*. With VB4, characters can now be stored in 2-byte units.

• The Get command is typically used with random files. You cannot use Input$, in Visual Basic, with random files. You'll get an error message if you try to do so.

• Input$, unlike Line Input #, throws away no characters. Line Input # pulls in text until it reaches a Carriage Return character. It throws out the Carriage Return character and an associated "Line Feed" character as well as any leading spaces, providing you with clean text Variables. Not so with Input$. It pulls in *all* characters until it has reached the amount you said you wanted. And it doesn't remove Carriage Return/Line Feed characters for you. If you want to put text into a Text Box exactly as the user typed it in, use Input$.

• You can put in a # symbol prior to the filenumber, if you wish:

```
Input$(22,#1)
```

Example Here we're going to precisely control the information we get from a file and the amount of it we want to view. In the Do...Loop, we say, "While we haven't reached the end of this file, and while we haven't reached a 'Line Feed' character code, print each character and print its character code in parentheses on the same line." Then we exit the Loop and bring in the next seven characters, print them and Close the file. (For more about character codes, see "Chr$.")

```
Sub Command1_Click ()

Open "C:\AUTOEXEC.BAT" For Input As #1

Do While Not EOF(1) And X$ <> Chr$(10)
    X$ = Input$(1, 1)
    Print "   "; X$, "("; Asc(X$); ")"
Loop

X$ = Input$(7, 1)
Print X$

Close

End Sub
```

Results in

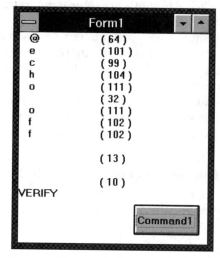

```
┌─────────────────────────────────────┐
│ ─        Form1           ▼  ▲        │
├─────────────────────────────────────┤
│  @           ( 64 )                  │
│  e           ( 101 )                 │
│  c           ( 99 )                  │
│  h           ( 104 )                 │
│  o           ( 111 )                 │
│              ( 32 )                  │
│  o           ( 111 )                 │
│  f           ( 102 )                 │
│  f           ( 102 )                 │
│                                      │
│              ( 13 )                  │
│                                      │
│              ( 10 )                  │
│ VERIFY                               │
│                        ┌───────────┐ │
│                        │ Command1  │ │
│                        └───────────┘ │
└─────────────────────────────────────┘
```

Figure I-17: Input$ gives you fine control over incoming characters: you can easily pick them off one at a time for examination.

The Carriage Return (ANSI code 13), Line Feed (ANSI 10) characters, and other special nontext characters can be embedded within files. Input$ gives you exact control over the *input stream* coming in from a file you are reading. You can use it to pick characters off the file one at a time, examine them and deal with them appropriately according to your task.

See also   Close; Line Input #; Open; Print # (use this one); Write # (avoid this one)

NPUTBOX($)

FUNCTION

Description   You may be tempted to use InputBox$ when other Controls such as Option Buttons, File List Boxes, etc., would be easier for the user. Input-Box$ has a most unpleasant effect: like MsgBox, InputBox$ halts the program until the user responds. It's rather like being arrested.

InputBox$ is sometimes necessary, perhaps, but the more you employ this command, the more you'll annoy the user. It's similar to MsgBox but requires the user to enter some text.

InputBox$ is commonly used when you need some specific information from the user, but the information is either too unpredictable or too infrequently needed to offer the user a list of choices via Command Buttons, Option Buttons, Menus or other, less intrusive approaches.

It's best to confine your use of InputBox$ to near-emergency situations where you feel you must demand that the user react. One example would be if the user attempts to shut down your program before having saved some changes he or she made to a Text Box. Another good use is to request that the user enter a password at some point in a program where you want access to be restricted.

Use Text Boxes for most text input from the user. Not only can you leave Text Boxes lying around on the screen for the user to work with when he or she chooses to, but Text Boxes also have a number of user-friendly features not available to InputBox$.

Variables   You can control five qualities of an InputBox$, but only the first one, *the prompt*, is required:

```
InputBox$(PromptMessageToUser$, TitleBar$, Default$, XPosition%, →
    YPosition%, helpfile, context)
```

PromptMessage ToUser$
The text message you provide to the user, often called a *prompt*.

TitleBar$
The text displayed in the Title Bar of the box (optional; if you put nothing in, the Title Bar will be blank).

Default$
Any text you want provided by default within the user's "edit box," the place where the user is to type in text. If you think you know in advance how the user will respond, perhaps you shouldn't be interrupting the program in the first place. It might be better to use Preferences Menus or Buttons. (Default text is optional and sometimes annoying to users, since they frequently have to delete what you've presumptuously entered for them.)

XPosition%
The location of the box measured over from the left side of the screen. (This is expressed in *twips*, a unit of measurement. There are 1,440 twips per inch. Optional.)

YPosition%
The location of the box as measured down from the top of the screen. (Also expressed in twips, also optional. See "ScaleMode" about twips.)

Helpfile
If you want a Help button to appear on your InputBox, add a text ("string") variable or expression that names the help file. You must also include a Context, as described below. Context This is a numeric variable or expression defining the "Help context number." This displays the appropriate topic within the larger Help file.

Uses
• Other methods of getting user input are less restrictive and more pleasant for the user: Text Boxes, Option Buttons, dragging Icons and so on. Since InputBox$ forces your program to halt until the user responds, it's an uncomfortable moment at best. MsgBox and InputBox$ are not really in the spirit of the open-ended, visually oriented and freedom-loving environments of Windows and Visual Basic.

There will doubtless be times when you can think of no better alternative; but a program filled with MsgBox and InputBox$ roadblocks should be redesigned. The idea is to allow the *user* to guide your program's behavior. At least this has been true in the past few years, once computers became powerful enough to support rich, supple graphical operating systems. This means that you can't keep slapping messages onto the screen, immobilizing the computer until the user acknowledges your message or provides the information you're demanding *now*.

Visual Basic is an Event-driven language. Its programs should not be *linear*, not a series of experiences that must happen in a strict order, like the Mad Hatter ride at Disneyland or the forms you fill out to get into North Korea. Older Basic programs were heavily linear; the programmer told the user what to do and in what order to do it.

The trend in computing, then, is that the programmer creates *opportunities* for the user, providing a well-designed vehicle and an appealing visual landscape. Control over the computer is gradually passing from the programmer to the user. Option Menus and Preference Menus are proliferating. Few elements of an Event-driven program are strictly cause-and-effect. The paradigm is a relaxing, generous self-serve buffet as opposed to a nerve-wracking, rigid formal dinner.

Windows and Visual Basic are important contributors to this altogether welcome development. There's even a symbolic difference between the *look* of the older two-dimensional, black-and-white programs and the colorful, three-dimensional Windows programs. Programmers should now try to create programs that behave in the spirit of the new freedom that Windows offers the user.

Cautions
• Your prompt text cannot be larger than 255 characters.

• To create a prompt with more than one line, you must add Carriage Return and Line Feed characters to any text Variable where you want to move down to the next line:

```
CR$ = Chr$(13) + Chr$(10)
MyPrompt1$ = MyPrompt$1 + CR$
MyPrompt2$ = MyPrompt$2 + CR$
```

• If you include the X position, you must also supply the Y position. Without both, the InputBox$ is placed one-third of the way down from the top of the user's screen and centered horizontally.

• If the user clicks on the Cancel Button or does not enter any text (and you have not provided any text in the Variables you supply to InputBox$), an empty text Variable is the result (""). You can check for this with the following: If X$ = "".

• The $ symbol is optional. InputBox works just as well.

Example

Figure I-18: An Input Box stops your program until the user responds.

The following code will put the first message into the "Prompt" zone of the box, "ATTENTION!" into the Title Bar, and "Enter Name Here!" into the user's input box zone. It will then paste the box 5,000 twips down from the top of the screen and 5,000 twips over from the left—about 3 1/2 inches:

```
Q$ = InputBox$("Enter Your Name. Now!", "ATTENTION!", "Enter Name →
    Here!", 5000, 5000)
```

See also   Text Box; and the various other Controls that accept user responses more smoothly, and far less coercively, than InputBox$. Also see MsgBox.

 I NSTR FUNCTION

Description   This is a remarkably handy Function when you need to *parse* some text (isolate, extract or search for some information from within a larger body of text). InStr can allow you to see if a particular word, for example, exists within a file or within some text that the user typed into the computer.

One common use for InStr is to make some necessary adjustments to the paths and filenames that you get back when a user selects from one of your File, Directory or Drive List Boxes (see the Example).

InStr looks through a text ("string") Variable, searching for a character, word or phrase. It tells you whether it found the target and, if so, the character position within the larger text where the target was located.

Used with Variables

Text ("string") Variables

```
L = (1, BigText$, Target$)
```

OR (if you want to search for Target$ starting from the first character in BigText$, you can optionally leave out the first Variable, the 1 that tells InStr at which character position within BigText$ to start searching):

```
L = InStr(BigText$, Target$)
```

OR

BigText$ and Target$ can be any text ("string") Variable or literal text enclosed between quotation marks:

```
L = InStr("ABCDEFGHIJ", "A")
```

Uses

- Search for a particular piece of text within a larger text Variable.
- Locate a piece of text, then remove unwanted surrounding text (see the Example below).

Cautions

- InStr stops at the first match it finds.
- InStr can't be used to access byte-sized string (text) arrays anymore with the VB4 32-bit version. (See "Chr$".)
- InStr is case-sensitive; it makes a distinction between *Upper* and *upper*. What if you want to know whether there is more than one Target$ within the BigText$? You can easily find them by using the result of a previous InStr search. InStr, when it finds a match, reports the location, the character position within the BigText$ where the Target$ was found. (For this example, we're going to use the UCase$ Function to make sure that capitalization won't affect the outcome. UCase$ converts everything into uppercase letters. Remember that InStr$ will not see a match if the letters are not all in the same "case.")

```
Sub Form_Click ()

Big$ = "Abracadabra"
Target$ = "bra"

Big$ = UCase$(Big$)
Target$ = UCase$(Target$)

Do
    X = Y + 1
    Z = Z + 1
    Y = InStr(X, Big$, Target$)
Loop Until Y = 0

Print "We found "; Target$; Z − 1; "times inside "; Big$
End Sub
```

Results in   We found BRA 2 times inside ABRACADABRA

Example   Let's construct a Form that will allow us to search for a particular piece of text within any file. Creating a program like this before Visual Basic came along would likely have taken many days of effort. However, we can easily do it in a couple of hours, thanks to Visual Basic's built-in features.

Because it is relatively complex, we'll step through the various Routines involved and show details about the visuals as well. There are a number of special effects here, including raised and sunken frames and a jewel icon. We'll explain precisely how to achieve each of these effects. When we're through you'll know how to create the graphic effects as well as how to use InStr and make various Controls interact intelligently with the user.

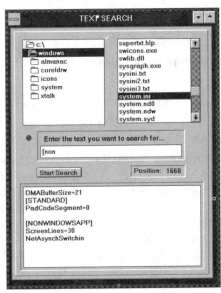

Figure I-19: This Windows program, which could take weeks to create in other languages, can be finished in an hour or two in Visual Basic.

The Form contains a Directory List Box on the top left, a File List Box, and a jewel-like icon—the only color on the Form. This icon participates in the shadows and highlights that fall across many of the elements of the Form. Here's what the icon looks like blown up. When this appears in its real size, against the background color of a window, it appears quite lifelike:

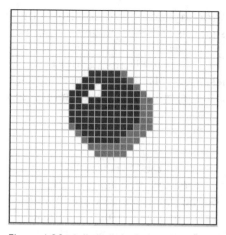

Figure I-20: A little light icon, designed with highlight and shadow for realism.

Shadows and Highlights: The background of this icon is set to the light gray used by all the frames on this Form. A dark gray circle forms the shadow, and a few pixels of white form the highlight. In most Windows programs, the shadows are on the bottom and right of an object; the highlights are on the top and left. The light source, in other words, is from the upper left of the screen.

If you want an object to appear *sunken*, depressed into the screen, reverse the highlight and shadow positions. Notice that we've done just that with the "Metallic Frames" inside the largest frame. You'd probably agree that these background frames create a professional look that's far preferable to simple background colors with no 3D qualities.

In the Form_Load Event, after we empty two Text Boxes (so their default text is erased) and then Show the Form, we create the frames:

```
Sub Form_Load ()

Text1.Text = ""
Text2.Text = ""

Show

Drawframeon Dir1, text2, "outward", 200
Drawframeon Label1, text1, "inward", 75
Drawframeon text2, text2, "inward", 75
Drawframeon label2, text3, "inward", 20
End Sub
```

(The DrawFrameOn Subroutine is explained in the entry for the Line command, which see.)

Next to the jewel icon is a Label, "Enter the text..." and Text1, a Text Box where the user types in the word he or she is looking for. Below is the Start Command Button and a "Position" Label next to Text3 Box. Finally, at the bottom, is a large Text2 Box where we'll show the results of the search.

The Text2.Multiline Property must be set to True in the Properties Window when you design this Form—MultiLine cannot be adjusted while a program runs.

Now for the instructions we place in the various Event Procedures underneath some of these Controls, to make the program work.

To make the File List Box respond to changes in the Directory List Box:

```
Sub Dir1_Change ()
     File1.Path = Dir1.Path
End Sub
```

This means that any change to the Directory List Box, such as the user double-clicking on a new directory, will automatically cause the File List Box's Path Property to be the same as the new Path in the Directory Box. The Directory Box itself automatically adjusts to mouse clicks on it, so you need not put anything in its Click or DblClick Event.

Double-Click as an Alternative: To make the program behave like a normal Windows program, we want the user to be able to double-click on a filename within the File List Box and cause the program to do its job. This is an alternative way to start the search, instead of having the user click on the Command Button labeled "Search." Since the search is carried out within the Command Button's Click Event, we simply direct the program there by naming that Subroutine:

```
Sub File1_DblClick ()
     Command1_click
End Sub
```

And we want to allow a *third* way for the user to start the search. Pressing the ENTER key within the user-input Text2 Box should also trigger the search. Having several alternatives like this is typical of the user freedom that Windows encourages. Let them do it their way.

This Event also prevents an unhappy byproduct of hitting the ENTER key within a Text Box—a brief unpleasant Beep in the user's speaker. By setting Keyascii to 0, we eliminate the Beep before going on to the search Routine in Command1's Click Event:

```
Sub Text1_KeyPress (keyascii As Integer)

If Keyascii = 13 Then
     Keyascii = 0
     Command1_click
End If

End Sub
```

Now for the *meat* of this program—the search Routine itself:

```
Sub command1_click ()

On Error Resume Next

If Text1.Text = "" Then Text1.Text = "Enter Search Text...": Exit Sub
```

```
If Right$(File1.Path, 1) = "\" Then
    TargetFile$ = File1.Path + File1.Filename
Else
    TargetFile$ = File1.Path + "\" + File1.Filename
End If

Open TargetFile$ For Input As #1
    If LOF(1) > 10000 Then
    Close #1
    Beep
    Text1.Text = TargetFile$ + " IS TOO LARGE TO SEARCH..."
    Exit Sub
End If

BigText$ = Input$(LOF(1), #1)

y = InStr(BigText$, Text1.Text)

If y = 0 Then y = InStr(UCase$(BigText$), UCase$(Text1.Text))

If y = 0 Then
    Text2.Text = Text1.Text + " NOT FOUND IN " + TargetFile$
Else
        L = Len(BigText$)
        T = 100
        If T > L Then T = L: s = 1
        If y > 50 And s <> 1 Then s = y – 50
        If s < 1 Then s = 1
        text2.Text = Mid$(BigText$, s, T)
        text3.Text = Str$(y)
End If

Close #1

If Err Then MsgBox (Error$(Err))
End Sub
```

Let's explicate.

As usual, when accessing the user's disk drive, the first thing we do is insert an On Error Resume Next command, which means that if something goes awry, just keep on going, move to the next instruction in this list of instructions. We'll handle the error later (at the bottom of the Event).

It's possible that the user will accidentally trigger a search even though no search word(s) have yet been entered into the Text2 Box. Clicking the Search Button, pressing ENTER or double-clicking on a filename in the File Box would send the program into this Event, so we need to make sure that there *is* something to search for. If Text2 is blank (""), then we print a message to the user and Exit this Event.

Path Adjustments: The next few lines of instructions are always necessary when you are working with File and Directory Boxes. If the user clicks on C:\ in the Directory Box, it will supply us with a Path of C:\; but if the user clicks on a subdirectory, we'll get no backslash "\" attached to the Path:

C:\DOS. So the full path for our target file must be constructed by testing to see if the "\" exists or not, and supplying it if it's missing. (See "Drive List Box" for more on file access.)

Now we attempt to open the Targetfile. We check to see if the file's LOF (Length of File) is larger than 10,000 characters. If it is, we close the file and tell the user that the selected file is just too big for our program to handle (because a single string Variable cannot hold mega amounts of characters). Then we exit the Event.

However, if the file is of reasonable size, we read the entire thing into the Variable BigText$ by using the Input$ Function. Now InStr does its job. InStr looks all through BigText$, searching for whatever the user entered into the Text2 Text Box. If InStr finds a match, then Y will hold the starting position of the first character where the match was found inside BigText$ (counting from the first character of BigText$). If InStr doesn't find a match, Y will be 0.

Recall that InStr is case-sensitive; it would not see a match between *West* and *west*, since the w's are different. We can get around this sensitivity by transforming both the search text and the BigText$ into all-capitals, using the UCase$ Function. Why not just do this the first time we use InStr? Most of the time case sensitivity will not cause a search to fail, since the cases will usually be lower and therefore will match. The program will search faster without transforming all these characters into uppercase. (UCase$ isn't *instantaneous* when you're transforming a large amount of text.) So we use UCase$ only when we must.

Now if we still fail to find a match, Y = 0 and we inform the user. Otherwise (Else), we did find a match, and we want to show the user the context of the found text. We want to show about 50 characters before and after the found text, but there are a couple of problems with this: what if the text was found only ten characters from the end of the entire BigText$ or too close to the beginning of BigText$ for us to show 50 characters?

Boundary Conditions: The following lines of instruction endeavor to check for these *boundary conditions* that are a frequent source of errors in computer programming. T is the total number of characters we want to display, L is the length of BigText$. Now we ask a series of If...Then questions and react to the answers we get.

If 100 is larger than the length of BigText$, then the total number of characters we will display should equal the length of BigText$. Furthermore, the character we will start with (S) is 1.

If the location of the found match within BigText$ (Y) is greater than 50, and we haven't already established that BigText$ itself is smaller than 100 characters long, then we make the start character (S) 50 characters earlier in BigText$ than the location of the found text match (Y).

Special situations could force our start to be less than 1 (it's impossible to have a negative position within a text string). If so, we make S = 1.

Now we extract the context, the 100 or so characters which surround our found text. The Mid$ command says, "Extract from BigText$, starting at the Sth character, T number of characters." We put the result into the large Text Box (called Text2) on the bottom of the Form; and since we know the position where the match was found, we might as well let the user know too. So we translate Y from a pure, computable *number* into a text digit with Str$, and then display it in the Text3 Text Box.

Finally, errors can cause a running Visual Basic to shut down. We don't want a disk access problem to shut down our program; we merely want to inform the user of the problem and allow the program to keep on running. Putting On Error Resume Next at the top of this Event told VB to ignore any errors until we decide to act on them ourselves. Here's where we act. VB's Err Variable contains the code number of the most recent error, if any. If there have been no errors, Err will be 0 and the If...Then structure won't react. We'll simply go to End Sub.

However, if Err does contain an error code, we display the message to the user by putting up a Message Box containing a text translation of the meaning of the error, provided to us by the Error$ Statement. Since *we*, the programmers, have handled this error instead of having Visual Basic handle it, our program will not stop running if a disk-access error occurs.

Idea to Result: It takes about as much time to write a program like this in Visual Basic as it does to explain it. Once you're comfortable with all the techniques and features of VB, you'll likely be amazed at how quickly you get from initial idea to finished, professional-looking results. So much functionality is built into VB: for example, a Directory List Box handles all mouse clicks by itself, automatically. So much visual design, so many Properties, so many ready-to-use Controls like Text Boxes, and such powerful built-in responses (the Events) are available to you by just selecting something from the Toolbox or the Properties Window.

Several years ago it would have taken a programmer considerable effort to write many of the elements of this program. When you get familiar with the Events, Properties and Controls provided by Visual Basic, you'll understand why programming in Visual Basic is such a slick, swift process.

See also   Len; UCase$

|NT

FUNCTION

Description   Int crudely "rounds off" a number that contains a fraction, making it a whole number with no fractional part. Int is crude because it just chops off the fraction and doesn't truly round the number off. As far as Int is concerned, 5.1 and 5.9 are both 5. (There is a way to compensate for this crudity. See "Rounding Numbers" later in this section.)

Int reduces the original number to the next lowest whole number. Positive numbers get their fractions chopped off, but negative numbers change to a different number.

Used with   Numeric Variables (X)

Groups of numeric Variables in a mathematical relationship (X + Y)

OR

Literal numbers (12.5)

Variables   Y = Int(X)

OR

Y = Int (X + Z)

OR

Y = Int (Z * 22.75)

(You can use Int with any *numerical expression*. See "Variables" for an explanation of "expressions.")

Uses   • You'll probably find that you rarely if ever use the Int command. Fractions and rounding just don't matter that much in most applications, even if Int *could* intelligently round off numbers. Int's one main use is with the Rnd command (which see).

Int does something similar to assigning a number to an Integer Variable type (see "Variables"). However, assigning a decimal number to an Integer Variable causes a true rounding effect:

```
Z = 4.7
Y% = Z
Print Int(Z)
Print Y%
```

Results in   4
5

The only even reasonably frequent use of Int is to round off the results when creating a random number. The Rnd Function—used often in games to simulate unpredictable behavior on the part of enemy aliens, dice, etc.— provides you with a fractional number, a "double-precision floating-point" number that has an extremely large range. This range, however, is between 0 and 1. Rnd gives a fraction. So to get, for example, random rolls of a die, you would multiply the random fraction, building it up beyond 1, then use Int to round off the result.

Int can also be useful for integer division: when you want to know how many 16s are in 243, you divide 243 by 16 to get 15. To get the remainder, use the MOD command, or the formula: $X-INT(X/Y)*Y$.

Rounding Numbers: There *is* a way to round numbers accurately:

    X = Int(N + .5)

By adding that .5 to whatever number we want rounded by the Int command, we can be sure that we'll get true rounding.

If the fraction is less than one-half:

    N = 4.226
    X = Int(N + .5)
    Print X

Results in   4

And if the fraction is more than one-half:

    N = 4.889
    X = Int(N + .5)
    Print X

Results in   5

Cautions   • Int rounds down. It's as if you just chopped off the fraction and handed back the whole number. See the Example below.

• Int also behaves badly with negative numbers, so VB includes another Function called Fix (which see, if any of this is of use to you).

Example   Int(5.2)

Results in   5

Example   Int(5.7)

Results in   5

What kind of "rounding" is *this*? To make Int round correctly when the fraction is higher than .5, you need to add .5 to the number you want rounded:

    Int(5.7 + .5)

See also   CInt; DefType; Fix; Rnd

INTERVAL

PROPERTY

Description   Interval is a Property of a Timer. Interval is a *duration*. The Interval determines how long the Timer must wait before it can carry out any instructions you've put into the Timer's Event. In other words, when a Timer Event is triggered, nothing happens until the Interval passes.

A Timer's Event (it has only one Event) is quite different from the other Events in VB. The commands within most Events are carried out as soon as the Event is triggered. Command1.Click is triggered the very moment the user clicks on that Command Button, for example.

A Timer is different. When its Event is triggered, it looks at its Interval Property. It then *waits* until that interval of time has passed before it carries out any instructions you've put into its Event.

The Interval Property describes extremely small increments of time—*milliseconds*. This means that you can do some pretty detailed measurements of the passage of time or can be pretty specific about how much time should pass before the commands inside a Timer's Event are carried out. Milliseconds are 1/1000th of a second. To specify a delay of two seconds: Timer1.Interval = 2000

Why Timers Are Confusing: It may be confusing at first that Timers are called Controls yet are unlike any other Visual Basic Control:

- Most Controls have more than a dozen Properties; Timers have only five.
- Most Controls have at least 10 Events they can respond to; Timers have only one Event.
- Most Controls are accessed and triggered by the user of the program; Timers work in the background, independent of the user. They are always invisible when a program runs.

Enabled and Interval are the most important of the five Timer Properties. And Timers are so distant from the user that they have only one Event! It doesn't help clear up our confusion that this Event is also called *Timer*:

```
Sub Timer1_Timer ()

End Sub
```

Ultimately, though, you'll understand Timers, after you work with them a few times.

A Timer's Purpose: It's best to think of a Timer as one of those kitchen timers that you wind, say, to 20; the Timer starts ticking and 20 minutes later it goes BING! The BING is whatever instructions you have put into the Sub Timer1_Timer( ) Event. The Interval Property is the number of minutes (actually, *milliseconds*) that you set the Timer to.

There's just one kink: unlike a kitchen timer, a VB Timer *resets itself after going BING* then starts counting down from 20 again. After 20 more minutes pass–BING! Reset. Count down 20 minutes. BING! And so on.

This resetting will continue forever unless the program is exited or your program deliberately turns the Timer off by setting the Timer1.Enabled Property to False. If you need the Timer again, turn it on again with Timer1.Enabled = True.

And remember that if you've given an Interval to a Timer, you must set the Timer's Enabled Property to 0 when you design the program (or right after the program starts running in the Form_Load Event of the Startup Form [see "Form"]). Otherwise the Timer will start running the minute its parent Form is Loaded. Timers are Enabled (they start running) by default. However, the Interval defaults to 0, so it won't be activated automatically unless there is some Interval set.

Used with   Timers

Variables   Often you set a Timer's Interval Property when you design your program, using the Properties Window:

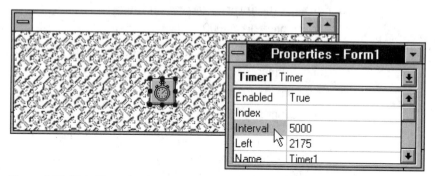

Figure I-21: This Timer is given a five-second Interval in the Properties Window while the program is being designed.

OR (to adjust a Timer's Interval Property to 3 seconds while the program runs): Timer1.Interval = 3000

OR (to use a Variable to set the Interval. In this case the Interval of another Timer): Timer1.Interval = Timer2.Interval

Uses
- Delay something (see the Example).
- Add clock-like features to your programs.
- Find out how long things take.
- Wait until a specified amount of time has passed, then remind the user that something needs to be done (a "kitchen-timer-with-brains" application). (See the Example.)

Cautions
- A single Timer can count down about one minute maximum. The maximum interval you can set a Timer to is 65,565 milliseconds, and there are 1,000 milliseconds per second. One minute, though, is sufficient for many programming situations (such as the Example animation that follows). And if you need a Timer to operate longer than one minute, it's easy enough to make it wait as long as you wish. Read on.

A Reasonably Accurate Timer: What if you want a Timer to alert you to the passage of more than a minute of time? If extreme precision isn't important, you could create a Global Variable as a counter. Let's make a "bell" go off in five minutes:

In a Module, type this:

```
Global Counter As Integer
Global TotalMinutes as Integer
```

Then, somewhere in your program (or directly while designing the program), set the Interval to one minute:

```
Timer1.Interval = 60000
```

Now, inside the Timer event, just increment the Counter:

```
Timer1_Timer

    Counter = Counter +1

    If Counter = TotalMinutes — 1 Then
            Beep:Beep:Beep
            Counter = 0
            Timer1.Enabled = False
    End If
End Sub
```

When your program starts, all numeric Variables are 0. We start off adding 1 to Counter: That's why we have to subtract 1 from the Total-Minutes requested from elsewhere in the program. VB gives every numeric Variable a 0 when a program starts running, and we also always reset Counter to 0 when the Event has done its job. (Counter = 0.)

One thing about Timers when used for measuring the passage of time—they temporarily stop counting down if the user moves a Form or if Windows itself performs certain actions. This doesn't happen often, but when you need great precision, such as when creating a clock, you'll want to have a Timer interact with the clock that is built into the computer. To do that, you can set Variables using the Now and Time$ commands (see "Timer").

How can you allow the user to specify a time for an alarm to go off? It will probably exceed one minute from now, so a simple Timer cannot be used–one minute is about all a Timer's Interval can handle.

One way is to check on the computer's internal time, which is maintained by a small battery-powered quartz "watch" in the computer. Even when you turn off the power, that little watch keeps ticking. The Time$ command can check to see the time as registered by that watch. The user enters the desired alarm time, and you compare that to Time$, the computer's time. You put the comparison within a Timer, and set its interval to 1000 so the Timer checks the computer's watch every second:

```
If Time$ > = UserAlarm$ Then
```

In other words, if the current time (Time$) is greater than or equal to the time that the user set, go ahead and ring the bell. Time's up. Luckily, you can compare *text* Variables in a quasi-arithmetic fashion. "A" < "B" means that the text character A is (alphabetically) "less than" B. Even *digits* (text representations of numbers) will compare accurately: "2" < "5" and "5" < "22" (the digit 2 is less than the digit 5, and the digit 5 is less than the digits 22). (See Appendix C for more on the way you can compare pieces of text using "operators" such as <.)

This approach works reasonably well; but unless the user has experience in the military, we are making him or her set an alarm in an awkward way. Time$ uses the military 24-hour format and the user must set the alarm to 13:00:00 (no deviations from this :00:00 format) simply to ask for an alarm at 1 PM.

Let Your Program Do It: It's often best to have your program anticipate and translate a wide variety of possible user responses: 1 PM, 1, 100, 1:00, etc. After all, if your program is well designed, the human will be using your program often–maybe for years. And you have to write this program only once, so it seems only fair that you make the program accommodate the user rather than the other way around.

Perhaps you could design a graphic that showed a clock face, and let the user drag the clock hands around to the alarm time. (Use MouseDown to tell where the user is pressing the mouse, and keep repainting the Picture Box as the user drags the hands.)

Or let the user select from two Picture Boxes that display all 24 hours and 60 minutes in an attractive Gothic typeface. The user could click on the desired numbers. (You could tell which numbers the user chose within the Picture Boxes by using the X and Y coordinates provided by the Mouse-Down Event.)

Let the User Specify a Delay: The user is permitted to specify a *relative delay* rather than the *precise time*. How many minutes do you want to pass before we ring the alarm? The user answers five, and your program handles the math.

To do this, set up a Global Variable. (Global Variables don't reset themselves to zero every time the program is not within the Event where the Variable is located. And Global Variables can be accessed anywhere in the program.) We'll name the Variable "ThisMinute." You would use the Minute Function (Thisminute = Minute(Now)). Then you would have the Timer Event check: If Minute(Now) − Thisminute >= 5 Then...

We're using the greater-than-or-equal-to symbol (>=) just in case the user moved a Form at the wrong time. Of course, even this won't deal effectively with crossing an hour boundary where ThisMinute might equal 58 and Minute(Now) might equal 2. To be reasonably accurate, we have to be a little more manipulative. Here's a kitchen timer imitation that works well:

Create several Global Variables in a Module:

```
Global Stoptime As Integer
Global Stopsc As Integer
Global Stopmn As Integer
Global Stophr As Integer
```

Then create this general-purpose Subroutine (see "Sub") that can accept whatever delay in minutes the program passes to it:

```
Sub Setcountdown (Delay As Integer)

stopsc = Second(Now)
stophr = Hour(Now)
stopmn = Minute(Now) + Delay

If stopmn > 59 Then
    stophr = stophr + 1
    stopmn = stopmn − 60
End If

StopTime = stophr + stopmn
Timer1.Enabled = True
Timer1.Interval = 1000

End Sub
```

We find out the current second, hour and minute from the Now Function. If the Now minute is larger than 60, we adjust the Variables stophr and stopmn–because that means our requested Delay crossed an hour boundary. Then we create a number that combines the hour and minute. This serial number will continue to grow larger for 24 hours, from 101 at 1:01AM to 2359 at one minute to midnight. This way we can compare the Stoptime to the current Now time in the Timer Event. (We also start the Timer and set it to check if the time is up every second by setting its Interval to 1000.)

Now, inside Timer1, here's how we check to see if it's time to ring the alarm:

```
Sub Timer1_Timer ()

sc = Second(Now)
hr = Hour(Now)
mn = Minute(Now)
st = hr + mn
    If st >= Stoptime And sc >= stopsc Then
        Timer1.Enabled = False
        Beep
        Print "TIMER UP!!"
End If
End Sub
```

We create another serial number by combining the Now hour and minute. Then we check to see if the Now time is greater than or equal to (>=) the Stoptime we had created earlier in our SetCountDown (Delay) Subroutine. AND we check to make sure that enough seconds have passed.

To use the Timer, you call on the SetCountdown (Delay) Subroutine and it does the rest:

```
Sub Form_Click
    SetCountdown 2
End Sub
```

(Also see "Timer.")

• A Timer's Event (remember Timers have only one Event, also called *Timer*, unfortunately) is a little perplexing when you first come across it. Most VB Events, such as a KeyPress Event, trigger an immediate response, performing at once those actions you have listed as commands within the KeyPress_Event Procedure:

```
Command1_KeyPress
    Print "OUCH!"
    Print "Press me again!"
End Sub
```

The instant the user clicks on Command1, the word OUCH! will be printed, and any other instructions in the Event will be carried out as well.

If, however, you enable a Timer (Timer1.Enabled = True), the *countdown* starts.

The Countdown: Recognize that this is a *countdown*. The instructions within the Timer1_Timer Event will not be carried out until the countdown is completed. No bell will ring until the Timer has counted down, until the time has passed until the number of milliseconds you put in its Interval Property has counted down to zero.

In truth, a Timer's Event *is* triggered immediately, but the Timer Event puts off doing its thing until the Interval has passed. And only then are your instructions carried out.

• You might want to display a message to the user but have the message become invisible automatically after a few seconds. This would often be an improvement over an InputBox$ or MsgBox, which intrudes on the user by holding the computer hostage until the user responds to the Box. Your program cannot continue (and the user cannot click anywhere on the screen) until the user reacts to the Box.

But how do you create a delay? How do you measure some time between displaying your message and making it automatically disappear? Timers offer facilities far superior to the techniques programmers formerly used to make a program pause for a certain amount of time. Here's how it used to be done:

```
For I = 1 to 5000
Next I
```

This Loop does nothing other than make the computer unresponsive for as long as the computer takes to count up to 5000. The problem here is that computers count at different speeds. Some run far faster than others.

The Same Delay for All: Today's computers come in many configurations, with many speeds. It might take one computer twenty times longer to run this loop than a faster model would take. However, the computer's system time (measured by its battery-powered internal quartz "watch") is realtime—time as it happens in the world, not dependent on the speed of the particular computer. Coupled with a Timer, the computer's internal clock provides a highly accurate way to measure duration or create a delay. A delay based on the internal clock and a Timer will be the same for someone running your program on a wizened 4 MHz XT or the latest 50MHz 586 model.

What's even better, a Timer works "in the background," meaning that other things can be done by the user while the Timer counts the passage of time. This can offer you, the programmer, some excellent ways to inform the user, without being pushy or annoying. This approach allows the user to ignore your information. You can update your message in an unobtrusive gray box at the bottom of the screen—to be there when the user needs the information or to be ignored when the user doesn't care about it.

MsgBox and InputBox$ *demand* a response. They effectively immobilize the computer. The user must respond to one of these Boxes before getting access to his or her computer again. See the Example below for a way to employ a Timer to both govern the duration of, and animate, a message to the user.

• Timer Events will slow down the computer if you set especially small Intervals. Use large Intervals, one second or larger, unless you have a real need for nearly constant activation of the instructions inside the Timer's Event, or unless you require great precision in the timing. Also note that very small Timer Intervals will not be precise or accurate anyway, due to the time involved in responding to the Timer and triggering its Event.

Example To inform the user that a file is being saved, we scanned in a picture of a mouth and put it into Picture1, Border Property set to None, Backcolor set to match the Form Backcolor:

Figure I-22: Here's how we'll let the user know that a file is being saved by our program.

In the Form_Load Event, type this:

```
Sub Form_Load ()
    Picture1.visible = False
    Timer1.enabled = False
End Sub
```

In this program the Timer defines the movement from left to right across the screen (and beyond, to make the image slide right past visibility):

```
Sub Timer1_Timer ()

Static c As Integer

c = c + 1

If c = 90 Then Timer1.enabled = 0: Exit Sub
    Picture1.left = c * 75
End Sub
```

The Left Property of the picture is urged farther right each time the Timer Event happens, moving 75 twips over to the right. Setting the Interval Property of Timer1 low, the mouth seems to glide smoothly across the Form and disappear when triggered by this:

```
Picture1.visible = True
Timer1.enabled = True
```

Note that the Timer shuts itself off:

Figure I-23: The window the user sees while a file is being saved.

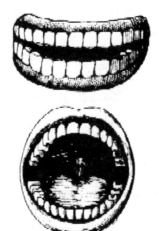

Figure I-24: Alternating two images (with the Visible command) and using a Timer to switch between the two would provide an animation while a file was being saved.

See also   Timer Control; Timer Event

S   OPERATOR

Description   The Is operator tells you if two Variable names refer to the same Control or Form. The Is command is highly specialized and is used with Arrays that keep track of Controls or Forms. It can also be used with the Data Control, the OLE Control, database and DLL (see "LinkMode") commands.

Used with   Arrays, Variables, Data or OLE objects and If TypeOf Then.

Variables   To test to see if two names refer to the same entity:

```
If A Is B Then...
```

OR (to test to see if an Array item has been used yet):

```
For i = 1 to 20
    If TheArray(i) Is Nothing Then
        Set TheArray(i) = AFormName
        Exit For
    End If
Next i
```

The "Nothing" Command: This command is a "reserved word" like True and False. VB uses Nothing to test to see if an object (a Form or Control) exists. It is similar to the reserved word "Empty" used with numeric and text Variables to indicate that a Variable name is not being used, has not been declared either implicitly (V = 12) or explicitly (Dim V As Integer).

You can also test for the existence of a Data object or an OLE object, like this:

```
If Data1.Recordset is Nothing Then...
(This means "if the Control Named Data1 doesn't currently have an
open database then...")
```

Uses
• The Is command is used to test when two Variable names (Array names) refer to the same object (a Form or Control).

Example
Create a new "instance" of Form1 by typing this into Form1's General Declarations section:

```
Dim Clone1 As New Form1
```

Put a Picture into the Picture Property of Form1 and type this into the Load_Event:

```
Sub Form_Click ()
    Clone1.Show
    Clone1.Left = Form1.Left + 5000
    If Clone1 Is Form1 Then Clone1.Caption = "Clone of Form1"
End Sub
```

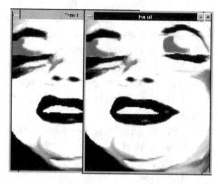

Figure I-25: A new "instance" of a Form is not equivalent to the Form. The second Form inherits the Properties like this image but the "Is" test fails because we haven't used Set.

When you press F5 and run this program, you'll see both Form1 and the new clone Form we created, as illustrated by Figure I-24. However, notice that the If...Is...Then line did not change the caption of the cloned Form. *The two Forms are not the same entity,* but the clone did inherit Form1's qualities.

Now, change the Click Event by adding one line that uses the Set command to make the two Forms the *same entity:*

```
Sub Form_Click ()
    Set clone1 = Form1
    clone1.Show
    clone1.Left = Form1.Left + 5000
    If clone1 Is Form1 Then clone1.Caption = "Clone of Form1"
End Sub
```

If you now run the example, you'll see that the caption of the clone does change. Clone1 *Is* Form1 because we used the Set command to make it the same entity. Also notice that only Clone1 or Form1 can be visible at a given time.

See also   Control Array; Multiple Document Interface (MDI) Form; Set

Is Queries

FUNCTION

(IsArray, IsDate, IsEmpty, IsError, IsMissing, IsObject, IsNull and IsNumeric)

Description   As we move toward object-oriented programming, there will be times, believe it or not, when the *programmer* will not know the data type of a Variable. A Variant Variable, like a shape-shifter, can morph into several different Variable types dynamically during run time. This can happen without the programmer's knowledge or consent. A Variant will accept *whatever* the user types in or loads in from disk, for example.

In the brave new world of Objects, even an application's user can be permitted to create new Objects in some situations. Parameters passed to procedures can be *optional.* What's more, with OLE Automation, one program can make use of another program's features (see "Objects"). And what about the fact that a Collection (which see) or Variant Array can hold items of various different data types?

One side effect of all this freedom (and the possible resulting mutations of your original expectations about Variable types when you designed the program) is that you, as a programmer, might sometimes have to ask your running program to tell you the type of a Variable.

Used with   Variables, Collections and Arrays

Variables Now you can specify that some or all of the parameters listed as "expected" by a procedure *can be optional*. You do this with the Optional command (Optional MyParameter). Then, the IsMissing function tells your program whether or not an Optional parameter has in fact been passed to a procedure. The following example either prints a single text "string" twice or, if the optional second string has been passed, concatenates both strings:

```
Function multiple(A, Optional B)
If IsMissing(B) Then
    multiple = A & A
Else
    multiple = A & B
End If
End Function

Sub Form_Load( )
    A = "Once"
    Print multiple(A)
End Sub
```

OR, to display any members of a Collection that are not numeric:

```
Dim SomeFacts As New Collection
Private Sub Form_Load( )
Show
SomeFacts.Add 1425.33
SomeFacts.Add "Misty"
SomeFacts.Add "Jeb said he would return late."
SomeFacts.Add 77 * 33
For Each Thing In SomeFacts
    If Not IsNumeric(Thing) Then Print Thing
Next
End Sub
```

Result in Misty
Jeb said he would return late.

Uses To tell you the type or contents of a Variant variable, Variant Array or Collection; tells you if an optional parameter has been passed to a Sub or Function.

Cautions • Empty and Null (which see) have special meanings. Null is what you typically think of as an "empty" Variable (A\$ = "" makes A\$ Null). Empty, by contrast, means that the Variable has never even been used in the program, has never been initialized at all.

• When testing for Null, you can't use something like: If Var = Null. (If an expression includes the Null command, the whole expression automatically becomes Null itself.) So, you must use IsNull to test for nullness.

Example   This example uses IsDate to check the user's input. The user's response is put into a Variant Variable, *x*, which will adapt itself to *whatever* Variable type can hold whatever the user might type in. (Any Variable you don't formally declare defaults to the Variant type. Variants will happily accept text or digits.) However, our program can avoid an error here if it can determine just what the Variant turned into. So we use the IsDate Function to let us know how to proceed:

```
Sub Form_Click( )
x = InputBox("Please type in the date of your birthday...")
If IsDate(x) Then
    z = (Now - DateValue(x)) / 365
    Print "You are " & Int(z) & " years old."
Else
    MsgBox "We can t understand " & x & " as a date..."
End If
End Sub
```

See also   Objects; TypeName; TypeOf; Variant

ITEM

See   Add, Remove

ITEMDATA

PROPERTY

Description   Using ItemData, along with the NewIndex Property, allows you to set up a kind of mini-database within a List or Combo Box.

ItemData is the name of a numeric Array that VB can maintain in parallel to the Array of items in a List or Combo Box. In other words, if you fill a List Box with all the names in your Rolodex, you can simultaneously fill the ItemData Array with the ZIP Code associated with each name. You could set up your own parallel Array, but if all you need is a single number associated with each item, ItemData makes the job easier.

The *NewIndex* Property is used with ItemData to keep the ItemData's index numbers straight. NewIndex always holds the index number of the item most recently added to a List or Combo Box. This matters only if you have set the Sorted Property to True, in which case VB puts each new item into the Box in alphabetical order. In that situation, you use NewIndex to find out which index number to use when creating a new item in the ItemData Array. (See the Example.)

Used with   Combo Box or List Box

Variables   **Variable type:** Long Integer

When you add an item to a List Box, you immediately also add an associated numeric item to the List Box's ItemData Array—"immediately" because you need to use NewIndex, which gives the position (the index) of the most recently added item:

```
List1.AddItem "John Durhan"
List1.ItemData(List1.NewIndex) = 91927
```

Uses   • Create a small database, like a Rolodex, which provides the ZIP Code when any item in the list is selected. (See the Example.)

• Create a more complex database. But use the ItemData Array to point to a separate Array that you maintain which could contain a whole group of related data associated with each item in a List or Combo Box. For instance, you could expand the Rolodex concept by setting up an Array that contained fields for phone number, address, birthday, favorite food, etc. (See "Type" for more on setting up multi-item Arrays.)

Cautions   • NewIndex holds –1 if an item has been deleted from a List or Combo Box or if there are no items in the Box.

• The ItemData Array can only hold *long integer* numeric data. Therefore, it can hold a number between –2,147,483,648 and 2,147,483,647. (Most phone numbers will not fit into this range.)

Example   We'll create a simple Rolodex-type list of names and use the ItemData Array to maintain a parallel list of each person's ZIP Code. When the user clicks on a name, the ZIP Code appears in a Label.

Select New Project from the File Menu and put a List Box on Form1. Set the Box's Sorted Property to True. Then type the following into the Form_Load Event:

```
Sub Form_Load ()

list1.AddItem "Bob Roberts"
list1.ItemData(list1.NewIndex) = 41542
list1.AddItem "Norris Temple"
list1.ItemData(list1.NewIndex) = 21519
list1.AddItem "Jill Chambers"
list1.ItemData(list1.NewIndex) = 61678
list1.AddItem "S. Trouband"
list1.ItemData(list1.NewIndex) = 80834
list1.AddItem "Darlene Railsback"
list1.ItemData(list1.NewIndex) = 91923
list1.AddItem "Sam Samson"
```

```
list1.ItemData(list1.NewIndex) = 61498
list1.AddItem "Dean Naples"
list1.ItemData(list1.NewIndex) = 71877
End Sub
```

Then, in the List1_Click Event, type this to display the appropriate ItemData when a name is clicked:

```
Sub List1_Click ()
    label1.Caption = list1.ItemData(list1.ListIndex)
End Sub
```

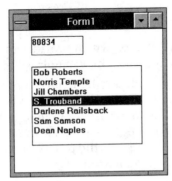

Figure I-26: ItemData is maintaining a parallel Array of ZIP codes.

See also   Combo Box; List Box; Type

KeyDown, KeyUp

EVENT

Description These Events are triggered when the user presses or releases a key on the keyboard.

When you press a key, the KeyDown Event in the Control that has the focus is triggered. (The focus is on only one Control at a time or on the Form itself if there are no Controls Enabled or Visible on the Form.) *Focus* means that this Control will receive anything that is typed on the keyboard. For example, if there are two Text Boxes, the one with the focus will display typed characters.

KeyDown and KeyUp tell you the full status of *every key on the keyboard*. That means the ALT, SHIFT, CTRL, function keys, arrow keys or any other key *or combination of keys*.

By contrast, the KeyPress Event only detects the ordinary letter and number keys and a few other keys, and is insensitive to key combinations. An advantage of KeyPress is that it is simpler to work with and uses the standard ANSI character code. KeyPress is most often used with Text Boxes, etc., for checking that the user is not entering things you don't want, or for changing intercepted characters such as forcing uppercase.

Far Finer Control: The advantage of KeyDown/KeyUp is precise control over which keys, or combinations of keys, are being typed by the user. KeyDown/KeyUp are used for such global activities as acting on function keys, macro keys (such as CTRL+S) or other combinations; for example, CTRL+SHIFT+F2. Many programs offer key combinations as shortcuts to menus or other actions. Most programs, for example, interpret the F1 key as a request for Help. If you want to provide such features in your programs, you'll need to use KeyDown to detect the pressing of nontext keys and combinations.

KeyUp is normally used to cause something to happen repeatedly as long as the KeyUp has not occurred. For instance, as an alternative to dragging, the user could hold down the Left arrow key to move a Picture Box left across the screen. When the user released the key, the KeyUp Event would be triggered, and we would put instructions in the KeyUp Event to stop the Picture Box at that point.

Used with Check Boxes, Combo Boxes, Command Buttons, Directory, Drive & File List Boxes, Forms, Grids, Horizontal & Vertical Scroll Bars, List Boxes, OLE, Option Buttons, Picture Boxes and Text Boxes

Variables The KeyDown and KeyUp Events provide you with two Variables: *KeyCode* and *SHIFT*.

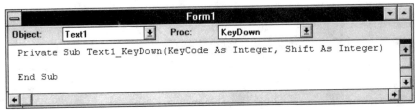

Figure K-1: You'll find that the built-in Variables *KeyCode* and *Shift* come in handy.

KeyCode provides a unique number for *every* key on the keyboard—even distinguishing between the 3 on the numeric keypad and the 3 in the row above the alphabetic keys. In this way, you can have your program react to *anything*—the arrow keys, the NUM LOCK key, etc.

This code is contained within a file called CONSTANT.TXT that is supplied with VB. The VB documentation encourages you to load this into your programs. (From the File Menu, choose Load Text, then choose Merge.)

However, most programmers use the elements within CONSTANT.TXT so infrequently that they just look them up by opening Notepad if they need information contained therein. CONSTANT.TXT contains a lengthy list of definitions that can be used in your programs.

For example, Key_Tab= &H9 is defined in CONSTANT.TXT so you can then use the word Key_Tab in place of 9 when you are testing a KeyDown:

    If KeyCode = Key_Tab

instead of:

    If KeyCode = 9

Here are the KeyCodes provided by the KeyUp and KeyDown Events:
(Note that the KeyCodes for uppercase and lowercase letters, A and a, for example, are the same. Also, the normal and shifted digits, such as 3 and #, are the same. To detect a shifted key, use the SHIFT Variable provided by the KeyUp and KeyDown Events.)

    8   BACKSPACE
    9   TAB
   12   5 (keypad)
   13   ENTER (keyboard and keypad)
   16   SHIFT
   17   CTRL
   18   ALT
   19   PAUSE (Break)
   20   CAPS LOCK
   27   ESC
   32   SPACE
   33   PgUp and 9 (keypad)

34	PgDn and 3 (keypad)
35	END and 1 (keypad)
36	HOME and 7 (keypad)
37	LEFT ARROW and 4 (keypad)
38	UP ARROW and 8 (keypad)
39	RIGHT ARROW and 6 (keypad)
40	DOWN ARROW and 2 (keypad)
45	INS and 0 (keypad)
46	DEL and decimal point
48	0 and)
49	1 and !
50	2 and @
51	3 and #
52	4 and $
53	5 and %
54	6 and ^
55	7 and &
56	8 and * (not keypad *)
57	9 and (
65	A
66	B
67	C
68	D
69	E
70	F
71	G
72	H
73	I
74	J
75	K
76	L
77	M
78	N
79	O
80	P
81	Q
82	R
83	S
84	T
85	U
86	V
87	W
88	X
89	Y
90	Z

96	INSERT and 0 (with NUM LOCK on)
97	END and 1 (keypad) (with NUM LOCK on)
98	DOWN ARROW and 2 (keypad) (with NUM LOCK on)
99	PgDn and 3 (keypad) (with NUM LOCK on)
100	LEFT ARROW and 4 (keypad) (with NUM LOCK on)
101	5 (keypad) (with NUM LOCK on)
102	RIGHT ARROW and 6 (keypad) (with NUM LOCK on)
103	HOME and 7 (keypad) (with NUM LOCK on)
104	UP ARROW and 8 (keypad) (with NUM LOCK on)
105	PgUp and 9 (keypad) (with NUM LOCK on)
106	* (keypad)
107	+ (keypad)
109	– (keypad)
110	DEL and decimal point (with NUM LOCK on)
111	/ (keypad)
112	F1
113	F2
114	F3
115	F4
116	F5
117	F6
118	F7
119	F8
120	F9
121	F10
122	F11
123	F12
144	NUM LOCK
145	SCROLL LOCK
186	; and :
187	= and + (same as keypad =)
187	= (keypad)
188	, and <
189	- and _ (not keypad –)
190	. and >
191	/ and ? (not keypad /)
192	` and ~
219	[and {
220	\ and	
221	] and }
222	' and "

There are other codes; keyboards do vary, and you may have keys not represented by this list. But these are the ones most users are likely to have. Going much beyond the above list is risky. Most keyboards won't have such keys as MENU and EXECUTE, for instance.

If you want to discover other codes, see the Example.

Detecting SHIFT, ALT, CTRL

KeyDown/KeyUp also lets you determine if a key is being pressed at the same time as the SHIFT, ALT or CTRL key, thus allowing you to create macros or other shortcuts within your program. A typical macro might allow the user to press CTRL+S, for example, to save his or her work as an alternative to accessing a menu or pressing a Command Button.

The Variable called *Shift* that is passed to you by a KeyDown or KeyUp Event tells you the status of the SHIFT, ALT and CTRL keys as follows:

```
SHIFT = 1
SHIFT + CTRL = 3
SHIFT + ALT = 5
SHIFT + CTRL + ALT = 7
CTRL = 2
CTRL + ALT = 6
ALT = 4
```

So, to tell if the user is pressing ALT+SHIFT+F3:

```
If Shift = 5 and Keycode = 114 Then
```

Uses • Allow custom keyboards and macros. You could trap all CTRL+C key-presses, and then cause a Cls command to clear a Text Box in response.

• Add special features triggered by function keys. (But see "KeyPreview" for a better approach.)

• Repeat something based on how long a key is held down. Allow the user to hold down a key and, until the KeyUp Event, keep moving a rocket ship that is pursuing an alien.

Cautions • Although the VB *Language Reference* says it doesn't happen, KeyDown and KeyUp Events do respond to the TAB key. If you press the TAB key in a Text Box, and there is no other Control on the Form to which the focus can go, then the KeyDown and KeyUp Events are triggered. If there *is* another Control that can get the focus, TAB will shift the focus to that Control, and no KeyDown or KeyUp Events are triggered.

• If you have set a Command Button's Default Property to –1, then the KeyDown/KeyUp Events will not be triggered by the ENTER key.

• If you have set a Command Button's Cancel Property to –1, then the KeyDown/KeyUp Events will not be triggered by the ESC key.

• If you want to trap the user's keypresses *before* they get a chance to trigger the KeyPress and KeyDown Events, use KeyPreview (which see). It is triggered first Formwide, so you can use it for macros and access or "shortcut" key combinations.

Example   This example will print any codes triggered when you press a key or combination of keys.

```
Sub Form_KeyDown (Keycode As Integer, Shift As Integer)
    Print "KeyCode is "; Keycode; "Shift is "; Shift
End Sub
```

See also   KeyPress; KeyPreview

 EY PRESS   EVENT

Description   A KeyPress Event is triggered when a key is pressed on the keyboard. If a key is held down, a KeyPress Event is repeatedly triggered. The KeyPress Event is triggered in the Control which has the *focus*. The focus is on only one Control at a time (or on the Form itself, if it has no Controls Enabled or Visible on it). *Focus* means that this Control will receive anything that is typed on the keyboard. For example, if there are two Text Boxes, the one with the focus will display typed characters.

Your alternative to KeyPress is the KeyDown Event. KeyPress, however, works primarily with the normal characters A–Z, 1–0, #, $, %, etc.—that is, characters that can be printed. It also detects a few others, such as the ENTER key (code 13) and so forth. But KeyPress Events are insensitive to CTRL, function keys, etc.

If all you need to do is *trap* the incoming keystrokes, use KeyPress. To simulate a typewriter, you could trap the ENTER key and send each line to the printer as the user types it in:

```
Sub Text1_KeyPress (Keyascii As Integer)

If Keyascii = 13 Then

    Printer.Print Text1.Text
    Text1.Text = ""
End If

Keyascii = 0
End Sub
```

In the above example, you must set KeyAscii to 0 before leaving the Event, or you will get a beep from the computer's speaker.

Used with   Check Boxes, Combo Boxes, Command Buttons, Directory, Drive & File List Boxes, Forms, Grids, List Boxes, Horizontal & Vertical Scroll Bars, OLE, Option Buttons, Picture Boxes and Text Boxes

Variables   The KeyPress Event provides you with a Variable called KeyAscii—a code number for the key that was pressed.

Here is the first half of the ASCII Code (the codes from 128–255 are graphics, special text, etc.):

0	NUL	32	Space	64	@	96	`
1	SOH	33	!	65	A	97	a
2	STX	34	"	66	B	98	b
3	ETX	35	#	67	C	99	c
4	EOT	36	$	68	D	100	d
5	ENQ	37	%	69	E	101	e
6	ACK	38	&	70	F	102	f
7	BEL	39	'	71	G	103	g
8	BS	40	(	72	H	104	h
9	Tab	41	)	73	I	105	i
10	LineFeed	42	*	74	J	106	j
11	VT	43	+	75	K	107	k
12	FF	44	,	76	L	108	l
13	Enter	45	-	77	M	109	m
14	SO	46	.	78	N	110	n
15	SI	47	/	79	O	111	o
16	DLE	48	0	80	P	112	p
17	DC1	49	1	81	Q	113	q
18	DC2	50	2	82	R	114	r
19	DC3	51	3	83	S	115	s
20	DC4	52	4	84	T	116	t
21	NAK	53	5	85	U	117	u
22	SYN	54	6	86	V	118	v
23	ETB	55	7	87	W	119	w
24	CAN	56	8	88	X	120	x
25	EM	57	9	89	Y	121	y
26	SUB	58	:	90	Z	122	z
27	ESC	59	;	91	[	123	{
28	FS	60	<	92	\	124	|
29	GS	61	=	93	]	125	}
30	RS	62	>	94	^	126	~
31	US	63	?	95	_	127	

Uses   • Intercept, examine and adjust characters as they are being typed in.

Printing the KeyAscii Variable returned to you by the KeyPress Event is possible by using the Chr$ Statement:

```
Print CHR$(KeyAscii)
```

But VB will automatically display things you are typing into Text Boxes, Combo Boxes and so forth. KeyPress is useful if you want to simultaneously store the keystrokes to a backup file, or send them to the printer.

But the real value of KeyAscii is that you can change the code before the character is printed onscreen—you are intercepting the keystrokes and can examine and adjust them. You could force them into a mathematical contortion for a password (see "PasswordChar"); you could ignore errors (such as a text character typed into a phone number field that wants only digits); or, if you want to avoid that annoying Beep when the ENTER key is pressed, substitute a 0 (a nothing):

```
If KeyAscii = 13 Then KeyAscii = 0
```

Cautions
• KeyPress cannot detect when an ESC, CTRL, NUM LOCK or other non-printable key has been pressed. Use KeyDown for that.

• If you want to trap keypresses *before* they get a chance to trigger the KeyPress and KeyDown Events, use KeyPreview (which see). It is triggered first Formwide, so you can use it for macros and access "shortcut" key combinations.

Example
Here's a way to ignore any alphabetic characters that the user tries to insert when asked for a telephone number:

```
Sub Text1_KeyPress (KeyAscii As Integer)
    If KeyAscii > 57 Then KeyAscii = 0
End Sub
```

The user can still enter such symbols as parentheses and the minus sign but cannot, for instance, enter one of those "memorable" half-text numbers like this one for a veterinarian: 454–MEOW.

See also
KeyDown; KeyPreview; KeyUp; PasswordChar

PROPERTY

Description
Using KeyPreview is the easiest way to make a general "keyboard handler" in VB. Use KeyPreview if you want VB to always alert the Form's keyboard-sensitive Events (KeyUp, KeyDown, KeyPress) in case the user presses F3 or a special key combination like CTRL+C.

KeyPreview lets you force the Form to be first to trap keypresses (before any of its Controls). If the user presses F2, for instance, the Form's Key-Down and KeyPress Events are triggered; *then* those same Events are next triggered in the Control with the *focus* (the one that reacts to keypresses).

If KeyPreview is set to False (the default), then the only way the Form's KeyDown or KeyPress Event can be triggered is if no Controls are on the Form.

If you want a general keyboard handler but don't use KeyPreview, you need to repeat the handler Routine in *each* Control that could get the focus.

Used with   Forms or Multiple Document Interface (MDI) Forms

Variables   You can set KeyPreview in the Properties Window.

OR (to set it while a program is running): KeyPreview = True

OR (to find out its status while the program is running): X = KeyPreview

Uses   • Allow custom keyboards and macros. You could trap all CTRL+C key-presses and then cause a Cls command to clear a Text Box in response.

• Add special features triggered by function keys.

• Repeat something based on how long a key is held down. Allow the user to hold down a key and, until the KeyUp Event, keep moving a rocket ship pursuing an alien.

Cautions   If a Form has no Controls, it automatically gets its KeyPress, KeyDown and KeyUp Events triggered, so KeyPreview has no effect.

Example   Create a New Project from the File Menu and put two Command Buttons on the Form. Into the second Button's KeyDown Event, type the following to cause a reaction when the user presses the F2 key:

```
Sub Command2_KeyDown (keycode As Integer, Shift As Integer)
    If keycode = 113 Then Print "Function Key #2 trapped by Command2"
End Sub
```

Run the program and notice that unless you give Command2 the *focus* by tabbing to it or clicking on it, Command1 is the entity that responds to keypresses. It was the first Control created and, therefore, *it*, not the other Control or the Form, reacts. However, our goal here is to react to F2 no matter what Control has the focus. In other words, we want all keypresses trapped initially by the Form itself. So, to make this happen, set the KeyPreview Property of the Form to True in the Properties Window and type the following into the Form's KeyDown Event:

```
Sub Command2_KeyDown (keycode As Integer, Shift As Integer)
    If keycode = 113 Then Print "Function Key #2 trapped by the Form"
End Sub
```

Now run the program again and note that the Form always takes precedence over any of its Controls.

See also   KeyDown; KeyPress; KeyUp

ILL

STATEMENT

Description   Kill deletes a file from a disk drive, just as the DEL command does in DOS.

Kill can also delete whole categories of files. Kill C:*.* would remove the CONFIG.SYS, AUTOEXEC.BAT and other important files from the user's root directory on the C: hard drive.

Kill is, it goes without saying, extremely risky to use without some failsafe mechanism to prevent massive damage.

Used with   Disk file management

Variables   Kill Filename$

OR (to use wildcards for the deletion of a class of files. This one deletes any filename that begins with the letters TEMP): Kill "C:\MYPROGDIR\TEMP*.*"

Kill permits the familiar DOS wildcards * and ?

Uses   • Automatic deletion of backup files within your program's private subdirectory. Let's assume that as your program runs, you regularly back up the user's work by creating a file with an extension of, say, .BAK. If nothing has gone wrong, you no longer need the file when the user quits your program. So, as part of the shut-down Routine, you delete all the .BAK files:

    Kill "*.BAK"

• Allow the user File Manager-like control from within your program.

Cautions   Some users are annoyed if asked "Are you sure?" every time they try to do something in a program. But file deletion is so potentially destructive that perhaps you ought to at least provide a query-on-deletion *option* within a program that uses the Kill Statement. If the user selects that option, you would perhaps display a set of Option Buttons and ask the question, Are you sure you want to delete STORY.WRI?

Example   If the user selects yes,

```
Sub YesOption_Click ()
    Kill filename$
End Sub
```

Delete
"TEMP.TXT" ?

◉ NO
○ YES

Figure K-2: A dramatic question mark asks the user to verify his or her request to eliminate a disk file.

See also   Drive List Box (for an example of a complete VB file management system); Name; RmDir (to kill an entire directory)

KILLDOC   METHOD

See   Printer

LABEL

Description

Figure L-1: The symbol for a Label in the Toolbox.

A Label informs the user of the meaning of something visible on a window. A Label normally has no border and appears to be printed on a Form (window). However, because you can drag Labels around while designing your program, using Labels is usually a more efficient way of attaching text to some other Control than printing directly on a Form's background.

Variables Labels are usually not changed while a program runs, although they can be. Often the Caption (the Label's displayed text) and its other Properties are adjusted while you design your program using the Properties Window:

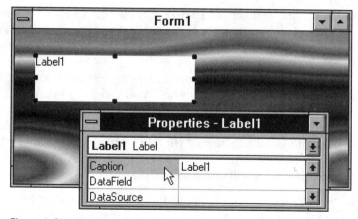

Figure L-2: Adjusting a Label's Properties in the Properties Window.

The UseMnemonic Property determines whether an ampersand (&) within the caption is printed or causes the following character to be underlined and become an *access key*. See "A Special Trick" below.

OR (to change a Property of a Label while the program is running):

```
Label1.Caption = "Loading Images..."
```

OR (to make a Label the same width as another Label):

```
Label2.Width = Label1.Width
```

Uses
• Print information on a Form but with greater flexibility than by using the Print command. It's easier to design the look of your Form with Labels than with Print. If you move a Picture Box, you can likewise drag its associated Labels, then position them the way that looks best. You can't see the location of printed text until you run your program.

• Add captions or other descriptive text to Controls that have no Caption Properties of their own—such as Scroll Bars.

• Apprise the user of changing conditions while your program runs: a file is being loaded, information is being sorted, etc.

• Provide a Status Bar—a line of helpful information, often found at the bottom of the screen in word processors and other programs. A Status Bar displays the name of the currently opened file, the X,Y position onscreen, the currently selected font, a description of a particular icon's purpose, etc. (Also see "Align" for more on Status Bars.)

A Special Trick: VB offers a feature called *access keys*. If the user presses ALT+K (if K has been made an access key), a Control or Menu designated "K" gets the focus. ALT+K in this instance acts as if the user clicked on that Control or Menu. (The Control "with the focus" reacts to any keys typed on the keyboard. If there are two Text Boxes on a Form, the one with the focus displays the characters when the user types.) Access keys offer the user an alternative to pressing the TAB key as a way of moving among the Controls on a Form.

Frames and Labels cannot get the focus, but they do have TabIndex Properties and Caption Properties. You can use a Frame or Label to give a *trick* access key to a Text Box, Picture Box or other Control that normally couldn't have one (because those Controls don't have a Caption Property).

Make the Label's Caption &Hit (<u>H</u>it). Then set the Label's TabIndex to a number one lower than the Text Box's TabIndex. When the user presses ALT+H, the focus will move to the Text Box.

Cautions

• The most important element of a Label is its Caption Property, which is where you put your descriptive text. The main purpose of a Label is to label something on your Form. Text Box Controls are also designed to handle text, but they also accept input from the user.

A Label wraps its text at its right edge. (It breaks lines at a space character.) You can take advantage of this fact to add multiline notations on forms. First, create a Label that is a couple of lines high, and type some words separated by spaces into its Caption Property. When you reach the edge of the Label, the words move to the next line. A Label is limited to 1,024 characters. A Label's Alignment, AutoSize and WordWrap Properties determine how text is displayed within the Label. (See the entries on those Properties for more.)

• Using Labels adds to the memory requirements of a program and takes away from the maximum of 255 Controls that are permitted per Form. If you ever need to conserve memory or Controls, use the Print command, although using Print makes designing the Form a little harder.

Example

Figure L-3: Mixing and matching font sizes and styles three Labels and a Picture Box.

Label Properties

Alignment • AutoSize • BackColor • BackStyle • BorderStyle • Caption
DragIcon • DragMode • Enabled • FontBold • FontItalic • FontName
FontSize • FontStrikethru • FontUnderline • ForeColor • Height
Index • Left • LinkItem • LinkMode • LinkTimeout • LinkTopic
MousePointer • Name • Parent • TabIndex • Tag • Top
UseMnemonic • Visible • Width • WordWrap

Label Events

Change • Click • DblClick • DragDrop • DragOver • LinkClose
LinkError • LinkNotify • LinkOpen • MouseDown • MouseMove
MouseUp

Label Methods

Drag • LinkExecute • LinkPoke • LinkRequest • Move • Refresh
ZOrder

See also   Text Box

LARGECHANGE, SMALLCHANGE

PROPERTY

Description   A window is frequently too small to display the entire picture, or text document, that it contains. The Windows system conventionally uses *Scroll Bars* so the user can move the document around, determining which part of the document is visible within the window at any given time.

It is also a Windows convention that if the user clicks on one of the small arrows at either end of a Scroll Bar, there is a *small* adjustment. Usually, clicking moves you to the next contiguous area of a document. For instance, if you were viewing a document, you would move down to the next line of text. This movement is governed by the SmallChange Property.

On the other hand, if the user clicks *within* a Scroll Bar, there is a larger shift. Depending on the size of the document, you might go to the beginning or end, fully to the right or left, or shift up or down by a single screenful of text. The shift, in this case, need not be contiguous although it usually is. This movement is governed by the LargeChange Property.

You, the programmer, determine the behavior of SmallChange and LargeChange by giving them values that interact with the Value Property of a Scroll Bar.

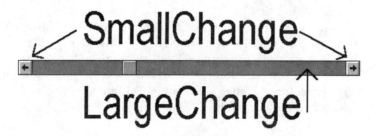

Figure L-4: A LargeChange is triggered when the user clicks *within* a Scroll Bar.

The Scroll Bars that automatically appear on List Boxes and Combo Boxes are controlled by Visual Basic. The optional ScrollBars Property of Text Boxes is also controlled by VB. VB sets the appropriate amount of movement for the small and large adjustments to the proportions of the text contained within them.

However, if you add a Horizontal or Vertical Scroll Bar Control to your program, you must set the increments by which the text or image shifts when the user clicks within or on the arrows of your Scroll Bar. The default LargeChange or SmallChange increment is 1. You can set the increment anywhere between 1 and 32,767. (You also establish the outer limits of the range that describes the shift, using the Max and Min Properties. You can restrict movement to a smaller area than the total size of the document under the window.)

Used with   Horizontal and Vertical Scroll Bar Controls

Variables   **Variable type:** Integer

Ordinarily, the SmallChange and LargeChange Properties are set in the Properties Window while you design the program:

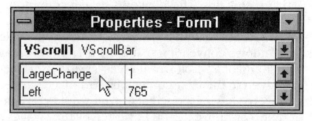

Figure L-5: Adjust the LargeChange amount in the Properties Window.

OR (to adjust the Properties while the program runs):

```
HScroll1.SmallChange = 1
HScroll1.LargeChange = 4
```

Uses • Give the user control over the position, size, color or other Properties of your Forms and Controls. The advantage of Scroll Bars is that the user can adjust qualities of your program and immediately see the results of his or her physical movements (if you provide such feedback by making a Picture Box or other Control react to the Scroll Bar's Change Event). The user will find choosing options by clicking on a Scroll Bar's arrows, clicking within the Bar or dragging the sliding lozenge (also called the Thumb or Scroll Box [see Cautions]) within the Bar is often far easier than entering 123,442 in response to an InputBox asking for BackColor.

• Allow the user to slide the visible window over a word processor document, database, picture or some other information that is too large to fit entirely within the window.

Cautions • The position of the square sliding lozenge (sometimes called the Thumb or Scroll Box) that moves within a Scroll Bar is represented in the Value Property; you check this Property to make your program respond when the user moves the thumb. You respond to a change in the Value within the Scroll Bar's Change Event:

```
Sub HScroll3_Change ()
      Picture1.FontSize = Hscroll3.Value
End Sub
```

• The Scroll Bars trigger their Change Event only *after* the user has finished sliding the thumb. If you want to display data *while* the user is dragging the thumb, use the Scroll Event (which see).

• *You* determine the range of numbers representing the thumb's extent of movement within a Scroll Bar. This range can be between –32,768 and 32,767. You will probably want to set the range to reflect whatever your Scroll Bar is controlling. For instance, an RGB color can range from 0 to 255, so you would set the Min Property of your Scroll Bar to 0 and the Max Property to 255. In the following example, we have a Scroll Bar that can change the FontSize in Picture Box1. For this, we set Min to 8 and Max to 150—the range of FontSizes that can comfortably fit with our particular Picture Box.

• If you don't set Min and Max, they default to 0 and 32,767, respectively.

• In a Horizontal Scroll Bar, Min is at the left; in a Vertical Scroll Bar, Min is at the top. This position reverses if you set Max to a lower number than Min.

Example The window in this example appears if the user selects a Command Button labeled OPTIONS. Several windows appear, including SELECT COLORS, SELECT WALLPAPER and SELECT FONTS. If the user decides to customize the size and style of the fonts, the user selects a font from a List Box. Then our View Fonts Window provides two Scroll Bars.

One bar permits the user to view the characters in the font; the other adjusts the size of the characters. When the user is satisfied with the selections, pressing the QUIT button changes the FontSize for the previously selected Control and also saves this preference to the program's .INI file on disk. That way, the customization becomes part of the program because that .INI file's settings are read by the program when it starts up.

Figure L-6: Allow the user to choose fonts and character sizes to use for elements of your program.

The QUIT button is an icon. Here's how to design it:

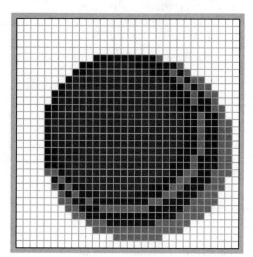

Figure L-7: One approach for designing a Button Icon.

The various raised and sunken frames around the Controls on this Form were created using the DrawFrameOn Subroutine described in "Line" (which see).

Adjusting the Extremities

When the Form loads, we draw several highlighted frames around the Controls and then print a sample letter "A" on the Picture Box. We set HScroll1.Max to 25, leaving Min at its default 0. This setting allows the user to scroll through the 26 letters of the alphabet. Then the user can click on the Arrow Icons at either end of the Scroll Bar, moving one letter forward or backward with each click. If the user clicks within the Scroll Bar, it moves forward or backward four letters of the alphabet.

Next, we adjust the extremities of the Scroll Bar that govern FontSize, allowing a minimum size of 8 and a maximum of 150. SmallChange permits the user to adjust the size in increments of 1. Because this range is so large, however, we set the LargeChange to increments of 16.

Finally, the Label just below the Picture Box is set to display the Font-Name—to both name it and exemplify it:

```
Sub Form_Load ()

Show
drawframeon picture3, picture4, "outward", 300
drawframeon picture3, picture4, "inward", 150
drawframeon picture2, picture2, "inward", 160
drawframeon hscroll1, hscroll1, "inward", 20
drawframeon hscroll3, hscroll3, "inward", 20
drawframeon label4, label4, "inward", 50
drawframeon label1, label1, "inward", 20
```

```
drawframeon label3, label2, "inward", 20
drawframeon label5, label5, "inward", 10
drawframeon picture1, picture1, "outward", 150
drawframeon picture1, picture1, "inward", 50

picture1.Print "A"

hscroll1.Max = 25
hscroll1.SmallChange = 1
hscroll1.LargeChange = 4

hscroll2.Min = 8
hscroll2.Max = 150
hscroll2.LargeChange = 16
hscroll2.SmallChange = 1

label4.FontName = picture1.FontName
label4.Caption = picture1.FontName
End Sub
```

If the user adjusts the letter of the alphabet Scroll Bar, we force the ASCII code to print the new letter by adding the Value (which will be 0 through 25) to 65. The ANSI code capital letters range from 65 through 90 (see "KeyPress"). Adding this value gives us the correct letter to print, but first we clear the Picture Box using the Cls command. Without using the Cls (Clear Screen) command, the letters would print one after the other and disappear from view. Cls resets the CurrentX and CurrentY coordinates to 0,0. Because we want the letters relatively centered within the Box, we add to the CurrentX Property:

```
Sub HScroll1_Change ()

    X$ = Chr$(hscroll1.Value + 65)
    picture1.Cls
    picture1.CurrentX = 100
    picture1.Print X$
End Sub
```

If the user adjusts the FontSize Scroll Bar, we set the FontSize of the Picture Box directly to the Value Property of the Scroll Bar. We translate the FontSize, which is a number, into a printable digit with the Str$ command and then put the result in the Label that shows the user the current FontSize. Because the HScroll1_Change Event does everything necessary to update the Picture, we just trigger it by naming it:

```
Sub HScroll2_Change ()

    picture1.FontSize = hscroll2.Value
    label2.Caption = Str$(hscroll2.Value)
    HScroll1_Change

End Sub
```

See also   Change; Max; Min; Scroll; Value; Vertical Scroll Bar

LBOUND

Description   LBound tells you the lower limit of an Array's index. You rarely use this function because you usually *know* when you are writing your program how big your Arrays are—you must define Arrays, including their range. (For more information, see "Arrays.") However, if you are writing a Subroutine (called from more than one location in your program or used by more than one program because you import it as a part of your "toolkit of useful Routines"), you may very well need to know the dimensions of a passed or Global Array.

```
Sub Form_Click ()

Static A (1 To 50) As String

X = LBound(A)
Print X

End Sub
```

Results in   1

LBound is also a *Property* of Controls, Columns, Forms, Objects, or a Control Array. But it is always zero, except for Control Arrays where it is usually zero (it's the Index value of the first Control).

Used with   Arrays

Variables   If you've defined an Array like the following: Dim Names (5 To 16, 12 To 12):

```
Sub Form_Click ()
    X = LBound(Names, 1): Print X
End Sub
```

Results in   5

```
Sub Form_Click ()
    X = LBound(Names, 2): Print X
End Sub
```

Results in   12

Uses   LBound can be used if an Array is redimensioned based on a range defined by the program's user. However, this information could just as easily be retained in a Variable at the time the Array is redimensioned.

Cautions   • The equivalent UBound Function tells you the upper limit of an Array's index while a program is running.

• You can omit the "dimension number" [the 2 in LBound(A,2)] if there is only one dimension. Dim A As String has only one dimension; Dim A (1 To 5, 1 To 7, 1 To 4) has three dimensions.

• When creating an Array—when *declaring* the Array with the Dim, ReDim, Global or Static commands—you don't need to use the To Statement. Dim A (15, 15) creates a two-dimensional Array, with space for items ranging from 0 to 15 in each dimension. You can, however, have the Array start at a different lower index by using Dim A (1 To 15), which creates a single-dimension Array with 15 items, ranging in index number from 1 to 15.

• If you use the Option Base Statement, you can force all Arrays to default to a lowest index number of 1 (Option Base 1). LBound then becomes meaningless.

Example

```
Sub Form_Click()

Static A (44)
X = LBound (A)
Print X

End Sub
```

Results in   0

See also   Arrays; Dim; Global; Option Base; ReDim; Static; UBound

LCase$ OR LCASE

FUNCTION

Description   LCase$ forces all the characters of a text (string) Variable to become lowercase letters. It changes "VIRGIL" to "virgil," for example.

Used with   Text Variables, text Constants, text expressions or literal text. See "Variables" for an explanation of these terms.

Variables

```
A$ = "Declaration of Independence"
B$ = LCase$(A$)
Print B$
```

Results in   declaration of independence

OR (because LCase$ is a Function, you can use it as part of an *expression*):

```
A$ = "Declaration of Independence $$$"

Print LCase$(B$)
```

Results in   declaration of independence $$$

Because the $$$ are not text characters, they remain unaffected by LCase$.

Uses   • Some VB commands are *case sensitive*. One frequently used command, InStr, makes a distinction between *This* and *this*.

   You cannot always know how users might capitalize the input when typing something into your program. To avoid a problem, you can force the user's text to all lowercase letters and not worry about unwanted mismatches. It's a good idea to build the LCase$ function into any general-purpose text-handling Subroutines and Functions you write. That way you don't need to worry about capitalization when providing Variables to the Subs or Functions. (See the Example.) However, VB also provides a Str-Comp command (which see) that can compare pieces of text and includes case-insensitivity as an option.

   • If you write a Routine that capitalizes the first letter of each word or the first letter of each word in a name, use LCase$ or UCase$ first to get all the words to a known state.

   • You can also use LCase$ when storing a text Variable that will later need to be matched (such as a password).

   • In searching through documents or databases for a match (using the InStr command), you could use LCase$ to make capitalization variations irrelevant to your search. (See the Example.)

Cautions   • Only alphabetic letters are affected by LCase$—not digits like 8 or symbols like &.

Example

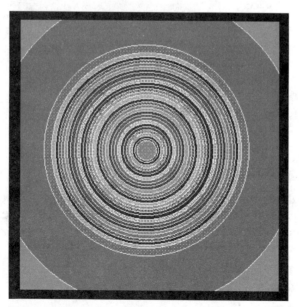

Figure L-8: The Subroutine in this program can accept uppercase, lowercase or combinations of the two when you "pass" it Variables.

For a program requiring that we frequently draw circles or boxes, we've written a general-purpose Subroutine that takes Size and Shape as Variables and then draws the requested image. Size, of course, is a number. But we want to use the words *circle* and *square* to define Shape. And we don't want it to matter whether the Sub is passed *Circle, circle, CIRCLE* or some other variation in capitalization.

Type the following into the General Declarations section of the Form:

```
Sub Drawshape (Size As Integer, Shape As String)

X$ = LCase$(Shape)

If X$ = "circle" Then
    Circle (2000, 2000), size, QBColor(15)
Else
    Line (2000, 2000)-(500 + size, 500 + size), , B
End If

End Sub
```

Notice that we first used LCase$ to remove any uppercase letters that were used in describing *Shape*. Then we can compare it to *circle* without concerning ourselves with any capitalization.

Now we call upon the Drawshape Routine. First, we pass *Circle* and then *circle*. Without LCase$, the first call to Drawshape would produce a square since the word *Circle* was capitalized and would fail to match *circle*.

```
Sub Form_Click ()

Fillstyle = 0

For i = 10 To 1 Step –2
    Fillcolor = i * 1500000
    Drawshape 400 * i + 100 / i, "Circle"
Next i

For i = 30 To 1 Step –1
    Fillcolor = i * 50000
    Drawshape 50 * i + 100 / i, "circle"
Next i

End Sub
```

We step down from 10 to 1 and from 30 to 1 to draw these bull's-eye designs because if you draw them starting with a small circle, each subsequent larger circle covers the smaller one. You end up with one big circle. Always draw larger items first if you expect to draw smaller images within them.

See also   StrComp; UCase$

LEFT

Description   The Left Property describes the distance between the left edge of a Control and the left edge of the Form (or another Control) which contains it.

As a Property of a Form, Left refers to the position of the left edge of the Form in relation to the left border of the screen.

Left, along with the Top Property, describes the *location* of an object within another Object. (An Object's Height and Width Properties describe the *size* of the Object.) Using these four Properties you can both position and size the Object. And there are times when you will use all four Properties together.

For example, there are no right or bottom Properties. If you want to draw a box around an Object with the Line command, you'll need to know the Object's right and bottom locations in addition to Top and Left. To find the right side of an Object, you add its Left and its Width Properties. To find the bottom of an Object, you add Top to Height. See "Cautions" below.

Used with   Everything except Timers

Variables   **Variable type:** Single

When you drag an item around the screen while designing your program, you are automatically affecting its Left Property. Visual Basic keeps track.

However, if you wish, you can set the Left Property directly in the Properties Window, though few people do:

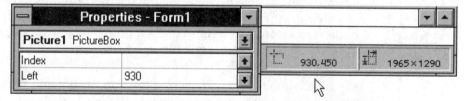

Figure L-9: The Properties Window is rarely used to set the Left Property.

Notice that the Left and Top Properties are always visible on the right side of the Toolbar when you are writing a program. And, next to them are the Width and Height Properties. You can see these four coordinates as you drag your Controls around. However, *seeing* the relative sizes and positions of Controls is much more meaningful than looking at those numbers. The numbers are rarely used.

OR (to find out the leftmost location of an Object while the program runs):

```
X = Picture1.Left
```

OR (to change the horizontal position of an Object while the program runs): Picture1.Left = 500

OR (to position an Object horizontally relative to another object):

```
Picture1.Left = Picture2.Left + 1000
```

OR (to use a numeric Variable):

```
Position = 500
Picture1.Left = Position
```

Uses
• Animate Controls by changing the Left Property directly, or by finding out the Left Property and providing it to the Move command for smooth diagonal movements. You would generally animate by putting the movement inside a For...Next Loop so you could Control the speed of the animation:

```
X = Picture1.Left

For I = X To X + 400 Step 20
    Picture1.Left = I
Next I
```

(Adjusting the Step size from 20 to 40 would make the Picture slide twice as fast. However, this method of animation—though easily programmed—is processor-dependent. That is, the speed of the user's computer will determine the speed of the animation. It's better to use a Timer, which see, to move Objects.)

• Format your screen by adjusting the relative positions of Controls, in response to current conditions in your program. Perhaps when the user clicks on an icon, you want to make it drop into a Text Box, then disappear, transforming from a graphic into a text statement of its purpose. See the Example below.

• Used in combination with an object's Top, Height and Width Properties, you can have complete control over both the size and location of an Object.

Cautions
• Left is expressed as a number, but precisely what the number means can change. Unless you have adjusted the Scale Method or the ScaleMode Property (which apply only to Forms, Picture Boxes and the printer), the number will be in *twips*. There are 1,440 twips per inch. There are several other "coordinate systems"—points, inches, millimeters, etc.—and you can even define a custom system. (See "ScaleMode.")

Within a Picture Box, Form, or printer page, the Left Property for all Objects is given in twips (or in an optional alternative system) and says, "My left side is 500 twips from the left border of my container (the Form or Picture Box or printed page)."

How to Tell if an Object Is Flush-Left With Its Container: If the Left Property is 0, that means that the Object is flush against the left side of its container.

How to Tell if an Object Is Flush-Right With Its Container: An Object is butted up against the right side of its container if its Left Property plus its Width Property equal the Width Property of the container, *minus* the Object's Left plus Width Properties:

```
X = Command1.Left + Command1.Width
If Form1.Width — X = X Then
```

How to Move an Object Flush-Right Within Its Container:

```
Command1.Left = Form1.Width — Command1.Width
```

How to Tell if an Object Is Butted Against the Top of Its Container: An Object is butted against the top of its container if its Top Property is 0.

How to Tell if an Object Is Butted Against the Bottom of Its Container: An Object is butted against the bottom of its container if its Top Property plus its Height Property equal the container's Height Property, *minus* the Object's Top plus its Height Properties:

```
X = Picture1.Top + Picture1.Height
If Form1.Height — X = X Then
```

• When an Object is moved to the far right side of a Form, part of it can disappear under the Form's frame unless the Form's BorderStyle is set to None. You'll need to adjust the Object's Left Property to take into account Frames with borders. However, if you use a Form's ScaleWidth Property instead of its Width Property, you can avoid worrying about the size of the border. ScaleWidth is a measurement of the interior dimensions of a Form (Picture Box, or the Printer). Width is a measurement of a Form's entire width, including any border.

• The video screen is the container for a Form, and in this situation, *the Left Property measurement is always expressed in twips.* There can be no other coordinate system for the Screen Object.

How to Center Objects Within Their Containers:

```
Picture1.Left = (Form1.Width — Picture1.Width) / 2
Picture1.Top = (Form1.Height — Picture1.Height) / 2
```

How to Center Text Horizontally Within an Object:

```
T$ = "Center This"
W = TextWidth(T$) / 2
CurrentX = (ScaleWidth / 2) — W
Print T$
```

(See "TextWidth" for more on this.)

How to Animate an Object: Adjust the Left Property if you want an instant change in an Object's position. Use the Move Method for a smoother animation, particularly if you are combining a horizontal movement with a vertical movement (a diagonal movement). However, you can retard the speed of either technique by placing the command within a For...Next Loop:

```
For I = Command1.Left To Command1.Left − 1500 Step − 50
    Command1.Left = I
Next I
```

Adjust the Step amount to adjust the speed of this animation.

The Strange Quality Called "Granularity": In the Windows Control Panel (Desktop item) there is an option you can adjust called *Granularity* which decides how closely Objects on the screen can get to each other and by what degrees Objects can be expanded or shrunk. This option isn't something you can adjust for the users of your programs, but you might ask them to set it to zero. If it's anything other than zero, the positioning and sizing commands in your Visual Basic programs will be relatively crude. Objects will *jump* in increments of Granularity * 16 pixels when their Left, Top, Height or Width Properties are adjusted. This might not seem like much of a jerking–16 pixels is not much space–but things are smoother when Granularity is set to zero. That eliminates the bumpy motion (at some small cost in speed).

Example   This is a complete electronic cookbook, affording the user several ways to access the recipes within. They can move the Scroll Bar at the bottom to reach any one of the hundreds of recipes in the "book."

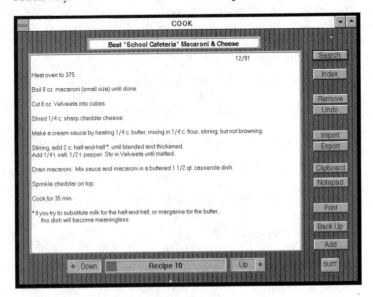

Figure L-10: An electronic cookbook.

Or they can click on the Index Command Button:

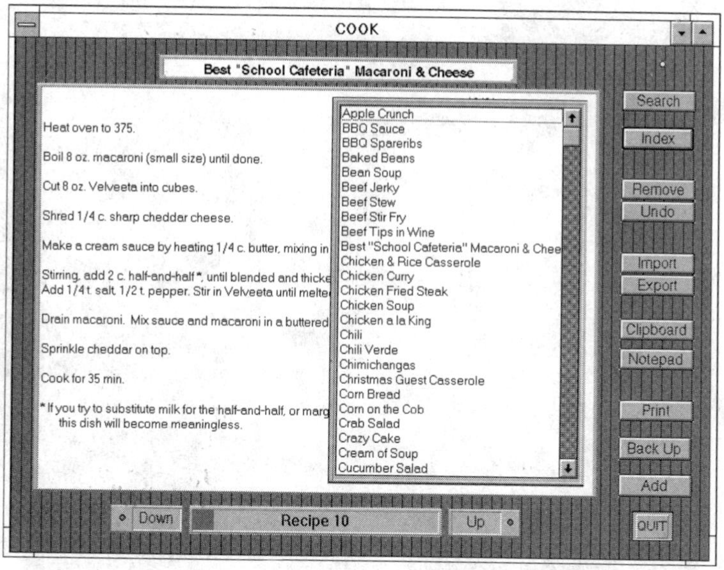

Figure L-11: An index feature offers an alternative to the Buttons on the bottom of the window.

This reveals a scrollable list of all the recipes. Clicking on any one of the recipes in the list brings that recipe into the main recipe window and collapses the index window.

But it's more fun to press the Search Button, because the effects are *animated*. This reveals a second, smaller window with a group of icons representing the various food categories and cooking methods–meat, microwave, American, pork, Mexican, etc. The user *could* type in various selection criteria in the Text Box at the top, but far more interesting is the process of combining the various icons.

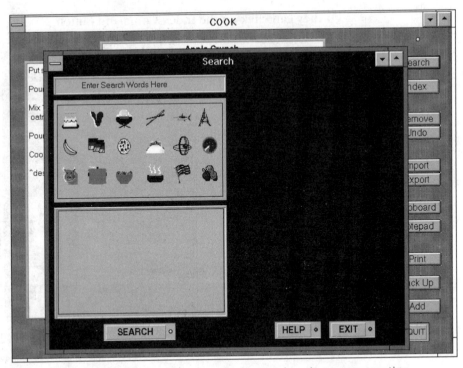

Figure L-12: Yet another alternative way to select recipes icons representing cooking categories.

Clicking on an icon visibly slides it down into the Criteria Box, below the icon collection. In the process, the icon transforms into text, showing the user's selection. Several icons could be dropped this way, narrowing the search criteria each time.

Want to find a list of Mexican-American dishes? Click on the taco and the American flag. Let's select all Mexican recipes that use the microwave. Click the taco and the atomic nuclear-accident symbols. They fall into the box, becoming text. You could further narrow your search by adding, say, the pig icon and the soup bowl. This would give us a list of all Mexican pork soup dishes that are microwaved. But, let's leave it at Mexican microwave, and click on the SEARCH button to reveal those recipes that qualify under these criteria:

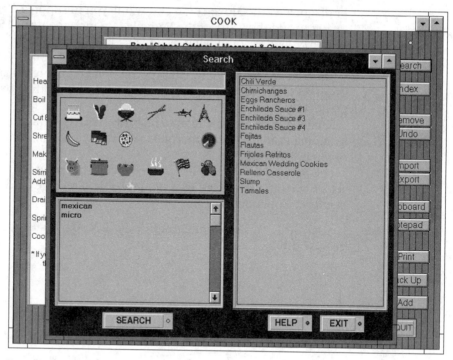

Figure L-13: When an icon is clicked, it falls into the box below and turns into a word.

Let's see how the Left Property of the taco icon helps us to slide it into the Text Box below:

```
Sub Picture6_Click ()

Pt = Picture6.Top

For i = 1 To 200 Step 15
    Picture6.Move Picture6.Left, Picture6.Top + i
Next i

Picture6.Visible = 0

Cust.AddItem inis(12)

Picture6.Top = Pt
End Sub
```

Clicking on the Taco

If the user clicks on the taco, Picture6, we first save its Top position, so we can restore it later within the collection of icons. Then we move it down 200 twips, 15 twips at a time. If you're moving left or right, you can simply adjust the Left Property because the Move command will work with only the Left Property specified. However, to move vertically, as we want to do, or diagonally, the Move command wants you to supply Left and Top. We're saying to add the value of the Variable i, in increments of 15, to the Top Property. We're not moving diagonally, just straight down, so we leave Picture6.Left unchanged each time this For...Next Loop cycles.

Then we make the Picture disappear, and add the text name we've assigned to this icon (Inis(12)) to the Cust List Box (the box of text below the icons).

Finally, we restore the icon to its proper place within the icon group by assigning Pt to its Top Property. Pt was the Variable in which we saved the original Top location.

The Scroll Bar in the main screen contains the *name* of the currently selected recipe. This feature is not available directly from VB (see more details in Appendix D).

See also   Height; Scale; ScaleHeight; ScaleLeft; ScaleMode; ScaleTop; ScaleWidth; Top; Width

LEFT

FUNCTION

Description   Left allows you to extract a specified amount of text from the left side of a text Variable:

X$ = "We Employ A Maid From Planet X."

Y$ = Left(X$,18)

Print Y$

Results in   We Employ A Maid

Y$ = Left(X$,9)

Print Y$

Results in   We Employ

A variation, the LeftB function, allows you to specify the length in *bytes* rather than *characters*. (Characters in VB is a two-byte unit in the 32-bit version.)

Used with   Text ("string") Variables

Variables   To put the first 15 characters of Large$ into Partial$:

Partial$ = Left(Large$,15)

Uses   • *Parse* some text—pull out the various elements of the text.

Left is used along with several other Functions that manipulate text–Right, Mid, Instr and Len–to isolate and extract a piece of text from within a larger group of characters.

Right pulls out a number of characters, counting backward from the right side:

```
X$ = "We Employ A Maid From Planet X."
Y$ = Right(X$,9)

Print Y$
```

Results in   Planet X.

Mid pulls out a piece of text anywhere from within a larger text. It has the format Y$ Mid(LargerText$, StartingCharacter, NumberOfCharacters). Use Mid when the target piece of text isn't flush against the left or right of the larger text:

```
X$ = "We Employ A Maid From Planet X."

Y$ = Mid(X$,23,6)

Print Y$
```

Results in   Planet

Len tells you the length, in characters, of a text ("string") Variable.

```
X$ = "We employ a maid from Planet X."

Print Len(X$)
```

Results in   31

Instr finds the location of the first character of a piece of text within a larger group of characters:

```
L = Instr(X$, "maid")

Print L
```

Results in   13

Instr will give back a 0 if it cannot find the text. Instr is case-sensitive; looking for "Maid" would give back a 0, meaning "not found," because the searched text does not capitalize the *m*.

Cautions   • The group of characters from which Left extracts a smaller piece of text will usually be a text ("string") Variable. However, it can also be a Constant (Const CALCAPITOL = "Sacramento"), or a *string expression*. (See "Variables" for a full explanation of *expression*.)

Briefly, an *expression* is a group of Variables, Constants, literals or

Functions connected together by operators such as + or >. An expression can be reduced to a single answer: True or False.

```
If Y$ = Left(X$,3) = "We " Then
```

This is not an expression because Y$ = Left(X$,3) = "We " cannot be evaluated into a single result by VB.

```
Left(X$, 2) + Right(X$, 3) = "We X."
```

This *is* an expression, because it can be evaluated as True or False (–1 or 0) and can therefore be used in a larger structure, such as If...Then.

```
X$ = "We employ a maid from Planet X."

If Left(X$, 2) + Right(X$, 3) = "We X." Then
    Print "Yes."
End If
```

Results in   Yes.

• The number of characters you are requesting Left to extract–the 15 in Left(X$, 15)–can be a literal number like 15 or a numeric Variable like N%.

• The number of characters you are requesting Left to extract from a larger piece of text can be as many as 65,535, but if you ask for more characters than exist in the larger piece of text, you get back the entire larger text.

Example

```
X$ = "1234567890"

For I = 1 to Len(X$)
    Print Left(X$,I)
Next I
```

Results in
```
1
12
123
1234
12345
123456
1234567
12345678
123456789
1234567890
```

See also   InStr; Len; Mid; Right; StrComp

LEN

Description   The Len command serves two unrelated purposes in Visual Basic.

1. Most often you use Len to tell you the length—the number of characters—in a text ("string") Variable.

2. If you need to find out how many bytes of the computer's memory (or a disk's storage space) *any kind of Variable* will take up—use Len (Variablename).

Used with   Text ("string") Variables, to determine their length.

OR User-defined *Type* Variables, to determine the amount of memory or disk space they use.

Variables   X = Len(A$)

Uses   • You use Len with text, when you don't know how long the piece of text is. This usually means that the user entered the text or your program is reading a disk file. You can make your programs more responsive to the user, more forgiving of variations in how the user might enter or request information—even more "artificially" intelligent. One way to do this is to use Len, along with other text-analysis commands such as Mid$ and Instr, to take a sentence apart. Once you have the individual words, your program can take a look at them, and react with a degree of understanding.

Let's say there is a general-purpose Text Box that the user can access anytime, entering a question that your program is supposed to answer. If the user enters any one of the words *costs, cost, expense, expenses, payment*, etc., you would switch to a special budget window that would list the months and years for which budget data exist in the program (or load in a disk file with that information).

Better yet, if the user has also entered the name of a month (Jan, January, Jan., etc.), your program notices that and provides the expense information for that month only. You can also check for other words that would further narrow the criteria and permit you to require the user to interact with fewer menus, submenus, command buttons. Your program could analyze the user's English-language request intelligently and zoom right in on the data the user requests. You might check to see if a subset of the budget request includes text like Car, 1990, All, Lowest and so on, making adjustments in how you present the data based on the meaning of these terms. See Example 1 below.

• Len's other primary use is to tell you how much space a user-defined Variable type takes up in memory or on disk. (See "Variables" for a discussion about *Variable types*.) Len is used in this way with random-access files and the associated Type command. (See "Open" for information on that technique. And see Example 2 below.)

Random & Sequential

Briefly, random-access files contain individual records that are of the same length. Because of that, the records can be accessed mathematically. If each record is, say, 35 bytes in size, then the computer can access record #10 by instantly moving 350 bytes into the disk file. Random files are also easier to manipulate: they allow the user to change the data in record #10, and you can replace it in the disk file without worrying that it might cover up data in record #9 or #11. The space for data is as predictable and uniform as an ice cube tray. The drawback is that all random file records must be as large as the largest record.

Sequential-access files are more efficient in some ways. Since data always takes up varying amounts of space (your name probably isn't the same length as mine), storing information sequentially allows you to use up only as much space on the disk as the data requires. It's like making a cassette tape—one song after the other, all of varying lengths. Searching for the fourth song requires that you check for silence between songs from the beginning of the tape until you reach the third silence. At the third silence you've found the start of the fourth song.

If you are using a random file, you can find out the number of records using this formula. (RecType is the defined Type structure, which see, for this file.)

    NumRecs = Lof(1) \ Len(RecType)

Cautions

• If you want to find out the memory or disk space requirements of a defined *Type* Variable, don't use Len with the original definition of the Type (the one in a Module).

Instead, use Len after you have declared a specific instance of this Type with the Dim, Static or Global command. The specific instance of a Type will give you the correct Len. The original Type...End Type name will not give you an accurate report on the space requirements. To see how this works, see Example 2 below.

If you want a byte count in 32-bit VB, use the LenB function. In 32-bit VB4, Len doesn't return the number of *bytes* because characters are 2-bytes large. See "Chr$" for more on this.

Example 1

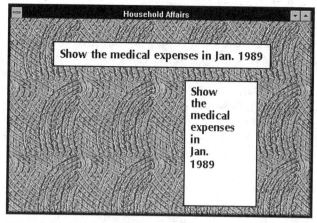

Figure L-14: Breaking a sentence into its components the first step in an analysis of the meaning of the user's request.

When the user types a question into the top box, our program prepares to analyze the question and respond intelligently. The first step is to break the sentence down into individual words. For purposes of illustration, we added the individual words to the List Box in the Example.

As soon as we have the words, we can look them up and have the program react. Using Select Case or If...Then, we can make the program switch to an expenses screen, get the data for the requested month and year, and even highlight the medical, insurance, auto, or whatever particular information the user might have requested.

Our program will often need to break a text Variable into its component words, so we write a Subroutine called Parse. Parse accepts a single text Variable and pulls it apart. We "pass" that single Variable to the Parse Subroutine when we use it: Parse "This piece of text." or Parse T$.

```
Sub Parse (A As String)

L = Len(A$)

For I = 1 To L
    P& = InStr(I, A$, Chr$(32))
        If P& = 0 Then Exit For
    T$ = Mid$(A$, I, P& — I)
    Box.AddItem T$
    I = P&
Next I

T$ = Mid$(A$, I, L — P&)
Box.AddItem T$
End Sub
```

First off, Len tells us the length of the passed Variable. Then, we use a For...Next Loop to extract each character.

P& holds the location of any space within A$. [Chr$(32) is the code for a space.] InStr looks for a space, but if P& is 0, then it did not find a space (A$ has only one word), or we've been through the Loop several times and have found all the spaces (and therefore all the words) already.

As soon as we *do* find a space, we assign the word to T$. We know where within A$ the Mid$ Function should extract the new word. The Variable I holds the starting position of the new word, and P& holds the position where we came across a space. So P&–I is the *length* of the new word. Finally we add T$ to the box so we can see it. Then we move our place marker, the I Variable, up to where we found the space and look for the next space.

Notice that when we've found no more spaces, we still have to add that one last word in A$ to the box. In this final situation, we use L, the length of A$, to provide the last character and subtract the most recent position (P&), so we know how many characters to tell our final Mid$ to extract.

Here's how we use the Parse subroutine, and how we "pass" A$ to it:

```
Sub Form_Click ()
    A$ = Text1.Text
    Parse A$
End Sub
```

The user can click on the Form to show that the program should go ahead and accept what has been typed into the top box, but it's always nice to provide several ways for the user to make himself or herself known. In addition to clicking, we allow the user to press the ENTER key, signaling the computer to proceed:

```
Sub Text1_KeyPress (Keyascii As Integer)
    If Keyascii = 13 Then
            Keyascii = 0
            Form_Click
        End If
End Sub
```

We watch every letter entered into the Text Box. If one of them has code 13, we know the user pressed ENTER, so we do two things. VB has an unfortunate habit of beeping the computer's speaker when it comes upon an ENTER character in a Text Box that is not set to permit multiple lines (with the MultiLine Property). Presumably this is to alert the user that it is foolish to continue to press ENTER, since this box only allows one line.

Prevent the Beep: Nevertheless, pressing ENTER can be a valid way of demonstrating completion. It is not always a deluded effort to force additional lines. So, by reassigning a 0 (the "nothing" character) to Keyascii, we prevent the beep. Then we make the program behave as if a Form_Click Event had taken place.

Example 2   The following example illustrates a completely different use of Len—telling us how much memory (in the computer, or on a disk file) is used by each unit (each "record") in a collection of records called a *random-access file*. There are several "types" of Variables built into VB—Integer, Double, etc. (see "Variables"). However, you can create your own Variable type.

Some people find this approach useful. It groups Variables into a kind of family. Type is useful if you want to collect several Variables together in a logical unit. It can make your program easier to understand if a family of related Variables is given the same "last name" in this way. (An Array, which see, is more often used for this purpose than are Type Variables.)

In a Module, you can create your own "programmer-defined" data type:

```
Type Expenses
    Insurance As Currency
    Medical As Currency
    Mortgage As Currency
    Car As Currency
    Food As Currency
    Paymentday As Double
    Weekday As Integer
End Type
```

Then, whenever you want to use the new Type, declare a Variable to be of that Type.

In the General Declarations section of a Form, let's declare the new Variable *January* to be of the "Expenses" type.

```
Dim January As Expenses
```

Now, whenever we use January (the "family name"), we can attach one of the Variable names, such as January.Medical.

To find out how much space a compound Variable like January will take up, we use Len:

```
Sub Form_Click ()
    Print Len(January)
    January.Insurance = 340.78
    January.Medical = 0
    January.Mortgage = 876.8
    January.Car = 407.88
    January.Food = 280
    January.Paymentday = Now
    January.Weekday = 12
End Sub
```

When you click on the Form, the Len Function shows that any Variable declared to be of the Expenses type (in this case the compound Variable *January*) will take up 50 bytes, 8 each for all the Currency and Double types, and 2 for the Integer at the end.

The size of the January family of Variables is useful information if you are working with a random-access file (see "Open").

See also   Chr$; Instr; Left; Mid; Open (for *random-access files*); Right; Type; Variables (for Variable *types*)

LET

STATEMENT

Description Let is no longer used. It is retained in Visual Basic for compatibility with extremely ancient programs. Let has not been used in Basic for over ten years.

In the very early days, though, Basic required Let when you were *assigning* a number or piece of text to a Variable.

```
Let MonthlyBudget = 800
```

OR

```
Let PowerCoName$ = "Duke Power"
```

However, it was quickly realized that the equals (=) symbol is never used by itself like this (outside of a larger structure), *except* when assigning to a Variable. Basic could figure out that when you said X = 15 or Y$ = N$ you were assigning, so Let got dropped.

Let also served what the designers of Basic thought was an important purpose: it helped people understand that *assignment* did not mean precisely the same thing as *equality*. Everyone who takes algebra learns that = means that the items on either side of the equals sign are equal to each other. This had to be unlearned to program a computer.

An equals sign is used in two different ways in computer programming:

1. *Assignment*. By itself, when simply connecting a Variable with a literal (Y$ = "No") or connecting a Variable with another Variable (X$ = Y$), an equals sign means "now let the item on the left be *assigned* (given) the value on the right." Prior to the assignment, X$ might have held any-thing– "MAYBE" or "Portland," or perhaps it had not been used yet and was an empty text Variable "". However, after assignment (X$ = Y$), X$ contains a piece of text, a copy of what was in Y$.

2. *Equality*. Used inside a larger structure, such as If...Then, an equals symbol *does* represent equality in the algebraic sense.

```
X = 12
Y = 12
If X = Y Then Print "They are Equal."
```

X = Y is called an *expression*, which means that Basic can "evaluate the truth of it." An expression is a group of Variables, Constants, literals and/or Functions connected to each other by operators (such as < or / or =). An expression can be reduced to True (–1) or False (0) after being evaluated by Basic.

```
X = 4: Y = 15
```

We can evaluate the expression X > Y (X is greater than Y), by putting it within an If...Then structure:

```
If X > Y Then
```

In this instance, the evaluation would result in a False (0), and whatever instructions followed the Then command would not be carried out. The expression Y > X would return a True (–1) result to the If...Then structure, and commands following Then in the structure would be carried out.

The differences between assignment and equality may seem rather trivial at first encounter, but they represent two essentially different uses of the equals sign in programming. After some experience communicating with computers, people quickly grasp the difference. They come to recognize that used by itself = gives something to a Variable. Used within a larger structure such as Select Case or If...Then, = comes closer to its algebraic meaning of equality. And thus the descriptive function of Let is not necessary.

Used with Not used.

Variables
```
Let X = 175
```

Uses None

Cautions None

Example
```
Let Z$ = "Nova Scotia"
```

is precisely the same as
```
Z$ = "Nova Scotia"
```

See also There is no referent for this dead command.

LIKE
OPERATOR

Description Like lets you compare a text ("string") Variable to a pattern using wild cards. This operator is similar to the wild cards you can use when asking for a directory in DOS: * or ?. Just as in DOS you can see all files ending with .DOC by typing Dir *.DOC, and you can compare text Variables, as follows:
```
A$ = "Rudolpho"
If A$ Like "Ru*" Then Print "Close Enough"
```

Used with Text ("string") Variables

Variables To compare against a *single* character in a particular position:
```
X = "Nora" Like "?ora": Print X
```

Results in   -1 (meaning "True")

```
X = "Nora" Like "F?ora": Print X
```

Results in   0 (meaning "False"–the first letter in *Nora* isn't F, the third letter isn't o, and so on).

OR (to compare when you don't care about a match between a series of characters):

```
If "David" Like "*d" Then
Print "Match"
Else
Print "No Match"
End If
```

Results in   Match

"D*d" or "**D*d" or "*i*" will all match "David"

OR (to find a match against a single digit (0-9), but *only* a digit):

```
If "99 Elide Rd." Like "???###" Then
```

Results in   No Match

"????##" would match, however.

OR (to match a single character in the text against a single character or range of characters in the list enclosed by brackets):

```
If "Empire" Like "??[n-q]*" Then
```

Results in   Match

You can also use multiple ranges such as: "[n-rt-w]."

OR (to match if a single character in the text is not in the list):

```
If "Empire" Like "??[!n-q]*" Then
```

Results in   No Match

Uses   • Make List Boxes more sensitive (see the Example).

• Allow "fuzzy" or approximate comparisons. Let your program excuse the user's typos and make intelligent guesses about the user's intent; this is particularly helpful during repetitive data entry. If the user has been typing *SnaDiego*, CA, for five entries into an address book, your program could change, or offer to change, *SnaDiego* to *SanDiego*.

Cautions   Like is case-sensitive: it sees a difference between *Money* and *money*– unless you use the Option Compare command (see "StrComp").

Example   Many programs, including the Search feature in VB's Help, adjust their list as the user types in each character. Here's an easy way to accomplish that. Start a New Project from the File Menu and put a File List Box and a Text Box on the Form.

In the Text Box's Change Event, we'll sense any additions to the word the user is typing and instantly react:

```
Sub Text1_Change ()
    m$ = text1.Text + "*"
    For i = 0 To file1.ListCount − 1
        If file1.List(i) Like m$ Then
            file1.TopIndex = i
            Exit For
        End If
    Next i
End Sub
```

There are other ways to accomplish this, but if you don't use the Like command, the programming is cumbersome.

See also   StrComp

L INE

CONTROL

Description   Using the Line Control is an easy way to add lines to your Forms for graphic effects. The more flexible Line *Method* requires you to provide a series of coordinates. However, when you use the Control, you can just drag and drop it wherever it looks good on a Form.

Figure L-15: The Line Control icon on the Toolbox.

Used with   Forms

Variables

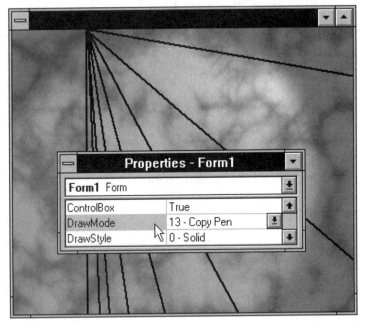

Figure L-16: You can set the Line Control's Properties in the Properties Window.

OR (to change a Property while a program is running): line1.BorderWidth = 5

Uses   • Create subtle, shaded frames behind or around your Controls. Most commercial software uses such frames, and VB provides one example in the Command Button. (See the Example below and the Examples under "Line" Method.)

• Create various background "Wallpaper" patterns.

• Draw visual frames around Control groups and use different line widths and colors to highlight portions of a Form. Even change the width, size, position and color properties while the program is running to clue the user of changes in the status of Controls, etc.

• Make Data Entry Boxes look like they are organized as a table. Or put a grid over a group of Boxes.

Cautions   In the current version of VB, the Move Method doesn't work with the Line Control, although it is mentioned in Help and does work with its sister, the Shape Control.

Example

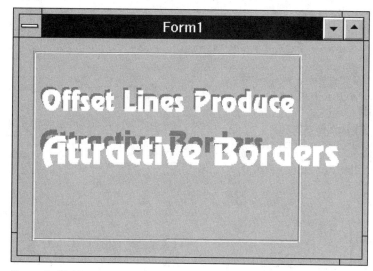

Figure L-17: You can create professional-looking frames by offsetting lines.

In this example, we used eight Line Controls, moving them into position by turning off "Align To Grid" in the Environment Options Menu. Then we set the color of four of the lines to a light gray and the other four to darker gray. The Form's BackColor was made gray as well. You could get this effect more quickly with two Shape Controls, but the result would look less professional where the squares intersected; a close observer would notice the superimposition of one box on another. The drop shadow effects for the lettering are created by overprinting each line, as illustrated in the following program:

```
Sub Form_Click ()

currentx = 300: currenty = 600
ForeColor = QBColor(8)
Print "Offset Lines Produce"
currentx = 320: currenty = 630
ForeColor = QBColor(15)
Print "Offset Lines Produce"

currentx = 300: currenty = 1200
ForeColor = QBColor(8)
Print "Attractive Borders"
fontsize = 24
currentx = 340: currenty = 1250
ForeColor = QBColor(15)
Print "Attractive Borders"
End Sub
```

Line Properties
BorderColor • BorderStyle • BorderWidth • DrawMode • Index
Name • Parent • Tag • Visible • X1, X2, Y1, Y2

Line Events
A Line has no Events.

Line Methods
Move • Refresh • ZOrder

See also   Frame; Line *Method*; Shape

L INE   METHOD

Description   Draws lines, Boxes and Filled Boxes. Using Line you can create attractive frames and other surfaces on your Forms. In this entry, we're going to do some worthwhile things with Line.

Used with   Forms, Picture Boxes and the printer

Variables   **To draw a single line:**

```
Line (StartX, StartY) —(EndX, EndY)
```

For instance,

```
Sub Form_Click ()
    DrawWidth = 3
    Line (300, 300)-(1000, 300)
End Sub
```

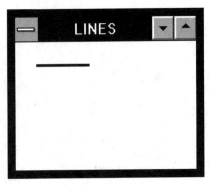

Figure L-18: A simple single horizontal line.

To define the color of a line:

```
Line(X,Y) - (EndX,EndY), QBColor(3)
```

To create a box:

```
Sub Form_Click ()
    DrawWidth = 3
    Line (300, 300)-(1000, 800), , B
End Sub
```

Notice that the coordinates (startingX, startingY) – (endingX, endingY) now define the upper left corner and lower right corner of a box.

Notice, too, that we left out the color definition but had to provide a space for it anyway by using two commas before the B. The B creates a box.

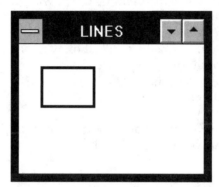

Figure L-19: The Line command can also draw squares and rectangles.

To draw a filled box:

```
Sub Form_Click ()
    DrawWidth = 3
    Line (300, 300)–(1000, 800), , BF
End Sub
```

The F causes the box to be filled with whatever color was used to draw the line. If no color is specified, the box is filled with the current FillColor Property (which defaults to black unless you specify otherwise).

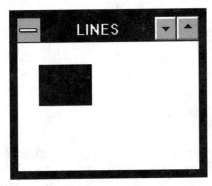

Figure L-20: You can fill rectangles with the current FillColor.

You can use B without F, which will fill your box with the current FillColor and in the current FillStyle. *Unless you change FillStyle, however, it defaults to "Transparent" and your box will not be filled. The background will show through.* Normally, to fill a box with color, you'll want to use FillStyle = 0 (which makes the fill style "Solid").

You cannot use F without also using B.

There is no comma between B and F.

To draw several boxes, each new box's location relative to the location of the previous box:

```
Sub Form_Click ()

DrawWidth = 3

For I = 1 To 5
    Line Step(75, 100)–Step(300, 200), , BF
Next I

End Sub
```

The Step command means move X and Y *away from the previous X and Y.* Without Step, the X and Y positions are relative to the container—the Form in this case—with 0,0 being the top left corner of the Form.

But *when the optional Step command is added*, a coordinate of 0,0 is the X,Y coordinate of the previously drawn box. To be precise, when using Step, the starting X,Y of the Box or Line will be CurrentX,Y *plus* whatever number you give to starting X,Y. The ending X,Y will be *relative* to the starting X,Y of that Box or Line.

The CurrentX and CurrentY Properties are updated each time a Box (or Line, Circle, PSet or Print command) is drawn. In the case of Lines, the endpoint X, Y becomes the new CurrentX and CurrentY. This is what Step uses to calculate the new offset for the next box. In this next example, the circle is drawn at CurrentX, CurrentY after the final box is drawn and establishes their new location:

```
Sub Form_Click ()
DrawWidth = 1
For I = 1 To 5
    Line Step(30, 200)–Step(200, 200), , B
Next I
Circle (currentx, currenty), 100
End Sub
```

Uses

• Create subtle, shaded frames behind your Controls. Most commercial software uses such frames, and VB provides one example in the Command Button. (See the Examples that follow for two valuable Subroutines you can add to your VB programs–DrawFrameOn and Emboss.)

• Create various background wallpaper patterns by enclosing the Line command within For...Next Statements. Using the For...Next Counter (the I in For I = 1 to 100), you can create various offsets for Step. You can create Mondrian-like effects by randomizing the X,Y positions, and by using Rnd with the colors as well.

• Draw visual frames around Control groups and use different line widths and colors to highlight portions of a Form.

• Make data entry boxes look like they are organized as a table. Or put a grid over a group of boxes.

• Use Line to draw graphs.

Cautions

• If you don't specify that the Line goes to a Picture Box or the printer (Picture1.Line or Printer.Line), the Line will be drawn on the Form.

• The measurements of X and Y are in twips, unless you specify otherwise using the Scale Method or the ScaleMode Property. There are 1,440 twips per inch. (See "ScaleMode.")

• The starting X,Y coordinates for a Line are optional. If you leave them out, CurrentX and CurrentY are used. The ending X,Y are required. Therefore, the most brief command to create a line is

```
Line –(150, 200)
```

which starts the line at 0,0 on the Form unless you have caused CurrentX or CurrentY to change by previously drawing something on the Form, or by directly changing CurrentX,Y:

```
Sub Form_Click ()
    DrawWidth = 5
    Line –(600, 300)
End Sub
```

Figure L-21: Drawing diagonal lines

• If you leave out the color you want used, a line will be drawn with the current ForeColor Property. A Filled Box (BF) will be filled with the Fore-Color. However, a regular Box (the B without the F) will be filled with the current *FillColor* Property—*and it will be invisible unless you also set the FillStyle Property to something other than its default 1 ("Transparent").* Try 0 for solid FillStyles, or 2–7 for various patterns such as crosshatches.

• You can create irregular geometric patterns by utilizing the fact that CurrentX and CurrentY are always the endpoint of the previously drawn Line:

```
Sub Form_Click ()

Randomize

For I = 1 To 40
X = Int(2000 * Rnd)
Y = Int(2000 * Rnd)

Line — (X, Y)

Next I

End Sub
```

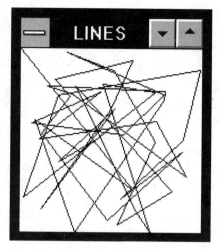

Figure L-22: Random, connected lines drawn with the Line and Rnd commands.

Adding , , B to the above Line command causes the Lines to shape into Boxes:

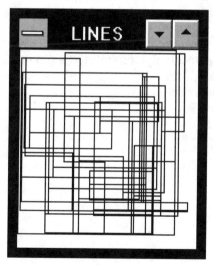

Figure L-23: When you add the B option to the Line command, box shapes occur.

(Note that if the AutoRedraw Property of the Form or Picture Box is off (0), then you need to redraw your lines in the Paint Event. If there are only a few lines, this is a better approach than having VB do the repainting automatically–the Paint Event would be faster and would use up less memory.)

Examples **How to Draw 3D Frames**

The following Subroutines can add a sophisticated, professional look to any of your Visual Basic programs.

They are variously called *Relief, Embossing, Metallic, "The 'Next' Look."* Whatever they're called, these attractive drawn lines and boxes lend a finished look to any application. Visual Basic's Command Button is an example of a simple raised frame; nearly all commercial programs employ them extensively.

The idea is, in principle, easily understood. *Set the BackColor of a Form and all objects within the Form to light gray* and draw a box around the objects, filling the box with light gray. Then draw a white line across the top and left sides, a similar dark gray line across the bottom and right sides. Then surround the whole thing with a thin, 1-pixel-wide black line.

There are several variations. To make the frame appear to recess into the Form, reverse the white and dark gray lines, and leave out the exterior black line. If you're framing something with a white interior, such as a Text Box, put the thin black line *inside* the white and dark gray lines.

You can draw one frame on top of another (as long as you draw the bigger frame first). To create a look like sculpted molding, draw several frames within a larger frame, adjusting their widths in various ways, and varying their styles ("inward" vs. "outward").

Figure L-24: Create attractive borders and frames around your graphics with the DrawFrameOn Subroutine described below.

An All-Purpose Framing Subroutine

Instead of figuring out the dimensions of each frame, and worrying about the other details of drawing these boxes, we'll use an all-purpose Subroutine. One of its advantages is that you don't have to measure anything or provide any coordinates. The Subroutine itself will draw all styles of embossed frames—you just tell it which Control or Controls you want framed, whether you want the frame "inward" or "outward" and how wide you want the frame to be.

Here is how the frames on the above example were created:

```
Sub Form_Load ()

Show

Drawframeon Picture6, Picture7, "outward", 200
Drawframeon Label4, Label4, "outward", 50
Drawframeon Picture5, Picture5, "outward", 150
Drawframeon Picture5, Picture5, "inward", 50
Drawframeon Picture2, Picture8, "inward", 20

End Sub
```

Sometimes you'll want to adjust the position of the Frames by adding additional Picture Boxes (or use Image Controls to speed up your program) but making their Visible Property 0. These Picture Boxes can't be seen when the program runs, but you can stick them around like Post-It Notes on the Form when designing and hang frames on them. This gives you finer control over the location and size of some framing jobs. In particular, when framing several Controls that are not lined up symmetrically, the Draw-FrameOn Routine may not produce the frame you are after. But it's simple to paste some invisible "pictures" around and give their names to the DrawFrameOn Routine. Here's how this looks while you are designing:

Figure L-25: Place invisible Controls around a graphic for special effects the DrawFrameOn Subroutine can frame invisible Controls as well as visible ones.

The DrawFrameOn Subroutine

Start a new project from the File Menu in VB. Type the following into a Form's General Declarations section.

Then, from the File Menu, select Save Text. Call it "Frame.txt" or something. Now you can use the Framing Subroutine in any program by selecting Load Text from the File Menu, then selecting Merge.

Make sure that this first line, starting with Sub and ending with Frame-width, is all on one line (don't hit the ENTER key). Likewise, put all the Variables following the Line command on the same line.

```
Sub DrawFrameOn (TopLeftControl As Control, LowestRightControl As →
   Control, Style As String, Framewidth)
' remember the drawwidth, fillstyle, and scalemode so we can restore →
   them at the end
dw = drawwidth
fs = fillstyle
sm = scalemode

drawwidth = 1
fillstyle = 1
scalemode = 1

st$ = LCase$(Left$(Style$, 1))

Lft = TopLeftControl.left
Toplft = TopLeftControl.top
Hite = TopLeftControl.Height

Rite = LowestRightControl.left + LowestRightControl.Width
Ritebotm = LowestRightControl.top + LowestRightControl.Height

'Use tallest Control as Y
If Ritebotm > Hite Then Hite = Ritebotm

'Draw a Thick Box
Line (Lft - Framewidth, Toplft — Framewidth)—(Rite + Framewidth,→
   Ritebotm + Framewidth), QBColor(7), BF

'Draw Highlight and Shadow lines
lt = 15: rb = 8

If st$ = "i" Then lt = 8: rb = 15
Line (Lft — Framewidth, Toplft — Framewidth) — (Rite + Framewidth,→
   Toplft — Framewidth), QBColor(lt)

Line (Lft — Framewidth, Toplft — Framewidth) — (Lft — Framewidth, Hite ↔
   Framewidth), QBColor(lt)

Line (Rite + Framewidth, Toplft — Framewidth) — (Rite + Framewidth,→
   Ritebotm + Framewidth), QBColor(rb)

Line (Rite + Framewidth, Ritebotm + Framewidth) — (Lft — Framewidth,→
   Hite + Framewidth), QBColor(rb)

If st$ <> "i" Then

Line (Lft — Framewidth — 25, Toplft — Framewidth — 25) — (Rite ↔
   Framewidth + 10, Ritebotm + Framewidth + 10), QBColor(0), B
End If

drawwidth = dw
fillstyle = fs
scalemode = sm
End Sub
```

This *is* a bit of typing, but you'll probably use this Subroutine quite often. (Be sure to remember to type the Line commands, with all their Variables, on a single line without hitting the ENTER key.)

Variations Using DrawFrameOn: *For the DrawFrameOn effects to work correctly, you must set the BackColor of your Form to light gray. This is the most commonly used color in Windows programs.* It is the gray right below white in the VB Color Palette. However, you can adjust the BackColor (and the QBColors inside DrawFrameOn) for special effects.

1. If you want a frame drawn around a single Control, give its Name twice:

    DrawFrameOn Text1, Text1, "Inward", 200

2. To draw a frame around two or more Controls, give the Name of the Control first in the upper left of the group, then the lower right Name. To frame a group of five Command Buttons, for instance:

    DrawFrameOn Command1, Command5, "Outward", 150

3. To superimpose frames, draw the bigger one(s) first:

    Sub Form_Load ()

    Show

    DrawFrameOn Command1, Command3, "Outward", 800
    DrawFrameOn Command1, Command3, "Inward", 100

    End Sub

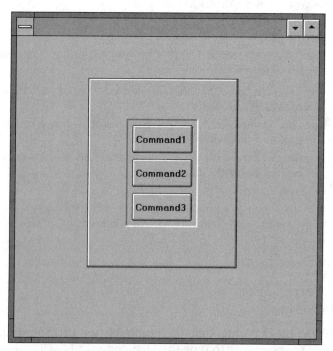

Figure L-26: You can create this effect by superimposing one frame on top of another.

4. For more dramatic frames, change the DrawWidth in DrawFrameOn from
   1 to 2:

   Drawwidth = 2

You can get a delicate effect by "commenting out" the final thin black
line. Commenting out means inserting a single-quote symbol in your program. Anything following the ' symbol on a line will be ignored by VB.
That's how you can add comments to your programs, and you won't have to
worry that VB will try to interpret them as if they were instructions it should
follow. Commenting out is also a good way to try different things without
having to remove and replace part of your programming. Here we'll comment out the outer black line so it won't be drawn:

```
If St$ <> "i" Then
'Line (Lft − Framewidth − 25, Toplft − Framewidth − 25) − (Rite →
   Framewidth + 10, Ritebotm + Framewidth + 10), QBColor(0), B
End If
```

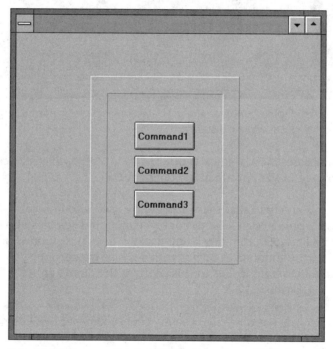

Figure L-27: You can fiddle with the DrawFrameOn Subroutine
to get subtle effects like this.

5. Create molding effects by giving several frames similar Framewidths:

Figure L-28: Moldings are generated by nesting several frames sizing them close to each other but at varying distances.

Frames nested within each other, 100 or 200 twips (see ScaleMode) difference in size, produce molding effects.

6. Here's an effect that's also frequently used in commercial applications to give a punched-in look to control panels and selection boxes. The DrawFrameOn thin black line usually looks best *moved inside* the frame, if you are framing an object with a white background. To do this, make the following changes to this piece of the DrawFrameOn Subroutine:

```
'If St$ <> "i" Then
    Line (Lft — Framewidth + 10, Toplft — Framewidth + 10) — (Rite ↔
        Framewidth — 25, Ritbotm + Framewidth — 25), QBColor(0), B
'End If
```

Note that we "commented out" the If...End If, since we do want the black line this time, even though we normally don't with "inward" frame styles. We also adjusted the +10s and –25s, to move the black line inside the frame.

For this effect, give DrawFrameOn a very small Framewidth, so the frame butts up against the contained object:

```
DrawFrameOn picture1, picture1, "inward", 10
```

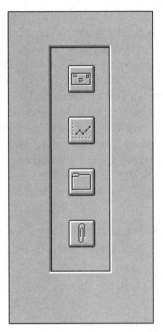

Figure L-29: A Button-Bar effect the sunken look is created by temporarily removing a line from the DrawFrameOn Subroutine.

7. Also try adjusting the DrawWidth, QBColor and other commands inside the DrawFrameOn Subroutine. For instance, to allow the background—perhaps a graphic on the Form itself—to show through a frame, change the BF (box fill) to a simple B (box). But do beware of using too many colors. Color theorists have said that riotous color on a window's Controls is not only confusing to the viewer, but also defeats the purpose of *occasional* subtle color that is used to draw attention to special situations and as an accent in the overall design. Also, try removing the line that sets the FillStyle to 0 ("Solid"). FillStyle will then default to "Transparent" (unless your program adjusts it before you get to the DrawFrameOn Subroutine).

8. To make frames when a group of Controls is arranged asymmetrically, or where there are no Controls, put two tiny Picture Boxes on the Form and set their Visible Property Off (0). Position them where you will, like Post-It Notes, and provide their Names as the argument for DrawFrameOn:

    DrawFrameOn Picture7, Picture8, "inward", 400

The Emboss Subroutine—Embossed or Etched Frames: *For the Emboss effects to work correctly, you must set the BackColor of your Form to light gray. This is the most commonly used color in Windows programs. It is the gray right below white in the VB Color Palette.*

This style of frame is also popular in commercial programs. It consists of very thin, three-dimensional lines which appear to have been raised out of (embossed), or carved into (etched), the window's background.

Here's another Subroutine you can type in and save as Text for importing into any VB program you are writing. Start a new project from the File Menu in VB. Type the following into a Form's General Declarations section. Then, from the File Menu, select Save Text. Call it "Emboss.txt" or something. Now you can use the Embossing Subroutine in any program by selecting Load Text from the File Menu, then selecting Merge.

Make sure that this first line, starting with Sub and ending with Integer, is all on one line (don't press the ENTER key). Likewise, put all the Variables following the Line command on the same line:

```
Sub emboss (DoWhat As Control, Style As String, FrameSize As Integer)
    ' First make sure that you set the Form's BackColor to light gray (the white
    ' frame in this Subroutine won't show up against a white background)
DrawWidth = 1
    ' Decide whether to make it "Embossed" or "Etched" based on the Style
    ' requested "inner" or "outer"
If Left$(LCase$(Style), 1) = "o" Then
    cg = 15: c2 = 8
Else
    cg = 8: c2 = 15
End If
    ' Set the frame distances relative to the Control
DoWhat.BackColor = QBColor(7)
x = DoWhat.left − 46 − FrameSize
y = DoWhat.top − 46 − FrameSize
x1 = DoWhat.left + DoWhat.width + 26 + FrameSize
y1 = DoWhat.top + DoWhat.Height + 26 + FrameSize
    ' Draw the first frame
Line (x, y) − (x1, y1), QBColor(cg), B
    ' Draw the second frame down and to the right
Line (x + 14, y + 14) − (x1 + 20, y1 + 20), QBColor(c2), B
    ' Add dots to make two of the corners look smooth
    ' (Only Used with the "embossed" style)
If cg = 15 Then
    PSet (x1, y + 14), QBColor(cg)
    PSet (x + 14, y1), QBColor(cg)
End If
End Sub
```

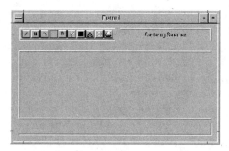

Figure L-30: A Button Bar surrounded by an "etched" style frame. Three other frames, two "embossed" and one "etched."

Figure L-30 was created with the following commands:

```
Sub Form_Load ()

w = picture1(0).width

For i = 1 To 9
    Load picture1(i)
    picture1(i).left = picture1(i − 1).left + w + 10
    picture1(i).visible = −1

Next i

picture1(1).picture = LoadPicture("c:\vbasic\bitmaps\toolbar\bld-up.bmp")
picture1(2).picture = LoadPicture("c:\vbasic\bitmaps\toolbar\arc-up.bmp")
picture1(3).picture = LoadPicture("c:\vbasic\bitmaps\toolbar\ →
  cnt-dwn.bmp")
picture1(4).picture = LoadPicture("c:\vbasic\bitmaps\toolbar\ →
  dblu-up.bmp")
picture1(5).picture = LoadPicture("c:\vbasic\bitmaps\toolbar\ →
  hlp-inac.bmp")
picture1(6).picture = LoadPicture("c:\vbasic\bitmaps\toolbar\jst-up.bmp")
picture1(7).picture = LoadPicture("c:\vbasic\bitmaps\toolbar\mcr-up.bmp")
picture1(8).picture = LoadPicture("c:\vbasic\bitmaps\toolbar\ →
  ovl-inac.bmp")
picture1(9).picture = LoadPicture("c:\vbasic\bitmaps\toolbar\prt-up.bmp")

Show

emboss frame1, "inward", 20
emboss frame2, "outward", 10
emboss frame3, "outward", 10
emboss frame4, "inward", 10

x = frame2.width / 2
a$ = "Centering Selected"
t = TextWidth(a$) / 2
currentx = (frame2.left + x) − t
currenty = frame2.top + 50
Print a$

End Sub
```

Metallic Gradients

Though not an effect created by the Line command, metallic gradients look so attractive that we wanted to describe the technique here.

One of the best ways to avoid dull-looking Forms is to use metallic shading. It's subtle and conservative enough for any business application, yet considerably more attractive than plain gray.

We've included on the disk for this book several gradients you can put into the Picture Property of 3D button Controls (Sheridan's 3D Controls) and Forms, but you can make your own with Corel Photo-Paint, Picture Publisher or most any photo-retouching program. It's easy to create gradients. Here's how to do it.

The best metallic gradient is a gradual shift between two shades: white and the typical Windows gray (the light 25% gray often used as BackColor; the same gray that's used on the VB Command Button and many other Controls). Another, somewhat more powerful, effect can be achieved by using the darker, 50% gray used to shadow Command Buttons and other Controls.

So to capture a gray that will fit in with VB's (and Windows's) color scheme, put a Command Button on a Form, and then press ALT+PrintScreen to capture the Form to the Clipboard. Then open a photo-retouching program like Photoshop or Corel's PhotoPaint. From the Edit menu, select Paste to bring in the Form.

All retouching programs have a "color picker" tool. It sometimes looks like an eyedropper. Use it to select the color of the Command Button's shadow, thereby placing it into the main color selection. Change the alternate color (sometimes called "backcolor" or "secondary color") to white. (If you don't want to use the picker, adjust the main color directly to shadow gray by setting RGB to 75% each, or to white, by setting RGB to 100% each. If you're specifying colors in CYMK rather than RGB, the percentages for gray are 25% for the first three and 0% for K.)

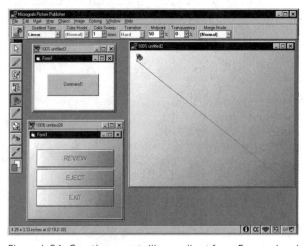

Figure L-31: Creating a metallic gradient for a Form s background.

Now create a new graphic (File|New Menu) and drag your gradient so that the gray shadow is strongest in the lower right corner and white is strongest in the upper left corner. Use the linear gradient option (not circular, radial or some other type). Save the results to disk as a .BMP file for later use. Also make several differing sizes of small gradients as .BMP files to load into the Picture Property of 3D Command Buttons.

Figure L-32: Metallic gradients are conservative yet sophisticated. Here we ve used 50% gray. For a less dramatic sheen, use 25% gray.

Figure L-32 illustrates how metallic gradients look on a Form and on 3D Command Buttons. To add gradients to a Sheridan 3D Panel (which has no Picture Property), just put an Image Control inside the panel and size it almost to the edges, but preserve the panel framing. Then load your gradient .BMP file into the Image.

See also   Circle; DrawMode; DrawStyle; DrawWidth; Line (Control); Print (to see how to create shaded text); PSet; Shape

LINE INPUT

STATEMENT

Description   Line Input # can be a useful way of getting information from a disk file. It reads in a single "line" of text—all characters up to the "Carriage Return." Line Input # strips off the Carriage Return (and Line Feed) codes and provides you with a clean, single line of text. (A Carriage Return plus Line Feed is a two-byte text code that indicates the user pressed the ENTER key, intending to move down one line.)

The practical alternative to Line Input # is Input$, which works much the same way but leaves the CR and LF codes. Using Input$ you get an exact image of the text. If you saved a Text Box's text to a disk file, you might want to read it back into a Text Box with the CR and LF codes where they were. Using Input$ you can read back the text because it doesn't strip off the codes.

Used with   • Sequential files containing text (character-based) information. This type of file has individual records of varying length. It is useful for storing word processor-type data and can also store numbers (but stores them in a printable, rather than computable, format).

To turn "printable" text numbers (digits) back into computable numbers so you can add, divide and otherwise manipulate them mathematically, you use the Val Function.

For more about the various kinds of disk files, see "Open."

Variables   Line Input #1, X$

Each time Line Input is used (within a Do...Loop or other structure), it pulls in the next piece of text from an Opened file, a file identified in this example as #1. Line Input # makes its decision about the length of the new line by stopping when it finds a pair of Carriage Return/Line Feed characters. These characters are added to a text Variable when the user hits the ENTER key, so this is a natural way to store information typed into a Text Box.

Line Input # *removes* the Carriage Return/Line Feed characters before storing the line in X$. Removing the characters allows you to analyze the line within your program without worrying about the existence of two extraneous characters at the end of each piece of data. You get the text Variable in its purest state. However, if you are pulling in X$ lines to print them, you will probably want to restore CR/LF to the end of each line so that the text will be printed with the line breaks where the user entered them:

```
CRLF$ = Chr$(13) + Chr$(10)
X$ = X$ + CRLF$
```

Uses
- Line Input # is used for reading information from a sequential file (see "Open"), especially when the information therein is stored as *text*.

- The Line Input # command works well for importing fixed-format data into a VB application. Say you have an old application you are converting to a VB program, but the data for that program is in an unknown format. First, have the old application save a copy of all its data to a disk file. Figure out how the pieces of data are separated (by commas, Carriage Returns, spaces, zeros or whatever). Then use Line Input # to read each line into your VB program and break the lines into the Variables you want to store them into inside your VB application.

Cautions
- Because Line Input # removes the Chr$(13) and Chr$(10) Carriage Return/Line Feed characters when it reads in a line from a file, you'll need to *put them back onto the line* if you want them to appear in a Text Box in the format the user originally intended. (See "Variables" above.) Reinserting Carriage Return/Line Feed characters is only necessary if you are building a single large Variable by adding each line to it. However, a Text Box requires this because it contains only one big text Variable–Text1.Text:

```
Do While Not EOF(1)
    Line Input #1, X$
        Text1.Text = Text1.Text + CRLF$ + X$
Loop
```

By contrast, you can use the Print command to display text on Forms, Picture Boxes and the printer. The Print command automatically adds a CR/LF each time you use it (if you don't append a comma or semicolon). If you Print each line as it comes in, you don't need to add a CRLF$. The following example Prints your SYSTEM.INI file to the printer:

```
Sub Form_Click ()

Open "C:\WINDOWS\SYSTEM.INI" For Input As #1

Do While Not EOF(1)

    Line Input #1, X$
    Printer.Print X$
Loop

Printer.EndDoc

Close

End Sub
```

Example
In this example, we tell the user which display driver is being used to control what he or she sees on the screen. That information is in the SYSTEM.INI file, following the words "display.drv=":

```
Sub Form_Click ()
On Error Resume Next
Open "C:\WINDOWS\SYSTEM.INI" For Input As #1
If Err GoTo Problem
Do While Not EOF(1) And I = 0
    Line Input #1, X$
L = InStr(LCase$(X$), "display.drv")
Loop
L = InStr(X$, "=")
X$ = Right$(X$, Len(X$) - L)
MsgBox ("The name of your display driver is: " + X$)
Close
Exit Sub
Problem:
    Close
    MsgBox(Error$(Err))
End Sub
```

Line Input # can pull in a single line at a time from a disk file.

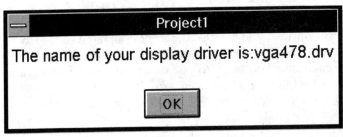

Figure L-33: Here we look in the SYSTEM.INI file to find out which video display driver is currently in use.

First, we tell VB what to do if there is a problem: simply continue down the list of instructions ("resume next instruction"). Normally, we would let Basic complete all the commands in the entire Sub and wait until the end to report any error with the following:

```
If Err Then MsgBox(Error$(Err))
```

However, because we are using a Do...Loop, the program would get hung up inside that Loop if the file cannot be opened. Perhaps the user has Windows on Drive D: or something. So we check for an error immediately after attempting to Open, but prior to entering, the Loop. If an error is found, we go down to the section we labeled Problem: and deal with it.

Otherwise, we continue to read in each line within the Opened file (that we named file #1) until one of two things happens—either we reach the end of the file (EOF) or our InStr pointer L no longer equals 0. The pointer will contain the position in a line if it finds a match to "display.drv." Because InStr will not match unless the capitalization is identical, we force X\$ to be all lowercase letters and search for "display.drv" with lowercase letters as well.

Information in .INI files is generally stored in this fashion:

```
display.drv=vga478.drv
```

Therefore, we move our pointer L to the location of the equals sign (=) and then extract the characters between L and the end, the length (Len) of X\$.

See also   Close; Input #; Input\$; Open; Print #

L INKCLOSE   EVENT

Description   This Event takes place when either side of a DDE conversation terminates the conversation and breaks the "Link."

The various "Link" commands work with *Dynamic Data Exchange* (DDE), a facility provided within Windows. This facility is rather like an automated Clipboard; DDE-ready programs can copy information between each other while they are running, exchanging text, pictures and even commands—independently of the user.

For example, instead of the user selecting some text, choosing the Edit Menu, choosing Copy, then switching to the target application, choosing Edit, choosing Paste—all of these steps can be automated.

Automating these steps has broad implications: in essence, it means that one program can control the behavior of another.

For a full discussion of Linking and DDE, see "LinkMode."

Used with   Forms, Picture Boxes and Text Boxes

Variables   The LinkClose Event is triggered when one of the programs that is engaged in a DDE conversation "hangs up the phone," breaking the Link. Because Link-Close is an Event, you can add programming within this Event if you choose.

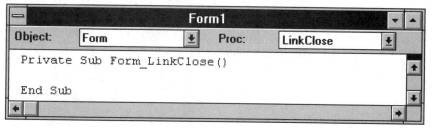

Figure L-34: LinkClose is triggered when one party "hangs up the phone" during a Link.

Uses   • You can build user control over Links into your programs. You can allow the user to establish Links or to break them.

You might want your program to notify the user that a Link has been terminated (the most common use for the LinkClose Event). However, because linking has wide-ranging possibilities, you might also want to use LinkClose to inform other parts of your program that a conversation has ended. You might want your program to respond by reestablishing the Link, for example, or otherwise reacting to the Event.

Changing the LinkTopic Property of either program engaged in a DDE conversation breaks the Link between them, causing a LinkClose Event.

Cautions   • Linking is an evolving feature of Windows. It has not fully stabilized, and only a few programs currently respond to Links—most notably Word for Windows, Excel, and any Visual Basic programs that have been written to include linking facilities.

Linking is not yet standardized. For instance, the Field Code for a Link was called "DDE" in Word for Windows V.1 and is called "Link" in Word for Windows V.2.

The naming convention—what you call each Link to identify it within the program that's receiving data over the Link—is also unstable at this time. The format for naming the Link always groups three names: Program/Topic/Item. This group is like a unique telephone number for a particular Link. It is composed of the program name, the name you gave the Link-Topic property and, finally, the LinkItem (which is the name of the Control that is providing information to be transferred across the Link).

However, different link-capable programs punctuate these three name elements differently. When establishing the location of a Link within a document in Word for Windows, a typical Link might be referred to as VBPROGRAM Phrase Text1. Excel would punctuate this differently: VBPROGRAM|Phrase!Text1. And VB has yet a *third* way of punctuating the full name of a Link: VBPROGRAM|Phrase.

Example   The simplest possible Link—and it is startlingly easy to create—involves using the Properties Window to set two Properties of the Form that *send* information and setting three Properties of the Control that *receive* that information. (This can be done while a program is running.) You know how easy it is to set Properties in VB. Let's create two programs that will instantly interact simply because a Link has been established between them.

• First, create a New Project from the VB File Menu. Put a Text Box on Form1 and in the Properties Window set the *Form's* LinkTopic to "Hello":

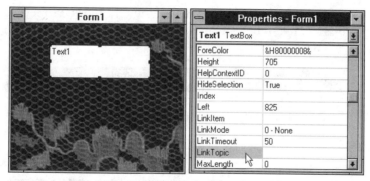

Figure L-35: To prepare for the simplest link conversation between two programs, set the LinkTopic of the Form that's going to *send* information.

• Second, set the Form's LinkMode to 1 to make this program the *server* or *source*; the program that's providing information to others (these others are referred to as the *clients, destinations,* or *containers*). Set Form1's Caption Property to "PROVIDER," just for clarity–it's not necessary.

That's it. From the VB File Menu, select Make EXE and call this program "Provider."

• Finally, we will create the client, a program that will "place a call" to Provider whenever the client is run. If Provider isn't running under Windows when the call is placed, a message will automatically inform the user that no Link could be established. This is why *you want a server to be running when a client is started up*–if you intend for them to link up.

Select New Project from the VB File Menu. Put a Label on Form1. Now, all we have to do is set three Properties of Label1 (note that in a destination program, we adjust the properties of the receptor *Control*, not the *Form*).

We want Label1 to receive data across the Link from the program we named "Provider," from the Text1 Control on Provider. Set Label1's Link-Topic Property to PROVIDER|Hello. The first name is the name of the server program; the second name is the LinkTopic we gave to Form1 in the server program. They are separated by the "pipe" character, a vertical line which, on most keyboards, is the shifted backslash (\) key.

Now set Label1's LinkItem to Text1 (the LinkItem is the Control on the Provider that will be the source of information sent across the Link). We want any changes to Provider's Text Box to appear in our new client program's Label. Set the Form's Caption Property to "CLIENT" and put the following into the LinkClose Event of Label1:

```
Sub Label1_LinkClose ()

MsgBox ("The Link from Provider Has Been Broken")
End Sub
```

Now, the mad scientist pulls the switch! In the Properties Window set Label1's LinkMode to 1. As soon as you do, you get a message right out of Star Trek:

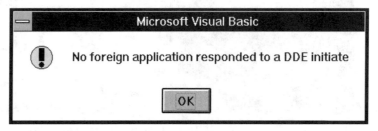

Figure L-36: The other program must be running for a Link to take place.

VB is a running program, and when you set a LinkMode Property to 1 (Automatic), the Link call is placed at once, even though you haven't run the client program yet. Because the VB design environment is a running program, you can test your Links—and you can use the Clipboard for testing as well because it acts as the "telephone exchange" during linking.

Ignore the message you see in Figure L-36. We must set the LinkMode in the running program, so put this in the Form_Load Event: Label1.LinkMode = 1. Now from the File Menu, select Make EXE File. Call this one "Client," and save it to disk. Now exit VB. Run Provider. Then Run Client. Watch what happens when you type things into Text1 on Provider.

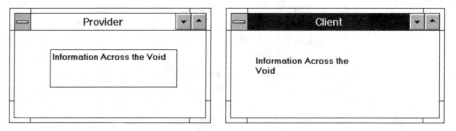

Figure L-37: One program sending a message to another program across a Link

Closing the Provider will trigger our LinkClose Event in the Label on Client:

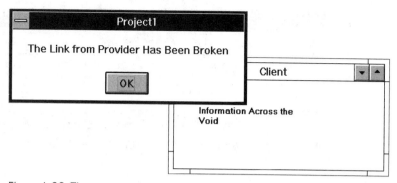

Figure L-38: The message says that the caller has hung up the phone.

See also   LinkError; LinkExecute; LinkItem; LinkMode; LinkNotify; LinkOpen; LinkPoke; LinkRequest (Event and Method); LinkSend; LinkTimeout; LinkTopic; OLE

LINKERROR

EVENT

Description   LinkError reports problems caused by *outside programs* linked to your VB program. Link problems caused by your VB program are handled in the normal way VB performs error handling—using On Error, Err and Error$ (which see).

However, VB cannot directly trap Link errors caused by foreign programs, such as Excel, when they are engaged in a "Link conversation" with your VB program. The LinkError Event, though, provides a way. See Cautions for a more complete description of the difference between normal VB error trapping and LinkError.

There are 12 errors that can be caused by an outside program during a Link, and, should such an error happen, the LinkError Event is triggered and reports which error it was. For a full discussion of linking and DDE, see "LinkMode."

Used with   Forms, Labels, Picture Boxes, Text Boxes

Variables   The LinkError Event returns a code, called LinkErr, which is a number between 1 and 12 identifying the type of Link error that triggered the Event. See the Example.

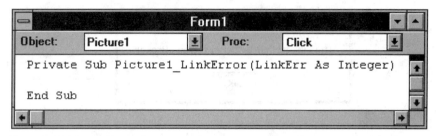

Figure L-39: The LinkError Event provides an error code if a problem occurs during a Link conversation.

LinkError Codes

1 The other application has requested data in the wrong format.
2 Another application requested data without first initiating a DDE conversation.
3 Another application attempted to perform DDE without first initiating a DDE conversation.
4 Another application attempted to change the Item for a nonexistent DDE conversation.
5 Another application attempted to poke data without first initiating a DDE conversation.
6 The other application attempted to continue performing DDE after you set the LinkMode on your server Form to 0.
7 Too many DDE Links.
8 A string was too long to be transferred through DDE and was truncated.
9 A client specified an invalid Control Array element as the Item in a DDE conversation.
10 Another application sent an unexpected DDE message.
11 Not enough memory for DDE.
12 The server application in a DDE conversation attempted to perform client operations.

Uses
• When you are testing your programs, LinkErr codes can provide you with valuable information about the nature of a Link problem.

• Inform the user of the nature of the linking problem, and permit him or her to make adjustments to correct the problem.

• Allow your program itself to make adjustments that will establish a viable Link.

Cautions
• LinkError Events cannot occur as the result of your Visual Basic program itself. They are problems generated by outside applications engaged in Link conversation with a VB program. LinkError Events do not occur when any VB program code is running.

Instead, and conveniently, a Link problem within your VB program is reported in the usual VB error-handling fashion—by triggering Err, Error$, etc. (which see). Link errors *interior* to your VB program are reported directly in the Err code as code numbers 280–297:

280 DDE channel not fully closed; awaiting response from foreign application.
281 No more DDE channels.
282 No foreign application responded to a DDE initiate.
283 Multiple applications responded to a DDE initiate.
284 DDE channel locked.
285 Foreign application won't perform DDE method or operator.
286 Timeout while waiting for DDE response.
287 User pressed ALT key during DDE operation.
288 Destination is busy.
289 Data not provided in DDE operation.
290 Data in wrong format.
291 Foreign application quit.
292 DDE conversation closed or changed.
293 DDE method invoked with no channel open.
294 Invalid DDE link format.
295 Message queue filled; DDE message lost.
296 PasteLink already performed on this Control.
297 Can't set LinkMode; Invalid LinkTopic.

However, because a Link is a two-way conversation, the program on the other end of the Link might not be a VB program. This error would be *exterior* to a VB program. Link Error Events are triggered when outside programs, such as Word for Windows, request an inappropriate Link Event or otherwise foul up a Link conversation. The outside program might try to send a picture to a Text Box, for example. Link Error is designed to recognize these errors coming from outside the VB program itself and allow you to respond.

Example If an outside program tries to get some text data from the following Picture Box, Case 1 would be triggered:

```
Sub Picture1_LinkError (Linkerr As Integer)

Select Case Linkerr
    Case 1
        m$ = "#1 Wrong data format requested."
    Case 2
        m$ = "#2 Data request prior to DDE initiation."
    Case 3
        m$ = "#3 Attempted DDE prior to DDE initiation."
    Case 4
        m$ = "#4 Attempted item change in nonexistent DDE conversation."
    Case 5
        m$ = "#5 Attempted Link Poke prior to DDE initiation."
    Case 6
        m$ = "#6 Attempted DDE after LinkMode = 0"
```

```
                    Case 7
                       m$ = "#7  Too many DDE Links."
                     Case 8
                       m$ = "#8  String too long. Truncated."
                    Case 9
                       m$ = "#9  Client requested invalid Control Array element."
                    Case 10
                       m$ = "#10 Unexpected DDE message."
                    Case 11
                       m$ = "#11 Not enough memory for DDE."
                    Case 12
                       m$ = "#12 Server attempted to perform Client operation."
                    Case Else
                       m$ = "Unrecognized DDE Code."
                  End Select

                  MsgBox ("DDE Error " + m$)

                  End Sub
```

See also   LinkClose; LinkExecute (Event and Method); LinkItem; LinkMode; LinkNotify;
LinkOpen; LinkPoke; LinkRequest; LinkSend; LinkTimeout; LinkTopic; OLE

LINKEXECUTE   EVENT

Description   The LinkExecute Event of a Form is triggered when another program—the
client or *destination* in a Link "conversation"—endeavors to control your
program. Your program must be the *server* or *source* in this conversation.

LinkExecute is the reverse of the normal way that data flows through a
Link. Normally, information flows across a Link from the source to the
destination. If you change some text in the source's Text Box, it causes the
Text Box in the destination to change simultaneously.

However, sending commands using LinkExecute works in the opposite
direction—the commands originate with the destination (using the LinkExecute Method, not the Event). The command flows from the destination to
the source, where it is detected in the source's LinkExecute *Event*. All this
is confusing at first, but a few examples will clear it up. It's worth learning
because linking (sending data and commands between programs) is an
especially powerful feature of Windows. And it is an important innovation.
Linking will be an increasingly common tool in future computing.

In any case, the LinkExecute happens when the destination program
sends a "command string" (not information, but an instruction, a command) to the source program. Your VB program, acting as a *source*, can
accept these commands and respond to them.

The reverse of the LinkExecute *Event* is the LinkExecute *Method* (which follows this entry). The Method sends a command to an outside program from your VB program, attempting to dominate the outside program with that command. See "LinkMode" for a general discussion about DDE and linking.

Used with   Forms only (and only those Forms designed to be "sources" in a DDE conversation)

Variables   Events are passive; they are triggered by things that happen while your VB program is running. The LinkExecute Event is triggered by an outside program (a destination program in the Link) trying to send a command to make your VB program (the source) respond by taking some action based on the command.

Two Variables are involved in the LinkExecute Event:

• *CmdStr* is a text Variable that the outside program sends to your VB program. Your program can then take action based on what that text command says.

• You *must* set Cancel to 0 within the source Form's LinkExecute Event; otherwise, there will be an error. *Cancel* is a number, an integer, which is sent back to the outside program (after the LinkExecute Event finishes) to inform it whether, or how, your VB program responded to the command. Although the VB *Language Reference* states that Cancel defaults to 0, it in fact defaults to –1. Unless you deliberately change it, Cancel will remain –1, signifying to the outside program that your VB program refused and did not respond to the command. If Cancel is anything other than 0, the outside program (the destination) is informed that the command was rejected by your VB program.

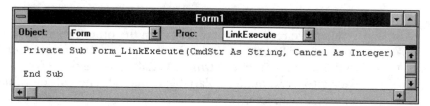

Figure L-40: The two built-in Variables available from within the LinkExecute Event CmdStr and Cancel.

Uses   Allow programs to send commands to each other while they are running. Normally, Links transfer information between two programs, but the LinkExecute Event (and Method) allow linked programs to control each other's behavior, not simply provide each other with graphics or text.

Cautions   • Cancel must be set to 0. (See the second item under "Variables" above.)

• You should always start the server program before the client program; this is true for any kind of linking.

• Because linking is still an evolving technology, there are no set standards for the punctuation and syntax of such elements as the CmdStr. Your VB program can receive a CmdStr, however, and analyze it any which way—responding appropriately.

Things get a bit more dicey when you are sending command strings to such programs as Excel and Word for Windows. They expect commands to arrive in their particular, and differing, macro language formats. See their respective reference books to learn how to send commands to which these programs will react.

• Because linking is still relatively unstable, you need to follow the instructions in the following example precisely. You cannot deviate until you more fully understand what is, and what is not, allowed during linking.

Example   We'll create two VB programs—a "source" that will accept commands within the Form's LinkExecute *Event* and a "destination" that will send commands by using the LinkExecute *Method*.

First, create a new project in VB and in the Form's Properties Window and set the LinkTopic to Ex. (You can use any name for a topic, but the second program's LinkTopic Property must match.) Then set the LinkMode to 1 (Source or Server). Now put a Text Box on the Form.

Put the following instructions into the Form's LinkExecute Event:

```
Sub Form_LinkExecute (CmdStr As String, Cancel As Integer)

Colr = Val(CmdStr)
BackColor = QBColor(Colr)

height = height + 200
width = width − 100

Cancel = 0
End Sub
```

When we receive a command from the other program, it will change the color of our Form and also make the Form taller and thinner. CmdStr comes to the server as a text ("string") Variable, as digits, so we have to change it back into a real numeric Variable using Val. The QBColor function requires a numeric Variable.

That's it. You've created a source program the color and size of which can be controlled by an outside program. Think of the potential this capability gives you—anything you can make a VB program do, you can allow a separate program to do to a source program.

Save this program as an EXE program called S.EXE.

Now we'll make the destination program. Create a new project in VB and put a Text Box on the Form. Change the Text Box's Text Property to "Press a number...." Then change its Name Property to "ClientText," so we can keep it separate in our mind from the source's text box.

Change the Text Box's LinkTopic Property to "S|Ex" (use no quotation marks). This refers to the name of the source (server) program, "S," and the name we gave the LinkTopic of the source, "Ex." They are separated by the "pipe" character (|), the vertical line symbol usually found as a shifted backslash (\) on your keyboard.

Change the Text Box's LinkItem to "Text1"—referring to the Control in the source program that is involved in the Link. Because we're using a Link to send commands in this example, we're not interested in changing the "destination" Text Box's text by typing into the source's Text Box. Creating a Text Box on the source is still necessary, however, because a Form has no LinkItem Property. And no Link can be established without a LinkItem.

Now, watch out. Change the Text Box's LinkMode Property to 1 (Automatic). Even though you're just designing a VB program, linking can still occur. You should now see an attempt to make a Link. The message in Figure L-39 should appear (because there is no source program running with the LinkTopic and LinkItem we are using). Just ignore this "nobody answers" message; we know that the source isn't running. In the Form_Load Event, put this: Text1.LinkMode = 1.

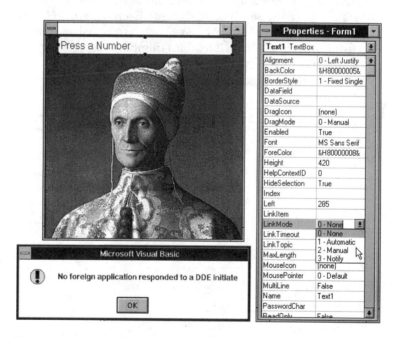

Figure L-41: Ignore this message for now.

Finally, put the following instructions into the Text Box's KeyPress Event. We will send commands from our destination (client) program to the dominated source (server) program with these instructions:

```
Sub ClientText_KeyPress (KeyAscii As Integer)
If KeyAscii < 48 Or KeyAscii > 57 Then
    KeyAscii = 0
Else
    K = KeyAscii — 48
    ClientText.LinkExecute Str$(K)
End If
End Sub
```

Here we are accepting keyboard input and translating it into a text ("string") Variable that we can send to the other program. When the user presses a key, we check the code of that key (see "KeyPress" for more on the ASCII code).

If the code is not a digit, we just ignore the keypress and End the Sub. If the pressed key is one of the number keys 0 through 9, we subtract 48 from the code, turning it into the correct real (non-text) number. Then we use the LinkExecute Method to send a text Variable to the source program. We had to translate the number into a text Variable using Str$ because the LinkExecute Method cannot send numeric Variables, only text ("string") Variables. Likewise, the LinkExecute Event cannot receive and interpret numeric Variables. But it's easy enough to translate numbers to strings (using Str$) and strings back into numbers (using Val).

Save this program as an EXE program called C.EXE.

To test transprogram domination, first run the S.EXE server program and then run the C.EXE program.

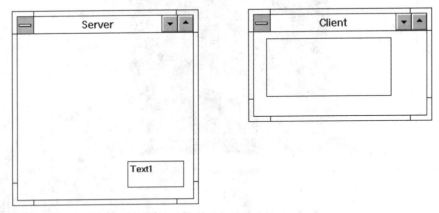

Figure L-42: First, run the source (server) program.

Then press some number keys into the destination (client) program's Text Box and watch the effect on the hapless source.

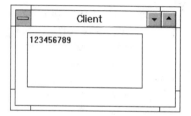

Figure L-43: The source (server) responds by changing colors and growing thinner.

For a more general discussion on the purpose and implications of linking, see "LinkMode."

See also   LinkClose; LinkError; LinkExecute (Method); LinkItem; LinkMode; LinkNotify; LinkOpen; LinkPoke; LinkRequest; LinkSend; LinkTimeout; LinkTopic; OLE

LINKEXECUTE

METHOD

Description   You use the LinkExecute Method to send a command from a "destination" (client) program to a "source" (server) program. (VB's terminology ["source" and "destination"] gets confusing with LinkExecute and LinkPoke because the ordinary direction of the data flow between linked programs is *reversed* in these two cases. In other words, LinkExecute sends a command *from* the "destination" *to* the "source" program.) Also, normally, we think of linking as allowing a change in some information—some text or graphics—within one program to update information automatically in a separate program. However, linking also permits the powerful capability of one program controlling another by sending commands to it.

A command tells the computer to *do something*, as opposed to conveying mere information such as text, which is useful, but, by itself, causes nothing to happen. Print is a command. "Larry" is information.

When you use the LinkExecute *Method* to send a command from a "destination" (client) program, the LinkExecute *Event* (which see) in the "source" (server) program receives that command and can react to it.

Linking is part of Dynamic Data Exchange (DDE), a powerful Windows capability. See "LinkMode" for more on DDE and linking.

Used with   Text Boxes, Picture Boxes, Labels

Variables   To send a text Variable:

```
Text1.LinkExecute "TurnOffButtons"
```

OR (to send a code for a command):

```
X$ = "[down]"
Label1.LinkExecute X$
```

When communicating between two VB programs, you can decide what command to send—how it is punctuated and what it means. However, if you are sending a command to a program such as Excel or Word for Windows, you have to follow the conventions of their macro languages, since it is their macro languages you'll be communicating with. See the manuals of non-VB programs for the punctuation and syntax required.

Uses   Allow one program to control the behavior of another—not pass text or graphics but, rather, issue commands describing how that program should *behave*.

Cautions   The command sent by LinkExecute must be sent as a text ("string") Variable, not a numeric Variable. However, you can transform a numeric Variable into a string with Str$( ) prior to sending it. Then, after it is received by the source (server) program in the Form's LinkExecute Event, the string can be translated back into a number with Val( ).

Example   See "LinkExecute Event"

See also   LinkClose; LinkError; LinkExecute (Event); LinkItem; LinkMode; LinkNotify; LinkOpen; LinkPoke; LinkRequest; LinkSend; LinkTimeout; LinkTopic; OLE

LINKITEM
PROPERTY

Description   There are two Properties which, together, identify a particular Link: LinkTopic plus LinkItem.

Combined, these Properties are similar to a telephone number that two linked programs can call. This "phone number" is unique to a particular Link.

In a VB program, the LinkItem is the Name of the linked Control in the *source* (*server*) program (the program sending information to another program across the Link). It must be either a Text Box, Picture Box or Label. No other Controls can be used for Links. The LinkItem Property is only adjusted in the *destination* (*client*) program. LinkItem tells VB which Text Box, Label or Picture Box in the source program will be sending data to the destination program.

You identify the LinkItem in the *destination* program, the program that will receive the information. You are changing the LinkItem Property of the *receiving* Control but naming the *sending* Control. It's like saying, "Information will be coming in from Text1 on the foreign program. Its Name is Text1, so I'm identifying it here in the LinkItem Property."

Note that more than one Link can share the same LinkItem (the same Control) as the source of the incoming data. However, a related Property, *LinkTopic*, cannot be shared by different Links. Individual Links are uniquely identified by the LinkTopic. You set the LinkTopic in both the source and destination programs; it is composed of the program name (such as "MyProg.EXE") of the source program plus the name you make up and put into the source's LinkTopic Property. LinkTopic names are separated by the pipe (|) symbol. Here's an example: MYSERVER|PhotoInfo

Although a number of Links can be active at any one time, each will have its own unique LinkTopic.

Linking is part of Dynamic Data Exchange (DDE), a powerful Windows capability. See "LinkMode" for more on DDE and linking.

Used with   Labels, Picture Boxes, Text Boxes

Variables   **Variable type:** Text ("string")

Normally, you set the LinkItem in the Properties Window when designing a destination (client) program:

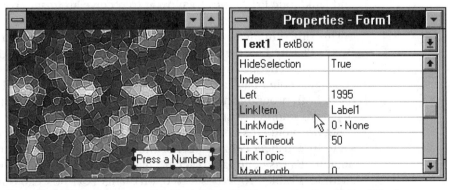

Figure L-44: You can name this Text Box's LinkItem in the Properties Window.

OR (to set the Property while the program is running):

```
Text1.LinkItem = "Label1"
```

OR If you are setting up a Link between your VB program (as destination) and a non-VB program such as Excel (as source), the LinkItem will not be a Control. Instead, it will be a spreadsheet cell (or range of cells). The Link-Item for Word will be "DDE_LINK1" or similar. To establish this kind of Link, see the manual of the non-VB program for details, or see "LinkMode."

Uses • Creating a LinkItem is one of three necessary steps in allowing a destination (client) program to receive data from a Control like a Text Box on a separate (source) program. You put the Name of the alien Control (the "source" of data) into the LinkItem Property of the destination. The other two steps are setting the LinkTopic and LinkMode Properties.

The LinkItem Property is adjusted in the destination program, but it refers to the Control on the source program—the program providing data to the Link (and through the Link, to the destination).

LinkItem identifies the source of information flowing from a source to a destination program. If you identify Text1 on the source (server) as the LinkItem, then typing new information into Text1 will instantly change the text in the destination's linked Text Box or Label.

Which Text Box (or Label or Picture Box) *receives* the new information depends on which of those Controls on the destination program you made receptive to a Link. To make a receptor for a Link, you change a Control's LinkItem, LinkTopic and, finally, activate the Link by turning on the target Control's LinkMode (LinkMode cannot be set in the Properties Window).

Cautions • It is possible to create a DDE *Loop*, the computer equivalent of a nervous breakdown. For instance, you cause a Picture Box to be a source (server) because it is on a Form whose LinkMode is set to 1 (source), and yet the same Box is identified by an outside destination program as the LinkItem. In addition, this same Picture Box has also been made the *destination* (*client*) of the other program because we set the Box's LinkTopic, LinkItem and LinkMode Properties to allow it to receive an image from the other program.

This situation means that when we Load a new image into the Picture Box, a Picture Box on the other program responds by changing to that image. This change triggers our original Picture Box to respond and "change," going back and forth like a pressed Ping-Pong ball. All activity halts, both programs heat up, and within seconds the computer itself begins to smolder (just kidding).

But *do* avoid Link Loops. Simply avoid using the same Control (or the same spreadsheet cell in Excel or the same field in Word) for bidirectional linking. It's easy enough to accept data from a Link into a special Text Box (with its Visible Property set to 0, off). This Text Box can obviously react and process anything it receives, sending the results to the other Text Box. Just don't make any single Control (or other "item" on a non-VB program) bidirectional. They can't handle it.

Example We'll create two programs, each with a Picture Box. Then we'll Link the Picture Boxes. Any .BMP, .WMF or .ICO files loaded into the server will also appear in the client. LoadPicture will affect both Picture Boxes.

(Drawing with PSet, Line, Circle or Printing will not appear in the server. These are *Methods*, and to send drawn graphics or Printed text across a Link you need to involve LinkExecute.)

• To create the *source (server)* program, select New Project in VB's File Menu. Put a Picture Box on the Form and set the Form's Caption Property to Server Picture. Then Load a picture into the Picture Box by using its Picture Property in the Properties Window, and put the following into the Form_Load Event:

```
Sub Form_Load ()
    LinkTopic = "Image"
End Sub
```

Then change the *Form's* LinkMode to 1 (source) in the Properties Window. A *source* program's LinkMode *cannot* be changed by writing commands within the program. You must use the Properties Window for this.

Save this program as an EXE file called S.EXE.

Note that we can choose any name we want for LinkTopic, but we must later use the same name in the destination (client) program's LinkTopic Property. There are also two other differences between sources and destinations:

▪ The LinkTopic goes into the source's *Form* LinkTopic Property.

▪ The LinkTopic goes into the destination's *Control* LinkItem Property (whichever Control is going to receive the linked data). Also, LinkTopic for the destination contains the name of the source program plus the LinkTopic name. (Note that the LinkTopic for the destination is put into Picture1 and is called "S|Image" instead of "Image.")

• Select New Project in VB's File Menu. Put a Picture Box on the Form and set the Form's Caption Property to Client Picture. Then put the following into the Form_Click Event:

```
Sub Form_Click ()
    picture1.AutoSize = 1
    picture1.LinkTopic = "S | Image"
    picture1.LinkItem = "Picture1"
    picture1.LinkMode = 1
End Sub
```

Save this program as an EXE file called C.EXE.

We set AutoSize to on, so that whatever the size of the server's image, our Picture Box will fit itself to the image. Then we set the three Properties that the Picture Box Control must have to become the destination of a Link. LinkTopic identifies the source program "S" and the name we gave this transaction, "Image." We could call "Image" anything we want, just so the source and destination references to it are the same. Then we identified Picture1 on the source (server) as the source of our data by setting the LinkItem Property. Finally, we turned on the Link by setting the LinkMode to 1 (Automatic).

• Now run S.EXE and then run C.EXE. Click on C.EXE's Form and watch the picture come through the Link like a spaceship through a worm hole.

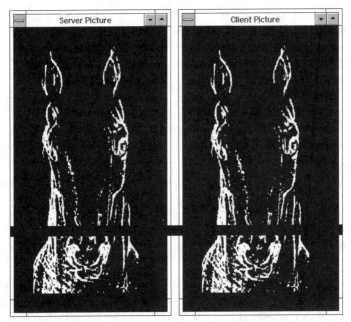

Figure L-45: The picture is copied from the source (server) program to the destination (client) program.

See also LinkClose; LinkError; LinkExecute (Event and Method); LinkMode; LinkNotify; LinkOpen; LinkPoke; LinkRequest; LinkSend; LinkTimeout; LinkTopic; OLE

LINKMODE

PROPERTY

Description The setting of this Property determines how, and if, a Link can occur. There are four possible settings: No Link, Automatic, Manual, Notify.

No Link (the default) means the program will not respond to efforts to link with it. Automatic means that it will respond instantly and continuously. Manual means that it will respond, but the user (or the program) must specifically request a response (with LinkRequest). The LinkNotify Event is triggered if the linked data changes (if the LinkMode is set to "Notify"). Whether or when your program responds to the changed data is up to you.

Linking is so dramatic, and so novel, that we should spend a little time exploring its purpose and implications.

The Concept of Linking: Windows is moving us toward the future of computing in ways more subtle and more powerful than simply its splendid *visual* features. Windows includes a capability called Object Embedding and Linking (OLE), which, when fully utilized, will revolutionize computing. OLE may well be a major step on the road to artificial intelligence.

Embedding means that you can create a picture in CorelDRAW and place it into a Word for Windows document. Later, if you want to make some changes to the picture while you're working in Word, you can click on the picture and CorelDRAW automatically appears with the picture loaded. You're ready to edit the picture in the program that created it. When you're finished, the updated picture appears where it should in your Word document. Thus, pictures and words more or less exist outside the programs that created them. They are available everywhere at once. The old approach of first running a program and then loading in something to work on is no longer necessary. That's one of the things that Bill Gates means by "information at your fingertips."

Embedding breaks down the barriers between data (like a picture) and application (CorelDRAW or Word). The computer has only one big program and you, the user, don't have to worry about loading a specific program that is optimized to create graphics or process text or recalculate a spreadsheet. You just work on something—graphics, numbers, data, words, music—and when you work, the best application automatically and silently appears around whatever you are working on.

Embedding is partially implemented in Windows 3.1, but its full potency is still being developed at Microsoft. For more on embedding, see "OLE." Linking, however, is fully available in Windows now.

Linking performs two services for programs that are *both currently running*. It can pass text or graphics between the two programs. This updating can be instantaneous and constant, or only when the user requests the update. (A program could also request an update, even at timed intervals if desired.)

The second service provided by linking is that one program can pass *commands* to another (see "LinkExecute"). What primarily distinguishes the kind of communication that linking offers from what embedding can do is that embedding does not require that both programs be running for the communication to take place. Embedding is more automatic in that it calls up whatever program created some data; it starts the program running without any intervention from the user and without any preconditions. The data simply invokes the right program.

Computer programs have only two fundamental qualities—instructions (commands) and information (data). PRINT "LAURA" is an example. *Print* is a command, an action. *"Laura"* is data, the stuff acted upon. This distinction is fundamental to all behavior. Shine sunlight. Put the book back. Eat. Even when data isn't specified, it's implied. Eat implies food. The Cls command implies clearing the screen of anything (any data) that's on it.

When two or more programs are linked, via the various Link commands available in some Windows programs and VB, the programs can instantly send *information* back and forth. This exchange is called a "conversation," and it is impressive. If you change text in Word, it appears simultaneously in your VB Text Box. But there's even more. For example, with the linking feature, one program can dominate another, making the dominated program perform as if a user were activating features of that program. This capability is similar to macro control—such as the Recorder that comes with Windows—but considerably more powerful.

Clearly a Breakthrough: Linking can be valuable and is clearly a breakthrough in computing; the divisions that traditionally separated one program from another are breaking down. This blending makes computers more intelligent and easier to use. After all, the various "programs" in our mind communicate with each other, sharing data and even dominating one another in, usually, effective chains of command. Of course, there are states such as panic when the behaviors go off the rails, but generally things work well in an integrated fashion.

Prior to linking, the activities of one program were essentially unrelated and unavailable to the activities and products of another program. The user had to translate the information in a file saved, for example, in WordPerfect format into information that Lotus 1-2-3 could utilize. Not only were these programs unable to run simultaneously (multitasking); they also produced information in proprietary formats. A WordPerfect file could not be read by Lotus, and vice versa. Often transferring information even required retyping. Now, with linking and other new facilities, these barriers are coming down.

Used with   Forms, Labels, Picture Boxes, Text Boxes

Variables   **Variable type:** Integer

You can set the LinkMode while you are designing your program by using the Properties Window triggering an attempted Link immediately and an error message if the Link cannot be achieved because the target of the Link isn't running:

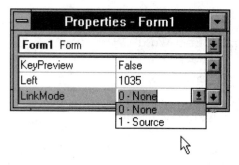

Figure L-46: Optionally, set the LinkMode in the Properties Window.

OR (to turn on a Link while the program is running): Text1.LinkMode = 1

OR: There is a special way of establishing Links using the Paste Link option in VB's Edit Menu.

As an example of this approach, we'll create two Links. In the first Link, any changes to text in a Word for Windows document are immediately reflected in the Text Box in our VB program (the client or "destination"). (Microsoft is now referring to the destinaiton as the container. For more on this terminology, see "OLE.")

In the second example, VB becomes the *server* or *"source"*; any changes we make in the VB Text Box are updated in the document in Word.

• **VB as Destination:** (VB receives data from an outside program.) To make your VB program receive data from Word, create a New Project from the VB File Menu. Put a Text Box on the Form.

Then run Word. Select some text in the document and use Word's Edit Menu to copy the text to the Clipboard.

Now click on the Text Box to give it the focus (its frame will have black "handles" around it). Select Paste Link from VB's Edit Menu. VB automatically adjusts the Text Box's LinkItem, LinkTopic and LinkMode Properties to point to the correct location in the correct Word document. To see this, click on Form1 in the Properties Window. Then click back to Text1. This updates the Properties Window.

These changes are *persistent*–the Link has been established as part of the VB program. If you make an .EXE a runnable program out of your VB program, the link information will stay in the program. Word has its own Paste Link command, as well as a way to insert and edit Field Codes for Links. (See the Word user's guide.)

• **VB as Source:** (VB provides data to an outside program.) To make your VB program provide data to Word, start running Word. Create a New Project from the VB File Menu. Put a Text Box on the Form and click on the Text Box. Choose the Copy command from VB's Edit Menu.

Click where you want to locate the Link in a Word document. Select Paste Special and then Paste Link from Word's Edit Menu. If you select the View Field Codes option from Word's View Menu, you'll see the following inserted into your Word document:

{DDEAUTO Project1 Trans Text1 * mergeformat \t}

Now, whatever changes you make to the Text Box in your VB program will also appear in the Word document.

Differences Between Destination and Source Programs: In a destination program, LinkMode defaults to 0 (No Link). Or you can set it to 1, the "Automatic" setting, meaning that the Link is always active and responds at once to changes in the source (server) program; or 2, the "Manual" setting, meaning the information is updated only after a specific request (using "LinkRequest") from the user or your program; or 3, the "Notify" setting, meaning the destination (client) program is informed when the data in the source changes and can use LinkRequest to receive the data when and if you wish.

In a destination program, the LinkMode is a Property of a Label, Picture Box or Text Box—but not of a Form.

In a source program, LinkMode defaults to 0 ("None"), but you can permit linking by changing the LinkMode to 1 ("Source"). If there is a Picture Box, Text Box or Label on this Form, it can act as the source of information to a destination program. To make one of these Controls the source of information, the destination program must put the Name of the Control in the destination's LinkItem Property.

LinkMode can be set to 0 (Off) in the source (server) program Form. In this case, none of the Controls on that Form can act as a source in a Link.

In a destination program, the LinkMode is a Property of a Form only. In other words, a source (the "server") uses a Form's LinkMode Property; the destination (the "client") uses a *Control's* LinkMode Property.

Here is how a typical DDE Link is established:

SOURCE (SERVER)

LinkTopic: **Trans.** Make up a name and type it into the source *Form's* LinkTopic Property. Let's call it *Trans* in this example. Also, set the *Form's* LinkMode to 1.

Put a Text Box, Label or Picture Box on the Form. This Control will act as the source, providing data across the Link to the destination program. Make an .EXE file called "PROVIDE" from the Files Menu and select New Project.

DESTINATION (CLIENT or CONTAINER)

Put a Text Box, Label or Picture Box on a Form. This Control will act as the destination, receiving data from the source program. Let's use a Text Box in this example.

Adjust three of this Text Box's Properties:

1. LinkTopic: **PROVIDE|Trans**. Add the name of the source program ("PROVIDE.EXE" for this example) plus the name you made up for the LinkTopic. In this example, we would put PROVIDE|Trans into the Text Box's LinkTopic Property. Note that the source program name is separated from the LinkTopic name by a pipe (|) symbol. It is usually found on the keyboard as a shifted backslash (\).

2. LinkItem: **Label1** Into the destination program's Text Box's LinkItem Property, type the Name Property of the Control on the source program that will be providing the information during the Link. (If you used a Text Box instead of a Label, use "Text1" as the LinkItem, etc.)

3. LinkMode: **1** Turn on the Link by setting the destination Control's LinkMode to "Automatic" (or, if you prefer, set it to 2, for "Manual"). This *must* be done within the program: Text1.LinkMode = 1. You cannot use the Properties Window to adjust the *destination* LinkMode, but you *must* use the Properties Window when adjusting the source's LinkMode.

Uses
• Turn on a Link so that two programs communicate.

• Find out while a program is running whether a Link is Automatic (always active) or Manual (activated by the user or program periodically) or Notify (lets you know when source/data has changed).

Example
We're going to Link to Word for Windows. Our VB program will be the *destination* (*client*), receiving any text that the user types into Document1. Word will be the *source* (*server*) in this Link.

This kind of Link would allow the VB program to analyze the text as it is typed into Word, which means that our VB program is *watching* what's happening as you write in Word. The VB program is sitting there, always aware of what's happening.

One useful application would be to create a list of frequently used phrases, assigning each one to a letter of the alphabet:

a = 415 Oak Ridge Ln., Clorox, CA 92672
y = Yours truly, L. D'Arabia
t = Thank you very much for your assistance in this matter.

Put these phrases into a separate Text Box (so the user can edit them). When the program ends, save the contents of the Text Box to an .INI file, so that any changes can be loaded in each time the program runs.

Have your VB program continually check the typing, watching for an "xx," which signals that the following letter should trigger a replacement text. So, if the user types xxa, your VB program sends your address into the Word document, replacing the xxa with:

415 Oak Ridge Ln.
Clorox, CA 92672

Here's how to establish the first Link to Word, the Link that allows us to watch what's being typed into Word.

First, create a Label and put text into it that tells the user how to establish the Link. Also create a Command Button and then a Text Box that will receive the Word text across the Link (set the Text Box's Visible Property to False):

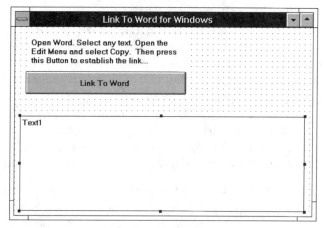

Figure L-47: Designing the Form that will establish a conversation with Word for Windows.

After the user selects some text in Word and copies it to the Clipboard, the Link can be established by clicking on the Command Button:

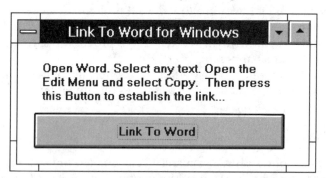

Figure L-48: The running link-to-Word program the user presses the Command Button to start the conversation.

```
Sub Command1_Click ()
w$ = clipboard.GetText(&HBF00)
If w$ = "" Then
    MsgBox ("You must select some text in Word, then Copy it.")
```

```
Else
    command1.visible = 0
    label1.visible = 0
    text1.visible = —1

    text1.LinkItem = Mid$(w$, InStr(w$, "!") + 1)
    text1.LinkTopic = Left$(w$, InStr(w$, "!") — 1)
    text1.LinkMode = 1
End If

End Sub
```

More Than Words: When any text is copied from Word into the Clipboard, not only the text gets copied. Word also inserts a special piece of Link information. If we use the GetText Method with the special code (&HBF00), we get back the Link information we need. W$ now holds the following text:

WinWord|Document1!DDE_LINK1

WinWord|Document1 is the LinkTopic. DDE_LINK1 is the LinkItem. We extract this information using InStr and put it in the respective Properties of Text1.

If there is no Link information in the Clipboard, the user has not copied anything from Word, so we advise him or her of that and exit the Sub. Otherwise, we hide the Label and Command Button, reveal the Text Box and, having already put the Item and Topic into Text1's Properties, we can now turn on the Link by setting LinkMode to 1 (Automatic).

From now on, anything typed into Word will be available to our VB program.

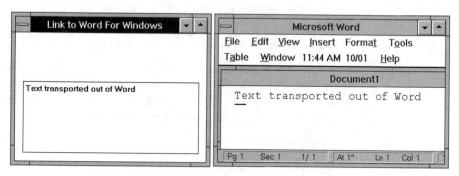

Figure L-49: Word sends text to our VB program across a Link.

See also   LinkClose; LinkError; LinkExecute (Method and Event); LinkItem; LinkNotify; LinkOpen; LinkPoke; LinkRequest; LinkSend; LinkTimeout; LinkTopic; OLE

LINKNOTIFY

EVENT

Description LinkNotify tells the destination (client) Control in a Link conversation that the data–a picture or text–in the source (server) Control has changed. In a "hot" Automatic Link, such a change would automatically result in an updating of the text or picture in the destination. However, if the destination (client) has its LinkMode Property set to 3, "Notify," then updating is not automatic. The destination is merely *informed* of the change: The destination's LinkNotify Event is triggered. It's up to you (or you can leave it up to the user) to decide whether or when to update the data in the destination Control.

Used with A destination Picture Box, Text Box or Label that is engaged in a "Notify style" (LinkMode = 3) Link conversation

Variables
```
Sub Text1_LinkNotify ()

End Sub
```

Inside this Event you type the commands telling VB how to react to the notification that data has changed (in the "source" program).

Uses • Notify the user that data has changed and let the user decide if the change should be sent across the Link at this time.

• Have your program immediately update the data (using LinkRequest, which see). However, this would be indistinguishable from setting the LinkMode to 1 (Automatic).

• Using a Timer, delay the transfer of the changed data.

Example To create the server (source) program, select New Project in VB's File Menu. Put a Text Box on the Form. In the Properties Window, set the Form's LinkMode to 1, "Source." Set the Form's Caption Property to Source. Then put the following into the Form_Load Event:

```
Sub Form_Load ()
    LinkTopic = "Tex"
End Sub
```

Save this program as an .EXE file called S.EXE (using the Make EXE File option on the File Menu).

Now, to create the client (destination) program, select New Project in VB's File Menu. Put a Text Box on the Form. Set the Form's Caption Property to Destination. In the Properties Window, set Text1's LinkTopic to "S|tex," its LinkItem to Text1 and its LinkMode Property to 3, "Notify." (Ignore the error message.)

And, in Text1's LinkNotify Event, type the following:

```
X = MsgBox("Notification of a Link")
```

Save this as an .EXE file called C.EXE. Now run S.EXE and then run C.EXE.

See also

LinkClose; LinkError; LinkExecute (Event and Method); LinkMode; LinkOpen; LinkPoke; LinkRequest; LinkSend; LinkTimeout; LinkTopic; OLE

L INKOPEN

EVENT

Description

LinkOpen is triggered when one program endeavors to link to another, to start a "conversation" between them, as it's called.

For general information on linking, see "LinkMode."

Used with

• A Form, when the VB program is to act as the *source* (*server*), the provider of information across a Link to a separate program. When the outside program "calls up" and requests a Link, the Form's LinkOpen Event is triggered.

• A Text Box, Picture Box or Label when one acts as the *destination* (*client*) in a Link, the receiver of information across a Link from a separate program. The Control's LinkOpen Event is triggered when this destination program's Control "places a call" to an outside program, attempting to start a conversation with this outside *source* or *"server."*

Variables

A Variable called *Cancel* controls whether or not the Link "conversation" is permitted or refused. You set Cancel to 0 in the LinkOpen Event, *after* whatever instructions in the Event are carried out. Setting Cancel to 0 allows the "conversation" to occur–allows the Link to be established. Setting cancel to –1 or anything other than 0 rejects the "conversation," thereby preventing the Link.

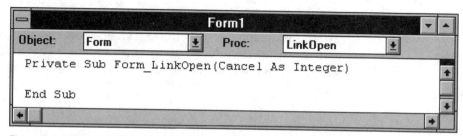

Figure L-50: The built-in Variable *Cancel* can reject a Link attempt from outside your VB program.

Uses
- Alert the user that a Link has been established.
- Allow your program to take some action, such as creating a new Control or making one visible.
- While debugging (fixing errors in your program), this Event allows you to know when a "Link" has worked.

Cautions
- The Variable *Cancel* will automatically remain 0, its default, unless you set it to –1 or any other value. If you do change it, the attempted Link is thwarted.
- The usual asymmetry between Link Properties of a Form and a Control apply to LinkOpen. The *source* Form's LinkOpen Event is triggered when an outside program attempts to "call"; the *destination* Control's LinkOpen Event is triggered when that Control itself makes a "call" to an outside program.

Example
- Put a Text Box on a Form. To make this Text Box a source, *in the Properties Window*, set the Form's LinkTopic Property to LOpen (you can use any name you want). Then set the Form's LinkMode to 1-Source. Save this program as an .EXE program named S.EXE.
- Create a New Project from the File Menu, and put a Text Box on the new Form. To make this new program the *destination* program in the Link, we must set three Properties of the Text Box. We'll do this when the Form is clicked:

```
Sub Form_Click ()
    text1.linkitem = "Text1"
    text1.linktopic = "S|Lopen"
    text1.linkmode = 1
End Sub
```

(For more information about these Properties, see "LinkItem.")

Now, in the Text1 LinkOpen Event, add the following:

```
Sub Text1_LinkOpen (cancel As Integer)

Print " THE LINK HAS BEEN ESTABLISHED WITH THE ALIEN PROGRAM."
End Sub
```

Save this program as C.EXE. Run S.EXE first (because sources should be operating when a destination tries to make a Link). Then run this destination program, C.EXE. Clicking on C.EXE results in the following:

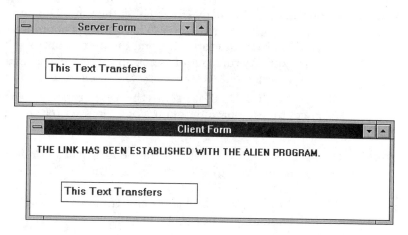

Figure L-51: The conversation is successfully established; the Link works.

See also LinkClose; LinkError; LinkExecute (Event and Method); LinkItem; LinkNotify; LinkPoke; LinkRequest; LinkSend; LinkTimeout; LinkTopic; OLE

LINKPOKE

METHOD

Description LinkPoke reverses the normal flow of information during a Link.

Usually, a *source* (*server*) program provides information to a *destination* (*client*) program. For instance, if the user changes some words in a Text Box on the source, those changes occur in the destination program's Text Box as well. It's like a transaction between a waiter (the server) and a customer (the client).

LinkPoke, though, allows a *destination* Text Box to give information to its *source*, reversing the normal flow of data between linked entities.

For an overview of linking, see "LinkExecute (Method)."

Used with A destination (client) and a source (server) during a Link

Variables To cause the contents of a Text Box (Text1.Text, for example) to be sent to an outside *source* program linked to this program:

    Text1.LinkPoke

Uses • LinkPoke provides a way that one program can affect another during a Link. LinkPoke allows you to respond with a message (or a picture) that flows back to the supplier of information (the source program).

• Modify some text or graphics in the destination program and send the results back to the source.

Cautions
• You can establish many Links. Using the same Link for bidirectional communications can result in a "Link Loop," a continuous batting of information back and forth, beyond the user's control. The computer, in this case, quickly runs out of "stack space" (a special area of memory), and an error is generated. To prevent a Link Loop, see the following Example.

• For a Text Box, LinkPoke sends the Text Property (Text1.Text, for instance) to the source program. For a Picture Box, the Picture is sent. For a Label, the Caption is sent.

Example
Create a Form with a Text Box. In the Properties Window, set the Form's LinkTopic Property to "Censor" and set the LinkMode to 1 (Source). Save this Property as S.EXE.

Select New Project again and put a Text Box on that Form as well. Put the following in the Form_Load Event:

```
Sub Form_Load ()
    text1.linktopic = "S | Censor"
    text1.linkitem = "text1"
    text1.linkmode = 1
End Sub
```

This Event will turn on the Link as soon as you start this program. (To understand the meaning of these Properties, see "LinkItem.")

Now put the following into the Text1_Change Event:

```
Sub Text1_Change ()

If LCase$(text1.text) = "bloody" Then
    text1.text = "That Word Is Not Allowed!"
    text1.LinkPoke
    text1.text = ""
End If
End Sub
```

Save this program as C.EXE.

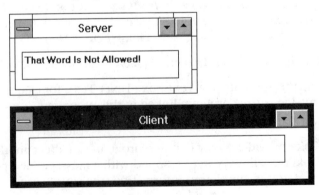

Figure L-52: LinkPoke sends messages in the opposite direction from the normal flow of information across a Link.

Now start S.EXE and then start C.EXE. As you type some words into S.EXE's Text Box, you'll see them appear instantly in C.EXE's Text Box. Backspace over anything you've typed, to clean out the Text Box. Try typing the word *bloody*. It will be refused. The message "That Word Is Not Allowed!" will be inserted into the source (server) Text Box, and the destination (client) Text Box will be cleaned out.

If you try to restore the destination text within its Change Event, you would create a Link Loop and the program would grind to a halt after a second or two of violence. The messages would be sent back and forth along the Link at the speed of light, continually causing LinkPokes. Here's the kind of structure that would cause a Link Loop:

```
Sub Text1_Change ()

If LCase$(text1.text) = "bloody" Then
    X$ = text1.text          'we save the word "bloody"
    text1.text = "That Word Is Not Allowed!"
    text1.LinkPoke

    'now we restore the word, triggering another change,
    'another LinkPoke, another restoration, in an endless
    ' circle.
    text1.text = X$

End If

End Sub
```

See also   LinkClose; LinkError; LinkExecute (Event and Method); LinkItem; LinkMode; LinkNotify; LinkOpen; LinkRequest; LinkSend; LinkTimeout; LinkTopic; OLE

LINKREQUEST

METHOD

Description   The LinkRequest command is used by the destination (client) in a link conversation between two programs. The destination program is asking the source (server) program to send information. A LinkRequest need only be sent when the programs are linked via a Manual (or "cold") Link. An Automatic (or "hot") Link provides information instantly and continuously. (For more about Automatic and Manual Links, plus an overview of linking in general, see "LinkMode.")

Used with   A destination Picture Box, Text Box or Label that is engaged in a "manual conversation" with a source program. A Manual Link only sends information from the source program to the destination program when requested to do so—hence LinkRequest.

Variables   Text1.LinkRequest

Depending on what has been linked to Text1–a Text Box or a Label on the source program–the Text1.Text or Label1.Caption information will be updated by this LinkRequest. A Picture Box must talk to another Picture Box; they can transfer .BMP, .WMF or .ICO graphics between each other via links.

Uses   • A Manual Link doesn't instantly and constantly change text (or graphics) on the destination (client) program when the contents change in the Control on the linked source program.

If you have established a Manual Link between two Controls on two different programs, LinkRequest can

- Allow the user to update the text or graphics in a Control on the destination program. The user has the option of deciding when to permit the update. For example, you could create a Command Button with the caption "UPDATE." Within it's Click Event, you could put: Text1.LinkRequest. Whenever the user clicked that button, the destination Text Box would be fed the source Text Box's contents.

- Allow your program to update in response to some condition.

- Allow your program to update periodically, by using a Timer to determine how often the LinkRequest should occur.

Example

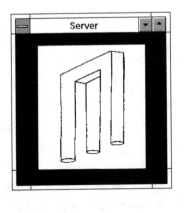
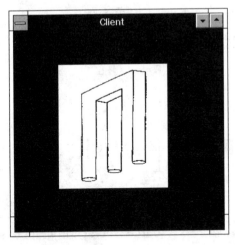

Figure L-53: LinkRequest tries to turn on a Manual Link. The other party is on hold.

• Create a source and a destination program.

- To create the source (server) program, select New Project from the VB File menu. Put a Picture Box on the Form. Using the Properties Window, type the word Cool into the Form's LinkTopic Property. We selected the name *Cool* for this link. You can use any name you wish, but make sure you use the same name again when setting the *destina-*

tion LinkTopic. Now save all this as S.EXE, creating a runnable .EXE program.

▪ To create the destination (client), select New Project in VB's File Menu and put a Picture Box on the Form. Type this into the Form_Load Event:

```
Sub Form_Load ()
    Picture1.LinkTopic = "S | Cool"
    Picture1.LinkItem = "Picture1"
    Picture1.LinkMode = 2
End Sub
```

(For more about these Properties of Picture1, see "LinkItem.")

By setting the LinkMode to 2, we have created a Manual Link—the picture in the source program's Picture1 will not flow across the link until we *make it flow* by provoking a LinkRequest.

We can do that in the Click Event of the destination Picture, but it doesn't have to be in this Event. It could be a Command Button that triggers the transfer of information, a click on the Form, whatever you want. Here we've chosen to send the request when the destination Picture is clicked:

```
Sub Picture1_Click ()
    Picture1.LinkRequest
End Sub
```

Save this program as C.EXE (for "destination").

Now run the S.EXE program, then run the C.EXE program. C.EXE's Picture will be blank until you click on it, stimulating the LinkRequest and causing Mr. Escher's design to flow across the link.

See also   LinkClose; LinkError; LinkExecute (Event and Method); LinkItem; LinkO-pen; LinkPoke; LinkSend; LinkTimeout; LinkTopic; OLE

LINKSEND

METHOD

Description   LinkSend causes a linked graphics image to be sent over the Link, from a Picture Box on the source (server) program to a Picture Box on the destination (client) program.

There is a problem sending graphics over a Link, a problem we don't have when sending text. Graphics generally involve far more data than text. It would be inefficient and it would slow down the computer if a Link had to update graphic data frequently. Using LinkSend, your program (or the user) explicitly decides when a linked graphic should be updated. Text, by contrast, is often "Automatically" Linked, which means that any slight change in the source program is immediately reproduced in the destination program.

As you have doubtless noticed, a text file on your disk takes up much less space than a graphics file. An entire 200-page *book* would take up about 300,000 bytes (200 pages x 250 words per page x 6 letters per average word). That's roughly 1/3 of a megabyte.

A Super-VGA high-resolution picture of a sun fish or Laura Dern or Keanu Reeves can use about 1,000,000 bytes, a full megabyte. Text is black and white, and there are a limited number of possible variations of text—only 26 letters in the alphabet, for example. When you type in a letter, you are adding only one byte to the data. When you fill an area of a picture with a color, you can add thousands of bytes, a flood of data.

Text Uses Much Less Space Than Graphics: A pixel (the smallest unit visible on a video screen) is far finer than a letter of the alphabet. And, what makes things worse—and finally proves scientifically that a picture is indeed worth much more than a thousand words—each pixel has to be described in terms of both color and luminance (what color is it and how dark is that color?).

Interestingly, VB handles bitmapped graphics—.BMP, .WMF, .ICO—in the normal fashion, the same way that text is handled, with the usual linking techniques. You cannot dynamically change these images. You can Load and UnLoad them, but you do not call upon Visual Basic to *draw* them while a program is running.

However, for graphics that are drawn—using the Line, Circle, PSet or Print command—LinkSend allows you to control when the image is transferred over the Link. Transferring a drawn graphic continuously while a program is trying to create it would result in unacceptably slow performance.

(For an overview of linking, see "LinkMode.")

Used with   Picture Boxes containing *drawn* (as opposed to *bitmapped*) graphics. See "Uses" below.

Variables   Picture1.LinkSend

Uses   • LinkSend is used to allow linking between *drawn* pictures. The PSet, Print, Circle and Line Methods *draw* on a Picture Box. This technique differs fundamentally from pictures that you import as *bitmaps* (.BMP, .WMF, .ICO images).

The bitmaps can be automatically linked and update the client program immediately whenever the source (server) program's graphic is changed by loading in a new .BMP file, for example. (See the first Example below.)

Drawn graphics cannot be automatically updated across a Link. You must use the LinkSend Method when you want a drawn image updated. The decision about when to update with LinkSend can be given to the user. (See the second Example below.) Or, for instance, your program can cause a LinkSend after it has finished creating a drawing, or use a Timer for periodic updates.

Cautions
- LinkSend will not work unless the source program's Picture Box Auto-Redraw Property is set to –1. (AutoRedraw defaults to 0.)

- LinkSend will also fail to work if you try to create a Manual Link by setting the destination (client) program's LinkMode Property to 2. A Manual Link can be updated only via the LinkRequest Method.

- If you run a source program, draw something on it, and then start the destination program running, *the drawn graphics will appear on the destination*. LinkSend is only necessary for updating changes made to the source after the destination program has started running.

Examples
We'll create two examples of linked graphics. The first involves an automatic type of Link that instantly updates the destination Picture Box when the .ICO image in the source changes. In this case, we don't need to use LinkSend. .ICO, .WMF and .BMP images can be automatically linked and, thus, update themselves. The second example will require LinkSend because it involves *drawing* (using the PSet, Circle, Line or Print command).

Linking Bitmapped Pictures

Source (Server): Create a new VB Project from the File Menu, and put a Picture Box and a File List Box on the Form. In the Form_Load Event, type the following:

```
Sub Form_Load ()

File1.Path = "C:\VBASIC\ICONS\OFFICE"
LinkTopic = "icons"
End Sub
```

This Subroutine makes a VB icon collection available to our program, and names the topic of our Link "icons." Now in the Properties Window, change the *Form's* LinkMode to 1-Source. Naming the LinkTopic (whatever name you want) for the Form and setting the LinkMode for the Form is all you need to do to make a source program capable of linking. (If your VB icons are located in a different path, change the path for File1.Path above.)
Now put the following into the File1_Click Event:

```
Sub File1_Click ()
    picture1.picture = LoadPicture(file1.path + "\" + file1.list(file1.listindex))
End Sub
```

This Event allows us to click on the File List Box and put different icon graphics into the Picture Box. Save this program as S.EXE using Make EXE File in the VB File Menu.

Destination (Client or Container): Create a new VB Project, and put a Picture Box on the Form. In the Form_Load Event, type the following:

```
Sub Form_Load ()
    picture1.linktopic = "S | icons"
```

```
        picture1.linkitem = "picture1"
        picture1.linkmode = 1
    End Sub
```

Here we've created an automatic-style Link; it will respond immediately to any new icon loaded into the source program. This, our destination program, will display whatever new icons are selected by the source. (For more on the Properties we set for Picture 1, see "LinkTopic.") Save this program as C.EXE.

Now, run S.EXE and then run C.EXE. Select various icons from S.EXE's File List. You'll see the Link in action as new icons also appear in C.EXE.

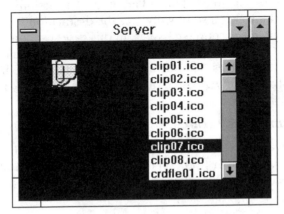

Figure L-54: Sending pictures across a Link

Linking Drawn Pictures

Source (Server): Create a new VB Project from the File Menu and put a Picture Box and a Command Button on the Form. In the Form_Load Event, type the following:

```
    Sub Form_Load ()
        LinkTopic = "Drawings"
        Picture1.DrawWidth = 4
        Picture1.AutoRedraw = True
    End Sub
```

The source's AutoRedraw Property must be set to True for the LinkSend to work. (AutoRedraw defaults to False; you must explicitly change it to True.)

In the Picture1.MouseMove Event, type the following:

```
    Sub Picture1_MouseMove (Button As Integer, Shift As Integer, X As Single,→ Y
        As Single)
        Picture1.PSet (X, Y)
    End Sub
```

And in the Command1 Click Event, type the following:

```
Sub Command1_Click ()
    Picture1.LinkSend
End Sub
```

Change the Form's LinkMode Property to 1-Source in the Properties Window. Save this program as S.EXE.

Destination (Client or Container): Create a new VB Project and put a Picture Box on the Form. In the Form_Load Event, type the following:

```
Sub Form_Load ()
    Picture1.LinkTopic = "S | Drawings"
    Picture1.LinkItem = "Picture1"
    Picture1.LinkMode = 1
End Sub
```

(See "LinkItem" for the meaning of these Properties.)
Now save this program as C.EXE.

Start S.EXE and then start C.EXE. As you move the mouse around and draw some lines on S.EXE's picture, you'll notice that these changes are not reproduced in C.EXE. Press the Update button, triggering LinkSend. At this point, the source sends the picture over the Link.

Remember to set the source's Picture Box AutoRedraw Property to True.

Before LinkSend:

Figure L-55: Preparing to send the drawing.

After LinkSend:

Figure L-56: The drawing makes it across the Link between these two programs.

See also   LinkClose; LinkError; LinkExecute (Event and Method); LinkItem; LinkMode; LinkNotify; LinkOpen; LinkPoke; LinkRequest; LinkTimeout; LinkTopic; OLE

LINKTIMEOUT

PROPERTY

Description   LinkTimeout permits you to extend the amount of time that a destination (client) program will wait for a source (server) program to respond when the destination "calls" the source. VB allows five seconds for a response unless you adjust the LinkTimeout Property.

Destinations and sources engaged in a *Link* are said to converse with each other after a Link is established. LinkTimeout is the amount of time that is allowed for the source to "pick up the phone" after a destination calls it. (For more on linking, see "LinkMode.")

Used with   Destination programs. LinkTimeout is a Property of a Text Box, Picture Box or Label.

Variables   **Variable type:** Integer

This Property can be set while you are designing your program. Here we'll change the default (50, which means five seconds) to 500, allowing the source program to take as much as 50 seconds to respond:

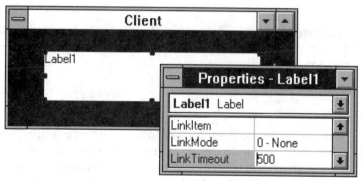

Figure L-57: Changing the amount of time allowed during a Link attempt.

OR (to adjust the grace period while your program is running):

Label1.LinkTimeout = 200 (now we'll wait up to 20 seconds for a source's response)

Uses • Allow a source to finish a lengthy task before responding to your destination program's request.

Setting LinkTimeout to –1 permits the source to take as long as it wants to respond. The computer will lock up until the source responds, although the user can get out of the lockup by pressing the ALT key.

Normally, source programs respond right away–well within the default five seconds. However, if your source program is creating a complex drawing, engaged in telecommunications, or some other lengthy activity, you might want to permit the source program to finish its job no matter how long that job might take, or at least give it a reasonable amount of time to answer.

Cautions • If you don't adjust LinkTimeout and the source program exceeds five seconds to respond to the destination program, VB will generate an error message.

• The durations measured by LinkTimeout are in *realtime*. A second is a second. This means that no accommodations are made for relative computer clock speeds. Older PCs might run at 6 or 8 MHz, newer ones run at 16, 20, 25, 33 and even 50 MHz. However, clock speed is not taken into account by LinkTimeout. So, if timing is critical in your application, you may want to set a longer LinkTimeout duration than you think is necessary. This allows older machines to have enough time to respond.

Example To illustrate LinkTimeout, we'll set the source (server) program a task that will take longer than the five seconds usually allowed for a response. A For...Next Loop will lock up our source program until the Loop is completed. (You *can* make a Loop interruptible by putting a DoEvents Function inside the Loop, but we want the source to be busy and to refuse outside messages for a time.)

Source (Server): Create a New Project in the VB File Menu and put a Text Box on the Form. First, we permit this program to act as a server by giving the Form a LinkTopic:

```
Sub Form_Load ()
    LinkTopic = "timetest"
End Sub
```

Also, change the *Form's* LinkMode to 1-Source in the Properties Window. When the destination program first establishes the Link, a LinkOpen Event is triggered in the source program. So we start our Loop, showing its progress by setting Text1.Text to reveal the value of the Variable *i* as it keeps incrementing within the Loop. When the Loop finishes, we report that in the Text Box:

```
Sub Form_LinkOpen (Cancel As Integer)

For i = 1 To 1000
    text1.text = "Link Established. Looping--" + Str$(i)
Next i

text1.text = "Loop Finished."
End Sub
```

Save this source program as S.EXE by selecting Make EXE File in the File Menu.

Destination (Client or Container): Create a New Project in the VB File Menu and put a Text Box on the Form. When the program is started, the Form_Load Event is triggered. It's here that we'll accomplish two-thirds of the Property settings necessary to create a linked destination program.

```
Sub Form_Load ()
    text1.linktopic = "S | timetest"
    text1.linkitem = "text1"
End Sub
```

(For more about these Properties, see "LinkItem.")

To start our test by clicking on the Form, we put the following in the Click Event:

```
Sub Form_Click ()
    text1.linktimeout = 900
    text1.linkmode = 2
    text1.text = "Requesting Update"
    text1.LinkRequest
End Sub
```

We change LinkTimeout from its usual default of 50 (five seconds) to 900 (90 seconds), giving the Loop in the source program a generous minute and a half to finish its counting.

Then we activate the Link by setting the LinkMode Property. At that point, the source program's LinkOpen Event is triggered because the Link has just been established between the two programs. We then report that our destination program is waiting for an update. As long as the destination program is waiting, its Text Box will read "Requesting Update." We formally request the update with the LinkRequest. Now we wait.

Save this program as C.EXE and then run the S.EXE program. Finally, run the C.EXE program and click on C.EXE to start the test. You'll see that the Text Boxes, although linked, differ. The source is counting its Loop, but the destination is not being updated—even though the destination has requested an update.

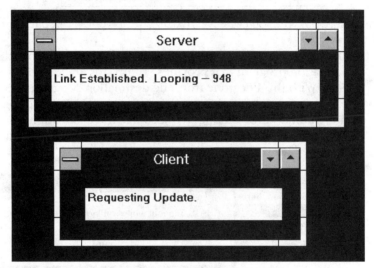

Figure L-58: The destination (client) is requesting data, and the Link has been established. However, the source (server) isn't prepared to respond.

When the source finally finishes its job, it notices the requested update and responds. Now both text boxes contain the same text.

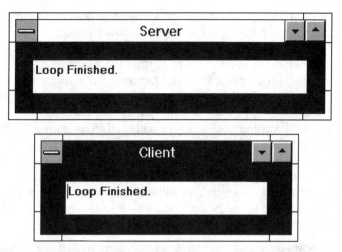

Figure L-59: The source (server) reacts, after its Looping is completed.

What if the Loop Cannot Finish Its Job? Try taking out the line in the destination program that provides 90 seconds grace period: text1.linktimeout = 900. With this line gone from the destination program, the grace period reverts to the default of five seconds for a source's response, not nearly enough time. After waiting five seconds, the destination disappears. An Error Message Box appears, and the destination program shuts itself down and its window vanishes.

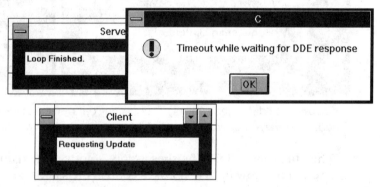

Figure L-60: The error message appears if a Link fails because the allotted time ran out.

There is a way to trap such errors while a program is running; see "LinkError."

See also   LinkClose; LinkError; LinkExecute (Event and Method); LinkItem; LinkMode; LinkNotify; LinkOpen; LinkPoke; LinkRequest; LinkSend; LinkTopic; OLE

LINKTOPIC

PROPERTY

Description   The *source (server)* program in a Link is the one that provides information (text or pictures) over the Link. The *destination (client)* program is the one that receives this information.

A LinkTopic is handled differently depending on whether it is the Link-Topic of a source, of a destination or of a non-Visual Basic program.

Source (Server) LinkTopic: *Bigtime* is an example of a *source* LinkTopic. You can use whatever name you want, but you must use the same name when you set the *compound* LinkTopic in the destination program.

In a source program, you set the LinkTopic of the *Form*.

Destination (Client or Container) LinkTopic: *MYPROG|Bigtime* is an example of a *destination* LinkTopic. The name of the source program (in this case, MYPROG.EXE) is added to the name of the source LinkTopic.

In the *destination* program, you change the LinkTopic of a Picture Box, Text Box or Label.

The program name is separated from the specific topic name by the pipe (|) symbol, usually found on keyboards as the shifted backslash (\) character.

Non-Visual Basic Programs: You'll need to see their manuals to learn how to handle Links and to set LinkTopics for programs such as Word for Windows and Excel. Link communication has not yet standardized enough to provide generic rules. Programs differ in their expectations for Link protocols.

For programs that were not created by Visual Basic, the destination's LinkTopic is usually composed by adding the name of the server program—Excel or WinWord—to the specific worksheet or document that is acting as the source, Document1, for instance. These names are separated by the pipe (|) symbol.

Excel, Visual Basic and Word for Windows all differ in the punctuation they expect for LinkItem names. Linking is still an unstable technique. If Microsoft applications all differ in their punctuation, what can we expect from independent software developers as their programs become link-capable?

Here are Microsoft's three different protocols for naming a source (server) LinkTopic:

Visual Basic: MYPROG|TOPIC (The LinkItem is not identified on a source Form; it's identified by the destination.)

Excel: MYPROG|TOPIC!R1C4 (The three elements—program name, topic and item—are separated by | and !)

Word: MYPROG TOPIC DDE_LINK1 (There are no separators, merely spaces to indicate that three elements are being named here.)

Used with   A Form acting as a source for a Link.

A Text Box, Picture Box or Label acting as a destination in a Link.

Variables   **Variable type:** Text (string)

You can set the LinkTopic in the Properties Window while designing your program:

Properties - Form1	▼
Form1 Form	▲
LinkMode	0 - None	▲
LinkTopic	Big	
MaxButton	True	▼

Form1	▼ ▲

Figure L-61: The Properties Window can be used to set the LinkTopic.

OR (most commonly you will set the LinkTopic in the Form_Load Event. This example sets a *source* (*server*) program's LinkTopic, so it is unnecessary to say Form1.LinkTopic. The source program in a Link *always* involves the Properties of the Form only, never the Controls on that Form):

```
Sub Form_Load ()
    LinkTopic = "Big"
End Sub
```

OR (to set the LinkTopic of the *destination* (*client*) program, we must specify the particular Control that will be receiving the data. The destination program in a Link *always* involves the Properties of a Control, never the Form. Also notice that there is no LinkItem involved in the example above; you do not specify a LinkItem in the source program. But here, because the example below is a destination program, we do specify a LinkItem [the Name of the specific Control on the *source* program that will be receiving our data]):

```
Sub Form_Load ()
    Text1.LinkTopic = "MYPROG | Big"
    Text1.LinkItem = "Picture1"
End Sub
```

Uses   Setting a LinkTopic is part of the process of establishing a Link between two programs.

Cautions
• The LinkTopic by itself does not establish a Link. It is a prerequisite. A Link will be established if four things are true:

▪ The source Form's LinkTopic has been named (to, say, "Big") and the *Form's* LinkMode has been set to 1-Source in the Properties Window.

▪ The destination Control's LinkTopic has been named by joining the source program name to the source LinkTopic ("MYPROG|Big").

▪ The destination Control's LinkItem names the source Control that will be receiving information across the Link ("Picture1").

▪ Finally, the Link is established when the destination Control's LinkMode Property is set (Text1.LinkMode = 1).

• The LinkTopic, together with the *LinkItem*, creates a unique name for a Link. (The LinkItem–as distinct from the LinkTopic–is the *Name* Property of whichever Control on the source Form will be receiving information across the Link.)

• Several destinations can receive data from the same source over the same Link. In this situation, there will be one LinkTopic because this is a single Link, fanning out its information to several destinations. There will be a single LinkItem, too. (See Example 1 below.)

More Than One Link Can Share a Topic: More than one Link can share the same LinkTopic. In this mode, the Links are connected to the same source Form, but different Controls on that Form are feeding information. The Links will then be distinguished by having different LinkItem names. (See Example 2 below.)

• A client can be linked only to one source at a time; destinations can have only one LinkTopic and LinkItem name at a time.

• If you change a Form's LinkTopic Property while a program is running (a Form LinkTopic always identifies the *source*), the Link is destroyed and all conversations on it are terminated. Of course, you can immediately set up different Links by setting new LinkTopics and allow destinations to connect with these new conversations.

• The first half of a destination LinkTopic is the name of the source program, with the .EXE omitted (WINWORD, not WINWORD.EXE).

• LinkTopics and LinkItems are not case-sensitive; it doesn't matter how or whether you capitalize some of the letters in these names.

Example 1
We'll set up a single source program with a Text Box. But we'll link three destination program Text Boxes to it. Notice that the Link sends the same content to each destination, but each destination's FontSize and FontName Properties remain unique. Qualities like FontItalic, etc., are not automatically conveyed over Links (although you could transmit them—or anything else—with the LinkExecute command, which see).

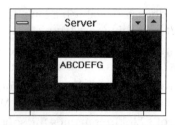

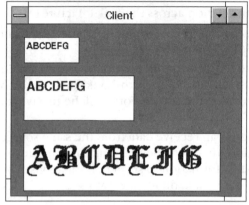

Figure L-62: Such Properties as FontName and FontSize are *not* transmitted over a Link when text is sent.

Source (Server): Create a source program by selecting New Project from VB's File Menu and put a Text Box on the Form. In the Form_Load Event, set the LinkTopic:

```
Sub Form_Load ()
    LinkTopic = "Big"
End Sub
```

Then change the *Form's* LinkMode to 1-Source in the Properties Window. Then save this program as S.EXE by using Make EXE File from the VB File Menu.

Remember, the LinkTopic can be any name you choose. It's like a Name Property; you decide what it should be. However, when you refer to it later in the destination program, you must use the same name.

Destination (Client or Container): Create a destination program by selecting New Project from VB's File Menu. Put three Text Boxes on the Form. In the Form_Load Event, type the following instructions:

```
Sub Form_Load ()

text1.LinkTopic = "S | Big"
text2.LinkTopic = "S | Big"
text3.LinkTopic = "S | Big"
```

```
text1.linkitem = "text1"
text2.linkitem = "text1"
text3.linkitem = "text1"

text1.linkmode = 1
text2.linkmode = 1
text3.linkmode = 1

text1.fontsize = 9
text2.fontsize = 12
text3.fontsize = 36

text3.fontname = "Linotext"
End Sub
```

Here we've set the LinkTopic of all three Text Boxes to "S|Big"–the filename of the source program (which is S.EXE) plus the source program's LinkTopic name "Big." The destination LinkTopic is the source's name plus its LinkTopic–separated by the pipe (|), usually found as a shifted backslash (\) on the keyboard.

Then we set the LinkItem, which is the Name Property (Text1) of the source of data, the Text Box on the source program that provides data over this Link.

Next, we turn on the Link by invoking LinkMode.

We set the FontSizes differently and adjust a FontName–just to show that these Properties are qualities of the destination and that they are not part of the information that comes across a Link. Now, save this as an .EXE program by selecting Make EXE File and call the program C.EXE. Now run S.EXE; then run C.EXE. You can even run a second "instance" of C.EXE. See "Objects" for more about "instance."

Properties Are Not Sent Across a Link: When you run these programs, you notice that text is transmitted but not the Properties of that text, such as its FontName.

Example 2   It's easy to change Example 1 into an example of two Links coming out of the same Form. In this situation, the Links will share the same LinkTopic but will have different LinkItems; different Controls on the source will be providing data over the Link.

Add a second Text Box to the source Form. And merely change this line in the destination's Form_Load Event:

```
text2.linkitem = "text2"
```

Now the middle Text Box on the destination is linked to the new Text Box on the source. This Link is entirely independent, although it does share a LinkTopic Property with the other Link. Links are distinguished by *both* the LinkTopic and the LinkItem.

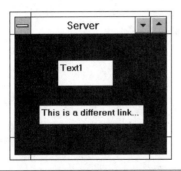

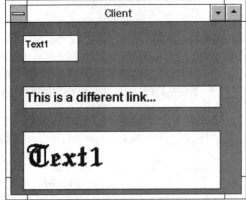

Figure L-63: An example of two Links emerging from the same Form. Each Text Box on the destination (client) program represents a unique, separate Link.

See also   LinkClose; LinkError; LinkExecute (Event and Method); LinkItem; LinkMode; LinkNotify; LinkOpen; LinkPoke; LinkRequest; LinkSend; LinkTimeout; OLE

(For an overview of linking, see "LinkMode.")

LIST

PROPERTY

Description   List provides one way for your program to find out which item in a Box-type Control has been selected by the user. The List Property is used in conjunction with the ListIndex number; List is a text ("string") Array containing all the items within a Box.

There are five types of Controls called "Boxes"—List, Combo, Directory, Drive and File Boxes.

The ListIndex Property points to the currently selected item in a Box. Therefore X$ = List(ListIndex) would provide your program with a text ("string") Variable, X$, which contained the currently selected item.

You cannot adjust the List Property for the file-related Boxes while you are writing your program, and you cannot adjust it while the program is running. (However, you can adjust the List Property for a Combo or List Box.) The three file-related Boxes do not allow you to change their Lists; these Boxes manage their Lists automatically with no intervention allowed by you, the programmer. Your program can, however, always find out various aspects of the Lists of any of the five Boxes while the program is running.

Used with   Combo Boxes, Directory, Drive & File List Boxes, List Boxes

Variables   **Variable type:** Text (string) Array

(To get item 6 from a List Box. Note that the first item in all Box-type Controls has a 0 index. Asking for (5) gives us the sixth item in the Box):

```
A$ = Combo1.List(5)
```

OR (to get the currently selected item): A$ = List1.List(List1.ListIndex)

OR (to display the currently selected item):

```
PRINT "You have selected "; List1.List(List1.ListIndex); " from the list."
```

(Be sure to identify the List and ListIndex by adding the Name Property of the Box involved.)

The different Box-type Controls utilize their List Properties in slightly different ways. The three disk-file Control Boxes (Drive, Directory and File) are automatically filled with the appropriate items. VB checks the computer and determines what items exist on the user's disk drive and, therefore, should be displayed within the Box.

The Combo and List Boxes are empty when a program starts running. You must use the AddItem command to place items within these Boxes (and RemoveItem to remove items). Normally, you would add items as part of your program's "initialization." You initialize your program when you properly set up the Variables and other housekeeping preparations for your program. Normally, you initialize right at the start—in the Form_Load Event—before the user even sees one of your program's windows. Initialization takes place during that pause when nothing seems to be happening after a program is first run.

Uses   • Find out which item in a Boxed-list-type Control has been selected by the user. Based on this information, your program can take appropriate action.

• Find out the status of the disk drive while a program is running—what is the selected drive and directory? What files are listed in the current directory? See "Drive List Box" for a complete discussion on disk file management using the three file-related Boxes.

Cautions   • The ListIndex number begins with the *zeroth* item in a List. If you attempt to identify the fifth item in a List, you should ask for List1.List(4).

Another consequence is that ListCount is the total number of items. List-Count –1 is the number of the last item.

This numbering system is an unhappy by-product of the way computers currently handle Arrays (which see).

To find out the name of the seventh item in a List:

```
X$ = List1.List(6)
```

To find out how many items are in the list:

```
X = List1.ListCount
```

• The ListIndex number works peculiarly for Directory List Boxes. The current directory (the active directory when your program starts running) is represented by –1. Directories *higher* (such as a parent directory) are represented by –2, –3 and so on–the higher the directory is in the structure, the lower its ID number. Conversely, subdirectories under the current directory count from 0 up to ListCount –1.

Example

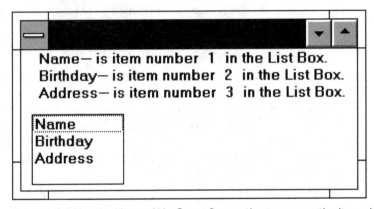

Figure L-64: Use the List and ListCount Properties to access the items in a List Box.

To put items into the List Box, you'll normally use the AddItem command within the Form_Load Event:

```
Sub Form_Load ()
    List1.AddItem "Name"
    List1.AddItem "Birthday"
    List1.AddItem "Address"
End Sub
```

If you want items alphabetized within the List Box, set its Sorted Property to –1.

To access and print the items in the Box, use the List Property:

```
Sub Form_Click ()
    For i = 0 To List1.ListCount – 1
        Print "   "; List1.List(i);
        Print "– is item number "; i + 1; " in the List Box."
    Next i
End Sub
```

Note the adjustments we had to make—subtracting 1 from ListCount and adding 1 to i—because ListCount starts counting at the zeroth item.

See also   AddItem; the five Box-type Controls: Combo, Directory, Drive, File and List; ListCount; ListIndex; MultiSelect; RemoveItem; and Selected

CONTROL

Figure L-65: The symbol for a List Box on the Toolbox.

Description   A List Box is the same as a Combo Box, except the user cannot type anything into a List Box. He or she can only click on one or more of the listed items, thereby selecting that item or set of items.

Variables   To add a literal piece of text to a List Box: List1. AddItem "New Option"

OR (to add a Variable):
```
X$ = "Paris"
List1.AddItem X$
```

OR (to remove an item from a list): List1.RemoveItem 5

OR (to find out the total number of items in a List Box):
```
Print "There are "; List1.ListCount; " items in the List Box"
```

OR (to detect and display the name of the item the user has selected):

```
Print "The user has selected the item in position "; List1.ListIndex + 1; →
   " in this List Box"
Print "The name of this item is "; List1.List(List1.ListIndex)
```

OR (if the MultiSelect Property is turned on, to find how many items are selected):

```
For i = 0 to List1.ListCount − 1
    If List1.Selected(i) Then x = x + 1
Next i
Print x " items selected"
```

We have to add +1 to the ListIndex to report its position to the user because it starts counting items with the first item, which is the zeroth item in the List Box.

Uses • Provide the user with a list of "hard-wired" choices reflecting your judgment about appropriate options. If you want the user to select between light, medium and dark blue for the BackColor of a Form, put only those names in a List Box. The user must follow your aesthetic rules; those are the only options you offered.

Figure L-66: A List Box takes on a different character when surrounded by graphics and framed.

(See "Line" to find out how to create frames like the ones in Figure L-66.)

• Provide the user with the only *possible* choices. There are only two choices for FontBold: bold or not. So your List Box would contain only those two options. If, however, there are only two choices, perhaps an Option Button or Check Box might be more easily recognized as a True/False, On/Off Control.

• Make a List Box more accommodating to the user. Add a Text Box or other Controls to the Form, as adjuncts to a List Box, offering the user more flexible control than what a lone List Box would normally offer. Let the user, for instance, select from Check Boxes or Option Buttons to "Add-Items" (which see) to your List Box.

• List Boxes can be made more efficient in some situations by adjusting their MultiSelect, Columns and TopIndex Properties (which see). Multi-Select permits the user to select more than a single item at a time; Columns displays more than a single vertical list of items; and TopIndex allows your program to *scroll* the list, independent of the user.

Cautions

• A Combo Box with its Style Property set to 2 is called a "Dropdown Combo Box" and is almost identical to a List Box. The user cannot type anything into the Box and is presented with a list of options. The one difference is that the Dropdown Combo shows only one item from the list plus an arrow the user can click on to reveal the entire list. If you have a particularly crowded screen, this capability can save space.

• Use a Combo Box when the user should have the option of adding new items to the list by typing them in. Use a List Box when the options are provided by your program.

• You can allow the user to add or remove items from your list (with the AddItem and RemoveItem methods). One approach would be to have a single click highlight an item, then a keypress of the DELETE key delete the item, and the INS key replace the item (or the plus key could pop up another list from which the user could select items to add).

• The Text Property of a List Box always contains the currently selected item (available as a text ("string") Variable). X$ = List1.Text would allow your program to examine and react to the selected item in the Box. The Text Property of a Combo Box, however, can contain something the user may have typed in, some text that is not part of the Box proper.

• The user can select an item from a List Box by clicking on it or by typing in its first letter. This triggers a Click Event, without using the mouse.

• By convention, List and Combo Boxes are usually accompanied by Option Buttons, Check Boxes or Command Buttons. These extra Controls define how the program will respond to a user selecting from the List Box—a click (to select) or a double click (to take action).

Example

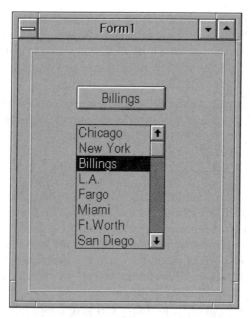

Figure L-67: To draw the thin frame, see the Emboss Subroutine under Line (Method). The lettering effect on the window's Title Bar was created with the "OSFrame" add-on product (see Appendix D).

Windows programs by convention use a single click on a List or Combo Box to highlight the clicked item, but no further action is taken. However, double-clicking causes action—a new window is opened, a file is loaded in or some such event.

In Figure L-67 a Command Button has been added to a List Box. This process is also common in Windows. Now there are two ways for the user to cause the program to respond—by double-clicking on an item in the Box or by clicking on the Command Button. The Command Button Click Event responds to whatever item in the list is highlighted at the time the user clicks. Within the List Box's Click Event, we put the command that changes the Button's Caption property:

```
Sub List1_Click()
    Command1.Caption = List1.List(List1.ListIndex)
End Sub
```

Notice, too, that if you design a List Box frame that is smaller than the list of items contained within the Box, VB automatically adds a vertical Scroll Bar.

List Box Properties
BackColor • Columns • DataField • DataSource • DragIcon
DragMode • Enabled • FontBold • FontItalic • FontName • FontSize
FontStrikethru • FontUnderline • ForeColor • Height • HelpContextID
hWnd • Index • ItemData • Left • List • ListCount • ListIndex →

MousePointer • MultiSelect • Name • NewIndex • Parent
Selected • Sorted • TabIndex • TabStop • Tag • Text • Top
TopIndex • Visible • Width

List Box Events
Click • DblClick • DragDrop • DragOver • GotFocus • KeyDown
KeyPress • KeyUp • LostFocus • MouseDown • MouseMove
MouseUp

List Box Methods
AddItem • Clear • Drag • Move • Refresh • RemoveItem • SetFocus
ZOrder

See also   AddItem; Combo Box; List; ListCount; ListIndex; MultiSelect; RemoveItem;
Selected; TopIndex

LISTCOUNT

PROPERTY

Description   ListCount works differently as a Property for the various Controls:

List Boxes and Combo Boxes. ListCount tells you how many items are in
the Box.

File List Box. ListCount tells you how many of the filenames listed in the
Box match the File List Box's Pattern Property (such as *.EXE). Therefore,
ListCount tells you how many filenames are displayed (or could be seen if
an attached Scroll Bar were used because the filenames exceed the visual
space of the Box).

Directory List Box. ListCount tells you the number of subdirectories that
exist below the current directory.

Drive List Box. ListCount tells you how many disk drives are in the
system (including "drives" in memory, such as those set up with
RAMDRIVE.SYS or network drives).

Used with   Combo Boxes, Directory, Drive & File List Boxes, List Boxes

Variables   **Variable type:** Integer

To find the total number of items in a List or Combo Box (see "Cautions"):
        X = Combo1.ListCount

Uses   • Manipulate the items in Combo and List Boxes by using ListCount along
with ListIndex, Selected, AddItem and RemoveItem.

• Find out how many files match a Pattern Property in a File List Box.

• Find out the number of subdirectories below the current directory in a Directory List Box.

• Find out the number of drives in the computer from a Drive List Box.

Cautions For Combo Boxes and List Boxes, the ListCount starts counting from the "zeroth" item. The only consequence of this oddity is that you must always remember to use ListCount –1 when manipulating the items in a Box (For I = 0 To ListCount –1).

Example

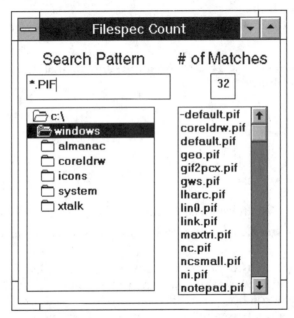

Figure L-68: Here's how to locate and count the number of files of a particular type.

The ListCount of a File List Box tells you the number of matches to a file specification. To achieve the result shown in Figure L-68, put two Labels, two Text Boxes, a Directory and a File List Box on a Form.

Whatever you type into Text1 becomes the Pattern Property for the File Box. Text2 displays the number of matches to that pattern. (In the example, we set *.PIF as the pattern. We used Str$ to change the number provided by ListCount into a text ("string") Variable because Text Boxes can display only string Variables.)

```
Sub Text1_Change ()
    file1.Pattern = text1.text
    text2.text = Str$(file1.ListCount)
End Sub
```

The following changes the File List Box when the user changes the selected Directory in the Directory List Box:

```
Sub Dir1_Change ()
    file1.path = dir1.path
End Sub
```

See also   AddItem; the five Box-type Controls: Combo, Directory, Drive, File and List; List; ListIndex; RemoveItem; and Selected

L IST INDEX

PROPERTY

Description   ListIndex provides an index number that points to the selected item in a List Box, Combo Box or one of the file-handling Boxes (File, Directory or Drive Box).

By using ListIndex, along with the List Property, you can find out what item in a Box the user has clicked on, then allow your program to respond in some fashion, e.g., X$ = Combo1.List(Combo1.ListIndex). Now X$ would contain the name of the selected item within the Combo Box.

The Text Property of a List Box or Combo Box, however, provides this same information more directly.

In addition, ListIndex provides special information that differs for each of the five Box-type Controls for which it is a Property. (See "Variables" below.)

Used with   Combo Boxes, Directory, Drive & File List Boxes, List Boxes

Variables   **Variable type:** Integer

```
Item$ = List1.List(List1.ListIndex)
Print "You have selected "; Item$; "from the List Box."
```

When your program first runs, the user has not yet intervened by selecting any item in any Box-type Control. While ListCount is in this pristine state, the meaning of ListCount varies:

List Box, Combo Box and File List Box. A ListCount of –1 means that no item has been selected.

Directory List Box. The ListCount will be –1, which is the index of the directory that was current when the program started. (See "List.")

Drive List Box. The ListCount will be a number that represents the drive that was current when the program started. (See "List.")

Uses   • Find out what the user has selected from within a Box-type Control.

• Find out which drive or directory was current (active) when your program started running.

Cautions

• For List Boxes and Combo Boxes, the ListIndex starts counting the items in the Box from the *zeroth* item. So you must add 1 to ListIndex to adjust the index to reflect reality. (For example, the fifth item is ListIndex = 4.)

To see how this works, put a Combo Box and a Command Button on a Form. Then type the following into their Click Events:

```
Sub Form_Click ()

combo1.AddItem "text1"
combo1.AddItem "text2"
combo1.AddItem "text3"
combo1.AddItem "text4"
combo1.AddItem "text5"
Debug.Print combo1.listcount

End Sub

Sub Command1_Click ()
    combo1.RemoveItem 4
End Sub
```

When you click on the Command Button, you'll notice that the item called *text5* is removed from the Combo Box even though you said "RemoveItem 4."

• If you want the items in a particular order within a List or Combo Box, use the AddItem command. Using it you can specify an index for the new item. This way, you can place an item where you want it. In this situation, leave the Box's Sorted Property set to 0, off. *Sorted* means that VB automatically keeps the items in alphabetical order.

If you adjust the ListIndex of a Combo Box, then the item identified by ListIndex will be the one that will show in the Box next to the arrow. If the user drops the Box down, then the ListIndex item will be highlighted. Using this technique, you can set ListIndex to a default selection (the most likely item to be selected) in the Combo Box but also allow the user to change it if needed.

To see how this technique works, put a Combo Box and a Command Button on a Form. Then type the following into their Click Events:

```
Sub Form_Click ()

combo1.AddItem "text1"
combo1.AddItem "text2"
combo1.AddItem "text3"
combo1.AddItem "text4"
combo1.AddItem "text5"
Debug.Print combo1.listcount

End Sub

Sub Command1_Click ()
    Debug.Print combo1.listindex
    combo1.listindex = 3
```

```
        Debug.Print combo1.listindex
    End Sub
```

You will see 0 and then 3 in the Immediate Window when you run this program. Then the text Variable *text4* will appear beside the arrow. If you drop the Box, *text4* will be highlighted.

• In a List Box or File List Box with the MultiSelect Property turned on, you would use the *Selected* Property–rather than the ListIndex Property–to find out which *group* of items the user had selected. See "Selected" for more.

Example In a very closely watched chicken farm operation, the owner keeps track of the types of poultry, as well as their individual statistics. In this example, we'll illustrate how ListIndex can be used in two different ways–to report the position of a selected item in a Box and to remove a selected item from a Box.

Create a Form with a List Box, a Combo Box (its Style Property set to 1, simple combo) and two Labels.

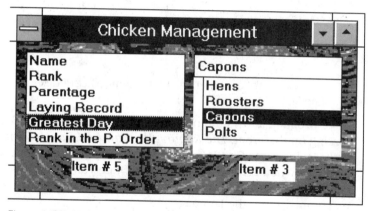

Figure L-69: A closely watched chicken farm

As usual, we do the initial housekeeping for our program in the Form_Load Event. In this case, we fill the Boxes with their various items:

```
Sub Form_Load ()
    List1.AddItem "Name"
    List1.AddItem "Rank"
    List1.AddItem "Parentage"
    List1.AddItem "Laying Record"
    List1.AddItem "Greatest Day"
    List1.AddItem "Rank in the P. Order"

    Combo1.AddItem "Hens"
    Combo1.AddItem "Roosters"
    Combo1.AddItem "Capons"
    Combo1.AddItem "Polts"
End Sub
```

We want the Labels to show the Item number selected when the user clicks within a Box. Note that we have to add 1 to ListIndex to get the correct position; remember that ListIndex starts counting items from the *zeroth* item.

The Zeroth Bugaboo: Computers at this point in their evolution, unfortunately, think of the first object in a series or group as being the *zeroth* object. Humans don't. We don't say, "My house is the zeroth house you'll see after you cross the bridge."

For now, though, starting at zero is what the computers want and what we must adjust to when dealing with *Arrays*. In computing, an Array is a series, or group, of related items (see "Arrays"). The List Property of a Box-type Control is an Array, and the ListIndex Property points to a specific item within that Array.

Also notice that ListIndex, being a number, must be translated by the Str$ command into a text ("string") Variable. Caption Properties can deal only with strings:

```
Sub List1_Click ()
    label1.caption = "Item #" + Str$(List1.ListIndex + 1)
End Sub

Sub Combo1_Click ()
    label2.caption = "Item #" + Str$(Combo1.ListIndex + 1)
End Sub
```

The program allows the user to remove an item from a Box by double-clicking on that item. *The RemoveItem and AddItem Methods relate to ListIndex as if the first item were the first item!* You don't need to add 1 to ListCount when using these methods. Once you learn these different techniques, it's easy to adjust your programming to fit the requirements of the computer and the language.

```
Sub List1_DblClick ()
    List1.RemoveItem List1.ListIndex
End Sub

Sub Combo1_DblClick ()
    Combo1.RemoveItem Combo1.ListIndex
End Sub
```

See also   AddItem; the five Box-type Controls: Combo, Directory, Drive, File and List; List; ListCount; RemoveItem; and Selected

 INKVIEW   CONTROL

See Windows 95 Controls

LOAD

Description   The Load Event is triggered when a Form is brought into being. Loading a Form makes its Event Procedures, Subroutines and Functions available for use by the rest of your program. Loading, however, does not necessarily make a Form visible to the user.

One Form in each program is special. It's called the *Startup Form*. Visual Basic will automatically Load the Startup Form when the program starts running, and the Startup Form will be automatically visible as well. If you don't want the Startup Form to be visible, set its Visible Property off (0). (You can make a Module govern the initial phase of your program by creating a Sub Main ( ) in the Module and then writing commands inside it that determine the Forms that should be loaded. In this case, there is no Statup Form.)

For other Forms, a Load can happen in two ways:

- When the Load Statement is used somewhere in your program, naming that Form and commanding it to become active.

- When a reference is made to an Event, Control or Property of that Form somewhere in your program. (Form 3.FontSize = 12, for instance.)

Note that a Form (other than the Startup Form) does not become visible in either of these situations. The Show Method makes a Form visible (and is a third way to implicitly Load a Form).

The Startup Form: The Load Event of the Startup Form is an important and specialized Event. It is the first thing that happens when your program starts running. Often you'll want to put some commands and instructions into this particular Load Event. Here you do any housekeeping preliminaries that are necessary for the rest of the program to perform as it should.

Early programming languages were far more *linear* than Visual Basic. In fact, each line of a program was *numbered* in sequence. When the program was started up, the lowest line number contained the instructions that were the first thing that happened. If, for example, the program needed some data placed into a box from which the user selected, you would often find a list of items following a DATA statement very near the start of the program.

Those linear and more primitive approaches to programming have been eclipsed by Visual Basic and other languages that share its spirit of extending freedom to the user. Visual Basic does not set up a fixed routine for its users. Instead, a set of tools, Forms, Controls and other options are simply placed on the screen. The user largely determines which tools are used and when they are used. The user, not the programmer, decides the order of events.

There's one exception. The user does not control the Form_Load Event of the Startup Form (or of the commands within a Sub Main ( ) in a Module, if you use that approach). Within this Load Event you can put anything that your program needs which you didn't, or couldn't, define during the design of the program. One example is the list of items in a List Box—because that list cannot be defined as a Property of the List Box. These items must be fed to the program when it starts running; preliminary housekeeping is the primary value and intended purpose of the Form_Load Event.

Changing the Startup Form: If your program has more than one Form (many don't), you can change which of the Forms is the Startup Form from the VB Tools|Options Menu. If you don't make this change, the Startup Form will be the first Form that appeared when you selected New Project from VB's File Menu and began creating your program.

Commands you placed within the Form_Load Event (or in VB4, the Form_Initialize Event) of the Startup Form will be the first to happen when the user runs your program. You *initialize* your program within the Form_Load Event. Initialization, in programming, means setting up preconditions, creating graphics, establishing Links, adjusting Properties that you didn't define while designing the program, filling List and Combo Boxes, or defining some of your Variables and Constants. None of these things *must* take place, but often you'll want to set up some things at the very start.

The Form_Load Event of the Startup Form is the one place in your program that the user cannot avoid. No matter what else the user might choose to do, the Startup Form's Form_Load Event will happen.

Used with   Forms only

Variables   When a Form is loaded, all its Variables are initially zero (or, in the case of text ("string") Variables, *empty* "" strings). This predictability is valuable to the programmer; you don't need to worry about random values accidentally occupying your Variables.

However, you will often want to use a Form_Load Event to initialize Variables, to give them their initial values. You can also use the Load Event to set Properties such as Width of Controls, position, colors, etc. Stuffing items into a List Box is another frequently necessary Variable initialization because there is no way to do that while designing your program:

```
Sub Form_Load ()
    List1.AddItem "US"
    List1.AddItem "Foreign"
    List1.AddItem "First Day Covers"
    List1.AddItem "Postcards"
    List1.AddItem "Airmail"

    List1.Left = 0
    List1.Top = 0
End Sub
```

Uses • Because a Form_Load (or Form_Initialize) Event is the first thing that happens when a program starts running, the Startup Form's Form_Load (or Form_Initialize) Event is the place to put necessary initialization. This will include creating Links, adjusting Properties that you didn't define while designing the program, filling List and Combo Boxes, or defining some of your Variables and Constants.

• When Visual Basic starts running a program, VB must do a number of things, such as accessing DLLs (Dynamic Link Libraries) and establishing the various qualities of Controls that you selected from the Properties Window when designing your program. VB performs these actions in addition to any initialization your program might also perform.

These initializations can create a delay that makes it appear to the user as if nothing is happening—as if the computer is "locked up." To keep from disconcerting the user, some programs change the mouse cursor to an hourglass. Others display a title and copyright window. To see one technique that lets the user know things are working as they should during startup, see the Example that follows.

Cautions • When any Form is Loaded, the following Events are triggered in the following order: Load, Resize, Paint, GotFocus.

• Load is related to the UnLoad Event. The user can cause UnLoad by clicking on the Form's Control Box—the button in the upper left-hand corner. Or Unload can be triggered by your program, using the UnLoad Statement.

In either case, the Form's visual elements disappear from the computer's memory. The Form is no longer visible. All its Variables are set to 0 or, for text Variables, empty "". This frees up some of the memory in the computer that the Form was using. Its Event Procedures, Subroutines and Functions, though, remain in the computer's memory. Can your program still access these elements of the UnLoaded Form? Can a still-loaded Form utilize the programming that's still there in memory? Yes and no. It's a somewhat torturous process and probably more trouble than it's worth.

You *can* access the *Properties* of Controls on other Forms, and in some cases, changing a Property will trigger an Event on the other Form. For example, try it with the Value Property. But you can't directly call an Event in another Form. If you need to do the same thing in two different Forms, put the commands in a Subroutine (see "Sub") in a Module. Then, when you want the commands executed, call that Sub from within either Form.

In any case, if you think a Form will have to be shown again while the program is running, it will take some time to Load its visible elements into the computer again. In this situation, using the Hide command is better.

• Hide and Show are commands that make a Form invisible or visible. If a Form has not been Loaded, Show automatically causes a Load. The Startup Form is always Loaded and always triggers a Show.

• The Show method Loads a Form if it has not yet been Loaded. Show also makes a Form visible, unless the Form's Visible Property is turned off (0).

Show can be either *modal* or *modeless*. You can provide an optional modal number following the Show command:

```
Form2.Show 1
```

Show with a 0 after it (or no mode number) is the normal "modeless" window.

Putting 1 after Show, however, creates a special situation: The user cannot access other windows until this "modal" window (Form) is closed. Other programs that are running can continue to process information, but the user cannot access them. The Visual Basic program, however, halts all activity until the modal Form is disposed of. MsgBoxes, InputBoxes and error warning windows are examples of modal Forms.

Example

Figure L-70: A Title screen for the user to watch while the program gets itself together.

We want this Title screen of our program to appear while the Startup Form is initializing and while VB is getting itself together to run the program. We'll set a Timer to display the Title screen for 10 seconds and then UnLoad it. When its job is finished, there's no reason to simply hide it. We won't need to make it visible again.

As a further visual clue to the user that things are happening, we'll change the mouse pointer to an hourglass. In the Startup Form's Form_Load Event:

```
Sub Form_Load ()
    Timer1.Interval = 10000
```

```
    Form2.MousePointer = 11
    Form2.Show

    Form2.FontSize = 48
    Form2.Currentx = 800
    Form2.Currenty = 300
    Form2.Print "GARDENING"

    Form2.Currentx = 800
    Form2.Currenty = Form2.Currenty - 300
    Form2.Print "DIARY";

    Form2.FontSize = 12
    Form2.Currenty = Form2.Currenty + 100
    Form2.Print Chr$(174)

  ' Here we would perform our Program's Initializations
  End Sub
```

First, we put a Timer on Form1, the Startup Form. We set Form1's Visible Property to 0, so it won't appear onscreen. Then we create Form2 (from VB's File Menu). We set Form2's BorderStyle to 3, Fixed Double, and set its Control Box Property to False (removing the button on the upper left of the Form).

Now, in the Startup Form's Load Event, we set the timer to 10 seconds (10,000 milliseconds). Recall that a Timer starts when its Form Loads, unless you turn its Enabled Property off (False).

Printing Special Symbols: Next, we change the mouse pointer from the default (0) to 11, which makes it look like an hourglass. Then we set a large FontSize and move the CurrentX and CurrentY properties of Form2 to where we want to print the word *GARDENING*. We again adjust the print position for the word *DIARY* and adjust it once more to print the Registered Trademark symbol. The FontSize is reset to small. Chr$ allows you to print symbols that cannot be enclosed in quotation marks (because they are not available on the keyboard, you can't type them in). To see which symbols you can print, and their codes, search VB's Help window for ANSI. ANSI will show you the list of character codes you can use with the Chr$ command.

After printing on Form2, we can perform whatever initializations our program might require.

The Timer, when it has finished counting 10 seconds, does the following:

```
  Sub Timer1_Timer ()
      Unload Form2
      MousePointer = 0
  End Sub
```

The Event will make Form2 invisible and remove it from memory. It also returns the mouse cursor to its default arrow shape.

It is possible that our program could take longer than 10 seconds to initialize (initialization varies depending on the program's needs and on the speed of the user's computer). However, you presented the Title Screen, and even if it disappears before your program comes visibly to life, the user is likely to remain calm.

An alternative approach would be to avoid using the Timer. You would simply put UnLoad Form2 at the end of the Startup Form's initializations. This approach, though, can cause the Title Screen to simply flash in front of the user if there is little initialization or if the user has a fast computer.

See also   Hide; Load (Statement); QueryUnLoad; Show; UnLoad

LOAD

STATEMENT

Description   The Load Statement is used in two unrelated ways:

• The first use of the Load Statement brings a Form into the computer's memory but does not make it visible. Load is rarely used for this purpose, however, because Show automatically Loads, as does any reference in your program to the Form or any of its Properties, Controls, Events, Subroutines or Functions.

In Visual Basic, a Form can perform two functions. It can be a visible window, a zone of the screen that informs the user or accepts input from the user. However, a Form is also a fundamental unit of organization for the programmer—roughly equivalent to a chapter in a book. Related Controls, Events and Subroutines are grouped together on a Form. In this way, Forms help the programmer arrange and order the program in a sensible, quickly understood fashion.

• A second use for the Load command involves Control Arrays (see "Control Array"). By creating a Control and giving it an Index Property, you let VB know that you may be adding additional Controls (of the same type). This group of Controls is called a *Control Array*, and all the Controls in the Array will share the same name but will be distinguished by having different Index numbers: Text1(0), Text1(1), Text1(2), etc. They will also inherit the Properties, the qualities, of the original member of the Array (unless you specifically change the offsprings' Properties). All members of the Control Array also share the same Events.

A second way to create a Control Array is to give two Controls the same name. VB will then ask you if you want to create an Array.

Control Arrays are useful in two ways:

1. The members of a Control Array share the same name but are uniquely identified by a different *number* that's attached to the name. This way they can be manipulated within a Loop. You can refer to each Control by using the Loop counter (I in this example):

```
For I = 0 to 3
    Text1(I).Visible = False
Next I
```

This approach is a more efficient way to make four Text Boxes invisible than the following way, where only their *names* can be used to identify them:

```
Text1.Visible = False
Text2.Visible = False
Text3.Visible = False
Text4.Visible = False
```

You should use Control Arrays if you will be frequently manipulating the Properties of a group of Controls or if you want to be able to *create* new Controls while your program is running. Also, because the members of a Control Array all share the same Event Procedures, additional efficiencies are possible. (See the Example.)

2. The only way to bring new Controls into existence *while your program is running* is to use a Control Array. (See the Example below.)

Used with   Forms and Control Arrays

Variables   To load in a Form:

```
Load Form2
```

OR (to create a new member of a Control Array. The Name Picture1 must have already been made into a Control Array while you were designing your program. See "Control Array"): Load Picture1(3)

Uses   • Bring a Form into action in the program, but don't make it visible.

For example, if you generate data from the activities on one Form and need to display the data on another Form, by Loading and not Showing the second Form, you can access its Properties, fill Text Boxes, etc. When the second Form is filled with the data, you are finished with the first Form, and you can then Show the second Form. Load is rarely used in this way, however, because setting a Form's Visible Property to False is usually more practical if you want to use the Form but don't want it seen.

The Show command—or any reference to a Form, anywhere in your program—will automatically Load in the Form.

• The most common use for Load is to bring new Controls into existence while a program is running. (See the Example.)

Cautions
• Your program cannot Load an already Loaded Form. Because there is only one of each Form, you can't Load a Form a second time unless you have UnLoaded it in the meantime. A Form is a single entity. In computer parlance: There should only be one *instance* of a Form at any given time—for the same reason that you can't put on your hat if it's already on your head. VB, nonetheless, *does* permit multiple instances of the *same Form*. However, you create multiple instances with the "Set" command or as a part of an MDI Form (see "Multiple Document Interface (MDI) Form").

• MsgBox and InputBox$ are special kinds of Forms; you create them by simply using them as commands, much the way you would Print something. Although technically Forms, they operate more like the Print command. Neither MsgBox nor InputBox$ works with the Form commands Hide, Show, Load or UnLoad.

Example
Let's see how to use the Load command to create members of a Control Array while a program is running.

Create a Picture Box and set its Index Property to 0 by using the Properties Window. Create a Label and set its Index to 0 as well. By setting these Index Properties, you create two Control Arrays. Put a button or bead-like icon into Picture1(0), by setting its Picture Property.

Now, in the Form_Click Event, enter the following:

```
Sub Form_Click ()

For I = 1 To 5
    Load Picture1(I)
    Picture1(I).Visible = True
    Picture1(I).Top = Picture1(I – 1).Top + 500

    Load Label1(I)
    Label1(I).Visible = True
    Label1(I).Top = Picture1(I).Top + 100
    Label1(I).Caption = "Choice #" + Str$(I + 1)
Next I

End Sub
```

Notice that we don't have to create a Picture for each of the new Picture Controls that are born here; Control Array babies share all the Properties of the parent Control (except Visible, Index and TabIndex).

A single Picture and Label are all that you created on this Form:

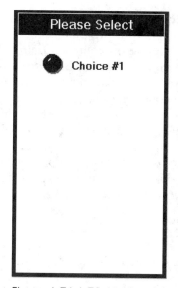

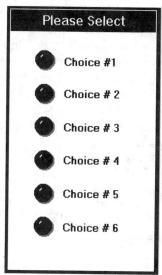

Figures L-71, L-72: Making clones of this single Picture creates a whole nest of Buttons.

When you click on the Form, the Arrays are created. The Load Statement, repeated five times within the Loop, fathers these new Controls.

See also   Array; Hide; Load (Event); QueryUnLoad; Set; Show; UnLoad

LOADPICTURE

FUNCTION

Description   You could do all of the things that LoadPicture does while you are designing your program. But the LoadPicture Function *allows you to do them while your program is running.*

LoadPicture puts a new graphic image into a Form, Picture Box, Image or the Clipboard. (This is the same as typing the filename of a graphic into the Picture Property of a Form or Picture Box using the Properties Window while designing your program.)

LoadPicture can also be used to give a Form a new icon. (This is the same as setting the Form's Icon Property.)

Finally, LoadPicture can give a Control a new "drag icon." (This is the same as setting a Control's DragIcon Property. All Controls except Timers or Menus have a DragIcon Property.)

Images and icons can be put into your program while you are designing the program, by setting the Picture and Icon Properties of Forms and

Controls. Such graphics become a permanent part of your program; they are embedded in the .EXE file that is your program.

Images and icons loaded in while the program is running, using the LoadPicture Function, *do not become a permanent part of the program.* They are visible and can be manipulated like embedded images, but when the program is shut down, they go away. (None of this has any effect on the files on disk from which the graphic was LoadPictured into your program. Copies are made for use in your program when LoadPicture is invoked.)

With LoadPicture, the graphics must be available on the disk; they are not part of your program. *And your program can be considerably smaller because it will not contain, but rather will import, bulky graphic images.*

Used with   Forms, the Clipboard and all Controls except Timers

Variables   (With Forms)   Picture = LoadPicture("C:\BMPS\LEGER.BMP")
                                                Icon = LoadPicture("C:\VBASIC\ICONS\FILE02.ICO")

   (Picture Boxes   Picture2.Picture = LoadPicture("DUBOIS.WMF")
   or Image Controls)

   (Controls' DragIcons)   Label1.DragIcon = LoadPicture("SHADOW.ICO")

   (The Clipboard)   Clipboard.SetData LoadPicture("ROSE.BMP")

Uses   • Allow the user to change the icons or background graphics used in your program. These changes don't become permanent features of the program, but they do allow some measure of temporary customization.

You *could* provide an .INI file, however, to accompany your program. If the user makes any changes to the graphics, Open that .INI file and record the changes. Then each time the program runs, it first checks its .INI file to see what graphics the user wants loaded in.

• Allow your program to respond graphically to conditions while the program is running. For instance, a family budget program might load in a picture of a bright, sunny day when the monthly budget is calculated and is in the black. If, however, more money went out than came in, a rainy day picture could be loaded.

• You can, of course, create a number of Image Controls, making them invisible by setting their Visible Property to 0. Then display them as the situation requires. This procedure is faster than LoadPicture—which must read from the disk—but if the graphics are large, this approach can quickly make your program enormous. .BMP and .WMF graphics images can be huge.

• **Erasing With LoadPicture:** Clear a Picture Box or the background graphic on a Form. By using LoadPicture with no filename, your Picture Box, Image, or the background of your Form will go blank. This procedure is the equivalent of using Cls to clear graphics that were *drawn* on Forms or Picture Boxes using the drawing methods PSet, Circle, Line or Print:

```
Picture1.Picture = LoadPicture()
```

• For graphics-intensive programs. If your program is going to allow a perusal of many different graphics (a "viewer" type of program), you will neither know which images the user wants to view nor could your program contain all of them and remain of reasonable size. Use LoadPicture for such programs and similar applications such as Icon Viewers, etc.

• Allow the user (or your program) to import pictures from the disk drive to the Clipboard:

```
Clipboard.SetData LoadPicture("CHEF.BMP")
```

• Allow the user to import pictures from the Clipboard into your program. Once in the Clipboard, they can then be placed into your program with the GetData Method:

```
Picture1.Picture Clipboard.GetData()
```

Cautions   • At this time, LoadPicture works with graphics saved only in .ICO, .BMP or .WMF (Windows MetaFile) file formats.

• As with any disk access, you should use On Error (which see), so that if the expected graphics file cannot be loaded in, your program will handle that gracefully and not shut down on the user. (See the Example below.)

• LoadPicture keeps the huge graphics images on the disk, and not in your program, where only a few of them could bloat the program to immense size. However, LoadPicture will slow up your program when it is used. It isn't nearly as rapid as Picture1.Visible = –1, as a way of showing something new to the user. For animation, though, you should use the Visible technique, even at the cost of making your program larger. And there is no reason not to include tiny .ICO files as invisible parts of your program, made visible as needed. Each .ICO adds only 766 bytes to your program.

Example   This program will allow you to view any .ICO, .BMP or .WMF file on your disk.

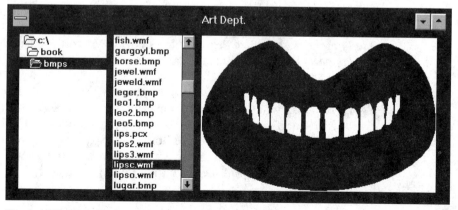

Figure L-73: With the LoadPicture command, you can create a graphics viewer.

Put a Directory List Box, a File List Box and a Picture Box on a Form. Set the Picture's AutoSize Property to –1, so it will expand and contract to fit the graphics Loaded into it.

Into the Directory List Box's Change Event, enter the following. (With this, the File List Box will respond to changes that user-clicking causes in the Directory Box):

```
Sub Dir1_Change ()
     file1.path = dir1.path
End Sub
```

Next, put the following into the File Box's DblClick Event, to allow the user to bring in whatever image is wanted:

```
Sub File1_DblClick ()
     On Error Resume Next

     f$ = file1.path + "\" + file1.filename
     picture1.picture = LoadPicture(f$)

     If Err Then MsgBox (Error$(Err))
End Sub
```

The backslash character is always used unless File.Path is *not* the root directory. One way to deal with this character is to see if a \ is the last symbol in a File1.Path Property (using the Right$ command), and then add one if necessary.

See "On Error" for more on error trapping, and see "Drive List Box" for more on how to access a disk drive using the File, Directory and Drive List Boxes.

As with any creative activity that you take seriously, a program is never really completed. You can always improve it, make it more pleasant for the user, add features, reduce its size or speed it up. Let's take this DblClick one step further.

Improvements: Although the AutoSize Property does embrace the dimensions of an imported graphic, the Form itself does not adjust to the size. There is no AutoSize Property for a Form. We will simulate a Form.AutoSize Property and also handle a freak quality of .WMF files. They don't work well with AutoSize at all.

.WMF graphics are very flexible; you can pull a .WMF graphic into a Picture Box while designing your program *and stretch or shrink the image at will.* But if you Load .WMF files dynamically while the program is running, and you have the Picture Box's AutoSize Property turned on, the .WMF images retract themselves and become very tiny. We want all the images to come in full size, like the one in Figure L-74:

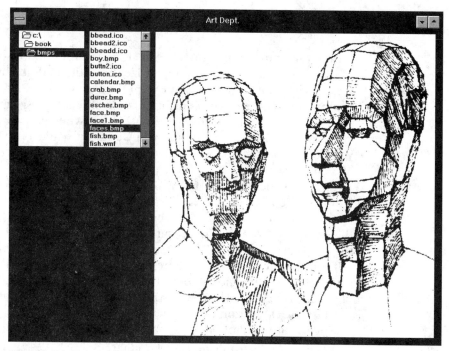

Figure L-74: Our graphics viewer window expands to the size of the image we select to view.

Here are the additions to the Sub File1_DblClick ( ) Event that will make things work better:

```
Sub File1_DblClick ()

width = 8640
height = 3648

On Error Resume Next

f$ = file1.Path
If Right$(f$,1) <> "\" Then f$ = f$ + "\"
f$ = f$ + file1.Filename
picture1.picture = LoadPicture(f$)

If UCase$(Right$(file1.filename, 3)) = "WMF" Then
    picture1.width = 4692
    picture1.height = 2892
    Exit Sub
End If

x = picture1.left + picture1.width + 300
y = picture1.top + picture1.height + 600

If x > width Then width = x

If y > height Then height = y
```

```
If Err Then MsgBox(Error$(Err))
End Sub
```

Each time this Event happens, each time the user double-clicks on the File Box, we tell the program what size the width and height were when we designed the Form. We don't want the Form or the Picture Box to respond to .WMF's dimensions because .WMF files really have *no dimension*. They can be made any size. That's great when you are designing—you can adjust them to whatever size you want. But when a program is running, you don't want them to establish their own size. They shrivel themselves like cold roses.

If the user tries to import a .WMF graphic type (we check the last three letters of the FileName of the File Box to find out), we set the width of the Picture Box to its original size when the Form was designed. Then we leave this Event via Exit Sub. This ensures that the imported .WMF will be a standard size. WMF graphics act as if AutoSize means *minimize yourself*.

If the graphic isn't a .WMF type, we go past that If...Then structure and make the Form expand or contract to accommodate the fixed size of .BMP files. This is our simulated AutoSizing of a Form. However, if the user Loads in a little .ICO, we don't want the Form to go microscopic.

We measure the imported graphic (adding some twips for a border):

```
x = picture1.left + picture1.width + 300
y = picture1.top + picture1.height + 600
```

Then we tell the program: If either of these x/y (width/height) measurements is larger than the designed Picture Box, expand the Picture Box—otherwise, leave it alone.

Where did we get the following default measurements?

```
width = 8640
height = 3648
picture1.width = 4692
picture1.height = 2892
```

Easy. When you are designing a Visual Basic program, the default dimensions—the *size* of your Form (or of its Controls)—are always available at the far right of the VB Menu Bar if the Toolbar option is turned on. Click on a Control or on the Form, and VB will report its size:

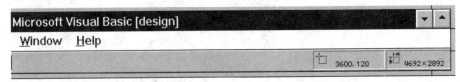

Figure L-75: Size and position information is available on the right end of the Menu Bar. You can see the dimensions and location of the selected object.

(The information immediately to the left of the size information tells you the *position* of the Form on the screen. For Forms, the size and position are always measured in *twips*. For Controls, the default is twips but can be inches, centimeters, pixels, points and other measurements—if you have fiddled with the ScaleMode Property of the host Form. See "ScaleMode.")

How about the amounts we added to create a border around the Picture Box? How did we figure the +300 and +600?

```
x = picture1.left + picture1.width + 300
y = picture1.top + picture1.height + 600
```

Easy again. VB, unlike more primitive languages, exacts no time penalty for trying different things and watching the results. You can adjust these border amounts, and then just press F5 to run the program to see if that's what you want.

See also   DragIcon; GetData; Icon; Picture; SavePicture; SetData

Loc

FUNCTION

Description   When you have Opened a disk file, Loc tells you your "current location" within that file.

When first Opened, the current location is the first byte in the disk file (the first text character, for example). However, the current location will change when you pull information into your program from the file or add information to the file. Loc tracks these changes.

Loc keeps track of any "reading" from the file (pulling information off the file) or "writing" to the file (putting information into the file). Because reading and writing can move you forward or backward in the file, Loc maintains a pointer to the current position within the collection of information in a file—like your finger moving down the Yellow Pages of a telephone directory. Your finger is always in a particular position within the data.

What Loc tells you depends on the kind of file you have Opened.

With *sequential files*, Loc tells you the current "byte position" divided by 128 (see "Cautions").

With *binary files*, Loc tells you the location of whichever byte (a small unit of computer memory that can, for instance, hold a single text character) was most recently accessed—either read from or written to.

With *random-access* files, Loc tells you the record number of whichever record was most recently accessed—either read from or written to.

(See "Input$" for an overview of sequential files. See "Open" for a general discussion about binary and random-access files.)

Note that there is a similar function called Seek. Seek tells you where the *next* read from, or write to, a file will take place. Although the results from Seek will usually be the same as Loc +1, the similarity isn't inevitable. Reading from or writing to a file *will* update both Loc and Seek within a file. However, there is also a Seek *Statement. Using the Seek Statement moves the pointer wherever you want within a file, without performing any reading or writing.* The Seek *Function* would be updated when the Seek *Statement* moved you to a different location within the file. The Loc Function would not know about this update because no reading or writing had taken place. (See "Seek.")

Used with Opened Disk Files

Variables   X = Loc(1)

Uses Using Loc you know the position within an Opened file of the most recent activity involving that file. This pointer is useful when you are updating a file because it allows you to always know the record location, record number or byte position of the most recent read or write. (All of this is true as long as the Seek Statement is not used.)

Loc is also somewhat similar to the way InStr works with text ("string") Variables–keeping you apprised of your "current location" within a larger piece of data. However, InStr also searches for a matching piece of text within a larger body of text. Loc merely lets you know where, in an Opened file, reading or writing last occurred.

Cautions • Loc is not the best choice when you are working with sequential files. Use Seek instead. The Seek Function has two advantages over Loc:

  ▪ The Seek Function is aware of changes made to the current location by the use of the Seek Statement.

  ▪ The Seek Function will provide a more precise pointer to the current location with files Opened in the popular sequential mode.

• Loc reports the byte-position within a file Opened in the binary mode, the record position for a file Opened in the random mode and the number of 128-byte chunks you are into a file Opened in the sequential mode.

Sequential–the method used most often for reading and writing text–has no fixed record size (as does random). You can read or write data of varying length (usually sentences or paragraphs). Because Loc, in this case, is imprecise, it is not generally useful with sequential files. Use *Seek* instead of Loc when you need to know the precise byte position.

Example
```
Sub Form_Click ()
Print "BINARY FILE ACCESS": Print
Open "C:\WINDOWS\SYSTEM.INI" For Binary As 1
For i = 1 To 6
```

```
        a$ = Input$(1, #1)
        x = Loc(1)
        Print "    Loc ("; x; ") = "; a$
    Next i

    Print
    Print "Now Loc is:"; Loc(1)
    Print "Now Seek is:"; Seek(1)
    Print

    Close 1

    Print "SEQUENTIAL FILE ACCESS": Print

    Open "C:\WINDOWS\SYSTEM.INI" For Input As 1

    For i = 1 To 6
        x = Loc(1)
        a$ = Input$(128, #1)
        Print "    Loc ("; x; ") = "; Left$(a$, 9)
    Next i

    Close 1

    End Sub
```

The preceding Subroutine demonstrates how Loc keeps track of the most recent file activity—in this case, reading information from the SYSTEM.INI file. We show Loc working with individual bytes (in the file Opened "For Binary") and in 128-byte chunks in the file Opened "For Sequential" access (by using the "For Input" command).

Here are the results:

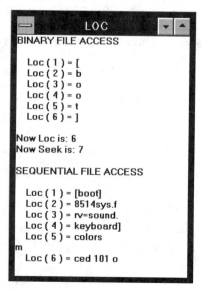

Figure L-76: Moving the "pointer" within an Opened file by using the Loc and Seek commands.

Notice the difference between the location reported by Seek and the location reported by Loc. Seek is virtually identical to Loc, except Loc tells you the position of the most recent activity within an Opened file, whereas Seek tells you the position where the next activity will take place.

See also   EOF (End Of File); Input$; LOF (Length Of File); Open; Seek

LOCK AND UNLOCK

STATEMENT

Description   Used within networks, Lock temporarily prevents access to a part (or all) of an Opened file. Used within Windows, Lock can prevent two running programs from trying to access an Opened file.

   If two people on a network, or two Windows programs, are changing an Opened file at the same time, problems can occur. Lock allows you to forbid multiple access to all, or some portion, of a given file. The Unlock command releases the protection and permits access to the file once again.

   It is important to always Unlock a previously Locked file (and Unlock it using the same values that you provided as Variables when you Locked it). If you don't, the file can be damaged.

Used with   Lock is used with files that are Opened in a network environment, or within Windows, where several computers or programs can access the same disk drive. These several accesses could potentially try to make changes to a given file simultaneously, creating an unstable and unpredictable situation. Lock prevents such simultaneous multiple access.

Variables   Lock works differently, depending on whether a file has been Opened as a binary, sequential or random file. (For more about sequential file types, see "Input$." For more on binary and random files, see "Open.")

To Lock an entire file:

   Lock #1 (substitute for the 1 whatever # the file was Opened with)

OR (to specify how many bytes—like text characters—from the start of the file to Lock in a *binary* mode file):

   Lock #1, V& (the Variable V& means that you can specify any number over a huge range—see "Variables")

OR (to specify a *range* of bytes within the file to Lock in a *binary* mode file, here bytes 12 through 450): Lock #1, 12 To 450

OR

Random Files: For *random* mode files, you can use the same syntax as above, but instead of byte ranges, you would be specifying *record* ranges.

OR

Sequential Files: For *sequential* mode files, the entire file is locked; even if you do try to specify a range, it is ignored.

OR

Unlock: Unlock uses exactly the same syntax as Lock. (See the third and fourth items in "Cautions" below.)

Uses   Prevent potentially damaging multiple access to a single file Opened on a network or by more than one Windows program.

Cautions   • Lock and Unlock cannot be used with DOS versions earlier than 3.1.

• You must run SHARE.EXE before using Lock and Unlock. See your DOS manual.

• Lock and Unlock must always be used together—just as when you Open a file, you must also Close it.

• The list of Variables you provide following an Unlock Statement must precisely match the list of Variables you provided its paired Lock Statement.

Example   Locking may at first seem puzzling—why would you Open a file and then promptly Lock it? Could *you*, the one who Locked it, access it? Yes. If your program Locks a file, your program can use the file freely, but others cannot get into it.

You Lock a file after Opening it to get exclusive access to the entire file. If your program will Open and use files that other programs may want to access, then you should do some kind of Locking. Conversely, if your program tries to Open a file that another application has Locked, you would get a "permission denied" message. If that happens, you could either try again and again until you get to the file, or inform the user and let him or her make some kind of decision about how to proceed.

Locking is especially useful when two applications will share the same data file, such as on a network. A partial Lock (specifying a range of the data, for example, records 1 through 200) allows two applications to access the same file without having to worry that both of them would try to do something with the same record at the same time, causing havoc.

```
Open "C:\WORD\DOC4" For Input As 1
Lock #1
```

This program would Lock all of "DOC4." Nobody else on the network nor any other program running under Windows could get access to it until you Unlocked it.

See also   Input$; Open

FUNCTION

Description LOF (Length Of File) tells you how large a disk file is, how many bytes it takes up on the disk.

This number is the same as you would get if you typed DIR within DOS:

DIR *.ICO

and got the following information on the screen:

SYSINFO.ICO   766   6-06-92 6:00a

The number 766 means that this icon uses up 766 bytes on the disk (or takes up that much RAM memory if this file is loaded into the computer's internal memory).

Used with Opened disk files

Variables   X = LOF(1)

(The 1 refers to the number you assigned that file when you used the Open Statement to gain access to this disk file: Open "Myfile" For Input As #1.)

OR (to use the LOF ( ) Function itself as a Variable within a larger expression. The following tells you how many fixed-length records exist within the file. For more on determining the number of records, see the third item in Uses below):

NumberOfRecords = LOF(1)\RecordLength

Uses • You can manipulate information—update records, search for a particular phrase in a text document, repaint a picture—far faster within the computer's RAM memory than while the information resides on the disk drive. Most programs Open or Load files before allowing you to word-process them, paint them or whatever.

Often you'll want to Load a file into RAM, make adjustments to it and then save it back to the disk drive with the changes you made to it.

If you are planning to pull in all the data at once from a disk file and put it into a single text ("string") Variable, you should check to be sure that the file is not larger than 32,767 bytes. A single text Variable will not be able to hold more than that number of bytes. You could, of course, use more than one text Variable for files with an LOF larger than 32,767. But you do want to check first to see if that might be necessary.

• If you are pulling data into an Array (which see), you'll also need to know in advance how many elements to create for that Array. (When you create an Array you must tell VB how big an Array it should be.) LOF will tell you the size Array you need.

• Determine *how many records* are in a random-access file. When using the random-access technique (see "Open") to manipulate a disk file, each *record* (each Name + Address + Phone Number + Birthday + Favorite Soup, each group of related information) *is a fixed size*.

That is, even if someone likes split pea and someone else likes Mongolian Hot Pot, the soup-preferences part of each record is still going to be the same size; each record is made large enough to accommodate the longest names and preferences. If someone likes pea soup, spaces would be inserted to make that record take up as much space as the Mongolian item.

Because the record length is known for a random-access file, a relationship exists between the record length and the total length of the file. The length divided by the record size tells us how many records are in the file:

```
RecordLength = 60
Open "C:\Myrelatives" For Random As 1
NumberOfRecords = LOF(1)\RecordLength
```

If, in this example, LOF(1) turned out to be 600, there would be 10 records in this file. The Variable *NumberOfRecords* would contain 10.

Recall that Functions can be part of larger "expressions" just as we have used the LOF function here.

We could have determined the number of records this way:

```
RecordLength = 60
Open "C:\Myrelatives" For Random As 1
X = LOF(1)
NumberOfRecords = X\RecordLength
```

But that extra step is not necessary. The phrase LOF(1), used within a larger expression, *will take the actions necessary to produce the answer*. So we don't need to assign the value of LOF(1) to a Variable; we can use a Function as if it were, itself, a Variable, and as if it already had the answer we want. (See "Variables" for more on "expressions.")

How Much Memory Is Needed in RAM? If you are bringing in a graphic file from the disk, LOF can let you know in advance how much memory the picture will require when loaded into the computer. It's possible, in older computers, that a single picture file would be too large for the available RAM memory.

• Just as the DOS command DIR tells you how large files are, if you write a File Manager-type program, you may want to provide that information to the user along with the filenames and other information. You may even want to provide the user with the option to view the files sorted according to size. LOF allows all this.

Cautions

• If a file has just been *created* (by Opening it For Output, for instance, using a filename that's not on the disk already)—LOF( ) will be 0 until something is written to the file.

• LOF doesn't really tell you the number of bytes that a file uses up physically on a disk; it tells you the size of the file itself (how many bytes it would take up if put into the computer's memory). File size is not the same thing as disk real estate used when a file is stored. Like the LOF command, asking for a *Dir*ectory in DOS also tells you the file size (not the consumed bytes). A file will actually consume more space than its file size—based on the *cluster size* used by the disk drive. A cluster is the smallest amount of space that can be allocated to a file. For instance, on a typical PC system the cluster might be 8,192, and therefore every file would consume at least 8,192 bytes on the disk drive. Any file larger than 8,192 would add to this in 8,192-byte chunks. If a file is reported by LOF to be 8,193-bytes-large, it would nevertheless take up 16,384 bytes on the disk.

Example

Let's see if your WIN.INI file is trim enough to fit into a single text Variable—or if it has swollen.

WIN.INI is the victim of force-feeding like a French goose. WIN.INI (the *WIN*dows *INI*tialization file) on your Windows directory is something like DOS's CONFIG.SYS file. Like many things in a graphical environment, WIN.INI can get big fast.

Many Windows programs and commercial applications use WIN.INI to store their startup defaults. They do this because they know Windows cannot run without WIN.INI, and if they made their own .INI files, you might erase them. Then you would run Windows and try to use their program. It would behave badly or crash. You would blame them. So the programs and applications stuff their startup info into WIN.INI.

Let's say you don't want to use a particular commercial program any more. You delete it from your disk so that it won't take up useless space. But *it's not completely gone*. Its remnants remain within WIN.INI like a residue.

Therefore, WIN.INI can grow in this way to unseemly size. And it can be somewhat risky to prune things inside the WIN.INI file. Unless you know exactly what you are doing—what references are no longer meaningful for active programs—you can cripple or immobilize programs you currently use by destroying their sections within WIN.INI.

Here's how to check WIN.INI's size:

```
Sub Form_Click ()

Open "C:\WINDOWS\WIN.INI" For Random As 1

Print "YOUR WIN.INI FILE IS"; LOF(1); " bytes big! That's pretty large."

If LOF(1) > 32767 Then

    Print "Sorry, it's gotten monstrously fat and we can't put it into a single →
Variable."
Else
    Print "We can still fit your WIN.INI into a Variable."
    Print "Try this test again in a few months."
    Print "Your WIN.INI is growing."
End If

End Sub
```

See also   EOF (End Of File); Input$; Loc; Open; Seek

Log

Description   Log is an advanced math function, like Cos and Tan, that you would find on a scientific calculator.

Log tells you the "natural logarithm" of a number.

Used with   Advanced mathematical calculations

Variables
```
X = Log(3)
?X
```

OR

```
X = 3
Y = Log(X)
? Y
```

OR

```
PRINT Log(3)
```

In all of these cases, the result is: 1.098612

If you know what this means, and know what to do with it, you remember more than I remember.

Uses   Advanced mathematical calculations

Cautions   Log returns a single-precision number if you provide it with a single-precision value or an Integer Variable. Otherwise, it provides a double-precision value. (See "Variables" for an overview of the several types of numeric Variables.)

Example
```
X = Log(.5)
Print X
```

Results in   –.6931472

See also   Exp; Sqr

LostFocus

EVENT

Description *Focus* means which Control on a Form is currently "active"—which Control is receptive, which one would respond if you pressed a key on the keyboard.

Focus is changed in three ways:

1. If the user clicks on another Control (or the Form), the focus then changes to the object clicked upon.

2. Pressing the TAB key shifts the focus.

3. Your program itself can move the focus by using the SetFocus Method.

Repeatedly pressing the TAB key while a program is running will cycle you through all the Controls on a Form, moving the focus each time TAB is pressed. The only exception to this is if you have changed the TabStop Property. Any Control with TabStop set to 0 (False) will be ignored while the TAB key moves the focus around the Form.

The LostFocus Event occurs when the user clicks on another Control or presses the TAB key, removing the focus from a Control that had the focus. At this point, the Control that *had* the focus loses it, and its LostFocus Event is triggered.

Which Control gets the focus next, if the user presses the TAB key, is determined by the TabIndex Property. Each Control on a Form has a TabIndex number, and pressing the TAB key cycles you up through these index numbers. When it reaches the Control with the highest TabIndex, it restarts at the Control with the TabIndex of zero.

Visual Basic assigns TabIndexes in the order in which you create new Controls on a Form, but you can change the index numbers while designing your program by using the Properties Window.

Used with Everything except Timers, Frames or Labels:
Forms, Check Boxes, Combo Boxes, Command Buttons, Directory, Drive & File List Boxes, Grids, Horizontal & Vertical Scroll Bars, List Boxes, OLE, Option Buttons, Picture Boxes and Text Boxes

Variables Within the LostFocus Event, you enter instructions telling your program how to respond when a Control, or Form, loses the focus:

```
Sub Command2_LostFocus ()
    Command3.Visible = True
    Command2.Enabled = False
```

```
        Text1.Width = Text1.Width * 2
        Text1.Height = Text1.Height * 2
    End Sub
```

Uses
• A LostFocus Event is usually triggered because the user has just moved to a different place in your program–has selected a different Control. This action by the user also triggers the *GotFocus* Event within the newly active Control (or Form).

You can provide your user with visual clues about which Control is currently active. You can, for example, turn off the Enabled Properties of Controls that do not have focus. Within the LostFocus Event you would set Command1.Enabled = 0 when that Command Button lost the focus. Turning Enabled off makes a Command Button pale gray. (See the Example.)

Similarly, you could dramatize shifts of focus by Hiding or Showing Forms; by making Controls visible or invisible; by adjusting colors, Pictures, or sizes of Controls; or by displaying a constantly updated Label, which described the purpose of the Control that currently has the focus. All of these techniques can be helpful to the user, and all are easily accomplished by putting appropriate commands within GotFocus and LostFocus Events.

• In some programs, you will allow the user to interact with a Control but then perform some housekeeping chores when the user is finished with that Control. For instance, if the user is typing information into a Text Box, you might want to save that data in a disk file, or at least to the Clipboard, when the user switches to some other Control. The LostFocus Event of the Text Box would contain instructions to make a safety backup. This way, if the user changes his or her mind, you can offer an Undo feature in your program.

• If the user is entering information or making a selection of some kind, you may need to confirm that the information was entered correctly or that the selection is a valid one. When a LostFocus Event occurred, you might want to authenticate what the user has done and provide a message if the user's actions have been inappropriate. Some kinds of user input are checked while the user types on the keyboard. For instance, you can use the Key-Press Event's KeyAscii Variable to make sure that only digits are entered when the user is supposed to type in a ZIP Code. If the user made a mistake, you could set the focus back to the Control where there is a problem (see "SetFocus").

LostFocus, however, permits you to wait until the user is finished working with a Control (or Form) and then check to see if what the user did was acceptable.

Cautions
• If you set a Control's Enabled Property to 0, the Control becomes unresponsive to mouse clicks or tabs. In fact, the user cannot restore focus to a disabled Control at all. Your *program* must re-enable the Control, often in response to a LostFocus Event within some other Control.

Setting the Control's Enabled Property creates something of a paradox. Let's say you want a set of Controls to behave like "radio buttons" (push one in and the others pop out—only one can be Enabled at a time). How, then, can the user click on another of the buttons in the group? It's disabled and won't respond. For one way to solve this dilemma, see the Example below.

• A Form can get the focus only if it possesses no Controls or if all Controls on it are disabled.

Example

Figure L-77: WordPerfect for Windows's row of "intelligent" buttons. The program disables (grays out) options that are unavailable in a particular context.

Many commercial programs provide "Button Bars" or other collections of icons or Command Buttons. WordPerfect for Windows, for instance, disables (grays out and freezes) any buttons that are currently inappropriate. When you select some text within a document, such option buttons as "Close," "Select Text" and "Preview" become disabled because performing these options is impossible while a piece of text is selected.

In other situations, you want only one button—a radio button in a group—to be Enabled at any given time. Visual Basic provides a Control that acts like radio buttons—the Option Button. Put several of these Buttons on a Form or Picture Box, and if the user selects one, all the others remain unselected.

The drawback to Option Buttons is that they are unattractive, plain objects. Commercial programs generally use more sculpted Controls, like VB's Command Buttons. Our task in this example is to create a set of Command Buttons that operate like Option Buttons—whenever the user selects one, all the others are disabled.

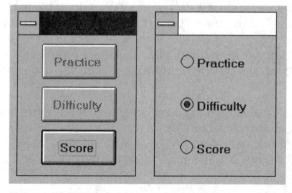

Figure L-78: The Form's MouseDown Event can be used to detect clicks on disabled Controls. Which version looks best to you?

The Paradox: The paradox we must solve here is that if we set a Command Button's Enabled Property to False, *the user cannot click on that Button*. The Button's Click Event will never happen, even if the user tries to click on it. The Form's *MouseDown* Event, however, responds to a click anywhere on a Form. What's more, that Event tells us the X,Y position, the horizontal and vertical location on the Form where the click happened. We can use this information to detect a click on a disabled Control:

```
Sub Form_MouseDown (Button As Integer, Shift As Integer, X As Single, y As
Single)

Select Case y
    Case Is > 1320
        Command3.Enabled = True
        Command3.SetFocus
    Case 720 To 1319
        Command2.Enabled = True
        Command2.SetFocus
    Case 120 To 719
        Command1.Enabled = True
        Command1.SetFocus
End Select

End Sub
```

What's happening here is that MouseDown is triggered when the user clicks, and we care about only the vertical position of the click. So we set up a Select Case structure (you could use If...Then, but it's less readable and a bit more clumsy).

This structure says: If Y (the vertical position of the click on the Form) is greater than 1320, the user has clicked in the area of the lowest Command Button. So we Enable it and give it the focus with the SetFocus Method. Similarly, if Y is between 720 and 1390, the middle button was clicked. A click between 120 and 719 is on the upper button.

How did we get these position numbers? While designing the program, we clicked on each button and read its Top Property from the information on the right side of the Toolbar.

Now we've taken care of Enabling a clicked Button and giving it the focus. But what about disabling the other two Buttons? We do that in their respective LostFocus Events. SetFocus in the newly focused Control triggers LostFocus in the one that had focus previously. So for each Button, we make the LostFocus Event disable that Button:

```
Sub Command1_LostFocus ()
    Command1.Enabled = False
End Sub

Sub Command2_LostFocus ()
    Command2.Enabled = False
End Sub

Sub Command3_LostFocus ()
```

```
        Command3.Enabled = False
    End Sub
```

Finally, so that only one of these Buttons is enabled when the Form first appears, put the following into the Form_Load Event:

```
Sub Form_Load ()
    Command2.Enabled = False
    Command3.Enabled = False
End Sub
```

See also   GotFocus; SetFocus; TabIndex; TabStop

LSET

STATEMENT

Description   LSet is used for two essentially unrelated purposes, but both involve text ("string") Variables, and both operate on a *fixed-length* text Variable.

First, LSet can move a piece of text all the way to the left within a text Variable, padding the right side with spaces.

Second, LSet can copy the entire contents of one user-defined Variable into another. (A user-defined Variable is something like an Array and is created with the Type command, which see.)

What a Fixed-Length String Is: A fixed-length string is one whose size cannot change. It is a text Variable with a fixed number of characters. Fixed-length string Variables are used with random-access files (see "Open") because each record in such files must be of the same, unchanging length. Fixed-length strings are also occasionally employed for some kinds of formatting; even if there are fewer text characters in a particular fixed string, it will still be padded with spaces so that the length should remain stable. However, now that computers and printers are most frequently utilizing proportional fonts (the characters vary in width), the value of this approach to formatting is passing into history. If you want things to line up in columns, use the CurrentX command and the TextWidth or Format$ command.

How to Create a Fixed-Length String: You can create fixed-length strings two ways:

Dim Name As String * 25   (This creates a fixed-length string that will be 25 characters long. You must use the Dim command in a Form's or Module's General Declarations section.)

Name$ = String$(50," ")   (This fills Name$ for the time being with 50 spaces and fixes it at that length. You can use the String$ command anywhere in your program.)

The Two Uses of LSet: First, to move part of a text ("string") Variable to the left, padding with spaces if necessary, so that the length of the Variable remains the same, use the following:

```
a$ = "Now. Move This Over."
Print a$, Len(a$)
```

Results in   Now. Move This Over.   20

```
LSet a$ = "Move This Over."
Print a$, Len(a$)
```

(After using LSet...)

Results in   Move This Over.   20

A companion RSet Statement right-justifies a piece of text-within-text in the same fashion, by padding it. However, RSet shoves text to the right, stuffing spaces into the left side of a text Variable.

The other purpose of LSet is to make a copy of a *user-defined* Variable.

Such Variables are created by using the Type...End Type structure in a Module. A user-defined Variable is similar to a "structure" in the C programming language or a "record" in the Pascal language. (See the Example further on, or see "Type.")

Used with   Fixed-length text ("string") Variables

OR

User-defined Variable structures

Variables   To put the text characters *Five* into a text Variable with 10 spaces in it. This retains the length of the original Variable a$, 10 characters long. But it puts the word *Five* against the left side a$:

```
a$ = String$(10, " ")
LSet a$ = "Five"
Print a$
Print Len(a$)
```

Results in   Five
10

OR (if the item being LSet into a text Variable is *longer* than the text Variable, then the item being LSet is chopped off on the right side to fit into the fixed-length text Variable):

```
a$ = String$(10, " ")
LSet a$ = "FiveFiveFiveFive"
Print a$
Print Len(a$)
```

Results in   FiveFiveFi
10

OR (to copy a user-defined Variable structure): LSet Thisrec = Thatrec

Uses   • Copy an entire user-defined Variable structure (which can contain a number of interior Variables). This is an efficient way to work with the records of a random-access file (see "Open"). Sometimes you will want to delete a record from a random-access file, too:

```
For I = DeletedRecordNumber To TotalRecordsInTheFile − 1
    LSet Record(I) = Record(I+1)
Next I
TotalRecordsInTheFile = TotalRecordsInTheFile −1
```

This Subroutine replaces the deleted record with the record one higher in the list (record 8 gets replaced by record 9). And it continues replacing each record up through the list with the next higher record. It runs out of possibilities at TotalRecords −1, and we reset the total.

• LSet could also be used to reset the effects of the RSet command (which see).

Cautions   • When working with a single Variable (not a user-defined structure), if the Variable being LSet is smaller than the target, it will be padded to the right with spaces:

```
A$ = String$(20,"*")    ' fills a Variable called A$ with 20 asterisks.
```

LSet A$ = "1234567890" ' results in A$ holding those 10 digits plus 10 spaces. The trailing asterisks are replaced with space characters.

If, however, the Variable being LSet is *larger* than the target, it will be *truncated* to the right. That is, characters will be chopped off on the right side of the original Variable to stuff it into the smaller target:

```
A$ = String$(5," ")  'fills A$ with 10 spaces
LSet A$ = "1234567890" 'results in A$ holding "12345"
```

• LSet copies entire user-defined Variable types (see "Variables"). It copies both numeric and text Variables, but any text Variables must be of fixed length.

• If two user-defined Variable structures are set up the same way (with text Variables defined as the same length), LSet copies the source structure precisely into the target structure. However, if the target Variable is shorter than the source Variable (the one being copied), some characters in the source Variable will be chopped off to make it fit into the target.

• LSet only works if both the copied and the copied-to user-defined text Variables are *fixed-length*. (See "Description.")

• You create a fixed-length string by describing its length in the process of DIMensioning (defining) it. To make one that's 45 characters long:

```
Dim Varname As String * 45
```

OR

 A$ = String$(30,"a") is another way to create a fixed-length string. Here we've filled a string with 30 *a*'s.

If you don't assign a length, a text Variable is not a "fixed-length" Variable. It defaults to the more common *dynamic* Variable, which means that the Variable expands and contracts as necessary, depending on what happens in the program and depending on the size of the text you assign to that dynamic Variable. Here's how a dynamic text Variable would be defined:

```
Dim Varname$
```

OR

```
Dim Varname As String
```

You don't even need to define (Dim) most text Variables that you are just going to use within a single Event Procedure, Subroutine or Function. Just assign some text to it, and it's a dynamic text Variable:

```
A$ = "Noisome"
```

The purpose of defining a fixed-length string is to stabilize it so it will always be the same size. (This is important when working with random-access files. See "Open.")

The purpose of defining other (Variable-length) strings, using Dim, Global or Static, is that you want them to *retain* their information outside a single procedure. Dim a string in a Module and the entire program can access the information in that string. If you Dim one in the General Definitions of a Form, everything in that Form can use the string's contents.

Example We'll create a user-defined Variable structure and then copy it using LSet.

First, in a Module, we define the two structures. Remember that this is merely a *definition*, a description of the qualities of these structures. It's as if you conjured up a whole new type of Variable and are setting out the rules for that genre of Variable. Later, you must define a specific instance of this type, using Dim. And, later still, you assign *values* (the actual data) to the name you Dimmed. Here's how it works (in a Module):

```
Type Personal
    Varname As String * 30
    Age As Integer
End Type

Type Back
    Bname As String * 30
    Bage As Integer
End Type
```

Now we have our two new Variable types and can describe specific Variables as being of these types. In the General Declarations section of the Form:

```
Dim One As Personal
Dim Two As Back
```

At this point we have a user Variable called "One" which is of the "Personal" type. That is, "One" has a structure, and that structure is a text Variable called "Varname," which can hold 30 characters and an Integer-type Variable called "Age." And we have a second structure called "Two," with "Bname" and "Bage" as subsidiary Variables. Now we can use these structures:

```
Sub Form_Click ()

one.varname = "Tommy Hanenshank"
one.age = 12

two.bname = "Nadia Compesatia"
two.bage = 14

LSet one = two

Print one.varname
Print one.age

End Sub
```

We assign a name and age to the two structures. Note that you punctuate user-type Variables with a period between the generic name and the specific subsidiary Variable name.

Then we LSet the entire "One" to equal "Two." The whole structure is copied from "Two" into "One." This is effective, particularly if your structure is large and contains many interior Variables. When we Print one.varname and one.age, we get the following:

```
Nadia Compesatia
14
```

This proves that "One" has been changed into a copy of "Two."

Note that user-defined Variables are somewhat like Arrays (which see). But one important difference is that there is no equivalent of LSet for Arrays, no swift single-copy command. Instead, to copy an Array you must run it through a For...Next Loop, copying each item, one at a time.

See also   Dim (As String); LTrim$; RSet; RTrim$; String$; Variables

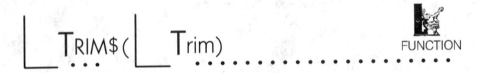

LTRIM$ (LTrim)

FUNCTION

Description   LTrim$ removes any spaces from the left side of a text ("string") Variable:

Andy Doodie

Changes to:

Andy Doodie

Used with Variables

Text ("string") Variables

```
A$ = "    Nobody home."
Print LTrim$(A$)
```

Results in

Nobody home.

OR (To assign the results to a text Variable):

```
X$ = LTrim$(A$)
Print X$
```

Results in

Nobody home.

Uses

• Clean up user input.

You can never tell what the user might do. When typing in a lot of data, the user might accidentally hit the TAB key or enter some extra spaces. If your program is going to alphabetize a list and one of the items has a space as its first character, that item will appear before the *A*'s as the first item in the list. To prevent this, you want to clean up any items that you are about to alphabetize (or are going to compare, such as If A$ < B$).

Use LTrim$ to make sure that you are comparing apples to apples and not dealing with some accidental leading spaces. And, while you're at it, you might as well eliminate random capitalization with the LCase$ Function, too. (For an alternative to LCase$, see "StrComp.")

• Clean up numbers translated by Str$.

You can transform a number into a text ("string") Variable (into printable digits rather than a pure number) by using Str$(X). However, Str$ inserts an extra space in front of a number to provide room for a minus sign. LTrim$ is a way of getting rid of this extra space. (See the Example below.)

• When reading text files, you can remove paragraph indentations, centering or other formatting that involves using space characters to achieve a visual effect.

Cautions

• LTrim$ works the same with either Variable-length or fixed-length text ("string") Variables. (See "Variables.")

Example

When you transform a positive number into a text ("string") Variable, Basic inserts an extra space to allow for a possible minus (–) sign. This has mystified programmers for a generation, but that's what happens. This space is inserted so that a column of numbers would line up when displayed if you add a space to positive numbers and leave negative numbers with their minus (–) sign intact. Contemporary computers no longer format columns, though, by counting character spaces. The characters now used are *proportional* (the characters vary in width), so it is useless to use characters as a way of formatting displayed text.

Nonetheless, Str$ still adds a space character to the left of a positive number. LTrim$ gets rid of the space. Here's an example:

```
Sub Form_Click ()
    x = 144
        Print x
    y$ = Str$(x)
        Print y$
        Print LTrim$(y$)

    x = -144
        Print x
    y$ = Str$(x)
        Print y$
        Print LTrim$(y$)
End Sub
```

Results in

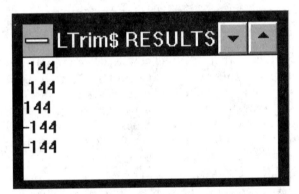

Figure L-79: Note that LTrim$ does not remove symbols like the minus sign.

See also   LSet; RSet; RTrim$

Max

Description   The position at the far right of a Horizontal Scroll Bar Control.

OR The position at the bottom of a Vertical Scroll Bar Control.

Figure M-1: When the interior tab reaches the far right of a Horizontal Bar, that's the Max.

(For a general overview of Scroll Bars, see "LargeChange.")

You determine the measurement system of your Scroll Bar Controls based usually on what information they slide the user through. For instance, if you are showing data about your family and there are five of you, set Max to 5. For a calendar, set Max to 12 if you want to allow the user to slide through pictures of each month. For a cookbook with 150 recipes, set Max to 150.

Any change the user makes by moving the lozenge-shaped button (called the Scroll Box or "Tab") inside a Scroll Bar will change that Scroll Bar's *Value* Property. Your program can use the Value to take appropriate actions. Normally, these actions are taken within the Scroll Bar's Change Event.

A Scroll Bar's Min and Max Properties set the limits that its Value Property can change.

The highest Max can be is 32,767. But an RGB color for a Control can range from 0 (black) to higher than 16 million (white = (32768 * 512) – 1). To handle ranges larger than 32,767, simply multiply the "value" of the Scroll Bar by whatever is appropriate. In this case, we could set Min to 0 and Max to 32,767. Then, to allow movement through RGB colors:

```
Sub VScroll1_Change ()
    R& = vscroll1.Value
    R& = R& + 1
    Form1.BackColor = (R& * 512) – 1
End Sub
```

Here we've created a Long *Integer* Variable by attaching the ampersand (&) symbol. This is necessary to hold numbers as large as 32768 * 512. (See "Variables.")

Then we pick off the current Value of the Scroll Bar, add 1 to it (because white is 32768 * 512, but the Max allowed for a Scroll Bar is 32767). Then we multiply the Value times 512 but subtract 1 because, again, there's a slight kink. A Color Property can handle an RGB number of 16,777,215 but chokes on 16,777,216. How did we figure this out? We kept trying numbers until we got white, the highest possible RGB value. You sometimes just get in there, abandon theory and fool around until you get the results you want.

Technically, each number in an RGB triplet can be as much as 255, but there is also 0 to figure on. (Remember that computers often prefer to start counting with zero; humans start with one.) This means there are 256 possible values for each of the R, G and B Variables. Therefore, the number of possible combinations is 256*256*256, which results in 16,777,216. Nonetheless, this number is the *total* of valid colors, yet the first color is color 0, so the last (highest) color value is 16,777,215.

Used with   Horizontal Scroll Bars and Vertical Scroll Bars

Variables   **Variable type:** Integer

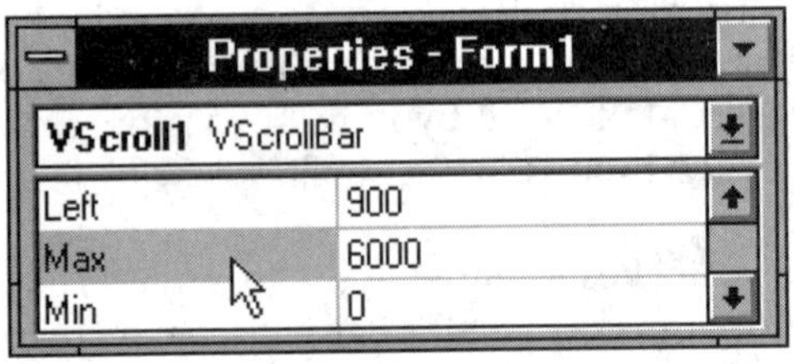

Figure M-2: You can establish the maximum value for a Scroll Bar in the Properties Window.

OR (to set it while the program is running): HScroll1.Max = 12000

Uses   Used in combination with the Min, LargeChange, SmallChange and Value Properties of a Scroll Bar, you can provide the user with an intuitive and vivid way to adjust various kinds of information—slide things around on-screen, resize things, change their colors, flip through the "pages" of an automotive manual, etc. Scroll Bars are an important user-input tool used by the graphical user interfaces on modern computers.

Cautions   • Both Max and Min Properties can be set anywhere from –32,768 to 32,767.

• If you don't change Max and Min, they default to 32,767 and 0, respectively.

• It is possible to reverse the direction of a Scroll Bar. Normally, Max is at the far right of a Horizontal Bar and at the bottom of a Vertical Bar. However, if you set the Max Property to a number *lower than* the Min Property, the Max flips and becomes the position at the far left of a Horizontal Bar and at the top of a Vertical Bar.

Example   You can adjust most any quality of a Control or Form via a Scroll Bar. Just create a relationship between the quality you want to adjust and the Min and Max numbers of the Scroll Bar. Usually, you'll spot the relationship right away. Then adjust the LargeChange and SmallChange Properties of the Scroll Bar to fine-tune the *amount of change* caused by clicking or dragging on the Scroll Bar.

In this example, we'll allow the user to expand or contract a Picture Box. Our first job is to figure out what Min and Max should be. The smallest size we want the picture to shrink to is about 3,000 twips—about two inches. (VB measures with "twips" by default, although you can change this. See "ScaleMode.")

Not the Easy Way Out: The graphic, however, is not absolutely square. It's longer than it is wide. We could set the Picture Box's AutoSize Property to –1. Then, we need to adjust only one of its other Properties—Width or Height—and the Picture Box automatically adjusts the other Property.

But we want this example to illustrate how to set up Max and how to make it interact effectively with LargeChange and SmallChange. So we'll adjust both Height and Width when the user moves the Scroll Bar:

Figure M-3: You can use a Scroll Bar to reveal text or graphics.

```
Sub Form_Load ()
    hscroll1.Max = 7450
    hscroll1.Min = 3252
    hscroll1.LargeChange = 500
    hscroll1.SmallChange = 75
End Sub
```

We found the preceding numbers while designing the Form. We pulled the Picture Box out until we reached the full size of the enclosed picture. Then, looking at the far right of the VB Design Bar, we could see that the Height was 7,450, so we set Max to that. We then shrank the Picture Box by dragging the lower right corner with the mouse. We decided that 3,252 was about as small as we wanted the Picture to ever get, so we set Min to that number.

Then, while testing the program, we found that a good compromise between speed and visual smoothness for LargeChange was about 500 twips. The LargeChange takes place when the user clicks *within* the Scroll Bar. SmallChange is caused when the user clicks on one of the arrows at either end of the Scroll Bar. By trying different values, we found that 75 produces a nice, smooth expansion or contraction of the Picture.

The only other thing we need to do is to create the relationship between the Scroll Bar's movements (its Value Property) and the Picture Box's Height and Width. We do this in the Scroll Bar's Change Event:

```
Sub HScroll1_Change ()
    Picture1.Width = .8 * Hscroll1.Value
    Picture1.Height = Hscroll1.Value
End Sub
```

We set Max to exactly the Height of the picture at its greatest extension. Because the picture is not square, we need to adjust the narrower Width somewhat less than we adjust Height whenever there is a change.

By pulling the picture out to its full size again, we find (at the far right of the VB Design Bar) that the Width is 6,000 and the Height is 7,450. Because we set Max to 7,450, there is a 1-to-1 ratio between any movement on the Scroll Bar and the adjustment of the Picture's Height Property.

To find the ratio for adjusting Width, divide the maximum desired Width by the maximum Height. Whenever you divide a smaller number by a larger number, you get the percentage that the smaller number is of the larger number. So, 6,000 / 7,450 is .80, or 80 percent. All we have to do, then, is multiply the Value by the percentage to maintain the right ratio of expansion or contraction in both the Height and the Width. And, at the maximum size, the picture will still be in proportion.

Figure M-4: Sliding the Scroll Bar reveals the entire face of Caesar.

See also   Horizontal Scroll Bar; LargeChange, SmallChange; Min; Scroll; Value

MaxButton

PROPERTY

Description   The MaxButton is the up-arrow button at the top right of a window (Form). The MaxButton Property of a Form determines whether or not that Form includes that Button.

When the user clicks on a MaxButton, the window expands to fill the entire screen. At that point, the MaxButton symbol changes to the Restore Button symbol. If the user clicks on it, the window shrinks back to the size it was before being maximized to full-screen size.

Figure M-5: Click on a Restore Button symbol to shrink a window.

Used with   Forms only

Variables   **Variable type:** Integer (Boolean)

Unless you change it, a MaxButton will be on any Form that has a Fixed Single or Sizable BorderStyle. You can remove the MaxButton, however, using the Properties Window.

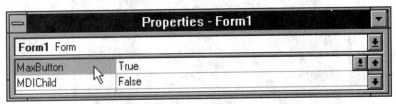

Figure M-6: The MaxButton Property cannot be adjusted while your program is running, so you cannot put MaxButton = 0 into your program.

Uses   Some Forms and some windows are not supposed to fill the entire screen— small message or user-response Forms, for example. In such cases, you can set the BorderStyle of the Form to no border or a "fixed double" border. Neither of these styles includes a MaxButton or MinButton. Alternatively, you can deliberately remove the MaxButton by setting the Form's Max-Button Property to 0, False.

Cautions   • If you want your *program* to maximize a window, you can do it this way: Form1.WindowState = 2.

• If you leave the MaxButton Property enabled, the user will be able to expand your Form to the full size of the screen. If your program does not respond to this possibility by adjusting the sizes and positions of the Controls, then the resulting display will not look professional (all the Controls will be too small and in the upper left area of the form). If you have designed a program so that everything is supposed to work with the Form at a fixed size, then disable the MaxButton so the user can't mess up the design that you worked so hard to create.

Example

Figure M-7: The position of the Max Button on a window.

See also   BorderStyle; ControlBox; MinButton; WindowState

MDI CHILD .... PROPERTY

See   Multiple Document Interface (MDI) Form

ME .... RESERVED WORD

Description   The word *Me* refers to the Form or *class* (see "Class Module") that is currently executing your program. If you have a Subroutine in a Module that does things for Forms in general, you can pass the identity of the calling Form with *Me*. (See the Example.)

   If you have several Forms (Form1, Form2, Form3, etc.), you can just use their Name Properties when calling a Subroutine. However, if you have created new "instances" of a single Form, all the instances will have the same Name, so *Me* identifies them individually.

Used with   Forms

Variables   To call a Subroutine, passing the ID of the calling Form: SomeSub Me

Uses   Use Me to identify the Form where the program is currently executing (or where a Subroutine was called from). This only applies to new "instances" of a single Form (see "Set" or "Multiple Document Interface").

Cautions
• You might think that Me is superfluous because you could resort to the Screen.ActiveForm Property (see "ActiveForm"). However, in rare cases, the Form from which a Subroutine is called can be different from the Form that currently has the "focus" (the Form that has a different-colored Title Bar and that will accept keystrokes when the user types something).

The most obvious case would be where a Form has a Timer running, but the user clicks on a different Form (thereby changing the focus to the new Form). However, when the Timer finishes its countdown, a Subroutine call within the Timer could send Me as the identifier of the Form. (See the Example.)

Example
Start a New Project from the File Menu, then set Form1's MDIChild Property to True. From the File Menu, select New MDI Form, and put this into its Load Event:

```
Sub MDIForm_Load ()
    Dim f as New Form1
    f.Show
End Sub
```

We're going to create a Subroutine that will reduce any Form by 10%, but we need to tell that Subroutine *which* Form is requesting this adjustment. Since our two MDI Child Forms share the same Name, we need to tell the Subroutine which of them is calling by sending the unique identifier *Me*. Now, create a new Module and type this Subroutine into it:

```
Sub Shrink (N As Form)
    N.Width = N.Width * .90
End Sub
```

Finally, in Form1's Click Event:

```
Sub Form_Click ()
    Shrink Me
End Sub
```

Since new "instances" of cloned Forms inherit all the commands of the original Form from which they were cloned, if you click on the original Form1 or the New Form1, either will call the Shrink Subroutine. Press F5 and try it.

See also
ActiveForm; Class Module; Multiple Document Interface (MDI) Form

Menu

Description Many Windows programs have a Menu Bar, a list of words on a strip across the top of the window. Visual Basic's Menu Bar is shown in Figure M-8:

<u>F</u>ile <u>E</u>dit <u>V</u>iew <u>I</u>nsert <u>R</u>un <u>T</u>ools <u>A</u>dd-Ins <u>H</u>elp

Figure M-8: A typical Menu Bar

Drop-down menus (as opposed to fixed, always visible menus) are hall-marks of a graphical environment—taking up screen space only when needed. Microsoft discourages the use of multiple controls on a form, encouraging instead the liberal use of drop-down menus.

However, menus are something of a throwback to the text-based computing of the DOS years, 1981–1990, before Windows offered an exuberant graphical alternative. Nonetheless, there is often nothing else that's practical, especially when there are dozens of hierarchical choices.

Visual Basic makes designing menus easy. Using the Menu Design Window, you can easily set up a series of menus. You provide a Caption and a Name Property for each menu (and for each item within each menu).

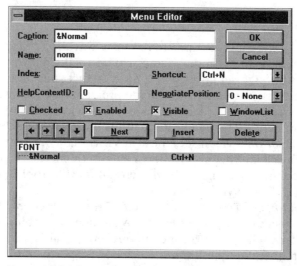

Figure M-9: Visual Basic provides this convenient Menu Editor for creating custom menus for your programs.

Each menu or menu item becomes a "new Control" just as if you added a Text Box to a Form. But menu items have only one Event—Click.

Used with Forms, Multiple Document Interface Forms and MDI Child Forms.

Variables Each menu and each menu item becomes a separate Control, just like a Picture Box or a Label. A menu has 11 Properties, some of which you can adjust in the Menu Editor. Others must be adjusted in the Properties Window (select the Menu "Control" from the list of Objects at the top of the Properties Window).

To bring up the Menu Editor, press CTRL+E or select it from the VB Tools Menu.

Or you can set menu Properties directly while your program is running: Fnt.Enabled = 0 (this menu item with a Name of Fnt will now become disabled; it will turn pale gray and not respond to any clicks from the user).

A menu item has 11 Properties:

- Caption
- Checked
- Enabled
- HelpContextID
- Index
- Name
- NegotiatePosition
- Shortcut
- Tag
- Visible
- WindowList

Most of these Properties operate the same way they do for other Controls. *Tag* is rather like an expanded Name. *Caption* is the text visible to the user. *Index* allows you to set up a Control Array so that your program or the user can add or delete menu items while the program runs (see "Control Array").

The *Checked* Property determines whether a given menu item has a check mark next to it—to indicate that it is the currently selected option. *NegotiatePosition* (which see), new in VB Version 4, tells VB how to handle things if another application's menus are merged into yours (during "in-place editing," an OLE trick whereby an outside application temporarily offers its services to your user).

The *WindowList* Property, if checked (True), works only for an MDI (Multiple Document Interface) Form. A Menu item with its WindowList Property True will display a list of all open MDI child Forms within the MDI Form. Note that the Caption, not the Name Property, of the child Form is displayed. This is a way to allow the user to switch between child windows, or to locate one that might be hidden.

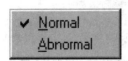

Figure M-10: A check indicates that a menu option is active.

Additional Menu "Properties": While not Properties properly speaking, there are three additional qualities of menus that you can adjust while designing your program: "separator bars" (menu division lines), "access keys" and "shortcut keys."

Separator Bars

Menus can be subdivided by a line, which is a way of grouping options visually. To add a line, insert a new menu item, give it a Name, and then, for Caption, simply type in a hyphen (-). (See the line between FONTS and OPTIONS in Figure M-14.)

Access Keys

Also, you can add an access key, a combination of the ALT key and another key (such as ALT+B). When you add an access key to a menu item, the user can then press, for instance, ALT+B to activate that menu item as an alternative to clicking on the item. To create an access key, place an ampersand symbol in front of the character you want underlined:

Results in   &Borders

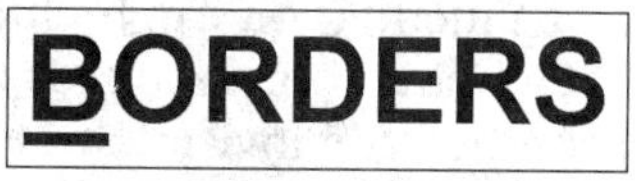

<u>B</u>ORDERS

Figure M-11: An underline indicates that the user can press ALT plus the underlined letter to activate that menu item.

Shortcut Keys

Finally, you can select a "shortcut key" from the drop-down list in the Menu Design Window. Just first select the menu item (in the window at the bottom of the Menu Editor) that you are giving the shortcut to, and then pull down the list of CTRL + key combinations to choose one. Shortcut keys work even if the menu item isn't visible to the user.

Uses   • It's sometimes better, in a graphical computing environment, to avoid menus. For example, if your program allows the user to choose the Font-Size, FontName and other properties of text, why not present him or her with a Picture Box and some Scroll Bars? In the Picture Box is some sample text, and the Scroll Bars allow the user to cycle through all the size, font and other options. Not only is this approach faster for the user, it's far more direct. What they see is what they get. In Windows 95, too, there is an excellent tabbed "Property Sheet" to allow users to adjust options and preferences.

Nonetheless, some situations do lend themselves to using menus. The most frequent uses for menus are as follows:

- A list of various approaches to the Help feature (Index, How To, Using Help, Definitions, Search)
- Window options (Tile, Cascade)
- Edit (Cut, Copy, Paste, Undo, Link)

- File (Open, Close, Save, Import)
- Preferences (features of your program that the user can customize. However, in many cases, adjusting the features and seeing the results graphically is preferable.)

Menus are sometimes preferable to a screen full of buttons. If an application has a large number of options or commands that can be selected, they may be better placed in a menu structure. If a Form needs only a couple of buttons to provide for all its features, then a menu is certainly extra, unnecessary work for the user.

Many Windows applications these days are using "Toolbars" (see the Emboss Subroutine under "Line" for a way to create Toolbars in your VB programs, or see "Align"). There's also a new Toolbar Control for the 32-bit Windows 95-compatible version of VB4.

Essentially, a Toolbar is a grouped collection of tiny icons that have three different looks—on, off and disabled. When turned on, they appear pressed into the screen (depressed when the user clicks on them); when off, they appear popped out; disabled, they are pale gray.

A Toolbar offers the advantages of a menu (you can include lots of options at little cost in screen space), but a Toolbar avoids the relatively awkward clicking and jumping around within invisible tree structures that are a drawback of menus.

Cautions • Every menu can have five levels of submenus. Submenus move down and to the right of the menus above them. If a menu has a submenu, it is visually indicated by a black triangle next to the Caption:

Figure M-12: This triangle symbol indicates that there is a submenu beneath the visible option.

• In the Menu Design Window, do not indent menus that should appear on the Menu Bar proper and thus always be visible when the program runs. These are the top menus in the menu hierarchy.

All submenus are indicated by indentation and dotted lines. The more indentation, the lower in the hierarchy. To create a submenu, simply indent further than the menu (or submenu) above it in the list.

• If a Form has a menu, you can use only BorderStyles of "Sizable" (style 2) and "Fixed Single" (style 1). If you select the "None" or "Fixed Double" styles, the fact that the menu exists causes VB to change the BorderStyle to "Fixed Single."

Example Both of the following illustrations are the same menu. First, Figure M-13 shows how it looks in the Menu Design Window, and then Figure M-14 shows how it looks while the program is running:

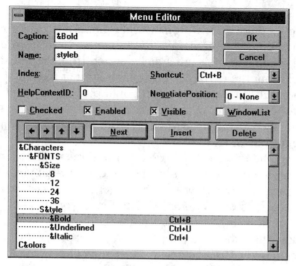

Figure M-13: The Menu Design Window, showing the indentation that defines the subordination of menus and submenus.

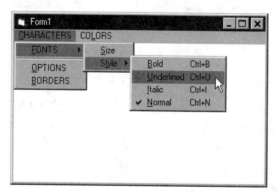

Figure M-14: The resulting menu while the program is running.

Menu Properties
Caption • Checked • Click • Enabled • HelpContextID • Index • Menu Events • Name • NegotiatePosition • Shortcut • Tag • Visible • WindowList

See also Checked; Control Array; NegotiateMenus

Mid

FUNCTION

Description   Mid extracts a piece of text from a larger piece of text. For instance, Mid could pull *penthouse* out of *Meet me in the penthouse suite at seven.*

The *Left* command pulls out a piece of text from the left side of a larger body of text, but the extracted piece must start at the left side of the larger text. In the preceding example, Left could pull out *M, Meet, Meet me* and so on, but the first letter of the extracted piece would have to be *M.* The Right command operates the same way but pulls pieces from the right side of the larger body of text.

Therefore, Mid is the most flexible of the three ways to extract words or phrases from larger bodies of text. The tradeoff is that you must supply Mid with two numbers: where within the larger text to start extracting and how many characters to extract. For Left and Right, you need only supply the number of characters, not the starting position.

A variation, the MidB Function, allows you to specify the Start and Length parameters in *bytes.* (Characters in VB are now expressed as two-byte codes in the 32-bit version of VB.) Mid specifies Start and Length in *characters.*

Used with   Text ("string") Variables

Variables

```
A$ = "This person, named Malia Borzini, was caught shoplifting."
B$ = Mid(A$, 20, 13)
Print B$
```

Results in   Malia Borzini

OR (to illustrate the various effects of putting Mid within a Loop structure):

```
Sub Form_Click ()
K$ = "1234567"

For i = 1 To Len(K$)
    Print Mid(K$, i, 1)
Next i

Print

For i = 1 To Len(K$)
    Print Mid(K$, 1, i)
Next i

Print

For i = 1 To Len(K$)
    Print Mid(K$, i, i)
Next i

End Sub
```

Results in

1
2
3
4
5
6
7

1
12
123
1234
12345
123456
1234567

1
23
345
4567
567
67
7

Uses
• Use Mid with the InStr command to find, then extract, a piece of text within a phrase, sentence, paragraph or larger body of text. InStr searches for a matching letter or word or phrase. If InStr finds what you've asked it to look for, InStr tells you the character *position*, within the larger text, where it found the match. You can feed this information to Mid as the starting position where it should begin extracting text. (See the Example.)

• Mid is often used in combination with one or more of these other text-manipulation commands:

• Mid (when used as a *Statement* instead of a *Function*, Mid *replaces* a piece of text within a larger body of text):

```
B$ = "Down by the old mill stream."
Mid(B$, 13, 3) = "new"
Print B$
```

Results in
Down by the new mill stream.

• Left (pulls out a number of characters from the left side of a piece of text)

• Right (pulls out a number of characters from the right side of a piece of text)

• Len (tells how long a piece of text is, how many characters it contains)

• InStr (tells where a letter, word or phrase is located within a piece of text)

By using these commands in various combinations, you can extract, search, replace, scramble, rearrange, edit or otherwise manage text.

Cautions   • Normally, you provide two numbers to Mid—the starting character position and the number of characters to extract. However, if you leave out the number of characters, Mid will extract all the text from the starting position to the end of the larger body of text:

```
A$ = "ABCDEFGHI"

Print Mid(A$,4)
```

Results in   DEFGHI

This is the equivalent of:

```
X = Len(A$)

Print Right(A$, X − 3)
```

• The larger body of text (the target text Variable) from which Mid will extract a piece cannot be larger than approximately 60,000 characters (bytes).

Example   One valuable use for Mid is to get rid of extraneous text. Assume we've got a police report, and we want the computer to locate a suspect's name (using InStr) and then provide an extraction (using Mid), just the immediate context, from a large report. It has been a busy night in Williamsport and we want only the brief facts about this one perp, Malia.

```
Sub Form_Click ()

A$ = "This person, named Malia Borzini, was caught shoplifting Bess →
Myerson's autobiography."

Search$ = LCase$(InputBox$("Please enter the perp's name..."))

StartPos = InStr(LCase$(A$), Search$)
If StartPos = 0 then MsgBox (Search$ + " didn't get into any trouble →
   yesterday."): Exit Sub

EndPos = InStr(StartPos, A$, ".")
Ingth = EndPos − StartPos + 1

Print Mid(A$, StartPos, Ingth)
End Sub
```

Note that we used LCase$ to make sure that we found a match, regardless of the capitalization in the police report or in the user's request (also see "StrComp" for an alternative to LCase$).

By having the user enter the name into the Variable Search$, we can then find the Search$ within the report (A$). If StartPos is 0, we tell the user that the name wasn't found in the report and exit the Subroutine.

Otherwise, we look for a period (.) so we can extract all the information between the search name and the end of the sentence where the name was located. This search gives us the end position for our extraction.

Mid wants the *length* of the extraction, the number of characters. So we subtract StartPos from EndPos, adding 1 to make it come out right. Then we print the results to the screen:

> Malia Borzini was caught shoplifting Bess Myerson's autobiography.

See also   InStr; Left; Len; Mid (Statement); Right; StrComp$

MID (OR MID$)

STATEMENT

Description   Mid used as a Statement replaces a piece of text within a larger body of text.

However, this Statement isn't very often useful—the text you are replacing *must be the precise length* of the text that you are replacing it with. Otherwise, you'll have to resort to less direct methods of editing a piece of text. (See the Example below.)

When used as a Statement, Mid accomplishes somewhat the reverse of what it does when used as a *Function*. As a Function, Mid extracts (makes a copy of) a piece of text from a larger body of text. As a Statement, Mid replaces text.

Used with   Text ("string") Variables

Variables
> Big$ = "Notions, linens and bath items are on the third floor."

We've rearranged the store. We must replace "bath items" with "appliances." Mid(Big$, 21, 10) = "appliances"

Results in   Notions, linens and appliances are on the third floor.

Note that the replacement text *must be the same length* as the replaced text. Mid does not automatically shrink or expand the large body of text to accommodate a difference in length because it doesn't know what you intend to replace. There is a solution to this problem, however. See the Example below.

Uses   • Edit text ("string") Variables.

• Search and replace text within a document (see the Example).

• Also see "Mid" (used as a *Function*).

Cautions • This Mid *Statement* isn't as useful as the Mid Function (which see). The Statement is only useful when the target text is exactly the same size as the replacement text, which doesn't happen often in the real world.

• Normally, you provide two numbers to Mid—the starting character position and the number of characters to replace. However, if you leave out the number of characters, Mid will use the entire replacement text.

```
Bigtext$ = "The danger zone."
Replacement$ = "Civil War"

Mid(Bigtext$, 5, 6) = Replacement$
Print Bigtext$
```

Results in The Civil zone.

Note that the 6 defines how many characters will be replaced; not all of Replacement$ was inserted into Bigtext$.

If you leave out the 6, the description of how many letters to replace, the whole Replacement$ is used:

```
Mid(Bigtext$, 5) = Replacement$
Print Bigtext$
```

Results in The Civil Warne.

Note also that if the replacement text is larger than the replacement zone (the distance between the starting location within the bigger text and the end of the bigger text), the replacement text will be cut off. A replacement cannot extend beyond the bigger text.

```
Mid(Bigtext$, 10) = Replacement$
Print Bigtext$
```

Results in The dangeCivil W

• The larger body of text (the target text Variable) into which Mid will place a piece of text cannot be larger than approximately 60,000 characters (bytes). The same size limitation applies to the replacement text as well.

Example To a Text Box we'll add a Search & Replace feature and allow the user to decide whether this feature should be case-sensitive (whether it cares about capitalization).

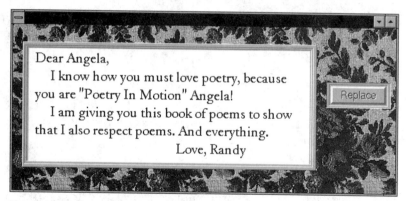

Figure M-15: An earnest love note.

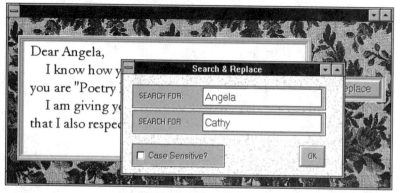

Figure M-16: The efficient suitor is prepared for a change of plans.

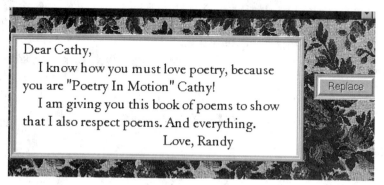

Figure M-17: The change is made.

First, create a New Project from Visual Basic's File Menu. Then create a Text Box and a Command Button with its Caption set to "REPLACE." Next, set the Form's BackColor to black and adjust the FontSize and FontName

Properties to please yourself. Set the Text Box's MultiLine Property to True. There is only one Event we need to respond to in this Form:

```
Sub Command1_Click ()
    Form2.Show
End Sub
```

Open a Module by clicking on New Module in the Project Window. Then type the following line in to create a text ("string") Variable that all Forms in the program can use and change:

```
Global Main As String
```

Create a New Form: Create a second Form by selecting New Form in VB's File Menu. On this Form, put two Labels, two Text Boxes, a Check Box and a Command Button. Position and caption them as shown in Figure M-16.

This Form, too, has only one Event it needs to respond to:

```
Sub Command1_Click ()
    Main$ = Form1.Text1.Text
    SearchReplace Main$, Form2.Text1, Form2.Text2
    Form1.Text1.Text = Main$
    Form2.Hide
End Sub
```

Here we are giving the Global Text Variable called Main$ the contents of the large Text Box on Form1—the place where the user writes a letter or whatever.

Then we call upon a Subroutine, providing it with the main body of text, and the contents of Text1 ("Search For") and Text2 ("Replace With"). When the Subroutine finishes searching and replacing, we change the large body of text by replacing it with the changes that the Subroutine made to Main$.

The Meat of the Program: Now we get to the real *meat* of this program, the engine that drives the whole thing. Create a New Module from VB's File Menu and type the following:

```
Sub SearchReplace (Main As String, Target As Control, Replacement As →
Control)

prev = 1

If Form2.CaseSensitive.Value = 0 Then
    Foundit = InStr(prev, LCase$(Main$), LCase$(Target.text))
Else
    Foundit = InStr(prev, Main, Target.text)
End If

Do While Foundit <> 0
        L = Len(Main$)
    If Len(Target.text) = Len(Replacement.text) Then
            Mid(Main, Foundit) = Replacement.text
    Else
```

```
            A$ = Left$(Main$, Foundit - 1)
            B$ = Mid(Main$, Foundit+1)
            Main$ = A$ + Replacement.text + B$
        End If

        prev =  Foundit + 1

    If Form2.CaseSensitive.Value = 0 Then
        Foundit = InStr(prev, LCase$(Main$), LCase$(Target.text))
    Else
        Foundit = InStr(prev, Main, Target.text)
    End If

    Loop

    End Sub
```

You can use this general-purpose Subroutine in your programs anytime you need a Search & Replace feature. You must set up a Global Text Variable (in a Module) as illustrated with Global Main as String. After that, you just supply this Subroutine with the name of the Global Variable and the Names of two Controls—the one holding the "search for" (target) and "replace with" (replacement).

Now let's describe what's happening in this Subroutine. First, we make a Variable called *prev* that will act like a finger moving through some text. When we come upon a match, the Variable *prev* will remember the location of that match. We must start off with prev = 1 so that InStr will start with the first character in the main body of our document (Main$).

If the user has not selected the CaseSensitive Check Box, we will ignore any variations in capitalization in the "search for" text and in the main text. We therefore make both the main text and the target text completely lowercase by using the LCase$ command. Otherwise ("Else"), we leave the text as it is.

Where We Found a Match: In either situation, when we finish with InStr's activity, the Variable called *FoundIt* contains the character position within the main text where we found a match. InStr puts a 0 into *FoundIt* if there was no match, and in that case, the entire Do...Loop structure would never activate itself. We would just leave the Subroutine, having no effect on the main text.

But let's assume that a match was found. We now tell the computer that as long as *FoundIt* doesn't hold a 0 (meaning that no match was found), we should adjust the main text.

We first put the length of the main text into the Variable *L*. Then we check to see if the length of the "search for" text is exactly the same as the "replace with" text. If so, we can use Mid. We go ahead and replace the text and then jump past the EndIf to see if there are any further matches in the main text.

But, as will usually be the case, if the searched-for text and the replacement text are not the same size, we must do a few gymnastics to keep the main text intact.

```
A$ = Left$(Main$, Foundit — 1)
B$ = Right$(Main$, L — Foundit — Len(Target.text) + 1)
Main$ = A$ + Replacement.text + B$
```

We'll have to break the main text in two and then stuff the replacement into the middle.

We store into the temporary text Variable *A$* all the text to the left of the location where we found a match, less one character (we don't want to include the first letter of the match).

Then we put the text to the right of the match in *B$*. The calculation of how many characters (counting back from the far right of the main text) should be included is rather obscure. But this formula always works, so if you program a lot, you might want to make a note of it somewhere. You subtract the length of the text you want to replace from the position where you found it. Then you subtract that number from the total length (*L*) of the main text. Then add 1. (It doesn't matter why you have to add 1, but you must.)

Splitting the Text in Two: Now we have sneaked up on the main text and *bifurcated* it before it knew what was going on. We split it into the piece to the left of the target text and the piece to the right. This split leaves a hole where the target used to be, but we'll fill that hole with the replacement text and then join the three pieces back together: Main$ = A$ + Replacement.text + B$. We envelop the replacement with our two pieces. Now the main text is whole again and contains the replacement.

Now we continue looking for any other targets that need to be replaced:

```
prev = Foundit + 1

If Form2.CaseSensitive.Value = 0 Then
    Foundit = InStr(prev, LCase$(Main$), LCase$(Target.text))
Else
    Foundit = InStr(prev, Main, Target.text)
End If

Loop
```

We must first update the Variable *prev* (our finger that moves through the text, keeping our place), so we will be one character past the previous match. We don't want to start searching from the location where we just found a match; otherwise, we'll find that same match again.

Now we go through the same process of searching the main text, just as we did before we entered the Do...Loop. If *Foundit* fails to find a match, it will contain 0, and the Do While Foundit <> 0 (do this Loop as long as Foundit doesn't equal zero) will send us past the Loop command, and we'll leave this Subroutine without further ado-loop.

Otherwise, the Loop will once again perform its replacement, once again search for another match, and so on until no more matches are found.

See also   InStr; Left; Len; Mid (Function); Right

Description

MIN

Figure M-18: When the interior tab is at the far left of a Scroll Bar, that's the Min.

The Min Property is the position at the far left of a Horizontal Scroll Bar Control or the position at the top of a Vertical Scroll Bar Control. (For a general overview of Scroll Bars, see "LargeChange.")

You determine the minimum and maximum values for your Bar Controls based usually on what information they slide the user through. For instance, if you are showing data about your family and there are five of you, set Min to 1 and Max to 5. For a calendar, set Min to 1 and Max to 12 if you want to allow the user to slide through pictures of each month. For a cookbook with 150 recipes, set Min to 1 and Max to 150.

Any change the user makes by moving the lozenge-shaped button (called the Scroll Box) inside a Scroll Bar changes that Scroll Bar's Value Property. Your program can use the Value to take appropriate actions. Normally, these actions are taken within the Scroll Bar's Change Event.

A Scroll Bar's Min and Max Properties set the limits that the Value Property can change.

The highest Max can be is 32,767. However, you can multiply what Value returns if you need a larger number for some reason.

    X = HScroll1.Value * 5.

Used with

Horizontal Scroll Bars and Vertical Scroll Bars

Variables

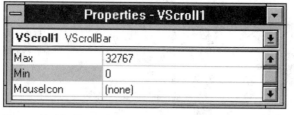

Figure M-19: If you know the Min Property you want while designing your program, you can set it in the Properties Window.

OR (to set it while the program is running): HScroll1.Min = 10

Uses

Used in combination with the Min, LargeChange, SmallChange and Value Properties of a Scroll Bar, you can provide the user with an intuitive and vivid way to adjust various kinds of information—slide things around onscreen, resize things, change their colors, flip through the "pages" of an automotive manual, etc. A Scroll Bar is an important user input tool in the graphical user interfaces on modern computers.

Cautions
• Both Max and Min Properties can be set anywhere from –32,768 to 32,767.

• If you don't change Max and Min, they default to 32,767 and 0, respectively.

• You can reverse the direction of a Scroll Bar. Normally, Max is at the far right of a Horizonal Bar and at the bottom of a Vertical Bar. However, if you set the Max Property to a number *lower than* the Min Property, the Max flips and moves to the far left of a Horizonal Bar and the top of a Vertical Bar. And, of course, the Min reverses position, too.

Example
We'll use three Vertical Scroll Bars to allow the user to select any date between 1–1–1900 and 12–30–2078. When the selection is made, the Label at the bottom reports the day of the week for that date.

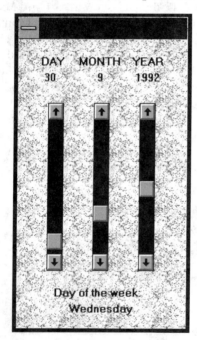

Figure M-20: A day-of-the-week calculator.

First, create a New Project and put three Vertical Scroll Bars and eight Labels on the Form. Then, in the General Declarations section of the Form, create the following Variables:

```
Dim serdate As Double
Dim yr As Integer, mon As Integer, dy As Integer
```

Next, in the General Declarations section of the Form, create the following Subroutine:

```
Sub translate ()

dateser = DateSerial(yr, mon, dy)

label2.caption = format$(dateser, "dddd")
End Sub
```

This Subroutine fills our Variable "dateser" with the "serial number" of the date the user has selected (see "DateSerial"). Then we use the Format$ Function to display the day of the week in Label2.

When the program first runs, we want the current date displayed, so put the following into the Form_Load Event:

```
Sub Form_Load ()
    dy = Day(Now)
    mon = Month(Now)
    yr = Year(Now)

vscroll1.value = yr — 1900
    label1.caption = Str$(1900 + yr)
vscroll2.value = mon
    label3.caption = Str$(mon)
vscroll3.value = dy
    label4.caption = Str$(dy)
translate

End Sub
```

We load our dy, mon and yr Variables with the correct current values (Now looks at the computer's built-in clock). Then we set each Scroll Bar to the proper position. (Years are measured from 1900 on with 0 representing 1900; we must add 1900 to the number in Variable yr.)

In addition, we change the captions of the Day, Month and Year Labels so that they will contain the correct numbers. Captions must show text, so we translate the numbers into text with Str$.

Now, using the VB Properties Window, set the Min and Max Properties for each of the Scroll Bars. Set the Day Bar to a Min of 1 and a Max of 31; the Month Bar, Min 1, Max 12; and the Year Bar, Min 0, Max 178. The Year Variable automatically assumes 1900 as the starting date, so 0 means 1900 and 178 means 2078.

The activity of each of the Scroll Bars' Change Events is similar. Here's the bar to adjust the day:

```
Sub VScroll3_Change ()
    dy = vscroll3.value
    label4.caption = Str$(dy)
    translate
End Sub
```

The Change Event Is Triggered: We find out the new Value that the user created when he or she moved the Scroll Box on the Scroll Bar. In this case, the Day Bar was moved, triggering its Change Event. So we take the Value, put it into the appropriate Label Caption and translate it into a weekday using the Subroutine described previously.

The month:

```
Sub VScroll2_Change ()
    mon = vscroll2.value
    label3.caption = Str$(mon)
    translate
End Sub
```

And the year:

```
Sub VScroll1_Change ()
    yr = vscroll1.value
    label1.caption = Str$(1900 + yr)
    translate
End Sub
```

See also   Horizontal Scroll Bar; LargeChange, SmallChange; Max; Scroll; Value

 INBUTTON

PROPERTY

Description   Allows you to remove the Minimize Button from the top right of a Form.

The Form's BorderStyle Property must be set to 1 ("Fixed Single") or 2 ("Sizable," the default) for a Minimize Button to appear. However, even for these border styles, you can refuse to allow the user to minimize (make into an icon) the window by removing the MinButton.

Used with   Forms only

Variables   **Variable type:** Boolean

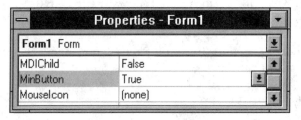

Figure M-21: The MinButton Property must be set while designing a program.

The MinButton Property can only be set using the Properties Window; it cannot be set while the program is running.

Uses   Prevent the user from shrinking a window into an icon. Many kinds of windows—short messages, preferences options, file access—are best made visible when the user needs them and left invisible otherwise. For these kinds of brief-life windows, there is little point to allowing iconization (or full-screen maximization, for that matter).

Cautions   • You can iconize (minimize) a window from within your running program by setting the WindowState Property to 1.

• When a window is minimized, it triggers a Resize Event on the Form.

Example

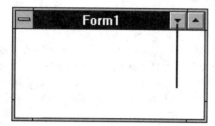

Figure M-22: The location of the Minimize Button on a window.

See also   BorderStyle; ControlBox; MaxButton; WindowState

INUTE

FUNCTION

Description   The Minute command tells you the minute of the hour, giving you a number between 1 and 59.

Minute can give you any hour between January 1, 100, and December 31, 9999, using Visual Basic's built-in "serial number" representation of date+ time. Visual Basic can provide or manipulate individual serial numbers *for every second* between those two dates. These serial numbers also include coded representations of all the hours, days, months and years between 100 A.D. and 9999. (For more on the serial number, see "DateSerial.")

Used with   Often used with the Now Function to tell you the current minute as registered by your computer's clock:

    Print Minute(Now)

The Now Function provides the serial number for the current date and time. Minute extracts the minute portion of that serial number.

Variables   X = Minute(Now)

Uses   • Create "digital" clocks.

• Create Timers, using Minute with the Timer Control.

M...**715**

Cautions   • The Format$ Function offers an extremely flexible and powerful method of displaying or printing date and time information. Use it to present the results of Minute, and other date+time Functions, in precisely the way you want them to appear.

Example
```
X# = Now
Y = Minute(Now)
Print X#
Print Y
```

Results in   33606.7413773148
47

Of course, the serial number, the X#, will always differ, based on what Now is. Every time you use Now, the serial number will be larger.

In fact, Visual Basic's serial number is unique for every second between January 1, 100, and December 31, 9999—the range over which VB can calculate date and time.

The number of seconds in a span of 325 years is obviously quite large. There are more than 30 million seconds in a single year, which is why we had to add a # symbol to the Variable X that would hold the serial number returned by the Now Function. The # symbol makes a Variable a "Double-Precision Floating-Point" type of Variable (see "Variables"). This kind of Variable is capable of holding an extremely large range of numbers.

The VB date+time serial number contains the day, month and year to the left of the decimal point, and the numbers to the right of the decimal point contain the hour, minute and second.

However, the meaning of the serial number is encoded. There is no direct way to examine the serial number and extract the various information contained therein. VB, therefore, provides various Functions—Second, Minute, Hour, Day, Month, Year—to decode that information for you.

See also   DateSerial; Day; Format$; Hour; Month; Now; Second; Weekday; Year

 KDIR

STATEMENT

Description   MkDir makes a new directory on a disk—floppy disks or hard drives. It's the equivalent of the DOS command MD (or Mkdir).

Used with   Disk drives

Variables   MkDir "C:\TEMP"

OR (to use a Variable):

X$ = "C:\TEMP\TEMP1"

MkDir X$

Uses
- Build into your program some of the features of a File Manager—allowing the user to create, remove, search and otherwise manipulate disk file directories.

- Check to see if a special directory exists for holding temporary data or whether a special directory is devoted to your program alone. If one of these directories doesn't exist and your program requires it, tell the user that you are about to create a new directory to make your program run more efficiently. (Always allow the user to overrule changes to his or her disk drive structure. How disk drives are organized is the personal responsibility of each user; your program shouldn't unilaterally change this organization.)

Cautions
- If you attempt to make a directory where one with the same directory name already exists, you'll get the following error message:

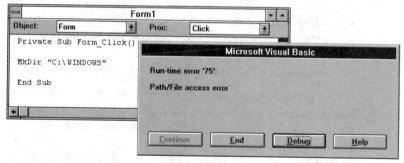

Figure M-23: You cannot create a duplicate directory name.

If the error message appears while a user is running your program, it will shut down your program. The program will disappear from the screen like a closed window. Therefore, you should always use error trapping during unpredictable activities such as disk manipulation. (See "On Error.")

Example   Two valuable techniques are illustrated in this example, in addition to MkDir.

- You'll find out how to learn the precise file path of the running program. If, for example, the user started your VB program from C:\WINDOWS and the name of your program is MYPROG.EXE, the technique illustrated in this example will provide you with "C:\WINDOWS\MYPROG.EXE." VB itself includes the Path and EXEName commands (which see) that allow a running VB program to tell you its location on the disk.

▪ You'll also find out how to make a program *self-modifying*. That is, the program will change itself, will contain information that it didn't have when you made it into an .EXE file. The first time the user runs this program, it will change forever. We force the program to identify itself as having been run. The program makes itself different from what it was in its virgin state. (Note that this technique is risky for several reasons and should be used with great caution, if at all. It is possible, for example, that a self-modification could cause virus-detection programs to go ballistic.)

Nevertheless, this technique can be valuable if you want the user to register or pay for your software, or if you want the software to contain a self-modifiable password of some kind. It's as if you give the program the capacity to evolve. The program will *know* if it is in its original state or if it has been run. And because the program is different, you can build in reactions to the change.

The simplistic way to make a program different is to create an external file, like an .INI file that contains the user's font and color preferences, for example. The great drawback of .INI files—for purposes of password security and program registration or author-control—is that they are simple files that anyone can read (or delete). Having a program capable of changing itself opens up a whole new level of control.

Creating Sufficient Space: How would you create space for large changes to a program, space that could contain significant information? One way is to declare a Variable of large size:

```
Myspace$ = "XXXXXXXXXX"
```

This procedure gives you bytes to work with. What is its location? Where would you Get and Put to it after you've Opened the program's .EXE file on the disk? You could use a file-examination program like the Disk Editor feature of the Norton Utilities.

Another approach would be to open the .EXE file itself on the disk from within the running program in binary mode. You would then search for the tagged data and change it. If you set the data to something unique like "Place System Startup Information Here," then you should be able to find it.

An alternative to modifying the program itself—and a better one from the point of Windows standards—is to use a private .INI file. If this file is named the same as the .EXE file, the user can easily identify it if moving or deleting the .EXE file. Many Windows programs use .INI files to store information they need from one run to the next. Many programmers believe that using self-modifying programs is a bad practice because it can be dangerous; if an error occurs, the disk structure itself could be damaged. If that happens, you could come close to creating something akin to a virus, and the user would not be amused.

However, if you want to take these risks, you can even make your program aware of *how often* the user has run the program. After they have used it 20 times, you could warn them that they will be allowed to run it five more times, but then it will destroy itself because they never sent you a payment.

Let's create a program called TEST.EXE to see how all this works. Start a New Project from VB's File Menu and then, in a Module, enter the following:

```
Declare Function GetClassWord% Lib "User" (ByVal HWnd As Integer, →
    ByVal nIndex As Integer)
Declare Function GetModuleFileName% Lib "Kernel" (ByVal HWnd As →
    Integer, ByVal filname As String, ByVal nSize As Integer)
```

These API Functions (see Appendix A) extend the power of VB. Just type them in exactly and put each Declare on a *single line*:

Right:

```
Declare Function GetClassWord% Lib "User" (ByVal  HWnd As Integer, →
    ByVal nIndex As Integer)
```

Wrong:

```
Declare Function GetClassWord% Lib "User" (ByVal HWnd As Integer, ByVal
nIndex As Integer)
```

Now, in the Form_Load Event, enter the following:

```
Sub Form_Load ()

On Error Resume Next

filname$ = Space$(100)
Module = GetClassWord(Form1.hWnd, −16)
Flen = GetModuleFileName(Module, filname$, 100)
progpath$ = Left$(filname$, Flen)

Open progpath$ For Binary As #1
    a$ = String$(1, " ")
    Get #1, 1069, a$
    b$ = "k"
    Put #1, 1069, b$
Close 1

If a$ = "k" Then Exit Sub

msg$ = "Please enter the path where you wish to keep this program."
i$ = InputBox$(msg$, "CREATE DIRECTORY", "C:\WINDOWS\MYPROG")
If i$ = "" Then Exit Sub

MkDir i$

If Err Then MsgBox (Error$(Err))
End Sub
```

Here the Declare statements in the Module allow us to use special built-in Windows Functions that go beyond what VB can do. We have effectively added a new command to VB by declaring these Functions.

Now we create a text ("string") Variable called *filname$*, giving it a length of 100 characters by using the Space$ Function. This Variable will hold the path of our VB program—no matter where the user might have put the program on his or her disk drive.

Then we find the "module," supplying that information to the GetMod-uleFileName Function. As our reward, GetModuleFileName provides us with the path of the currently running program (which goes into filname$) and also the length of that path (how many characters are in it). We put this information into progpath$ by stripping off any leftover spaces from filname$ using the Left$ Function.

Self-Modifying at the 1069th Byte: Now we know what drive, directory and program names were used to start the current program running. At this point we can self-modify the program because we know precisely where, on the user's disk drive, the program resides. We open it, create a single byte string Variable *a$*, get the 1069th byte from the program on the disk and put the letter *k* into the 1069th position in the VB program on disk.

Why the 1069th Byte? Our task here is to change a VB program but not to cripple it. Two types of data are in any program—information and com-mands. The commands make the program take various actions. All the Functions, Statements, Methods, etc., in this book are commands. VB takes some action when you use them, like Print X, or Width = 500. However, there are also zones within programs that contain *information*: A$ = "Robert Prior." Robert Prior is information.

If we made our VB program self-modify one of its commands, the pro-gram would behave erratically or even shut itself down. If we self-modify information, however, we merely change "Robert Prior" to, perhaps, "Robert Xrior." This change doesn't affect the way the program runs. We want to find a place within VB programs where there is information and where it is always in the same location within every VB program. There are several places.

In every VB program, an embedded message is shown if the user tries to run the program from DOS, outside Windows. Windows programs need Windows; they cannot run in the old DOS environment. Each VB program is prepared to print the following message on the screen if the user tries to run the program from DOS:

"This program requires Microsoft Windows."

In all VB 3.0 programs, the *q* in *requires* occurs as the 1069th byte within the .EXE program. In all VB 2.0 programs, *q* occurs at the 1036th byte. In VB 1.0, it occurs at the 94th byte.

In most commercial Windows programs, the *q* occurs at the 530th byte. And a few commercial Windows programs contain this message:

"This program cannot be run in DOS mode."

We're interested only in VB-created programs, and we'll always find our *q* at the 1069th position in every VB .EXE program with VB 3.0. We can change this character and check, when the program loads in, to see if it *has* been changed. If it's been changed, the program has been run once.

Our intent here is to find out if this is the first time this program has been run. If it is, we want to create a special directory for the program. We'll offer the user our suggestion (C:\WINDOWS\MYPROG) but allow a different path:

```
Open progpath$ For Binary As #1
    a$ = String$(1, " ")
    Get #1, 1069, a$
    b$ = "k"
    Put #1, 1069, b$
Close 1

If a$ = "k" Then Exit Sub
```

We opened our VB .EXE program as a binary file (see "Open"). That way, we can look at individual characters (single bytes) within the program. We create a single byte text ("string") Variable by using String$ and make the string 1 byte long. The Get statement returns a Variable of whatever size is requested; because a$ has been made a single-character size, it is assigned the character at the 1069th position.

Keeping the character in a$, we stuff a *k* into the 1069th position, *self-modifying* the program. Then we close the program on the disk.

If a$ holds a *k*, we know that this program has been run before, so we just exit the Subroutine. We want to set up a special directory only the first time this program runs.

If a$ holds something else (it would be a *q*), we know that the program is being run for the first time. In this case, we don't exit the Subroutine. Instead, we make the directory of the user's choice, suggesting that it be C:\WINDOWS\MYPROG:

```
msg$ = "Please enter the path where you wish to keep this program."
i$ = InputBox$(msg$, "CREATE DIRECTORY", "C:\WINDOWS\MYPROG")
If i$ = "" Then Exit Sub

MkDir i$
```

How would you allow the user to run the program 10 times before reminding him or her to send you some money?

Z is 10 letters in the alphabet beyond *q*:

```
Open progpath$ For Binary As #1
    a$ = String$(1, " ")
    Get #1, 1069, a$
If a$ = "z" Then
msgbox ("Well, you seem to be enjoying this program, having used it →
    10 times!")
Close 1:Exit Sub
End If
    c = asc(a$)
    c = c + 1
```

```
        b$ = chr$(c)
        Put #1, 1069, b$
    Close 1
```

To Never Ask for the Number Again: How would you allow the user to register your program, after you have received payment for the program? How can the program be modified to never again request a registration number from the user?

When your program first loads, you could check to see if it is a registered or unregistered version:

```
Sub Form_Load ()

Open progpath$ For Binary As #1
    a$ = String$(1, " ")
    Get #1, 1069, a$
    Close 1
If a$ = "q" Then
    Show
    Print "Please type in your registration number..."
Else
    Form2.Show
    Form1.Unload
End If
End Sub
```

If a$ is still *q*, the program hasn't been registered. If a$ has been modified, then the user has registered it, and we move on to the main program that starts in Form2.

If we must ask the user to type in the registration number, however, Form1's KeyPress Event looks for the correct sequence of keypresses:

```
Sub Form_KeyPress (keyascii As Integer)

Static reg As String
reg = reg + Str$(keyascii)
If reg = "114 101 103" Then
    Open progpath$ For Binary As #1
        a$ = "r"
        Put #1, 1069, a$
    Close 1
    Cls
    Print "Thank you for registering."
End If
End Sub
```

By defining reg$ as Static, we make sure that it retains its information. Otherwise, reg$ would be "re-created" for every KeyPress Event and could thus never hold more than the data about a single keypress.

The KeyPress Event returns the code of the key that was pressed, keyascii. We add the text Variable *reg* to itself, plus each new keycode: *reg* = reg + Str$(keyascii). The Variable *reg* accumulates the key codes of whatever sequence of keys the user presses. When the user pays for the program, we tell them that the secret registration code is "reg." So, the next time the user runs the program, he or she can type in that sequence. We then open the program, change the *q* to *r* and thank the user.

Now, when Form1_Load looks for *q* in the 1069th position, it finds an *r* instead—and knows that it has been registered.

See also   ChDir; CurDir$; RmDir

Module

See   Sub

Month

FUNCTION

Description   The Month command tells you the month of the year, giving you a number between 1 and 12.

Month can provide an accurate date and time for any day between January 1, 100, and December 31, 9999, using Visual Basic's built-in serial number representation of date+time. Visual Basic can provide or manipulate individual serial numbers *for every second* between those two dates. Each serial number includes a coded representation of a particular second of a minute of an hour of a day of a month of one of the years between 100 A.D. and 9999. Needless to say, there are many serial numbers available, and each is unique.

(For more on the serial number, see "DateSerial.")

Used with   Often used with the Now Function to tell you the current month as registered by your computer's clock:

```
Print Month(Now)
```

The Now Function provides the serial number for the current date and time. The Month Function extracts the month portion of the serial number.

Variables   X = Month(Now)

Uses   • Create calendar programs.

• Create "to-do" scheduler programs, keeping track of appointments by comparing Year(Now), Month(Now) and Day(Now) against the information stored when the user first identified a particular appointment. You create a serial number for a date by using either the DateSerial or DateValue Function. (See the Example below.)

• Date-stamp data. Add the serial number to information stored by your program (data the user types in, a picture the user creates, whatever is being saved to disk for future use). You can get the current serial number by entering: X# = Now. Then, if you save X# to a disk file along with the other data, you'll always have a precise record of the exact second when that data was created and stored.

Cautions • The Format$ Function offers an extremely flexible and powerful method of displaying or printing date and time information. Use it to present the results of Month, and other date/time Functions, in precisely the way you want them to appear.

• Here's how the serial number works:

```
X# = Now
Y = Month(Now)

Print X#
Print Y
```

Results in 33608.132349537
1

Of course, the serial number, the X#, will always differ, based on what Now is. Every time you use Now, the serial number will be larger.

In fact, Visual Basic's serial number is unique for every second between January 1, 100, and December 31, 9999—the range that VB provides for date+time calculations.

The number of seconds in a span of 9899 years is obviously quite large. There are 31,536,000 seconds in a single year. Therefore, we add a # symbol to the Variable X that would hold the serial number returned by the Now Function. The # symbol makes a Variable a "Double-Precision Floating-Point" type Variable (see "Variables"). This kind of Variable is capable of holding an extremely large range of numbers.

The VB date+time serial number contains the day, month and year to the left of the decimal point, and the numbers to the right of the decimal point contain the hour, minute and second.

However, the meaning of the serial number is encoded. There is no direct way to examine the serial number and extract the various information contained therein. VB, therefore, provides various Functions—Second, Minute, Hour, Day, Month, Year—to decode that information for you.

Example We'll sketch out a to-do program, a scheduler that allows the user to keep a diary of reminders. We'll design the Form and the necessary components, and make suggestions on how it can be expanded if you want to create a full-fledged application. The amount of programming involved would be larger than the scope of the examples in this book, but the program would require only some additional features typically found in a simple database application.

Create a Form and load in a picture via the Picture Property. Set the Form's FontSize to 56, FontBold to Off and FontName to Garamond (or whatever font is available that looks pleasing). Add a Text Box (set its MultiLine Property to –1). Then add a Horizontal Scroll Bar (set its Min Property to 1 and its Max Property to 31).

Scrolling through the Bar changes the date, the day of the week and the Form's caption.

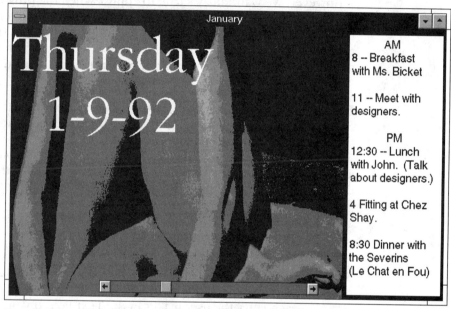

Figure M-24: A scheduler program.

All the action takes place in the Horizontal Scroll Bar's Change Event:

```
Sub HScroll1_Change ()

m = Month(Now): y = Year(Now)
d = hscroll1.value
ds# = DateSerial(y, m, d)

Dt$ = Format$(ds#, " m-d-yy")
Dt1$ = Format$(ds#, "dddd")
dt2$ = Format$(ds#, "mmmm")

Cls
Form1.Print Dt1$
Form1.Print Dt$
Form1.caption = dt2$
End Sub
```

We pick up the current month and year from the Now Function, which fetches that information from the computer's built-in clock. Then we find out where (between 1 and 31) on the Scroll Bar the user moved the button—the day the user wants. We set the Variable *d* to the correct day of the month. The DateSerial Function uses the year, month and day information to create a serial number.

Now we can use the Format$ Function to translate the serial number into the three formats we are interested in displaying—numeric month-day-year; text day name; text month name. Then we clear out the previously displayed date information from the Form with Cls, print two pieces of information to the Form and put the name of the month in its caption.

However, we want today's date to appear when the program first runs; we don't want to wait until or if the user moves the Scroll Bar. To set up today's date, we establish which day is "now" and then set the Scroll Bar to that value. We don't have to specifically activate the printing Routines within the Scroll Bar's Change Event by naming that procedure:

```
hscroll1_change
```

Either the User or Your Program: Changing the Scroll Bar's Value Property triggers its Change Event; it doesn't matter whether the user or the program makes the change.

If you print or draw (with the Circle, PSet, Line or Print commands) within a Form's Load Event, you must first force it to show itself. Otherwise, the drawing or printing will not show up when the Form first appears.

```
Sub Form_Load ()
    Show
    hscroll1.value = Day(Now)
End Sub
```

Suggested Options: A scheduler program would operate like a typical database, with the added information of a serial number that you could attach to each entry the user makes in the Text Box. If you want to build this program into a complete application, you should provide additional Controls to permit the user to scroll through months, perhaps even years. Each time the user moves to a new date, the Text Property of the Text Box, plus the currently active serial number, should be saved to a data file on disk. This data file will preserve the user's text notes when the program is not actively running.

Useful additions to the program might include a special options Form that allows the user to insert "alarm" symbols (such as *) next to items that should be announced a day or two before they happen. When the program first loads, it could check for such special notifications by simply searching through the information after it has been loaded in from the disk (see "Open"). (For a general-purpose search routine, see "InStr.")

You could also incorporate a month-at-a-glance feature that would be a separate window showing which dates had been annotated by the user.

Clicking on such a date could bring back the original data-entry screen illustrated previously.

You also could call upon a series of pictures (see "Load *Method*") to illustrate different months. Another nice touch would be draggable icons that can be placed next to special dates–a cake to signify a birthday, a heart attached to February 14, etc. Your program could illustrate known holidays, and a "box" of draggable icons could be made available for the user's personal special occasions.

See also   Day; Format$; Hour; Minute; Now; Second; Weekday; Year

MouseDown, MouseUp   EVENT

Description   The MouseDown and MouseUp Events are triggered when the user clicks the mouse (or releases a pressed mouse button) on the Form or on one of the Controls that is sensitive to this Event.

A Click Event occurs when the user *presses and releases* the mouse button. MouseDown reacts to the press; MouseUp, to the release–giving you finer control over position and duration as the user maneuvers the mouse about a window.

MouseDown and MouseUp provide more information than does a Click Event. Click generally means only that the user selected something. Double-click is frequently used as a way of causing your program to react to something the user did. But where a click is like a finger pointing to a vase, MouseDown and MouseUp (along with MouseMove) are like using pressure, position and duration to build a vase out of wet clay–there's much more fine control over the activity of the mouse.

MouseDown and MouseUp provide three kinds of information:

- which button was pressed.
- whether or not the user simultaneously pressed the SHIFT, CTRL or ALT key (or any combination of them) when the mouse button was pressed.
- the current X,Y location within the Form or Control where the MouseDown or MouseUp Event occurred.

This distinction between Click and MouseDown/Up is similar to the one between KeyPress (which merely provides the code for a text-type single character that the user pressed) versus the KeyDown and KeyUp Events (which tell you about the status of the SHIFT, CTRL and ALT keys, plus Function keys, arrow keys and other special, non-printable keys like ESC).

Used with Check Boxes, Command Buttons, Directory List Boxes, File List Boxes, Forms, Frames, Grids, Images, Labels, List Boxes, OLE, Option Buttons, Picture Boxes, Text Boxes

Variables

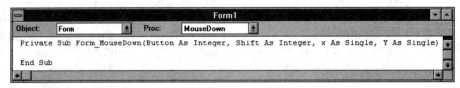

Figure M-25: The MouseDown Event has several built-in Variables that provide you with information.

Button: To detect which button has been pressed, look at the Button Variable.

1–the left button was pressed.

2–the right button was pressed.

4–the middle button was pressed.

```
Sub Form_MouseDown (Button As Integer, Shift As Integer, X As Single, →
    Y As Single)

Select Case Button
  Case 1
    Print "Left Button Just Pressed"
  Case 2
    Print "Right Button Just Pressed"
  Case 4
    Print "Middle Button Just Pressed"
End Select
End Sub
```

SHIFT, CTRL, ALT: The Shift Variable provides codes that can tell you all possible combinations of the SHIFT, CTRL and ALT keypresses when they are being held down at the same time that the user presses a mouse button:

No key pressed	0
SHIFT	1
SHIFT + CTRL	3
SHIFT + ALT	5
ALT	4
ALT + CTRL	6
CTRL	2
SHIFT + CTRL + ALT	7

X,Y: These coordinates provide the current location within the Control or Form, the horizontal and vertical positions where the MouseDown or MouseUp Event was triggered.

Uses
- Drag icons in Picture Boxes, or drag other Controls around a window.
- Allow your user to modify a picture that is the background of one of your Forms.
- Create a drawing program.
- Respond to the mouse in a more sensitive and varied way than is possible via the Click or DblClick Event.

Cautions
- The X and Y information is provided as twips (1,440 per inch) unless you have adjusted the ScaleMode or one of the other Scale Properties of the Form or Control involved. (See "ScaleMode.")
- Once the mouse button is pressed, VB assumes that any MouseMoves, the MouseDown and any associated SHIFT, CTRL or ALT keypresses, and the final MouseUp Event all take place within the Form or Control in which the MouseDown Event took place. That is, if you press the mouse while its pointer is over the Form, the Form's mouse-related Events all register mouse activity until the mouse button is released.

  If, for instance, you click on a Picture Box, hold the button down and drag the mouse *outside the Picture Box onto the Form,* the Picture Box nevertheless continues to report the X,Y coordinates. If you release the mouse on top of the Form, the *Picture Box's* MouseUp Event will be the one triggered, not the Form's.

  It is important to remember this encapsulation by the object first getting the MouseDown Event trigger. This encapsulation doesn't restrict your programming, but it can cause confusion if you forget about it. To detect when the mouse has moved beyond the borders of the Picture Box and onto the Form, check the coordinates inside the MouseMove Event of the Picture Box. To left or above the Picture Box border, *the X or Y coordinate will become negative.* A negative coordinate is clearly impossible; normally, (0,0) is the upper left point within any Control's coordinates. To test for moves beyond the right or bottom borders, check the X or Y value against the Width or Height Properties of the Picture Box. (Note that if you have adjusted some of the Scale Properties of the Control, you'll have to adjust these rules as well. See "ScaleMode.")

- If the user presses more than one mouse button (without releasing the first button pressed), the rules outlined in the second "Caution" in this section apply until *all buttons are released.*

- For MouseDown and MouseUp, the Button Variable provides information about only one of the buttons on the mouse—whichever button initially triggered the Event. The *MouseMove* Event provides information on the state of *all* the buttons. In other words, MouseMove tells you if the left, right and middle buttons are being depressed and in what combination.

Example We'll illustrate the second item in Cautions and also show how MouseUp and MouseDown work.

First, create a New Project. Put four Picture Boxes on the Form and set Picture1's Picture Property in the Properties Window so that you load in a charming picture like this languid 16th-century Correggio:

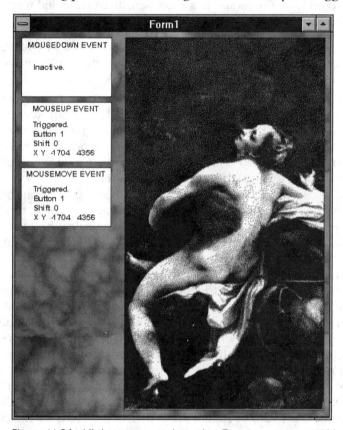

Figure M-26: All three mouse-detecting Events are reported by this program.

Notice here that the X position reported by both the MouseUp and MouseMove Events is *negative* 1704. X positions do not normally become negative because the leftmost coordinate of an object is 0.

This negative result demonstrates that our mouse cursor has moved beyond the Correggio woman Picture Box and over into the space of the Form. Therefore, because it's the Picture Box's Mouse Events that we are reporting here, the X position has gone below zero.

(Unfortunately, we cannot show you the cursor, although it's right below the MouseMove –1704. Most current screen capture programs cannot capture a mouse cursor.)

Here's the program. The commands we are giving to the MouseDown, MouseUp and MouseMove Events of Picture1 are virtually identical. So, once you've typed in one of them, select it using the SHIFT+Down arrow keys and then copy it with the CTRL+INSERT combination. Stuff it into another of the three Events with SHIFT+INSERT. Then take advantage of VB's Replace feature in the Edit Menu.

Each Mouse Event that happens within Picture1 is displayed in Picture-Boxes 2–4. Here's what happens in Picture1.MouseDown:

```
Sub Picture1_MouseDown (button As Integer, shift As Integer, x As →
    Single, y As Single)

Picture2.Cls
Picture2.Print "MOUSEDOWN EVENT"
Picture2.Print
Picture2.Print "MouseDown"
Picture2.Print "Button"; button
Picture2.Print "Shift"; shift
Picture2.Print "X Y"; Str$(x); " "; Str$(y)
Picture3.Cls
Picture3.Print "MOUSEUP EVENT"
Picture3.Print
Picture3.Print "Inactive."
End Sub
```

We clear out what has been previously printed with Cls, show the title of this Picture Box (MOUSEDOWN EVENT), add a space between the lines and then notify the user that a MouseDown Event did, in fact, just occur. Then we show the status of the three Variables in the MouseDown Event. Finally, we clear out anything printed in Picture3, the MouseUp Event report. Because MouseDown and MouseUp are mutually exclusive, we simply announce that MouseUp is "Inactive" because MouseDown has happened.

The MouseUp Event is similar:

```
Sub Picture1_MouseUp (button As Integer, shift As Integer, x As Single, y →
    As Single)

Picture3.Cls
Picture3.Print "MOUSEUP EVENT"
Picture3.Print
Picture3.Print "Triggered."
Picture3.Print "Button"; button
Picture3.Print "Shift"; shift
Picture3.Print "X Y"; Str$(x); " "; Str$(y)
Picture2.Cls
Picture2.Print "MOUSEDOWN EVENT"
Picture2.Print
Picture2.Print "Inactive."
End Sub
```

The MouseMove Event also resembles the other two but doesn't clear out their report boxes because MouseMove can happen during either Mouse-Down or MouseUp. MouseMove is continuously being triggered, even if you start another program and use it for a while. If you move the mouse over the Picture Box, it will trigger MouseMove:

```
Sub Picture1_MouseMove (button As Integer, shift As Integer, x As →
    Single, y As Single)

Picture4.Cls
Picture4.Print "MOUSEMOVE EVENT"
Picture4.Print
Picture4.Print "Triggered."
Picture4.Print "Button"; button
Picture4.Print "Shift"; shift
Picture4.Print "X Y"; Str$(x); " "; Str$(y)

End Sub
```

See also   Click; DblClick; MouseMove

MOUSEMOVE   EVENT

Description   Whenever the user moves the mouse, MouseMove reports that fact—along with whether the mouse buttons are being pressed; whether any of the CTRL, ALT or SHIFT keys are being pressed; and the current position on the Control or Form of the mouse cursor (usually shaped like an arrow).

Used with   Check Boxes, Command Buttons, Directory List Boxes, File List Boxes, Forms, Frames, Grids, Images, Labels, List Boxes, Option Buttons, OLE, Picture Boxes and Text Boxes

Variables   The four Variables provided by MouseMove are available to your program from within the MouseMove Event:

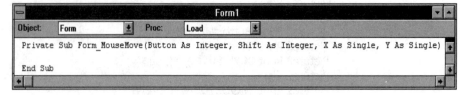

Figure M-27: The MouseMove has four built-in Variables.

Button: To detect which button has been pressed, look at the Button Variable for one of these values:

Left button is pressed	1
Left + right	3
Left + middle	5
Middle	4
Middle + Right	6
Right	2
Left + Right + Middle	7

```
Sub Form_MouseMove (Button As Integer, Shift As Integer, X As Single, Y →
  As Single)

Select Case Button
  Case 7
    Print "All Buttons Depressed on Mouse"
  Case 4
    Print "Only the Middle Button Depressed"
End Select

End Sub
```

SHIFT, CTRL, ALT: The Shift Variable provides codes that can tell you all possible combinations of the SHIFT, CTRL and ALT keypresses when they are being held down at the same time that the user presses a mouse key:

No key pressed	0
SHIFT	1
SHIFT + CTRL	3
SHIFT + ALT	5
ALT	4
ALT + CTRL	6
CTRL	2
SHIFT + CTRL + ALT	7

X,Y: These coordinates provide the current location within the Control or Form, the horizontal and vertical positions where the MouseMove Event was triggered. These Variables will change rapidly as the user moves the mouse around. Even a small mouse movement triggers the MouseMove Event repeatedly and often. Depending on how quickly the user moves the mouse, moving across one inch of space could generate as many as 100 MouseMove Events. Perhaps the average range would be between 40 and 100 triggered MouseMove Events per inch. The Events are triggered by the clock, not by the distance moved—that's why the number of Events triggered will vary depending on the speed of the movement.

Uses
- Drag icons in Picture Boxes, or drag other Controls around a window.
- Allow your user to modify a picture that is the background of one of your Forms.
- Create a drawing program.
- Respond to the mouse in a more sensitive and varied way than is possible via the Click or DblClick Event.
- Provide a continuously updated display of the X,Y coordinates of the mouse's location.

Cautions
- The X and Y information is provided in twips (1,440 per inch) unless you have adjusted the ScaleMode or one of the other Scale Properties of the Form or Control involved. (See "ScaleMode.")

- Once the user presses the mouse button, VB assumes that any Mouse-Moves, the MouseDown Event and any associated SHIFT, CTRL or ALT keypresses, and the final MouseUp Event all take place within the Form or Control in which the MouseDown Event took place. That is, if you press the mouse while its pointer is over the Form, the Form's mouse-related Events all register mouse activity until the mouse button is released.

  If, for instance, you click on a Picture Box, hold the button down and drag the mouse *outside the Picture Box onto the Form,* the Picture Box, nevertheless, continues to report the X,Y coordinates. If you release the mouse on top of the Form, the *Picture Box's* MouseUp Event will be the one triggered, not the Form's. (For more information, see "Cautions" under "MouseDown.")

- If the user presses more than one mouse button (without releasing the first button pressed), the rules outlined just above apply until *all buttons are released.*

- For MouseMove, the state of all the buttons is available from the Button Variable via a code. In other words, MouseMove tells you if the left, right and middle buttons are being depressed and in what combination. (See "Variables" above.)

  For MouseDown and MouseUp, the Button Variable reports only one button–the one that initially triggered the Event.

Example
For this example, we'll create a painting program, or at least the start of one. We use MouseDown, MouseUp and MouseMove in combination to allow the user to draw a new picture or to touch up an existing one.

Figure M-28: Use the mouse-detecting Events as the basis for a drawing program.

First, adjust a Form's Picture Property from the Properties Window to load in some image. Then put three Control Buttons, a Text Box and a List Box on the Form. The Command Buttons will provide the user with the ability to adjust the width; change the mode—black, erase (white); copy the current setting of the pen and invert; and remove the changes with Undo.

The Width Command Button will either make the Width Text Box visible or register what the user typed in as the new width:

```
Sub Command3_Click ()
    If WidthText.visible = 0 Then
        WidthText.visible = -1
    Else
        WidthText_KeyPress = 13
    End If
End Sub
```

The associated Text Box allows the user to specify the DrawWidth Property:

```
Sub WidthText_KeyPress (keyascii As Integer)
    If keyascii = 13 Then
        keyascii = 0
        Form1.drawwidth = Val(WidthText.text)
        WidthText.visible = 0
    End If
End Sub
```

M . . . **735**

If the user presses the ENTER key, we change the keyascii Variable to 0 (to prevent the speaker from clicking) and set the DrawWidth to the value of the text the user entered into the Text Box. Val changes text digits into a pure number that can be used for computation by the computer. Then we make the Text Box disappear.

The Mode Button simply makes its associated List Box visible:

```
Sub Command4_Click ()
    modebox.visible = True
End Sub
```

This List Box provides the user with four choices of DrawModes to select by clicking:

```
Sub Modebox_Click ()

Select Case modebox.listindex
    Case 0
        drawmode = 1
    Case 1
        drawmode = 6
    Case 2
        drawmode = 13
    Case 3
        drawmode = 16
End Select

modebox.visible = False
End Sub
```

The DrawMode of the Form is set and then this List Box is made invisible.

The Undo button simply performs a Cls on the Form, which has the effect of leaving the original image but removing anything the user drew on the image:

```
Sub Command2_Click ()
    Cls
End Sub
```

Now for the mouse activity, set up a Variable that all the Form's Events can use in common in the General Declarations section of the Form:

```
Dim DoIt As Integer
```

In the Form_Load Event, we'll insert the various options into the Draw-Mode List Box:

```
Sub Form_Load ()

modebox.AddItem "1. Black"
modebox.AddItem "2. Invert"
modebox.AddItem "3. Copy"
modebox.AddItem "4. White"
modebox.AddItem "5. No Change"

End Sub
```

The Signal to Draw: In the Form's MouseDown Event, we turn the DoIt Variable on—the signal to MouseMove that it should draw. When the button isn't being held down, movements of the mouse will not draw anything on the picture:

```
Sub Form_MouseDown (Button As Integer, Shift As Integer, X As Single, →
  Y As Single)
    DoIt = −1
End Sub
```

The MouseUp Event turns *off* the possibility of drawing:

```
Sub Form_MouseUp (Button As Integer, Shift As Integer, X As Single, →
  Y As Single)
    DoIt = 0
End Sub
```

The MouseMove Event draws on the Form (with the PSet Method) while the mouse button is being depressed:

```
Sub Form_MouseMove (Button As Integer, Shift As Integer, X As Single, →
  Y As Single)

If DoIt =−1 Then
    PSet (X, Y)
End If

End Sub
```

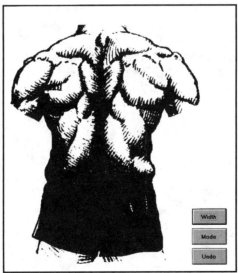

Figure M-29: Leonardo would be displeased with our touch-up.

Saving the Picture: You can save the changes that you made by creating a Command Button and giving it a Name "Save":

```
Sub Save_Click ()
    SavePicture Form1.Image, "c:\mypict.bmp"
End Sub
```

In the current version of VB, *the Form's AutoRedraw Property must be on (True) while you are drawing.* Unless you have a very fast computer, drawing will be quite slow. Every change that you make to the picture–no matter how finite–must then be saved to memory. Saving to memory is relatively fast, but picture files are relatively large. These two speed factors cancel each other out and the drawing gets sluggish; what you intended to be a smooth line can be a series of dots, the spaces between the dots representing the times the computer saved your work.

Also, you would have to change the Cls method for undoing changes with AutoRedraw on. (You could periodically copy the Form1.Picture to an invisible Form2 or to the Clipboard. See "SetData.") The only purpose of copying to an invisible Form would be to hold a backup copy of the altered graphics that could be copied back onto Form1 as required.

See also   Click; DblClick; MouseDown; MouseUp

MOUSEPOINTER

PROPERTY

Description   The MousePointer Property can change the mouse pointer (sometimes called the mouse *cursor*) to a different shape. Figure M-30 shows the available shapes:

Figure M-30: The 12 available mouse pointer shapes

Used with Everything except Timers, Shapes, Lines, OLE, Grids and Menus. Also used with the "Screen Object" (see "Screen"), which means that you can define the mouse pointer shape that will appear only if the mouse moves *outside* your VB program's windows. Any mouse movement, however, outside your VB windows will return the pointer to the default arrow shape. (See the first item in "Cautions" below.)

Variables **Variable type:** Integer (enumerated)

You can set the MousePointer Property from the Properties Window:

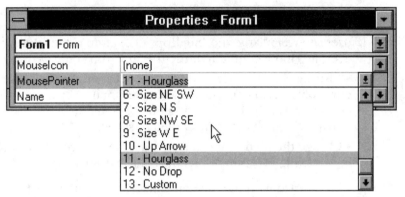

Figure M-31: Select a pointer while designing your program if you want.

OR (to change the pointer directly within your running program):

    Label1.MousePointer = 3

OR (to find out the current pointer assigned to a Control while the program is running): X = Picture1.MousePointer

Here are the Variables you can assign to the pointer:

0   Each Control's MousePointer Property determines the shape of the mouse cursor when it is located over that Control.

1   The default arrow—forced to appear everywhere—ignores Controls' individual MousePointer settings.

2   Cross-hair.

3   I-Beam.

4   Rectangle-within-rectangle. Used to represent an "icon".

5   Resize in all directions. Arrow pointing in four directions. Preserves aspect ratio of an object being stretched or shrunk.

6   Resize arrows NE–SW. Stretch object along an upper right, lower left axis.

7   Resize arrows NS. Stretch an object along a top–bottom axis, vertical stretch.

8   Resize arrows NW–SE. Stretch object along an upper left, lower right axis.

9   Resize arrows WE. Stretch object along a left–right axis, horizontal stretch.

10   Dark up arrow. Sometimes used as a pointer to select objects.

11   Hourglass. (The computer is busy. You must wait.)

12   The user cannot drop the dragged item into the current zone on-screen.

Uses   Some conventions have arisen in Windows about the typical meaning of the various pointer symbols.

• Visually clue the user about the current status of the program. The hourglass signifies that the program is busy and will return control to the user soon. Similarly, the "no-drop" (12) often means the same thing. However, it is more common to use the "no-drop" only during a drag operation.

• Visually clue the user about features currently available or capabilities currently available to the user. The I-Beam usually means insert text; the cross-hair usually means draw a line or, sometimes, enclose and thereby select a visual object to be copied or saved.

• Change the pointer whenever you want to zero in on an X,Y position, as in a drawing program or picking a color from a part of a drawing.

Cautions   • When used with the "Screen Object" (see "Screen"), the shape of the MousePointer Property of the screen will be unchanged everywhere on the screen. The pointer will not change, regardless of the MousePointer settings for Forms or Controls. However, outside your program's windows on the general Windows screen, the mouse pointer will revert to the default arrow if the user moves the mouse.

• Set Screen.MousePointer = 0 to activate the local pointer shapes as defined by each Form's and Control's MousePointer Properties.

Example   Create a New Project and put a Timer on the Form. Put the following into the Timer Event. The result will be that all 13 MousePointer Properties will be displayed in turn, changing every two seconds:

```
Sub Timer1_Timer ()

Timer1.Interval = 2000
Static x As Integer
Cls
Print "Mousepointer Property is now "; x
Form1.MousePointer = x
x = x + 1
If x = 13 Then x = 0
End Sub
```

Note that a Timer's Interval Property is normally set in the Properties Window while you are designing your program or set in the Form_Load Event as one of the first things that happens when the program runs. There is no advantage to resetting the Interval each time the Timer is activated, but it does no harm either. We simply do it here for illustration purposes—that way we don't have to show a separate Form_Load Event.

Static is a useful command. Normally, the value of X would be reset to 0 every time the program left this Event (End Sub). Local Variables like X are active only while the Event within which they reside is active. Static, however, defines this Variable X as *persistent*—it will not reset to zero, but, rather, it will retain its value. That's how we can use it as a counter and still go in and out of the Timer Event. X, however, cannot be "read" (accessed to see what it holds) or "written to" (changed in value) by any command outside of the Timer Event. X is still "local in scope" to the Timer Event. Static merely makes X persistent.

 OVE METHOD

Description   Move relocates or resizes a Form or Control smoothly. You can relocate objects by merely changing their Left and Top Properties, but that causes abrupt, uneven *diagonal* movements. (Horizontal and vertical movements are smooth using either technique.)

Likewise, you could stretch or shrink an object by changing its Width and Height Properties. But if you want to resize the object *in both directions at once,* then Move produces smoother effects.

Move is usually placed within a For...Next Loop to create a series of blended, small moves rather than a single, large move. Move is normally used for special animation effects, and without delaying it in a Loop, the effect is lost on faster computers. These two examples would produce the same effect: the Label would seem to leap from its original location to the new location, rather than slide down to it. We'll put the Label at the top left and then move it:

```
Label1.Left = 0
Label1.Top = 0
Label1.Move 300,300
```

Or try replacing the preceding Move command with the following:

```
Label1.Top = 300
Label1.Left = 300
```

However, the following will produce a smooth animation effect, as if the Label were gliding down to its new position:

```
lx = label1.left      '(get its current x position)
ly = label1.top       '(get its current y position)
```

```
For I = 0 to 300 Step 5
    Label.Move lx + i, ly + i
Next I
```

Used with Forms and all Controls except Timers and Menus

Variables Picture1.Move Left, Top, Width, Height

Only Left is required (to move the Picture horizontally).
To add any of the other specifications, you must always include any
Variables to its left:

Right: Picture1.Move Left, Top, Width

Wrong (because it's missing the Top specification):
Picture1.Move Left, Width

OR (to move the Picture up or down but not sideways from its current
location): Picture1.Move 0, 400

The movement caused by the Move command *is absolute, not relative.*
Move describes a particular location on the Form to which the Control will
move. It does not describe how far to move from the current position of
the Control. This movement is like the difference between telling somebody to run to the police station (absolute) or telling him or her to run
three blocks left (relative to their current location).

In other words: Move to the X position horizontally within the Form and
the Y position vertically within the Form (Command1.Move X,Y). We are
not saying to move X distance from your current position horizontally and
Y distance vertically.

Another way of understanding this distinction is to watch how Move is
used, as it usually is, within a For...Next Loop:

```
For I = 0 to 3000
    Command1.Move I,I
Next I
```

This example would move the Command Button from the upper left
corner of the Form, down and across 3,000 twips. If the Command Button
is *not* located in the upper left corner, it will be moved there with the first
Move command. A *relative* system would start the moving from the current
location of the button.

Moving Forms Versus Controls: Remember that when moving a Form, the
movement is within the Screen coordinates of the video monitor. When
moving a Control, the movement is within the coordinates of the host Form:

Picture1.Move 300,500 (moves the picture from its current position to
coordinates 300,500 within the Form)

Picture1.Move 0,0,Picture1.Width — Picture1.Width /2 (makes the Picture
half as wide)

Picture1.Move 300, 500, 100, 100 (both moves the Picture to position 300, 500 within the Form, and resizes it to 100 twips wide and tall)

Uses
- Create animated effects. For instance, you can use Move with the Drag commands to allow an icon to travel smoothly across a Form. However, using a Timer is preferable so the speed of the particular computer won't have an effect on the speed of the animation.

- Shrink or enlarge a Control in response to current conditions in the program. One interesting effect would be to make an icon shrink when it cannot be clicked on because it is inappropriate. Before a user has done any drawing in your paint program, leave icons (such as an image that says "SAVE") tiny. Then, as soon as the user draws something, enlarge SAVE to indicate that it can be used.

To try out this example, first create a picture in PaintBrush or some other drawing program and add the word "SAVE" to it. Save the picture as a .BMP file, not an .ICO, which has a limited size. Then, to enlarge the picture, put it into a Picture Box and make the Box as small as you wish it to appear initially. Then enter the following:

```
Sub Form_Click ()

x = picture1.left
y = picture1.top
h = picture1.height
w = picture1.width

For i = 1 To 500
    picture1.Move x, y, w + i, h + i
Next i

End Sub
```

Notice that we didn't change X and Y, the *position*. We only change Height and Width, the *size*.

This method of enlarging or shrinking a graphic doesn't *really* blow it up or reduce it. If you use Move to make a graphic larger, you are merely making the border larger and, in effect, *revealing* hidden portions of a larger graphic. To truly enlarge or shrink a graphic—like a photograph being blown up or reduced—see the description and example of how to use the API StretchBlt Function under "Declare."

- Alternatively, set up a group of icons representing different vacation destinations and modes of travel. Put a picture of a bulletin board on the window. Then, when the user clicks on the New York City icon, it seems to move over and attach itself to the board (and simultaneously appears as the words "NEW YORK CITY" in a List Box or Label, for example). Next, the user could click on a Fly icon, and it would slide onto the bulletin board and appear as text. Clicking on a Command Button labeled Calculate would open up a new window showing the options and costs for a plane trip to NYC.

Cautions   • Only the Left Variable is required, but if you want to specify more, you must supply preceding Variables. (In other words, to specify Width, you must supply Left and Top as well.)

> Picture1.Move 300,500, 100,100 (using both moves the Picture to position 300,500 within the Form, and resizes it to 100 twips wide and tall)

These are all the possible Variables for Move:

> Picture1.Move Left, Top, Width, Height

If you don't want to change the Height, you can leave it off because it's to the right of the Variables you do want to specify:

Right: Picture1.Move Left, Top, Width

Wrong: Picture1.Move Left, Width

Here we left out Top, so VB would think that Width is what we are specifying for Top.

• All moves inside a frame or moves of a Form within the "Screen Object" (see "Screen") are described in twips. There are 1,440 twips per inch (see "ScaleMode").

All other moves are also calculated in twips, unless you have changed the scale (see "ScaleMode").

Example   This example will illustrate the difference between animation by changing Top and Left Properties and the smoother animation via the Move Method.

First, create a New Project and put two Picture Boxes on it. Put the same icon in each Picture Box by using its Picture Property. We're using a small, polished ruby.

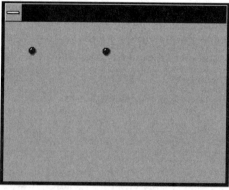

Figure M-32: Two ruby-like icons, ready for animation.

Here's how the ruby and its highlight and shadow were created in an icon drawing program:

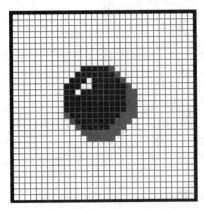

Figure M-33: The design of the ruby as viewed in an icon-drawing program.

Here are the measurements for the Form:

```
Sub Form_Load ()
      width = 4400
      height = 3400
End Sub
```

And following is how one ruby is sent down via Move and the other is animated via its Left and Top Properties:

```
Sub Form_Click ()

p1x = picture1.left 'get the current coordinates of these two Picture Boxes
p2x = picture2.left
p1y = picture1.top
p2y = picture2.top

For i = 1 To 2000 Step 50   'Animate the first one by changing its Left →
   and Top Properties
      picture2.left = p2x + i
      picture2.top = p2y + i
Next i

For i = 1 To 2000 Step 50   'Animate Picture1 with Movepicture1.Move
      p1x + i, p1y + i
Next i

End Sub
```

You'll see at once why Move is better for diagonal animated motion. The first ruby seems to be bouncing down a staircase; the second seems to be rolling down an incline.

The smaller you make the Step, the less difference there will be in the smoothness of the animation. But using smaller Steps slows up the movement.

To see how Move loses its value when you don't use it inside a For...Next Loop, put a single quotation mark symbol (') in front of the Loop and try running the program again. (The single quotation mark tells VB to ignore every command following it on a line in your program.) Then give an absolute position for the Move (i + 2000):

```
For i = 1 To 2000 Step 50   'Animate Picture1 with Movepicture1.Move
    p1x + 2000, p1y + 2000
Next i
```

Move has no value unless you slow it up by using a For...Next Loop. It's indistinguishable from changing the Top and Left Properties.

Now let's see what happens when we use Move to grow or shrink a picture. This second example creates a dramatic effect: the picture seems to unfold.

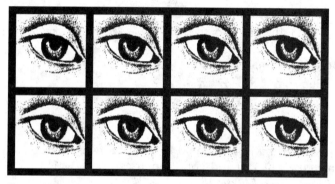

Figure M-34: The Move command can also be used to reveal or conceal graphics.

First, create a New Project from the VB File Menu. Set the Form's Backcolor to black and put a Picture Box on the Form. Set the Picture Box's Index Property to 0 and load a .BMP graphic into the Picture Box using its Picture Property. Then select a BMP that is about 2 inches square. Now resize the Picture Box; adjust it with the mouse until it is only about ¼ of an inch square and located about ¼ inch from the top and left of the Form.

Because we set the Picture Box's Index property to 0, we can use the Load Method to bring in seven clones of the original Picture Box, using a *Control Array* (which see).

Now set the Picture Box's BorderStyle Property to 0 (no border), and type the following into the Form_Load Event:

```
Sub Form_Load ()

For i = 1 To 3
    Load picture1(i)
    picture1(i).left = picture1(i − 1).left + 2500
Next i
```

```
        For i = 4 To 7
            Load picture1(i)
            picture1(i).top = picture1(0).top + 2500
            picture1(i).left = picture1(i — 4).left
        Next i
        End Sub
```

In the first For...Next Loop, we create three clone pictures. When a Control Array is activated as a program runs, the baby clones all inherit the Properties of the original Control (except for TabIndex, Index and Visible). These babies will be the same size and contain the same graphic as the original Picture Box.

The only thing we want to be different about the babies is their Left Property (so they will line up in a row instead of piling up on top of the original). To make them line up, we make each one move to the right by 2,500 twips (measuring from the previous picture by i –1). The *i* counter is acting as an index as each baby is born. As *i* goes up from 1 to 3, Picture1(1), Picture1(2) and Picture1(3) are born, simply by using the Load command.

Lining Up the Second Row of Babies: Similarly, we create Picture1(4) through Picture1(7), and this time we want them to line up in a second row beneath the upper four pictures. We set their Top Properties to move them down the screen by 2,500 twips. Then we pick their Left Properties from the pictures on the upper row, by referring to the index number (i –4). If *i* is 4, we'll copy the Left Property of Picture1(0); if *i* is 5, we use Picture1(1).Left, and so on.

Now here's where the action starts. In the Form_Click Event, type the following:

```
        Sub Form_Click ()

        cx = picture1(0).width
        cy = picture1(0).height

        For i = 0 To 7
            picture1(i).visible = —1
        Next i

        For i = 400 To 2000 Step 400
            For j = 0 To 7
                    picture1(j).Move picture1(j).left, picture1(j).top, cx + i, cy + i

        Next j, i
        End Sub
```

First, we get the current Width and Height measurements of each picture. Then we make them all visible, and we grow them by using Move.

Next, we set up two For...Next Loops, one nested within the other. The outer Loop uses the counter Variable *i*, and it keeps feeding a larger Width and Height measurement to the Move command. Each time the outer Loop acts, it grows the pictures by 400 twips. We grow the pictures from their original size to a final size of 2,000 twips (plus the original size) by using CX + i and CY + i. Step 400 means that we add 400, 800, 1,200, 1,600 and 2,000 in turn as the outer Loop cycles.

Because we don't want Move to cause these pictures to change position on the Form, we give the Move command their original position each time—Picture1(j).Left and Picture1(j).Top.

The *inner Loop*, governed by the counter j, merely cycles through all eight pictures, growing them in turn. The action here is as follows:

```
make i = 400
do the commands inside the j loop 8 times
now i = 800
do the commands inside the j loop 8 times
now make i = 1200
do the commands inside the j loop 8 times
```

and so on until *i* reaches its final value of 2,000, and we stop Looping and End Sub.

See also   Arrays; Control Array; For...Next; Height; Left; Objects; ScaleMode; Top; Width

 SG BOX   FUNCTION AND STATEMENT

Description   A MsgBox appears onscreen and waits until the user clicks on it (or presses the ESC key).

A MsgBox won't go away, and the user cannot access any other windows in your program until the MsgBox is clicked. (MsgBoxes and InputBoxes are *modal*, which means that they freeze the action until the user acknowledges them.)

As a Statement: You can use a MsgBox in its *Statement* mode (you can even omit the parentheses) if you merely want to tell the user something and don't care about the user's reaction:

MsgBox ("Please enter your name before requesting budget information.")

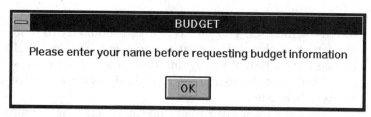

Figure M-35: A Message Box that merely informs the user.

As a Function: Functions always return some information to your program, so they are always in the form of an "equation":

X = MsgBox ("Are you sure you want to quit the program?"), 4

Use the "Function" style of MsgBox when you want information back from the user. Here we added the ,4 to the MsgBox command, causing it to display Yes and No Buttons for the user to click. Without ,4 the MsgBox would have displayed the single OK Button, which is the default.

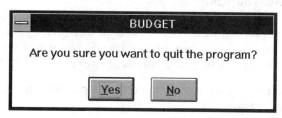

Figure M-36: This style of Message Box expects the user to supply a yes or no answer.

If the user clicks on the Yes Button, X will contain 6, and clicking on the No Button returns 7 to X. Therefore, your program can use X to decide what to do based on the user's response:

If X = 6 Then End

Used with   Use MsgBoxes in places in your program *where you want to force the user to respond to the program.*

Whenever possible, you should avoid using a MsgBox or the InputBox$ because they violate the spirit of user-control freedom that Windows brings to PC computing. Perhaps the only reasonable use for a MsgBox is when your program is trying to access files. (See "Cautions.")

Windows programs—unlike the rigidly designed programs of years past—provide the user with a set of objects and tools that he or she can manipulate. The user expects to be able to manipulate these objects to the extent, and at the time, that he or she chooses.

Objects can be moved around the screen, resized, even hidden or ignored—by the user. This means that you should try to write your programs in such a way that the user can participate in the design of the program, can customize how the program looks and how it behaves. You provide a set of tools, and the user arranges and selects the tools that are appropriate to his or her goals.

MsgBox and InputBox$ freeze up the program and demand a response before they release the program and the user from captivity. In certain emergency situations you may need to resort to MsgBox or InputBox$—if the user is about to erase a disk file that has not been backed up, for instance. But you should probably check carefully to make sure there isn't a preferable alternative to freezing the program. Perhaps you could have your program automatically create that backup file and provide an Undo Button to retrieve it for the user.

Most users, most of the time, know what they are doing. And most users quickly grow tired of a program that carps, that repeatedly asks some variation of "Are you SURE?"

Visual Basic's rich set of Controls provides a great variety of ways for your program to interact with the user—to accept or provide information. When you are tempted to use MsgBox or InputBox$, you might want to see if there is a better approach. There almost always is.

Variables **Used as a Statement:** You *don't* need to use parentheses with the *Statement* version of MsgBox.

```
Msg$ = "Attention! Program is sorting data."
MsgBox Msg$
```

However, you *do* need parentheses if you are including the text in the *MsgBox command proper* (not using a text Variable):

```
MsgBox ("Attention! Program is sorting data.")
```

Used as a Function: A Function-style MsgBox *always* requires parentheses around the text, whether it's literal text within quotation marks or a text Variable. That—and the fact that a Function gives back a Variable to tell your program how the user responded—are the only two differences between the Function and Statement approaches to MsgBoxes.

```
X = MsgBox ("Attention! Program is sorting data.")
```

Additional Variables You Can Provide: The fully armed MsgBox looks like the following:

```
X = MsgBox ("Please confirm that you intend to delete this item from the
list.", 4, "ALERT!" Helpfile, Context)
```

The 4 puts a set of Yes and No Buttons on the MsgBox, and the "ALERT!" is put into the Title Bar of the Box:

Figure M-37: The fully armed MsgBox.

Your choices for which Buttons should be displayed are as follows:

0	OK (the default)		
1	OK	Cancel	
2	Abort	Retry	Ignore
3	Yes	No	Cancel
4	Yes	No	
5	Retry	Cancel	

You also can include icons built into MsgBox that symbolize the meaning of the message. To include these, you *add* the icon's number to the Button's number:

16   Critical Message (a red stop sign)

Figure M-38: A serious warning.

32   Warning, plus question mark (a question mark inside a green circle)

Figure M-39: A quizzical warning message.

48   Warning alone (an exclamation point enclosed within a yellow circle)

Figure M-40: Alert.

64   Information (a lowercase *i* inside a small, blue circle)

Figure M-41: Information only.

To display OK and Cancel Buttons plus a Warning icon, add 1 to 48:

MsgBox ("Are you sure?"),49

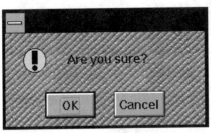

Figure M-42: You can create any combination of symbols and Command Buttons.

Finally, you have three possible ways to *focus* the Buttons—focus means which Button will respond if the user presses the ESC or ENTER key (rather than clicking on a particular Button):

   0   First Button (the default)

256   Second Button

512   Third Button

The Meaning of the Variable Showing Which Button the User Clicked: X = MsgBox ("Please Answer",2). When the user clicks on a Button, X holds one of the following values and thereby tells your program how to respond to the user's selection:

1 OK

2 Cancel

3 Abort

4 Retry

5 Ignore

6 Yes

7 No

Note that if the MsgBox contains a Cancel Button, pressing the ESC key *is the same* as clicking on the Cancel Button: X will contain a 2.

If you want a Help button to appear on your MsgBox, add a text ("string") Variable or expression that names the help file. You must also include a Context, as described below. Context This is a numeric variable or expression defining the "Help context number." This displays the appropriate topic within the larger Help file.

Uses
• When the user is about to do something dangerous, something that could irretrievably destroy data or a disk file, for instance.

• When the program is doing something that could generate a functional error, such as attempting disk access. If you are using Err and On Error Resume Next, that part of your program might benefit from MsgBox. If the door is open on drive A: and the user is trying to read that disk, your program cannot proceed until the door is closed. This situation generates an error message in the program, and you may well want to respond by putting a MsgBox in front of the user:

```
On Error Resume Next

Open "A:\TEST" For Input As #1
Close
If Err Then MsgBox (Error$(Err))
```

• MsgBoxes are sometimes used when the program has to pause for some length of time to, for example, search through a large amount of information. Users become uneasy if the program seems to be doing nothing—even for a few seconds. They may even look to see if the disk is active, fearing that something is terribly wrong and may be trashing their files. To assuage this concern, when a program does something that will take time, a Msg-Box is displayed, remarking that the user should be patient.

Nevertheless, a MsgBox is not the best or even the second best choice in this situation. Perhaps the nicest way to keep the user calm is to show the progress of the task with a gauge: by showing percentages, such as 10% and

20%, you can update the user as the program finishes its task. (See "Refresh" for a method that creates attractive gauges in VB.) Your second best choice might be simply to display a window that says "Searching," for example, and then have your program remove that window when the job is done.

Cautions
• If you don't include the title Variable for a MsgBox, then the name of your project (the name of the .MAK file in the Project Window) will be inserted into the Title Bar of the MsgBox.

• If you don't *want* anything in the Title Bar, provide an empty piece of text, two quotation marks around nothing, which is sometimes called a *null string*:

```
MsgBox ("Careful!"),0," "
```

• You can put as many as 1,024 characters into a MsgBox, and the lines will automatically be arranged correctly within the Box. If you want to end a line before it reaches the right side of the Box (for formatting purposes), add the following code for Carriage Return/Line Feed to your message:

```
cr$ = chr$(13) + chr$(10)
msg$ = "Break the line here" + cr$ + "and start the next line here."
msgbox (msg$)
```

• The user can either click on one of the Buttons on your MsgBox, press the ESC key or press the ENTER key. Any of these approaches gets rid of the MsgBox.

• Once your program has displayed a MsgBox or InputBox, the program itself cannot make it disappear. The user *must* respond. A friendlier way to inform the user is to show a Form with a message on it and then unload the Form after a few seconds–setting a Timer to, say, 3,000 for three seconds. Alternatively, the message Form could disappear whenever the user simply moved the mouse, reacting to the MouseMove Event.

• Visual Basic will decide where the MsgBox appears onscreen and how large it is. Neither you, the programmer, nor the user has any control over this.

Example
This MsgBox informs the user of a disk problem, specifically that the B: disk drive is unresponsive:

Figure M-43: The Ignore and Retry Buttons allow the user to fix a simple problem, such as a drive with no disk in it, and then make another attempt.

You would check the values returned by the MsgBox and call again upon the Sub OpenFileButton_Click, depending on which Button was clicked by the user.

```
Sub OpenFileButton_Click ()

On Error Resume Next

Open "B:\MYFILE" For Input As #1
Close #1
    If Err Then MsgBox (Error$(Err)), 2, "Disk Access Error"
End Sub
```

See also   Error$; InputBox$

 ULTILINE

PROPERTY

Description   The MultiLine Property determines whether a Text Box can accept or display more than a single line of text. You must explicitly set MultiLine to True to allow the user to type in (or permit your program to display) multiple lines in the Text Box.

Oddly, MultiLine defaults to Off (False). If you want more than one line to appear in a Text Box, you must specifically change this Property. The creators of VB explain this by pointing out that MultiLine makes your program run more slowly and should be avoided unless you need more than one line. But it doesn't, in fact, run noticeably more slowly.

Used with   Text Boxes only

Variables   **Variable type:** Integer (Boolean)
You must set MultiLine in the Properties Window. You cannot change it while the program is running.

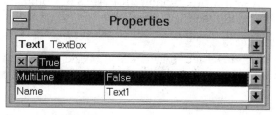

Figure M-44: There is no alternative to the Properties Window for adjusting the MultiLine Property.

OR (It *is* possible, however, to find out the status of this Property while the program is running): X = Text1.MultiLine

Uses
- Setting MultiLine to True activates the word-wrap feature that is built into every Text Box. When the user types up to the right side of the Box, the text jumps down to the next line, without breaking a word. "Word wrap," as it's called, separates the text on a space character.
- Create word processor-like applications. A Text Box has a number of built-in Windows-style word processing features—the HOME and END keys, the arrow movement keys, INSERT, DELETE, BACKSPACE, etc. You can even add Scroll Bars to it by setting the Text Box's ScrollBar Property.

Cautions
- A Text Box defaults to MultiLine *Off*. If you want multiple lines, you have to set this Property explicitly in the Properties Window.
- Without MultiLine On, the more the user types, the more text disappears off the left side of the box. The text isn't *gone*; it's still in the Text Box's Text Property, and the user can still access it by going backward through the single long line with the Left arrow, Backspace or HOME key. But it's like the sign on Times Square with thousands of light bulbs that displays the news—it scrolls horizontally but never wraps onto another line.

Even a visually deep Text Box with MultiLine = False will never wrap to the next line, even though there's plenty of space for more lines to be visible.

However, if MultiLine is set On (True) for a Box that's only a single line high, the text will only scroll horizontally because there is no room to move vertically down to the next line.

If MultiLine is set to False, any time the user presses the ENTER key, that keypress is ignored.

If a Horizontal Scroll Bar is "attached" to the Text Box via the Text Box's ScrollBar *Property*, then the text will only move horizontally—regardless of MultiLine's setting. However, if you want the ENTER key recognized by such a Text Box, you must set MultiLine = True.

Pressing ENTER normally moves you down to the next line in a Text Box with MultiLine set on. However, if the Form has a Command Button with its Default Property set to –1, the user must press CTRL+ENTER to move down a line. Because pressing CTRL+ENTER is cumbersome for the user, you should avoid setting any Default Properties of Command Buttons to –1. Fortunately, the default (for the Default Property) is 0.

A Text Box can contain up to about 32,000 (32k) characters.

Example
This example illustrates that MultiLine also breaks apart text Variables that are assigned to Text Boxes. It doesn't merely work on text that is typed in by the user:

```
Sub Text1_Change ()
    Text2.Text = Text1.Text
End Sub

Sub Form_Click ()
    Text1.Text = "Whether text wraps around to the next line depends on
how MultiLine is set."
End Sub
```

You set up two Text Boxes and change the MultiLine Property of Text1 to True to turn it on. Leave MultiLine off in Text2.

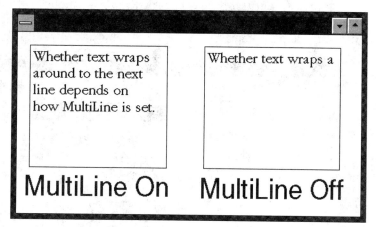

Figure M-45: Text Boxes with MultiLine on and off.

See also   ScrollBars Property; Text Box

MULTIPLE DOCUMENT INTERFACE (MDI)

TYPE: A Special Kind of Form

Description   An MDI Form is a container for other Forms. Like multiple open documents in Word for Windows or WordPerfect, the parent window (Form) encloses child windows (other Forms).

Child windows can be opened, iconized, resized, moved and otherwise treated as if they were normal windows. However, the child windows always remain within the parent window: they cannot be dragged outside the parent. Even when you turn them into icons, they do not move to the bottom of the screen but rather to the bottom of the parent window. The child windows are contained within the parent window as if the parent were the entire monitor screen.

An MDI Form has only 23 Properties (a normal Form has 54); this is because an MDI Form is intended to act as a background for child Forms and Controls. There is no need for a group of Font Properties, for instance, for an MDI Form. In addition, you cannot put any Controls on an MDI window; you put your Controls inside the child window(s). The single exception is the Picture Box Control, which can be placed directly on an MDI window to allow you to create a Toolbar. (You also put Image Controls holding .ICO or .BMP graphics on the Picture Box.) An MDI Form does, however, have a new Picture Property in VB4.

Figure M-46 illustrates how Form1 becomes an icon within the parent MDI window and how a Picture Box aligned at the top of the MDI Window can serve as a Toolbar.

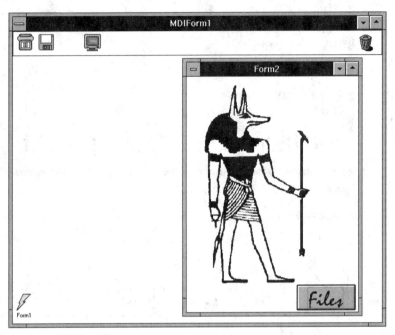

Figure M-46: MDI is an efficient way to organize multiple documents or related windows. Notice the Toolbar at the top.

Used with   Child windows, to create a kind of Windows within Windows—a desktop that mimics the larger Windows desktop

Variables

Figure M-47: You create an MDI Form by selecting that option from the Insert Menu.

An MDI Form's Properties can be set during program design in the Properties Window; or they can be set directly while the program runs: MDIForm1.Caption = "Access Opened"

One command peculiar to the MDI Form, Arrange, allows you or the user to determine whether the child windows will be of random sizes and in random positions, will be tiled (arranged so that each is visible and of the same size) or will be cascaded (overlapping each other like slices of ham on a deli plate). The Example shows how to use Arrange.

New in VB4 is an AutoShowChildren Property. It determines whether or not child windows are visible when they are loaded into an MDI Form. Loading an ordinary form (Load Form4) brings it into RAM memory, but doesn't make it visible to the user. To do that, you must use the Show command.

By contrast, child windows within an MDI Form become visible merely by being Loaded. The AutoShowChildren Property of an MDI Form is True. Therefore, if for some reason you want child windows (child Forms) to remain unseen when loaded, set the AutoShowChildren Property to False. You can do this during design time with the Properties Window. Or, to do it during runtime: MDIForm1.AutoShowChildren = False

The ActiveForm Property tells you which child Form has the focus while your program is running.

Uses

• An MDI Form is like a micro-version of Windows within your Windows screen. The MDI can include multiple child windows that behave the same way that ordinary windows act in the Windows desktop. For word processing, file management, graphic file viewing and other applications, it's often useful to contain related windows within a larger window. It's a kind of visual organization that users can immediately understand.

The "child" windows within the MDI Window "desktop" container are fully functional, and the user can adjust them in all the various ways: close, resize, iconize, maximize, tile, cascade or move within the MDI. If the collective children inside the MDI get larger than the size of the MDI window, VB attaches Scroll Bars to the MDI. But a child window cannot be dragged beyond the MDI Window; when iconized, the icon appears at the bottom left of the MDI Window.

Cautions

• There can be only one MDI Form in a VB program.
• If you want a Form to be a "child" of the MDI and contained within it, turn on that Form's MDIChild Property in the Properties Window. However, you cannot change an existing Form into a child Form while a program is running.

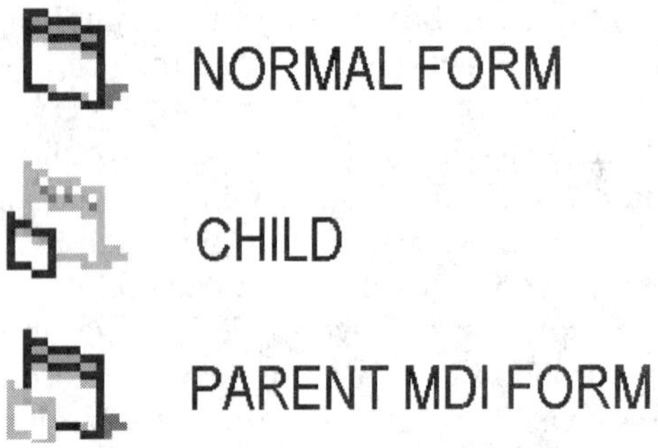

 NORMAL FORM

 CHILD

 PARENT MDI FORM

Figure M-48: In the Project Window, you can tell which Forms are Normal, MDI child or MDI parent because of their distinctly different icons.

• You can dynamically clone a Form while your program is running using the Set command (see the Example). This technique is similar to creating clone Controls in a Control Array (which see) on the fly. You can create as many clone Forms as you want.

Note that when you do create clone Forms, the clones inherit the Controls, Properties and any programming within the original Form on which the children are based. This programming inheritance could give you problems. Let's say that you have the following programming in the Click Event of the original Form:

```
Form1.Caption = Active Window
```

Then you create five clone Forms. Each of the clones will have the same line of programming in their Click Events, too. This is not what you intend because clicking on the clones will set only Form1's Caption. To avoid this, change the line as follows:

```
Caption = Active Window
```

By leaving off the Form1 identifier, each clone's Caption will now be affected when that clone is clicked. Alternatively, you could identify the intended Form by using the Me command (which see).

• While you are designing an MDI-style program, the child windows (Forms with their MDIChild Property set to "True") will not cluster within the parent MDI Form. The child Forms will seem to behave just like any normal Form. But when you run the program, all the children will gather within the parent.

• If your program needs to determine whether a particular Form is a child-type, do this: X = Form1.MDIChild

If X is 0, the answer is no; if X is –1, then yes, it is an MDIChild.

• You cannot use the Hide, Enabled = 0 or Visible = 0 technique to make a child Form inactive or make it disappear from the parent MDI Form. To get rid of child Forms, you can use UnLoad (which wipes out Variables, Property settings, things printed or drawn on the child, etc.). An alternative approach, which preserves the state of the child, is to slide it offscreen by setting its Left Property to something radical like 20,000.

• If your program explicitly Loads an MDI child Form (or implicitly loads it by referring to one of its Properties—Form3.BackColor = QBColor(4)), then the MDI parent Form is also Loaded; therefore, the child Form is always contained. By contrast, Loading the MDI parent doesn't automatically Load its child Form(s). Also, Windows will decide how large and where on the screen a Loaded child Form will appear. However, you can take control of size and position by setting the child's Top, Left, Height and Width Properties.

• The QueryUnLoad Event can be used to alert all child windows or the MDI window that any one of them is attempting to shut down (the user is closing the window, the user is shutting down Windows itself, etc.). The MDI window and each child's QueryUnLoad Events are triggered in turn before any of their UnLoad Events are triggered. This allows you to take steps from within any window if any other window is being closed. See "QueryUnLoad" for more information on this.

Example
Just as a Control Array (which see) creates clones of a particular Control and the clones inherit the original Control's Properties, you can create clone Forms (new "instances" of a Form) that inherit the Properties plus any Controls and programming that the original Form contained.

This example illustrates how to use the Set and New commands to clone Forms—a particularly useful technique with MDI. If you have a number of child Forms, it's easier to access and modify their behavior or appearance if the children are members of an Array of Forms. In this case, the Forms all share the same name, identified only by a different index number. You can then use Loops to access the entire group of Forms efficiently, as we'll see.

Figure M-49: Eight child windows tiled within an MDI window.

Start off by selecting New Project from the File Menu, and also select New MDIForm, New Form and New Module. Select New Form again and change its Name Property to Form10. This will be our File Manager, so put a File List Box and a Directory List Box on Form10.

As usual, if we need some global Variables, we must put them in a Module. So type this into Module1:

```
Global PicForm(9) As Form1
Global picount As Integer  The current total of pictures
```

The *picount* Variable will keep track of how many pictures we've loaded; it's a pretty typical Variable, just an integer. But PicForm( ) is quite a novelty in computer programming; it's a user-defined Variable of a Form1 type. Therefore, any additional "Variables" of this type that we might create will include the qualities (and any Controls) of Form1. PicForm is also an Array (which see).

Put an Image Control on Form1, stretch it to nearly fill the Form, and we'll build eight clones of Form1. Each clone will have an Image Control of the same size. In the MDIForm_Load Event, type the following:

```
Sub MDIForm_Load ( )
For i = 2 To 9
    Set PicForm(i) = New Form1
    Load PicForm(i)
Next i
Arrange 2
picount = 1
End Sub
```

We make eight copies of Form1 by using the Set and New commands (see "Set"). Cloned windows are not loaded or visible until you specifically Load them, so we do that right after creating them.

Next, we use the Arrange command (notice it doesn't need an = sign, it's a Method of the MDI Form) to make the child windows within the MDI Window tile. There are four styles of Arrange: 0 (Cascade), 1 (Tile horizontally), 2 (Tile vertically), 3 (Arrange Icons). Finally, we set our counter for the number of clone windows with pictures loaded to 1. (We created PicForm's 2 through 9, so we want to bypass Form1 when the user selects Add Picture from our menu.) It's time to create that menu.

In the Project Window, click on MDIForm1 and then click on View Form. Now, from the Window Menu, select Menu Design and fill it in as shown in the figure:

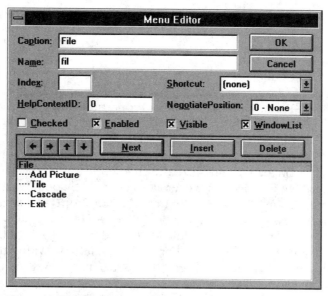

Figure M-50: The Menu Design Window.

Note the Window List option; check it and VB automatically provides a list of the number of child windows in the MDI, as well as showing which one currently has the focus.

Now, go through and put the various necessary commands within each of our menu items. Add Picture brings up Form10, by setting its Window-State Property to 0 (Normal). The real action of adding a .BMP picture will take place in Form10's List1 DblClick Event.

```
Sub AddP_Click ( )
    Form10.WindowState = 0
End Sub
```
If the user wants to tile or cascade the child windows inside the MDI Form, we offer those commands:
```
Sub Til_Click ( )
    MDIForm1.Arrange 2
End Sub
Sub Casc_Click ( )
    MDIForm1.Arrange 0
End Sub
```
The Exit option is self-explanatory:
```
Sub exi_Click ( )
    End
End Sub
```

Form10 is where the main action takes place, once the clone windows have been created in the MDI Form. First, ensure that changes the user makes to the Directory List update the File List:

```
Sub Dir1_Change ( )
    file1.Path = dir1.Path

End Sub
```

You Can't Hide Child Windows: There's a special reason for reminding
the File List Box of the Pattern Property we want it to have. When you
UnLoad a Form, it loses track of its Properties (they reset to their defaults).
And, we have to UnLoad Form10 each time the user selects a picture
because you can't get rid of child windows (child Forms) that are within an
MDI Form by using the Hide method or its equivalent Visible = 0. Instead,
you must UnLoad or minimize the child Form's WindowState Property,
thus making it an icon. A clever alternative that would make a child Form
temporarily invisible would be to set its Left Property radically beyond the
MDI Window's visible space (Form10.Left = 30000). That would move it
into the void beyond the visible MDI Window until you called it back by
resetting its Left Property to 0 or 300 or something within the visible space.
In any case, we'll UnLoad Form10, so we have to reset the Pattern Property
each time Form10 Loads:

```
Sub Form_Load ( )
    file1.Pattern = *.bmp
End Sub
```

Last, type the following into the DblClick Event of the File List Box,
where we let the user fill the child windows with pictures:

```
Sub File1_DblClick ( )
picount = picount + 1
    pa$ = file1.Path
    If Right$(pa$, 1) <> \ Then pa$ = pa$ + \
pa$ = pa$ + file1.List(file1.ListIndex)
PicForm(picount).Image1.Picture = LoadPicture(pa$)
UnLoad form10
End Sub
```

First, we raise picount, the counter that keeps track of which child
window should next be filled with a picture. Then we make sure we've got
the right syntax for the path and filename of the picture the user has
selected (see "Drive List Box" for more on this). Finally, we use the Load-
Picture command to bring in the graphic. Notice how many specifications
we use to identify the child window: PicForm(picount).Image1.Picture
(Array name, Array index, Control, Control's Property).

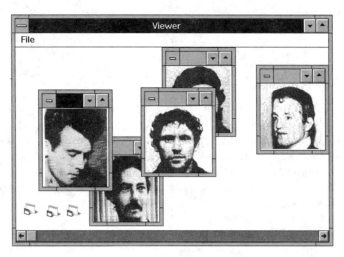

Figure M-51: The user can close, resize, iconize, maximize, tile, cascade, or move child windows within the parent MDI window.

MDI Properties
ActiveControl ActiveForm • Auto3D • AutoShowChildren • BackColor • Caption • Enabled • Height • HelpContextID • Icon • hWnd • Left • LinkMode • LinkTopic • MousePointer • Name • NegotiateToolbars • Picture • ScaleHeight • ScaleWidth • ScrollBars • Tag • Top • Visible • Width • WindowState

MDI Events
Activate • Click • DoubleClick • Deactivate • DragDrop • DragOver • Initialize • LinkClose • LinkError • LinkExecute • LinkOpen • Load • MouseDown • MouseMove • MouseUp • QueryUnLoad • Resize • Terminate • UnLoad

MDI Methods
Arrange • Hide • Move • SetFocus • Show • ZOrder

See also   Control Array; New; Set

PROPERTY

Description   MultiSelect allows the user (or your program) to select more than one item in a List Box or File List Box. Selecting means clicking on an item in the list, at which time the item reverses to white lettering against a black background. Clicking again deselects. You can also select from the keyboard by moving the "preselect focus"—a small gray frame—with the Up arrow and Down arrow keys, then selecting with the Spacebar. Your program can select items, too.

Used with   File List Boxes and List Boxes

Variables   **Variable type:** Integer

MultiSelect must be adjusted in the Properties Window. This property cannot be changed while a program is running.

MultiSelect offers the following three options:

0   Only one item at a time can be selected (the default). The previously selected item is deselected.

1   Simple multiple selection. Clicking on an item selects it, adding it to any other items already selected.

2   Extended multiple selection. Clicking while holding down the SHIFT key selects all items between a previously selected item and the one clicked upon. SHIFT+Up/Down arrow operates the same way from the keyboard. CTRL+click selects or deselects a single item in the list.

To find out which item(s) have been selected, you can use the Selected Property like this:

```
For i = 0 To List1.ListCount — 1
    If List1.Selected(i) = True Then
        Print List1.List(i); " is selected."
    End If
Next i
```

Uses   • Allow the user to delete, copy or move a *group* of files from within a File List Box.

• Allow multiple documents or Forms to be displayed, printed or otherwise manipulated by your program.

Example

Figure M-52: With MultiSelect the user can select any number of items in a File °List °Box.

See also   Columns; File List Box; List Box; Selected

Name

PROPERTY

Description   The Name Property is the unique identifier of each object in VB. VB and the programmer use the Name Property to refer to specific entities such as the Name *Form1* in Form1.BackColor or the Name *Text1* to identify a particular Text Box. Unlike most Properties, the Name isn't of any use to, or seen by, the user of a program.

Name Properties can be combined, separated by a period (.), to specify on which of several Forms a particular Control is located: Form1.Text1 as opposed to Form2.Text1. References to Names often include references to Properties, again separated by a period: Form1.Label2.Width.

Used with   The App object, all Controls, all Forms, all Menus and Menu items.

Variables   **Variable type:** Text (string)

VB automatically assigns a unique Name to all Forms and Controls each time you create a new Form or Control. VB uses the generic name of the object and adds a unique digit, starting from 1. For example, when you double-click five times on the Picture Box icon in the Toolbox, five (super-imposed) Picture Boxes will appear in the center of your form. Their Names will be Picture1, Picture2, Picture3, Picture4 and Picture5.

For Many Programmers, VB's Names Work Fine: You can change Names to whatever you wish, but many people find that the default Names given by VB work well. If you want to make the purpose of a Control clearer, give it a Name that reflects its function: you might use ExitButton as a Name for a Command Button. An advantage of descriptive Names is that the list of "Objects" on a Form's Object Menu will reflect the purpose of each Control, and the Event names will likewise reveal your intentions about that particular Control.

VB will automatically give the first Command Button you created on a Form the Name "Command1." If you change the Name, the Events for that Control will be more descriptive. This would be the VB default Name:

```
Sub Command1_Click ()
End Sub
```

But if you change the Name for this Button, all its Events are renamed by Visual Basic:

```
Sub ExitButton_Click ()
End Sub
```

Similarly, if you change the Name of a Form, the new Name will show up in the Project Window. When you first run Visual Basic or when you select

New Project from the File Menu, VB creates an initial blank Form and assigns it the Name Form1. Subsequently, if you add another Form to your program by selecting New Form from the File Menu (or clicking on the New Form icon in the Toolbar), VB automatically assigns it the Name Form2. For many programmers, this scheme is perfectly workable, and they never change the Name Property of their Forms.

Programmers who do not alter the Forms' or Controls' Names argue that it's one less thing to keep track of while designing a program. You can focus on the real issues: how your program should look and work. One of the signal advantages of Visual Basic is that it handles so many of the details of programming for you. Why not let it also name your Forms and Controls?

However, if you prefer, you can assign different Names from the Properties Window, giving each Form a Name that describes its purpose. The approach you use is a matter of personal taste and programming preference.

You must make any adjustments to a Name Property in the Properties Window while designing your program:

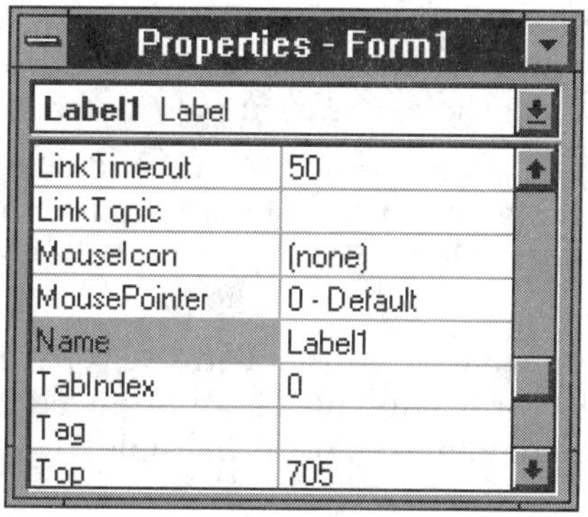

Figure N-1: A Name is like any other Property but must be unique for each Control.

A Name cannot be changed while the program is running.

Uses • Because an object like a Picture Box is uniquely identified by its Name, you use Names to adjust the Properties of all your Controls:

```
Picture1.Width = Picture2.Width
```

• Events are Subroutines (see "Sub"). Therefore, you can "call" an Event, cause it to be triggered from elsewhere within the same Form in which the Event resides. If, for example, Command1.Click clears a window (Cls) and performs some other tasks that you want done by the Form_Click Event, you have two choices. You can either reproduce the Cls and other commands within the Form_Click Event, or you can "call" the Command1 Click Event, triggering its commands as if the user had clicked on the

Command1 Button with the mouse. To "call" an Event, use the Name plus the Event's name, separated by an underline (_) character:

```
Sub Form_Click()
Command1_Click
End Sub
```

Now, whatever you've programmed to happen within the Command1's Click Event will also happen when the Form's Click Event is triggered. This is precisely as if the user had clicked on Command1. In this case, though, your program, not the user, triggered the Command1 Click Event.

• While designing your program, you can change one Control's Name to the same Name as another Control of the same type (for instance, you could give two Text Boxes the Name Text1). You would make this change in the Properties Window; if you do, you will create a *Control Array* (which see). You can efficiently manipulate many Controls using this technique because all such arrayed Controls are *clones* of the original; they share the same set of Events, Properties and *the same Name*. The Controls are identified by a unique index number for each Control, so you can use Loops like For...Next to affect the entire group of Controls at once.

• You can set up an Array of Forms, too. Cloned Forms share the same Name without any distinguishing index number (you use the Me command or Object Variables to distinguish the Forms). For more on Form Arrays, see "Set" or "Objects."

• Use a Form's Name if you want to adjust a Form's Properties or use Subroutines and Functions (or Events) on a Form from a different Form (or Module). Here's how you could make Form1 invisible, by a command from within Form2:

```
Sub Form2_Click ()
    Form1.Hide
End Sub
```

It is unnecessary to use a Form's Name when adjusting Properties or using Subroutines and Functions within that same Form—for the same reason it is unnecessary to add U.S.A. to letters mailed from within the U.S. to another place within the U.S.—it is understood. Let's say that you want to change the Caption Property of Label1 from within a Command Button's Command1_Click Event. Both of these Controls are within Form1:

```
Sub Command1_Click ()
    Form1.Label1.Caption = "Milton"
End Sub
```

This is equivalent to leaving off the Name *Form1:*

```
Label1.Caption = "Milton"
```

The Form's Name is entirely optional here.

Likewise, if you want to run an Event (utilize a Function or Subroutine Procedure) from another Event on the same Form, you can just supply the Event_Name. The Form's Name is optional here, too:

```
Sub Command1_Click ()
    Label1_Click
End Sub
```

This causes whatever instructions you have placed inside Label1's Click Event to be carried out. In this next example, clicking on the Command Button causes a Beep in the speaker because we triggered Label1's Click Event by naming it:

```
Sub Label1_Click ()
    Beep
End Sub
```

A Form's Name is also optional when adjusting a Property of the Form itself from within one of the Form's own Events. This Sub changes the Form's Caption:

```
Sub Form_Click ()
    Caption = "NewFormName"
End Sub
```

Cautions • Names are not the same as Caption or Text Properties. Captions and Text display information to the user; the user does not see Names. They are identifiers that you and Visual Basic use to refer to Controls and Forms and to manage them within the program itself. Names are not public information.

An apparent exception to this rule is the fact that a Form's Name and Caption both default to Form1, Form2 and so forth, as VB automatically assigns these Properties. However, Name and Caption are distinct Properties. The Caption is what appears in the bar across the top of the Form; the Name is the unique ID. You can freely change either Property while designing your program.

• You cannot change Names while a program is running.

• If your program has more than one Form, you can use the same Control Names in the first and second Forms. (This duplication of Names on separate Forms does not create a Control Array, which see.) In this situation, you distinguish between the duplicated Names by adding the Form's Name to the Control's Name: Form1.Picture1 vs. Form2.Picture1. If you don't add the host Form's Name to a Control's Name, VB assumes you are referring to the Picture1 on the current Form (the Form within which you are using the Control's Name). Text1.BackColor = QBColor(4) will turn a TextBox *in the same Form* red. Form3.Text1.BackColor = QBColor(4) will change the color of a TextBox on Form3—regardless of where in your program you have written these instructions.

• A Name can have as many as 40 characters; it cannot be one of VB's words (like Print); and it must start with a letter of the alphabet. However, a Name can include digits and the underline (_) symbol. If you give a Form a Name longer than eight characters, the name will be truncated in the Project Window and also when saved to disk (to deal with the filename size limitation of DOS—eight characters plus a three-character extension: ABCDEFGH.FRM).

Example   Label1

See also   Caption; Control Array; Objects; Text

 AME

STATEMENT

Description   The Name Statement can be used in two ways: renaming files and directories or moving a file.

• The Name Statement allows your program, or the user, to change the name of a disk file or a disk directory. Used this way for files, Name is the equivalent of the DOS file command RENAME (or REN).

• The Name Statement can also be used to *move* a file from one directory to another on the disk. The file is copied to the target directory; then the original is deleted from the source directory. DOS has no equivalent move.

   Recall that if you want to *create a new file*, you use the Open and Close Statements (with a unique filename). (See "Open" for more information.)

Used with   Disk files and disk directories

Variables   **To Rename a File:**

   Name "MYFILE.OLD" As "MYFILE.NEW"

OR (to use Variables):

   Oldname$ = "MYFILE.OLD"
   Newname$ = "MYFILE.NEW"
   Name Oldname$ As Newname$

To Move a File:

   Name "C:\DOS\UNZIP.EXE" As "C:\WINDOWS\UNZIP.EXE"

(By providing a different path, C:\WINDOWS\ vs. C:\DOS\, the file is copied to the WINDOWS directory, and then the original file in the DOS directory is deleted.)

To Move and Rename a File at the Same Time:

   Name "C:\DOS\UNZIP.EXE" As "C:\WINDOWS\DOUNZIP.EXE"

(By providing both a different path *and a different filename*, the original is both moved and renamed.)

To Rename a Directory:

Name "C:\TEMP" As "C:\TEMPOLD"

Uses
• Use the Name command to rename files or directories, or to move files (copy and then delete the original).

The Name Statement is one of the many tools that Visual Basic provides for dealing with disk drives and the files on them. This set of tools is so generous that you can design an effective alternative to the File Manager and can add it as a feature of your VB programs. This way, the user doesn't have to rely on the rather clumsy File Manager provided with Windows and doesn't have to move out of your program to manage his or her disk.

Cautions
• An error will be generated if the file you are trying to rename doesn't exist on the disk (as it was specified in your Name Statement).

• An error will be generated if the new Name you are trying to give this file already exists on the disk (as it was specified in your Name Statement).

• Name cannot move files across disk *drives.* You cannot use Name "C:\MYFILE" As "D:\MYFILE" to move it from drive C: to drive D: .

You would need to use Open, Kill and ChDrive in combination to achieve a trans-drive move.

• You cannot use Name while the file involved is open. If your program has used the Open Statement to expose a file to access by your program, you must close that file before trying to use Name with it. (See the Example below.)

• As always, when your program accesses the user's disk drive, use On Error (which see) to prevent your program from shutting down if the unexpected happens.

Example
This program allows the user to edit his or her AUTOEXEC.BAT file. Before permitting the editing, we first use the Name command to make a safety backup in case something untoward happens.

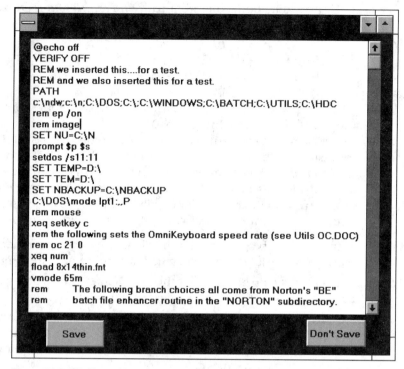

```
@echo off
VERIFY OFF
REM we inserted this....for a test.
REM and we also inserted this for a test.
PATH
c:\ndw;c:\n;C:\DOS;C:\;C:\WINDOWS;C:\BATCH;C:\UTILS;C:\HDC
rem ep /on
rem image
SET NU=C:\N
prompt $p $s
setdos /s11:11
SET TEMP=D:\
SET TEM=D:\
SET NBACKUP=C:\NBACKUP
C:\DOS\mode lpt1:,,P
rem mouse
xeq setkey c
rem the following sets the OmniKeyboard speed rate (see Utils OC.DOC)
rem oc 21 0
xeq num
fload 8x14thin.fnt
vmode 65m
rem        The following branch choices all come from Norton's "BE"
rem        batch file enhancer routine in the "NORTON" subdirectory.
```

[Save]   [Don't Save]

Figure N-2: We'll use Name to make a backup before any changes can be made to the important AUTOEXEC.BAT file.

Put a Text Box on a Form, set its MultiLine Property to –1 (in the VB Properties Window) and add two Command Buttons. Into the Form_Load Event, type the following:

```
Sub Form_Load ()

On Error Resume Next

Name "C:\AUTOEXEC.BAT" As "C:\AUTOEXEC.BAK"

Open "C:\AUTOEXEC.BAK" For Input As #1
    x = LOF(1)
    a$ = Input$(x, 1)
    text1.text = a$
Close

If Err Then
    MsgBox (Error$(Err))
    Name "C:\AUTOEXEC.BAK" As "C:\AUTOEXEC.BAT"
    MsgBox ("Problem encountered. Exiting Program.")
    End
End If
End Sub
```

First, we rename AUTOEXEC.BAT to .BAK because we're going to save a new AUTOEXEC.BAT file, modified by the user, but we want to retain the original just in case. By renaming it, we'll have a copy of it when we create a new AUTOEXEC.BAT in the Command Button labeled "SAVE" described in the following paragraphs. (See "Error$" for the error handling here.)

Then we find out the LOF (Length Of File) and assign the entire text contents of the file to a$. We put a$ into the Text Property of our Text Box, making it available to the user. Then we close the disk file. If there is some kind of error, we rename the .BAK file to restore the contents as they were on the disk before our program intervened. And we shut the program down with End.

In the Command1 Button_Click Event, the Button with the caption "SAVE," type the following:

```
Sub Command1_Click ()
On Error Resume Next

Open "C:\AUTOEXEC.BAT" For Output As 1
    Print #1, text1.text
    Close 1

If Err Then MsgBox (Error$(Err))
End Sub
```

This Click Event creates a new file called AUTOEXEC.BAT and stuffs the modified text into it.

Finally, if the user wishes to abort the proceedings, enter the following into the Command2_Click Event, the Button labeled "Don't Save":

```
Sub Command2_Click ()
    Name "C:\AUTOEXEC.BAK" As "C:\AUTOEXEC.BAT"
End Sub
```

Here we simply undo the renaming that we did in the Form_Load Event—restoring the disk to its original state.

See also MkDir or Open (to create directories and files); RmDir or Kill (to delete directories or files)

Here is an alphabetical list of all the disk- and file-management commands that Visual Basic offers:

AppActivate; Archive; Change; ChDir; ChDrive; Close; CurDir$; Dir$; Drive; EOF; EXEName; FileAttr; FileName; FreeFile; Get; Hidden; Input$; Input #; Kill; Line Input #; List; ListCount; ListIndex; Loc; Lock; LOF; MkDir; Normal; On Error; Open; Path; PathChange; Pattern; PatternChange; Print #; Put; ReadOnly; Reset; RmDir; Seek; Shell; System; Unlock; Write #

NAMED ARGUMENTS   PARAMETERS

Description   Unfortunately, the new style of naming parameters, found in VBA and WordBasic, has only been implemented in VB4 in a highly limited way (with the Add and Opendatabase Methods, and to a degree within the With...End With structure). (We're going to use the terms *argument* and *parameter* interchangeably here.)

The versions of Basic built into Word, Excel(VBA) and Project(VBA) now name their parameters. This means you can list the parameters in any order. To define the typeface as 9 points large, not underlined, and turn strikethrough on, in WordBasic you can do this:

```
FormatFont .Points = "19", .Underline = 0, .Color = 0, .Strikethrough = 1
```

Notice that each parameter (argument) has a label, a name. For example, the label Underline = 0 means that underlining is not turned on. The virtue of named arguments (aside from the clarity they lend to your programs when you try to read them) is that you can mix and match parameters, moving the arguments around any way you want. Because the arguments are named (identified), VB can accept them in any order. And you don't have to do the old comma repetition to place a parameter in its proper location if you want to use the default parameters for the rest of the arguments: Circle (10,12),1222, , , 144.

The punctuation of named parameters currently used by Word differs from the way VBA and VB4 punctuate parameters. In Word you assign a named argument with a simple equals sign:

```
param = value
```

In VBA (Excel and Project at this time) or VB4 you use := (a colon + equals sign) and the spaces go away around the equals sign too:

```
param:=value
```

Used with   The various arguments (parameters) which describe a Property or Method. Named arguments are pervasive in Microsoft Project, Excel and Word. In VB4, they are currently in limited use. However, because they are the wave of the future, we should get used to them. They have distinct advantages over the older positional arguments syntax.

In VB4, one style of named parameters is found inside the With...End With structure. However true named parameters are found in the syntax of the Add and the OpenDatabase Methods.

Variables   If you are interested in setting the size, italic, and strikethrough parameters of a Font Property, you could simply write this:

```
Private Sub Form_Load( )
With Text1.Font
    .Italic = True
    .Strikethrough = True
    .Size = 24
End With
End Sub
```

(You're not mentioning many of the Properties of a Text Box. For example the default for underlining, or the current status of underlining, is what you want. So you don't mention the Underline Property.)

Notice that you can alternatively nest levels of parameters inside the With...End With:

```
Private Sub Form_Load( )
With Text1
    With .Font
        .Italic = True
        .Strikethrough = True
        Size = 24
    End With
End With
End Sub
```

True Named Parameters

Although With...End With mimics named parameters, true named parameters are found in the Add Method of the Collection Object:

```
MyNames.Add item:= Name  & I, key:= Key#  & I
```

Or, since you can change the order of named parameters:

```
MyNames.Add key:= Key#  & I, item:= Name  & I
```

Uses
• Named arguments are most useful with Methods like Line, rather than Properties like Font. This is because the traditional way of assigning values to Properties in VB is both readable and can be in any order:

```
Text1.FontStrikethru = True
Text1.FontItalic = True
```

Named arguments used inside With...End With merely streamline the process by eliminating the need to keep repeating the Object's name, Text1.

However, if you could name the arguments for, say, the Line Method, you'd get some real advantages over the old style:

```
Line (350, 350)-(1500, 1500), , B
```

Because the new style names each element, it's both clearer and easier (to eliminate those spacer commas):

```
Line .X1 = 350 .Y1 = 350 .X2 = 1500 .Y2 = 1500 .Style = B
```

But named parameters for most Methods aren't implemented in VB at this time. So let's take a look at the advantages named parameters offer to WordBasic (or see the entry on "Add," a VB Command that does permit named parameters):

The order of these parameters is also irrelevant when they are labeled. This line . . .

```
FormatFont .Points = "9" .Strikethrough = 1
```

does the same thing as . . .

```
FormatFont .Strikethrough = 1 .Points = "9"
```

By contrast, in Visual Basic and previous Basics, there are such labels. When you want to describe a series of parameters for a Method, you have to include them all and in the correct order. (You can leave out the defaults, but you still have to include spacers, or commas, to create the correct position for each item.)

Word, being a word processor, has a mania about fonts—there are 18 possible parameters. Obviously, turning on italics, the final item in Word-Basic's parameter list for Font, is cumbersome in the old WordBasic style where position matters:

```
FormatFont "9", , , , , , , , , , , , , , , , 1
```

Yet it is very simple in the new style:

```
FormatFont .Italic = 1
```

Cautions • With VB4, there are now three different words used in three different contexts for the idea of Strikethrough. This might be too much of a good thing, claritywise.

#1: STRIKETHROUGH, with named arguments inside With...End With:

```
With Text1
    With .Font
        .Italic = True
        .Strikethrough = True
        .Size = 24
    End With
End With
End Sub
```

#2: STRIKETHRU, with traditional VB parameter assignment:

```
Text1.FontStrikethru = True
Text1.FontItalic = True
```

#3: STRIKEOUT, in the Properties Window under Font.

Wouldn't be so bad if they were all synonyms to VB, and it accepted each with good grace. But use any one of them in the wrong context and you get an error message.

• Since parameters/arguments are used in several contexts in VB (during procedure calls to pass values to a Sub or Function, as qualifiers for Methods, as qualifiers for Properties), one could hope that the punctuation will eventually be the same for any parameter in any context. For now, though, you have to remember whether or not to use parentheses, spaces, commas, periods, equal signs, colons+equal signs, quote marks and even exclamation points. As yet, the semicolon, single quote, and the tilde aren't involved.

Examples

For With...End With:

When the user clicks on this Form, it shrinks to 25% of its original size:

```
Private Sub Form_Click( )
With Form1
    .Width = Width / 2
    .Height = Height / 2
End With
End Sub
```

For the Add Method:

Here we'll use two parameters, Item and Key, to Add to a Collection. Notice that the Key is a text variable that can be later searched (the actual Item of data can't be automatically searched for by the Add or Remove Methods, though you could write a loop to search through each item for a match). Here we just add a "k" to the actual data, to create the Key:

```
Dim MyFriends As New Collection
Private Sub Form_Load( )
Show
x = 1
Do
    x = InputBox( What s the name of a Friend? )
    MyFriends.Add Item:=x, Key:= k  & x
Loop Until x =
For Each whatever In MyFriends
    Print whatever
Next
y = InputBox( Type in a name to remove... )
On Error Resume Next
MyFriends.Remove ( k  & y)
If Err Then
    MsgBox  Can t locate   & y
Else
Print  RESULTS
For Each whatever In MyFriends
    Print whatever
Next
End If
End Sub
```

See also   Collection

NEGOTIATEMENUS

PROPERTY

Description   There's a new technique, *in-place editing*. This OLE phenomenon occurs (thanks to the operating system) when the user double-clicks on a linked or embedded Object. For example, say you put an OLE Control on a Form, then embed a graphic in your Form. When the user double-clicks on this embedded (or linked) Object, the originating application's facilities are made available. If your user's system includes CorelDRAW, then some of Draw's menus can appear on your Form.

There's the NegotiateMenus Property of a Form determines whether these menus from the outside application will be, in fact, permitted to be added to any menus you might have put on the Form in VB. NegotiateMenus defaults to True.

Used with   A Form (or a "Forms Collection")

Variables   NegotiateMenus cannot be changed while the program is running. Change it in the Properties Window during program design.

There's another Property which interacts with NegotiateMenus. The *NegotiatePosition* Property (it's a Property of each individual Menu Control) governs which of your Form's top-level menus (the one's you see on the Menu Bar itself) are displayed (or made invisible) when the menus of the "active" (editable) Object are being displayed. Here are the possible settings for the NegotiatePosition Property:

0   None. The Form's menu isn't displayed on the Menu Bar when the linked or embedded Object is active (this is the default).

1   Left. The Form's menu is moved to the left side of the Menu Bar when the Object is active.

2   Middle. The Form's menu is positioned in the middle of the Menu Bar when the Object is active.

3   Right. The Form's menu is positioned to the right side of the Menu Bar when the Object is active.

Uses   • With OLE 2.0, it's possible to *combine* applications dynamically in various ways. For instance, while running Excel, you could temporarily "add" facilities from Word. When Word appears like this "within" Excel, Word's menus (and Toolbar buttons) can be temporarily added to Excel's menus and buttons. This phenomenon, this blending of two "Objects," is called in-place editing.

In VB, a Form's NegotiateMenus Property governs whether or not the menus of an active Object on the Form will be permitted to share (negotiate) space with the Form's menus.

Cautions • An MDI Form doesn't have the facility to display outside menus.

• To use the NegotiateMenus feature, a Form must at least *have* a menu (even if that menu isn't visible).

Example Place an OLE Control on a Form. Select "Create from File" when the Insert Object dialog window appears. Choose a .BMP file. Then press CTRL+E and add a menu named Add Object to your Form. This will be a VB menu. Then, with the Menu Editor still visible, select "Right" in the "Negotiate Position" drop-down menu. Now press F5 to run the program. When you double-click on the graphic, menus from a graphics editing program will push our Add Object Menu all the way to the right (except for Help, which always is rightmost). Precisely which menus appear during this in-place editing depend on which graphics editing program is "associated" with .BMP files in the user's computer.

Figure N-3: Add Object is our VB-created menu on this Form.

Figure N-4: When the user double-clicks on the graphic Object, our menu item is pushed all the way to the right to make room for the outside application s menus.

See also   Menu, NegotiateToolbars

See   NegotiateMenus

Description   There's a new technique, *in-place editing.* This OLE phenomenon occurs (thanks to the operating system) when the user double-clicks on a linked or embedded Object. When the user double-clicks on an Object embedded (or linked) into one of your *MDI Child Forms,* the originating application's toolbar can appear at the top of your VB MDI Form.

The NegotiateToolBars Property of an MDI Child Form determines whether these Toolbar(s) from the outside application will be, in fact, permitted to appear in the MDI Parent (container) Form when the embedded/linked Object is double-clicked (activated) by the user. NegotiateToolbars defaults to True.

The *Negotiate* Property determines whether or not a Picture Box or Data Control (the only Controls with the Negotiate Property) remain visible when an outside application's Toolbar(s) becomes visible. The reason for this is that a Picture Box can be used to create a Toolbar in VB by setting its Align Property (which see). Negotiate defaults to False.

Used with   An MDI Child Form

Variables   NegotiateToolbars cannot be changed while the program is running. Change it in the Properties Window during program design.

Uses   Permit an outside application to insert its Toolbar(s) when an embedded/linked object is activated (double-clicked) by the user.

Cautions   • A regular VB Form doesn't have the facility to display outside Toolbars.

• If NegotiateToolbars is set to False, it's still possible that the outside application's Toolbar will be displayed, but it will be a "floating" Toolbar rather than fixed into the Parent MDI Form, as shown in Figure N-5. How the outside application behaves in this situation is up to that application.

Example   Place an OLE Control on a Form. Select "Create from File" when the Insert Object dialog window appears. If you have Word for Windows, choose a .DOC file. Press F5 to run the program. When you double-click on the text document, Word's Toolbars will appear at the top of the MDI Parent (container) Form as you can see in Figure N-5. Precisely which Toolbars appear during this in-place editing depend on which word processor is "associated" with .DOC files in the user's computer.

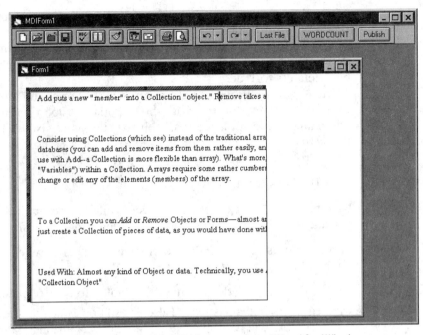

Figure N-5: The Toolbars in this MDI Form are from Word for Windows.

See Also   NegotiateMenus, Align

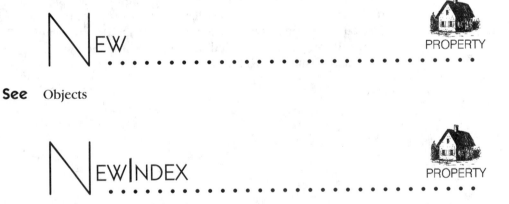

New

See   Objects

NewIndex

See   ItemData

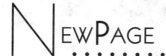

METHOD

Description   NewPage forces the printer to move to the next sheet of paper. This command is sometimes called a *hard page*, a *forced page* or a *page break*.

Used with   The printer

Variables   Printer.NewPage

Uses   • Eject the current sheet of paper at whatever point you want the text to end.

If you are at the end of a logical division in your work—a major section, a chapter—you might not want it to flow across two pages when it's printed. NewPage allows you to specify page breaks.

All word processors include a "hard page" feature, so the user isn't at the mercy of his or her printer's rather crude formatting (printers keep printing until they run out of space on a page).

If you are creating a program that includes a Text Box for word processing, you might want to offer the user the option to force a page break. One way would be to use the Text Box's KeyDown Event to detect the F8 key. You've told the user that pressing F8 will insert a page break. If that function key is pressed, you can then insert a code into the Text Box. When the Text Box's Text Property is printed, your program will detect this code and invoke NewPage to eject the current sheet from the printer. (See the Example.)

• Used with the EndDoc Method, NewPage prevents the printer from ending a printing job with a blank last page. To accomplish this, send the printer these two commands after sending all your text :

    Printer.NewPage
    Printer.EndDoc

Cautions   • NewPage *increments* the Printer.Page Property (adds 1 to it).

Example

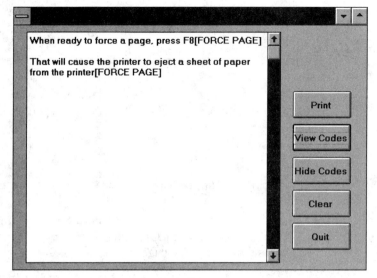

Figure N-6: This Text Box includes a reveal-codes option. We're embedding force-page codes (invoking the NewPage command wherever these codes are encountered within the text).

This example is a mini-word processor, and it includes a special feature. If the user presses F8, a force-page code is inserted into the text. This example also illustrates the EndDoc Method and how to use an invisible Text Box as a convenient buffer to back up a visible Text Box.

First, create a Form and put two Text Boxes on it. Set Text1.MultiLine to –1 and set Text2.Visible to False. Put five Command Buttons on the Form, and label them as shown in Figure N-3. Use their Caption, not their Name, Properties.

We want to filter the user's keypresses, looking at each one to make sure it isn't the F8 key. Therefore, we put the following into Text1's KeyDown Event:

```
Sub Text1_KeyDown (keycode As Integer, shift As Integer)

If keycode = 119 Then
    p = text1.SelStart
    l = Len(text1.text)
    lft$ = Left$(text1.text, p)
    rgt$ = Right$(text1.text, l – p)
    text1.text = lft$ + Chr$(187) + rgt$
    text1.SelStart = p + 1
End If
End Sub
```

SelStart is a Property of Text Boxes that tells you the current location of the cursor, the I-Beam symbol that indicates where the next letters will be displayed. We cannot assume that the user will always press F8 at the very end of the text. This will sometimes be the case, but other times the user might want to insert a forced page somewhere within the text.

We find out where the user pressed F8 and put that character location into the Variable *p*. Then we find out how many characters there are in the text (using Len). Left$ extracts all the characters to the left of the cursor and stores them in a Variable. Right$ extracts all the characters to the right of the cursor (length–position).

Chopped in Two Pieces: In this way, we've chopped the text into two pieces, at the location where the user pressed F8. Now we can put it together again but also insert Chr$(187), which we're using to indicate a forced page. You can use any kind of special character you want. (See *ANSI* in VB's Help Window to pick out a different one.) A more sophisticated approach would be to simply keep track of the position of the forced page but not make anything visible to the user, unless the user requested to see the codes.

Our next job is to respond when the user presses Command2, requesting to view the codes in the text:

```
Sub Command2_Click ()

text2.text = text1.text
l = Len(text1.text)
p = 1
p = InStr(p, text1.text, Chr$(187))

Do Until p = 0
    x$ = Left$(text1.text, p − 1)
    y$ = Right$(text1.text, l − p)
    text1.text = x$ + "[FORCE PAGE]" + y$
    l = Len(text1.text)
    p = InStr(p, text1.text, Chr$(187))
Loop
End Sub
```

Here we use the invisible Text2 to store a copy of the text. The user will only be viewing the codes temporarily, so we'll copy Text2 back into Text1 when the user presses the Hide Codes Button.

After making our copy, we find the length of the text and set pointer Variable *p* to 1. (You can't use InStr with a zero pointer.) Now we look for Chr$(187) inside the text. If it isn't found, the Do Until Loop never happens—VB bounces off it because *p* will equal 0 if InStr found no Chr$(187).

Otherwise, if a 187 code was found, *p* will hold the character location of the hit. So we divide the text at that point into x$ and y$. We recombine it, inserting the phrase [FORCE PAGE]. Setting Text1.Text automatically updates it onscreen.

What if There Are More Than 187 Codes? There may be *more* than 187 codes. That's why we have this Loop. We change the length of the text (it's gotten longer with the insertion of [FORCE PAGE]), and we run another InStr to see if there are any more. Loop forces the program back up to the Do command, but if InStr made *p* = 0, the Do Until test will fail, and it will bounce us past Loop to exit the Subroutine. If *p*, however, contains any-thing other than 0, we've hit yet another 187 code further into the text. This Looping keeps up until, at some point, InStr finds no more matches, gives *p* a 0, and we bounce past the Loop.

Now we'll look at three Buttons that have simple jobs to perform. The Button with the caption "Hide Codes" restores the original text from the invisible buffer, Text2, where we put it before messing around with Text1 in the "Show Codes" Subroutine:

```
Sub Command5_Click ()
    text1.text = text2.text
End Sub
```

The Button with the caption "Clear" sets Text1.Text to an empty Variable (nothing between the quotation marks):

```
Sub Command3_Click ()
    text1.text = ""
End Sub
```

And the Button with the caption "Quit" ends the program:

```
Sub Command4_Click ()
    End
End Sub
```

Now, how do we pick up the 187 force-page codes while we're printing the document? If the user presses the Print Button:

```
Sub Command1_Click ()
    text2.text = text1.text
    l = Len(text1.text)
    p = 1

p = InStr(p, text1.text, Chr$(187))

If p = 0 Then printer.Print text1.text: printer.EndDoc: Exit Sub

Do Until p = 0
    x$ = Left$(text1.text, p − 1)
    y$ = Right$(text1.text, l − p)
    printer.Print x$
    printer.NewPage
    text1.text = y$
    l = Len(text1.text)
    p = InStr(p, text1.text, Chr$(187))
Loop

printer.Print y$
```

```
text1.text = text2.text
printer.EndDoc
End Sub
```

This Subroutine is somewhat like the text-searching we did when the user wanted to view codes. We save the text, get its length and set pointer p to 1—so it points to the first character in the text.

Now we search for code 187. If we don't find any such codes, we merely print the document and exit the Subroutine. We use EndDoc to make the printer aware that nothing more is coming (and that it can eject the page), and the Print Manager can shut itself down as well. EndDoc means no pending printing, nothing in the pipeline. Notice that EndDoc is different from NewPage (which means "go to the next sheet of paper but expect more text coming down the pipeline").

If we find a 187 code—if p isn't 0—we split the text in half at the point where the 187 code was found. We print the left half of the text, use NewPage to eject the sheet of paper, and change the text so it's now *only the right half* of its former self. We find the new length and search again for code 187. We'll keep Looping until we don't find any more codes. Then we "fall through" the Loop and print that last (codeless) piece of text. We put the original text back into the visible Text Box (because we've been chopping up the text, we need to restore it). Then we notify the printer that the document has finished. The printer will eject the page for us; we don't need a NewPage if we send EndDoc.

See also   EndDoc; Page; Print; Printer

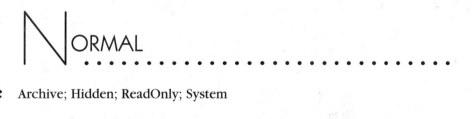

NORMAL

See   Archive; Hidden; ReadOnly; System

NOTHING

See   Is

Now

FUNCTION

Description   The Now command checks the computer's clock and provides a "serial number" that represents the current date and time.

The serial number returned by the Now command is one of a large list of unique numbers calculated by Visual Basic. There is a different serial number for every *second* between January 1, 100 A.D., and December 31, 9999. One implication of this splendid profligacy is that whenever you request a serial number by using the Now command (which tells you the current moment), the serial number will be a higher number.

The serial number encodes the second, minute, hour, day, month and year.

After being translated into a serial number, the current time can be *manipulated mathematically* with the serial numbers of other times and dates. (See "DateSerial" for more information.)

Used with   Various VB commands can extract specific information from the serial number:

    X = Month(Now)

Results in   (if the current month is February, X will be 2)

The Functions that can extract information from the Now serial number are as follows: Second, Minute, Hour, Day, Month, Year and Format$.

To create text (such as "February") out of the numbers extracted from the serial number, use Format$.

Variables   To find out the current year:

    X = Year (Now)

OR (to use a Variable):

    X = Now

    Print Minute(X)

Uses   • Create calendar programs, or timer programs, that pop up with reminders at the appropriate times.

• Create "to-do" scheduler programs, keeping track of appointments by comparing Year(Now), Month(Now) and Day(Now) against the information stored when the user first identified a particular appointment. You create a serial number for a date by using either the DateSerial or DateValue Function. (See the Example.)

• Use date-stamp data. Add the serial number to information stored by your program (data the user types in, a picture the user creates, whatever is being saved to disk for future use). You can get the current serial number by using X# = Now. Then, if you save X# to a disk file along with the other data, you'll always have a precise record of the exact second when that data was created and stored.

Cautions   • The Format$ Function offers an extremely flexible and powerful method of displaying or printing date and time information. Use it to present the results of Month and other date/time Functions, in precisely the way you want them to appear. However, Print Format$(Now, "mmmm") responds with a typo if it's October, producing *Octoler.*

• The mathematics that translate a serial number into meaningful date and time information are complex. Visual Basic, therefore, provides Functions, such as Day and Second and Format$, to translate information for you. You can *directly* manipulate the serial number that Now provides, but perhaps it's not worth the trouble because VB does it so well for you.

Technical Note: If you do want to get into direct manipulation, the whole-number portion of a date+time serial number represents the date portion, and it is calculated by this formula:

TheYear*365 + fix(TheYear/4) + 2 + DayOfYear.

For example, March 28, 1992, would give 33691. (Use the 92 in 1992 for TheYear.)

About 0.000011574 Each Second: The decimal portion of the serial number contains the time since midnight of the date. The value increases by about 0.000011574 each second, so you could divide the fractional portion of the serial number by this number to get the number of seconds that have elapsed since midnight. The serial number is only updated each second, as can be seen by repeatedly getting the value. There is really no need to know the method of storing and calculating with the serial number because VB provides a wealth of commands to extract the portion you need.

• The date/time serial numbers cover an enormous range of numbers, as if you had a roll of theater tickets, each stamped with a unique serial number, that stretched to the moon and back. Therefore, Now and other commands that work with these serial numbers are often transformed into double-precision floating-point numeric Variable types by adding the # symbol to the Variable's Name: X# = Now. X# can hold much larger numbers than a plain X Variable.

(For more on Variable types, see "Variables.")

Example   This example shows three approaches to the same timed event. We'll have the computer count up to 20,000 and see how long it takes:

```
Sub Form_Click ()

A! = Timer
B# = Now
C = Second(Now)
For t = 1 To 20000: Next t

X! = Timer
Y# = Now
Z = Second(Now)

Print "Elapsed time: "; X! - A!; " seconds."
Print
Print "First Timer "; A!
Print "Second Timer "; X!, "Difference: "; X! — A!
Print
Print "First Now "; B#
Print "Second Now "; Y#, "Difference: "; Y# — B#
Print
Print "First Second "; C
Print "Second Second "; Z, "Difference: "; Z — C

End Sub
```

First, we fill the Variable A! with the current Timer number. The Timer Function (it's not related to the Timer Control) keeps an extremely precise record of the time that has passed since midnight. This Function can be useful for measuring how long things take or for creating a feature that counts down and reminds the user to do something (like a kitchen timer does). (To find out the meaning of the different Variable symbols—! and #— used here, see "Variables.")

Then we put the Now serial number into Y# and extract the Second from Now, putting it into Z. For...Next counts from 1 to 20,000, and we report the amount of time the Loop took to count that high.

Results in Elapsed time: 2.470703 seconds

First Timer 31297.86
Second Timer 31300.33   Difference: 2.470703

First Now 33613.3622337963
Second Now 33613.3622685185   Difference 3.472222230629996D—05

First Second 37
Second Second 40   Difference 3

The number that the Now command returns to your program, like all date/time serial numbers, holds the date information to the left of the decimal point and the time information to the right. Somewhere to the right of the decimal are the data that Visual Basic can examine to extract hours, minutes and seconds.

By subtracting these two serial numbers, we get a result that resembles the other answers, but note the D-05. This notation means we must move the decimal point over five places (adding zeros) to get rid of the D-05. The actual result of subtracting the first Now result from the second one is

.0000347222230629996

As you can see, this result is remarkably precise. *Precision*, however, is not the same as *accuracy*. You can be highly precise and still wrong, as some bureaucrats and statisticians frequently demonstrate.

The Magnetron Death Tube Clock: The accuracy of the timing results we get are the best our computers can provide, and they are pretty good indeed. But we aren't tapped into the U.S. Naval Observatory relativity-corrected, uncertainty-compensated, cesium atomic Magnetron Death Tube Clock buried under the Rockies near Boulder. That clock has an accuracy based on the vibration of a cesium-133 atom—9,192,631,770 vibrations per second. The Death Tube Clock keeps an eye on the atom as it vibrates. It is a precise and accurate clock. We can't be *that* precise!

Using DefInt: It's worth recalling, as an aside, that you should insert the DefInt Statement in the General Declarations of any Form or Module where you want to make a program run faster. If we up the ante in the previous example, asking the computer to count to a million:

```
For t = 1 To 1000
For j = 1 To 1000
Next j, t
```

With DefInt A–Z in the General Declarations section of the Form, this count takes five seconds (on a 33MHz computer). Without DefInt, the same job takes nearly two minutes. (See "DefType.")

See also   Day; Financial Functions; Format$; Hour; Minute; Month; Second; Timer; Year

OBJECT BROWSER

Description Press F2 and you'll see something that appeared for the first time with Version 4 of VB. You've opened a door to a new kind of help file. It lists *Objects* in, or available to, your VB program.

Objects are self-contained entities that have Properties and Methods. A Form is an Object. It has qualities (Properties) and behaviors (Methods). A "Class" is a generic description of the qualities and behaviors of particular Objects. (You can use the general class to create a specific, particular Object.) Now, in Visual Basic, you can build your own Objects, using a "Class Module."

The purpose of the Object Browser is to provide a list of the classes available to be used in a program. Beyond that, the Browser also lists the Methods and Properties of each Class or Class Module, with an example of the syntax and a brief description of the purpose of the Method or Property.

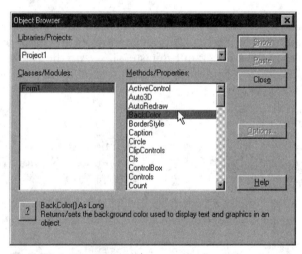

Figure O-1: The Object Browser displays Libraries, Classes, Properties and Methods.

The term *Library* refers to a collection of classes (Object templates). What appears in the Library list depends on what custom controls you've added to your current project. You'll always see your current Project (program) listed, along with VB and VBA (Visual Basic for Applications). Beyond that, it depends. Figure ON2 shows that the current program has added to the Toolbar two libraries of custom Controls: the Sheridan 3D set and the Microsoft Data Control (the database engine).

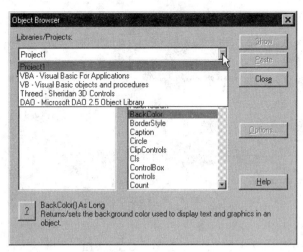

Figure O-2: VB, VBA and your current program are always included as Libraries. What else appears depends on what you ve added to your Toolbar.

How to Use the Object Browser

Notice in Figure O-2 that the VB entry says "objects and procedures." The VB lists include all the standard Controls, along with Forms, Screen, Print, OLE and other Objects. There's also a listing of Constants, hundreds of them, which are now built into VB4. This means, for example, that you can assign to a backcolor the Constant VBBlue instead of specifying an RGB value:

    BackColor = vbBlue

When you select the VB library then select Constants from the Classes/ Modules list box, you'll see the entire set of built-in Constants. Each begins with vb. When you select one of the constants by clicking on it, the Paste button in the Object Browser becomes active. Clicking on Paste will insert that Constant's name into your programming at the point where the insert cursor was when you activated the Object Browser. Therefore, you can type this:

    MousePointer =

Then you press F2 to activate the Object Browser. Select VB then Constants and find the name of the pointer style you're after. Then click on paste and the Object Browser inserts the Constant into your program:

    MousePointer = vbCrosshair

The VBA library contains sets of classes for math, financial, file manipulation and other programming commands. You'll also find a set of VBA Constants.

The Options button on the Object Browser remains inactive unless you have a Class Module in your program. If so, you can add a brief description of any Subs or Functions in your Class Module. Click on the Options button and you'll see the window shown in Figure O-3:

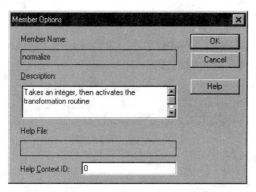

Figure O-3: Here s where you can add a brief description of procedures in your Class Module.

This description will appear in the Object Browser when the procedure is selected in the Methods/Properties list box.

See also Objects

OBJECTS   OBJECT

Description Several years ago structured programming was the rage. Largely an effort to wean programmers from bad habits that caused bugs (such as the now-disgraced GoTo command), structured programming is so widely accepted today that it isn't mentioned much anymore. These days, the buzzword is *object-oriented programming (OOP)*, which, although it can mean somewhat different things to different people, represents another step away from low-level communication with computers.

VB includes aspects of OOP. An underlying concept of OOP is interchangeable parts: the idea is that we could purchase a grammar checker, a standard file-access window or a standard music-synthesizer control routine and then attach these "Objects" to our programs. Instead of handmade individual programs, you build a program from existing parts that can just be "plugged in." This should make things easier for the user because all file access should be the same for every program in Windows.

It also should make things easier for the programmer because the disk-access or music-control part of a program is already written, tested and ready to screw onto the program. Clearly, VB's prewritten Controls are a step in this direction.

With Version 2.0, VB expanded its OOP components, including five "system" Objects: Printer, Screen, Debug, Clipboard and "App" (the program). These commands are global—you can access them anywhere in your program. The Printer and Screen Objects tell you information about the user's equipment (available fonts, etc.) and allow you to access and control the printer and screen. The Debug Object allows you to print to the Debug Window to locate errors while designing a program. The Clipboard is Windows's temporary storage zone. The App is the running program, and you can query it for information about where the program has been stored on the user's disk (X$ = App.Path) or if the user has renamed the program (X$ = App.EXEName).

Beyond this, however, Forms and Controls can also be manipulated as Objects. This provides you with efficient ways to access, manage and create copies of Forms and Controls. Several intriguing, metaphysical-sounding commands were added to VB 3. These commands represented new concepts in the Basic language: Variant, Is, Set, New, Null, Empty, Nothing, Me. And, although initially as confusing as the streets of Boston, these new concepts can add efficiency to your programming. Some of them are optional—you can do the same thing other ways but perhaps less efficiently (Variant data types). Some of them offer techniques that could be written no other way (creating clones of Forms, multiple "instances," with New; tracking the behavior of multiple Controls or Forms by using normal Variable Arrays in parallel to the Controls or Forms).

Then the Lid Blew Off
With VB 4 the language came apart. It's no longer possible to list its few Objects—most anything can be used as an Object now. Beyond this, you can create new Objects with their own Methods and Properties (see "Class Module.")

Object-oriented Programming purports to bring three primary new ideas to programming: *inheritance*, *polymorphism* and *encapsulation*. A brief explanation of these ideas doesn't do them justice, but an extended examination of the theory of OOP is beyond the scope of this book.

As a summary, then, inheritance means that you can copy and reuse objects, and the copies inherit the Methods and Properties of the original (the "class" template that describes the behaviors and qualities of these particular Objects). VB4 does not permit full OOP inheritance. Polymorphism means that you can add new Methods and Properties to an Object, but you don't get in and actually mess with the original programming of the Object, the class. Instead, you "subclass" an Object to cleanly make adjustments. This way, you avoid modifying the original template and thereby causing potential problems with other programming that uses that template (class) and depends on the stability and predictability of Objects created by the template. Encapsulation means that Objects are sealed black boxes—you can't get inside them and fool around with the programming. An Object has a set of Methods and Properties you can access from the outside, but the interior mechanisms of the Object are protected from modification.

You can modify and customize the way an Object behaves, but you're customizing a copy of the class, not the class itself. You modify a "child" Object by setting its Properties, passing parameters to its Methods, or subclassing ("replacing" with your own programming one of the Object's Methods)—rather than actually changing the code within the original Object. A subclass only substitutes your modifications for one or several Methods in the original class. The class remains unaffected and can be used in the future to stamp out (instantiate) new Objects indistinguishable from all the others it has produced or will produce. Your particular subclass Object is customized, but the class remains stable and unchanged.

After you experiment for a while, you'll probably begin to see uses for Objects, ways they can help you extend your programming capabilities. We'll go through some examples here. For additional examples, see the entries for the Object-related commands elsewhere in this book.

Quick Xerox: If you have used Control Arrays (which see) in your VB programs, you know how easy it is to clone a Picture Box or Text Box. All the clones automatically inherit most of the Properties of the original Control, just as a Xerox copy has the qualities of the original. In addition, all the clones share a single set of Events (and you specify which or how many of them should react to an Event by using their individual index numbers).

Creating copies of Forms or Controls as Objects is similar to creating a Control Array—the new Objects inherit the Properties, commands and, in the case of copied Forms, any Controls on the original Form. When you copy a Form or Control, the copies are called new instances of the original. This concept is a similar to clicking on Notepad in Windows and then clicking on it again—launching a second instance of Notepad. The two running programs come from an identical source (the NOTEPAD.EXE file on the disk), but now you have two independent, functional, running instances of this program.

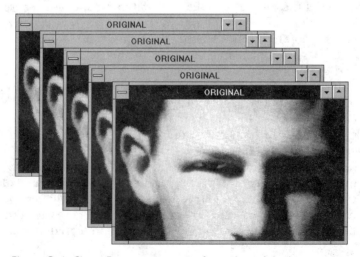

Figure O-4: Clone Forms propagate from the original.

To create an Array of Forms, start a New Project from the File Menu; then use the Form's Picture Property to bring in a graphic and change the Form's Name Property to "original." Then type the following into the Form's Click Event:

```
Sub Form_Click ( )
Static clones(3) As New original
clones(0).Left = original.Left + 600
clones(0).Top = original.Top + 400
clones(0).Show
For i = 1 To 3
    clones(i).Left = clones(i − 1).Left + 600
    clones(i).Top = clones(i − 1).Top + 400
    clones(i).Show
Next i
End Sub
```

This is similar to the way you create Control Arrays, but there are differences. To create new "instances" of a Form or Control Object and make an Array, you use the standard commands that create Variable Arrays: Dim, ReDim, Static or Global (see "Arrays").

Object Variables: As you can see, creating an Object Variable is much like creating a normal Variable. Here's how to create a single instance of a Form (as opposed to an Array). Select New Project from the File Menu, put a Label on the Form. The Form's Name should be Form1. Then put this in the Form's General Declarations section:

```
Dim NewOne As New Form1
```

We've told VB that there is a New type of object (it's a Form1 object, or more technically: a new object of the Form1 "class"), and its name is NewOne. Now we can change its Properties, just as if it were a normal Form. And we can make it visible with Show. Type the following into the Form1's Click Event:

```
Sub Form_Click ( )
    NewOne.Left = Left + 2500
    NewOne.Label1.Caption = I m a CLONE!
    NewOne.Show
End Sub
```

We're still writing our commands within Form1's Events. We can't get access to the Events in new instances of Form1; they will all respond to Events just as Form1 would. We can, however, adjust the new instances' Properties (their qualities, such as their locations onscreen). To keep this straight, just think of multiple copies of Notepad running at the same time—all the ways that Notepad behaves (its "Events," so to speak) do not change. However, we could move and resize a new instance, changing the Properties of each instance, and bring in different data to read and edit.

We set the NewOne's Left Property to 2,500 twips to the right of the left position of Form1 (*Left* with no identifier refers to the host Form, Form1). Try clicking on the clones, and they'll behave exactly as if you had clicked on the original. They'll create another instance.

What Use Is This? Think of Notepad again. If you create a Form that allows the user to view and modify .BMP pictures, you might want to propagate a clone, so the user could view two different .BMPs and cut and paste between them.

However, because clones must share Events, how could we make a clone react individually in any way? How can we create a Subroutine to enlarge the FontSize for any Form that calls the Sub, but not for all instances of that Form? In other words, a Text Box in a Control Array can identify itself by its index number, although it has the same Name as all its brother clones. But when you use Object Variables, the clones share the same Name yet do not have index numbers to differentiate them. To identify a particular Form among several instances, you use the new Me command.

Figure O-5: Use the Me command to identify an individual in a group of clones.

Select New Project from the File Menu and put this in the Form's General Declarations section:

```
Dim NewOne As New Form1
```

Reveal the clone by typing the following into the Form_DblClick Event:

```
Sub Form_DblClick ( )
    NewOne.Left = Left + Width
    NewOne.Show
End Sub
```

Then select New Module from the File Menu and type this Sub into it:

```
Sub BiggerFont (N As Form)
    Static f As Integer
    f = Not f
    If f Then
        N.FontSize = 18
    Else
        N.FontSize = 9
    End If
End Sub
```

This Subroutine will toggle the FontSize between 18 and 9 for any Form that calls it. This is exactly the way you would write this Subroutine for a normal Form. However, we identify the Form that's calling this Sub not by its Name Property but by the word Me. Type the following into the Form's Click Event:

```
Sub Form_Click ( )
    Cls
    BiggerFont Me
    Print  Make it Different
End Sub
```

The Set Command: You create Form and Control (Object) Variables in much the same way that you create normal Variables–with Dim, ReDim, Static or Global commands. Add the New command to make a clone of an existing object and all its qualities; leave out New, and you create a reference to the general Object Form (the "class"), and this reference can be used later via the Set command to apply to whatever Form(s) you want.

You manipulate Object Variables somewhat differently than normal Variables. There is one primary distinction to remember: Normal Variables *contain* their data; Object Variables *refer to* an Object. When you assign some value to a normal Variable, it holds that data:

```
A$ =  Some other thing :B$ = A$:A$ =  This
Print A$:Print B$
```

Results in This
Some other thing

In other words, assigning the contents of A$ to B$ creates a copy of the words *Some other thing* in B$. It's like making a copy of a letter from your lawyer, then putting the copy in an envelope labeled B$ and leaving the original letter in an envelope labeled A$. You've got two letters now: Changing A$ after making the copy has no effect on the contents in B$.

However, when using Object Variables, assigning A to B merely tells B where to look for data–it's like telling someone the location of the lawyer's letter. No copy is made, there is only one item and changes to that item can be detected by either A or B because they both refer to the same entity. You "assign" to an Object Variable with the Set command in addition to the = symbol. Put a Label on a Form; then type this into the Form's Click Event:

```
Sub Form_Click ( )
    Dim A As Control, B As Control
    Set A = Form1.Label1
    Set B = A
    A.Caption =  This
    Print A.Caption
    Print B.Caption
End Sub
```

Results in   This

This

Object Variables A and B both point to the same entity: Label1 on Form1. So reading or writing some data from or to a Property, such as the Caption, will be the same data for both A and B.

Forms and Controls Collections, Built-In Arrays: VB keeps a list of all the Forms in a program and all the Controls on each Form. This is similar to the items in a List Box VB maintains in an Array that you access via the List and ListCount Properties. Why do you need to know how many Forms and Controls your program has? You wrote the program, created the Forms and put the Controls on them, so you should know what's in the program, right? The problem is that in OOP you can't always know these things while designing the program.

Take an MDI (Multiple Document Interface) Form, for example. You allow the user the option of opening as many as six windows, each containing a different text document to work on. The user might open five or two or none. And perhaps the FontSize or some other Property of these various windows will be at the user's option as well. There must be a way of keeping track of what the user has done in situations like this. For one thing, when the user shuts down the program, you'll want to make sure that any edited text in any of the windows is saved to disk (or at least ask the user about it).

The syntax for accessing Forms (and their Properties) is as follows:

```
For i = 0 to Forms.Count -1
    Print Forms(i).FontSize
Next i
```

Here's an example of using the Controls Array to make all the BackColors of each Control on a Form red:

```
Sub Form_Click ( )
    For i = 0 To Controls.Count - 1
            Controls(i).BackColor = QBColor(4)
    Next i
End Sub
```

This approach is faster than naming each Control.

And as usual in VB, this activity is bidirectional—if you can query something, you can often change it:

```
Form(2).Caption =  A New Me
```

This tactic is dangerous, however, for several reasons. Primarily, you must remember that the Form and Control Arrays are unstable; the index numbers shift around when Forms are unloaded. If Forms(3) is unloaded, then Forms(4) becomes Forms(3). If you want to track the Forms, create a Global Array of Form Object Variables (see above), and use the Set command to assign each Form to a member of the Array.

Object Variables are stable. These "parallel Arrays" are useful when you allow the user to create or destroy windows (Forms) or Controls while your program runs.

Cautions   • **Cascades:** You can create a cascading (infinitely repeating) behavior if you do something like this:
In the General Declarations of Form1:

```
Dim NewOne As New Form1
Sub Form_Load ( )
        NewOne.Left = Left + Width
        NewOne.Show
End Sub
```

Each clone Form will create a new instance each time it is Loaded. You'll quickly get an Out Of Stack Space error message. For a solution, see the example under Inheritance, immediately below.

• **Inheritance:** One of the cornerstones of Object-oriented programming (OOP) is the capacity to create new Objects out of existing ones but make a few changes in the process. Recall that a class is like a template—it describes the nature and contents of a whole type of Object. For example, the class "Form" in VB describes how a Form should have the ability to be minimized by the user; to be stretched or dragged; to contain a picture—in other words all the Properties and Methods, the qualities and behaviors, of which Forms are capable.

A class is rather like a genetic code—a detailed description of the appearance and capabilities of something. When you click on the New Form button on the VB toolbar, VB brings a particular Form into being based on the class Form description. This particular Form is an Object. You can now add Controls to the Form, change its color, etc.

What, though, if you want to skip a step? Let's say that you have a Form that's well-designed to display pictures to the user. But you want the user to be able to compare two pictures at the same time. You need two of these display forms. You could start from scratch, from the class, then stretch the new form to match the size of the already designed display form. You could add the same controls, position them, and so on. But since you already have an excellent display form, why not just copy it. After you clone it, the second form will inherit all the qualities and behaviors of the original display form. These display-form Properties and Methods don't exist in the Form class (you added them), but they are all nice and tested in the display form. (So, in this sense, you can think of the display form as a new genetic code, a new "class" of its own.)

What's also useful about inheritance is that Objects can be templates for other Objects, which are then in turn modified to perform perhaps similar but not identical jobs. And, of course, you can keep on going—using modified Objects as templates for other Objects.

VB4 doesn't implement inheritance in the same, complete way that you would find it in C++. However, you can create temporary new Objects. These Objects aren't permanent (persistent). They'll work while the program is running but go away when the program stops. (You could mimic persistence by storing information about the Object in a disk file, though.)

For example, we'll start with a Form that contains an Image Control with a picture of apples at sea. Then we'll create a new instance of Form1. This second Form will inherit all the Properties and programming from the original Form. To tell them apart we'll promptly change Form2's Caption to "CLONE." Then we'll change the Picture in the Image Control. (To make the second Form's Properties—in this case its Picture Property—persistent, you could save the name of the new picture in an .INI file that the program reads every time it's run.)

Because we're putting the cloning activity into the Form_Load Event, it will be repeatedly triggered. We'll get cascading, never-ending clones because each new clone will run its Form_Load Event as it comes into existence. Then, it will bring yet another clone into existence, and so on. To prevent this, we created a Public variable in a Module (all Forms can read this variable). Then, after creating a single clone, we set that variable to True and test it, exiting the Form_Load Event if it is True.

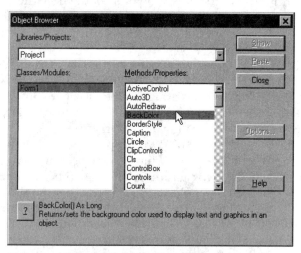

Figure O-6: We can change the Picture in Form2, a new instance of Form1.

```
Private Sub Form_Load( )
Show
If stopit = True Then Exit Sub
Dim form2 As New Form1
stopit = True
form2.Top = Form1.Top + Form1.Height + 100
form2.Caption =  CLONE
```

```
form2.Image1.Picture = LoadPicture( C:\A.BMP )
form2.Show
End Sub
```

• You can declare a Form Object Variable that is "generic" (Dim NewOne As Form) or "specific" (Dim NewOne As New Form1). However, you can only declare Control Object Variables that refer to a type of Control (Dim NewC As TextBox), not a particular existing Control such as Form1.Text1. You can also create an Object Variable that could refer to any type of Control (Dim NewC As Control). If you need to clone a particular Control and its Properties, see "Control Array." You should avoid using generic Form and Control Object Variables (Dim NewOne As Form or Dim NewC As Control) because they make programs run slower. Instead, create Variables that refer to a specific existing Form or a type of Control.

• The New command is only used to declare copies of existing Forms (cloning). It cannot be used to declare generic Form Object Variables or Control Object Variables of any kind.

• Within Subs that service various kinds of Controls, you sometimes need to know what kind of Control is calling the Sub (Text Boxes have Text Properties, but Labels have Captions). You can find out what kind of Control is calling by using the Is and Typeof commands (see "If...Then...Else"). However, you cannot use Typeof with a Select Case structure or with the Or or And command. Each Typeof comparison must be on a line of its own in your program.

• If your program no longer needs an Object Variable, free up computer memory and other resources by "emptying" the Variable in this fashion: Set Myobjvar = Nothing

• If your program propagates some clone Forms, all the clones share any commands you have put into the original ("prototype") Form's General Declarations section or within its Events. The clones also inherit all the Properties, Controls and Variables declared with Dim or Static and thus made persistent and Formwide in their scope. However, these Properties, Controls and persistent Variables can be changed independently for each clone. Each clone has a copy of these items—they're not shared, just inherited. The moral of this story is that if you want to have the clones act in unison on some data, create Global (Public) Variables. Their "Module-level" Dim- or Static-created Variables are not "in common."

• You cannot create Arrays of Object Variables.

See also   Arrays; Class Module; Is; LinkMode; Me; Multiple Document Interface; OLE; OLE Automation; Set; Variables

CT$

Description The Oct$ command is rarely used. It gives you a text ("string") Variable that contains a translation of a regular decimal number into an *octal* number. Translating numbers into octal numbers has few real uses in contemporary programming.

Numbers are always numbers—7 is 7. The computer understands what 7 represents; we understand, too.

But, to manipulate numbers mathematically, the computer prefers to work with the powers of two: 2, 4, 8, 16, 32 and so on. This creates a conflict because we humans prefer to use a system that manipulates and expresses numbers in groups of ten: 10, 100, 1,000. Our *decimal* system is not terribly compatible with the computer's *binary* system. The numbers remain the same, but the approach to them differs.

The decimal system has 10 symbols, 10 "digits," 0 through 9, but the octal system has only eight, 0 through 7. When we reach 9 and run out of symbols, we move over a place and use two columns, 10, and then start repeating the symbols. We are in effect saying: 1 of the "tens" and none of the "ones." In octal, "10" means eight items.

A Few Used Octal: A few early programming languages operated in octal. (Most early languages operated in hexadecimal (base 16), see "Hex$.") The decision of which numerical base to use seems to have been whimsical—the DEC PDP 11 series of early computers were based on octal, yet the successor to these machines, the VAX, were based on hexadecimal.

Fortunately, programming has become more human-oriented. You no longer have to deal with anything other than the decimal system for anything beyond the most arcane computing tasks. However, "low-level" computing—where you get right down into the innards and manipulate things directly—can still require that you calculate in number bases other than ten. The Windows API (see Appendix A) uses hex values to reference Constants in its calls. The use of binary (base two) counting systems is absolutely necessary when working at the hardware level with a program. One advantage of octal is that it is relatively easy to see that 0x42 or octal 102 means that bits 1 and 6 are high. It's not so easy to see the same thing with the decimal number 66. Also, hex numbers are still used in many situations, including port addresses (2F8, 3F8, etc.).

Used with Numbers translated to text for display onscreen or to a printer and rare mathematical calculations

Variables X = Oct$(19)

OR

    Q = 8
    X = Oct$(Q)

Cautions • Oct$ rounds off the number you ask it to translate to the nearest whole number. It does not express fractions, numbers involving decimal points.

Example   ? Oct$(8)

Results in   10

See also   Hex$

O LE .... CONTROL

Description

Figure O-7: The Object Linking and Embedding Control in the Toolbox.

Like the Data Control, the OLE Control is a shortcut. The OLE Control doesn't offer all the commands and options for Object Linking and Embedding that are available in VB. But the OLE Control is a quick way to set up communications between your VB program and other Windows applications. It's more than *OLE Lite*, but less than a fully *programmatic* approach.

What Is OLE?

OLE isn't finished yet, it's evolving. It's a new technology with exciting possibilities, but it's still being designed. Like high-definition television, OLE will be great when it's finally working. At this time, though, OLE is a set of specifications—more a list of goals and hopes than a smoothly working system.

Yes, VB includes dozens of OLE-related commands, Methods, Properties, etc. And yes, a few Windows applications can respond to some of these commands. But before you get very far into OLE programming, you'll realize that much about this technology remains unfinished. One side effect of this partial implementation is that the terminology is still fuzzy (in the past year, the answering application in an OLE communication has been called, successively, *client*, *destination* and *container*). Recently, the terms *producer* and *consumer* have been used. Worse than shifting terminology is the current overlap in competing OLE techniques—*there are three different ways to set up an icon that will bring up an outside application via OLE.*

In the Examples below, we'll demonstrate how to contact CorelDRAW and Word for Windows with the VB OLE Control. As you'll see, both of these outside programs respond differently to an OLE "call," and even the protocols for initiating communication with them differ. OLE programming today, even with the simplifications that the OLE Control provides, is not for the timid.

The Purpose of OLE

On the simplest level, OLE and DDE (*Dynamic Data Exchange*) are ways to pass data between programs, an attempt to bypass the need to copy something to the Clipboard from one application and then paste it from the Clipboard into another application.

Microsoft describes the goal of OLE this way: it will provide seamless integration between applications. Users can drop Excel spreadsheets into a VB application, and when they click on the spreadsheets, Excel runs in the background as a server providing them with Excel functionality without their knowledge. They don't have to exit and run Excel, and then go back to VB (or Word, or whatever). Instead, the tools and facilities of one application can be made available to another application.

OLE and DDE will eventually make communication between programs instantaneous and efficient, and will free data from being "located" within particular applications. A picture can exist *simultaneously* in your VB program, in a Word document, in CorelDRAW, etc. If you make changes to a picture in any of these applications, the change appears in all of them. Likewise, if you click on a picture in Word that was created in CorelDRAW,

CorelDRAW starts running and displays that picture for you to edit (because CorelDRAW has better facilities for editing pictures than does Word). This isn't precisely the same as "invisible background" behavior or "seamless integration." You do see the originating application pop up onscreen, but it is a taste of things to come.

All of these features have great potential and will be terrific when fully implemented. For now, though, OLE, DDE and particularly the new OLE 2.0 standard are cumbersome. At the time of this writing, VB and Publisher 2.0 are the *only* Windows programs that are capable of OLE 2.0. Even when you're using OLE 1.0 commands and the DDE commands built into VB, you'll still get unexpected results. All of this points to a technology that is in the process of being constructed, not a finished tool you can just pick up and work with easily.

The Goals of OLE

Microsoft has projected impressive goals for OLE and the related technology of OLE Automation. Programmers can plug prewritten, pretested modules (Objects) into programs that they are creating. Programming will be more efficient and the resulting programs can be richer and contain more features. Also, as the barriers that currently separate one application from another—and data from applications—come down, it will eventually seem as if there is just one amorphous "program" in the computer. Programs will be able to pass data, messages, etc., back and forth freely. You'll be able to drag something from one program and drop it into another program: therefore those two programs will seem to be merely two opened windows of the same program. One program will be able to utilize the features of another program, further blurring the distinction between the two programs. When these goals are realized, OLE and automation should be most valuable for both programmers and users. But that day is not yet here.

Lifting the Haze

The terminology is especially confusing at this point. DDE does some of the things that OLE does, but OLE cannot do some of the things that DDE can do. OLE *linking* is very similar, from the user's point of view, to OLE *embedding*; in both cases, clicking on data brings up the application that created that data. In both cases, the user can click on a graphic representation of the data (rather than a simple icon) to bring up the originating application. Then there is a *separate* category of interprogram communication called *DDE* with its own variety of *linking* and *embedding*.

Another way of contrasting OLE and DDE is to compare *how* DDE and OLE exchange information. OLE uses an object, which can reside in the VB application (embedded), or on disk with a link to the object from VB (linked). DDE, by contrast, essentially hooks up a pipe (or link) between two applications and when the data changes in one application, it is updated, through the pipe, in the other application. During DDE, both applications have copies of the same data.

In the next few paragraphs we'll try to lift some of the haze so you can, if you want, work with the OLE Control and perhaps also write some programs involving DDE linking (see "LinkMode"). If you intend to work with OLE in the future, perhaps wrestling with it now will give you a good foundation. You'll at least get a feel for creating programs using what will eventually be exciting and valuable techniques for breaking down the barriers between applications, and the barriers between programs and their data.

Embedding means that the Object data is actually in your program; that you can create a picture in Paintbrush and place it into a VB program. Later, if you want to make some changes to the picture while you're working in the VB program, you can click on the picture, and Paintbrush automatically appears with the picture loaded. You're ready to edit the picture in the program that created it. While you're editing (if the Update-Options Property of the OLE Control is set to 0, "Automatic," the default), the changes will also appear in the picture in your VB program. Thus, pictures and words more or less exist outside the programs that created them. They are available everywhere at once. The old approach of first running a program and then loading in something to work on is no longer necessary.

OLE linking means that the object data is in a file on disk, that VB knows the filename and path of a particular file (and the name of the application that created it). But unlike embedded OLE objects, the data of a linked OLE object is not *contained* within the VB program. (Therefore, linked OLE results in smaller VB .EXE programs unless the embedded object is created while the program is running. But the linked data cannot be *directly* manipulated within the VB program.) One advantage of linking is that if the file is updated, many other applications linked to that file will show the change.

Two Kinds of Linking

Unfortunately for the purposes of trying to dispell the haze surrounding OLE, there are two kinds of *linking*: OLE linking and DDE linking. To users, OLE linking is virtually indistinguishable from OLE embedding. Double-click on an embedded *or* linked OLE Control (which will contain a sample of the data or an icon), and the outside application that created the data will appear with the data loaded and ready for editing. From the user's point of view, there appears to be no difference. However, after some changes have been made to the data, a linked OLE Control might still look the same. (This depends on the setting of the UpdateOptions Property, which see later in this section.)

The data (if you aren't using an icon) that is visible to the user of a *linked* OLE Control is merely a *picture*, not all that different from an icon. It merely *symbolizes* some data as it would look in the originating application—so that the user can remember what will happen if the symbol is clicked. This is more or less a superior kind of icon, and a VB program containing a linked OLE Control is merely acting as a program-launcher—a kind of advanced Shell.

With OLE linking, the data (text or picture) is controlled and manipulated *by the program that created it*. For example, if you link a Word for Windows document, that document is edited, saved, etc., by Word (not via your VB OLE Control). The only information in VB is the path and filename (the SourceDoc Property of the OLE Control) and perhaps some other information (such as the optional SourceItem Property).

With OLE embedding, however, the data is contained *within* your VB program and is saved *by* your VB program. In practice, though, any editing is still done in the outside application that created the original data file. Activating an OLE embedded or linked object still brings up the outside application for the actual manipulation of that data.

But how do you cause *instant communication*? How do you make a change in a Text Box and have that change instantly appear in a running Word for Windows document? You can use OLE linking or embedding (with the UpdateOptions Property set to 0, Automatic, the default). Or you can use programming commands called *DDE linking*, for Dynamic Data Exchange.

DDE linking performs two services for a pair of programs running simultaneously. It can pass text or graphics between the two programs. This updating can occur either instantaneously and constantly, or only when the user requests the update. (A program could also request an update, at timed intervals if desired.) The second service provided by linking is that one program can pass commands to another (see "LinkExecute").

What primarily distinguishes DDE linking from DDE embedding is that DDE embedding (like OLE linking) does not require that both programs be running for the communication to take place between them. Embedding is slightly more automatic in that it calls up whatever program created the data; it starts the program running without any intervention from the user and without any preconditions. The data simply invokes the right program.

DDE vs. OLE 2.0

DDE (non-OLE) linking (see "LinkMode") is the most dynamic of these various techniques at this time because it is the most mature. You can link a VB Text Box to a Word text file, open Word and watch both copies of the text change as you edit in the VB Text Box. Non-OLE linking (called DDE) is as yet the only way to allow the user to edit text or graphics *within* your VB program. In addition to that, because VB contains the actual data, you can use all of VB's facilities and commands (such as InStr to search for particular words in the text) to affect, display or manipulate the data however you wish. Essentially, DDE gives you the *programming commands* to work with linked data *directly* (if you fully understand the outside application's format). However, OLE 2.0 promises to make this process more efficient in the future, via *OLE Automation* (see the "OLE Automation" entry).

OLE 2.0

Version 2.0 of OLE (it first appeared in Visual Basic 3.0) adds several new *potential* capabilities and expands the power and stability of OLE. Most notable is *OLE Automation*, which, in theory, will allow you to utilize features of OLE-capable applications in your VB programs and vice versa. For example, you could request, via OLE Automation, that the contents of a VB Text Box be checked for correct grammar—*by the grammar checker built into Word for Windows,* or you could create an object with VB that would provide services to an outside application (see "Class Moduule"). Being able to borrow facilities from outside applications is an exciting possibility. At the time of this writing, however, the only OLE 2.0-capable application extant is Publisher 2.0 (not Word, Excel, Access nor any applications from outside Microsoft). Visual Basic is the first product to have OLE 2.0, Publisher the second. As soon as other applications get OLE 2.0, VB can have conversations with them. For now, Visual Basic and Publisher have the only phones in town. Word can be contacted, too.

Cautions   • If you want to utilize the "Insert Object" Window with an OLE Control that is already placed on a Form, click on it using the right mouse button and select "Insert Object." (A user can also click on an OLE Control with the right mouse button and a pop-up menu will appear, listing appropriate actions, called *verbs*, that can be performed by the Control while the VB program is running.)

Terminology

In Visual Basic 1.0, the program in an OLE "conversation" that supplied data was called the *server*, and the program that received data (and perhaps displayed it) was called the *client*. New, somewhat clearer terminology was used in VB 2.0: *server* became *source*, and *client* became *destination*. Now, with VB 3.0 and VB4, the *client* is called the *container* application.

Similarly, when referring to the types of links, VB 1.0 used the term *hot link* for what is now called an *automatic link*. Also, what VB 1.0 called a *cold link* is now called a *manual link*.

Finally, the data in outside applications is broken down into "classes" or types of data. Excel 5.0, for instance, had three "classes"—spreadsheets, charts and macro sheets. And their "class names" were "ExcelWorksheet," "ExcelChart" and "ExcelMacrosheet." These class names, however, changed in Excel 7.0. You can expect more changes in terminology as OLE technology evolves. Aside from the inconvenience this instability creates, it also means that a VB program you write today using OLE is unlikely to work without modification in the future.

Which Applications Are OLE-capable?

You can't launch all applications via OLE: a Windows program must have OLE capability built into it by the program's manufacturer. (Note that although only VB and Publisher 2.0 are OLE 2.0-capable, several applications are OLE 1.0-capable, and the OLE Control can contact and manipulate them.) Which of your programs are OLE-capable? To find out, start a New Project from the File Menu; then put an OLE Control on the Form and the Insert Object Window will pop up, containing a List Box with the names of all OLE-responsive applications currently registered with your Windows.

The OLE Control is a "Custom Control," which means it is not built into VB and thus requires a special file to be Loaded into your VB. OLE requires the MSOLE2.VBX file. If it isn't listed in your Project Window, use Add File from the File Menu to add MSOLE2.VBX before using an OLE Control. (MSOLE2.VBX is in the WINDOWS\SYSTEM directory.)

Moreover, if you create a VB .EXE program that contains an OLE Control and give the program to someone else to use, you must make sure that eleven files exist in the user's WINDOWS\SYSTEM directory: COMPOBJ.DLL, MSOLE2.VBX, MSOLEVBX.DLL, OLE2.REG, OLE2.DLL, OLE2CONV.DLL, OLE2DISP.DLL, OLE2NLS.DLL, OLE2PROX.DLL, STORAGE.DLL and VBOA300.DLL. Beyond that, the DOS program SHARE.EXE must be in the user's AUTOEXEC.BAT file and OLE2 itself must be "registered" with the computer. You can accomplish all this by using the VB Setup Wizard, or you can check to see whether the file OLE2.DLL is installed in the user's WINDOWS\SYSTEM directory. If it isn't, you must copy all the files named above into the WINDOWS\SYSTEM directory and then instruct the user to register it by typing the following in Windows's File/Run dialog box:

```
REGEDIT /S OLE2.REG
```

For information on how to do this in Windows 95, see "Cautions" under "OLE Automation."

Examples

We'll look at two examples here, one illustrating embedding, the other illustrating linking.

Embedding

Using the OLE Control to embed and link is easier than accomplishing those tasks through programming alone. With the OLE Control, you can embed and link in several ways, although at the time of this writing, OLE communication to outside programs is unpredictable. Let's do what we can, though, to illustrate the OLE Control's capabilities. First, we'll use the Insert Object Window, which automatically pops up. Put an OLE Control on a Form, and you'll see the window shown in Figure O-8.

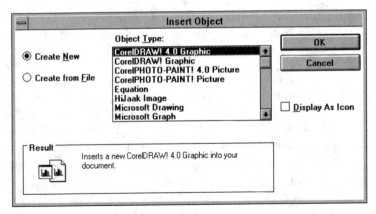

Figure O-8: The Insert Object Window.

Create New File

The default in this window is "Create New" (embed) and display the data (not an icon). Double-click on one of the programs listed under "Object Type," and the selected outside application will appear, ready for you to type in a new file or create a new graphic. We'll select a CorelDRAW! 4.0 graphic for this example. Within CorelDRAW, we load a clip art picture into a CorelDRAW drawing surface. If you attempt to close CorelDRAW at this point, you will be reminded that this picture is communicating with an outside program, that closing it will "close the connection," and you'll be asked if you want to "Update" it. Answer yes, or simply select "Update" from the outside application's File Menu and don't close the outside application. (Some applications will display different messages; some will not automatically list "Update" as an option on their File Menu. OLE is a new and, as yet, inconsistent facility.)

Now minimize the outside application, and you should see the data displayed within your OLE Control. Set the OLE Control's SizeMode Property to AutoSize so that the entire datum will be displayed. (The default SizeMode is "Clip," which means that part of the datum can be hidden from view, but the datum will be its correct, original size within the OLE Control. The third SizeMode is "Stretch," which allows you to drag the image to whatever size you wish.)

Figure O-9: The OLE Control filled with data from an outside program (Clip Art courtesy of CorelDRAW!)

Try pressing F5 to run your VB program. Double-clicking on the OLE Control will load the outside application from disk (or switch to it if it's currently running). The data will automatically be loaded into the outside application, ready for editing.

If, when you first put an OLE Control on a Form, you select "Display as Icon" in the Insert Object Window, instead of the data, an icon representing the outside application will appear when the VB program is run. Otherwise, everything else behaves the same as if the data is showing.

Create From File

The alternative way to embed an outside object via the OLE Control is to click on the "Create from File" option when the Insert Object Window appears. You'll see no difference in VB's behavior; you're still embedding. Double-clicking on the embedded data (or icon) will still bring up the outside application with the data loaded. The only difference between embedding via "Create New" and "Create from File" is that the *from File* option starts things off with a picture or text that already exists in a disk file. Also, you don't define the size, color or whatever other qualities can be defined for a new object in the outside application. Instead, with "Create from File," your object will be using that file as the template.

Linking

To *link* using an OLE Control, start a New Project in VB's File Menu and place an OLE Control on the Form. In the Insert Object Window, select "Create from File" and click on the Link option. Then browse or type in the filename of the file you want to link to VB and to the outside application that created it.

For this example, we're going to use a .DOC file, so the outside application will be Word for Windows. You are supposed to see an image of the data—part of a text file in this case (unless you select the "Show as Icon" option in the Insert Object Window). Nevertheless, at the time of this writing, you will see a Word for Windows icon in your OLE Control, no text.

Running your VB program and then clicking on the OLE Control will bring up Word for Windows with the text file loaded and ready for editing. You would get precisely the same result if you clicked on an OLE Control with an *embedded* data object.

The primary distinction is that the data in an OLE Control from an embedded object is the actual data; data displayed in an OLE linked object is just a symbol of the data, essentially an icon. At this point in the development of OLE technology, though, particularly from the user's point of view, the differences are largely academic. For more information on the implications of *embedding* versus *linking*, see "Description" above.

The OLE Pop-Up Menu
When an OLE Control contains some data, clicking with the *right* mouse button on the Control while designing your program will bring up a pop-up menu, as shown in Figure O-10.

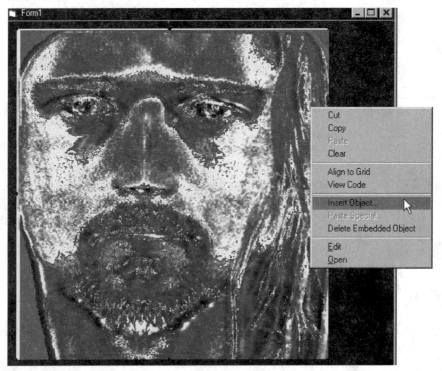

Figure O-10: You can define or modify the contents of an
OLE Control during program design.

This menu has several options. Insert Object brings up the Insert Object Window. Paste Special will insert data that has been copied to the Clipboard from a running OLE-capable program like Word for Windows. Delete Embedded Object does just what its name says. Activate Contents mimics the behavior of clicking on the OLE Control while the VB program is running. Edit Package brings up Windows's Package Editor. Note that Activate Contents and Edit Package are below a separator bar in the pop-up menu. They are *verbs* (actions the application can take during OLE conversations). Verbs are not necessarily the same for all applications. Anything below the separator bar in the pop-up menu is a verb.

Programmatic OLE

A whole set of VB commands allows you to manipulate Object linking and embedding (and Dynamic Data Exchange) *while a program is running*. You don't need to utilize an OLE Control to create links; you can use a Text Box, for example (see "LinkMode").

Programmatic means done via programming commands while a program runs. You can use this approach (or combine it with setting some Properties in the Properties Window during program design).

Here are the steps to embed a Word for Windows document via programming:

1. Put an OLE Control on a Form. When the Insert Object Window comes up, select Cancel.

2. In the Form_Load Event, type the following:

```
Sub Form_Load ()
    Show
    Ole1.Class = "WordDocument"
    Ole1.SourceDoc = "C:\WINWORD\EXIT.DOC"
    Ole1.Action = 1
End Sub
```

The SourceDoc should be your path to some Word document that exists on your disk drive. The Action determines what kind of OLE takes place, in this case (1), which means create a link. The difference in this programmatic approach is that you're writing commands to set three Properties instead of answering questions in the OLE Control's Insert Object Window and then letting the OLE Control set the Properties for you.

OLE Control Properties

Some of the OLE Control's Properties behave the same way they do with other Controls: BackColor, BorderStyle, DragIcon, DragMode, Height, Left, Name, Tag, Top, Visible and Width. See these entries for more on these Properties.

However, many Properties of an OLE Control are unique. Following is a list of the Properties that apply only to the OLE Control.

Action

An OLE Control can do a variety of things (Paste Special, Link, etc.). Setting the Action Property while a program is running causes the Control to take a particular action.

For example, Ole1.Action = 1 creates a link.

Here are the settings:

0   This setting creates an OLE embedded object. You must first set the Class and OleTypeAllowed Properties, to tell VB what kind of outside application will be involved and that we're doing an embed. Set OleTypeAllowed to 1 (Embedded) or 2 (Either). To see what the Class Property can be set to, click on the ellipsis (...) in the Properties Window after clicking on Class. You'll see the list.

1   This setting creates an OLE linked object from a file on the disk drive. You must set the OleTypeAllowed Property to 0 (Linked) or 2 (Either). And the SourceDoc Property must be the path and filename of the file you intend to serve as the data for this link. Optionally, you can specify which *part* of the file is linked by setting the Source-Item Property.

4   This setting puts a copy of the contents of the OLE Control (whether linked or embedded) into the Clipboard. Both the data and link information about that data go to the Clipboard.

5   This setting puts a copy of the contents of the Clipboard into your OLE Control. You first must set the OleTypeAllowed Property, and you should make sure that the PasteOK Property is True or –1. This PasteOK number tells you that there *is* something in the Clipboard that can be put into your OLE Control.

6   This setting updates the OLE Control, as if the user had clicked on Update in the outside application's File Menu. The data in the application, even if it's been modified, will now appear in its current state within your OLE Control. This setting interacts with the Up-dateOptions Property, which see later in this section.

7   This setting activates the OLE Control. The outside application will come up, and you can edit the data (just as if the user had double-clicked on the OLE Control). You could put Ole1.Action = 7 in a Command Button, for example. The Action Property interacts with the Verb Property (see later in this section).

9   This setting "closes" an *embedded* OLE Control—breaking the connection with the outside application. It does nothing if this OLE Control is linked. This "closing" mimics what happens if the user clicks on "Exit" or otherwise shuts down an outside application.

10 This setting "deletes" or removes the current data in an OLE Control. The picture or text goes away, and the Control is left empty.

11   This setting "saves" the data in an OLE Control to a disk file. You first must set the Filenumber Property and the file must also be Opened for binary access (see "Open").

12   This setting "reads" the data from a disk file that was saved using option 11. You first must set the Filenumber Property and, again, the file must also be first Opened for Binary Access (see "Open"). There is an example of how to use this setting in VB's online help.

14   This setting displays the Insert Object Window. The user can then use this window to create an OLE connection, either linked or embedded. The OleTypeAllowed Property can control which type of connection is the default.

15   This setting displays the Paste Special Window. Now the user can paste data from the Clipboard to the OLE Control. The data must have first been "Copied" from an OLE-capable outside application.

17   This setting updates the list of Verb Properties that an OLE Control's data permits.

18   This setting saves data in the old OLE 1.0 file format.

AppIsRunning

This Property tells you whether the outside application that created the data in the OLE Control is now running. It is either True or False (–1 or 0).

AutoActivate

This Property determines how the OLE Control is triggered. In other words, it determines when the Control brings up the outside application with the appropriate text or picture to be edited.

Here are the settings:

0   The user cannot activate the OLE Control. Your program must activate it, perhaps in response to the user clicking on a Command Button: Ole1.Action = 7.

1   The OLE's action will trigger when the OLE Control gets the focus, for example, via the SetFocus command. If the user clicked it *once*, that would give the Control the focus. This setting doesn't work at the time of this writing because there aren't any applications that support it yet. Soon, this technique will have interesting uses. For one thing, it enables what is known as "in-place activation"—editing something right in VB without having to go to a separate window.

2   With this setting, the Control will be activated when the user double-clicks on the OLE Control (the default).

AutoVerbMenu

This Property is either True (the default) or False. It determines whether a pop-up menu appears when the user clicks the right mouse button on the OLE. Clicking will give the user various choices (the Control's *verbs*), such as Activate Contents, Edit Package, etc.

Class

This Property tells VB the "class name" of the data in an OLE Control. Excel version 4.0 has three "classes"—spreadsheets, charts and macro sheets. And their "class names" are "ExcelWorksheet," "ExcelChart" and "ExcelMacrosheet."

To see what class names are registered as available on your computer, click on the ellipsis (...) in the Properties Window with the Class Property highlighted.

When you put data from an outside application into the OLE Control by using the Insert Object Window, VB automatically inserts the Class Property, so you don't have to worry about it. Why worry? Three reasons: Class names are unstable at this point; you can't know what the user might have available on his or her computer; *and these names will change when OLE 2.0 is fully implemented.*

Data

This Property provides a "handle" (see "hDC") to the data. With this Property, you can transmit data to an outside application. Beware: This Property requires highly sophisticated programming.

DataText

This Property can receive or transmit a text ("string") Variable to or from an OLE Control. Beware: This Property is highly sophisticated and highly problematic at the time of this writing.

DisplayType

This Property is set to 0 (the default) or 1. When it's set to 0, the Insert Object Window "Display as Icon" Check Box is not selected. When it's set to 1, the Check Box is selected. If 0, the OLE Control will try to show the true visual representation of the object data as would be seen in the host application. If 1, just an icon is displayed.

To *program* this decision (to let the user choose, for example, between the options), use the Action Property (setting 14 or 15).

FileNumber

You use this Property in conjunction with the Action Property (when it's set to 11 or 12, save or read a file). FileNumber specifies the filenumber and must be a file Open for Binary Access (see "Open"). You can use the FreeFile command (which see) to get an unused filenumber.

Format

This Property is a text ("string") Variable that reports to your program (or changes) the format that will be used to transmit data between an outside application and your VB OLE Control.

You use Format with the Data and DataText Properties, and the same warning that applies to them applies to this Property. Beware: Format is highly sophisticated and highly problematic at the time of this writing.

HostName

This Property is the title of a window that the user will see when editing OLE data. Some applications don't support HostName. The HostName appears, for example, when you go to Word for Windows to edit your OLE object—the title bar in Word says "Object in ..." Whatever you set for the HostName will replace the ... (ellipsis) in this example.

lpOleObject

This Property provides the *address* of the OLE object. Some OLE 2.0 Dynamic Link Libraries require the address of your Control. Using this Property is similar to passing an hDC (which see) during any other API call.

ObjectAcceptFormatsCount

This Property tells your program the number of formats that OLE Control can *receive*. This Property is an index for the ObjectAcceptFormats Property text Array. It is to ObjectAcceptFormats what ListCount is to List. You use it with the Data and DataText Properties.

ObjectAcceptFormats

This Property tells your program which formats an OLE Control can receive. It is an Array Variable (like ListBox.List), and it tells you the acceptable formats that you can specify for the OLE Format Property. If the OLE Control doesn't contain any data, trying to access this Property will cause an error. The only ObjectAcceptFormat for an OLE Control containing a Word for Windows document is "Native." You use it with the Data and DataText Properties. This Property lets your program find out what formats can be used to send data to an Object.

ObjectGetFormatsCount

This Property is similar to ObjectAcceptFormatsCount, but ObjectGet-FormatsCount tells you the number of formats the OLE Control data can *provide* or *send* to the communicating outside application. You use this Property with the Data and DataText Properties.

ObjectGetFormats

This Property is a text ("string") Array that your program can read to find out which formats the OLE Control can *send* to the communicating outside application. You can use this information to set the Format Property when you want to receive data via the Data and DataText Properties. The Object-GetFormats for an OLE Control containing a Word for Windows document are Native, CF_METAFILEPICT, CF_DIB, CF_BITMAP and CF_TEXT. You use this Property with the Data and DataText Properties.

Object

You can use this "Object" to specify the OLE Control's data (its "object") if you are attempting the currently unavailable *OLE Automation* (which see below).

To find out what Properties and Methods you can use with a particular Object (like a Word for Windows document), you have to check the manual for that Object's parent application.

ObjectVerbFlags

This text ("string") Array lists the current status of the *verbs* (the actions an OLE Object can take). If you want to show the user a menu or list of an OLE Object's verbs, you use the ObjectVerbFlags Array to detect which verbs were currently checked, unavailable, etc. (Your menu would be a duplicate of the pop-up menu that appears when the user clicks the *right* mouse button on an active OLE Control.)

In other words, this Property tells you *how* to display each verb in your menu. The *ObjectVerbs* Property provides the Array of actual verbs; the *ObjectVerbFlags* Property tells you the status of each of these verbs while a program is running.

Here are the possible settings:

0   Enabled
1   Grayed
2   Disabled (but not grayed)
8   Checked
2048 Display a separator bar

ObjectVerbsCount

You can use this Property to list the number of *verbs* (behaviors) that can be performed by data embedded or linked within an OLE Control. In other words, you use ObjectVerbsCount to find out how many *verbs* the Object has. You use this Property with the ObjectVerbs Property.

ObjectVerbs

This text ("string") Array lists the actions (verbs) that are currently possible for a given OLE Control Object (the data in the Control). For an OLE containing a Word for Windows document, the verbs are "&Activate Contents" (bring up Word with the document loaded) and "&Edit Package" (bring up the "Edit Package" Window). Use the ObjectVerbsCount Property to know how many verbs you can list for this particular OLE Control. The *Action* and *Verb* Properties can then be used to perform one of the actions.

The first item in the ObjectVerbs Array, OLE1.ObjectVerbs(0), is the default. When the user clicks on the OLE Control (or your program activates it by using OLE1.Action = 7), this default verb will be the action taken.

Note that this is a way for you to *duplicate* via programming the pop-up menu that automatically appears when the user clicks with the right mouse button on an OLE Control. Similarly, many OLE-capable outside applications will include an "Object" option in their Edit Menu during an OLE conversation. Clicking on this option will bring up the menu of verbs from which the user can choose.

OleTypeAllowed

This Property governs whether the OLE Control can contain a linked or an embedded object or both. The default is "either," meaning that either type is allowed.

Here are the settings:

0   Linked only

1   Embedded only

2   Either linked or embedded

This Property is useful if you are allowing the *user* to establish a connection between your OLE Control and an outside application, and you want to control which kind of OLE the user will be permitted to create. The user can click on an OLE Control with the right mouse button and, usually, create a new OLE communication, delete the current object, etc. (Right-clicking displays a pop-up menu with the list of verbs for that OLE object.) However, you can disable this pop-up menu by setting Ole1.AutoVerbMenu = 0. In that case, the user cannot manipulate the OLE Control's object by clicking the right mouse button.

OleType

This Property tells you the status of an OLE Control while the program is running: X = Ole1.OleType. The value of X will tell you:

0   There is a linked object in the OLE Control.

1   There is an embedded object in the OLE Control.

3   There is no object in the OLE Control.

PasteOK

This Property lets you know while your program is running whether data in the Clipboard can be pasted into your OLE Control.

    X = Ole1.PasteOK

If X is True (–1), things will work out fine if you try (or the user tries) to paste data from the Clipboard with Ole1.Action = 5.

If X is False (0), you'd better not try it. Perhaps you included a Paste option in your VB program. If X is False, you should gray or disable that option.

SizeMode

How this Property is set determines how data (or an image of data if you are linking) will appear within the OLE Control. It is similar to the Stretch Property of the Image Control.

Following are the three possible settings for the SizeMode Property:

0   Clipped. The data is displayed in its actual size, regardless of how big or small you've made the OLE Control on the Form. If the data is larger than the OLE Control's boundaries, the user will not see part of the data; it will be *clipped* off. This setting is the default.

1   Stretched. The data will be forced to fill the OLE Control's frame. This setting can distort data by changing its aspect ratio.

2   Autosize. The OLE Control's frame is made to conform to the actual size of the data being displayed. If the size of the data changes, the size of the OLE Control on the Form will change correspondingly (this change can mess up the design of your Form while the program is running). However, you'll get some warning: the OLE Control's ReSize Event will trigger before the resizing actually becomes visible. You could react within the ReSize Event if you wish. Perhaps the safer course, though, would be to set Ole1.SizeMode = 1; the size of the OLE Control will then remain stable on your Form, regardless of what the user might do in the outside application to modify the data.

Note: The OLE Control's ReSize Event contains these two Variables:

```
Sub OLE1_Resize (HeightNew As Single, WidthNew As Single)
End Sub
```

These Variables tell you—before any actual changes take place—the new height and width of the OLE Control. You could therefore forbid this change to take place if it would ruin the design of your Form or cover up some other Control. (Forbidding the change is only necessary if the OLE Control's SizeMode Property is set to AutoSize.)

You can *redefine* the HeightNew or WidthNew Variable within the OLE_Resize Event:

```
Sub OLE1_Resize (HeightNew As Single, WidthNew As Single)
    If HeightNew > 1200 Then HeightNew = 1200
End Sub
```

This example would have the effect of clipping off the bottom of the data displayed within the OLE Control.

SourceDoc

This Property is a text ("string") Variable that names the path (directory\filename) of the disk file that holds the linked or embedded data. When you use the OLE Control, the Insert Object Window automatically specifies the SourceDoc Property.

SourceItem

You can optionally *link* to only part of a file—a paragraph in a large document, a set of cells in a spreadsheet. The SourceItem property is a text ("string") Variable that defines this subset of a file. The syntax used to describe the subset varies from application to application, and you should look at the program's manual for the correct wording.

When you're linking to Excel, you can specify an individual cell (A2B2), a range (A2B2:A5:B5) or a named range ("costs").

UpdateOptions

This Property governs whether a linked Object is updated immediately when data is changed, only when the data is saved to disk, or only when the update Action (Ole1.Action = 6) or an Update menu option is selected. You cannot change this Property while a program is running.

Here are the settings:

0 Automatic Update (the default). When the data is changed, such as editing a Word document, the linked data also changes.

1 Frozen Update. The linked data only changes when the file is saved to disk from within the outside application.

2 Manual Update. The linked data only changes when the user selects "Update" from an outside application's File Menu, or your program sets the Action Property to 6.

No matter which method is used, when an update *does* take place, the Updated *Event* is triggered.

Verb

When the user double-clicks an OLE Control (with the left mouse button), the Control can be *activated*. (Whether you can activate the Control depends, however, on the setting of the AutoActivate Property, which see.) Or your program can activate it by using Ole1.Action = 7. Precisely what *happens* when an OLE Control is activated depends on the setting of the Verb Property.

Most outside applications will respond to the "Edit" verb, meaning that you can change the OLE data; the outside application appears and the data is loaded into it, ready for editing. However, all OLE-capable outside applications can have their own custom set of verbs. (See the ObjectVerbs Property; it is a list of the permitted verbs for a particular application. However, the following standard verbs *may not be listed* in the Object-

Verbs Property's list. Nonetheless, all OLE-capable applications are supposed to react, at a minimum, to the following verbs.)

0   Whatever is the default behavior for OLE data with this outside application.

1   Data is made ready for editing. If an outside application supports it, this will trigger in-place activation.

2   A separate window is displayed, with the data inside and (if applicable) ready for editing.

3   The outside application is hidden (used with OLE embedding only).

Whatever positive number is entered corresponds to the verb (in that index position) that you would find in the ObjectVerbs list.

If the AutoVerbMenu Property is set to True, the user can see a list of an outside application's verbs by *right-clicking* on the OLE Control.

OLE Control Events

All but one of the OLE Control's Events behave as they do for other Controls: Click, DblClick, DragDrop, DragOver, GotFocus, KeyDown, KeyPress, KeyUp, LostFocus, MouseDown, MouseMove, MouseUp and Resize. For more on these Events, see their entries elsewhere in this book.

The Updated Event, however, is unique to the OLE Control.

Updated

This Event is triggered when OLE data is edited or changed.

```
Sub OLE1_Updated (Code As Integer)
End Sub
```

The Variable *Code* tells you what kind of change occurred to the linked or embedded data, according to the following list:

0   The data has been modified. Note that the Updated Event can be triggered quite often—every time the user draws a line in CorelDRAW or fills an area with a new color, etc.

1   The outside application saved the data to disk.

2   The outside application has closed the file that contains the data (which doesn't necessarily mean the data has been saved). This setting can be triggered if the user closes the outside application by pressing Alt+F4 or any other method.

3   The outside application has renamed the file that contains the data.

Your VB program may need to respond to one or more of these conditions. Essentially, you would be trying to prevent a loss of data if the user had modified something and that modification should be saved to disk. However, most outside applications would not allow a modified file to be closed, for example, without first asking the user if the changes should be saved to disk.

OLE Control Methods

The Drag, Move, Refresh, SetFocus and ZOrder Methods all behave as they do with other Controls. See their entries elsewhere in this book. The OLE Control has no unique Methods.

See also LinkMode; Objects; OLE Automation

OLE Automation

CONTROL

Description OLE Automation is a highly sophisticated set of techniques. It isn't limited to linking or embedding, *per se*. The term OLE has broadened to include several, somewhat vaguely related, concepts—in-place editing, object oriented programming, OLE "container" Controls, and "OLE" Automation.

With OLE Automation you can accomplish three jobs. First, you can use outside applications' features—such as Word's word counter or spell checker—for your own purposes within a VB program. For example, you can pass the contents of a Text Box to Word, and ask Word to pass back statistics about that text—the number of paragraphs, words, etc.

Second, you can use VB to closely control the behavior of outside applications and their data. For example, you could trigger macros in Excel. Or you could make Word load a particular file, format it a particular way, print five copies of it, then shut down.

Third, you can create new Objects in VB (by using the new VB4 "Class Module") that perform services for outside applications. In this section we'll provide examples of the first two automation techniques. See "Class Module" for an example of the third—how to turn a VB program into an Object.

At the time of this writing, OLE Automation is part theoretical, part usable. Only a handful of applications currently support OLE 2.0—notably Excel and, to a degree, Word—and that support is a requirement for Automation. (Applications must "expose their Objects" to outside contact, among other things.) But when OLE is all finished and working smoothly—when most applications and even Windows itself are OLE-compliant—the techniques will be quite useful. OLE will take us way past the capabilities of, for example, the SendKeys command or DDE. With OLE Automation, you enter the alternative reality of free-floating Objects.

What Are Objects?

The term Object is so broad that it's hard to get a handle on it. What, we might ask, is *not* an Object? In common parlance, an Object is something in the material world, something you could look at or touch, like a pen or a walnut. A non-Object is something non-material, such as greed.

In Visual Basic, even this distinction breaks down because many VB Objects are simply clusters of information, and information isn't material—although it can be expressed by, or contained in, material things. Perhaps the easiest way to visualize a VB Object is to think of it as a bundle of information which might include data, Methods, Properties, or a combination of them.

In VB, an Object can be almost anything—a piece of data; a whole database; a representation of a database; a range of data plus details about its filename, its subdivisions (fields, indexes, whatever) and so on. Then there are Screen Objects, and you can find out information about such Objects while a program is running by using Print Screen.ActiveControl.Caption. And there is a Printer Object, and an Object representing your program itself (the "App" Object).

Also, each Form and Control is considered an Object; they are listed under "Object:" in VB programming windows when you double-click on a Form. And you can create Object Variables representing Controls or Forms. This kind of Object Variable symbolizes the Control or Form, and you can clone the Object, creating new "instances" of the Object.

For databases, there is a Tabledefs "collection," a group of Objects, each of which can have Properties. Objects can contain or "nest" other Objects. A Tabledefs collection contains one or more Tabledef Objects; a Tabledef Object has a Fields collection; a Fields collection contains one or more Fields Objects. And these collections and their Objects can have individual Properties and Methods. For more on this subject, see the entry on "Objects."

During OLE Automation, outside applications are said to "expose" their internal Objects (such as their text files, spell checkers, macros) to Visual Basic. When an Object is exposed, VB has "access" to the Object and can manipulate it or utilize its features as if VB were a ghost user of the application. The concept is similar to creating macros, where the computer imitates a user's behavior with an application. But OLE Automation goes far beyond macros.

An outside application's Objects, once exposed, will have Methods (actions the Object can perform) or Properties (qualities) that VB can manipulate or query, or both. You need not contact an application's Objects via linking or embedding (or via the OLE Control), and no copy of the data (or icon) need appear in VB. In fact, during automation VB doesn't necessarily contain any data from the outside application; VB can manipulate the application directly, without linking to it. The reverse is also true: you can write a special kind of VB program and put Objects into it that can be exposed to outside applications (or other VB programs) for their use (see "Class Module"). (To get to the Properties and/or Methods of an Object that's in an OLE Control, use the Object Property of the Control. See "Ole Control.")

VB includes several commands that work with OLE Automation: Dim, Set, CreateObject, GetObject, Close and Quit.

OLE Automation permits virtually unlimited manipulation of outside "Objects" (typical Objects would be an equation editor, a word counter, and so on). It doesn't matter that these Objects are part of a separate, outside application. With OLE Automation, you get essentially unrestricted access to the innards of any application that permits its Objects to be used.

With DDE (see "LinkMode") and ordinary OLE, the user often has to manually activate and specify the links. With Automation, you, the programmer, set up the entire process of sharing data, or features ("Objects," as they are called). Then, the user merely clicks on an icon in your Visual Basic Form to have the spelling of a Text Box checked, the words counted—whatever services and functionality that Word for Windows provides for its own documents can be "borrowed" by your VB program. The user doesn't have to care how the functionality is implemented, doesn't have to specify the outside document or feature. You, the programmer can automate this process.

In sum, with OLE Automation you can do two new and very valuable things. First, you can directly employ any of the tools in an OLE-capable application (heightening contrast in a photo, sending email, or whatever tasks that application performs). You can employ those tools from the outside, from within a separate application (for example, a VB application that you write). Second, you can have these services performed automatically between applications. This combination of inter-app communication (OLE) and automation is the essence of OLE Automation.

One way to find out what Objects you can utilize from an external application is to drop down the Tools menu, and select "References." You'll see a list of "libraries" of applications. Click on those you're interested in. Then press F2 to look at the Object Browser. With the Object Browser you can look at the individual Objects that an application makes available ("exposes") to outside manipulation. However, at the time of this writing, few applications' Object libraries appear in the Tools|References list. For more on this topic, see "Object Browser."

Example #1: Borrowing Word s Spell-checker

It can be surprisingly easy to construct an OLE Automation. Let's try one. We'll have Word for Windows do a spell-check of the text in a VB Text Box. VB doesn't have a spell checker, so we'll borrow the services of the one that comes with Word for Windows 6.0. Fortunately, Word exposes all of the WordBasic macro language to outside manipulation. In effect, you can have VB make Word do whatever you could make it do via Word's own WordBasic—which is a lot.

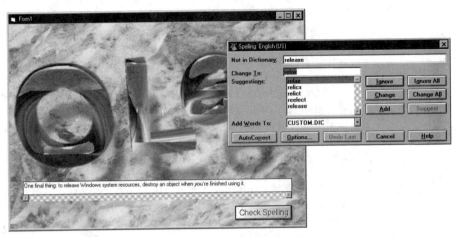

Figure O-11: Word for Windows s spell checker points out an error in our
VB Text Box.

The CreateObject Command

How do you contact Word? Create an Object. Objects can be virtually
anything, but in this example, the Object will be Word's macro language,
WordBasic. Here's how to create the WordBasic Object:

```
Dim Wordobj As Object
Set Wordobj = CreateObject( word.basic )
```

Once the Object is created, we can use all the commands and facilities of
WordBasic from within VB. But which WordBasic commands should we
use to manipulate our text? That's easy, too: just record a macro in Word-
Basic, then copy the result to the Clipboard. WordBasic will do the main
work itself, providing the necessary WordBasic commands and their
parameters. We'll just paste the result into a VB Sub or Function, then do a
little translation to help VB understand what's wanted.

Recording the Macro

Let's create our spell-check automation, step by step:

1. Start Word, and then type in a few lines of text. Highlight (select) these
words by dragging the mouse across them.

2. Copy the highlighted words to the Clipboard by pressing CTRL+INS.
(We'll send our VB Text Box's contents to Word via the Clipboard, so we
want something that can substitute for the actual text while we're recording
this macro.)

3. Turn on Word's macro recorder by pressing ALT+T, M.

4. Type in the macro name *ForVB* (or whatever name you want to give the
macro).

5. Press ALT+O, ENTER to start recording the macro.

6. Now, with WordBasic recording your every move, do this:

- Press ALT+F, N to create a new document.
- Press SHIFT+INS to paste the Clipboard text into the Word document.
- Invoke the SpellCheck by pressing ALT+T, S, ENTER.
- To select the entire document, press ALT+E, L. Then press ALT+E, C to copy the spell-checked text back into the Clipboard.
- Finally, close the document by pressing ALT+F, C, and stop the macro from recording by pressing ALT+T, M, ALT+O.

At this point, we want to see the results, so press ALT+E to Edit the ForVB macro. You should see this:

```
Sub MAIN
FileNew .Template =  Normal , .NewTemplate = 0
EditPaste
ToolsSpelling
EditSelectAll
EditCopy
FileClose
End Sub
```

In our VB Sub, we can use this entire piece of programming as is, except for the first line. VB doesn't understand named parameters like .Template = "Normal", so our next task will be to translate the FileNew command so that VB will know what to do with it.

How VB Handles Parameters

A parameter (sometimes called an argument) is a modification or list of specifications for a command. For example, the VB Move command has four parameters: left, top, width and height.

```
Move left[, top[, width[, height] ] ]
```

The actual names of the parameters (left, top, width and height) never appear in your programming. You merely list the values of any parameters you use:

```
Move 400, 200
```

Moreover, you have to get the order of the parameters right or there will be problems. And if you want to change the last parameter in the list, you have to include commas as spacers for any parameters you omit.

Named Parameters

To make Basic more programmer-friendly, products like Excel, Microsoft Project and Word 6.0 now feature named parameters. Named parameters describe or label each parameter in English. Therefore, your intentions can still be understood by the application even if you list them "out of order" or omit some of them. A parameter's name is listed with the parameter's value, separated by an equals sign (The parameter name is preceded by a period.) It looks like this

```
Object .Parametername = value, .Parametername = value, →
    Parametername = value
```

rather than the traditional:

```
Object value, value, value
```

Basic is not only the highest-level computer language today, but it is also perhaps receiving the most attention, creativity and care. Basic is evolving faster than any other language. The latest versions of Basic in Word, Excel and Microsoft Project have moved ahead of VB in at least this named-parameters respect. For more on this topic, see "Named Arguments."

In any case, in VB you write a parameter list like this:

```
ToolsWordCount = 0, "1","3","9","1","1"
```

If you don't care about any of these parameters except the fourth one, you still must preserve the order by using spacer commas:

```
ToolsWordCount 0, , ,"9"
```

The new style (not yet in VB, alas) avoids all this by giving names to each parameter; this line

```
ToolsWordCount .Characters = "9", .Lines = "1"
```

works the same as this:

```
ToolsWordCount .Lines = "1", .Characters = "9"
```

Notice, too, that there is no = sign between the command and the parameters, but there is an = sign between each parameter name and its value.

Tip: VB requires that you surround with brackets any WordBasic commands which return a text (string) variable. There aren't all that many such commands, nor are most of them useful in OLE Automation, but you should be aware of this anomaly. As an example of this, though, the little routine that follows uses WordBasic's Time$( ) function to return a text (string) Variable to VB which is then printed in a Message Box. Note that the command [Time$] must be bracketed.

```
Sub Command3D1_Click ( )
Dim WordObj As Object
Set WordObj = CreateObject("Word.Basic")
MsgBox WordObj.[Time$]( )
Set WordObj = Nothing
End Sub
```

Translating WordBasic Into VB

Now back to our spell-check automation. How do we translate WordBasic into something that VB can understand? Because the current version of VB doesn't use parameter names, we must strip those off. VB does not recognize this new VBA-style of parameter listing:

```
FileNew .Template = "Normal", .NewTemplate = 0
```

But it does accept the traditional ("Normal" and 0 are the default parameters for FileNew, so we can leave them off):

```
FileNew
```

So let's copy the WordBasic macro. Select the text in Word's Macro Edit screen and press CTRL+INS (don't copy the Sub Main or End Sub). Now switch over to VB and put a Command Button and a Text Box on a Form. Double-click on the Command Button to bring up its Click Event. Then paste the WordBasic right into VB:

```
Private Sub Command3D1_Click ( )
    Dim Wordobj As Object
    Set Wordobj = CreateObject("word.basic")
    FileNew .Template = "Normal", .NewTemplate = 0
    EditPaste
    ToolsSpelling
    EditSelectAll
    EditCopy
    FileClose
End Sub
```

Now we go through and translate the WordBasic into VB 3.0-compatible programming. First, strip off the unneeded default parameter list (.Template = "Normal", .NewTemplate = 0). Then, to let VB know that each command should be sent to the WordBasic object, add "Wordobj." to the start of each command:

```
Private Sub Command3D1_Click ( )
    Dim Wordobj As Object
    Set Wordobj = CreateObject("word.basic")
    Wordobj.FileNew
    Wordobj.EditPaste
    Wordobj.ToolsSpelling
    Wordobj.EditSelectAll
    Wordobj.EditCopy
    Wordobj.FileClose 2
    Set Wordobj = Nothing
End Sub
```

One final thing: to release Windows system resources, destroy an Object when you're finished using it. The final line sets our object to Nothing, which makes the object evaporate. More on this below. (Then we add a 2 to the FileClose command; adding that 2 eliminates certain problems that can occur if you use FileClose alone. You just have to remember this kink.)

Now all that remains is to insert the VB commands that will copy the Text Box's contents to the Clipboard and, at the end, paste the spell-checked result back into the Text Box. Here's the finished Automation routine:

```
Sub Command3D1_Click ( )
    On Error Resume Next
    Dim wordobj As object
    Set wordobj = CreateObject("Word.Basic")
    clipboard.Clear
    clipboard.SetText text1.Text, 1
    wordobj.FileNe
    wordobj.EditPaste
    wordobj.ToolsSpelling
    wordobj.EditSelectAll
    wordobj.EditCopy
    wordobj.FileClose 2
    Set wordobj = Nothing
    text1.Text = clipboard.GetText( )
End Sub
```

Why Not Just Exit?

Setting the object to Nothing (Set wordobj = Nothing) when an automation is done accomplishes two things. It releases any Windows system resources that were used by the Object, and it shuts down Word (or whatever application you've automated) if that application wasn't running when the OLE Automation started. You cannot exit an OLE Automated server application by using the Exit command on its File menu. This will not work:

```
Wordobj.FileExit
```

The reason for this is that OLE Automation very sensibly assumes that if an instance of Word was running prior to the automation activity, it should be the user's responsibility to shut down that instance of Word. After all, the user started that application and perhaps the user wants to continue using it. However, if the automation started Word (because Word was not already running), then the Set Wordobj = Nothing will, as it should, shut Word down.

Also note that when you use the CreateObject command, VBA looks to see if Word is already running. If Word is running, OLE Automation uses that copy of Word rather than starting a new "instance" of Word. This is why you'll usually want to use the Wordobj.FileNew command to display a new, blank document in Word. You generally won't want your automation to potentially interfere with an existing document that the user might be working on, independent of your automation activities.

Under Windows, you can start more than one copy, or "instance," of Word and some other applications, such as Notepad, at the same time. Some applications permit multiple instances of themselves; others don't. OLE Automation, though, is not designed for multiple-instance automation and never starts a new instance if an application is already running.

It is, of course, regrettable that we must use the Clipboard as a postal service for our Automation activities. Rather a throwback, all things considered. For now, we must send the contents of a Text Box to the Clipboard so Word can later be told to import it (EditPaste). Then, after Word has done its job, we must export the text back to the Clipboard (with Word's EditCopy command), and import it to the Text Box.

You can avoid the sending, by directly importing the Text Box contents with WordBasic's Insert command:

```
Wordobj.Insert Text1.Text
```

However, there is no comparable way to export data back from Word to VB; the Clipboard is required. Using the Clipboard as a way station isn't exactly as automatic as we'd like things to be. In the future we can look forward to directly describing the location of the text or other data that we want manipulated or imported. After all, the data does reside inside the computer, so we can point to its location rather than making a copy of it. But not yet. OLE Automation, remember, is just in its infancy.

The GetObject Command

If you want to create an Object from a file, use GetObject. GetObject can also be used in conjunction with CreateObject, as we'll illustrate shortly. When you use GetObject, you can provide merely the disk location, the path, of a file. Based on it's extension .DOC, .BMP or whatever, the correct application will be automatically contacted:

```
Dim wordobj As Object
Set wordobj = GetObject(, "c:\winword\alarm.doc")
```

Alternatively, you can create an "empty" Object of a particular type by using the "class" (the comma is necessary):

```
Dim wordobj As Object
Set wordobj = GetObject(, "word.document")
```

If you supply the class, note that it has at least two parts, separated by a period: applicationname.objecttype.

Here's how to combine GetObject with CreateObject. In this example, we create an Object out of a particular Word for Windows file ("alarm.doc") and then embrace that Object with a Word.Basic Object. Then, using WordBasic commands, we select the entire document, copy it to the Clipboard, close the File and destroy the Object. Finally, we transfer the text from the Clipboard to the Text Box.

Put a Text Box on a Form, then type this into the Form_Load Event:

```
Private Sub Form_Load( )
    Dim wordobj As Object
    Set wordobj = GetObject("c:\winword\alarm.doc")
    Set wordobj = CreateObject("Word.Basic")
    wordobj.EditSelectAll
    wordobj.EditCopy
    wordobj.FileClose 2
```

```
Set wordobj = Nothing
text1.Text = Clipboard.GetText( )
End Sub
```

Cautions

• If you're looking for exposed Objects (and the correct names to use when attempting to access them as servers), you can use the Windows Regedit program. For example, if you run an .EXE Object program that you create in VB (see "Class Module"), the fact that you RUN it under Windows 95 registers it. You'll find it when you run Regedit under HKEY_LOCAL_MACHINE\SOFTWARE\Classes\ and the name that you gave it as a "Project Name" in the Tools menu, "Project Options." It works well with VB4, but it doesn't always work well yet with other applications that expose their Objects.

Type Regedit in the Run option in Windows. Regedit differs between Windows 3.1 and Windows 95, but the correct names for exposed objects appear in both. However, given that OLE is an ongoing, evolving technology, things aren't always what they are listed as. For example, in Windows 95, if you look in the following path for Word for Windows's exposed Objects, you'll see

```
Registry: HKEY_LOCAL_MACHINE\SOFTWARE\Classes\.doc gives
"Word.Document.6"
```

But if you try to grab that Word.Document.6 Object:

```
Private Sub Form_Load( )
Dim wordobj As Object
Set wordobj = GetObject(, "Word.Document.6")
```

you'll get an error message which isn't too helpful:

```
-2147221021
```

Technically, we were trying with the above example to open an "empty" Word document using GetObject (in VB4/32-bit under Windows 95). In other words, we wanted to provide the class, but not a specific path to a particular Word .DOC file. We looked in the registry and found that the only class registered for a .DOC file is "Word.Document.6" Then, trying to use that class, we got that really strange error number.

The answer: You can contact Word 6.0 in two ways for OLE purposes. There are two classes that you can use to CreateObject or GetObject with Word 6.0. The best way is to activate the WordBasic object:

```
Set x = CreateObject("Word.Basic")
```

This gives you a direct link into all the rich language of WordBasic itself—via which you can pretty much make Word dance to your tune. In fact, WordBasic is the only part of Word that can be automated. The second Object, "Word.Document.6" is only going to give you a naked Word Object. If you want to OLE Automate with Word, you'll have to take the extra step of getting the WordBasic Object off of the Application Object:

```
Set x = CreateObject("Word.Document.6")
Set y = x.Application.WordBasic
```

So there's really no point to contacting Word.Document.6. It's indirect and unnecessary.

The moral? Look at the documentation for any application whose Objects you want to contact. Regedit—at this time—is only a crude guide.

When You Can't Use a Macro . . .

As we've seen, you can generally find the WordBasic parameters you need, and their correct order, by simply recording a macro. However, some things cannot be recorded because they either aren't on Word's menus or aren't otherwise accessible to the user except as pure WordBasic commands. Often you'll find a complete parameter list by looking at Word's WordBasic Help file. One problem with these parameter lists when you want to use them with VB 3.0: The parameters are sometimes listed in the "wrong" order. Recall that position is irrelevant when you're using named parameters. However, for VB, the order does matter. The order is the only way that VB can know which parameter is which.

Fortunately, Microsoft provides a self-extracting file called POSITION.EXE which contains the information (positional information) in this format:

```
EditReplace
    [.Find = text]
    [.Replace = text]
    [.Direction = number]
    [.MatchCase = number]
    [.WholeWord = number]
    [.PatternMatch = number]
    [.SoundsLike = number]
    [.FindNext]
    [.ReplaceOne]
    [.ReplaceAll]
    [.Format = number]
    [.Wrap = number]
```

You can obtain POSITION.EXE from the Microsoft Software Library on CompuServe (GO MSL), from the Microsoft Software Library on Internet (ftp.microsoft.com cd softlib), or directly from the Microsoft Download Service (206) 936-MSDL.

Your OLE Automation might fail or behave strangely if too many other applications are running at the same time, using up memory and system resources. When memory is low, strange behavior occurs in any kind of Windows activity, not just OLE Automation. You may, for example, notice odd screen redraws or sluggish behavior (it takes 30 seconds for something to happen while the madly paging disk drive whirrs). If this or other unusual activity occurs, see if you have too much going on at once. Shut down some of the applications (or better yet, restart the computer). Then try Automation again.

An application's customized start-up behavior can also cause problems. You might have defined your Word Normal.Dot file so that certain things happen when Word is first fired up. Or you might use an Autoexec macro (a macro named Autoexec automatically runs when Word first starts). For example, some people are annoyed that Word doesn't always start full-screen, maximized and ready for them to type something in. To ensure that Word is always maximized on start-up, you could create this WordBasic macro and name it Autoexec:

```
Sub MAIN
x = AppMaximize( )
If x = 0 Then
    AppMaximize
EndIf
End Sub
```

This tests the window size status of Word. After "reading" the AppMaximize( ) function, the Variable x contains a zero if Windows isn't filling the screen. In that case, the AppMaximize command is used to make Windows full-screen.

Any other instructions that you've programmed into this macro with the special name, Autoexec, will also be carried out when Word first runs. Recall that OLE Automation directed to Word will start Word if it's not already running. This, of course, will trigger any behaviors specified within an Autoexec macro.

So if things seem strange when you try OLE Automation, see if some start-up conditions are being carried out by the target (server) application. To test this, just start the application manually before trying the OLE Automation. (Start Word by clicking on its icon in Program Manager, rather than having OLE Automation start it. Or, if you're using Windows 95, start Word in Explorer.) If the automation problem you were having goes away, that points to start-up behaviors as the source of the difficulty. Or look in Word's Tools/Macros menu for a macro named Autoexec, then click on the Edit button to read it and see what it does.

Which Apps Can Automate?

There are two ways an application can use (or be used by) OLE Automation, just as there are two distinct roles in an employer-employee relationship. The application that initiates communication to a second application is called the *controller*. Microsoft calls the second, target application the OLE Automation Object or, in popular usage, the *server*.

Regardless of what you call them, these two applications are clearly distinguished during their OLE Automation relationship. One application contains the procedure (Sub, Function, macro or Module that starts and then controls the OLE Automation). This is the active, "caller," application. The other application is passive ("called"), and it provides services, like its spell-checker, to the controller application. The passive application exposes its Objects to outside access from an OLE Automation controller application.

In other words, the OLE Automation "Object application" includes the technology (an "interface") that permits its various features to be manipulated from the outside. It is possible to see this behavior in nature, too, in almost any field or forest in the spring.

But how do you know which applications can be controllers, which expose their Objects, and which do both? Presumably most applications will be able to do both in the next couple of years. However, OLE Automation, and objectification in general, are emerging technologies. At this point, only some applications "expose their Objects" and can thus be used as the target, or server, during automation. Others, like VB, can take advantage of exposed Objects but don't yet expose their own.

However, more applications are becoming OLE Automation-capable all the time. In fact, eventually Windows itself will expose its Objects—its menus, dialog boxes, and all the rest of the things that the Windows shell can do. This will permit extensive manipulation and control of the operating system itself.

Triggering Macros

So far we've recorded macros as a shortcut to generate the commands necessary to automate. But we can also just use an application's existing macros, activating them by Automation like any other feature of a server application.

If you have a macro in Word that you want to trigger via OLE Automation, use this syntax:

```
WordMacro.ToolsMacro "Publish", True
```

Provide the name of the macro in quotes and add the "True" parameter.

Note that the same line in WordBasic is:

```
ToolsMacro .Name = "WordMacro", .Run
```

To edit rather than run the macro, the syntax would be:

```
ToolsMacro .Name = "WordMacro", .Edit
```

Since VB doesn't yet support named parameters, you must put the parameters in the correct position, separated by commas. (True is VB's substitute for .Run, .Edit or Yes in whatever other yes/no options appear in a parameter list):

```
WordMac.ToolsMacro "WordMacro", True
```

But to trigger the Word macro editing window, which is the third parameter, for VB you must insert an extra comma to preserve the .Edit parameter's position in the parameter list:

```
WordMac.ToolsMacro "WordMacro", ,True
```

Using Dialogs

Here's how to get statistics about the text in a VB Text Box. On a new Form, place a Text Box (with its MultiLine Property set to True) and a Command Button. In the Button's Click Event, type this:

```
Sub Command3D1_Click ( )
On Error Resume Next
Dim wordcontact As object, dlg As object
Set wordcontact = CreateObject("Word.Basic")
clipboard.Clear
clipboard.SetText text1.Text, 1
wordcontact.FileNewDefault
wordcontact.EditPaste
wordcontact.ToolsWordCount
Set dlg = wordcontact.curvalues.ToolsWordCount
c = dlg.characters
w = dlg.words
p = dlg.paragraphs
cr$ = Chr$(13)
n$ = "Characters = " & c & cr$
n$ = n$ & "words = " & w & cr$
n$ = n$ & "paragraphs = " & p
msgbox n$
wordcontact.FileClose 2
Set wordcontact = Nothing
End Sub
```

The valuable trick in this word-counting example is an unassuming little powerhouse named *curvalues*. You can use it to "read" (find out) the values or information contained in any Word dialog box. We requested the number of characters, words and paragraphs from Word's WordCount feature. We could have asked for lines and pages, too, since the Word-Count dialog box also provides those statistics.

Going the Other Way

We've seen several examples of how VB can control, or borrow tools from, outside applications. You can also do the opposite—create tools and features, Objects, in VB, and provide them as servers to be exploited by outside applications. For an explanation and examples of this technique, see "Class Module."

Why Bother?

OLE can be rather sluggish on anything less than a Pentium. And it's certainly complex at this point in time for the programmer—so many exceptions, so many application-specific quirks and restrictions. But OLE is obviously an excellent idea and will be increasingly important as computing moves forward toward ever more user-friendly, more intelligent software. OLE is worth learning to use even if the programming sometimes leaves you nonplused and the results are sometimes rather clumsy.

See also   Class Module; LinkMode; Objects; OLE

STATEMENT

Description   On Error tells Visual Basic what to do if an error happens while your program is running.

On Error must tell VB to do something with the "procedure" in which it resides. On Error *cannot* refer to some Label, line number or Subroutine *outside* of the current procedure (Event, Sub or Function). Errors *must* be dealt with *inside* the procedure where the error occurred.

A procedure is the space between a Sub and its matching End Sub command, or a Function and its matching End Function. (An Event is a Sub procedure.)

You should probably avoid setting up a special, stand-alone Subroutine or Function to handle errors that happen across your entire program. VB isn't designed to work this way. Error handling must be located within each potentially offending procedure. You could, however, create a Function that does something based on an error code. Then you would call that Function from your local error routine and pass the error code to the Function. Such a Function could be called from within various other Subroutines and could handle general errors. Perhaps its only job would be to display a custom error window that you've created to match the look of your program. This Function must, however, eventually return to the Sub that generated the error for the completion of the error handling. (See "Sub" for more on Subs and Functions.)

When to Use On Error: You will generally want to include the On Error Statement whenever your program accesses something outside itself—the Clipboard, another running program, the printer and, especially, the user's disk drive. So much is unpredictable about the user's disk drive. Is the drive B: door open (by accident) when the program tries to read a file on B:? Has the file your program is looking for been renamed or erased? Likewise, is the printer turned on? Is the Clipboard empty? When you are trying to link to another program, is that program currently running in Windows? There is much you cannot know when going outside your program, and On Error is the way that VB reports unexpected events to your program. And this way you can prevent your program from shutting itself down should an error occur.

If you don't include On Error and something goes awry, Visual Basic will present an Error Message Box to the user, *and shut down your program.* You don't want to punish the user simply because the drive door was left open or the wrong drive was being accessed. Instead, you want to allow the user to continue to use your program after fixing the problem. Your program should wait for the user to close that door, not collapse and crash.

Used with   Any situation where something unexpected might result in an error:

- Massive use of memory, causing an "Out of Memory" error (Visual Basic Error Code 7)
- Printing or drawing of massive amounts of data onto a single Form—"Overflow" (6)
- A linking activity that took too long (286)
- Printer problem (82)
- Clipboard problem (520, 521)
- Disk-access problem (52 through 76)
- Any program error that slipped by your testing methods

You can find a complete list of the errors that you can access via On Error by selecting "Trappable Errors" from VB's Help Menu.

Note that many of the errors that occur while a program is running involve the program's effort to communicate with a device or object *outside* the program. When trying to go outside your program, you'll want to insert On Error to deal with surprises. Because you test-run your program within the Visual Basic design environment, most of the errors that could occur *inside* the VB program are reported during the test runs. You can correct them before you make a final .EXE version of your program. (See Appendix B for information on debugging.)

An example of a typical design error is trying to change a Text Box's MultiLine Property from within your program (MultiLine can be adjusted only during program design by using the Properties Window). When you try to run a program that includes an attempt to change MultiLine within the program itself, Visual Basic responds with the following:

MultiLine Property cannot be set at runtime.

And you can change the offending line in your program.

When you are writing your program, you cannot know the configuration of the user's disk drive, much less whether or not he or she has inserted a disk into a floppy drive when your program wants to open a file on that drive. The On Error command is designed to make it possible for your program to react gracefully to such contingencies. Visual Basic shuts down your program if an error occurs while the program is running and you haven't included any On Error provisions.

Variables

Once you include On Error in one of the Events or other procedures in your program, all the commands that follow it—that lie between On Error and End Sub (or End Function)—will be handled by that On Error command. However, no errors that occur in other Subroutines or Functions or Events, or *above* the On Error—between the Sub and the On Error command—can be dealt with by On Error's instructions.

On Error Resume Next

On Error Resume Next is the most common use of On Error, and it means: "If there is a problem, just go to the next line and keep the program running." Normally, you will put On Error Resume Next at the top of a Subroutine that tries to work with the disk drive or is otherwise risky because it reaches outside your program.

After telling VB to keep running the program with On Error Resume Next, we might put the following into the line that follows any command that attempts to access the disk:

```
Open "A:\DATA.TXT" For Input As #1
If Err = 71 Then
    MsgBox ("Your disk drive reports that it is not ready for access. Please →
    fix it; then click OK.")
    Exit Sub
End If
```

In this case, we simply leave the Subroutine, expecting the user to fix the problem and click again on the Save Command Button or whatever got us into this Subroutine in the first place. (Error 71 means "Disk Not Ready.")

OR

```
On Error Resume Next

Open "A:\DATA.TXT" For Input As #1
A$ = Input$(LOF(1),#1)
Close 1
For i = 1 to 500
(read in the data...)
    Next i
```

```
If Err Then MsgBox (Error$(Err))
End Sub
```

This technique is perhaps the *second most common* way to deal with errors. It says: "If there's a problem (or more than one problem), just keep on going with the program. We'll deal with it when we get around to it. At the bottom of the Subroutine, we'll check for any kind of error that might have happened."

If the drive A: door is open, we would generate three errors in this example:

- by failing to open the file

- by failing to input from it

- by failing to close it

Because On Error Resume Next tells VB to simply keep chugging away, ignoring any errors, these three problems don't shut down the program.

Instead, our program does whatever it's instructed to—goes right down the list of commands, blithely ignoring errors. Finally, at the bottom of the Subroutine, we handle the errors. The built-in VB Variable Err holds the code number of the most recent error. When, in the previous example, we said *If Err* (if Err doesn't = 0), we were testing to see if there were some error. If so, the Error$ Function provides a text description of what the error code means when you present Error$ with an error code (Err).

OR

```
On Error GoTo Fixit
```

This method is probably the *third most common* way of trapping an error. We are directing VB to immediately go to a zone within this procedure that we have labeled Fixit. This zone will deal with the error and then either Exit Sub or jump back up to another Label, as here:

```
Sub Form_Click ()

On Error GoTo FIXIT

OPENIT:

X$ = InputBox$("Please Enter New Directory")
ChDir X$
Exit Sub

FIXIT:

If Err Then MsgBox (Error$(Err))

c = c + 1

If c = 2 Then Exit Sub

GoTo OPENIT

End Sub
```

Results in   If there is no directory that matches the user's input, VB responds by jumping down to FIXIT as soon as this problem is encountered. It doesn't *resume next*, ignoring the error. It jumps right away to the target Label FIXIT. And then the error-handling area causes this message to be printed in a message box:

PATH NOT FOUND

We set the counter *c* to increment each time we get into this area of the program labeled FIXIT, giving the user two chances before we Exit Sub.

Note the Exit Sub command prior to FIXIT. This is the usual way of preventing the program from falling into an error-handling area. Put these areas at the bottom of your procedure, just before the End Sub, to get them out of the way of the normal commands. And put an Exit Sub command just above the error-handling area in case there are no errors and the program goes through all the commands and arrives at this area. We don't want the program to carry out the error handling if there were no errors.

A Different Approach: As a variant of the preceding approach, where you *don't* want to give the user more than one chance to rectify a problem, put the Resume Next Statement *within* the error-trapping area:

```
FIXIT:

If Err Then
    MsgBox (Error$(Err))
    Resume Next
End If

End Sub
```

This Subroutine would send VB to execute the command immediately following the ChDir X$. The ChDir$ command caused the problem and triggered OnError in the first place. Therefore, "Resume Next" means continue running at the next line following the error. In this case, the Resume Next would put us at the Exit Sub command.

OR

```
On Error GoTo 0
```

A GoTo 0 turns off error trapping. Recall that *where* you place the On Error Statement determines where it starts taking effect:

```
For i = 1 to 1500
Next i

On Error Resume Next
Open "A:\DATA" For Output As #1
Close1
On Error GoTo 0

For i = 1 to 12000
Next i
```

Results in   The two For...Next Loops are not error trapped. The file access is.

Any error occurring *outside* On Error Resume Next (which turns the error trapping on) and On Error GoTo 0 (which turns the error trapping off) will not be handled by the On Error command.

Note that you can separate On Error from the Resume Next command (see the preceding variant). Visual Basic turns on error handling when it encounters On Error. It turns off error handling when it encounters On Error GoTo 0 *or* when it encounters a Resume Next. However, more than one error can occur, and more than one error-handling On Error can be competing for attention if several errors have occurred in succession. (See "The Royal Succession..." in "Cautions" below.)

OR

    On Local Error Resume Next

This word *Local* is merely included because some people may have written programs in older versions of Basic such as QuickBasic, and they want to import such programs into VB without having to retype them.

All error trapping in VB is local to a single procedure. Each Sub or Function, therefore, needs its own error trapping if such trapping seems advisable. The word *Local* is not needed in any program written in pure Visual Basic.

Uses   • When your program is going to contact something outside itself—the printer, a disk drive, another program via a Link, the Clipboard—you are in some danger that the outside entity will be contacted incorrectly, contacted too slowly or called upon after it has been killed, deleted or otherwise taken out of existence.

On Error is like those prerecorded messages that the phone company provides when you try to call a friend whose line has been disconnected. On Error lets your program deal with failed attempts.

Without On Error telling Visual Basic what you want done in the event of a blunder or misfire, VB will completely shut down your program. That's a rude, intense way of telling users that they mistyped a filename.

Cautions   • On Error doesn't, itself, trap an error. In other words, it tells VB how to *respond* if an error occurs—where to go, whether to react—but On Error is not itself a response. You cannot put On Error just below a potential trouble spot and expect the error to be caught.

This computer has no drive E:, so this attempt to change to that drive name will cause an error. Here the On Error comes *after* the problem and, because error handling is *turned on* by the On Error command, the program will shut down. On Error was not in effect when ChDrive "E:" occurred.

Wrong:

    ChDrive "E:"
    On Error GoTo Fixdiskproblem

Right:

```
On Error GoTo Fixdiskproblem
ChDrive "E:"
```

• Error handling uses VB's built-in Variable Err to provide an error code and another built-in Variable, a text Variable (*Error$*), to translate that code into a text description of the error. But Err, like any other Variable, can hold only one piece of information at a time. If multiple errors occur, Err will hold only the code for the most recent of the errors. This means you should handle errors near where they might occur. Otherwise, if another error happens, Err will change to contain the code of the new error.

• If you give line numbers to each line in your program (no one does this anymore), you can provide a line number instead of a Label as the target of an On Error GoTo:

```
On Error GoTo 350
```

• **The Royal Succession in the Kingdom of Ur:** A complex set of rules determines which On Error takes precedence if several On Error Statements are concurrently triggered. Few of us will need to worry about this degree of error handling. (It would suggest, for one thing, that the program is poorly designed.)

However, if you *do* need to know how Visual Basic reacts to synchronous errors, I invite you to try to translate the paragraph in the *Visual Basic Language Reference* that describes it. If you can create an English-language version of that paragraph, I'd be grateful if you would send me a copy via CompuServe. This murkiness isn't the fault of the author of that book. The Visual Basic order of succession for errors seems to be as convoluted and sinister as the plan that described the royal succession in the kingdom of Ur.

• On Error—and its associated instructions about how and where to respond to a problem—are ignored when the program leaves the Subroutine or Function in which that On Error resides. In other words, On Error is actively watching for trouble only while the VB program *is in* (is executing commands within) the same Sub or Function or Event in which the On Error command resides.

Example Few people are likely to have 15 disk drives. So attempting to change to drive O: will likely generate an error. That will be our example, and we can rest assured that it will trigger an error when we run this program on most systems. (Note, however, that drive names are not always sequential. Network drives usually assign a letter higher in the alphabet than non-network drives—to eliminate potential conflicts. However, for this example, we'll assume that drive O: doesn't exist.)

```
Sub Form_Click ()

On Error Resume Next

ChDrive "O:"
```

```
Print "We probably have an error here, unless this is the Pentagon."
Print
Print "Anyway, here are some of the weird characters you can print..."

For I = 174 To 221
Print Chr$(I);
Next I

If Err Then MsgBox (Error$(Err))
End Sub
```

This example demonstrates that the program does, in fact, ignore the error and simply resumes—simply carries out the command following the one that triggered an error. The error is ignored by the program until we decide to take it up further down—when we ask: If Err...

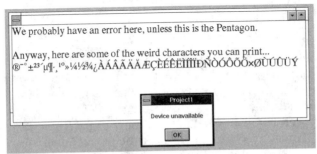

We probably have an error here, unless this is the Pentagon.

Anyway, here are some of the weird characters you can print...
®¯°±²³´µ¶·¸¹º»¼½¾¿ÀÁÂÃÄÅÆÇÈÉÊËÌÍÎÏÐÑÒÓÔÕÖ×ØÙÚÛÜÝ

Project1

Device unavailable

OK

Figure O-12: We try to change to disk drive O:, which is sure to generate an error. We can see how Visual Basic delays its response when we use the On Error command.

See also   Appendix B; Err; Error$; Resume
For a complete list of VB's error codes, see "Trappable Errors" in VB's Help Menu.

ON GOSUB, ON GOTO STATEMENT

Description   The On GoSub and On GoTo commands are not used much anymore. They both create a structure that lets a program *branch* to different locations. They send the computer to different locations within the program, depending on current conditions.
The On GoSub command was used in programs that didn't have lots of *Objects* for the user to work with. Such old style programs could consist of perhaps 300 lines—one long list of commands, subdivided by Labels.

Typically, the program would respond after the user was presented with a printed menu on a blank screen:

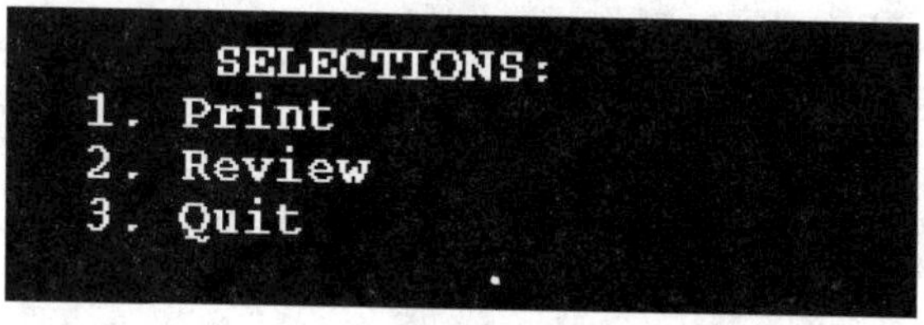

```
      SELECTIONS:
  1. Print
  2. Review
  3. Quit
```

Figure O-13: An old-fashioned DOS program

Here's what the program would look like:

```
Selections:
PRINT    " SELECTIONS:"
PRINT "1. Print"
PRINT "2. Review"
PRINT "3. Quit"

Input "Your choice?"; x

On X GoSub PrintIt, ReviewIt, QuitThis

GoTo Selections

PrintIt:
Print...
Return

ReviewIt:
Text1.Visible = −1
Return

QuitThis:
End
Return
```

The program branched to the appropriate Subroutine after the user responded to the menu. The user's 1, 2 or 3 response caused the program to look for the first, second or third Label following the On X GoSub.

Then, when the Subroutine was finished, the Return command sent us back up to the line following the On GoSub, and that line, GoTo Selections, bumped us back up to the menu again.

In Visual Basic, by contrast, there is no monolithic list of instructions. Instead, virtually *everything* in a VB program is a Subroutine. A VB program's user branches by clicking on one Command Button, for example, out of a group of Command Buttons. Selecting this Button would immediately activate the Subroutine within that Button's Click Event. There is generally no need for a VB program to set up an On GoSub structure because the Subroutines are encapsulated underneath each Button that the user can select.

The same program in VB might look like Figure O-14 and have no need for the On GoSub structure:

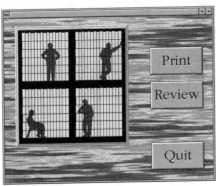

Figure O-14: The monochromatic text of Figure O-13 becomes dimensional and colorful here as a Windows program.

The On GoTo command is similar to On GoSub, but there is no set of Return commands to send the program back to the On GoTo location within the program. Instead, On GoTo causes a program to jump to the appropriate target Label where some command would direct the program where to go next.

Again, there is no need for On GoTo in VB programming. One preferable alternative to On GoTo is the Select Case command (which see).

Used with   Older-style, pre-Visual Basic programs

Variables

```
X=2
On X GoSub TargetOne, TargetTwo
```

(Because X is 2 here, the *second* Label in the list of Labels following GoSub identifies the location where the program now goes. Whatever commands exist beneath the TargetTwo Label are carried out. Finally, the program comes upon a Return command and goes back up to carry out the commands following the original On GoSub.)

```
X=1
On X GoTo TargetOne, TargetTwo
```

(In this case X is 1, so the program will branch to TargetOne or whatever Label is listed *first* in the list of Labels following GoTo. The results are as described for On GoSub, but there will be no Return command. Instead, another GoTo or some other command will direct the program as to what to do after it reaches the TargetOne Label location in the program.)

Uses   • None in Visual Basic.
Formerly used for redirecting a program in older styles of programming languages. Created a structure called *multiple branching*; based on

user-input or current conditions in the program, the program would go to one of several targets listed (as line numbers or Labels) following the On GoTo or On GoSub command.

Select Case is available for any situation in VB where multiple branching seems appropriate.

Cautions
• The Y in On Y GoTo (or GoSub) can be any number between 0 and 255. If 0 (or if larger than the number of targets listed after the GoTo), the program ignores the list of targets following GoTo (or GoSub) and merely carries out the instructions in the line below the On Y GoTo.

• Any negative number or number larger than 255 for the Y in On Y GoTo generates an error.

Example

```
A = 2

On A GoTo RADIO, PHOTO, TV

RADIO:

PHOTO:

TV:
```

(Because A = 2 in this case, we branch to the location in the program labelled "PHOTO.")

See also
GoSub; GoTo; Return; Select Case

PEN

STATEMENT

Description
Open is your gateway to the computer's disk drive and the files thereon. Using Open is like pulling a file drawer open—now you can put new folders (files) into the cabinet or take out existing files for inspection or modification.

Disk files hold all kinds of information—pictures, budget data, even programs that can be run. However, the Open command works with *data* (information of some kind), not runnable programs. And you would use the LoadPicture and SavePicture commands for images. So what's left? Information, usually in text form—records of tax payments, lists of birthdays and anniversaries, short stories, whatever kinds of data a program generates or manipulates and wants to save for later use. Data saved in the computer's memory is only available while the computer's power is turned on and a program is active that deals with that data. As soon as that program is shut down or the computer itself is turned off, data in memory disappears. Data is saved permanently on disk files.

There are three modes, three ways to open a disk file: *binary, sequential and random*. They represent different degrees of automation, different degrees of computer control over the data. The *binary* mode is the least automated but offers the programmer the greatest flexibility.

The Quantity Depends on Both the Mode and the Command: How many characters are read in from or written to a file depends both on the mode with which the file was opened and the particular command you are using to read from or write to the file. Line Input # reads in a whole sentence at a time, Get # can read a single byte, and Input$ could read an entire text file into a single text ("string") Variable. (The Input$ command cannot be used with random-mode files—only binary and sequential mode.) Here we're opening a file in sequential mode and using Input$ to read in the entire file:

```
Open Filename$ For Input As #1
    n = LOF(1)
    a$ = Input$(n,#1)
Close 1
```

LOF tells you the length of the file, the total number of characters it contains. After the preceding commands were carried out, the Variable *a$* would hold all the characters in whatever disk file was called *Filename$*.

The various file-reading and file-writing commands—Line Input #, Input$, Input B, Input #, Get, Print #, Write #, Put—are somewhat interchangeable. You can use the Input$ command, for instance, with files opened in either sequential or binary modes (but not random). Depending on what you are trying to accomplish and on the nature of the file involved, you can construct the appropriate combination of Open mode and read or write commands to do anything you need to do.

Let's look at the three modes you can use with the Open command. We'll go a little more deeply into binary and random here. For a more complete discussion of sequential—arguably the most popular mode for smaller non-professional programs—see "Input$."

Binary: When you Open Filename$ For Binary, you can "read" (get data from the file) or "write" (put data into the file) at *any* location within that file. Information is stored on disk as individual characters (bytes). The word *normal* would use up six bytes of space on the disk because there are six letters in *normal*. Using the Get and Put Statements, you can specify which particular character, or group of characters, to read or write.

We'll demonstrate this by reading in the first 40 characters of your WIN.INI file:

```
Sub Form_Click ()

Open "C:\WINDOWS\WIN.INI" For Binary As #1
x$ = String$(1, " ")
```

```
For i = 1 To 40
   Get #1, , x$
   Print x$;
Next i

Close 1

End Sub
```

Results in

```
[windows]
LOAD=c:\ndw\sleeper.exe
RUN=
```

We set x$ to a single character using String$. The Get # pulls in as many characters as there are in the Variable you offer it. If you entered x$ = String$(50, " "), putting 50 blank characters (50 spaces into x$), then the Get # would bring in 50 characters in one operation, and you could eliminate the For...Next Loop in the preceding example.

Sequential: Visual Basic assists you with managing the data transfer (in or out) of a file that was opened using Open Filename$ For Input (to read), Open Filename$ For Output (to write) or Open Filename$ For Append (to write by adding new data to the end of the file). Using the *For Input, For Output* or *For Append* command automatically opens a disk file in the sequential mode.

The assistance provided to you in sequential mode is greater than in the binary mode but less automatic than in the random mode.

Although you can use the Input$ command to pull in a single character, or Input B to get a single byte, sequential mode is more commonly used to read in (or write out) entire lines at a time. Reading or writing entire lines automates the process because you can use Line Input # to get an entire text ("string") Variable at one time—not just an individual character, but a whole sentence or paragraph, or even the entire file if it's not longer than 32,767 bytes.

Sequential mode also means that Visual Basic keeps track of *where you are* in the process of reading information from (or writing to) the file. In other words, if you've just used Line Input # with the first line from an Opened file, you don't need to describe the position within the file for the *second* line. Just use Line Input # again, and you'll automatically get the second line. Let's try this procedure to see how it works:

```
Sub Form_Click ()

Open "C:\WINDOWS\WIN.INI" For Input As #1

For i = 1 To 4
   Line Input #1, x$
   Print x$
Next i

Close 1

End Sub
```

Results in   [windows]
LOAD=c:\ndw\sleeper.exe
RUN=whiskers.exe
Beep=yes

Here we pulled in the first four lines. Line Input # knows when a line ends because it pulls in all characters until it reaches a Carriage Return. Carriage Return symbols (which are not visible) are inserted into text when the user presses the ENTER key.

Rather than read and write individual bytes (as in the binary approach), a file opened for sequential access usually manipulates data in larger chunks—whole sentences, paragraphs or, indeed, the whole file can be read into a text ("string") Variable. (For more on sequential mode, see "Input$.")

Random: The name "random" is somewhat misleading because this is the most rigid, most computer-controlled of the three modes with which you can Open a file. It's called random because items are stored as "records" of fixed size. Because you know in advance that each record in a particular file is, say, 50 characters long, the computer needs only to multiply to figure out the exact location of record number 12. (It will be at byte-position 600, the 600th character counting from the first character in the file.) The computer, therefore, need not search through such a file *sequentially*, looking for Carriage Returns or some other code to let it know when it has a complete chunk of data. Instead, it can *randomly* access the records in the file. The location of record number 12 is known and its length is known because each record is the same size in a random-mode file.

Visual Basic handles this multiplication, this random access, for you. When you Put to or Get from a random file, you merely provide the record number and that record is automatically written to (or read from) the disk file.

The advantages to random mode are that the programmer has to do somewhat less programming than with the other modes. And, because all the records are the same length, random access can be the fastest mode when you only want to get at particular parts of a file (for editing or reading only a single piece or a few pieces of information in the file). With sequential mode, you often read in the whole file and sometimes need to use the InStr command or some other method to search for particular pieces of information.

Also, it's easier to replace information within a random file—easier to update the file while it resides on the disk. Because all the records are of uniform length, you can put a revised record #34 right into the slot that the old #34 occupied—without disturbing or overwriting #33 or #35.

There are, however, some drawbacks to random mode. It takes up more room on the disk; the size of *every* record must be as big as the *longest* record. And, because of the rigid size and structural requirements of the random technique, the program's user can be restricted by the program. What if a street address is too long, for example?

In addition to being strict with the user about the amount of information he or she enters, the program may also enforce rules about the *order* in which that information is entered. If a record is set up with the expectation that last month's cost of baby clothes is entered first, then entertainment expenses and then gas, the user had better follow that pattern. Or else. (See the Example for an illustration of random mode.)

A Rather Totalitarian Mode: That the user can be restricted to a predetermined length and order of entry for responses to the computer's questions strikes some people as a somewhat totalitarian quality of the ironically named *random* mode. Perhaps *disgust* is too strong a word, but some programmers and users are turned off by the strictures imposed by the random mode. Users can be alienated (they mistakenly blame the computer itself for the restrictions) by programs built in the "random" style. Of course, a well-designed program can get around these problems, but all too often the random mode has resulted in programs that are rigid and awkward.

The speed advantages of random are becoming something of a nonissue because of ever-faster disk drives and ever-larger computer memory. The speed efficiencies are essentially negated when a file is Loaded—as most now at least partly are—into the computer's memory before being updated or read by a program.

Working with data in the computer's RAM is so much faster than any disk could ever be that many programmers now endeavor to bring data, or at least part of it, into RAM before manipulating it. Although the purpose of a disk is *storage*, disks may not be the best places to *make use of* the things they store. So you might want to stay with the sequential mode for disk access unless your program requires the random mode for its particular efficiencies. The sequential mode is particularly suited to word processing applications; the random mode is often used with database and spreadsheet applications. (See "Input$" for sequential mode options and techniques.)

Business Is Another Matter: In some business and scientific applications, the random-access approach is preferred. Business and financial data must be ordered in a well-structured manner so that you can efficiently perform multifield comparisons (queries); assign fields to reports and mailing labels; sort information; and pack data in predefined formats (numbers of any range can be packed to a few bytes, whereas they can be enormous if stored as straight ANSI text where each digit must take up a byte of space).

You also will probably want to use "field types" to allow data validation: a phone field, for example, controls the size and format of the entries. It allows only properly formatted entries such as (999) 999-9999, and ZIP code fields ensure that the user enters 99999 or 99999-9999. Boolean fields allow up to eight yes/no fields to be packed into a single byte.

With string Variables limited to 32k and Arrays limited to 64k, you obviously cannot manipulate databases of any significant size in the computer's RAM .

Also, business applications can require that users be able to import data written by other programs like spreadsheets and dBASE files that are structured random-access files.

Finally, *if a program is well-designed*, the user will rarely feel limited by a database stored in structured random access. A well-designed user interface is not limited by any particular storage-and-access technique, but it can make a big difference in efficiency and practicality.

For these and other situations, rely on the random-access mode instead of sequential.

Used with   Disk files, to permit a program to get information from a disk file (to "read" it) or put information into a disk file ("write to" it)

Variables   Open filename [For mode] [Access access] [lock] As [#] filenumber →
[Len = recordlength]

Random Mode

    Open "C:\TEST" As 5

This command opens a file called "TEST" on the root directory of drive C:. The file is random mode (the default unless a mode command is used). Unless this file remains open from a previous Open command that defined the type of access (Read, Write or Read/Write), the access will be Read/Write, allowing you to either get data from or put data into the file. The length of the records in this file has not been specified with the optional *Len* Statement, so the record lengths will be 128 bytes, the default.

OR

    X$ = "C:\TEST"
    Open X$ As 5

This command is the same as the preceding command, but we are using a text ("string") Variable instead of explicitly naming the file.

Future references to this file will involve its filenumber 5: Get #5

OR

To specify that this is a random-mode file (it's not necessary but it's easier to read the intention): Open "C:\TEST" For Random As 3

OR

To specify that we are going to be putting data into the file but *not* reading information (with Get) from the file. (Use Access Read to read information. Use Access Read Write to permit both.):

    Open "C:\TEST" For Random Access Write As 5
    Put #5, RecordNumber, Variable

OR

To specify that the size of the records in this particular file is 231 bytes (without this, the default is 128 bytes):

```
Open "C:\TEST" For Random Access Read Write As #2 Len = 231
Get #2, 15, a$
```

The # symbol is always optional with Get, Put or Open but does make clear that the number refers to the filenumber. In the preceding example, we are reading from file #2, the 15th record, and putting it into the Variable *a$*. The records in this file are 231 bytes long. We can either read from or write to the file.

The optional *Lock* command controls access to this file by other programs or computers (see "Lock").

Sequential Mode

To open a file from which you want to read data, use *For Input*:

```
Open "C:\TEST" For Input As #2
```

OR (to use a Variable instead of just naming the file):

```
A$ = "C:\TEST"
Open A$ For Input As #2
```

In these examples, a file called TEST is opened in the root directory of drive C:. It is opened in sequential mode because the *For Input, For Output* or *For Append* command triggers the sequential mode.

(*For Append* is a special version of For Output. When you use For Append, a sequential file is opened and will *add* any data it gets via Print # or Write # to the end of the file. That is, Append causes the file to grow in size by adding new information to the end of the file.)

We have Opened our example file "As #2"; therefore, its identifying filenumber will be *2*, and any reference to this file by other commands should include the *2* to distinguish it from other files which might also be open at the time:

```
Input #2 (avoid )
Line Input #2 (use sometimes, to read text files)
Input$, numberofbytestoread, #2 (use most of the time. See "Input$" for
```
the reasons these three approaches are not equally useful.)

OR (to open a file to which you want to write data, use *For Output*):

```
Open "C:\TEST" For Output As #14
```

This file is now opened to *receive* information and has the filenumber 14. You can now send data into it using

```
Print #14
```

Print # works precisely like Print does when putting information on the screen. If you want a line printed to the screen, you write Print "Hello": Print "You" and you get the following:

```
Hello
You
```

If you write Print "Hello ";: Print "You", you get:

Hello You

The ; holds the "You" onto the same line as the "Hello." A comma causes a tab. Using no punctuation you skip down to the next line. Print # works precisely the same way, saving data to the disk already formatted for printing to the screen. Because data is often printed to the screen, you'll normally want to use Print # with sequential files.

Print # puts into the file only the exact numeric value or the exact text character(s) that are in the Variable you supply, plus the punctuation. If you enter A$ = "abc": Print #14, A$, then only *abc* will go into the file.

The alternative to Print #14 is Write #14, which used to be an important technique, but has been replaced by Print #. Write # inserts commas between items and quotation marks around text ("string") Variables.

Binary Mode

Binary mode gives you, the programmer, the greatest, most precise control over file access. You, not Visual Basic, decide where you want to be within the opened file and how much data you want to manipulate at any given time.

The trade-off is that you have to do more programming to earn this control over the situation. But, when dealing with files you didn't create, particularly if they are not text files, binary mode is the best approach. You can explore data piece by piece and have fine control over the data.

Likewise, use binary if you want to store text in a proprietary format of your own devising (you normally shouldn't, though, because the Clipboard, Notepad, Linkage and other Windows benefits are thereby negated).

Perhaps you will want to store data via binary mode if you want to encrypt it—if you want it inaccessible unless a password is provided.

Open "C:\TEST" For Binary As #2

OR (to use a Variable instead of just naming the file):

A$ = "C:\TEST"
Open A$ For Binary As #2

Now you can move to a particular byte position within this file. Binary allows you precise control over *where* in a file you want to read or write information. Binary mode also allows you to define how *much* data you will read or write—from a single character to the entire file.

OR (to open a binary-mode file for reading only):

Open "C:\TEST" For Binary Access Read As #4

(You can also use *Access Write* or *Access Read Write*.)

In a Network or Multitasking Environment: More than one person might attempt to read or write a file at the same time, or in a multitasking environment like Windows, more than one program might attempt access simultaneously. When more than one computer tries to open the same file at the same time, the "Lock" command provides a way to control the traffic. Lock is optional, but if it's used it should be placed immediately before the As command:

Open "C:\TEST" For Binary Access Lock Read Write As #3

This lock prevents any other computer or program from reading or writing this file. Any attempt is responded to with a "Permission Denied" message.

You can use four types of Lock:

• Lock Read Write (no access permitted to your opened file)

• Lock Read (another computer or program can write to, but not read from, your opened file)

• Lock Write (another computer or program can read from, but not write to, your opened file)

• Lock Shared (all access, either reading or writing, is permitted other computers or programs)

If you leave out the Lock command, it defaults to Lock Read Write, forbidding any other program or outside computer from any kind of access.

Uses   • Any time you want your program to be able to store or retrieve data from the files on the computer's disk drive.

Random file access is an excellent technique for simple database applications such as customer lists, inventory records, etc. Using For Random you can get a record out of the file in one shot, and with no other manipulation, you can access the individual portions of the record such as customer name or quantity in stock.

Likewise, to delete a record, you can simply mark it as deleted and then clean it out later during a periodic file save or data compress. You can quickly sort records within the file. The primary drawback to random mode is that it requires that the size of file records and fields be defined and fixed at a certain size or format. This requirement not only uses up extra space, but also can require the user to interact with the data in a restrictive way. For instance, the user cannot add *more* information than is permitted by the predetermined size of the records.

Cautions   • The Len command is used in two ways:

The Len command is normally used to describe the size of the records in a random-style file, but can also be used with sequential files to define the size of the "buffer." A buffer is an area within the computer's RAM where portions of an opened file's data are temporarily stored for quicker access than through the disk drive itself.

The Open command itself, however, stores data into a buffer (and flushes it back to the disk when the Close command shuts the file). Likewise, such disk cache programs as SmartDrv also buffer data. So Len is rarely used with sequential files.

If you do use Len with a sequential file, Len describes the size of the buffer that Open will create to temporarily store data. Visual Basic uses a default buffer of 512 bytes unless you specify otherwise with the Len command.

When used with random files, Len can be any size between 1 and 32,767, and it specifies that the length of the records equal the number of bytes described by Len =. If you specify no record length, it defaults to 128 bytes.

Files opened in binary mode do not use the Len command.

• Filenumbers (the As #15) can be any number between 1 and 255. All subsequent reading from and writing to that opened file (via such commands as Put and Input$) must refer to the filenumber–it's like an abbreviation or Label for the filename.

Each filenumber must be unique; it cannot currently be in use as a Label of an already opened file. If your program has lots of opened files at the same time or if the user is allowed to open files, your program may not know which filenumbers have already been used. If your program needs to be given an unused filenumber so it can open another file, use the FreeFile command.

• To create a new file on the disk drive, use a filename that isn't currently on the disk directory specified. If you Open "C:\UTILS\QZ" For Output As #6, and *there is no file called QZ* in the UTILS directory, *a file called QZ is created*. This procedure works when you use Open with For Output, For Binary, For Random or For Append. It does not work when you Open a file For Input.

Random Is the Default: If you do not specify the mode (For Random, For Binary, For Input, For Output or For Append), the opening defaults to random mode: Open "C:\NEWFILE" As #3 would be a random-mode file.

If the Access command (Access Read, Access Write, Access Read Write) is omitted (as it usually is) when you are opening a file in binary or random mode, VB will try to open the file three times. First, it tries Read Write, then Write and then Read.

Note that sequential mode defines the type of access in its mode command (For Input, For Output or For Append) and thus does not need the Access command at all. However, the For Append technique can coexist with the Access Read Write command.

Access only works for versions of DOS 3.1 or later, which permit networked environments. If you use any versions of the Lock command, the DOS program SHARE.EXE must have been run prior to the Open attempt. Usually, if a computer needs SHARE, SHARE is run in an AUTOEXEC.BAT file or by the networking software itself when the computer is turned on.

A particular file can be opened any number of times, without first closing it. That is, at several places in your program you can access a file in different ways, by opening it each time with a unique filenumber:

```
Open "C:\TEST" For Input As #2
Open "C:\TEST" For Binary As #7
```

The preceding procedure is a valid way to make C:\TEST available to both sequential and binary access simultaneously.

However, this multiple-opening is *not* allowed with files opened in the sequential modes For Output or For Append. In these two cases, you must first close the file before opening it again with a different filenumber.

The Input$ command cannot be used with files opened in the random mode.

Example   To illustrate the random-access mode, we'll create a file that is organized with fixed-length records. The usual suspects—WIN.INI, CONFIG.SYS—will not work because they are not random. Each contains information organized in phrases of varying lengths, so reading them, for instance, cannot be efficiently accomplished by pulling in the same size chunk of data each time. The predictable size of its records is the hallmark of the random-access file mode.

Often the records in random files are subdivided into smaller pieces of data called *fields*. Along with each name, for instance, you might want to include address, city, state and ZIP. This information is merely a convenience for the programmer; the data is stored in chunks that have organizational meaning to us, but on the disk they are simply unlabeled, just raw data.

In any event, when you want to create records with fields, you may want to use a Type Statement in a Module (see "Type"). Type Variables are frequently used with random files. For this example, type the following into a Module:

```
Type testrecord
    varnam As String * 30
    address As String * 50
    citystate As String * 50
    zip As Integer
End Type
```

You must also Dim a Type Variable, just like any normal Variable. Here we'll Dim it in the General Declarations section of our Form:

```
Dim tr As testrecord
```

Now we can use the Variable *tr*, knowing that it's of the "Type" test record and can contain three text ("string") Variables, plus an Integer Variable. You access Type Variables by naming their Dimmed name (tr.address) plus the subordinate name, separated by a period.

Here's the routine that creates a random file for this example:

```
Sub Form_Click ()

Open "C:\TESTRAND" For Random Access Write As #1 Len = Len(tr)
```

```
For i = 1 To 30
    a$ = Chr$(i + 64)
    tr.varnam = String$(30, a$)
    tr.address = String$(50, a$)
    tr.citystate = String$(50, a$)
    tr.zip = i + 16000

    Put 1, i, tr
Next i

Close 1

End Sub
```

Len Is Necessary: We need to add a Len statement at the end of our Open clause to tell VB how long each record will be. We use the command Len(tr) to tell us how long the Variable is. The Len of our Type Variable *tr* is 132 bytes: one text Variable 30 bytes long, two text Variables of 50 bytes, and a two-byte Integer.

Now we put 30 of these compound Variables into the file. We're just making up data, stuffing 30 text characters into tr.varnam, 50 into tr.address, and so on. These characters will be AAAA the first time through the Loop, BBBB the second time, etc. String$ creates a text Variable filled with whatever character we want. We get these characters by adding the Loop counter *i* to 64; this is the ASCII code (see "Chr$") in which A is code 65, B is 66, etc. The ZIP will be 16001, 16002, etc.

Each fake record is put, at position *i*, into the file. Notice that we don't need to go through all the subordinate Variables within the composite Type Variable, tr. We can just Put tr. This is another reason for going to the trouble of defining a Type Variable. You can later manipulate Type Variables as big, single units. (You can even copy one entire Type Variable into another; you need not copy each element individually. See "LSet.")

A Program to Read a Random-Mode File: Now we have created a random-mode file on the disk. Let's create a program that will allow the user to slide through the records with a Scroll Bar to illustrate the randomness of the random mode and the fact that it can quickly locate any requested record.

Use the same program we just created to save the file to the disk. This way, we won't have to reenter the Type Variable structure. But *remove* the Open command from the Form_Click:

```
Open "C:\TESTRAND" For Random Access Write As #1 Len = Len(tr)
```

Put four Text Boxes on the Form, a Label for each, a Command Button and a Horizontal Scroll Bar. Set the Scroll Bar Min Property to 1 and its Max Property to 30, allowing it to access all 30 records in the file. Also, put a Label on top to display the current record number.

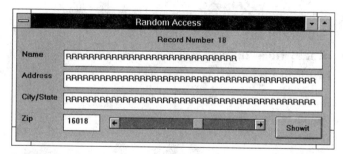

Figure O-15: Viewing the records and fields of a random-access file. Typically, database programs separate the fields into individual boxes for the user to view or modify.

We'll Open the file in the Form_Load Event, so we'll be ready to be read from it right from the start:

```
Sub Form_Load ()
    Open "C:\TESTRAND" For Random Access Read As #1 Len = Len(tr)
End Sub
```

The only difference between this approach and the way we opened this file in the preceding example about writing is that an *Access Read* command has replaced *Access Write*.

In the Command1_Click Event, put the following:

```
Sub Command1_Click ()

recnum = hscroll1.value

Get #1, recnum, tr

text1.text = tr.varnam
text2.text = tr.address
text3.text = tr.citystate
text4.text = Str$(tr.zip)
End Sub
```

Here we find out the position of the tab inside the Scroll Bar (its Value Property) and then get that particular record. Your hard drive light doesn't go on because the computer usually loads small files like this one entirely into RAM when they are first opened, making access faster.

After getting the record identified by the Type Variable *tr*, we break it down into its various fields and put them into the appropriate Text Boxes:

```
Sub HScroll1_Change ()
    label1.caption = "Record Number " + Str$(hscroll1.value)
End Sub
```

When the Scroll Bar is changed by the user, the Record Number Label shows the current record number.

See also   Close; EOF; FreeFile; LOF; LSet

For more about the individual access modes, see also:

For sequential files–Input$; Input B; Input #; Line Input #; Print #; Write #

For binary files–Input$; Seek

For random files–Get; Len; Put; Type

OPENDATABASE .... METHOD

See   Data Control

OPTION BASE .... STATEMENT

Description   Option Base allows you to make the lowest item in an Array 1 instead of the default 0.

If a computer is working with a list of items, it almost always thinks of the first item in the list as the *zeroth* item. Humans prefer to think of that first item as item #1. (We don't say, "We should probably start chilling the shrimp, Sonja. Our zeroth guest will be here soon.")

An Array is a collection of data, of pieces of information, which are in some way related. (See "Arrays" for more on this useful programming technique.)

Unless you use Option Base 1, the first piece of information will be indexed as item 0. Here's how it works. In the General Declarations section of a Form, type the following:

```
Dim Nme$(3)
```

This command creates an Array of text ("string") Variables, each of which will be called Nme$ and will differ only because each will have a unique index number. Even though you said Dim (3), there are actually *four* spaces inside this Array because there is a zeroth item. (Counter-intuitive, no?)

You identify and manipulate the items in an Array by providing the Array name plus the index number, enclosed in parentheses:

```
Sub Form_Click()

Nme$(0) = "Bob"
Nme$(1) = "Sara"
```

```
Nme$(2) = "Sonny"
Nme$(3) = "Jim"
End Sub
```

Option Base to the Rescue: *Notice that there is a Nme$(0) here.* The *second* item in the Array has the index number *1*. Option Base attempts to fix this awkwardness by allowing you to tell the computer that you want all Arrays to start with item 1. In the General Declarations section of a Form, type the following:

```
Option Base 1
Dim Nme$(4)

Sub Form_Click()

Nme$(1) = "Bob"
Nme$(2) = "Sara"
Nme$(3) = "Sonny"
Nme$(4) = "Jim"

End Sub
```

Now you can work with the Nme$( ) Array, knowing that there is no Nme$(0) item. The lowest Nme$( ) is now indexed as 1. And when you Dim this Array, you create it with the number of items you intend, Dim Nme$(4), not one less than your intended total if there is a zeroth item.

Remember, however, that there *is* another way to accomplish this. When an Array is created (using the Dim, ReDim, Global or Static commands), you can define the lower and the upper limits of the Array at the same time:

```
Static A$(1 To 3)
```

OR

```
Static A(1 To 3) As String
```

This approach is more descriptive than Option Base 1 (and the description is right next to the Dim that creates the Array, rather than off in the General Declarations section of the Form). In addition, you can even specify odd starting points if you want:

```
ReDim A$(5 To 10)
```

The Dim (1 To 3) is preferable to using Option Base. Specifying the range of index numbers for an Array is more commonly handled this way than with the Option Base command.

Used with   Arrays (which see)

Variables   The Option Base command can be used only in the General Declarations section of a Form or Module:

```
Option Base 1
```

(Also, this is the only possible way to use Option Base; it cannot have any numbers other than 0 or 1.)

Uses   Make working with Arrays easier

Cautions   • You must reissue the Option Base command in the General Declarations section of each Form or Module you want to use it in. You cannot put it in a Module to make it apply to the entire program.

• Option Base must be used before creating any Arrays with Dim, ReDim, Static or Global commands.

Example   In the General Declarations section of a Form:

```
Option Base 1
```

See also   Arrays; Dim; Global; LBound; ReDim; Static; UBound

CONTROL

Description

Figure O-16: The symbol for Option Buttons in the Toolbox.

Option Buttons allow the user to select one choice from a group of mutually exclusive choices. That is, selecting one Button turns off any of the other Buttons in the group.

This kind of Control is frequently referred to as a *radio button group* because it operates the way the buttons do on your car radio—if you press one radio button, the button previously down pops out. Only one of these buttons can be active at any given time.

Check Boxes are another VB Control frequently used in groups, but any number of Check Boxes can be On at a given time.

You could use a group of Option Buttons if you wanted to offer the user a choice of possible BackColors for a Form. Because there can be only one background color on a Form at a time, the choices are mutually exclusive. If the user clicks on Magenta, then whatever Button was previously active should pop out and become inactive.

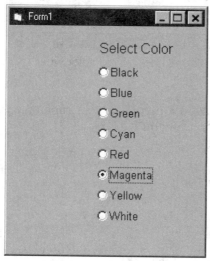

Figure O-17: A set of Option Buttons (see the Example).

Used with   Option Buttons are placed directly on a Form or grouped within a Picture Box or Frame. If you want to create a group of Option Buttons that will cause each other to pop out when a new one is selected, they must all be on the same Form or *within* the same Picture Box or Frame.

To draw one Control within another, first draw a Picture Box and then click (don't double-click) on the Option Button symbol in the VB Toolbox. Then move your mouse to the Picture Box and press and hold the left button as you "draw" the Option Button within the Picture Box.

Clicking on the Toolbox is different from double-clicking, which merely assigns the Button to the Form. A single-click and then drawing has two effects. The group of Buttons you draw on the Picture Box will all move together if you move the Picture Box. And, more important, the Buttons are now part of a team and pressing one will automatically pop out any of the others.

Variables You can set the various Properties for a Control Button in the VB Properties Window while you are designing your program.

OR (to change the Properties while the program is running):

```
Option1.FontBold = False
```

OR (to work with the Events to which the Option Button responds, place instructions within the appropriate Event):

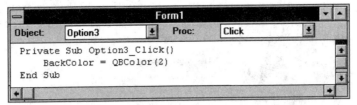

```
Private Sub Option3_Click()
    BackColor = QBColor(2)
End Sub
```

Figure O-18: We adjust the Form's background color when the user clicks on the different Option Buttons.

An Option Button's Value Property tells your running program whether that Button is currently "on" or "off":

```
X = Option1.Value

If X = True Then
    Print "Option 1 is ON"
Else
    Print "Option 1 is OFF"
End If
```

Uses Use Option Buttons when you want to offer the user a set of choices, but only one selection at a time can be active. A Form's FontSize, for example, could be selected via a group of Option Buttons because there can be only one FontSize active at any given time for a particular Form or Control.

Cautions • An Option Button is often used as part of a group of Option Buttons. See the "Used with" section to find out how to group them physically so that they will act in a coordinated fashion.

• When grouped within a Picture Box, Frame or Form, it's sometimes easier to manipulate Option Buttons if they are also grouped as part of a *Control Array* (which see).

Example To create the "Select BackColor" group of Option Buttons described in the preceding paragraphs, start a New Project from VB's File Menu and place a Picture Box on the Form. Now, using the single-click draw technique described under "Used with", put a Label and eight Option Buttons on the

Picture Box. The Buttons (having been embraced within the same Picture Box) automatically form a "group" that will work in concert. VB takes care of the details so that clicking on one of the Buttons deselects the other Buttons in the group.

The only commands you need to provide are within the Click Event of each Option Button, as in the following:

```
Sub Option1_Click ()
    BackColor = QBColor(0)
End Sub

Sub Option2_Click ()
    BackColor = QBColor(1)
End Sub
```

. . . and so on. Then set their Caption Properties to describe the appropriate colors.

You could expand this example to include a Check Box with the Caption "LIGHTEN." QBColor (which see) will provide lighter versions of the colors we are using here by merely adding 8 to the darker color. QBColor(1) is blue; QBColor(9) is light blue. Add a Check Box to the Form and then change the Click Event of each Option Button to

```
Sub Option2_Click ()

X = 1
    If Check1.Value = 1 then X = X + 8
BackColor = QBColor(X)
End Sub
```

The Value of a Check Box is 1 if it's selected, 0 if not. If the user clicks on the Check Box, we add 8 to the Variable X that we provide to QBColor.

Manipulating a group of Option Buttons can be considerably easier if you use a Control Array (which see). A Control Array would avoid much of the repetition that you can see in this example—we have to deal with eight separate Events, one for each Button. With a Control Array, we would deal with only one Click Event for all eight of the Buttons. They would all respond to *the same Event* if we put them into a Control Array.

Option Button Properties

Alignment • BackColor • Caption • DragIcon • DragMode • Enabled FontBold • FontItalic • FontName • FontSize • FontStrikethru FontUnderline • ForeColor • Height • HelpContextID • hWnd Index • Left • MousePointer • Name • Parent • TabIndex • TabStop Tag • Top • Value • Visible • Width

Option Button Events

Click • DblClick • DragDrop • DragOver • GotFocus • KeyDown KeyPress • KeyUp • LostFocus • MouseDown • MouseMove • MouseUp

Option Button Methods
Drag • Move • Refresh • SetFocus • ZOrder

See also Check Box; Control Array

Option Compare

STATEMENT

See StrComp

Option Private

STATEMENT

See Objects

Optional

STATEMENT

See IsQueries

PROPERTY

Description Page keeps track of the number of pages printed on the printer.

Page is a Variable that keeps incrementing (going up by 1) each time the printer ejects a sheet of paper. Printers automatically eject when given enough text to fill a page. (You can also force an ejection by using the NewPage command or the EndDoc command, which both ejects and signals that a document is complete.)

Used with The printer

Variables **Variable type:** Integer

To print the current page number on the sheet of paper in the printer:
```
Printer.Print Printer.Page
```

OR (to insert the picture that fills Form 2 into page 7 of the document):
```
If Printer.Page = 7 Then
    Form2.PrintForm
End If
```

OR (to find out the current page): X = Printer.Page

Uses • Put page numbers on the sheets of paper during printing.

• Specify on which page to insert a particular text or graphic.

Cautions • Page is automatically adjusted by Visual Basic while your program runs. You cannot assign a page number to it (Printer.Page = 3 doesn't work).

• If you are using the drawing methods to create designs that you are sending to the printer (the PSet, Circle, Line commands) and the design is too large for the sheet of paper, the design will be *cropped*, cut off where it exceeds the dimensions of the paper. Cropping does not increment the Page Property.

Text larger than the sheet of paper causes the printer to eject the page and continue printing the remaining text, which *does* generate the next Page number (increments the Page Variable).

The Printer.NewPage command ejects the current sheet of paper and increments Page.

The Printer.EndDoc method *resets* the Page Variable to 1, so it can again begin keeping track of the current sheet of paper in the printer. The EndDoc command forces a page eject and makes it possible to start printing a new document.

Example   This example shows how to print the page number at the bottom of each page, centered, and in this format: – 2 –

```
Sub Form_Click ()

For i = 1 To 2
        For j = 1 To 55
                Printer.Print i; "."; j
        Next j
    Pageno$ = "– " + Str$(Printer.Page) + " –"
    lengthofpagenumber = Printer.TextWidth(Pageno$)
    Printer.Currentx = (Printer.scalewidth / 2) – (lengthofpagenumber / 2)
    Printer.Print "– "; Printer.Page; " –"
    Printer.NewPage
Next i

Printer.EndDoc

End Sub
```

We set up an "outer Loop" that counts up to 2, so we'll print two pages. The inner Loop prints 55 sample lines. Then, because we want to center the page number, we need to find out how big our – 2 – is on the printer, how much space it takes up. We put it into a text ("string") Variable; then we use the Printer.TextWidth Property to measure the size of this 2 as it will be when printed using the currently active Printer.FontSize and Font-Name. The Variable *lengthofpagenumber* now holds the size of the 2.

To Be Really Precise: We move the printer to the center of the page by setting the printer's CurrentX Property to the width of the page (Printer.ScaleWidth) divided by two. To be really precise, we also move a little farther left on the sheet of paper—one-half the size of the 2. This process may seem painstaking, but it does make the results symmetrical and accurate.

Finally, we print the Printer.Page at the location on the sheet of paper that we have calculated and moved to via the CurrentX command. And we eject the page. When finished with this document, we use EndDoc.

Note: You can center printed text on the printer, a Form or a Picture Box by using the ScaleWidth, ScaleHeight, TextWidth and TextHeight Properties as illustrated in this example. (For more information on formatting text, see "TextHeight.")

See also   EndDoc; NewPage; Print (Method and Object); Printer; PrintForm

PAINT

EVENT

Description

Paint should probably have been named *TimeToPaint*. The Paint Event is triggered when a window is moved after having covered one of your Forms or Picture Boxes. Paint is also triggered when your Form or Picture Box itself is enlarged. Any of these actions can *erase* designs that were drawn on a Form or Picture Box (by using the PSet, Circle or Line command) or text that was Printed on them (using the Print command).

To avoid erasing designs, you can put all drawing or printing activity within the Paint Event—so the designs or text are repainted whenever they should be.

A Serious Drawback: Unfortunately, using Paint has a serious drawback—the repainting can be slow and quite visible to the user. Using the Paint Event in this fashion can add a cheesy, amateurish look to your Windows application. There is a simple solution, though: use the AutoRedraw Property and forget about the Paint Event.

Use the Paint Event when you need to control the painting. For example, use Paint if the painted graphic is supposed to be relative to the Form's size or to a chart drawn with lines and text. Without the AutoRedraw Property on, graphics drawn on a Form are "temporary" and must be redrawn every time a Paint event occurs. This gives you, the programmer, more control over what is displayed. When AutoRedraw is on, VB maintains a "device context" with the image drawn onto it; then, when it's time to Paint, VB *BitBlts* the image back to the screen. This approach is much faster than recalculating and creating the drawing all over again.

Normally, you won't bother with the Paint Event. Simply set Form and Picture Box AutoRedraw Properties to True and let Visual Basic solve the problem. The Paint Event is never triggered when AutoRedraw is on, and AutoRedraw does everything Paint would do—except it does it instantly and smoothly.

AutoRedraw does use up some of the computer's memory. If your computer has a very small amount of memory—less, say, than two megabytes—you might have to leave AutoRedraw in its default state (0, off) and insert drawing and printing housekeeping commands into the Paint Event.

Because most people using Windows have more than enough memory for AutoRedraw and because memory is increasingly less expensive, the Paint Event is usually something you can safely ignore.

A Second Fatal Flaw: The Paint Event is also triggered when a Form is enlarged by the user. But Paint has another fatal flaw: Paint is *not* triggered when the user shrinks a Form, only when it is dragged larger. If you want some text or a design to be redrawn (and thereby kept proportionate) to a resized Form, use the Resize Event, which see. Using Paint also allows you, the programmer, to use a variation of the commands that you use to draw to the screen to draw something on the printer.

Technically, Paint is analogous to the WM_PAINT message in the Windows API (see Appendix A for more on API). Paint only occurs when some portion of the "client" area has become "invalid." If a Form has been reduced, there is nothing that needs to be updated (as far as WM_PAINT is concerned), nothing that needs to be repainted on the screen. If the Form is increased in size, there must be a PAINT; otherwise, some of the screen would be white.

The ClipControls Property determines the *way* that a Paint Event behaves. (Should Paint blindly repaint everything or only those areas that really need to be repainted?) See "ClipControls" for more details.

Used with   Forms and Picture Boxes

Variables

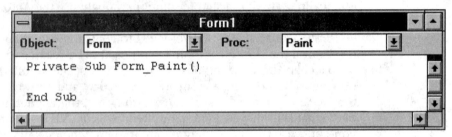

Figure P-1: Paint is an Event, so you put commands within its "procedure," its Subroutine.

Uses   • Perhaps one use for the Paint Event might seem of value—at least if you want your programs to behave in a sophisticated fashion. You might want text or designs to be repainted in a larger size if the Form is stretched, and, conversely, to shrink if the Form is made smaller. Paint is triggered when the user has stretched a Form, making the Form larger onscreen. But, again, Paint has a fatal flaw: What happens if the user shrinks the Form? *Paint is completely insensitive if a Form is reduced in size.*

If a Form is shrunk, you can use the Resize Event to trigger a Paint Event. You could, therefore, handle all the redrawing with only one piece of programming.

Aspect Ratio: If you want to maintain the *aspect ratio* (a ratio of height and width that parallels that of the host Form) of drawn designs and printed text, you can use the Resize Event, which is sensitive to any resizing—enlargement or shrinking. However, Resize is *insensitive* to other Forms or windows, erasing your Form when placed on top of it. To deal with every possible situation, you would want to call upon the Resize Event from within the Paint Event:

```
Sub Form_Paint ()
    Form_Resize
End Sub
```

Then put your redrawing inside the Resize Event:

```
Sub Form_Resize ()
    Cls
    centerform = scalewidth / 2
    FontSize = centerform / 80
    centertext = (TextWidth("RESPONDS")) / 2
    Currentx = centerform — centertext
    Print "RESPONDS"
End Sub
```

If you have drawn a design on the Form with Circle, PSet or Line, you may want to redraw *to make the design fill the Form with larger or smaller design elements*. Rectangles 1 inch in size would become 2 inches or .5 inch, adjusting their size in proportion to changes in the Form's ScaleHeight and ScaleWidth Properties. (See the Example under "Resize.")

• Use the Paint Event along with the Resize Event if you want to redraw proportionate designs or text when a Form is resized by the user. See "Resize."

Cautions • Setting the AutoRedraw Property to True (On) is preferable to working with the Paint Event. AutoRedraw is faster at redrawing and also handles all possible situations where redrawing is necessary. AutoRedraw defaults to 0 (Off), so you must explicitly change it within the Properties Window while designing your program or by using Form1.AutoRedraw = True while your program is running.

If you wanted to draw an X,Y chart that changed as data was modified, you could set AutoRedraw to Off and then use Line commands to draw it. This would allow you to wipe out lines with invert mode (see "Draw-Mode," option 6) and draw new lines without causing a screen refresh. Deleting and redrawing an image would trigger a screen refresh.

If AutoRedraw is left set to Off (False)—the default—and the user or your program enlarges the Form, first the Resize Event is triggered, and then the Paint Event is triggered.

Computers use two kinds of graphics: *Bitmap* pictures (.BMP, .ICO and .WMF files are the ones used in VB) contain a point-by-point *copy* of the graphic. Some kinds of compression are possible; however, an .ICO file, like the image of a floppy disk in Figure P-2, would require nearly as many bytes to hold the copy of the icon as there are dots in the picture:

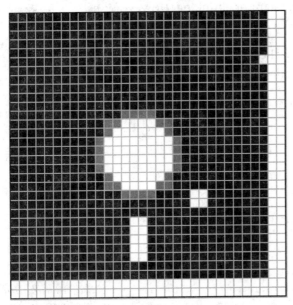

Figure P-2: If you blow it up enough, you can see the *bits* in a bitmapped graphic.

Black-and-white bitmaps take up the least amount of memory, and as you add more colors (16-color or 256-color), the pictures take up increasingly more memory. Bitmaps redraw very fast onscreen, but they do take up space on a disk or in the computer's memory while a program is running.

The alternative is to provide mathematical descriptions of a graphic and then redraw the graphic each time it is needed (as opposed to simply moving the mass of bytes in a picture saved as a bitmap onto the screen). The drawback to this technique is that calculating and displaying such graphics can be slow. It is often visible to the user as the computer goes through all the math involved:

```
For i = 1 To 200
    Line (x + i, y + i) — Step(x + 1200, y + 1200), , B
Next i
```

A Xerox of Your Bitmap: You don't want your drawn graphics or printed text to be erased when a window is resized or temporarily covered by another window. With the AutoRedraw Property set to True (On), VB creates a *temporary bitmap* of anything you print or draw in a Picture Box or Form. This bitmap is saved in memory while your program is running—and is automatically copied back into the Form or Picture Box when something covers and then uncovers part of the image.

For a *Form* (if the Form's BorderStyle Property is set so that the Form is resizable), VB saves a bitmap *of the entire screen,* which does use up memory rather quickly. For a *Picture Box*, only the drawn or printed data within the borders of the Box is saved to memory. The result of these two approaches is that you can draw or print *larger than the current size of a Form, and even the invisible parts of the drawing will be saved in case the Form is later enlarged.* Anything drawn outside the borders of a Picture Box, though, is not saved to memory.

The implication of the preceding Caution is that you can conserve memory by creating a Picture Box as large as you want your graphic to be and set its AutoRedraw Property to True. But you should leave the Form's AutoRedraw Property at the default of False. Then use the image in the Picture Box for your designs.

• The AutoRedraw Property can be *turned on and off* while a program is running. If you draw or print while AutoRedraw is on (True), using the Cls command does not clear the graphics or text. Try turning AutoRedraw on and off at various points within your drawing activity and observe the various effects you can achieve. (See "AutoRedraw.")

Example   When this Form is enlarged or reduced in size, its Paint Event is triggered, and the graphic is redrawn to a larger size. With this technique, the graphic will always remain proportionate to the Form:

```
Sub Form_Paint ()

Cls

For i = 0 To scalewidth Step scalewidth / 32
    Circle (i / 2, i / 3), i / 2
Next i

End Sub
```

Without the Cls to clear out the previous graphics, remnants of earlier drawings will show up under each repainting. (See "Circle" for more on setting coordinates for designs.)

Note: If you want your drawing to respond proportionately to changes in the size of the Form, you must adjust the size of your drawing *in terms of both the ScaleWidth and ScaleHeight Properties.* Here we're only making the drawing resize in proportion to changes that are horizontal.

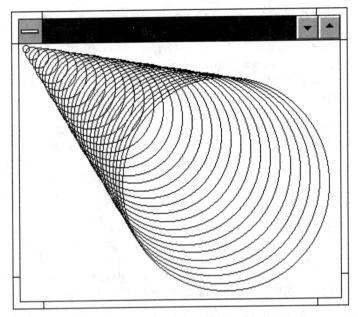

Figure P-3: This drawing will expand or contract horizontally if the user stretches the window.

See also   AutoRedraw; ClipControls; Refresh; Resize

PAINTPICTURE

METHOD

Description   New to VB4, PaintPicture allows you to copy, invert, resize, reposition, combine and otherwise manipulate graphics. This facility isn't new to Windows. PaintPicture is merely a VB command which triggers the Stretch-Blt API function described in Appendix A and in the entry on "Declare." PaintPicture, though, is somewhat easier to use than the API call because with the API function, you first have to first Declare it before VB can use it. Also, PaintPicture runs about five times faster than the API call, though both are plenty fast.

Used with   Forms, Picture Boxes or the Printer

Variables   The following copies the graphic from within a Picture Box to the Form (see the Example). It means: copy the picture in Picture1 to Form1.

(All this must be typed on a single line):

> Form1.PaintPicture Picture1.Picture, DestXPosition, DestYPosition, DestWidth, DestHeight, SourceXPosition, SourceYPosition, SourceWidth, SourceHeight, copymode

DestXPosition and **DestYPosition** describe the *position*, the starting points in the *Form* (the upper left hand corner) where the graphic will be drawn. To fit it snug against the top and left of the Form, you would use 0, 0 for these parameters. You are required to enter these parameters, but all the rest of the parameters listed below are optional.

DestWidth and **DestHeight** describe the *size* of the copied graphic. To make it fill the entire Form, use Form1.Width and Form1.Height. These are optional parameters and default to the Width and Height Properties of the *source* Object. In other words, you get by default an exact copy the same size as the source. (In our example, the source is the Picture Box and the target is the Form. But you could just as easily be copying *from* the Form to a Picture Box, or from one Picture Box to another.)

SourceXPosition and **SourceYPosition** (along with SourceWidth and SourceHeight) describe how much of the source graphic you want to copy. SourceXPosition and SourceYPosition describe a location in the upper left of the graphic in the *Picture Box* (the source graphic). In other words, you don't have to copy the entire graphic—you could specify a region within the graphic by changing these parameters from their default (0,0). If you use (10,0) you wouldn't copy a bar of 10 units from the left side of the graphic (the *units* are whatever ScaleMode is in effect for your Form). These are optional parameters and default to 0,0.

SourceWidth and **SourceHeight** also describe how much of the source graphic you want to send to the target Object. To quit before copying the bottom 400 units (whatever units are the Form's ScaleMode) in our example, you would use Picture1.Width, Picture1.Height - 400.

Copymode The various *copymodes* are identical to those described and illustrated in Table AA-1 in Appendix A and in the entry on "Declare." The default is an ordinary direct copy.

```
Global Const SRCCOPY = &HCC0020        ' (DWORD) dest = source
Global Const SRCPAINT = &HEE0086       ' (DWORD) dest = source or
                                       ' dest
Global Const SRCAND = &H8800C6         ' (DWORD) dest = source AND
                                       ' dest
Global Const SRCINVERT = &H660046      ' (DWORD) dest = source XOR
                                       ' dest
Global Const SRCERASE = &H440328       ' (DWORD) dest = source AND
                                       ' (NOT dest )
Global Const NOTSRCCOPY = &H330008     ' (DWORD) dest = (NOT source)
Global Const NOTSRCERASE = &H1100A6    ' (DWORD) dest = (NOT src)
                                       ' AND(NOT dest)
```

```
Global Const MERGECOPY = &HC000CA      ' (DWORD) dest = (source AND
                                       ' pattern)
Global Const MERGEPAINT = &HBB0226     ' (DWORD) dest = (NOT source)
                                       ' OR dest
Global Const PATCOPY = &HF00021        ' (DWORD) dest = pattern
Global Const PATPAINT = &HFB0A09       ' (DWORD) dest = DPSnoo
Global Const PATINVERT = &H5A0049      ' (DWORD) dest = pattern XOR
                                       ' dest
Global Const DSTINVERT = &H550009      ' (DWORD) dest = (NOT dest)
Global Const BLACKNESS = &H42&         ' (DWORD) dest = BLACK
Global Const WHITENESS = &HFF0062      ' (DWORD) dest = WHITE
```

Uses   Manipulate graphics in a variety of ways. Picture Boxes can be made
              invisible (and used with PaintPicture as quick ways to change the back-
              ground graphic on a Form). Also, don't forget that you can load icon (.ICO)
              files into a Picture Box as well as .BMP or .WMF graphic files.

Cautions • You cannot use the new Named Parameters (which see) with PaintPicture.
              • You cannot use an Image Box with PaintPicture.
              • Recall that unless the target Object (the Form or Picture Box to which
              you're copying the graphic) has its AutoRedraw Property set to True,
              minimizing the Form or otherwise covering the target object will erase the
              copied graphic.

Example   Put a Picture Box on a Form, then enter this in the Form Load Event:

```
Sub Form_Load( )
    Show
    Form1.PaintPicture Picture1.Picture, 0, 0, ScaleWidth, ScaleHeight
End Sub
```

Figure P-4: The Picture Box is blown up to fill the entire Form.

Or, to flip the image, put the start-copy point at the lower right of the source graphic (Picture1.ScaleWidth, Picture1.ScaleHeight in the following example) and then copy *backwards up to 0,0* in the source graphic (-Picture1.ScaleWidth and -Picture1.ScaleHeight) by using negative values for the SourceWidth and SourceHeight, like this:

```
Sub Form_Load( )
Show

sw = -Picture1.ScaleWidth
sh = -Picture1.ScaleHeight

Form1.PaintPicture Picture1.Picture, 0, 0, ScaleWidth, ScaleHeight,
Picture1.ScaleWidth, Picture1.ScaleHeight, sw, sh

End Sub
```

There are many additional transformations you can manage with Paint-Picture. For additional examples, see the entry on Declare or Appendix A.

See also   Declare; Appendix A

 ARENT

PROPERTY

Description   The Parent Property identifies the Form that holds a particular Control. When you are designing your program and you put a Label on it, you obviously *know* which Form you put that Label on. However, there is a specialized use for the Parent Property: it can come in handy when your program has several Forms, and you want to use a single Subroutine that can affect all the Forms.

Say that you have three Forms and you want each of them to respond by turning into icons and flashing when the user presses a button marked "CLOSE." You could write the same procedure in each of the three Command Button Click Events. Or, using Parent to identify which Form has been clicked, you could write a single, general-purpose Subroutine in a Module.

This Subroutine would service each Form the same way, and it knows *which* Form to manipulate based on the Parent Property of the Control that is "passed" to the Subroutine. (See the Example.)

Used with   Any Control, including Timers and Menus

Variables   **Variable type:** Built-in Form Variable

To Hide the Form that the Command Button named Command1 is on:

```
Command1.Parent.Hide
```

P ... **881**

Uses   Parent allows a single, independent Subroutine (in a separate Module) to affect various Forms. It knows which Form to affect because Controls can be "passed" to Subroutines; and within the Subroutine, Parent will tell us the Control's host Form. (See "Sub.")

Cautions   • You cannot adjust Parent, either during program design or when the program runs. You cannot say "Command1.Parent = Form2."

Nor can you directly quiz Parent to get the Form Name of the parent like this:

```
X$ = Command1.Parent
```

You can, however, use

```
X$ = Command1.Parent.Caption
```

to get the Caption, or any other Property that can be "read" while a program is running.

Example   We want all the Forms in this project to minimize and flash briefly when the user clicks on the Command Button labeled Close. Create three Forms and put a Command Button on each. To make all the Forms visible when the program starts, put the following in Form1's Load Event (Form1 is the default "Startup Form"):

```
Sub Form_Load ()
    form2.Show
    form3.Show
End Sub
```

In each of the three Command Button Click Events, put the following:

```
Form1:
```

```
Sub Command1_Click ()
    shutdown form1.command1
End Sub
```

```
Form2:
```

```
Sub Command1_Click ()
    shutdown form2.command1
End Sub
```

```
Form3:
```

```
Sub Command1_Click ()
    shutdown form3.command1
End Sub
```

Now create a new Module (from VB's File Menu) and put this general-purpose Subroutine into it:

```
Sub shutdown (whichone As Control)
```

```
whichone.parent.WindowState = 1
whichone.parent.visible = 0

For i = 1 To 2000
    Next i
whichone.parent.visible = —1
End Sub
```

You can put Subroutines (and Functions) that are designed to service more than one area of a Form into the Form's General Declarations section. However, to allow a Subroutine to service your whole program, you need to put the Subroutine into a Module. Modules, although some programmers don't use them much in Visual Basic, are designed to provide a place to put Subroutines and Functions that will be available to perform a task from anywhere in a multi-Form program.

Passing a Name: You "pass" the name of the Control that "called" the Subroutine by merely providing a name (any name you want) in the parentheses following the Sub command. Here we're naming it *whichone*. Then, to show that the item we're receiving in the Sub's list of Variables is a particular *Control*, we use the phrase "As Control." Using this phrase lets the Subroutine know that a *Control* has been "passed" rather than something else, such as a text or numeric Variable.

Now we can use the Parent Property to find out which of the three Forms this Control is located on. We set it to icon size (WindowState = 1), make it invisible, count to 2000 to create a brief delay and then make it visible again. Note that each of these buttons is named *Command1,* but VB can distinguish between them with the Parent Property.

See also   Module

PROPERTY

Description   When you assign a character to a Text Box's PasswordChar Property, VB intercepts all characters typed into the Text Box and changes them into a special character before displaying them onscreen. It is common practice not to echo passwords to the screen, in case someone nearby is *watching.* It is also a convention to use the asterisk (*) as the password character.

Used with   Text Boxes only

Variables

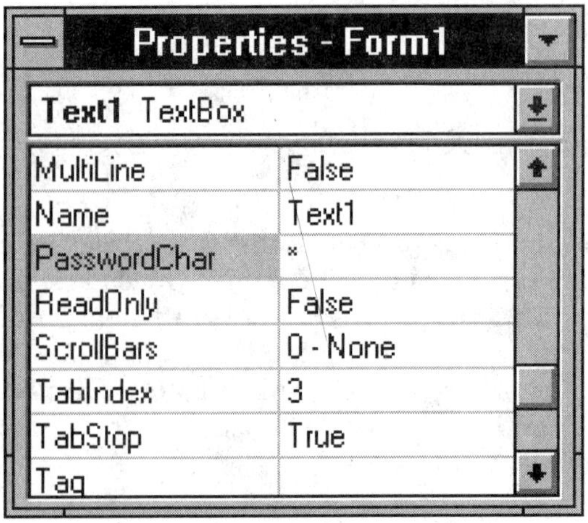

Figure P-5: You can adjust the PasswordChar in the Properties Window.

OR (to set the character while the program is running):

```
Text1.PasswordChar = "*"
```

Uses   Prevent typed characters from appearing onscreen in a Text Box to keep others from seeing a secret password as it is being typed in. You can refuse access to your program (or portions of your program) to those who do not know the password.

Cautions   • The KeyAscii, KeyCode and Shift built-in Variables used by the KeyPress and KeyDown Events are unaffected by setting a PasswordChar. The Text Box's Text Property is also unaffected.

• The PasswordChar defaults to Off, holding empty text "". To turn off the effect of PasswordChar, reset it to empty text: PasswordChar = "".
This will not work if the Text Box is MultiLine.

Example   We'll create a typical password-entry window. Put a Text Box on a Form and type this into the Form_Load Event:

```
Sub Form_Load ()
    Text1.PasswordChar = "*"
    Text1.Text = ""
End Sub
```

By defining the PasswordChar as "*", we've prevented the characters the user types from appearing onscreen. Now we want to detect each character and match the user's input against the password. Type the following into the Text Box's KeyPress Event:

```
Sub Text1_KeyPress (KeyAscii As Integer)

Static Tries As Integer
Static User As String
```

```
        User$ = User$ + Chr$(KeyAscii)
    If Len(User$) = 4 Then
        Tries = Tries + 1
        If Tries > 2 Then Text1.Text = "": End
        If LCase(User$) = "yess" Then
            Text1.PasswordChar = ""
            Text1.Text = "PASSED!  ADMITTED."
            KeyAscii = 0
        Else
            Text1.Text = ""
            User$ = ""
            KeyAscii = 0
        End If
    End If
```

We make a Static integer Variable called Tries, which will count how many times the user types in a four-letter word. We'll give the user three tries. We also make a Static text Variable to hold and accumulate the user's keypresses. Static is required if you are using Variables that are not Global (which see) and you want the Variables to retain their contents. Then we add each new character the user types to User$ and, if the length of User$ reaches four characters, we raise the count of Tries and shut down the program if there have been three tries. If not, we test it against the secret word *yess*. If they match, we announce the fact. If they don't match, we erase the text, reset User$ to no-text and give a "nothing" to KeyAscii to prevent a phantom character from appearing in the Text Box.

See also   Static

PATH

PROPERTY

Description   • The Path Property tells your program the current "path" of a Directory List Box or a File List Box. The path is the drive plus directory (plus any subdirectories) that the Box is currently pointing to. For example, C:\DOS is the path of the DOS directory on drive C:.

• Also, the App Object ("application," VB's lingo for current program) has a Path Property, which can report where on the user's disk drive your program is located. In other words, if you finish a VB program and create an .EXE file (from the File Menu), you might name it QUICK.EXE. If the user puts your file in his or her Windows directory on drive C:, Print App.Path would result in C:\WINDOWS. What if the user has renamed your program? You can find out the name by using X$ = App.EXEName.

• Your program can *change* the Path Property of a Directory List Box or a File List Box while the program is running. Drive, Directory and File List Boxes are normally used together to provide the user with a way of navigating around the disk drive and also allowing files to be saved or retrieved. When used this way, it is common practice to react to a change in the Directory List Box. This means that the user has clicked on a new directory, so we put the following into the Change Event. This will adjust the *File List* Box to display the files in the new directory the user has selected:

```
Sub Dir1_Change ()
    File1.Path = Dir1.Path
End Sub
```

(For a complete discussion on adding a full file-management feature to your VB program, see "Drive List Box.")

Used with Directory and File List Boxes and the App (application) Object

Variables **Variable type:** Text ("string")

To find out the current path as registered in a Directory List Box:

```
X$ = Dir1.Path
```

OR (to have your program, not the user, change the path in a Directory List Box): Dir1.Path = "C:\WORD"

OR (to find out where the running .EXE program itself is located on the disk): X$ = App.Path

Uses • Changing the Path Property is like using the ChDir Statement in Visual Basic or the ChDir (CD) command in DOS.

• Manipulate files on the disk drive—save, open or otherwise access files.

• Show the attributes of files or display selective lists of files when used with the Pattern Property.

• When used with the App Object, knowing where the user has put your program on his or her disk drive comes in handy for self-modifying programs (see the Example under "ChDir"), for creating subdirectories during a Setup/Installation and for saving data in the same location as the program.

Cautions • When your program is first started up, the "current" path is the default. One disk drive path is always "current" when the computer is running. What's "current" depends on whether the path was changed by starting VB, whether you have recently used File Manager, etc.

• Assigning the drive name only (C:) to the Path switches to the "current directory" on that drive.

• Path returns the *full path,* including the drive name. See "Drive List Box" to find out how to extract, or compose, directory+subdirectory+filenames.

• Changing Path triggers a PathChange Event in File List Boxes but triggers a Change Event in Directory List Boxes.

• The Path Property of a Directory List Box is not the same thing as its List(ListIndex) Property. See the Example.

Example   Directory List Boxes are somewhat automated by VB. When the user clicks on a directory, the Box responds appropriately by changing visually. However, only a double-click will change the Path Property.

(File List Boxes are not automated. Their only automatic behavior is to highlight a clicked or double-clicked file; you have to provide additional instructions in the File List Box's Click or DblClick Event to make these Boxes respond as they should to the user's needs.)

A Directory List Box's Path and List(ListIndex) Properties react somewhat differently. To see the variations, try this example. First, create a Form and then put a Directory List Box and a File List Box on it.

Then put the following into the Directory List Box's Change Event:

```
Sub Dir1_Change ()

Print
Print "CHANGE  "
Print "PATH"; Dir1.path
Print "LIST  "; Dir1.List(listindex)
End Sub
```

Next, enter the following into the Click Event:

```
Sub Dir1_Click ()

Print
Print "CLICK  "
Print "PATH"; Dir1.path
Print "LIST  "; Dir1.List(listindex)
End Sub
```

Now run the program and observe the effect of clicking and double-clicking on directories within the Box.

See also   See "Drive List Box" for a lengthy example of file management using all three file Control tools—Drive, Directory and File List Boxes.

Visual Basic provides a wealth of ways to view, access and manage disk drives and the files that are on them. Here is a complete alphabetical list of the VB commands related to file management:

AppActivate; Archive; Change; ChDir; ChDrive; Close; CurDir$; Dir$; Drive; EOF; EXEName; FileAttr; FileName; FreeFile; Get; Hidden; Input$; Input #; Kill; Line Input #; List; ListCount; ListIndex; Loc; Lock; LOF; MkDir; Name; Normal; On Error; Open; PathChange; Pattern; Pattern-Change; Print #; Put; ReadOnly; Reset; RmDir; Seek; Shell; System; Unlock; Write #

PATHCHANGE

EVENT

Description

The PathChange Event isn't often needed.

PathChange is triggered in a File List Box whenever its Path or FileName Properties are changed (by the program itself, not by the user clicking on something).

A File List Box's path does *not* change when the user clicks within the Box; there are only filenames in there, not *paths*. You have to respond when a user clicks or double-clicks in a File List Box by putting instructions within the Click and DblClick Events of the Box. You can change the path that way, but user-clicking itself won't work.

How a PathChange Is Triggered: A File List Box works in concert with a Directory List Box; in the Directory Box's Change Event (it's changed when the user has clicked on a different directory name) you should respond by adjusting the Path Property of the File List Box:

```
Sub Dir1_Change ()
    File1.path = Dir1.path
End Sub
```

This resetting of the File Box's Path or FileName Properties triggers the Box's PathChange Event, and you can react to that if you want. Few applications for this Event suggest themselves, however. If you gave the user a box to type in a filename within a FileOpen Dialog Box, he or she could type a file path that wasn't the one selected in the Directory List Box. This entry would trip a PathChange Event and your program could then update its current path. Here's an example:

```
Sub Text3_LostFocus ()
    File1.Filename = Text3.Text
End Sub

Sub File1_PathChange
    Dir1.path = File1.path
End Sub
```

This Subroutine will take the text typed into the File Descriptor Box (Text3) and transfer the paths into the File and Directory Boxes. If the user typed \mydir*.doc, then the Directory Box would change to \mydir and the File Box would show all the .doc files. This approach allows the user to get to his or her files by typing on the keyboard (versus using the mouse) if he or she knows the location of the desired files. Typing the directory name can be faster than traversing a large tree structure by having to click through directories and subdirectories. You could also use this technique to prevent a user from accessing certain directory paths on a disk.

Used with File List Boxes

Variables PathChange is an Event, something that happens while your program is running:

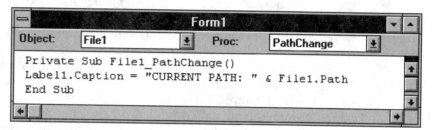

Figure P-6: You put instructions within this Event if you want the program to respond to changes in the Path.

Uses There's not much that you will want to do with PathChange. It's informational, and you can create a separate Label to always hold the current Path and show the user where he or she is when navigating through the disk drive.

However, a Drive List Box is almost always on a Form that has a File List Box. And a Drive List Box visually displays the Path, so a separate display of the Path would be redundant.

Cautions • The PathChange Event is *not triggered* when the user clicks or double-clicks on a filename within a File List Box. It can be triggered only by changing the File Box's Path Property from within a running program:

```
Sub Dir1_Change ()
    File1.path = Dir1.path
End Sub
```

OR by explicitly assigning a complete path (including a filename) to the File List Box's FileName Property:

```
File1.Filename = "C:\DOS\SORT.EXE"
```

Example In this example, put a Label, a Directory List Box and a File List Box on a Form. Put the usual cause-effect trigger into the Directory Box's Change Event:

```
Sub Dir1_Change ()
    file1.Path = dir1.Path
End Sub
```

Then put your reaction to this change in the Path within the File List Box's PathChange Event:

```
Sub File1_PathChange ()
    Label1.Caption = "CURRENT PATH:" + File1.Path
End Sub
```

This Subroutine will display the path in the Label, but note that the user can already see the path highlighted in the Directory List Box.

See also See "Drive List Box" for a lengthy example of file management using all three file Control tools—Drive, Directory and File List Boxes.

Visual Basic provides a wealth of ways to access, view and manage disk drives and the files that are on them. Here is a complete alphabetical list of the VB commands related to file management:

AppActivate; Archive; Change; ChDir; ChDrive; Close; CurDir$; Dir$; Drive; EOF; EXEName; FileAttr; FileName; FreeFile; Get; Hidden; Input$; Input #; Kill; Line Input #; List; ListCount; ListIndex; Loc; Lock; LOF; MkDir; Name; Normal; On Error; Open; Path; Pattern; PatternChange; Print #; Put; ReadOnly; Reset; RmDir; Seek; Shell; System; Unlock; Write #

 ATTERN PROPERTY

Description Pattern works exactly like Dir *.TXT does in DOS.

It creates a filter that causes a File List Box to show only those files that match the pattern. You can use * or ?, just as in DOS, to limit the files that are listed.

When no Pattern has been set up, a list of the filenames in a directory might look like this:

```
RUN.EXE
NAME.TXT
SIGN.BAT
JACK.TXT
MACRO.PIF
```

With a Pattern set to *.TXT, the list of filenames would become

```
NAME.TXT
JACK.TXT
```

Used with File List Boxes

Variables **Variable type:** Text ("string")

You can adjust the Pattern while designing your program by using the Properties Window:

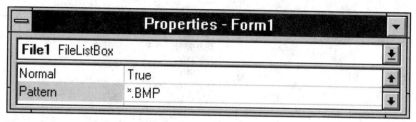

Figure P-7: Optionally, you can set the Pattern from the Properties Window.

OR (to change the Pattern while the program is running):

    File1.Pattern = Text1.Text

OR (to find out what the Pattern is): A$ = File1.Pattern

Uses
• Allow the user to specify which kinds of files will appear in a File List Box:

> *.* (all files)
>
> *.TXT (only files ending in .TXT)
>
> B*.* (all files whose names begin with B)

• Provide a "suggested list" of filenames, based on current conditions, from which the user chooses. If your program is preparing to launch *Word For Windows*, you might set the File List Box Pattern Property to *.DOC because *Word* saves files with this extension.

Cautions
• Setting a default Pattern for the user can be overdone. You should probably avoid having your program control what the user will see in a File List Box. Allow the user to set a Pattern, but don't be presumptuous enough to assume that all users like to append all their word processed documents as .DOC, or that every program name ends in .EXE. Some end in .COM or .BAT.

Let the user set a filter, but don't create a default filter. Always show all the files in a File List Box, unless the user specifies otherwise by changing the Pattern Property.

• File List Boxes also have a PatternChange Event that can react to any change your program, or the user, makes to the Pattern Property.

Example
Pattern is most commonly used by attaching a Text Box to the top of a File List Box. The user can type in any kind of pattern and then press ENTER. That sends a new pattern to the File List Box, which responds with a new list of files.

First, create a Form with a Directory List Box, a File List Box and a Text Box right above, butted against the File List Box.

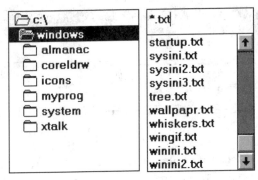

Figure P-8: The Pattern here is *.TXT, so only files with that extension are displayed in the File List Box.

Then make the File Box respond to changes in the Directory Box by putting this Subroutine in the Directory Box's Change Event:

```
Sub Dir1_Change ()
    File1.path = dir1.path
End Sub
```

In the Text Box's KeyPress Event, watch to see when the user presses the ENTER key (ANSI code 13):

```
Sub Text1_KeyPress (keyascii As Integer)

If keyascii = 13 Then
    keyascii = 0
    File1.Pattern = text1.text
End If

End Sub
```

Setting an ANSI code from 13 to 0 prevents the speaker from clicking. The speaker clicks if a Text Box's MultiLine Property is off (False), and pressing the ENTER key cannot, therefore, send us down one line. But we're not interested in the Carriage Return anyway; hitting ENTER is just a way for the user to indicate that the Text Box has been satisfactorily changed and the new Pattern is ready to be given to the File Box. So, when the user presses ENTER, we assign Text1.Text to File1.Pattern and are done.

By the way, this approach technically violates the CUA (Windows's "Common User Interface"). The CUA is a list of standard ways that Windows programs should behave when dealing with user input and output. The ENTER key is defined as selecting the default Command Button. The TAB key is used for exiting or terminating text entry.

See also　Dir$; Path; PathChange; PatternChange

See "Drive List Box" for a lengthy example of file management using all three file Control tools—Drive, Directory and File List Boxes.

Visual Basic provides a wealth of ways to access, view and manage disk drives and the files that are on them. See "PathChange" for a complete alphabetical list of the VB commands related to file management.

PATTERNCHANGE

EVENT

Description PatternChange is triggered when a File List Box's FileName or Pattern Property is changed.

PatternChange has few uses; perhaps the only use worth mentioning is to display the current Pattern in a Label or Text Box. However, the user normally changes the Pattern anyway, and the Pattern is therefore already visible in the Text Box where the user made the change.

Used with File List Boxes

Variables PatternChange is an Event, so you provide instructions to the computer within the Event Procedure as to how it should respond if this Event is triggered while the program is running.

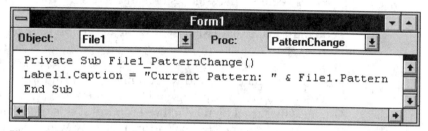

Figure P-9: Here you tell the computer what to do if there's a change in the Pattern.

Uses Provide the user with information about a change to the Pattern in a File List Box, although that is generally unnecessary because the user initiates the change.

Cautions • PatternChange is triggered when either the FileName or Pattern Property changes in a List Box.

Example
```
Sub File1_PatternChange ()
    Label1.Caption = "Current Pattern: " + File1.Pattern
End Sub
```

When the Pattern Property of the File List Box is changed, this Label is updated to show the new pattern. (If you wanted to restrict the user from accessing certain files, you could use the Change Event to detect a forbidden pattern and reset the pattern if necessary to keep the user away from places he or she isn't allowed to go on the disk.)

See also Dir$; Path; PathChange; Pattern
   See "Drive List Box" for a lengthy example of file management using all three file Control tools—Drive, Directory and File List Boxes.
   See "PathChange" for a complete alphabetical list of the VB commands related to file management.

 ICTURE

PROPERTY

Description Using the Picture Property you can display graphics on the background of a Form or within a Picture Box, Image or OLE Control. The Picture Property operates much like the Windows *wallpaper* feature that is adjusted in Windows's Control Panel. You decide what graphic you want and use the Properties Window to assign its filename to the Picture Property (except for the OLEClient; see "OLE").

   (You must make this assignment while designing your program; the Picture Property cannot be changed while a program is running. However, you *can* change the image in a Form, Image or Picture Box with the Load-Picture or GetData command while a program is running. See "Picture Box" for a description of the options and technique.)

   Graphics files used by the Picture Property at this time can be .ICO (icon), .BMP (the same "BitMaP" format used by Windows wallpaper) and .WMF (Windows MetaFile—a special, versatile format that allows the BackColor to show through and can be freely resized). Additional graphics file formats will doubtless be usable with Picture Boxes in the future.

   Visual Basic can display high-resolution graphics. Some Windows wallpaper scenes of Yellowstone Park or the rings of Saturn are breathtakingly photo-realistic when viewed on good video monitors.

Used with Forms, Images, OLE and Picture Boxes

Variables To assign a graphic to the Picture Property, use the Properties Window while you are designing your program:

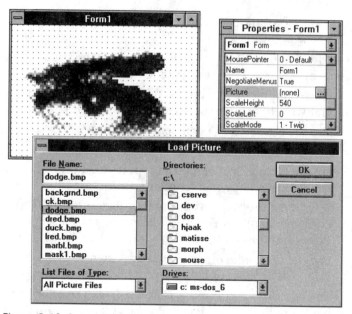

Figure P-10: Put a .BMP file onto a Form for a wallpaper background.

OR (to import an image from the Clipboard while the program is running. See "GetData"): Picture1.Picture = Clipboard.GetData (2)

OR (to put a copy of a Picture Box's Picture onto a Form. Copies can also be made of a Form's Picture into a Picture Box, or of one Picture Box into another or between Image Controls and Picture Boxes or Forms):

    Picture = Picture1.Picture

OR (to put a copy of a Form's Image Property into a Picture Box. The Form's AutoRedraw Property must be set on (True) for there to be an Image. You can also make copies of a Picture Box's Image into a Form or from one Picture Box into another): Picture1.Picture = Image

OR (to put a copy of an Icon—or DragIcon—of a Control into a Picture Box):

    Picture1.Picture = Form1.Icon

OR (to Load an image from a disk file into a Form while the program is running): Picture = LoadPicture ("C:\WINDOWS\SUNSET.BMP")

Uses
- Create more attractive programs by adding graphic images to your program's windows.
- Allow the user to select the wallpaper for the backgrounds of your program's Forms. (Use the LoadPicture command.)
- Change graphics dynamically. While a program is running, you have several ways to change the image in a Picture Box:
  - Use the LoadPicture command to get a disk file.
  - Use the GetData command to transfer a graphic from the Clipboard.
  - Set the Picture Box's Picture Property to another Control's icon (or DragIcon) to copy that icon into the Picture Box.
  - Set the Picture Property to another Picture Box's Picture Property to copy that graphic. You can freely copy graphics between Forms, Picture Boxes and Image Controls: Image1.Picture = Form2.Picture
  - Use the Cls command to erase any drawn or printed images, and use Print, Circle, PSet or Line (all of which see) to draw new graphics.
  - To copy *drawn* graphics (using the Line, Circle or PSet command) between Forms and Picture Boxes, you use the Image Property in conjunction with the Picture Property: Picture1.Picture = Picture5.Image
  - Use the various Link commands (which see) so that two programs can dynamically affect each other's graphics.
  - Use a Picture Box to create Toolbars and Status Bars within an MDI Form. See "Multiple Document Interface."

Cautions
- Image Controls are often preferable to Picture Box Controls because they use up fewer resources in the computer while a program is running. An Image Control is not designed to accept drawn graphics (using the Line, Circle or PSet command) or printed text (using the Print command). A Picture Box has 53 different Properties, many of them relating to the active drawing of graphics while a program is running (versus the importing of already created .BMP, .ICO, .WMF or .RLE [run-length encoded, one of the more than dozen graphics file formats] graphics files). An Image Control has only 18 Properties. Among other things, an Image cannot engage in Dynamic Data Exchange (see "LinkMode"). Nonetheless, for displaying graphics files, you should use the Image Control, and your programs will run more efficiently.

  Even 16-color graphics can take up large amounts of memory. If you adjust the Picture Property of a Picture Box or Form, whatever image you assign to the Picture Property *becomes part of the finished program*. (This is true only if the Picture Property is assigned while you are designing your program.)

  In other words, a copy of the disk file that you assigned to the Picture Property will be placed into the program when you make an .EXE version of the program that can be run under Windows. This can make your programs considerably larger than they would be without the embedded images. One alternative is to load in images from the disk while the program is running (see "LoadPicture"). Another is to *draw* graphic designs using the Line, Circle and PSet commands.

A .WMF file has two advantages over a .BMP or .ICO file. .WMF files can be stretched to any size or shape; the other graphic types are a fixed size. (.BMPs will be whatever size you saved them as into a file; .ICO files are always the same icon size.)

However, the Image Control permits you to stretch *any* graphic—see "Stretch."

The BackColor Property of a Picture Box works properly with a .WMF file. The image is *superimposed* on the BackColor. An .ICO or .BMP file is rectangular, and the BackColor Property of the Picture Box will appear only if you stretch the Box beyond the size of the .ICO's or .BMP's rectangle.

At this point, though, .WMF (Windows's MetaFile) images are rare. You can, however, create them with CorelDRAW. Oddly, the PBrush program that comes with Windows cannot create .WMF graphics because .WMF pictures are object-oriented (created by formulae rather than bit-by-bit copies of an image). You *cannot* create such files with a bitmap paint program. Some programs can translate between the two approaches. For instance, you can use an autotrace program to convert a bitmap to an object file like an .EPS (Encapsulated PostScript), .CDR or .WMF file.

The one drawback to a .WMF is that it takes longer to display because, unlike a .BMP that is copied to the screen, a .WMF is *drawn*. .WMFs contain drawing commands; .BMPs are predrawn and are thus ready to be blasted directly onscreen.

You can create a number of exciting graphic effects if you access the Windows API. (See Appendix A for examples of dynamic graphic manipulation using the StretchBlt Function. Also see "Declare.")

The Necessary Show Command: Graphics *drawn* in a Picture Box (as opposed to imported from a disk as .BMP, .ICO or .WMF files) are usually drawn while your program is setting itself up just after the user has started the program running. This means that the drawing commands (Print, PSet, Line, Circle) are in the Startup Form's (which see) Form_Load Event.

However, because that Event goes on invisibly while a newly started program gets itself together, *you must use the Show command* to prevent drawn graphics from being invisible when the Form is finally displayed. (See "Show.") The only exception to this rule is if you set the Picture Box's AutoRedraw Property on (-1), which preserves an image of the graphic in memory but slows down the program. In effect, setting AutoRedraw on creates an Image Property (see "Image").

The AutoSize Property will make a Picture Box fit snugly around the graphics file you place into it (.ICO, .BMP or .WMF). Then the Box will neither be larger than its picture—with some white space potentially around the right or bottom sides—nor will it be smaller, clipping off part of the image. However, .WMF files are resizable. The AutoSize feature will make them extremely small—selecting a very conservative size.

If you use the LoadPicture command to bring in a graphics file while your program is running, be sure that the graphics file exists on the disk drive where the program expects to find it. (As usual, when accessing the disk drive from within a program, you should use the On Error command, which see, in case the unexpected happens.)

Example

Figure P-11: This butterfly image was created with *Deluxe Paint II*.

The frame around this example was drawn with the DrawFrameOn Sub routine (see "Line").

Here is the programming that centers the Picture Box on the Form, Loads in the image and draws two subtle frames around the picture:

```
Sub Form_Load ()

Show
x = scalewidth / 2
y = scaleheight / 2
picture1.left = x — (picture1.width / 2)
picture1.top = y — (picture1.height / 2)

picture1.filename = "c:\picture\butrfly.bmp"

drawframeon picture1, picture1, "outward", 550
drawframeon picture1, picture1, "inward", 10

End Sub
```

See also   GetData; Image; LoadPicture; PaintPicture; Picture Box; SaveData; SavePicture

CONTROL

Description

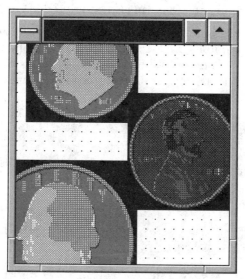

Figure P-12: Three .WMF files from Microsoft's Professional Toolkit for Visual Basic (see Appendix D).

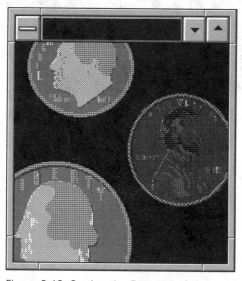

Figure P-13: Setting the Form's BackColor blends the three Picture Boxes into a single design.

Picture Boxes and Image Controls are the two primary ways to display graphics in Visual Basic; there are two types of graphics:

1. Graphics files—.BMP, .WMF, .ICO—which are imported via the Picture Property or via the LoadPicture command. These images can range from those drawn in paint programs, such as Pbrush.Exe, all the way up to high-resolution photographs.

2. Designs drawn while the program is running by using the Line, Circle or PSet (which see) command. Text can also be Printed in Picture Boxes.

Figure P-14 is an example of a VB Picture Box displaying an image in 16-color versus 256-color in Figure P-15. You'll notice the blur and the loss of detail in the 16-color rendition. When you view these images side-by-side in color, the difference is striking—as different as a newsprint comic is from a glossy photograph.

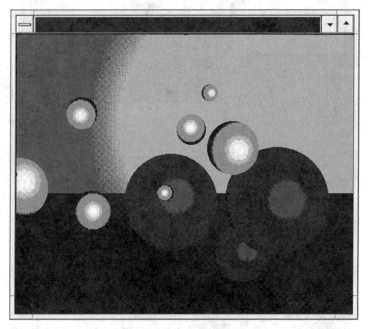

Figure P-14: A 16-color graphic in a Picture Box.

Figure P-15: A 256-color graphic displays far finer detail.

Notice the larger balls in the two figures. They are drawn in red, and a 16-color graphic can display only two shades of red. The result is that you get a gross approximation of a highlight–a lighter red circle surrounded by a dark red circle. Between the two shades is a thin zone of *dithering*–a checkerboard pattern that mixes individual dots of the two shades to simulate a transition shade. Similarly, the background should be a smooth gradient, but with 16-color you get two large areas washed with a single shade, separated by a dithered transition zone. Some of the smaller balls are drawn in gray, and Visual Basic features several shades of gray. Therefore, you get more bands in the gradient, but the effect is still a rather crude bull's-eye pattern rather than a smooth, realistic gradient.

Variables   Because a Picture Box is a Control, you will often adjust its Properties, its qualities, in the Properties Window while designing your program:

Properties - Form1		
Picture1 PictureBox		
Name	Picture1	
Negotiate	False	
Picture	(Bitmap)	...
ScaleHeight	1020	
ScaleLeft	0	
ScaleMode	1 - Twip	

Figure P-16: Selecting a graphics file for a Picture Box.

OR (to make changes to its Properties while the program is running):

```
Picture1.FontSize = 16
```

OR (to make changes by using a Variable while the program is running):

```
Picture1.BackColor = Picture2.BackColor
```

OR

```
N = 700
Picture1.Width = N
```

Uses
- Display graphics to make your programs more visually appealing.
- Animate graphics (see the Example).
- Controls can be *grouped* onto a Picture Box (as they can on a Frame). You can place them within the Picture Box or Frame and then move them as a unit while designing your program. The other implication is that grouped Option Buttons will behave like the buttons on a car radio—press one in and the others pop out.
- Several different graphic images can be combined into a design on a Form by using multiple Picture Boxes. See Figures P-12 and P-13.
- Icons can be added *within* a Form by importing an .ICO file into a Picture Box. Or you can reate a Toolbar filled with icons—see "Align."
- Change graphics while a program is running by using the LoadPicture command.
- Use LoadPicture to allow the user to select which graphics will be displayed. You can also load graphics from the Clipboard with the GetData command. You can save a Picture Box's graphics to the Clipboard with the SetData command, or save to a file with the SavePicture command.
- Change graphics dynamically. While a program is running, there are several ways to change the image in a Picture Box:
  - Use the LoadPicture command to get a disk file.
  - Use the GetData command to transfer a graphic from the Clipboard.
  - Set the Picture Box's Picture Property to another Control's icon (or DragIcon) to copy that icon into the Picture Box.
  - Set the Picture Property to another Picture Box's Picture Property to copy that graphic.

  You can freely copy graphics between Forms, Picture Boxes and Image Controls: Image1.Picture = Form2.Picture
  - To copy *drawn* graphics (using the Line, Circle or PSet command) between Forms and Picture Boxes, you use the Image Property in conjunction with the Picture Property: Picture1.Picture = Picture5.Image
  - Use the Cls command to erase any drawn or printed images, and use Print, Circle, PSet or Line to draw new graphics.

- Use one of the various Link commands (which see) so that two programs can dynamically affect each other's graphics.

Cautions
• Image Controls are often preferable to Picture Box Controls because they use up fewer resources in the computer while a program is running. An Image Control is not designed to accept drawn graphics (using the Line, Circle or PSet command) or printed text (using the Print command). A Picture Box has 44 different Properties, many of them relating to the active drawing of graphics while a program is running (versus the importing of already created .BMP, .ICO, .WMF or .RLE graphics files). An Image Control has only 15 Properties. Among other things, an Image cannot engage in Dynamic Data Exchange (see "LinkMode"). As a rule, using the Image Control for displaying graphics files makes programs run more efficiently.

A .WMF file has two advantages over a .BMP or .ICO file. First, .WMF files can be stretched to any size or shape; the other graphics types are fixed in size. (.BMPs will be whatever size you saved them as into a file. .ICO files are always the same icon size.) Second, the BackColor Property of a Picture Box works properly with a .WMF file. The image is *superimposed* on the BackColor. An .ICO or .BMP file is rectangular, and the BackColor Property of the Picture Box will appear only if you stretch the Box beyond the size of the .ICO's or .BMP's rectangle.

At this point, though, .WMF (Windows's MetaFile) images are rare. You can, however, create them with CorelDRAW. (Oddly, the Pbrush program that comes with Windows cannot create .WMF graphics.)

Figure P-17: The same .WMF file in two different Picture Boxes and on the Form.

You can shape .WMFs while designing your program or distort them while the program is running.

You can achieve a number of exciting transformations with graphics if you access the Windows API. (See Appendix A for examples of dynamic graphic manipulation using the StretchBlt Function. Also see "Declare.")

Graphics *drawn* in a Picture Box (as opposed to imported from a disk as .BMP, .ICO or .WMF files) are usually drawn while your program is setting itself up just after the user has started the program running. This means that the drawing commands (Print, PSet, Line, Circle) are in the Startup Form's (which see) Form_Load Event. However, because that Event goes on invisibly while a newly started program gets itself together, *you must use the Show command* to prevent drawn graphics from being invisible when the Form is finally displayed. (See "Show.")

The only exception to the above Caution is if you set the Picture Box's AutoRedraw Property on (–1 or True) to preserve an image of the graphic in memory; but this slows down the program.

The AutoSize Property will make a Picture Box fit snugly around whatever graphics file you place into it (.ICO, .BMP or .WMF). The Box will then neither be larger than its picture—with some white space potentially around the right side or the bottom—nor will it be smaller, clipping off part of the image. However, .WMF files are resizable. The AutoSize feature will make them extremely small—selecting a very conservative size.

Example   You can achieve one kind of animation by moving several Picture Boxes and manipulating their Visible Properties at the same time.

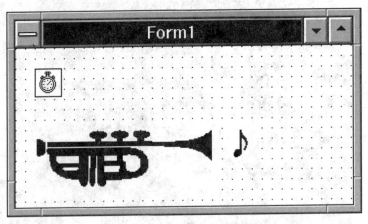

Figure P-18: Animation by toggling the Visible Property.

Put two Picture Boxes and a Timer on a Form. Fill one Box with a musical instrument and the other Box with a note symbol. Set the BorderStyles of both Boxes to "none." Set the Index Property of the Box with the note in it to 0 to create a Control Array (see "Arrays").

Now, in the Form_Load Event, type the following:

```
Sub Form_Load ()
timer1.interval = 200

For i = 1 To 6
    Load picture2(i)
Next i

End Sub
```

And, in the Timer Event, type the following:

```
Sub Timer1_Timer ()

For i = 1 To 6
    picture2(i).visible = 0
Next i

For i = 1 To 6
    x = Int(6 * Rnd + 1)
    y = Int(6 * Rnd + 1)
    picture2(i).left = 2600 + (200 * x)
    picture2(i).top = (y * 200) + 200
    picture2(i).visible = -1
Next i

End Sub
```

When this program is run, the notes will appear in random patterns, seeming to dance around the window in a loose cloud near the mouth of the horn.

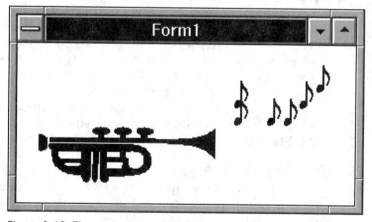

Figure P-19: The notes appear to dance onscreen.

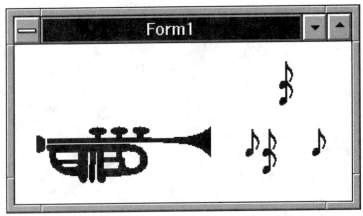

Figure P-20: The horn remains still, but the notes flutter in front of it.

In the Form_Load Event, we set the Timer to go off every 1/5 of a second to achieve a smooth animation. (If you set the Interval to 1,000 [one second], the notes appear and disappear in a jerky fashion.) Then we use the Load command *to create six new Picture Boxes* while the program is running. Each new Box will contain the same graphic as the original Picture2 Box. This technique is efficient for animating graphics (see "Arrays").

Then the animation proper takes place within the Timer Event. It will change the position of the notes five times per second. First, we make all the notes invisible. This happens fast enough that it appears to the user that new notes are simply appearing; it's not noticeable that the old notes are being erased. Then we find random numbers between 1 and 6 for horizontal and vertical positioning of the new notes. We move each new note to a random horizontal position that is *at least* 2,600 twips over from the left side of the Form. (Moving the notes like this prevents them from covering up the horn.) Then we add a random distance further to the right by multiplying whatever Rnd gave to Variable x by 200. Because x can range from 1 to 6, the horizontal distance we add to the 2,600 will range between 200 and 1,200 twips.

Keep the Notes Within a Visually Appealing Zone: Similarly, we position the new note vertically at least 200 twips down from the top of the Form *plus* anywhere between 200 and 1,200 twips farther down. This approach positions the notes randomly but within a graphically attractive zone. We don't want the notes appearing *anywhere* on the Form; we want them to seem to emerge from the mouth of the horn. Finally, after they have been repositioned, we make each note visible once again. (For more about twips, see "ScaleMode.")

The Timer will repeatedly trigger this animation until the program is shut down. You could, of course, stop the animation from within the program by putting Timer1.Enabled = 0 inside the Click_Event of the Form or inside a Control such as a Command Button. Or just use a second Timer to turn off the first Timer.

Picture Box Properties
Align • AutoRedraw • AutoSize • BackColor • BorderStyle • ClipControls • CurrentX • CurrentY • DataField • DataSource • DragIcon DragMode • DrawMode • DrawStyle • DrawWidth • Enabled FillColor • FillStyle • FontBold • FontItalic • FontName • FontSize FontStrikethru • FontTransparent • FontUnderline • ForeColor • hDC Height • HelpContextID • hWnd • Image • Index • Left • LinkItem LinkMode • LinkTimeout • LinkTopic • MousePointer • Name Parent • Picture • ScaleHeight • ScaleLeft • ScaleMode • ScaleTop ScaleWidth • TabIndex • TabStop • Tag • Top • Visible • Width

Picture Box Events
Change • Click • DblClick • DragDrop • DragOver • GotFocus KeyDown • KeyPress • KeyUp • LinkClose • LinkError • LinkNotify LinkOpen • LostFocus • MouseDown • MouseMove • MouseUp Paint

Picture Box Methods
Circle • Cls • Drag • Line • LinkExecute • LinkPoke • LinkRequest LinkSend • Move • PaintPicture • Point • Print • PSet • Refresh Scale • SetFocus • TextHeight • TextWidth • ZOrder

See also Align; AutoRedraw; Image (Control and Property); LoadPicture; Picture; SavePicture; Show

 OINT

METHOD

Description Point tells your program the color of a particular dot on the screen.
Where exactly this dot is located depends on the X,Y coordinates you supply to the Point command, and on the ScaleMode Property of the Form or Picture Box involved.

Used with Forms and Picture Boxes

Variables The following tells you the color of the point on a Picture Box that is 12 points over from the left and 15 points down from the top (of the Picture Box, not the Form):

```
Color& = Picture1.Point (12, 15)
```

The following line tells you the color of the point on the Form that is at the top left of the Form:

```
X& = Point (0, 0)
```

Visual Basic allows for a huge number of colors (see "RGB"). To accommodate such a large number of possible responses to the Point command, we add the ampersand (&) symbol to a Variable used with it. Adding the & to a Variable creates a "Long Integer" Variable type. It has no decimal, no fractional part, but can hold a huge range of numbers—from about minus 2 billion to plus 2 billion. (For more about Variable *types*, see "Variables.")

Uses   • Use Point with the PSet command to selectively replace colors.

Offer the user a selection of optional colors, and then, using the X and Y coordinates supplied by the MouseDown Event, see which color the user clicked on. You could put several swatches of color into a Form by filling Picture Boxes with a single BackColor. (The Click Event of each Box would then reveal which of the colors the user clicked on.)

An alternative would be to create a spectrum of color bars within a single Picture Box. Then Point could report the color of the bar the user clicked on.

```
Sub Form_Load ()
h = picture1.height
For i = 1 To picture1.width Step 200
    picture1.Line (i, 0) — (i + 200, h), i * 500, BF
Next i

End Sub
```

• Use Point in drawing programs for touching up, magnification and special effects. Changes of any significant size take a long time to finish. (See the Example.)

You would want to take a vertical line of perhaps 20 sample points from one of these bars because they are not solid colors.

Cautions   • Whereas PSet can change more than one *pixel* at a time (based on how large you set the DrawWidth Property), the Point Method will always provide the color of only a single *pixel*, not of a larger dot. *A pixel is the smallest dot of information on a video screen.* You can sometimes see them in the background of a Scroll Bar, but they are not the same as "dithered" colors (two colors combined in a checkerboard pattern). Dithering is the computer's attempt to imitate a color that your monitor or Visual Basic cannot directly display as a pure color. Pixels are the smallest unit of measurement, of color information, on your particular screen or available in a particular program. Visual Basic permits 256 pure (undithered) colors. Any other requested color is simulated by mixing additional colors, which creates patterns. You can see examples of these patterns in the VB Color Palette Window.

For Now, Twips Are Overkill: The default ScaleMode in VB is "twips." There are 1,440 twips per inch. (See "ScaleMode.")

You will have more twips than pixels—unless you have a huge monitor. So unless you specifically change the ScaleMode of your Form or Picture Box to ScaleMode = 3 (pixels), the Point Method will not work as quickly as it could. (It's slow, in any case, because it must deal with so much information to report on the colors in even a small area of the screen.)

Point tells you about the colors of the dots that it can be positioned on. If you set the ScaleMode to *inches*, you could test perhaps only 150 or so total dots on the entire screen, depending on the size of your screen. *The ScaleMode determines where and how finely you can test colors. Set ScaleMode to Pixels for the finest, most detailed testing of your screen, based on your screen's particular resolution.*

Example   Transforming a picture via Point and PSet can take a lot of time. On a typical 15-inch monitor, there are more than 130,000 pixels in a 4-inch-square Picture Box. There are far faster ways of transforming pictures (inverting the colors, etc., via the special StretchBlt Function—see Appendix A). A graphics aficionado, for example, is willing to present his or her computer with a ray-trace image to create, and wait 36 hours for the computer to compose the image. You won't have to wait very long to try the following example; it takes about four minutes on a 33Mhz 386 computer.

First, we'll put a black-and-white picture into the Picture Box. We're going to change its blacks to neon green and leave its whites alone. Type the following into the Form_Click Event:

```
Sub Form_Click ()

picture1.scalemode = 3

For x! = 0 To picture1.scalewidth
    For y! = 0 To picture1.scalewidth
        q = DoEvents()
        C& = picture1.Point(x!, y!)
            If C& < 5000 Then
                        picture1.PSet (x!, y!), 125000
            End If

    Next y!, x!
End Sub
```

Figure P-21: The statue entirely in black, white and grays.

Figure P-22: The black and gray pixels on the left half of the statue have been replaced by green pixels.

We first set the Picture Box's ScaleMode to Pixels and then create a nested Loop (see "For...Next") that will contact every pixel within the Picture Box.

The DoEvents Function allows other programs to run and allows the user to turn off this program, resize windows, etc. Without DoEvents, a For...Next Loop will lock up the computer until it has finished its work.

Next, we find out the color of the pixel; if it's black (less than 5,000), we change it to neon green (color 125,000). Otherwise, we leave it alone.

See also   Appendix A; PSet

PopupMenu

Description
A PopupMenu is something of a combination of an ordinary menu and an InputBox. A PopupMenu displays a list for the user to select from, like a regular menu. In fact, a PopupMenu merely duplicates the list within an already existing menu. But you can position a PopupMenu onscreen at the current mouse location or at a specified X,Y coordinate. Ordinary menus have to stay at the top of a window and be *pulled down*.

Variables
PopupMenu *nameofmenu*, location/behavior-flag, xposition, yposition. The *nameofmenu* Variable is the name of an existing menu on the Form. The x and y positions are optional. If you leave them out, the menu pops up at the current position of the mouse pointer.

The flags can be as follows:

0   The default; the left side of the menu will be at the location specified by the X coordinate (if you choose to specify it). And the menu will only respond to a left-mouse-button-click on one of the items in its list.

2   The menu will respond to a left- or right-mouse-button-click on one of the items in its list.

4   The menu will be centered at the location specified by the X coordinate (if you choose to specify it).

8   The right side of the menu will be at the location specified by the X coordinate (if you choose to specify it).

You can combine more than one of the flags by using the Or command: PopupMenu *nameofmenu*, flag OR flag, xposition, yposition.

Uses
• To have free-floating menus (rather than the traditional style that is attached to the top of a Form).

Cautions
• Your program can respond to the user's selection of one of a Popup-Menu's items by instructions you place within that menu item's Click Event. (See the list of Objects in the Form's programming window; the name of each menu item will be a separate Object.)

Only one menu can pop up at a time. The user can have the option of displaying a PopupMenu by clicking the *right* mouse button: just put the PopupMenu command within a MouseDown Event. That Event reacts to both mouse buttons, but it has a Button Variable that tells you which was clicked. You can therefore force it to respond only to a right-button click as follows:

```
If button = 2 Then PopupMenu Popper
```

Example

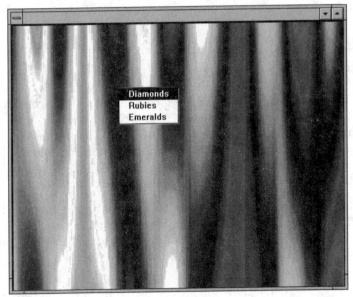

Figure P-23: This menu can appear anywhere you decide (or the user decides) to display it.

Select New Project from the VB File Menu; then select Menu Design from the Window Menu. Create a menu (see "Menu" for more information). Name your menu **Popper** (the name will be the Name Property you give to the first item in the list). You should indent the subsequent items from the first name because a PopupMenu requires at least one submenu. Turn off the "Visible" option so that there will be no menu at the top of this Form; we only want our PopupMenu to show.

Now, in the Form's Click Event, type the following:

```
Sub Form_Click ()
    PopupMenu Popper
End Sub
```

See also Menu

 RESERVE ·
PROPERTY

See ReDim

PREVINSTANCE

Description
PrevInstance is a Property of the "App" Object. App is a special word that refers to the program itself. App, short for *application,* means the currently running application. It is used to identify qualities of the program, much the way a program uses the word Screen (for Screen "Object") to find out qualities of the user's monitor.

App.PrevInstance tells your program if the user has other "instances" of the same program currently running. Some programs let you to run several copies of the program at the same time. For example, a graphics file viewer might allow you to repeatedly click on its icon in Program Manager—launching it over and over so you can view and compare different images in each "instance" of the program. Word for Windows, however, refuses to share its resources with a second "instance" of itself. If you want your program to refuse to have more than one copy running at a time, in the Startup Form's Load Event put the following:

```
If App.PrevInstance Then MsgBox ("This program is already running"):End
```

Used with
App, the "application" Object

Variables
To find out if another copy of the program is currently running:

```
If App.PrevInstance Then...
```

Uses
• Prevent the user from running more than one copy of your program at a time because your program is large or uses many of Windows's resources, and you don't want several copies gobbling up what's left of the stack or memory.

Your program might already contain provisions for opening several documents at the same time (a Multiple Document Interface, which see). In that case, multiple instances of the program would be redundant.

Networks have special traffic jam problems to overcome, as several copies of the same program could be trying to access the same file at the same time (see "Lock"). You don't want to wrestle with the resonance bugs or data collision problems that bedevil networks. So if your program allows the user to access the disk drive, you might want to prevent the user from launching more than one instance of your program.

Cautions
• You cannot adjust PrevInstance while you are designing your program (it's not in any Properties Window). And, while the program is running, you can only *query* PrevInstance; you cannot *change* it.

• You must always use the word App when using PrevInstance:

```
App.PrevInstance
```

• PrevInstance doesn't tell you *how many* other copies of your program are running—just whether other copies are running.

Example   Create a New Project from the File Menu. Put this in the Form_Load Event:

```
Sub Form_Load ()
    Show
    If App.PrevInstance <> 0 Then
        Print "At least one other copy is running."
    End If
End Sub
```

Now, from the File Menu, select Make EXE File and save it on your disk. Then, from Program Manager or File Manager, launch the program several times to see how PrevInstance reports the existence of other "instances" of the program.

See also   App

PRINT

METHOD

Description   The Print command prints text on the screen or to the printer. Don't confuse it with Caption or Text Properties. Print is in the same family as the VB drawing commands PSet, Circle and Line.

Used with   The Debug Object, Forms, Picture Boxes and the printer

Variables   Print, by itself with no Control's Name, will print to the Form, even if the Print command is inside one of the Picture Box Events. This example prints to the Form:

```
Picture1_Click ()
    Print "New Information."
End Sub
```

OR (to print to the Picture Box, attach the Name of the Picture Box to the Print command): Picture1.Print A$

OR (to print a text Variable): Print A$

OR (a comma places a "tab" between the two pieces of text, moving over eight spaces to the right before printing B$): Print A$, B$

OR (a semicolon puts the text of B$ right up next against the text of A$):

```
Print A$;B$
```

OR (successive Print commands print on separate lines):

```
Print A$
Print B$
```

OR (to print a numeric Variable): Print N

OR (to print to the printer): Printer.Print A$

OR (with nothing following it, Print inserts a line—moves the printing down one line. The following would print A$, then a blank line and then B$):

```
Print A$
Print
Print B$
```

OR (you can use an abbreviation for Print. VB will translate a "?" into the *Print* command):

```
?

? A$
```

Uses
• Place text or numeric Variables on a Form or Picture Box (numeric Variables do not need to be translated with Str$ before being Printed).

 The text will appear at the location described by the CurrentX and CurrentY Properties. VB handles this automatically, increasing CurrentX as a new character is added to a line. When a new line is started, VB resets CurrentX to 0 and adds a specified amount to CurrentY. However, you have more control over the appearance of printed text by directly manipulating CurrentX and CurrentY yourself.

• Print text to the printer. To print an entire Form, graphics and all, use the PrintForm Method.

Cautions
• The FontName, FontSize, FontItalic, FontBold, FontStrikeThru, FontTransparent and FontUnderline Properties govern the size and appearance of Printed text.

 However, if you try to print the contents of a Text Box to the printer, you can run into problems because a Text Box wraps text around to the next lower line as necessary. No text is cut off on the right side if a line is too long; instead, it is moved down (if the Text Box MultiLine Property is set to "True"). But no line break codes are inserted when the text wraps, which means that a single line may appear to be many lines in the Text Box but when printed to the printer will be cut off (no Carriage Return codes are contained in a wrapped line).

 The solution is a special call to the API (see Appendix A). Here's an example of printing the lines in a Text Box exactly as they appear on-screen.

 In a Module, type the following (put each Declare on a single line; do not hit the ENTER key):

```
Declare Function GetFocus% Lib "user" ()
Declare Funtion SendMessage% Lib "user" (ByVal hWnd%, ByVal wMsg%, →
    ByVal wParam%, ByVal lParam As Any)
```

Then set up a Text Box with a Name of Text1 and set its MultiLine Property to True. Add a Command Button and put the following inside the

Click Event of the Button:

```
Dim ii As Long
    printer.currenty = printer.currenty + 400
    Text1.SetFocus
    Inz% = SendMessage(GetFocus(), &H40A, 0&, 0&)

For ii = 0 To Inz%
    printer.CurrentX = 1000    '
    Text1.SetFocus
    tem$ = Space(80)
    w% = SendMessage(GetFocus(), &H414, ii, tem$)
    printer.Print tem$
Next ii
```

Using this technique, you must control the Printer.CurrentX and Printer.CurrentY properties, but the SendMessage API call handles the rest. The first time we use it (with a value of &H40A), SendMessage tells us how many lines are in the Text Box when it is visible onscreen (as opposed to how many Carriage Return codes are found within its Text Property). Then we set up a For...Next Loop that prints each line. We get the line by using SendMessage, a multipurpose API call. We have to set the vertical position (CurrentY) only once; thereafter we worry only about keeping CurrentX stable. Also note that API calls are picky about the Variable types. That's why we had to define the Loop Variable *ii* as Long—the SendMessage wants a Long number in that location in its arguments.

Unlike a Text Box with its MultiLine Property set on (–1), a Form or Picture Box will not automatically scroll text up to make room for text that won't fit within its boundaries. Instead, the text will be cut off where it meets the bottom or right border. The printer will scroll to accommodate text that is *longer* than the page but will cut off text that is wider:

```
A$ = String$(200,"*")
Printer.Print A$
```

The 200 characters in the preceding command will be cut off at some point. Where it will be clipped depends on the font and font size currently active in the printer.

```
A$ = String$(400,"*")
Printer.Print A$
```

Trying to print a text Variable 400 characters long will generate the Visual Basic error message "Overflow."

• Print # is to disk text files what Print is to Picture Boxes, Forms and the printer. Print # sends an exact copy of the text to the disk; it's a very useful command for saving data that you will later want to print onscreen or on the printer. Print #, used with sequential files (see "Input$"), is valuable for word processing applications.

• You can use the Spc and Tab Functions to replace the comma and semi-colon as ways of formatting printed items.

Example

Figure P-24: These frames were created with the DrawFrameOn Subroutine included in this book (see "Line").

When the Form in Figure P-23 Loads, we describe the various qualities for the printed text:

```
Sub Form_Load ()

Show

picture1.filename = "C:\BOOK\BMPS\WORLDS.BMP"
fontname = "mystical"
fontsize = 60
forecolor = QBColor(15)
backcolor = QBColor(8)

A$ = "WORLDS"
textw = TextWidth(A$) / 2
currentx = scalewidth / 2 — textw
currenty = 50
Print A$

drawframeon picture1, picture1, "outward", 300
drawframeon picture1, picture1, "inward", 20
End Sub
```

To center the text *WORLDS*, we find its width and divide it in half. Then we subtract the result from the exact center of the Form (the Form's ScaleWidth Property divided by two). Then we move the horizontal coordinate for printing–CurrentX–to the resulting position, and set the vertical position 50 twips down from the top. Although you can govern the formatting of a Print statement in a number of ways, manipulating CurrentX and CurrentY is a precise way to place your printed items on the host object.

TextHeight / 2, along with ScaleHeight, will assist in centering Printed text on the vertical axis.

Etch & Emboss—Two Functions That Create Etched or Shadowed Text Effects: These Functions will come in handy whenever you want to print text that looks embossed or etched. First, start a New Project from the File Menu. Select Module from the Insert Menu. Type these Functions into the Module. When you've finished typing, select Save File As from the File Menu and save this Module, naming it PrintEffects.Bas or something similar. Thereafter, you can add these effects to any of your programs by using the Load File feature in the File Menu.

```
Function Etch(fname As Form, a$, x, y)
    fname.CurrentX = x
    fname.CurrentY = y
    fname.ForeColor = QBColor(15)
    fname.Print a$
    fname.CurrentX = x - 28
    fname.CurrentY = y - 20
    fname.ForeColor = QBColor(8)
    fname.Print a$
End Function
Function Emboss(fname As Form, a$, x, y)
    fname.CurrentX = x
    fname.CurrentY = y
    fname.ForeColor = QBColor(15)
    fname.Print a$
    fname.CurrentX = x + 6
    fname.CurrentY = y + 8
    fname.ForeColor = QBColor(8)
    fname.Print a$
End Function
```

Figure P-25: An example of the Etch Function. Experiment with the values subtracted from X and Y to get the best-looking shading. Here we've changed the second ForeColor command from QBColor(8) to QBColor(0).

Figure P-26: The embossed effect, which makes the characters look as if they were protruding slightly from the background.

Figure P-27: Here you can see both etched and embossed effects.

The most subtle, attractive effects are usually created when you leave the QBColors at 15 and 8.

Here's how you can call these Functions (using the Me command to identify the calling Form):

```
Private Sub Form_Load()
    Show
    FontSize = 14
Etch Me,  Bobby , 200, 200
Emboss Me,  Betty , 200, 800
End Sub
```

See also   CurrentX, CurrentY; Debug; Me; PrintForm; TextHeight; TextWidth

RINT #

STATEMENT

Description   Print # sends *an exact copy* of text to an Opened file on the disk.

The Print # command is, to a disk file, what the Print command is to the screen or printer. A copy of text saved to disk with Print # can later be read off a disk file and printed directly to the screen or printer with all the appropriate line breaks, tabs or other formatting intact.

Print # is usually preferable to the alternative, Write #, because Write # inserts commas between the individual pieces of saved text and adds quotation marks to text ("string") Variables. All these extra symbols have to be extracted by your program before the data can be properly printed onscreen, or manipulated by your program.

Used with   Files Opened in the sequential mode (see "Open" for a complete general discussion of files in VB; see "Input$" for an explanation of the very useful sequential mode).

Variables   To save the text ("string") Variable to a file opened As #1:

```
Print #1, A$
```

OR (to save literal text): Print #1, "DONE"

OR (separated by semicolons, the text in each of these Variables will butt up against the previous text in the file, just as they would butt up against each other if Printed to the screen separated by semicolons):

```
Print #1, A$;B$;C$
```

OR (separated by commas, the text would be saved to the disk with eight space characters inserted between each Variable): Print #1, A$,B$,C$

OR (to save numeric Variables): Print #1, N,M

Uses   • Print exact copies of text or text Variables.

• Print the entire contents of a Text Box. The text can then be retrieved exactly as it was formatted and appeared on the screen:

```
Open "C:\TEST" For Output As #1
    Print #1, Text1.Text
Close 1
```

```
Open "C:\TEST" For Input As #1
    Input #1, A$
    Text1.Text = A$
Close 1
```

Cautions   • Database management—the organizing, updating, storage and retrieval of information—is approached differently than word processing. With a word processor, your primary goal is to reproduce text in a manner that is faithful to the user's original—sentences and paragraphs intact.

When managing a database, you might want to offer such features as lists sorted by ZIP Code or operations that require information to be divided into smaller data units than the sentence.

Because Print # inserts no special characters of its own into the data sent to a disk file, you may need to add some special characters in a database-management situation. For instance, if you want to keep Name separate from Address, you may want to add a 0 between them. This 0 is not a text character 0, nor is it the digit. Rather, it is a nonprintable code (see "Chr$"):

```
Finaltext$ = Name$ + Chr$(0) +Address$
```

Also, pressing the ENTER key inserts a Carriage Return (ASCII code 13) and a Line Feed (ASCII code 10) that can also be used as separators for data (delimiters). In this case, the user would simply put each unit of data on a different line. Or, pressing ENTER would move the user from a Text Box for "NAME" to a separate Text Box for "ADDRESS." (In each Text Box's KeyPress Event, you would put: If KeyAscii = 13 Then Text2.SetFocus.)

Rather than twist Print # into carrying out jobs it is not optimized for, you might want to use the random-access file mode and its associated disk-writing and -reading commands. (See "Open.") Or purchase the Professional version of VB which includes additional, specialized commands for database management.

Example

```
Sub Form_Click ()
Open "C:\TEST" For Output As #1
    Print #1, "Line 1", "Tab "; "Space"
    Print #1, "Line 2"
Close 1
Open "C:\TEST" For Input As #1
    Line Input #1, A$
    Print A$
    Line Input #1, A$
    Print A$
Close 1

End Sub
```

See also

Close; Write #

See "Open" for a general discussion of file handling techniques. See "Input$" for an overview of the sequential-file technique.

RINTER

OBJECT

• •

Description

Using the Printer object you can draw graphics (using PSet, Circle, Line), print high-resolution pictures (using PaintPicture, which see) and print text (using Print) on your printer. Normally, the Print, PSet, Circle or Line command will send results to the screen. By adding the word *Printer*, separated by a period, to one of these commands, the results go to the printer instead. Similarly, if you use the FontSize command, it normally changes the appearance of the text on a Form or Control: Text1.FontSize = 12. However, Printer.FontSize = 12 changes the text printed on the printer.

Used with   Your printer

Variables   To send text to the printer. (The Print command, without Printer.Print, would send the text to the screen.)

```
Printer.Print A$
```

OR (to print literal text):

```
Printer.Print  THIS
```

OR (a comma places a "tab" between the two pieces of text, moving over eight spaces to the right before printing B$):

```
Printer.Print A$, B$
```

OR (a semicolon puts the text of B$ right up next against the text of A$):

```
Printer.Print A$;B$
```

OR (successive Print commands print on separate lines):

```
Printer.Print A$
Printer.Print B$
```

OR (to print a numeric Variable):

```
Printer.Print N
```

OR (with nothing following it, Print inserts a blank line—moves the printing down one line on the page. The following would print A$, then a blank line and then B$):

```
Printer.Print A$
Printer.Print
Printer.Print B$
```

OR (to draw a circle with the printer):

```
Printer.Circle (700, 700), 500
```

OR

There is also a Printer *Collection* (an Object Array) representing all printers attached to the user's computer, if more than one. Here's how you can find out the status of a printer's Properties:

```
n = Printers(3).Orientation
```

Or, if you want to change a Property of a printer, you must first make that printer the currently active one:

```
Dim P As Printer
Set P = Printer
P.Orientation = vbPRORLandscape
Printer.Print  HELLO
```

The Count Property tells you how many Objects (printers) are in the Collection (attached to your computer). LBound and UBound tell you the lower and upper index numbers you can use with this collection. LBound is always zero, because the first printer in the Printers collection is Printers(0).

Uses
• Print text or graphics to your printer.
• Print *drawn* graphics (using PSet, Circle or Line) to your printer.

New in VB4

PaintPicture
• You can now, in VB4, also Print bitmap images (.BMP, .ICO or .WMF files), using the PrintPicture Method:

```
Private Sub Form_Click( )
Printer.PaintPicture Form1.picture, 0, 0
End Sub
```

The syntax for PaintPicture requires three arguments: the Picture Property (of a Form or Picture Box), and the offset from the top left (expressed as horizontal, then vertical) of the paper. That is, when the picture is printed, how far down or over on the paper do you want it to appear (in addition to the printer's inherent margins). The ScaleMode of the Printer determines the measurement of the offset.

PaintPicture also has seven additional, optional arguments:

```
PaintPicture picture, x1, y1, width1, height1, x2, y2, width2, height2, opcode
```

Width1 allows you to distort or resize the image. Width1 specifies the width of the picture when printed on paper. As with all the rest of these position and size arguments, the ScaleMode Property of Printer determines the unit of measure used (it defaults to "twips," as it does for a Picture Box or Form). Also, all of these arguments are Single-Precision Floating-point Variables. If Width1 is larger or smaller than Width2 (below), the graphic will be stretched or compressed when printed.

Height1 behaves the same as Width1.

The x2, y2 coordinates describe an offset within the original graphic (onscreen). This way, you could print only part of a graphic.

Width2, Height2 signify the width and height of the original graphic (if you omit this argument, the entire width and height of the Picture Property is assumed). Combine these arguments with x2 and y2 and you can print any zone within the source (onscreen) Picture.

opcode is a Long numeric Variable that specifies a "bit-wise" transform should take place on the graphic. For a complete list of these optional transformations, see Table AA1 in Appendix A.

If you provide negative arguments for Height1 or Width1 or both, you can flip the graphic.

Just like Controls and Forms, the Printer Object has a complete set of Properties. These Properties can control formatting, orientation, fonts and drawing qualities like DrawWidth. Unlike Controls and Forms, though, there is no VB Properties Window for the Printer within which you could select options for the printer.

Instead, you adjust the Properties for the Printer by specifically assigning Variables when designing your program. Then, when the program runs, these Properties are communicated to your printer. The Form_Load Event is a good place to put such specifications. Windows maintains a list of your printer's capabilities and will translate your specifications into codes to which the printer can react.

How to Find Out Which Fonts Are Available: A special Property of the Printer Object will provide a list of the fonts that a printer can reproduce. Using the Printer.Fonts command you can let the user of your program select which of the possible fonts will be used for printing to his or her printer. See the Example.

Regardless, a Printer may ignore or "interpret" some of the specified Properties. An attempt to describe a FillColor to a printer that cannot print color will be approximated to the best of the printer's ability—but there won't be any color unless there's a miracle.

• Eject the current page (at a position of your choice within the text) with Printer.NewPage; use Printer.EndDoc to end the printing of a long document (also use EndDoc to prevent an extra blank page at the end); use Printer.KillDoc to cancel printing immediately; or add page numbers with Printer.Page.

Cautions The Printer might ignore or "interpret" Properties that you attempt to assign to it but cannot manage. Most current printers are not able to produce colors, so ForeColor = QBColor(4) will not result in red text (as it would on a Form or Picture Box if its ForeColor Properties were set to QBColor(4)). While some printers will ignore this request, others will create a simulated red by picking a gray that they think is red-like in relation to black.

Example We'll locate the center of the sheet of paper in the printer and draw various "colored" circles. They'll likely be several shades of gray because that's how most printers display color. Then we'll move back up to the top of the sheet and print some text.

First, create a Form, and put a Text Box, a List Box and a Command Button captioned "PRINT" on it.

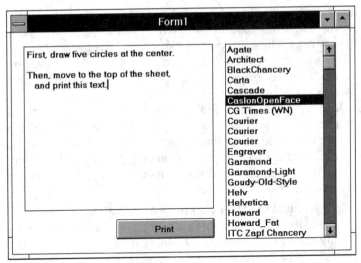

Figure P-28: Display the available fonts so the user can select one.

We now create the list of available printer fonts by using the Fonts and FontCount Properties of the Printer Object:

```
Sub Form_Load ( )
    For i = 0 To printer.fontcount – 1
        List1.AddItem Printer.Fonts(i)
    Next i
End Sub
```

When the user makes a selection in the List Box, we assign the printer's FontName Property:

```
Sub List1_DblClick ( )
    c$ = List1.List(List1.ListIndex)
    Printer.FontName = c$
End Sub
```

Finally, a click on the Command Button starts the printing process by setting several Printer Properties:

```
Sub Command1_Click ( )
x = Printer.scalewidth / 2
y = Printer.scaleheight / 2
Printer.currentx = x
Printer.currenty = y

Printer.Circle Step(0, 0), 1500

Printer.fillstyle = 0
Printer.currentx = x
Printer.currenty = y + 800

For i = 0 To 4
    Printer.fillcolor = QBColor(i)
```

```
      Printer.Circle Step(0, —800), i * 200 + 100
   Next i
   Printer.currentx = 0
   Printer.currenty = 0
   Printer.fontsize = 24
   Printer.Print text1.text
   Printer.EndDoc
   End Sub
```

First, we locate the exact center of the sheet of paper by dividing the ScaleWidth and ScaleHeight Properties of the Printer by two. Then we set the CurrentX and CurrentY Printer Properties to this center position and draw an unfilled circle.

Now, by setting FillStyle to 0, future drawn circles will be filled. We reset the CurrentX, CurrentY to the center but add 800 to the vertical position because each of our vertical Steps in the Circle command below will subtract 800 from the previous circle's position. (We want the first filled circle to also be in the exact center of the sheet of paper.)

Now we draw five circles, filling each with a different QBColor, moving each 800 twips higher on the paper and making each somewhat larger than the circle below it.

Finally we reset the X,Y coordinates to 0,0–the upper left corner of the paper. The FontSize is set to 24, the text in the Text Box is printed, and the Printer is informed that the document is finished. EndDoc will also feed the paper out of the printer.

**First, draw five circles at the center.
Then, move to the top of the sheet,
   and print this text.**

Figure P-29: The results of the example show how to control position of printed graphics and text.

Printer Properties
ColorMode • Copies • Count • CurrentX • CurrentY • DeviceName
DrawMode • DrawStyle • DrawWidth • DriverName • Duplex FillColor
FillStyle • Font • FontBold • FontCount • FontItalic • FontName • Fonts
FontSize • FontStrikethru • FontTransparent • FontUnderline • ForeColor
hDC • Height • Lbound • Orientation • Page • PaperBin • PaperSize • Port
PrintQuality • ScaleHeight • ScaleLeft • ScaleMode • ScaleTop • ScaleWidth
TrackDefault • TwipsPerPixelX/Y • Ubound • Width • Zoom

Printer Methods
Circle • EndDoc • KillDoc • Line • NewPage • PaintPicture • Print • PSet
Scale • ScaleX/Y • TextHeight • TextWidth

See also   EndDoc; FontCount; Fonts; NewPage; Page; Print; Collection

PRINTFORM

OBJECT

Description   PrintForm is like making a photocopy of a window. It prints a complete
copy of the text and graphics on a Form. Just how close the printer can
come to the screen image will depend on your printer's capabilities—its
resolution and if it can print color. The printed image also includes the
border and Caption Bar of the window.

A Print option in the VB File Menu will print the programming in a
Project (a program). When you ask Visual Basic to print a Project, it asks if
you want the Forms printed along with the text of your program. If you
request that the Forms be printed, VB automatically utilizes PrintForm in
the process.

Used with   The printer

Variables   PrintForm

OR (to specify which of several Forms to print): Form3.PrintForm

Uses   • Save copies of the visual and design aspects of your projects.

• Print pictures. Either set a Form's Picture Property to bring in a .BMP,
.ICO or .WMF image, or enlarge a Picture Box and fill it with an image.

• Offer printouts of selected windows in your programs.

Cautions   • Unless you set the Form's AutoRedraw Property on (True), any drawn
graphics (using PSet, Circle or Line) will *not* print. .BMP, .ICO or .WMF
images will, however, print—even if AutoRedraw is left off, its default.

You will generally get better quality results if you can use the Print command to print text and the drawing commands PSet, Circle and Line to create graphics on the printer (see "Printer"). However, PrintForm does a reasonable job of approximating the look of a window.

Example Here is a way to easily print copies of any of your .BMP, .ICO or .WMF picture files. First, create a Form and put a Directory List Box, a Command Button captioned "PRINT," a File List Box and a large Picture Box on the Form. Set the Picture Box's AutoSize Property on (True).

We want any changes to the Directory List Box to also influence the File List Box, to change, in effect, the directory and display a different list of files:

```
Sub Dir1_Change ()
    file1.path = dir1.path
End Sub
```

When the user double-clicks on a file in the File List Box, we want a new picture loaded into the Picture Box:

```
Sub File1_Click ()
    x$ = file1.list(file1.listindex)
    If right$(x$,1) <> "\" then x$ = x$ + "\"
    picture1.picture = LoadPicture(x$)
End Sub
```

And, when the user clicks on the PRINT Button:

```
Sub Command1_Click ()
    x = width
    y = height
    width = picture1.width
    height = picture1.height
    PrintForm
    width = x
    height = y
End Sub
```

We temporarily store the size of the Form in the x and y Variables. Then we reduce the Form to the size of the Picture Box. We've set the Picture Box's AutoSize Property on, so it will exactly fit whatever image is put into it. Then, because we don't want to print the nongraphic portions of this Form, we set its width and height temporarily to the same size as the Picture Box and then PrintForm. After the printing is finished, we expand the Form to its original size.

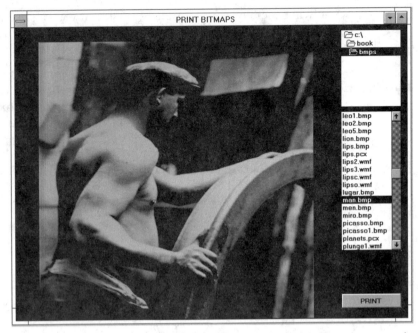

Figure P-30: Print graphics on the printer with a single PrintForm command.

See also   AutoRedraw; AutoSize; Print; Printer

PRIVATE

See   Public

PROGRESSBAR

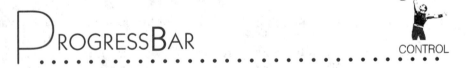

CONTROL

See   Windows 95 Controls

PROPERTY LET, GET & SET PROCEDURE

Description   These three new entities are *procedures*, like a Function or a Subroutine. But they're a bit unconventional. They change a Property of an Object (Let), find out or "read" the value of a Property of an Object (Get), or create a reference to an Object (Set). Before getting into the behavior of these new procedures, let's briefly review the meaning of *procedure.*

Until now, there were only two types of *procedures:* Functions and Subs. The essential difference between these two procedures is that a Function, after it does its job, can return a value to the place in your program from where you call it:

```
X = MyFunction ( )
```

This puts some "value" (a piece of text or a number) into that X. A Sub, by contrast, returns nothing.

However, the purpose of both of these kinds of procedures is to take some action, to *do something,* and that something can be done over and over, as often as needed, from anywhere in your program. Say, for example, that you frequently want to display a custom "message box." Rather than repeating the programming that displays this box over and over, in various places in your program, you just write a single reusable procedure:

```
Sub ShowBox M$
    Form5.Show   this Form is our custom Box
    Form5.Text1.Text = M$  This is the message we want to display
End Function
```

Simple enough: now we can display our Message Form anywhere in our program by merely "calling" (using the name of the procedure as if it were a command in the language). When we call this procedure, we're providing it with the message we want displayed, and it does the job:

```
ShowBox  Please enter the zipcode...
```

A New Kind of Procedure

The new *Property* procedures, however, are intended to provide quite a different service to the programmer. They are mainly useful with a Class Module (see "Objects"). When you create an object, it's somewhat as if you are creating a custom Control, like a new kind of Command Button or something like that. A Control has Methods and Properties, and you can give them to your Objects, too.

In other words, your new Object can have *Methods* (actions it can perform) as well as *Properties* (*qualities:* how the Object looks; its size and position; what color it is if it's visible; the fontsize of any text; and so on). If you want the outside world (users or other programmers) to be able to change a Property of your Object, write a Property Let procedure. If you want to give the world the ability to find out the status (value) of a Property of your Object, write a Property Get procedure. To let the world set a reference to an Object, write a Property Set procedure. Object Variables can be used to assign references to particular Objects, or to copy references from one Object Variable to another. Set works similarly to the way the equals (=) symbol works with regular text or numeric Variables. (For more on the utility of "setting a reference to an Object" see the entry on "Set.")

Notice that these three Property procedures mimic the behavior of ordinary variables. Property Get finds out the current value of a Property. It's similar to this typical VB query of a Property:

```
X = Form1.FontSize
```

Property Let changes the current value of a Property. It's similar to this:

```
Form1.FontSize = X
```

However, a Property Let procedure must contain behaviors and actions that *accomplish* whatever the Property is supposed to do. For example, if your Property Let procedure governs your Object's color, you would have to write programming within the Property Let procedure that would change the color, based on whatever argument was passed to the Property Let procedure and whatever rules or limitations you might have imposed on this particular Property. In other words, when you create an Object, *you* decide what qualities (Properties) it has, how many variations are possible, and how the outside application must interface with (provide arguments to) this Property to make any changes.

Property Set refers an Object Variable to a particular object. It's similar to this, which makes the Object Variable *MyCtlObj* refer to the particular Object Text1:

```
Set MyCtlObj = Text1
```

With Property Set, you would do the same thing a different way, by first "calling" the Property Set procedure:

```
Form1.AssignTextBox = Text1
```

and then, having passed the object to which you want the Object Variable *MyCtlObj* to now refer, the procedure does the job for you:

```
Property Set AssignTextBox(Ob As Object)
    Set MyCtlObj = Ob
End Property
```

One use for Property Set would be to provide Parent or Application Properties for your Object.

What s the Use?

Why bother with Property Procedures at all? They seem to be merely a more indirect way of doing what you could more simply accomplish with ordinary variables and ordinary procedures (to change something). The short answer is that in normal, traditional Forms and Modules, Property procedures have no use. You can merely create a Public Variable and then assign values to it or read its values; or you can adjust the Properties by writing to built-in VB Properties like the Height Property of a Picture Box.

From other Forms or Modules in your program, you could contact (assign or read values) a Public Variable by adding the Form's Name to the Variable's name. This is a way to read or change the "Properties" (the Public Variables) of the Form from another Form or Module:

```
X = Form1.MyPubVar
```

OR

```
Form1.MyPubVar = x
```

Likewise, you can use a Form's Public Subs or Functions from another Form or Module in your program. This is the way to use the Form's "Methods" (its procedures) from within another Form or Module. And it's also a way to pass arguments back and forth between Forms without resorting to Public (formerly "Global") variables:

In Form1 there is a Public Function:

```
Public Function Anx1(Nert As Integer) As Integer
    Anx1 = Nert * 2
End Function
```

From Form2, we call this Function, passing an argument and getting a result back:

```
Private Sub Command3_Click( )
    Print Form1.Anx1(5)
End Sub
```

So why, even in a Class Module, would you use Property procedures at all—when you can just use a Public Variable? The answer is that you *can't* just use a Public Variable to *change* a Property of an Object you create. Unlike a VB Form's Properties which are built into every Form, your own Objects must be taught (by your programming) how to respond to a request to change a Property. A *procedure* can trigger activities, can have one or more lines of programming within it which are carried out when that procedure is "called." A variable, though, doesn't trigger any activities when you change it.

Think of an ordinary Property of a Form. To change the Height, you can just assign a new value to the Height Property, which is pretty much like assigning a value to a Variable. But the programming that *achieves* this change in the height is built into VB. Therefore, when you create your own *custom Property*, create a Property for a new Object that you've defined in a Class Module, you can't just assign a value to this Property. You have to write some programming that will change the Height or whatever Property you're dealing with. *You* wrote this new Object and decided that its Height would be a changeable Property of the Object—it's not built in as it would be for a VB Form. So, you need to write a *procedure*, a Property procedure, within which you put the lines of programming that will accomplish the task of changing this Property when it's called upon while the program is running.

Property Let Up-Close

The Property Let procedure is something like a Function, but its purpose is to permit you or a user to change the value of a Property of an Object. In other words, when you create an Object (see "Objects") you'll sometimes want to give it some qualities, some Properties, which are user-adjustable or programmatically adjustable.

Here's how it works. In VB, a Form has a list of Properties (BackColor, Caption, etc.). There are 41 Properties of a Form in VB4 (more, if you consider that the Font Property contains its own set of Properties such as FontBold, FontName, etc). Anyway, Properties are the *qualities* of an object that can be adjusted. The user can adjust them if you, the programmer provide a Command Button or List Box or some other interface which permits the user to make these adjustments. Or you, the programmer, can adjust them during program design within the Properties Window or during program execution by assigning values to Properties. How the Form looks, its size and location, and some of its capabilities (like AutoRedraw) are all Properties of that Form.

When you create your *own* Object in a Class Module, you might well want to give that Object adjustable Properties. Again, these can be adjusted by a user or by programming, but you, as the designer of the Object, must first define these Properties and provide a way for an outsider to adjust them. To permit changes to a Property, you write an Property Let procedure. (By doing this, you are in effect *creating* a Property of your Object.)

Since you can both write ("Let") and read ("Get") most Properties, there is a facility for finding out what value a Property procedure contains. (You can also put a Public Variable into a Class Module to hold the current status of a Property.)

To permit a query of the status (value) of a Property, you write a Property *Get* procedure.

Notice that this word *Let* harkens back to the very early days of Basic when to assign a value to a variable, you had to use the Let command:

```
Let MyVar = 1254
```

Quickly, though, it was realized that *Let* was unnecessary and it was made optional. Nobody uses it these days, but it's still in VB (see the entry for "Let" elsewhere in this book). The Property Let has a similar meaning: *assignment*, giving something a new value, such as changing the FontSize to 15.

Used with   Class Modules and Forms

Variables   You create a Property Let procedure as you would create a Function, except instead of writing:

```
Function ItsName ( )
    (programming goes here)
End Function
```

you create a Property procedure by writing:

```
Property Let ItsName ( )
    (programming goes here)
End Property
```

After you do this, you have a new Property of that Form or Module. (It wouldn't make much sense to put it into a normal Module. They are receptacles for Subs and Functions and declarations that you want to give projectwide scope. Ordinary Modules don't have *qualities* as such, so they don't need Properties. Instead, put your Property procedures in Forms or Class Modules. Note that you can add Properties to ordinary Forms using Property Let and Get, if you wish.)

All the usual optional commands can be used with a Property Let (or Property Let or Property Set) procedure:

```
[Public|Private] [Static] Property Let ItsName [(arguments)] [As Variable-
Type]
```

Calling Property Get

You query (read) a Property Get Property just as you would a normal built-in VB Property, such as Width.

```
X = PropertyGetName
```

OR (calling a Property Get from within an expression):

```
If PropertyGetName = 5 Then...
```

OR , (in cases where you have to identify the Object involved):

```
X = Class1.PropertyGetName
```

Calling Property Let

Likewise, you change a Property Let procedure the same way you'd change a normal built-in VB Property:

```
PropertyGetName = 5
ItsName = 125
```

Or, in cases where you have to identify the Object involved:

```
Form1.ItsName = 125
```

However, there is a peculiarity. You *can* pass more than a single value to a Property procedure (or, put another way, you can create a Property procedure with more than one argument):

To pass multiple arguments when you call a Property procedure, you have to use a unique, we might say *weird*, syntax. Put all but the final argument in parentheses, then use an equals sign for the final argument:

```
Form1.ItsName (one, two, three) = four
```

This passes four arguments to

```
Property Let ItsName (one, two, three, four)
    (programming goes here)
End Property
```

Arrays in Property Procedures

You might have noticed in VB4 that some Properties which were separate in VB3—FontName, FontSize, FontUnderline, FontItalic, FontBold and FontStrikeThru Properties—have collapsed into a single Font Property in the Properties Window. You can still address them within your programming as separate entities: FontBold = True. However, they are treated in the Properties Window as a collection of related data under the main idea of *Font*. In other words, they're like an Array. A "Collection."

Likewise, you can gather related entities into one of your Object Properties. A Property procedure can, in other words, handle Arrays, with a little help from you. It's done the same way that you maintain a Public Variable in your Class Module that has the purpose of holding (remembering) the current value of one of your Properties. (When the Property Let procedure changes the value of one of your Properties, within that Let procedure you assign the new value to the "holder" Public Variable. The associated Property Get procedure merely queries this Public Variable and returns it.)

To do the same kind of thing with Arrays, you Declare an Array Variable (make it a Variant type), and declare an associated "counter" (it's just another Variable that, in this case, has the job of holding the total number of elements in your array). In a Class Module:

```
Private MyArray( ) As Variant
Private MyArraysIndex As Integer
```

Then you dimension the Array in a Form_Initialize or Form_Load Event, or a Class Module's Initialize Event (Class Modules don't have typical Events as such, like the Click Event or the ReDraw Event of a normal Form. However, Class Modules do have two "Events": Initialize and Terminate.) Notice that we'll just create a one-element Array here. In the Property Let procedure we'll expand it as necessary each time we add a new element to the Array:

```
Private Sub Class_Initialize( )
    ReDim MyArray (1)
End Sub
```

Now, within a Property Let procedure, you can manage this Array by updating the counter (MyArraysIndex) and by, for example, adding a new element. Here we'll assume that our Array is holding a set of names and that this Property Let procedure adds a new name to the Array:

```
Property Let AddOne (NewName As Variant)
    If UBound(MyArray) > 1 Then this isn t the first element
        My ArraysIndex = My ArraysIndex + 1
        increase the size of the array by 1 and
        preserve the contents of the array
        ReDim Preserve MyArray (My ArraysIndex)
```

```
        EndIf
        add new name to array
        MyArray(My ArraysIndex) = NewName
    End Property
```

Uses
• Property procedures aren't limited only to Class Modules, to Objects. You could add new custom Properties to add to the Properties which Forms already possess (see Example 1). Since Forms themselves are Objects, you can now with VB4 also *pass arguments to and retrieve return values from* Forms. This way, you can create Forms which are detachable from the program within which they are written. (In Object-oriented programming parlance, the Form would be *encapsulated,* meaning that it could be plugged into some other program quite easily. Traditionally, in VB3 and earlier, you would communicate between Forms using Global Variables. However, as you can well imagine, this ties the Form to the Project within which it resides and makes a Form less transportable to other projects. If, however, you can pass arguments (messages) back and forth to the Form, you can avoid the hard-wiring that results from the use of Global (Public) variables.

You can affect or query a Form's Properties with Property procedures. Likewise, you can provide the Form with the equivalent of *Methods* by accessing from the outside the Forms Public Subs or Functions (its behaviors). However, there is no Object equivalent of a Form's or a Control's *Events* (though a Form's Subs or Functions could trigger its or its Controls' Events).

But the real utility of Property Procedures for most programmers will be to define Properties of Class Modules (see Example 2). A Class Module (whether or not, because it needs a visible component, it involves an associated Form) must have a way to let the outside world contact its qualities (Properties) and its behaviors (Subs and Functions).

With programmer-defined tubes of communication (the Object's Public Functions or Subs, and Property Procedures), messages can be sent back and forth between the Object and an outside application. The Object, then, can be useful to some other application, or that application could be useful to the Object. However, there is no need to establish special common data zones (such as Public Variables) because data can freely pass back and forth between the entities. An Object which "exposes" some or all of its interior Methods and Properties thus floats within the Windows operating system as a self-contained entity. It can be temporarily "attached" to other applications and provide services for them. (It could also use services exposed by other applications or Objects.)

In short: if you create an Object, you want to give it Methods, and sometimes Properties as well. And you often want to allow the outside world to modify some of the Object's qualities or activate some of its behaviors and capabilities. To provide a gateway into your Object's behaviors, you write

Public Subs or Public Functions. To provide a gateway into your Object's Properties, you write Property procedures.

Cautions • The variable types must match between associated Let and Get and Set procedures. When you give two or three Property procedures the same name, they become "associated" and are intended to represent the same Property. For example:

```
Private SizeStatus As Boolean  Variable to hold status of Property
Property Get Sizer() As Boolean    Returns value of Property
   Sizer = SizeStatus
End Property
Property Let Sizer(x As Boolean)   Changes value of Property
If x = True Then
  SizeStatus = False
  Width = Width / 1.5
Else
   SizeStatus = True
  Width = Width * 1.5
End If
End Property
```

Notice that these two Property procedures are both named "Sizer" and therefore work with a single Property. TheVariable types must match between associated Let and Get and Set procedures. Because the Let accepts a boolean variable type, the Get must *return* a boolean type as well. If you just say Property Get Sizer( ) it will default to a Variant Variable type, and you'll get an error message when you try to run it.

• Even if you use the Static command to make a Property Let procedure retain the contents of its internal variables, this isn't a *Global* or *Public* set of Variables that you can query. Property Let doesn't return any arguments. You are supposed to use Property Get when you want to find out the status (value) of a Property in an Object. In other words, you can't for example query the Property Let procedure to find out the BackColor of your Object. The BackColor variable within Property Let, if the procedure is Static, does remember that value. However, Property Let has no facility with which to provide you that information.

So, you should usually create paired procedrues—Get and Let—for a particular Property of your Object. You should use an associated Property Get procedure to permit querying the value (the text or number) of a Property Let entity. (We call this "associated" because it is suggested that when you write a Property Let procedure you also write a Property Get procedure *with the same name*. This duplication of names won't cause a problem—VB expects you to do this and graciously permits it. But, you might well ask, what could you write, what programming could you put into a Property Get procedure that would provide value of the BackColor Property? Good question. You have to establish a Variable *outside* the Property Get procedure. This Variable will hold the information you're after! (Shades of Global Variables again.)

The Variable that holds the status of your Object's Property, however, isn't really Global (or *Public*, as the older, pre-VB4 *Global* scoping is now called). The Variable's scope should normally be made Private, so that its scope is only within that Module, within your Object. You *could* make the variable Public if you wanted to, but that would go against the "encapsulation" that is supposed to shield an Object's innards from all but necessary contacts with the outside world. The idea is that you build an Object and put all its mechanisms together in a Class Module. Then you put only those *few and necessary* tubes to the outside that allow certain properties or Methods to be manipulated. Other Properties and Methods and Variables are supposed to remain *private* to your "black box" Object.

You don't want the average person or outside application or programmer to muck around with the interior structure of your Object. You want to maintain stability; you want your Object's features and the commands which manipulate those features to remain fixed and unchangeable. The only things that can be changed by outsiders are those things that you *permit* to be adjusted. And these should be the minimum necessary knobs on the outside of your black box.

The reason for all this concern is the same reason that a radio might expose only three knobs to the user: volume, tuning and on/off. You want the rest of the radio–its variable capacitors, its internal trim pots, its RF modulator–kept off-limits from the user. So when you make an Object, you label the few knobs that the user or another application can adjust (Public Subs, Public Functions and Public Property procedures). You tell the outside world what arguments these exposed entities can accept, and what, if any, arguments they pass back as verification, error notification, or other information. The rest of the innards of your black box are then sealed off from outside tinkering. You pour hot black plastic over the entire thing, leaving only those few conduits exposed. That way, the integrity of your machine is ensured and it can be used endlessly, without fail, as it was intended to be used.

So, we've established that Property Let changes a Property of your Object. And we've also pointed out that Property Get has no information about the activities of Property Let, unless you help it out by using a Variable to hold the current status of the Property. Therefore, here's how to make a pair of Let and Get procedures work together harmoniously. In your Class Module, at the top so it's not within any procedure, you establish a Modulewide, but Private, Variable:

```
Private FontSiz as Integer
```

Now we'll insure that this Variable will always contain the current status (value), the number describing the FontSize of your FontSize Property for this Object. We'll update this Variable whenever the program, the user or an outside application changes this particular Property of our Object. How? In that Property's Property Let procedure:

```
Property Let ChangeFontSize (X As Integer)
    FontSiz = X   here s where we remember this change to this property.
    Form1.Text1.FontSize = X   we make the actual change.
End Property
```

Now, any query of this Property takes place in the associated Property Get procedure, which also contacts the FontSiz Variable. Within our program (or from some outside agent like another application or Object or the user) we could "read" the status of FontSize by calling on the Property Get like this:

```
Fsize = ChangeFontSize ( )
```

And the Property Get procedure responds this way, by simply accessing and returning the value in that Variable, *FontSiz*, which exists only to hold the current status of our object's FontSize:

```
Property Get ChangeFontSize ( ) As Integer
    ChangeFontSize = FontSiz
End Property
```

• Remember to write a Property procedure outside of any existing Property...End Property structures. Like all procedures, Property procedures cannot be nested within other procedures.

• The Property Get procedure is the only Property procedure which returns a value (so it's like a function in this respect). The other two, Let and Set, operate more like Subs.

• You can use the familiar modifiers that you would use with Subs or Functions to define the *scope* of a Property Procedure:

Public – the Procedure can be used from anywhere in your program and can be accessed from the outside by other applications or other objects. Put another way, making a Property procedure Public is the way that you *expose* this Property of your Object to the outside world. Public is the default for Property procedures.

Private – can be used only from within the Form or Module where the procedure resides.

• You can declare a Property procedure as Static (which see).

• Property Set *must* have at least one argument—the Object that the procedure will assign an Object Variable to. If Property Set has more than one argument, the *final argument* must be that Object.

• The Exit Property command (like Exit Sub or Exit Function) causes the program to leave the procedure immediately, without executing any of the programming below the Exit Property command. Your program's execution is returned to the command following the original *call* to that procedure.

• You might well wonder what use the Property Get procedure is. After all, it usually just returns the contents of a Variable—so why not just directly query that Variable instead of going through the indirect extra step of having a Property Get procedure do this querying for you?

To answer this, let's see how Property Let actually works in practice. Recall that to maintain the value of an Object's Property, you store it in a Variable. In other words, when the Object's Property changes (via a Property Let procedure), you assign this new value to the "holding" Variable. This way, something in your program always knows the current value of the Property.

However, when you want to query that Property's value, you aren't supposed to just directly read that Variable. Instead, you are supposed to call a Property Get procedure. Here's how you're supposed to create a custom Property. First, you declare a "holder" Variable (it can be Public or Private) like this:

```
Public PropVal As Integer
```

Then, you write a Property Get procedure which returns the contents of the "holder Variable:

```
Property Get ItsValue ( )
    ItsValue = ProPVal
End Property
```

Then you query the Property's current value from the outside by calling the Property Get procedure:

```
X = Object.ItsValue
```

OR, if the Object is implicit:

```
X = ItsValue
```

However, since all Property Get does is assign the Public Variable to be returned via the Get procedure, why not just query that PropVal Public Variable directly and avoid the indirection?

```
X = Object.PropVal
```

It is easy to overlook the virtue of establishing this special type of procedure, Property Get, for the sole purpose of reading a Property's value. A procedure (unlike a Variable) permits you to do three things: receive a return value, send arguments, and also to write code within the procedure to carry out some task. What is confusing here is why, when simply *reading* a value, one would ever want to pass arguments *to* the procedure or execute some lines of programming. There are, in fact, obscure cases where you might want to react if the user tries to read your Property (for example, your Property might be an Array of Properties, like VB4's Font Property, so you would have to handle the indexing and searching of this Array). However, perhaps the most compelling reason is the new Object Browser which informs the user of your Object's Methods and Procedures. The Object Browser does not list the Variables used in your Object, but it does show Property procedures. If you want the user to be aware that a Property is readable, you must use the Property Get procedure.

Also, for consistency with the way VB in general handles Property queries, calling on Property Get preserves the syntax.

• Avoid unintentional recursion. When you think about Properties, you might assume that you can change one by just assigning a new value to the Property name. For example, say that you have a Property that is supposed to read or write (find out or change) the current size of Form1. Is it Minimized, Maximized or Normal? The Windowstate Property of the Form can be used to tell us this, or to change the size. You might start out by setting up paired (associated) Let and Get Property Procedures:

```
Property Let currentsize(z As Integer)  restore form to normal size
    currentsize = z
End Property
Property Get currentsize() As Integer
    0 = Normal, 1 = minimized 2 = maximized
    currentsize = Form1.WindowState
End Property
```

Then you could invoke the Let (intending to change the windowstate of Form1 to Normal) by:

```
Sub SetSize()
    currentsize = 0
End Sub
```

The problem is that this would force the computer into a nosedive, and you would get an out of stack space error. Your Let procedure *is calling itself*...infinitely cycling through a loop. Whenever you get an out-of-stack error message, check the Calls option on the Tools menu. You'll likely see one procedure called over and over.

The solution: you must use a Variable to hold the status of a Property, and your Let procedure should *change* something, in addition to adjusting that Property:

```
Public WindowStat As Integer
Property Let currentsize(z As Integer)  restore form to normal size
    Form1.WindowState = z
    WindowStat = z
End Property
```

Example #1   First let's look at a simple, non-OLE, example. This isn't a Class Module; it's not intended to be an "Object." We're just going to add a new Property to a Form. Here we'll give a Form (and all the Controls on it) the ability to be resized and repositioned to become roughly twice as big, or to be restored to the original dimensions. Notice that the entire shift in the Form's appearance is triggered by a single *assignment* of the value True or False to the new Property we've created called *sizer*. It's as if we've added a new Property to this Form (along with the built-in VB Properties such as Back-Color and FontSize). Now this Form and its contents will be large or small depending on the "sizer" Property.

Put three Command Buttons on a Form. Then type the Variable that will hold the current status of our Property:

```
Private SizeStatus As Boolean
```

Now type in the procedure that lets you read (Get) the Property:

```
Property Get Sizer() As Boolean
    Sizer = SizeStatus
End Property
```

and write (Let) the Property:

```
Property Let Sizer(x As Boolean)
If x = True Then
  SizeStatus = False
  Width = Width / 1.5
Else
   SizeStatus = True
  Width = Width * 1.5
End If
End Property
```

Now two Command Buttons that write to (change) the Property:

```
Private Sub Command1_Click()
 Reduce size by setting sizer property to false:
Sizer() = False
End Sub
```

```
Private Sub Command2_Click()
 Enlarge Form by setting sizer property to True:
Sizer() = True
End Sub
```

And, finally, the Command Button that reads the Property:

```
Private Sub Command3_Click()
 Query the Property
  If Sizer = False Then Print  It s small.
  If Sizer = True Then Print  It s big.
 OR
x = Sizer
Print x
End Sub
```

Example #2   An Object With Properties

For the second example, let's construct a timer. It will be like those kitchen timers that you set for, say, an hour from now and then it goes off (keeps going bong, bong, bong) until you shut it off. This will be useful for those of us who get lost while working on the computer and have to be forcefully reminded that it's time to take a break.

It's said that those of us used to "procedural" programming (traditional programs based on Subs, Functions and If...Then) should approach OOP, Object-Oriented Programming by trying to construct Objects that imitate the real world. These Objects can be thought of as user-defined data types, but with a twist—they hold more than just data, they also contain behaviors that can act on data. They're like little self-contained computers—they have raw data (such as the fact that A comes before B in the alphabet) as well as the ability to process that data (such as the ability to concatenate A&B and display the string AB). They're little highly dedicated computers that imitate some limited, real-world ones. So let's give it a try.

We have to remember that we won't scatter our procedures all over the place in our program. Instead, we'll put them (as "Methods") *within* the Objects they act upon. So we'll talk about the components of our timer as if they each encapsulate both qualities (Properties) and actions (Methods).

Let's describe our Timer. How we want it to look, sound and behave:

It will have the ability to be set to a delay. It can be turned off before or after it starts ringing. It can ring repeatedly. It will display the remaining time to the user. It can be large (about 2 inches square) or small (icon-sized, but still displaying the remaining time). It checks the current time against the remaining time every second.

Now break this down into Properties and Methods:

Properties:
1. Size (large or small)

2. Ringing (yes or no)

3. Remaining time (duration expressed in seconds)

Methods:
1. Set delay (user interface to establish remaining time initially)

2. Turn off (user interface to cancel timer, or cancel ringing; double-click does this)

3. Ringing (interval of bongs)

4. Resize (toggle between big and small, single-click does this)

5. Regularly check time (interval of seconds)

Let's implement the Properties:

```
Private Remaining As Long  end-time, the relative time
                    that the ringer should go off
                    in seconds
Private Active As Boolean  is timer running?
Property Let Running(x As Boolean)   is the coundown active?
Active = x
End Property
Property Get Running() As Boolean
Running = Active
End Property

Property Let duration(x As Long)   establishes duration (in seconds)
Remaining = x
End Property
```

```
Property Get duration() As Long
duration = Remaining
End Property


Sub SetDelay(x As Integer)  accepts duration, in minutes
duration = x * 60  stores it as seconds
End Sub

Public Sub Startcountdown()  starts the timer running ; button press calls
this
Running = True
Form1.Command1.Caption = STOP
SetDelay Form1.Text1
Form1.Timer1.Interval = 1000  timer to count 1 second
End Sub

Sub DownOne()  timer has counted 1 second, so decrement
duration = duration - 1
Form1.Label1 = duration
Form1.label2 = Format(duration / 60,  ###0.00 )  express it in minutes
If duration = 0 Then StartBongs: Exit Sub  Alert User if time s up
End Sub

Private Sub StartBongs()  Time s up
Form1.Timer1.Interval = 0  turn off countdown timer
Form1.Timer2.Interval = 1000  turn on bong timer
 currentsize = 0  restore form to normal size
Form1.Command1.Caption = Start
End Sub

Public Sub StopBongs()  user has clicked OFF button or time s up
Running = False
Form1.Command1.Caption = Start
Form1.Timer1.Interval = 0  turn off countdown timer
Form1.Timer2.Interval = 0  turn off bong timer
Form1.Label1 =
Form1.label2 =
End Sub
```

In the Form:

```
Public obj As New Class1

Private Sub Command1_Click()
If obj.Running = False Then
obj.Startcountdown
Else
obj.StopBongs
End If
End Sub

Private Sub Timer1_Timer()
obj.DownOne  decrement counter
End Sub
```

```
Private Sub Timer2_Timer()
Beep
Form1.Print  . ;
End Sub
```

See also   Class Module, Objects

SET

METHOD

Description   PSet prints a dot on a Form, Picture Box or the sheet of paper in the printer.

Used with   Forms, Picture Boxes and the printer

Variables   (To try the following examples, set the DrawWidth Property of a Form to 6 to make the points easier to see: DrawWidth = 6.)

To draw a dot on the Form about one inch from the left and about two inches down from the top if the ScaleMode is in the default measurement of twips (see "ScaleMode"):

```
PSet (1440,2880)
```

OR (to draw a dot in the same position relative to the left and top of a Picture Box): Picture1.PSet (1440,2880)

OR (to draw a dot in the same position relative to the left and top of a sheet of paper in the printer): Printer.Pset (1440,2880)

OR (to draw a light green dot in the Form): PSet (120, 3000), QBColor (10)

OR (to draw several dots, each one positioned 300 twips to the right *of the previous dot*. Using the Step command causes the position described by the X,Y coordinates to be *relative* to the position of the previous dot—or the previous Line, Circle or Print command. Without Step, the X,Y coordinates describe the position in terms of the host Form, Picture Box or sheet of paper in the printer):

```
DrawWidth = 6
For i = 1 to 6
    PSet Step(300,0)
Next i
```

Results in

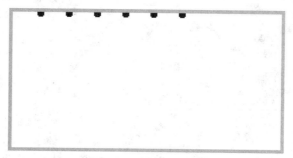

Figure P-31: Adjust DrawWidth to make the dot whatever size you wish.

(If we removed the Step command in the preceding example, all six dots would be printed at the same position, namely, 300 twips over from the left side of the Form and at the very top.)

OR (to draw six points that start at the 300th twip and move down vertically. We'll have to avoid Step and use Loop counter Variable *i* to cause each point to move down the screen. Notice that without the Step command the horizontal position remains unchanged at 300 twips over from the left of the Form):

```
For i = 1 to 6
    PSet (300, i * 200)
Next i
```

Results in

Figure P-32: You control the position of the dots.

OR (to draw diagonals, use Step and provide steps in both horizontal and vertical directions):

```
For i = 1 to 6
    PSet Step(300,100)
Next i
```

Results in

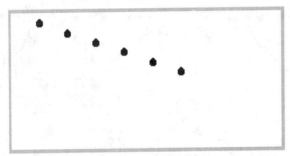

Figure P-33: Add the optional Step command to PSet to draw diagonally.

Uses
• Like the other drawing commands, Line and Circle, you can use PSet to create attractive backgrounds for your Forms, at no cost in memory.

The alternative to these *drawn* designs is bitmap files. You load bitmap pictures (.BMP, .ICO or .WMF files) into your programs by setting the Picture Property of a Form or Picture Box (or via the LoadPicture command while the program is running). For all their versatility and beauty, bitmaps can use up lots of memory on the disk, in the computer (when your program is running) and in your finished VB programs if they are embedded in an .EXE file.

Drawing, by contrast, merely describes lines, circles and dots mathematically. The graphics are created when the program runs and thus take up virtually no memory on disk, in memory or within the .EXE program. There are two drawbacks to drawing. Complex drawings, for example, can require many calculations that can slow up the program. Often the user can see the drawing as it is painted, which doesn't look professional. *Note that if the AutoRedraw Property is "on," the graphics appear only after they have finished drawing.* In this instance, you need not worry that the user will see the initial drawing activity when the program first starts up.

The other drawback is that the results of drawing methods will always be abstract, wallpaper-like designs—never realistic or photo-realistic images that could come close to the impact of bitmaps.

• Create various kinds of "painting," "drawing," or even photo-retouching applications. (See "DrawWidth" and "Point.")

Cautions
• Drawn images will be erased if another window covers them up or if their host Form is resized. To prevent this, set the AutoRedraw Property to On (True). AutoRedraw defaults to Off (False). Setting the AutoRedraw Property on saves a copy, in the computer's memory, *of the entire screen* in the case of Forms or just the image of a Picture Box. This setting does use up memory, but redisplaying such images is virtually instantaneous, and it is better than the slow-redraw alternative of putting the drawing commands within the Paint or Resize Event of the Form or Picture Box.

The DrawWidth Property Governs the Size of a PSet: How large a point is drawn when you use PSet depends on the setting of the DrawWidth Property. The default is 1, which will turn on the smallest unit your screen can display, *a pixel*. If you set DrawWidth larger than one, the dot is positioned–based on the *200,400* coordinates in PSet(200,400)–at the exact center of the dot. If you put dots close enough together or make them wide enough, they will overlap, creating a scalloped effect.

Exactly which distances are described by the coordinates, the *400,500* in PSet(400,500), depends on the setting of the ScaleMode Property (which see). Unless you have altered it, the ScaleMode defaults to twips (there are 1,440 twips per inch).

The color of the drawn point will be the ForeColor Property, unless you specify a different color when using PSet (see "QBColor"):

```
PSet (240, 1500), QBColor(15)
```

OR

You can use RGB colors, which number in the millions (see "RGB").

DrawMode (which see) provides various ways that PSet (and Circle and Line) will interact with any colors they are covering up on the background. You can invert, cover completely, and so forth. You'll usually want to use the default mode–"cover completely" (DrawMode = 13).

To erase a drawn point, specify its location and use the BackColor Property as the color. Here we'll draw a fat dot, delay briefly with the For...Next Loop and then erase the dot:

```
DrawWidth = 12
PSet (300,600)
X& = Form1.BackColor

For i = 1 to 1200
Next i

PSet(300, 600),X&
```

Example   This example demonstrates the variety of effects possible by selecting random colors, DrawStyles and DrawWidths. Put the following in the Form_Load Event:

```
Sub Form_Load ()

Randomize
Show

xs! = scalewidth
ys! = scaleheight

For i = 1 To 300
    cl = Int(16 * Rnd)
    dw = Int(35 * Rnd + 1)
    dm = Int(16 * Rnd + 1)
    xpos! = Int(xs! * Rnd)

ypos! = Int(xs! * Rnd)
    drawwidth = dw
    drawmode = dm
    PSet (xpos!, ypos!), QBColor(cl)
Next i
End Sub
```

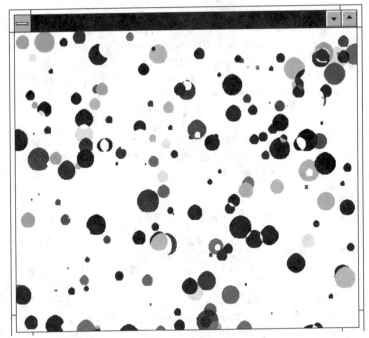

Figure P-34: Hardly a threat to abstract painters (the results are a little *too* random), we can create attractive splattered backgrounds for windows using the Rnd and PSet commands.

When you use the Randomize Statement at the start of a program, you ensure that later use of the Rnd Function will produce different sequences of random numbers each time the program runs. This randomness may or may not suit your needs when drawing backgrounds. If you want the same background design each time the program is run, omit the Randomize command.

You must put a Show command in the Form_Load Event when you use drawing commands within Load. Otherwise, the Form will not become visible until the commands within the Event have been completed. Unless the AutoRedraw Property of the Form is set to on (True), the drawn graphics will be erased before the user even sees them. AutoRedraw = True will also delay revealing the graphics until they are drawn; the user will not see the process of the drawing while the computer accomplishes it.

Next, we find the dimensions of the Form from the ScaleWidth and Scale Height Properties.

The QBColor Range: A For...Next Loop is set to produce 300 points of various sizes and colors, located at random positions on the Form. Each time we cycle through this Loop, the Variables for color (cl), DrawWidth (dw), DrawMode (dm) and the position on the Form are given random values within their respective ranges.

The Variable *cl* is given a random value between 0 and 15, which is the range of colors possible for the QBColor Function. The Variable dw is given a random value between 1 and 35 because we decided that 35 was the fattest dot we wanted. The DrawWidth Property range is up to you.

DrawMode (dm) can range between 1 and 16. Finally, we set an X coordinate and a Y coordinate based on the measurements we earlier made of the width and height of the Form involved. You establish the range of numbers from within which Rnd selects a random number by first providing the upper limit–16, 35 or a Variable like a Form's ScaleWidth Property. Then, if you want the range to be from 0 to one less than the upper limit, leave out the +1 following the Rnd command.

The QBColor command expects numbers between 0 and 15. However, because DrawMode wants numbers between 1 and 16, we use +1 to bump the supplied number up one. Then we'll never get a zero.

Finally, the PSet command puts the dot onscreen. Its position, color, size and DrawMode (inversions, pure white, etc.) are all randomly determined each time through the Loop.

For variety, try limiting the range of color and extending the number of times through the Loop (to 800, for instance). Also, you can sometimes achieve alarming effects by using only DrawMode 6, Invert, and drawing on top of a bitmap picture loaded in with the Picture Property. This technique can sometimes be too much of a good thing: Splattering inverted dots on a Van Gogh results in especially tasteless backgrounds.

See also   Circle; CurrentX, CurrentY; DrawMode; DrawWidth; Line; Point; QBColor; RGB; ScaleHeight; ScaleMode; ScaleWidth

PUBLIC

STATEMENT

Description   The Public command creates a Variable (or Constant or procedure) that will be available to all parts of your program. Public can be used only in a Module. If you try to put it into the general declarations section of a Form, you'll get an error. Public replaces the *Global* command which was nearly identical in behavior and was used in VB 3.0 and earlier. Global is still recognized by VB, for compatibility with programs written in earlier versions of VB.

If you don't declare a Variable as Public, it will be available for use only within a single Form (or Module), or even only within a single Event– depending on where you first name it (*declare* it) or first use it. In other words, variables have a range of influence which can be as limited as a single procedure (Event, Sub or Function) or as large as the entire program.

Variables can have different zones of influence–they can differ in how widely throughout the program the Variable can be read (to find out what it contains, its *value*) or written to (to change its value). The way that you declare them determines their range, from the narrowest, ReDim (procedure-level), through Dim (Form- or Module-level), up to programwide range established with the Public command.

A Variable declared (using ReDim) within a single Event, Subroutine or Function can be read or written to only within that Event, Sub or Function. Unless it is an Array (which see), you don't even have to officially declare it with ReDim; you can just use it.

A Variable declared (using Dim) within the General Declarations section of a Form or Module is available to all the Events, Subs or Functions within that Form or Module. But a Variable declared using Public is available to every section of your entire program.

The range of a Variable's influence is called its *scope*. You determine scope by the location where you declare a Variable. And where you declare it governs which of the three Variable declaration commands you can use: Public, Dim or ReDim. (Static is a fourth way of declaring Variables and Arrays and is a special case. See "Static.")

An entire *procedure* (an Event, Sub or Function) also has scope. In other words, a Private procedure can only be called (see "Sub") from within the same Form or Module. A Public procedure can be called from anywhere in the entire program. You may have noticed that VB4 supplies the Private statement automatically in front of every Event, whenever you double-click on a Control or Form (or click on the dropdown list under Proc. in the VB editor). The reason for this is that procedures are Public by default, but VB wants them to be "Private" so it inserts the word Private in front of each of them. (You would think that if the default was supposed to be Private, that would be made the default and VB wouldn't have to insert "Private" in front of everything.)

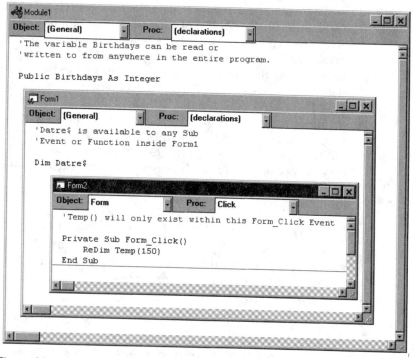

Figure 35: The three ranges of scope Programwide, Form/Modulewide, or Eventwide.

Used with   Variables, Arrays (which see) and procedures (see "Sub")

Variables   If you just provide the Variable's name with no specification about its Variable *type,* the Variable defaults to a Variant type. (See "Variables" to learn about the Variable types): Public MyVariable

OR (you can declare a Variable type other than the default by stating the type as a word, with the As command): Public Reminder As String

OR (you can declare a Variable type other than the default by attaching the type's symbol to the Variable name. This Variable becomes a text "string" Variable because $ is the text symbol): Public Reminder$

OR (you can declare an Array [which see]. An Array is a special kind of Variable. It is actually a cluster of Variables of the same type.)

OR declare an Array, the index numbers of which range from 1 to 50:

Public Names (1 To 50) As String

OR declare a fixed-length string (text) Variable. Unless you specifically declare a string as fixed, all string Variables are dynamic and adjust in size to accommodate whatever length of text you store in them. Certain special situations require fixed-length strings. (See Appendix A or "Get.")

Notice that the above Public Declarations involving strings created space for strings (text Variables) of varying size (in other words, "dynamic Variables" that can resize themselves while a program runs). Public Names (1 To 50) would allow you to put the Name William P. Sanderson, III into a single one of the 50 "cells" we created in the preceding example Array. (However, you can't use Public to declare a fixed-length string in a *Class Module*.)

Characters, not Items: However, when you declare a fixed-length string, you are defining the number of *characters* that this Array can hold, not the number of Variable-length text items. Fixed-length strings are a special type of Variable and are not true Arrays at all. This example creates a string 75 characters in length:

```
Public WelshForHelp As String * 75
```

OR declare a multidimensional Array—one having 12 rows and 3 columns.

This is a way to link related information, such as 12 names, each with an address and phone number Variable associated with it. VB allows you to create as many as 60 dimensions for a single Array:

```
Public Names$ (1 To 12, 1 To 3)
```

OR define a *dynamic* Array. These are handy because they conserve memory. Dynamic Arrays come into existence in your program when they are needed, but then go away as soon as you leave the Event, Sub or Function in which they reside. The ReDim Statement is used within an Event, Sub or Function to bring a dynamic Array to life, but you can optionally declare them using Public with empty parentheses:

```
Public Ages( ) As Integer
```

OR you can combine several declarations on one line following a Public Statement:

```
Public A, B( ), Counter as Integer, X$, L (12 To 4)
```

Uses
- Use Public to make the contents of a Variable (or Array or Constant) available to your entire program. (You can also declare *an entire procedure, a Subroutine, Event or Function* to be Public, and then it can be called from anywhere.)
  After being declared Public, your Variables are accessible from any location in your program. Any instructions in any Event Procedure in any Form—or any Function or Subroutine anywhere in your program—can find out what's currently in the Variable (its current "value") or *change* that Variable's value.

Cautions
- *Note this: Public in Forms doesn't really make a variable or procedure completely global in scope. You are also required when writing or reading this Variable outside the "home form" to type the Form's Name in front of the name of the procedure: Form1.Variablename.* The solution

to this little kink is to put your public variables or procedures in a Module where that prepended location name isn't needed.

You can use Public in Forms as well as Modules. However, if you want to utilize a Public Variable or Procedure defined as Public in Form1 (from within Form2, for instance) you must provide Form1's Name first:

In Form1:

```
Public MyVariable$

Private Sub Form_Click( )
 MyVariable$ = Fred
 Form2.Show
End Sub
```

In Form2:

```
Private Sub Form_Click( )
 Print Form1.MyVariable$
End Sub
```

Note that prepending Form1. to MyVariable$ is required—even though you made this variable Public. This won't work:

In Form2:

```
Private Sub Form_Click( )
 Print MyVariable$
End Sub
```

Similarly, if you've got a Public Event, Sub or Function in Form1 that you want to trigger from Form2, you must prepend Form1's name. This works:

In Form1:

```
Sub Shrinkit( )
 Form2.Height = Form2.Height / 2
End Sub
```

In Form2:

```
Private Sub Form_Click( )
 Form1.Shrinkit
End Sub
```

This doesn't work:

In Form2:

```
Private Sub Form_Click( )
 Shrinkit
End Sub
```

However, you're supposed to put general-purpose (programwide-accessible) Subs or Functions in a Module. In that case, you don't have to prepend the Module's Name, you can just call the procedure without any fuss:

In Module1:

```
Public Sub movit(n As Form)
  n.Left = n.Left - 300
End Sub
```

In Form1:

```
Private Sub Form_Click( )
     movit Me
End Sub
```

• Most versions of Basic allow you to implicitly create an Array by just using it, like this:

```
Sub Form_Click
For I = 1 To 8
    A(I) = I
Next
End Sub
```

This is not permitted in VB. VB requires that you formally declare all Arrays using Public (in a Module) or Dim (in Forms' or Modules' General Declarations sections) or ReDim (in Event Procedures, Subs, or Functions). However, ordinary non-Array Variables can be implicitly declared by simply using them.

You can use Public with the special *Type* Variable structure (see "Type").

• It's not a good idea to overuse Public Variables. Sure it's convenient to have a Variable that's available to all Events, Subs and Functions. But no Subroutine (which see) can create a new Variable with the same name as a Public Variable.

If you like to build programs from a personal "toolkit" of Subroutines, you don't want to have to check to see if there are duplicated Variable names whenever you add a Public Variable. Also, because you can implicitly ReDim a Variable in a Sub or Function, you may inadvertently be referencing a Public Variable rather than what you thought was a local, privately held Variable. This could result in inexplicable behavior when you run your program. It's best to be conservative with Public Variables. Or use very strange names, such as adding "P" to the end of each Public Variable name: "NameP$," for instance, to identify the Variable as Public. Be aware that you can create havoc if you import Subroutines that share Variable names with Public Variables.

Example

Figure 36: Two separate Forms, but each can refer to and manipulate the same Public Variable when the user presses one of the Command Buttons.

These two Forms can both contact the Public Variable *Choice*—because we declare it Public in a Module.

Declare the Variable *Choice* Public in a Module:

```
Public Choice As Boolean
```

Clicking on the Command Button in Form1 sets Choice to True:

```
Sub Command1_Click ( )
    Choice = True
End Sub
```

Clicking on the Button in Form2 copies the picture from Form1 to Form2.

The important thing here is that two Forms can refer to, and adjust, the same Variable. If *Choice* had been *declared Private* (given its name and, optionally, its "type"), we could not work with it from any Form other than the Form in which *Choice* was declared. But it was declared Public, so we can utilize it anywhere in the program.

```
Sub Command1_Click ( )
If Choice = True Then
    Form2.Picture = Form1.Picture
End If
End Sub
```

If you try this example, be sure to put a Form2.Show command within the Form_Load Event of Form1. That's the way to make multiple Forms visible from the very start of your program. Form1 is the Startup Form and defines what happens at the beginning when your program runs. (You can select which Form has this privilege from VB's Tools Menu, Project Options.)

Notice, too, that separate Forms are truly isolated. In this case, we've got two Command Button Controls, and they are both named Command1. It would be impossible to have two Controls with the same name within a single Form (unless you created a Control Array, which see).

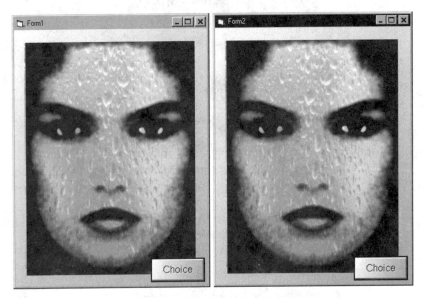

Figure 37: We copied the graphic from Form2 into Form1 s Picture Property.

See also   Arrays; Const; Dim; Module; Option; Private; ReDim; Static; Sub; Variables

Put

STATEMENT

Description   Put saves a piece of information into an Opened file. It is normally used with files Opened in random mode, but can also be used with binary mode, and even sequential-mode files.

(See "Open" for a general discussion of file types and file management. See "Input$" for a general discussion of the sequential mode.)

Used with   Files Opened in the random mode; sometimes with files Opened in the binary mode; hardly ever with files Opened in the sequential mode

Variables   For a file Opened in random mode, this example places the text ("string") Variable A$ into the file where record #12 is located. A$ must be less than or equal to the size of the records in this random file (all records in a random file are exactly the same size). A$ replaces any current record #12.

For a file Opened in binary mode, this example places A$ at the 12th byte (character position) into the file. Subsequent bytes are covered over by A$, to the length of A$:

```
Put #1, 12, A$
```

OR

Visual Basic keeps track of the current location within an Opened file, so you can feed several Variables to an Opened file without having to specify the record number (random files) or the byte position (binary files). Thus, you can omit the 12 in Put #1, 12, A$ if you are feeding a series of Variables to a file; however, you do need to include the comma:

```
Open "C:\TEST" As #1 For Binary

For i% = 0 to 100 Step 10
     Put #1, ,i%
Next i%
Close 1
```

The preceding routine places the numbers 0, 10, 20, 30, 40, 50, 60, 70, 80, 90, 100 into the first, third, fifth, etc., byte positions in the file. Where a single text character like *m* takes up only one byte, numeric Variables can take up several bytes, depending on the *type* of the numeric Variable (see "Variables"). In the case of an *Integer* type, signified by adding a percentage (%) symbol, each number will take up two bytes. That's why these numbers are placed in the first, third, fifth, etc., byte positions in the file.

Similarly, a filed Opened for random-mode access with no record number specified will stuff records into the file, one record after the next, starting with the first record position in the file:

```
Open "C:\TESTRAND" For Random As #1 Len = 2

For i% = 0 to 100 Step 10
     Put #1, ,i%
Next i%
Close 1
```

The preceding example of random-mode file access produces a file that is indistinguishable from the previous example that Opened a file in binary mode. The approach is different, but the result is, in this case, the same.

Uses
- Put is most often used with random-mode files.
- Create a new random-mode file by placing records into an Opened file.
- Update a random-mode file by replacing records previously stored in the Opened file.
- Put Variables of any length or type into a file Opened in binary mode.

    (See "Open" for a general discussion of files and of the random mode and its uses, in particular.)

Cautions
- Variables Put into a random-mode file must be the same size, or smaller, than the record size for that file. The record size is described by the Len command used with the Open Statement when a random-mode file is created. The size of a user-defined Variable type usually determines record sizes (see "Type").

    Because Visual Basic adds a special two-byte code to any text ("string") Variable that's not a *fixed* size (see "Variables"), you will need to be sure that such Variables are at least two bytes less than the record size. Simply working with program-defined Variable types (see "Type") is easier; then you need not worry about this detail.

- If you leave out the record number (or, for binary files, the byte number)—the 44 in Put #2, 44, A$—Visual Basic will Put the Variable at the record (or byte) position following the most recent Put to the file. (If you use the Get or Seek Statement prior to using a Put, the Variable will be Put immediately following the most recent Get or Seek.)

    If you do leave out the record (or byte) number, you must still use two commas: Put #2,,A$

- Files Opened in binary mode Put as many bytes as necessary into a file—as many characters as are in a text ("string") Variable or as many bytes as the numeric Variable type requires to store its number. (See "Variables.")

Example
Here we'll put 100 numeric Variables into a binary-mode file. Then we'll check the length of the file to see how many bytes this Variable uses.

```
Sub Form_Click ()

Open "C:\TEST" For Binary As #1

For i = 1 To 100
    Put #1, , i
Next i

x = LOF(1)

Close 1

Print "Length of file is: "; x; ". Each Single-Precision Floating-Point Variable requires "; x / 100; " bytes for its storage."

End Sub
```

Results in   Length of file is: 400. Each Single-Precision Floating-Point Variable requires 4 bytes for its storage.

See also   Get; Open; Seek

See "Open" for a general discussion of file management and binary files.

FUNCTION

Description

QBColor provides one of 16 colors for use with such Properties as Fore-Color and BackColor, and drawing Methods like PSet, Line and Circle.

QBColor is a holdover from an earlier Microsoft version of Basic (Quick-Basic). In the days when most computer monitors could display only 16 different colors, the QBColor command was added to provide a quick way to specify a full range of useful colors. However, VB4 now also provides a set of built-in Constants such as vbBlue and vbWhite. (See "Constants.")

A Useful Shortcut: QBColor is still a handy shortcut for many tasks. The alternative, RGB, can specify nearly 17 million colors, but they are not contiguous like a rainbow. You can't memorize RGB zones as you could if all the blues were in the first two million values. So, although RGB is (considerably) more precise, you'll often simply want to resort to the quick alternative, QBColor. Many users' video hardware exhibits only 16 pure colors; any other colors are "dithered," which means they are displayed with checkerboard or dot patterns to simulate in-between colors. In many kinds of graphics applications, the 16 pure QBColors will be all that you will need. But 256 colors or more are much preferred if the hardware supports them.

Used with

Any Control or Form to which you can assign color Properties.

The drawing commands—PSet, Line and Circle—to simplify defining which colors should be used.

FillColor, to define what color will be used to fill rectangles, circles or ovals drawn with the Line and Circle commands. (Remember that FillColors do not show up unless you set FillStyle to 0. FillStyle defaults to 1, transparent, and no colors will be visible until you set FillStyle to 0.)

Variables

Variable type: Integer

```
BackColor = QBColor (2)
```

OR

You can use a Variable to define the color on the fly while your program is running. Here we'll provide a fairly large DrawWidth (so we can better see the dots drawn by PSet), and we'll start the dots down 200 twips (see "ScaleMode") from the top of the Form:

```
Sub Form_Click ()

DrawWidth = 12
Currenty = 200

For I = 0 To 15

    PSet Step(300,0), QBColor(I)

Next I

End Sub
```

QBColor's 16 Possible Colors (depending on your hardware):

0   Black
1   Blue
2   Green
3   Cyan (blue-green)
4   Red
5   Magenta (purple)
6   Yellow (actually, a kind of army green)
7   White (actually, light gray)
8   Gray (darker gray)
9   Light Blue
10   Light Green
11   Light Cyan
12   Light Red
13   Light Magenta
14   Light Yellow (true yellow)
15   Bright White (real white)

Uses

• QBColor is simpler to use than the alternative, RGB, for specifying the color of objects and design elements of drawings.

• Assign the ForeColor and BackColor Properties and other color Properties of a Form or its Controls.

• Assign the colors of shapes drawn with Line, Circle and PSet.

Cautions

• Visual Basic works with RGB (which see) color specifications only. QBColor supplies to VB the equivalent RGB number when you use the QBColor Function. QBColor is a shortcut because it "knows" the values of the eight most common colors and lighter shades of those same colors.

Here is a list of the 16 RGB equivalents of the QBColors. There *is* a pattern here, albeit obscure. Four of these numbers are an exact power of two; three of them are one less than a power of two; and others are a power of two *minus or plus* another power of two. In spite of this "pattern," it's unlikely that you'll ever memorize RGB numbers. After you program in VB for awhile (or if you're used to QuickBasic), you're bound to recall that QBColor(0) is black, QBColor(15) is white and remember some others in between. (RGB values must be passed to the RGB Function as three different numbers: one each for red, green and blue.)

```
For i = 0 To 15
    x& = QBColor(i)
    Print i, x&
Next i
```

Results in

0   0
1   8388608
2   32768
3   8421376
4   128

5	8388736
6	32896
7	12632256
8	8421504
9	16711680
10	65280
11	16776960
12	255
13	16711935
14	65535
15	16777215

If you want, you can adjust the preceding program by inserting Print i, Hex$(x&). This will show the color as it will be seen in other places in Visual Basic, such as the BackColor Property. The individual values for QBColor(7) are 0xC0, 0xC0, 0xC0 for use with the RGB Function.

• Because the QBColors are matched with lighter shades of the same colors, you can simply subtract 8 to go from light to dark, or add 8 to go from darker to lighter shades. (QBColor(4) is red; QBColor(12) is light red.)

Example   For each of the 16 possible QBColors, this example prints the Variable value you provided to QBColor; the RGB value that QBColor then provides to Visual Basic; and an example of the color that Visual Basic puts on-screen.

This example also illustrates how you have to fool around with spaces inside quotation marks and CurrentX and CurrentY to achieve a horizontally aligned look. The Tab command, though, won't help you here.

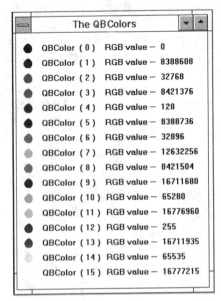

Figure Q-1: Each QBColor and its equivalent RGB value.

The Tab command doesn't line up graphics; CurrentX and CurrentY position graphics. If you want to mix text and graphics, you have to spend some time adjusting the CurrentX or CurrentY Property. We're going to describe, in some detail, how and why these drawn and printed data in Figure Q-1 line up in vertical columns. It's something you'll need to wrestle with from time to time because there is no direct way to combine drawn graphics and printed text into neatly organized rows and columns.

Here's the list of commands that line up the items horizontally in Figure Q-1:

```
Sub Form_Click ()

DrawWidth = 15

For i = 0 To 15
    x& = QBColor(i)
    currentx = 300
    currenty = currenty + 200
    Print "   QBColor ("; i; ") ";

            If i > 9 Then offset = -90
    currentx = currentx + offset
    Print "RGB value "; x&; " ";

    currentx = 150
    PSet Step(100, 100), x&
Next i

End Sub
```

We're looping through all 16 possible QBColors here, by going from 0 to 15. We attach the ampersand (&) symbol to the Variable x because we want to find out which RGB color QBColor is providing, since RGB colors can range from 0 to 16,777,215.

The Long Integer Type: Such a large range of numbers must be held within a Variable type that can handle that range. The Long Integer type, created by attaching an ampersand (&) symbol to a Variable's name, is just what we need. Its range is minus two billion to plus two billion, give or take a hundred million or so (Long Integers can hold numbers from −2,147,483,648 to 2,147,483,647). Our RGB color range will fit comfortably within the space provided by a Long Integer.

Numeric Variables in Visual Basic default to Variant types, which could also be used here (see "Variant"). Nevertheless, we attach an & symbol to the Variable x—x&—and make it into a Long Integer type. (See "Variables" for more about the different numeric types that you can create to handle extremely large or small numbers.)

We set the current horizontal position (CurrentX) to 300 twips. This is because we don't want the first items on our Form to print smack against the left side of the Form. We need to leave some room for the dot of color, too. We then move the current vertical position (CurrentY) *an additional 200 twips downward.*

Absolute Versus Relative Distances: Note that the CurrentX is an *absolute* distance from the left side of the Form, while the CurrentY is a *relative* distance from the previous CurrentY. (This difference isn't *always* true, but it is here because of our example's design.) This difference between these two coordinates results from the fact that we are moving down the Form, rather than across it. The horizontal position will remain stable, absolute. The vertical position will increment *relative* to the previous vertical position for each successive printed item.

Now, having correctly positioned ourselves, we display the QBColor presently involved and put a semicolon after the printed text, causing the CurrentX and CurrentY to remain at the end of this text. *Without the semicolon, the computer would move down one line.* Print with no semicolon causes the screen to "scroll" down to the next line.

The digits from 0 to 9 take up a single column onscreen, so we need to adjust for the digits from 10 to 15. We do that by using an If...Then, which creates a Variable called *offset*. This Variable subtracts 90 twips from any printed digit greater than 9–effectively lining up the column of digits.

The Invaluable Semicolon: The text about RGB is printed, the RGB numeric Variable is printed, and we again invoke the invaluable semicolon to keep the computer from scrolling down one line. This freezes CurrentX *on the current line.* We next set an *absolute horizontal location* for the position of the PSet dot of color (CurrentX = 150). Then, using Step (a *relative* movement of the position of the drawn dot), we anchor it to the absolute CurrentX. In other words, the Step isn't relative to the previously drawn dot. Instead, via the semicolon that held us on this line and the CurrentX that positioned us 150 twips from the left side of the Form, we can now put our dot exactly where we want it.

Nobody, not even a nuclear scientist, could imagine these tortured relationships in advance. Nobody could take out a tablet, mull over this problem and write down these commands while riding a bus. To achieve these results, you have to be at your computer, and you have to try different Properties and formatting commands until you *see* the effect you are after.

See also   DrawMode; RGB

QUERYUNLOAD   EVENT

Description   QueryUnLoad is supposed to act as a global alarm system, telling *each* Form in a VB program that a *particular* Form is being shut down. This is useful if you want your program to respond in a general way to the closing of any of its windows (Forms). QueryUnLoad doesn't yet work quite like this, however.

Each Form has an individual *UnLoad* Event that is triggered when that Form is closed and unloaded. If you need to ask the user if the text in a Text Box on that Form should be saved to disk, you can ask in the UnLoad Event. But if you want Form2 to know that Form1 is being unloaded, in theory you would put the commands that respond to that situation into Form2's QueryUnLoad Event. The QueryUnLoad Events of *all other Forms in a program* are supposed to be triggered *before* any Form's UnLoad Events are triggered.

Say you have four Forms in a program and the user tries to shut down the program or shut down Windows itself. This is the order in which the Events in your VB program are supposed to be triggered:

```
Form1_QueryUnLoad, Form2_QueryUnLoad, Form3_QueryUnLoad,
Form4_QueryUnLoad, Form1_UnLoad, Form2_UnLoad, Form3_UnLoad,
Form4_UnLoad.
```

Warning—It's Not Working Yet: There are five ways an individual Form can be shut down (unloaded): (1) The user selects "Close" from the Control-menu box on the upper left corner of the Form (or double-clicks on this box). (In Windows 95, the user can also click on the X in the upper right of a window.) (2) The programmer has used the UnLoad command within the program. (3) The user is shutting down Windows itself. (4) The user is closing the VB application (and thus UnLoading all its Forms) from the Windows Task Manager (in Win95, the Taskbar). (5) An MDI Form (see "Multiple Document Interface [MDI] Form") is forcing the unloading of a child Form because the MDI Form is being closed.

At the time of this writing, QueryUnLoad doesn't work in situations 1 or 2 above but does work in 3, 4 and 5. In situations 1 and 2, Form1 can be unloaded without ever triggering any other Form's QueryUnLoad Event. Perhaps this is fixed so that it works in the VB version you use. Test it by creating two Forms and putting the following into the QueryUnLoad Event of Form2:

```
X = MsgBox("An alien Form is attempting to close")
```

Then run the program and double-click on the Control-menu box on the upper left of *Form1*. If Form2 responds before Form1 can be closed, you'll know that QueryUnLoad has become the global alarm that makes it useful outside of MDI Forms (where it currently works).

Used with Forms. Currently useful mainly with Multiple Document Interface Forms.

Variables QueryUnLoad also provides a useful Variable to your program, UnLoad-Mode, which tells you *how* the Form's UnLoad Event was triggered:

0   The Control-menu box on the Form.

1   The UnLoad command was used in the VB program itself.

2   Windows itself is being shut down.

3   Task Manager is being used to shut down the VB program.

4   An MDI Form is being closed, forcing the closure of all child Forms within it.

You may want your program to respond differently, depending on whether the user is shutting down an individual window (Form) in your program or the entire program. Also, you might want to know *how* the user is shutting down your VB program. If your VB application is a program-launcher like Windows's Program Manager, you'd want to know if the application itself, or just a window within it, was being unloaded by the user.

Stop Everything With Cancel: Also, like UnLoad, QueryUnLoad has a Variable called *Cancel*; if you set this Variable to anything other than its default 0, it will abort the closing of a window (Form) or the entire application. If you want to be cruel in a program that makes a student practice typing for 30 minutes, put Timer (which see) into a Global Variable.

In a Module:

```
Global Notyet
```

In the Form_Load Event:

```
Sub Form_Load ( )
    Notyet=Timer
End Sub
```

Then, in the Form's QueryUnLoad Event:

```
Sub Form_QueryUnLoad (Cancel As Integer, UnLoadMode As Integer)
    x = Timer–notyet
    If x < 1800 Then Cancel=True
End Sub
```

The student users can't close the window, they can't close the program, and they can't even close Windows itself unless they press CTRL+ALT+DEL twice or shut off the power.

Uses   • If you want your program to react to an attempt to close *any one* of its windows (Forms), put the reaction inside the QueryUnLoad Event of any Form. When QueryUnLoad is fully operational, no window can be shut down without *triggering all the Forms' QueryUnLoad Events*. If you don't care about this, put specific reactions to the shutting down of individual Forms in each of their UnLoad Events. The primary value of UnLoad and QueryUnLoad is to alert the program that some data (a changed picture, edited text or adjusted options from your Options Menu) needs to be saved to disk. Both UnLoad and QueryUnLoad give your program this last chance to perform any necessary duties for an orderly shut-down. However, only QueryUnLoad is sensitive to the closing of *any* window within the entire program.

- Respond differently based on *how* the user is closing down the program (by closing down the main window vs. shutting down Windows itself, for example).

- Prevent shut-down by using the Cancel Variable.

Cautions　At the time of this writing, QueryUnLoad is not triggered if the user shuts down a window from the window's Control-menu box or if the program uses the UnLoad command.

Example　We'll demonstrate how a child Form can prevent the closing of its MDI host Form (see "Multiple Document Interface"). Start a New Project and set Form1's MDIChild Property to True. Then, from the File Menu, select New MDI Form. Type the following into the QueryUnLoad Event of Form1, the child Form:

```
Sub Form_QueryUnLoad (Cancel As Integer, UnLoadMode As Integer)
    x = MsgBox("Should we shut down the program?", 4)
    If x = 6 Then End
    Cancel = 1
End Sub
```

Now press F5 and try to shut down the host MDI Form by double-clicking on the box in the upper left of its window. The child responds and can prevent the program from shutting down.

See also　Multiple Document Interface (MDI) Form; Terminate; UnLoad

R AISE

See Err

R ANDOMIZE

Description   Use Randomize as the first command in your program if you want the program to be able to produce truly random numbers. Randomize makes your program produce a *different* series of random numbers each time the program runs.

   The computer can provide a series of random numbers when you use the Rnd Function. However, each time you run a program, the series will repeat itself unless you use the Randomize Statement at the start of the program to provide a truly random "seed" for the Rnd Function.

Arbitrary and Erratic? The Rnd Function uses a complex series of calculations to create a random number out of another number. The original number that Rnd transforms is called the *seed*. Each time you use Rnd, it saves the result and uses that result as the seed the next time you use Rnd. Such a series of numbers will appear to be erratic and arbitrary, but because it is based on mathematical calculations designed to produce one random number from a previous number, it is not a truly random series *unless the first seed is itself randomly selected*. The Randomize Statement uses the Timer to provide just such an initial, chance seed.

   Computers are relentlessly logical and orderly. Nonetheless, games, simulations, aspects of art and other situations require a random element. The Rnd Function provides your program with numbers picked at random. You can then imitate the randomness of a shuffled deck of cards, of a cloud pattern, of splattered paint.

Technical Note: Random numbers are created with a routine that imitates a shift register with feedback. Bits shifted out are fed back into the register at a certain bit position.

Used with   The Rnd Function. Randomize insures that Rnd will produce a unique series of random numbers every time a program is run.

Variables   To make the Rnd Function behave in a completely random fashion from the start of your program, put Randomize as the first command in your program. Randomize will then create a truly random seed for the Rnd Function when it is used later in the program:

Randomize

OR

If you provide a particular number to Randomize, it saves that number as the seed for the next use of the Rnd Function. If N is always the same, the seed will always be the same. Subsequent use of the Rnd Function will produce a random series of numbers, but each series started by the same seed will be the same *series*.

Randomize N

In other words, if N = 12, the Rnd Function might generate .637310206890106 as its random number based on the seed of 12. *Rnd will always generate the same number from a seed of 12.* The next time Rnd is used in a running program, it uses .637310206890106 as the seed to generate a new number. Then the result becomes the seed, and this process continues each time Rnd is used in a running program. However, if the series of random numbers starts from a seed derived from 12, the series, though internally random, will always be the same series.

You may want to allow the user to "save a simulation." In other words, you want the random famines, wars and other events in an Egyptian Economy game to repeat in the same sequence in the next game. This would be a use for Randomize N.

A Unique Number: Most of the time you want nonrepeating sequences of random numbers. That's why you usually employ the *Randomize command with nothing after it*. As the first command in a running program, Randomize picks a seed from the unique serial number calculated from the computer's clock. This serial number will not repeat itself except once every 100 centuries—it combines the date and time into a unique number. Randomize thereby gets a unique seed that will differ every time a program is started.

Uses   • Randomize allows a program to use the Rnd Function to produce different random series of numbers each time the program runs.

Use Randomize if you want randomness that is entirely based on chance, for such things as drawing various spots on a window's background in chance locations; for creating alien spaceships that appear at random times and in random places in a game; for simulating the shuffling of cards or the rolling of dice; etc.

• Use Randomize N—with some number after it—when you want repeatable series of random numbers.

Cautions

• Randomize should usually be the first command in a program where you use random numbers, which generally means that you will put it as the first command in the Form_Load Event of your Startup Form. The Startup Form is usually Form1, the first Form you work on when building a VB program. (You can change the Startup Form from VB's Options Menu.)

• Sometimes you might want to create a drawing or a simulation that *is* always the same pattern, that repeats the random moves each time a program is run. In these cases, don't use Randomize alone, but follow it with a number (see "Variables" above).

• **There May Be No Such Thing:** The Rnd and Randomize commands do not produce *true* random numbers. In fact, number theorists say that there may be no such thing as a truly random series. The transcendental number *pi* has, so far, been calculated out a couple of million decimal places using high-speed computers, and pi hasn't yet revealed any discernible pattern. Therefore pi would appear to be a good example of randomness. But no one can prove that pi is, in fact, random. Nobody has been able to demonstrate that God hasn't put a message within pi. Pi could start producing a letter-for-letter copy of the Bible or the Koran when it's calculated to three million decimal places.

Mathematicians cannot yet even agree on a definition of *randomness*. For our purposes, though, for rolling dice—instead of something tougher like simulating global weather patterns—Rnd and Randomize suffice. These commands produce results that are random enough for most programs.

Example

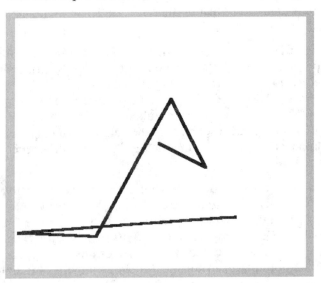

Figure R-1: Every time the following program is run, it will produce this same design.

```
Sub Form_Click ()

drawwidth = 4
currentx = scalewidth / 2
currenty = scaleheight / 2

For i = 1 To 5
    x = Int(Rnd * 5000)
    y = Int(Rnd * 5000)
    Line Step(0, 0)–(x, y)
Next i

End Sub
```

We set the DrawWidth so the lines will be fairly thick and then position the first line to start in the center of the Form.

Then we draw five lines at random. Using (0,0) as the starting point for each line will connect it to the previous line. Then, where the line goes next, both its direction and its length are determined by the X and Y coordinates generated by Rnd.

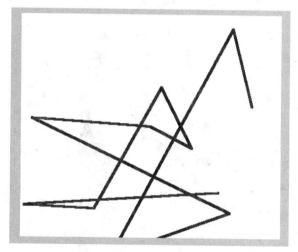

Figure R-2: Click again on this Form and you'll get five more random lines.

Now, stop the program and then run it again. The first click produces exactly the same design; the second click draws exactly the same five additional lines.

To produce *different* drawings each time the program runs, insert the Randomize Statement into the Form_Load Event:

```
Sub Form_Load ()
Randomize
End Sub
```

Now, the results will always differ. Now, not only are the lines random within each series, but also *the series themselves have become random*.

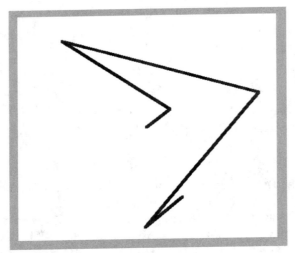

Figure R-3: With the Randomize command, the design changes each time you run the routine.

Figure R-4: Running the program again produces another novel design.

See also   Rnd

READONLY . . . .

See   Archive, Hidden, Normal, System

STATEMENT

Description ReDim sets aside space in the computer's memory to temporarily hold an Array (see "Arrays").

ReDim works only within an Event Procedure of a Form, or within a Subroutine or Function placed in the General Declarations section of a Form or a Module. ReDim brings an Array into existence between the Sub...End Sub or the Function...End Function commands. ReDim temporarily cordons off some of the computer's memory to hold an Array, but when that particular Subroutine or Function is finished doing its work, the set-aside memory is released back to the computer for general use.

Arrays that bloom and fade like this within a single procedure are called *dynamic Arrays*, as opposed to the permanent storage offered by *static* Arrays (see "Static," "Dim," or "Global").

Used with Used within a procedure (a Sub or Function or Event) to declare—to create—an Array.

There are several ways to declare Variables and Arrays:

You can declare (set aside memory for and describe the type of Variable) *a Variable that can be used by the entire program* if you use the Global command in a Module.

If a Variable must be *used only within a single Form*, declare the Variable by using the Dim command in the General Declarations section of that Form.

If a Variable is needed only within a single procedure, but *should not be created and destroyed each time the Sub or Function is used*, declare the Variable inside a procedure with the Static command. Static ensures that if you declare these Variables Static, the Variables' "values" (John Williams held in A$, for instance, or 155.3 held in N) will remain after you leave the procedure. The next time you use this procedure, any Static Variables still have their information intact.

Brief Lives like Mayflies: If your Array is needed by only a single procedure and *needed only while that procedure is active*, declare it with ReDim. Such Arrays spring into life and die quickly, like mayflies.

ReDim can also *redeclare* an Array that has previously been declared using Global or Dim with empty parentheses. Such a Global or Dim command alerts VB that this will be an Array but doesn't declare the size of the Array (how many elements it should be sized to hold). In such cases, however, you can ReDim no more than eight dimensions for the Array. If there is no previous Global or Dim referring to this same Variable (by using the same name to declare it), you can use ReDim to create an Array with as many as 60 dimensions.

Variables   In this following example, we are defining *N* as an Integer-type Array (see "Variables" for more about types).

> ReDim N(22) As Integer

OR

The following is the same as the preceding example, except we are declaring that *A* represents a text ("string") Array. Now we can use it within this procedure without having to add the $ symbol. However, this is not usually a good idea. You want to be able to see that a Variable is a text type.

> ReDim A(75) As String

OR

The following creates an Array with 45 individual items, numbered 1 to 45. Such an Array may previously have been declared by a Global or Dim Statement. Previously declared Arrays cannot have more than eight *dimensions.*

> ReDim F(1 To 45) As Integer

OR

This next example also creates an Array but with 700 individual elements.

> ReDim F(1 To 700) As Integer

OR

The following version has no To statement, so the first element of this Array will have an index of 0. F(0) will be its name and the way you refer to it within the program as you use it. The second element will be called F(1). The last element will be F(59). F must not have been previously declared by a Global or Dim Statement if it is to have more than eight elements. Previously undeclared ReDims can have as many as 60 elements.

> ReDim F(59) As Integer

OR (to change the size of an Array *while preserving its contents*—see "Uses" below for more on this technique): ReDim Preserve F(60) As Integer

OR (to declare a series of Arrays following a single ReDim Statement): ReDim datArray(12) As String, Numbs(15) As Integer, towns(3) As String

Uses   • Create temporary storage space for an Array that you need to use only while a particular procedure is active.

The virtue of temporary Arrays is that they don't use up the computer's memory by taking space that can be otherwise used while a program is running. Normally, space isn't much of an issue, but some programs are data-intensive and need to manipulate large amounts of information. In such cases, being able to create and then destroy dynamic Arrays can be of value.

You *can* preserve the data within a dynamic Array by using the Preserve command. Ordinarily, each time you use the ReDim command all the contents of the Variables within the Array are lost. (If an Array has been declared to be *static* with Static, Dim or Global, use the Erase command [with the same Array name] to destroy the contents of the Array and free up computer memory.) If you ReDim a dynamic Array, all its "cells" are set to 0 (if it's a numeric Array), to "" empty text (if a text Array) or to "Empty" (if a Variant Array). However, what if you merely want to change the size of the Array but preserve its contents? Here's the syntax:

```
ReDim Preserve F(60) As Integer
```

Cautions
• You can use the To command to define a range of elements in an Array:

```
ReDim S (1 To 2)
ReDim S (1 To 3, 1 To 4)
```

• If you've used Option Base (which see), you could achieve the same effect illustrated in the preceding Caution item like this:

```
ReDim S(2)
ReDim S(3,4)
```

• The range of elements defined for an Array—the index of this Array—can be negative. An index can range from –32,768 to 32,767.

• If the same Variable name was previously declared by using a Global or Dim command, the maximum number of dimensions in a ReDimmed Array is eight.

  If this Variable is being declared for the first time by ReDim, however, there can be as many as 60 dimensions.

• Unless you use the optional Preserve command, ReDim resets (empties) all the elements of a numeric Array to 0, and all elements of *s* string (text) Array to empty strings (""). The fields of a user-defined Variable type (see "Type") are similarly reset.

• The number of elements in a ReDimmed Array can be changed at any time:

```
ReDim This$(4)
This$(3) = "Nadia C."
Print This$(3)
ReDim This$(5)
This$(4) = "Thomas R."
```

The preceding procedure is perfectly legal. However, while you can change the number of elements, you *cannot* change the number of *dimensions* in the Array:

Wrong:

```
ReDim This$(4)
This$(3) = "Nadia C."
Print This$(3)
ReDim This$(5, 2)
This$(3,1) = "Thomas R."
```

The second ReDim attempted to create a two-dimensional Array out of one already declared as single-dimensional.

Likewise, you cannot change Variable type by ReDimming:

Wrong:

```
ReDim This$(4)
This$(3) = "Nadia C."
Print This$(3)
ReDim This (5) As Integer
```

This$ started out as a text Array, and you attempted to redeclare it as an Integer (numeric) Array.

The Distinction between Elements and Dimensions: The number of elements in an Array is the number of individual items of data it can contain. How many text or numeric Variables can the Array hold? Elements are defined as a *range*: C(1 To 50), for instance, or F$(44) is a range from 0 to 44, or 45 total elements.

An Array's *dimensions* are how many of these ranges it contains. Many Arrays have only a single dimension: Z$(1 To 50) is a single-dimensional Array with 50 elements. A(5,6,7) is a three-dimensional Array with 6, 7, and 8 elements (a total of 21 elements). This Array could describe a cube—over 5, up 6, in 7 would be a cell position within the cube.

Example

This example fills a temporary (dynamic) Array and then shows what information is held within that Array. We'll illustrate how to create a temporary Array, and help you visualize how an Array stores pieces of data the same way mail is stored in the boxes in a post office.

```
Sub Form_Click ()

ReDim Nameaddr$(1 To 4, 1 To 2)

Nameaddr$(1, 1) = "Bobby Jones"
Nameaddr$(2, 1) = "Marcia Delobia"
Nameaddr$(3, 1) = "Sam Missile"
Nameaddr$(4, 1) = "Bertha Vanation"

Nameaddr$(1, 2) = "Arlington, VA"
Nameaddr$(2, 2) = "Wilmington, DE"
Nameaddr$(3, 2) = "Azuza, CA"
Nameaddr$(4, 2) = "Bukon City, AL"

Currenty = 400

For i = 1 To 4
        Currentx = 300
    For j = 1 To 2
                Array$ = "Nameaddr$(" + Str$(i) + "," + Str$(j) + ") "
                Print Array$ + Nameaddr$(i, j);
                currentx = 3500

    Next j
        Print
```

```
                    Print
        Next i
        End Sub
```

We create a temporary text ("string") Array, capable of holding a total of eight Variables. An Array helps you manipulate relationships between the Variables within its structure. In this example, we are providing two pieces of information (name and address) about four people. The first "dimension" of the Array (1 To 4) will contain the names of the four people. The second dimension (1 To 2) will contain each person's address.

We assign that information to the Array Variables. Each Variable within an Array is uniquely identified by the index numbers (1,2) or (3,1) and so on. The point here is that we can manipulate such names *mathematically* within a For...Next Loop. Once all the information is in this Array, we don't need to keep referring to each individual Array element by some text name.

We move down from the top of the Form by resetting the CurrentY Property. Then we create a Loop that will go through all four of the names. Each time we pull a new name out of the Array, we want to have a left margin on the Form, so we set CurrentX to provide a slight offset.

The Inner, Nested Loop: Then, we print the name and the address (using the inner, "nested" Loop For j = 1 To 2: see "For...Next"). We want to print the Variable name of each element within the Array and then the Variable. So we set up a text Variable that will print something like this example: Nameaddr$(2,3). We then print that data along with the actual Variable from that location within the Array.

CurrentX = 3500 works better than the Tab Command; CurrentX moves us precisely where we want to be near the center of the Form.

Then, the second time through the *j* Loop, we pull each person's address out of the Array. We move down the Form two lines by using the Print command twice and then go back to fetch any more names from the Array.

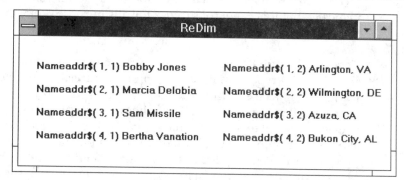

Figure R-5: The Array made visible

See also   Arrays; Dim; Global; Option Base; Static; Variables.

REFRESH

METHOD

Description   The Refresh command is rarely used because Visual Basic automatically "refreshes" (updates the visual content of) Forms and Controls whenever the program isn't actually doing something.

Programs spend most of their time waiting for the user to type or move the mouse. Then there is usually a rapid series of actions as the computer carries out whatever commands have been programmed to respond to the user's actions. Following that is another long delay while the program remains idle, waiting again for the user. Even the most agile mousist or typist leaves lots of computer idle time between keypresses. Computers are so much faster than humans that you will generally never need to use Refresh.

Nonetheless, there are calculations so huge, files so large, or other computing tasks so intensive that they do tie up the computer. A For...Next Loop, for instance, does lock up the computer. Also, if you are dynamically redrawing graphics (see "Resize"), Refresh is useful.

DoEvents Prevents Freeze-Ups: The DoEvents command interrupts whatever might be going on in your program to allow the user to move the mouse or open and close windows, to allow other programs to perform *their* calculations, etc. Large For...Next Loops are prime targets for including DoEvents, so the computer doesn't freeze up, thwarting Windows from one of its primary features—multitasking several programs at once.

Similarly, by using Refresh you can update a Control or a Form while the VB program is otherwise busy.

(DoEvents provides VB with an opportunity to refresh the screen automatically, but it is dangerous to use for this purpose. Refresh is preferable. See "Cautions" below.)

Technical Note: Because Windows 3.1 uses a somewhat inefficient "cooperative" type of multitasking, programs are allowed to decide when to yield their access to the processor (the computer's "brain," its CPU, such as an Intel Pentium chip) to allow other running programs to have access and get a chance to accomplish their goals. The DoEvents() command allows other programs to check in, to interrupt, and use some of the processor's time if they have anything they need to do. Other systems, such as UNIX, use *preemptive* multitasking, which means that the processor itself allocates its brain-time and will break into the activity of a program and make it wait while another program takes a turn. This is a more efficient approach to the problem of sharing the computer's brainpower and is used in OS/2 and Windows NT.

The Auto-Generating Self-Feedback Redundancy: DoEvents merely allow Windows applications to execute "messages in their queues." When you use the DoEvents command, you should be careful that you don't put it within an Event in a way that would *trigger that same Event*. One example of this would be calling the Refresh Event from within a Paint Event and using the DoEvents command at the same time. This would send the computer into an infinite Loop—an unending feedback—where it continually self-triggers, auto-generating Event after cascading Event.

Used with
Forms and Controls, to update them visually, on the screen. Is not used with Timers, Menus or MDI Forms (but can be used with MDI child windows—see "Multiple Document Interface").

Variables
Refresh (refreshes the Form)

OR

Label1.Refresh (refreshes Label1)

Uses
If your program will be tied up performing massive calculations—loading or saving a huge file or otherwise locking out the user for longer than you feel is wise—use Refresh to update text or graphics on a Form or one of its Controls.

Frequently, you'll simply use this technique to announce to the user that a significant delay is about to take place. You can send up a Message Box "LOADING..." just before bringing in that big file, for example. However, you could also use the Refresh Method to show the progress of your program's activities, to, for instance, move a gauge (see the Example below).

If you leave the AutoRedraw Property off, your program will have to redraw any drawn (Circle, PSet and Line commands) or Printed text on a Form or Picture Box. Use Refresh inside a Resize Event. This is also a way of keeping graphics and text proportionate to a user-stretched or -shrunk Form (see "Resize").

Cautions
• DoEvents allow a VB program to extend the courtesy of computer time to other programs, but DoEvents can also be "recursive." That is, it can give itself computer time. That's bad. If the user clicks on something and thereby starts some time-consuming task in VB, that same task *could be clicked again during the recess provided by the DoEvents command itself*. Clicking twice on a Control could create an infinite feedback Loop where multiple instances of an Event within that Control were lined up behind each other, waiting for computer time. You should disable (Enabled = 0) any recursion-susceptible Command Button or other Control in these cases. In other words, don't allow a Control to remain Enabled if it includes DoEvents. Re-Enable it when the danger has passed.

Also, DoEvents can be overkill when all you want to do is show that a lengthy process is underway. Put something on the screen to show the user the progress. DoEvents really slows your program down, so you might want to use Refresh instead.

• Refresh can interact with the Paint Event of a Form or Picture Box (see "Paint").

Example

Figure R-6: Create a gauge that shows the user the progress of something that ties up the computer.

This example shows a simple way to let the user watch the progress of anything that's tying up the computer—a Picture Box fills in, illustrating the percentage of the task that's currently completed.

We'll pull in each byte from your KERNEL.EXE file—everyone with Windows has this file. It contains crucial Subroutines that Windows uses when it runs (see Appendix A). We're not going to *do* anything with this information, just use it as an example of a lengthy task for which the Refresh command is appropriate.

No Gross Signs: This file is large, and it will take the computer some time to get each of its bytes, one at a time. But we're in Windows, so we don't want to just put up a crude sign that says "WORKING..." or "PLEASE WAIT..." Let's give the user something to look at; let's provide a gauge that fills and also reports what percentage of the task has completed. This is more Windows-like and looks more professional.

First, create a Form, put two Picture Boxes on it and a small Label right next to the Picture Box you will use for the gauge. We also add Picture3, an icon that starts things off when clicked.

To create the frames behind the gauge and the portrait, load FRAME.TXT into the General Declarations section of the Form. If you don't yet have FRAME.TXT, see "Line" to learn how to create this extremely useful file.

Figure R-7: Here's how this Form looks during design.

Into the Form_Load Event, enter the following:

```
Sub Form_Load ()

Show

Picture1.Picture = LoadPicture ("C:\BOOK\BMPS\HARRIET.BMP")

drawframeon picture1, label1, "outward", 100
drawframeon picture1, label1, "inward", 10
drawframeon Picture1, Picture1 "outward", 200
End Sub
```

We load the portrait into the Picture Box and then draw two frames around the gauge and one around the portrait.

Now, put the rest of the program into Picture3's Click Event:

```
Sub Picture3_Click ()

On Error Resume Next

picture1.fillstyle = 0
picture1.backcolor = QBColor(7)
```

```
picture1.forecolor = QBColor(8)
pictheight = picture1.height

Open "C:\WINDOWS\SYSTEM\KERNEL.EXE" For Binary As #1

For i& = 1 To LOF(1)
     Get #1, i&, n%

          If i& Mod 4000 = 0 Then
                    percen = i& / LOF(1)
                    boxsize = Int(picture1.width * percen)
                    percen = Int(percen * 100)
                    picture1.Line (0, 0)–(boxsize, pictheight), , BF
                    label1.caption = Str$(percen) + " %"
                    label1.Refresh

          End If
     Next i&
Close 1

If Err Then MsgBox (Error$(Err))

End Sub
```

We set up the usual error trapping as a precaution when accessing the disk drive (see "On Error"). Then we ensure that we'll be able to see the boxes we draw onto Picture1 to make it look like a thermometer gauge smoothly filling up. Because FillStyle is normally "transparent," we must set it to 0 (solid) so we can see the results of our drawing. We make the BackColor light gray and the ForeColor dark gray. And we'll want to draw our gauge box so it fits the Picture Box vertically. To do this, we'll need the measurement of the height of the Picture Box, which we put into the Variable *pictheight*.

Now we open the file and create a Loop that will get each byte in succession from the first to the last (1 to LOF). (LOF means Length Of File.)

Mod Interrupting Byte-Grabbing: We interrupt this byte-grabbing every 4,000 bytes, so we can update the gauge. The Mod command gives us any remainder when one number is divided by another. In this case, we're saying: "If the current value of i&, our Loop counter, can be divided precisely by 4,000—if the Mod, the remainder, is 0—then do the following update of the gauge." Mod is the command to use if you want something to happen periodically.

We find out how much of the file we've currently read by dividing the current byte (i&) into the total length of the file, its total number of bytes. Then we create an appropriate width for our box and put it into the Variable boxsize. This width will be the *same percentage of the Picture Box* as is the number of bytes read as a percentage of the total bytes. Then we get a rounded off percentage number we can print to the Label as text. The line percen = Int(percen * 100) changes the percentage from a fraction into a whole number and also rounds it off to the nearest whole number.

Now we are ready to move the gauge over slightly to reflect how much of this file we've read so far:

```
picture1.Line (0, 0)—(boxsize, pictheight), , BF
```

Fitting the Fill to the Gauge: The *BF* means Box Fill, which causes the coordinates of the Line command to be filled in, drawing a filled box. The first coordinates are the horizontal, vertical points on the Picture Box Control where the upper left corner of our filled box should be. We want it flush against the top and left of the Control, so we put 0,0. The second set of coordinates are the horizontal, vertical location of the lower right corner of the filled box.

How far over into the Control we should draw keeps changing as the percentage completed goes up. So, we use the *boxsize* we calculated earlier. We also want our moving gauge to fit against the top of the Picture Box, so we use *pictheight*, the Variable we previously defined as pictheight = picture1.height. We could use picture1.height instead here, but it's slightly faster if the computer doesn't have to look up the Control's Property each time.

Finally, we put the text description of the percentage completed into the Label. And then we refresh the Label. Without Refresh, the Label would never change until the entire job was finished. Because we want the Label to constantly show the current percentage, Refresh is required. The last command concludes the error handling (see "Err").

See also   DoEvents; Paint

STATEMENT

Description   Short for *rem*ark, Rem tells Visual Basic to ignore everything following the Rem command on the current line. Use the Rem command to attach comments to your program, without worrying that VB would try to interpret those comments as commands. And fail.

Rem is another holdover from earlier versions of Basic. The ' (single quotation mark) symbol is generally used instead and serves the same purpose. The ' is, of course, easier to use, and ' has the added advantage of not requiring a colon to separate it from any previous commands on the same line, as does Rem (see the third item under "Cautions" below).

Used with   Any place in your program where you want to attach an explanatory note to the commands. Some people feel that such notes make it easier:

• To read a program, to understand the purpose of the nearby commands as you read through the program.

• To maintain a program, to make adjustments and changes to improve the program or keep it current.

• To team-program, to allow others to read and maintain the program.

• To debug the program, to track down and fix errors.

Variables

```
If B$ = "Martha" Then        ' If B$ is "Martha" print her an invitation to the →
ball.
    PrintInvite "Martha Blivings"
End If
```

OR

```
' ................................ PRINT A BALL INVITE FOR MARTHA..........
'
'
If B$ = "Martha" Then
    PrintInvite "Martha Blivings"
End If
'
'
' ......................................................................................................
```

Some programmers like to put ' at the start of lines and, as illustrated above, to create elaborate zones in their programs, visually separating the various sections with dots or underline symbols. In this way, each part of the program is described and also framed into a quickly recognized functional unit. Such approaches are perhaps not as necessary as they once were—programs used to be just one long series of commands from start to finish, like a mystifying insurance policy. Visual Basic, however, naturally encapsulates commands into Events and Procedures, so there is less need to utilize drastic cryptographical Rem statements.

Uses

• If, or how much, *Remarking* you do to your programs is essentially a matter of personal preference.

Just as some composers can read a score as easily as they read the daily paper, some programmers can read programs with great facility. To them, commented programs are annoying, cluttered, and the comments superfluous. These programmers understand computer language well and don't need the purpose of the commands paraphrased in English.

Others find program syntax, and even the meaning of various commands, obscure or hard to remember. This doesn't mean that these people are necessarily inferior programmers. Just because some people have a hard time remembering names doesn't mean they cannot be convivial or a success at parties. It's often merely that a part of their brain doesn't work as well as, perhaps, other parts do. For these people, lots of commenting serves the same purpose as notes in a Latin textbook—a handy English translation of the original.

Why We Don't Use Comments: In this book, we have rarely used comments. There are two reasons for this. First, each program is thoroughly paraphrased in a text explication immediately following the program. Second, when you are typing in a program from a book, comments *are* clutter.

If you frequently find yourself unable to understand the meaning or purpose of a program that you've written, comment as much as possible. If you find it easy to read programs, perhaps you'll want to comment only when a particular section or command is especially obscure.

Cautions

• Once you have inserted a ' or a Rem, everything after that on the same line is ignored by Visual Basic.

• You can follow ' or Rem with spaces, symbols, anything that you wish.

• If you *do* choose to use Rem instead of the ' symbol, remember that Rem requires a colon to separate it from any previous commands on that line:

Right:

```
PRINT N$: REM print Nancy's name and address
```

Wrong:

```
PRINT N$ REM print Nancy's name and address
```

When using the ' symbol, a colon is unnecessary, another reason for preferring ' over Rem.

Right:

```
PRINT N$ ' print Nancy's name and address
```

Example

Some programmers like to tab over until all their comments line up on the page, like a running commentary of the program:

```
Sub Form_Click ()

drawwidth = 4        ' We want these lines to be fairly thick.
currentx = scalewidth / 2      ' This positions the first drawn or printed item
currenty = scaleheight / 2     ' at the exact center of this Form

For i = 1 To 5        ' Draw five lines
    x = Int(Rnd * 5000)      ' The horizontal position of the END point → will
                             be between
    y = Int(Rnd * 5000)      ' 1-5,000 and so will the Y, the vertical position.
    Line Step(0, 0)–(x, y)   ' Now draw the random line, relative to the →
                             previous endpoint
                             ' of the previously drawn line. This way, the →
                             lines connect.

Next i

End Sub
```

REMOVE

See Add

REMOVEITEM

Description RemoveItem deletes one of the entries in a List Box or Combo Box, or removes a row from a Grid Control.

Used with Grids, Combo Boxes and List Boxes

Variables To remove the *fourth* item in a List Box (the items are counted from 0, so an item with an index of 3 is really the fourth item in the Box):

```
X = 3
List1.RemoveItem X
```

OR (to remove the last item in the Combo Box):

```
Combo1.RemoveItem Combo1.ListCount
```

OR (to remove the first item in the List Box): List1.RemoveItem 0

OR (to completely empty the Box of the items within it): List1.Clear

OR (to remove the *fifth* row from a Grid Control—note that the top row is Row(0)): grid1.RemoveItem (4)

Uses • Allow the user to control which items are removed from a Combo or List Box.

• Allow your program to remove items within Combo or List Boxes.

• Remove entire rows from a Grid Control.

Cautions • List and Combo Boxes maintain an Array (which see), called the "List." A List Box with a Name of List1 would be called List1.List. List is a Property of List and Combo Boxes (as well as of the three file-handling boxes, File, Directory and Drive Boxes).

Two other Properties work with List to allow you to manage these Boxes:

▪ *ListIndex* holds a number that identifies the currently selected item in the Box—the item that appears blackened, reversed, on the screen. You can get the item into a Variable by using X$ = List1.List(List1.ListIndex). *The repetitions of "List1." are necessary.* When working with these Properties, most errors are attributable to forgetting to identify which Box by adding its Name to the Property.

- *ListCount* counts the items in the Box: X = Combo1.ListCount. But be aware that if you work with a Loop, you must use ListCount –1 because the first item in a list is the *zeroth* item: For I = 0 to List1.ListCount –1.

The List Property is an indexed list of all the items in a Box. The List Array is numbered from 0 to ListCount –1. You must remember to subtract 1 from the actual item you want. The fifth item you see on the screen in the List Box is List1.List (4).

To clear out an entire Box: List1.Clear

Example

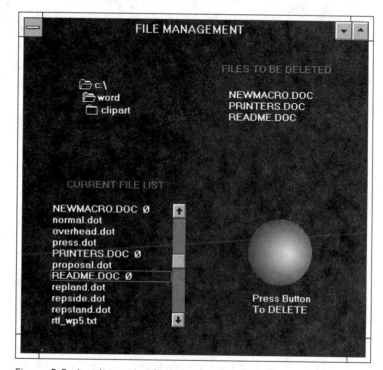

Figure R-8: An alternative file-access window.

This example illustrates how you can build special versions of standard Controls. Instead of the usual File List Box, we've transferred the contents of an *invisible* File List Box to the visible List Box, allowing us to change the names in the List Box—something we can't do with a File Box. Sometimes making a Control invisible is a handy technique. You can *use* the Control, taking advantage of many of its Properties and Events, but the user doesn't see the activity behind the scenes.

To try this example, put two List Boxes on a Form, a File List Box, a Directory List Box and a Picture Box.

Add three Labels and set their Caption Properties as illustrated in Figure R-8. Set the File List Box's Visible Property to 0 and set List1's Sorted Property to –1. (Sorted keeps the filenames listed alphabetically within the List Box.) We also decided to make the BackColors of the Controls black and their ForeColors either white or, for the Labels, blue. Select a large .BMP as the Picture Property of the Picture Box. We're using a graphic of a globe.

Now, in the Form_Load Event, type the following:

```
Sub Form_Load ()
Show
dir1_change
End Sub
```

The Kill Command: We fill List1 with the contents of the File List Box by activating the commands contained in the Dir1_Change Event:

```
Sub dir1_change ()
file1.path = dir1.path
List1.Clear
List2.Clear
For i = 0 To file1.listcount − 1
    list1.AddItem file1.list(i)
Next i
End Sub
```

First, when the user double-clicks on a Directory Box, VB automatically updates its Path. We want this update to also change which files are listed in the File List Box, so any change to the Path Property of the Directory Box is now assigned to the Path of the File List Box, too.

Then we clean out both of our visible List Boxes. After that, we fill the left List Box with the filenames in the invisible File List Box; our List Box mimics the contents of the File List Box.

Two Things Should Happen: When the user clicks on one of the filenames in the left List Box, we want two things to happen: the name should become uppercase and a special symbol should be added to the name. This way, the user can easily see which files have been selected. Also, we want the filenames to be added to the second List Box—"To Be Deleted."

In File1's Click Event, enter the following:

```
Sub List1_Click ()

y$ = list1.list(list1.listindex)
y$ = Left$(y$, Len(y$) − 3)

For i = 0 To list2.listcount − 1
    If y$ = list2.list(i) Then Exit Sub
Next i

z$ = Chr$(32) + Chr$(32) + Chr$(216)

x$ = UCase$(list1.list(list1.listindex)) + z$
```

```
list2.AddItem UCase$(list1.list(list1.listindex))
list1.RemoveItem list1.listindex
list1.AddItem x$
End Sub
```

The first few lines here prevent the user from repeatedly clicking on the same name in the List Box that holds all the filenames. We put the filename clicked by the user into y$ and then strip off the three rightmost characters (in case this filename had been previously selected and had the special character added to it). Now we check through List2 to see if the names match. If they do match, this file has already been added to List2, so we Exit the Subroutine.

An Uppercase Version: Now we put two spaces and the special identification character into z$. Then we add z$ onto the end of the selected filename, which is also made uppercase with UCase$.

Then we add an uppercase version of the selected filename to the "To Be Deleted" Box, remove it from the original List Box and replace it with the uppercase + special character version.

The "To Be Deleted" list should work just the opposite when the user clicks—a name should be removed from that list and restored to its original condition (lowercase, no special character) to the filename's List Box. Put the following into the Click Event of List2:

```
Sub List2_Click ()

x$ = list2.list(list2.listindex)

For i = 0 To list1.listcount − 1
    y$ = list1.list(i)
        If Left$(y$, Len(y$) − 3) = x$ Then
                list1.AddItem LCase$(x$)
                list1.RemoveItem (i + 1)
                list2.RemoveItem list2.listindex
        End If
Next i
End Sub
```

We put the selected name into x$ and then check every item in List1, the original filename's Box. We put each filename from List1 into y$. Then we check to see if y$ (stripped of special characters) matches x$. If it does match, we put the filename (lowercase) into List1, remove the uppercase + special character version from File1 and remove the clicked filename from the "To Be Deleted" Box.

See also   AddItem; Clear; Grid; List; ListCount; ListIndex

RESET

Description   Reset closes any files that your program has opened on the disk drive.

Reset does exactly the same thing as using the Close command with no filenumber. Close #1 closes only the file that was previously opened as #1. However, Close, by itself, closes all files. Few programmers use Reset, trusting the Close command and the computer's operating system will correctly save any changes made to the file by your program or the user.

However, there is the matter of *buffers*. Both VB and the operating system create buffers when a file is opened. These are areas in the computer's memory that temporarily hold some or all of a file's contents while your program is actively accessing it. The purpose of using buffers is speed. It's far faster to read and write data to a memory buffer than to a disk drive.

Flushed, as It's Called: When you use the Close command, all files are closed and the data in the buffers are sent to the operating system (OS) buffers. Reset, by contrast, not only closes the files, it also sends the contents of the OS buffers to disk—they are *flushed,* as it's so colorfully called. Any changes you made to the contents of the file are saved by flushing these buffers.

If you want to be absolutely sure that all changed data are updated on disk, use the Reset command instead of the Close command. A power failure then could not destroy data resting in the OS buffers. In practice, however, the Reset command is not used by most programmers.

Used with   Reset is theoretically appropriate as a precaution to ensure that data is safely and completely saved to disk.

Variables   Reset

Uses   Only for the most conservative.

Cautions   The example offered in the *Visual Basic Language Reference* is erroneous. It will not work because a Reset is used to Close #1 and then later an attempt is made to read from #1. You cannot read from a closed file. That particular example will generate an error message.

Example
```
Sub Form_Click ()
Open "C:\TEST" For Random As #1 Len = 5

For i = 1 To 40
    x$ = Str$(i)
    Put #1, , x$
Next i
```

```
Get #1, 14, c$
Print c$

Close #1
Reset
End Sub
```

We open a random-mode file, store text versions of the numbers 1 through 40 in it, then read record number 14 and print it on the Form. Then we close and reset the file. Unless the computer loses power, though, the results here would be the same without the Reset command.

See also

Close; End

See "Open" for a general discussion of disk and file management.

RESIZE

EVENT

Description

A Resize Event is triggered when a Form first becomes visible onscreen and also when the user (or your program) stretches or shrinks the physical size of the Form or Picture Box.

Used with

Forms and Picture Boxes only

Variables

Because this is an Event, you put commands within the Resize Event Procedure. These commands will tell Visual Basic how you want to react if the Form or Picture Box is resized.

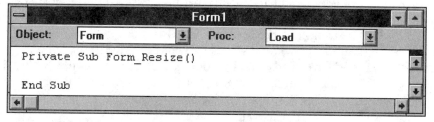

Figure R-9: Your program can react to resizing within the Resize Event.

Uses

• Allow your program to react to changes in the size of a Form. In particular, designs that have been drawn (using PSet, Circle or Line) may need to be redrawn. If the AutoRedraw Property of the Form is off (0), shrinking a Form will erase any drawn graphic or text that was Printed (as opposed to Caption Properties, etc., which are persistent and do not get erased).

Alternatively, if your program does not care if drawn or Printed items have been covered by shrinking a Form, you could ignore the change.

Shrinking triggers the Resize Event, and the program could keep track of the Width and Height Properties in a Global Variable. Then, seeing that one or both of those Properties had grown smaller, the program could ignore the need to repaint.

• Preserve the relative size or position of drawn graphics or Printed text if a Form changes size. You might want, for example, to make a FontSize smaller if a Form is shrunk. Or you might want to keep some text or graphics centered on the Form, even if the user makes the Form narrower by dragging it in with the mouse. (See "Cautions" and the Example below.)

• Preserve the relative size, shape or position of a Control–such as a Text Box–when the size, shape or position of a Picture Box or Form that contains the Control changes.

• Perform the above services for the relationship between child windows and an MDI Form that contains them. See "Multiple Document Interface."

Cautions   • You might want text or designs to be repainted in a larger size if the Form is stretched, and, conversely, to shrink if the Form is made smaller. The Form's Paint Event is triggered when the user has stretched a Form, making the Form larger onscreen. But Paint has a fatal flaw when used for this purpose. What happens if the user shrinks the Form? *Paint is completely insensitive if a Form is reduced in size.*

A Paint Event is generated only when some part of a Form is uncovered by an object that previously covered the Form or if the Form grows larger. If your program draws (or prints text) to a nonpermanent surface (AutoRedraw is off), then you must respond to Paint and Resize to figure out what you need to do to restore the graphics or text that may have been affected.

Maintaining the Aspect Ratio: If you want to maintain the *aspect ratio* (a ratio of height and width that parallels that of the host Form) of drawn designs and printed text, you can use the Resize Event. It is sensitive to any resizing–enlargement or shrinking. But *Resize is insensitive* to other Forms' or windows' erasing your Form when placed on top of it. So, to deal with every possible situation where erasures could occur, you would want to call upon the Resize Event from within the Paint Event:

```
Sub Form_Paint ()
    Form_Resize
End Sub
```

Then put your redrawing inside the Resize Event:

```
Sub Form_Resize ()
    Cls
    centerform = scalewidth / 2
    FontSize = centerform / 80
    centertext = (TextWidth("RESPONDS")) / 2
    Currentx = centerform – centertext
    Print "RESPONDS"
End Sub
```

Example   We'll see how to draw a design on the Form with Circle, PSet or Line and then redraw as necessary *to make the design react* by expanding or reducing its size when the Form's dimensions are changed. Rectangles 1 inch large become 2 inches or .5 inch, maintaining a constant relationship with the Form's height and width (its ScaleHeight and ScaleWidth Properties).

Let's draw some rectangles on a Form and make them respond to changes in the Form's size—maintaining the *aspect ratio*, the proportions of width to height. We'll also make some text respond as well, growing when the user enlarges the Form and shrinking when the Form is shrunk.

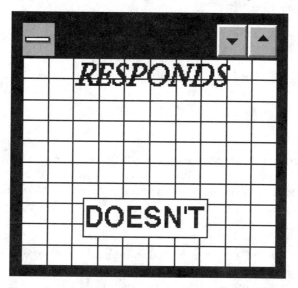

Figure R-10: When this Form is resized, the drawn rectangles and the printed text respond; the Label does not.

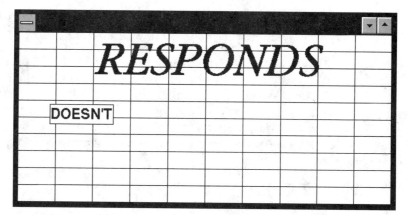

Figure R-11: "Doesn't" will not react when this Form is stretched.

First, put a Label on a Form and set its Caption to "DOESN'T." Then, in the Form's Resize Event, enter the following:

```
Sub Form_Resize ()

Cls
centerform = scalewidth / 2
FontSize = centerform / 80
centertext = (TextWidth("RESPONDS")) / 2
Currentx = centerform − centertext
Print "RESPONDS"

x = scalewidth
y = scaleheight
tx = x / 10
ty = y / 10

For i = 0 To x Step tx
    For j = 0 To y Step ty
            Line (i, j)−Step(tx, ty), , B
    Next j, i
End Sub
```

First, we use Cls to remove any previous drawing and to reset the CurrentX and CurrentY Properties to 0,0 (the upper left corner of the Form). Then we figure out the exact horizontal center of the Form by dividing its ScaleWidth property in two. We then set the FontSize to be 1/80 of the result. (You'll want to fiddle with this number, but 70 to 80 works well on my screen.)

Then we use the TextWidth Method to find out how wide the word *RESPONDS* will be when printed on the Form in the current FontSize. Subtracting one-half of the width of this word from the horizontal center of the Form allows us to set the current X printing position where the word *RESPONDS* will be in the exact center.

Rectangles, All Over the Form: Now we prepare to draw rectangles all over the Form as a background design. We get the width and height of the Form and also get one-tenth of these measurements. We use a *nested Loop* with *Step* (see "For...Next"), which allows us to fill the Form with rectangles. (Also see "Line" to discover how Step works with the Line command to make drawing *relative* to something previously drawn, rather than *absolute* and based on the coordinates of the Form itself.) In this task, we want the endpoint of each rectangle to be one-tenth of the size of the Form, *relative* to the starting point of the rectangle. Step(tx, ty) does this for us.

See also   ClipControls; Maximize; Minimize; Paint; Refresh

RESUME

Description   Resume tells Visual Basic what to do after you've dealt with an error that happens while a program is running.

You tell Visual Basic how to handle errors by inserting an On Error command. If an error does happen, Visual Basic jumps to the instructions located where you told it to go. You deal with the error and then tell Visual Basic where to go next with the Resume Statement.

Used with   Resume is always paired with the On Error command (which see). An On Error without a matching Resume causes VB to respond with an error message.

Variables   There are three ways you can tell VB where to go after an error has been handled:

1. Resume (Visual Basic goes to the line in the program that caused the error.)

OR

Resume 0 (same as above)

2. Resume Next (Visual Basic goes to the line *following* the line in the program that caused the error.)

This is the most common structure for On Error...Resume; it means, "If there is a problem, just ignore it for now and go to the next line and keep the program running." You normally put this statement at the top of a Subroutine that tries to work with the disk drive or is otherwise risky because it accesses something outside of the program itself (like the Clipboard). Accessing anything outside the program is precarious because you cannot tell if a floppy disk is in drive A:, etc.

After telling VB to keep running the program with On Error Resume Next, we might put something in the line following the command that attempts to access the disk:

```
On Error Resume Next

Open "A:\DATA.TXT" For Input As #1

If Err = 71 Then
    MsgBox ("Your disk drive reports that it is not ready for access. Please → fix
        it and then click OK.")
    Exit Sub
End If
```

In this case, we simply leave the Subroutine if the problem occurs, expecting the user to fix the problem and click again on a Save Command Button or whatever got us into this Subroutine in the first place. (Error 71 means "Disk Not Ready.")

3. Resume Morestuff (*Morestuff* is whatever word you've used to label the location you want VB to go next. You can use any word you want for a Label, as long as it isn't a word in the VB language, like *Load* or *FontSize.*)

On Error Resume Morestuff (a labeled line in your program)

Morestuff: (the Label where VB is supposed to go after handling an error)

OR

Resume 150 (VB goes to line 150, if you still use line numbers. This statement is simply a variant of Resume *Label* described above.)

Don't Let Blunders Shut Down Your Program: Without On Error telling Visual Basic what you want done in the event of a blunder or misfire, *VB will completely shut down your program*–a rude way of telling users that they mistyped a filename or left a floppy disk drive door open when your program tried to access the disk.

Uses   Resume is only used when paired with the On Error command. You should use On Error when your program is going to contact something outside itself–a disk drive, another program via a Link, the Clipboard. You are in some danger that the outside entity will be contacted incorrectly, contacted too slowly, or called upon after it has been killed, deleted or otherwise taken out of existence.

On Error is like a warning light that goes on in your car when the oil pressure is low. It allows you to inform the user of a problem but doesn't turn off the ignition and stop the car.

Cautions   • On Error does not, itself, trap an error. It tells VB how to respond if an error occurs but is not itself a response. You therefore cannot put On Error just below a potential trouble spot and expect the error to be caught. On Error would not be active when the error occurs. You must use On Error to describe a response, a location that VB should go to if an error happens. Then Resume tells VB where to go after the error has been dealt with.

• "Program flow" is programmer lingo for the path that the computer follows when carrying out your commands. Normally, the program flows from left to right across a line and then down the page to the next line. It flows just the way you would read a book.

However, some commands interrupt program flow: GoSub, On GoSub, Return, GoTo, On GoTo, Exit Sub, On Error and Resume. Inserting the name of a Subroutine or Function also redirects program flow, sending the program to the location in the program where that Sub or Function is located.

Making Your Program Jump: On Error GoTo *HandleIt* makes the program do something it normally would not. Instead of performing the tasks you have listed on the next line, it jumps to the location of the Label *HandleIt*. Flow is interrupted. Any commands between the GoTo and the HandleIt are not read or carried out by VB.

Likewise, Resume redirects program flow to the target you provide following the Resume command.

• Handle errors within the same Sub, Event or Function where the On Error command resides. Do not try to set up a separate error-handling Subroutine. Deal with any errors locally, within the same procedure. This approach avoids a whole jungle of confusing program flow pathways and execution prioritizing when errors are not locally resolved.

• If you use an On Error command, *you must provide a matching Resume* command.

Example

This example is a typical error-handling setup. We tell Visual Basic to go immediately to the commands following the Label called *Problem:* if an error occurs:

```
Sub Form_Click ()
On Error GoTo Problem
x$ = Dir$("A:\*.*")
Print x$

quit:
Exit Sub

Problem:
Print "Look, either there is no disk in drive A:, or you forgot to close the → drive
    door!"
Resume quit
End Sub
```

If an error occurs, our error handler then prints a warning to the user, and the Resume command tells Visual Basic where to go next. In this instance we go to the Label called *quit*, which exits the program.

Note that you'll often want to put the error handler at the end of the Event or Subroutine, so you'll usually have to precede the error-handler section with an Exit Sub command. That tells VB that if there *is no error*, it should skip past the error-handler section and leave the Subroutine.

See also

Err; Error$

See "On Error" for a complete discussion of error handling.

RETURN

STATEMENT

Description   Return redirects Visual Basic to the command following a GoSub command. Return is always used with a GoSub.

In Visual Basic and other modern languages, though, you are unlikely to use GoSub...Return much, if at all. These commands are remnants of an earlier style of programming. Instead, you will create Sub...End Sub entities. And, to use a Subroutine, you will not say GoSub—you will provide the name of the Sub (or Function) that you want to perform some task. The End Sub will automatically return you to the command following the "call" to that Sub. (Return is the old-style equivalent of End Sub.)

Program Flow: "Program flow" is programmer lingo for the path that the computer follows when carrying out your commands. Normally, the program flows from left to right across a line, then flows down to the next line, and then across that line, and so on until it reaches an End Sub or End Function command. A program flows through your commands just the way you would read a book.

However, some commands interrupt program flow: GoSub, On GoSub, Return, GoTo, On GoTo, Exit Sub, Exit For, On Error, Resume, etc. Inserting the name of a Subroutine or Function will also interrupt flow, sending the program to the location in the program where that Sub or Function is located. The location of a Sub or Function is *not* the following line.

GoTo *Privilege* would send the program to the label named *Privilege:*, where it would start carrying out the commands following that label.

The GoSub...Return pair of commands have largely been replaced by Sub...End Sub in Visual Basic. To access a Subroutine, you don't say GoSub, you just *name* the Subroutine. If you have written a Subroutine called *Search*, use it by providing its name. You don't need to say GoSub Search; just say Search. (See "Sub.")

The Search Sub would likely be in a Form's General Declarations section or in a Module (if you want the Sub available to the entire program). And, instead of ending the VB Sub with the Return command, End Sub is used to return the program to the command immediately following the location where you named *Search* as a way of going to that Sub. This process of naming a Sub to redirect program flow is sometimes referred to as *calling* a Subroutine (or a Function).

Used with   The GoSub Statement

Variables   Return

Uses • Few

In earlier versions of Basic, the GoSub...Return pair were used frequently. They were used the same way we now utilize Event Procedures, Subroutines and Functions in Visual Basic—to put a small group of instructions together that perform some specialized task.

This helps organize a program and makes it easier to track down errors. When each entity is relatively small, you can feed it data and watch the results, noting whether or not the results were what you expected.

Smaller Subs Are Easier to Debug: Testing is easier when parts of a program can be tested as if they were little black boxes that got something in and pushed something out, but performed a relatively finite transformation on the data. If a black box does 15 things in one big Event to the word *palatine*, it's hard to figure out which of those 15 things caused it to pop out *lapitaen*. But, if you have 15 black boxes, each of which performs a discrete single transformation, the job of finding out where the word is being mangled is simplified.

The Value of Subroutines in General: Another virtue of Subroutines is that you don't have to duplicate tasks. Say that you want your program to respond initially the same way when the user clicks on each of several Command Buttons. You want the program to first display the name of the clicked button in an animated Picture Box. You could write the commands that activate the Picture Box *in each Click Event of each Command Button*. Or, because the list of commands would be the same for each button (except for the name of the clicked button), you could write a general-purpose Subroutine that was "called" from each Click Event.

Into the General Declarations section of a Form, enter the following:

```
Sub showbuttonname (WhatButton As String)

Picture1.AutoRedraw = True
Picture1.Cls
Picture1.Visible = True
Picture1.Print WhatButton

For i = 1 To 400
    Picture1.Move Picture1.Left + 1
Next i

For i = 1 To 400
    Picture1.Move Picture1.Left − 1
Next i

Picture1.Visible = False
End Sub
```

First, we set AutoRedraw to On (–1 or True) so that when the Picture Box moves, the printed text will remain visible. We use Cls to position the printing in the top left of the Box. We make the Box visible and print whatever Caption was "passed" to the general-purpose Subroutine. Then we slide the Picture Box to the right and return it back to the left. Finally, we make it invisible again.

Then, in all the Click Events of all the Command Buttons that use this Subroutine, you simply provide its name (to call the Subroutine) and provide the Caption of the Command Button (to pass the text ("string") Variable to the general-purpose Subroutine):

```
Sub Command1_Click ()
    x$ = command1.caption
    showbuttonname x$
End Sub
```

Cautions • The Return command must be within the same procedure (Event, Sub or Function) as the GoSub with which it's paired. That is, the GoSub...Return structure must reside within a single Sub...End Sub or Function...End Function. You cannot use GoSub to refer to a location outside the procedure where the GoSub...Return is located. This is quite unlike traditional programming, where a GoSub could take you anywhere in the entire program.

• When VB encounters a Return Statement, it goes back to the location immediately following the originating GoSub command and begins carrying out the subsequent commands.

Example (See Uses above for the way Subroutines are generally handled in Visual Basic.)

If you do, for some reason, want to use GoSub...Return, here's how. (The only meaningful use of GoSub...Return in VB is when you need do the same thing several times within a procedure and you don't want to repeat that series of commands):

```
Sub Form_Click ()

x$ = "This is the message."

GoSub Findit

If y = 0 Then
    Print "Not found"
Else
    Print "Found"
End If

Exit Sub
Findit:
    y = InStr(x$, "message")
Return

End Sub
```

Note that we could simply replace the GoSub with y = InStr(x$, "message") and not bother with GoSub...Return. Because Visual Basic procedures are usually short, it makes little sense to embed GoSub...Returns within them.

When you *do* use a GoSub, it will be inside a procedure (nearly everything in VB is inside a procedure). So, when you use GoSub...Return in an Event, Sub or Function, you are, in effect, *putting one kind of Subroutine within another*. The tactic rarely has any value.

See also   Function; GoSub; GoTo; On GoSub; Sub

RGB

FUNCTION

Description   RGB provides your program with a highly specific definition of a color—specific because the RGB command will accept any number between 0 (black) and 16,777,215 (white). Within this nearly 17 million range are all the colors of the visible universe. There are zones within this rainbow within which human eyes cannot distinguish any change of color. But Microsoft is planning ahead, looking toward ever more excellent video and willing to build in redundancy now so that programs written in Visual Basic will still run when we all have ultra-high-definition wallscreen TV.

On many current computer systems, 16 is the maximum number of colors that the graphics hardware can display. The other 16,777,200 colors available via VB's RGB capabilities will force the video hardware to resort to textured ("dithered") approximations.

The QBColor Function provides only 16 different colors, but that's enough for some computer monitors and for many current VB applications. VGA, Super VGA and new standards to come, however, can display 256 or more colors at the same time. For precision work with color, you'll need to use RGB.

Red, Green, Blue: RGB stands for *Red Green Blue*. Mixing these three colors in various proportions will produce all the other colors. If you mix none of the colors—RGB (0,0,0)—you get black, the absence of color. If you use all three at full strength, you get white: RGB (255,255,255). And if you push one all the way up, you'll get that color at its purest: RGB (0,0,255) results in pure blue.

You provide the RGB Function with three numbers, each ranging from 0 to 255, and each number signifies how much red, green and blue to mix into the final color. RGB then combines these three numbers into a single large number that Visual Basic will recognize as a valid color. This larger number is a "Long Integer" (see "Variables").

Used with   BackColor, FillColor, ForeColor Properties
Line, Circle, PSet—these drawing Methods accept optional color specifications

R...**1003**

Variables   **Variable type:** Long

To mix various amounts of the three colors:
```
X& = RGB (12, 24, 234)
```

OR (to use Variables to describe the mix):
```
R = 12
G = 24
B = 234

X& = RGB (R,G,B)
```

Uses
- Any activity involving adjusting colors can potentially use RGB, but the ultimate quality of the colors depends on each user's video hardware.

  Many computer monitors cannot display very many colors; 256 simultaneous colors–Super VGA–is considered quite advanced these days. The latest video cards can handle more than 30,000 colors, and some very expensive ones can go into the millions. But it will be a few years before the high resolution and depth afforded by millions of colors will be widely available. Yet the RGB command stands ready to accommodate Visual Basic programs when this happy day arrives.

  Color limitations are generally not a factor of the display monitor but of the video card. Currently, for about $1,000, you can buy a 24-bit graphic card (TrueVision is one), which will display 16.7 million colors on analog color monitors.

  RGB's Purpose: The purpose of RGB is to accept three Variables, one each for red, green and blue. Each of these Variables can range from 0 to 255. The RGB Function simply compresses the three Variables into one larger Variable. If the user is adjusting three Scroll Bars representing red, green and blue, your program could respond to these adjustments by using the RGB Function to set the selected color (see the Example below).

  If you have three independent Variables that can each vary from 0 to 255, the total number of combinations is 256^3, which means 256 * 256 * 256– 16.7 million or thereabouts.

- Assign the ForeColor, FillColor and BackColor Properties of a Form or its Controls.

- Assign the colors of shapes drawn with Line, Circle and PSet.

- Create drawing, painting or photo-retouching applications.

Cautions
- Visual Basic works with RGB colors only. The purpose of the 16-color alternative command *QBColor* (QuickBASIC color) is to supply an RGB number. QBColor is a shortcut because it "knows" the values of the eight most common colors and eight lighter shades of those same colors. These are the colors used in programs written in Basic for DOS. When you use X& = QBColor(2), the X& Variable contains the number 32,768. (See "QBColor" for more on the interaction between it and RGB.)

```
Sub Form_Click ()
    x& = QBColor(2)
    backcolor = x&
    Print x&
End Sub
```

Results in   32,768

(and the Form turns green)

• If you provide RGB with any numbers larger than 255, it assumes you meant 255 and uses that.

• You'll often notice patterns in the colors on your screen. These patterns—dots, *X*s, checkerboard patterns, etc.—are called *dithering* and are the computer's attempt to approximate a color that Visual Basic or your monitor cannot display. By printing mainly light blue with white dots in it, you get a slightly lighter blue. Sort of.

This compromise is temporary, and computers with 24-bit color should become affordable fairly soon. Describing colors in 24 bits is exactly what RGB does. A byte is eight bits; a byte can hold any number from 0 to 255. So, ganging three bytes together to represent a single color allows a range of colors between 0 and 16,777,215. RGB combines a byte-sized number for R, G and B into a three-byte-long number.

Another unpleasant yet temporary video effect is called *aliasing*—the stair-step, jagged pattern that appears when two colors border each other diagonally. Because the screen is made up of many tiny "tiles" like a mosaic, it cannot draw truly diagonal lines. When two colors meet, such as the black lines of the < symbol meeting the white background of a Text Box, there is some inevitable "stair-stepping."

Anti-Alias or Why They Stopped Making Suits out of Herringbone-Patterned Cloth: Some programs contain an "anti-aliasing" feature that attempts to blend colors at the notorious diagonal borderline, softening the stair-step effect. You see a similar artifact when someone wears a diagonally striped blouse or diagonally patterned tie on TV—the pattern seems to vibrate. This is called *dot crawl* by video people who always advise talk-show guests to wear a plain blue blouse or a plain solid-colored tie.

You'll see paisley, you'll see polka dots, you'll even see vertical and horizontal stripes. You'll *never* see someone wearing a herringbone-patterned fabric on television. (/\/\/\/\/\/\/\). It makes a TV screen go crazy. It crawls up and down. It looks as if the clothing had come alive. Fashion industry experts connect the virtual disappearance of the once-popular herringbone pattern directly to the advent of television.

However, these artifacts, too, will eventually disappear as ever finer pixels are used on monitors and TVs, and as circuits are included in TV sets to stabilize, and compensate for, dot crawl. Herringbone, because it is inherently attractive, will doubtless then come back into fashion.

Like Fish Gills: Many graphic artists and the production departments of any publishing house that's attempting to computerize its images are familiar with the dreaded *moiré* pattern. These patterns are created when analog diagonal lines come up against the filtering effect of digital storage and display. Moiré patterns look like fish gills–radiating, often oval, lines superimposed on an image. This, too, will pass. Moiré is also a matter of resolution. As soon as storage media and the computers that control them are sufficiently fast and large, the problem of moiré patterns will, for all practical purposes, disappear.

However, because they are essentially mathematical events, moirés will never go away completely. They will happen in any resolution. Take two tea strainers or splatter screens and look through them both, rotating one; you'll see the cause of moiré. Moiré patterns are on the molecular level; they are responsible for the rainbow colors on bubbles and oil slicks, among other things.

• The DrawMode Property (which see) can affect colors by creating inter-actions between background and foreground colors when you use the drawing methods–PSet, Line and Circle.

• Far more serious is *artifacting*: a fine line drawn against a strongly con-trasting color will flicker on many monitors–usually standard Super VGA monitors in 1024x768 resolution. Some dithered colors are checkerboards and flicker quite badly. If you are writing programs that you intend to sell to the IBM audience at large, be sure to look at a Super VGA screen to see how your programs will fare at this resolution on this type of monitor. These monitors usually boast that they are "noninterlaced," but the fine print reveals that they interlace beyond the 800x600 mode of resolution.

Interlacing is caused when the video card doesn't have the raw speed to draw all the video lines of the display in the time limit imposed by the scanning speed of the monitor: 70 times per second for Super VGA. So the video card just draws in the even-numbered lines in one pass which begin to fade, and follows up with the odd-numbered lines in the next pass. The contrast in brightness between the already fading pixels and the brighter new ones sets up a beating, vibrating pattern unless the images on adjacent rows are similar in contrast. (Screen phosphors light only while stimulated by the CRT electron death beam, hence the need for constant repainting.)

Example   Many professional programs allow the user to adjust the colors of the windows and other elements of the program. You can add a Form like the one in this example, which would pop up whenever the user selects one of your Preferences or Options Menus. The user can then pick any color he or she wishes, and your program can save the choices in its .INI file, a special initialization file that it checks in the Form_Load Event of the Startup Form.

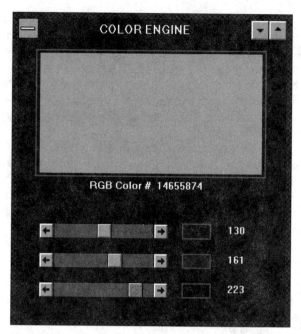

Figure R-12: You can add this window to any program to allow the user to select colors for the background or other elements of the program.

On a new Form, put three Horizontal Scroll Bars. Set each one's Max Property to 255. Then put three small Picture Boxes and three Labels next to these bars. Create one large Picture Box and put a larger Label underneath it.

The main action takes place in a separate Subroutine we created called "adjustcolor" and put in the General Declarations section of the Form. This Subroutine will service each of the Scroll Bars whenever its Change Event is triggered:

```
Sub adjustcolor ()
    r = hscroll1.value
    g = hscroll2.value
    b = hscroll3.value

    x& = RGB(r, g, b)

    picture4.backcolor = x&

    label4.caption = "RGB Color # " + Str$(x&)
End Sub
```

To be technically correct, you might want to change the final line in the above example to:

```
label4.caption = "RGB Color # " + "0x"+ string$(6—len(hex$(x&)),"0") +→
hex$(x&)
```

This line uses Hex$(x&) to give the RGB value in the form in which it is normally shown. We add the leading "0x0" and pad with another "0" to give true representation (for instance, QBColor(4) would be displayed as: 0x000080).

Each of the three RGB Variables is read from the Value Property of each of the Scroll Bars. Then we use the RGB Function to provide a Long Integer. RGB colors can range from 0, black, to white, 16,777,215, at the other extreme of the RGB range.

(By adding the & symbol to a Variable's name, you make it a Long Integer, a Variable that can hold a number with an enormous range from more than minus two billion to more than plus two billion. See "Variables.")

Then we set the large Picture Box to the particular color that was selected and show the color's RGB number in the large Label. Each of the Scroll Bar Change Events is functionally identical. The only differences are the names of the small Picture Boxes and small Labels, plus the *position* of the R, G or B Variable provided to the RGB Function:

```
Sub HScroll1_Change ()

adjustcolor
picture1.backcolor = RGB(hscroll1.value, 0, 0)
label1.caption = Str$(hscroll1.value)

End Sub

Sub HScroll2_Change ()

adjustcolor
picture2.backcolor = RGB(0, hscroll2.value, 0)
label2.caption = Str$(hscroll2.value)

End Sub

Sub HScroll3_Change ()

adjustcolor
picture3.backcolor = RGB(0, 0, hscroll3.value)
label3.caption = Str$(hscroll3.value)

End Sub
```

In each case, we call upon the *adjustcolor* Subroutine to do its work with the large Picture Box and Label and then reset the associated small Picture Box and small Label next to each bar. This demonstrates the utility of Subroutines—you use them when several Events need the same thing done. That way, you don't have to repeat the same commands within each Event. Just write the commands once in a Sub, and use that Sub whenever it's needed (see "Sub").

You also can use a single Scroll Bar to move through the RGB colors if you wish. However, because a Scroll Bar's Max Property cannot go higher than 32,767, you would have to do a little multiplying to allow the user to scroll from black (RGB 0) to white (RGB 16,777,215). Here's how: In the Scroll Bar's Change Event, enter the following:

```
Sub HScroll1_Change ()
R& = HScroll1.Value
R& = R& + 1
picture1.backcolor = (R& * 512) − 1
label1.caption = Str$(R&)
End Sub
```

Nonetheless, this approach is not recommended. For one thing, the Scroll Bar now skips all values except multiples of 512. Also, there's too much of a gradient, too much data being controlled by a single Scroll Bar. Who has enough control over a mouse to slide it along a desk and precisely stop at location number 12,000,075? There aren't that many twips anyway.

See also   DrawMode; QBColor

CONTROL

See   TextBox

FUNCTION

Description   Right$ extracts a piece of text from the right side of a larger piece of text. Right does the same thing but returns a *Variant* rather than a text Variable type (see "Variables").

A variation, the RightB function, allows you to specify the length in *bytes* rather than *characters*. (Characters in the 32-bit version of VB are two-byte units.)

```
Print Right$("ABCDE", 2)
```

Results in   DE

Text Variables are called *strings* in computerese. When using Right$, you specify how many characters you want extracted, and Visual Basic counts over that far from the right side of the larger text and provides you with the piece of text you requested.

Used with   • Text ("string") Variables, Constants or expressions (see "Variables," or the "Cautions" below, for a definition of *Constants* and *expressions*).

Right$ can also be used with *text literals*. A "literal" means that you provide the actual text rather than a Variable:

```
X$ = "Pour the soup, Sam"
X$ (is a Variable)
```

"Pour the soup, Sam." (is a literal)

However, there is no real reason to use Right$ with a literal. If you want the rightmost three characters from the preceding literal, then just use "Sam" and you have no need for Right$.

• Right$ is often used in conjunction with Left$. Together, they enable you to divide a larger text into two smaller pieces. The Mid$, InStr and Len commands are often used with Right$ as well. See the descriptions under "Uses."

Variables To put the rightmost five letters from A$ into Result$:

```
Result$ = Right$(A$, 5)
```

OR (The Variable N determines how many text characters Result$ will get from the right side of X$):

```
Result$ = Right$(X$, N)
```

OR

```
Result$ = Right$("This message", 4)
```

Right$ is used here with a text literal—although you would more likely just enter Result$ = "sage" than go to the trouble of having your program calculate what you can plainly see in the "literal." (See "Variables.")

Uses *Parse* some text—pull out the various elements of the text.

Right$ is used along with several other Functions that manipulate text— Left$, Mid$, Instr and Len—to isolate and extract a piece of text from within a larger group of characters.

Left$ pulls out a number of characters, counting from the start of the larger text:

```
X$ = "Montenegro is rising."
Y$ = Left$(X$,10)
Print Y$
```

Results in Montenegro

**Mid$** pulls out a piece of text anywhere from within a larger text using the format Y$ Mid$(LargerText$, StartingCharacter, NumberOfCharacters). Use Mid$ when the target piece of text isn't flush against the left or right of the larger text:

```
X$ = "We Employ A Maid From Planet X."
Y$ = Mid$(X$,23,6)
Print Y$
```

Results in Planet

> **Len** tells you the length, in characters, of a text ("string") Variable.
> ```
> X$ = "We employ a maid from Planet X."
> Print Len(X$)
> ```

Results in 31

> **Instr** finds the location of the first character of a piece of text within a larger group of characters:
> ```
> X$ = "We employ a maid from Planet X."
> L = Instr(X$, "maid")
> Print L
> ```

Results in 13

> Instr will give back a 0 if it cannot find the text. Instr is case-sensitive—looking for "Maid" would give back a 0, meaning "not found."
> To left-pad a string with spaces or other characters, use X$=RIGHT$("****"+B$,4). Asterisks (*) are used like this by companies and banks for check-protection.

Cautions • Right$ usually extracts a smaller piece of text from a text ("string") Variable.

> However, Right$ can also extract from a Constant (Const CALCAPITOL = "Sacramento"), or a string expression. (See "Variables.")

• The number of characters you are requesting Right$ to extract—the 15 in Right$(X$, 15)—can be a literal number like 15 or a numeric Variable like *N*.

• The number of characters you are requesting Right$ to extract from a larger piece of text can be large as 65,535. If you ask for more characters than there are in the larger piece of text, you get back the whole larger text.

Example Right$ is often used together with Left$ and InStr to break a piece of text into pieces. For instance, you could pull in an .INI file from the disk and put each of its lines into a separate Array Variable (see "Arrays"). Then your program could examine the contents of the .INI file in detail.

> Another way that Right$ can help is when you need to stuff information into an Array (or items into a List Box) but don't want to do it the normal Visual Basic way:
> ```
> ReDim NolteMovies$(1 To 9)
>
> NolteMovies$(1) = "Return To Macon County"
> NolteMovies$(2) = "The Deep"
> NolteMovies$(3) = "North Dallas Forty"
> NolteMovies$(4) = "Heart Beat"
> NolteMovies$(5) = "Cannery Row"
> ```

and so on until you've assigned all nine members of this Array.

This approach is (slightly) faster when the computer runs than the traditional approach, but it is certainly more trouble for the programmer. Traditionally, there were two commands in Basic—DATA and READ—but they are unavailable in VB.

Using DATA and READ, you could accomplish the same thing as in the preceding example:

```
DATA "Return To Macon County", "The Deep", "North Dallas Forty", "Heart Beat",
"Cannery Row", "48 Hours", "Under Fire", "Teachers", "Grace Quigley"

For I = 1 To 9
    Read NolteMovies$(I)
Next I
```

We can use Left$ to provide an acceptable substitute for the READ command. Using Left$ you can easily build an Array with data while the program is running.

In a Module, enter this declaration to make the information available to the entire program:

```
Global NolteMovies(1 To 9) As String
```

Then, in the Startup Form's Form_Load Event, add the following:

```
Sub Form_Load ()

D$ = "Return To Macon County, The Deep, North Dallas Forty, Heart Beat,
Cannery Row, 48 Hours, Under Fire, Teachers, Grace Quigley"

L = InStr(D$, ",")

Do While L
    c = c + 1
    NolteMovies$(c) = Left$(D$, L − 1)
    D$ = Right$(D$, Len(D$) − L − 1)
    L = InStr(D$, ",")
Loop

c = c + 1
NolteMovies$(c) = D$

End Sub
```

This approach may *seem* like the long way around, but if you have a lot of data and you want it embedded within your program (as opposed to reading it in from a disk file), this little Subroutine can be very handy indeed. Instead of dozens of NolteMovies$(18) = "Name of Movie" you can just use this Loop.

Technical Note: VB has no provision for extending a line. In other words, the entire D$ data must be on the same line. However, you can get around this restriction by:

```
D$ = "Return To Macon County, The Deep, North Dallas Forty,"

D$ = D$ + "Heart Beat, Cannery Row, 48 Hours, Under Fire, Teachers, → Grace
    Quigley"
```

The preceding routine first gets the location (L) of the first comma in the data (D$). Then we enter a Loop which that says: "Keep looping while L (is not zero). If L is zero, we would not find any more commas."

Inside the Loop, we keep a counter (c), which will increase each time through the Loop and provide a unique index number for each item in the Array (NolteMovie$). We pull the Left$ from D$. Left$ will contain everything left of the comma—in other words, the name of the first movie. Then we use Right$ to strip off that first movie name. Now D$ will contain all the remaining movies but not the first one. With each use of Left$ and Right$, we subtract 1 from the location (L). That avoids including the comma in either the new small piece of text or in the remaining larger piece of text.

Then we keep repeating, splitting pieces of D$ off until we've reached a point where there are no more commas left, and we exit the Loop and, one more time, insert the last movie name into the Array.

See also   InStr; Left$; Len; Mid$

RmDir

STATEMENT

Description   RmDir deletes an entire directory from the disk drive. It does the same thing as does the DOS command Rmdir (rd).

Used with   Disk Drives

Variables   To remove the C:\TEMP directory:

```
RmDir "C:\TEMP"
```

OR (to use a text Variable instead of the literal text):

```
X$ = "C:\TEMP\TEMP1"
RmDir X$
```

Uses   • Build into your program some of the features of a File Manager—allowing the user to create, remove, search and otherwise manipulate disk file directories.

If you are writing a large, polished program in VB, you may want to offer the user the ability to manage disk files and even directories while your program is running.

Cautions   • RmDir, like the Kill command that deletes individual files, can be risky for the user.

RmDir, like its DOS equivalent, will not delete a directory if there are any files within that directory. Nonetheless, it does make a major change by removing an empty directory.

As always when accessing the user's disk drive, use the On Error command (which see) to prevent your program from shutting down if anything goes wrong.

Example   We'll create and then destroy a directory. First, put a Directory List Box on a Form, so we can watch the new directory come into existence while we build a file inside it; and then we will remove the file and directory.

Put the following into the Form_Click Event:

```
Sub Form_Click ()

On Error GoTo Problem

D$ = "C:\TEMP1"
MkDir D$
Dir1.path = D$

Open D$ + "\TESTFILE" For Output As #1

Dir1.Refresh

For i = 1 To 5000
    Print #1, Str$(i)
Next i

Close #1

Open D$ + "\TESTFILE" For Input As #1

For i = 1 To 1425
    Line Input #1, A$
Next i

Close #1

Print A$

Kill D$ + "\TESTFILE"

RmDir D$

Dir1.path = "C:\"
Dir1.Refresh

Exit Sub

Problem:

If Err Then MsgBox(Error$(Err))

Close

End Sub
```

Several of the preceding commands and structures are typical of file and directory management. First, we tell VB what to do if one of our manipulations causes an error. Maybe the directory "TEMP1" already exists, for instance. If there is an error, we go down to the Label *Problem:* and show the user a text description of the error (Error$), close any opened file, and leave the Subroutine.

We make a directory called TEMP1 on drive C: and adjust the Path Property of the Directory List Box so that it shows the new directory. Then we create a file in that directory, refresh (reprint the information inside) the List Box and fill the test file with text versions of all the numbers from 1 to 5000. Then we reopen this test file to make sure it exists and pull in each item until we reach the 1425th item. Each time we use the Line Input # command, A$ gets the next text number that we stored—one way to find a particular item inside a sequential-mode file (see "Input$"). The fact that A$ is rapidly being filled with each item and then having that item replaced is not a problem for a Variable. Variables are designed to *vary*, so A$ won't heat up from all this activity.

Now we print A$ on the Form to verify that the file was created, contains all those items and exists within C:\TEMP1. Then we Kill the file, which is the same thing as typing "del testfile" in DOS. (We normally have to Kill all the files in a directory before we can destroy the directory itself.) Now we remove the directory with RmDir, change the Path of the Directory List Box and again refresh the Box; the user can see that TEMP1 no longer exists on drive C:.

See also ChDir; CurDir$; Dir$; Kill; MkDir; On Error

See "Drive List Box" for a way to build general-purpose disk management into your programs, a disk manager like a simplified version of the File Manager in Windows.

ND

FUNCTION

Description Rnd provides your program with random numbers. This Function is very useful in a variety of situations. With a random number, you can draw a card out of a deck, make aliens unpredictable in a space game, create "abstract" designs that never repeat and accomplish many other tasks. Randomness is particularly important when you are creating simulations, games and some kinds of graphics.

Use the Randomize command (which see) as the first command in your program if you want Rnd to produce truly random series of numbers. The computer can provide a series of random numbers when you use the Rnd Function. However, each time you run a program, *the series will repeat itself* unless you use the Randomize Statement at the start of the program to provide a truly random "seed" for the Rnd Function.

Used with The Randomize Function. Randomize ensures that Rnd will produce a unique series of random numbers every time a program is run.

Variables   The following is the most common way to use Rnd. You decide what range of numbers you want and then multiply that number by Rnd. Adding 1 makes the result range between 1 and the upper limit. The Int Function rounds off any fractional part of the result. This example provides a random number between 1 and 50:

```
X = Int(Rnd * 50 + 1)
```

OR

(to provide a range between 0 and an upper limit, supply as an upper limit a number one higher than you actually want. And don't add 1 inside the parentheses. This example provides a random number between 0 and 50):

```
X = Int(Rnd * 51)
```

OR

(Rnd is *supposed* to be random, but you can make it behave predictably, nonrandomly. There is no known use for this technique, but you *can* provide numbers or numeric Variables in parentheses following the Rnd Function. If you provide a number, Rnd will always produce the same result each time you run the program. However, subsequent uses of the Rnd (.2233) in this example, while the program runs, will produce varying numbers):

```
X = Rnd (.2233)
```

OR

(if you provide 0 in parentheses following Rnd, you will get the *previous* random number that was generated by Rnd in the program):

```
X = Rnd(0)
```

Uses   Use Rnd whenever you want things to happen by chance—for games, simulations, statistical analysis or art—anytime you want to introduce unpredictable results into the relentlessly orderly world of the computer.

You may want to draw lines or splash spots on a window's background in chance locations. If you are doing an economic simulation, you might want to crash the stock market every 60 or 90 years, causing hardship for nine years thereafter. But exactly *when* the crash occurs should be unpredictable and should be different every time the program runs (see "Randomize"). Each time a "year" passes in the economic simulation, you use X = Int(Rnd * 60 + 1): If X = 42 Then...CRASH. (You can have any of the numbers between 1 and 60 trigger the crash because each number will randomly occur with a probability of 1 in 60 each "year.") For card games, shuffle an Array of cards with Rnd, etc.

Cautions   • In most situations you won't have to worry, but Rnd is capable of generating a huge range of random numbers. Most of the time you'll use it to toss a coin (range 0 to 1); or to determine which direction a dangerous asteroid wanders across the screen, threatening your space ship (range probably 1 to 8); or to roll dice (range 1 to 6). In these cases, don't worry about Variable types.

Rnd creates a fraction between 0 and 1. That's why you multiply and round off Rnd to get a whole number you can use for things like tossing a coin.

Rnd Gives Good Fractions: The fraction produced by Rnd has an enormous range of possibilities, as you can see by this example:

```
For i = 1 To 20
    Print Rnd
Next i
```

Results in
```
.705547511577606
.533424019813538
.579518616199493
.289562463760376
.301948010921478
.774740099906921
.014017641544342
.76072359085083
.814490020275116
.709037899971008
4.53527569770813D-02
.414032697677612
.862619340419769
.790480017662048
.373536169528961
.961953163146973
.871445834636688
5.62368631362915D-02
.949556648731232
.364018678665161
```

(If D-02 follows a number, you should move the decimal point over two spaces to the left, adding zeros if necessary. Therefore, 4.53527569770813D-02 means .0453527569770813.)

With this much variability in the series of digits that Rnd can supply, you can generate random numbers over an enormous range, should you ever need to.

• You should generally use Randomize as the first command in a program. This means that you will put it as the first command in the Form_Load Event of your "Startup Form." The Startup Form is usually Form1, the first Form you work on when building a VB program. You can change the Startup Form from VB's Options Menu if you want.

Example   In this example, five bunnies are going to race each other several thousand times. Each time a bunny wins the race, we'll add one to her score and start another race. After a couple of hours, we'll check the scores. If Rnd is doing its job, each rabbit should win roughly as often as the others.

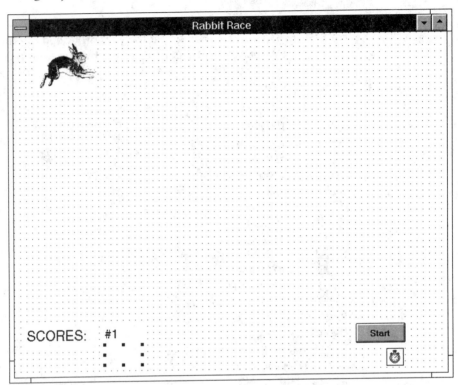

Figure R-13: The rabbit race program while being designed (note that we need only one rabbit).

First, put a Picture Box in the upper-left corner of a Form. Set the Picture Box's AutoSize and AutoRedraw Properties to True (On). Set the Box's BorderStyle Property to 0 (no border). Put a .BMP or .ICO into the Box using the Picture Property. Then set the Index Property to 0, thereby creating a Control Array (which see).

Next, put a Label about one inch in from the bottom and left of the Form. Make sure that its Name Property is set to Label1. Then set its Index Property to 0 and its Caption Property to #1.

Put another Label just to the left of the first one and set its Caption to "SCORES." Make sure its Name Property is Label2.

Put a third Label just below the first, erase its Caption Property, set its Index Property to 0, and then make sure its Name is Label3. Also put a Command Button in the lower right corner of the Form and set its Caption Property to "Start."

Put a Timer anywhere on the Form, but set its Interval Property to 2,000 so it will "go off" every two seconds. Timers default to Enabled.

When you put a Timer onto one of your Forms, it becomes a nag. If you set its Interval Property to anything greater than the 0 default, it goes off independently of anything else that's happening in the computer at the time.

Any commands you put into the Timer Event will happen as often as the Timer's Interval Property specifies. In this program, we haven't disabled the Timer anywhere (by setting its Enabled Property to False), so this Timer will do its thing every two seconds as long as the program runs.

Timers Can Cause Delays, Too: Timers have another capability, too, aside from their wonderful ability to float outside a program and touch down from time to time to intervene in whatever is happening. They can *delay* things as well. When you set a Timer's Enabled Property to On (-1 or True), it waits until its Interval passes and then carries out the instructions you have placed between . . .

```
Sub Timer1_Timer ()
```

. . . and

```
End Sub
```

(To see all the things you can do with Timers, see "Timer.")

In the General Declarations section, define a Variable *t* that will be accessible from anywhere in the Form. The Timer and the Command Button will both use this Variable *t* to tell us whether the user wants to start or stop the rabbits.

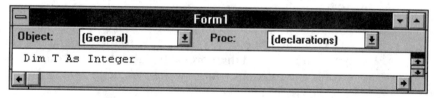

Figure R-14: If you define Variables in the General Declarations section, they'll be available everywhere in that Form.

As always, we make preparations—the preliminary housekeeping for the program—in the Form_Load Event:

```
Sub Form_Load ()

Randomize

width = 8700: height = 7000

For i = 1 To 4

    Load picture1(i)
    picture1(i).visible = −1
    picture1(i).top = picture1(i − 1).top + 900
```

```
        Load Label1(i)
        Label1(i).visible = —1
        Label1(i).caption = "#" + Str$(i + 1)
        Label1(i).left = Label1(i — 1).left + 1000

        Load Label3(i)
        Label3(i).visible = —1
        Label3(i).left = Label3(i — 1).left + 1000

    Next i
    End Sub
```

The Randomize Statement, as the first command that gets carried out when this program runs, ensures that each sequence of random numbers generated by Rnd will start with a truly random number. Therefore, each time we run this program, there will be a unique race.

Then we set the Form to the size that we want it and create three or four new members of our Control Array (which see). In essence, a Control Array can create new Controls while the program is running. The Load command brings to life four Picture Boxes, four Labels that identify each rabbit's score and four Labels that will change as the scores change. These Controls are not placed onscreen by you or otherwise designed when you are programming; instead, they are created by VB each time the program runs. In each case, we make the newborn Control visible (they arrive invisible), and we position each one to some offset of the previous Control (otherwise, they would pile on top of each other as they came on board).

Now, as you've doubtless discovered, Visual Basic allows you to create Subroutines (see "Sub") in the General Declarations section of a Form. As you do this, VB makes room for it and adds it to the list of any other existing Subs. Such a Sub is available to perform tasks as requested by any other section of that Form. Let's put the commands that make the rabbits jump and race into a Sub called "Race." Go to the General Declarations section, type Sub Race, and then press ENTER. Instantly, you see that VB has created the basics of your new Subroutine:

```
    Sub race ( )

    End Sub
```

Between these two commands, add the following:

```
    Sub race ( )

    L = scalewidth — 200
    L1 = label2.top — 200
    drawwidth = 4

    Line (L, 0)—(L, L1)
    Line (0, L1)—(L, L1)

    z = scalewidth — 2000
```

```
     Do
          r = Int(5 * Rnd)
          x = picture1(r).left
          picture1(r).Move x + 400
     Loop Until picture1(r).left > z

     caption = "Rabbit #" + Str$(r + 1) + " Wins !!!"
     c = Val(Label3(r).caption): c = c + 1
     Label3(r).caption = Str$(c)

     End Sub
```

This is the heart of the program. Here's where we make the rabbits leap to the finish line, and then announce the winner and update the cumulative score for each bunny. First, we draw two lines to give the rabbits a (purely visual) enclosure for the race. Then we establish the "finish line" by subtracting 2,000 from the right side of the Form (z = scalewidth – 2000). (See "ScaleWidth.") We'll use *z* later to let us know when one bunny has been victorious.

Making the Bunnies Jump at Random: Now we create a Loop that will keep on going, making the bunnies jump at random toward the finish line: Until picture1(r).left > z. This line translates into English: "Keep going back up to the Do command and executing each command that makes the bunnies jump *until* one of these Picture Boxes arrives at a position, as measured by its Left Property, which is greater than (>) our finish line (z)."

Each time through this Loop, we first "roll the dice of Rnd" to decide which of the five creatures will bound forward this time. Our bunnies are known to the program as Picture1(0) through Picture1(4), so by using Int(5 * Rnd) we are supplied each time through the Loop with a number between 0 and 4.

When one of the rabbits finally gets to z, the finish line, we fall through the Loop to change the Caption of the Form to announce the winner. Because the five Label3( )'s hold the current score of each rabbit, we use that to add 1 to the winner's total and then display it.

Note that you can put F = DoEvents( ) inside the Do...Loop, permitting interruption of a race in progress. Adding this command will slow the program down somewhat and will also permit the Timer to "go off" during a race.

These things happen for each race. But what triggers the races? Pressing the Start Button:

```
     Sub Command1_Click ()

     If t = 0 Then
          t = 1
          command1.caption = "Stop"
          race
```

```
Else
    t = 0
    command1.caption = "Start"
End If
End Sub
```

This simple "toggle" structure is either on or off like a light switch. When the user first starts the program, all numeric Variables are 0. So, the first time the user clicks on the Command Button, t = 0. Recall that we defined the Variable *t* in the General Declarations section so it would be available to all areas, all Events, within this Form. If the Formwide Variable *t* is 0, we change it to 1, change the Caption to "Stop" and start the race by merely mentioning the name of the Subroutine called *race*.

However, if the race is going on, *t* will equal 1, so a click on the Command Button then will cause *t* to be toggled back to zero and the caption to be reset to "Start." But we *do not*, this time, say "race." The user has requested that the race should stop.

Timers Just Keep Going Off: What, though, is watching all the time and can check the status of *t* to see if a race should continue to run or should be stopped? The best Control to use for monitoring continuous activity—for looking after things the whole time a program is running—is a *Timer*. Timers keep going off at regular intervals determined by what you put into their Interval Property. But—like a teacher during a test, or a homunculus— Timers keep on watching *no matter what is going on elsewhere in the program*. They can, therefore, intervene at regular intervals or can react to a change in any Variable. We'll have our Timer look for changes in the *t* Variable and also pause for two seconds at the end of each race so that the user can see who was the winner:

```
Sub timer1_timer ()

If t = 0 Then Exit Sub

For i = 0 To 4
    picture1(i).left = 480
Next i

caption = "Rabbit Race"

race
End Sub
```

This Timer's Interval was set to 2,000 (2-second intervals). Every 2 seconds it will look at conditions in the program and respond according to the commands we've put inside this Event. If *t* is 0, the user clicked on the Command Button to stop the program, so we exit this Subroutine but do nothing else. Exiting the Subroutine puts the program into "pause"— nothing goes on. It stops.

However, if *t* is not zero, then the Command Button has not been pressed, and the user doesn't want the action to stop. This means that the race was finished, so we put all the rabbits back to the starting line, located at 480 twips (see "ScaleMode"). And we change the Form's Caption to its generic title, replacing the announcement of the winner that was put into the Caption at the conclusion of the "race" Subroutine.

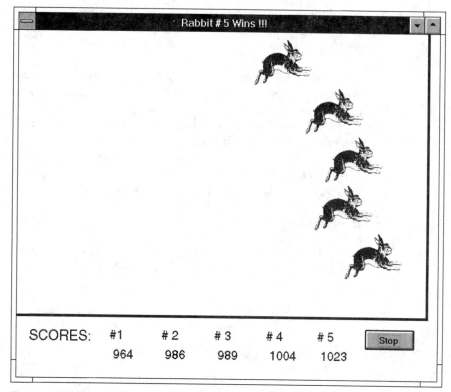

Figure R-15: The results are in after thousands of races.

Note that the rabbits are, over time, running essentially random races: no one rabbit has a significantly better record than another. And, every time you run the program, the results, to the extent that they *do* skew, will skew differently.

Running this program as an icon greatly speeds it up because the computer no longer has to keep redrawing the screen.

See also   Randomize

RSET

Description   RSet moves a piece of text all the way to the right within a "fixed-length" text Variable, padding the left side with spaces. The primary use for RSet is with random-mode files (see "Open").

What Is a Fixed-Length String: A fixed-length string is a text Variable whose size cannot change. Such Variables are used for random-access files (see "Open") because each record must be the same, unchanging length. Fixed-length strings are also useful for some kinds of formatting: If there are fewer text characters in a particular fixed string, it will still be padded with spaces so that the length remains stable. However, now that computers and printers are most frequently using proportional fonts (the characters vary in width), the value of that approach to formatting is passing into history.

How to Create a Fixed-Length String: You can create fixed-length strings by using Dim Name As String * 25 (which creates a fixed-length string that will be 25 characters long). You can also use Global and Static—other ways of declaring text Variables of stable length.

OR

Name$ = String$(50," "), which fills the Variable Name$, for the time being, with 50 spaces and fixes it at that length.

Used with   Fixed-length text ("string") Variables that are used with random-mode files (see "Open")

Variables   To replace the text in A$ with a new, padded piece of text:

```
A$ = String$(25," ")        'create a text Variable with a fixed length of → 25
                              characters
A$ = "More's the Pity"      'put some characters into the Variable
RSet A$ = "Just this."      'replace with new padded text
Print A$;A$
```

Results in   Just this.   Just this.

(Note that A$ is padded with spaces on the left side.)

OR (to take a piece out of A$ itself and replace the original with the padded piece):

```
A$ = String$(25," ")        'create a text Variable with a fixed length of → 25
                              characters
A$ = "More's the Pity"      'put some characters into the Variable
```

```
Cut$ = Left$(A$, 12)        'pull out a piece of A$, the 12 leftmost →
                             characters in this case.
RSet A$ = Cut$              'replace A$ with the piece
Print A$;A$
```

Results in   More's the P More's the P

Uses   • Move part of a text ("string") Variable to the right, padding with spaces if necessary, so that the length of the Variable remains the same. RSet is used mainly with random-mode files (see "Open").

A companion LSet Statement left-justifies a piece of text-within-text in the same fashion.

Cautions   • RSet is not useful for extracting a piece of text out of a larger text Variable (instead, use Mid$, Right$ or Left$).

• Unlike LSet, RSet cannot be used to copy user-defined Variables (see "Type").

• If the Variable being RSet is smaller than the target, it will be padded to the left with spaces, covering up some of the original characters:

```
A$ = String$(20,"*")        ' fills a Variable called A$ with 20 asterisks
RSet A$ = "1234567890"
Print A$
```

Results in   1234567890

A$ now holds 10 space characters followed by those 10 digits. The original first 10 asterisks are covered by space characters.

OR

If, however, the Variable being RSet is *larger* than the target, it will be truncated to the right. That is, characters will be chopped off on the right side of the original Variable to stuff it into the smaller target:

```
A$ = String$(5," ")   'fills A$ with five spaces
RSet A$ = "1234567890"
Print A$
```

Results in   12345

Example
```
a$ = "Now. Move This Over."
Print a$, Len(a$)
```

Results in   Now. Move This Over.   20

```
RSet a$ = "Now."
Print a$, Len(a$)
```

After RSet

Results in   Now.   20

R...**1025**

(A$ is still 20 characters long, but the left side is padded with spaces, moving the text to the right.)

See also   Left$; LSet; LTrim$; Mid$; Open (for random-mode files); Right$; RTrim$; Type; Variables

FUNCTION

Description   RTrim$ removes any spaces that might be on the right side of a text ("string") Variable.
It changes "U.S.A.   " into "U.S.A."

Used with   Either Variable-length or fixed-length text ("string") Variables (see "Variables").
The RTrim command does the same thing but returns a *Variant* rather than a text Variable type (see "Variables").

Variables   To remove the five trailing spaces from the text Variable A$:

```
A$ = "ABCDE      "
X$ = RTrim$(A$)
Print Len(A$)
Print Len(X$)
```

Results in   10
5

Uses   • Clean up user input.
You can never tell what the user might do. When typing in a lot of data, the user might accidentally hit the TAB key or some extra spaces. Use RTrim$ if you want to clean up any accidental trailing spaces. And while you're at it, you might want to eliminate random capitalization with the LCase$ Function, too.
You'll sometimes see a triple-command cleanup of text Variables. The following removes any leading or trailing spaces and all capitalization:

```
A$ = " Not tYped in too WELL "
Print A$
A$ = LCase$(LTrim$(RTrim$(A$)))
Print A$
```

Results in   Not tYped in too WELL
not typed in too well

• Clean up text from random-mode files (see "Open").

Every item in a random-mode file must be the same length, so some text Variables may have been padded with spaces (using LSet) before being stored. The Type command also pads text. Therefore, prior to printing or otherwise manipulating text Variables that were read from a random file, you might want to use RTrim$ to get rid of the padding.

Cautions RTrim$ works with either variable-length or fixed-length text ("string") Variables. (See "Variables.")

Example
```
A$ = "123" + "   "
B$ = RTrim$(A$)
Print Len(A$), Len(B$)
```

Results in 6   3

Here we add three spaces to the right side of A$. We RTrim$ the spaces off of A$ and put the result into B$. Then we print the length of the two text Variables.

See also LSet; LTrim$; Open (random-mode files); RSet

SAVEPICTURE

STATEMENT

• •

Description   SavePicture saves a graphic image from a Form, Image Control or Picture Box into a file on disk.

   The images can be designs you've drawn using the drawing Methods (Line, Circle, PSet). You can also save images that were imported by setting the Picture Property of a Form or Picture Box or via the PaintPicture Method or via the LoadPicture Function; these imported images can be .BMP, .ICO or .WMF graphics files.

Used with   Forms, Image Controls and Picture Boxes

Variables   To save the graphics on a Form:

       SavePicture Image, "C:\TEST.BMP"

   OR (to save the graphics on a Picture Box):

       SavePicture Picture1.Image, "C:\TEST.BMP"

Uses   • In your own painting applications or in other programs involving graphics, use SavePicture to save the results to disk files. This way, you can later view or modify them. SavePicture is to graphics what Open and Print # are to text.

   Unless your program modifies .BMP, .ICO or .WMF graphics, there would be no point to using SavePicture with them because they will already exist on the disk.

Cautions   • The AutoRedraw Property of the Form or Picture Box *must* be set to –1 (On). Otherwise, you will save a blank picture when you use the SavePicture command.

   • Drawn graphics (using the Line, Circle, PSet or Print command) that are saved using the Image Property are always saved as .BMP files. However, if you imported the graphic by using the Picture Property of a Form or Picture Box, or via the LoadPicture Function, then the SavePicture Statement saves the graphic in the same format as it was when imported (.BMP, .ICO or .WMF).

   The Image Property is an "hBitmap" (bitmap "handle"), which identifies a particular bitmap graphic (see "Image" for more information). You could also use the Picture Property with SavePicture.

Example

```
Sub Form_Click ()

On Error Resume Next

picture1.drawwidth = 5
picture1.autoredraw = -1

wd = picture1.scalewidth
ht = picture1.scaleheight

For i = 1 To 500
    x = Int(Rnd * wd)
    y = Int(Rnd * ht)
    colr = Int(Rnd * 16)
    picture1.PSet (x, y), QBColor(colr)
Next i

SavePicture picture1.image, "C:\TEST1.BMP"

If Err Then Msgbox (Error$(Err))
End Sub
```

To try the preceding example, we put a Picture Box on a Form. We set the DrawWidth Property to 5 so that the dots will be moderately large. AutoRedraw *must* be set to On for any picture you intend to save.

Then we find the measurements of the Picture Box and use them to draw 500 dots in random locations and in random colors. Then we save the picture to the disk.

As usual, when accessing the disk drive, we bracket the activities with On Error Resume Next and If Err... (see "On Error") to prevent mishaps from shutting down the program.

See also   Image; LoadPicture; PaintPicture; Picture; SetData

SCALE

METHOD

Description   Using Scale you can set up a "coordinate system" of your own design. You can then use the coordinates for

- drawing graphics (with PSet, Line and Circle)

- placing Controls, for formatting (centering objects, making objects the same size, positioning them in a row, etc.)

- moving or animating Controls

(See "ScaleMode" for a general discussion of coordinate systems.)
With the Scale command you can establish a *relative* coordinate system. Visual Basic provides several optional coordinate systems, including inches, for example. But all of VB's systems are *absolute* measurements. Absolute

S ... **1029**

coordinates will create different effects on Forms of varying sizes. However, if you use the Scale command, changes in the size of a Form will be reflected in the coordinates you set; the coordinates become relative to the size of the Form (or Picture Box or sheet of paper in the printer).

Although Visual Basic provides a default coordinate system of twips (1,440 per inch) and other options such as millimeters or inches, using the Scale command you can create your own coordinate system for special purposes. And the most important feature of the coordinates created with the Scale command is that the coordinates will be sensitive to the shape that contains them.

What Is a Coordinate System? A *coordinate system* utilizes two sets of measurements, like the typical city map with *A B C D* across the top and *1 2 3 4*, etc., across the left side. By saying C-3, you provide two "coordinates" and thereby specify a particular location on the map. In VB the coordinates are a pair of numbers, the X (horizontal) and Y (vertical) coordinates.

By convention, the horizontal coordinate is always given first and then the vertical coordinate. PSet (14, 2000) puts a dot on the Form 14 twips from the left side of the Form and 2,000 twips down from the top. Coordinates are often expressed in the following way:

```
X = 14
Y = 2000
PSet(X,Y)
```

Visual Basic provides several built-in coordinate systems from which you can choose (inches, points, pixels, etc.; see "ScaleMode"). The default system—"twips"—is a very precise unit of measurement; there are 1,440 twips per inch. To put a dot on a Form roughly one inch from the left side and two inches down from the top, using the default twips:

```
PSet (1440, 2880)
```

If you set the coordinate system to *inches*, though, the same dot would be drawn in the same spot with the following:

```
ScaleMode = 5 '(this changes the coordinate system to inches)
PSet(1,2)
```

What's Different About "Custom" Coordinates? When you use the Scale command, you create a "programmer-defined" coordinate system, and this new system is *relative to the size of the Form, Picture Box or paper in the printer.* All other coordinate systems (those set with ScaleMode or with the default twips) are *absolute.* They do not change with different sizes of Forms, Picture Boxes or sheets of paper in the printer. Put another way, if you choose inches, one of the built-in ScaleMode systems, an 8- x 11-inch sheet of paper would have 8 coordinates horizontally and 11 vertically. A smaller 5- x 5-inch sheet would have 5 horizontal and 5 vertical coordinates.

If you use the Scale command and set it to five—Scale (0, 0) - (5, 5)—*both an 8- x 11-inch and 5- x 5-inch piece of paper would have five coordinates in both directions.* The point of all this is that you can then draw on these two pieces of paper or position items on them, knowing that the drawing and positioning will be in proportion. Using the coordinates to draw three overlapping circles near the center of the larger paper would be reproduced in proportion if you changed the size of the paper. The circles would be smaller, but they would appear to have been simply *reduced* in a photocopier. Their relative positions would remain the same, regardless of the size of the paper being used.

Used with   Forms, Picture Boxes and the printer

Variables   Scale (Horizontal Starting Position, Vertical Starting Position) —(Horizontal Ending Position, Vertical Ending Position)

To create your own custom coordinate system starting from 0 and going to 10, both horizontally and vertically:

Scale (0, 0) —(10, 10)

Your coordinates would look like the following:

```
0     1     2     3     4     5     6     7     8     9     10
1
2
3           2,3
4
5
6                                               8,6
7
8
9
10
```

OR

(to create a system from 0 to 100, in both horizontal and vertical directions): Scale (0, 0) —(100, 100)

OR

(to create a coordinate system on a Picture Box, with 8 horizontal and 3 vertical coordinates): Picture1.Scale (0, 0) —(8, 3)

```
0     1     2     3     4     5     6     7     8
1
2
3
```

OR

(to use Variables to create a coordinate system):

```
X = 15:Y = 30
Scale (0, 0) — (X, Y)
```

Uses
- When using the drawing Methods—PSet, Line and Circle—describe the shape, size and location of the drawn objects.
- Position Controls on a Form by adjusting their Top and Left Properties.
- Size or resize Controls using their Height and Width Properties.
- Animate and reposition Controls using the Move Method.
- Position, size or move a Form on the screen, using Screen.Height and Screen.Width, and the Form's Top, Left, Height and Width Properties.

Cautions
- For special purposes, you can create any scale of your preference, starting at –300 if you want. Or you could make the horizontal scale different from the vertical, starting at 500 horizontally but at 100 vertically, for example.
- Changing the Scale automatically resets the ScaleMode, ScaleLeft, Scale-Top, ScaleWidth and ScaleHeight Properties:

  Scale (0, 0) – (10, 10) would change these other Properties as follows:

  > ScaleMode becomes 0 (meaning "user-defined").
  > ScaleWidth and ScaleHeight both become 10.
  > ScaleTop and ScaleLeft both become 0.

- You can create *negative* ScaleWidth and ScaleHeight Properties. When this happens, the coordinates increase from bottom to top, and from right to left—the opposite of the normal way of counting coordinates.

  Scale (3, 3) – (–1, –1) would look like the following:

```
3    2    1    0    –1
2
1
0
–1
```

Example
To illustrate a variety of user-defined coordinate systems, we will draw a line between each coordinate, as on a city map. That way, the coordinate system itself will become visible.

The following Subroutine creates a coordinate system on a Form. The system has 10 vertical and 10 horizontal positions:

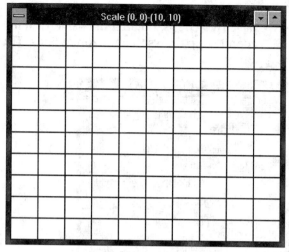

Figure S-1: Scale (0, 0) — (10, 10).

Type the following into the Form_Load Event:

```
Sub Form_Load ()
Show
Scale (0, 0)—(10, 10)
x = scalewidth: y = scaleheight
drawwidth = 2
For i = 0 To x
    Line (i, 0)—(i, y)
Next i
For i = 0 To y
    Line (0, i)—(x, i)
Next i
a$ = "Scale (0, 0)—(10, 10)"
caption = a$
End Sub
```

All the following examples are created using the preceding commands; the only difference is that the line with the Scale command (Scale (0,0) – (10,10)) will be changed.

(Whenever you are putting some drawing into a Form_Load Event, you must use the Show command before doing the drawing. It doesn't matter if you are in the Startup Form or not. The only exception is if you've set the AutoRedraw Property to On (–1), but that slows up the drawing.)

We set the scale to start at 0 and go to 10 in both the horizontal and vertical directions. We find the measurements of the Form, which will be

10 for both X and Y in this case. We thicken the lines slightly with Draw-Width. Then we have two Loops: the first draws vertical lines at each coordinate; the second Loop draws the horizontal lines. Then we show the scale in the Caption of the Form.

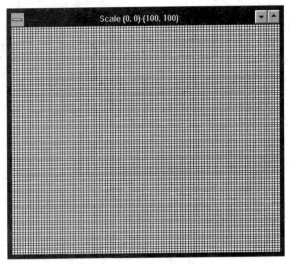

Figure S-2: Scale (0,0) — (100,100).

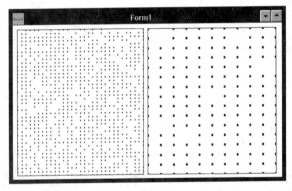

Figure S-3: Scale (0, 0) — (20,4).

For a Picture Box with a different scale than its Form, use the following:

```
Scale (0, 0) — (5, 5)
Picture1.Scale (0, 0) — (8, 16)
```

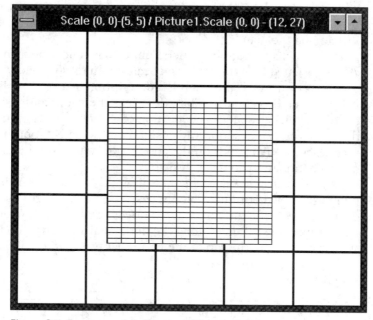

Figure S-4: Because each Form and Picture Box has its own ScaleMode, you can set different coordinates for each.

See also ScaleHeight, ScaleWidth; ScaleLeft, ScaleTop; ScaleMode; Screen

SCALEHEIGHT, SCALEWIDTH PROPERTY

Description See "ScaleMode" for a general overview of coordinate systems.

ScaleHeight and ScaleWidth are most often used to center text or graphics.

Uses • The second most common use for these Properties is to change coordinates. Either during the design of your program or while the program is running, you can *change* the "coordinate system" of a Form, Picture Box or the sheet of paper in the printer.

Each of those objects has a "coordinate system," and the ScaleHeight describes how many coordinate points (or, simply, *coordinates*) exist for vertical measurements within a Form, Picture Box or sheet of paper. ScaleWidth describes the horizontal coordinates.

A *coordinate system* utilizes two sets of measurements, like the typical city map with *A B C D* across the top and *1 2 3 4*, etc., across the left side. By saying C-3, you provide both "coordinates" and specify a particular location on the map.

Using the map example, ScaleHeight tells you how many numbers exist along the left side of the map, and ScaleWidth tells you how many exist across the top. So, ScaleHeight is a description of a vertical distance, of the height of the object. ScaleWidth describes the width and, using the two together, you can specify the location of a unique point on the object. In this way, you can describe any position on the object, but the precision of that description depends on the coordinate system you define, on how many coordinates you make available.

When you change ScaleHeight, ScaleWidth or both, you automatically establish a new coordinate system based on the number you provide. (The default coordinates are no longer in effect.) Setting ScaleWidth to 10, for instance, creates 10 units along the horizontal axis, as if you had placed a special ruler along the top of the Form that was marked off in 10 units:

ScaleWidth = 10

Figure S-5: Establishing a custom coordinate system.

If you do not adjust the ScaleHeight or ScaleWidth Property, Visual Basic sets up a coordinate system of its own based on *twips* (there are 1,440 per inch). Having this many coordinates allows you to very precisely describe the size, shape and position of Controls, Forms and things sent to the printer. But changing the ScaleWidth or ScaleHeight Property (or using the Scale Method, which see) to accomplish the same thing can be useful in a variety of situations where you want to make the mathematics involved in drawing or positioning objects reflect the goals you have in mind. What's more, changing the coordinates in this fashion makes the coordinates *relative* to their container (see "Scale" for the implications of this.)

Use ScaleHeight and ScaleWidth to Reveal Current Coordinates: If you use ScaleHeight, you can also *find out* how many coordinates exist along the left side of a Form, Picture Box or the piece of paper in the printer. You can say X! = ScaleHeight, for instance, to find out how many coordinates are along the left side of the "map" of the Form—this would tell you how vertical positions within the Form are measured. Normally, though, you would not need to find out the coordinate system—you are writing the program, so you know which ScaleMode is in effect.

Used with   Forms, Picture Boxes and the printer

Variables   **Variable type:** Single
(The following examples also work the same way with ScaleWidth.)

To change the Form's coordinates:
```
ScaleHeight = 400
```
OR
```
Picture1.ScaleHeight = 30
```
OR
```
Printer.ScaleHeight = 50
```
OR
```
X = 5000
ScaleHeight = X
```
OR
```
F! = 450000
ScaleHeight = F!   (see Variables for the meaning of the ! symbol)
```
OR (to find out the current ScaleHeight of the Form): Z! = ScaleHeight

Uses   • The most common use of ScaleHeight and ScaleWidth is to measure the *internal* size of a Form—*minus its border or frame.* You can remove a Form's border by changing its BorderStyle Property, but most Forms have some kind of frame around them to enable the user to move them, change their shapes or reduce them to icons. When you are trying to draw graphics, position printed text, animate objects or place Controls on a Form, you often want to know the internal size of the Form. You don't want to be bothered trying to figure in the extra dimensions of the window's border. ScaleHeight and ScaleWidth tell you how tall and wide the Form is—*measured from inside its border.* (The Height and Width Properties tell you the dimensions *including the border.*)

(See "TextHeight" for an example showing how ScaleHeight and Scale-Width are employed to create symmetry.)

The various Scale-related Properties are used for the following purposes:

• When using the drawing Methods—PSet, Line and Circle—describe the shape, size and location of the drawn objects.

• Position Controls on a Form by adjusting their Top and Left Properties.

• Size or resize Controls using their Height and Width Properties.

• Animate and reposition Controls using the Move Method.

• Position, size or move a Form on the screen, using Screen.Height and Screen.Width, and the Form's Top, Left, Height and Width Properties.

Cautions   • Changing *either* the ScaleHeight *or* the ScaleWidth Property leaves the other Property in the default mode. For instance, changing ScaleWidth to

100 will reset the horizontal axis to 100 coordinates but leave the vertical axis (the Y axis along the left side) in twips. Notice which Properties are affected by changing ScaleWidth to 100 in the following:

```
Sub Form_Click ()

Print scalemode
Print scalewidth
Print scaleheight
Print scaleleft
Print scaletop

scalewidth = 100

Print
Print scalemode
Print scalewidth
Print scaleheight
Print scaleleft
Print scaletop

End Sub
```

Results in

```
1
6660
2736
0
0

0
100
2736
0
0
```

Notice that the ScaleMode changed from 1 (the default twips) to 0 ("user-defined"). Although the ScaleWidth changes, the ScaleHeight remains as it was when the twips were in effect. To change both Properties at the same time, using the Scale Method is the most efficient approach (see "Scale").

(The actual numbers reported for the twips in the preceding example will depend on the size of the Form. Note that the new user-defined coordinate, however, will *not* depend on the size of the Form. ScaleWidth will now *always* be 100, regardless of how big or small the Form.)

• You can set up coordinates that start at 10, –30 or anything you want, by setting the ScaleLeft and ScaleTop Properties or by using the Scale Method. You can even use fractions. However, the default for the upper left corner of an object is ScaleLeft = 0, ScaleTop = 0; that usually makes the most sense.

Don't assume that setting the ScaleLeft to 30 will create a *margin*. You'll need to set the CurrentX or CurrentY Properties to create a margin. You cannot lie about the actual *dimensions* of a Form, Picture or sheet of paper. If you set ScaleLeft to 30, that 30 is *still the left edge of the paper*. Calculations, formatting or drawing, therefore, will use 30 as the starting point, the leftmost point, on the sheet. To make a left margin on a sheet of paper in the printer, use something like CurrentX = Printer.ScaleLeft + 20.

The Differences Between the Scale and Measurement Properties: The various Scale Properties are related to the *measurement Properties*–Left, Top, Height and Width. Yet there are some differences:

▪ The measurement Properties of a Form, Picture Box or the printer are *always expressed in twips* (see "ScaleMode"). You can express a Form's ScaleTop Property in inches (because you can change the internal measurement system of a Form), but its *Top* Property remains measured in twips. This discontinuity is not possible, though, for Controls.

▪ The measurement Properties of a Control are always expressed in the coordinate system of the Form or Picture Box within which it resides. For instance, if you put a Command Button on a Form and the Form's Scale-Mode has been set to inches, then the Left, Top, Height and Width of that Button are expressed in inches and fractions of inches. (However, if a Control is placed on a Frame, the mode will be twips, even if the underlying Form is using pixels or some other unit of measurement. A Frame has no ScaleMode.)

▪ The Height and Width of the Screen Object (which see) are expressed in twips. There are no Top and Left Properties for the screen because that is relative to the world outside the computer's domain (the universe).

▪ The measurement Properties describe *external* qualities of an Object: Height and Width describe the size of the Object; Top and Left describe its position relative to a larger Object that contains it. The Scale Properties describe an *internal* grid, which is a way of describing the location and size of things printed or drawn *within* a Form (excluding its border), Picture Box or sheet of paper in the printer.

▪ A Form's measurement Properties *include* its borders and its Title Bar; a Form's Scale Properties do not.

• For Forms and Picture Boxes, the coordinate system describes only the interior; it does not include borders or the Form's Title Bar. However, the coordinate system extends to the ends of the sheet of paper in the printer.

• It is possible to create *negative* ScaleWidth and ScaleHeight Properties. When this happens, the coordinates increase from bottom to top, and from right to left–the opposite of the normal way of counting coordinates:

```
3    2    1    0    -1
2
1
0
-1
```

- Setting either ScaleHeight or ScaleWidth, or both, automatically sets the ScaleMode Property to 0 (user-defined mode).

- Setting the ScaleMode to one of the built-in optional coordinate systems resets ScaleHeight and ScaleWidth to one of these coordinate systems. It also sets ScaleLeft and ScaleTop to 0 and moves the CurrentX and CurrentY to the new coordinates—to the lower right corner, in fact. If you are going to dynamically adjust coordinate systems while your program runs—few will—you might want to look at the effects as illustrated in the Example for ScaleMode.

- Using the Scale Method (which see) resets the ScaleLeft, ScaleTop, Scale-Height, ScaleWidth and ScaleMode Properties in one fell swoop.

- When you iconize a Form, if the Form's AutoRedraw Property is off (0), ScaleHeight and ScaleWidth are changed to reflect the true measurements of the icon. However, if AutoRedraw is on, those two Properties stay the size of the window at its "normal" larger size.

Example These three Picture Boxes will have their coordinate systems altered, but two will have a coarse system with only 150 coordinates, while the other will have 1,200. You can see the coordinate systems start to become visible after randomly drawing on these objects.

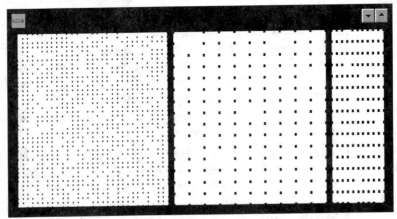

Figure S-6: The coordinate systems become clear after random dots begin to fill in the pattern.

```
Sub Form_Load ()
Show

Picture1.Scale (0, 0)–(30, 40)
Picture2.Scale (0, 0)–(10, 15)
Picture3.Scale (0, 0)–(10, 15)

Picture1.DrawWidth = 2
Picture2.DrawWidth = 4
Picture3.DrawWidth = 4

For i = 1 To 1500
    x = Int(Rnd * 31)
    y = Int(Rnd * 41)
    Picture1.PSet (x, y)
Next i

For i = 1 To 500
    x = Int(Rnd * 11)
    y = Int(Rnd * 16)
    Picture2.PSet (x, y)
Next i

For i = 1 To 500
    x = Int(Rnd * 11)
    y = Int(Rnd * 16)
    Picture3.PSet (x, y)
Next i
End Sub
```

First, put three Picture Boxes on a Form. Then use the Show command to make the Form visible so you can see the graphics.

The first picture is given a coordinate system of 30 x 40. The other two pictures are treated identically in this program, except that the shape of the third picture is narrow, which illustrates how setting a custom, user-defined coordinate system makes the coordinates *relative* to the shape of the object. The narrower picture has exactly as many coordinates as the middle picture, but their relative positions are deformed by the shape of the picture itself.

Appropriate DrawWidths Are Set: Picture1 will have a total of 1,200 coordinates; the other two pictures have 150 coordinates, so we give those two pictures larger dots.

Now Picture1 is filled randomly with dots. However, if you create enough random dotting, then the underlying grid, the coordinate system, is revealed. We get a random X (horizontal) position between 0 and 30, and a Y (vertical) position between 0 and 40 (see "Rnd"). Then we put a dot on that position. And we keep on doing this 500 times. You'll get an error message, "Overflow," if you try to draw to a coordinate that's not available. In this case, an X higher than 30 or a Y higher than 40 would be "off the coordinate system" and is illegal.

S . . . **1041**

The other pictures are similarly filled with random dots, and the shape of their coordinate system emerges.

See also   Scale; ScaleLeft, ScaleTop; ScaleMode; Screen

PROPERTY

Description   Coordinates are like the marks on a ruler that you place across the top of a sheet of paper. ScaleLeft describes which number is at the left side of an object—which number you start measuring with. You normally position a ruler so that 0 is at the left side of the paper, the 1-inch marker is one inch over, and so on. In Figure S-7, ScaleLeft = 0:

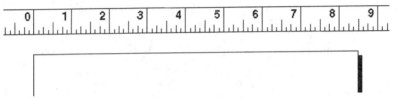

Figure S-7: You normally place a ruler so that the left side of the page starts at 0.

(In this example, the ScaleMode Property is "inches," and the ScaleWidth Property is 8.5 for a typical 8 1/2- x 11-inch sheet of paper.)

However, you might prefer to adjust where you start measuring—you might want to slide the ruler over. Figure S-8 is an example of ScaleLeft = 2, so we've repositioned the ruler. The first inch over from the left side of the paper is 3. As you can see, changing ScaleLeft doesn't affect the size of the Object, or even the number of "units" or coordinates that measure it—there are still 8 1/2 inches. But now that the ruler has been moved, ScaleLeft = 2 and all the other "horizontal coordinates" (the inch markers) are similarly offset. The rightmost coordinate is now 10.5, not 8.5:

Figure S-8: You *can* shift the starting point for measurement. Here we began at the second inch on the ruler.

ScaleLeft describes the first "horizontal coordinate," the number used to describe the first measurement on the left side of a Form, Picture Box or sheet of paper in the printer. ScaleTop describes the first measurement on the top. Using ScaleTop is like placing a ruler along the left side of a Form, which allows you now to describe vertical coordinates.

Usually both ScaleLeft and ScaleTop are zero—the default in Visual Basic. (See "ScaleMode" for a general overview of coordinate systems.)

Using ScaleHeight and ScaleWidth to Change the Starting Point Coordinates: Either during the design of your program or while the program is running, you can *change* the "coordinate system" of a Form, Picture Box or the sheet of paper in the printer. Each of those Objects has a coordinate system to describe locations inside the Object.

A *coordinate system* utilizes two sets of measurements, like the typical city map with *A B C D* across the top and *1 2 3 4*, etc., across the left side. By saying C-3, you provide both "coordinates" and specify a particular location on the map.

Using the map example, ScaleHeight tells you how many numbers exist along the left side of the map, and ScaleWidth tells you how many exist across the top. So, ScaleHeight is a description of a vertical location; ScaleWidth, of a horizontal location. And the two together provide the location of a unique point on the Object; but the precision of that description depends on the coordinate system (set by ScaleMode), on how many coordinates are available.

ScaleLeft and ScaleTop determine whether the first coordinates (the leftmost and topmost coordinates) are zero or something unusual. (They could be negative or fractional as well.)

The Default Coordinates Are Replaced by Your New System: When you change ScaleHeight, ScaleWidth or both, you automatically establish a new coordinate system based on the number you provide. (The default coordinates are no longer in effect.) Setting ScaleWidth to 10, for instance, creates 10 units along the horizontal axis, as if you had placed a special ruler along the top of the Form that was marked off in 10 units. Then, setting ScaleLeft to 6 would mean that there were 10 "markers" along the top, starting at 6 and ending at 16. If you then said PSet (11, 0), a dot would appear on the Form in the middle—11 is half the distance between 6 and 16. The other coordinate here, 0, would cause the dot to appear at the top of the Form, 0 vertically.

If you do not adjust the ScaleMode, ScaleHeight or ScaleWidth Property, Visual Basic sets up a coordinate system of its own based on *twips* (there are 1,440 twips per inch). Having this many coordinates allows you to very precisely describe the size, shape and position of Controls, Forms and things sent to the printer. But changing the ScaleMode, ScaleWidth, or ScaleHeight Property (or using the Scale Method, which see) can be useful in a variety of situations where you want to make the mathematics involved in drawing or positioning Objects reflect the goals you have in mind or the range of the data you are displaying. Changing ScaleLeft or ScaleTop is less common, though, because you usually calculate positions starting from 0. How far is it to Washington from here? You don't think of "here" as 30 miles. You calculate the distance by using your current location as 0 and counting up.

Using ScaleLeft and ScaleTop to Find Out What Coordinates Are in Effect: If you use ScaleLeft you can also *find out* which is the first coordinate. You can say X! = ScaleLeft, for instance, to see if 0 is the first unit of measurement in the currently active coordinate system. You can use ScaleTop to do the same thing, but with it you are counting down vertically from the top of the Form (or other Object). Normally, though, you would not need to find out the coordinate system this way—you are writing the program, so you know that ScaleMode, ScaleLeft and all the rest of the Scale Properties are in effect.

Used with Forms, Picture Boxes or the sheet of paper in the printer

Variables **Variable type:** Single

(To change the ScaleLeft Property of a Form): ScaleLeft = 100

OR (to change the ScaleLeft Property of a Picture Box):

Picture1.ScaleLeft = –10

OR (to change the ScaleTop Property of the printer): Printer.ScaleTop = 5

OR (to use a Variable):

X = 5000
ScaleTop = X

OR

F! = 450000
ScaleLeft = F! (see Variables for the meaning of the ! symbol)

OR (to find out the current ScaleTop of the Form): Z! = ScaleTop

Uses • When using the drawing Methods—PSet, Line and Circle—describe the shape, size and location of the drawn objects.

• Position Controls on a Form by adjusting their Top and Left Properties to coordinates of the Form.

• Size or resize Controls using their Height and Width Properties in relation to the coordinates of their Form.

• Animate and reposition Controls using the Move Method.

• Position, size or move a Form on the screen, using Screen.Height and Screen.Width, and the Form's Top, Left, Height and Width Properties.

Cautions • You can set up coordinates that start at 10, –30 or anything you want, by setting the ScaleLeft and ScaleTop Properties or by using the Scale Method.

You can even use fractions. However, the default for the upper left corner of an Object is ScaleLeft = 0, ScaleTop = 0; that usually makes the most sense.

• The various Scale Properties are related to the *measurement Properties*—Left, Top, Height and Width. Yet there are some differences:

▪ The measurement Properties of a Form, Picture Box or the printer are always expressed as twips (see "ScaleMode"). You can express a Form's ScaleTop Property in inches (because you can change the internal measurement system of a Form), while its *Top* Property will remain measured in twips. This discontinuity is not possible, though, for Controls.

▪ The measurement Properties of a Control are always expressed in the coordinate system of the Form or Picture Box within which they reside. For instance, if you put a Command Button on a Form and the Form's Scale-Mode has been set to inches, then the Left, Top, Height and Width of that Button are expressed in inches and fractions of inches.

▪ The Height and Width of the Screen Object (which see) are expressed in twips. There are no Top and Left Properties for the screen because that is relative to the world outside the computer's domain (the universe).

▪ The measurement Properties describe *external* qualities of an Object: Height and Width describe the size of the Object; Top and Left describe its position relative to a larger Object that contains it.

▪ The Scale Properties describe an *internal* grid, which is a way of describing the location and size of things printed or drawn within a Form, Picture Box or sheet of paper in the printer.

▪ A Form's measurement Properties *include* its borders and its Title Bar; a Form's Scale Properties do not.

• Leave ScaleLeft and ScaleTop to their default value of 0 unless you have a special reason to change them. When you do change them, you drift into a geometry that is not easily or intuitively understood by humans. Computers have no problem—it's all the same to them. But humans prefer to think of an 8- x 10-inch photo as meaning that the first horizontal inch is, in fact, one inch from the left edge of the photo. Resetting ScaleLeft or ScaleTop changes all this.

• For Forms and Picture Boxes, the coordinate system describes only the interior; that is, it does not include borders or the Form's Title Bar. However, it extends to the ends of the sheet of paper in the printer.

• It is possible to create *negative* ScaleWidth and ScaleHeight Properties. When this happens, the coordinates increase from bottom to top, and from right to left—the opposite of the normal way of counting coordinates:

```
3    2    1    0    -1
2
1
0
-1
```

• Setting either ScaleHeight or ScaleWidth, or both, automatically sets the ScaleMode Property to 0 (user-defined mode).

• Setting the ScaleMode to one of the built-in optional coordinate systems resets ScaleHeight and ScaleWidth to one of these coordinate systems. It also sets ScaleLeft and ScaleTop to 0, and moves CurrentX and CurrentY to the new coordinates–to the lower right corner, in fact. If you are going to dynamically adjust coordinate systems while your program runs–few will– you might want to look at the effects as illustrated in the Example for ScaleMode.

• Using the Scale Method (which see) resets the ScaleLeft, ScaleTop, ScaleHeight, ScaleWidth and ScaleMode Properties in one fell swoop.

Example The large dot in the Picture Box shown in Figure S-9 moves when you adjust the Scroll Bars and leaves a trail of small dots to show where you've been as you move about the coordinate system. ScaleLeft and ScaleTop are both zero, the default, so X or Y in the Label at the top will be 0 when you are at the left or top of the Picture.

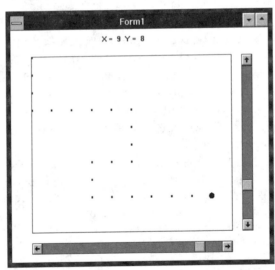

Figure S-9: Move through the coordinate system, revealing it as you go.

Some preliminary conditions are set up in the Form_Load Event. The coordinate system is set to 10 x 10–ten units vertically and ten horizontally. And the units of measurement for the Scroll Bars are also set to ten:

```
Sub Form_Load ()

picture1.ScaleWidth = 10
picture1.ScaleHeight = 10

hscroll1.max = 10
vscroll1.max = 10

End Sub
```

Moving the vertical Box replaces the large dot with a small dot and then draws a new large dot in the new position, the new coordinate:

```
Sub VScroll1_Change ()

Static lastx As Integer
Static lasty As Integer

picture1.drawmode = 6
picture1.PSet (lastx, lasty)

picture1.drawmode = 1
picture1.drawwidth = 3
picture1.PSet (lastx, lasty)
picture1.drawwidth = 10

x = hscroll1.value
y = vscroll1.value
label1.caption = "X = " + Str$(x) + " Y = " + Str$(y)
picture1.PSet (x, y)

lastx = x
lasty = y
End Sub
```

First, we establish two Static Variables (they will hold their information even when Visual Basic leaves this Sub). These Variables, *lastx* and *lasty*, tell us the coordinates of the previously drawn large dot. We now want to cover it up, so we set the DrawMode to 6 (this "inverts" the ForeColor with the BackColor—in this case, turning black to white and therefore erasing the large dot).

Now we want to leave a small dot behind to show where we've been, so we set the DrawMode back to the default (1 means to draw using black) and make the DrawWidth fairly small, 3. After drawing the little dot, we set the DrawWidth back to 10.

We find the current coordinates by looking at the values of the two Scroll Bars, then display their respective values in the Label at the top and draw the large dot. Finally, we save the current position.

Changing the Horizontal Scroll Bar should have the same effects as changing the Vertical Bar: replace the dot, print a new dot and update the Label. Because the effects are identical, we can simply name the VScroll Change Event in the HScroll Change Event—treating the VScroll Change Event as if it were a Subroutine (see "Sub"). Events are, in fact, Subroutines by another name and can be "called" by simply providing their name:

```
Sub HScroll1_Change ()
    VScroll1_Change
End Sub
```

See also   CurrentX, CurrentY; Scale; ScaleHeight, ScaleWidth; ScaleMode; Screen

SCALEMODE

Description   ScaleMode determines which of the seven built-in Visual Basic "coordinate systems" will be used for a Form, Picture Box or the sheet of paper in the printer.

A *coordinate system* utilizes two sets of measurements, like the typical city map with *A B C D* across the top and *1 2 3 4*, etc., down the left side. By saying C-3, you provide both "coordinates"–a horizontal and a vertical coordinate–and thereby point to a particular location on the map.

By convention, the horizontal coordinate is always given first and then the vertical coordinate. PSet (14, 2000) puts a dot on the Form 14 twips over from the left side of the Form and 2000 twips down from the top.

Visual Basic provides several built-in coordinate systems from which you can choose–inches, millimeters, etc.–but the default system is twips. It is a very precise unit of measurement because there are 1,440 twips per inch.

If you have not changed the coordinate system (by adjusting ScaleHeight, ScaleWidth or using the Scale Method), you would draw a dot on a Form one inch from the left side of the Form and two inches down from the top, like this:

```
PSet (1440, 2880)
```

(Because there are 1,440 twips per inch, two inches for the vertical measurement is 2,880.)

If you set the coordinate system to *inches*, though, the same dot would be drawn in the same spot with the following:

```
ScaleMode = 5   '(this changes the coordinate system to inches)
PSet(1,2)
```

(Screen resolutions and sizes vary, so the actual position may not be precisely 1 x 2 inches. However, a printer will accurately position items coordinated via twips.)

Used with   Forms, Picture Boxes and a sheet of paper in the printer

Variables   **Variable type:** Integer (enumerated)

There are seven built-in ScaleModes and one "user-defined," meaning that you decide:

```
ScaleMode = one of the following
```

0 User-defined (the ScaleMode is automatically set to 0 if you create your own coordinate system by using the Scale Method or by adjusting any of the following Properties–ScaleWidth, ScaleHeight, ScaleLeft, Scale-Top.)

1 Twips (the default, 1,440 per "logical" inch. *Logical* in this context means that there are 1,440 twips per inch when using the printer. However, because monitor screens differ both in size and in resolution, 1,440 may or may not be precisely an inch on your screen.)

2 Point (72 points per logical inch. Points are a measurement used by typographers and printers to describe the size of different character fonts.)

3 Pixel (the smallest point that your monitor can display. You can usually see a pixel if you look closely at a light gray or at a color gradient—a place where two colors are being blended on the screen. On my monitor, there are 120 pixels per logical inch.)

   To find out how many pixels per logical inch your monitor has, enter the following:

```
Sub Form_Click ()

X! = ScaleWidth
ScaleMode = 3
Y! = ScaleWidth
Inches! = X! / 1440
Print "The Form is currently "; Inches!; " inches wide."
Print "It is "; X!; " Twips wide."
Print "It is "; Y!; " Pixels wide."
Pixels! = Y! / Inches!
Print "Your monitor has "; Pixels!; " pixels per logical inch."

End Sub
```

4 Character (120 twips wide, 240 twips high. Character-based text and graphics are a holdover from earlier computer operating systems, like DOS, where each character printed onscreen was exactly the same size. Also, in some DOS screen modes, attempts at graphics were confined to this same feeble and gross granularity. Efforts to create attractive screens in DOS are disappointingly cartoon-like because of the lack of resolution when you have space for only 80 x 25 pieces of information: 2,000 cells are not many. DOS displays are usually 80 characters per line by 25 lines. However, Windows offers high resolution graphics as well as proportional character fonts. Windows characters are usually of varying widths and heights. The width of the letter *i* is, for instance, less than the width of *m*. The only common exception in Windows is the "Courier" font, which is derived from typewriters and is nonproportional, sometimes also called *monospaced*.)

5 Inch

6 Millimeter (roughly 25 per inch)

7 Centimeter (roughly 2.5 per inch)

To change the ScaleMode Property, you can adjust it from within the Properties Window for a Form or a Picture Box (the printer must be set from within your program).

To change the ScaleMode while your program is running:
To set the Form to twips, the default:

ScaleMode = 1

OR (to set a Picture Box's coordinate system to inches):

Picture1.ScaleMode = 5

OR (to set the printer to a millimeter system):

Printer.ScaleMode = 6

OR (to find out what a ScaleMode is while your program is running):

X = Picture1.ScaleMode

Uses
• You can use ScaleMode to set up a new coordinate system quickly because Visual Basic automatically responds to one of the seven possible ScaleMode options.

The various Scale-related Properties are used for the following purposes, and all involve *internal* (borders and Title Bars are ignored) locations within an Object.

• When using the drawing Methods—PSet, Line and Circle—you can describe the shape, size and location of the drawn Objects.

• You can position Controls on a Form by adjusting their Top and Left Properties to coordinates of the Form.

• You can size or resize Controls using their Height and Width Properties in relation to the coordinates of their Form.

• You can animate and reposition Controls using the Move Method.

• You can position, size or move a Form on the screen, using Screen.Height and Screen.Width, and the Form's Top, Left, Height and Width Properties.

Cautions
• When you change the ScaleMode, the ScaleWidth and ScaleHeight Properties are reset to appropriate values representing the Form's width as measured by the new coordinate system (likewise for a Picture Box or the sheet of paper in the printer). In the same fashion, the CurrentX and CurrentY Properties (which are like a "cursor," pointing to the location where the next Printing or drawing would occur) are reset to reflect the new coordinate mode. Finally, the ScaleLeft and ScaleTop Properties are reset to 0.

For Forms and Picture Boxes, the coordinate system is only for the interior; that is, it does not include borders or the Form's Title Bar. However, it extends to the ends of the sheet of paper in the printer.

The various Scale Properties are related to the *measurement Properties*—Left, Top, Height and Width. Yet there are some differences:

▪ The measurement Properties of a Form, Picture Box or the Printer are always expressed as twips (see "ScaleMode"). It is possible for you to express a Form's ScaleTop Property, for example, in inches (because you can always choose to change the internal measurement system of a Form), yet its *Top* Property must remain measured, as a Form's Top Property always is, in twips. This discontinuity is not possible, though, for Controls.

▪ The measurement Properties of a Control are always expressed in the coordinate system of the Form or Picture Box within which they reside. For instance, if you put a Command Button on a Form and the Form's Scale-Mode has been set to inches, then the Left, Top, Height, and Width of that Button are expressed in inches and fractions of inches.

▪ The Height and Width of the Screen Object (which see) are expressed in twips. There are no Top and Left Properties for the screen because those coordinates are beyond the computer; the position of the monitor is relative to the universe itself.

▪ The measurement Properties describe *external* qualities of an object: Height and Width describe the size of the Object; Top and Left describe its position relative to a larger Object that contains it.

▪ The Scale Properties describe an *internal* grid, which is a way of describing the location and size of things printed or drawn within a Form, Picture Box or sheet of paper in the printer.

▪ A Form's measurement Properties *include* its borders and its Title Bar; a Form's Scale Properties do not.

• You can set up coordinates that start at 10, 30 or anything you want, by setting the ScaleLeft and ScaleTop Properties or by using the Scale Method. You can even use fractions. However, the default for the upper left corner of an Object is ScaleLeft = 0, ScaleTop = 0; that generally makes the most sense.

• Using the Scale Method (which see) resets the ScaleLeft, ScaleTop, ScaleHeight, ScaleWidth and ScaleMode Properties in one fell swoop.

Example   Setting the ScaleMode to one of the built-in optional coordinate systems resets ScaleHeight and ScaleWidth to that new coordinate system. It also sets ScaleLeft and ScaleTop to 0, and moves the CurrentX and CurrentY to the new coordinates—to the lower right corner, in fact. If you are going to adjust coordinate systems dynamically while your program runs (few will) you might want to look at the effects as illustrated in Figure S-10:

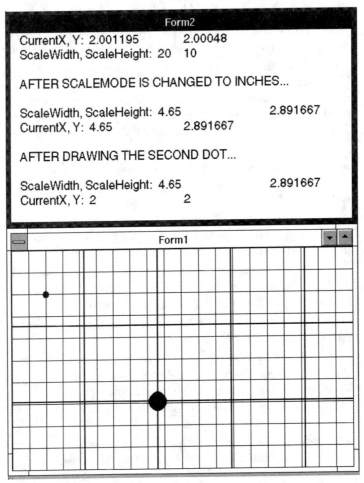

Figure S-10: Although few situations call for this, you *can* change the coordinate system while a program is running. (Don't try to decipher this figure unless you think you might need dynamic coordinate systems.)

This program starts out with a user-defined custom coordinate system, prints a dot and then prints current Scale Properties on Form2. Next, the ScaleMode is changed to inches (option 5). Then the Properties are printed again and another dot PSet, at the same coordinates (2, 2). But now the coordinates are expressed as inches, so the dot goes to a different place. Once again we print the Properties.

For both systems, we draw a grid showing the coordinate system in its entirety. (See "Scale Method" for an explanation of the Loops that reveal the grid.)

```
Sub Form_Click ()
Form2.Show
DrawWidth = 10
ScaleHeight = 10
ScaleWidth = 20
PSet (2, 2)
Form2.Print " CurrentX, Y: "; CurrentX, CurrentY
Form2.Print " ScaleWidth, ScaleHeight: "; ScaleWidth, ScaleHeight
DrawWidth = 1
x = ScaleWidth: y = ScaleHeight
For i = 0 To x
    Line (i, 0)— (i, y)
Next i
For i = 0 To y
    Line (0, i)— (x, i)
Next i
ScaleMode = 5
Form2.Print
Form2.Print " AFTER SCALEMODE IS CHANGED TO INCHES... "
Form2.Print
Form2.Print " ScaleWidth, ScaleHeight: "; ScaleWidth, ScaleHeight
Form2.Print " CurrentX, Y: "; CurrentX, CurrentY
x = ScaleWidth: y = ScaleHeight
DrawWidth = 2
For i = 0 To x
    Line (i, 0)— (i, y)
Next i
For i = 0 To y
    Line (0, i)— (x, i)
Next i
DrawWidth = 30
PSet (2, 2)
Form2.Print
Form2.Print " AFTER DRAWING THE SECOND DOT... "
Form2.Print
Form2.Print " ScaleWidth, ScaleHeight: "; ScaleWidth, ScaleHeight
Form2.Print " CurrentX, Y: "; CurrentX, CurrentY
End Sub
```

(Drawing the grid and printing the Properties are repeated. Repetitive tasks like this are usually put into a Subroutine to save space and to simplify the structure of a program. But for purposes of clarity here, we've left them "as is." See "Sub.")

See also   CurrentX, CurrentY; Scale; ScaleHeight, ScaleWidth; ScaleLeft, ScaleTop; Screen

CALE WIDTH

See   ScaleHeight

CREEN   OBJECT

Description   The Screen Object can provide several pieces of information while your program is running:

• What is the width or height of the screen (as measured in "twips," see "ScaleMode")?

• Which Form is currently active (which one has the "focus," meaning, which Form is lit up and can react to keys that the user might press)? Or which Control is active (ActiveControl)?

• How many screen fonts, styles of characters, are available to be printed on the screen?

• What are the names of those fonts?

• What MousePointer is active on the screen?

The Screen Object could be thought of as an all-encompassing entity that can tie into Controls in your program. The Screen Object is seldom used in most programs. The Screen command offers you a method of accessing a Form or Control without knowing or using the actual Name of the Form or Control. You could also use the Screen command to change the screen mouse pointer, change the font, etc., of a Form or Control while the program is running.

Screen.ActiveControl cannot be changed while a program is running, the way other Properties can. ActiveControl is used to reference a Property of a Control. In other words, X$ = Screen.ActiveControl: Print X$ would result in "Command1" if Command1 is the active Control. (See "SetFocus" for the meaning of active in this context.) With ActiveControl you can access only the active Control on the current Form; you can't, however, *make* a particular Control active, cannot give it the focus—likewise your program cannot change the ActiveForm Property.

Used with   Subroutines usually

Variables   To access a Property of the currently active Control. (Assume you have three Text Boxes on a Form. The following will print the text from the Text Box that has the "focus" (see "GotFocus")):

```
Sub Form_Click ()

x$ = Screen.ActiveControl.Text
Print x$
End Sub
```

OR (to paste the contents of the Clipboard into the Text Box with the "focus"): Screen.ActiveControl.SelText = Clipboard.GetText()

OR (to find out about a Property of the Form which has the "focus"): X = Screen.ActiveForm.Backcolor

OR (to find how many fonts are available to be displayed on the screen, using the FontName Property of a Form or Control): X = Screen.FontCount

OR (to get a list of all the font names that are available for display using the FontName Property of a Form or Control):

```
For i = 0 to Screen.FontCount −1
    Print Screen.Fonts(i)
Next i
```

OR (to find out the height or width of the user's computer screen, a measurement *always* expressed in twips, 1,440 per inch. See "ScaleMode"):

```
X = Screen.Width
Y = Screen.Height
```

OR (to change the Screen mouse pointer while the program is running. See "MousePointer"): Screen.MousePointer = 5

OR (to find out what the Screen mouse pointer is): X = Screen.MousePointer

Uses   • Let a Subroutine or Function know which Form or Control has the focus. This use of Screen involves the ActiveControl Property, which see.

• Offer the user the option of changing the default character font. See the example of Screen.Fonts in the preceding section.

• Find out where to place windows (Forms) or how many can be displayed on the user's monitor by getting the Screen.Height and Screen.Width.

• Find out or change the Properties of the Form or Control that currently has the "focus" (see "GotFocus") while the program is running.

• Change the appearance of the mouse pointer when it moves away from a window and onto the background screen.

• Center a Form on the screen with this technique and its variations:

```
Sub Form_Load ()
  x = .9 '(this will make the form fill 90% of the screen)

  Form1.Height = x * Screen.Height
  Form1.Width = x * Screen.Width
  Form1.Left = (Screen.Width − Form1.Width) / 2
  Form1.Top = (Screen.Height − Form1.Height) / 2

End Sub
```

Cautions
• The Printer "Object" operates in a fashion similar to the Screen Object. See "Printer."

• If your program has more than one Form, you will have to involve the SetFocus or GotFocus commands to access individual Controls when using the Screen.ActiveControl or Screen.ActiveForm commands.

Example
If you want to center a Form on the screen, use this formula:

```
Sub Form_Load ()
    left = (screen.width − width) / 2
    top = (screen.height − height) / 2
End Sub
```

To make the Form a certain percentage of the screen size:

```
percent = .75
height = screen.height * percent
width = screen.width * percent
```

Screen Properties
ActiveControl • ActiveForm • FontCount • Fonts • Height • MousePointer Width

See also
GotFocus; Printer; SetFocus

SCROLL .... EVENT

Description
The Scroll Event repeatedly triggers if the user drags (slides) the "thumb" (or "Scroll Box") inside a Horizontal or Vertical Scroll Bar.

This is distinct from a Scroll Bar's Change Event, which reports if the user clicks on one of the tabs on either end of a Bar, or within the Bar. In fact, Change is triggered only *after* the user releases the thumb. By contrast, the Scroll Event is *continually triggered during the dragging.*

Used with
Horizontal and Vertical Scroll Bars only

Variables

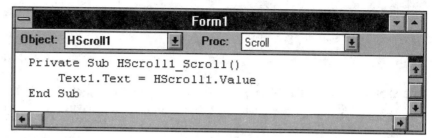

Figure S-11: Place any commands that you want continually updated within the Scroll Event, not the Change Event.

Uses

The Change Event is not triggered *while* the user drags the thumb within a Scroll Bar, but the *Scroll* Event is. In fact, Scroll is repeatedly triggered. This allows you to provide the user with continually updated graphic, color display, numeric or text data. The user can then get another view of the degree of change he or she is causing by dragging the thumb. (See the Example.)

Example

To graphically see the distinction between the Scroll and Change Events, put a Text Box and a Horizontal Scroll Bar on a Form. In the Form_Load Event, set the Min and Max Properties:

```
Sub Form_Load ()
    hscroll1.Min = 0
    hscroll1.Max = 200
End Sub
```

Then cause a "change" or "scroll" to report its status in the Text Box:

```
Sub HScroll1_Change ()
    text1.Text = "Change " + HScroll1.Value
End Sub
```

```
Sub HScroll1_Scroll ()
    text1.Text = "Scroll " + HScroll1.Value
End Sub
```

Press F5 and run the program. Notice that when you *click* anywhere on the Scroll Bar (on the Bar itself or on the tabs at each end), you only trigger the Change Event. However, clicking and holding down the mouse button while you slide the thumb along the Scroll Bar repeatedly triggers a Scroll Event. The Change Event triggers only once—after the user finishes sliding the thumb and releases the mouse button.

See also

Change; Horizontal Scroll Bar

SCROLL BARS

CONTROL

Description A Scroll Bar is an *analog* Control, like the volume knob on a stereo. The position of an analog Control is an analogy, a symbol that shows the status of the thing it adjusts.

Such Controls can be "turned all the way up" or "all the way down" or can be moved gradually between the extremes. Scroll Bars are, therefore, appropriate for allowing the user to adjust things that have a range of possible states, such as background color. This range of states should also be contiguous, like the way the colors of a rainbow blend into each other across the spectrum.

There are Horizontal and Vertical Bars, but there is no functional difference between the two. Their orientation is strictly a matter of convenience for the user—"turning the pages" of a diary would suggest a Horizontal Bar. Moving vertically through scrolling text would suggest a Vertical Bar, as would a temperature gauge, in imitation of thermometers.

Variables Scroll Bars have the usual assortment of Properties, such as Enabled, Height and Visible. You can set them in the Properties Window when designing a program, or change them while a program is running.

Five Properties are unique to Scroll Bars—Max, Min, LargeChange, Small-Change and Value.

Value: The *Value* Property tells you the current numerical equivalent of the position of the movable square (sometimes called the "thumb" or Scroll Box) within a Scroll Bar. The Min and Max Properties determine the range of numbers possible for the Value Property.

Max and Min: By default, Min is 0 and Max is 32,768. You normally adjust Max (and sometimes Min) to reflect the range of whatever the bar is supposed to control. If there are 214 entries in your "Car Repair" computerized handbook, you would set Min to 1 and Max to 214.

There are 256 possible shades of the color red in Windows. To let the user select a particular red, put a Picture Box and a Horizontal Scroll Bar on a Form. Then set the Max Property in the Form_Load Event:

```
Sub Form_Load ()
    hscroll1.max = 255
End Sub
```

Then adjust the RGB color from within the Scroll Bar's Change Event:

```
Sub HScroll1_Change ()
    picture1.backcolor = RGB(hscroll1.value, 0, 0)
End Sub
```

The amount of red will now change relative to the Value Property of the Scroll Bar. If the user moves the tab inside the bar, the color changes.

LargeChange and SmallChange: A Scroll Bar in Windows can be moved three ways. The user can drag the interior "thumb" to position it anywhere within the bar. Clicking on the arrows at either end of the bar moves a small amount (defined by SmallChange). And clicking *within* the bar moves a large amount (LargeChange).

The LargeChange and SmallChange Properties default to 1, but this number is often too little, especially for LargeChange. You'll usually want to set LargeChange to, say, 1/10 or 1/20 of the Max Property.

Uses
• Some people have used Scroll Bars to report visually the status of something, like a gauge that keeps moving up in proportion to how many records have been saved to disk. If you are saving 150 records, you can have a Scroll Bar reflect the progress of the storage activity. You would set the Max Property to the number of records involved, and then, inside the Loop that saves the records, add this:

```
Max = NumberOfRecords

For I = 1 to NumberOfRecords
    Put #1, Record(I)
    HScroll1.Value = I
Next I
```

Using a Scroll Bar in this way, however, results in a crude visual image. What's more, most people are used to seeing Scroll Bars employed to adjust something, not to display the condition of some changing event. You'd do better to construct a gauge that looks like a proper gauge, using the Line command to slowly fill a Picture Box, for instance. To see how to create attractive gauges, look at the Example under "Refresh."

Cautions
The Change Events of Scroll Bars Are Too Sensitive: *Setting any of the Properties of a Scroll Bar while the program is running will trigger the Scroll Bar's Change Event.* This can create unsettling effects, particularly if you are printing or drawing (with Circle, Line or PSet) to a window. You don't want the window repeatedly drawn while you're just trying to define some of the Properties of a Scroll Bar and get the program started. Rapid, repeated triggering of Events while drawing and printing will make the screen spasm and undulate as the computer struggles to redraw the same graphic elements over and over.

An aside: Some programmers have suggested that Events should never be triggered by anything that happens within the program itself; only clicking or other actions by the user should cause an Event to react. This would indeed simplify things for the programmer (you wouldn't have to set up a Global Variable to keep track of whether the user or the program had triggered an Event), but it would also eliminate efficiencies such as triggering one Event from within another just as you would "call" a Subroutine.

The usual solution to the problem of rapid, repeated triggering of Events while drawing and printing is to use the Properties Window to adjust the Properties of a Scroll Bar while you are creating the program.

However, sometimes you are forced to set the Value Properties of a Scroll Bar while the program is running. For instance, if a Scroll Bar is to represent the current month, you cannot know in advance what the current month will be. Thus, you can't set the Max and Min Properties to the correct number of days in that month (see the Example under "Weekday").

To prevent triggering a Scroll Bar's Change Event, set up a Global Variable in a Module or, as shown here, a Formwide variable in the General Declarations section of the Form:

```
Dim Startup As Integer
```

Then, in the Form_Load Event, where you are adjusting a Scroll Bar's Properties, set the Variable Startup to 1:

```
Sub Form_Load ()

Startup = 1
HScroll1.Max = 29
HScroll1.Min = 1
HScroll1.LargeChange = 2
Startup = 0
HScroll1.Value = 4

End Sub
```

By putting 1 into the Variable *Startup*, you can prevent a Change Event from performing its jobs (drawing, in this example) *until we reset Startup to 0*. As the first command in the Change Event, enter the following:

```
Sub HScroll1_Change()

If Startup = 1 Then Exit Sub
```

You will exit this Event if the Variable Startup contains a 1. Notice that in the Form_Load Event we finally changed Startup = 0, after we have finished establishing the Properties of the Scroll Bar and can safely allow its Change Event to trigger. We *do* want the screen drawn once, so we let the adjustment to HScroll1's Value trigger its Change Event.

Dealing with a Huge Range: The highest you can set the Max Property is 32,767. However, an RGB color for a Control can range from 0 (black) to higher than 16 million (white = (32768 * 512) – 1).

You can cover a huge range with a Scroll Bar, but the coverage will have to skip some of the possible values within the range—in other words, the coverage will be rather rough (heavy-duty "granularity"). In the following example, for instance, each SmallChange to the bar will increase the value by 512, so we will be able to select only every 512th number.

To handle ranges larger than 32,767, you can multiply the "value" of the Scroll Bar by whatever is needed to cover the range you want. In this case, we could leave Min at 0 and set Max to 32,767. Then, to allow movement through all possible millions of RGB colors, enter the following:

```
Sub VScroll1_Change ()
    R& = vscroll1.Value
    R& = R& + 1
    Form1.BackColor = (R& * 512) − 1
End Sub
```

Here we've created a *Long Integer* Variable by attaching the ampersand (&) symbol, which is necessary to hold numbers as large as 32768 * 512. (See "Variables.")

Next, we pick off the current Value of the Scroll Bar and add 1 to it (because white is 32768 * 512, but the Max allowed for a Scroll Bar is 32,767). Then we multiply the Value times 512 but subtract 1 because there's a slight kink. A Color Property can handle an RGB number of 16,777,215 but chokes on 16,777,216.

Note that because the preceding Subroutine hits only every 512th number within this range, finding another way to deal with such huge ranges would probably be better if you want fine control. Perhaps dividing this task among *three* Scroll Bars—each would need to range only from 0 to 255—is the ticket. See the example under "RGB."

Scroll Bars provide the user with an intuitive and vivid way to adjust various kinds of information—slide things around onscreen, resize things, change their colors, flip through the "pages" of a "book," etc. Scroll Bars are an important tool for graphical user interfaces.

You can set both Max and Min Properties anywhere from −32,768 to 32,767.

If you don't change Max and Min, they default to 32,767 and 0, respectively.

You can reverse the direction of a Scroll Bar. Normally, Max is at the far right of a Horizontal Bar and at the bottom of a Vertical Bar. However, if you set the Max Property to a number *lower than* the Min Property, the Max flips and becomes the far left of a Horizontal Bar and the top of a Vertical Bar.

Example   We'll make a diary for Becky. She'll be able to move through the "pages" by using a Scroll Bar, and the current date will appear at the top of each page.

First, put a Picture Box, a Text Box, a Label and a Horizontal Scroll Bar on a Form. Then create a "cover" for the diary and put it into the Picture Box:

Figure S-12: The cover of Becky's diary a program that simulates a daily record of a life.

In the General Declarations section of the Form, define a "Formwide" Variable called *dy* to hold the current day (from 1 to 365) and another called *today* to keep track of the "serial number" of the current day (see "DateSerial"). We use a "Double" Variable because this number can be quite large (see "Variables"):

```
Dim dy As Integer
Dim today As Double
```

We'll set up the positions of the Text Box and the Label, and do some other preliminary tasks in the Form_Load Event:

```
Sub Form_Load ()

Label1.Visible = 0
Label1.Top = Picture1.Top
Label1.Left = Picture1.Left
Label1.Width = Picture1.Width
Label1.Height = Picture1.Height * .1

text1.Visible = 0
text1.Left = Picture1.Left
text1.Top = Label1.Top + Label1.Height
text1.Width = Picture1.Width
text1.Height = Picture1.Height * .9
text1.FontSize = 9
text1.FontBold = 0
```

```
hscroll1.Min = 1
hscroll1.Max = 365
hscroll1.LargeChange = 7

Show

drawframeon Picture1, Picture1, "outward", 200
drawframeon Picture1, Picture1, "inward", 30
drawframeon hscroll1, hscroll1, "outward", 50
drawframeon hscroll1, hscroll1, "inward", 20

dy = Day(Now)
mon = Month(Now)
yr = Year(Now)
today = DateSerial(yr, mon, dy)
End Sub
```

We're going to replace the picture of the diary's "cover" with a Label and a Text Box. For now, we'll leave them invisible, but we'll set their positions and dimensions relative to the size of the Picture Box. Note that we make the Label 10 percent of the size of the Picture and the Text Box 90 percent.

Because this Scroll Bar will move us through a year of pages in the diary, we set its Min and Max Properties to 1 and 365. We leave SmallChange at the default of 1; clicking on the arrows in the bar will move us one day forward or backward. We adjust LargeChange so that it will move us a week in either direction.

Next, we Show the Form (so the activities of the *DrawFrameOn* Subroutine will be visible). See "Line" for information on how to create frames around Controls using DrawFrameOn.

Then we use some of the built-in date Functions to find the current day, month and year, according to the computer's clock. We put the current "serial number" of today's date into the Variable *today*.

Now the Form is ready for use. Clicking on either the Scroll Bar or the Picture will start things off. Clicking on the Picture Box merely sends the program to the commands that respond to clicking on the Scroll Bar:

```
Sub Picture1_Click ()
    HScroll1_GotFocus
End Sub
```

Now we create a Static Variable because we want the following commands carried out only *once*, the first time the user moves from the Picture to the Text Box. This Variable will not lose its contents, like local Variables do when Visual Basic moves out of the Sub in which the Variable resides.

All Variables Are "Empty" When a Program Is Started: All numeric Variables are 0 when a program first runs. Text Variables similarly have no characters; they contain ""—nothing between the quotation marks. So, the first time this Event is triggered, the Variable Stopit will = 0 and will react accordingly with the commands following the If. However, from then on, Stopit will = 1 and we will ignore the fact that the Scroll Bar GotFocus. At the bottom of this Sub, we set Stopit to 1 so that we don't keep repeating the commands in this Sub while the program is running:

```
Sub HScroll1_GotFocus ()

Static Stopit As Integer

If Stopit = 0 Then
    d$ = Format$(today, "dddd   mmmm d yyyy")
    hscroll1.value = dy
    Label1.caption = d$
    Picture1.Visible = 0
    Label1.Visible = −1
    text1.Visible = −1
    text1.SetFocus
End If

Stopit = 1
End Sub
```

In the Form_Load Event we found the serial number for the current day, month and year by using the DateSerial Function. Now we use the Format$ Function to display the date in the Label. We also move the button to the proper position inside the Scroll Bar by setting its Value Property to the current day. The Picture now becomes invisible and is replaced by the newly visible Label and Text Box.

Our Assumptions about Becky: We have assumed that the user, Becky, in this case, will normally want to start writing in her diary when the program first starts up. That's why we open it to the current day's "page" and set the focus on the Text Box. Set the Text Box's MultiLine Property to On (–1 or True) when designing the program. This MultiLine Property, unlike most Properties, cannot be adjusted from within a running program.

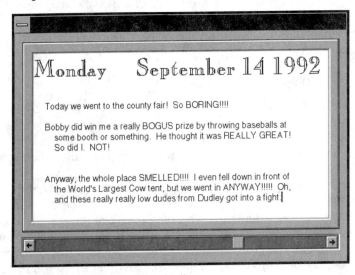

Figure S-13: An entry in Becky's diary.

All that's left to do is to react when Becky clicks on the Scroll Bar—triggering a Change Event:

```
Sub HScroll1_Change ()

dy = hscroll1.value
today = DateSerial(yr, mon, dy)
d$ = Format$(today, "dddd   mmmm d yyyy")
Label1.caption = d$
End Sub
```

Here we reset the Variable *dy*—the one that holds the "current" day from 1 to 365. This is a way that the Scroll Bar Min and Max Properties can interact with the quantities and ranges for which the Scroll Bar is an analogy. When Becky changes the Scroll Bar, we know that she is requesting a different page, a different day of the year. So we change the "current" *dy* and *today* Variables. Then we put a new Caption into the Label.

To flesh out this program into a fully functional diary, you would want to add commands within this Change Event to move to a different item within the Array that holds the entire diary (see "Arrays"). And you would have to add file-loading and -saving to the program—a provision to automatically read and update the disk file that holds the diary (see "Input$").

Scroll Bar Properties
DragIcon • DragMode • Enabled • Height • Index
LargeChange • Left • Max • Min • MousePointer • Name • Parent
SmallChange • TabIndex • TabStop • Tag • Top • Value
Visible • Width

Scroll Bar Events
Change • DragDrop • DragOver • GotFocus • KeyDown • KeyPress
KeyUp • LostFocus

Scroll Bar Methods
Drag • Move • Refresh • SetFocus

See also   LargeChange, SmallChange; Max; Min; ScrollBars (inside Text Boxes)

PROPERTY

(Inside Text Boxes, Grids & MDI Forms)

Description   The ScrollBars Property of a Text Box, Grid or MDI Form allows you to add Vertical, Horizontal or both types of Scroll Bars to the Object.

Used with   Text Boxes, Grids and MDI Forms

Variables   **Variable type:** Integer (enumerated)

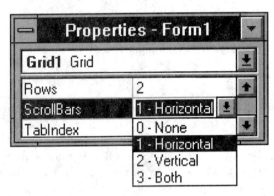

Figure S-14: Select one of the ScrollBar options from the Properties Window.

You must adjust the ScrollBars Property in the Properties Window while designing a program. There are four possible settings of the ScrollBars Property:

    0 No ScrollBars (the default)
    1 A Horizontal Bar
    2 A Vertical Bar
    3 Both Bars

Uses   • If your application is to include a word processor-like component—allowing the user to enter or read text—a Vertical Scroll Bar is a handy feature. It provides an alternative to the direction keys as a method of moving through text that is larger than the Text Box can display.

Horizontal Bars are not frequently used because text is not easy to read when it is cut off on the right side of the screen. Horizontally scrolled text is rare except in the Orient.

For Grids, a Scroll Bar will appear on the Control if all of its contents cannot be seen within the visible size of the Grid. For an MDI Form (see "Multiple Document Interface"), a Scroll Bar will appear if one of the child windows is partly hidden behind the MDI Form's border.

Cautions   • Even if you set the ScrollBars Property and attempt to add one or both Scroll Bars to a Text Box, they will not be added unless the Text Box's MultiLine Property has been turned on (set to True). If MultiLine is turned on, but you have not added a Horizontal Scroll Bar to a Text Box, the text will automatically "wrap" (move to the next line as appropriate). It doesn't matter in this case whether or not you have the WordWrap Property turned on.

• When a Horizontal Scroll Bar is added to a Text Box, text the user types will keep moving off to the right unless the user presses the ENTER key.

Normally, a multiline Text Box automatically *wraps* the text–and moves down to the next line when the text reaches the right side of the Text Box.

Similarly, text loaded into a Text Box from a disk file will also move off the right side of a Text Box that has a Horizontal Scroll Bar. New lines will appear only when there is a paragraph break–the keycode for the ENTER key, Chr$(13), plus the Line Feed code Chr$(10); see "Chr$".

• Neither the MultiLine Property nor the ScrollBars Property of a Text Box can be set while a program is running. You must set them with the Properties Window while designing your program.

If the contents of an Object are entirely visible within the Object, Scroll Bars will not appear on the Object–even if the ScrollBars Property is on, set to True.

Example   For this example, put a Text Box on a Form and, using the Properties Window, set the ScrollBars Property to 2 and the MultiLine Property to True. Now position the Text Box so that it fills the interior of the Form. Type the following into the Form_Load Event:

```
Sub Form_Load ()

Caption = "AUTOEXEC.BAT VIEWER"

CR$ = Chr$(13) + Chr$(10)

Open "C:\AUTOEXEC.BAT" For Input As #1

Do While Not EOF(1)
    Line Input #1, X$
    Text1.Text = Text1.Text + X$ + CR$
Loop

Close

End Sub
```

We first put a Caption on the Form. Then we create a special text Variable to hold the combined Carriage Return/Line Feed codes. We must add these codes to the text file that we are going to read with Line Input #. Line Input # strips off these two codes, and, without them, the text appears as a single long line rather than as separate lines. (See "Input$" for a solution.)

Because we've set MultiLine to True and have not used a Horizontal Scroll Bar, the text would wrap within the Text Box even if we didn't use the CR$ Variable. However, it would be virtually unreadable because the lines would not be separated as they were in the original.

Then we Open the AUTOEXEC.BAT file and read in each line until the EOF Function tells us that we have reached the End Of File. When each line is read in, it is added to the Text Property of the Text Box, and a CR/LF code is also put between each line.

See also   MultiLine

 ECOND
FUNCTION

Description   The Second Function tells you the second of the minute. It gives you a number between 0 and 59.

You can locate any minute between January 1, 1753, and December 31, 2078, using Visual Basic's built-in "serial number" representation of date+time. Visual Basic can provide or manipulate individual serial numbers for *every second* between those two dates. These serial numbers also include coded representations of all the minutes, hours, days, months and years between 1753 and 2078.

Used with   • Second is often used with the Now Function, to tell you the current second as registered by your computer's clock:

Print Second(Now)

The Now Function provides the serial number for the current date and time. Second extracts the second portion of the serial number.

• You can use Second with any of the commands in VB that produce a "serial number" for date+time (see "DateSerial").

Variables   X = Second(Now)

Uses   • Create "digital" clocks.

• Create Timers, using Second with the Timer Control.

Cautions   The Format$ Function offers an extremely flexible and powerful method of displaying or printing date and time information. Use it to display the results of Second, and other date+time Functions, in precisely the way you want them to appear.

Example

Figure S-15: Seconds change every second via the Timer.

For this example, create a Form and put a Picture on it. Also put two VB Picture Boxes on the Form to display the digital Hour:Minute and a separate Box for seconds. Then add a Timer.

Put the following in the Form_Load Event:

```
Sub Form_Load ()

Show

Picture1.Picture = LoadPicture("c:\book\bmps\clock.bmp")
End Sub
```

In the Timer, enter the following:

```
Sub Timer1_Timer ()

Picture1.Cls
picture2.Cls

Picture1.Print Format$(Now, "h:mm/PM")
picture2.Print Str$(Second(Now))
End Sub
```

Next, set the FontSize of the Picture Boxes to whatever looks best. Then set the Timer's Interval Property to 1000 so it will update the digital numbers every second.

The Timer uses the Cls command to remove the previously printed digits and then prints the current time information, which is taken from the Now Function. We use the Format$ Function to print the hour with no leading zero, the minute with a leading zero and either AM or PM. The Second Function returns a number, so we have to translate it into a printable text form using the Str$ Function.

See also   Day; Format$; Hour; Minute; Month; Now; Weekday; Year

 EEK

FUNCTION

Description   Seek tells you the current position within an Opened disk file.

VB keeps track of the location in a file of the last byte read or written (for binary- and sequential-mode files) or the last record (for random-mode files).

The Seek Function tells you the byte position—the location of the text character, for instance—where the next file access will take place. This *access* could be either reading in or writing out information from or to the file in question, or using the Seek *Statement.*

If a file has been opened in binary mode, the Loc Function would also provide location information—but it tells you the position of the *last byte* read or written. Seek describes the byte Loc +1 (the *next byte* to be read or written).

(See "Open" for a general discussion of file types, file management and the binary mode, with which Seek is most often used. See "Input$" for a general discussion of the sequential mode.)

Used with Seek is used most often with files opened in the binary mode—where you, the programmer, control precisely how the file is accessed. If you want to update a binary file or to move around in a nonsequential fashion, you could use the Seek Function (and its companion, the Seek *Statement*).

Variables X = Seek(1)

(X now contains the current position within a file that had been Opened with #1 as its filenumber.)

Uses • The Seek Function can tell you about your current location. For instance, you could subtract what Seek tells you from the LOF (Length Of File) and know how many bytes remained in the file beyond the current position.

Used with the random mode, Seek can give the number of records remaining to be accessed in the file (by subtracting the number provided by Seek from the total number of records in the file). However, a program Variable is more common for keeping track of the current record number.

(See "Open" for a general discussion of files and of the binary mode and its uses, in particular.)

Cautions • Seek, when used with random-mode files, provides the next *record* to be read or written, rather than the next byte.

• Seek can report numbers up to 2,147,483,647.

Example
```
Sub Form_Click ()
Open "C:\test" For Binary As #1
For i% = 1 To 28 Step 2
    Put #1, i%, i%
Next i%
x = Seek(1)
Print x
Close 1
End Sub
```

Results in 29

Here we Opened a binary-mode file and put 14 integers into it (see "Variables"). Integers take up two bytes each, so when we put 14 of them into this file, the next byte position is 29.

See also Get; Loc; Put; Seek (Statement)
See "Open" for a general discussion of file management and binary files.

SEEK

Description   The Seek Statement moves the "current position" in an opened file to the location you specify.

Visual Basic maintains a "pointer" when you access a file to indicate the position where the last activity occurred within the file. The pointer is something like the cursor in a word processor. If you read something from or write something to an opened disk file, the pointer moves to the position just past the item you accessed.

With Seek, you can deliberately reset the position of that pointer causing the next read or write to occur at the new position, rather than the position just after the previous access. (The Loc command, however, will not notice this change and will continue to report the most recent access.)

Used with   Most often, Seek is used with files opened in the binary mode.

(See "Open" for a general discussion of files and of the binary mode and its uses, in particular.)

Variables   To position yourself at the sixth *record* of a file Opened in random mode or the sixth *byte* of a file Opened in any other mode. (This file was Opened As #1 and that's how we identify it):

    X = Seek 1, 6

OR (using this approach is clearer, it's preferred):

    X = Seek #1, 6

Uses   Files you access in the binary mode allow you the greatest control and flexibility but are more complicated to manage than random- or sequential-mode files. However, you can use Seek to position yourself anywhere within a file—for reading from or writing to that file at the new position.

Cautions   • Seek, when used with random-mode files, positions you at the next *record* to be read or written, rather than the byte. However, a Put or Get command will cancel the effect of the Seek command. The Put and Get commands, which are used primarily with random-mode files, contain their own positioning information.

Writing information to a position *greater than the size of the file* will append that information to the file. For instance, if a file contained:

    1 2 3 4

and you used X = Seek #1, 25: Print #1, "HERE" you would get something like the following:

    1 2 3 4   HERE

Example

```
Sub Form_Click ()
    Open "C:\test5" For Output As #1
    For i% = 1 To 15
        Print #1, Chr$(i% + 64);
    Next i%
    Close 1
    Open "C:\test5" For Input As #1
    Seek #1, 11
    a$ = Input$(1, #1)
    Close 1
    Print a$
End Sub
```

Results in   K

Here we Opened a new file called "TEST5" and printed the letters *A* through *0* (the first 15 letters of the alphabet) into this file. We added 64 to the value of the i% Variable because the capital letter *A* has an ASCII code of 65, B is 66, and so on. (See "Chr$" for more on the ASCII code.)

Then we reopen this file, For Input, and use the Seek command to position ourselves at the 11th text character in this file. When we pull in the next item from the file, we get a *K*, the 11th letter of the alphabet.

Most file-reading and -writing commands do not specify the location within the file where they will perform their duty (the Get and Put commands are the exceptions). Most file commands rely on the "position pointer," a cursor-like movable pointer that VB keeps track of internally, to know where to next access the file.

The Pointer Starts Off at the First Byte: When you first Open a file, the position pointer is located on the first byte in the file. Without Seek, the first attempt to read this file after it has been Opened–Input$(1, #1)–would provide the letter *A*. Then another access–Input$(1, #1) again–would pull in the next character *B*, and so on. Each access shifts the position pointer forward. The Seek command summarily changes the position pointer. In this example, we used Seek to move ahead in the file to the 11th character.

Note that Basic still isn't entirely consistent in its syntax. The position of the filenumber is reversed in these two commands:

```
Seek #1, 11
a$ = Input$(1, #1)
```

See also   Get; Put; Seek (Function)
See "Open" for a general discussion of file management and binary files.

SELECT CASE

Description   Select Case is similar to the If...Then structure, but Select Case is generally used for multiple-choice situations. If...Then is primarily designed for True-False situations, but can also contain multiple choices. These Select Case and If...Then structures can often be used interchangeably, but Select Case is somewhat easier to grasp for those times when there are more than one or two possible "cases."

The general distinction between If...Then and Select Case goes something like this:

If it's raining, *Then* take your umbrella.

```
Select Case Weather
      Case Raining
            Take your umbrella.
      Case Sunny
            Wear light clothing.
      Case Snowing
            Wear snowshoes.
      Case Hot
            Wear cotton.
End Select
```

(You could also set up a similar structure for If...Then using repeated ElseIf commands.)

Select Case works from a list of possible "answers." Your program can respond to each of these answers differently.

If you use Select Case, you can make your programs look something like ordinary English. For that reason, Select Case is often better in multiple-choice situations than the If...Then structure.

Used with   Situations where If...Then is too restrictive or becomes obscure because there are so many possible choices.

Select Case is useful if you have several possible conditions you must respond to, so you want to list a variety of causes and a variety of effects.

Variables   To react to what is in a numeric Variable:

```
Select Case X

Case 4
  (put one or more commands here)
Case 8
  (put one or more commands here)
End Select
```

OR (to react to a text ("string") Variable):

```
Select Case X$

Case "blue"
   (put one or more commands here)
Case "green"
   (put one or more commands here)
Case "money"
   (put one or more commands here)
End Select
```

For the following examples, you must imagine what the Select Case Statement would say at the top of the structure. Each of the following is a variation of the "multiple choices" that you can put underneath the Select Case (something) command:

OR (to react to a range of literal numbers): Case 5 To 5000

OR (to react to an alphabetic range, here reacting to any letter between *a* and *f*): Case "a" To "f"

OR (to combine several items, each of which should be responded to in the same way–use commas to separate the items): Case "a" To "q", "francis", N$

OR (use the special *Is* command to test for):

1. greater than (>)
2. less than (<)
3. equals (=)
4. doesn't equal (<>)
5. is greater than or equals (>=)
6. is less than or equals (<=)

Here are some examples of how you can use the six "operators" with the Is command. (For a definition of operators, see Appendix C.)

```
Select Case Z

Case Is > 1200
   (put one or more commands here)
Case Is > 1600
   (put one or more commands here)
Case Is <> 55
   (put one or more commands here)
Case Is = X
   (put one or more commands here)
End Select
```

(Note that this "Is" command is entirely distinct from the "Is" operator (which see). The Is operator tells you if two Variable names refer to the same Control or Form.)

Uses
• Use Select Case when you think that multiple If...Then structures (or If...Then with interior IfElse commands) are more confusing than Select Case.

Select Case tests something against a whole list of possible matches. Each element in the list is followed by one or more commands that are carried out in the event of a match. In this way, the program can respond in multiple ways to the current state of a numeric or string Variable, or an *expression*. (See Appendix C for a definition of *expression*.)

The Select Case structure acts the same as a series of If...Then structures, but Select Case simplifies the process:

```
If X = 4 Then Print "Four"
If X = 5 Then Print "Five"
If X = 6 Then Print "Six"
```

OR (the same program expressed differently by using the ElseIf command):

```
Sub Form_Click ()

a$ = InputBox$("number please?")
x = Val(a$)

If x = 4 Then
    Print "Four"
ElseIf x = 5 Then
    Print "Five"
ElseIf x = 6 Then
    Print "Six"
End If

End Sub
```

Both of the preceding examples are the same as the following:

```
Select Case X

    Case 4
            Print "Four"
    Case 5
            Print "Five"
    Case 6
            Print "Six"
End Select
```

Cautions
• The match can include several items, separated by commas. The following would Print "Odd" for any odd number between 1 and 10:

```
Case 1,3,5,7,9
    Print "Odd"
```

The match can be a range, either alphabetic or numeric. This Case would be triggered by any word that lies between *aardvark* and *czar* in the dictionary:

```
Case "aardvark" To "czar"
```

If you are testing an alphabetic range, *a* is "lower than" *b*, which is "lower than" *c*, and so on. But capitalization throws things off because the ANSI codes (see "Chr$") for capital letters *are lower than* the codes for lowercase letters. It's often a good idea to force a text Variable into all-lowercase and then write out all the possible matches in lowercase, too. The LCase$ Function forces all letters in Name$ here to be tested as lowercase letters:

```
Select Case LCase$(Name$)
    Case nancy
    Case donald
    Case roy
```

The match can be one of the "relational operators" (greater than, less than, etc., see Appendix C), but the command *Is* is then required. Here, if the current value of X is less than 15, the match is triggered:

```
Select Case X
    Case Is < 15
```

Each of the preceding matches can be mixed within a single test Case. Here the match is triggered if X is less than 15, is 44, or is the same as the Variable Y:

```
Select Case X
    Case Is < 15, 44, Y
```

You cannot start with a text Variable and try to match it against a numeric Variable or a number:

Wrong:

```
Select Case A$
    Case 5
```

Likewise, you cannot start with a numeric Variable and try text matches as Cases.

Furthermore, which numeric Variable "type" that you start with (Integer, Long, etc.—see "Variables") determines how the matches are tested. If you start with an Integer, for example, all the matches will be tested as if they were Integers. Here X% is an Integer, and Y! is a Floating-Point number (it can have a fractional part, a decimal point). However, because X% is what we are testing against, the fractional part of Y! is ignored. Y! is treated as if it, too, were an Integer:

```
X% = 5
Y! = 5.332

Select Case X%
    Case Y!
            Print "This did trigger a match"
End Select
```

Case Else: You can use a Case Else command at the end of a Case Structure. Case Else will be triggered if no match is found in the list of Cases above it. The following would trigger the Case Else:

```
X = 5
Select Case X
     Case 4
          Print "Match"
     Case 6
          Print "Match"
     Case Else
          Print "No Match"
End Select
```

If you don't use a Case Else and no match is found, the program moves to the line following End Select and resumes the instructions found there. In other words, none of the commands inside any of the Cases will be carried out, and nothing will happen at all in the entire Case structure.

Case Else is equivalent to the Else command within an If...Then structure:

```
X = 5
If X = 4 OR X = 6 Then
          Print "Match"
     Else
          Print "No Match"
End If
```

Results in   No Match

• You can *nest* Select Case structures, but nesting would quickly get rather confusing. Nesting means putting one thing inside of another, as in the following:

```
Select Case Name1$
     Case "A" To "C"
          Select Case Name2$
               Case "Rose"
                    Print "This could be Audrey Rose..."
          End Select
End Select
```

Example   In this example we ask the user to describe how big a character font he or she wants to use on this window. First, put a Label on a Form, change its Caption Property to "Enter Font Size..." and then add a Text Box where the user can type in the desired font size. When he or she types a recognized word, the FontSize changes and prints an example.

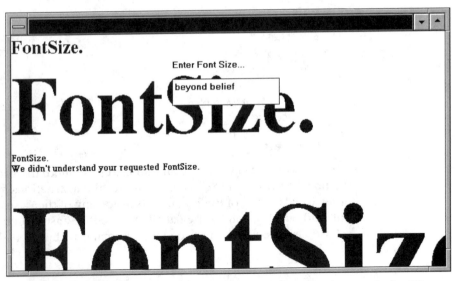

Figure S-16: Use a little artificial intelligence in your program to interpret a FontSize that is specified in plain English.

Into the Text Box's_KeyPress Event, type the following:

```
Sub Text1_KeyPress (keyascii As Integer)

If keyascii <> 13 Then Exit Sub

Select Case LCase$(Text1.Text)

Case "tiny", "really small", "mousetype"
  FontSize = 7
Case "small"
  FontSize = 9
Case "medium", "average"
  FontSize = 18
Case "large", "big"
  FontSize = 36
Case "really big", "huge", "immense"
  FontSize = 76
Case "beyond belief"
  FontSize = 126
Case Else
  Print "We didn't understand your requested ";
End Select

Print "FontSize."

End Sub
```

Notice that we use an If...Then to react to a True-False situation. Here, we want to trigger the Select Case if the user presses the ENTER key (which has an ASCII code of 13—see "Chr$").

If the user presses ENTER, we move into the various "Cases" in the Select Case structure. We want to determine how to act based on the contents of Text1.Text. So, we put the Text after the Select Case command. To eliminate the problem of variations in capitalization, we force the Text1.Text to all lowercase with LCase$. Then we'll test against only lowercase possible answers.

Each Case command is followed by a possible choice or choices. You can separate synonyms with commas ("couch", "sofa").

Between the Case instructions are the reactions the program should take if it finds a match. If the user types *huge*, it matches the "Case" that lists "huge" as a possibility, and the FontSize is set to an appropriate number.

If no matches are found, the program executes the command or commands following "Case Else." In this example, Print "We didn't understand your requested "; follows.

See also   If...Then; IIf; Choose; Switch

 ELECTED
PROPERTY

Description   Selected is an Array (a list of related Variables) that reveals which, if any, items have been selected within a File List Box or List Box. If the user is allowed more than one selection (see "MultiSelect"), the Selected Array tells you which items have been chosen by the user.

Used with   File List Boxes and List Boxes

Variables   To test if the fourth item is selected in a List Box, recall that the first item in all Box-type Controls has a 0 index number. So asking here for index (3) gives us the fourth item in the Box:

    X = List1.Selected(3)

OR

    If List1.Selected(3) = True Then Print "Item Four is selected"

OR (to have your program select an item instead of the user):

    List1.Selected(3) = True

You'll most commonly use a Loop to go through all items in a Box and identify all selected items (see the Example).

Uses   • Both File List Boxes and List Boxes have a MultiSelect Property, which allows the user to click and highlight (select) more than one item in the Box. The Selected Property maintains a list of highlighted items, so your program can take action on those items the user wants to affect.

- Perform some service for the user on the items he or she has selected within a List Box.
- Move, copy or delete the group of files selected in a File List Box.
- Have *your program* select items in a list, based on criteria the user has specified (all people over a certain age, all travel destinations costing less than $400 airfare, etc.).

Cautions
- As always, you have to deal with the unfortunate fact that the first item in a Box-type Control has an index of 0. See "Variables" above.
- The Properties of List and File Boxes must always include the Name of the Box. For instance, you must use A$ = List1.List(List1.ListIndex) rather than A$ = List1.List(ListIndex).
- The ListIndex Property returns the selected item if a Box's MultiSelect Property is set to Off. However, if MultiSelect is set to On, the item with the "focus rectangle" (whether selected or not) is returned by ListIndex. When MultiSelect is on, the user can move the focus rectangle within the Box by using the arrow keys. This movement doesn't select any items; clicking or pressing the Spacebar does.

Example
Put a Command Button and a List Box on a Form. Set the MultiSelect Property of the List Box to Simple. Then fill the List Box by typing the following into the Form_Load Event:

```
Sub Form_Load ()
    For i = 1 To 20
            List1.AddItem "Item " + i
    Next i
End Sub
```

When the user clicks on the Command Button, all selected items are reported by using a Loop to test the Selected Property of each item in the Box:

```
Sub Command1_Click ()
Cls
For i = 0 To List1.ListCount − 1
    If List1.Selected(i) = True Then
            Print List1.List(i); " is selected."
    End If
Next i
End Sub
```

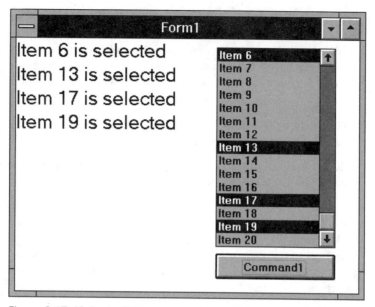

Figure S-17: "Selected" lets your program know which items the user has chosen.

See also   File List Box; List; List Box; ListCount; ListIndex; MultiSelect

SelLength, SelStart, SelText

Description   The SelLength, SelStart and SelText Properties together describe the current cursor position within a Text or Combo Box, as well as any text that the user has highlighted by dragging the mouse across it. This is useful for cut, copy and paste operations.

SelLength describes how many characters are highlighted, if any.

SelStart points to the character position of the first highlighted character. If no characters are highlighted, SelStart points to the current cursor position within the text.

SelText contains whatever text has been highlighted. (It is like a text "string" Variable.)

Used with   Text Boxes or Combo Boxes, often with the Clipboard

Variables　　**Variable type:** Long (for SelLength and SelStart), text ("string") for SelText

To find out the current cursor position within the text in the Text Box. Or, if SelLength isn't 0 because the user has selected text by dragging the mouse across it, SelStart points to the first selected character:

```
X = Text1.SelStart
```

OR (X will be 0 if no characters have been selected. If some characters are selected, X holds the number of selected characters): X = Text1.SelLength

OR (A$ will now contain whatever characters the user has selected. If no characters have been selected, A$ will be an "empty string" ("")):

```
A$ = Text1.SelText
If A$ = " " Then Print "Nothing Selected."
```

Alternatively, you can *cause your program to select text*, to move the position of the cursor or even to *insert* (to "paste") text.

To paste text, set SelStart to where you want the new piece of text inserted. Then put the replacement text into the SelText Property.

If the original text is "HOW ARE YOU?"

```
Text1.SelStart = 4

Text1.SelText = "NEW PIECE"
```

Results in　　HOW NEW PIECE ARE YOU?

OR (to have the program highlight some text, set the SelStart and SelLength Properties):

```
SelStart = 6
SelLength = 12
```

Uses　　• Allow cutting, copying and pasting of text. Just like a word processor, your Text Box can permit mouse-controlled editing in the typical Windows style. Usually, you add a menu and offer Cut, Copy and Paste options. The selected text can then be held in the Clipboard (which see). You send text to the Clipboard with SetText, and you retrieve it with GetText.

• Provide for some automated (program-controlled) word processing effects. For instance, you could react to special situations by repositioning the cursor, selecting some text, highlighting text or automatically removing pieces of text.

Cautions　　• Changing the SelText Property from within a running program automatically *inserts* the new SelText into the Text Property of the Text Box or Combo Box. The new text does not replace existing text; rather, VB makes room for it within the existing text.

• SelLength can be any number from 0 to the total number of characters in the Text Box's or Combo Box's Text Property. You can find the number of characters with: X = Len(Text1.Text).

SelStart also can be any number from 0 to the total number of characters in the Text Property.

If the user or your program changes SelStart, then SelLength is, at least temporarily, set to 0. Any selecting, however, adjusts SelLength to the length in characters of the selected text.

Example

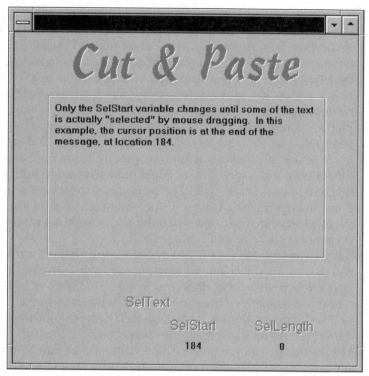

Figure S-18: Here no text is selected, so SelLength is 0 and SelText is empty. However, the cursor position is reported to be at character position 184.

This program will demonstrate all three Sel Variables. First, put a Text Box and three Labels on a Form. When the user types into the Text Box, the SelStart Property keeps a current record of the position of the cursor. Usually, the cursor is at the end of the text as the user types. However, clicking within the text moves the cursor to the current position, and SelStart adjusts to reflect the new position. To track SelStart, SelLength and SelText, we'll update the Caption Properties of the three Labels:

```
Sub text1_change ()
label1.caption = text1.SelText
label2.caption = Str$(text1.SelStart)
label3.caption = Str$(text1.SelLength)
End Sub
```

Note that if the user types something or changes the position of the cursor by clicking within the text, those actions trigger the Change Event in the Text Box. However just selecting text (by clicking and then holding down the mouse button and dragging), *does not trigger the Change Event in a Text Box.* (Selecting does affect the SelLength and SelText Properties.) How can you, the programmer, know when the user wants something to be done with selected text? Usually you'll employ a menu: The user must pull down the menu and choose something like Cut or Copy from that menu. You would react to the menu selection, which *does* trigger a Click Event in the selected menu item, by putting your commands within that Click Event. Alternatively, you could put a Command Button on the Form that, when clicked on, would cause copying to take place. (The instructions for copying would then reside within that Command Button's Click Event.) Just remember that when the user simply *selects* text, that action triggers *no* Visual Basic Events at all.

For keyboard users, Text Boxes *automatically* perform selecting, cutting and pasting via the Windows conventions–SHIFT+arrow key selects, SHIFT+INS pastes, CTRL+INS copies and SHIFT+DEL cuts.

In this example, we use the Form_Click Event to simulate a menu or COPY Command Button. A click on the Form will update the Captions of the Labels, thereby revealing the current state of the three Sel Properties. In an actual program, you would probably use an Edit Menu instead to allow the user to choose Cut or Copy. Those menu items' Click Events would contain the commands necessary to put the selected text (the SelText Property) into the Clipboard (see "SetText").

```
Sub Form_Click ()
   text1_change
End Sub
```

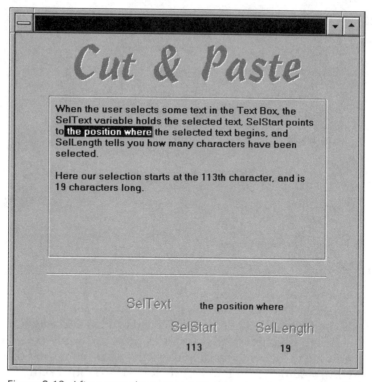

Figure S-19: After you select some text, this program shows you its length and how to use the SelText Property to cut or copy this text to the Clipboard.

Etched and Embossed Visual Effects: The remaining activity in this example takes place in the Form_Load Event and is not related to the Sel Properties. The following illustrates how to create etched and embossed effects. (See "Line" for more information on drawing various kinds of 3D frames. See "Print" for the Raiseit Subroutine that adds etched, embossed and drop-shadow effects to printed text.)

```
Sub Form_Load ()

Show

Emboss text1, "inward", 75

x = text1.left – 146: x1 = text1.left + text1.width + 126
y = text1.top + text1.height + 400
Line (x, y)–(x1, y), QBColor(8)
Line (x, y + 6)–(x1, y + 6), QBColor(15)

fontsize = 48
fontname = "cascade"
fontbold = 0
x = 1000: y = 50
a$ = "Cut & Paste"

GoSub Raiseit
```

```
fontsize = 12
fontname = "helv"

x = 2000:y = 4500:a$ = "SelText": GoSub Raiseit

x = 2800: y = 4900: a$ = "SelStart": GoSub Raiseit

x = 4300: y = 4900: a$ = "SelLength": GoSub Raiseit

Exit Sub

Raiseit:

currentx = x
currenty = y
ForeColor = QBColor(15)
Print a$
currentx = x — 12
currenty = y — 12
ForeColor = QBColor(8)
Print a$

Return

End Sub
```

The instructions here in the Form_Load Event create the various etched and embossed lines and text of this program. As always, when drawing or printing to a Form, you should use the Show command unless you turn the Form's AutoRedraw Property to On (–1 or True). We then use the Emboss Subroutine to draw an etched line around the Text Box. (See "Line" for this Subroutine.)

The next four lines in the program illustrate how to draw an "etched" line below the Text Box. You first draw a medium gray line and then slightly offset a white line. Following a similar principle, we etch the main title "Cut & Paste" as well as the smaller printed identifiers at the bottom of the Form.

The rest of the Event utilizes the Raiseit Subroutine (see "Print"). The Raiseit Subroutine produces the shadowed text. You provide the Subroutine with the X,Y location where you want the text printed, and also the text you want printed (A$)–the Subroutine does the rest.

See also   Clipboard; GetText; SetText

SENDKEYS

STATEMENT

Description   SendKeys allows your VB program to send keystrokes *to another Windows program*, just as if the user were typing those keys. In other words, Send-Keys slips into the pipeline between the keyboard and a Windows program, and the program cannot tell that a user isn't simply typing away.

This technique allows your VB programs to communicate with each other or even to communicate with non-VB Windows programs. (You cannot use SendKeys with DOS programs.)

The alternative interprogram communication technique is called DDE (Dynamic Data Exchange). Not many Windows programs yet support DDE, but your Visual Basic programs can talk to each other across a DDE Link. DDE allows one Windows program to communicate with another; changing text or graphics in one program can cause changes in the other simultaneously. (DDE is described at length in the various Link commands in this book.) Some of Microsoft's Windows programs can connect with your VB programs using DDE—notably Excel and Word. (Also see the entry on "OLE" for yet a third way for programs to communicate.)

Used with   A Visual Basic program and/or another Windows program.

Variables   The target program must be running at the time SendKeys attempts to "type" something into it. You can use the Shell Function to start an external program running from within your VB program.

Also, you must switch to the outside program (set the "focus" to it, as if the user had clicked on it and made it the "active" window). You can use the AppActivate command to switch the focus to an outside program. (See "Shell" and "AppActivate," or see the Example below.)

To directly send the following twelve text characters:

    SendKeys "MESSAGE SENT"

OR (to cause your VB program to pause until the outside program has digested—"processed"—whatever keys you have sent, add –1):

    SendKeys "MESSAGE SENT" , –1

OR (to repeat an individual key, specify the number of repeats with a space between the key and the number of times you want it sent. Put both items in braces. To print seven *Z*s): SendKeys "{Z 7}"

OR

You can also send the "nonprinting" keys, the keys which cause actions to take place rather than text to be printed—F1, ENTER, PgDn, etc. Many programs recognize and respond to special keys like the Function keys, ALT+key combinations, and so on. To "press those keys" with SendKeys, you provide the name of the special nonprinting key and put it inside braces ({}) using the following list. It doesn't matter how you capitalize—*Enter* is the same as *enter* or *ENTER*.

{Backspace} or {Bksp} or {Bs}

{Break}

{Capslock}

{Clear}

{Delete} or {Del}

{Down}

{End}

{Enter} or ~

{Esc} or {Escape}

{Help}

{Home}

{Insert}

{Left}

{Numlock}

{Pgdn}

{Pgup}

{Prtsc} (for Print Screen)

{Right}

{Scrolllock}

{Tab}

{Up}

{F1} through {F16}

OR

You can simulate the CTRL, ALT or SHIFT keypresses in combination with other characters.

For **SHIFT**, put the + (plus) symbol before the character you want shifted: +E

OR (Many commercial programs Save to the disk after the ALT+F, S keys are pressed, activating their File Menu and selecting the Save option):

For **ALT**, put the % (percent) symbol before the character you want "pressed" simultaneously with ALT: %F S

For **CTRL**, put the ^ (caret) symbol before the character you want "pressed" simultaneously with CTRL: ^F

OR (to "hold down" the SHIFT, ALT or CTRL key while several other keys are pressed, put the other keys in parentheses. To print shifted *ABC*): SendKeys "+(abc)"

Using "+abc" would only shift the *A* resulting in *Abc*.

Uses   • The SendKeys technique, although sometimes useful, is nonetheless limited. The DDE (see "LinkMode") technique is superior because, among other things, you have more control over the communication, and, via DDE, the communication can go in both directions. With SendKeys, your program can "talk to" another program, but the other program cannot talk back.

• Bringing up the Notepad is a quick way to give the user a simple Help screen for your programs. You could use Shell to activate the Notepad and then SendKeys information to the Notepad. See the Example below.

• You could give the user the option of running Word for Windows or some other application. Your program could then use WFW's translation facilities, for example, to save text files in a variety of formats. Using another application's facilities in this way, however, is an indirect and not entirely a satisfactory technique. Your program would then be able to do nothing for people who didn't have WFW.

Shell could be used to load your favorite program and SendKeys (with – 1) to skip past its opening screen by typing the keyboard shortcut that closes the initial dialog box. You can use this method to bypass, for instance, the required typing on the opening of some shareware programs. Or you can activate the menus of a remote program by sending the keyboard shortcuts like ALT+F, S to save a document from the File Menu. You could then use a Timer in your "controlling" VB program to automatically save your files every so often.

Cautions • SendKeys works only with the currently active Windows application. If your VB program is *active* (is the one that has been clicked on most recently), the keystrokes will go back into the VB program. Use AppActivate or Shell to make another program active.

Because the braces characters are used in a special way, if you need to send one of them, enclose *it* in braces, {{}.

Because the +, % and ^ characters are used to indicate SHIFT, ALT and CTRL, enclose them in braces if you want to send one as a character, as printable text. To print the symbol for percent, use {%}.

If the program to which SendKeys is instructed to send keystrokes is not running or hasn't been given the focus with AppActivate, the keystrokes are sent back *to your Visual Basic program* as if the keys were being typed into *it*. This permits you to simulate keystrokes that the user might have typed while the VB program is running. This approach would be one– albeit indirect–way of testing the program. (Why not just type the keys in yourself?)

DOS programs cannot receive from SendKeys. Only Windows programs can.

The "keystrokes" sent by SendKeys are not sent if your VB program is doing something at the time–working within a For...Next Loop, for example. When that Loop is finished, the keys will be sent. You can always add a DoEvents Function inside the Loop, though, and the keys will be sent. Normally, sending keys wouldn't be a problem because you likely will not put SendKeys inside a Loop or within some other structure that will keep VB tied up.

Example

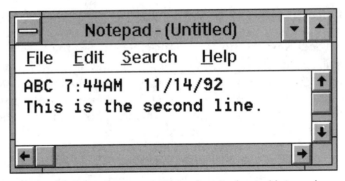

Figure S-20: Our program sent these keystrokes to Notepad.

```
Sub Form_Click ()
x = Shell("C:\WINDOWS\NOTEPAD", 1)
SendKeys "ABC %ed {enter}This is the second line."
End Sub
```

This example starts the Notepad running and opens it to a "normal size" window with the number 1 (see "Shell" for other options). Then we send the letters *ABC*, use ALT+E, which opens the Edit Menu, and send *d*, which inserts the date. Then SendKeys simulates pressing the ENTER key and prints a second line of text.

Shell makes the loaded program the "active" window. If the program is already running, you can use AppActivate to switch from your VB program to the program to which you want to SendKeys:

```
AppActivate "Notepad"
```

See also   AppActivate; LinkMode; OLE Automation; Shell

SET
STATEMENT

Description   Using Set you can assign an object, Form or Control to an *Object Variable*. Before using Set, you must first declare an Object Variable of the correct type:

```
Dim MyFormObj As Form1
```

OR

```
Dim MyCtlObj As TextBox
```

(Note that we can use a *particular* Form (Form1), but must use a *general* Control type–TextBox, not Text1.)

Then, when the Object Variable has been declared, you can use the Set command to attach a particular Control to the Object Variable:

Set MyCtlObj = Text1

Now you can use MyCtlObj to query or change Properties of Text1: MyCtlObj.BackColor = QBColor(4). And if you have another Object Variable of the same type, you can assign the Object of one Variable to the other: MyCtlObj = MyOtherCtlObj.

OR (to use the New command with Set to create a new "instance" of Form1): Set MyFormObj = New Form1

Forms and Controls already have their *Name Property:* What's the point of giving them a Variable name? VB allows the creation of new "instances" of Forms and Controls while a program is running. These clones inherit the *same* Name along with the other Properties of the original Form or Control, so there's no way for your program to keep track of them unless you use Set to give them unique Variable names as a method of identification.

Clones are called "instances" of the original prototype Form or Control. It's like Notepad; you can have more than one "instance" of Notepad running at the same time under Windows. It's still the same program, but the user can bring different text into each instance.

If your program propagates some clone Forms, all the clones share any commands you have put into the original ("prototype") Form's General Declarations section or within its Events. The clones also inherit all the Properties, Controls and Variables declared with Dim or Static and, thus, made persistent and Formwide in their scope. However, these Properties, Controls and persistent Variables *can be changed independently* for each clone. Each clone has a copy of these inherited items.

Forms and Controls are called *Objects.* When you declare a Variable of the "Form" type, you are creating an *Object Variable.* You can use an Object Variable much the way you would use a normal Variable, but Object Variables "point to" or "refer to" a single entity (their Object, such as ObjName.Text1.Text). Object Variables do not *contain* data the way a nor-mal text or numeric Variable does. (For more on this, see "Objects.")

However, merely declaring an Object Variable does not create a new "instance" of an Object. Set is also used with the New command to create new "instances."

For a complete discussion of how Objects are used in VB (and several examples), see "Objects."

Used with   Object Variables, to assign references to particular Objects, or to copy references from one Object Variable to another. Set works similarly to the way the equals (=) symbol works with regular text or numeric Variables.

Variables   First, you must declare an Object Variable. This doesn't create a new "instance" of a Form. In this example, it merely defines a new Variable to be of the "Form1" type. Declaring a Control Object Variable also merely defines a new Object Variable of the Label type. Start a New Project in the

File Menu and put a Label on the Form. In Form1's General Declarations section, type the following:

```
Dim newlabel As Label
Dim cloneform As form1
```

Then, to assign a particular Label Control to our Variable *newlabel* and to create a new instance of Form1, type the following into the Form's Click_Event:

```
Sub Form_Click ()
    Set newlabel = Label1
    Set cloneform = New Form1

    newlabel.Caption = "I've Changed."
    cloneform.Left = left + width
    cloneform.Show
End Sub
```

Run this program by pressing F5 and then click on the Form. Notice that the New command, used with Set, created a whole new "instance" of Form1, and we used *newlabel* to adjust the Caption Property of Label1.

OR (if you have object Variables that your program no longer needs, use the *Nothing* command to release the computer's resources that were used by the Variables): Set cloneform = Nothing

Uses
• Use Set to assign an Object Variable to an Object or to another Object Variable.

• Use Set with New to create clone Forms (see "Objects").

• Use Set to create an Object Variable Array that acts as a shadow of a set of clone Forms. You don't know when the program is being designed how many clones the user might create (though you could enforce a *range* by refusing to go beyond a limit). Likewise, you might need to keep track of whether or not the user had used one of the clones for any purpose (and should the Form's data be saved to disk when the user exits the program?). The shadow Array can keep track of these things by holding information about the number of clones and their Properties and contents.

Knowing the status of clone Forms can allow you to make your program more intelligent. For example, say you have six Forms in a financial program, but the user never clicks on the "Amortization" or "Bonds" Forms. They are available as icons onscreen and as menu items, but the user never utilizes them. You could have your program store this information in an .INI file and leave them accessible in the menu but not continue to display the icons.

You can adjust object Variables to point to different Objects as the program runs. If you want to keep track of the user as he or she creates new clone Forms, for example, set up an Array of Form Object Variables (see "Objects"). Then, when the user creates another clone, you create another Array item because the following Sub is in the Form_Load Event of *all* the clones. To do this, you need only to put these commands within the prototype, original Form that is giving birth to these clones; they will all inherit any commands in the Events of the prototype.

```
Sub Form_Load()
    For i = 1 To totalclones
            Set Formsarray(i) = Formsarray(i+1)
    Next
    Set Formsarray(1) = Me
End Sub
```

The Me Command: The Me command refers to whatever clone these commands are executing within. Remember that all the clones will have the same *Name* Property, so you need to use Object Variables to refer to the clones. Me tells VB which particular clone is being added to your Array.

The Is Command: Is lets you query whether a member of a Form Array is, in fact, pointing to a Form. One use for this is to see which item in the Array is empty and available for use:

```
For i = 1 To 20
    If Formsarray(i) Is Nothing Then
            Set Formsarray(i) = Me
            Exit For
    End If
Next
```

Cautions   See "Cautions" under "Objects."

See also   Arrays; Is; Me; Multiple Document Interface; Objects

See   GetAttr

Description   You use SetData to send a graphic on a Form, Image Control or Picture Box to the Clipboard. Or you can use SetData to place a graphic image from a disk file into the Clipboard.

Used with   Forms, Image Controls and Picture Boxes

Variables   To send the picture in a Picture Box to the Clipboard:

```
Clipboard.Clear
Clipboard.SetData Picture1.Picture
```

OR (If your picture is in a format other than .BMP, you must specify which format. .BMP, Bit-Mapped Picture, is the default. To send a picture on the current Form as a .WMF—Windows Metafile Format):

```
Clipboard.Clear
Clipboard.SetData Picture, 3
```

OR (to send the Image Property instead of the Picture Property):

```
Clipboard.SetData Picture1.Image
```

The four possible formats are as follows:

Picture, 2	(.BMP, the default)
Picture, 3	(.WMF, Windows Metafile; see "Picture")
Picture, 8	(.DIB, Device-Independent Bitmap)
Picture, 9	(Color Palette)

Note: If you don't add this optional specifier, VB does it for you.

OR (to load a disk file graphic into the Clipboard):

```
Clipboard.Clear
Clipboard.SetData LoadPicture("C:\WINDOWS\DOUG.BMP")
```

Uses   • Temporarily back up the user's efforts in a drawing application. The picture saved to the Clipboard can be an image that has been imported into the VB program via LoadPicture or imported while you are designing your program by modifying the Picture Property of a Form, Image or Picture Box.

An image that was drawn with the drawing commands PSet, Line or Circle, or something printed with Print, can also be sent to the Clipboard. However, the AutoRedraw property must be set to On (True), and you *must* use the Image, not the Picture, Property.

• Export graphics to other programs. In the other program's Edit Menu, select Paste. If the formats match, the other program should be able to import your picture.

Cautions   • You must first use Clipboard.Clear to remove anything that currently resides in the Clipboard; otherwise, SetData won't work (except when importing from a disk file).

Unlike Notepad and many other Windows programs, only one Clipboard can be running at a time. If the Clipboard contains something, such as text, your Picture or Image Property will not be saved. If, however, the *format* of the Clipboard's contents match the format of the graphic you are trying to save, the old graphic will be replaced in the Clipboard. You can use

X = Clipboard.GetFormat (1) to find out the current format of anything in the Clipboard. In this case, X will be –1 if there is text in the Clipboard, or X will be 0 if not. (See "GetFormat.")

To make certain that your picture is saved, first use Clipboard.Clear to remove anything that might be in the Clipboard.

• GetData can pull in four kinds of graphics from the Clipboard—.BMP (Bit-Mapped Picture), .WMF (Windows Metafile Format), Color Palette or .DIB (Device-Independent Bitmap). There are many other PC graphics file types such as .TIF, .GIF, EPS. However, the Clipboard can accommodate only the .BMP, .WMF and .DIB types.

Use GetFormat to find out if the Clipboard contains the graphics type that you are requesting to be imported into VB.

• If you want to save a drawn image (one created with PSet, Line, Circle or Print), you must turn AutoRedraw on (True) and Clipboard.SetData *Image*. You cannot use the Picture Property to save drawings.

Example

Figure S-21: A graphic three ways   as a Picture Property of the Form (on the left); as a Picture Box (on the right); and after being copied to the Clipboard.

```
Sub Form_Click ()
clipboard.Clear
clipboard.SetData Picture
End Sub
```

Here we have a Form with a picture, a Picture Box with the same picture in 256 colors, and the results of sending the Form's image to the Clipboard.

The Picture Box is in 256 colors and the Form has been given a 16-color version. You can see some smearing and false color patterns typical of 16-color images (compare the gloves).

See also   Clipboard; GetData; GetFormat; GetText; Image; SetText

SetFocus

METHOD

Description   SetFocus enables your program, while running, to shift the focus to a different Control or Form. Ordinarily, the user moves the focus by clicking on a File List Box or some other Control, but your program can also adjust the focus.

When a Control, such as a Text Box, *has the focus*, any typing on the keyboard will appear in that Text Box. Only one Control at a time can have the focus, just as only one window in Windows can be *active* (able to receive input from the user) at any given time.

The user can change the focus by using the TAB key to cycle the focus among all the Controls on the active Form. The order in which the focus cycles is determined by how the Controls' individual TabIndex and TabStop Properties are set. Clicking on a Control also shifts the focus to that Control.

Used with   Forms (see the second item in "Cautions" below), Check Boxes, Combo Boxes, Command Buttons, Directory, Drive and File List Boxes, Horizontal and Vertical Scroll Bars, List Boxes, OLE, Option Buttons, Picture Boxes and Text Boxes.

The only objects that *cannot* have the focus and, thus, are not susceptible to SetFocus are Frames, Labels, Lines, Shapes, Timers and Menus.

Variables   Text1.SetFocus

OR

Form2.SetFocus

Uses   • Make your program react intelligently to current conditions. If you are creating a database application, for instance, there may be several Text Boxes on a Form for different kinds of data—date, invoice #, balance, inventory, etc. If the user clicks on a Command Button to retrieve some unrelated information for a moment, you may want to restore the focus to where it was before the interruption.

Controls are arranged in a particular order of focus, established by the order in which you created them. This order is contained in their TabIndex Property. Your program can change the TabIndex order, but that won't directly affect the current focus—only the order in which pressing the TAB key cycles through the Controls.

Use SetFocus to deliberately give one Control the focus because it's most likely to be accessed next by the user. This approach eliminates some inefficiencies. If the user is typing, he or she would probably prefer to have the program intelligently adjust focus as appropriate, rather than having to reach for the mouse or press TAB to cycle through the Controls.

Cautions
• SetFocus adjusts the focus among the Controls and Forms (the windows) in your VB program. To change the focus to a separate program running under Windows, use AppActivate.

• A Form itself can get the focus, but only under special conditions: either there must be no Controls on that Form, or any extant Controls must be disabled (their Enabled Property set to 0).

• Your program knows when an object gets the focus—that object's GotFocus Event is triggered. And the LostFocus Event is triggered when the focus shifts to another object.

• A Control's Keydown, KeyPress or KeyUp Event can be triggered *only* if that Control has the focus.

• A Control cannot get the focus if its Enabled or Visible Property is off (set to 0). If a Control's TabStop Property is set to False, the user cannot tab to it (but it can still get the focus by clicking or SetFocus).

Example
The visual clues as to which Control has the focus are subtle, but we wouldn't want them to be intrusive. The active Text Box has a "caret" at the insertion point—the place where the next keystroke will insert a character. (This used to be called a *cursor*, but in Windows parlance the cursor is the *mouse pointer*.)

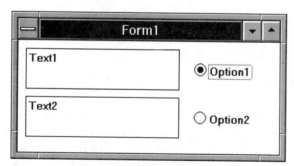

Figure S-22: An active Option Button (the one with the focus) has a thin gray line around it. On this Form, the first Option Button currently has the focus.

We can change the focus to Text Box 2 in Figure S-23 by this method:

```
Sub Option2_Click ()
    text2.SetFocus
End Sub
```

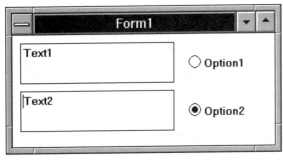

Figure S-23: Now the caret appears in the lower Text Box after the user clicks on Option2. The focus has changed.

See also   GotFocus; Label; LostFocus; TabIndex; TabStop

S ETTEXT

METHOD

Description   You use SetText to place text in the Clipboard.

Used with   The Clipboard

Variables   To send the text in the text Variable A$ to the Clipboard:

    Clipboard.SetText A$

OR (to use the format that is used for DDE, Dynamic Data Exchange. Note that a special format is required for DDE; see "LinkMode" for more information): Clipboard.SetText A$, &HBF00

OR (to send a literal piece of text, not a Variable):
Clipboard.SetText "THIS GOES INTO THE CLIPBOARD"

Uses   • Export text that was *copied* or *cut* from your VB program by using the SelLength and other Sel Properties (which see) to other programs. Once text has been copied from your program into the Clipboard, it is available via the Edit Menu Paste option in many other Windows programs or via SHIFT+INS.

• Provide an *undo* feature. Before allowing the user to modify text in a Text Box, first temporarily store it in the Clipboard:

    Clipboard.SetText Text1.Text, 1

Then, if the user presses a Command Button you've labeled *Undo,* the instructions in the Command Button are as follows:

```
Sub Command1_Click ()
    Text1.Text = Clipboard.GetText(1)
End Sub
```

Cautions

• Unlike Notepad and many other Windows programs, only one Clipboard can be running at a time. If the Clipboard contains something, such as a graphic image, your text will not be saved.

If, however, the Clipboard contains text, the *format* of the Clipboard's contents is set to "text" and the previous text will be replaced. You can use X = Clipboard.GetFormat (1) to find the current format of anything in the Clipboard. In the case of GetFormat(1), X will be –1 if there is text in the Clipboard, or X will be 0 if not. (See "GetFormat.")

To make certain that your text is saved, first use Clipboard.Clear to remove anything that might be in the Clipboard.

Example

For this example, put a Text Box and a Command Button on a Form. Into the Command1_Click Event, type the following:

```
Sub Command1_Click ()
    Clipboard.SetText Text1.Text
End Sub
```

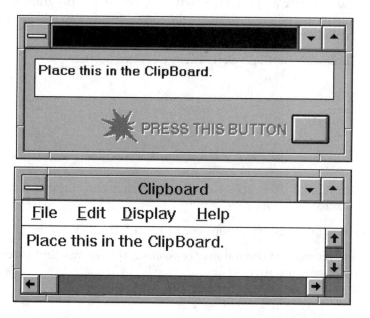

Figure S-24: The Clipboard must receive properly addressed messages. The correct address of this message is Clipboard.SetText Text1.Text.

Every time the button shown in Figure S-24 is clicked, the Clipboard will contain whatever text you have typed into the Text Box. Just position the Clipboard on the screen so you can watch the action.

The other part of this program is in the Form_Load Event, and it creates the Form's appearance when the program runs:

```
Sub Form_Load ()

Show

fontname = "helv"
x = 1500: y = 900: a$ = "PRESS THIS BUTTON"
    Raiseit a$, x, y

fontname = "carta"
fontsize = 18
x = 1000: y = 500: a$ = "&"
    Raiseit a$, x, y

End Sub
```

You must always use Show when you are going to Print on a Form in the Form_Load Event. Otherwise, the printed items (or drawn items created by PSet, Circle or Line) will not be visible.

The Raiseit Subroutine (described in "Print") gives the embossed look to the message "PRESS THIS BUTTON" and the symbol printed in the symbol set called "CARTA." Notice that you can adjust the Properties of the printed text—the size and even the font itself—while the program runs. This is the way to use different fonts on the same object or to add symbols like the exploding star in this example.

See also   Clipboard; GetData; GetFormat; GetText; SetData

 GN

FUNCTION

Description   The Sgn Function tells you whether a numeric Variable is positive, negative or zero.

Used with   Numeric Variables (as opposed to text "string" Variables)

Variables   Sgn returns 1 if the number is positive, 0 if the number is zero, and –1 if the number is negative.

```
Z = 55

X = Sgn(Z)

Print X
```

Results in   1

Uses   None. Sgn is a semi-useful "shortcut." You can find the sign of a number this way as well:

```
X = -2
Select Case X
    Case Is = 0
            Print "The Number is zero."
    Case Is < 0
            Print "The Number is negative."
    Case Else
            Print "The Number is positive."
End Select
```

You could also use If...Then to react to the sign of a number.

To learn the sign status of a number, you can use Sgn to do it in an abbreviated, slightly more efficient way, but some would say that is hardly a reason to add a word to the Basic language:

```
If Sgn(X) = 0 Then Print "It's Zero"
```

You could just as easily enter the following:

```
If X = 0
```

Example
```
Z = 45
Print Sgn(Z)
```

Results in 1

SHAPE

CONTROL

Description The Shape Control is a shortcut. It can allow you to create designs more easily and quickly than using the Line and Circle commands (which see). Although Line and Circle are more flexible, for simple design work you might prefer to use Shape to add rectangles, circles and ellipses, or to frame other Controls.

Figure S-25: Use the Shape Control to add simple designs to your Forms.

Used with   Forms

Variables

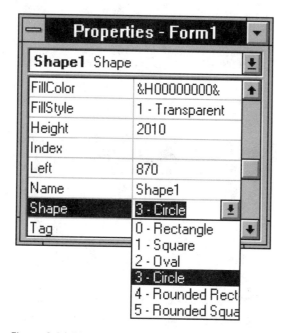

Figure S-26: You can set the Shape Properties in the Properties Window.

OR (to change a Property while a program is running):
```
shape1.BorderWidth = 5
```

Uses
• Create attractive frames around various objects in your Forms. By layering one Shape on top of another and playing around with their BorderWidth, FillStyle, Shape and Color Properties, you can give depth and graphic charm to your work.

• Change the appearance of Command Buttons and the like, depending on whether or not they are currently appropriate to the user's task at hand (as an alternative to the Enabled Property).

• Highlight parts of images or text (see the Example).

• Separate zones of a Form into logical areas, reflecting the purposes of the different parts of the Form.

Cautions
• Unlike the drawing commands—Line, Circle and PSet—moving a Shape (Shape1.Left = 500) does not effect the CurrentX and CurrentY coordinates.

If you place one Shape on top of another, it will remain the uppermost graphic. In other words, you can build multiple-Shape layered frames and designs from the background out to the foreground.

Example
This program shows all six available Shapes:
```
Sub Form_Click ()
    fontsize = 12
    currentx = 350: Print "0";
For i = 1 To 5
```

```
                    Load shape1(i)
                    shape1(i).Left = shape1(i − 1).Left + 600
                    shape1(i).Shape = i
                    shape1(i).Visible = −1
                    currentx = currentx + 400
                    Print i;
              Next i
              End Sub
```

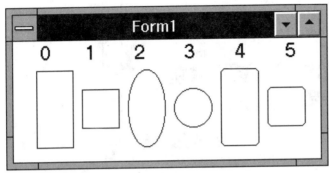

Figure S-27: There are six built-in Shapes you can add to your Forms.

Shape Properties
BackColor • BackStyle • BorderColor • BorderStyle • BorderWidth
DrawMode • FillColor • FillStyle • Height • Index • Left • Name
Shape • Tag • Top • Visible • Width

Shape Events
A Shape has no Events.

Shape Methods
Move • Refresh • ZOrder

See also   Circle; Frame; Line (Method); Shape (Property)

 HAPE

PROPERTY

Description   The setting of the Shape Property determines which of six possible shapes—square or rectangle (each with a "rounded" variant), circle or ellipse—appears when you place a Shape *Control* (which see) on a Form.

Used with	The Shape Control only
Variables	You can set the Shape Property in the Properties Window.

OR (to change the Shape to a circle while the program is running):

```
shape1.Shape = 3
```

There are six possible settings for the Shape Property:

0 Rectangle (the default)
1 Square
2 Oval (ellipse)
3 Circle
4 Rounded Rectangle
5 Rounded Square

Uses	See "Shape *Control*."
Cautions	See "Shape *Control*."
Example	This example is part of a physics program that demonstrates aspects of balance. At a certain place in the program, we want to highlight the point of greatest stress where Don balances Betty. First, we create some background frames—put a rounded rectangle Shape on a Form, and set its FillStyle to Solid and its FillColor to black. Then we add a thin second Shape with a BorderColor of light gray. Finally, on top of these frame Shapes, we place an Image of Don and Betty and their trick. Because we used an Image Box (instead of a Picture Box), we can adjust the size of the graphic to suit our needs by changing the Image's Stretch Property.

Now, to create a highlight, we put another Shape around the contact point between Don's hands and Betty's hips. We set that Shape's Border-Color to white and its Shape Property to circle. If you wanted to illustrate various aspects of this photo, you could place dozens of such highlights around on the image and set all their Visible Properties to Off (0). Then, at appropriate times, you could selectively turn on the Visible Properties.

Figure S-28: You can use Shapes to highlight key areas in a graphic or photo.

See also   Frame; Line; Shape (Control)

Shell
FUNCTION

Description   With Shell your Visual Basic program can start another program running.
  If the new program accepts one, you can also provide a "command string extension," a filename to load into the new program or a series of options. A "command string extension" would be the *REPORT.DOC* in "C:\W\WORD.EXE REPORT.DOC"
  The new program can either get the "focus" (become the "active" program) or your Visual Basic program can retain the focus, as you wish.

Used with External programs

Variables Because Shell is a Function, you must put it inside a larger structure. Here we use X =. After the Shell command is carried out, the X will contain a "Task ID" number for the newly started program. This ID is not used by Visual Basic directly. Technically, the Task ID is the "Instance handle" of the Shelled application. It can be used with "API calls" (see Appendix A), which require the hInstance or task handle.

The name of the program that you are starting with Shell can end in .COM, .EXE, .BAT or .PIF.

```
X = Shell("C:\WINDOWS\WRITE.EXE")
```

OR (to start a program and also put a file into it using a "command string extension"):

```
FNAME$ = "C:\WINDOWS\NOTEPAD.EXE C:\WINDOWS\SYSTEM.INI"
X = Shell(FNAME$)
```

OR (to start a program and control its "WindowState"– whether it is minimized, maximized, has the focus, etc.)

The example just above would start Notepad running and automatically load in the System.INI file. Notepad would appear as an icon and would have the focus because we didn't add an optional "WindowState" number.

The default WindowState is *Minimized, with focus.*

You can add an optional number that controls the new program's appearance on arrival. The 1 in the following example causes the program to load in at a "normal" size and to have the focus. (Normal means that it is neither an icon, nor fills the entire screen, but is somewhere in between):

```
X = Shell("Notepad.Exe", 1)
```

WindowState Options

1   Normal size, with focus
2   Minimized (icon), with focus; the default, if you omit the Window-State number
3   Maximized (fills entire screen), with focus
4   Normal size, without focus (your VB program remains active)
5   Minimized, without focus

Uses • Create a File Manager-like component in your programs to allow the user to launch additional programs from within your running VB program. There is a way for your VB program to know when a Shelled application has been shut down by the user.

Example The GetModuleHandle routine tells you which applications are currently running in Windows. In this example, all we want to know is whether or not Microsoft's Word for Windows is running.

In General Declarations:

```
Declare Function GetModuleHandle Lib KERNEL (ByVal App →
As String) As Integer
```

In an Event:

```
Sub Form_Load( )
    handle = GetModuleHandle( WINWORDEXE )
    If handle = 0 Then
            MsgBox Word isn t running.
    Else
            MsgBox Word is running.
    End If
End Sub
```

• Load a "help file" for your program into Notepad as an easy way to provide onscreen assistance to the user. (See the Example below.)

• Automatically run an outside program as needed. For instance, if you want to allow the user to create a design, Shell Paintbrush. For text work, Shell Notepad or Write.

• Govern the behavior of a Shelled program with the SendKeys command (which see).

Cautions
• As always when communicating outside your running VB program, you should provide for the possibility of an error. Perhaps the program you are trying to Shell isn't on the disk, for example. See the Example below for a way of handling unexpected errors.

• An alternative to Shell, for some jobs, is Object Linking and Embedding (see "OLE").

Example
Rather than write an elaborate, hypertext Help feature, we're simply going to provide a .WRI file and Shell Write.Exe, the word processor that comes with every copy of Windows. We'll automatically load our help file into Write, and the reader can scroll through it and get program assistance.

Since there is a possibility that the user of our program might not use Write and might have erased it from his or her disk, we need to put an error handler into this part of our program as well.

To try this example, put a Command Button on a Form and find the name of some sample .WRI file that you want to use to simulate a Help screen. We've also put a Picture on the Form, just for visual appeal.

Figure S-29: When the user clicks on Help, he or she will fire up the *Write* word processor, filled with our help info (see Figure S-30).

```
Sub Command1_Click ()

On Error Resume Next

X = Shell("C:\WINDOWS\WRITE.EXE TESTHELP.WRI", 1)

If Err Then
    MsgBox(Error$(Err))
End If

End Sub
```

When the user clicks on the Command Button labeled HELP, the Write.Exe word processor is loaded and run. The help file is then loaded into Write and becomes visible. The Write window will be "normal size" and will have the focus because we added the ,1 option at the end of the Shell command.

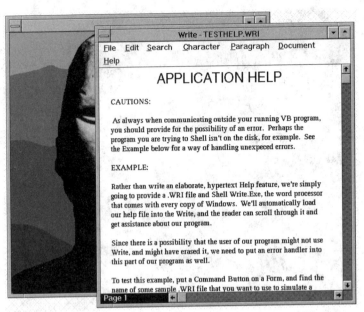

Figure S-30: Using "Shell Notepad" is an easy way to add a Help feature to your programs. (To create a traditional "hypertext" Windows Help feature, see Microsoft Professional Toolkit in Appendix D.)

On Error Resume Next tells VB to continue if it cannot find Write.Exe and Shell it for us. Without this error trap, VB would present the user with a message but shut down our program. After Shell, we check the built-in VB Variable called *Err*, which will be zero if things went well or will contain an error number if something went wrong. This error number can be offered to the Error$ command, which will report the problem to the user but not shut down our VB program. (See "On Error.")

An Error That's Not Trapped: On Error will trap a problem trying to Shell Write.Exe, but *will not trap* the error if "Testhelp.Wri" is missing or for some reason cannot be loaded into Write because Write itself is loading in "Testhelp.Wri," not our VB program. How such an error is handled when there is a problem in the "command string extension" depends on the error handling built into the program that you Shelled. With Write.Exe, the user is told that the file cannot be found and is asked to put a disk into drive A:. This error handling doesn't crash your VB program, or Write. The user could simply select the Cancel Button on Write's Error Message Box, then shut down Write and return to your VB program.

See also   AppActivate; OLE Automation; SendKeys

SHOW
··
METHOD

Description

The Show command makes an invisible Form (window) visible.

The Form will also be Loaded (from the disk into the computer's memory) if it hasn't already been Loaded.

Show is sometimes used as the first command in a VB program because you might draw a graphic design or Print some text directly on the first visible window (normally, this is the first Form). Unless Show forces VB to reveal the window, the drawn graphics (using PSet, Circle or Line) or anything that's Printed to the Form cannot show up. When the Form appears, the drawn or Printed items will not be on the Form (unless the Form's AutoRedraw Property is set to "True").

Printed or drawn objects cannot normally be created when their Form is invisible. The user will never get to see these objects unless you force a Show prior to the execution of the commands that draw or Print. An alternative is to set the Form's AutoRedraw Property on (True), but this both slows down the program when the graphics are first drawn and takes up computer memory. (See "AutoRedraw" for more on this trade-off.)

To make Show the first command executed when a program is run, put Show into the Form_Load Event of the "Startup Form." One Form is always the first Form that VB executes when a program starts. By default, the Startup Form will be the first Form you created, called Form1 unless you've renamed it. You can also make a different Form the Startup Form by selecting Set Startup Form from VB's Options Menu.

Used with

Forms only

Variables

To display the current Form:

        Show

OR (to display a different Form from the one that contains the Show command): Form4.Show

OR (to make a Form *modal*): Show 1

Modal Forms: A *modal* Form means that your VB program freezes until that Form is either hidden (with the Hide command) or UnLoaded (with the UnLoad command). A Message Box (created with the MsgBox command) is a modal Form.

A modal Form prevents the user from accessing other parts of your program—other windows—until a message is acknowledged. Other Windows *programs* can be accessed, but your VB program will accept neither mouse clicks nor keypresses from the user until the modal Form has been dispensed with.

Primarily, you Show a modal Form if you want to display custom Message or Input Boxes. Perhaps you want to make these Boxes match the visual look of your program, rather than use the generic VB MsgBox or InputBox$ Functions.

Uses
• If your program has several windows, several Forms, you can switch among them as appropriate by Hiding and Showing them. Why not UnLoad them and free up some memory in the computer? You can UnLoad if you're certain the Form won't be needed by the program again. A fancy opening title screen is a perfect candidate for UnLoading.

Forms actively used by a program should be left hidden, but not UnLoaded, when they aren't currently needed. You can then make them visible again much more quickly via Show than via Load. And they will retain any Variables, such as Static Variables, that are remembered by the program while it is running (see "Variables").

• Use Show prior to any drawing or printing, unless the Form's AutoRedraw Property is set on (True). See the Description above.

Cautions
• If you Show a modal Form, no commands after the Show command in your program will be carried out until you have used a Hide or UnLoad command to remove the modal Form. The normal, modeless Show, however, does not have this effect. Visual Basic will carry out any commands that follow a normal Show in your program.

For a Control, like a Text Box, the equivalent of Show is setting that Control's Visible Property to On (–1 or True).

If a Form is not currently Loaded, Show will force a Load to take place before making the Form visible.

There is no difference between setting a Form's Visible Property to On (–1) and using the Show command. Likewise, there is no difference between setting a Form's Visible Property off (0 or False) and using the Hide command.

Show triggers the Form's Activate Event, which see.

Example
Many programs provide the user with something to look at while the program prepares its Variables, fills List Boxes with text information, etc. This "title screen" also lets the user know that nothing has gone wrong—that the program is running, is getting itself together, and will soon interact with the user when it displays its first working window.

The first things that happen when a VB program runs are any commands you've put in the Form_Load Event of the Startup Form (see "Description" above).

In this example, we'll Load in a title screen (Form2) and then Print "TAX RECORDS" on top of a textured .BMP graphic that we've already set into Form2's Picture Property.

First, create two Forms and put a Timer on Form2. Then put the following into Form1's Form_Load Event (Form1 is the Startup Form):

```
Sub Form_Load ()
    Hide
    Load Form2
End Sub
```

All we do here is make the Startup Form invisible and then Load Form2.

Figure S-31: A title screen provides an attractive visual and prevents the user from worrying that something is wrong.

Into the Form_Load Event of Form2, enter the following:

```
Sub Form_Load ()

Timer1.Interval = 4000
Timer1.Enabled = 0

Show

fontsize = 148
    Raiseit "TAX", 20, 200
fontsize = 55
    Raiseit "RECORDS", 400, 2700

Timer1.Enabled = —1

End Sub
```

Here we set the Timer to a four-second interval, but you should disable it. The Timer will act as a time bomb once Enabled—it will UnLoad Form2, the very Form that hosts it. Timer1 will destroy itself and everything else in this now-unneeded Title Screen Form.

Then we Show Form2 and Print "TAX RECORDS" using the Raiseit Sub-routine, which creates drop-shadows (see "Print"). Remember that we must use the Show command *before* printing the text or the text will not be visible. Try removing Show to see what happens.

Finally, we turn on the Timer. It will count down four seconds and then carry out whatever commands are in its "Timer" Event:

```
Sub Timer1_Timer ()
Hide
Form1.Show
Unload Form2
End Sub
```

Making the Window Look Smoother: At once, the Timer makes Form2, the title screen, invisible. This isn't necessary because the UnLoad Form2 below will not only make Form 2 invisible, but will also remove it from the computer's memory as if it had been detached from the program. However, Hide makes the move between Form1 and Form2 look smoother to the user. Without the Hide command, Form1 appears briefly on top of Form2.

Form1 is then made visible and would contain the first working window of the program. Finally, Form2 is destroyed.

See also   Hide; Load; UnLoad; Visible

 IN

FUNCTION

Description   Sin gives you the sine of an angle expressed in radians.

You can use a number, a numeric Variable, a numeric Constant or a numeric "expression."

You can get the sine of any type of Variable—Integer, Floating-Point, etc. (See "Variables" for more on Variable types and expressions.)

Variables   Print Sin(x)

OR

F = Sin(.3)

Uses   Trigonometry

Cautions   If the Variable or Constant you use with Sin is an Integer or Single-Precision number, the result will be Single-Precision. All other data types are calculated in Double Precision. (See "Variables.")

Example   z = Sin(.3)
Print z

See also   Atn; Cos; Tan

Slider

CONTROL

See Windows 95 Controls

Sorted

PROPERTY

Description   When you set its Sorted Property to On (–1 or True), the text items within a List or Combo Box will be automatically alphabetized by Visual Basic. Additions and deletions to the Box—by the user or by the program—will be inserted into their correct alphabetical position in the list.

Visual Basic also adjusts the *index* of each item to reflect any changes in the order of the items (see "ListIndex").

Used with   List Boxes and Combo Boxes

Variables   **Variable type:** Integer (Boolean)

You cannot set the Sorted Property while a program is running. You must explicitly adjust it from VB's Properties Window.

By default, Sorted is off (0 or False). If you want the items in a Box in alphabetical order, you'll have to adjust the Sorted Property in the Properties Window while writing your program.

Uses   Most kinds of lists that you will put within List and Combo Boxes are easier for the user to work with if they are sorted. The Sorted Property automatically maintains an alphabetized list.

Cautions   • While the program is running, using the AddItem command to insert a new entry into the list (or using RemoveItem to delete one) will not violate the alphabetization that Sorted carries out for you. The list will be maintained in correct order. *But there is one exception involving AddItem.*

AddItem allows you the option of specifying exactly where within the list the new item should be placed. List1.AddItem "John" will put "John" in the correct alphabetical position if Sorted has been turned on. List1.AddItem "John", 4 will force "John" into the fifth position in the list, ignoring Sorted, because lists start counting at 0. (See "AddItem" and "ListIndex.")

RemoveItem has no effect on the alphabetization of the items in a list.

Example

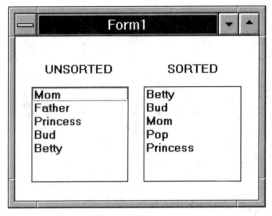

Figure S-32: The Andersons, ordered and disordered.

```
Sub Form_Load ()

Show
currenty = list1.top − 350
Print "   UNSORTED      SORTED"

list1.AddItem "Mom"
list1.AddItem "Father"
list1.AddItem "Princess"
list1.AddItem "Bud"
list1.AddItem "Betty"

list2.AddItem "Mom"
list2.AddItem "Pop"
list2.AddItem "Princess"
list2.AddItem "Bud"
list2.AddItem "Betty"

End Sub
```

We have two List Boxes here, and List2's Sorted Property was set to True using the Properties Window while the program was being designed. Because we are printing on the Form, we must first use a Show command (see "Show") to display the printed titles.

Then we move to where we want the titles printed above the boxes. The CurrentY Property of the Form is the vertical location; we arrive at this location by subtracting from the Top position of the first List Box. There are many ways to format Printing. In the Print line, we adjust the horizontal positions of the titles by simply adding spaces until it looks right.

Then we add the same list of items to each Box. The first Box displays them in the order they were added; the second Box sorts them and then displays them in alphabetical order.

See also   AddItem; Combo Box; List Box; ListIndex; RemoveItem

SPACE$

FUNCTION

Description   Space$ creates a text ("string") Variable with nothing in it except the number of spaces you specify.

Space$ is not often, if ever, used in Windows programming but is retained to enable you to import older DOS Basic programs into VB.

Used with   The Print command for crude formatting of text Variables to "pad" them to a particular desired length. There are other preferable approaches to formatting that do not involve Space$.

Variables   To create a text Variable with 23 space characters in it:

```
A$ = Space$(23)
PRINT "X" + A$ + "X"
```

Results in   X   X

OR (to make a text Variable a particular length, in this case, 50 characters long):

```
G$ = "Nob Hill"
Print Len(G$)
G$ = G$ + Space$(50 — Len(G$))
Print Len(G$)
End Sub
```

Results in   8
50

Here we changed G$ by making it equal (=) a new version of itself with the spaces added. The number of spaces was calculated by subtracting the current number of characters in G$ (its Len) from the desired size, 50.

Uses   **Creating Text Variables of a Particular Size:** When using the random-mode file technique (see "Open"), your program is expected to provide text Variables of predictable length. You can use Space$ to "pad" a too-short piece of text into the desired number of characters and length. However, alternative approaches work better (see "Type").

Formatting Screen or Printer Output: Space$ is rarely, if ever, used for formatting in Windows. A decade ago, typewriters were more common than printers, and computer screens imitated typewriters. Machines work more easily with text characters if the characters are all the same size. The familiar "Courier" typeface was widely used because its letter *W* is exactly the same width as its letter *i*. Although this nonproportional text is easier for machines to print, it is harder for humans to read. You have fewer visual clues when each letter is the same width.

When, in the DOS programming world of the 1980s, most of the text onscreen was nonproportional (all letters were the same size), Space$ was used sometimes instead of Tab. Space$ could provide finer adjustments to the formatting of the text onscreen (or on early printers). However, even then, there were other, better, approaches to this formatting problem. Two such flexible commands are the Spc and Tab Functions.

Spc prints a desired number of spaces over from the current (cursor) position. Print Spc(10), for example, prints 10 spaces. Tab *moves* the cursor but doesn't print spaces on top of intervening text.

Now that Windows, and most printers, use the more attractive and more easily read proportional fonts, Space$ is of little value in formatting.

Cautions   • The String$ Function can imitate Space$, but String$ is more flexible. It will create a text Variable containing a specified number of *any* character—including spaces. It thus makes Space$ redundant, even if Space$ did offer any utility when programming for Windows.

```
X$ = String$(35, " ")
```

The preceding line produces the same X$ as

```
X$ = Space$(35)
```

The number of spaces requested of Space$, the 35 in Space$(35), must not be larger than 65,535.

Example   The Len command shows that Z$ is 14 characters long.

```
Z$ = Space$(14)

Print Len(Z$)
```

Results in   14

See also   CurrentX; Open; Spc; String$; Type

 PC

FUNCTION

Description   Spc prints a number of blank "space" characters to the screen, printer or a disk file. It has few uses.

If you intend to format your work, you'll want to *move* the cursor, the current print position, but not print space characters. The Tab Function does this (which see). But the best approach in VB is to format printed text with the CurrentX and CurrentY commands. They can position text with a fine degree of control.

Used with	The Print command for the screen (a Form or Picture Box) or a printer; the Print # command for disk files
Variables	Print Spc(10) "HERE"
Results in	HERE

OR

Print Spc(20)

Results in   HERE

OR (to put spaces into a disk file): Print #1, Spc(5) A$

Uses   None. (This command has no uses in Visual Basic; the reasons are discussed in the similar command, Space$.)

Cautions   • Spc cannot print more than 32,767 spaces. And it cannot print negative spaces.

• Spc does more than merely "move the cursor," advancing the current position where the next character will be printed. *It prints space characters.* Any text between the current cursor position and the number of Spcs will be covered up.

• Most Windows and printer fonts, "Courier" being the notable exception, are proportional. That is, the characters in most Windows and printer fonts vary in width–the *i* being narrower than the *w*–which eliminates any possible uses Spc might have in formatting text onscreen. The actual horizontal distance of a space printed by Spc is an average of the width of all the characters in that particular font at that particular font size.

• You do not need to put a semicolon after a Spc command. Spc will not cause a new line to be printed.

• If you are thinking of using Spc with random-mode files, you may want to approach the job of creating fixed-length text Variables instead. See "Type" and "Open" for a discussion of random mode.

Example   Print "HERE" Spc(30) "TO HERE"

Results in   HERE   TO HERE

See also   CurrentX; Open; Space$; String$; Tab; Type

S_{QR}

FUNCTION

Description   Sqr provides the square root of a positive number. (The number cannot be negative.)

Used with
Variables

Any positive *numeric expression* (see "Variables" for a definition)

To use a literal number:

```
X = Sqr(144)
```

OR (to use a Variable):

```
Z = 144
X = Sqr(Z)
```

Uses

Use with arithmetic calculations.

Cautions

The Sqr Function will not work with zero or negative numbers.

Example

```
Print Sqr(144)
```

The opposite of the square root is raising a number to the power of two:

```
Print 12 ^ 2
```

See also

Abs; Sgn (the other two arithmetic Functions in Basic)

Description

If your program has more than one Form (window), one of the Forms is designated the *Startup Form*. This Form will be the first place that VB will start carrying out any commands that you have written. In a program with one Form, it's automatically the Startup Form.

When the user runs your VB program, any commands you have placed within the Form_Load Event of the Startup Form will be carried out first.

By default, the Startup Form is the Form that appears when you begin working on a VB program (or select New Project from VB's File Menu). When you first run VB, it presents you with a blank Form named "Form1."

If you write your entire program within the default Form1, you don't need to worry about Startup Form because Form1 will be the only Form. And the program will fire it up first.

Longer programs can benefit from several Forms, several windows. If you add new Forms by selecting New Form from the VB File Menu, these additional Forms will also be part of your program, but Form1 will still be the Startup Form.

If you later decide that you want to add, say, a special window that merely displays the title of your program, you will probably want that newly created Form to be the Startup Form. To change which Form is to be the Startup Form, change the Startup Form name in the Tools/Project Options Menu.

Sub Main Instead of Startup Form: You don't *have* to use a Startup Form. You could create a Module and in it put a special Subroutine called Sub Main( ). Then select Sub Main as the Startup Form in the Tools Menu "Project Options." VB would then use this Subroutine as the first place it looked for commands when the program starts running. Some programmers like to put commands within Sub Main, which, for example, could check initialization Variables in an .INI file that goes with the program. Then, based on what options the user might have previously selected when the program was installed (or later from an Options Menu), this Sub Main would decide which of several Forms to Load and display.

Used with   Forms

Variables   Change the Startup Form in the Tools/Project Options Menu:

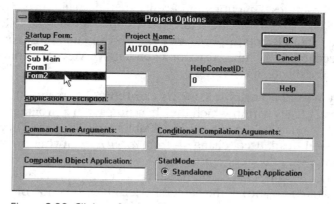

Figure S-33: Click on Startup Form to make a different Form the first thing that happens when your program runs.

STATIC

STATEMENT

Description   The Static command can be a useful tool. It preserves the contents of a Variable or of an Array.

Static is used most frequently in two situations:

1. To *keep a count* of how many times an Event has been triggered—how many times the Event happens while the program runs:

```
Sub Form_Click()
    Static Counter
    Counter = Counter + 1
    Print "This Form has been clicked on ";Counter;" times so far."
End Sub
```

2. To *toggle* something—to turn it off if it's on, and vice versa. Say you have a Command Button that, when clicked, changes the text in a Text Box to bold. When clicked again, it turns off bold. If clicked again, it turns bold back on, and so on—toggling boldface each time it's clicked:

```
Sub Command1_Click()
    Static Toggle
    Toggle = Not Toggle
    If Toggle = 0 Then
            Text1.FontBold = True
    Else
            Text1.FontBold = False
    End If
End Sub
```

(Subroutines, Functions and Events are the small units of programming in VB. Collectively, they are referred to as *procedures*. The following comments about Events apply as well to Subs and Functions. For more on procedures, see "Sub." Also, for a general overview of Variables and Arrays, see "Variables" and "Arrays.")

Why Would a Variable Lose Its Contents? In essence, Variables can have several ranges within which they have impact in a program. Some Variables are defined as Public in a Module (Public N As Integer). They can be accessed—read, used, changed—from *anywhere* in your program, and they always retain their contents.

Other Variables have a narrower range of impact. Those defined (with the Dim command) in the General Declarations section of a Form (or Module) can be accessed only by Events, Subroutines or Functions *within that Form or Module*. Other Forms cannot check to see what such a Variable contains, nor can they change the contents. In fact, these other Forms can have a Variable with the same name but holding different contents. Such Variables are said to be "Form-wide" or "Module-wide" in their scope, their influence. These Form-wide Variables, though, like Public Variables, always retain their contents.

The Narrowest Range of Influence: The Variables with the smallest range of influence are those you never define with Public or Dim commands. They are generally named within an Event (or Subroutine or Function). And they *do not retain their contents*. These local Variables have brief lives. They come into existence whenever their Event is triggered (or their Sub or Function). However, as soon as that Event is finished—when the program moves out of the procedure because it reaches the End Sub or End Function command—the Variable's contents disappear. A local Variable gets recreated each time an Event or other procedure is activated but loses its contents when that Event is finished. This has two virtues:

1. It conserves computer memory because when local Variables (in particular, local Arrays) die, they release the memory that they used.

2. It prevents you from creating bugs by inadvertently using the same Variable name for two different purposes in separate zones of a program.

You *can* make one or more of these "local" Variables remember its contents, though, using the Static command. In Figure S-34 we're using two Labels on a Form. Both Labels have the same commands in their Click Events, but the one on the right, Label2, has defined its X Variable as static:

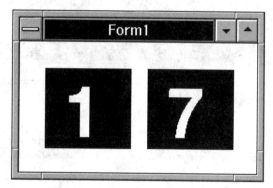

Figure S-34: The information in the Label on the right will be persistent preserved because it's been defined as static.

```
Sub Label1_Click ()
    x = x + 1
    label1.caption = Str$(x)
End Sub

Sub Label2_Click ()
    Static x
    x = x + 1
    label2.caption = Str$(x)
End Sub
```

Every time you click on the left Label, it shows 1. Every time you click on the right Label, the one with the Static command, it raises the number by one. In Figure S-34, both Labels were clicked on seven times, but the one with the Static X is the only one that can remember the previous value of X and then, when X = X + 1, increment X.

Used with Either text or numeric Variables to preserve their contents

OR Entire Subroutines can be declared static; then all the Variables within that Subroutine will preserve their contents:

```
Static Sub MySub ( )
```

OR Events can be declared static, too. Events are simply built-in Subroutine structures, waiting for you to put commands inside them. To make an Event static, just type Static in front of the Event name:

```
Static Sub Command1_Click ( )
```

Variables　To make a numeric Variable static: Static Z

OR (to make a text Variable static): Static X$

OR (to make all the Variables inside a procedure become static):
　　Static Sub MyRoutine ( )

OR (to make all the Variables in an Event static, insert the Static command before the name of the Event): Static Sub Form_Click ( )

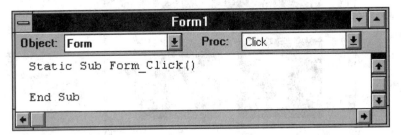

Figure S-35: You can make all the Variables within an *entire Event* (or Subroutine or Function) static. Just insert the word *Static* in front of the procedure.

OR (to make all the Variables in an Array static. See "Arrays" for the various permutations of Array declarations that you can use. Static can create as many different kinds of Arrays as can the Dim or Public commands): Static Name$(12)

OR (to use the *As* command when defining the Variable type. In this example, HomeTown becomes a text ("string") Variable. It is the equivalent of adding the Variable type symbol to the Variable name: Static Home-Town$. See "Variables" for more on Variable types): Static HomeTown As String

Uses　• You primarily use Static to allow things to *accumulate*–that is, to allow a numeric Variable to keep increasing each time an Event is triggered (thus acting as a counter) or allowing a text Variable to keep getting larger. Both of these uses are illustrated in the Example below.

• Static Variables are also useful if some condition should *toggle,* should switch between two states like italic or not-italic. Use Static in any situation where the Variables should be persistent, any time you need to know the value of a Variable as it was when the Event (or Sub or Function) was previously activated.

　　There may come a time when you want to change the size of an Array but also want to preserve its contents. In that situation, use the ReDim Preserve command. (See "ReDim.")

Cautions • When you declare an entire Subroutine static, all the Variables in the Sub, including Arrays, then become static. That is, their contents remain in existence throughout the life of the program, but they are only available to be queried or changed within their Event, Sub or Function procedure. They are still *local*.

If you don't use Static, all Variables (including Arrays created with the ReDim command) within a Subroutine would be temporary, "dynamic Variables," brought to life when the Subroutine is run but extinguished when the program moves on to another Event.

With Static, however, the Variables within are permanent as long as the program is running. That is, they can, of course, *vary* in what numbers they hold, but the memory space they reserve *and their contents* will not be destroyed when the program moves on to other events. Using Static is the only way to use a Dim Statement to build an Array within a Subroutine or Event. Without Static, you have to use ReDim to create dynamic, temporary Arrays.

In addition to using the Static command, you can also create permanent Variables and Arrays by putting a Dim Statement in the General Declarations section of a Form (or Module), thereby making a Variable or an Array available for use by all procedures (Events and Subroutines or Functions) within that Form.

Or, to make Variables and Arrays available to *all* areas—all Forms and Modules in your program—declare an Array using the Public command. You must type this declaration into a Module. (For more information, see "Arrays" or "Variables.")

Example Perhaps the most common use of Static is to allow your program to count the number of times a particular Event has happened while the program is running. In this example, we'll ask the user to type in a password before we allow the program to proceed.

We're going to put the password-testing commands inside the KeyPress Event of a Text Box. The KeyPress Event is triggered every time a key is pressed by the user, and it tells us which key. We want to *intercept* the keypresses, so we can check them against the password, "AEON," and so we can prevent the typed characters from becoming visible in the Text Box. It is common practice not to echo passwords to the screen, in case someone is watching over the user's shoulder.

Note: With the introduction of VB 2.0 a special Property was added to the Text Box Control, PassWordChar (which see), that provides a simpler way to address this problem of prying eyes.

In addition, keypress interception allows us to give the user only three chances to enter the password. Most people feel that this is a sufficient number of tries, no matter what condition the user might be in.

Figure S-36: We'll give the user three tries to get the password right. After that, the End command shuts down the program.

First, put a Text Box on a Form. Also put a Label on the Form but set its Visible Property off (False). We'll be using the Label later in the Form_Load Event described below. The Label is used only for the formatting of the embossing and framing that gives this window its look.

In the Text Box's KeyPress Event, type the following:

```
Sub Text1_KeyPress (KeyAscii As Integer)

Static PWord As String
Static Counter As Integer
Static numberoftries As Integer

numberoftries = numberoftries + 1
If numberoftries = 12 Then End

Counter = Counter + 1
PWord = PWord + Chr$(KeyAscii)
KeyAscii = 0
Text1.Text = String$(Counter, "*")

If LCase$(PWord) = "aeon" Then
    Load Form2
    Unload Form1
ElseIf Counter = 4 Then
    Counter = 0
    Text1.Text = ""
End If

End Sub
```

First, we make all three of the Variables in this Event static. We are going to allow the user to type in 12 characters—three tries at the four-letter password *AEON*. Each time the user presses a key, this KeyPress Event is triggered. We want these Variables to retain their contents, and making them static is a way to preserve their values.

We could accomplish the same thing by declaring this entire Event static, and thereby making all its Variables static: Static Sub Text1_KeyPress (KeyAscii As Integer).

Each time the user presses a key, we raise the total counter, "number-oftries," by 1. When it reaches 12, the user has had his or her three tries, and we shut down the program with the End command.

Accumulating Characters into a Variable: If the user hasn't gone that far yet, we raise the password's character-counter and add the just-pressed character to the PWord Variable. Chr$ transforms the KeyAscii numeric Variable into a text character that can be added to PWord. If the user knows the password, PWord will be *a* after the first key is pressed, then *ae*, then *aeo* and finally *aeon*. We're *accumulating* characters.

Next, we set KeyAscii to 0 to prevent VB from displaying the typed character in the Text Box. Instead, we make the text show * (asterisk) characters. The number of * that we display matches the number of key-presses. This convention allows the user to see how many characters of the password have been typed.

Now we test to see if PWord matches the password. We use LCase$ to make all the letters lowercase in PWord. That way, we can allow the user to type in all caps, or whatever, and still match the password. If there is a match, we Load in the second Form, the window that starts our program. We remove Form1 from the computer; its password-checking job is done.

It's possible that the Counter has reached 4, which means that the user has tried, and failed, to enter the four-letter password. In this situation, we blank out the **** from the Text Box and reset the Counter to 0 again.

Embossed Letters and Frames: You can achieve the Edwardian calling-card look of this window by using three Subroutines included in this book. The framing Subroutines—DrawFrameOn and Emboss—and their variations are fully described in the entry for the Line command. The etched letters are created with the Raiseit Subroutine described in the entry on Print. Here is how they were used in this program:

```
Sub Form_Load ()

Show
FontSize = 12

drawframeon label1, label1, "inward", 200
drawframeon label1, label1, "outward", 150

emboss Text1, "inward", 5
emboss label1, "inward", 10

raiseit "Please Enter Your", 500, 400
FontSize = 16
raiseit "Password...", 750, 650

End Sub
```

See also   Arrays; Dim; Erase; Function; Global; Option Base; ReDim; Sub

STATUSBAR

CONTROL

See Windows 95 Controls

STOP

STATEMENT

Description   Stop halts a running program. You should not use it in the final version of a program, but some programmers use it to test a program being designed. Most programmers, though, never use Stop because Visual Basic's "break-point" feature is more powerful and flexible when you are testing your programs (see "Debug" or Appendix B).

Years ago, Stop was used while testing a program for errors. The Stop command is a holdover from earlier versions of Basic, which, unlike Visual Basic, did not have single-stepping, Watches or breakpoints as part of a suite of "debugging" tools.

Used with   Testing programs, ten years ago

Uses   None

Cautions   • One danger in using Stop to test your program is that you might put the command in some out-of-the-way Event in your program. This Event might be rarely triggered while the program is running—a Subroutine that allows the user to adjust the FontSize of a Text Box, for instance. If you leave that Stop command in the program when you make your final version (the Make EXE File option in VB's File Menu), Stop will lurk in the program, waiting for someone to adjust the FontSize. Then it will mysteriously crash the program and the user will see a message box that says "Stop Statement Encountered!" which would puzzle most people.

When Stop is encountered while you are testing your program during its design, Stop behaves as if you had pressed F9 on the same line and, thereby, set a "breakpoint" (see Appendix B). The program halts and the Immediate Window appears. There is no advantage in using Stop instead of breakpoints, and several disadvantages.

If you do use Stop, you can restart the program with the Continue option in VB's Run Menu or by pressing the F5 key.

Example

Figure S-37: The Stop command halts a running program and pops up the "Debug Window."

When you put Stop into a program that you are designing, it halts execution of the program, shows you the location where the Stop occurred in the "Code Window," and brings up the "Debug Window" in case you want to check the status of some Variables. Breakpoints do all this, and they do it better (see Appendix B).

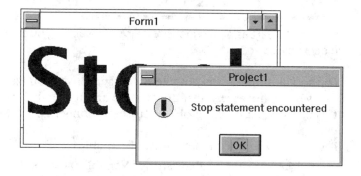

Figure S-38: Don't leave a Stop command in a completed program or the user will get this inexplicable error message.

If you leave a Stop command in a program others will use, the program will crash. When you finish designing your program, you turn it into a normal, runnable Windows program by selecting Make EXE File from the VB File Menu. If Stop is in your program, the user will see the error message in Figure S-38. Clicking on OK isn't OK. It proceeeds to remove your offending program from the computer, leaving nothing on the screen. The user will have no further communication from your program beyond that *Stop Statement Encountered.*

See also   Appendix B; Debug

Description   Str provides you with a text version of a number. It translates a pure
number into a character (or series of characters); *digits* that can be displayed but cannot be manipulated mathematically.

In previous versions of Basic, if you used a pure number in a text environment, like the following:

    Text1.Text = 5

Basic would respond with:

Figure S-39: Visual Basic 1.0 remonstrates in this fashion if you attempt to force a
number into a text context.

The actual *number* 5 is not a text character to Visual Basic 1.0. The digit
"5" is. VB 2.0, however, introduced the Variant Variable type (see "Variant") and now many of the old strictures no longer apply. First, some
background.

There are two fundamental kinds of Variables:

• Text Variables (often called "string" Variables) can be printed to the
printer, printed on the screen, and are made up of the *symbols* that we call
the English language. You cannot divide or use text Variables to calculate
the amount of linoleum that you would need to redo your kitchen floor.
Text is for *communication,* not calculation.

• Numeric Variables can be printed. (Print 5 or X = 5: Print X is the same as
Print "5" as far as what the user will see on screen.) Numeric Variables are
used to calculate things; they are really numbers rather than symbols. The
12 on top of a carton of eggs is *text* and the actual number of eggs in that
carton is *numeric,* a real number.

Str mediates between the two kinds of numbers. It translates a real
number into a text digit that can be displayed. Can you translate a text
Variable like "5" back into a real number that you could multiply? Yes, you
use the Val Function for that. It can turn "1992" into 1992 for you.

(Val cannot translate *words* like "Nineteen hundred and ninety-three." You have to do a lot of programming to change words into real numbers. But Val can translate digits—characters that stand for numbers.)

Visual Basic is wonderfully inventive: VB 2.0 introduced to computer languages a special Variable type called *Variant*, which more or less allows you to forget about Variable "types." A Variant *embraces* text and numeric as well as date/time and all other Variable types into a single "Variant" type. VB then handles things for you; VB decides how to manipulate the Variable based on the context. Are you multiplying? VB will treat the Variant as a numeric Variable. Are you putting it into a Caption? VB changes it to text. The Variant is VB's *default* Variable type. Unless you specifically use Public, Dim, Static, ReDim or DefInt commands (or use a Variable type symbol such as $) all your Variables will be of the Variant type.

The price you pay for Variants is that they slow down the program somewhat (while VB checks out what's going on and how the contents of the Variable should be used), and they consume more memory than *any* other kind of Variable. Nonetheless, if your Variable is a Variant type, you need not bother using Variable-type translator commands as Str and Val, or that esoteric group of numeric Variable type manipulators: CDbl, CInt, CLng, CSng (CInt "forces" a number to become an integer, for example).

Used with Text Boxes, Forms and other entities that have a Caption or Text Property. Captions and Text (and such things as the items in a List Box) require that the numbers displayed on them be in a *text* format. Str changes real numbers into displayable text.

You *can* use real numbers with the Print command. You can feed Print a numeric Variable containing 4 or the literal text "4." Print displays text on a Form, Picture Box or the printer. X = 4: Print X works the same as Print "4." (You cannot say Form1.Caption = X or Form1.Caption = 4.)

Variables To turn a real number into a text Variable: N$ = Str(15)

OR (to use Str within an "expression"): Print Str(x)

OR (to translate a numeric Variable into text):

```
X = 12
Label1.Caption = Str(X)
```

Str can translate any *numeric expression* into text (see "Variables" for a definition of *expression*).

Uses • Display numbers in the Caption Properties of Labels, Command Buttons, etc.; or in a Text Box, List Box or MsgBox. If a Variable isn't a Variant, you must use Str to translate the numbers into printable text format.

• Text displayed (or sent to the printer) with the Print command *does not need the services of Str.* The Print command—which prints on a Form, Picture Box or the printer—*can* print numeric Variables:

```
S = 14: Print S
```

Print can also print *literal numbers*: Print 14 will work.

Print can even print complicated *expressions* that it "solves" before translating the result into symbolic text characters, which it can show on the screen or printer:

```
Picture1.Print 144 * 23
```

Results in   3312

Cautions   • When you are using Str, you usually intend to display the results. Visual Basic adds a space character to the left of the text it creates out of a number "to leave room for a minus sign." (See the Example below.)

If you do not want this extra space, use Str in combination with LTrim$. LTrim$ removes any "leading spaces" from text:

```
N = 122
Print Str(N)
Print Ltrim$(Str(N))
```

Results in   122
122

The powerful Format command also translates numbers into displayable text. Format has many special features for printing in columns, for special formatting and for displaying scientific numbers, dates and time.

Example   This example prints a mixed batch of positive and negative numbers. In the two lists of numbers, some will have a minus sign. Because Visual Basic adds a space character to the left of positive numbers, the lists will line up neatly in a vertical column:

```
Sub Form_Click ()

For i = 1 To 20
    x = Int(10 * Rnd + 1)
    Print i — x, x — i
Next i
End Sub
```

We are printing two columns of 20 numbers each. The Rnd Function provides us with a random number between 1 and 10. We then create one list by subtracting the Loop counter Variable *i* from the random number, and the other list by reversing the subtraction. All the numbers, though, line up on the Form in two clean columns.

See also   Format; LTrim; Val; Variant

StrComp

Description StrComp is a slight variation on the normal way of comparing text ("string") Variables. Ordinarily, you would use the < operator for less than (meaning alphabetically lower: *cat* is less than *dog*), > for greater than and = for equal.

StrComp does the same thing but produces a *Variant* Variable type (see "Variables"), which tells you how the text Variables compare. Aside from this, the only virtue of StrComp is that it includes an option that eliminates the need to use the LCase or UCase command to force VB to ignore capitalization (case-sensitivity) during a text comparison.

Used with Text ("string") Variables

Variables To find out how a$ compares to b$:

```
X = StrComp(a$,b$)

If X is
    −1     then a$ is less than b$
     0     then a$ equals b$
     1     then a$ is greater than b$
   NULL  then one of the two pieces of text is a Null (which see).
```

OR (to specify that the comparison should *not* be case-sensitive, should not pay attention to how or if the words are capitalized): X = StrComp(a$,b$,1)

OR (to specify that the comparison *should* be case-sensitive):
X = StrComp(a$,b$,0)

Option Compare: If you leave out the "case-sensitivity" Variable, then StrComp defaults to case-sensitive *unless* you have specified that all string comparisons are not case-sensitive by using the Option Compare Text command. You can place this command in the General Declarations section of a Form or Module. It forces all string comparisons in the Form or Module to ignore capitalization. A related command, Option Compare Binary, is the default for VB—comparisons are case-sensitive.

Uses • StrComp, because of its optional control over case-sensitivity, allows you to compare items of text without resorting to the UCase$ or LCase$ command. String comparisons are done when alphabetizing lists, testing for a match to passwords, and so forth. Although VB defaults to case-sensitive comparisons, you most often want them insensitive.

Example Put two Text Boxes and a Label on a Form. Select New Module from the File Menu and type the following into the Module:

```
Sub updatelabel (ByVal a As String, ByVal b As String)
x = StrComp(a, b)
Select Case x
   Case -1
      Form1.Label1.Caption = a + " is less than " + b
   Case 0
      Form1.Label1.Caption = a + " is equal to " + b
   Case 1
      Form1.Label1.Caption = a + " is greater than " + b
End Select
End Sub
```

We created a Subroutine and because we put it into a Module, any of the Forms or Events in our program can access the Sub. We will "pass" the Text Property of both Text Boxes to this Sub, and it will make its report on how they compare by setting the Label's Caption. When you pass *Properties,* you must use the ByVal command. When passing ordinary text Variables, you would just use (a As String, b As String) and forget the ByVal command.

Now, type this same thing into both Text1's and Text2's KeyPress Events:

```
Sub Text1_KeyPress (KeyAscii As Integer)
   If KeyAscii = 13 Then
            updatelabel text1.Text, text2.Text
      End If
   End Sub
```

When the user presses the ENTER key (code 13, see "Chr$"), we call the Sub and pass the two items of text that are in the Boxes.

Figure S-40: StrComp compares two items of text.

See also   InStr; Variables

STRETCH

Description The Stretch Property determines whether a picture placed into an Image Control will expand or contract so it fits the size you've made the Image Control (Stretch = True) or the Image Control will adjust itself (like a Picture Box with AutoSize on) to the size of the imported picture.

The Stretch Property and the fact that Image Controls use fewer system resources justify the existence of the Image Control (given the functionality and extra Properties and features available to Picture Boxes).

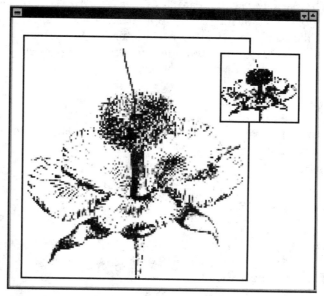

Figure S-41: On the left, Stretch is turned off (False); on the right, it's on (True).

Used with The Image Control only

Variables You must set the Stretch Property in the Properties Window while designing your program; you cannot change Stretch while a program is running.

OR (to find out the Stretch Property while the program is running):
X = Image1.Stretch

Uses The value of Stretch (and the Image Control itself) is that you can make any .ICO, .DIB or .BMP picture act like a .WMF picture. That is, you can decide how large and what shape a picture file should be in your program (by adjusting the Image Box), and VB will force the picture to grow, shrink or stretch to fit the size of your Image Box.

Normally (when it is imported into a Picture Box or Form), a picture file in .ICO, .RLE or .BMP format cannot be any larger, smaller or wider than it was when designed or scanned. In other words, these types of graphics files have a fixed size and shape. However, the Image Control does some tricks (if you set Stretch to False). The Image Control then does not adjust to the size of the Picture; instead, the Picture is forced to fill the size and shape of the Image Box.

Caution See Appendix A for ways to use the API to accomplish Stretching and additional special graphics effects (such as inversion, obversion and reversion) using normal Picture Boxes instead of Image Boxes.

Example One of many uses for the Image Control is if you want to build an application where the user can create .ICO files (icons). You can show the user a blown-up version of the icon graphic designed by the user (or those saved as .ICO files on disk). Take an .ICO picture to gargantuan proportions so that each pixel is visible. Icons all measure 32 x 32 pixels. This example, forcing icons into massive size onscreen, reveals those 1,024 pixels quite clearly.

Start a New Project from the File Menu. Then double-click on an Image Box and a Picture Box on the Toolbox to place them on the Form. Move them away from each other and then type the following into the Form_Load Event:

```
Sub Form_Load ()

image1.Width = 4200
image1.Height = image1.Width
image1.Stretch = 0
image1.BorderStyle = 1
image1.Picture = LoadPicture("C:\VB2\ICONS\ELEMENTS\MATCH.ICO")
picture1.Picture = LoadPicture("C:\VB2\ICONS\ELEMENTS\MATCH.ICO")
picture1.AutoSize = −1

End Sub
```

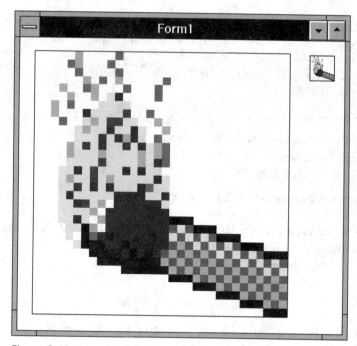

Figure S-42: An .ICO reveals its pixels when stretched in an Image Control.

We want the Image Box to be square, so we first make its Width and Height Properties equal to each other. Then we force the .ICO file to fill the entire (large) Image Box by refusing to allow the Image Box to conform to the .ICO's normal small size.

If you don't call the directory with your VB icons "C:\VB2\ICONS," substitute whatever name you use. Or give LoadPicture some other .ICO path and filename of your choice.

See also Appendix A; AutoSize; Image; PaintPicture; Picture Box

STRING (STRING$)   FUNCTION

Description String provides you with a piece of text that is filled with a particular character. You specify the character and how many of them you want:

```
Print String(20, "*")
```

Results in ********************

Used with Text Variables and text expressions (see "Variables" for a definition of *expression*)

Variables First, you tell String how many characters you want and then which character. You can use a *text literal*, an actual character enclosed within quotation marks:

```
A$ = String(15, "-")
Print A$
```

Results in ———————-

OR (you can use a text Variable):

```
A$ = "#"
Print String(25, A$)
```

Results in #########################

OR (you can provide the ANSI code for the desired character—see "Chr$" about this code—instead of a text Variable or text literal):

```
Print String(30, 47)
```

Results in //////////////////////////////

(47 is the ANSI code for the / (slash) character. See "Chr" for a list of codes.)

Uses • Create simple design elements when displaying text by printing a line of periods, hyphens, underline characters, etc.

• "Pad" text ("string") Variables so they are all the same length for use with random-mode files. However, there are better ways to do this (see "Open"). When using Get or Put for random-mode disk file access, you will need to use a "fixed-length" text Variable. Create one by using A$ = String(20," "), which causes A$ to have 20 space characters. A more common way to create a fixed-length string, however, is by using Dim A As String * 20.

Cautions • If you provide a text Variable that has more than one character, String will use the first character:

```
A$ = "ABCD"
Print String(9,A$)
```

Results in AAAAAAAAA

The number of characters that you request can be between 0 and 65,535.

If you provide a character code instead of a literal character, the code number you provide can be any numeric expression but must be between 0 and 255, the limits of the ANSI code. (See "Chr.")

Example

```
Sub Form_Click ()

Design$ = String(150, ".")

Print Design$
Print , "   SIMPLE FORM DESIGNS VIA TEXT"
Print Design$

End Sub
```

Results in

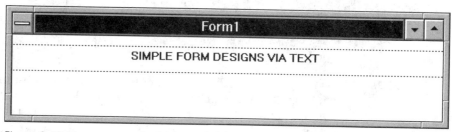

Figure S-43: You can create old-fashioned designs text-based efforts to create graphics with String.

In Figure S-43 a typical DOS-type design element is created by printing two lines of dots around a title. The title itself is centered on the page by adjusting tabs (the comma) and spaces within the title text.

This approach is crude by Windows standards. The drawing facilities in Visual Basic—Line, DrawStyle, the Shape Control, etc.—are capable of sophisticated design effects. Centering a piece of text, for instance, would be precise using the TextWidth Method, which see.

See also   Open; Space; Spc; Tab; Type

 TYLE

PROPERTY

Description   Style selects one of the three possible types of Combo Boxes.

Used with   Combo Boxes only

Variables   **Variable type:** Integer (enumerated)

The Style Property cannot be adjusted while your program is running, so you cannot put it into the program as a command. Instead, you must select it from the Properties Window while designing your program:

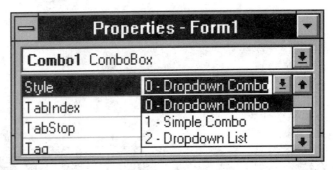

Figure S-44: You must change the Style Property from within the Properties Window.

Uses
• Use a Combo Box when you want to offer the user a list of choices but also accept alternative items that the user would type into the box.

Combo Boxes are similar to List Boxes. However, a List Box simply provides a list of preselected options from which the user must choose. A Combo Box offers its list but also allows the user to *type in* additional choices. (In one of the three Combo Box styles, the user is not allowed to type in additional items. See the Example below for the three Combo Box styles.)

You can detect the user's mouse-clicked selections within the Box's Click Event. You detect that the user has *typed* something in because typed text will trigger the Box's Change Event.

Cautions
• Of the three possible "styles" of Combo Boxes, Style 1, the "Simple Combo," is probably the most useful and would be most appealing to users. Here is a brief rundown of the qualities of each Style:

Style 0—Dropdown Combo: With the Style Property set to 0, the default, you get a full "Dropdown Combo" Box with all the attributes associated with a Combo Box—a list of choices, clicking to select a choice, double-clicking to cause some action in the program and a small Text Box at the top where the user can enter an alternative selection (something that's not on the list). Style 0, though, has, in the opinion of some programmers, a serious drawback. Its arrow must be clicked before the user can see the choices in its list.

In Style 0, the arrow button is separated from the Text Box portion. When the box first appears, only its user-entry Text Box appears (unfortunately), and to select from the options the user must click on the arrow.

But there are always two sides to every question, and you'll find that other programmers prefer Style 0. They argue that it is the "cleanest" one because it can show the most likely choice to the user, but allow that choice to be changed if the user wishes. By not showing the entire list, the screen looks neater. In fact, Style 0 is used in many Windows applications to provide a list of selections. If your VB program sets the ListIndex

Property to the most likely selection, then the user can quickly accept it if it is the correct choice. For example, in a program that contains a feature to add an address for a company to the customer list, the most likely choice could be the state that the user resides in. So, set this state name as the default position for the ListIndex Property of the Combo Box.

Style 1—Simple Combo: This style is oddly named because it is probably the most functional of the three for many situations. With the Style Property set to 1, the Combo Box becomes a "simple" Box, and in this style the list is always displayed. There is no arrow button. This may be the best choice, unless your Form is terribly crowded and you need to conserve space by requiring the user to click on an arrow to see the suggested options. In that case, use Style 0.

Style 2—Dropdown List: You'll probably want to avoid Style 2. With its Style Property set to 2, the Combo Box becomes a "Dropdown List Box" and combines the weaknesses of a List Box (the user cannot type in any alternatives to the items on the list) with the drawbacks of the Dropdown Combo Box (the user must click on the arrow button to get information on the options).

A Style 2 Combo Box does not recognize the Change Event because you cannot type anything into it. The Click Event (not DblClick) and the Drop-Down Event are the only things to which it can respond. (DropDown is triggered when the user tries to display the list. That gives you an opportunity to update the list before allowing the user to see it.)

Unlike the other Combo Box styles, you cannot modify the Text Property of a Style 2 Box. The one raison d'être offered for a "Dropdown List" is that it, as the manual says, "conserves screen space"—at the expense of user comfort and convenience. Style 0 also saves screen space.

Example

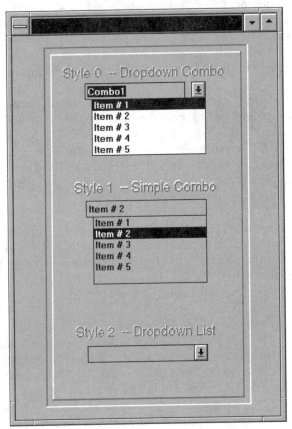

Figure S-45: The three Combo Box "styles" are not equally useful.

We put three Combo Boxes on the Form and then set their Style Properties to 0, 1 and 2. The Style Properties were set manually, as they must be, using the Properties Window. Then we filled them with lists inside the Form_Load Event:

```
Sub Form_Load ()

For i = 1 To 5
    n$ = "Item #" + Str$(i)
    combo1.AddItem n$
    combo2.AddItem n$
    combo3.AddItem n$
Next i

Show
drawframeon combo1, combo3, "inward", 750
drawframeon combo1, combo3, "outward", 630

fontsize = 12
fontbold = 0
```

```
raiseit "Style 0   Dropdown Combo", 900, 500
raiseit "Style 1   Simple Combo", 1100, 2500
raiseit "Style 2   Dropdown List", 1100, 5000
End Sub
```

The DrawFrameOn Subroutine makes frames around the Combo Boxes. This Subroutine is described in "Line" in this book. The embossed letters are produced by a Subroutine called Raiseit, which you can find under "Print."

See also   Combo Box; List Box

$\mathcal{S}$UB

STATEMENT

Description   The Sub command announces that you are creating a Subroutine, a structure that, in many ways, is like adding a new command to Visual Basic.

A Subroutine is like a little program within your larger program—performing some limited task and available to be called upon to execute that task from anywhere in the program.

Subroutines are

- available anytime

- part of a larger structure (your program)

- limited but useful

Visual Basic uses the Sub...End Sub structure for Subroutines. (The structure commonly found in earlier versions of Basic—GoSub...Return—is strictly limited to tiny zones within a Sub...End Sub structure (or Function). As a result, GoSub...Return has little, if any, utility in Visual Basic.)

Visual Basic relies much less on classic Subroutines than do older computer languages. Earlier, a program of any size had many Subroutines, and you used GoSub often. Subroutines are, of course, an inherent part of programming and will always exist as long as people need to communicate with computers. Subroutines are fundamentally efficient because they extend the language in much the same way that abbreviations and acronyms extend human language. We use *U.S.A.* for the same reason Romans used *SPQR*—shortcuts that save time but express a complete idea.

Just how Subroutines work in any particular computer language, though, can differ considerably. VB's design essentially eliminates the need for traditional Subroutines to which you would GoSub and then Return. Each Event in VB is a Subroutine. In place of GoSub...Return, VB offers a programwide coagulation of all instructions into Sub...End Sub structures. Essentially the only programming you do outside Subroutines (or their cousins, Functions), is defining Constants and Variables.

Traditional Subroutines: GoSub...Return: A typical traditional program was structured as follows:

```
(Main Program)
10 GoSub Reset
20 ? "HELLO"
30 GoSub Ask
40 If A$ = "Y" Then End
50 GoSub Reset

(Subroutine #1)
400 Reset:
410  CLS
420  A$ = "    "
430 Return

(Subroutine #2)
500 Ask:
510 Input "Do you want to quit now? (Y/N) "; A$
520 Return
```

The GoSub command temporarily transfers control of your program to a Subroutine. The preceding example of a traditional program structure started by going to a Subroutine in line 400, which cleared the screen and cleared a Variable. Then, that Subroutine having finished its job, the Return command caused the program to go back to the line following the GoSub, line 20.

Notice that lines 10 through 50 are not within a Subroutine. In VB, by contrast, nothing, no commands, can be outside of a Sub, an Event Procedure (which is a Subroutine by another name), or a Function (which is quite similar to a Subroutine). The only exception is declarations, such as Global, which define Variables (or a few other similar items such as Option-Base). Declarations, however, are not commands like Print that make the computer take some overt action while a program runs. All the action in VB takes place within Sub...End Sub (or Function...End Function) structures.

Visual Basic Subroutines: Typically, you write Subroutines to save yourself from having to repeat the same instructions over and over in various locations in your program. Instead, if there is some task that you'll need to have done repeatedly from different places in your program (such as alphabetizing several Arrays of names), you create a single, general-purpose sorting routine and then use it wherever it's needed. Thus, writing a Subroutine is something like adding a new command to VB, a command that your program needs to use repeatedly but that doesn't come supplied with the language.

Often, you put Subs into Modules (that way they are available to the entire program). Modules are similar to Forms, but they never become visible and they have no Events because they have no Controls. Instead, the purpose of a Module is to contain Subroutines or Functions and to declare Variables or Arrays that you want available to the entire program using the "Global" command. In addition to helping you organize your programs, you can access Subs in Modules from anywhere in your program. And a Sub in a Module can run marginally faster because a Form is keeping track of additional objects such as Controls.

An Example of a Typical Subroutine: Let's say that your program will often need to clean off whatever may have been printed on its various Forms and restore the Forms to a uniform BackColor and a uniform size. You could put the commands for this task directly into the several places in your program where you want the Form restorations to happen. But creating a single Subroutine is more efficient. You would write the commands only once, your program would be smaller and, once placed inside a Module, this part of your program will run faster than if it were put into a Form. Also, once a Subroutine is inside a Module, that Sub becomes available to all Forms in your program.

Open a new Module and type the following into it:

```
Sub ResetForms (Formnm As Form)

    Formnm.Cls
    Formnm.BackColor = &H00FF00FF
    Formnm.Height = 3000
    Formnm.Width = 3000
End Sub
```

This general-purpose routine (a Subroutine) works with any Form because you "pass" to it the Names of whichever Forms you want it to affect. The special Variable type "As Form" enables you to pass any Form's Name to a Sub for servicing. Whenever you want to clean off a Form, from anywhere within your program, you can simply name the Subroutine (as if it were a command in VB) and pass the Name of the Form you want cleaned:

```
ResetForms Form3
```

You create a Subroutine to avoid writing commands like Form1.Cls:Form1.BackColor each time your program needs to clean its Forms. This approach not only saves you time, but it also makes your finished program smaller.

Used with   For a Sub that will be available from anywhere within a Form, put the Sub into the General Declarations section of the Form.

To make a Sub available from anywhere in your program, put the Sub into a Module. Select New Module from VB's File Menu:

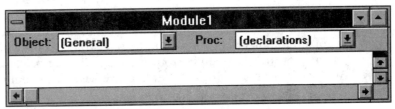

Figure S-46: Subroutines and Functions in a Module are accessible from anywhere within your entire program (unless you use the "Private" command).

Variables

Some of the following commands, the ones [enclosed in brackets], are optional. But the full syntax for a Sub is as follows:

[Static] [Private] [Public] Sub MySubsName [(Variables passed to the Sub)]

The special command, *Private,* prohibits other Modules from using the Sub. Without *Private,* a Sub (or Function) in a Module is available for use by the entire program. *Private* is also used with Subs that you put in the General Declarations section of a Form, which also prevents their use outside their Form. The Public command permits them to be accessed from any location. See ("Public").

The *Static* command prevents VB from destroying the contents of the Variables used between Sub and End Sub. Normally, Variables within an Event, Sub or Function (unless declared Formwide by the Dim command in a Form's General Declarations section or declared programwide with the Global command in a Module) are as fragile as fireworks—they come into existence while VB is within a given Sub or Function but are extinguished when VB reaches the End Sub or End Function command. (See "Static.")

You can create a simple Subroutine by simply naming it and entering commands into it. You put Subroutines that are to be used only by a single Form into the General Declarations section of that Form. You should put Subroutines that you want available to all the Forms in a multi-Form program into a Module. (You must explicitly create a Module by selecting New Module from VB's File Menu or clicking on the Toolbar. A Module will then be added to any Forms or other Modules that are listed in the Project Window.) You can put as many Subroutines as you wish into a Module.

To practice creating a new Subroutine, type this line into the General Declarations section of a Form:

Sub MyNewSub

As soon as you press the ENTER key, Visual Basic makes room for this Subroutine and adds both the End Sub command and ( ) in case you didn't add them (every Sub has parentheses, in case you'll want to "pass" something to it when you use the Sub). VB has also added the name of your Sub to the Proc: list of the Form. Now you can put commands into the Sub structure, just as you would into an ordinary Event:

```
Sub MyNewSub ()
    Print "It Works."
End Sub
```

Now, from some other place in the program, you activate this Sub by merely naming it:

```
Form1_Click ()
MyNewSub
End Sub
```

Clicking on this Form after pressing F5 to start the program running will result in the Subroutine doing its job:

It Works.

OR (to allow a Subroutine to accept Variables, to "pass" Variables to a Sub):

Often you will want to "pass" information to a Sub. Unless you use the special ByVal command (see the first "Caution"), any Variables that you "pass" to a Subroutine can be changed by that Subroutine.

Tell the Sub Which One to Shrink: If you create a Subroutine that will shrink any of your Controls to one-third its former size, for example, you would "pass" the name of the Control and then the Sub would know which one to shrink. The Sub has the general facility of being able to shrink Controls; you tell it which specific Control you want shrunk whenever you call on the Sub. You can refer to the passed item with any Variable name you wish. Here we'll call it WhichCtl:

```
Sub Shrinkit (WhichCtl As Control)

WhichCtl.Height = WhichCtl.Height / 3
WhichCtl.Width = WhichCtl.Width / 3

End Sub
```

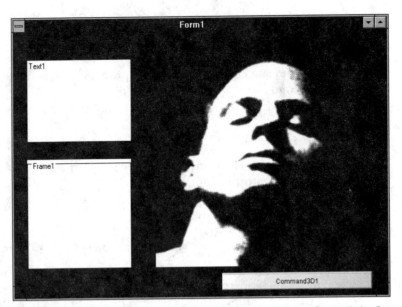

Figure S-47: We'll tell a Subroutine to shrink each of these Controls by "passing" their names. (Also see Figure S-48.)

Now, in the Form_Click Event, you can specify the Controls to shrink by "passing" their Names to the Sub:

```
Sub Form_Click ()

shrinkit Text1
shrinkit Command1
shrinkit Picture1
shrinkit Frame1

End Sub
```

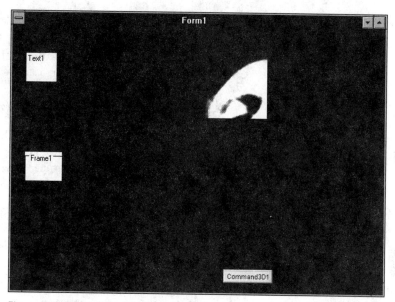

Figure S-48: Shrink any Control through the services of a single Subroutine.

Imagine how much more typing we would have had to do if we hadn't used the Subroutine and were forced to redefine the Width and Height Properties individually to shrink each Control.

OR (to pass more than one Variable to a Sub):

```
Sub Shrinkit (WhichCtl As Control, HowMuch As Integer)

WhichCtl.Height = WhichCtl.Height / HowMuch
WhichCtl.Width = WhichCtl.Width / HowMuch

End Sub
```

Here we are adding flexibility to the Subroutine by allowing the amount of shrinkage to be specified, along with the name of the Control to shrink.

You can add as many "arguments," the Variables that can be passed to a Sub, as you wish. But when calling on this Sub, you must provide all the Variables it will expect to receive. Note that you enclose the "arguments" in parentheses when creating a Sub, but you do not use parentheses when calling on that Sub to do its job. In both cases, though, you must separate the items by commas.

OR (to pass the name of a Form): Sub Shrinkit (WhichForm As Form)

OR (to pass any Variable "type"):

Numeric Variables come in several "types" (see "Variables"). They can all be passed to a Sub and can be declared with their symbols (Numb%) or with their official type names (Numb As Integer). Here we'll mix and match the two approaches:

Sub Display (Cntrol As Control, FntName$, FntBold%, FntSize)

You must follow the same rules for naming these "passed" items as you would for creating new Variable names: You cannot use names already in use by VB. We use *Cntrol* for the specific Control the user wants affected by this Sub.

FntName$ is identified as a text ("string") Variable type by adding the $ symbol for text Variables. FntBold was identified as an Integer (no decimal points) type. Finally, we didn't identify the Variable type of FntSize because it doesn't matter whether it's an Integer or a "Floating-Point" Variable. If you don't add a type symbol or spell out As Typename, VB assumes you want the default VB Variable type–Variant (which see).

Variable Types Are Often Interchangeable: FntBold would have worked just fine with Visual Basic's default numeric Variable type–Variant. There is some interchangeability. For much of your computing, you can just stick to the default Variant if you wish. If you need to speed up a program, use the "Integer" types. For more on Variable types, see "Variables."

OR (to pass an Array, which see, add empty parentheses to identify the Variable as an Array): Sub Sort (Appointments())

You cannot pass a fixed-length string (text) Array. If you want to sort such an Array, you could declare it Global in a Module. Then the Array would be available from anywhere in the program, including available for manipulation by your Sorting Subroutine. In this case, you wouldn't "pass" the Array, but your Subroutine could still sort it. (See "Arrays" for more on fixed-length strings and the Global command.)

OR (to preserve the values of the Sub's own local Variables):

Static Sub Sortnames

The Variables inside a Subroutine–the ones used by the Sub, not passed to it–are all "local." They come into existence each time the Sub is called, each time it's activated from somewhere in the program. All the Variant Variable start out holding an "Empty" value, all the numeric Variables start out holding a 0, and all text Variables are empty ("") with no characters inside them. Variables inside a Sub come into existence when the Sub is activated and disappear when the Sub is finished with its job. They therefore lose all their contents–they "forget" the values, the text or numbers that they held.

If you want the Variables inside a Sub to retain their values between calls to the Sub, use the Static command. (Also see "ReDim.")

OR (to leave the Sub prematurely, to refuse to carry out the rest of the commands in it, use the Exit Sub command):

```
Sub StretchPicture (ThePic As Control, HowMuch)

TargetSize = ThePic.Width * HowMuch

If TargetSize > Form1.Width Then
    Exit Sub
End If
ThePic.Width = TargetSize
End Sub
```

Here, the amount to stretch a Picture Box is passed to this Sub. If the amount to stretch it (the Variable HowMuch multiplied by the Width Property of the Box) causes the Picture Box to get wider than the Form, we abort with Exit Sub.

If you have more than one Form and you put this Subroutine in a Module, the Sub would not know which Form you were referring to if you just typed Width. Here we named the Form inside the Sub as Form1, but that makes the Sub less generic than Subs really should be. To make this Sub truly general-purpose, you would want to pass it the Form Name (As Form) along with the other information that's passed.

OR (to restrict access to the Sub): Private Sub Sort ()

A special command, Private, is optional but can be used with Sub. If you use Private, VB will "restrict access" to that Subroutine to the Module within which the Sub resides. The Sub cannot be called from within any other Module. (Private is unnecessary for Subs within Forms; no other Form or Module can access a Form's Subs.)

Optional Arguments

New in VB4 is the ability to extend the usefulness of a procedure (Sub or Function) by specifying that one or more of the arguments are optional and need not be passed. For example, you might create a Sub that multiplies two numbers together, but can optionally multiply a third. You would describe the third as optional, by preceding it with the Optional command. Then, within your Sub, you could test the existence of the third argument using the IsMissing command:

```
Sub Mult(first As Integer, second As Integer, Optional third)
    n = first * second
    If Not IsMissing(third) Then
            n = n * third
    End If
    Print n
End Sub
```

Now, when you call this Sub and provide only these two arguments, you get the result 36:

```
Private Sub Form_Load()
    Show
    Mult 12, 3
End Sub
```

But if you choose to multiply three numbers, you can, getting, in this case, the result 144:

```
Private Sub Form_Load()
    Show
    Mult 12, 3, 4
End Sub
```

Note that an optional argument must be the last one in the argument list (though you can add additional arguments after the first optional one, they must also be optional) and it must be a Variant Variable type.

Extreme Flexibilty

ParamArray: When You Don't Know How Many Arguments: Objects, among their other side effects, can result in strange situations—where you the programmer don't know how many items are going to be involved in a programming situation when the program is run by the user. Beyond that, you might want to make a Sub or Function even more flexible than the Optional command (described above) permits. Using the new ParamArray command you can pass *any number of arguments, and they can be of any variable type.* Talk about flexibility. Here's how the example above would be written to permit any number of arguments. Note the use of For...Each (which see):

```
Sub Mult(ParamArray Numbers())
    n = 1
    For Each x in Numbers
        n = n * x
    Next x
    Print n
End Sub
```

Now, when you call this Function you can as many or as few arguments as you wish:

```
Private Sub Form_Load()
    Show
    Mult 5, 3, 4, 2
End Sub
```

Note that you can also mix and match variable types with the ParamArray feature:

```
Private Sub Form_Load()
Dim a As Integer, b As Long, c As Variant, d As Integer
a = 5: b = 3: c = 4: d = 2
  Show
    Mult a, b, c, d
End Sub
```

All in all, ParamArray is an exceptionally flexible way of passing arguments to a procedure.

Named Arguments

Now you can freely rearrange the order of argments supplied to a Sub or Function that you write. Because they can be *named* (using the names in the procedure's argument list) when you call that procedure, you can rearrange the order. However, all arguments must be provided, unless the procedure defines one or more of the arguments as Optional (see above):

```
Sub Add(firstvar, secondvar)
  Print firstvar + secondvar
End Sub
```

```
Private Sub Form_Load()
  Show
    Add secondvar:=6, firstvar:=5
End Sub
```

For more on this, see "Named Arguments"

Uses • Use a Subroutine whenever you will want a task performed in several places in your program. If the task isn't trivial, like simply changing a FontSize, but involves a series of actions, such as manipulating seven different Properties of a Control or alphabetizing a list of names, a Subroutine is the ideal solution.

Subroutines are not used as often in Visual Basic as in more traditional kinds of programming because every action in Visual Basic is inside a Subroutine (all Events are Subroutines) or, sometimes, inside a cousin of Subs, the Function. If the job performed by a Control's Event Sub is needed somewhere else in the same Form, you can "call" that Event by merely naming it. The following is precisely the way you would activate a normal Sub:

```
Sub Label2_Click()
  Command1_Click
End Sub
```

(This Subroutine would carry out whatever instructions you had placed inside Command1's Click Event when the user clicked on Label2.) However, in larger programs, you might find that it's more convenient to put the bulk of the programming in Modules (inside Subs or Functions). The Events would then be largely devoted to the user interface (getting and giving information between the program and the user). One scuba diver logbook program we've seen has about 25k of its substance in Events, and the bulk, the meat of the program, resides in about 120k worth of Modules.

How Functions Differ From Subroutines: A Function is the same thing as a Subroutine, with a single exception: a Function directly returns a result (a value) to the caller. You must use a Function inside an expression, but you cannot use a Subroutine inside an expression. A Subroutine must be a separate command, whereas a Function is part of one or more additional commands that "evaluate" to something simpler (see *expression* under "Variables").

Following is an illustration of the distinction between Subroutines and Functions:

(Subroutine)

```
Sub PrintBackwards (What as String)
    For i = Len(What) to 1 Step —1
        Print Mid$(What,i,1);
    Next i
End Sub
```

This Sub prints any text Variable backward. It loops from the length of the text Variable back down to 1, stepping back down 1 each time through the Loop. This has the effect of pointing to each character in the Variable, starting with the last one and working back to the first.

Mid$ uses the value of *i*, the Loop Variable, to know which particular character to print each time through this Loop.

```
PrintBackwards "Norway"
```

Results in   yawroN

(Function)

You create a Function as you would a Subroutine, except you must provide the Variable type that the Function returns. You can do this in two ways: by attaching the Variable type symbol to the Function's name:

```
Function PrintBackwards$ (What as String)
```

or by explicitly naming the Variable type at the end of the declaration line:

```
Function PrintBackwards (What as String) As String

    For i = Len(What) to 1 Step —1
        Print Mid$(What,i,1);
    Next i
End Function
```

You "call" a Function by making it part of an "expression," even if you don't pay any attention to the results of that expression. Here we don't care what's in A$, but we nevertheless must create an expression. Also, unlike a Subroutine, you must enclose the Variable or Variables that you are "passing" to a Function in parentheses:

    A$ = PrintBackwards ("Sweden")

Results in   nedewS

(For more examples of how you can use Functions, see "Function.")

• Use Subroutines in more than one program. If you spend some time to come up with a useful Subroutine, you should save it in a disk file by using the Save Text or Save File option in VB's File Menu. Then use Load Text to import it into other programs that you write. This approach expands Visual Basic's vocabulary. (See the DrawFrameOn and Emboss Subroutines in "Line." Or see the Raiseit Subroutine in the entry on "Print," or the technique for creating gauges in "Refresh." These four Subs allow you to easily beautify any Control or group of Controls with elegant, professional-looking frames, add attractive design elements and sink or extrude text in subtle ways.)

• Events are Subroutines. If one of your Events does something that you also want to be done when another Event is triggered, just provide the name of the first Event inside the second. See the Example below.

Cautions   • There is a new Optional command in VB4. If you want to permit the user to optionally leave out an argument when calling a procedure (a Sub, Function, etc.) add this command:

    Sub Shrinkit (WhichForm As Form, Optional Factor)

Note that any Optional argument *must be a Variant Variable type.*

• The special ByVal command prevents a Subroutine from changing the contents of a Variable. ByVal puts a lock on a Variable's contents. You can provide information to a Subroutine by sending it that Variable, and the Subroutine might even make changes to the Variable while doing its job. Nonetheless, you don't want this Variable permanently changed by whatever happens inside the Sub. You want the Variable to remain unchanged when the program has left the Subroutine. The ByVal command does this.

In the following example, we prevent any changes to the TodaysDate Variable:

    Sub Adjust (Name$, Time, ByVal TodaysDate)

• Subroutines can be recursive, can call themselves. This advanced technique, though, can lead to an endless Loop, an echo-chamber effect, an infinite regression or worse. If you understand and use recursion, you don't need it explained here. If you don't, avoid using Subroutines in this fashion. The following is a recursive Subroutine:

```
Sub Endless ()
    Print "One more time around."
    Endless
End Sub
```

This Sub includes its own name and thus calls itself, again and again.

• You cannot use a Variable type symbol when creating a Subroutine (as you might with a Function):

Wrong:

```
Sub Sort$ ()
```

Right:

```
Sub Sort ()
```

Nor can you use an explicit declaration of Variable type:

Wrong:

```
Sub Sort () As String
```

Right:

```
Sub Sort ()
```

Unlike Functions, Subroutines do not have a "Variable type" of their own. (See "Variables" for more on the types.)

• You cannot put one Subroutine inside another; Subroutines cannot be "nested."

Wrong:

```
Sub FirstSub
    Sub SecondSub
    End Sub
End Sub
```

If you do want to set up a structure like this, you can use the GoSub...Return command inside a Sub or Event or Function. See "GoSub...Return."

• All Variables inside a Subroutine are "local"; they are created when the Sub is called and die when the program reaches the End Sub (or Exit Sub) command. The exceptions are Variables declared with the Global command, Formwide (with Dim) or Static. (See "Variables.")

Example

Figure S-49: The user can click either on this Picture Box or on the Form itself to end this program.

You can use any Event as a Subroutine. Visual Basic's Events are Subroutines and can be called from other Events within the same Form. You can use this Event-calls-Event technique when you want to allow the user to click on more than one Control to accomplish the same thing. Why, for instance, should the user have to click only on a Picture Box to display the next graphic? Or to end the program? Or to move the program to some other task?

Why not let the user click on the Picture or the Form? Indeed, why not let him or her click or double-click? Here we've drawn a frame around the picture of fighters. (See "Line" for more on how to create effects like this matted look behind the graphic.)

The drawn frame in this example is not part of the Picture Box, but we want to allow the user to click on the frame (which is on the Form itself) as well as within the Picture Box to end this program. We also want to permit the user to double-click on either the Form or the Picture Box to exit the program. This example is simple, but if you have a number of commands you want carried out, putting them all in one Event or Subroutine is a time-saver—and makes your program smaller, too.

```
Sub Form_Click ()
    MsgBox ("Thank you for using my program.")
    End
End Sub
```

Now we can simply use the Form_Click Subroutine in all the other Events in the program where we want the same effect. All we have to do is provide the name of the Event that contains the actions we want imitated elsewhere: Form_Click (that underline character is part of the name of an Event):

```
Sub Form_DblClick ()
    Form_Click
End Sub

Sub Picture1_Click ()
    Form_Click
End Sub

Sub Picture1_DblClick ()
    Form_Click
End Sub
```

Now all four soldiers obey the same commands.

See also   Call; Function; GoSub...Return; Static; Variables

SWITCH

FUNCTION

Description   This strange Function tests several (up to seven) expressions and then returns the associated expression of the first one that's true (going from left to right). The Select Case command (or even If...Then...Else) would be far easier to work with for jobs like this one.

In essence, within the Switch Function you list a series of expressions, alternating the tested expression with the action to take if the test is true: Ifthisistrue, DoThis, Ifthisistrue, DoThis, Ifthisistrue, DoThis, Ifthisistrue, DoThis....

Variables   X\$ = (TestExpression, ResponseIfTrue,TestExpression, ResponseIfTrue, →
TestExpression, ResponseIfTrue,...)

Uses   Select among a list of possible responses. The Select Case structure is more easily programmed, however, and less likely to generate an error.

Cautions   • With text Variables, Switch is case-sensitive, so you might want to use the UCase Function to force matches if you want to ignore capitalization.

• Switch, like its cousin Functions IIF and Choose, evaluates *each* tested expression no matter what. Therefore, multiple MsgBoxes are triggered if you put several of them into the "Ifthisistrue" parts of the expression list.

Example   The following lines will choose the appropriate text Variable, based on the user's input:

```
Sub Form_Click ()
N = InputBox("How many days of vacation are you due?")
A$ = Switch(N > 20, "ten years", N > 10, "five years", N > 5, "two years", N < 5,
"one year")
Print "You are required to have worked here for " + A$
End Sub
```

Notice that your program would generate an error if you left off the final test (N < 5) and the user entered a number less than 5. An easier, clearer, less error-prone way to do this same thing is with the Select Case structure:

```
N = InputBox("How many days of vacation are you due?")

Select Case N
    Case > 20
            A$ = "ten years"
    Case > 10
            A$ = "five years"
    Case > 5
            A$ = "two years"
    Case Else
            A$ = "one year"
End Select

Print "You are required to have worked here for " + A$
```

See also   Choose; If...Then...Else; IIF; Select Case;

SYSTEM

See   Archive; Hidden; Normal; ReadOnly

TAB

FUNCTION

Description   Tab moves the cursor a specified distance from the left side of the screen or page of paper in the printer. It was useful in DOS programs for setting up neat columns and tables of text or numbers.

You can also use Tab with the Print # Statement for saving data to a disk file. (See "Print #" for more on this technique.)

Tab is a holdover from the early days of information processing. Just as teletype machines were used as printers and hand-cranked adding machines were used as calculators—many contemporary computer formatting techniques (and the words we use to describe them) are modeled on the typewriter.

Typewriters had a number of metal clips that you could position along the roller. Pressing the TAB key moved the carriage over to the next clip. This was a way of making columns of numbers or words line up vertically on the page. In Visual Basic, you can use the Tab Function for the same purpose. In practice, the CurrentX command is preferred because it affords finer control over the horizontal position of "printed" data.

Used with   Printing columns or tables of text or numbers onscreen or on the printer.

Also, though rarely, used with Print # for formatting data sent to a disk file (see "Print #").

Variables   When you use Tab, Visual Basic draws an imaginary grid over the screen, or over the paper in the printer, like graph paper. The width of each cell (or column) is the same. (It's the average width of the characters in whatever font and font size you are using.)

You can then use Tab to move the "cursor" to the place where the next character will be printed. The cursor is moved horizontally, to the column number you specify. It's as if each column in the invisible grid were numbered, starting with 1 against the left side of the screen or paper, and going up to whatever number is possible based on the width of the target. The paper in the printer has a finite number of possible columns. There is no practical upper limit for Tabs involving a Form or Picture Box, but if you go crazy and try to Tab 20,000, you'll get an "Overflow" error message.

To move the print position to the third column from the left side of the Form, Picture Box or printer paper:

```
Tab(3)
```

OR (to use a Variable to specify the Tab position): Tab(N)

Uses   • Use Tab to line up columns and tables horizontally when Printing on a Form, Picture Box or to the printer. Tab is an alternative to manipulating the CurrentX Property of these printing targets. But Tab is cruder than

CurrentX because Tab uses an average of the width of the characters of the currently active font.

• There is another variety of Tab. You can append two symbols to a Printed item: the semicolon and the comma (a variant of Tab). A semicolon keeps the cursor from moving down to the next line after the item is Printed.

To stay on a line, use a semicolon:
```
B$ = "Wayne": N$ = " Netski"

Print B$;
Print N$
```

Results in Wayne Netski

Without a semicolon:
```
Print B$
Print N$
```

Results in Wayne
Netski

You can use a comma following a Print command to advance the cursor 14 "columns." A column is 14 times the average width of the characters in your current FontName and FontSize– the equivalent of Tab(14).

To tab with a comma:
```
Print B$, N$
```

Results in Wayne   Netski

Cautions • If the cursor–the current position where the next text character will be printed–is greater that the column number used with Tab, then Tab moves the cursor to the next line below and over to the column you specified. Here's how this works.

If we print all 26 letters of the alphabet, we have moved the cursor past the 11th column on that line. By using Tab(11), we cause the next printed text to appear on the following line and at the 11th column in that line:
```
Print "ABCDEFGHIJKLMNOPQRSTUVWXYZ" Tab(11) "HERE IS THE CURSOR"
```

Results in ABCDEFGHIJKLMNOPQRSTUVWXYZ
          HERE IS THE CURSOR

If you use zero or a negative number, Tab assumes you mean the first column. The result will be the same as using Tab(1).

Example

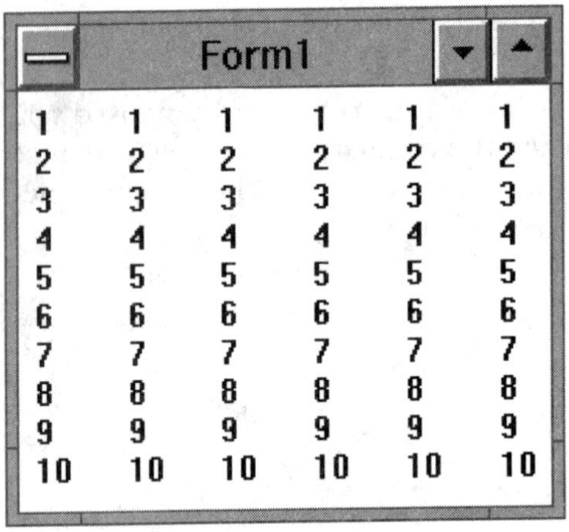

```
                    Form1
1   1   1   1   1   1
2   2   2   2   2   2
3   3   3   3   3   3
4   4   4   4   4   4
5   5   5   5   5   5
6   6   6   6   6   6
7   7   7   7   7   7
8   8   8   8   8   8
9   9   9   9   9   9
10  10  10  10  10  10
```

Figure T-1: The Tab command can line data up in columns.

On the Picture Box shown in Figure T-1, we display a table by using Tab inside a Loop, which would be one way to format an Array (which see):

```
Sub Form_Click ()

For i = 1 To 10
    For j = 1 To 30 Step 5
        picture1.Print Tab(j); i;
    Next j
    Print
Next i

End Sub
```

This Subroutine is a nested Loop structure—one Loop is nested inside another (see "For...Next"). The "outer" Loop governed by the counter *i* determines the number of lines of information printed and creates a new line by using the Print command. By itself, Print merely moves you down one line onscreen or on the printer.

The "inner" Loop is where we create the columns of data. We are allowing for 30 columns. The Step 5 command positions us at intervals of five: 1 To 10 Step 5 results in 1, 5, 10, 15, 20, 25. Those are the numbers we give Tab as it moves us across the page. Then, to simulate some data for the purpose of this example, we Print the *i* counter.

The semicolon following *i* is important: when you Print something, a semicolon holds you on the same line. Without it, Print would move to the next line below where we Printed.

See also   CurrentX; Print; Print #; Space$; Spc

TabIndex

PROPERTY

Description   The TabIndex is a unique number identifying each Control on a Form. A Control's TabIndex determines the order in which that Control will "get the focus" and become active if the user presses the TAB key. Pressing TAB cycles the user among the Controls on a Form while a program is running. (Pressing SHIFT+TAB cycles in the opposite direction.)

Using the TAB key to move among the objects on a window is a Windows convention. If the user is typing into a Text Box, for instance, pressing TAB to move to another Text Box or Command Button is often easier than reaching for the mouse, thus removing a hand from the keyboard.

"Moving to another Control" makes it the active Control—the one with the focus, the one capable of reacting to something the user types on the keyboard. Of three Text Boxes on a window, only one has the focus at any given time and can thus display what the user types.

The user can move to any of the Controls on a Form by pressing the TAB key, which is an alternative to using the mouse to click on a Control and make it active.

There are two exceptions to the rules involving TabIndex:

▪ Frames and Labels cannot "get the focus" although they do have a TabIndex Property. (See "Uses" for a special trick involving the TabIndex Property of Frames and Labels.) Frames and Labels will nonetheless be skipped over, ignored, when the user presses the TAB key to move among the objects on a Form (window). Menus and Timers do not have a TabIndex Property at all.

▪ Any Control that is disabled (its Enabled Property set to 0) or invisible (its Visible Property set to 0) will also be skipped during user tabbing.

If there are three Text Boxes on a window, pressing the TAB key moves you from the first, to the second, to the third, and back to the first, and so on. Which Text Box is "first," "second" or "third" is determined by its TabIndex number. Pressing TAB cycles through the Controls on the window. The order in which the user moves through the Controls on a window is also determined by their TabIndex Properties.

You can ignore the TabIndex Property. Visual Basic automatically assigns a TabIndex number to each Control in the order in which you create the Controls. If you first draw a Command Button on a Form, then a Text Box and then an Option Button, their TabIndex Properties will be as follows:

Control	TabIndex
Command1	0
Text1	1
Option1	2

(Note that the first item in the list has a TabIndex of zero, not one.)

You are allowed to change the TabIndex Property because there are situations where you might want to change the order. You might want to adjust the TabIndex so that pressing TAB cycles more intelligently through related Controls. See the Example.

Used with   Check Boxes, Combo Boxes, Command Buttons, File, Directory and Drive List Boxes, Frames, Grids, Horizontal and Vertical Scroll Bars, Labels, List Boxes, Option Buttons, Picture Boxes and Text Boxes

Variables   **Variable type:** Integer (enumerated)

(Usually, you'll use the Properties Window while designing your program to set a TabIndex).

OR (to set the TabIndex while the program is running):

Text1.TabIndex = 3 (this makes the Text Box the fourth in the tab index list of this Form because TabIndex starts counting from 0.)

OR (in a rare case where you want to find what the TabIndex is while the program is running): X = Label1.TabIndex

Uses   • By adjusting the TabIndex order, you can make your program behave more intelligently. Many people are good typists. And many computer applications involve typing lots of data. At least the first few times the user works with your program, he or she may have to enter plenty of information—perhaps the entire list of birthdays and anniversaries for his or her extended family.

The program will save this information to the disk for permanent use. But someone does need to enter it into the program at some point. Perhaps you have a Text Box for the user to type in birthdays and a separate Text Box for typing in anniversaries. There should be a relationship between the TabIndex and the order in which most users will want to move among the Controls on a Form. This way, the user can quickly accomplish saving, updating, paging forward or backward through the data—all without removing the hands from the keyboard to use the mouse when a particular Command Button should be pressed.

In the Birthday-Anniversary Box example, the TabIndex of the Anniversary Box should be one higher than the TabIndex of the Birthday Box.

Look for a Pattern: When you are designing a program, think about the various Command Buttons or other Controls on your program's windows. See if the user will access these Controls in a particular pattern. Will the user be likely to use the Backup Button before the Quit Button? If you see a likely pattern, adjust the TabIndex Properties of the Controls to conform to the user pattern. In most of the programs you will write, you'll often add Controls after your initial design. You'll likely want to adjust the TabIndex Properties so the Controls will end up in a logical sequence.

Sometimes you'll want a particular Text Box (or some other Control) to have the focus as soon as the window becomes visible. Let's assume that in a program the user starts typing information right away into a Text Box. The user shouldn't have to click on the Box because some other Control has the focus. The focus should devolve immediately to this Text Box. To make this happen, set that Text Box's TabIndex to 0 (either in the Properties Window when designing your program or within the Form_Load Event).

Using Access Keys Instead of TAB: You can assign an access key to a Control to offer the user an alternative to the TAB method of moving among the Controls on a Form. Another Windows convention is pressing the ALT key with a designated access key to automatically move the focus directly to a specific Control.

You can assign any Control with a Caption Property to an access key. The Controls with Captions are Forms, Check Boxes, Command Buttons, Frames, Labels and Option Buttons. (Menus can also have access keys.)

In Figure T-2, a Command Button has an ALT+E access key, made clear to the user by the underlined *E* in its Caption:

Figure T-2: The underlined *E* indicates that this Command Button has an "access key." In this case, pressing ALT+E will have the same effect as clicking on the Button with the mouse.

You create an access key by placing an & (ampersand) in front of the letter you want to be the access key:

```
Command1.Caption = "&EXIT"
```

OR you can place an ampersand by using the Properties Window while designing your program.

Special Trick: Frames and Labels *cannot* get the focus, but they *do* have TabIndex Properties. They also have Caption Properties. You can use Frame or Label to give a trick access key to a Text Box, Picture Box or other Control that normally couldn't have one (because those Controls don't have a Caption Property).

To attach a trick access key to a Text Box, first make sure that the Frame or Label you are using has its TabIndex Property set to one number lower than the Text Box's TabIndex. Then assign your access key to the Frame or Label. When the user presses the access key for the Frame or Label, the focus will not go to that Frame or Label because they cannot get the focus. However, the focus will move to the next Control in the TabIndex order. That's the trick.

Eliminating a Control From the TabIndex List With the TabStop Command: You may also want to look at the TabStop Property. It can eliminate Controls, such as Picture Boxes, from the list of Controls that Tab will hit. This way, if there is no reason for the user to ever need to access a Picture Box; it can be ignored when the user tabs around.

Cautions
• The TabIndex is not affected by manipulations of "ZOrder" (which see).

You can assign any number between zero and the total number of Controls on a Form (minus one) to a TabIndex Property. Minus one because the first Control in the Tab order has a TabIndex of 0.

VB automatically assigns TabIndices to each Control as you add it to a Form, starting with 0 and working up. If you change a Control's TabIndex Property, VB automatically adjusts the TabIndex Properties of the other Controls. You can make changes to the TabIndex order either while creating your program or while the program is running, by inserting some variation of Command1.TabIndex = 4 into the program proper.

Labels and Frames—as well as any Control that is currently not Visible or not Enabled—cannot get the focus, but do remain part of the Tab order.

• Because the TAB key is used in Windows programs as a way of maneuvering around a window, it cannot serve its traditional purpose within a Text Box. In a Text Box, the user cannot use the TAB key to move the cursor over as a way to indent paragraphs or create tables. The TAB key performs these jobs in most word processors (and typewriters).

Instead, Visual Basic permits CTRL+I to cause a "tab" within a Text Box.

Example

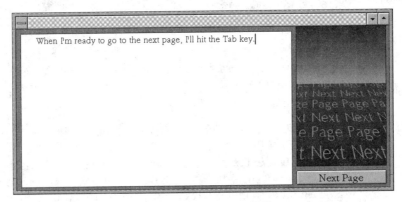

Figure T-3: The user can either click on the Next Page Button or press the TAB key. Tabbing allows typists to keep their hands on the keyboard.

Let's assume that we have a Picture Box on a window, and it was created right after we created a Text Box. (We double-clicked on the Text Box symbol in the VB Toolbox and then we double-clicked on the Picture Box symbol.) The Picture Box would then come after the Text Box in the TabIndex order. Because the Text Box was created first, VB would give it a TabIndex of 0 and then give the Picture Box a 1.

After that we add a Command Button captioned "Next Page" (VB would assign it a TabIndex of 2). The user cannot get to the Next Page Button until the TAB key is pressed twice. He or she will have to "tab through" the Picture Box before getting to the "Next Page" Button.

Your Program Isn't Acting Intelligently: Most users will want to finish typing something into the Text Box and then press the Next Page Button. This Command Button "flips the page"; it saves whatever the user typed into the Text Box to a disk file and then presents the user with a new page by emptying out the Text Box's Text property: Text1.Text = ""

Clearly, the user would rather press TAB once to get to the Next Page Button, instead of having to press twice to get past the picture. So we will give the Command Button a TabIndex right above the Text Box:

```
Command1.TabIndex = Text1.TabIndex + 1
```

(This way, we don't even need to know what TabIndex that Text1 might have. We just make the Next Page Button the Control after the Text Box in the Tab order by giving the Command Button the next higher Tab-Index number.)

As another way of being considerate to the user, we will also make sure that the Text Box gets the focus after the Next Page Button is pressed and has cleared the Text Box for more typing: Text1.SetFocus

In the Form_Load Event, type the following:

```
Sub Form_Load ()

Show
Command1.TabIndex = Text1.TabIndex + 1
End Sub
```

In the Command1_Click Event, you would enter the following:

```
Sub Command1_Click ()
```

(Put a file-saving routine here. See "Open.")

```
Text1.Text = ""
Text1.SetFocus

End Sub
```

See also   Label (for more about access keys); TabStop; ZOrder

TabStop

PROPERTY

Description   You use TabStop when you want your program to skip past a Control.

The user can press the TAB key to cycle among the Controls on a Form, activating each in turn. If you don't want a Control to be activated by the TAB key, set its TabStop Property off (0).

Using the TAB key to move around the items on a window is a Windows convention. If the user is typing into a Text Box, for instance, pressing TAB to move to another Text Box or Command Button is easier than leaving the keyboard to reach for the mouse.

"Moving to another Control" makes that the active Control—the one with the focus and capable of reacting to something the user types on the keyboard. Of three Text Boxes on a window, only one will have the focus at any given time. Only one will display what the user types.

The user can move to any of the Controls on a Form by pressing the TAB key, which is an alternative to using the mouse to click on a Control. (Pressing SHIFT+TAB moves through the Controls in the opposite order.)

The order in which Tab moves through the Controls is determined by the TabIndex Property of each Control (which see). Setting a Control's Tab-Stop Property to Off (0) means that this Control will not be activated (get the focus) when the user presses TAB to move among the Controls. This Control will be skipped over.

Turning off the TabStop, though, does not remove the TabIndex of the Control. The Control remains part of the Tab order, but it is skipped. Turning TabStop on and off while a program is running has some uses. See "Uses" below.

Used with Check Boxes, Combo Boxes, Command Buttons, File, Directory and Drive List Boxes, Grids, Horizontal and Vertical Scroll Bars, List Boxes, Option Buttons, Picture Boxes and Text Boxes

Frames and Labels cannot get the focus, so they will never be tabbed to. They therefore don't have a TabStop Property. They do have a TabIndex Property, however, and this allows you to use them for a special trick (see "Uses" under "TabIndex").

Variables **Variable type:** Integer (Boolean)

You can turn a TabStop Property off (the default is "on") while designing your program by using the Properties Window.

OR
You can turn the TabStop Property on and off while the program is running:

> Command1.TabStop = False (this Command Button is now prevented from getting the focus during Tabbing.)

OR (to restore the Command Button's ability to get the focus via pressing TAB): Command1.TabStop = True

Uses • You have several ways to make your Controls react intelligently while your program runs. For example, you can make a Control move (see "Move"); you can make it change size or shape (see "Width"); you can make it invisible (see "Visible"); you can make it go pale gray and become unresponsive (see "Enabled").

Or you can make the Control unable to get the focus when the user presses the TAB key to move among the Controls on the Form. Making a Control invisible or not Enabled automatically makes the Control unresponsive to Tab (so you don't need to set its TabStop Property as well).

(See "Uses" under "TabIndex" for a complete discussion of how the TAB key is used, and some alternative approaches as well.)

Cautions
• Any Control that is not Visible or not Enabled cannot get the focus. Therefore, you need not set TabStop Properties for invisible and disabled Controls. Such Controls do, however, remain part of the Tab order as defined by their TabIndex Property.

Labels and Frames cannot get the focus under any circumstances although they do have a TabIndex Property. They are always skipped while the user presses the TAB key to cycle among Controls on a Form. Labels and Frames have no TabStop Property at all.

Example
Let's assume that you put a Picture Box on a Form for purely decorative purposes. You don't want the picture to ever get the focus if the user presses TAB. TAB is for moving among Text Boxes, Command Buttons and other Controls that the user types things into, activates by pressing ENTER, or otherwise interacts with. To turn off this Picture Box's sensitivity to the TAB key, enter the following:

```
Picture1.TabStop = 0
```

See also
TabIndex

TAGSTRIP

CONTROL

See Windows 95 Controls

TAG

PROPERTY

Description
Tag is something like a Post-It note that you can attach to any Control, providing information to you, the programmer, about a particular Text Box or whatever. The Tag Property is a text ("string") Variable, like the Name and Caption Properties.

Tags are not very useful, though. The Rem command (which see) is a more direct and effective way of annotating your programs. You could use the Tag Property of a Form to hold the same text Variable as the Form's Name Property. Then the program could get access to the value of the Form's Name Property for some uses (the Name Property is not available to your program while the program is running). But such uses are, obviously, limited.

The primary use for Tag is to allow you to identify the "calling" Control or Form when a Subroutine or Function is invoked. You can then use the Tag Property to let the Sub or Function know which Form or Control is involved, in case the Sub or Function is supposed to react differently based on the identity of the caller. You could, though, use the TypeOf or Me command instead.

Tags, unlike most of the other Properties, do not cause some change to the qualities of the Control. You can adjust its Width Property to make a Picture Box thinner, and BackColor can change the color, but Tag is merely informational, merely a note about the Picture. It's like an extended Name Property— not just a name for the Control, but perhaps also a description as well.

Used with   Everything: Forms, Check Boxes, Combo Boxes, Command Buttons, File, Directory and Drive List Boxes, Frames, Grids, Horizontal and Vertical Scroll Bars, Images, Labels, Lines, List Boxes, Menus, OLE, Option Buttons, Picture Boxes, Shapes, Text Boxes and Timers

Variables   **Variable type:** Text ("string")

You can create a Tag from the Properties Window while designing your program:

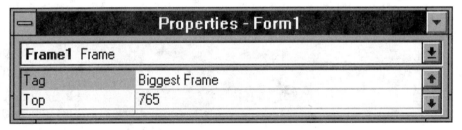

Figure T-4: You can adjust a Tag in the Properties Window.

OR (to change a Tag while the program is running):

Command1.Tag = "This Option Button is used only for reducing the font size."

OR (to find what a Tag is while the program is running): X$ = Command1.Tag

Uses   The VB *Programmer's Guide* suggests using a Tag to "pass" the name of a Control to a Subroutine, something like the following:

' (You would put this in an Event, such as Form_Click:)

Text1.Tag = "Text1"   ' put the Name of this Text Box into its Tag Property

Something Text1   ' call the Subroutine

' (in a separate Subroutine, created in the General Declarations section of the Form, you put the following):

```
Sub Something (T as Control)
    Print "The name of this Text Box is: " T.Tag
End Sub
```

What's the point of this? You cannot access some Properties—Name is one—while a program is running. Not only can you not change a Name, you cannot even find out what it is:

```
X$ = Text1.Name
```

This line does not work.

Tag provides you with a way of including and attaching information about a Control or Form that you can access while a program is running. When calling Subroutines or with MDI Forms (see "Multiple Document Interface") or new instances of Forms (see "Set"), this facility comes in handy.

Cautions None

Example
```
Label1.Tag = "This label identifies the suite of Command Buttons for disk access."
```

See also Me; Multiple Document Interface; Set

AN

Description You use Tan to give you the tangent of an angle expressed in radians. The argument can be a number or a numeric Variable or a numeric Constant.

You can get the tangent of any type of Variable—Integer, Floating-Point, etc. (See "Variables" for more on Variable "types.")

Variables
```
Print Tan(x)

F = Tan(.3)
```

Uses Use Tan in Trigonometry.

Cautions If the Variable or Constant you use with Tan is an Integer or Single-Precision number, the result will be Single-Precision. All other data types are calculated in Double-Precision. (See "Variables.")

Example
```
Print Tan(.01745)
```

See also Atn; Cos; Sin

TEXT

PROPERTY

Description A Text Property contains the contents of a Text Box, Combo Box or List Box. Text is similar to the Caption Property of other Controls, but Text can hold as many as 32,766 characters (however, if a Text Box's MultiLine Property is set to False, the limit is about 22,000 characters). Text can be changed by your program and can also be directly modified by the user. (The text cannot be modified in a Dropdown Combo Box [style 2] or a List Box, but the Text Property of these Controls can tell your program which item in the list the user has selected.)

Text is a text ("string") Variable. The Text Property behaves and is used like any text Variable (see "Variables"). Text is used in a specialized way with a List Box or a Combo Box, with its Style Property set to 2 (Dropdown List). In these two cases, Text contains the *selected item,* the highlighted item, in the Box. To have your program change the selected item's text, use the following:

        List1.Text = "New name."

OR (to have your program find out which item is currently selected within the Box): X$ = List1.Text

(However, a more common approach to finding out the currently selected item is to use the List(ListIndex) commands, which see.)

Used with Combo Boxes and List Boxes, Grids; Text Boxes

Variables **Variable type:** Text ("string")

To enter some default text while designing your program, you can use the Properties Window:

Figure T-5: Notice that the characters appear in a Text Box itself as you type them into the Properties Window.

OR (to put some text into a Text Box while the program is running):

        Text1.Text = "The bear is loose in the tent."

OR (to find out what text is currently in a Text Box, so you can manipulate it or save it to a disk file): X$ = Text1.Text

OR (to use the Text Property as a text Variable when you want to save it to a disk file, for example): Print #1, Text1.Text

OR (to use the Text Property in the same way that you use a normal text ("string") Variable; see "Variables"): If Text1.Text = "Mona Lisa" Then

OR (to find the contents or change the contents of the currently selected item in a List Box or Combo Box (Style 2)):

X$ = List1.Text

List1.Text = "New name."

Uses
- A Text Box is like the Notepad program that comes with Windows—a simple but effective word processor.
- Use Text Boxes for data entry or any situation where the user needs a convenient way to type something.
- Use Text Boxes to display information, such as a disk file that the user will want to view or edit.
- Use List and Combo Boxes to display lists of options from which the user can select.

Cautions
- If a Text Box's MultiLine Property is left in its default state (False), the Text Property can contain around 22,000 characters. If you set MultiLine on (you must do this in the Properties Window, you cannot do it while the program is running), then Text can contain 32,766 characters.

   If more than one line is in the Text Property, then text will contain two special characters called "Carriage Return" and "Line Feed" mixed in with the normal characters you can see. The "CR/LF" characters indicate where the line break is within the text. You can break down text into its component lines (see "InStr") and remove this pair of formatting characters if you wish. However, saving them along with the rest of the text to a disk file preserves the original formatting. See the Example below.

- The Text Property behaves just like a text ("string") Variable (see "Variables").

   (Also see "Asc" and "Chr$" for text Variable manipulations involving the ANSI code that is used in Windows to handle text characters. And see the Example below.)

- You can use the KeyDown Event of a Text Box to intercept characters as they're typed in. This allows you to control user input—refusing to accept letters, for example, if the user is supposed to be entering a phone number. You can also add shortcut commands, such as detecting when the user presses CTRL+Q for Quit.

- To add a cut, copy and paste feature to a Text Box, see "SelText."

- By default, the Text Property will initially contain the Name of its Text Box or Combo Box. Usually, you'll want to present the user with a clean Text Box into which he or she can type, just like a word processor. To remove this default Name, either delete it in the Properties Window, or put the following line somewhere early in your program:

```
Text1.Text = ""
```

A List Box's Text Property defaults to an empty string.

• You cannot add a boldface or italics feature, or include varying typefaces or font sizes within a single Text Property. These variations of character appearance and size are set for the entire Text Box, so you cannot mix and match them in the text inside the Box.

Example

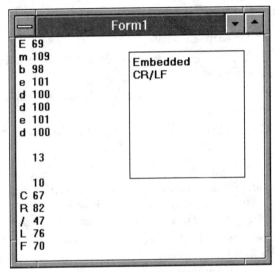

Figure T-6: Each letter used in Windows text has a code, called the ANSI code. (See "Chr$" for more on ANSI code.)

In Figure T-6, we are showing how an embedded line break is mixed in with the normal, viewable text characters. A Text Box knows when to move down to the next line when it comes upon a pair of codes called "Carriage Return" and "Line Feed." These codes become part of a Text Property if the MultiLine Property of its Text Box is set to On.

In Figure T-6, you can see the code for each viewable character, and also the 13 for CR and 10 for LF. We printed the codes on the Form, using Mid$ to pick off each character and Asc to translate them into their respective codes. Notice that when we printed the CR and LF, no actual characters were printed, *but they did move the text down a line* on the Form.

To try this example, first put a Text Box on a Form and set the Box's MultiLine Property to On (True) by using the Properties Window. Enter the following commands, then run the program and type in some characters. Press ENTER to insert a CR/LF, as well:

```
Sub Form_Click ()

For i = 1 To Len(Text1.Text)
```

```
         a$ = Mid$(Text1.Text, i, 1)
         currentx = 50
         Print a$;
         currentx = 200
         Print Asc(a$)
      Next i

      End Sub
```

Here we used the CurrentX and CurrentY Properties of the Form to position each character and code precisely where we wanted them. CurrentX and CurrentY are often preferable to using a comma (to create a "Tab" effect) when lining up columns.

See also   Asc; Chr; Combo Box; KeyDown; List Box; SelText; Text Box; Variables

CONTROL

Description   A Text Box is a simple, though surprisingly functional, word processor.

It responds to all the usual editing keys—DELETE, INSERT, Backspace, PgUp and PgDn. It automatically "word wraps" (detects when the user has typed to the right side of the Box and moves the word down to the next line without breaking it in two.)

You can add Scroll Bars (via that Property of a Text Box). By manipulating the SelText and related Properties, you can create a cut, copy and paste feature. By using the KeyDown Event, you can capture characters as the user types them and thus add special, additional features triggered by CTRL or ALT or Function keys.

You cannot add a selective boldface or italics feature, however, or include varying typefaces or font sizes. These Properties are set for the entire Text Box, so you cannot mix and match them in the text inside the Box.

With VB4, a more advanced TextBox (TB) Control makes its appearanceóthe RichTextBox (RTB). This Control does permit formattingóitalics, boldface, various typefaces and typesizes, bulleted lists, even color. You can import and export .RTF files, thereby retaining the formatting (most word processors recognize the RTF codes). In Windows 95 (which the RTB requires), the user can drag an .RTF file from Explorer or a Folder right into the RTB. And last but not least, the RTB has a useful built-in find utility.

We'll look first at this new Control, then discuss the general TB features that both the TB and RTB have in common (see "Variables" below).

What are the major distinctions between the TB and the new RTB? First, the TB was limited to 64K worth of text; the RTB is not. And, mercifully, the RTB defaults to MultiLine = True and doesn't insert the Text Property

(Text1). This way, you no longer have to start out erasing the Text and adjusting the MultiLine Properties each time you put a text input box on a Form.

Adjusting Format

How does the user adjust the Font Properties of a RTB? You, the programmer, have to supply that functionality. For example, it's a Windows convention that Ctrl+I toggles italics and Ctrl+B toggles boldface. However, Ctrl+I inserts a Tab in the RTB (Tab itself cycles you among the Controls on the Form). However, you could use a different shortcut. We'll use Alt+I and Alt+B here:

```
Private Sub RichTextBox1_KeyDown(KeyCode As Integer, Shift As Integer)
If Shift And 4 Then  Alt key depressed

Select Case KeyCode
Case vbKeyB
RichTextBox1.SelBold = Not RichTextBox1.SelBold
Case vbKeyI
RichTextBox1.SelItalic = Not RichTextBox1.SelItalic
End Select

End If
End Sub
```

You can, of course, also put RTB formatting options on a Toolbar (see "Windows 95 Controls"), within menus, or display a CommonDialog Font dialog Box (see "Common Dialog").

Recall that the CommonDialog Control's Font incarnation requires that you set the Flag to 1 (for Screen Fonts) or 2 (Printer) or 3 (both). Otherwise you get an error message:

```
Private Sub Command1_Click( )
commondialog1.Flags = 1
commondialog1.ShowFont
RichTextBox1.SelBold = commondialog1.FontBold
RichTextBox1.SelItalic = commondialog1.FontItalic
RichTextBox1.SelFontSize = commondialog1.FontSize
RichTextBox1.SelFontName = commondialog1.FontName
End Sub
```

Saving & Loading

To save and load files in the .RTF format, you can follow the usual Open...Close file saving tactics (see "Open"), but instead of the Text Property, use the TextRTF Property to preserve the RTF codes:

```
Open  SAMPLE.RTF  For Output As 1
    Print #1, RichTextBox1.TextRTF
Close 1
```

In addition to the "Open" technique for saving and loading .RTF files demonstrated above, you can also use the RTB's SaveFile and LoadFile Methods:

```
RichTextBox1.LoadFile  D:\SAMPLE.RTF
```

If you look inside an .RTF file, it contains lots of codes. This text "This is our test of italics and our test of boldface!!!" translates into this RTF file:

```
{\rtf1\ansi\deff0\deftab720{\fonttbl{\f0\fnil MS Sans
Serif;}{\f1\fnil\fcharset2
Symbol;}{\f2\fswiss\fprq2 System;}{\f3\fnil\fprq2 MS Sans Serif;}}
{\colortbl\red0\green0\blue0;}
\deflang1033\pard\plain\f0\fs17 This is our \plain\f0\fs17\i test of italics
\plain\f0\fs17 and our test of \plain\f0\fs17\b boldface!!!\plain\f0\fs17
\par }
Printing
```

You might think you could just send the Text or TextRTF contents of an RTB to the printer, like this:

```
Printer.Print RichTextBox1.Text
```

That does print the text, but doesn't preserve any of the formatting. This next attempt also fails. It prints the codes for the formatting rather than formatting the actual text:

```
Printer.Print RichTextBox1.TextRTF
```

To print formatted text, you must use the SelPrint Method:

```
Private Sub Command1_Click( )
Printer.Print
RichTextBox1.SelPrint (Printer.hDC)
End Sub
```

Note that you must first "seed" or wake up the printer object by sending a null string "". In addition, you are sending your RTF package of text to a "device" (the printer object) and therefore the "device context" (hDC) is required. (See "hDC".) Note also that no EndDoc command is requiredóthe printer will eject the page. Finally, if some of the text has been selected within the RTB, only that will be printed. Otherwise, by default, the entire contents of the RTB will go off to be printed.

The Find Method

The RTB contains a fully functional search capability. You invoke Find and, depending on the parameters you specify, the target text is searched for within a selected zone, or the entire text. Then, if found, the target is highlighted.

```
RichTextBox1.Find(string, start, end, options)
```

The string parameter is required and is whatever text the user is interested in locating.

Start is optional. Every character within an RTB has a unique integer index number. The first character is 0. If you choose to specify Start, the search will begin with the character identified by its index.

End is also optional and specifies the index of the character where the search should end.

The Options parameter is optional. Note that you can add these options together to create additional filtering. You can use either the built-in constant, or the numeric equivalent:

Constant	Value	
rtfWholeWord	2	(will not trigger a match unless the entire word matches)
rtfMatchCase	4	(the search is case-sensitiveócapitalization matters)
rtfNoHighlight	8	(suppresses the highlighting of found matches)

Here's an example. Put a RTB and a CommandButton on a Form. In the Button's Click Event, type this:

```
Private Sub Command1_Click( )
x$ = InputBox( Look for... )
IndexLocation = RichTextBox1.Find(x$, , , rtfWholeWord)
End Sub
```

Additional Notes on the RichTextBox:

The user can also format a zone of text by selecting it, then triggering a change by whatever method(s)óToolbar, CommondDialog, shortcut keystroke or menuóthat you've offered them.

The RTB has a Locked Property which makes the contents of the Box into read-only.

The RTB's HideSelection Property can prevent any selected text from being deselected if the RTB loses the focus (if the user clicks, for example, on a CommandButton).

If you want to provide additional functionality to the user, take a look at the RTB's Span Method. It's a way to control selected text so you can, for example, allow the user to press a shortcut key combination to select the entire paragraph where the cursor resides.

Variables

Because a Text Box is a Control, you usually adjust its Variables, its qualities, in the Properties Window while designing your program.

OR (to make changes to its Properties while the program is running):

```
Text1.Text = "Please enter your name..."
```

OR (to make changes by using a Variable while the program is running):

```
Text1.Text = File1.Path
```

OR

```
N = 700
Text1.Width = N
```

OR (to set a limit on the number of characters the user can type into a Text Box): Text1.MaxLength = 30

(You must adjust some of the Properties of a Text Box, such as MultiLine, from the Properties Window. They cannot be changed while the program is running.)

Uses
• A Text Box is like the Notepad program that comes with Windows—a simple but usable word processor.

• You can use Text Boxes for data entry, or any situation where the user needs a convenient way to type something into your program.

• If you want to limit the number of characters the user is permitted to enter into a Text Box, use the MaxLength Property. It can be set in the Properties Window or while the program is running. When not 0 (the default), a Text Box will refuse to accept—will not print onscreen or add to the Text Property—any further characters typed by the user.

• You can also use Text Boxes to display information, such as a disk file that the user will want to view or edit.

Cautions
• The MultiLine Property—which allows a Text Box to display more than one line—is off by default. You need to set it to On (True) by using the Properties Window (see "Variables" above).

Also, if you add a Horizontal Scroll Bar with the ScrollBars Property, all text will be on a single line. This single line can contain up to 255 characters. Any additional characters that the user attempts to type in—or your program attempts to add to the Text Property—will be ignored. It's therefore usually practical to use only a Vertical Scroll Bar, both Horizontal and Vertical Bars, or none. A Horizontal Bar by itself is restrictive. If there is only a Horizontal Bar, there will be no way to move down through multiple lines if CR/LF (see "Chr$") gets added.

If the MultiLine Property of a Text Box is True, the maximum size of the Text Property becomes roughly 32,000 characters. That is the size of a disk file that the user could view or edit with a Text Box or the size of a document the user could type in.

• A Text Box's Text Property (Text1.Text, for instance) behaves just like a text Variable (see "Variables"):

(Also see "Asc" and "Chr$" for text Variable manipulations involving the ANSI code that is used in Windows to handle text characters.)

• You can use the KeyDown Event of a Text Box to intercept characters as they're typed in, which allows you to control user input—refusing to accept letters, for example, if the user is supposed to be entering a phone number. You can also add shortcut commands with this technique, such as CTRL+Q for Quit.

• To add a cut, copy and paste feature, see "SelText."

• Windows uses the TAB key as a way of moving between the items, the Controls, on a window. Pressing TAB cycles you through the various Option Buttons, Command Buttons or whatever Controls are on a Form (see "TabIndex"). In a Text Box (unless it is the only Control on the Form which can respond to tabbing), the user cannot use the TAB key to move the cursor over, as would be possible in most word processors (and type-writers). CTRL+I, however, will tab in a Text Box.

Example

Sometimes a bit of animation adds an extra touch to your programs. We're going to let this Text Box slide in from the left side of the Form. Also, it's never necessary to explicitly define in your program all the Properties that we've listed in this program. You can adjust most Properties in the VB Properties Window and so they need not be written into your programs. However, several of the Properties of the Command Button, Text Box and Form interact in this program, so we'll want to illustrate how. Also, center-ing Controls and animation are both often best accomplished by setting Properties in a program. In this way, for instance, you can divide the ScaleWidth Property of the Form in half to get the horizontal center of the window. Here we want to center the Command Button.

First, select New Project from the VB File Menu, so you have a fresh start. Put a Text Box, a Command Button and a Timer on the Form. Then—so the following will be the first things that happen when this program starts running—we'll put these commands into the Form_Load Event:

```
Sub Form_Load ()

width = 7008
height = width

command1.left = (scalewidth / 2) — (command1.width / 2)
command1.top = scaleheight — 300
command1.fontbold = 0

text1.visible = 0
text1.text = ""
text1.width = 1
text1.height = scaleheight — 800
text1.top = 400
text1.left = 0

backcolor = QBColor(9)
command1.backcolor = backcolor

text1.fontsize = 12
text1.fontname = "Arial"
text1.fontbold = 0

End Sub
```

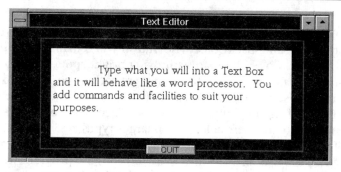

Figure T-7: A typical text-entry box that can be added to a VB program

The preceding series of commands establishes the look of the window. First, we make it square by setting the Width Property of the Form to a size that we want and then set the Height Property to equal the Width.

Putting It in the Precise Center: We want the Command Button at the bottom of the window and centered within the window. To accomplish this, we set its Left Property to one-half of the ScaleWidth (of the Form). ScaleWidth is the interior width of the Form, excluding the frame. (The Width Property includes the frame.) Then, to adjust for the size of the Button itself, we subtract one-half the width of the Command Button. Now the Button will appear in the precise horizontal center of the window. Then we move it up 300 twips (see "ScaleMode"), which puts it about halfway between the frame and the Text Box. Finally, we turn off its FontBold Property because we prefer a subtle lettering in its Caption. (We set the Caption with the Properties Window to read "Quit.")

The Text Box gets our attention next. Because we want it to appear to slide into the window from the left, we make it invisible at first. We remove any text in it by giving its Text Property an empty text Variable (""). We make it 1 twip wide. Note that a Text Box cannot get less wide than a single blank character, so it will not really be 1 twip wide. But that forces it to get as thin as possible, which will help with our animation effect.

The size and position of these Objects, the Text Box and Command Button, are obviously a matter of personal preference. But often you'll want Objects somewhat symmetrical relative to each other. The Text Box looks neater if things are lined up or equidistant from the window's frame.

To position the Text Box, we decided to use several numbers divisible by 400. We want the Box to be 800 twips shorter than the window's Scale-Height. Then we move it down 400 twips from the top of the window, centering it vertically within the window. We position this now tall, thin Text Box flush against the left side of the window—so it will appear to emerge from the left as we adjust the Text Box's Width Property in the Timer.

Now we set the BackColor of the window to blue and give the Command Button the same BackColor. The button will remain gray, but giving it the Form's BackColor eliminates annoying bright spots in the corners of the button. Finally, we make the characters within the Text Box 12 pt. Arial Normal. (Use whatever FontName you prefer.) Unfortunately, the FontBold Property of all Controls defaults to boldface. This font looks rather crude on most screens, particularly with larger typesizes. You'll likely find yourself turning FontBold off (setting it to 0) rather often.

When the user presses the "Quit" Button, the program will end, so we put that command into the Command1_Click Event:

```
Sub Command1_Click ()
    End
End Sub
```

To make this program a fully functional text editor like Windows's Notepad, you would want to add a menu that includes file-saving and -loading features. (See "Drive List Box.")

Animation: To make our Text Box move over into position from the left side of the window, we'll put the following Subroutine into the Timer. We want the user to see the window for a couple of seconds and then the Text Box will slide in. Set the Timer's Interval Property in the Properties Window to 2,000 to give us a two-second delay. A Timer is active by default when its Form Loads, so the Timer will automatically perform any commands in it after the delay in its Interval.

Now put the following into the Timer's Timer Event:

```
Sub Timer1_Timer ()

timer1.enabled = False

x = scalewidth - 1200
text1.visible = True

For i = 1 To x Step 400
    text1.width = i
    Refresh
Next i

text1.left = 600
text1.SetFocus

x = text1.left - 200: y = text1.top - 200
x1 = x + text1.width + 400
y1 = command1.top + (command1.height / 2)
drawwidth = 2
Line (x, y)-(x1, y1), QBColor(3), B
End Sub
```

First, we turn off the Timer so that this animation won't keep happening every two seconds while the user is trying to type something into the Text Box. We want to animate the Box only once, when the program first runs. Then we figure out how wide we want the Text Box to grow (the window's internal size, less 1,200 twips), making the right side of the Box the same distance from the surrounding window frame as its left side. And we suddenly make the Text Box visible and begin the animation within a Loop.

X is how wide we want the Box to grow, and the Loop counter i will move from 1 to X in steps of 400. This Step command isn't necessary, but it speeds up the animation so that the Text Box appears to slide rapidly, rather than to flow, onto the window. You can fiddle with the Step size to determine how big a Step looks best for the effect you prefer. X is, in fact, 5,592 twips in this example. The Loop counter Variable i will be 1 the first time through the loop, then 401, then 801, etc., in Steps of 400, all the way up to the ultimate width of 5,592. Inside the loop we keep changing the Width Property of the Text Box, which makes it appear to slide in. When the Loop is finished, though, the Box is still flush against the left side of the window. That's how we positioned it in the Form_Load Event. We immediately move it over 800 twips, and, to the user, this appears to be a seamless part of the overall animation.

The next five lines in the program calculate where to draw that thin blue box around the Text Box, for a simple design. The goal was to make the thin line appear to go right through the middle of the Command Button—a common visual effect used by Windows programs. To find the vertical center position of the Command Button, we add one-half its height to the location of its top. (The technique for drawing this box is explained in the entry for the Line command, in the section on the *Emboss* Subroutine.)

At the very end, we SetFocus (which see) to the Text Box, and the user can start typing.

Text Box Properties

Alignment • BackColor • BorderStyle • DataChanged • DataField DataSource • DragIcon • DragMode • Enabled • FontBold • FontItalic FontName • FontSize • FontStrikethru • FontUnderline • ForeColor Height • HelpContextID • HideSelection • hWnd • Index • Left LinkItem • LinkMode • LinkTimeout • LinkTopic • MaxLength MousePointer • MultiLine • Name • Parent • PassWordChar ScrollBars • SelLength • SelStart • SelText • TabIndex • TabStop Tag • Text • Top • Visible • Width

Text Box Events

Change • CLick • DblClick • DragDrop • DragOver • GotFocus KeyDown • KeyPress • KeyUp • LinkClose • LinkError • LinkNotify LinkOpen • LostFocus • MouseDown • MouseMove • MouseUp

Text Box Methods
Drag • LinkExecute • LinkPoke • LinkRequest • Move • Refresh
SetFocus • ZOrder

See also   KeyDown; Label; SelText; Text

TextHeight

METHOD

Description   TextHeight tells you how much space will be taken up (vertically) when some text is printed on a Picture Box, a Form or the sheet of paper in the printer. TextHeight, along with the TextWidth command, allows you to position text precisely–to center a title, for example.

Used with   Forms, Picture Boxes and the printer

Variables   To find out the width of this literal text when it is printed:

    X = TextHeight("MY SENIOR PROM")

OR (to use a Variable instead of a text "literal"):

    A$ = "The Title of my Report"
    X = TextHeight(A$)

OR (to find out the TextHeight as it would be printed by the printer):
X = Printer.TextHeight(A$)

Uses   Use TextHeight to position text vertically. You can use it along with TextWidth, which positions text horizontally. See the Example below.

Cautions   • The TextHeight is the size of the currently selected FontName Property in the currently selected FontSize *plus* the spacing between the lines, the *leading*. The spacing is called "leading" because of the bars of lead that typesetters used to wedge between lines of text. Both the leading above and below the text is figured into the TextHeight measurement.

The TextHeight's unit of measurement is the ScaleMode Property of the host entity–the Picture Box, Form or printer. This measurement is usually the default, twips (there are 1,440 twips per inch). You can change the mode by adjusting the ScaleMode (which see).

The text that you are measuring can be any kind of "text expression." It can be a text Variable (A$), a literal ("VACATION DAYS"), a Variable plus a literal (A$ + "MONDAY"), and so on. See "Variables."

Example   • You can vertically center printed text on a Form by finding the center of the Form: Center = ScaleHeight / 2

The CurrentY Property is the vertical location where the next text will be printed. In this example, we'll set CurrentY to one-half of the ScaleHeight (the interior height minus any framing) of the Form:

```
Sub Form_Click ()

currenty = scaleheight / 2

Print "CENTERING A TITLE"

End Sub
```

Results in

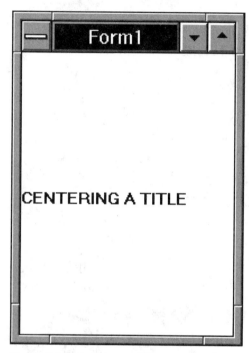

Figure T-8: This line won't be centered until we take into account the *text* itself.

But this result is not quite right. The text is slightly off-center, slightly too low. We must also take into account the fact that printed text itself has height. CurrentY positions at the *top* of the text. In other words, the text starts printing *down from* CurrentY.

To precisely center our text, we must also figure out its height and subtract that from the center of the Form:

```
Sub Form_Click ()

th = TextHeight("CENTERING A TITLE")

currenty = scaleheight / 2 − th

Print "CENTERING A TITLE"

End Sub
```

Results in

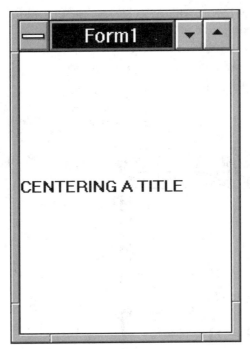

Figure T-9: This text is now centered on the vertical axis, but more remains to be done if we want it centered horizontally as well.

To format text both vertically and horizontally, we'll need to use Text-Width and ScaleWidth as well. See the next example.

Figure T-10: Center text with the ScaleWidth, ScaleHeight, TextWidth and TextHeight commands.

Example We want to add a title to a graphic. In this example, we're creating a program that will act like a visual scrapbook of the pictures we took on our trip to Europe. This first Form is going to be the title screen. We want the main title "EUROPE" to be in the horizontal center of the space reserved for it on the right of the window. And we want it to start one-third of the way down from the top. To position the title, we will use ScaleHeight / 3 along with TextHeight / 2.

All our commands—most of which position and draw the text—are put into the Form_Load Event so they will be the first thing that happens when this window in Figure T-10 appears:

```
Sub Form_Load ()

left = 0
top = 0
height = 8000
backcolor = QBColor(7)

Show
picture1.left = 0
picture1.top = 0
picture1.height = scaleheight
picture1.width = 7200

fontsize = 24

currenty = 100

a$ = "OUR"
    GoSub sinkit
a$ = "TRIP"
    GoSub sinkit
a$ = "TO"
    GoSub sinkit

fontname = "CaslonOpenFace"
fontsize = 36

th = TextHeight("E") / 2
currenty = scaleheight / 3 — th

n$ = "EUROPE"
For i = 1 To 6
a$ = Mid$(n$, i, 1)
GoSub sinkit
Next i

Line (7950, 2000)—(8900, 7000), QBColor(8), B
Line (7965, 2015)—(8915, 7015), QBColor(15), B

Exit Sub

sinkit:

    halfway = (scalewidth — picture1.width) / 2
    halfway = halfway + picture1.width
```

```
        tw = TextWidth(a$) / 2
        x = halfway — tw

        y = currenty
        currentx = x
        forecolor = QBColor(15)
        Print a$

        currentx = x — 14
        currenty = y — 14
        forecolor = QBColor(8)
        Print a$

    Return

    End Sub
```

First, we position the window on the screen at position 0,0—against the top and left of the screen. Then we make it 8,000 twips high (see "Scale-Mode") and turn the backcolor gray. Next, we Show the window, so the printed text and the line drawn around Europe will be visible. Then we position the Picture Box.

The Sinkit Subroutine: Now we set the FontSize to 24, moderately large characters, and position ourselves slightly down from the top of the window by setting CurrentY to 100 twips. Next, "OUR TRIP TO" is printed using a technique that manipulates a shadow to make the text appear engraved into the window's background. To accomplish this, we use a Subroutine (see "GoSub") called *Sinkit*. This Subroutine also centers each of the words between the edge of the graphic and the right side of the window.

The font is now changed to *Caslon,* a more fussy, formal-looking typeface than the default Helv that we've been using. And we enlarge the characters to 36. The following commands position the word *EUROPE* one third of the way down the window:

```
    th = TextHeight("E") / 2
    currenty = scaleheight / 3 — th
```

Here we take a sample letter, get its TextHeight and then divide that by two. This way, we know the precise middle of the letter *E* in the Caslon typeface at a size of 36. Then we adjust CurrentY—the "cursor," the next position where a character will be Printed—to one-third of the total height of the interior of our window. A further, fine adjustment is accomplished by subtracting one-half of the height of the letter *E.*

Using TextHeight in this fashion is less critical when you are positioning at 1/3 or 2/5 or some other odd fraction. People won't notice slight errors with odd fractional positions. However, if you are trying for symmetry, putting something exactly in the center of a window, the eye will be quick to notice if you don't use TextHeight / 2 along with ScaleHeight / 2.

Then we use a Loop with Mid$. Mid$ will pick off each of the characters in *EUROPE* in turn and send them individually down to the *Sinkit* Subroutine to be printed on separate lines. And we draw an embossed box design around the word *EUROPE*. (For more about this technique and its variations, see the *Emboss* Subroutine in the entry on the Line command.)

Now we come to the Subroutine that centers text horizontally and highlights it so that it appears to sink into the background. When you put a Subroutine into an Event, you need to precede it with Exit Sub because you want the Subroutine to be used only when you "call" it by giving its name. You don't want VB to run the Subroutine one last time when the program finishes with the commands above it in this Event.

First, we determine the horizontal center of the space between the Picture Box and the right side of the window. We subtract the size of the Picture Box from the total interior size of the window and divide that by two. This number tells us how far over from the edge of the Picture Box to move. And we add the result to the position of the right edge of the Picture Box (by adding Picture1.Width). This works because we earlier set the Picture Box's Left Property to 0, putting it up against the left edge of the window. Now we know the exact middle of our title zone.

To know where to print each letter in *EUROPE* as it arrives in the Subroutine, we subtract half of the width of that letter from the center of the zone. Now we can set CurrentX, the "horizontal print location cursor."

The engraving effect is achieved by printing a white version of the characters first, then moving slightly up and to the left, and *overprinting* in dark gray. (This technique and variants are described in the entry on Print, in a Subroutine called *Raiseit*).

Because Printing automatically moves you down to the next "line," we need to remember the CurrentY, the vertical "cursor" position. We save this position in the Variable *y*. And, we also need to remember the CurrentX, the horizontal position. The values of CurrentX and CurrentY are saved in the Variables *x* and *y* so that we will know where we were when we printed the white highlight. We move up and left 14 twips from that position—just a slight offset—and overprint a dark gray version of the same character. QBColor(15) is white; QBColor(8) is dark gray.

See also   CurrentX, CurrentY; Print; ScaleHeight; ScaleMode; ScaleWidth; TextWidth

T EXTIDTH

METHOD

Description   TextWidth tells you how much space will be taken up (horizontally) when some text is printed on a Picture Box, a Form or the sheet of paper in the printer. Using TextWidth, along with the TextHeight Method, you can position text precisely—to center a title, for example.

Used with   Forms, Picture Boxes and the printer

Variables   To find the width of a literal piece of text:

X = TextWidth("The Hidden Causes of the Franco-Prussian Conflict")

OR (to use a Variable instead of a text "literal"):

A$ = "The Title of the Book"
X = TextWidth(A$)

OR (to find out the TextWidth of the paper in the printer):
X = Printer.TextWidth(A$)

Uses   Use TextWidth to position text horizontally. You can use it along with TextHeight, which positions text vertically. See the Example below.

Cautions   • The TextWidth is the horizontal size of text. It reflects the currently selected FontName Property in the currently selected FontSize.

• The TextWidth's unit of measurement is the ScaleMode Property of the host entity—the Picture Box, Form or printer. This measurement is usually the default, twips (there are 1,440 twips per inch). You can adjust the scale by changing the ScaleMode (which see).

• The text that you are measuring can be any kind of "text expression." It can be a text Variable (A$), a literal ("Composed Salad"), a Variable plus a literal (A$ + "Fish"), and so on. See "Variables."

Example

Figure T-11: This example demonstrates how to put a title in the precise center of a Picture Box.

To experiment with TextWidth and the other Print formatting commands, create a Form and put a Picture Box on it. Then put the following into the Form_Load Event:

```
Sub Form_Load ()

Show

width = Picture1.width
height = Picture1.height

Picture1.fontname = "BlackChancery"
Picture1.fontsize = 48
a$ = "GARGOYLES"

tw = Picture1.TextWidth(a$) / 2
hcenter = scalewidth / 2
Picture1.currentx = hcenter — tw

th = Picture1.TextHeight(a$) / 2
vcenter = scaleheight / 2
Picture1.currenty = vcenter — th

x = Picture1.currentx
y = Picture1.currenty

Picture1.Print a$

Picture1.currentx = x + 50
Picture1.currenty = y + 50

Picture1.ForeColor = QBColor(15)

Picture1.Print a$
End Sub
```

First, we Show the window because printed text won't appear if you don't use Show inside Form_Load (unless the AutoRedraw Property is set to True). Then we make the window fit the size of the Picture Box exactly. We select an appropriately creepy font, *Black Chancery*, set its size to 48 points and define our title, "GARGOYLES."

We now use TextWidth to find out how wide the word *GARGOYLES* is in Black Chancery at this point size. We divide the Variable *tw* in half because we want half of the word to the left of the horizontal center of the Picture. We find the horizontal center of the Picture by dividing ScaleWidth by two. Because we made the window fit the Picture, both of their ScaleWidths will be identical. (We could have used Picture1.ScaleWidth here as well.)

Then we set the CurrentX Property, the location where the next text will be placed (horizontally) to the horizontal center, less one-half of the width of the word *GARGOYLES*.

Following exactly the same steps, we locate the *vertical* position where the next Print should take place. Then we print it. The color defaults to black. We'll use this as a drop-shadow and print on top of it in white to create a dimensional effect.

Notice that we saved the CurrentX and CurrentY positions before printing in black. Printing causes the CurrentX to reset to the far left of the Picture and CurrentY to move down one line, just like pressing the ENTER key while typing. We want to move a little down and to the right, and overprint in white. To accomplish this, we must memorize the first printing position in the Variables *x* and *y*. Now we move CurrentX and CurrentY an offset of 50 twips (see "ScaleMode") down and 50 to the right, and print *GARGOYLES* again.

We've Covered the Monster's Eyes: The effect shown in **Figure T-11**, though, isn't what we want. The text is covering up the monster's eyes. It would look far better if the text were printed only one-fourth of the way down the window. Adjusting horizontal or vertical position by any fraction is easy. Just divide ScaleHeight or ScaleWidth by the desired number. In this case, we want to be one-fourth of the way down, so we change this line and leave everything else as is:

```
vcenter = scaleheight / 4
```

Thus, we get this more attractive result:

Figure T-12: Graphics often look better if accompanying text isn't ruthlessly *symmetrical.* Here we improve on Figure T-11 by positioning the title higher up on the window.

(See TextHeight for a thorough examination of formatting with all the interacting commands that position for printing–CurrentX, CurrentY, TextWidth, TextHeight, ScaleWidth, ScaleHeight.)

See also CurrentX, CurrentY; Print; ; ScaleHeight; ScaleMode; ScaleWidth; TextHeight

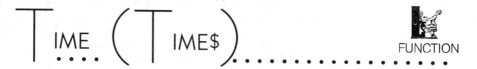

TIME (TIME$)
FUNCTION

Description Several Functions in VB give you information about your computer (such as CurDir, which tells you the currently active drive and directory, and Date, which tells you the current date).

Time tells you what time the computer thinks it is, based on the battery-driven clock inside the machine. Time is similar to typing in DOS: C:> TIME

The Time command is identical to Time$, but instead of providing a text ("string") Variable, Time returns a "Variant" Variable (see "Variant").

A Better Alternative to Time: Time functions as a text Variable that contains the hours, minutes and seconds in a HH:MM:SS format–13:12:22. The hours are in "military" format, with 13 being 1PM, 17 being 5PM, etc.

Because most people prefer to use the 12-hour format, you will probably want to avoid using Time in your programs. Instead, use the Now Function, along with the Format Function. Together, they can describe time in the familiar AM/PM fashion. Also, Format is quite flexible. It offers you many options for displaying time, date and other information. (See the Example below.)

In addition, the components of time are easily available by using the Hour, Minute and Second Functions, along with the Now Function.

Variables To put Time into a Variable:

    X$ = Time

OR (to use Time itself as if it were a normal text Variable): Print Time

Results in 13:55:38
(meaning 1:55 PM and 38 seconds)

Uses • Stamp the time on Printed documents.

• Use for calendar or datebook-like features within databases, word processors or other applications.

Cautions • You can change the computer's time with Time (used as a *Statement*, which see). Time as a Function is merely a text Variable used to display the time.

Because Time contains three pieces of information, you may want to extract just the hour, minute or second. To do this, use the InStr Function. See "CurDir" for an example of extracting compressed information. However, the Now and Format Functions are more flexible for this purpose. (See the Example below.)

Example
This example illustrates the difference between Time and the preferable Format(Now) approach to displaying time:

```
Sub Form_Click ()

Print Time
Print Format(Now, "h:m:ss AM/PM")

End Sub
```

Results in
14:35:14
2:35:13 PM

See also
Date; Format; Hour; Minute; Now; Second; Time (Statement)

T IME$

STATEMENT

Description
With the Time$ *Statement*, you can change the computer's idea of what time it is. You can set the computer's battery-backed internal clock to a different time.

Used with
The computer's internal clock

Variables
To set the time to 4 AM:

```
Time$ = "04"
```

OR (to set the time to 1:55 PM): Time$ = "13:55"

OR (to set the time to 1:55:23 PM): Time$ = "13:55:23"

OR (to use a text Variable instead of the literal text, a Variable, for instance, that was set by the user while the program is running):

```
T$ = InputBox$("Please enter the adjusted time", ,Time$)
Time$ = T$
```

Uses
Provide a feature in your program that allows the user to adjust the time as remembered by the battery-powered clock in his or her machine. You may also want to use the Date$ Function to offer a similar option concerning the date.

Cautions   • The *Visual Basic Language Reference* says that using Time$ to change the time in the computer's battery-powered clock is only temporary. In fact, most contemporary IBM-style computers make this change permanent, at least until you use Time$ again or reset the clock from the DOS command line by typing TIME. The *Language Reference* cautions that the time will reset to its original value when you turn off the computer, but this is not usually the case. The change is permanent in most machines.

Time$ as a Statement affects the time stored in your computer's battery-powered clock. Time$ used as a Function (which see) simply checks and reports the stored time.

If a partial text Variable is entered, then Time$ assumes the rest of the items are zero:

08:. becomes 08:00:00
08:12 becomes 08:12:00

Example   This example illustrates how Time$ adjusts the current time as registered by the computer's built-in battery-powered clock:

```
Sub Form_Click ()

Print Time$
Time$ = "16"
Print Time$
Print Format$(Now, "hh:mm:ss AM/PM")

End Sub
```

Results in   15:23:04
16:00:00
04:00:00 PM

Here is a special window that you could add to one of your programs. This window, an InputBox, allows the user to reset the time, just as the TIME command in DOS resets the time. When the user clicks on the Command Button, he or she gets the current time and is shown the format for changing it:

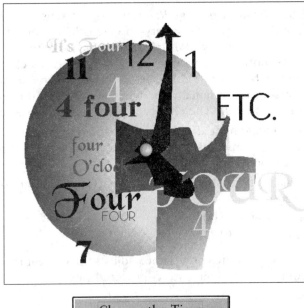

Change the Time

Figure T-13: The user can click on the Command Button to change the computer's clock.

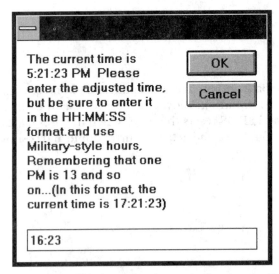

The current time is
5:21:23 PM Please
enter the adjusted time,
but be sure to enter it
in the HH:MM:SS
format.and use
Military-style hours,
Remembering that one
PM is 13 and so
on...(In this format, the
current time is 17:21:23)

OK

Cancel

16:23

Figure T-14: This Input Box instructs the user on the proper format for adjusting the computer's clock.

```
Sub Command1_Click ()

On Error Resume Next

info$ = "The current time is "
info$ = info$ + Format$(Now, "h:m:ss AM/PM")
info$ = info$ + ". Please enter the adjusted time, but be sure to enter it in →
    the HH:MM:SS format."
info$ = info$ + "and use Military-style hours, "
info$ = info$ + "Remembering that one PM is 13 and so on..."
info$ = info$ + "(In this format, the current time is " + Time$ + ")"

T$ = InputBox$(info$)

Time$ = T$

If Err And T$ <> "" Then
    Print "You failed to enter the time in a format we can understand. →
        Please try again."
End If

End Sub
```

It is not unlikely that the user will make an error entering the time. Time$ is very strict about the acceptable format: HH:MM:SS. So, we take into account the possibility of a problem by using the On Error Resume Next structure. This structure tells VB to keep going if there is a problem when we assign the user's input to Time$ (by: Time$ = T$).

Now we *build* the message that the user will see when the InputBox appears. Sometimes the easiest way to create text for a Text Box or Input-Box is to write several shorter pieces of text and add them together as you go, like stringing pearls.

After the text is built into the text Variable *info$*, the InputBox is displayed and waits for the user to enter something. Then the data entered into the InputBox is put into Time$ to make the change to the computer's clock. If the built-in error-detecting VB Variable *Err* is anything but 0, there was a problem. *Time$* rejected what we tried to assign to it with *T$*.

Possibly, the user clicked the Cancel Button in the Input Box. In this case, *T$* would be empty, a blank text Variable (""). Because we don't want to display the error message in that situation, we also include If T$ <> (does not equal) "" (an empty string). In other words, this If...Then structure says: "*If* there is an Err and *If* T$ isn't empty, *Then* show the error message."

How Your Program Can Assist the User: If you allow the user to change the clock from within one of your programs, you will probably want to make things less strict than the format required by Time$. Have the program make adjustments to what the user might enter–add any necessary leading zeros, and turn PM or AM into the 24-hour time that Time$ wants. To make the program more accommodating to the user, we'll add some commands to the second example. These new commands analyze what the user types and try to translate it into the format Time$ expects.

It is often good practice to make allowances for a wide variety of possible user responses. Your program should endeavor to accept this variety, and, if necessary, make corrections. We're going to illustrate how to take the user input apart and make sure that it conforms to the HH:MM:SS format that Time$ wants. (You could accomplish this more easily by using the TimeValue Function. However, the following techniques are useful in many situations, so we'll do things the hard way here to demonstrate a typical approach to fixing user input.)

```
Sub Command1_Click ()

On Error Resume Next

info$ = "The current time is "
info$ = info$ + Format$(Now, "h:m:ss AM/PM")
info$ = info$ + ". Please enter the adjusted time."

t$ = InputBox$(info$)

hr$ = Left$(t$, 2)
suspect = Asc(Right$(hr$, 1))
If suspect < 48 Or suspect > 57 Then t$ = "0" + t$

z$ = LCase$(t$)
If InStr(z$, "p") Then
    x = Val(Left$(t$, 2))
    x = x + 12
    t$ = Right$(t$, Len(t$) − 2)
    t$ = LTrim$(Str$(x)) + t$
End If

l = Len(t$)

For i = l To 1 Step −1
    testchar = Asc(Right$(t$, 1))
            If testchar > 58 Or testchar = 32 Then
                    t$ = Left$(t$, l − 1)
                    l = Len(t$)
            End If
Next i

Time$ = t$

If Err And t$ <> "" Then
    MsgBox "You entered the time in a format we cannot understand. Please try again."
End If
```

Here our first job is to add a leading zero if the user didn't—changing 4 into 04 in the hour section, the first two characters entered.

Let's follow the progress of our fix-up job as it grapples with a user entry of 4 PM. There are three problems with this entry as far as Time$ is concerned:

1. There is no leading zero (04 PM).
2. It is not in military time (16 PM).
3. There should be no text (16 is an acceptable entry for Time$; PM is not).

As soon as we have the user's entry in the Variable *t$*, we look at the two leftmost characters. We put those two characters into the text Variable *hr$*. Then we pick off the right character to see if it is anything other than a number. In that case, there is a colon or a space (4:00 AM or 4 PM or something). We'll want to add a 0 to that.

The Asc command tells us the ANSI code of the suspect character (see "Chr$"). Digits fall between 48 and 57 in the ANSI code, so if our suspect is less than 48 or greater than 57, it's not a digit and we add a "0" to the text. This transforms 4:00 PM into 04:00 PM.

Time$ Wants It Military-Style: So far, so good. But that *PM* also requires that we adjust the digits. 04:00 PM should become 16:00 PM, military-style time, the way Time$ wants it. We use LCase$ so we can ignore "pm" versus "PM" and put the entire thing into a new Variable *z$*. If we do find a *p* in the user's text, we extract the leftmost two characters (04, in our example) and find their numeric value (with Val). We add 12 and use Str$ to translate the result back into text characters. Then we remove the leftmost two characters from *t$* (turning it from 04:00 PM into :00 PM). Because the Str$ command adds a leading space character when it translates a number into text digits, we use LTrim$ to remove the leading space and add the text to *t$*. Now we have 16:00 PM, and all we need to do now is remove any characters that aren't digits or colons. We want to present Time$ with 16:00, which it can understand, not 16:00 PM.

To strip off any alphabetic characters, we set up a Loop structure that will look at each character in *t$*. Nondigit characters are likely to be on the right side of the text, so our job will be easier if we begin from the right side and remove whatever characters we find. To do this, we go through the text backward, starting with the rightmost character. The Loop moves from the length of the text down to 1, Stepping backward (–1). We again use Asc to see if the rightmost character is a letter of the alphabet, which would be an Asc value greater than 58. The colon and all the digits have codes less than 58, so we will leave them alone. We also check for any spaces, which have a code of 32.

If we find something other than a digit or a colon, we remove the right-most character from *t$*. By the end of this process, we've turned the user's 4 PM into 16:00. Time$ recognizes 16:00. The several adjustments that this program can perform will take care of a variety of potential user entries and translate them into the correct format.

Put the Burden on Your Program, Not the User: Ideally, if the computer requires a rigid and essentially nonhuman format, your program should accept a range of typical user responses and fix them before presenting them to the computer. The burden should be on your program, not on the user. You write your program once, but the program will potentially be used many times by many people. The preceding example illustrates the general approach you can take to analyze and fix user input.

Visual Basic includes a TimeValue Function (which see), an alternative command that makes solving the HH:MM:SS problem easier. The user can enter either 13:15 or 1:15PM and TimeValue translates that into a serial number. You can then build HH:MM:SS from the serial number by using the Format$ Function. See the Example under "TimeValue."

See also   Date; Format; Hour; Minute; Now; Second; Time (Function); TimeValue

TIMER
CONTROL

Description

Figure T-15: The symbol for a Timer on the Toolbox

A Timer is a powerful and sophisticated clock. It is accurate to a millisecond—1/1,000th of a second. To specify a delay of two seconds, you would set the Interval to 2,000: Timer1.Interval = 2000.

Once started, a Timer works independently and constantly. No matter what else might be happening in your Visual Basic program or in Windows, your Timer keeps ticking way. This is the meaning of *multitasking:* more than one thing happening at the same time.

The Interval Property of a Timer is a *duration.* The Interval determines how long the Timer must wait before it can carry out any instructions you've put into the Timer's Event. In other words, when a Timer Event is triggered, nothing happens until the Interval passes.

This Timer Event is quite different from the other Events in VB. The commands within most Events are carried out as soon as the Event is triggered. Command1_Click is triggered the very moment the user clicks on that Command Button, for example.

A Timer is different. When its Event is triggered, it looks at its Interval Property. It then *waits until that interval of time has passed before it carries out any instructions you've put into its Event.*

Why Timers Are Confusing at First: Timers are a little confusing if you haven't yet worked with them. They are called Controls, but they are unlike any other Visual Basic Control:

- Most Controls have more than a dozen Properties; Timers have eight.

- Most Controls have at least 10 Events they can respond to; Timers have only one Event.

- Most Controls are accessed and triggered by the user of the program; Timers work in the background, independent of the user. They are always invisible when a program runs.

- Most Controls' Events are triggered instantly; Timers don't carry out the instructions you've put into their Events until their Interval (the duration) passes.

How to Visualize a Timer's Purpose: It's best to think of a Timer as one of those kitchen timers that you wind to, say, 20 and then the Timer starts ticking. Twenty minutes later it goes BING! The BING is whatever instructions you have put into the Sub Timer1_Timer() Event. The Interval Property is the number of minutes (or *milliseconds*) that you set the Timer to.

There's just one kink to remember: unlike a kitchen timer, a VB Timer *resets itself after going BING.* And then it starts counting down from 20 again. After 20 more minutes pass—BING! Reset. Count down. BING!

This resetting will continue forever unless you stop the program or deliberately turn off the Timer by setting the Timer1.Enabled Property to False while your program is running. If you need the Timer again, turn it on again with Timer1.Enabled = True.

Figure T-16: Drag this Timer symbol onto a Form when you want to delay, repeat or control the duration of events in your programs.

Timers Are Superior to Loops for Measuring Duration: If you create a Loop structure in one of your programs, the amount of time the Loop takes to finish will depend on the speed of the user's computer:

```
For I = 1 to 20000
Next I
```

A few years ago, programmers inserted a delay like the one above into their program so that the user could, for instance, view a message onscreen. After the Loop was completed, the program made the message go away. But the delay caused by a Loop is so computer-dependent, that this approach is particularly useless these days. IBM computers using Windows can have speeds that range between 15 and 50 MHz.

A Timer is far superior to a Loop because the Timer will delay the same amount of time on any machine. It uses the computer's vibrating crystal clock, so the time it measures is absolute. Well, pretty near absolute.

What Timers Do: When you put a Timer onto one of your Forms, it can keep interrupting whatever else might be going on—even if the user is doing something that's not in your VB program.

If you set a Timer's Interval Property to anything greater than 0, which is the default, the Timer operates independently of anything else that's happening in the computer at the time. The Timer will repeatedly do what you tell it to do, carrying out any commands you put inside the Timer_Timer Event until your program turns off the Timer (Timer1.Enabled = False). Timers are both relentless and system-wide in their effects. You could make one that collapses the Windows operating system itself, like a bomb (see Appendix A for an example of this).

Remember that the commands you place inside a Timer's Timer Event are carried out *after* the Interval Property elapses. And they are carried out *every time* the Interval Property elapses. You can make a Timer do pretty much anything you want that involves duration, delay, repetition—by using the Interval and Enabled Properties in various ways.

The Job You Give to a Timer: A Timer, once turned on, becomes an alien robot agent loose in Windows. It has its instructions, and it knows how often you want the job done. Its instructions are the commands you have given it in its Timer Event between:

```
Sub Timer1_Timer ()
```

and . . .

```
End Sub
```

Doing the Job on Schedule: Of a Timer's eight Properties, Enabled and Interval are the most important.

When you want the Timer's job done is determined by the time between when your program turns on the Timer (Timer1.Enabled = True) and the Timer's Interval Property (Timer1.Interval = 6000)–six seconds in this case. Unless you specify otherwise (by setting its Enabled Property to Off (False) in the Form_Load Event), a Timer will start counting when your program starts (if its Interval Property has been changed from the default 0).

For the Timer to do its job only once, include Timer1.Enabled = 0 within the Timer Event:

```
Sub Timer1_Timer ()

MsgBox ("This Timer has done its job for you.")

Timer1.Enabled = 0
End Sub
```

A Timer is activated when your program starts; its Enabled Property defaults to On. If you've given it an Interval and you don't want a Timer to start counting until you tell it to, put Timer1.Enabled = 0 into the Form_Load Event of the Startup Form. That way, it will remain dormant until you turn it on somewhere else in the program.

A Timer's Interval Property, the amount of time it can measure, ranges between 0 and 64,767 *milliseconds.* This means that the longest time an unassisted Timer can regulate is 1.079 minutes. You can, however, magnify the amount of time that a Timer will delay. You can make it wait until next Wednesday if that's what you want.

To measure time in longer intervals than the one minute limit of a Timer's Interval Property, use a Static Variable within the Timer Event and raise it by one each time the Event is triggered. Recall that a Timer *keeps going off, triggering its Timer Event,* until it's turned off (Timer1.Enabled = 0). To wait two hours, set the interval Property to 60000 (one minute) and then enter the following:

```
Sub Timer1_Timer

Static Counter as Integer
Counter = Counter + 1
If Counter >= 120 Then
    Print "TIME'S UP!"
    Timer1.Enabled = 0
End If

End Sub
```

Timers have another capability, too, aside from their wonderful ability to float within Windows and touch down from time to time, intervening and doing what you want them to do in spite of whatever else might be happening. They can *delay* things as well. When you set a Timer's Enabled Property to On (True), it waits until its Interval Property passes and *then carries out the instructions* you have placed between:

```
Sub Timer1_Timer ()
```

and . . .

```
End Sub
```

Variables
Because the Timer is a Control, you can set its Properties from the Properties Window while you are creating your program. A Timer has the following Properties:

Name, Enabled, Index, Interval, Parent, Top, Left and Tag

The most commonly used Timer Properties are the *Interval*, which determines how long the Timer waits until doing something, and *Enabled*, which turns a Timer on or off. Each time Enabled is turned on, the Interval starts over again. If you turn off a Timer before it has finished counting and then turn it back on, the Interval will restart from the beginning.

OR (to adjust a Timer while the program is running): Timer1.Interval = 2000

OR (to start a Timer ticking while the program is running): Timer1.Enabled = True

Uses
• A Timer can perform a variety of jobs in your programs. We'll illustrate each of the following applications in the Examples below:

1. It can act like *a traditional kitchen timer*—counting down from a preset time and then ringing a bell (or doing whatever you want) after the preset interval has elapsed.

2. It can *cause a delay*, so a window with a message appears onscreen for four seconds and then disappears, for example.

3. It can cause events to *repeat at prescribed intervals,* like a digital clock changing its readout every second. Or it could save the user's work to disk every 10 or 20 minutes, or whatever "backup interval" the user selected in an Options Menu in your program.

4. It can look at the computer's built-in battery-powered clock to *see if it is time to do something*. In this way, you can build reminder programs, to-do schedulers, that will display a message or take some other action based on the current time. In this application the Timer looks at the computer's clock at regular intervals, independent of what the user might be doing or what is going on in Windows.

5. It can show the user the time at regular intervals, and thus you can *make a clock*.

6. It can *measure the passage of time,* acting like a stopwatch and reporting the time that something took to complete its behavior.

Cautions

• You can place a Timer anywhere on a Form. Unlike other Controls, it is never visible when the program runs.

• By default, a Timer's Enabled Property is *on* when a program starts running. Therefore, a Timer will start its countdown when a program starts, unless one of three things has happened:

- You have not set its Interval Property yet. (The Interval defaults to 0, and a Timer will not become active until the Interval is greater than 0.)

- You turn off the Timer's Enabled Property from the Properties Window while designing your program.

- Your program turns off the Timer's Enabled Property (Timer1.Enabled = False) while the program is running.

• Unless turned off, Timers continue to run, even after their Interval has finished. When the Interval is over, a Timer resets itself and starts counting the Interval again, then carries out whatever commands are in its Timer Event. When the Interval is finished, the Timer again resets itself then carries out the commands. This cycle—countdown, reset, carry out commands—continues until the program ends or until you turn the Timer off from somewhere within the program by adding Timer1.Enabled = False.

• If you set a Timer to do something every second (Interval = 1000), it may occasionally fail to go off *precisely on the second.* The computer may have been tied up doing something that briefly took complete control of the machine (so the Timer couldn't react when its Interval was over). Even though it might be temporarily prevented from carrying out the commands in its Timer Event, however, the Timer *will keep counting.*

A related issue is the frequency with which the Timer counts. If you need extremely fine control over timing, set the Interval Property very small, say 100 (1/10th of a second). The tradeoff here is that setting a small Interval will somewhat slow down the computer because it must service your Timer so often. If you want the Timer's Event to happen every second, yet you have set the Timer's Interval to 100, use a Static Variable to count up to 10:

```
Sub Timer1_Timer

Static Counter as Integer
Counter = Counter + 1

If Counter >= 10 Then
    Print "TIME'S UP!"
End If

End Sub
```

A For...Next Loop will tie up the computer until it's completed, and so will loading or saving files from the disk drive, and a few other activities. You can, however, allow interruptions within a For...Next or similar structure by inserting a DoEvents command (which see). DoEvents, though, will slow down the computer while the DoEvents is active inside the Loop.

Inaccuracies Can Occur at Extremely Small Intervals: The computer itself must do a few things each time it activates a Timer (or any other) Event. As a result, if you set the Timer's Interval Property to a very small value (attempting to time something precisely), the accuracy is not certain.

• Because of the potential for slight inaccuracies, always use *greater than or equal,* rather than equal, when checking against a Variable. This way, on the odd chance that the computer was otherwise occupied (some other program was saving a file to the disk or something) when your Variable reached its target, your Timer will still respond as soon as it can. In the preceding example, the Counter could get up to 9 and then a disk file is saved, tying up the computer. When the Timer Event can next check, the Counter is up to 11 or greater . Therefore, the Timer would never see Counter = 10. Counter >=10 solves this problem.

• A Timer has only one Event, also called, unfortunately, *Timer:* Sub Timer1_Timer (). And its name isn't the only thing about it that is a little perplexing. Most VB Events, such as a Click Event, trigger an immediate response—performing at once those actions that you have listed as instructions within the Click_Event Procedure:

```
Command1_Click
    Print "OUCH!"
    Print "Press me again!"
End Sub
```

Here the instant the user clicked on Command1, the word *OUCH!* would be printed, and the other instructions in the Event would be carried out.

When you enable a Timer (Timer1.Enabled = True), that triggers the Timer Event. The Timer's *countdown* starts, but the instructions within the Timer1_Timer Event *will not be carried out until the countdown has finished.* No bell will ring, no message will print, no commands within the Event will be carried out until the Timer has counted down from the number of milliseconds you put in its Interval Property—to zero.

You can use as many as 16 Timers on a given Form.

Example   The following examples will demonstrate how to use a Timer for each of the six purposes described under Uses above. These examples are the main applications for Timers in Visual Basic.

The Kitchen Timer: A Timer can act like a traditional kitchen timer—counting down from a preset time and then ringing a bell (or doing whatever you want) after the preset Interval has elapsed.

First, put a Timer and a Command Button on a Form. Then type the following into the Timer's Event:

```
Sub Timer1_Timer ()
    Print "20 Seconds has elapsed."
End Sub
```

Then put this into the Command Button's Click Event. This turns on the Timer and sets it to go off in 20 seconds:

```
Sub Command1_Click ()
    Timer1.Interval = 20000
End Sub
```

Recall that you use a Timer's Enabled Property to turn a Timer on and off. Because Enabled defaults to "True," you need not specifically turn the Timer on; unless you turn Enabled "off," the Timer will be active when your program starts running. Why doesn't the Timer start counting, then, as soon as the program starts running? A Timer's *Interval* Property defaults to 0, and a Timer will remain inert until something greater than zero is put into its Interval. Therefore, when we set the Interval to 20000 in the Command Button's Click Event, *that* activates the Timer.

Note: The Timer will continue to "go off" every 20 seconds in this example, repeatedly printing its message at that interval. Because we want to turn on the Timer only when the user presses the Command Button, we need to turn off the Timer in its Event so that it works only when the user wants it:

```
Sub Timer1_Timer ()
    Print "20 Seconds has elapsed."
    Timer1.Interval = 0
End Sub
```

Making Your Program Pause: A Timer can cause a delay. For example, it could display a window with a message onscreen for four seconds and then disappear.

Figure T-17: Timers can display a message for a short time then remove it.

For this example, put a Timer and a Command Button on a Form. In the Properties Window, turn the Timer's Enabled Property off. Add a second Form to the program and set its BorderStyle Property to "None." Then type the following into the Timer's Event:

```
Sub Timer1_Timer ()
    Form2.Hide
    Timer1.Enabled = 0
End Sub
```

The Timer in this example behaves almost the opposite of the kitchen timer. In that example, we wanted the Timer to *wait* until several seconds had elapsed and then show something. In this example, we want the program to do something (show a message) and then have the Timer *stop doing, stop showing* what our program started. The primary difference between these two jobs is that now nothing really happens within the Timer Event— the Event stops something from happening that's been going on.

In the Command Button Click Event, we set up the position and visual elements of Form2, the message that we will display:

```
Sub Command1_Click ()

Form2.FontSize = 36
Form2.FontName = "Modern"
Form2.BackColor = QBColor(13)
X$ = " Brief Message."
Form2.Left = Form1.Left + 200
th = TextHeight(X$) / 2
Form2.Top = Form1.Top − th + Form1.ScaleHeight / 2

Form2.Show
Form2.Cls
Form2.Print X$

Timer1.Interval = 3000
Timer1.Enabled = True

End Sub
```

The first seven lines in this Click Event define the look of the message and position it roughly in the center of Form1, the main window. Then we make Form2 visible with the Show command and use Cls to reset the CurrentX and CurrentY position on the Form. Without Cls, the first time we printed our message things would be fine, but repeatedly pressing the Command Button would cause the message to go below the visible window (see "Cls").

Now we set the Timer's Interval (you could do this from the Properties Window while writing the program) and turn the Timer on. When its three-second Interval is over, the Timer will Hide Form2 and Form2 will disappear.

• **Making Events Happen at Regular Intervals:** A Timer can cause events to repeat at prescribed intervals–like a digital clock changing its readout every second. Or a Timer could save the user's work to disk every 10 or 20 minutes, or whatever "backup interval" the user selected in an Options Menu in your program.

First, put a Timer and a Label on a Form. This example will show how to make the program beep every second and display the elapsed seconds since the program was started. Because a Timer's Enabled Property defaults to "on," the Timer will start when the program starts. You just need to set the Timer's Interval to 1000 (use the Properties Window) and then put the following into the Timer's Event:

```
Sub Timer1_Timer ()

Static c As Integer
c = c + 1
label1.caption = Str$(c)
Beep
End Sub
```

If you try this example, you'll notice that you can use other programs, move around Windows, etc., and the digital clock keeps ticking away. Only a few things—most notably disk access—will interrupt the clock. Even then, the Timer will show the correct number of elapsed seconds. It keeps counting even during disk access but is temporarily unable to display the changing seconds or sound its beeps.

Do Something at a Particular Time of Day: A Timer can look at the computer's built-in battery-powered clock to see if it is time to do something. You can build reminder programs or to-do schedulers that will display a message or take some other action based on the current time.

The job of the Timer in this example is to take a look at the computer's clock at regular intervals, independently of what the user might be doing or of what else is going on in Windows. When it is 7 AM, the Timer will remind us to feed the swans. If you put this program in your WIN.INI file on the RUN = line, the program would automatically pop up with its reminder every day at 7 o'clock. The swans would stay white and plump.

First, put a Timer on a Form and set its Interval to 30000. We need to check the time only every 30 seconds because high precision isn't important in this application. A large Interval allows the computer to run more efficiently than if we were checking dozens of times a second.

Put the following into the Timer Event:

```
Sub Timer1_Timer ()

hr = Hour(Now)
mn = Minute(Now)

If hr = 7 And mn < 2 Then
    MsgBox ("It's 7 AM. The swans are hungry.")
End If
End Sub
```

Notice that we give ourselves a little range between 7:00 and 7:02, just in case a huge file was being saved right at 7:00 or some other event was tying up the computer. We can't use mn >= 0 because then the message would display every 30 seconds for the entire hour between 7 and 8. We don't have to worry about 7 *PM* because the Hour Function acts like a 24-hour "military-style" clock; 7 PM will be 19.

However, the condition we have set up to display the message (hour is 7 and minute is between 0 and 2) will cause this message to display several times. To prevent that, put a Static Variable into the Timer Event and change the If...Then:

```
Static x as Integer

If hr = 7 And mn < 2 And X = 0 Then
    MsgBox ("It's 7 AM. The swans are hungry.")
    x = 1
End If
```

By making x = 1 after we show our message, we prevent a repeat of the message. An alternative would be to use the End command in place of x = 1, shutting the program down once the user had clicked on the MsgBox.

Create a Clock: A Timer can show the user the time at regular intervals, and thus you can make a clock.

For this example, put a Timer and a Label on a Form. Set the Timer's Interval Property to 1000 (1 second) in the Properties Window. Then put the following inside the Timer Event:

```
Sub Timer1_Timer ()
    label1.caption = Time$
End Sub
```

To make the clock less austere, more like an ordinary clock instead of military-style time, use Format$ with the Now Function, which see.

Create a Stopwatch: A Timer can *measure* the passage of time, acting like a stopwatch and reporting the time that something took to complete its behavior, or reminding the user that an interval has elapsed. See the example in "Timer *Event*."

Timer Properties
Enabled • Index • Interval • Left • Name • Parent • Tag • Top

Timer Events
Timer

See also   Timer *Event*; Timer *Function*

TIMER

· ·

EVENT

Description   A Timer, unlike other Controls, *has only one Event.* (Unhappily, the Timer's Event is also called *Timer*–Sub Timer1_Timer ( ).)

Any instructions contained within this Event will be carried out *after the Timer's Interval has passed.* That is, if you set the Interval Property of the Timer to 10 seconds and put a Print command (Print "Sunrise!") inside the Timer's Event, when the Timer's Event is triggered, the Timer *will wait* 10 seconds. Then it will print *Sunrise!*.

You trigger a Timer Event (you turn on a Timer) by setting its Enabled Property to "True," and you turn it off by setting its Enabled Property to "False." But when you turn it on, *it won't carry out the commands inside the Event until its Interval has elapsed.*

This delaying behavior is the reverse of most Events. If you click on an Option Button, the commands within its Click Event happen immediately.

Also, a Timer will remain inert if its Interval Property is 0. The Interval defaults to 0, and Enabled defaults to "True." Another way of turning on a Timer is to change its Interval Property, to assign some Interval. (For an in-depth discussion of Timers and their many uses, see "Timer *Control.*")

Variables   The Timer Event is used just like other Events–you put commands inside the Event Subroutine:

```
Sub Timer1_Timer
    Print "It's time to back up your work."
End Sub
```

OR (to turn a Timer on or off from elsewhere in your program. In this example we're adjusting its Enabled Property to turn the Timer on):

```
Timer1.Enabled = True
```

OR (to turn the Timer off): Timer1.Enabled = False

Uses   For an in-depth discussion of Timers and their many uses, see "Timer" *Control.*

Cautions   See all but the first and last items in Cautions under "Timer *Control.*"

Example   This example is a useful reminder program. You tell it when you want to be reminded, and you provide an optional message. The program will pop up on top of a full-screen word processor–or interrupting anything else that's happening in Windows–to let you know that the time is up.

341

Figure T-18: When iconized, the program displays the seconds ticking down.

To create the program, first define four Global Variables in a Module—thus making them available to all locations in the program:

```
Global start As Single
Global totalseconds As Single
Global msg As String
Global beginning As Integer
```

Then create a Form and put three Labels, two Picture Boxes and a Timer on it.

The small Picture Box will hold an icon. We're using a simple bead-like icon with a white highlight and a color (deep blue) that matches the background color—an attractive alternative tactic if you're tired of the common Command or Option Buttons.

Add the "TIMER01.ICO" from the "Miscellaneous" collection of icons that comes with VB. Use the Properties Window to assign this icon to the Form. Now we're ready to draw the visuals in the Form_Load Event:

```
Sub Form_Load ()

Show

label1.caption = "START / STOP"
label3.caption = ""
label2.caption = ""

drawframeon picture1, picture1, "outward", 300
drawframeon picture1, picture1, "inward", 20
timer1.interval = 1000
timer1.enabled = 0
beginning = 1

End Sub
```

We make Labels 2 and 3 invisible. (All BackColor Properties have already been set with the Properties Window so they match the BackColor of the Form—deep blue). And we add the Caption to Label1. The FontSizes and FontNames are a matter of personal preference. We set them here to Garamond, not bold, using the Properties Window to adjust each Label. Label1's FontSize is 7.2, Label2's is 12, and Label3, where we'll show the elapsed time, has a FontSize of 16.2.

Next, we draw two frames around the clock graphic, creating a green velvet effect. We use the DrawFrameOn Subroutine that is listed and explained in the entry on the Line command.

Now we make the Timer perform its job every 1 second: 1000 milliseconds = 1 second, and a Timer counts in milliseconds. But we don't want the Timer to start until the user starts. The Timer's default is "True" when the program starts, so we set its Enabled Property to "False" to make it inert until the red bead is pressed by the user.

Paint, Resize and Load Are All Triggered: The Global Variable *beginning* prevents the Form's Paint Event from triggering. When a Form appears, the Paint (and Resize) Events usually are triggered along with the Form_Load Event. We've duplicated some of the frame-drawing in the Paint Event, so the frames will appear if the user iconizes the Form and then restores it, or if some other window covers up the Form. However, we don't want some of the commands in the Paint Event to happen when the program first starts. And we need not draw the frames twice. By setting the Global Variable *beginning* to 1 here, we can check for it in the Paint Event (If beginning = 0 Then Exit Sub). All Variables start out with 0, so until we set it to 1 here, it will be 0 and Paint won't activate. After that, Paint will always activate.

The Paint Event occurs when a Form is iconized, stretched, covered up by another window or otherwise adjusted so that it must be redrawn on the screen. Most of the graphics, the Controls and colors will automatically refresh themselves. But things you've printed (or, as here, the frames drawn with the Line command) will not be refreshed. They will be erased. If you set the Form's AutoRedraw Property to True, that prevents this problem. However, the program would run more slowly and take up more memory.

In the Paint Event, we duplicate much of the drawing we did in the Form_Load Event. This Paint Event will be triggered if the window is of "normal" size (see WindowState) and if this isn't the start of the program:

```
Sub Form_Paint ()

If windowstate = 0 And beginning <> 0 Then
    drawframeon picture1, picture1, "outward", 300
    drawframeon picture1, picture1, "inward", 20
    Line (100, 3200)-(3100, 3600), QBColor(11), B
    drawwidth = 3
    Line (110, 3220)-(3120, 3620), QBColor(9), B
    drawwidth = 1
    caption = Timer
End If
End Sub
```

In the Paint Event we also draw an embossed line around the "Seconds Remaining" Label at the bottom. We restate the Form's Caption because if the user Iconized the program, we use the Caption Property to display the countdown. Nonetheless, when the window is a normal size, the Caption should read "TIMER."

Figure T-19: The Timer running full size onscreen.

Finally, we put the bulk of this program into the Label1_Click Event—so the user can click on the red bead and start or stop the program. This Label has the Caption "START/STOP." The purpose of this Event is to show the user an Input Box. This Box is where the user will enter the desired delay and an optional message that will be displayed when the delay is finished. If the program is *already* counting down, however, when the user clicks, the user intends to stop the Timer prematurely. We check the Variable toggle to tell us which of these two meanings the user's click could have:

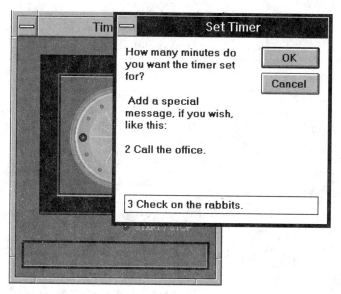

Figure T-20: The pop-up Input Box. The user enters the duration for the Timer program and an optional message to be displayed when the Timer goes off.

```
Sub label1_click ()

Static toggle As Integer

If toggle = 0 Then
    toggle = 1
    cr$ = Chr$(13) + Chr$(10)
    m$ = "How many minutes do you want the Timer set for?"
    m$ = m$ + cr$ + cr$ + " Add a special message, if you wish, like this:"
    m$ = m$ + cr$ + cr$ + "2 Call the office."
    usernum$ = InputBox$(m$, "Set Timer")
        If usernum$ = "" Then GoTo Cancel
    p = InStr(usernum$, " ")
        If p <> 0 Then
                msg$ = Right$(usernum$, Len(usernum$) — p)
                usernum$ = Left$(usernum$, p — 1)
        End If
    unum = Val(usernum$)
    totalseconds! = unum * 60
    start! = Timer
    timer1.enabled = True
    label2.visible = True
    label3.visible = True
```

```
        Line (100, 3200) — (3100, 3600), QBColor(11), B
        drawwidth = 3
        Line (110, 3220) — (3120, 3620), QBColor(9), B
        drawwidth = 1
    Else

    Cancel:
        toggle = 0
        timer1.enabled = False
        label3.visible = False
        label2.visible = False
    End If

    End Sub
```

The Variable *toggle* determines whether the user intended to start the Timer, or stop it, when clicking on the red bead. If toggle is zero, the Timer isn't running, so we go through the steps to start the Timer. In the process, we also set toggle to 1, to show that the Timer *is* now running. This flag tells us how to react if the user clicks on Start/Stop once again.

We create the necessary codes to cause our message—that we will print in the Input Box—to move down a line. We have several lines of instruction we want displayed, so we want to be able to insert codes that will mimic pressing the ENTER key (See "Chr$"). Now we build the message by adding it to itself, plus new items and the cr$ (move-down-a-line) codes.

The User Could Have Done Three Things: The text Variable usernum$ will contain whatever the user typed into the Input Box. There are three possible entries that the user might have typed. Perhaps the user typed nothing, either hitting the ENTER key or clicking on the Cancel Button. If that occurs, usernum$ will have nothing in it ("") and we go lower in the Event to the Cancel: Label just below the Else command. The program resets itself if the user clicked on the Start/Stop Button while the program was running. No Timer is set, nothing happens. It's just as if the program had been run for the first time.

Another possibility is that the user might have entered both a number of minutes for the Timer and a message. We use InStr to find any space characters in usernum$. There will be no spaces if the user typed a number but no message. If there is a message, though, we need to divide usernum$ into the number of minutes delay requested and the attached message. We put the message into msg$ and leave the number in usernum$.

Now we find out what to tell the Timer Control. Val tells us the numeric value of whatever digits the user typed for the delay. The user enters his or her requested delay as minutes, so we must multiply the request by 60 to get seconds. Then we put the requested number of seconds into the Global Variable *totalseconds!* (see "Variables" for the meaning of the ! symbol). And we put the current time into another Global Variable called *start!*. These Variables, being Global, can be used anywhere in the program. In particular, the Timer Event will use these Variables, as we'll see.

It's a little confusing, all these Timers–the *Event*, the *Control* and, now, we come to the *Function*. The Timer Function tells you *the number of seconds that have passed since midnight.* (See "Timer *Function.*") It measures durations against the computer's clock, but only within a given day and resets to 0 at midnight. (See "Now" for an alternative technique for measuring duration.)

In this program, we want to know the number of seconds that have passed since midnight. And we want to know the number of seconds the user wants the Timer to delay. This is how we can let the Timer Event decide when to act. The Timer Event will continually check to see if start! + totalseconds! is the current time, which is like saying, "It's 1 PM now; I want to be awakened in 20 minutes. Keep glancing at the clock and let me know when it's 1:20."

Now We Know What the User Wants from Us: To return to the matters at hand, we now know what delay, and possibly what message, the user wants. So we turn on the Timer, make the "Seconds Remaining" Labels visible, and draw the embossed line around them. The Timer will fill in their Captions almost instantly; it has a rapid, one-second Interval.

The remaining commands are the alternative to all the commands just discussed. Following the Else (and the Cancel: Label), we do the things necessary if the user presses the Stop/Start Button intending to *stop* an active Timer. Again, we reset the toggle to show that the next time Start/Stop is pressed, the user intends to *start* a Timer. We turn off the Timer Control and make the lower two Labels invisible.

It's usually a good idea to allow the user to click on a Label as well as its associated button. That's why we put all the commands to start or stop the Timer into the START/STOP Label's Click Event. Now we make the red button have the same effect as clicking on the Label:

```
Sub Picture2_Click ()
    label1_click
End Sub
```

At last we get to the commands inside the Timer Event itself. The Timer will do these things every second as long as it is Enabled. Its primary job is to keep checking to see if the time the user entered has elapsed yet. And, if so, to react, to display its message and then turn itself off:

```
Sub timer1_timer ()

currentsecond! = Timer
X! = currentsecond! − start!

If X! >= totalseconds! Then
    label3.visible = 0
            For i = 1 To 50
                    Beep
            Next i
    timer1.enabled = 0
    label2.caption = "TIME'S UP"
```

```
            If windowstate = 1 Then windowstate = 0
            If msg$ <> "" Then MsgBox (msg$): End
        Else
            Z = X! — totalseconds!
            t$ = Str$(Abs(Int(Z)))
            label2.caption = " Seconds Remaining"
            label3.caption = t$
            If windowstate = 1 Then caption = t$
        End If
        End Sub
```

Recall that in the Label1_Click Event we put the user's requested delay into the Global Variable totalseconds!. And we also checked the time at that point—the number of seconds that had elapsed since midnight—and put that into the Global Variable start!.

Here we again check the current total number of seconds passed since midnight and put that number into a Variable:

```
    currentsecond! = Timer
```

Then we subtract the Variable start! from the Variable currentsecond! and put the result into X!. This subtraction is like saying: "It was 3450 when the user started the Timer, and now is 3650. Subtracting 3450 from 3650 we get 200 and put that into X!. 200 seconds have therefore passed since the user started the Timer." The Variable totalseconds! contains the user's requested number of seconds to delay.

If X! is greater than or equal to (>=) the number of seconds the user requested, *Then* do the following:

1. Hide the Label containing the seconds remaining.

2. Beep 50 times (VB runs so fast this beep will sound like a brief buzz).

3. Turn off the Timer.

4. Put the notice "TIME'S UP" into the Label that used to say "Seconds Remaining."

5. If the Timer has been iconized, make it return to normal size.

6. If the Global Variable msg$ contains a user message, display it in a Message Box. Then stop the entire program.

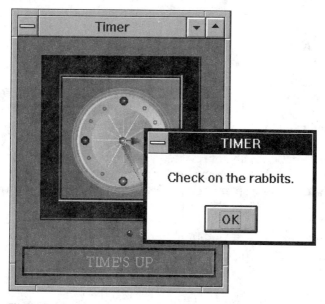

Figure T-21: When the Timer goes off, an optional message appears onscreen in front of whatever other programs the user may have running at the time.

Keep on Checking: But *If* X! is something *Else* than >= (in other words, *less than*) the delay the user requested, *Then* the Timer must keep on checking until the delay has elapsed. We do the following things to update the "Seconds Remaining" display for the user:

1. Calculate the number of seconds remaining and put the result into the Variable *Z*. We turn it into an Integer Variable with Int because the Timer Function returns a number that includes unwanted fractions.

2. Translate the numeric Variable into text digits that can be used in a Caption and put the result into the text Variable *T$*. We update the "Seconds Remaining" Label and put *T$* into the Caption of the Label next to it. Then, if the user has iconized the program, we put *T$* into the *Form's* Caption property; this has the effect of displaying, and updating, the elapsed time just under the icon. This technique is a quick way to display ongoing information even in an icon.

See also   Timer (Control and Function)

TIMER

FUNCTION

Description In Visual Basic, several entities are referred to by the name *Timer*. The Timer *Function* tells you how many seconds have elapsed since last midnight. There are 86,400 seconds in 24 hours, so the Timer *Function* provides a unique number between 0 and 86,400.

This Function is an abbreviated version of the Now Function, which provides a serial number as well, but one that offers a unique number for each second for a span of centuries before and after the current moment.

Variables X! = Timer

OR (because this is a Function, you can use it directly in *expressions*; see "Variables"): Print Timer

OR

If Timer < 43200 Then Print "It's still morning."

Uses • Use the Timer to measure short durations. You could use it to see how long a portion of your program took to execute. The following example tells us that counting from 1 to 20,000 takes a little over two seconds:

```
Sub Form_Click ()

Start! = Timer

For i = 1 To 20000
Next i

Ende! = Timer
Cls
Print "Elapsed time", Ende! — Start!

End Sub
```

Results in 2.308294 (results will vary depending on each computer's speed)

The example for the entry on the Timer *Event* includes another way to measure short durations with a program that acts like a kitchen timer.

• Use the Timer command to "seed" the Randomize Statement—Randomize(Timer). This method will generate a different random pattern of numbers from the Rnd Function (which see) each time the Randomize Statement is utilized. However, the Randomize command uses the Timer Function anyway to get its seed—Randomize with nothing following it checks the Timer for the seed and is therefore equivalent to Randomize(Timer).

Cautions Don't confuse this Timer *Function* with a Timer *Control* or a Timer *Event*. The Timer Function is utterly unrelated to the Control and its Event.

Example

```
Sub Form_Click ()

x! = Int(Timer)
Print x!; " seconds have elapsed since midnight."
Print "This translates into:"
Print Int(x! / 60); "minutes."
Print Int((x! / 60) / 60); "hours."
End Sub
```

The Timer Function provides a number that includes a fraction, so here we stripped the fractional part off with the Int Function.

Results in

56,880 seconds have elapsed since midnight. This translates into:

948 minutes.
15 hours.

See also

Hour; Minute; Now; Second; Time$ (Function); TimeSerial

TIMESERIAL
FUNCTION

Description

You provide the TimeSerial command with an hour, minute and second, and it provides you with a unique Visual Basic "serial number" that represents the described time. A serial number is a number within a series of numbers, like a number from a roll of movie tickets. Each number is unique, and each points to a particular position in the roll. The TimeSerial number is a unique number from among the 86,400 seconds in a day.

TimeSerial is the close relative of the DateSerial command. DateSerial does the same thing, but reports a unique serial number for any date between January 1, 100 A.D., and December 31, 9999.

TimeSerial is also a close relative of the TimeValue Function. TimeValue does the same thing as TimeSerial. But where TimeValue translates a *text* expression of the time (like 1 PM), TimeSerial translates a *numeric* expression of the time (like 13,0,0) into three numbers—hour, minute and second.

TimeSerial provides a fractional number.

DateSerial provides a whole number between –657,434 and 2,958,465.

Put the two together and you get *a range of unique serial numbers for every second between the years 100 A.D. and 9999.*

The Now command also provides a serial number with this combination of date and time; however, Now gets its data from the computer's built-in clock. These various "date+time serial numbers" can be the basis for calendar programs and other applications. Visual Basic takes the intelligent approach to time and dates by creating a huge range of unique numbers in a series to represent each second, minute, hour, day, month and year over a span of 98 centuries.

Because this range is a series of numbers, you can perform arithmetic. You can't subtract "12 Feb." from "18 Jan." But if you get their serial numbers, you *can* find out how many days there are between these two dates.

Variables

Variable type: TimeSerial returns a "Variant" (which see) and stores the data as a Double-Precision Floating-Point.

To translate literal numbers representing the hour, minute and second into a serial number:

```
X = TimeSerial(9,22,0)
```

OR (to use Variables instead of literal numbers):

```
hr = 9:mn = 22: se = 0
X = TimeSerial(hr,mn,se)
```

OR (to use an *expression*; see "Variables"): X = TimeSerial(hr−1,mn + 10, se)

Note that the hour number must be in 24-hour format, a range between 0 (midnight) and 23 (11 PM). The minute and second numbers must range between 0 and 59.

Uses

• Allow the user to adjust the computer's clock (see the Example for "TimeValue").

• Create to-do programs, calendars and other applications involving manipulation of time and dates *as if they were numbers in a series.*

• Use TimeSerial or DateSerial to generate a "registration number" the first time a customer uses your program. That number could be put into your program's .INI file and displayed on the startup screen (the way VB does). This may act as a mild deterrent on people copying programs.

Example

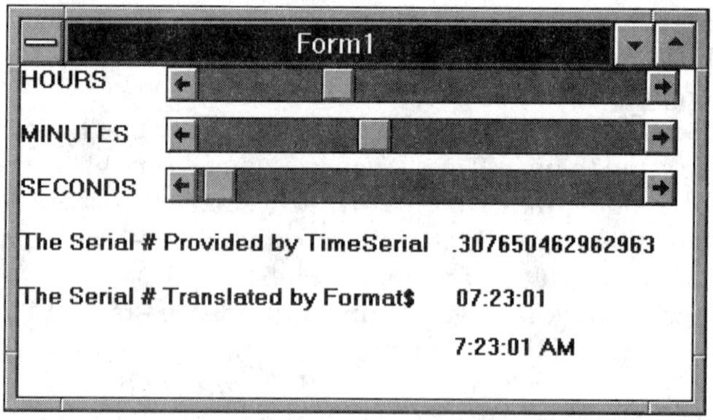

Figure T-22: Serial numbers created by the TimeSerial command and translated by Format$.

This example shows how TimeSerial translates three numbers for hour, minute and second into a serial number representing that time. Then, Format$ turns the serial number into a readable display.

First, put three Horizontal Scroll Bars and three Labels on a Form. Then put the following into the Form_Load Event:

```
Sub Form_Load ()

hscroll1.max = 23
hscroll2.max = 59
hscroll3.max = 59

Print "HOURS"
Print
Print "MINUTES"
Print
Print "SECONDS"
Print
Print "The Serial # Provided by TimeSerial"
Print
Print "The Serial # Translated by Format$"
End Sub
```

Note that we set the maximum values of the Scroll Bars to the maximum possible number of hours, minutes and seconds that TimeSerial can translate. When the slider (also called thumb or Scroll Box) is all the way to the right, the Hours Bar will have a Value Property of 23, and the other two bars will have values of 59. The Min Property of a Scroll Bar defaults to 0, so we have the correct range now: 0 to 23, 0 to 59, 0 to 59.

Then put the following into the HScroll1.Change Event to display the results when the user moves the sliders in the bars:

```
Sub Hscroll1_Change ()

hr = hscroll1.value: mn = hscroll2.value: sc = hscroll3.value

z# = TimeSerial(hr, mn, sc)
label1.caption = Str$(z#)

x$ = Format$(z#, "hh:mm:ss")
label2.caption = x$

x$ = Format$(z#, "h:mm:ss AM/PM")
label3.caption = x$
End Sub
```

When this Horizontal Scroll Bar is moved, its Change Event is triggered. First, we get the positions of the sliders in each bar and put them into Variables for hour, minute and second.

Next, we create our serial number by using TimeSerial, and put the result into the Variable z#. The # symbol makes z into a numeric Variable that can hold an extremely large range of numbers (see "Variables"). Then we display the serial number in Label1, after using Str$ to change the number into text characters.

Using Format$, we take the same serial number and display it as 24-hour time and as ordinary AM/PM style (see "Format$").

See also   DateSerial; Hour; Minute; Now; Second; TimeValue

TimeValue

FUNCTION

Description   You provide TimeValue with time expressed as *text* (either literal text, 2 PM, or a text Variable, T$). Then TimeValue provides you with a unique Visual Basic "serial number" that represents the described time. A serial number is a number within a series of numbers, like a number from a roll of movie tickets. Each number is unique, and each points to a particular position in the roll. In this instance, TimeValue will give you a unique number from among the 86,400 seconds in a day.

TimeValue is the close relative of the DateValue Function. DateValue does the same thing but reports a unique serial number for any date between January 1, 100 A.D., and December 31, 9999.

TimeValue is also a close relative of the TimeSerial Function. TimeValue does the same thing as TimeSerial, but TimeValue translates a *text* expression of the time (like 1 PM). TimeSerial translates a *numeric* expression of the time (like 9, 5, 0) into three numbers–hour, minute, and second.

TimeValue provides a fractional number.

DateValue provides a whole number.

Put the two together and you get a range that is capable of assigning a unique serial number to *every second* between the years 100 A.D. and 9999.

The Now command also provides a serial number with this combination of date and time; however, Now gets its data from the computer's built-in clock. These various "date+time serial numbers" can be the basis for calendar programs and other applications. Visual Basic creates a huge range of unique numbers in a series to represent each second, minute, hour, day, month and year over a span of 98 centuries.

Because this range is a series of numbers, you can perform arithmetic. You can't subtract "12 Feb." from "18 Jan." But if you get their serial numbers, you *can* find out how many days there are between these two dates.

Variables   **Variable type:** TimeValue returns a "Variant" (which see) and stores the data as a Double-Precision Floating-Point.

TimeValue is surprisingly forgiving in the variety of formats it will accept. It will see 5 as 05:00:00, 5.25 as 05:25:00, nothing (an empty text Variable "") as 00:00:00 (midnight). It will accept uppercase or lowercase AM and PM.

TimeValue also ignores extraneous information. It will translate 2 PM Tuesday into the correct serial number for 2 PM and pay no attention to *Tuesday.* TimeValue also ignores extra spaces.

To provide a literal text expression of a particular time:

```
X = TimeValue("1:00")
```

OR (to use am or PM): X = TimeValue("1 PM")

OR (to use a Variable):

```
T$ = "05:23:15"
X = TimeValue(T$)
```

OR (to use an *expression*; see "Variables"):

```
T$ = "5":V$ = "pm"
X = TimeValue(T$ + V$)
```

Uses
- Allow the user to adjust the computer's clock (see the Example below).
- Create to-do programs, calendars and other applications involving manipulation of time and dates *as if they were numbers in a series.*
- Use TimeValue or DateValue to generate a "registration number" the first time a customer used your program. That number could be put into your program's .INI file and displayed on the startup screen (the way VB does). This may act as a mild deterrent on people copying programs.

Cautions
- TimeValue accepts text Variables in either military format (24-hour time like 17:05:15) or normal AM/PM style (5:05:15 PM).

TimeValue can accept a range between 00:00:00 and 23:59:59, or 12 AM and 11:59:59 PM.

Example

```
Sub Form_Click ()

On Error Resume Next

info$ = "The current time is "
info$ = info$ + Format$(Now, "h:m:ss AM/PM")
info$ = info$ + " Please enter the adjusted time."

t$ = InputBox$(info$)

If t$ = "" Then Exit Sub

x = TimeValue(t$)

If Err Then
    info$ = "We did not recognize the format you entered"
    info$ = info$ + "Please adjust your entry to this format:"
    info$ = info$ + "2:55 PM"
    t$ = InputBox$(info$, "Please Try Again", t$)
    x = TimeValue(t$)
End If

t$ = Format$(x, "hh:mm:ss")

Time$ = t$

If Err Then MsgBox ("There is still a problem with the way you are →
entering the time.")

End Sub
```

You can use the Time$ command to adjust the computer's built-in clock. Time$, though, requires military-style (24-hour) time in an awkward HH:MM:SS format. In an example under "Time$," we demonstrated a technique that lets your program take a detailed look at how the user entered the time—and compensate for a variety of user errors and translate the input into HH:MM:SS format.

The example here does the same thing, but more efficiently. TimeValue allows the user to enter time in the more common 5:24PM format.

First, we tell VB to keep going if there is an error—not to stop the program. We will deal with errors ourselves, and VB need not react (see "On Error"). Then we build a text Variable that will be displayed in an Input Box. Building text Variables by repeatedly adding text is a common approach if you are dealing with relatively small messages.

Then we display the Input Box. If the user clicks Cancel or presses the ENTER key without typing anything into the Box t$, then the text Variable returned by the Input Box will be empty ("") and we quit the Subroutine.

What if TimeValue Can't Understand What the User Typed? If the user did enter something, we use TimeValue to translate it and place the resulting serial number into the Variable *x*. There might be a problem at this point, however. TimeValue might not be able to understand some odd format that the user tried to enter. If so, we display another Input Box to give the user a second chance. This time, we display *t$*, the user's mistake, in the Box so the user can see the problem and perhaps edit it. Then we again use TimeValue to put the user's second try into the Variable *x*.

The Format$ Function can translate a serial number into many different formats, among them HH:MM:SS, which is what we request here. Then we reset the computer's clock by using the Time$ Statement. An error is unlikely at this point, but we nonetheless include one last "If Err" message anyway to check the built-in VB error-reporting Variable. If Err returns anything but zero, an error was made.

See also   DateValue; Hour; Minute; Now; Second; TimeSerial

TITLE

PROPERTY

Description   Title is a Property of the "App" Object. App is a special word that refers to the program itself. App, short for *application,* means the currently running application. It is used to identify qualities of the program, much the way a program uses the word Screen (for Screen "Object") to find out qualities of the user's monitor.

Title tells your running program what name identifies your program in Windows 3.1's Task Manager, or, in Windows 95, the Taskbar.

Used with   App, the "application" Object

Variables   **Variable type:** Text ("string")

To find out the Title of your running program:

```
X$ = App.Title
```

Uses   Use the Title when creating DDE Links between programs. See "Link-Mode."

Cautions   • You can change this Property while your program is running, but it will not remain a permanent change once the program is exited. You can also assign a Title in the Make EXE File Dialog Box in VB's File Menu.

• You must always use the word App when using Title: App.Title.

• The Title cannot be longer than 40 characters.

Example   In the Form_Click Event, type the following:

```
Sub Form_Click ()
    Print App.Title
End Sub
```

Results in   Project1

See also   App; LinkMode

TOOLBAR
CONTROL

See   Windows 95 Controls

TOP
PROPERTY

Description   Top describes the position of the top edge of a Control in relation to the Form (or other Control) that contains it. The Top Property of a Text Box is the vertical location of the top of the Box.

The Top Property of a Form refers to the position of the top edge of the Form in relation to the top of the screen.

Left and Top describe the *location* of an Object within another Object. An Object's associated Height and Width Properties describe the *size* of the Object. Using these four Properties you can both position and size any Object. And there are situations when all four Properties are used to provide you with additional information.

For example, there are no "right" or "bottom" Properties. If you want to draw a box around an Object, you need to know its right and bottom locations in addition to Top and Left. These are important positional qualities, particularly when drawing boxes and frames with the Line command. To work with these qualities, you need to involve Width and Height in addition to Left and Top. See "Cautions" below.

Used with
Everything–Forms, Check Boxes, Combo Boxes, Command Buttons, Directory, Drive and File List Boxes, Frames, Grids, Horizontal and Vertical Scroll Bars, Images, Labels, List Boxes, OLE, Option Buttons, Picture Boxes, Shapes, Text Boxes and Timers

Variables
Variable type: Single

When you are dragging items around onscreen while designing your program, you are automatically affecting the Top Property of those items. Visual Basic keeps track. When you finally stop dragging an item, its Top Property will contain a description of its location automatically. The Top Property is expressed in "twips." There are 1,440 twips per inch (unless you have changed this default measurement system with the ScaleMode command, which see). The upper border of a Form is 0, so if a Text Box's Top Property is 1,440, the Box is about one inch down from the upper border of its Form. (The Top Property of a *Form* itself–which is relative to the upper edge of the video screen–is always expressed in twips.)

You could set the Top Property directly in the Properties Window, although few people do:

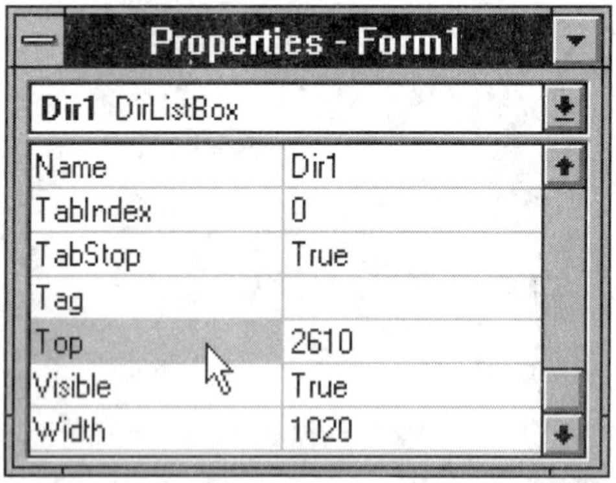

Figure T-23: In a few situations, you may want to set the Top Property in the Properties Window.

The Left and Top Properties are always visible on the right side of the VB Design Window when you are writing a program. They are reported on the right side of the Menu Bar where Left & Top, and Width & Height are always visible. You can watch these four coordinate numbers change as you drag your Controls around a Form. However, *seeing* the relative sizes and positions of Controls is much more meaningful than those numbers.

OR (to find out the topmost location of an object while the program runs):

```
X = Picture1.Top
```

OR (to change the vertical position of an object while the program runs):

```
Picture1.Top = 500
```

OR (to reposition an object vertically relative to itself, in this case moving it upward): Picture1.Top = Picture1.Top − 400

OR (to position an object vertically relative to another object):

```
Picture1.Top = Picture2.Top + 1000
```

OR (to use a numeric Variable):
```
Position% = 2300
Picture1.Left = Position%
```

Uses
- Animate Controls by adjusting the Top Property directly, or by finding out the current Top Property and providing it to the Move command.

- Format your screen by adjusting the relative positions of Controls in response to current conditions in your program. Perhaps when the user clicks on a Picture, you want it to slide into the bottom of the window and disappear. See the Example below.

- Used in combination with an object's Left, Height and Width Properties, you can have complete control over the object's size and location.

Cautions
- Top is expressed as a number, but precisely what this number means can change. Unless you have adjusted the Scale Method or the ScaleMode Property (which apply only to Forms, Picture Boxes and the printer), the number will be in *twips*. There are 1,440 twips per inch. Several other "coordinate systems" are available in VB–points, inches, millimeters, etc.

Within a Picture Box, Form or printer page, the Top Property for all objects is given in twips (or in an optional, alternative system) and says: "My top side is 500 twips from the top border of my container (the Form or Picture Box or printed page)."

Is an Object Flush Against the Top of Its Container? If the Top Property is 0, the Object is flush against the top of its container.

Is an Object Flush Against the Bottom of Its Container? An Object is butted up against the bottom of its container if its Top Property plus its Height Property equal the ScaleHeight Property of the container *minus* the Object's Top plus Height Properties:

```
X = Command1.Top + Command1.Height
If Form1.ScaleHeight − X = X Then
```

ScaleHeight provides the *inner* dimensions of a Form, Picture Box or the paper in the printer. It is really only useful with a Form because a Form can have a Border. By contrast, the Form's *Height* Property tells you the total dimensions of the Form, including its Border. The Form's ScaleHeight Property tells you the inner dimensions, excluding the Border, and is therefore more useful when positioning Controls than the Height Property.

To Move an Object Flush Against the Bottom of Its Container:

```
Command1.Top = Form1.ScaleHeight — Command1.Height
```

If you use a Form's Height Property to position an Object, part of an Object can disappear under the Form's frame unless the Form's BorderStyle is set to None. You'll need to adjust the Object's Top Property to take into account Forms with Borders. Or use the Form's *ScaleHeight* Property (rather than its Height Property) to eliminate this Border problem.

The video screen is the container for a Form, and in this situation, *the Top Property measurement is always in twips.* There can be no other coordinate system for the Screen Object.

To Center Objects Within Their Containers:

```
Picture1.Top = (Form1.Height — Picture1.Height) / 2
Picture1.Left = (Form1.Width — Picture1.Width) / 2
```

To Animate an Object: Adjust the Top Property for an instant change in an Object's position. Use the Move Method for a smoother animation, particularly if you are combining a horizontal movement with an adjustment to the vertical position (a diagonal movement). However, you'll almost always want to retard the speed of either technique by placing the command within a For...Next Loop:

```
For I = Command1.Top To Command1.Top — 1500 Step — 50
    Command1.Top = I
Next I
```

Adjust the Step amount to adjust the speed of this animation.

The Strange Behavior of Windows's "Granularity": In the Windows Control Panel (Desktop item), you can adjust the *Granularity* option, which decides how closely Objects on the screen can get to each other and by what degrees objects can be expanded or shrunk. You might ask your programs' users to set it to zero. If Granularity is set to anything other than zero, the positioning and sizing commands in your Visual Basic programs will be relatively crude. Objects will *jump* in increments of Granularity * 16 pixels when their Left, Top, Height or Width Properties are adjusted. This jerking movement might not seem like much—16 pixels is not much space— but animated graphics and other effects are smoother when Granularity is set to zero. Setting zero Granularity eliminates the bumpy motion (at some small cost in speed).

Example

1230 ... T

We'll make this picture drop off the Form in Figure T-24, as if it had come off its nail and slid down behind a desk.

Figure T-24: This graphic will appear to fall off the window.

We first use Top to move the entire Form against the top of the screen:

```
Sub Form_Load ()
    Form1.top = 0
End Sub
```

Then we use the Move command to make the Picture Box appear to slide off the Form:

```
Sub Form_Click ()

l = Picture1.Left
sh = Form1.ScaleHeight + 400

For i = 1 To sh Step 200
    Picture1.Move l, i
Next i
End Sub
```

The Move command requires that you specify Left and then Top. We first find the current Left Property of the Picture Box and put the result into the Variable *l*. Next, we figure out how far down to push the Picture Box. We are going to use the Step command to make the picture move fairly rapidly. We also add 400 to the ScaleHeight of the Form, just to make sure that the last Step (of 200 twips) is sufficient to push the picture off the bottom.

See also Height; Left; Scale; ScaleHeight; ScaleLeft; ScaleMode; ScaleTop; Scale-Width; Width

TopINDEX

PROPERTY

Description TopIndex allows your program to move (scroll) the items within a List or File List Box. By specifying which item in the Box should appear as the first visible item in the Box, TopIndex determines how the items will appear onscreen. (TopIndex has no effect on the contents of the Box other than to shift the list visually—as if the user had clicked on a Scroll Bar. The items remain in the same *order* in the list; the whole list just moves.)

Used with List Boxes and File List Boxes

Variables You can set the TopIndex only while a program is running.

To make the fifth item in the list move to the top of the Box, as if the user had scrolled the list to move it there:

    List1.TopIndex = (4)

To move the fifth item to the top of the Box, recall that the first item in all Box-type Controls has a 0 index number. So requesting TopIndex (4) actually moves the *fifth* item to the top.

Uses • Give your program (or user) control over what shows in a File List or List Box.

• Substitute for a Scroll Bar a different kind of control over the scrolling in a Box (perhaps a set of up and down arrows or buttons).

• Have your program move the items in a Box to display the data most likely of interest to the user. For instance, if the user has been working in a database on various names beginning with the letter *M,* move the list in the Box to reflect this (see the Example).

• Adjust a disk File List or other list alphabetically as the user types in each character (like the VB's Search feature in Help). See the Example in "Like."

Cautions • TopIndex will try to move an item in the list to the top of a Box (which has its Columns Property set to 0, Off). Nonetheless, if the item is so near the end of the list that moving it would leave space at the bottom of the Box, the scrolling will halt so the Box remains filled.

If the Columns Property is turned on (True), the item moved by TopIndex stays in the same spot within its column, but all the columns move horizontally to position the TopIndex item against the left side of the Box.

As always, you have to deal with the unfortunate fact that the first item in a Box-type Control has an index of 0. See the Example.

The Properties of List and File List Boxes must always include the Name of the Box. For instance, you must use A$ = List1.List(List1.ListIndex) rather than A$ = List1.List(ListIndex).

Example

To show how TopIndex scrolls the items in a Box, put a List Box and a Text Box on a Form. We'll first create a set of 26 "words," each of which starts with a different letter of the alphabet:

```
Sub Form_Load ()
    For i = 65 To 90
    list1.AddItem Chr$(i) + "-word"
    Next i
End Sub
```

Then, in the Text Box's KeyPress Event, type the following:

```
Sub Text1_KeyPress (KeyAscii As Integer)

text1.Text = UCase$(Chr$(KeyAscii))
KeyAscii = 0

For i = 0 To list1.ListCount − 1
    If (Left$(list1.List(i), 1)) = text1.Text Then
        list1.TopIndex = i
    End If
Next i

End Sub
```

First, we make whatever key the user presses into an uppercase, printable character (see "Chr$") and then assign it to the Text Box. Next, we loop through the entire list of items and, if one of the items begins with the same letter, we scroll the list so that item moves to the top of the Box.

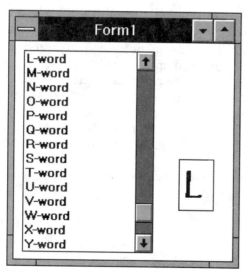

Figure T-25: Your program can freely scroll the items in a List Box.

See also

File List Box; List; List Box; ListCount; ListIndex

TreeView

CONTROL

See Windows 95 Controls

TwipsPerPixelX,
TwipsPerPixelY

PROPERTY

See   Appendix A

Type

STATEMENT

Description   You generally use the Type Statement to create a customized cluster of Variables for use with the random-access file technique (see "Open").

A random-access file stores pieces of information *of fixed sizes,* within "records" of a fixed size (and records are themselves subdivided into "fields" of fixed sizes). You decide what amount of information these subdivisions will contain, how many characters in each piece of text, for example. However, you must then make all the records and fields that same size.

Ordinarily, you cluster the Variables used with a random-access file into a group of related information:

Name

Address

Telephone Number

When used with a random-access file, the smallest unit of data (each Variable)–the name, the address or the phone number–is called a *field.* Together, they are called a *record.* The easiest way to manipulate these records is to put the fields together into a user-defined Variable with the Type command.

Because text Variables ("strings") by default can be of varying length, you can fix their length by using the * *N* technique. (Using Dim Mytext As String * 30 is one approach. The Type command can also create fixed-length strings.)

You can use the Type command only in a Module (see "Variables" below).

In a sense, the Type command enables you to create a special kind of Array (see "Arrays"). A normal Array is a collection of Variables, but they must all be the same kind of Variable. (The new Variant Variable type (see "Variant") allows you to get around this rule.) You can make an Array of text Variables or an Array of a particular type of numeric Variable, such as Integers, etc. (see "Variables"), but you cannot make an Array with mixed Variable types (except for Variants). However, using the Type command you can create a custom grouping of mixed Variables, called a "user-defined data type." The one kind of Variable *that cannot be used as part of a Type structure* is the Object Variable type (see "Objects").

Used with

Random-access files (see "Open").

Create a specialized custom data structure to help you, the programmer, organize information into a group of related items with meaningful Variable names.

Variables

You can use the Type command only within the General Declarations section of a Module.

```
Type AddressBook
    Nam As String * 50
    Address As String * 200
    Phone As String * 12
    Age As Integer
End Type
```

Three Things You Must Do to Create a Type Structure: Creating and using a Type Variable structure requires that you follow three steps:

1. Define the general Type structure in a Module as illustrated above.

2. Create a *particular* Variable of that type (Dim NewVar As Address Book, for example).

3. Manipulate the Variable as if it were an ordinary Variable (add, change or examine the data). The only difference between this and ordinary Variables is that the NewVar we created has four interior Variables. You manipulate them by using the name NewVar separated by a period (.) from the name of one of the interior Variables: NewVar.Nam = "Rusty Wheels" or Print NewVar.Age.

Let's define a particular Variable as being of the "AddressBook" type. *Once the general Type has been defined, you must then give a name to a particular Variable that will be of that type.*

You can use three "Variable defining" commands to make a particular Variable a *type*:

1. The Global command (you must use it in a Module).

2. The Dim command (you must use it in the General Declarations section of a Form). (You can also use ReDim, which see.)

3. The Static command (you must use it within an individual Event, Subroutine or Function).

Using any of these three declaration commands creates a Variable and defines its structure as being of the custom Type. In other words, this new Variable has the interior Variables Nam, Address, Phone and Age.

Only after you have declared this new Variable can you then use the custom structure. You *cannot* use the name of the Type (AddressBook) directly within commands that save, retrieve, print or otherwise manipulate data. The Type is a structure that you define; then later you can define *other Variables* as being "of that type." The word *AddressBook* is *only* used when you are defining a new Variable to be of the "AddressBook Type."

In other words, you establish a Type by describing the kinds of Variables it contains, and the order in which they reside within the structure. You *define* a structure in a Module:

```
Type AddressBook
    Nam As String * 50
    Address As String * 200
    Phone As String * 12
    Age As Integer
End Type
```

Then, in an Event, Subroutine, Function, General Declarations section of a Form, or a Module, you announce that a Variable is of that already-defined structural Type.

To complete this example, we'll announce that a Variable called *PersonnelRecords* is to be constructed like the AddressBook structure we have already defined as containing Name, Address, Phone and Age. *PersonnelRecords* will be a structure with four interior Variables of an already described Variable type and length:

```
Dim PersonnelRecords As AddressBook
```

PersonnelRecords has now become a Variable structure. How do you manipulate the interior Variables in this structure? You use a period (.) to separate the name of the structure from the name of one of its subsidiary Variables. PersonnelRecords can now be used in the following fashion.

(To put literal information into the structure):

```
PersonnelRecords.Nam = "Alice Dragonnette"
PersonnelRecords.Address = "2455 West Circle Drive"
PersonnelRecords.Phone = "929-4549-9090"
PersonnelRecords.Age = 45
```

OR (to use Variables to put information in the structure):

```
PersonnelRecords.Nam = N$
```

OR (to get information from the structure):

```
Telephone$ = PersonnelRecords.Phone
```

OR (if you are really attracted to Type Variables as a concept, you could make a more complex structure—*an* Array *of a user-defined Type Variable*): Dim PersonnelRecords(1 To 30) As AddressBook

Now you would have an *Array of structures,* with all the usual benefits of Arrays (which see).

```
PersonnelRecords(12).Age = 45
```

OR (you can put Arrays inside a Type structure. In a Module, define the Type):

```
Type CDCollection
    Jazz (300) As String
    Classical (1 to 600) as Variant
    Rock (400,400) As String
End Type
```

Then, in the General Declarations section of a Form:

```
Dim cds As CDCollection
```

Then, to use one of the internal Arrays:

```
Sub Form_Click ()
    cds.jazz(3) = "Miles Davis"
End Sub
```

Notice that an item in an *internal* Array within a Type structure is referenced by putting the index in parentheses after the internal name of the Array: cds.jazz(3). By contrast, if you're using an Array of Type structure, you put the parentheses after the structure name, but before the interior Variable name: PersonnelRecords(12).Age = 45.

Uses
• The Type command can be used to create fixed data structures, similar to Arrays, which are then used with random-access files (see "Open").

One significant advantage of a Type Variable structure is that you can manipulate the entire structure with one command. You can copy or save a structure as a total entity without having to specify each of its internal Variables. For instance, if you are storing the following structure into a random-access file, you don't go through and store each separate element of the structure:

```
Put #1, PersonnelRecords.Nam
Put #1, PersonnelRecords.Address
Put #1, PersonnelRecords.Phone
Put #1, PersonnelRecords.Age
```

Instead, you simply save the entire structure as a single item:

```
Put #1, PersonnelRecords
```

Likewise, you can copy this cluster-Variable *PersonnelRecords* into another Variable of the same Type. (You must have previously defined some *other* Variable as being of the AddressBook Type—Dim Backup As Address-Book, for example.) Then, to copy all the information stored in the interior Variables of *PersonnelRecords* into the parallel structure of the Variable *Backup*, you use the LSet command:

```
LSet Backup = PersonnelRecords
```

• Some programmers like to use Type Variable structures in other ways. Random-access files aren't the only way to use this handy technique. If you like to organize your data in this quasi-Array fashion, you might use the Type command often. If you want to define custom groupings of Variables for some special purpose, use Type. However, ordinary Variables and Arrays are usually simpler to manipulate. The structures of Variables created by the Type command are similar to the "records" used in the Pascal programming language or to "structures" in C.

• Type structures are also used to pass structures to the API (see Appendix A). Bitmap API Routines, for instance, such as GetDIBits, require structures as arguments when you "call" the API Function.

• Type structures can pass a group of Variables to a Subroutine (see "Sub").

Cautions • You *can* create Type structures that include Variable-length text ("string") Variables (just leave off the * 25 in Newname As String * 25). However, you cannot then use such a structure with random-access files. (See "Open.")

• You can build complicated structures by using one Type structure as a Variable *within another* (in a Module, for instance):

```
Type Directions
    North As String * 10
    South As String * 10
    East As String * 10
    West As String * 10
End Type

Type Mileage
    Car As Integer
    Bus As Integer
    Trailer As Integer
    Distance As Directions 'this is a Type structure
End Type
```

(We put this Type-within-Type technique under "Cautions" rather than "Uses" because this structure-within-structure could get too complex to be easily visualized and could become a source of programming errors.)

- You can use "Static" (which see) *Arrays* within a Type structure.
  Note: You cannot define the dimensions of a Static Array within a Type structure by using Variables:

  Wrong:

  ```
  Children (Start To Total)
  ```

- You cannot use Line Labels or line numbers inside a Type structure definition.
- You cannot use "Object" Variables within a Type structure (see "Objects").

Example In a Module, enter the following:

```
Type InvoiceType
    Date as String * 10
    InvNumber as Integer
    PastDue as Integer
End Type
```

In an Event, enter the following:

```
Sub Form_Click ()

Static Billthem As InvoiceType

Date$ = "07-19-1992"

Billthem.Date = Date$
Billthem.InvNumber = 1552
Billthem.PastDue = 30

Print Billthem.Date
Print Billthem.InvNumber
Print Billthem.PastDue

End Sub
```

Results in 07-19-1992
1552
30

See also Arrays; Open (about random-access files); Variables

TypeName

Description   TypeName tells you what kind of variable you're dealing with. Variables have types (Text (string), Integer, Date). For more on this, see "Variables." But you wrote the program, so why don't you already know the Variable type? A Variant Variable type (which see) can change type, depending on what kind of data is stored in it. Also, when you're programming with Objects, it's possible that you'll not know while writing your program what kind of object is being passed to a procedure. Clearly, if your procedure were designed to manipulate one kind of data or Object—it's important that the procedure be able to query the data or Object type being passed.

Further, an application's user can be permitted to create new Objects in some situations. Or when you're utilizing OLE Automation (which see "OLE"), one program can make use of another program's features. And what about the fact that a Collection (which see) or Variant Array can hold items of various different data types?

The TypeName Function returns a text ("string") describing the type of data in a Variable. It will also identify an Object, providing its "class." Since each Form is a separate class, you'll get the Form's Name. However, asking the TypeName of Controls will return only a generic class (you'll get Picture-Box rather than Picture1). For more on classes and Objects, see "Objects."

Used with   Variables, to determine the kind of data they hold.

Variables
```
Y = 100
Z = one hundred
Print TypeName(Y)
Print TypeName(Z)
```

Results In
```
Integer
String
```

The possible results when you use TypeName are: Byte, Integer, Long, Single, Double, Currency, Date, String, Boolean, Error, Empty, Null, Object, Unknown, Nothing.

"Object" means an OLE Automation Object. "Unknown" means an OLE Automation Object that's not known (registered) with Windows.

You can also get a Form's Name (each of your program's Forms is a "class"):

```
Sub Form_Click( )
Dim Formobj As Form
```

```
        For Each Formobj In Forms
            Print TypeName(Formobj)
        Next
        End Sub
```

Results in
Form1

By contrast, the Controls collection provides generic class names for any Controls you have on a Form:

```
        Sub Form_Click( )
        Dim Controlsobj As Control
          For Each Controlsobj In Controls
            Print TypeName(Controlsobj)
          Next
        End Sub
```

Results in
CheckBox
FileListBox
CommandButton
CommandButton
(a list of whatever Controls are on your Form).

Uses
When you have to know what kind of data—text, object, currency, whatever—is in a Variable.

Cautions
If you query the data type of an array, TypeName responds as it would to a simple Variable, but adds ( ):

```
        Dim N( ) As Integer
        Print TypeName(N)
        RESULTS IN:
        Integer( )
```

There is a quite similar Function, VarType, which returns a code number rather than a text string. It provides essentially identical information as TypeName, with a few exceptions. VarType doesn't return "Nothing" or "Unknown." However, it does make a distinction between OLE Automation Objects and other, "ordinary" objects. It also returns a specific code for "Array" and for a Variant Array. For more on VarType, see "Variant."

Example
Here we ask the user to type in a number, then add one to it. Because the Variable x has not been specifically assigned a type ($x\%$ or Dim x As Integer), it defaults to a variant type. However, when we perform math on it, the Variant changes into a numeric type. (Without the $x = x + 1$, the Variant would accept the user's typing as a text "string" Variable.)

```
        Private Sub Form_Click( )
```

1242 . . . T

```
                    x = InputBox( Type a number )
                    x = x + 1
                    Print TypeName(x)
                End Sub
```

Results in   Double

See also   Variant, IsQueries.

TypeOf

See   "If...Then...Else"

UBOUND

Description UBound tells you the upper limit of an Array's index (see "Arrays").

You will probably use this command rarely because you *know* when you are writing your program how big your Arrays are—you have to define Arrays, including their range. And if you should ReDim an Array based on some Variable affected by the user while the program was running (or a Variable loaded from disk or some other outside source), you could none-theless just check that variable to know the size of the Array.

Here is how UBound works:

```
Sub Form_Click ()

Static A (1 To 50) As String

X = UBound(A)
Print X

End Sub
```

Results in 50

But, there is always that specialized situation where you have allowed the user to specify the size of an Array or have a Subroutine or Function that accepts various Arrays—to search for something in them, for instance. Knowing an Array's size would be useful to a Sub that sorted several different Arrays. If you are working with dynamic Arrays, which could be of varying sizes, UBound would allow you a simple, direct way of finding out how big one of these Arrays is. You might use this approach:

```
For I = LBound(ArrayName$) To UBound(ArrayName$)
```

Used with Arrays

Variables **Variable type:** Integer

The complete syntax of UBound is:

```
X = UBound(Arrayname [,Dimension])
```

The dimension is optional and defaults to 1.

(Assume that you've defined an Array like this: Dim Names (5 To 16, 2 To 12) in the General Declarations section of a Form):

```
Sub Form_Click ()
    X = UBound(Names, 1): Print X
End Sub
```

Results in 16

OR (to get the upper limit of the second "dimension" of this Array):

```
Sub Form_Click ()
    X = UBound(Names, 2): Print X
End Sub
```

Results in 12

Uses When you cannot know, while designing your program, the size of an Array. Perhaps you allow the user to define the size, or perhaps you are using a multipurpose Subroutine that performs a job for several Arrays of different sizes.

Cautions • An equivalent Function, LBound, provides the lower limit of an Array's index. Recall that Arrays need not start with their first item as the zeroth index number (although Arrays default to zero as the lowest item's index). You can define the start: Dim A$(1 To 300). Or you can use the Option Base command to force all Arrays to default to a lowest index number of 1: Option Base 1.

• You can omit the "dimension number"–the 2 in UBound(A,2)–if there is only one dimension. Dim Z As String has only one dimension; Dim A (1 To 5, 1 To 7, 1 to 4) has three dimensions. In the second case, the Array *A* has more then one dimension so you must specify which dimension you are interested in. To find out the upper limit of Array A, third dimension:

```
N = UBound(A,3)
```

• When creating an Array–when *declaring* the Array with the Dim, ReDim, Global or Static Statements–you need not use the *To* Statement. Dim A(15, 15) creates a two-dimensional Array, with space for items ranging from 0 to 15 in each dimension; in other words, you can store *16* items in each dimension of this Array–a total of 32 items. You can, however, have the Array start at a different lower index by specifying the lower index. Dim A(1 To 15) creates a single-dimension Array with 15 items, ranging in index number from 1 to 15.

• There is also a UBound *Property* which tells you the number –1 of Objects in a Collection (see "Collections") of Columns, Controls, Forms or Printers. (This Property is always the same as the Collection's Count –1.) The Ubound Property of a Control Array also gives back the total –1 and is equal to the Index Property of the last Control in the Array.

Example

```
Sub Form_Click ()

Static A(44)
X = UBound(A)
Print X

End Sub
```

Results in 44

See also Arrays; Dim; LBound; Option Base; Public; ReDim; Static

FUNCTION

Description   UCase forces all the characters of a text ("string") Variable to become uppercase letters. For example, it changes "homer" to "HOMER." UCase works the same way but provides a "Variant" (which see) rather than a text Variable.

Used with   Text Variables, text Constants, literal text or text expressions (see "Variables" for an explanation of these terms)

Variables   To turn a text Variable into all-uppercase letters:

```
A$ = "Monetary Policy Debated By Monkey Boys"
B$ = UCase(A$)
Print B$
```

Results in   MONETARY POLICY DEBATED BY MONKEY BOYS

OR (because LCase is a Function, you can use it as part of an *expression*; see "Variables"):

```
A$ = "\\ Donkeys Found Alive In Grand Canyon \\"
Print UCase(A$)
```

Results in   \\ DONKEYS FOUND ALIVE IN GRAND CANYON \\

Notice that the \\ symbols, not being characters, remain unaffected by UCase; they are not shifted to pipe (|) symbols.

Uses   • Some commands in Visual Basic and other elements of programming are *case-sensitive*. They make a distinction between *This* and *this*. Sometimes when the user is providing input, you cannot know how he/she might capitalize the input. If your program needs to analyze the user's input, capitalization issues can cause errors. For instance, the InStr command will fail to find a match between *This* and *this*.

To avoid a problem, you can force the user's response to all-uppercase letters and then not worry about unwanted mismatches. Using UCase in general-purpose Subroutines and Functions that you write is a good idea. That way, you don't need to worry about capitalization when providing Variables to them. See the Example.

Cautions   • Only alphabetic letters are affected by UCase—not digits, nor symbols like & (the ampersand) or the backslash.

• A companion command, LCase, forces all characters into lowercase.

VB has a string-comparison (compares one piece of text to another) command called StrComp (which see) that can optionally be case-insensitive. In some situations, you can use StrComp as an alternative to UCase or LCase.

Example InStr is a useful command when you need to search for something within a text Variable. In this example, the user answers a question posed by our program, and our program checks to see if the answer contains any detectable impatience on the user's part. Because we can't know whether the user might capitalize some letters—particularly if the user is irate—we will force all letters to uppercase. InStr would not report a match if the capitalization doesn't match. InStr is thus said to be *case-sensitive*. *Heck* doesn't match *heck*, and neither matches *HECK*.

```
Sub Form_Click ()
reply$ = InputBox("Shall we proceed?")
reply$ = UCase(reply$)
If InStr(reply$, "HECK") Then
    MsgBox ("Tch. Tch. Tch.")
End If
End Sub
```

Our Message Box will become visible if the word *heck* is found *any-where* within the text Variable reply$. The value of the UCase$ command in this example is that it doesn't matter how the user might capitalize *heck*—all possible variations will match *HECK* once all the characters have been made uppercase within reply$.

See also LCase; StrComp

UNLOAD
EVENT

Description The UnLoad Event is triggered *just before* a Form is unloaded—is removed from the computer's memory—which allows you to signal the user that the Form is about to go away or to perform other tasks in response to the impending removal of the Form.

However, VB includes a more flexible and powerful alternative—the QueryUnLoad Event (which see). For most situations where you are tempted to use the UnLoad Event, QueryUnLoad works better.

The UnLoad Event is triggered by two actions:

- Your program used the UnLoad Statement (which see) to remove the Form.

- The user closed the Form (the window) by pressing ALT+F4; by clicking on the "Control-menu Box," the small tab in the upper left corner of most windows; by clicking on a Command Button which contains an End command; or otherwise by shutting down a window.

The contents of the Form (any programming that you've put in it) are not removed from memory when UnLoad occurs. However, the graphics are removed: graphics use up far more memory than the text that you insert as the commands in your program. UnLoad also causes all the numeric Variables on that Form to be reset to zero or empty text Variables ("") or Variants containing Empty values.

Used with Forms only

Variables UnLoad is an unusual Event in that you can prevent it from triggering. UnLoad includes a built-in Variable, called *cancel.* By setting *cancel* to anything other than the default 0, *the Form cannot be UnLoaded.* If the user tries to shut down a Form with its cancel = 1, the Form will refuse to close. If the user goes further and clicks open the Control Menu itself and selects Close, the Form will still refuse to close.

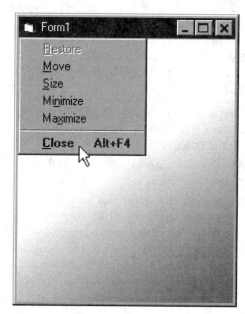

Figure U-1: When the built-in Variable cancel is set to anything other than zero in an UnLoad Event, the user cannot close the window even by selecting Close from the window's Control Menu, shown here.

```
Sub Form_UnLoad (cancel As Integer)
cancel = 1
Print "NOT"
End Sub
```

Uses   • Use the UnLoad Event to perform cleanup and safety procedures. For example, perhaps the user has been typing information into a Text Box. You can use the UnLoad Event to check that anything the user typed into this Text Box or other important Variables has been safely saved to the disk drive. You can make sure that editing or other information has been preserved.

The Last Thing That Happens in a Program: The UnLoad Event in the Startup Form (which see) is *the last Event that happens before the entire program shuts down* (and loses all its Variables). However, the *End* command bypasses the UnLoad Event. If you allow your program to be shut down via End, UnLoad is never triggered. Therefore, the safest approach to shutting down one of your programs is to put any prophylactic commands within the Startup Form's UnLoad Event. And, if you want to, say, provide the user with a Command Button labeled "Quit," redirect the program to the UnLoad Event rather than use the End command. See the Example below.

Inform the user that the window is being shut down and allow him or her to take measures, if necessary, to refuse to close the window—or to specify other actions such as saving data to disk.

Use the Variable *cancel* in the Form_UnLoad Event to refuse to allow the window to be closed.

Cautions   • The *End* command bypasses the UnLoad (and QueryUnLoad) Events. When you use End, no UnLoad Event is triggered in any of the Forms in the program (see the Example below).

• UnLoad makes unavailable the Controls in a Control Array that were created while the program was running.

• If their Form is UnLoaded, the Controls that were created while you were writing your program still exist in the computer's memory, but any *changes* made to their Properties or Variables are lost. You could get at the Properties from an active Form, but Events are to be used within the particular Form within which the Events reside (one Form's Events are not designed to be used by another Form).

• UnLoad erases any changes made to a Form's Properties while the program was running.

• You can use UnLoad to remove Controls in a Control Array that were created while the program was running. You cannot use UnLoad, however, with Controls in a Control Array that were created while you were *writing* the program.

• UnLoad resets all the Properties of a Form or a Control in a Control Array to their original state. Using UnLoad, followed by Load, can be a quick way to return a window to its original startup condition.

Example   If you want to prevent the user from accidentally shutting down a program—and perhaps losing valuable information before it is saved to disk—you can arrange to display a warning Message Box. In this example, a

Command Button labeled "QUIT" transfers the program to the Form_UnLoad Event. (If you used the End command within the QUIT Click Event, the UnLoad Event would never be triggered.)

There is now no way for the user to exit the program without triggering this UnLoad Event. Neither double-clicking on the Control Box on the window, nor selecting Close from the Control Box's menu, nor pressing ALT+F4, nor any other approach will bypass the UnLoad Event.

First, put a Command Button on a Form, and put the following in the Button's Click Event:

```
Sub Command1_Click ()
    Form_UnLoad 0
End Sub
```

Here the 0 following our call to the Form_UnLoad Event is required. That 0 is the (Cancel as Integer) value that an UnLoad Event expects. The Event wants to know if we want to allow UnLoading to take place. If we pass something other than 0, that Form cannot be UnLoaded (the user can't shut down the window). However, any commands within the UnLoad Event will nevertheless be carried out. And, if there is an End command within the UnLoad Event, the program *will* shut down, regardless of the status of the Cancel Variable.

Then put the following in the UnLoad Event:

```
Sub Form_UnLoad (cancel As Integer)
    x = MsgBox("Are you sure you want to end the program?", 4)
    If x = 6 Then End
End Sub
```

A MsgBox can display various kinds of choices for the user and then return information about the user's selection. Putting the 4 at the end of the message causes "YES" and "NO" to be the options in the Box. If the user clicks "YES," the Box returns a 6.

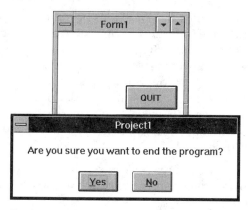

Figure U-2: You can react to an UnLoad Event by asking if the user truly wants to shut down the window perhaps a Button Labeled *QUIT* was clicked by accident.

See also   Hide; Load; QueryUnLoad; Show; UnLoad (Statement); Visible

STATEMENT

Description   The UnLoad command is used in two ways:

UnLoad Used With Forms: The UnLoad command is the opposite of the Load command. UnLoad removes a Form from the computer's memory while your program is running. You can UnLoad a Form if your program no longer needs a Form's services. If some of the Events, Variables or the window (the Form) itself might be needed later by the program, simply make the Form invisible by using the Hide command or by setting the Form's Visible Property to Off (False).

The UnLoad command is thus to your program what double-clicking on the button in the upper left corner of a window is to the user—it causes the window to collapse and disappear.

UnLoad destroys all Variables (resets numeric Variables to 0, resets Variants to Empty or, in the case of text Variables, to an empty string ""). Loading a Form into the computer later will also slow things down because it must be read off the disk. A Form merely hidden with the Hide command will come back into view quite quickly.

Note that UnLoad removes only the visual elements of the Form, not the commands, the programming within the Form. However, the visual elements take up much more memory than the programming.

The Load command causes a Form to be brought into being (to be transferred from the disk drive into the computer's memory). The Form's Event Procedures, Subroutines and Functions become available. Loading, however, does not necessarily make a Form visible to the user (except in the case of the Startup Form, which see).

The UnLoad command partly reverses the Load process. It causes a Form's visual elements to be extinguished (to be removed from the computer's memory). The Form still exists on the disk drive, of course, and its visuals can be Loaded in again. However, any Variables, Controls or other elements that were created, or Properties that were changed *while the program was running,* are lost.

UnLoad Used With Control Arrays: You can also use UnLoad to remove items in a Control Array if the items were added to the Control Array while the program was running.

Control Arrays are created when you are designing your program. The Array cannot be created while the program runs, but you can add new Controls to the Array while the program runs.

By giving an Index Property to a Control, you let VB know that you may be adding additional Controls (of the same type). This Control is the essence, the genesis, of what is called a *Control Array,* and any Controls you add to the Array will share the same Name Property but will be distinguished by having different index numbers: Text1(0), Text1(1), Text1(2), etc. They will also inherit the Properties, the qualities, of the original member of the Array (unless you specifically change the offspring's Properties). All members of the Control Array also share the same Events. (See "Control Array.")

A second way to create a Control Array is to give two Controls the same Name Property. VB will then ask you if you want to create an Array.

Control Arrays are useful in two ways:

Because the members of a Control Array share the same name and are identified *by a number,* you can manipulate them within a Loop. You can refer to each Control by using the Loop counter (*I* in this example):

```
For I = 1 to 4
    Text1(I).Visible = False
Next I
```

This approach is a more efficient way to make four Text Boxes invisible than the following:

```
Text1.Visible = False
Text2.Visible = False
Text3.Visible = False
Text4.Visible = False
```

If you are going to be frequently manipulating the Properties of a group of Controls, you should consider using Control Arrays.

Also, because the members all share the same Event Procedures, additional efficiencies are possible. With a Control Array you've got a group of precision dancers, joined together, kicking in unison like a chorus line. (See the Example below.)

The only way to bring new Controls into existence *while your program is running* is to use a Control Array. (Actually, you can indirectly create new Controls with the Set command, which see.)

Used with   Forms and items in a Control Array

Variables   To remove a Form's visual elements (and reset its Variables) while a program is running:

```
UnLoad Form3
```

OR (to remove an item in a Control Array): UnLoad Command1(4)

Uses   • Free up some of the computer's memory when the visual elements of a Form will no longer be needed by a program. One type of Form that would be a good candidate for UnLoading is a title screen that only appears when the program first starts.

• Remove one or more Controls that are members of a Control Array.

• Use UnLoad to reset all the Properties of a Form or a Control in a Control Array to their original state. Using UnLoad, followed by Load, can be a quick way to return an object to its original condition.

Cautions
• UnLoad makes unavailable the Controls in a Control Array that were created while the program was running. In other words, your program cannot use the Events within such Controls after UnLoad.

• If their Form is UnLoaded, the Controls that were created while you were *writing* your program remain available, but any changes made to their Properties or Variables are lost.

• UnLoad erases any changes made to a Form's Properties while the program was running.

• You can use UnLoad to remove Controls in a Control Array that were created while the program was running. UnLoad cannot remove Controls in a Control Array that were created while you were *writing* the program.

Example
This example illustrates how UnLoading a Form can free up some of the computer's memory. The Command Button on Form1 will Load and UnLoad Form2. Form2 has no programming in it, just a graphic put on it by setting its Picture Property while the program is being written.

To try this example, create two Forms. Put a Command Button and a Label on the first Form. Use the Properties Window to put a .BMP graphic into Form2.

We want to show how much of the computer's memory is used when Form2 is loaded and unloaded. No command built into Visual Basic shows free memory, but we can use the one that's built into Windows itself. (To find out how to access the over 600 special features built into Windows, the "API," see Appendix A. For how to do this using 32-bit VB4, see the end of this example.)

We use the built-in Windows 3.1 "Free Memory" feature by declaring a Function in the General Declarations section of a Module. Just type the following into the General Declarations section, making sure it is all on a single line:

Right:
```
Declare Function GetFreeSpace Lib "Kernel" (ByVal wFlags As Integer) As →
    Long
```

Wrong:
```
Declare Function GetFreeSpace Lib "Kernel"
(ByVal wFlags As Integer) As Long
```

Then, in Form1's Form_Load Event, type the following:

```
Sub Form_Load ()
    form2.Show
End Sub
```

With the Show command, we make Form2 visible when the program first starts running.

Now, type the following into the Command Button's Click Event:

```
Sub Command1_Click ()

Static toggle As Integer

If toggle = 0 Then
    toggle = 1
    command1.Caption = "Load Form2"
    UnLoad form2
    x = GetFreeSpace(0)
    Label1.Caption = "Free Memory: " + Str$(x)
Else
    toggle = 0
    command1.Caption = "UnLoad Form2"
    Load form2
    form2.Show
    x = GetFreeSpace(0)
    Label1.Caption = "Free Memory: " + Str$(x)
End If

End Sub
```

Here we create a "persistent" Variable called *toggle*, which will switch between 1 and 0 each time the user clicks the Button. (See "Static.") Depending on the status of *toggle*, we either Load or UnLoad Form2. Then we switch the value of *toggle*, change the Caption on the Button, and either Load or UnLoad Form2 as appropriate.

Finally, we use the special Function from Windows that reports the free memory in the computer. Then we display the results in the Label. When Form2 is unloaded, there are 4,696,928 bytes free, about 4.5 megabytes:

Figure U-3: What's the effect on the computer's memory when you UnLoad a window? Here's the amount of free memory before Form2 is Loaded in from the disk.

With Form2 loaded, there are 4,495,552 bytes free, about 200,000 bytes are being used up in the computer when Form2 is in memory:

Figure U-4: After Form2 is Loaded, it uses up about 200,000 bytes in the computer's memory. (.BMP and .WMF graphics use up a fair amount of memory.)

An empty Form with no programming and no graphics uses up about 1,000 bytes when loaded. But add some bitmap graphics and memory is used up rapidly. The .BMP file we used on Form2 in this example takes up 201,078 bytes on the disk. Try running the example with no Picture in Form2. You'll see that about 1,000 bytes are used up by a blank Form.

The 32-Bit API

There are differences between the APIs (the "application programmers interface") for Windows 3.1 and Win95 (see "Appendix A" for more). Usually, the only change you have to make when calling one of the built-in API Functions or Subs is to merely rename the library from, for example "Kernel" to "Kernel32." However, other API calls have either been re-named or restructured, or both. The "GetFreeSpace" Function that we're using in this example doesn't exist in the 32-bit API. Instead, it's been replaced by a Sub that provides much more detailed information about the status of the user's memory. Here's how to adjust our example if you're using the 32-bit version of VB4:

Instead of

```
Declare Function GetFreeSpace Lib  Kernel  (ByVal wFlags As Integer) →
    As Long
```

In a Module, type:

```
Declare Sub GlobalMemoryStatus Lib  kernel32  (lpBuffer As  →
    MEMORYSTATUS)
```

Then add this Type structure—where the information will be dumped—to the Module:

```
Type MEMORYSTATUS
  dwLength As Long
  dwMemoryLoad As Long
  dwTotalPhys As Long
  dwAvailPhys As Long
  dwTotalPageFile As Long
  dwAvailPageFile As Long
  dwTotalVirtual As Long
  dwAvailVirtual As Long
End Type
```

Then, in the General Declarations section of Form1, type this:

```
Dim mymem As MEMORYSTATUS
```

And, finally, replace

```
x = GetFreeSpace(0)
Label1.Caption =  Free Memory:  + Str$(x)
```

with

```
GlobalMemoryStatus mymem
Label1.Caption =  Free Memory:  & Str$(mymem.dwAvailPhys)
```

See also   Control Array; Hide; Load; QueryUnload; Show; UnLoad (Event); Visible

Use Mnemonic

PROPERTY

See   Label

Val

FUNCTION

Description   Val changes a text number into a real number, a number that the computer can use in arithmetic. You cannot multiply "5" times "5" because data inside text Variables like A$ or literal text inside quotation marks are only *text*—only *digits, not true numbers.*

To transform "5" into a real number, use Val:

```
X = Val("5")
```

Now X can be used in calculations by the computer:

```
Print X * X
```

Results in   25

```
Print Val("5") * Val("5")
```

Results in   25

The Val command is the opposite of the Str$ command. Str$ changes a true number into a text digit: X = 5: Print Str$(X).

Used with   Text ("string") Variables

Variables   To change a literal text of digits into a true number:

```
N$ = "124"
X = Val(N$)
```

OR (because Val is a Function, you use it as part of an *expression;* see "Variables"): Print Val(N$)

OR

```
If Val(N$) > 50 Then
```

OR (Val translates from the left side of a piece of text until it reaches a non-digit character or the end of the text. A space is not considered a non-digit character):

```
X$ = "5 10-gun salutes"
Print Val(X$)
```

1256 . . . V

Results in   510

OR (a period is translated as a decimal point):

    X$ = "5. 10-gun salutes"

    Print Val(X$)

Results in   5.1

Uses   • Change numbers from text characters (digits) into true numbers.

The most common use of Val is to translate numeric input from the user (which is, by definition, text typed at a keyboard) into numbers that the computer can compute with.

Visual Basic is wonderfully inventive: VB 2.0 introduced to computer languages a clever Variable type called *Variant* (which see) that more or less allows you to relax about numeric Variable "types." A Variant *embraces* text and numeric as well as date/time and all other Variable types into a single "Variant." VB then handles things for you; VB decides how to manipulate the Variable based on the context. Are you multiplying? VB will treat the Variant as a numeric Variable. Are you putting it into a caption? VB changes it to text.

The price you pay for Variants is that they slow down the program somewhat (while VB checks out what's going on and how the contents of the Variable should be used), and they consume more memory than other kinds of Variables. Nonetheless, if your Variable is a Variant type, you usually need not bother using such Variable-type translator commands as Val and Str$, or that esoteric group of numeric Variable type manipulators: CDbl, CInt, CLng, CSng (CInt "forces" a number to become an Integer, for example).

When used in conjunction with other Variable types, Variants *can* cause errors or ambiguities. See "Cautions" in the "Variants" entry.

Cautions   • If you print a text Variable and a numeric Variable, they can seem to be the same thing:

    X% = 144
    Z$ = "144"

    Print X%, Z$

Results in   144   144

Nonetheless, these Variables are quite distinct from the computer's point of view. To the computer, a text ("string") Variable is merely a grouping of characters *strung* together. Each character is represented by a code number (see "Chr$"), but the computer cannot perform mathematics on these strung-together codes. It simply holds them as a group of symbols that can be printed and will mean something to the user.

Text Variables have no intrinsic meaning to the computer. They are sets of symbols that, at best, can be organized or compared alphabetically. No

V . . . **1257**

other even quasi-mathematical manipulations can be performed on text. Numeric Variables, however, are *real numbers to the computer.* They can be manipulated mathematically—added, multiplied and so forth.

Val Translates Digits Until It Runs Into a Non-Digit: If Val finds a digit (a symbol between 0 and 9) in a text Variable, Val translates it into an actual number. If Val finds another digit at the next character in the text, it translates the two of them, multiplying the first one by 10 and adding the second one. If you give Val the digits "19," it will change the "1" into 1 and then see if there are more digits. In this case, it finds "9," so it multiplies 1 * 10 and adds the 9 to get 19. Val goes on picking off digits until it comes to a character that is not a digit, like the letter *f*, or reaches the end of the text.

• Val ignores any leading spaces (blanks), Tab characters or "Line Feed" character symbols (see "Chr$"). Val also ignores internal space characters and translates a period into a decimal point:

```
X$ = "45 57th St."
Print Val(X$)
```

Results in   4557

• Val reacts to &H and &O, the symbols for hexadecimal and octal numbers (see "Hex$"). It correctly interprets numbers following these special (though now rarely used) mathematical symbols:

```
X$ = "&H1F"
Print Val(X$)
```

Results in   31

• Val returns a Double-Precision Floating-Point number (symbolized by #). If you assign the result of a Val Function to some other type of numeric Variable, the result will be transformed into that other type of Variable. (See "Variables.")

Example

```
Sub Form_Click ()

x$ = InputBox$("Enter a number")
z = Val(x$)
Print z

End Sub
```

See also   Str$; Variables; Variant

Value

PROPERTY

Description   The Value Property is used in two ways:

• The Value Property of a Scroll Bar tells you the position of the tab (the sliding "thumb") inside the bar.

• As a Property of a Check Box, Value indicates that the Box is Unchecked, Checked or Grayed (unavailable). For an Option Button, Value tells you whether the Button has been selected. For a Command Button, Value tells you whether the Control has been clicked.

You can also have your program *set* the value of a Scroll Bar's thumb, put a check in a Check Box to trigger a Command Button's Click Event or select an Option Button—thereby changing their status, just as if the user had done so with the mouse or keyboard.

Used with   Check Boxes, Command Buttons, Horizontal & Vertical Scroll Bars, and Option Buttons

Variables   **Variable type:** Integer Enumerated (more than two states) 0, 1, 2 for a Check Box; Boolean (two numbers) True or False for Command and Option Buttons

To find the status of a Check Box. Is its check mark visible, gray, or is the Box blank?

    X = Check1.Value

OR (to change the status of a Scroll Bar's thumb): HScroll1.Value = 14

The Value Variable With Scroll Bars
The Value Property will range from –32,768 to 32,767. (This is the potential range of a Scroll Bar's Value. Normally, you leave the Min Property to the default 0 and set the Max to whatever is meaningful in the situation. If a Scroll Bar is supposed to move the user through a calendar application, you would set Min to 1 and Max to 12. Then the Value could be any number between 1 and 12, depending on the thumb's position in the Scroll Bar.)

The Value Variable With Check Boxes

    0   Off (the default)
    1   On (check mark)
    2   Gray (see the Example)

The Value Variable With Option Buttons

False (0)   Off (the default)
True (–1)   On (black dot in center)

The Value Variable With Command Buttons

False (0)   Not being clicked at the present time (the default)

True (-1)   Clicked (this is the same as a Command Button's Click Event. If you set a Command Button's Value to -1 while the program is running, you will trigger that Button's Click Event.)

Uses   The uses for the Value Property vary, depending on which Control is under consideration:

• The Value Property is used most often with Scroll Bars. Using Value you find out how much, and in which direction, the user has moved the thumb inside the bar.

• You can use Value to have your program adjust a Scroll Bar's thumb to display, for instance, the percentage of a file saved. The user could then view the Scroll Bar as a gauge. However, there are more visually appealing ways to do this. See "Refresh" for a way to create attractive, professional-looking gauges.

• Using Value your program can act like "invisible fingers," putting a black dot into an Option Button or a check in a Check Box. You would use this approach if something in the program made it likely that the user would want the option activated. For instance, you might offer an option that a Text Box could increase its FontSize to 14 from your default of 12. You would have an Option Button that allowed this larger size type. However, if the user moves to another Text Box on the same window that is to act as the title of the text, your program would automatically "turn on the option" when the user started typing. The user would probably *want* larger type in the Title Box, and your program would anticipate this change:

```
Option1.Value = —1
```

You could also have Check Boxes that displayed defaults (for example, create a backup file) if the user is editing an existing file rather than creating a new file.

• Normally, when the user clicks—to turn Option Buttons and Check Boxes on or off—your program finds out how to react by looking at the commands you wrote in these Controls' Click Events. However, you *may* want to delay your program's reaction or put the commands elsewhere in the program. The Value Property of these Controls can always be checked to find out the status—selected or unselected—of the Controls.

• **A Special Case:** Command Buttons are like the buttons on your mouse—you push them in, but they spring right back out. They don't stay "selected" like Option Buttons and Check Boxes. With Value, though, you can make a Command Button "sticky," causing something to, say, move across the win-dow. (Normally, the Value of a Command Button is only briefly True (-1) while the user is clicking on the Button. When the commands within the Click Event have been carried out, the Value returns to its default, False (or 0), which means that the Value Property is functionally indistinguishable from the Click Event. In fact, if your program sets a Command Button's Value Property to On, that setting generates a Click Event.)

```
Sub Command1_Click ()

Do While command1.value = −1
    Picture1.left = Picture1.left + 3
Loop

End Sub
```

Figure V-1: While the user *holds down* the Command Button, Vermeer's pensive man moves gradually to the right across the window.

Example   This example demonstrates the effects that the Value Property has on the various Controls that use Value.

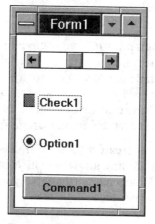

Figure V-2: This example program shows the various effects the Value Property has on Scroll Bars, Check Boxes, Option Buttons and Command Buttons.

```
Sub Form_Click ()

hscroll1.max = 35
hscroll1.value = 20
check1.value = 2
option1.value = True
command1.value = True

End Sub
```

See also   Scroll Bars

ARIABLES

Description   An important tool in computer programming, you create Variables for the same reason that you might write *VISA* on a manila envelope and put your most recent Visa statement inside. Each time you get a new bill, you throw out last month's bill and put the new bill into the envelope.

The amount you owe *varies* from month to month, but this particular envelope, called *VISA*, always "contains" the value (the amount) of the current bill. If someone asks to know your current balance, you could just hand them the envelope. In other words, the thing named *VISA* contains the data about your credit card account. In a computer program, you can then use the *Variable's name* in place of the number it contains:

```
Print 704.12
```

is the same as:

```
CurrentBill = 704.12
Print CurrentBill
```

You put the current Visa total each month in your envelope. You can always go to your stack of envelopes and look for the one labeled VISA to find out how much you owe. Similarly, once you create a Variable in a running program, a location in the computer's memory always contains the Variable's name and its "contents," the information that this label "holds" until, or if, the contents are changed by the running program.

How to Create a Variable: You can create a Variable by assigning some value to a Variable name, in any procedure anywhere in your program. This act simultaneously creates the Variable's name (the label you give it) and assigns some value to it:

```
Donkeys = 15
```

Here you have provided a label (a Variable name)—Donkeys—and said that there are 15 of these entities. Your program's user won't ever see this label, *Donkeys*. You use it when you are programming, and you give it a name that means something to you. Most programmers give Variables names that help them to understand the meaning of the contents. A Variable named X is less useful than one named *MasterCard* when you later read, test or modify your program. However, when the meaning of a Variable is obvious, you can use brief labels like *X* or *Y* or *N*.

You can use any label you want when creating a Variable, but the label cannot be the name of a word that VB uses, like *Print* or *Show* or *End*. VB will tell you if you make this error; it won't allow you to assign a value to one of these "reserved words."

Formal Declarations

Alternatively, you can create a Variable by formally "declaring" it with one of the three primary commands in VB that declare Variables—Public, Dim and Static.

There are three different ways to declare a Variable because Variables can have different levels of impact, different ranges of influence in a program. Sometimes called "scope," this range of influence determines whether a Variable can be used or recognized *everywhere* in the program (Public); only within a particular Form or Module (Dim); or only within a particular Event, Subroutine or Function (Static).

Public Variables: Everything in your program can access a Variable if, within a Module, you declare the Variable with the Public Statement Global MyVariable. Then commands within any Event, Subroutine, Function, Form or Module can get information about what is in Myvariable, and any of them can *change* Myvariable as well.

If you declare a Variable Public in a Form (as opposed to a Module), the Variable can also be accessed from. But you must identify the Form along with the Variable's name: X = Form1.MyVariable or Form1.MyVariable = "Fred"

Note: The command *Global* was used in Visual Basic Versions 1–3. *Public* has replaced Global in Version 4.

Formwide Variables: One step down in "scope" from Public are Variables that you declare in the General Declarations section of a Form or Module, using the Dim command. These Variables will be available to all Events (or Subroutines or Functions) that are part of that Form or Module. However, other Forms or Modules cannot access such Formwide Variables.

Procedure-Only Variables—For Use in a Single Event, Sub or Function: At the lowest level—within Events (or Subroutines or Functions)—Variables are like insects that live only briefly, do their duty and then die. Variables created inside Events pop into existence only when the program is running *within that Event* and disappear again as soon as the program goes on to some other Event. The next time the Event is triggered, the Variable comes back to life–and any value you assigned to it while writing commands within that Event (A$ = "Norman") will be *reassigned*.

Three Advantages of Locally Restricted Variables

You can use the same Variable name over and over should you wish (in different procedures [Events, Subroutines or Functions]) without an untoward effect. Each instance of this Variable label will be a unique Variable, specific to its procedure.

This use of local Variables makes for an efficient use of memory. You could create a large Array of information, for instance, and then manipulate it within a procedure. When you're done, the Array collapses, returning the memory space it used to the computer for other uses. (See "Arrays.")

Local Variables also eliminate one of the most frequent–and hardest to track down–errors in traditional programming: two Variables with the same name that are interacting and messing each other up as a program runs. You need not declare Variables at the procedure level; you can just use them. Y = 2346 creates a numeric Variable and puts the number 2,346 into that Variable.

Static Variables: Variables declared with the Static command are a special type of local Variable. Unlike other procedure-level Variables, Static Variables *do not lose their value (their contents)* when the program goes elsewhere and leaves their procedure. When you come back to the procedure, a Static Variable still retains whatever was in it when you last left the procedure. How is this different from Y = 9, which will always be reassigned that 9 each time the Event is triggered?

A Static Variable can be *changed* within the Event and *retain that change*. An ordinary procedure-level Variable will always lose its contents each time the program exits its procedure (or, as here, get reassigned the same value each time the program enters the procedure). Here you can see the difference between the ordinary Variable *Y* and the Static Variable *Z*:

```
Sub Form_Click( )
    Y = 9
    Static Z
    Z = Z + 1
    Print Y, Z

End Sub
```

Results in   The first time this Form is clicked: 9   1

The second time it's clicked: 9   2

and so on. (See "Static" for its practical uses as a counter and a toggle.)

Variables Interact: Variables can interact, as follows:

```
Donkeys = 15
Monkeys = 3
TotalAnimals = Donkeys + Monkeys
```

In other words, you can use the *Variables' labels* ("Variable names") as if they were the same as the contents of the Variables. If you say Monkeys = 3, then you have made them *equal* each other. You can thereafter use Monkeys just as you would use the number 3:

```
TotalAnimals = Donkeys + Monkeys
```

The preceding line is the same as the following:

```
TotalAnimals = Donkeys + 3
```

"Expressions": What is an *expression*? If someone tells you she has *a coupon for $1 off a $15 Mozart CD*, you immediately think *$14*. In the same way, VB reduces the several items linked into an "expression" into its simplest form.

The phrase "numeric expression" means anything that represents or results in a single number. Strictly speaking, the expression "evaluates" into a single number. When an intelligent entity hears an expression, the entity collapses that expression into its simplest form.

In plain English, if you type 15 – 1 into one of your programs, Visual Basic reduces that group of symbols to 14. Visual Basic simply evaluates what you've said and uses it in the program as the essence of what you are trying to say.

We humans always reduce things, too. Sometimes we call it *intuition*; sometimes we call it *putting two and two together*. But the result is the essence of a more complicated expression or idea.

5 * 3 is a numeric expression and, as far as Basic is concerned, 5 * 3 is just another way of expressing 15 (a single number). 5 * 3 collapses into 15 inside the program and is essentially that single number.

There are many kinds of numeric entities that you can combine into expressions:

- A numeric Variable
- A numeric Variable in an Array
- A Function that returns a number
- A literal number (12 is a literal number, as opposed to a Variable)
  - Print Sqr(12)–literal number
  - Print Sqr(N)–variable
- A numeric Constant, like Const Pi = 3.14159265358979
- A combination of literal and Variable numbers:
  - ?X + 14

Any combination of the preceding examples that can evaluate to a single numeric value *is an expression*. An expression is made up of two or more of the preceding items connected *by one or more* "operators." The plus symbol in 2 + 2 is an operator. Altogether there are 23 operators. (See sections on Operators that follow, or see Appendix C.)

Variable Expressions: When you combine Variables with other Variables, you create a *Variable expression*. An expression is a collection of items, which–seen as a unit–has a single value. This value can be either numeric or text ("string"). If the Variable *Days* has the value 7 and the Variable *Hours* has the value 24, this expression has the value 168:

```
Days * Hours
```

You can assign the preceding expression to another Variable:

```
HoursInAWeek = Days * Hours
```

You can also use the expression within a structure, such as If...Then, to test its "truth."

Expressions True and False: An expression can be evaluated by Visual Basic as either 0 (False) or not 0 (True). Let's see how this works:

```
BobsAge = 33
BettysAge = 27
If BobsAge > BettysAge Then Print  He s Older
```

BobsAge > BettysAge is an expression making the assertion that BobsAge is "greater than" BettysAge. The "greater than" (>) symbol is one of several "relational operators." Visual Basic looks at the Variable BobsAge and at BettysAge and at the relational operator that combines them into the expression. VB then determines whether or not your expression is True. The If...Then structure bases its actions on the truth or falsity of the expression.

Relational "Comparison" Operators

<	Less than
<=	Less than or equal to
>	Greater than
>=	Greater than or equal to
<>	Not equal
=	Equal
Is	Do two object variables refer to the same object? (see "Is")
Like	Pattern matching (see "Like")

Notes: You can use the relational operators with text as well. When used with literal text (or text Variables), the operators refer to the *alphabetic* qualities of the text, with *Andy* being "less than" *Anne*.

The relational operators are *comparisons*, and the result of that comparison is always True or False.

Arithmetic Operators

^   Exponentiation (the number multiplied by itself: 5 ^ 2 is 25 and 5 ^ 3 is 125)

–   Negation (negative numbers, such as –25)

*   Multiplication

/   Division

\   Integer Division (Division with no remainder, no fraction, no "Floating-Point" decimal point: 8 \ 6 is 1. Integer division is easier, and the computer performs it faster than regular division.)

Mod   Modulo arithmetic* (See "Special Note on Mod" below.)

+   Addition

–   Subtraction

&   String Concatenation ("Tom" & " Jones" results in: Tom Jones)

Variant Variables can be combined in a similar way to the traditional text Variable concatenation:

```
A$ = This :B$ = That :Print A$ + B$
```

Results in   ThisThat

However, you are urged to use the + operator only with arithmetic operations (to add numbers). To concatenate text, use the & operator:

```
Print A$ & B$
```

When you use *Variants* (recall that unless you specify otherwise, VB defaults to Variants):

```
x = 5:a = This :Print x & a
```

Results in   5This

Variants are in an indeterminate state, like Schroedinger's Cat, until they are used. For example, if you add two Integer Variable types, you'll get an overflow error if the result is larger than 32767, the biggest number that an Integer type can hold:

```
Dim x As Integer, y As Integer
x = 32760
y = 22
x = x + y
Print x
```

Results in   **Overflow Error**

However, if you don't use the Dim command, the variables will be Variants (or you can Dim x as Variant). When a Variant is assigned a value, it turns into the "subtype" appropriate to the number. In the following, both Variants *x* and *y* become Integer subtypes:

```
x = 32760
y = 22
x = x + y
Print x
```

Results in   32782

The TypeName command can tell you what "subtype" a Variant currently is. Notice in the following how the Variant Variable *x* changes from an Integer type into a Long type, to accommodate the addition which results in a number greater than an Integer can hold:

```
x = 32760
Print TypeName(x)
y = 22
x = x + y
Print x
Print TypeName(x)
```

Results in   Integer
32782
Long

Logical Operators

Not	Logical Negation
And	And
Or	Inclusive OR
XOR	(Either but not Both)
Eqv	(Equivalent)
Imp	(Implication–first item False or second item True)

In practice, you'll likely need to use only *Not, And, XOR* and *Or* from among the logical operators. These four operators work pretty much the way they do in English:

```
If 5 + 2 = 4 Or 6 + 6 = 12 Then Print  One of them is true.   (one of  →
these expressions is True, so the comment will be printed. Only one  →
OR the other needs to be True.)
```

```
If 5 + 2 = 4 And 6 + 6 = 12 Then Print  Both of them are true.   (this is  →
False, so nothing is printed. Both expressions, the first AND the second,  →
must be True for the Printing to take place.)
```

Use the XOR operator to change an individual *bit* within a number, without affecting the other bits. See the Example under "GetAttr" for the way to use XOR.

*Special Note on Mod: The Modulo (Mod) operator gives you any remainder after a division—but not the results of the division itself. This operation is useful when you want to know if some number divides evenly into another number. That way, you could do things at intervals. If you wanted to print the page number in bold on every fifth page, for example, you could enter the following:

```
If PageNumber Mod 5 = 0 Then
    FontBold = -1
Else
    FontBold = 0
End IF
```

15 Mod 5 results in 0.
16 Mod 5 results in 1.
17 Mod 5 results in 2.
20 Mod 5 results in 0 again.

The Text Operator

+ Adds pieces of text together (though you are encouraged to use the & operator instead)

```
N$ = Lois
N1$ = Lane

J$ = N$ +    + N1$
Print J$
```

Results in   Lois Lane

(You can also use the "relational operators" to compare the alphabetical relationship between two pieces of text.)

Operator Precedence: When you use more than one operator in an expression, which operator should be evaluated first?

```
Print 3 * 10 + 5
```

Does this mean first multiply 3 times 10, getting 30? And then add 5 to the result? Should VB Print 35?

Or does it mean add 10 to 5, getting 15? And then multiply the result by 3? *This* would result in 45.

Expressions are not necessarily evaluated by the computer from left to right. Left to right evaluation would result in 35 because 3 would be multiplied by 10 before the 5 was added to that result.

Instead there is an "order of precedence," a hierarchy by which various relationships are resolved between numbers in an expression. For instance, multiplication is carried out before addition. To make sure that you get the results you intend when using more than one operator, use parentheses to enclose the items you want evaluated first. If you intended to say 3 * 10 and then add 5:

```
Print (3 * 10) + 5
```

By enclosing something in parentheses, you tell VB that you want the enclosed items to be considered a single value and to be evaluated before anything else happens.

If you intended to say 10 + 5 and then multiply by 3:

```
Print 3 * (10 + 5)
```

In complicated expressions, you can even *nest* parentheses to make clear which items are to be calculated in which order:

```
Print 3 * ((9 + 1) + 5)
```

If you work with numbers a great deal, you might want to memorize the following table. Although most people just use parentheses and forget about this problem, here's the order in which VB will evaluate an expression, from first-evaluated to last:

Arithmetic Operators in Order of Precedence

- ^   Exponents (6 ^ 2 is 36. The number is multiplied by itself X number of times.)
- –   Negation (Negative numbers like –33)
- * /   Multiplication and Division
- \   Integer Division (Division with no remainder, no fraction, no "Floating-Point" decimal point. 8 \ 6 is 1.)
- Mod   Modulo Arithmetic (Any remainder after division. 23 Mod 12 is 11. See "Mod.")
- + –   Addition and Subtraction

The Relational Operators

The Logical Operators

Given that multiplication has precedence over addition, our ambiguous example would be evaluated in the following way:

```
Print 3 * 10 + 5
```

Results in   35

Expressions Combined into Larger Expressions: You can put expressions together, building a larger entity that, itself, is an expression:

```
Z$ = Tom
R$ = Right$(Z$,2)
L$ = om
N = 3
M = 4
O = 5
P = 6

If N + M + O + P = 18 AND Z$ = Tom  OR R$ = L$ Then Print  Yes.
```

Expressions Can Contain "Literals" and Constants, as Well as Variables: You can include literals as well as Variables when making an expression. Z$ is a Variable, but "Tom" is a literal. *M* is a Variable in the preceding example, and *4* would be a literal. You can mix and match. You could also create the preceding example with some literal numbers mixed in:

```
If 3 + M + 5 + P = 18 And Z$ = Tom  Then Print  Yes.
```

Expressions can also include *Functions*:

```
A$ =  44 Rue Madeline
If Val(A$) <> 55 Then Print  The text Variable doesn t start with the  →
digits 55.
```

Variables Versus Constants

A Variable's label, its name, remains the same. But the contents of a Variable can *vary*, which is how a Variable differs from a Constant.

Constants are not changed while a program runs; they are a known quantity, like the number of donuts in a dozen:

```
Const MONTHSINYEAR = 12
```

Variables vary:

```
MyVisaBillAtThisPoint = 1200.44
```

(but a month later...)

```
MyVisaBillAtThisPoint = 1530.78
```

In practice, some programmers love Constants, and some avoid them. If you read some people's programs, you can see they are making their programs more *readable*, more English-like, by including several Constants:

```
BackColor = WHITE
```

The preceding line is preferred by many people to the following line:

```
BackColor= QBColor(15)
```

Visual Basic (Versions 3.0 and earlier) provide a large text file called Constant.Txt, which contains many predefined Constants. To import this file into your programs, click on New Module in the VB File Menu. The Constants in Constant.Txt are defined as Public, so you must put them into a Module. Then select Load Text from the File Menu. (Be sure to select the Merge option, or you can wipe out some of your programming.) The Constant.Txt file contains definitions like the following:

```
Public Const RED = &HFF&
Public Const GREEN = &HFF00&
```

With these Constants, you can program

```
BackColor = RED
```

instead of

```
BackColor = QBColor (4)
```

and so forth.

Visual Basic 4.0 includes many Constants built into the language. You can just use them. You don't have to declare them—they're just there. To see what Constants are built in, press F2 to get the Object Browser. Then select VBA, VB or DAO in the Libraries/Projects list. Then click on "Constants" in the Classes/Modules list.

The Case against Constants: Some programmers feel that because Constants are known and stable numbers, you can just use the number itself. To calculate your average monthly bank interest, for example, you would use two Variables and the number 12:

```
MyAverageMonthlyInterest = MyTotalInterestThisYear / 12
```

rather than:

```
Const MONTHSINYEAR = 12
MyAverageMonthlyInterest = MyTotalInterestThisYear / MONTHSINYEAR
```

Constants can certainly make programs more readable and can make odd things like *&HFF00&* (green) more easily understood. Nevertheless, a contingent of the programming community finds that there's rarely any compelling reason to use Constants.

The Case for Constants: Many other programmers, though, like to use Constants. They argue that in the interest of program maintainability (being able to go back and more easily change the program later) it is always better to use Constants to define a number that would otherwise not be obvious. This is especially true for programmer-defined values (e.g., CONST NUMBEROFSTATES = 50). That way, if you need to alter the value, you need to change it only in one place in the program, rather than track down every occurrence where 50 refers to the number of states. Memory or disk storage to store a program is cheaper than the hours a programmer would spend trying to decipher somebody else's code that had numbers or text Variables "hard-coded" (used literally, like the digits *50* instead of the Constant NUMBEROFSTATES).

The general convention is to capitalize the first letter of a Variable name and capitalize the entire name of a Constant.

Arrays—Cluster Variables

Arrays, unlike Constants, are universally regarded as extremely useful. Arrays are Variables that have been clustered together into a structure, and they enable you to manipulate the items in the cluster by using Loops.

By giving a group of Variables all the same name, distinguished only *by an index number*, you can manipulate the group by referring to the index number. This approach might look like a small savings of effort, but imagine that your program will probably have to use these Variables in many situations. And eventually you'll have to save them to disk. (See "Arrays" for ways to utilize this important programming tool.)

Text and Numeric—The Two Basic Kinds of Variables: Following are two fundamental kinds of Variables (plus a couple added in VB Version 2.0—Variant and Object Variables):

- Text Variables (often called "string" Variables) can be used in Captions, Text Boxes and so on. Text Variables are made up of the *symbols* that we call the English language. They cannot be divided or used to calculate the amount of linoleum that you would need to redo your kitchen floor. Text is for *communication*, not calculation.

- Numeric Variables cannot be set into Caption or Text Properties. They are used to calculate things; they are numbers rather than symbols. The 12 stamped on top of a carton of eggs is *text*, and the number of eggs in that carton is *numeric*.

(The Print command, however, will accept numeric or text Variables for printing on a Form, Picture Box or to the printer. In Windows, those three destinations accept everything as a *graphic*, and to them numbers are just another picture to be drawn.)

How do you change a text Variable into a numeric Variable and vice versa? The Str$ and Val commands mediate between the two kinds of numbers. Str$ translates a true number into a text digit, or series of digits, that can be displayed. Val does the opposite: it turns a text digit like "5" into a real number that you could multiply. Val can turn "1992" into 1,992 for you.

There is only one kind of text Variable, but there are several "types" of numeric Variables because there are several ways of expressing numbers to a computer. VB refers to numeric Variable types as "data types," which means the same as "Variable types" or "classes" of Variables.

Variant—A Special New Variable Type: The "Variant" Variable type is new to the Basic language, and it has been made the *default* Variable type in VB. Default means that unless you deliberately specify a Variable's type, all Variables will be of the *Variant* type. (For a complete discussion of the Variant type and its advantages and disadvantages, see "Variant.")

Variants Allow You to Be Ambiguous About the Nature of Variables: Are the following Variables text or numeric types? If these Variables are *Variants*, then the *context defines the type*. If your program tries to manipulate them mathematically, they will behave like numbers. If your program tries to Print them as text, they will act like text:

```
A = 12
B = 3
Print A
Print A & B
Print A + B
Print A / B
```

Results in
12
123
15
4

Notice that in the first two times we Print, we are printing text *digits* (characters), not actual numbers. Then the Variables are used as *actual numbers* to arrive at arithmetic results: 15 and 4.

You Can't Mix and Match
For Variants to shift their type during arithmetic or text activity, however, all the Variables involved must actually be Variants. For example, you can get an overflow error if you try to add an Integer Variable to a Variant Variable. Here we'll try to exceed the 32767 upper limit permitted for an Integer type:

```
Dim x As Integer
Dim y As Variant
x = 32000
y = x
Print TypeName(y)
y = y + x
Print y
Print TypeName(y)
```

Results in
Integer
64000
Long

However this causes an overflow error:

```
Dim x As Variant
Dim y As Integer, z As Integer
y = 32760: z = 32760
x = y
Print TypeName(x)
x = y + z
Print TypeName(x)
Print x
```

A Variant used by itself, or in combination with other Variants, works quite well. A Variant looks at what you are doing, the context, and sort of "knows" for instance that you need some precision (some numbers beyond the decimal point): X = 15/40 will result in .375 as the answer.

In other words, when you assign 15/40 to a Variant, the Variant "understands" that an Integer variable type can't be used—Integers can't hold decimals. The Variant turns itself into a "Single" Floating-Point Variable type to accommodate the fractional number. Variants aren't brilliant, though. Always remember that ambiguity and error can result when you calculate using Variants in combination with other Variable types, such as Integers. (See the "Cautions" in the entry on "Variants.")

Object Variables—Forms and Controls as Variables: In addition to the new Variant type, VB 2.0 and 3.0 enable you to manipulate Forms and Controls as Objects and "Variables." This provides you with efficient ways to access, manage and create copies of Forms and Controls. Several meta-physical-sounding commands have been added to VB to support Object Variables. These commands represent new concepts in the Basic language—*Is, Set, New, Null, Empty, Nothing, Me*. These new concepts can add efficiency to your programming. Some are optional—you can do the same thing other ways but perhaps less efficiently. Some of them offer techniques that you could write no other way (creating clones of Forms, multiple "instances," with New; tracking the behavior of multiple Controls or Forms by using normal Variable Arrays in parallel to the Controls or Forms).

For an in-depth discussion of Object Variables, see "Objects."

• Different Variable types take up different amounts of space in the computer's memory (and on disk files). VB defaults to the Variant type unless you specify otherwise, and Variants use up more memory than any other Variable type and make programs run more slowly (30% more slowly isn't uncommon). You could use DefInt (which see) to make Integer the default type (some programs run *much* faster when most of their Variables are integers). Then, if you have to deal with huge numbers or tiny fractions, just define (Dim) those particular Variables individually as being of numeric Variable types that can accommodate those large ranges or highly precise numbers.

• If your application can get by with primarily using the Integer numeric type, you can make the program run as much as 25 times faster. See "DefType" for an example of how to do it. This increase in speed also applies to 486, Pentium, future 1086 and even 9986 microprocessors because the underlying reasons that Integers are so swift have nothing to do with a computer's clock speed. Fractions and division are hard for computers to manipulate for the same reasons that they are hard for humans to learn. It's just easier to give three friends six cookies than it is to give them seven cookies.

Computers calculate in different ways with different numeric Variable types. They can do arithmetic faster with Integer types than with Floating-Point types because Integers have no decimal point and no bothersome fractions to the right of that decimal point like Floating-Point numbers do.

Why? The simplest explanation is found in the fact that elementary school teachers have to spend much more time teaching *division* than teaching multiplication. These operations—addition, subtraction, multiplication and division—are not symmetrical: multiplication is pretty easy to get once you understand the idea of *addition*. And anyone who has written a list for Santa or made a stack of cookies understands addition. Subtraction, too, is clear enough—older brother steals some cookies from the stack.

But division is in a class by itself. Division can cause something to go below unity, below one, into the problematic world of fractions. Suddenly, two simple digits like 3 and 1 can expand into a list of digits bigger than the universe, .3333333333333333333 infinitely long, if you try to divide 1 by 3. And there are those *remainders*, unsettling things left over after the arithmetic is supposedly finished.

Computers have exactly the same problems working with division—there's more to consider and more to manipulate. Just like us, the computer calculates more slowly when you use numeric Variable types that can have fractions. If you want to speed up your programs, allow the computer to use Integers as a Variable type. Integers don't produce fractions. If you don't need the precision fractions offer—and most of the time you don't—use Integers.

Here is a list of the numeric Variable types that you can use in Visual Basic—along with their symbols, the range of numbers they can "hold" and the amount of space each requires in the computer to store a number of that type:

Name	Symbol	Range	Storage Required
Boolean	None	True or False	2 bytes
Byte	None	0 to 255	1 byte
Integer	%	-32,768 to 32,7672	2 bytes
Long Integer (or "Long")	&	-2,147,483,648 to 2,147,483,647	4 bytes
Single (Single-precision floating-point)	!	-3.402823E38 to -1.401298E-45 (negative numbers)	4 bytes
Double (double-precision floating-point)	#	-1.79769313486232E308 to -4.94065645841247E-324 (negative numbers)	8 bytes
Currency (scaled integer)	@	-922,337,203,685,477.5808 to 922,337,203,685,477.5807	8 bytes
Date	None	January 1, 100 to December 31, 9999	8 bytes

Name	Symbol	Range	Storage Required
Object	None	Any Object	4 bytes
Text ("String")* (a string of variable length)	$	1 to roughly 2 billion (roughly 65,400 for Windows 3.1).	The length of the text, plus 10 bytes.
Text ("String") (a string of fixed-length)	$	1 to roughly 2 billion (roughly 65,400 for Windows 3.1).	Length of string. The length of the text.
Variant (when holding a number)	None	Any number. Can be as large as a Double.	16 bytes
Variant (when holding text)	None	1 to roughly 2 billion (roughly 65,400 for Windows 3.1).	The length of the text, plus 22 bytes.
User-defined Variable (see the "Type" command)	None	The size of the defined contents (you, the programmer, establish the range).	Whatever is required by the contents.

Numeric Type Symbols and Examples

X% Integer (No decimal points. Can only include whole numbers between –32,768 and 32,767. Can make mathematical parts of your programs *run up to 25 times faster*.) See "DefInt."

Attaching the percent (%) symbol to a Variable forces it to include *no digits to the right of the decimal point*. In effect, there is no decimal point, and any fraction is stripped off.

X% = 1 / 20 results in X% becoming 0
X = 1 / 20 is .05

X% = 15 / 4 results in X% being 4 (it gets rounded off)
X = 15 / 4 makes X 3.75

X& Long Integer (No decimal points. Same as regular Integer but larger range. Can range from –2,147,483,648 to 2,147,483,647.)

Using & with a Variable strips off any fractional part, but the Variable is capable of calculating with large numbers.

X! Single-Precision Floating-Point (Huge range.)

X# Double-Precision Floating-Point (Same as Single-Precision Floating-Point but extremely huge range.)

X@ Currency (Ranges from –922,337,203,685,477.5808 to 922,337,203,685,477.5807) Has a *Fixed Point* rather than a Floating Point (although it does have a fractional component of four decimal points). The Currency numeric Variable type is superior in its accuracy. (*Accuracy* is not the same thing as *precision*. Someone could give you an incorrect, yet very precise, description of how to go about placing a call to London.)

X Variant (No type symbol; the default Variable type in Visual Basic. Adjusts itself as appropriate to the data assigned to it. Transforms the data—its contents—based on how it is being used in the program at the time. Memory space, potential ambiguity and program execution penalties balance the blessings this automation and versatility confer on the programmer. See "Cautions" under "Variant.")

Fixed-Length Versus Dynamic Text Variables
A text ("string") Variable can be either a specific, predefined size, or it can change its size to accommodate the different pieces of text you might assign to it. Each type has its advantages and uses.

You create a *fixed-length string* by describing its length in the process of dimensioning (defining) it. To make one that's 45 characters long:

```
Dim Name As String * 45
```

OR another way to create a fixed-length string. Here we've filled a string with 30 a's:

```
A$ = String$(30, a )
```

If you don't assign a length a string Variable will be *dynamic* and will expand and contract as necessary, depending on what data you assign to it while the program is running. These following two string Variables are not given a specific length, so they become *dynamic*, Variable-length strings:

```
Dim Name$
```

OR

```
Dim Name As String
```

If you are just going to use a text Variable within a single Event Procedure, Subroutine or Function (and you want it to be dynamic, an expandable length to fit the size of whatever text is assigned to it), you don't need to define, to Dim, the Variable. Just assign some text to it, and it's a string Variable:

```
A$ = Noisome
```

Defining a fixed-length string stabilizes it so that it will always be the same size (which is important when working with random-access files). See "Open."

Practical Advice: All Variables that you don't specifically define otherwise default to the Variant type in VB (see "Variant").

To define a Variable that will not be of this default type, attach a symbol to it: Mynum& makes the Variable named *mynum* into a Long Integer type.

OR, define Variable types by using the Public, Dim or Static commands:

```
Public mynum As Integer
Public mynum%
Dim mynum As Double
```

(When you define a Variable in this fashion, you can either use the type symbols or the As command to spell out the type.)

Unless you want to speed up a program (you often will), you can just ignore Variable types and let them default to "Variant" without worrying about it.

However, the computer can manipulate Integers arithmetically much more quickly than other Variable types. If you require math only within the range offered by Integers (–32,768 and 32,767), then use Integer (%) or Long Integer (&) Variables where possible (see "DefInt" for a quick way to define groups of Integers without using the symbols each time). Even something as simple as *adding* requires more computing when your numbers are of the default Floating-Point type.

Mostly, You Need Not Concern Yourself With Types: Most programmers use DefInt A–Z in the General Declarations sections of each Form and Module in a program to make Integer the default Variable type. Most of the things you'll be working with–unless you're Bill Gates working on his income tax or a rocket scientist plotting a precise trajectory–fall within the range of the Integer type. If you are calculating astronomic interest income or gravitational slingshots for interplanetary explorations, on the other hand, you might need to specifically define some of your Variables so they have a larger range or greater precision. Or, if you wish, take advantage of the new simplicity offered by the Variant type, which see.

See also   Appendix C; Arrays; DefType; Dim; Public; ReDim; Static; Type; Variant; VarType

VARIANT

Description

The "Variant" Variable type was first added to the Basic language with VB Version 3. And it made the *default* Variable type in VB. Default means that unless you deliberately specify a Variable's type, all Variables will be of the *Variant* type.

You can specify Variable types in three ways:

1. By attaching a Variable-type symbol to a Variable name—A$ or N!, for instance.

2. By using the As command with Global, Dim or Static—Dim A As String or Static N As Single. (You can also Dim with a type-symbol: Dim A$)

3. By using DefType, which see.

Traditionally, there have been two main types of Variables, numeric and text ("string"). Text Variables cannot be arithmetically *divided* by each other, for instance, because they are *characters*—letters of the alphabet or character-digits like "123." Clearly, it is meaningless to divide *Cadillac* by *marble*. If you tried to divide one text Variable by another like this:

```
A$ = 12
B$ = 3
Print A$ / B$
```

you would get a "Type Mismatch" error message because it makes no sense to try to divide letters of the alphabet or digit symbols mathematically. Text characters are just *graphic symbols* to the computer—important containers of information to humans; impossible to manipulate for arithmetic purposes to the computer. The Str$ and Val commands in the VB language "translate" numeric-to-text and text-to-numeric Variables, respectively. This translation is sometimes necessary. For example, if you use the InputBox Function to get the user to type in his age, the InputBox provides you with a *text* Variable: "35" rather than the number 35. If you want to use this data mathematically, to find out how much older the user is than someone else, you have to use the Val command to change the text into a numeric Variable.

Variants Allow You to Be Ambiguous About the Nature of Variables: When you don't use Dim or attach a Variable type symbol to a Variable's name, it defaults to a Variant type. Let's try an experiment. Are the following Variables, A and B, text or numeric types? They aren't Dimmed and they have no type symbol, so they are Variants. If these Variables are *Variants*, then *the context defines the type*. If your program tries to manipulate them mathematically, they will behave like numbers. If your program tries to Print them as text, they will act like text:

```
A = 12
B = 3
Print A
Print A & B
Print A + B
Print A / B
```

Results in
12
123
15
4

Notice that the first two times we Print, we are printing *text* digits (characters), not actual numbers. Then the Variables are used *as actual numbers* to arrive at arithmetic results: 15 and 4.

Variant Variables shift some of the burden of worrying about Variable types from the programmer to VB. Variants automatically *change type* depending on the context in which they are used. They are sensitive to the way you are using them at any given time (though there are exceptions—see "Cautions"). For example, if you use the & command, Variants will know you intend to combine "text" Variables as if you placed two pieces of text next to each other (123123), but if you use the + command, the *same Variables behave as if they are numeric,* and addition takes place:

```
Sub Form_Click ( )
    a = 123
    Print a & a
    Print a + a
End Sub
```

Results in
123123
246

Sensitive to Numeric Types, Too: This chameleon behavior is interesting and valuable (it makes the computer do more of the work). As we've seen, Variants can, at least in a limited way, cross the traditional border separating text from numeric data.

There is only one style of text Variable, but there are many kinds of numeric Variables. And a Variant can also sense which of the seven *numeric Variable types* you want to use, based on which kind of number you give it. For instance, an Integer type can only hold whole numbers up to 32,767. So, we'll test this by assigning a number that will be an Integer and another number that must be a *Long Integer* type (this Variable type can hold numbers up to 2,147,438, 647). Then we'll use the "VarType" command that reports to us how VB is handling these Variables—which type it thinks each is:

```
Sub Form_Click ( )
    a = 15          This could be an Integer
    b = 123456      This is too big; must be a Long Integer
    Print VarType(a)
    Print VarType(b)
End Sub
```

Results in   2
                 3

The VarTypes: The VarType Function tells you what kind of Variable is involved:

0	Empty
1	Null
2	Integer
3	Long Integer
4	Single
5	Double
6	Currency
7	Date
8	Text (String)
9	OLE Automation Object
10	Error
11	Boolean
12	Variant (Variant Array only)
13	Object (Not an OLE Automation object)
17	Byte
8192	Array

Before the Variant type was available, you would have had to explicitly Dim a Long Integer or add the Long Integer symbol to the Variable name. The important point here is that you need not specify that the number 123456 be of a Long Integer type (because it's too big to fit into a regular Integer type). VB's new Variant data type has the brains to understand this and makes the adjustment by itself.

(You might also take a look at the new TypeName Function which provides similar information to that provided by VarType, but TypeName returns a text description instead of the code returned by VarType.)

IsDate, IsEmpty, IsNumeric, IsNull: These commands can also tell you the status of a Variant Variable. To see if you can use a Variant type in a mathematical calculation:

```
A = N123
B = 456
If IsNumeric(A) Then Print A + 1
If IsNumeric(B) Then Print B + 1
```

Results in   457

Here the *N* in N123 prevents it from being seen as a number, and the IsNumeric Function reveals this fact. For more on this, see the entry on "Is Queries."

Warning—No Free Lunch: Variants aren't angels. When used in the same calculation with other Variable types (like Integers), Variants can cause ambiguity and errors. Variants use up more memory than any other Variable type (16 bytes when holding numbers, 22 bytes, plus the string, when holding text "string" Variables). They can also retard your program's speed (compared to the Integer type) because VB has to do extra work to analyze context. See "Cautions."

Used with   Variables (see the entry "Variables" or Appendix C)

Uses   • The most obvious use for this novel addition to computer languages is to relax and let Variants manipulate the various Variable types, more or less without you, the programmer, worrying much about types at all. However, see "Cautions."

• Arrays (which see) will also default now to the Variant type unless you specify otherwise. You can therefore *mix* text, numbers and date/time data within the same Array. This, too, is new to computer programming and, let's admit, would be pretty terrific if not for the penalty described in the first and second Cautions below.

• Arrays of other Arrays. In VB 4, you can now assign regular Arrays to a Variant Array. Not only are you thereby creating an "Array of Arrays" but, again, you can mix and match the data types of the various Arrays you assign to the Variant Array:

```
Private Sub Form_Load()
Show
Dim MyFirstArray(4) As String
For I = 1 To 4
   MyFirstArray(I) = Chr$(I + 64)  put a few letters into the array
Next I
Dim MySecondArray(4) As Integer
For I = 1 To 4
   MySecondArray(I) = I  put a few numbers into the array
Next I
Dim MyArrayOfArrays(2) As Variant
MyArrayOfArrays(1) = MyFirstArray()
MyArrayOfArrays(2) = MySecondArray()
For I = 1 To 4
   Print MyArrayOfArrays(1)(I);
   Print MyArrayOfArrays(2)(I)
Next I
End Sub
```

Notice the unique double set of parentheses used when accessing an Array of Arrays.

Cautions
• Variants work pretty much as you would hope, *as long as all the Variables involved in the situation are, in fact, Variants.* But if you try to mix in other types, try to get a Variant to absorb or interact with another type, the results aren't yet always predictable. Here are two examples where you might expect the Variant to behave more intelligently. Perhaps these problems will be fixed in the future, but at this time Variants, when mixed in with other Variable types in some situations can generate sometimes obscure errors.

The Variant can get mixed up about the + operator. In this example, the first + is correctly interpreted as an *arithmetic* plus. If the user responds 45 as his age, VB will print 50. However, if the user types in 45 to the second InputBox, VB prints 4545. In this case VB thinks that we're trying to concatenate (push together) two pieces of text.

```
Private Sub Form_Load( )
Show
x = InputBox( How old are you? )
Print  In five years, you ll be  ; x + 5
x = InputBox( How old are you? )
Print  When twice as old, you ll be  ; x + x
End Sub
```

The solution to this would be to reserve the + operator to *only* arithmetic activity and reserve the new & operator to only text activity. But VB doesn't yet do this. It can interpret + two ways and thus sometimes gets things wrong.

There are also some erroneous behaviors when working with the various numeric data types. A Variant's main job when handling a number is to use a Variable type large enough to hold the number. VB Help on Variants remarks that Variants can *promote* themselves to larger numeric types as necessary: "...if you assign an Integer to a Variant, subsequent operations treat the Variant as if it were an Integer. However, if an arithmetic operation is performed on a Variant containing a Byte, an Integer, a Long, or a Single, and the result exceeds the normal range for the original data type, the result is promoted within the Variant to the next larger data type. A Byte is promoted to an Integer, an Integer is promoted to a Long, and a Long and a Single are promoted to a Double."

For example, you would expect that exceeding the limit of the Integer (can hold only 32,767) would result in the Variant adjusting (promoting) itself to a long (can hold billions). Sometimes. But not always.

Of the three examples below, the first works (the Variant promotes itself from Integer to Long), the second causes an overflow error because the Variant stubbornly refuses to promote itself. The third is perhaps the strangest—it's logically identical to the first example, yet it too fails.

Example #1

```
Dim x As Variant
Dim y As Integer, z As Integer
y = 32760: z = 32760
x = y
x = x + y + z
Print x
```

Example # 2

```
Dim x As Variant
Dim y As Integer, z As Integer
y = 32760: z = 32760
x = y
x = y + z
Print x
```

Example #3

```
Dim x As Variant
Dim y As Integer, z As Integer
y = 32760: z = 32760
x = y
x = y + z + x
Print x
```

Moral: be careful when introducing other data types into situations where you're using a Variant. You can't assume that the Variant will react appropriately except when it's working with other Variants.

• Variants are an exciting new capability—let the language handle the Variable type details. VB can generally figure out a Variant Variable type on the fly based on the context and how you, the programmer, are using the Variable. If you are putting a number into a Caption Property, VB will sense this and transform it to a text "string" Variable type for that operation (so you can forget the Str$ command). But if you then use the same Variable to calculate some arithmetic result, the Variable is treated as a pure numeric Variable.

Good for the programmer, but bad for the user. Until computers are faster and have more memory, you should consider the cost of using the Variant type. Variants use up more memory than other Variable types. More important, Variants cause programs to execute more slowly than Integer (the swiftest of all types) and other Variable types (see "DefType"). The speed penalty isn't, however, too severe.

• Variants introduce some new Variable data types. The Null type is different from the Empty type (when using VarType to quiz a Variable about what type it is). Null means that it is deliberately empty:

```
X = 0
```

OR

```
X =
```

These commands create a zero number or a text Variable with nothing in it.

However, an "Empty" Variable, by contrast, *has not yet been used* in the program in *any* fashion (even to fill it with emptiness). An Empty Variable has not been declared either implicitly (V = 12) or explicitly (Dim V As Integer).

Null Is Special: The Null type has another unique quality you need to remember–it always makes an expression *False*. For example:

```
z = Null
If z = Null Then Print  Yes.
```

This will not print Yes. Null more or less *infects* ("propagates") an otherwise True expression, turning it False.

To find out if a Variable is of the Null type, use the following:

```
If IsNull(z) Then Print  Yes.
```

Note that the other predefined VB Constants *True* (–1) and *False* (0) do not "propagate" and can be freely used as if they were normal numbers:

```
z = True
If z = True Then Print  Yes ,
If z = –1 Then Print  Yes ,
If z Then Print  Yes ,
```

Results in Yes   Yes   Yes

Nulls are useful in some kinds of database programming (where "" empty text variables or zero numeric variables don't mean the same thing as Null).

• If you use the DefInt command, then all Variables in the Form or Module where you used DefInt will default to the Integer type. This speeds up your programs and many programmers use the technique. After using the DefInt A–Z command in the General Declarations section of a Form or Module, Variant would no longer be the default Variable type; Integer would be. In this situation, you can still declare specific Variables to be of the Variant type (Dim N As Variant), but any Variables that you merely use ("implicit declaration") instead of declaring will default, now, to Integers.

• In general, with the exceptions noted above, you can let VB worry about the Variants. However, if you try to perform math with Variants that hold text (such as "Word"), or at least text that cannot be translated by VB into a numeric Variable ("z12" cannot be translated; "12" can), then you'll generate an error. If you are unsure whether a Variant holds text, add this line:

```
If IsNumeric(A) And IsNumeric(B) Then X = A + B
```

Example This example program shows the first nine Variant VarTypes. Note that none of these Variables is Dimmed into a particular Variable type, nor is a

Variable type symbol (like $, %, &) appended to any Variable's name. Therefore, each Variable defaults to a Variant, and will configure itself according to the data that we assign to it. Note also that we didn't define, or even *use* the Variable *a*. Nothing was assigned to *a* so it's in the cleanest possible state—it is reported as an "Empty" VarType, meaning it's never been used in the program.

```
Sub Form_Click ( )
b = Null
c = 55
d = 123456
e! = .2
f = .222222222
g@ = 7777777777.7777
h = Now
i =  hello
Print VarType(a)
Print VarType(b)
Print VarType(c)
Print VarType(d)
Print VarType(e!)
Print VarType(f)
Print VarType(g@)
Print VarType(h)
Print VarType(i)
End Sub
```

See also   DefType; TypeName; Variables

See   Variant

With Version 4, Visual Basic has undergone a sea change. Much is new. One change is the absorption of Visual Basic for Applications (VBA) into VB. VBA originally appeared within Excel, as Excel's macro language.

While much of VBA will be familiar to the VB programmer, some of it is novel. Of necessity, in Excel many of VBA's commands are application-specific and, thus, don't appear in VB 4. In Excel, for instance, you can look under Help's "Programming with Visual Basic" and find a list of Objects. Most are useful only within Excel (Axis, WorkBook, etc.) and don't appear in VB 4. However, other VBA/Excel Objects are familiar to any VB programmer (TextBox, Option Button, etc.).

VBA didn't kill off Excel's familiar built-in macro language. Instead, it offered an alternative way to program macros for Excel. But this alternative is superior so we can predict that, over time, all the application-specific (and wildly incompatible) macro languages, like WordBasic and Access Basic, will atrophy. Most Microsoft products should eventually be able to communicate with each other using the same language—VBA.

VBA will likely also be built into Windows itself as well. Like DOS, with its batch language, we can expect Windows to incorporate a script language, but one that goes far beyond batch programming. The most obvious candidate is VB/VBA. A version of Visual Basic will probably become an essential part of the operating system itself.

Press F2 to look at VB's Object Browser. You'll notice listed under the heading "Libraries/Projects" that there is a separate library for VB and VBA. The primary categorization here is that VB includes all the Controls along with their Properties and Methods. The VBA library in includes commands not directly related to VB Controls—financial functions; date and time functions; file management commands; mathematical functions; string manipulation commands like UCase; and miscellaneous commands like Shell, DoEvents and so on.

From the VB programmer's point of view, it is essentially irrelevant that a command like Rnd is now considered part of the VBA library where the Refresh Method remains in the VB library. It's likewise of little import that certain commands new in VB 4 (For...Each, Collections, etc.) first appeared in VBA in Excel months ago.

General Changes
Here's a brief look at four examples of changes which first appeared in VBA/Excell and that are now qualities of VB 4 as well.

Text Variables Disappearing
Some changes that have occurred since VB 3.0 are subtle. For example, the distinction between the text ("string") Variable and numeric Variable is giving way to the new polymorphous Variant Variable. The major impact of this on VBA's diction is that the ancient string-manipulating commands like Left$ are dropping the string symbol, $, to become Left, Chr, Right, LCase, Ucase, Ltrim, Rtrim, Space, String and Trim. (Some of the commands in this group made this change in VB3.) Indeed, most any command which used to end with $ now has it stripped off (MsgBox, for instance). But the older name, MsgBox$ is still recognized.

For example, before

```
N$ =  Well, OK
Print N$
Print Trim$(N$)
```

Resulted in   Well, OK
                    Well, OK

Now we get the same result with:

```
N =  Well, OK
Print N
Print Trim(N)
```

Box Help

MsgBoxes and InputBoxes now have two additional, optional parameters: HelpFile and Context. HelpFile identifies the Help file to be available when the dialog box is visible. If you use the Helpfile parameter, you must also provide the Context parameter (the "Help context number" pointing to the correct topic in the Help file).

A Boolean Data Type

There's a new Boolean data type (which, odd as it might seem, uses two bytes in memory to store what could be stored in a single bit). However, it returns the words True or False when you Print it. For example

```
Dim n As Boolean
Print n
```

Results in   False

You can assign the older true/false values (–1 and 0, respectively) to a Boolean variable. It will accept them, but will always report with the words True or False. However, if you convert a Boolean into another data type, True does change to –1 and False to zero. For example:

```
Dim n As Boolean
Dim r As Integer
n = -1
Print n
Print TypeName(n)
r = n
Print r
```

Results in   True
                   Boolean
                   –1

And should you ever need to force another data type to compute as if it were Boolean, there's the new command CBool.

(Note that VB 4 now has single-byte data type, *Byte*. If you want to pull bytes in one by one off a disk file you no longer have to resort to defining a single-byte text string Variable—Dim C As String * 1— and then slow things up by translating each text variable as it comes in into computable numeric Variable types.)

Named Properties

VBA first introduced grouped Properties, using the new With...End With structure. This streamlines your programming and also makes reading the source code easier. Here's the old style:

```
Text1.Text =
Text1.Left = 12
Text1.Top = 100
Text1.FontBold = False
Text1.FontSize = 12
Text1.Width = Text2.Width
```

Now you can eliminate all those repetitive references to Text1:

```
With Text1
    Text =
    Left = 12
    Top = 100
    FontBold = False
    FontSize = 12
    Width = Text2.Width
End With
```

Whither VBA?

Visual Basic and VBA are cross-fertilizing. When a new edition of VBA comes out, it will include features that are not in the current version of Visual Basic. Likewise, each new version of Visual Basic will have capabilities not yet in existing implementations of VBA. VB is the world's most rapidly evolving language. Leap-frogging like this, VB and VBA should incorporate one another's facilities while adding new commands to the language they share. Ultimately, they are likely to converge into a single language.

VERTICAL SCROLL BAR
CONTROL

See Scroll Bars

VISIBLE

PROPERTY

Description Adjusting the Visible Property can make any Control or window (Form) appear or disappear on the screen. You can change this Property while designing your program or while the program is running.

You can also quiz the Visible Property while the program is running to find out whether a Control or window is currently visible.

Used with Everything except Timers—Forms, Check Boxes, Combo Boxes, Command Buttons, Directory, Drive and File List Boxes, Frames, Grids, Horizontal & Vertical Scroll Bars, Images, Labels, Lines, List Boxes, Menus, OLE, Option Buttons, Picture Boxes, Shapes and Text Boxes

Variables **Variable type:** Integer (Boolean)

While designing your program, you can set the Visible Property of a Form or Control to Off (it defaults to "True"):

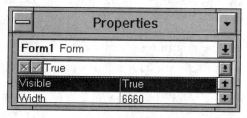

Figure V-3: You can make an object visible or invisible while designing your program. However, if you set the Visible Property to False, the object will still remain visible in the VB design environment until your program runs.

OR (to make something invisible while the program is running):

    Text1.Visible = False

OR (to find if something is currently visible while the program is running):

    V = Picture1.Visible
    If V = True Then...

OR (to use the Property within an "expression"; see "Variables"):

    If Picture1.Visible = True Then ...

Uses • Having Controls appear or disappear in an intelligent way while a program is running makes an impression on the user. If the user clicks on a Command Button captioned "OPTIONS," perhaps a whole row of other Command Buttons could suddenly appear, captioned Font Size, Type Style, Font Color, Bold, Italic. This approach is a pleasing alternative to menus. Visual Basic makes it easy to bring whole suites of Controls instantly into view and just as swiftly make them go away.

The Little Man Dances: When you are animating a Control, you can often achieve special effects by combining the Move command with manipulations of the Visible Property. For instance, if you want something to appear to fly off the top of the window, create a For...Next Loop. But, at the end, when the Control is nearly off the window, make it invisible. Or Move several similar icons, rotating their visibility, so a little man appears to dance across the window.

• Forms also have a Visible Property, although the Show and Hide commands do precisely the same thing as setting Visible to True or False.

If your program has several windows, several Forms, you can switch among them as appropriate by setting their Visible Properties to On and Off. Why not UnLoad them and free up some memory in the computer? You can UnLoad if you don't plan to use the Form again while the program runs. An opening title screen is a perfect candidate for UnLoading.

Forms actively used by a program should be left hidden, but not Un-Loaded, when they aren't currently needed. They will reappear more quickly via Form2.Visible = True than via Load. And they will retain any Variables, such as Static Variables, or changed Properties that the program may need to remember while it is running (see "Variables"). Loading in an UnLoaded Form while a program is running requires that all the visual elements (the bulk of a Form) be dragged in from the disk drive. This creates an unseemly, unprofessional *pause* while your program waits for the visuals to return to the computer's memory.

• If you are filling a Text Box with a lot of information, the Box can flicker on the screen. The solution is to make the Box invisible prior to filling it. It will fill faster that way and won't flicker. You can temporarily put a second empty Text Box in its place, so the user won't know that you made the real Box temporarily invisible.

Cautions   Use Show or Form1.Visible = True prior to any drawing or printing, unless the Form's AutoRedraw Property is set to On (True). Otherwise, things drawn or printed (with Circle, Line or PSet commands, or Print) will be erased before the Form eventually becomes visible.

Example

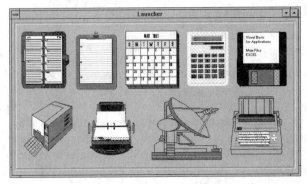

Figure V-4: When the user selects an icon, this launcher collapses into an icon and then starts running another application.

This program launches other programs. It includes a dramatic black curtain that falls quickly and smoothly down the entire window, just before the window collapses into an icon. As soon as the user clicks on one of the icons representing a calculator, disk drive, Clipboard, etc., all the icons become invisible and the window is rapidly covered in black.

First, put several Picture Boxes or Images on a Form to hold the icons. Then, in the Form_Load Event, type the following Subroutine. The icons we're using here are actually .WMF graphics supplied with the *Professional* version of VB. (For more information, see Appendix D.)

Set the Picture Box's Picture Properties in the Properties Window while designing your program.

```
Sub Form_Load ()

Show

drawframeon picture3, picture6, "inward", 250
drawframeon picture10, graphic1, "inward", 250

End Sub
```

(The DrawFrameOn Subroutine creates the frame around the pictures in this program. See "Line.")

Then, in each of the smaller Picture Box Click Events, type a variation of the following:

```
Sub Picture2_Click ()

collapse
x = Shell("C:\windows\playroom\smplcalc.exe", 1)

End Sub
```

Shell whatever programs you want. The Collapse Subroutine is "called" from each Picture Box (and described in the following paragraphs).

Create a New Module from the VB File Menu, and type this Subroutine into it:

```
Sub collapse ()

form1.picture1.visible = False
form1.picture2.visible = False
form1.picture3.visible = False
form1.picture4.visible = False
form1.picture5.visible = False
form1.picture6.visible = False
form1.picture7.visible = False
form1.picture8.visible = False
form1.picture9.visible = False

form1.scalemode = pixels
form1.drawwidth = 8
x = form1.scalewidth
y = form1.scaleheight
```

```
For i = 1 To y Step 80
    form1.Line (0, i)–(x, i)
Next i

form1.windowstate = 1

End Sub
```

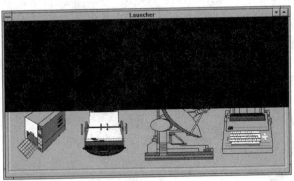

Figure V-5: The curtain's coming down a good transition between windows.

If you try this example, you'll be surprised at how fast and smooth the "falling black curtain" effect is. It's an intriguing way to shut down a program or to move from one window to another. You could also use it to briefly conceal a Form while you updated List Boxes or brought in new graphics with the LoadPicture command.

The Subroutine first goes down the list of Picture Boxes—making each one invisible. (An alternative approach would be to create a Control Array of Picture Boxes. See "Control Array.")

Then we change the ScaleMode to pixels, just for convenience, and make each line we're going to draw 8 pixels wide so we can quickly cover this large window. Then we find the interior width and height of the window. Finally, we draw enough lines, one after another, to cover the window completely. The commands inside the For...Next Loop say: "Draw a line on Form1 horizontally from 0 (far left) to x (the total width), and vertically at Variable *i* (*i* will keep getting lower as we keep cycling through the Loop)."

Then we make the window into an icon. The program then reverts to whichever Picture Box Click Event sent us to this Subroutine. At that point the desired application is launched.

Technical Note: A program-launcher like the one illustrated in this example may need to know if the user has closed (quit) one of the programs that was launched. In addition, knowing whether a program is currently running in Windows would be useful information. Both of these items of information can be accessed through the API (see Appendix A).

See also   Hide; Show

 EEKDAY

FUNCTION

Description
The Weekday command tells you the day of the week by giving you a number between 1 (Sunday) and 7 (Saturday).

Which week? Any week between January 1, 100, and December 31, 9999, using Visual Basic's built-in "serial number" representation of date+time. Visual Basic can provide or manipulate individual serial numbers for *every second* between those two dates. These serial numbers also include coded representations of all the minutes, hours, days, weekdays, months and years between 100 A.D. and 9999.

Weekday is much less frequently used for this purpose than the Format$ command, which see.

Used with
You can use Weekday with the Now Function to tell you the current weekday as registered by your computer's clock. You would set up an Array (which see) and then fill it with the names of the weekdays. To find which item in the Array to use, get the day-of-the-week number from Now by using the Weekday Function. However, as this example illustrates, this is more easily accomplished with the powerful Format$ Function, which can directly provide a day name if you use the Format$ dddd option:

```
Sub Form_Click ()

Static Daynames$(8)

Daynames$(1) = "Sunday"
Daynames$(2) = "Monday"
Daynames$(3) = "Tuesday"
Daynames$(4) = "Wednesday"
Daynames$(5) = "Thursday"
Daynames$(6) = "Friday"
Daynames$(7) = "Saturday"

x = Weekday(Now)
Print "Today is "; Daynames$(x)

y = Now
Print "Today is "; Format$(y, "dddd")

End Sub
```

Results in
Today is Friday
Today is Friday

The Now Function provides the serial number for the current date and time. Weekday extracts a number between 1 and 7, which represents the day of the week.

Variables To find the number representing the current day of the week as reported by your computer's built-in clock:

```
X = WeekDay(Now)
```

OR (to find the day of the week from a text representation of some past or future date):

```
T$ = "September 30, 1992"
x = Weekday(DateValue(T$))
Print T$; "falls on the"; x; "th day of the week."
```

Results in September 30, 1992 falls on the 4th day of the week.

Uses • Among the many options it offers, the flexible Format$ Function can display the name of the day of the week. (Using the dddd option can produce, for instance, *Thursday*.) You would likely use Format$ when you want to display a time or date.

Weekday does, though, have a specialized use: calendar or scheduler programs, where you need to *physically* show the days of the week on a grid. (See the Example below.) When you are creating a calendar, you need to know *on which "numerical" weekday the first of the month falls.* Weekday can give you that information.

Cautions The Format$ Function offers a flexible and powerful method of displaying or printing date and time information. Use Format$ to display the results of Visual Basic's many date+time Functions, in precisely the way you want them to appear.

Example We'll create a calendar that will display any month between January 100 A.D. and December 9999. The Weekday Function performs the important service of telling us which day of the week is the first day of a month. A calendar is a fixed grid with stationary labels for each day. The first day of the month slides around on this grid from month to month. We need to know the cell in which to place the number 1. Everything else follows from that. Each month can have seven possible "starting cells" within the calendar. Weekday is the only Function in Visual Basic that can directly supply us with this position.

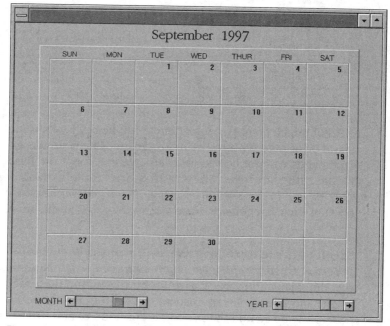

Figure W-1: This example is a fully functional calendar that covers nearly 100 centuries between 100 A.D. and 9999.

First, put two Horizontal Scroll Bars on a Form. Using the Properties Window, set HScroll1's Min Property to 1 and its Max Property to 12 (this bar will allow the user to adjust the month). HScroll2 adjusts the years, so set its Min to 100 and its Max to 9999—the range of years that Visual Basic's date calculations can embrace. Then set HScroll2's LargeChange Property to 10, so the user can click within the bar and move an entire decade if so desired.

In the General Declarations section of the Form, type the following:

```
Dim dt#
Dim startup
```

These two Variables are *declared* in the General Declarations section so you can use them anywhere in the entire Form. The Variable *dt#* will hold the "serial number" generated when we provide the positions of the Scroll Bar "tabs" (their lozenge-like, visible "thumbs," as they are called) to Date-Value. This serial number will uniquely identify the month and year the user wants to see displayed.

Scroll Bars' Change Events Are Hypersensitive: The Variable *startup* is used to prevent a triggering of the Scroll Bars' Change Events. Scroll Bars' Change Events are hypersensitive, as we'll see in the Form_Load Event.

In the Form_Load Event, type the following:

```
Sub Form_Load ()
Show
startup = 1
hscroll1.value = Month(Now)
startup = 0
hscroll2.value = Year(Now)
End Sub
```

All of the elements of our calendar are being drawn with the Line command or printed with the Print command. The products of both of these commands will not be visible unless we first force the Form itself to be visible with Show (see "Show"). Now we set the Variable *startup* to 1. As the first line in the HScroll1_Change Event, we put the following—to prevent the Change Event from being triggered at this time:

```
If startup Then Exit Sub
```

Scroll Bars are too Sensitive: *Setting any of their Properties while a program is running triggers their Change Events.* Note that we did not set the Min, Max and LargeChange Properties within the program—each would trigger the Change Event. Instead, we set them with the Properties Window while designing the program. This kind of auto-triggering—where changing something in VB triggers one of VB's Events—is the price we pay for the advantages that same behavior confers in other situations (see "Drive List Box" for an example of how you can put this domino effect to good use.)

All the drawing of the calendar takes place within the Change Event, and we don't want the calendar repeatedly drawn while we're just trying to get the Properties set up and the program started. Rapid, repeated triggering of drawing and printing will make the screen spasm and undulate as the computer struggles to redraw the same graphic elements over and over.

However, we *must* at least set the Value Properties of the Scroll Bars while the program is running. These Value Properties tell our program which month and year to display. And we want the program to start off displaying the current month and year. Obviously, we cannot know, when writing the program, what the current month will be when the program is run. So, to prevent triggering HScroll1's Event, we Exit Sub if the Variable *startup* contains 1.

We *do,* though, want the screen drawn once, so we let the adjustment to HScroll2's Value trigger its Change Event.

The Meat of This Program: Now to the main part of the program, the place where we create the entire calendar. Every time the user adjusts one of the Scroll Bars, we need to create a new calendar display. Type the following into the HScroll1_Change Event:

```
Sub hscroll1_change ()
```

```
If startup Then Exit Sub
Cls
drawframeon label1, label2, "outward", 1100
Line (800, 800)—(scalewidth − 800, scaleheight −800), QBColor(8), B
Line (814, 814)—(scalewidth − 786, scaleheight −786), QBColor(15), B
x = (scalewidth − 1600) / 7
For i = x + 800 To scalewidth − 800 Step x
    Line (i, 800)—(i, scaleheight − 800), QBColor(8)
Next i
For i = x + 814 To scalewidth − 786 Step x
    Line (i, 814)—(i, scaleheight − 786), QBColor(15)
Next i
y = (scaleheight − 1600) / 5
For i = y + 800 To scaleheight − 800 Step y
    Line (800, i)—(scalewidth − 800, i), QBColor(8)
Next i
For i = y + 814 To scaleheight − 786 Step y
    Line (814, i)—(scalewidth − 786, i), QBColor(15)
Next i
D$ = "SUN      MON       TUE       WED   "
D$ = D$ + "  THUR      FRI       SAT"
currenty = 600
currentx = 1100
fontbold = 0
    Print D$

fontsize = 9
currentx = hscroll1.left − 700: currenty = hscroll1.top + 25
    Print "MONTH"
currentx = hscroll2.left − 600: currenty = hscroll2.top + 25
    Print "YEAR"

hv = hscroll1.value
dt# = DateSerial(hscroll2.value, hscroll1.value, 1)
da = Day(Now)
mn = Month(Now)
ye = Year(Now)
dy = Day(dt#)
mo = Month(dt#)
yr = Year(dt#)
wd = Weekday(dt#)

fontsize = 16
fontname = "garamond"
moyr$ = Format$(dt#, "mmmm yyyy")
mtw = TextWidth(moyr$) / 2
currentx = (scalewidth / 2) − mtw
currenty = 50
```

```
            Print moyr$
        fontbold = −1
        fontsize = 7.8
        fontname = "helv"

        n = 1
        x = (scalewidth − 1600) / 7
        z = (scaleheight − 1600) / 5

        For y = 1350 To scaleheight − 800 Step z
            For i = x + 1200 To scalewidth − 400 Step x
                c = c + 1
                curdate# = DateSerial(yr, mo, n)
                    If da = n And mn = Month(curdate#) And ye = Year(curdate#)→
                    Then
                        currenty = y − 500
                        currentx = i − 700
                            If da = n And mn = Month(curdate#) Then
                                fontsize = 14
                                fontbold = 0
                                currentx = currentx − 150
                                Print n: n = n + 1
                                fontsize = 7.8
                                fontbold = −1
                        Else
                                Print n: n = n + 1
                        End If
                End If
            Next i
        Next y
        End Sub
```

   You should first invoke the Cls command, which clears the window, removing all the lines and printed dates and text. Printing and drawing can be superimposed. If you print one number on top of another number, you get a muddy combination of the two. We want to draw and print with a clean slate each time. Using Cls gives us a blank sheet.

   Next, we draw the embossed frame a short distance out from the calendar proper (see the DrawFrameOn Subroutine in the entry for the Line command to find out how this is done). The next two lines draw an "embossed" line around the outer perimeter of the calendar proper (see the Emboss Subroutine in "Line" for more on this technique).

   Because there are seven days in a week, we want to draw seven boxes horizontally. We find how wide the window will be (ScaleWidth) and then subtract 1,600 twips (see "ScaleMode") to give us an 800-twip border on each side of the window. We don't want the calendar filling up the entire window, so we provide this space. Then we find how wide each box should be by dividing the result by seven:

```
        x = (scalewidth − 1600) / 7
```

Now we can draw the vertical lines, moving over by *x* seven times. The following For...Next Loop does this:

```
For i = x + 800 To scalewidth − 800 Step x
    Line (i, 800)−(i, scaleheight − 800), QBColor(8)
Next i
```

Here the first line says: "Start 800 twips from the left side of the window (x + 800) and move to 800 twips from the right side, in increments of *x* (the width of each box)." Now the Variable *i* will provide the next horizontal position each time through this Loop.

Line (i, 800)–(i, scaleheight – 800), QBColor(8) actually draws the vertical lines. It says: "Start each line at the top at position *i* horizontally, and 800 twips down from the top of the window vertically. Then draw the line down straight (still *i* horizontally), and stop at the twip 800 up from the bottom of the window."

The ScaleHeight is the total interior height (minus frame) of the window, so subtracting 800 from that puts us 800 up from the bottom. Use QBColor(8), a dark gray.

Slightly, Almost Imperceptibly: The following three lines do exactly the same thing, but *slightly*, almost imperceptibly (only 14 twips), lower and to the right. And we use white as the color to create a line that appears to be etched into the background. This approach is more attractive than a simple single black line. Simple lines look printed; subtle offsets look sculpted. (See Figure W-1.)

```
For i = x + 814 To scalewidth − 786 Step x
    Line (i, 814)−(i, scaleheight − 786),  QBColor(15)
Next i
```

The next seven lines in the example do exactly the same thing that we've just done, except they draw the *horizontal* lines. We want five boxes going down, representing the weeks, so we divide the adjusted ScaleHeight by 5 and proceed to draw the etched lines across the screen.

Following that, we print the days of the week across the top of the calendar and label each Scroll Bar. When you are adjusting the CurrentX and CurrentY Properties to print Labels like this, *it's all a matter of trial and error.* Just keep guessing what might look right; then press F5 to run the program and see what happens. Mathematicians would call this approach *successive approximation*, but we call it *carving, hacking pieces out of the block of marble until it looks nice.* A signal advantage of a language like Visual Basic—and the reason that languages like Visual Basic will always be the most popular as long as people need to talk to computers—is that you can make a change in the program and almost instantly see the effect.

When to Use Simple Math for Visual Effects: Hacking is usually faster than trying to figure out a mathematical way to adjust the text on a Form. However, there are some valuable mathematical techniques, valuable because they are easily understood and easily applied to the job at hand. To center text, see "TextWidth." Likewise, you can effortlessly create various kinds of symmetries by ordinary mathematical manipulations of Controls (see "Top"). For example, you might want to use the Top or Left Property of a nearby Control to provide a location, as we've done with the Labels for the Scroll Bars. (This way, you have the added advantage of moving the Controls around to create a pleasing window without worrying about the associated Labels. The location of Labels becomes *relative* to the position of the Control they've been "attached to.")

Now we find the position of the tabs, the thumbs, inside the Scroll Bars. The Value Properties of the Scroll Bars tell us which month and year the user wants to see. And we use several of Visual Basic's date Functions to gather information we're going to need to print the day number within the calendar.

Knowing, at this point, which month and year the user wants to see, we can print the month and year at the top of the window.

At last we get to the technique that tells our program where to put the first digit, where to position each digit and when to stop printing digits (which day is the last day of this month?). What's more, we've decided that if the user has requested the *current* month, we want to highlight the current *day* by making it larger than the other digits.

The Variable *n* will hold the digits for each day of this month, so we start it off with a 1. Then we calculate the position onscreen where each day should be printed (*x*) and the vertical location of each row of days (the weeks) and put that into the Variable *z*.

Now we start two Loops, one inside the other. Many programmers find reading a program easier if structures are indented as we've done here. Indenting shows Loops and If...Then structures graphically:

```
For y = 1350 To scaleheight – 800 Step z
    For i = x + 1200 To scalewidth – 400 Step x
        c = c + 1
        curdate# = DateSerial(yr, mo, n)
            If c >= wd And Month(curdate#) = hv Then
                currenty = y – 500
                currentx = i – 700
                    If da = n And mn = Month(curdate#) Then
                        fontsize = 14
                        fontbold = 0
                        currentx = currentx – 150
                        Print n: n = n + 1
                        fontsize = 7.8
                        fontbold = –1
                    Else
                        Print n: n = n + 1
                    End If
            End If
    Next i
Next y
```

The outer Loop, governed by the *y* Variable, controls the position vertically as we move through the screen printing each number. Some of the specifications we used in these Loops–1,350, for instance–were a matter of trial-and-error, trying to find the most pleasing location for the digits within each box. Experimentation indicated that the first row of digits should be about 1,350 twips down from the top of the window, give or take a twip.

When we drew the boxes earlier, we provided a border of 800 twips between the calendar and the window. That's where we end. We already calculated *z* earlier: it's the vertical distance between each day's digits. Step will push us down that distance each of the five times through this outer Loop.

The inner Loop will happen seven times, once for each day of the week. Again, the distance between each row, the 1,200, was discovered by experimentation. Together, the two Loops will execute the commands inside the Loops a total of 35 times (7 days * 5 weeks). This is more than enough to fill a month of days.

Which Box Gets the First Digit? The Variable *c* will keep track of each time we go through the Loop. *C* will count from 1 to 35, so we know which box we're currently poised to print to. *C* helps us solve that nagging problem: which box should get the first digit? Which box holds the *first* day of this particular month?

The Variable *curdate#* tells us the serial number of the month and year the user wants to see. We'll use that in a minute.

Earlier in this Event we set up two Variables, *wd* and *hv*. *Wd* is the weekday of the first day in the month and year that the user has requested to see. *Wd* will be a number between 1 and 7, and will tell us in which box to start printing digits for this month:

```
dt# = DateSerial(hscroll2.value, hscroll1.value, 1)
wd = Weekday(dt#)
```

Note that we put a 1 as the "day" part of the DateSerial Function. The DateSerial (year, month, day) command then gives us the serial number of a particular date. We use that serial number to find which day of the week was day 1 of this month. (See "DateSerial" for more on how date+time serial numbers work in VB.)

When to Stop? The If structure here says that if we have gone through the Loop (repositioning ourselves each time in the next box) a number of times equal to or greater than the weekday, then go ahead and print the digits. This way, no digits are printed until we have moved over to the box that should display 1, the first day of this month.

```
If c >= wd And Month(curdate#) = hv Then
```

But how do we know when to *stop* printing digits? How do we know which is the *last* day of this month?

DateSerial provides the serial number of a particular day after you tell it three things: DateSerial (year, month, day). Earlier we memorized the user's requested year and month in the Variables *yr* and *mo*. We can now use DateSerial to find if we've crossed into the next month:

```
curdate# = DateSerial(yr, mo, n)
```

The *n* here is a Variable that is incremented *each time we print digits to show a day.* It always knows which digits we are about to print (1, 12, potentially *34* because we are going to touch down in each of this calendar's 35 boxes). We don't want to print *34* because that's an impossible date, nor do we want to print 30 if it's February. In other words, we need to know if, in this month, the digits contained in *n* are possible. When we provide the current year, month and *n* to DateSerial, we can then check the *month* in the *curdate#* Variable to see if it matches the month requested by the Value of the Scroll Bar. That's what Month(curdate#) = hv means.

The Variable *hv* contains the current value of HScroll1, the Scroll Bar that shows us what month the user is requesting. If the Scroll Bar's Value matches the month reported by *curdate#,* we are still in the requested month and should proceed to print the digits. If not, we have *moved past the requested month* and should not print anything. We should go down to the matching End If, ignoring all the commands in between that print digits. (Another approach to this last-day issue would be to set up an Array that contained the last day of each month. But you'd then have to calculate for leap year and leap centuries.)

A Matter of Experimentation and Taste: All that remains is to print the digits for each box. However, we want the current day's digits printed in a larger font if we're printing the current month according to the computer's clock. We position the "cursor" where we think it looks good inside the box. The 500 and 700 are a matter of experimentation and taste, offsetting the digits from the lines of the box.

Now we ask one more If...Then question. The Variable *da* was earlier given the Day (Now), so *da* contains 22 if this is the 22nd of the month, according to the computer's clock. If that date matches the Variable *n*—the one that always knows which day it is as we go through the month printing digits—then we should increase the FontSize and make a minor adjustment to CurrentX so these larger digits won't print on top of a line. Larger font sizes often look nicer when not bold, so we also turn FontBold off.

Oh, and one other thing—this requested month and year must be the month and year *now* before we will enlarge the font. The Variables *mn* and *ye* were earlier told the current month and year according to the computer. We compare them to the month and year the user is requesting to see. If all these tests pass, we enlarge the font. Otherwise (Else), we just print the digits normally. Note that we restore the font size and boldface after printing this one special day. Also note that this is where the Variable *n* is incremented. It always knows which digits we have just printed, and we use it to find out whether or not to enlarge a particular day's digits:

```
If da = n And mn = Month(curdate#) and ye = Year(curdate#) Then
                        fontsize = 14
                        fontbold = 0
                        currentx = currentx — 150
                        Print n: n = n + 1
                        fontsize = 7.8
                        fontbold = —1
                Else
                        Print n: n = n + 1
                End If
        End If
```

Optionally Printing the Calendar to the Printer: You can add a feature that prints the calendar, but you'll have to set the AutoRedraw Property of the Form to On (True), and this will slow down the program. Put an icon into a Picture Box to trigger printing and then type the following into the Picture's Click Event:

```
Sub Picture1_Click ()

picture1.visible = 0
hscroll1.visible = 0
hscroll2.visible = 0

PrintForm

picture1.visible = —1
hscroll1.visible = —1
hscroll2.visible = —1

End Sub
```

Here we hide the Controls and then print the Form.

See also   Date$; Day; Format$; Hour; Minute; Month; Now; Time$; Weekday; Year

WHILE... WEND

STATEMENT

Description   While...Wend is like the For...Next structure, except that it doesn't use a counter to decide how may times to *loop*, how many times to perform the commands within it. Instead, While...Wend keeps looping as long as the "condition" you give it remains True. This While...Wend will loop seven times because we are saying: While X does not equal 7, do the commands inside:

```
While X <> 7
    X = X + 1
    Print X,
Wend
```

Results in   1   2   3   4   5   6   7

While...Wend isn't used by most programmers. The Do...Loop structure, which see, offers you more options and is easier to use.

Why Is Do...Loop Usually Superior to While...Wend? With Do...Loop you can easily set up various interior tests and quit the Loop with Exit Do. In other words, you can create several conditions that will cause the computer to quit the Loop. Do...Loop is more flexible and more readable.

Also, you can place the condition to be tested for at the beginning or end of the Loop; this allows you to determine whether the Loop will stop immediately or repeat one more time after the condition has been satisfied.

Do...Loop also permits two kinds of conditional tests: *While* or *Until*. The distinction is often merely one of approach–sweep *until* the porch is clean vs. sweep *while* the porch is dirty. Nonetheless, putting the condition one way or the other can clarify the meaning of the condition.

While...Wend is a less powerful version of Do...Loop. While...Wend merely continues looping while a condition is True. WHILE X < 100: X = X + 1: ? X: WEND.

- While...Wend has no built-in Exit feature similar to Exit Do in a Do...Loop.
- While...Wend is limited to a test at the start of the Loop.
- While...Wend does not permit you to clarify things with a distinction between *while* and *until*.

Used with   Infrequently used, but can be employed for some of the simpler tasks performed by the more powerful Do...Loop structure

Variables   You provide the *condition* that must become True for the computer to leave the Loop, to stop repeatedly executing the commands between the While and the Wend. The condition can be any "expression" that the computer can evaluate as being True (–1) or False (0):

While S = 5

OR (B doesn't = 4): While B <> 4

OR (as long as the text Variable N$ still contains the text *Frank*):

While N$ = "Frank"

OR (expressions can be complex. The following says "Loop as long as the Variable A holds a larger number than the Variable C, and the Variable G is less than 3): While A > C And G < 3

(See "Variables" for more about expressions. See Appendix C for more on "operators," the symbols such as >, < and such commands as And and Or.)

Uses   • Use While...Wend when you want something done repeatedly but don't know the *number* of times you want it done. You know a *condition* that must be satisfied rather than the precise number of times the task should be performed. (For instance, continue to show a flashing arrow until the user clicks on a choice.)

However, the Do...Loop structure is superior for any situation in which you might be tempted to use While...Wend.

Cautions

• While...Wend can cause peculiar errors that are difficult to track down if you ever use GoSub or GoTo to move to a Label within the While...Wend.

• While...Wend, like If...Then and Do...Loop, takes control of the computer until the condition of the While...Wend is satisfied. In other words, using this Statement would prevent the user from using another Windows program, from mouse-clicking anything or from communicating with the computer in any fashion:

```
X = 12
While X = 12
    Cls
    Print X
Wend
```

Because X will never = 12 (nothing inside the Loop would ever allow X to become 12), the preceding lines become an "endless Loop" and lock up the computer. The only way to regain control is to press CTRL+BREAK.

One solution is to put an "interruption" within Loops, which keeps checking to see if any keys are being pressed, the mouse has been clicked or some other currently running program wants to do something:

```
While X = 12
Cls
    Print X
    Z = DoEvents()
Wend
```

(See "DoEvents.")

• The *condition* of a While...Wend must happen before the computer can leave the Loop or move past the Wend. The condition is the *A$ <> "AB-CDE"* in the following:

```
n = 64
While A$ <> "ABCDE"
    n = n + 1
    A$ = A$ + Chr$(n)
    Print A$
Wend
Print "DONE"
```

Results in

A
AB
ABC
ABCD
ABCDE
DONE

Here we said: "As long as A$ does not equal "ABCDE," keep looping." (See "Chr$" for the way that this command translates a number from built-in ANSI code into a text character.)

• While...Wend, like If...Then, can be *nested,* one structure placed inside another:

```
F = 11
While F > 2
    While X < 15
            Print Str$(X);
            X = X + 1
    Wend
    F = F − 1
    Print F;
Wend
```

Results in   0 1 2 3 4 5 6 7 8 9 10 11 12 13 14 10 9 8 7 6 5 4 3 2

You can nest as many While...Wends as you are capable of understanding.

Example   In this example, shown in Figure W-2, While waits until the arrow bumps into the stop sign.

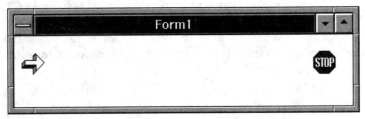

Figure W-2: The arrow zooms across the window until it hits the stop sign.
In other words, the arrow moves *While* it hasn't hit anything.

This animation is simple. First, put two Picture Boxes on a Form. Using the Properties Window, set their AutoSize Properties to On (True) and their BorderStyles to "none." Then type the following into the Form_Click Event:

```
Sub Form_Click ()

hitpoint = picture2.left

While picture1.left + picture1.width < hitpoint
    picture1.left = picture1.left + 25
Wend

For i = 1 To 10
    picture1.visible = x
    x = Not x
Next i

End Sub
```

Here we find the point of contact, the Left Property of the stop sign, and put that into a Variable called *hitpoint*. Now we use While, which says: "As long as the arrow's left side plus its width—in other words, the right side of the arrow—is less than the hitpoint, keep moving the arrow."

Visual Basic always keeps track of the position of Objects on a window, measuring by using twips (there are 1,440 twips per inch). Each Control has several Properties that tell you where it is at any given time. (See "ScaleMode" for more information.)

We move the arrow 25 twips at a time, resulting in a reasonably smooth and rapid glide across the window.

Finally, when the condition of the While...Wend structure is satisfied—when the arrow bumps into the stop sign and its right side is no longer "fewer twips" than the hitpoint—we flash the arrow on and off 10 times. Flashing makes it look like the arrow bumps into the sign. (See Appendix C for more about the Not command.)

See also   Do...Loop; For...Next; For Each

WIDTH
PROPERTY

Description   Using the Width Property you can find out the width of a Form or Control, or change it. Width is also a Property of the Printer "Object" and tells you the horizontal size of the paper. And Width is a Property of the Screen "Object" and can tell you the physical dimensions of the user's screen.

Used with   Forms, Check Boxes, Combo Boxes, Command Buttons, Directory, Drive and File List Boxes, Frames, Grids, Horizontal and Vertical Scroll Bars, Images, Labels, List Boxes, OLE, Option Buttons, Picture Boxes, Shapes, Text Boxes, the user's video screen and the printer

Variables   **Variable type:** Single

Usually, you establish the width of a Form or Control while designing your program—by dragging a side of the object with the mouse:

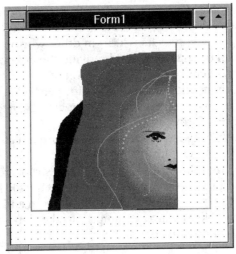

Figure W-3: You normally adjust the width of something by dragging its borders with the mouse. This picture needs to be a little wider to reveal the entire image.

OR (to make one Control the same width as another while the program is running): Picture2.Width = Picture1.Width

OR (to make a Control square): Picture2.Width = Picture2.Height

OR (to find how wide this Form is because the user might have stretched it): X = Form3.Width

OR (to change the width while the program is running): Text1.Width = 400

OR (to use a Variable to set the Width):

```
X = 400
Text1.Width = X
```

OR (to make a Control fill the entire window):

```
Picture1.Width = ScaleWidth
Picture1.Height = ScaleHeight
```

OR (to make a window fill the entire screen):

```
Width = Screen.Width
Height = Screen.Height
Left = 0
Top = 0
```

OR (to center the window within the screen):

```
Left = (Screen.Width − Width) / 2
Top = (Screen.Height − Height) / 2
```

OR (to make the window 80% the size of the screen and centered):

```
Width = .80 * Screen.Width
Height = .80 * Screen.Height
```

```
Left = (Screen.Width — Width) / 2
Top = (Screen.Height — Height) / 2
```

OR (to find where on the screen you should place an Object that you want to be flush against the right side of List1):

```
RightBeside = List1.Left + List1.Width
```

OR (to center asymmetrical objects, see the Example.)

Uses
- Restore related Controls to a uniform size (even if the user has changed them).

- Draw objects on the Form for a background, using Line or Circle. Width provides you with one of the dimensions of a Form within which you must do your drawing. (However, ScaleWidth, which see, is more useful in this situation.)

- Animate objects by enlarging them while the program is running. (Leave the Form and Picture Boxes' AutoRedraw Properties off (False); otherwise, you'll slow things up with this technique.)

- Open a "panel" of buttons. For example, you could adjust the size of a Form, uncovering a set of Controls based on some action the user took while the program was running. If the user clicks on a Command Button labeled "FORMAT," the Form could expand to reveal a set of optional graphics file formats (.BMP, .PCX, etc.). After the user makes his or her selection, the Form recedes to its normal size.

- Use the Width and Height Properties to change the design of the Form based on the resolution of the screen being used. A program designed for a 640x480 screen looks pinched on a screen with 1024x768 resolution. Perhaps you could give the user the option of resizing and repositioning the Controls to fit his or her particular screen.

Cautions
- If you're going to work in a visual environment, memorizing how X,Y coordinates are used to describe the size and location of Objects is valuable. X and Y together describe a particular point on the screen (or within a Form or printed page)—a point in the Object they are contained within.

X is always described first and then Y. *Y* looks like an arrow pointing down; that's how to remember that it represents the *vertical* position; X represents the horizontal.

While you're designing a program, VB provides you with two continually updated X,Y descriptions of the currently selected Object. The box on the far right always shows the X,Y *size* of an Object; its Width and Height. The box just to its left shows the X,Y *position* of the Object within its container (a Control is contained by a Form; a Form is contained by the monitor screen).

Position

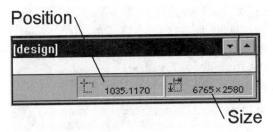

Size

Figure W-4: Few programmers use the position and size information on the far right of the Menu Bar.

Dragging Things Around: Nice as this constant report of size and position is in theory, few people design their programs with it. Dragging screen items around visually is so easy that the numbers displayed in VB's Design Bar are, mostly, ignored by programmers. The exception is when you need to insert those literal numbers into a program (see the Example).

You might have trouble getting the precise width you want; VB will seem to prefer certain widths and snap your Objects to those sizes. It's almost as if the widths are being rounded off by some secret, hidden agent. In fact, this resizing happens because the "Align to Grid" feature is turned on in the Options Menu. If you want finer control over Height (or Top, Left and Width) turn off "Align to Grid." You can also change the size of the Grid itself.

Width, like Top, Left and Height, can be measured in different ways. The *ScaleMode* Property of the current Form determines which "mode" is in effect for the Objects on that Form. ScaleMode (which see) defaults to a measurement called *twips*— there are 1,440 per inch (an inch measured on paper, not necessarily an inch of your screen space). This is why you see measurements in the *hundreds (of twips)* for Objects whose Widths don't seem all *that* big.

You can change the ScaleMode to:

Points (description of text size used by book designers and printers; there are 72 points per inch)

Pixels (the tiny dots of light, virtually invisible on today's monitors)

Characters (120 twips wide, 240 twips high)

Inches

Millimeters

Centimeters

Or you can define your own coordinate system by directly changing the ScaleHeight plus ScaleWidth or the ScaleLeft plus ScaleTop Properties.

The Strange Behavior of Windows's "Granularity": In the Windows Control Panel (Desktop item), you can adjust the *Granularity* option, which decides how closely Objects on the screen can get to each other and by what degrees Objects can be expanded or shrunk. You cannot adjust this option for your programs' users, but you might ask them to set it to zero. If Granularity is anything other than zero, the positioning and sizing commands in your Visual Basic programs will be relatively crude.

Objects will *jump* in increments of Granularity * 16 pixels when their Left, Top, Height or Width Properties are adjusted. Although 16 pixels might not seem like much movement, graphics are smoother when Granularity is set to zero, eliminating the bumpy motion (at some small cost in speed).

The *ScaleWidth* Property is similar to the Width Property but is often more useful. ScaleWidth (which see) tells you the *internal* dimensions of a Form or the paper in the printer—minus any border, margin or Title Bar. This is the measurement you most often need when formatting or positioning Objects within a window (Form) or on the printer.

Example

Figure W-5: The interior graphic is not square. We'll use the Width Property (among others) to determine the shape of the window itself so that the window will symmetrically enclose the image.

There are a variety of uses for the Width Property, usually in combination with the Height Property. We'll illustrate several of them here. Our goal is to center an asymmetrical picture, but to make the border, the size of the Form, match that asymmetry so there is an even border all around the graphic. We also want to draw a frame around the window and another frame around the picture. Finally, we are going to print the word "Windows" in a decreasing FontSize as a design behind the Picture.

First, put a Picture Box on a Form. Set the Form's BorderStyle Property to 0 (none). Then type the following into the Form_Load Event:

```
Sub Form_Load ()
x = 6972 + 2000
y = 5412 + 2000

width = x
height = y

backcolor = QBColor(4)
forecolor = QBColor(0)

left = (Screen.width − width) / 2
top = (Screen.height − height) / 2

Picture1.left = (scalewidth − Picture1.width) / 2
Picture1.top = (scaleheight − Picture1.height) / 2

Show

fontsize = 76
fontname = "garamond"
fontbold = 0
tx$ = "WINDOWS"

For i = 1 To 7
    fontsize = fontsize − i * 1.4
        If i = 7 Then
            currenty = currenty − 250
        ElseIf i = 1 Then
            currenty = currenty − 400
        Else
            currenty = currenty − (i * 40)
        End If

    currentx = currentx − 400
    Print tx$; tx$; tx$; tx$
Next i

drawwidth = 10
forecolor = QBColor(0)

Line (20, 20)−(x − 20, y − 20), , B

drawwidth = 8
forecolor = QBColor(15)

Line (Picture1.left, Picture1.top)−(Picture1.left + Picture1.width, →
    Picture1.top + Picture1.height), , B
End Sub
```

We will be printing and drawing on this window, so we must use the
Show command; otherwise, the two frames and the word *Windows* will
not be visible (unless you make AutoRedraw True). Often Show is the first
command in a Form_Load Event. Here, though, we want to center the
window on the screen, so we delay Show until that has been accomplished. This way, the window doesn't require redrawing and looks clean-
er; it just appears in the center of the monitor.

First we assign the Width and Height of the picture to the Variables *x* and *y*; we found those figures on the right side of the VB Design Bar when the picture was clicked. We add 2,000 to each dimension, so the background will make an even border all around the picture. Then we set the window's Width and Height to the dimensions we just calculated.

Next, we make the window's backcolor red and the forecolor–the color that will be used for printing or drawing lines–white.

By using Screen.Width and Screen.Height Properties, we center the entire window within the computer screen. The Width of the screen minus the Width of the picture divided by two gives us the correct horizontal position to center the window. Next, we perform the same calculations to center the picture within the window using ScaleWidth (a Form's Width minus any border). After all this repositioning and resizing activity has been performed behind the scenes, we finally Show the results to the user.

There Was No Inductive Reasoning Here: Now we prepare to print the word *Windows*. By decreasing the FontSize by a factor of 1.4 * i each time through this For...Next Loop, we achieve a pleasing effect. No *inductive reasoning* lead to choosing a reduction value of 1.4. in the sense that we sat back and said, "I believe a reduction of 1.4 times the value of i will look right." Instead, when working with programs like this, you can just keep adjusting the factors until you get a result–or a nice surprise–that pleases you.

Note that we didn't like the effect this 1.4 had on the first and last printed text. There's nothing wrong with putting an If...Then adjustment into your program to fine-tune things and get the result you're after. Try removing the two If...Thens to see how the background becomes less attractive.

Recall that the Variables *x* and *y* contained the Left and Top positions of the window. To draw our black outer frame, we set the DrawWidth to a size that looks good and then draw a box around the window. To draw a box, you provide the upper left and lower right positions, and VB figures out the rest. But we want the frame slightly inside the window's actual physical dimensions, so we add 20 at the top left and subtract 20 at the bottom right (see "Line" for more on Boxes and Frames).

Similarly, we draw a white border around the Picture itself with the following:

```
Line (Picture1.left, Picture1.top)–(Picture1.left + Picture1.width, →
    Picture1.top + Picture1.height), , B
```

Here the first position is simply the top and left of the picture. The lower right is calculated by adding its Left Property to its Width, and its Top Property to its Height.

See also   Height; Left; ScaleWidth; TextWidth

WIDTH

STATEMENT

Description Width # is a holdover from earlier versions of the Basic language and is not used in Visual Basic programming. It determines where a line of text should *wrap*, where it should go down to the next line as if the user had pressed the ENTER key while typing.

On old monochrome computer screens, Width # was sometimes used to switch between the default 80-character line and the other option, a 40-character line where the characters were wider. Switching line width was frequently a vain effort to create some visual excitement in a computer program before Windows came along with its powerful and versatile graphic capabilities.

Width # was also used to specify line breaks for data in disk files, so the data would "wrap" as desired when pulled in from a disk file and displayed. However, VB doesn't allow Width # to be used for displays, only files. And VB permits this command only because it might be a command it needs to recognize within a program written in an earlier version of Basic. VB includes it for compatibility. If a programmer wants to reuse an old program by importing it into VB, any Width # commands used with disk files will work.

In Visual Basic, you can use Width # only when you are writing data to an opened disk file. It specifies how many characters should be saved into the file before a CR/LF code (see "Chr$") is added, signifying that a new line should be created when the text is displayed.

The various VB file-access commands, such as Print #, write text to a file *exactly as it would appear onscreen,* including the formatting information such as where a line break should occur. The codes for a line break are included in the text sent to the file. Print # saves a literal "image" of screen text, including any tabs, line breaks, etc. And the companion "file-reading" commands—Input$, Input # and Line Input—efficiently handle formatting when they receive information from a disk file.

Used with No longer used, but recognized by VB if Width # is used for writing text to disk files, thus making old Basic programs compatible with Visual Basic.

Variables To announce that each line is 80 characters long, so a line break code (CR/LF, see "Chr$") should be inserted after 80 text characters have been sent to an opened file:

```
Open "C:\TEST" For OutPut As #1
Width #1, 80
```

Uses None

Cautions
- In earlier versions of Basic, you could use Width # to describe the length of text lines on a computer's screen or printer, or where to put line break codes into a disk file. VB allows Width # to be used only with disk files.
- Unlike all the other file-access commands in Visual Basic, the # in Width #3, 60 is not optional.
- Width # can specify that lines of text can range from 1 to 255 in length as they are being saved to disk. You can have the computer insert a code for a line break after each text character, after each 255th character or any size line in between.
- If you provide Width # with a 0 (Width #1, 0) as the desired length, it assumes that no line breaks should be inserted into the characters that are being sent to the disk file. This 0 is the default for Width # if you specify no number (Width #1).
- Width # is not to be confused with the valuable Width Property (which see).

See also   Open; Print #

See   Menu

Description   With WindowState you can change or find the current status of a window (Form).

Windows have three "states," and the WindowState Property will contain one of these numbers at any given time:

   0   Normal. The window neither takes up the entire screen nor is shrunk down to an icon. This setting is the default. The "normal" size starts out as the size you made the Form when you were designing your program. The exact size of a window, though, depends on whether or not the user adjusted its size with the mouse or your program has adjusted it by changing its Width and Height Properties. You can always find the size by having your program check the Width and Height Properties.

1 Minimized. Iconized, turned into an icon.

2 Maximized. Fills the entire screen.

Used with   Forms (windows) only

Variables   **Variable type:** Integer (enumerated)

(To find whether the user has turned the window into an icon and, if so, restore it to normal while your program is running):

```
If WindowState = 1 Then WindowState = 0
```

OR (to make the window fill the screen when the program starts running, or if this isn't the Startup Form, to make it fill the screen when it's Loaded by the program):

```
Sub Form_Load
    WindowState = 2
End Sub
```

OR (to use the Properties Window while designing the program to make the window fill the screen when Loaded:

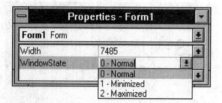

Figure W-6: You can select one of the three WindowStates from the Properties Window.

Uses   • Find out if the user has iconized or maximized a window, and restore it to normal size if appropriate.

• Have the program react to current conditions by automatically iconizing itself. For example, if the user decides to use the Notepad by clicking on a Command Button you have set up for that purpose (see "Shell"), you might want to minimize your program temporarily to make the Notepad the primary object on the screen. Then display the Notepad.

• It is generally considered Windows protocol for your programs to start off in a "normal" WindowState. This way, the user neither has to bring them to life by clicking on your icon nor reduce them to see other windows that might be onscreen at the time.

Going Down to DOS: You could make a VB program that sends you to DOS when it is double-clicked. You would want to use WindowState to keep this icon *always an icon.* Double-clicking would expand the icon to a normal window otherwise. In this case, the icon *is* the program, and you never want to use it as anything other than an onscreen button that you can use to Shell (which see) to DOS.

Here's a program that you can put on your desktop to Shell to DOS (get back to Windows by typing EXIT). In the Form_Load Event, type the following:

```
Sub Form_Load ()
    windowstate = 1
End Sub
```

Then, in the Form_Resize Event, type the following:

```
Sub Form_Resize ()
    If windowstate <> 1 Then
        windowstate = 1
        Ival = Shell("Command.com", 2)
    End If
End Sub
```

Then just make an .EXE file out of this program (from the File Menu) and add it to your other Windows icons by selecting New in the *Windows Program Manager*'s File Menu.

WindowState = 1 makes a window into an icon. We do that when this program starts running by putting the command into the Form_Load Event. Then, because double-clicking would automatically cause the window to grow to normal size onscreen, we prevent that by checking the WindowState during the Form_Resize Event. If the WindowState is anything other than iconized (<> 1), we force it to stay an icon. Then we Shell to DOS, using DOS's "program name"– Command.Com.

• **Shrink It Down and Then Pop It Back Up:** WindowState is also useful if your program is going into a lengthy computing process like sorting a huge Array. You could shrink the program into an icon, finish the job and then pop the window back to normal after the job was finished. Changing the Form's Caption Property while the Form is iconized might also be nice—feeding a report on the progress of the job: 10%, 11%, 12% and so on. This text would print beneath the icon on the screen so the user could see how things were going while the program was no longer visible as a normal window.

• If you create a reminder program, it could pop up from an icon when it's time to go to a meeting, for instance, and then display that message in a normal window.

Cautions • A Form's BorderStyle can affect how much control a user will have over the WindowState. The "None" (0) and "Fixed Double" (3) BorderStyles do not provide a way for the user to adjust the WindowState (see "BorderStyle"). However, as is usually the case in Visual Basic (and Windows, for that matter), many are the paths to paradise. You can program around this restriction; you can add custom WindowState Buttons to a borderless window. See the Example.

• Making a window *modal* (see "Show") will also prevent the user from iconizing or maximizing a window.

Ordinarily, though, the Windows 3.1 user will find two arrows in the upper right corner of any Form in a "normal" (0) WindowState. The down arrow will iconize the window; the up arrow will maximize it:

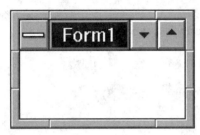

Figure W-7: The "normal" Windows 3.1 WindowState the most common style offers the user the options of minimizing, maximizing and resizing it. It also has a Control Menu icon on the upper left corner.

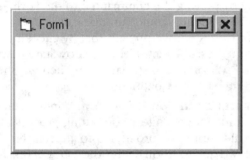

Figure W-8: The Windows 95 buttons differ: an icon appears in place of the Control Menu Button and on the right are changed Minimize, Maximize Buttons and a new instant Close X.

• An icon has no arrows, but when clicked or double-clicked it can be restored to normal size.

• If a window has been maximized to fill the entire screen, it also has two arrows in the upper right corner. The down arrow will, in most programs, turn the window into an icon; the double arrows will return it to "normal" size:

Figure W-9: A maximized window (one that fills the entire screen) has a double-arrow button, which will return the window to its "normal" size.

Figure W-10: The new Windows 95 Minimize and Normal Buttons.

Example   If you want to control the WindowState directly from within your program, you can set up your own system, using your own graphics for the corner arrows, etc. In this example, we are using a window with no border and, consequently, no WindowState arrow symbols appear automatically in the upper right corner. To permit the user to iconize the window or fill the screen with it, we attach our own tabs.

Figure W-11: We're adding custom window-sizing icons to this otherwise borderless window. A Form whose WindowState has been set to "Borderless" normally has no resizing icons for user manipulation.

First, put three Picture Boxes on a Form. Set the Form's BorderStyle to "none" (0) from the Properties Window. It doesn't matter where you put the Picture Boxes—the program will adjust their positions—but set their AutoSize Properties to On (True) and their BorderStyle Properties to none (False).

For the up and down arrows, we used two icons that come with Visual Basic: "ARW01DN.ICO" and "ARW01UP.ICO." We put the down arrow into Picture1 and the up arrow into Picture2. Double-arrows, which appear only on a maximized window, will restore the window to "normal" size if clicked. We followed the style of the VB icons to create a new icon:

Figure W-12: The design of the double-arrow icon.

We'll create a general-purpose Subroutine (see "Sub") that will be used to create a "normal" window in two instances: when the program is first run and when the user clicks on the double arrow to return a maximized window to "normal."

In the General Declarations section of the Form, type the following:

```
Sub makenormal ()

picture2.visible = True
picture3.visible = False

picture2.top = False
picture2.left = scalewidth — picture2.width

picture1.top = False
picture1.left = picture2.left — picture1.width + 20
End Sub
```

Here we make Picture2 visible (it's the up-arrow icon and will be made invisible when the user maximizes the window). Then we make the double-arrow invisible because it doesn't appear on a "normal" window.

Because It Looks Tighter: Now we position the up arrow at the top far right of the Form. To put Picture2 up against the right side of the Form, we subtract its own width from the ScaleWidth of the Form (the Form's interior width minus any border). Then we position Picture1, the down arrow, just to the left of Picture2. And we move them a little closer together by adding 20, just because that spacing looks tighter onscreen.

We want the window to appear normal-sized when the program first starts running, so type the following into the Form_Load Event:

```
Sub form_load ()
    makenormal
End Sub
```

All that's left to do is to make the Picture Box icons react when the user clicks on one of them. Picture1 is the down arrow and will turn the window into an icon. Type the following into Picture1's Click Event:

```
Sub Picture1_Click ()
    windowstate = 1
End Sub
```

Picture2 is the up arrow that will fill the screen with the window, requiring that we make the double-arrow icon visible and make the up arrow invisible:

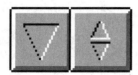

Figure W-13: Our custom-designed window-sizing icon at normal size.

```
Sub Picture2_Click ()

windowstate = 2

picture2.visible = False

picture3.top = False
picture3.left = scalewidth – picture3.width
picture1.top = False
picture1.left = picture3.left – picture1.width + 20

picture3.visible = True
End Sub
```

First, we maximize the window and make the up arrow invisible. Then we adjust the positions of Picture3 and Picture1, just as we did for Pictures 1 and 2 in the *Makenormal* Subroutine described previously. Finally, we make the double-arrow icon visible.

For the double-arrow icon, we just make the window normal-sized and use our Subroutine to place the appropriate icons on the window:

```
Sub Picture3_Click ()
    windowstate = 0
    makenormal
End Sub
```

That's it. We need not do anything about an iconized window. Visual Basic automatically detects when a user clicks on an icon—and restores the window to "normal" or maximized, depending on which of those states the window was in when it was turned into an icon.

See also   BorderState; Height; ScaleHeight; ScaleWidth; Show; Width

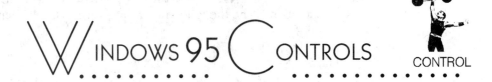

WINDOWS 95 CONTROLS

CONTROL

Description   VB4 includes 8 special new Controls designed for compatibility with new user-interface features found in the Windows 95 operating system. From the top left in Figure W-14 they are: TabStrip, ToolBar, StatusBar, Progress-Bar, TreeView, ImageList, ListView and Slider.

If you don't see these Controls on your VB4 Toolbox, click on the Tools menu and select Custom Controls. Then select Microsoft Windows Common Controls. If that option isn't available to you, you don't have the COMCTL32.OCX file installed in your Windows\System directory, or you're using a version of VB that doesn't support these Windows 95 32-bit Controls. (For information on the new Rich Text Control, see "Text Box.")

Figure W-14: The eight new Windows 95 Controls.

Some of these Controls supplement already existing Controls. For example, you can create a Toolbar—albeit a limited one—using the traditional Picture Box (see "Align"). But just as Windows 95 is more than merely a minor redesign of Windows 3.1, these new Controls are for the most part more than merely minor enhancements. As a way of organizing user-options, the TabStrip (called a "Property Sheet" in Windows 95 parlance) is a considerable improvement over anything VB offered for this purpose before—namely menus or separate Forms.

So let's take a look at each new Control and explore its uses and any unusual Properties or Methods that it features.

ImageList and ListView

The ImageList is an array that holds graphics. It's used in combination with other Controls to supply them with images they can display. These images can be either icon (.ICO) or regular graphics (.BMP or .WMF), but they should all be of the same size. You can use an ImageList with any Control that has a Picture Property, or also with several new Controls—the List-View, ToolBar, TabStrip, and TreeView Controls. You attach an ImageList (Microsoft calls this "binding" or "associating") to a susceptible Control. This is done by setting the ListView Control's Icons or SmallIcons Properties to specify the particular ImageList Control or Controls that you want bound. For the TreeView, TabStrip, and Toolbar Controls, you set their ImageList Property to an ImageList Control. This can be done in the Properties Window during design time, or dynamically while a program is running via a line like:

```
ListView1.Icons = ImageList1
```

as shown in the example below.

Then the ImageList is available to that Control; it can provide graphics to it. In this example, we'll demonstrate how to fill a ListView Control with graphics from an ImageList. (For another example, see TreeView below.)

When you place an ImageList on a Form, it's not visible when the program runs. Like a Timer, it provides an invisible service.

Put an ImageList on a Form, then click on the Custom entry in the Properties Window. Here you'll find the property sheet where you can add graphics to the ImageList. First you can select the size of the icons, or choose Bitmap. Then, on the second tab, you actually specify the images themselves. When you click on Insert Picture, the new graphic will appear to the right of the currently selected slot. If you insert more than the seven visible slots, a Horizontal Scroll Bar will appear, so you can scroll through them.

Note that the array of graphics in an ImageList *begins with an index of 1*. Also note that you can't just use the AddItem Method (as you would to insert to items into a traditional ListBox, for example). No, now you're expected to use the Object-oriented approach involving first creating a ListItem object, then setting it to refer to your ListView.ListItems "Collection" and announcing that the action you're about to take is *Add*. For more on this new syntax (Dim-Set-Add), see "Collections."

Now put a ListView Control on your Form, then type this:

```
Private Sub Form_Load()
    Dim AnItem As ListItem
    ListView1.View = 0  large icons
    ListView1.Icons = ImageList1
    For i = 1 To 8
Set AnItem = ListView1.ListItems.Add()
AnItem.Icon = i
```

```
AnItem.TEXT = ListItem  & i
    Next i
End Sub
```

Cautions • You can mix icons in with .BMP graphics, but remember the rule that all images in an ImageList must be of the same size. Most graphics programs (like CorelDRAW or PaintShop) have a resizing facility with which you can make all your images the same size.

Example • You can use the ImageList's Overlay Method to combine two images. To the above, add an Image Control, then add this line just above "End Sub":

```
Set Image1.picture = ImageList1.Overlay(5, 7)
```

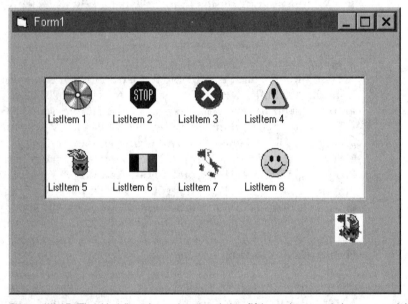

Figure W-15: The ListView in action, and the fifth and seventh icons combined in an Image Control.

When using the Overlay or Draw methods, you can set the ImageList's MaskColor Property to determine how the two images will combine. If you want a particular zone within an image to be transparent during the combine, set the MaskColor to that color.

An ImageList is a natural tool to produce simple animations. To try it, put a Timer, an ImageList and an Image Control on a Form. With the ImageList selected, double-click on the Custom entry in the Properties window and insert two similar icons to the pictures contained in the Control. (There are sets of icons supplied with VB that are designed to be animated, such as the mailbox with its flag up and down set in the ICONS\MAIL subdirectory.)

Now, put this into the program:

```
Private Sub Form_Load()
Timer1.Interval = 1000
End Sub
Private Sub Timer1_Timer()
Static t As Integer
If t = 1 Then
t = 2
Else
t = 1
End If
Set Image1.picture = ImageList1.ListImages(t).picture
End Sub
```

TreeView

The new TreeView Control is useful when you want to present the user with an organized, hierarchical list–something like an outline. In appearance, it's rather like a menu, with items subordinated to more general categories. However, the TreeView permits you considerable freedom to design the look–including associating an ImageList with it to add graphics to the text items.

To try it out, put an ImageList and a TreeView on a Form. Following the procedure described above (click on "Custom" in the Properties Window), add five icons to the ImageList. Then click on "Custom" for the TreeView. You'll see the property sheet shown in Figure W-16.

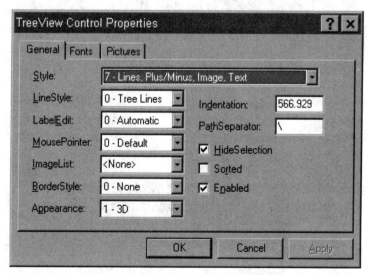

Figure W-16: Here s where you can adjust several Properties of a TreeList Control.

We'll leave most of the Properties set to their defaults, but do click on ImageList entry and set it to ImageList1. Now the ImageList is "bound" to our TreeView Control. You manipulate the TreeView by utilizing its Nodes Collection. As with other Collections, you can Add, Clear, Remove and, in the case of the TreeView, use the EnsureVisible Method (which expands a collapsed tree, or moves to a particular location within a tree so large that a Scroll Bar has to be used). For more on Collections and how to manage them, see "Collections." Now type this into the Form Load Event:

```
Private Sub Form_Load()
Dim nod As Node
    Set nod = TreeView1.Nodes.Add(, ,  Rt ,  Areas of Experise , 5)
    Set nod = TreeView1.Nodes.Add( Rt , tvwChild, ,  Bob (Fuels) , 1)
    Set nod = TreeView1.Nodes.Add( Rt , tvwChild, ,  Janice Prello (Trans-
port) , 2)
    Set nod = TreeView1.Nodes.Add( Rt , tvwChild, ,  Sandy (Space Explora-
tion) , 3)
    Set nod = TreeView1.Nodes.Add( Rt , tvwChild, ,  Joy DellaRobia (Main-
tenance) , 4)
nod.EnsureVisible
End Sub
```

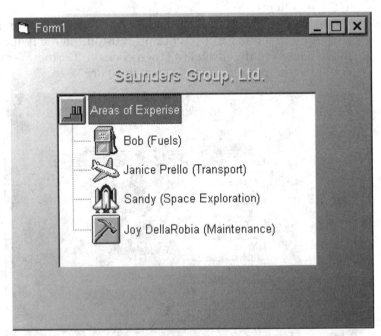

Figure W-17: A TreeView of a company s various managers complete with graphics showing their expertise.

The syntax when adding items to a TreeView is:

```
Objectname.Add(relative, relationship, key, text, image, selectedimage)
```

The *relative* argument is optional, but if you want to subordinate items down the list, you'll need to use it. It can be either the "key" or the index number of another Node object. Just how you want this node to appear in relation to that other Node object is defined by the *relationship* argument. Notice that in the example above, the top item (Areas of Expertise) omits both the relative and relationship arguments because it is a primary node—with no relationship to superior nodes. (But the commas are required nonetheless in the argument list.)

Relationship is also optional. It describes how the Node object will be positioned relative to the other Node object specified in the *relative* argument. There are these several possible relationships:

tvwFirst	First Sibling.
tvwLast	Last Sibling.
tvwNext	Next sibling.
tvwPrevious	Previous sibling.
tvwChild	Child.

Siblings are essentially equal (like brothers and sisters), whereas Child objects are subordinated.

If, for instance, you change this line to tvwFirst, this Node will appear at the top of the list:

```
Set nod = TreeView1.Nodes.Add( Rt , tvwFirst, , Janice Prello (Transport) , 2)
```

The *key* argument is optional and provides a way of using text to refer to an item in a Collection, rather than using an index number. (See "Collections.")

The *text* argument is required. It appears as the label for that Node when the user views it.

The *image* and *selectedimage* arguments are optional. They refer to the index number of a particular graphic contained within an associated ImageList Control. *Selectedimage* can refer to a separate graphic if you want the icon or picture to change when the user clicks on a Node, or the Node is otherwise selected.

Cautions

• Note that each time you add a Node object to a Nodes collection, that particular Node is automatically given an index number. You can use this as a way to manipulate the nodes while the program is running. Here we'll cause the third Node to disappear:

```
Private Sub Form_Click()
TreeView1.Nodes.Remove (3)
End Sub
```

StatusBar, ProgressBar & Slider

You can imitate the features of a StatusBar and ProgressBar using SSPanel Controls, and you can accomplish something similar to the Slider with a Scroll Bar, but these new Controls are Windows 95-style and also don't require that you resort to any special tricks or workarounds.

The StatusBar

The StatusBar is that optional information zone on the bottom of many windows (including Explorer in Windows 95). It contains information about the window's contents or other useful data—the name or number of files or selected files, the status of keys like Caps Lock, the date and time, or whatever seems likely to be of value to the user.

The current graphic is saved on disk as SOLUTION.BMP

Figure W-18: A Single-Panel style is quite simple to construct and manipulate.

You can choose between two Style Properties, the Single-panel style as shown in Figure W-18, and the default multiple panels. When you use the Single-panel style, you can use the SimpleText Property to provide the information that the user will see:

```
Private Sub Form_Load()
fnam$ = SOLUTION.BMP
StatusBar1.SimpleText = The current graphic is saved on disk as   & fnam$
End Sub
```

The Multiple Panels style, however, permits as many as 16 different zones, each individually adjustable and programmable, and each of which can contain either text or graphics.

Figure W-19: A StatusBar need not be short and you can include as many as 16 zones.

Put a StatusBar Control on a Form. Then in the Properties Window click on the Custom Property item and choose Panels. If your text seems crowded, or a graphic doesn't fill its panel, adjust the Minimum Width. With text panels, the Center alignment option is usually preferable to the default Left. The Style option includes several built-in displays, including time and date as well as the status (dark or grayed type) of toggle keys like Caps Lock and INS). The Bevel option makes the panel appear to extrude, and you could use it to draw attention to some information. However, no known Windows 95 application extrudes a Status Bar panel, so you might want to avoid that temptation.

The Autosize option has three possible settings. The default None or 0 keeps the panel at the size of its Width Property, no matter what the contents. The new Spring option (1) resizes the panel (along with any other panels set to "Spring") if the user makes the window larger or smaller. However, the panel will never be made narrower than its MinWidth Property (the value you specify in the Minimum Width box in the Panels page of the StatusBar property sheet, or establish by specifying the Min-Width Property in the program itself). The final Autosize option (2) causes the panel to adjust its size to fit whatever graphic or text you put into it. If this setting doesn't seem to work with text, make sure that the Minimum Width Property is set quite low—to 100, for example.

The ProgressBar
The ProgressBar is similar to the older VB Gauge Control—it displays how much of a particular task is completed. For example, if your program is loading 10 large files from disk, you could show the user the progress of the job by setting the ProgressBar's Min Property to 0 and its Max to 10. Then, after each file is loaded, increase the Value Property by 1.

Note that a ProgressBar is filled with blocks, from left to right, as a way of displaying the amount of the task that's been completed at any given time. The number of blocks depends on how high and how wide you make the ProgressBar on your Form. Also, unlike the Gauge Control which moves continuously, the ProgressBar advances block by block, discontinuously. Nonetheless, even though they're less precise indicators, ProgressBars are used about as often as Gauge-type Controls in Windows applications.

To try one out, put a Timer and a ProgressBar on a Form. Then type this:

```
Private Sub Form_Load()
Timer1.Interval = 500
End Sub
Private Sub Timer1_Timer()
Static counter As Integer
counter = counter + 1
ProgressBar1.VALUE = counter
End Sub
```

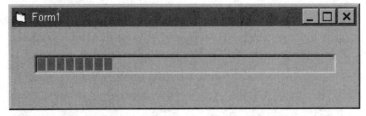

Figure W-20: The ProgressBar in action.

Note that if you click on the Custom option in the Properties Window of a ProgressBar, you'll see an option for Pictures. At the time of this writing, this option does nothing. Likewise, the BackColor and ForeColor Properties do not change anything at this time.

The Slider

Just as the ProgressBar is a kind of discontinuous Gauge, the Slider is a discontinuous Scroll Bar. The user moves it in discrete steps.

Put a Label and a Slider on a Form. Then type this into the Slider's Scroll Event:

```
Private Sub Slider1_Scroll()
Label1.Caption = Slider1.VALUE
End Sub
```

You might be tempted to change the Label's caption by using the Click Event, but then nothing would happen if the user moved the Slider with the arrow keys or the PgUp and PgDown keys. Sliders can be moved by mouse clicking, dragging or via the keyboard.

Use a Slider instead of a Scroll Bar if the activity the Slider will control or reflect takes place in discrete steps. For example, if you allow the user to adjust the font size between 8, 11, 14, and 22, you can set a Slider's Min Property to 0 and its Max to 3, thereby creating 4 states.

Like a ScrollBar, the Slider has LargeChange (triggered by clicking anywhere within the Slider or by pressing PgUp or PgDn) and SmallChange (triggered by using the arrow keys) Properties. The TickFrequency Property determines how many tick marks will appear. This interacts with the range—the difference between the Min and Max Properties. For example, if you set Min to 10 and Max to 50 and TickFrequency to 10, there will be 5 tick marks. Note that the user, however, can still press the arrow keys to move in smaller steps—the number of steps is governed by the SmallChange Property.

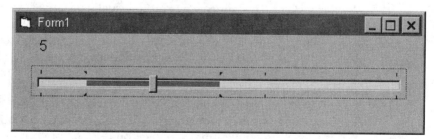

Figure W-21: The Slider can also display a range.

If you set the Slider's SelectRange Property to True, you can then establish a visible range within the Slider, determined by the SelStart and SelLength Properties. This could be useful if, for instance, you decided that a font size of 8 would be unreadable in the current context. You could then set the range from 11 to 22, with 8 left out of the range.

TabStrip

Among the most useful of the new Windows 95 Controls is the TabStrip. It organizes information in a way similar to a cardfile of 3x5 cards, with divider tabs to indicate logical divisions.

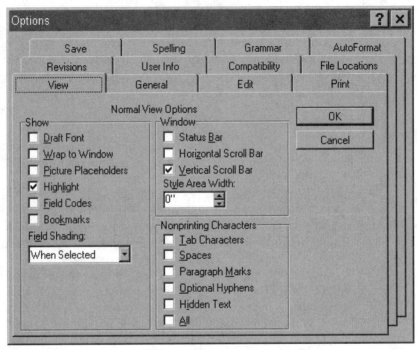

Figure W-22: The trend in Windows 95 applications is to display options with this tabbed 3x5 card box metaphor.

Windows 95 calls a set of TabStrips, like those shown in Figure W-22, a *property sheet*. This approach is more visually intuitive and easier to use than the traditional menu approach to changing and application's options.

A TabStrip Control is a visual rather than physical organizer. In other words, you must use Picture Boxes or Frames to contain Option Buttons, Check Boxes, List Boxes or whatever—for each page that you're presenting to the user. The best approach is to create a Control Array (which see) of your container Control, switching them on an off (with their Visible Property, or as we'll demonstrate, by using ZOrder). Let's build an example.

Put a TabStrip on a Form, then click on the Custom option in the Properties Window. Click on the "Tabs" tab and insert four new tabs.

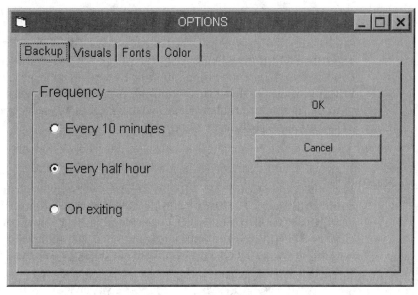

Figure W-23: Note that the Option Buttons are *contained* within a Frame Control. The Command Buttons, however, are actually on the background Form.

Now put a Frame onto the Form and set its Index Property to 0, thereby creating a Control Array. Now add three addition Frames as part of the Contol Array. Put the Frames in the same location on the TabStrip, and use the Bring To Front and Send To Back options on the VB Edit menu to add appropriate Controls to each one. In each Frame, customize it as you wish with whatever Controls you need. Then use the Edit Menu|Bring To Front to position the correct Frame on top.

Now, in the TabStrip's Click Event, type this:

```
Private Sub TabStrip1_Click()
Frame1(TabStrip1.SelectedItem.Index - 1).ZOrder 0
End Sub
```

ZOrder 0 means put the particular Frame on top of the others visually. Which Frame is described by the index number within parentheses, calculated by finding out the Index Property of the currently selected (clicked on) Tab, then subtracting one. The Index of most new Controls starts with 1 and counts up. Unfortunately, Control Arrays start with zero and count up. That's why you have to subtract 1. Aside from this, you have to remember when designing your Frame Controls to match the tabs that tab 1 will go with Frame1(0), tab 2 will display Frame1(1) and so on.

A TabStrip can also be set via its Style Property to resemble a row of Command Buttons (with no visible client area—though that location for a container still exists). However, we've never seen this style used in any Windows application.

If, for some reason, you need to get the measurements of the client area (the zone within which you put your container PictureBox or Frame or other container Control)—query the ClientLeft, ClientTop, ClientHeight, and ClientWidth Properties. You, the programmer, establish the actual size of a TabStrip Control by dragging it or by setting its Top, Left, Height, and Width Properties. However, when the program is run, VB can provide you with the usable internal area if you ask for those Client-Properties (x = TabStrip1.ClientLeft, for example).

ToolBar

Arguably, the ToolBar Control vies with the RichTextBox (see "TextBox") as the best new Control in VB4. In previous versions of Visual Basic, you could construct a ToolBar by setting a Picture Box's Align Property. However, the new ToolBar Control is a considerably better approach.

You add captions or images to buttons in a way similar to the technique for adding them to TreeView Controls, as described above. Here's the syntax for Buttons:

```
objectname.Add(index, key, caption, style, image)
```

The *index* is optional. It describes the position within the row of buttons where you want to insert a button. If you leave it out, the button will be put at the far end.

Key is also optional. It's a text string that can be used to identify that particular button object. Most people would just use the index number automatically assigned to any collection.

The *caption* is an optional text description of the button that will be placed at the bottom of the button. This is not generally done on Windows 95 button bars. Instead, you should probably use ToolTips that will appear if the user hovers his or her mouse over the button. Leave the ToolBar ShowTips Property True (its default) and then enter a tip for each button in the Custom Property, Buttons Tab, ToolTip Text text box.

Style is optional. The possible styles are (you can use either the Constant name or the value):

Constant	Value	Description
tbrDefault	0	(Default) The typical pushbutton style.
tbrCheck	1	Like a CheckBox. It doesn't *look* like a CheckBox, but does behave like one. When the user clicks on it, the button stays depressed until the user clicks on it again or, if it's in a "ButtonGroup" (value 2), until the user clicks on another button in its group. This style of button is often used in a formatting toolbar to indicate, for example, whether the current text includes italics or boldface. (See Figure W-25 below.)

tbrButtonGroup	2	Like OptionButton Controls, when the user clicks on one in the group, it remains down until another is pressed.
tbrCheckGroup	3	A combination of CheckBox and OptionButton: it stays checked until another button is clicked.
tbrSeparator	4	This is a spacer—just a blank space to allow you or the user to group buttons on a ToolBar in logical sets. It's always 8 pixels wide.
tbrPlaceholder	5	The same as a spacer, but its width can be adjusted. Note that a Placeholder can be enlarged and act as a container for other Controls—such as a ListBox. (See Figure W-25 below.)

The Image argument is also optional. An integer (or key if you've given the graphics each a text key) that identifies a particular graphic within an ImageList Control that's been "associated" with the ToolBar (either by setting it within the Custom Property item, or assigning the name of the ImageList to the Toolbar's ImageList Property).

Example   Put an ImageList and a ToolBar on a Form. Fill the ImageList with graphics or icons, as described above under "ImageList." Then, click on Custom in the Property Window for the ToolBar and set ImageList1 as the associated ImageList. Insert as many buttons as you want, and add ToolTips as well. Then, in the Form Load Event, type this:

```
Private Sub Form_Load()
For i = 1 To 3
Toolbar1.Buttons(i).Image = i
Next i
For i = 5 To 8
Toolbar1.Buttons(i).Image = i - 1
Next i
End Sub
```

Note that our Button(4) is a placeholder style, so we had to create two loops here to fill the images onto the buttons from the ImageList Control. And notice that –1; when we skipped button 4, we got out of phase with the ImageList indices.

Figure W-24: A ToolBar Control is highly flexible, yet easy to program.

Reacting

What do you do if the user clicks on a button while the program is running? Each button is supposed to trigger some behavior. Here's how you can respond:

```
Private Sub Toolbar1_ButtonClick(ByVal Button As Button)
Select Case Button.Index
    Case 1
MsgBox  Button 1 was clicked
    Case 2
MsgBox  Button 2 was clicked
    Case 3
MsgBox  Button 3 was clicked
End Select
End Sub
```

Of course, in the real world, you'd replace those message boxes with some suitable programming, something your program would *do* in response to the user's selection of that button.

Specialized Properties

There are four *additional* Properties of the ToolBar Control, Properties that are peculiar and specialized. The AllowCustomize Property, which is True by *default*, allows the user to hold down the Shift key and drag buttons to new positions, or off the ToolBar entirely. Likewise, if they double-click on the ToolBar, a dialog box pops up, allowing them to remove or rearrange the buttons, or add new buttons.

The Wrapable Property determines whether, if the user makes the Form narrow by dragging it, the button bar will adjust itself into two (or more) rows of buttons. It also defaults to True.

The Align Property allows you to place the ToolBar along the right or left sides of the Form, or at the bottom. It defaults to the typical position—along the top.

The MixedState Property is, to put it mildly, highly specialized. It's used to indicate that selected text, for example, contains both boldface and normal text. In other words, the selection is "mixed." When this happens, you can then supply a new graphic for that button to signal to the user that there is this mixed state. (Word for Windows, though, simply ignores mixed states—leaving the button extruded as normal when normal plus boldface text is selected.)

Figure W-25: A typical formatting toolbar features drop-down lists, Check style buttons, and can also display mixed states like the grayed B below indicating that the current selection includes, but isn t exclusively, boldface characters.

To see how MixedState works, try this example. Put a ToolBar, an Image-List and a Rich Text Box on a Form. Put a couple of graphics into the ImageList that indicate boldface and italics. And add a third graphic that will indicate that the current selection is a mixture of bold and normal text (see Figure W-26).

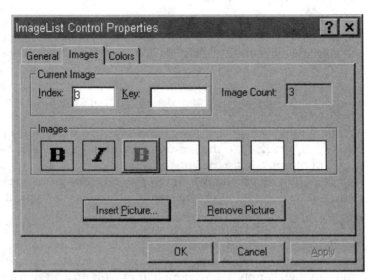

Figure W-26: Adding three graphics in the (Custom Property Window option) to the ImageList to represent bold, italics and *mixed* (bold+normal or bold+italics).

Click on Custom in the Properties Window for the ToolBar, set its Image-List Property to ImageList1, and add a couple of buttons (set their Style to "Check").

Put the images into the buttons with this programming in Form Load:

```
Private Sub Form_Load()
For i = 1 To 2
Toolbar1.Buttons(i).Image = i
Next i
End Sub
```

Then, in the ButtonClick Event of the ToolBar, type this to let the user adjust the text formatting between normal, boldface and italics:

```
Private Sub Toolbar1_ButtonClick(ByVal Button As Button)
static togglebold as boolean
static toggleital as boolean
Select Case Button.Index
Case 1
        togglebold = not togglebold
    RichTextBox1.SelBold = togglebold
Case 2
        toggleital = not toggleital
    RichTextBox1.SelItalic = toggleital
End Select
End Sub
```

And in the RichTextBox's SelChange Event, type this to change the look of the boldface button from normal to "mixed:"

```
Private Sub RichTextBox1_SelChange()
If IsNull(RichTextBox1.SelBold) Then  mixed
        Toolbar1.Buttons(1).MixedState = True
        Toolbar1.Buttons(1).Image = 3
Else
        Toolbar1.Buttons(1).MixedState = False
        Toolbar1.Buttons(1).Image = 1
End If
```

WITH...ENDWITH   STATEMENT

Description   Allows you to change or query a group of Properties at the same time, without having to repeat the name of the object which owns those Properties. Rather useful.

Used With   Objects, and Forms and Controls (Forms and Controls are Objects)

Variables   To first change, then query (and Print), some Properties of a Command Button Named Command1:

```
Private Sub Form_Load( )
Show
With Command1
    .Caption =  Never
    .Top = 300
End With
With Command1
 Print .Caption
End With

End Sub
```

Uses   Simplify your programming and make it more readable.

Cautions   • You have to use a dot (.) in front of each Property name.

You can nest one With structure within another, if the Properties are themselves subsets of the outer structure. Right now, the Font Property contains its own subsidiary set of Properties, so

```
With Form1
    .Left = 50
    .Caption =  My Own Form
    With .Font
            .Italic = True
    End With
End With
```

Example   The new VB4 With...End With structure can streamline your programming and also make reading the source code easier. If you want to adjust several Properties of a Text Box, here's the old style:

```
Text1.Text =
Text1.Left = 12
Text1.Top = 100
Text1.FontBold = False
Text1.FontSize = 12
Text1.Width = Text2.Width
```

Now you can eliminate all those repetitive references to Text1:

```
With Text1
    .Text =
    .Left = 12
    .Top = 100
    .FontBold = False
    .FontSize = 12
    .Width = Text2.Width
End With
```

See Also   Named Parameters

PROPERTY

Description   WordWrap determines how a Caption in a Label will appear onscreen. WordWrap interacts with the AutoSize Property. AutoSize should be turned on (set to True; it defaults to False) for WordWrap to work right.

When off (False), WordWrap stretches the width of a Label to whatever message you've placed into its Caption Property. The Label will expand horizontally to the longest line in your Caption and vertically to the number of lines if you create several lines by inserting the CHR$(13) command (see "Caption"). In other words, everything shows. This is similar to the way an Image Control can arrange itself to embrace whatever graphic you load into it.

If you turn WordWrap on (True), the Label will not grow wider than you originally drew it; rather, it will force your Caption into the number of lines necessary to fit within the width of the Label you designed. The Label does, however, grow in height to embrace the entire text of the Caption. This is similar to the automatic word-wrapping that occurs in a Text Box with its MultiLine Property turned on.

Used with   Labels only

Variables

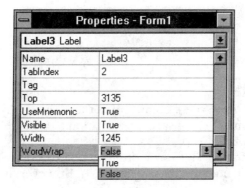

Figure W-27: You must adjust WordWrap in the Properties Window.

Uses • Conditions change while a program is running, and you cannot always know when designing a program what the data will be or what the user might do. For these reasons, some Controls should be permitted to grow and stretch as the program runs–so they don't clip or cut off some text or image.

Use WordWrap–in conjunction with the Alignment and AutoSize Properties–to prevent text in a Label from being hidden from view because its Font-Size or the number of words are too much for the original size of the Label.

Cautions Set AutoSize to "True"; otherwise, WordWrap won't work correctly. If AutoSize is "False" and your Label has little vertical space (height), the text will be clipped no matter how you set WordWrap.

Example

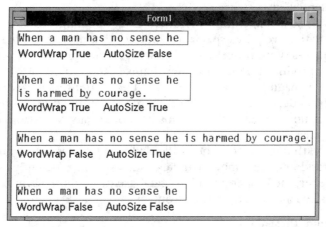

Figure W-28: The four possible variations of WordWrap with AutoSize. The original size of the Label is shown in the first and fourth examples.

See also Alignment; AutoSize; Caption; Label

RITE #

STATEMENT

Description   Programmers used the Write # command in the early days of computing for database applications. Write # saved information to a disk file as discrete chunks of a fixed size.

You can use Write # in VB to save ordinary text to a disk file that was Opened in the sequential mode (see "Input$"). However, in practice, Write # is now almost completely ignored by programmers.

The alternative commands *Print #* or *Put* are preferred because Print # saves *exactly* what would be seen onscreen when using the Print command to display text. Print # is to a disk file what the Print command is to the screen or printer. In other words, Print # saves the formatting—the tabs, line breaks, etc.—to the disk file (an important feature that Write # lacks). When you later read back text saved by Print #, the text can be printed to the screen *as an exact image of how it looked before it was saved to the disk* by Print #. And Put is useful with database applications.

Write #, by contrast, is a remnant, debris still in the language but no longer of any real use. Programmers used Write #, like its companion command, Input #, to save data to disk as individual records of a fixed size. For database applications, this approach speeded up access to the data and made replacing or updating an individual record more efficient than "sequential" data storage.

Database management—the organizing, updating, storage and retrieval of information—requires special techniques that differ from the way you store and access word processing text. With a word processor, your primary goal is to reproduce text in a manner that is faithful to the user's formatting. When managing a database, you will likely offer features such as lists sorted by ZIP Code. (Operations that require the information can be divided into smaller units of data and can thus be more easily sorted and otherwise manipulated.)

Now, though, a technique called *random-access* files is built into Basic. The random-access mode handles database jobs efficiently (see "Open"). However, the best approach to database programming by far is the VB database language. See "Data Control."

Used with   Nothing, these days

Variables   Open "FILENAME" For Output As 1:
Write #1, A$

OR (to combine numbers and text Variables):
Write #1, A$, N, Tax

Uses   No longer used. Print # or Put are used instead.

Cautions   • When Write # stores data in a file, it puts literal quotation marks characters around text Variables, stores numbers *as text* and inserts commas to separate the stored items of data (in the same places that you insert commas). See the Example below.

Perhaps most peculiar of all—when the last piece of data has been written to the file, Write # inserts a "new line" code (the numbers 13 and 10), three space character codes (32) and the number 16 (which has no meaning) at the end of the file.

In other words, if you have used Write #, the final six bytes of the file will contain these numbers, appended to whatever actual text data was saved:

```
13 10 32 32 32 16
```

• Write # can be used only with files Opened in the sequential-access mode. You must use either the For Output or For Append commands to use this file mode. (See "Open.")

• You can provide any number of text or numeric Variables or "expressions" for Write # to put into a file (see "Variables"). You must separate the Variables by commas if there is more than one Variable used after a Write # command. If you use Write # with no Variables (with nothing following it), a "new line" character code will be inserted into the file. This is analogous to using the Print command with nothing following it to move down a line when displaying text onscreen:

```
Print "Here"
Print
Print
Print "Two lines down."
```

Results in   Here

Two lines down.

Example
```
Sub Form_Click ()

Open "C:\TESTFILE" For Output As 1

X$ = "Send this message to the file."
Y = 12
Z = 14

Write #1, X$, Y, Z

Close 1

End Sub
```

Results in   "Send this message to the file.", 12, 14

(Note that the text "string" Variable was enclosed by quotation marks when saved to the disk file by Write #. Also, commas were inserted between the numbers, and, oddly, *the numbers were saved as text digits, not as true numbers.*)

See also   Input #; Print #; Put

See "Open" for a general discussion of random-mode file-handling techniques. See "Input$" for an overview of the sequential file technique.

EAR

FUNCTION

Description   The Year command tells you the year, any year between 100 A.D. and 9999, using Visual Basic's built-in "serial number" representation of date+time. Visual Basic can provide or manipulate individual serial numbers for *every second* between those years. These serial numbers also include coded representations of all the seconds, minutes, hours, days and months between 100 and 9999.

Used with   The Year command is often used with the Now command, to tell you the current year as registered by your computer's clock:

```
Print Year(Now)
```

The Now Function provides the serial number for the current date and time. The Year command extracts the "year" portion of that serial number.

OR (if you are building a calendar or similar application, you can create your own serial numbers using Visual Basic's various built-in date- and time-manipulation commands—see "DateSerial." Then you can provide that serial number to Year to find out which calendar year the user wants to see):

```
Sub Form_Click ()
    X$ = InputBox$("Please enter a date using the format Nov 24, 1990")
    CurYr# = DateValue(X$)
    Print "The year is:"; Year(CurYr#)
End Sub
```

Results in   The year is: 1996
(if the user entered something like Jan. 5, 1996)

Variables   X = Year(Now)

Uses   • Create calendar programs (see the Example under "Weekday").

• Create "to-do" scheduler programs, keeping track of appointments by comparing Year(Now), Month(Now) and Day(Now) against the information stored when the user first identified a particular appointment. (For an example of the elements of a scheduler program, see "Month.")

You can create a serial number for a date by using either the DateSerial or DateValue Function. (See the example above.)

• Date-stamp data. Add the serial number to information stored by your program (data the user types, a picture the user creates, whatever is being saved to disk for future use). You can get the current serial number by using X# = Now. If you save X# to a disk file along with the other data, you'll always have a precise record of the exact second when that data was created and stored. You can use the Year, Month and Day commands to extract and display the date from the number you saved. Use the Second, Minute and Hour commands to display the time.

Cautions
• The Format$ Function offers an extremely flexible and powerful method of displaying or printing date and time information. Use it to present the results of Year, and other date+time Functions, in precisely the way you want them to appear.

• Here's how the date+time serial number works:

```
X# = Now
Y = Year(Now)

Print X#
Print Y
```

Results in
```
33658.4246759259
1992
```

Of course, the serial number, the X#, will always differ, based on what Now is. Every time you use Now, the serial number will be larger.

In fact, Visual Basic's serial number is unique for every second between January 1, 100, and December 31, 9999–the range that VB provides for date+time calculations.

The number of seconds in this span of 9,899 years is obviously quite large. There are 31,536,000 seconds in a single year. That is why we added a # symbol to the Variable *X* that would hold the serial number returned by the Now Function. The # symbol makes a Variable a "Double-Precision Floating-Point" type Variable (see "Variables"). This kind of Variable is capable of holding an extremely large range of numbers. Alternatively, the Variant Variable type would accept Now and automatically treat it as a "Date" type of number (see "Variant").

The VB date+time serial number contains the day, month and year to the left of the decimal point, and the numbers to the right of the decimal point contain the hour, minute and second.

However, the meaning of the serial number is encoded. There is no direct easy way to examine the serial number and extract all the information contained therein. So VB provides various Functions–Second, Minute, Hour, Day, Month, Year–to decode that information for you.

Example
Here's a trick you can use to find out if a date exists within a particular month. In this case, we want to let the user know which years in the current century are leap years. We test each year to see if it has a February 29. If it does, we announce that it is a leap year:

```
Sub Form_Click ()

Print "LEAP YEARS IN THIS CENTURY"

For y = 1900 To 2000
    z# = DateSerial(y, 2, 29)
    If Month(z#) = 2 Then Print Year(z#)
Next y

End Sub
```

Here we set up a Loop that will let the Variable *y* count up from 1900 to 2000 so that we can check each year. Then we create a date+time serial number for February 29 of each year and put the serial number into the Variable z#. This serial number will actually contain a code *for the month of March* if the year in question has no February 29. This way, we can check to see if the Month command gets a 2 for February out of the serial number. If it does, we print the Year because this must be a leap year.

See also   Day; Format$; Hour; Minute; Month; Now; Second; Weekday

ZORDER

METHOD

Description   The ZOrder determines which Control in a group of overlapping Controls appears visually "on top" of the group—in other words, which Control looks like it's been placed on top of the pile like a card placed on top of a deck. You can also use ZOrder with Forms—for instance, the child Forms in a Multiple Document Interface (which see). With a little fiddling, ZOrder can also place an object at the bottom of a group of overlapping Controls— but cannot directly adjust their order other than putting one on the top or the bottom of a pile. Adjust the ZOrder several times, however, and you can arrange a pile in any fashion. For instance, in a pile of four objects, you could move the top object to the third position by first moving the third object, and then the second, to the top.

ZOrder only works among a group of Controls in the same *graphics layer*—among a cluster of Picture Boxes and Images, for instance. You cannot use ZOrder to move a Picture Box on top of a Command Button. There are three graphics layers in VB; at the back are Printed text or graphics drawn with Circle, Line or PSet commands. This layer is covered by Objects in the middle layer—Picture Boxes, Labels or Frames. The top layer covers both lower layers and includes all other Controls except Timers, which are always invisible, and Menus, which hang down from the Title Bar and cover whatever is under them—no matter what. For more about graphics layers, see "ClipControls."

Used with   Forms and all Controls except Menus, OLE Controls, Data Controls and Timers

Variables

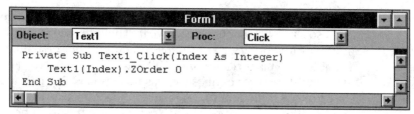

```
Form1

Object:   Text1  ▼       Proc:   Click  ▼

Private Sub Text1_Click(Index As Integer)
    Text1(Index).ZOrder 0
End Sub
```

Figure Z-1: You describe the ZOrder within an Event, usually the Click Event or a menu item's Event, and assign it a 0 to pop the Control to the top of a pile.

Because ZOrder is a Method, you use no equals sign (=) when changing the ZOrder of a Control. To bring a Text Box to the top of a pile of overlapping Controls:

Text1.ZOrder 0

OR (to push it to the bottom): Text1.ZOrder 1

Uses

Allow the user (or your program) to make a Control appear visually on the top or bottom of a pile of overlapping Controls. ZOrder affords you an alternative to the Visible or Enabled Property as a way of indicating which Controls are currently active (focused) while the program is running. It also offers an alternative to traditional menus or separated Controls, as a way for the user to select among various program options or features.

Cautions

Use only two Variables with ZOrder: 0 and 1 (top and bottom of a pile, respectively). (As is nearly always the case, alas, this numbering is counter-intuitive.) Other numbers will result in an Illegal Function Call error.

ZOrder is not like an Index number or the Tab Property or other indices to groups of Controls. You cannot directly specify that a Control should assume the second position in a pile by ZOrder, though you can manipulate the ZOrders of the Objects in a pile until you get the arrangement you are after.

Example

This example illustrates how to adjust the ZOrder of two Control Arrays simultaneously. We'll frame an Image Box with a Shape Control. Then, if the user clicks on a particular Image Box, it comes to the fore and brings the associated Shape up with it.

Start off with a New Project in the File Menu; then put an Image Control on the Form and also drag a Shape Control around it. Set the Shape Control's BorderColor to light gray. Set the Image Control's Picture Property to whatever .BMP you want and set its Stretch Property to True. Then give it an Index of 0 so we can use it as the seed for our Control Array. Also give the Shape Control an Index of 0.

Now, in the Form_Load Event, type the following:

```
Sub Form_Load ()

Show

For i = 1 To 3
    Load image1(i)
    image1(i).Height = image1(i − 1).Height * 1.5
    image1(i).Width = image1(i − 1).Width * 1.5
    image1(i).Top = image1(i − 1).Top + 400
    image1(i).Left = image1(i − 1).Left + 700
    image1(i).Visible = −1

    Load shape1(i)
    shape1(i).Height = shape1(i − 1).Height * 1.5
    shape1(i).Width = shape1(i − 1).Width * 1.5
    shape1(i).Top = shape1(i − 1).Top + 400 * .85
    shape1(i).Left = shape1(i − 1).Left + 700 * .85
    shape1(i).Visible = −1
Next i

End Sub
```

Here we're cascading both the Images and their Shape frames. As always, the clones created by this technique inherit most of the Properties of the original Control, including the Picture Property (see "Control Array"). We make each new instance of the Image 150% larger than the previous one by multiplying it by 1.5, and we move it down (Top Property) less than to the right (Left Property).

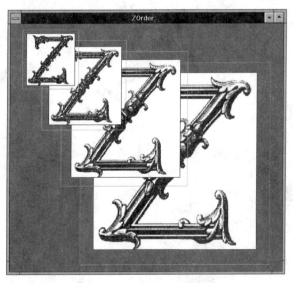

Figure Z-2: When the program starts, the pictures are spread like cards.

Now, to make the Controls adjust their ZOrder when the user clicks on the image:

```
Sub image1_Click (index As Integer)
    image1(index).ZOrder 0
    shape1(index).ZOrder 0
End Sub
```

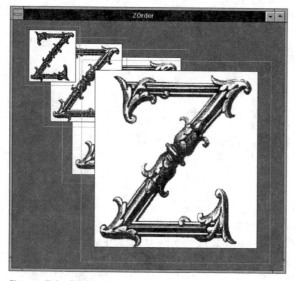

Figure Z-3: Clicking brings an Image to the top of the pile.

See also   Control Array; ClipControls

SECTION III

APPENDICES

A
B
C
D

THE WINDOWS APPLICATION PROGRAMMING INTERFACE

Now we're going to take a brief excursion beyond Visual Basic itself. The reason for this side trip is that there are things that Windows can do that are simply not in VB's vocabulary. For example, there is no VB command to crop or reverse or smear a picture. To do things like this, you'll want to have direct access to Windows itself. Fortunately, getting to the inner workings of Windows is quite easy via VB. And many of the extra features Windows offers are extraordinarily powerful.

Actually, we're not going *beyond* VB as much as *below* it. We'll get the key to the engine room under Windows, a place where more than 600 tools govern what happens in Windows. It's surprisingly simple, once you know the way, and you'll be able to add many new features to VB and take control over the way your Windows environment works.

There are occasional references to API Functions (Application Programming Interface) throughout this book. The VB Beep command, for instance, is so feeble that we explore the API alternative, which offers you elaborate control over audio effects. In this Appendix, we're going to focus on what the API collection of tools can do for you. Sometimes an API tool is preferable to a VB command (because the tool is faster or does something VB *cannot do*). Once you've absorbed a couple of rules, there's nothing particularly difficult about using the API, as you'll see.

Using the API

Windows's API is a collection of more than 600 prewritten program fragments. These Functions and Routines are in your computer already, hidden below Windows, just waiting for you to make use of them to add power to any Visual Basic program you write. And it's relatively simple to make a VB program temporarily turn control over to an API Routine. It's usually as simple as calling a Subroutine. We'll go through several examples in this Appendix.

Unique Features

Using the API is often the *only* way to get something done. The API GetTempDrive Routine, for example, looks around and reports which drive is the fastest one on the computer (maybe there's a RAM drive that would be faster than the hard drive). If one of your programs needs to store and retrieve temporary information, knowing which available drive is the fastest is quite useful. And even if the user doesn't have a RAM drive set up, it would still be useful to know where temporary files can be stored.

Near the end of this Appendix, we'll build a short program called "Quit-Win," by using several API Routines that illustrate how to do things via the API. QuitWin is a practical utility in its own right: if you double-click on the QuitWin icon, you'll get an animated picture of a window slamming shut. Then Windows instantly closes itself, landing you back in DOS. Instead of having to mouse around closing down various application windows and answering questions from Program Manager or some other shell, you're just *gone*.

With Visual Basic (VB) alone, you cannot do two of the things that QuitWin does with its API calls:

• Enlarge an icon to a bitmap 20 times the icon's original size (which uses up much less memory and disk space than would be used by a full-blown bitmap image). You could, however, use an Image with its Stretch Property set to True.

• Instantly exit Windows. (VB has the END command, but that only closes down the current VB application; it doesn't collapse all of Windows and return you to DOS.)

A Little Background

To understand how (and why) to use the API, we should first take a quick look at programming languages in general. If you are an experienced programmer, you might want to skip ahead in this Appendix to "Hands-On: API."

All computer languages fall into two primary categories: *interpreted* and *compiled* languages. Although the distinctions can sometimes be rather artificial, they are nonetheless important.

A compiled language is like a railroad track: before the train leaves the station (the user runs the program), all the instructions and decisions about how to get from Washington to Baltimore have been made. Tunnels have been drilled, curves carved out of mountains and left and right turns incorporated into the track to guide the train to its destination.

Using an interpreted language, on the other hand, is like driving a car from Washington to Baltimore for the first time. A number of decisions must be made *during* the trip—maps consulted, signs looked for, information looked up while you're on the way. This way to travel is obviously slower, but it does have its advantages.

Interpreted Languages Versus Compiled Languages: Interpreted languages require the computer to make extra calculations when a program is running ("runtime"). Compiled languages require less of the computer during runtime, so they generally run faster. Sometimes this is irrelevant: most word processing tasks involve waiting for the user to type things at the keyboard, and the computer is fast enough to be able to handle this, regardless of whether the word processor program was written in an interpreted or compiled language.

Interpreted languages are somewhat limited in handling time-consuming tasks such as sorting a large database. However, they can make the job of writing, of *designing* ("design time") a program more efficient than can compiled languages. When you type in a line of commands, such as PRINT "THIS," you can press F5 in VB and see the result instantly. A compiled language, such as MASM (an assembly language program for PCs), cannot provide this instant feedback. After you type in your commands, you must then run some other programs (compilers and linkers) before your program is ready to be understood by the computer. Also, compiled languages cannot offer Immediate Windows like VB's, or interactive debugging, where you can correct errors and restart the program to see if it works.

Solutions? Mixing two languages is one solution. Programmers have often designed a program in high-level Basic and inserted low-level assembly-language routines in key places within the Basic program where speed is an issue, such as in searching and sorting. Some third-party developers sell collections of prewritten assembly-language routines for just this purpose (such as Crescent Software, Inc., 32 Seventy Acres, West Redding, CT 06896, which sells "QuickPak for Windows." See Appendix D for a list of add-on products for VB).

Microsoft's solution is to throw its considerable resources behind Basic, believing, as I do, that of all computer languages Basic is the easiest to program, can be as efficient as any other language and promises to be the preferred language of the future. Over the years, Microsoft's versions of Basic have evolved to embrace some of the best features of competing languages such as Pascal and C while retaining Basic's essentially under-standable syntax and design-time efficiencies.

So, when you want to do something that VB cannot do, or when you need to speed up a portion of a program, call an API Routine. The API will give the computer a list of direct instructions it can understand at once.

Library Dynamics

Many compiled languages use "libraries" of prewritten code. During the process of compiling, one or more libraries are *Linked* in, so that the compiler can fetch Routines from within the libraries and patch them into the finished .EXE program. The .EXE program, the runnable program, is the product of the compilation process.

VB works a little differently with libraries: it links to them *dynamically* during runtime, every time a user runs your VB .EXE program. When Windows loads in a program from disk to be run, it first looks to see if any library's Functions have been declared within the program. If so, it supplies the program with the addresses of the declared items so that when the program needs to run one of these Functions, it knows where to tell the computer to find the necessary instructions. That's why these libraries are called *DLLs* (Dynamic Link Libraries). DLLs are a general feature of Win-dows and not limited to VB.

Advantages of DLLs

Among the advantages of the dynamic linking approach are modifiability and memory efficiency. DLLs are modifiable because you can add features to the main program without modifying it. For example, a manufacturer can put features of a new printer into an improved driver without having to recompile the original .EXE program to include them.

DLLs are memory-efficient in two ways: (1) several programs can access a single DLL rather than having to duplicate its Routines within all the programs; and (2) the Windows SETUP program can select just the particular driver you need for your printer, rather than storing a huge, multi-printer driver on your hard disk. If you have a Hewlett-Packard LaserJet III, you'll find that Windows's SETUP program selected the HPPCL.DRV for your SYSTEM directory.

DLLs in Action

Although a DLL cannot be executed like a regular program, it is like a regular program in many of its components: it can have an area of memory set aside for data, can contain executable segments of code (instructions for the computer to follow) and so forth. Libraries, though, do not have a "stack."

Most DLLs are best visualized as collections of small Routines that your programs can use after you provide the name of the API library and the address (a particular Routine's name), which tells the computer to look for instructions during runtime.

What happens when a DLL is requested by a Windows program (because the program declared that library or otherwise called on a library)? First, the DLL is loaded into memory as if it were an executable program. Then it announces its existence to the system (so multiple copies of the DLL don't have to use up RAM). It sets up its Global Variables like a regular program, and it does some housekeeping relative to the various Routines contained within it. Windows keeps track of which program(s) are using this DLL, and, when all of those programs have been shut down, the DLL is removed from memory. Some DLLs (the general Windows API libraries–KERNEL, USER, GDI) are in memory whenever Windows is running and don't need to be loaded or unloaded when VB programs use them.

Compared to VB, the API also offers you more control over, and more possible effects within, any program you write. You can give an API Function some information, such as the location of a bitmap picture, and it can perform quick manipulations on that picture. You can, for example, replace it with another picture in a way that seems to blend them like a video dissolve, or push one out of the frame with another, like a video wipe.

You can select an area *within* a window or Control and cut, copy or *smear* the chosen rectangle. We illustrate this interesting "ScrollWindow" feature later in this Appendix under "Smearing & Sliding." You can also control the speed of the effect and other aspects of Windows, such as color inversions.

Windows 95

If you're using VB4 (32-bit version) to write programs for Windows 95, there are some special considerations when calling the API. There are a few things to be aware of when translating API calls from their 16-bit versions that work with VB3 under Windows 3.x and their 32-bit versions that work with VB4 (32-bit version) under Windows 95. For the correct syntax for 32-bit API calls, you can cut and paste them from the file "WIN32API.TXT" supplied with VB4. However, here is a list of the four main adjustments to make when turning a 16-bit Windows 3.x API Declare into a 32-bit Windows 95 Declare:

• The primary change is that a library name gets "32" appended to it. Often, this is all you have to do to make a Windows 3.x API call work for Windows 95:

```
Declare Sub BringWindowToTop Lib  User  (ByVal hwnd%)
```

becomes

```
Declare Sub BringWindowToTop Lib  User32  (ByVal hwnd%)
```

• Also, if an API Function is an Integer type, it generally becomes a Long type under Windows 95:

```
Declare Function GetCaretBlinkTime Lib  User  ( ) As Integer
```

becomes

```
Declare Function GetCaretBlinkTime Lib  User32  ( ) As Long
```

or the alternative syntax, which is the eqivalent to "As":

```
Declare Function GetCaretBlinkTime& Lib  User32  ( )
```

• Arguments also change from Integer to Long, so you must make that change as well:

```
Declare Function arc% Lib  GDI  (ByVal hDC%, ByVal xa%, _ ByVal ya%,  →
ByVal xb%, ByVal yb%, ByVal xc%, ByVal yc%, _ ByVal xd%, ByVal yd%)
```

changes to

```
Declare Function Arc Lib  gdi32  (ByVal hDC As Long, ByVal X1 As Long,  →
ByVal Y1 As Long, ByVal X2 As Long, ByVal Y2 As Long, ByVal X3 As  →
Long, ByVal Y3 As Long, ByVal X4 As Long, ByVal Y4 As Long) As Long
```

However, it doesn't matter if you permit the return Variable to be an Integer, when you *call* a long Function:

```
x% = GetCaretBlinkTime( )
```

will work as well as

```
x&= GetCaretBlinkTime( )
```

• The final adjustment is required when you are working with API calls involving text ("string") variables. You append an "A" to the name of the API procedure to indicate that this is an "ASCII" code text. Windows 95 works with the new two-byte character code called UniCode, whereas ASCII holds each character code in a single byte.

```
Declare Function SystemParametersInfo% Lib User (ByVal Action As →
Integer, ByVal Param As Integer, Returned As Any, ByVal ChangeIni As →
Integer)
```

Changes to:

```
Declare Function SystemParametersInfo Lib user32 Alias →
SystemParametersInfoA (ByVal uAction As Long, ByVal uParam As →
Long, lpvParam As Any, ByVal fuWinIni As Long) As Long
```

Where To Put Them

Another thing: Whereas in VB3 you could put Declares into a Form's General Declarations section, in VB4 32-bit you put them in a Module. Otherwise, you'll get a mystery error message: "Constants, Fixed-length strings and Arrays not allowed as public members of a Class Module." Since you're not using any Constants or strings or Arrays here, nor are you in a Class Module, you might well pause when you see this message. (Perhaps it has been fixed, but at the time of this writing you'll get that message.) If you do want to put your Declare into the General Declarations section of a Form, add the word Private to the start of the Declare:

```
Private Declare Function GetCaretBlinkTime Lib User32 ( ) As Long
```

and all will be well.

Hands-On: API

There are a few rules to learn if you want to use the API (and you may crash your computer a few times in the process), but using the API is not all that hard once you get past the initial confusion.

Using API calls is like using VB commands, but a little more exacting. The main difficulties are: (1) error messages aren't specific; (2) when you send Variables, the types have to be what the API expects; and (3) the one available reference book on the API is written in terse computerese and offers few examples.

To fully exploit the API, you need to get a copy of the *Microsoft Windows Programmer's Reference*, a giant $40 book available at most bookstores. In it you'll find all the API Routines described alphabetically.

You can cut and paste from the API Declares listed in a file that comes with VB:WIN32API.TXT for Windows 95, VB4, or WINAPI.TXT for earlier versions.

Descriptions of API Routines in the *Microsoft Windows Programmer's Reference* are a bit cryptic. For example, the ExitWindows Routine looks like this:

```
BOOL ExitWindows(dwReserved, wReturnCode)
```

You are told that dwReserved is a DWORD, that it "is reserved and should be set to zero," and that wReturnCode is a WORD and passes its value to DOS when Windows shuts itself down. (Windows 95 doesn't include the ExitWindows function—this function only works in Windows 3.x.)

To use ExitWindows, you need to translate that information into the following lines in VB. In the General Declarations section of a Form, type *on a single line*:

```
Declare Function ExitWindows% lib "User" (ByVal L as Long, ByVal I as →
    Integer)
```

And in the Form_Click Event:

```
Static L As Long
Static I As Integer
GoAway = ExitWindows (L,I)
```

We'll get into some technical details about using the *Microsoft Windows Programmer's Reference* at the end of this Appendix. For now, let's take a look at some of the more useful or intriguing API Routines.

It's not necessary to understand fully how the API works. Fiddling with Variables and a monkey-see-monkey-do approach will usually get you the results you want.

Drawing Rounded-Edge Rectangles

Let's try some examples. The first rule to remember about using the API is that Declarations *must be on a single line in a Module (or the General Declarations section of a Form).* And some of the API Declarations can be quite long. However, you just keep typing and VB will scroll the Module's window as you type. Don't hit the ENTER key until you've typed the entire Declare and all its Variables.

The API has many special-purpose, built-in Functions. If you want to draw rounded-edge frames that look like lozenges, try RoundRect:

On one line in the General Declarations section of a Form, type the following:

```
Declare Function RoundRect Lib "GDI" (ByVal hdc As Integer, ByVal X1 →
    As Integer, ByVal Y1 As Integer, ByVal X2 As Integer, ByVal Y2 As →
    Integer,  ByVal X3 As Integer, ByVal Y3 As Integer) As Integer
```

Then we provide the same coordinates for this Function as we would if we were drawing a box with VB's Line command:

```
Line (left position, top position) – (lowerright,bottom),,b
```

Then substitute these same positions (x1, y1) – (x2, y2) in the RoundRect Function, adding two numbers at the end for the width and height of the ellipse that you want to use (the amount of curvature for the corners).

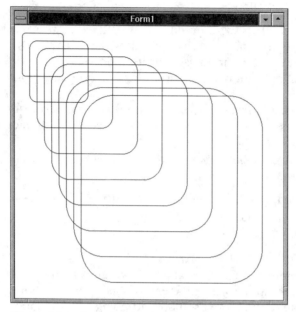

Figure AA-1: Rounded Rectangles.

```
Sub Form_Click ()
For i = 100 To 500 Step 50
    j = j + 15
    x = RoundRect(hdc, i, i, j, j, j, j)
Next i
End Sub
```

In this Loop, we make i go from 100 to 500 in steps of 50—in other words, 100, 150, 200, 250 and so on until it reaches 500. Each time through the Loop, the value of the Variable j increases by 15. We are using i to locate the upper left corner of each rectangle, and j to serve as both the lower right location and the amount of rounding. The rounding will get progressively more extreme for each new rectangle drawn.

TwipsPerPixel: Measurement Units for API Routines

Note that almost all API drawing Routines use pixels rather than twips, the VB default (for Line, Circle and Pset commands). In the API, pixels are the default "MAP_Mode." (You *can* change the MAP_MODE using the API SetMapMode Function.) Using pixels instead of VB's twips means only that you have to reduce the numbers you are used to (the twips) by dividing them roughly by 10. In other words, where you might use the following in twips:

```
Line (10,10) – (5000, 5000),,B
```

You would use this for an API rectangle:

X = RoundRect(hdc,1,1,500,500,5,5) (The last two numbers are the width and height of the curve that rounds the corners.)

This divide-by-10 rule can only be an approximation because computer monitors differ in the number of pixels they have. To get a precise translation for use with API Routines, use the TwipsPerPixelX and Y Properties of the Screen and Printer Objects:

Print screen.TwipsPerPixelX, screen.TwipsPerPixelY

might result in:

12   12

in which case you would be dividing VB's twip values by 12 for both horizontal and vertical coordinates that you supply to the API. Because this ratio varies on different screens (and printers), you might want to use Screen.TwipsPerPixelX and Y directly in your program to get the ratio while the program is running. That way, the results will be appropriate no matter whose computer is running your program.

If you ever need it, the API Function GetDeviceCaps will also give you the "LOGPIXELSX & Y" in use by the current "Device Context," the *DC* (for example: PostScript printer = 300). For more information, see the *Microsoft Windows Programmer's Reference.*

Printing Text

The "X and Y" coordinate position used in API Functions is similar but not identical to the CurrentX and CurrentY Properties in VB. Also, unlike VB, an API Function will not update the X,Y position to the new position after the Function is used. (When you use the Circle command in VB, for instance, the center of the drawn circle becomes the new CurrentX and CurrentY coordinate. Not so for the API Routines.)

The API contains a number of text-printing Routines, including the following one, which includes X and Y positioning within the Routine.

In the General Declarations section, put the following on a single line:

```
Declare Function TextOut Lib "GDI" (ByVal hDC As Integer, ByVal X As →
   Integer, ByVal Y As Integer, ByVal lpString As String, ByVal nCount As →
   Integer) As Integer
```

Then enter the following:

```
Sub Form_Click ()

s$ = "PRINT THIS TEXT on the screen."
l = Len(s$)

For i = 1 To 400 Step 12
X = TextOut(hdc, 12, i, s$, l)
Next i

End Sub
```

The Variables within the TextOut command represent the following:

TextOut (hDC, widthposition, heightposition, the text Variable to print, the number of characters in the text Variable)

This approach is essentially the same as using the VB Print command, along with CurrentX and CurrentY. However, the API has a wealth of typeface- and text-manipulation Routines. You could, for instance, overcome the limitation that all characters in a Text Box must either be normal or italic. Using the API, you could mix and match typefaces, type sizes and type styles—just as a word processor does.

Working With Windowswide Settings

There are hundreds of tools in the API that give you direct control over how Windows itself behaves. You could provide users with these fine-tuning adjustments as part of an Options Menu.

The WIN.INI file (and SYSTEM.INI) is to Windows what CONFIG.SYS and AUTOEXEC.BAT are to DOS—a place that Windows looks for initial settings when it first starts running. There is a setting in WIN.INI that tells Windows how quickly the user prefers a double-click—how sensitive Windows should be when the mouse button is pressed twice.

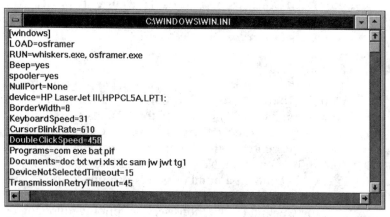

Figure AA-2: Windows stores configuration information in the WIN.INI file.

This setting is user-adjustable between 100 and 900 milliseconds from within the Windows Control Panel:

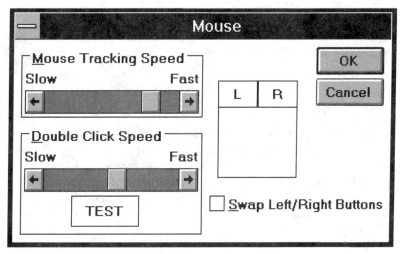

Figure AA-3: The Windows Control Panel mouse adjuster.

We can add this feature to our programs, allowing the user to adjust the double-click speed while our program is running:

Figure AA-4: Our mouse double-click adjuster.

Put a Horizontal Scroll Bar and five Labels on a Form, as shown in Figure AA-4. Type the various text messages into the Labels' Caption Properties using the Properties Window. Then, in the General Declarations section of the Form, type these two Declares, remembering that *Declares must be on a single line*:

Wrong:

```
Declare Function GetDoubleClickTime
Lib "User" () As Integer
```

Right:

```
Declare Function GetDoubleClickTime Lib "User" () As Integer
Declare Sub setdoubleclicktime Lib "User" (ByVal wCount As Integer)
```

Note: A few of the API features are Subroutines (see "Sub") instead of Functions. The primary difference for our purposes is that with a Sub you don't use the X = technique; instead, you just use the name of the Sub, followed by any Variables it wants. The other difference between a Sub and a Function is that *you don't enclose the Variables in parentheses* for a Subroutine:

(to use an API Function):

```
X = GetDoubleClickTime ()
```

(to use an API Subroutine):

```
SetDoubleClickTime 300
```

Now, type the following in the Form_Load Event, to try out the program:

```
Sub Form_Load ()

Show

x = GetDoubleClickTime()

hscroll1.min = 900
hscroll1.max = 100
hscroll1.largechange = 100
hscroll1.smallchange = 10
hscroll1.value = x

End Sub
```

See "Horizontal Scroll Bar" for the meaning of these Properties. In essence, we set the range of the Scroll Bar to be between 900 milliseconds for the slowest double-click and 100 for the fastest. This is the same range that the Windows Control Panel offers. Then we use the API call to put the current value of the double-click speed into the "Value" Property of the Scroll Bar. This positions the tab (the "thumb") in the Scroll Bar to the current Windows setting.

When the user slides the tab, we react by doing these things:

```
Sub HScroll1_Change ()

hv = hscroll1.value
setdoubleclicktime  hv
label5.caption = Str$(hv) + " milliseconds."
End Sub
```

We find out how much the tab has moved, set the Windows double-click speed to that new value, and report the change in milliseconds to the user.

In imitation of the Control Panel, we've included a Label that will change color when it detects a double click. This allows the user to test the different settings:

```
Sub Label3_DblClick ()

Static toggle
toggle = Not toggle

If toggle Then
    label3.caption = "Click Me Twice!"
Else
    label3.caption = "Do it again!!"
End If

End Sub
```

This test acts like the Control Panel, but instead of switching the text Label between black and white, we have it display messages by changing its Caption Property. To learn how the Variable *Toggle* acts like a light switch, going up and down each time this Event is triggered, see "Static."

These changes to the double-click sensitivity are not permanent. They will apply only while your VB program is running. You've probably noticed that there is a brief delay when you close the Windows Control Panel after making an adjustment to the mouse, the colors or something else. During this delay Windows changes the WIN.INI file to make a permanent record of your new preferences. Our program does not affect the WIN.INI file, so the adjustments apply only to your VB program.

If you are interested in making permanent changes to the WIN.INI file, you can use the API Function WriteProfileString. Proper use of this Function also requires sending the WM_WININICHANGE message to all top-level windows so that they can update any parameters they use from the WIN.INI file. See *Programming Windows* (Microsoft Press) for more on this technique.

hWnd & hDC "Handles"

Many of the API Functions need to know which window (which Form) you want affected by the Function. To know your intentions, you provide the "hWnd" (handle-to-the-window) or the "hDC" (handle-to-the-device-context). In other words, if you are printing text via the API to a window, you need to first find out what its hDC is and provide that information to the text-printing API Function.

The API TextOut Function was described previously. When you declare that Function in the General Declarations section of a Form (or in a Module), you can see that when activated it will want the hDC, among other things. The meaning of the Variables within the TextOut command are as follows

TextOut (hDC, widthposition, heightposition, the text Variable to print, the number of characters in the text Variable)

Visual Basic provides the hDC and hWnd commands, which give you a window's handles. Because the information contained in hWnd and hDC can change at any time while a program is running, it's best to use the actual words *hDC* and *hWnd* directly in the list of Variables following an API call, rather than assign their contents to a Variable. (The hDC or hWnd could have been changed by the time you call on the API Function.) Here's how the hDC is used in practice:

```
Sub Form_Click ()
s$ = "PRINT THIS TEXT on the screen."
X = TextOut(hDC, 1, 1, s$, Len(s$))
End Sub
```

To Get the hWnd of a Control
Most of the time, you can just use the hDC and hWnd Properties of Forms and Controls that are built into VB. VB provides an *hDC* Property for Forms, Picture Boxes and the printer. If you want to print text via the API to a Picture Box, for example, you need to provide the Box's hDC, not the hDC of the Parent window.

Visual Basic also includes an hWnd Property to give you that handle for almost every Control that you would want to use the API with: MDI Forms, Check Boxes, Combo Boxes, Command Buttons, Directory, Drive and File List Boxes, Frames, Grids, List Boxes, OLE, Option Buttons, Picture Boxes and Scroll Bars.

However, if you ever need the hWnd of a Control that doesn't have a VB hWnd Property, there is an easy way to get it. Type the following into the General Declarations section of a Form or into a Module:

```
Declare Function GetFocus Lib "User" () As Integer
```

Then, whenever in your program you need the hWnd of a Control (in this case, a Picture Box named Picture1), type the following:

```
Picture1.SetFocus
Picture1hwnd = GetFocus()
```

To Get the hDC of a Control
Here's how to get the hDC of Controls other than a Picture Box (the only Control that VB provides an hDC for). We'll expand our earlier example in this Appendix that utilized the API TextOut Function. Here, we'll use TextOut with a Text Box, even though TextOut requires an hDC and VB doesn't provide it for a Text Box. Type the following Declares into the General Declarations section of a Form (remember each Declare must be on a single line; do not press ENTER until finished with each Declare):

```
Declare Function Textout Lib "gdi" (ByVal hdc As Integer, ByVal x As →
    Integer, ByVal y As Integer, ByVal lpstring As String, ByVal ncount as →
    Integer) As Integer
```

```
Declare Function getfocus Lib "user" () As Integer
```

```
Declare Function getdc% Lib "user" (ByVal hwnd As Integer)
```

Then put a Text Box on a Form, and type the following into the Form_Click Event:

```
Sub Form_Click ()

text1.SetFocus
thwnd = getfocus ()
thdc = getdc (thwnd)
s$ = "Print This"
l = Len(s$)
For i = l To 400 Step 30
    z = textout(thdc, 12, i, s$, l)
Next i

End Sub
```

Smearing & Sliding

Among other things, the ScrollWindow API Subroutine can quickly and smoothly move any rectangle within any window. Here we'll have a piece of a graphic slide down and to the right, leaving two different kinds of trails behind it. Although you can use the Move command to animate your programs, ScrollWindow is faster and smoother; what's more, you can define whatever size rectangle you want to move, leaving the rest of an image, or piece of text, intact.

Here's our graphic before ScrollWindow affects it:

Figure AA-5: The graphic in its innocent state.

ScrollWindow requires that you set up a new data type (see "Type") that contains four coordinates to define your rectangle—left, top, right and bottom. This is precisely the same way you describe drawing a box using the Line command in VB.

Put a graphic into a Form by setting the Form's Picture Property. Then type the following into a Module, to set up the new "type" of Variable called *rect*.

In a Module:

```
Type rect
    x1 As Integer
    y1 As Integer
    x2 As Integer
    y2 As Integer
End Type
```

In the General Declarations section of your Form, define two rect-type Variables:

```
Dim lprect As rect
Dim lpcliprect As rect
```

And type in these three API definitions, making sure that each of the three is on its own single line. You should have only three lines of text for the following:

```
Declare Sub scrollwindow Lib "User" (ByVal hWnd As Integer, ByVal →
    XAmount As Integer, ByVal YAmount As Integer, lprect As rect, →
    lpcliprect As rect)

Declare Sub updatewindow Lib "User" (ByVal hWnd As Integer)
Declare Function GetFocus% Lib "User" ()
```

In the Form_Load Event, we'll print a title on top of the graphic, using some vibrant colors:

```
Sub Form_Load ()

Show
forecolor = QBColor(13)
backcolor = QBColor(0)
scalemode = 3
fontname = "blackchancery"      'Note, use whatever font you wish from
                                'those available in your computer.
fontsize = 78
currentx = 20
currenty = 12
Print "DECO";
fontname = "paradox"            'Use your own choice of font here as well.
forecolor = QBColor(11)
currenty = currenty + 19
currentx = currentx − 100
Print "in Motion"

End Sub
```

Finally, to activate the animation, type the following in the Form_Click Event:

```
Sub Form_Click ()

lprect.x1 = 0                    'defines the rectangle to move
lprect.y1 = 0
lprect.x2 = 1350
lprect.y2 = 1400

lpcliprect.x1 = 0                'defines the window that will clip the rectangle.
lpcliprect.y1 = 0
lpcliprect.x2 = 1050
lpcliprect.y2 = 1000

For i = 1 to 20
    scrollwindow hWnd, i, i, lprect, lpcliprect
Next i

End Sub
```

The preceding program smears the rectangle we want to move. Note that you define two rectangles. The first one, which we called *lprect* here, is the rectangle to be moved. The second rectangle defines the space that can be affected—that can be covered over or moved at all. What *is* this distinction?

The Glassine Window

It's as if you were moving a stamp within a business envelope that has a glassine window. The stamp is *lprect*—the thing that can slide, the image that will move. The portion of the envelope that is transparent defines how far the stamp can slide before it disappears (is clipped off) from view. A number of interesting effects are possible by adjusting the relative sizes of these two "windows within windows."

Figure AA-6: A total smear.

Adding the Updatewindow API call to this Loop and making adjustments to the spacing result in a different kind of smear:

```
Sub Form_Click ()

lprect.x1 = 84              'defines the rectangle to move
lprect.y1 = 58

lprect.x2 = 1350
lprect.y2 = 1400

lpcliprect.x1 = 0           'defines the window that will clip the rectangle.
lpcliprect.y1 = 0

lpcliprect.x2 = 1050
lpcliprect.y2 = 1000

For i = 1 to 14
scrollwindow h, i, i, lprect, lpcliprect
updatewindow hWnd
Next i

End Sub
```

This program causes the following:

Figure AA-7: A staggered smear.

Windows Within Windows—LPRECT Versus LPCLIPRECT

In the preceding examples, we cut a piece of a picture and smeared it over the background image. You define two rectangles: the piece that's being cut out and the space on the "background" that can be covered by the scrolling piece.

To understand how the two rectangles interact, we'll conclude our brief look at the API Scrollwindow Routine by drawing two boxes with the Line command and then showing the effect of using their coordinates to scroll one of them.

Type into a Module and the General Declarations section of a Form the same commands as in the preceding example. This defines the rect data type, defines two Variables that use it and declares three API Routines. But instead of the commands we used above in the Form_Load and Form_Click Events, type the following into Form_Load, which will draw two rectangles and set the Form's ScaleMode to pixels (the unit of measurement that the API's Scrollwindow uses):

```
Sub Form_Load ()

Show
scalemode = 3
Line (75, 30)–(450, 95), QBColor(13), BF
Line (45, 30)–(350, 75), QBColor(9), BF

End Sub
```

The preceding Sub results in these two Boxes:

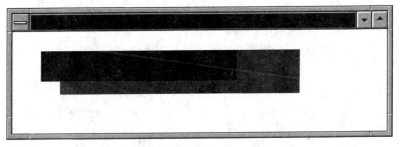

Figure AA-8: The rectangle and its "clipping window."

The larger Box in Figure AA-8 represents the "clipping window"–the space within which Scrollwindow is allowed to move the graphic. This is analogous to the Variable we're using called *lpcliprect*. The smaller Box is analogous to our Variable *lprect*, the rectangle we're selecting to move.

Now put the following into the Form_Click Event:

```
Sub Form_Click ()

lprect.x1 = 45            'defines the size of the rectangle to move
lprect.y1 = 10
lprect.x2 = 350
lprect.y2 = 75

lpcliprect.x1 = 75        'defines the "window" within which the above
lpcliprect.y1 = 10        'rectangle can move
lpcliprect.x2 = 450
lpcliprect.y2 = 95

scrollwindow hWnd, 150, 0, lprect, lpcliprect

End Sub
```

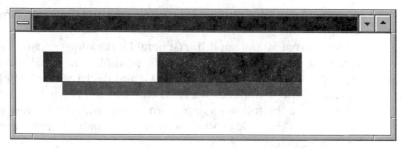

Figure AA-9: Only space that is not "clipped" can be scrolled.

Note that we are moving 150 pixels to the right and staying the same vertically—like sliding a bolt on a door. The rectangle we want to move starts at 45 pixels (from the left side of the window). But the *permitted* window of movement, *lpcliprect.x1,* starts at 75 pixels. That's why part of the original rectangle does not get moved. These two items—the definition of the rectangle you want to scroll and the permitted scrolling space—work together to determine the exact scrolling effect achieved.

QuitWin Shutting Windows Down

Now we'll create a complete VB program that you might find useful (note that Windows 95 doesn't include the ExitWindows function, so this example will only work under Windows 3.x). It's an icon that when touched shows an animated window slamming closed, then shuts Windows down and returns you to the DOS C:\ prompt. If you have anything pending, such as an unsaved file in Write, you'll be asked if you want to save it. Otherwise, Windows will just go away (without any menus and mouse clicks that you normally need to worry about).

Make a couple of icons—one that shows an opened window, one a closed window:

Figure AA-10: The opened window icon.

Figure AA-11: The closed window icon.

Then put two icon-sized Picture Boxes on a Form; then add one large Picture Box and a Timer. Set the Name of one of the small Picture Boxes to "SrcOpen" and Load in the opened window icon using the Box's Picture Property. Follow the same procedure with the other small Picture Box, but Name it "SrcClosed" and Load in the closed window icon. Set the Form's Visible Property to Off (False) and put the closed window icon into the Form's Icon Property.

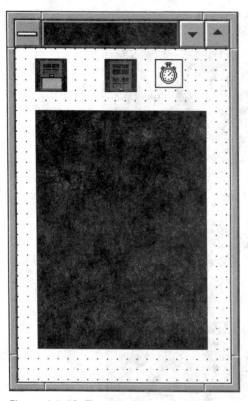

Figure AA-12: The two icon-sized Picture Boxes, the target Picture Box
and the Timer.

When this program runs, we'll blow up the opened window icon then
put it into the large Picture Box and then set the Timer for a half-second.
When the Timer Interval is over, the commands inside the Timer "Timer
Event" will be triggered, and we'll blow up the closed window icon and
shut down Windows itself. This will create an interesting animated effect
that seems to slam a window shut, while Windows itself collapses into
ordinary DOS.

Blow Up or Shrink a Picture to Any Size

You'll learn here how to take a picture of any size and resize it—larger or
smaller. This not only saves memory (because large .BMP pictures take up
huge amounts of disk and RAM space), but it is also a good way to manipulate images for special effects.

When the opened window icon is enlarged, it will look like Figure AA-13
on your screen. You won't see the enlargement process because it happens
in a flash.

Note: StretchBlt affects the apparent resolution of a bitmap graphic. StretchBlt cannot create extra visual information that is not already in the original picture. So, blowing up a picture can, as it does in photography, result in increasing *grain* or apparent loss of resolution.

Figure AA-13: The opened window icon after it has been blown up.

Now let's create our program. (Remember, you don't need to type in the comments, the lines that follow the ' symbol.) And, remember, too, that all you need to do is *copy* this stuff; *you don't need to understand everything here.* It works. If you want to make adjustments in the sizes or locations of the images, just change the appropriate Variables. If you want to use different pictures, Load them into the Picture Properties of the small Picture Boxes.

As always when using the API, we first need to declare our API Functions. Type the following into the General Declarations section of the Form, remembering to put all the Variables following a Declare on a single line:

```
Declare Function StretchBlt% Lib "GDI" (ByVal hDC%, ByVal X%, ByVal Y%, →
    ByVal nWidth%, ByVal nHeight%, ByVal hSrcDC%, ByVal XSrc%, ByVal →
    YSrc%, ByVal nSrcWidth%, ByVal nSrcHeight%, ByVal dwRop&)
```

```
Dim CopyMode As Long
Dim SrcWidth As Integer, SrcHeight As Integer
Dim DestWidth As Integer, DestHeight As Integer
```

Declare Function ExitWindows% Lib "User" (ByVal L As Long, ByVal I As →
Integer)

```
Dim L As Long
Dim I As Integer
```

Into the Form_Load Event, type the following:

Sub Form_Load ()

```
'    When the Form is loaded, this will center our animated window.
'        (regardless of what screen size the user has)
```

Move (screen.width − width) / 2, (screen.height − height) / 2

```
'    This tells Windows to perform a direct copy. (You have other choices for
'    CopyMode, such as producing a negative image. [See Table AA-1 below
'    for your options].)
```

CopyMode = &HCC0020

```
'    Set the width and height of the source images (the icons we're going to
'    blow up).
```

```
SrcWidth = SrcOpen.ScaleWidth
SrcHeight = SrcOpen.ScaleHeight
```

```
'    Set the width and height of the destination image (the size the icons will
'    become).
```

```
DestWidth = DestOpen.ScaleWidth
DestHeight = DestOpen.ScaleHeight
```

```
'    Set the location of the final, blown-up images.
```

```
DestOpen.top = 0
DestOpen.left = 0
```

```
'    Make everything visible to the viewer at this point.
```

Form1.Visible = 1

```
'    Blow up the opened window icon.
```

X% = StretchBlt(DestOpen.hDC, 0, 0, DestWidth, DestHeight, Srcpen.hDC, →
0, 0, SrcWidth, SrcHeight, CopyMode)

```
'    Start the timer to allow a half-second between the opened and closed
'    windows animation.
```

```
Timer1.interval = 500
Timer1.enabled = 1
```

End Sub

The following list is taken from a large file of API Functions, Variables and Constants. This file is called "WINAPI.TXT" and is available from Microsoft by calling (206) 637-7099. The file is included in the Professional version of VB. In our program, we set CopyMode to &HCC0020, a direct copy of the source graphic into the destination graphic. Experiment with these other options:

Table AA-1: Possible CopyModes

Global Const SRCCOPY = &HCC0020	' (DWORD) dest = source
Global Const SRCPAINT = &HEE0086	' (DWORD) dest = source or ' dest
Global Const SRCAND = &H8800C6	' (DWORD) dest = source AND ' dest
Global Const SRCINVERT = &H660046	' (DWORD) dest = source XOR ' dest
Global Const SRCERASE = &H440328	' (DWORD) dest = source AND ' (NOT dest)
Global Const NOTSRCCOPY = &H330008	' (DWORD) dest = (NOT source)
Global Const NOTSRCERASE = &H1100A6	' (DWORD) dest = (NOT src) ' AND(NOT dest)
Global Const MERGECOPY = &HC000CA	' (DWORD) dest = (source AND ' pattern)
Global Const MERGEPAINT = &HBB0226	' (DWORD) dest = (NOT source) ' OR dest
Global Const PATCOPY = &HF00021	' (DWORD) dest = pattern
Global Const PATPAINT = &HFB0A09	' (DWORD) dest = DPSnoo
Global Const PATINVERT = &H5A0049	' (DWORD) dest = pattern XOR ' dest
Global Const DSTINVERT = &H550009	' (DWORD) dest = (NOT dest)
Global Const BLACKNESS = &H42&	' (DWORD) dest = BLACK
Global Const WHITENESS = &HFF0062	' (DWORD) dest = WHITE

Now, in the Timer1_Timer Event, we'll slam the window shut and close down Windows itself:

```
Sub Timer1_Timer ()

X% = StretchBlt(DestOpen.hDC, 0, 0, DestWidth, DestHeight, →
  SrcClosed.hDC, 0, 0, SrcWidth, SrcHeight, CopyMode)
Z = ExitWindows(L, I)
End Sub
```

Please Remain Calm

The only truly alarming and confusing thing in this whole program is this line:

```
X% = StretchBlt(DestOpen.hDC, 0, 0, DestWidth, DestHeight, →
    SrcOpen.hDC, 0, 0, SrcWidth, SrcHeight, CopyMode)
```

Fortunately, you don't need to know how this works to use it, any more than you need to know how a piston turns a camshaft to drive your car. We have no use for the X%, nor do we worry about the 0's. *StretchBlt* is the name that Windows uses for the wonderful tool that manipulates pictures in all kinds of ways. See the entry on "Declare" for more examples that use the valuable *StretchBlt* Function. We only need to tell it several things:

• The name of the picture we're manipulating (SrcOpen.hDC)

• The location where we want the picture to end up (DestOpen.hDC)

• How wide and high the source and target pictures are (DestWidth, DestHeight, SrcWidth, SrcHeight)

• The way we want the source picture copied to the target (CopyMode)

Now there's nothing magic about the names I've given to these Variables. You could call them anything that makes sense to you. For example, you could decide that it's more descriptive to use names like *SmallOpenedWindow* and *BigOpenedWindow*. The only difference, then, between your program and mine would be this:

```
SrcWidth = SmallOpenedWindow.ScaleWidth
SrcHeight = SmallOpenedWindow.ScaleHeight

DestWidth = BigOpenedWindow.ScaleWidth
DestHeight = BigOpenedWindow.ScaleHeight

BigOpenedWindow.top = 0
BigOpenedWindow.left = 0

X% = StretchBlt(BigOpenedWindow.hDC, 0, 0, DestWidth, DestHeight, →
    SmallOpenedWindow.hDC, 0, 0, SrcWidth, SrcHeight, CopyMode)
```

The names have changed, but the effect remains the same. To get the hDC, you give some information to a Variable:

```
BOW.TOP = 0
```

Then you just use it in the command:

```
X% = StretchBlt(BOW.hDC, 0, 0, DestWidth, DestHeight, →
    SmallOpenedWindow.hDC, 0, 0, SrcWidth, SrcHeight, CopyMode)
```

Use Whatever Names You Want

DestOpen, BigOpenedWindow, BOW–they're all the same thing, as long as you're using the same name again inside the parentheses of the X%= command. Just be consistent. The one thing you *can't* do is make up a new name inside those parentheses. There must be some previous reference to and description of what this thing is. In the case of SrcHeight, the computer wants to know how high the little picture is, so we tell it this way:

```
anynameyouwant = 100
```

Then we use that same name when we invoke the tool:

```
X% = StretchBlt(BOW.hDC, 0, 0, anynameyouwant, DestHeight, →
    SmallOpenedWindow.hDC, 0, 0, SrcWidth, SrcHeight, CopyMode)
```

Notice that these things are just tags, just names we're attaching. So you can use any name you want. Just put some value into the name and then use the name again in the command. (Capitalization doesn't matter, but spelling does. If you get an error message from VB, check first that you haven't got a typo, a different name for the Variable than you've used when Declaring that Function.)

You Can't Hurt the Computer

That example will make the width of the blown-up picture 100 screen pixels (the dots that make up a TV image).

Because you can't hurt hardware with software (for the same reason that you can't hurt an oven with food), you should experiment with various things. Just try 100. VB makes this easy. Press the F5 key, and you'll see the results of that 100 you gave to *anynameyouwant*. The image would be pencil-thin. So change it to ANYNAMEYOUWANT = 1000. Then press F5 again. Better! You have infinite control over these things by merely changing the numbers and then trying them out.

Using the Microsoft Windows Programmer's Reference

If you want to strike out on your own to investigate the API, you'll be referring to the *Microsoft Windows Programmer's Reference* mentioned earlier. You might also want to get a copy of the companion tutorial book *Programming Windows* (also from Microsoft Press). It contains some of the things you should know when exploring the API.

Recall that to access an API Routine, you first "declare" it with the General Declarations section of a Form or in a Module (the same places where you create Form-wide or Global Variables). You type Declare Function followed by specific information about the Function's name, Variable type, library and any Variables the Function needs. (Sometimes you will declare Subs, but they are not as common as Functions in the API.)

Here is the example we explored earlier, QuitWin. Here's what you'll find about this Function in *Microsoft Windows Programmer's Reference*:

```
BOOL ExitWindows(dwReserved, wReturnCode)
```

You are told that dwReserved is a DWORD and "is reserved and should be set to zero." wReturnCode is a WORD and passes its value to DOS when Windows shuts itself down.

To use this Function in VB, the easiest approach is to look up the way VB wants it typed. You'll find it in the "WINAPI.TXT" file, mentioned earlier in this Appendix. Essentially, the Microsoft API reference book is designed for C or Pascal programmers, so there are some differences for VB. Here's how to use the ExitWindows Function in VB.

In the General Declarations section:

```
Declare Function ExitWindows% lib "User" (ByVal L as Long, ByVal I as →
   Integer)
```

(Note that the "User" in the above example refers to a Dynamic Link Library. Each API call specifies the library where the called Routine can be found. The ExitWindows Function resides in the "User" DLL.)

And type the following into the Form_Click Event:

```
Static L As Long
Static I As Integer

GoAway = ExitWindows (L,I)
```

By convention, the descriptions in the *Microsoft Windows Programmer's Reference* tell you a Variable's type in lowercase just before giving a suggested Variable name (for example, dwReserved). The dw signifies a Variable type called "long, unsigned integer" (see "Variables" in the reference section of this book for more on Variable "types" and see the API/VB translation table earlier in this Appendix).

Get the Types & Libraries Right

You don't have to use Microsoft's Variable *names* (we changed Microsoft's *dwReserved* to L, for example, in the preceding illustration). And you don't have to pay any attention to capitalization (Reserved, RESERVED and reserved are all the same), but you *do* have to get the Variable *types* correct. For example, # doesn't substitute for &.

You also have to get the name of the API Routine right (ExitWindows, for instance, or ScrollWindows). That's how the computer looks up the Routine within the API library. (Some few Functions add the kink of using reference *numbers* instead of names. These are called *ordinal numbers.*)

The word *lib* means library; it refers to several files, usually within your WINDOWS/SYSTEM directory. In Windows, the words *Library* and *DLL* mean the same thing. DLLs have filename extensions like .DLL, .EXE and .DRV. They include USER.EXE, GDI.EXE, KEYBOARD.DRV, KERNEL.EXE, SOUND.DRV, MOUSE.DRV and others related to such things as communications, your video card and your printer. Even those .FON files that come with Windows are DLLs, but they contain neither ordinary data nor executable Functions. Instead, they are maps of fonts. Taken together, these libraries are the API. (Technically, a library with only data and no executable Functions or Subs is called a *resource library.* The .FON files and the library called CARDS.DLL (used for graphics in card game applications) are examples of resource libraries.)

When you Declare a Routine in VB, you must mention the name of the library where that Routine can be found. Unfortunately, the *Microsoft Windows Programmer's Reference* doesn't list the libraries, but again, call Microsoft for the free disk mentioned previously.

Unknown Libraries

To find out about the Functions lurking within new or custom libraries, you can use a file-peeking utility (such as Norton's Disk Editor in the Norton Utilities or the view window in Norton Desktop for Windows). You'll find the list of the included Routines fairly close to the top of the file in ALL CAPS. (Other options include using "EXEHDR" included with Microsoft's C language or "TDUMP" included with Borland's C.) As for what Variables are wanted by these mystery Functions—exactly what they do and how to go about using them—you should contact the DLL's creator.

By the way, VB itself, as you might expect, relies on its own library. It's called VBRUN300.DLL, and it must be in the PATH of any computer that expects to be able to run a VB.EXE program. Unlike the self-contained, compiled .EXE programs we're used to in the DOS world, VB's .EXE programs need VBRUN300.DLL while they are running.

ByVal Versus by Reference

"ByVal" in VB means that information (a Variable) is being passed from one place to another *by value*. The alternative to "by value" is *by reference* (which is the VB default unless you specify otherwise by using the "ByVal" command).

The difference is that "by value" sends a *copy* of some information (the text "bell," the number 12, whatever the Variable being passed contains). The essential point is that the recipient (in this case, the DLL Routine) cannot *change* the Variable; it's only for the recipient's information. The difference between passing information by value and passing information by reference is the difference between showing your new girlfriend's picture to the town Romeo and giving him her phone number.

Two Conventions for Variable Types

Programmer's Reference

The Variable types mentioned in the *Microsoft Windows Programmer's Reference* and what you should use when calling the API from VB are as follows:

b	Boolean	(% or Integer in VB)
c	Character	(% or Integer in VB)
dw	Long (32 bits, unsigned integer)	(& or Long in VB)
f	bit flags within a 16-bit integer	(% or Integer in VB)

h	a 16-bit handle	(% or Integer in VB)
l	Long (32 bits, signed integer)	(& or Long in VB)
lp	Long (32 bits, pointer)	(& or Long in VB)
n	Short (16 bits, signed integer)	(% or Integer in VB)
p	Short (16 bits, pointer)	(% or Integer in VB)
pt	x and y coordinates within an unsigned 32-bit integer	(& or Long in VB)
rgb	RGB color within an unsigned 32-bit integer	(& or Long in VB)
w	Short (16 bits, unsigned integer)	(% or Integer in VB)

(The lack of a prefix indicates a short signed integer [Integer in VB].)

Visual Basic

The Variable types used in VB are as follows:

- % Integer (16 bits, signed integer)
- & Long (32 bits, signed integer)
- ! Single (32 bits, *floating-point* [can include a decimal point]
- # Double (64 bits, floating-point)
- @ Currency (fixed decimal point, for currency)
- $ String ("words and letters or digits within quotation marks," text rather than numerical values)

  Variant (no type symbol; the VB default. See "Variant.")

When working with the API from VB, you'll need to worry about only three Variable types—Integer, Long and String. (Some Functions use a Variable structure, created with the Type command. See the example of ScrollWindows under "Smearing & Sliding" earlier in this Appendix.)

If you get truly serious about using the API, there are also a few kinks about using strings, handles, Properties and Arrays that you should read about in the VB *Programmer's Guide*. Bon API!

B GETTING RID OF BUGS

"Bugs" (errors in computer programs) are almost inevitable. You can be enormously careful, tidy and thoughtful, but if your program is more than 50 lines long, errors are likely. If it's longer than 100 lines, errors are virtually certain.

There are three types of errors in computer programming:

- Typos
- Runtime errors
- Logic errors

Class Modules & OLE

Special debugging techniques are required with OLE Automation—when you're allowing one program to control another, or utilize objects inside another. For one thing, you can run two instances of the VB4 programming environment simultaneously. This allows you to watch the interaction between the two programs, using VB's debugging aids. For information about object debugging techniques, see "Class Module."

Typos

Visual Basic provides a suite of tools that track down and eliminate bugs. Typos are the easiest errors to deal with. Visual Basic knows at once that you've mistakenly typed *prjnt* instead of *print*: if it doesn't recognize the word, it can detect the error.

Also, impossible commands are easily noticed; for example, *Open a Door*. Visual Basic cannot digest this command, so it reports the problem. It understands the word *Open*, but it expects a text Variable or a filename in quotation marks following Open. Not finding that, it reacts with an error message.

Related to typos are errors in providing the amount or type of information necessary for VB to carry out a command:

Line (10,20)

This information is incomplete; you've given only the upper left starting point of the line. Visual Basic will see this and respond as follows:

Figure BB-1: A typical VB response to a typo.

This response indicates that something is mistyped or is missing. In this case, a hyphen is missing, VB requires more information before it can carry out the following command:

```
Line (10, 20)-(30, 50)
```

To get specific, informational error messages, turn on the "Display Syntax Errors" option in the Tools Menu, Environment Options. This feature annoys many people because it displays an error message window every time you mistype something. But some of its messages are more helpful than those you get with the messages displayed when you press F5 and try to run the program. In the case of Line (10,20), the error message you see with the "Display Syntax Errors" option turned on is: "Expected: List separator" (in other words, a hyphen and some additional info).

Tip: Whether or not you choose to leave the "Display Syntax Errors" option turned on, Visual Basic will always highlight syntax errors by changing the text to red. (Red is default, but you can change it in the Tools Menu, Format Options.) Another clue that a line of programming is wrong: VB won't capitalize commands or space the line correctly when you press ENTER or press the Down arrow key, to move to the next line. If you type in a line like this then press ENTER:

```
line(10,20)-(30,50)
```

VB recognizes that its syntax is correct (VB understands this line), but it helps you by adding some spaces and capitalizing the command Line:

```
Line  (10,  20)-(30, 50)
```

However, if you've made a mistake, VB neither capitalizes nor spaces the line, but VB does turn the whole thing red:

```
line(10,20)-(3050)
```

Another kind of error

A third variety of easily detected, easily fixed error is an inconsistency of some kind between parts of your program. If you have a Subroutine that expects three Variables:

```
Sub Numbers (a, b, c)
End Sub
```

and you try to call it, but provide only two numbers:

```
Numbers a, b
```

VB can't catch the error right away (these lines of programming are both syntactically correct), but it will catch the inconsistency when you try to run the program. It will again provide as much help as it can by specifying what it thinks is causing the error. In response to this, VB replies: "Argument Not Optional." (Note that prior to VB4, you would have seen "Argument-count mismatch" as the error message. However, there's now a new Optional command, which see.)

If the word argument makes no sense to you, press F1. VB's online Help feature will pop up and tell you the possible reasons for this kind of error in greater detail. In this case, VB elaborates with the following comments:

Argument not optional (Error 449)

The number and types of arguments must match those expected. This error has the following causes and solutions:

Incorrect number of arguments: Supply all necessary arguments. For instance, the Left function requires two arguments, the first representing the character string being operated on, and the second representing the number of characters to return from the left side of the string. Because neither argument is optional, both must be supplied.

Omitted argument is not optional: An argument can only be omitted from a call to a user-defined procedure if it was declared Optional in the procedure declaration. Either supply the argument in the call, or declare the parameter Optional in the definition.

For additional information, select the item in question and press F1.

This advice is specific and helpful. You are calling a Subroutine, and you have provided an incorrect number of "arguments" (Variables). Even better, VB offers to take you directly to the Subroutine (procedure), so you can see how you have failed.

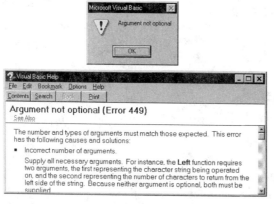

Figure BB-2: Getting help from VB's built-in answer man.

Alas, VB cannot always be such an effective assistant. Some typos and inconsistencies can be caused by several possible flaws so that VB can't pinpoint the particular problem. And some of VB's Help messages are in heavy-duty computerese. However, if you don't understand an error message, it's always worthwhile to press F1 while the error message remains displayed onscreen to get a fuller explanation of the potential cause(s). And often that's all you'll need to spot the problem.

Runtime Errors   Strictly speaking, runtime errors are not bugs, but they are failures on your part nonetheless. These errors are difficulties your program encounters while a user is running it. You need to prevent such errors as well as the gross errors that entirely stop your program from running. It's no good having a smoothly running program that crashes if the user has, say, forgotten to put a disk into drive A: or failed to close the drive door. (Some third-party add-on products include prewritten routines you can use in your VB programs. For example, add-on packages from companies like Sheridan and Crescent can check disk size, used space, drive door open, printer ready, etc., before your VB program takes any action involving the disk or printer.)

Runtime errors include all those unexpected situations that can come up when the program is running. There are a number of things you cannot know about the user's system. How large is the disk drive? Is it already so full that when your program tries to save a file, there won't be enough room? Are you creating an Array so large that it exceeds the computer's available memory?

Watch Out When You Reach Beyond VB: Whenever your program is attempting to interact with an entity outside the program—disks, the Clipboard, the user's RAM, or even using the Link or OLE commands to communicate with other running programs—you need to take precautions

1388

by using the On...Error structure. This structure allows your running program to deal effectively with the unexpected (see "On Error" for a full discussion of the available techniques). Visual Basic keeps track of any problems that occur, putting the Error Code of the problem into an internal VB Variable called Err. There is also an Error$ Function that can translate the Err code into text you can show the user.

Many runtime errors cannot be *corrected* by your program. For instance, you can let the user know only that his or her disk drive is nearly full. The user will have to remedy this kind of problem, but your program should report it. If you don't use On Error, Visual Basic will provide an error message to the user *but will then shut down the program.*

Because there is no drive Z, the following input will cause an error:

```
Sub Form_Click ( )
Open "Z:\MYFILE" For Output As #1
Print #1, x
Close #1
End Sub
```

When this program is run, the following message will appear to baffle the user; then the program will shut down:

Figure BB-3: The generic message box.

However, if you insert an error-handling structure (as follows), a similar message will appear, but your program will continue to run:

```
Sub Form_Click ( )
On Error Resume Next
Open "Z:\MYFILE" For Output As #1
If Err Then MsgBox (Error$(Err)): Close : Exit Sub
Print #1, x
Close #1
End Sub
```

Figure BB-4: Your Error Message Box doesn't frighten the user with a weird error message, like "Run-time Error 68," nor does the program crash.

You can even test to see how effectively your program reacts to runtime errors by feeding fake error codes into it while you are creating it. (See "Error" or "Raise.") And you can see if your program responds correctly to start-up information ("command line" arguments) by using the Command Line Argument option in the Tools Menu, Project Options (see the "Command$" Function).

Logic Errors

The third major category of programming bugs, logic errors, is the most puzzling of all. Some can be so sinister, so well concealed, that you might think you will be driven mad trying to locate the source of the problem.

A logic error means that you have followed all the rules of syntax, made no typos and otherwise satisfied Visual Basic that your commands can be carried out. You, and VB, think everything is shipshape. However, when you run the program the entire screen turns black; or every time the user enters $10, your program changes it into $1,000.

What To Do: Visual Basic's tools help you track down the problem. The key to fixing logic errors is finding out *where* in your program the problem is located.

Some computer languages have an elaborate debugging apparatus, some-times even including the use of two computer monitors—one shows the program as it runs, the other shows the lines of programming of the run-ning program. That is a good approach because when you are debugging logic errors you want to see beneath the surface of a running program. You want to locate the command or commands in your program that are caus-ing the problem.

You can see the symptoms: every time the user enters a number, the results are way, way off. You know that somewhere your program is man-gling the numbers—but until you X-ray the program, you can't find out where the problem is located.

Another kind of logic error is unique to Event-driven languages like VB—repeated triggering of an Event. (Try putting the Beep command within a Form's MouseMove Event.) These kinds of machine gun repeating errors can occur if, for example, you intend to do something only once while the program is running but you've put that command within the GotFocus or Resize Event which triggers quite often.

Let VB "Watch" While a Program Is Running

One of VB's best debugging tools is the Add Watch feature in the Tools Menu. In our example above, you could instruct Add Watch to stop the program if the $10 ever grows larger than, say, $200. Then, when the $10 is transformed into $1,000—our logic error—VB will halt the program and show us exactly where this problem is located.

The Debug Window pops up whenever you press F5 to run and test your VB program. The Debug Window has several handy features. The lower half is the Immediate Window and you can directly query or change Variables within it by just typing **? X** to find out the current value of the Variable X, or typing **X = 20** to assign 20 to X.

You can also launch procedures (Events, Subs or Functions) from inside the Immediate Window by typing their names and pressing the ENTER key. VB will execute the procedure and then halt again. This is a good way to feed Variables to a suspect Subroutine and watch it (and it alone) absorb those Variables. That way, you can see if things are going awry within that Sub. Perhaps that's the Sub that's changing $10 into $1000, so feed it 10 (x = 10) and see what happens by typing the sub's names, then looking at the value of x by typing **?x** and pressing ENTER.

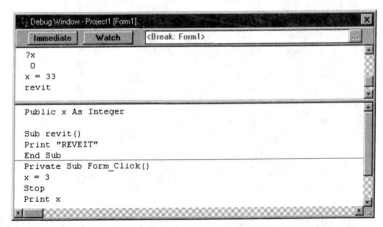

Figure BB-5: Use the Debug Window to check a Variable, change a Variable or test a Sub.

The Debug.Print (which see) commands send their results into the Immediate Window also. And, you can type any executable commands that can be expressed on a single line into the Immediate Window to watch their effects. Notice that this is all done while the VB program is halted during a run. Run by pressing F5, selecting Run from the Run Menu, or clicking on the green right-triangle button. There are several ways to break (halt) a program. You can type the Stop command somewhere within your programming or insert a *breakpoint* (select Toggle Breakpoint from the Run Menu or press F9). You can stop a program dynamically by pressing CTRL+Break, selecting Break in the Run Menu, or clicking on the Break button—the two vertical bars symbol. During a break, you can test conditions from within the living, running program. This approach is often a more direct way to locate problems than by examining a nonrunning program. When not running, all the program's Variables will be empty, etc.

The Watch Pane: If you have used the Add Watch option in the Tools Menu, VB keeps an eye on whatever you have asked it to watch. You can watch a Variable, an expression, a Property or a Function call, and you can watch as many of them as you want. The Watch pane replaces the Immediate pane (click on "Immediate" or "Watch" to switch between them) and shows the current status of any watched expressions. To add a watch while the program is halted, select (highlight with the mouse) a Variable or expression in the Code Pane (below the Watch/Immediate Pane in the Debug Window), and VB will add it to the Watch pane. Alternatively, you can just type in the Variable or other item you want watched, as shown in Figure BB-6.

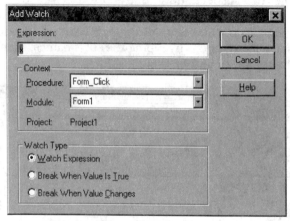

Figure BB-6: The Add-Watch Window. Here's where you can type in something you want watched; specify the scope of the watch (only during a particular procedure, or the entire program); and choose to trigger two kinds of breaks.

To add a watch while designing the program, select Add Watch from the Tools Menu and choose the scope and nature of the watch (see "Variables" for more on scope). Note that you might get a "Variable Not Defined" message when running a program to which you have added a watch. Yet you know the program contains this Variable. The error message means that you have violated a scoping rule; the Variable isn't in existence as far as VB is concerned because the program is running outside of the scope of that Variable as you specified it in the Add Watch Window. You'll never get this message for Variables defined with the Public command in a Module, but other Variables (local to a Form or procedure) can produce this response. You should go to the Edit Watch option in the Debug Menu and reduce the scope from Global to Form/Module or from Form/Module to Procedure.

Watch can continually display the value of a Variable or expression. In this case you could use F8 to step through the program line-by-line and constantly observe the value of the Variable. Alternatively, you can have VB halt the program when the Variable is in the state that you've defined in an expression (Z$ = "Norma" or X < Y). A third option is to have VB halt the program the instant a Variable's contents (or an expression's validity, its truth or falsity) have become True (or non-zero). A forth option is to trigger a halt when there's any change in the Variable or expression being watched.

Another tool in the Tools Menu (or by clicking on the eyeglasses icon in the Toolbar) is the Instant Watch option. If you select (highlight) an expression or Variable in your programming in the Code Pane of the Debug Window (during a Break of a running program), and then choose Instant Watch, VB will show you at once the current contents or status of that expression or Variable. VB also gives you the option of adding that item to the watched items.

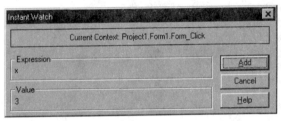

Figure BB-7:Instant Watch shows you the value of a selected item, and let's you optionally "Add" it to the watched items in the Debug Window.

A Colorful Alternative: An alternative to VB's built-in debugging windows is to make your own custom debugging screen. This would allow you, for example, to display current conditions graphically (you could literally send up a red flag). The Debug Window, good as it is, can't do graphics. What if you were trying to track down something going wrong with a Picture Box? With the following technique, you could show the Picture Property of a Picture Box, even if the Form on which it resides were currently hidden from view.

To demonstrate this technique, we'll create a Form to display the status of key Variables while the program runs. This little program calculates the cost of gas for a trip. The user types in miles traveled, MPG, and the price of a gallon of gas. The program calculates the total cost.

But it has a logic bug. It reports that a trip of 500 miles costs only 5 cents. And, stranger still, that a trip of 300 miles costs 9 cents. There's a flaw.

Create two Forms. Form1 is the real program. Put three Text Boxes on it and three Labels to describe the meaning of the Text Boxes. Finally, add a fourth Label to display the results of the calculations. We'll use Form2 to continually display all the Variables in the program, so we can watch them change.

In the General Declarations section of Form1, we put the calculation routine and the report to Form2. We calculate only if all three Text Boxes have something in them. Otherwise, we can get "Divide by Zero" errors or other anomalies:

```
Sub calculate( )
x = Text1.Text
y = Text2.Text
z = Text3.Text
If x <> "" And y <> "" And z <> "" Then
result$ = "Gas expense of this trip... $"
gascost = Val(x)
miles = Val(y)
mpg = Val(z)
totalcost = gascost / miles * mpg
Label4.Caption = result$ & Str$(totalcost)

Form2.Print "gascost ="; gascost
Form2.Print "miles = "; miles
Form2.Print "mpg = "; mpg
Form2.Print "totalcost ="; totalcost
Form2.Print
End If

End Sub
```

Following is what happens in the Text Boxes where the user enters figures:

```
Sub Text1_KeyPress(KeyAscii As Integer)
If KeyAscii = 13 Then
  KeyAscii = 0
  calculate
End If
End Sub
```

Each Text Box contains the same programming. They find out if the user pressed the ENTER key and then goes to the calculate Subroutine if that happens. The rest of the program is in Form_Load and merely makes Form2 visible:

```
Private Sub Form_Load( )
Show
Form2.Show
End Sub
```

Watching the Variables: When we run the program, we'll see the internal state of the Variables as they change:

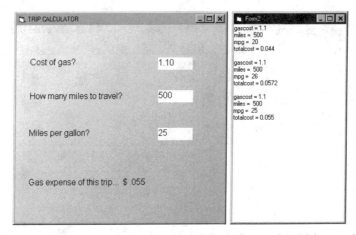

Figure BB-8 You can devote a special window to Variable-watching.

In this program, you can follow the changes in all the Variables by watching what is displayed in Form1—all of the Variables in this program are visible. Most programs, though, contain a number of internal Variables that you never see, and that's when a running display like the one in Form2 (or a Watch Pane) can sometimes show you where things go off track.

By watching the errors appear in Form2, it is clear that something is wrong with the calculate Subroutine. Our math is wrong. The gas cost should be divided by the MPG, and then that result should be multiplied by the miles traveled:

totalcost = gascost / mpg * miles

Other Debugging Tools

If watching Variables as they change doesn't do the trick, there are other approaches. You can press CTRL+BREAK to stop your program at any time (or click on the double vertical lines icon in the Toolbar). Then use the Immediate Window to type in Print X, and you can see the value of X at the point where you broke into the program.

Breaking into a program stops it in its tracks—right at the spot where your program was busy (or idle) when the break occurred. VB automatically shows you the line you broke into by circling it with a gray box, as you can see in Figure BB-9. You can see your "break location" in both the programming editor and the Debug Window.

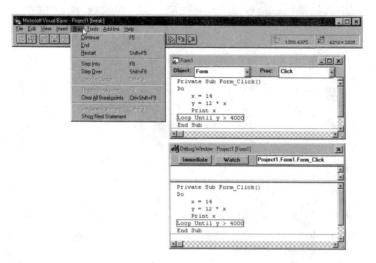

Figure BB-9: Some of Visual Basic's debugging tools

Visual Basic 4 spreads its set of debugging tools across two Menus—the Run and Tools menus. If, during a break, you pull down the Run or Tools Menu, you'll see VB's full collection of debugging tools. Let's discuss the rest of these tools.

The Run Menu

Continue: Visual Basic is rare among languages in that it lets you make direct changes to your program while that program is running. If you break into the program, you can change one or more of the lines to see if that fixes a problem. Then, selecting Continue (or pressing the F5 Function key) will cause your program to take up where it left off. This can be a useful way to see the effects of any changes you make, particularly if the program is long and you don't want to go back to the beginning, rerunning it each time just to adjust the distance a Control travels, say, during some animation late in the program. You want to keep running the program from the place where you broke into it—not waiting for all preceding commands to finish before you can see the effects of adjusting the Variables for Move. You want to pick up where you left off.

End: This option shuts your program down. It's as if the program had come upon an End Statement within itself, except you are shutting it down externally. There is no Function key combination that will cause an End, but you can click on the black box icon in the Toolbar (or the X icon in the upper right side of the main Form). End works the same way whether a break has occurred or if the program is still actively running. The program stops running.

Restart: This is not the same as Continue. Use Restart if you do want to restart a program from the beginning while in a "break," select Restart (or press SHIFT+F5). This has the same effect as choosing End and then Run. Your program will behave the same way that it would if the user started it running from scratch.

Step Into (or "Single Step"): This option is perhaps the most radical of the debugging features. Using it allows you to move through the program line-by-line. You single-step by pressing F8. Each time, the program carries out what's on the line and then moves to the next line. You can watch what's happening visually on the Form, look at the Watch pane or switch to the Immediate Window to query Variables by typing **? X**, etc.

Single Step is radical because it combs through a program in such great detail that it can take a long time to get to the problem. The next few tools provide some ways to speed up the process of getting to the root of a problem.

Step Over (or Procedure Step): If you are about to single-step into a Subroutine, Function or Event that you know is not the location of the problem, then press SHIFT+F8, and you will step over the entire Subroutine, Function or Event. This option gets you past areas in your program that you know are free of bugs but would take a lot of single stepping.

Step to Cursor: VB will execute all your programming between the current location in the program lines (wherever the program was halted) and the new location of the cursor (you click somewhere within your programming to establish a new cursor location). This is similar to Step Over, but works with any programming lines (Step Over merely bypasses a procedure). Step to Cursor has the same effect as setting a breakpoint (pressing F9 while on a line of programming where you want to stop).

Step to Cursor, like Step Over and setting breakpoints, is a way to avoid tedious and unnecessary single stepping through lines of programming that you know are OK.

Toggle Breakpoint: As you know, you can press CTRL+BREAK and stop a running program in its tracks. But what if it's moving too fast to stop just where you want to look, if it's alphabetizing a large list, for example, and you can't see what's happening? You can set one or more "breakpoints" in your program. While running, the program will stop at a breakpoint just as if you had pressed CTRL+BREAK. The Code Window will pop up so you can see or change commands, and the Debug Window will be available. It automates the process of breaking into a running program, and it allows great specificity.

You set a breakpoint by selecting the Toggle Breakpoint item from the Debug Menu or by pressing F9—while your cursor is on the line where you want to halt the program. The line of programming gets reversed (white lettering on a dark red background by default), showing that this line is a breakpoint. (You can change the colors signaling a breakpoint in the Tools Menu, Format Options.)

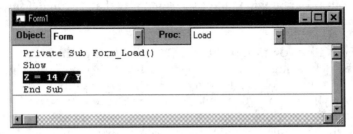

Figure BB-10: Z = 14 / Y is *reversed*, so it's a breakpoint.

You can set as many breakpoints as you wish. You turn off a breakpoint by again pressing F9, or selecting Toggle Breakpoint in the Debug Menu.

Another use for breakpoints is when you suspect that the program is never running some of your commands. Sometimes a logic error is caused because you think a Subroutine, Function or Event is being used, but, in fact, the program never reaches that section. Whatever condition is supposed to activate that zone of the program never happens. Possibly you are trying to call a Subroutine from a Text Box's Change Event. To activate the Subroutine, you put the following commands to respond when the user presses the ENTER key:

```
Sub Text1_Change( )
If KEYASCII = 13 Then
GoDoSubroutine
End If
End Sub
```

The GoDoSubroutine will never be activated. The Change Event does not recognize the KeyASCII Variable; therefore the If will never happen. (You meant to put these commands inside the Text1_KeyPress Event, where the KEYASCII variable exists.)

To find out if, as you suspect, Text1_Change is not responding, you would set a breakpoint, as follows:

```
Sub Text1_Change( )
If KEYASCII = 13 Then
GoDoSubroutine
End If
End Sub
```

Then run the program. The program will run, but never break—proving that the GoDoSubroutine command is never triggered. No break, even though you've typed text in the Text1 Box and pressed the ENTER key, supposedly triggering the GoDoSubroutine. Knowing that this isn't happening will lead you to realize your mistake eventually—that you should have put this KEYASCII test in the KeyPress, not Change, Event.

Clear All Breakpoints: If you've set lots of breakpoints, this option allows you to get rid of all of them at once without having to hunt them all down throughout your program, then toggle each off individually with F9.

Set Next Statement: With this command, you can move anywhere in your program and restart running from there. While the program is halted (in pause or "break" mode), go to the location in your code window where you want to start from, and click on a line in the Code Window. The clicking gives this line the cursor, as if you wanted to type in a modification to the line. Instead, select Set Next Statement option in the Run Menu (or press Ctrl+F9). This moves the gray box to that line. The gray box indicates at which line the program is currently paused.

Now, pressing F8 will single-step from that line forward in the program. (Or, pressing F5 will continue normal-speed execution from that new location.) If you know that things are fine in some Events but suspect a particular location in the program, move to that place with Set Next Statement and start single-stepping again. Or, if you have gone into a For...Next Loop with 100 Loopings, you might not want to press F8 100 times to single-step through that Loop. Move the cursor by clicking on the line below the Loop and start pressing F8 again to single-step on down.

Show Next Statement: If you've been moving around in your program, looking in various Events, you may have forgotten where in the program the next single step will take place (or where "Continue" will pick up execution). Pressing F8 would show you quickly enough, but you might want to get back there without reactivating the program. Show Next Statement moves you to the window, and you can see the next Statement; it will have a gray box around it.

The Tools Menu

Watches: The first three items on the Tools Menu allow you to keep an eye on suspect variables, Properties or expressions. See "The Watch Pane" earlier in this appendix.

Calls: You might break (pause) a running program when it's down at the bottom of a series of layered calls. The Calls option provides a list of still-active procedures (Events, Subroutines or Functions). Procedures can be "nested" (one can call on the services of another, which, in turn, calls on yet another).

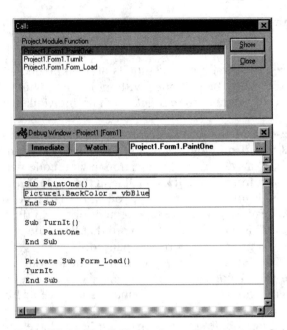

Figure BB-11: The Calls window tells us that the PaintOne procedure is called by (nested in) the TurnIt procedure. At the outermost level is the Form_Load Event—enclosing both procedures.

For example, if you wrote a Sub named TurnIt, that called another Sub named PaintOne, PaintOne would be "nested." The Calls option gives you the name of the procedure that called the current Function. And if your calling procedure was itself called by yet another procedure, Calls will give you a complete history of what is calling what.

APPENDIX C

OPERATORS

Before we start exploring what *operators* do and how we use them, let's focus on some everyday words that take on special meanings when used in a computer programming context.

Operators: An operator creates a relationship between two things: In the statement "Bob loves Stephanie," the word *loves* is the operator. Once the relationship has been established, the entire expression can be thought of as a single entity, an entity that can be "solved" into something simpler.

For example, plus (+) is the operator that creates a relationship between 4 and 7 in this expression:

```
4 + 7
```

In this case, the expression 4 + 7 is the entity 11.

There are 23 operators (which you'll find listed in "The Order of Precedence" on page 1405).

Expressions: When you combine Variables with other Variables (or with Constants or "literals"), you create an expression, which is a collection of items that has a single value when seen as a unit. This value can be either numeric, Variant or text (string).

Constants: A Constant is an unchanging value, like the number of days in a week. Const Days = 7. A *literal* is literally something, not represented by a Variable name or a Constant name, but the thing itself: Print "7" or Print "The number of days in a week is"; Str$(7).

If the Variable *Days* has the value 7 and the Variable *Hours* has the value 24, then the following expression has the value 168:

```
Days * Hours
```

You can assign the above expression to another Variable:

```
HoursInAWeek = Days * Hours
```

Or you can use the expression within a structure, such as If...Then, to test its truth. An expression can be evaluated by Visual Basic as either 0 (False) or not zero (True) when you use one of the *relational "comparison" operators*. Let's see how this works:

```
BobsAge = 33
BettysAge = 27
If BobsAge > BettysAge Then Print "He's Older"
```

"BobsAge > BettysAge" is an expression. It asserts that BobsAge is "greater than" BettysAge. The > (greater than) symbol is one of several relational operators. Visual Basic looks at the Variables, *BobsAge* and *BettysAge*, and at the relational operator with which you've combined them into the expression. It determines whether or not your expression is True. The If...Then structure bases its actions on the truth or falsity of the expression. Relational operators are almost always used in this fashion, within an If...Then structure, to allow Visual Basic to make a decision.

(Sometimes relational operators are used in other decision structures too, such as Select Case. However, the purpose of many expressions is to test the truth or falsity of some relationship, and have the program respond differently depending on the result of the test.)

Combining Expressions

You can put expressions together to build a larger entity that in itself is an expression:

```
Z$ = "Tom"
N = 3
M = 4
O = 5
P = 6

If N + M + O + P = 18 And Z$ = "Tom" Then Print "Yes."
```

The Twenty-Three Operators

Relational Operators

<	Less than
<=	Less than or equal to
>	Greater than
>=	Greater than or equal to
<>	Not equal
=	Equal
Is	Do two object Variables refer to the same object? (see "Is")
Like	Pattern matching (see "Like")

Notes

• The relational operators can be used with text as well as with numbers. When used with literal text (or text Variables), the operators refer to the *alphabetic* qualities of the text, with *Andy* being "less than" *Anne*.

- The relational operators are *comparisons* of two entities, and the result of that comparison is always True or False: Is a dozen less than or equal to the number of days in a month? (True.)

Arithmetic Operators

^	Exponentiation (5 ^ 2 is 25. 5 ^ 3 is 125)
–	Negation (Negative numbers, such as –25)
*	Multiplication
/	Division
\	Integer Division (Division with no remainder, no fraction, no "Floating-Point" decimal point: 8 \ 6 is 1. Integer division is much easier for the computer and can be calculated faster than regular division.)
Mod	Modulo arithmetic*
+	Addition
–	Subtraction
&	String Concatenation

Variant Variables can be combined in a similar way to the traditional text Variable concatenation:

```
A$ = "This": B$ = "That": Print A$ + B$
```

Results in   ThisThat

When you use *Variants* (recall that unless you specify otherwise, VB defaults to Variants):

```
x = 5: a = "This": Print x & a
```

Results in   5This

Variants are in an indeterminant state, like Schroedinger's Cat, until they are used. Also, when you use the & operator, VB will convert a numeric Variable into a Variant. If both Variables used with & are text Variables, the result will be a text "string" Variable. Otherwise, the result will be a Variant type.

Logical Operators

NOT	Logical Negation
AND	And
OR	Inclusive OR
XOR	(Either, but not both)
EQV	(Equivalent)
IMP	(Implication–first item False or second item True)

In practice, you'll likely only need to use AND, NOT, OR and XOR from among the logical operators. They work pretty much the way they do in English, and they are often used when you are comparing *two* smaller expressions within a single large (compound) expression like this:

If 5 + 2 = 4 Or 6 + 6 = 12 Then Print "One of them is True." ' (one of these expressions is True, so the comment will be printed. Only one OR the other needs to be True.)

If 5 + 2 = 4 And 6 + 6 = 12 Then Print "Both of them are True." ' (this is False, so nothing is printed. Both expressions, the first AND the second, must be True for the Printing to take place.)

The XOR operator is used to change an individual *bit* within a number, without affecting the other bits. See the Example under "GetAttr" for the way to use XOR.

Special Note on Mod: Mod gives you any remainder after a division—but not the results of the division itself. This is useful when you want to know if some number divides evenly into another number. That way, you could do things at intervals. If you wanted the page number in bold on every fifth page, you could do this:

```
If PageNumber Mod 5 = 0 Then
    FontBold = -1
Else
    FontBold = 0
End IF
```

15 Mod 5 results in 0
16 Mod 5 results in 1
17 Mod 5 results in 2
20 Mod 5 results in 0 again.

The Text Operator

+   Adds pieces of text together:

```
N$ = "Joan"
N1$ = "Rivers"

J$ = N$ + " " + N1$
Print J$
```

Results in   Joan Rivers

Operator Precedence Use Parentheses

When you use more than one operator in an expression, a problem can arise about which operator should be evaluated first:

```
Print 3 * 10 + 5
```

Does this mean multiply 3 times 10, then add 5 to the result? Should VB Print 35?

Or does it mean add 10 to 5 and then multiply the result by 3? Is the answer 45?

Expressions are not evaluated from left to right, which would make this 3 times 10, then add 5. *To make sure that you get the results you intend when using more than one operator, use parentheses to enclose the items you want evaluated first.* If you intended to say 3 * 10, then add 5:

```
Print (3 * 10) + 5
```

By enclosing something in parentheses, you tell VB that you want the enclosed items to be considered a single value.

If you intended to say 10 + 5, then multiply by 3:

```
Print 3 * (10 + 5)
```

In complicated expressions, you can *nest* parentheses to make clear the order in which items are to be calculated:

```
Print 3 * ((9 + 1) − 5)
```

People who work with numbers a great deal might want to memorize the following section. Operators have an "order of precedence" that VB uses to decide the order in which operators are evaluated.

Most people use parentheses, though, and forget about order of precedence. Not only can you safely ignore order of precedence when you use parentheses; it is also easier to read the expression and see the intention, because the parentheses display it visually. The next section details the order in which VB evaluates a parenthesis-free expression.

The Order of Precedence

The Arithmetic Operators

^	Exponents (6 ^ 2 is 36.)
−	Negation (Negative numbers like –33)
* /	Multiplication and Division
\	Integer Division (Division with no remainder, no fraction, no "Floating-Point" decimal point. 8 \ 6 is 1)
Mod	Modulo Arithmetic (The remainder after division. 23 Mod 12 is 11. See "Mod.")
+ −	Addition and Subtraction
&	String Concatenation

The Relational Operators

= > < <> >= <= Like, Is   The Relational Operators (Comparisons of numbers or text. Results in "True" or "False.")

The Logical Operators

NOT   Logical Negation

AND   And

OR   Inclusive OR

XOR (Either, but not both)

EQV (Equivalent)

IMP   (Implication–first item False or second item True)

Given that multiplication has precedence over addition, our ambiguous example above would be evaluated in the following way:

```
Print 3 * 10 + 5
```

Results in   35

Technical Details on the Logical Operators

Here is an overview of the ways that the logical operators operate:

NOT

NOT changes the bits in a numeric expression in the following fashion:

Numeric Expression	NOT	Results in:
0		1
1		0

NOT reverses the bit values of any expression. If it was anything other than 0, it becomes 0. If it was 0, it becomes 1. Many programmers use NOT to toggle a Variable. Each time the following Event is triggered, the Variable *Switch* goes from 0 to –1 (or if it's –1, it goes back to 0):

```
Sub Form_Click()

Static Switch
Switch = Not Switch

End Sub
```

This is the same as:

```
If Switch = 0 Then
    Switch = –1
Else
    Switch = 0
End If
```

VB Properties (and other elements in the language) generally use 0 to mean "False" or "off" and use –1 to mean "True" or "on." You can therefore use a toggled Variable to make something switch between two states. For instance, if you put this in the above example:

```
Label1.Visible = Switch
```

The Label would alternate between being visible or invisible each time the user clicked on the Form.

Some programmers also use NOT to find out the status of something in a way that makes the statement sound like English:

```
If NOT PrinterReady Then
    Wait_Some_More
End If
```

(This is the same as If PrinterReady = 0 Then...)

AND

AND works the way it does in English.

AND reports that a compound expression is True if the internal expressions are True (–1). If any one of the smaller expressions is not True, then the entire expression is False (0).

```
X = Joan Crawford Won An Academy Award AND the Sun is Hot AND
Food is Necessary
```

X would be True, –1, because all three expressions are True.

AND changes the bits in two numeric expressions in the following fashion:

Expression 1	AND	Expression 2	Results in
0		0	0
0		1	0
1		0	0
1		1	1

(**Technical Note:** AND is also used to "strip bits within a byte." This can be useful in such applications as communications over a modem. For example: Character\$ AND &H7F will strip the "high bit" and leave a 7-bit character behind.)

OR

OR works the way it does in English. If any expression in a group of expressions is True, then the entire thing is True. If none of the expressions is True, then the thing is False.

```
X = Joan Never Got One OR Food is Necessary
```

X would be True, –1, because one of the expressions is True.

OR changes the bits in a numeric expression in the following fashion:

Expression 1	OR	Expression 2	Results in
0		0	0
0		1	1
1		0	1
1		1	1

XOR

XOR says that if one of the expressions is True, but not both, then the entire entity is True. It's kind of a compromise:

TRUE (X = –1 in this example):

> X = China has 1/6 of the World's Population XOR Sinatra Can't Sing

FALSE (X = 0 in this example):

> X = China has 1/6 of the World's Population XOR Sinatra Can Sing

(If both expressions are True, then XOR paradoxically calls the entire compound expression False.)

XOR changes the bits in two numeric expressions in the following fashion:

Expression 1	XOR	Expression 2	Results in
0		0	0
0		1	1
1		0	1
1		1	0

EQV

EQV tells you if two expressions are identical. This is like asking If X = Y or If "BOB" = "BOB"

The uses for EQV are limited. EQV results in 1 (True) if two expressions are identical, and 0 (False) if they aren't. (EQV is the inverse of XOR.)

Expression 1	EQV	Expression 2	Results in
0		0	1
0		1	0
1		0	0
1		1	1

IMP

If you thought EQV was rarified—wouldn't be used all that often—IMP is even more arcane.

IMP says that a compound expression is True, taken as a whole, if the *first* expression is False and the *second* expression is True. Any other relationship (first True, second False, both True, both False) results in IMP reporting that the compound expression is False. Try to imagine a use for IMP.

> X = Water is wet IMP Evil is a Bad Thing

The above would be considered an Untrue statement by IMP, because the first expression is True. Even though we know that both expressions are palpably True.

Anyway, here's what IMP does to bits in numeric expressions:

Expression 1	IMP	Expression 2	Results in
0		0	1
0		1	1
1		0	0
1		1	1

D ADD-ON PRODUCTS FOR VISUAL BASIC & WINDOWS

Visual Basic is an *extensible* language—it can be extended. As with Windows, third-party manufacturers can sell special products that improve VB's performance or add new features. The most common way to extend Visual Basic is to add new Buttons to the Toolbox.

After trying many such add-on products for Windows and Visual Basic, we have found the following to be the most desirable.

Plug-In Subroutines

Including more than 400 prewritten Routines—everything from superfast sorting to enhanced Scroll Bars—the QuickPak Professional for Windows is a collection that could save you hours of time when developing a complex program. Many of these Routines are written in assembly language and are, therefore, lightning-fast when you want, for example, to search or sort a large Array. You can load in some of these Routines via the Edit Window's Load Text option and then just use them as you would any other Subroutine. Others are accessed via a library or are loaded into the Toolbox by the Add File option on VB's File Menu.

> QuickPak Professional for Windows
> Crescent Software, Inc.
> 11 Bailey Ave.
> Ridgefield, CT 06877
> (203) 438–5300
> $169

Dimensional Windows

Adding shadows and highlights can make the windows, Scroll Bars, Buttons and other elements of the Windows environment look more attractive. A Windows add-on called Makeover offers a great variety of control over both the colors and the apparent *dimensionality* of Windows. In this book, we demonstrate ways to add this dimensionality in your VB programs. (See the Frame and Emboss Subroutines described in the entry on the "Line" command, and the Emboss Subroutine in "Print.")

However, if you want to customize the look of Windows itself (and receive some additional utilities in the bargain), you might want to consider Makeover. Figures DD-1 and DD-2 show how different the windows appear with and without Makeover:

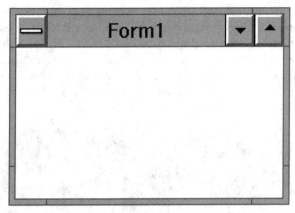

Figure DD-1: Windows appears rather flat using the default settings.

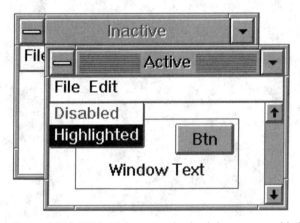

Figure DD-2: With Makeover, the look is more sophisticated, more dimensional, more attractive.

Makeover
Playroom Software
7308-C East Independence Blvd., Suite 310
Charlotte, NC 28227
(704) 536–3093
$49

Computer-Generated Art

A number of the pictures in this book were generated with Electronic Arts's DeluxePaint II. This is a DOS-based program, but it is to-date unmatched in the IBM computing world for the power and variety of its computer-assisted graphics design capabilities. Unlike such popular drawing programs as CorelDRAW, Deluxe Paint II is not primarily designed to create graphic art of the traditional sort. Instead, Deluxe Paint II offers a powerful suite of "computer-art" tools—automatically generated perspective and planar effects, gel overlays, colorization, translucence, elaborate fills and the concept that "anything can be used as a brush." (For example, you can select a photo of your dog's face and then *paint* with that face as if it were a brush.) The textural and pattern effects that this concept offers are both "computer-art" in their look and very easy to achieve. Here's a graphic that took only minutes to achieve (Deluxe Paint II calculates the dimensional elements and fills using the selected "brush"):

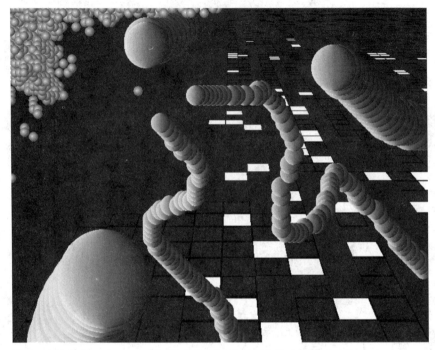

Figure DD-3: "Computer-art" effects are easy with Deluxe Paint II.

Deluxe Paint II
Electronic Arts
P.O. Box 7578
San Mateo, CA 94403
(415) 572-2787

Most of the Best

Many developers have come out with excellent add-ons for Visual Basic. Microsoft has collected most of the best into a product called Microsoft Visual Basic, Professional Edition. This is a collection of valuable tools. It includes several additional Controls that can be added to the Toolbox— among them: animated and 3D buttons and other user-input Controls; bitmap clipping; multimedia and communication Controls.

Beyond the added Controls, there is a report-generating add-on that can transform data into standard formats—such as mailing labels. There is an online reference to the API, and a facility for creating your own Controls (if you can program in C or C++).

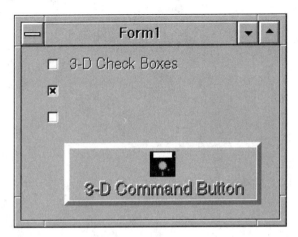

Figure DD-4: The 3-D Option and Command Buttons. Note that you can include embossed or etched text effects and add a graphic to the Command Button.

The Professional Edition is available from Microsoft or software resellers.

COMPANION DISK SNEAK PREVIEW

Visual Basic is an uncommonly rich language. There are hundreds of commands and many thousands of options that shade the meanings of those commands. As the culmination of years of refinement on the original Basic language, Visual Basic gives you the tools to communicate with your computer efficiently and in highly sophisticated ways. With VB 4.0, you can compile conditionally, use Collections instead of Arrays, and create OLE server programs. In some ways this richness creates complexity; that's why a companion disk is available for this book.

This efficiency and sophistication has a price. There is so much built into VB that learning and exploring the language can seem a daunting task. Even if you study it for months you'll know only a part of what VB can do. But Basic is arguably easier to understand than any other computer language. The commands are usually in English. PRINT "THIS" is pretty easy to understand. On the other hand, VB, like every other computer language, is not yet "fuzzy." (The new Variant Variable–VB's default Variable type–is an exception. It is fuzzy. Like subatomic waves, a Variant remains vague until observed or used. See "Variant.")

In general, though, computers are quite literal in their interpretations of words. If you say, "hot," the computer cannot assess the context of your remark to distinguish between "popular," "feverish" or other possible meanings of the word.

Or press the wrong key on your keyboard and you'll find your commands misunderstood or entirely unrecognized by the machine. The companion disk for this book helps reduce these problems: you get all the programming in the book.

What s on the Companion Disk

We've translated all the examples in this book into plain ASCII text and put them on the disk. They are organized by command, so you need only load the file into any word processor and search for, say, "grid," and you'll have the example for the Grid Control at your disposal. To plug that example into VB for experimenting, testing or building a new application–just drag the mouse over the text and press CTRL + INSERT to copy it. Then press SHIFT + INSERT and you've got the programming loaded into VB, typo-free.

What s Not on the Companion Disk

The companion disk contains all the examples; all the complete, ready-to-paste subroutines like "DrawFrameOn" (see "Line"), "Gauge" (see "Refresh") and all the other routines in this book. However, space limitations prohibit inclusion of most graphics. Graphics just take up too many bytes. The graphics in this book would fill dozens of disks. Instead, we've given you the programming and left the visuals up to you. Paste the companion disk's programs into VB, then select your own images and arrange your own Controls on Forms. It's quite easy to manipulate the visuals. However, since there was some room, we've included the best 256-color .PCX images on the disk.

COLOPHON

This book was produced on a Power Macintosh 8100/80 using Aldus PageMaker 5.0.

Page proofs were printed on a Hewlett-Packard LaserJet 4 and a LaserWriter Pro 630. Final film was output using a Linotronic 330 imagesetter.

Typefaces used are Digital Typeface Corporation Garamond (body), Bernhard Fashion (heads) and Kabel (heads).

NOTES

NOTES

Power Toolkits & Visual Guides

PowerBuilder 4.0 Power Toolkit 🌐

$49.95, 600 pages, illustrated

As the IS world moves to client/server technology, companies are leaning on PowerBuilder to build versatile custom applications. This advanced tutorial and toolkit addresses both Enterprise and Desktop Editions, and features application design tips and an overview of custom controls to aid in quick, efficient development. The companion CD-ROM contains all the applications from the book, plus sample controls, demos and other useful tools.

Visual C++ Power Toolkit 🌐

$49.95, 832 pages, illustrated

Add impact to your apps using these 10 never-before-published class libraries. Complete documentation plus professional design tips and technical hints. The companion CD-ROM contains 10 original class libraries, dozens of graphics, sound and toolbar utilities, standard files and demo programs.

Visual Basic Power Toolkit 🌐

$39.95, 960 pages, illustrated

Discover the real force behind Visual Basic's pretty face with this unique collection of innovative techniques. Hundreds of examples, images and helpful hints on data security, color manipulation, special effects and OLE automation. Demystify fractals and master multimedia as you push the power of VB! The companion CD-ROM contains all the routines from the book, sample Custom Controls, animated clips, MIDI music files and more.

The Visual Guide to Visual FoxPro 3.0

$34.95, 600 pages, illustrated

This complete tutorial covers Tables, Queries, Forms, Reports and more, with application design tips and advanced techniques for the most popular Xbase database software available for Windows. The disk includes all sample files from the book, ready for use.

The Visual Guide to Visual C++

$29.95, 888 pages, illustrated

A uniquely visual reference for Microsoft's next-generation programming language. Written for both new and experienced programmers, it features a complete overview of tools and features in each class of the "Visual C++ Foundation Class Library"—including names and prototypes, descriptions, parameters, return values, notes and examples. Ideal for day-to-day reference! The companion disk contains code examples, including programs and subroutines from the book.

The Visual Guide to Paradox for Windows

$29.95, 692 pages, illustrated

A pictorial approach to Paradox! Hundreds of examples and illustrations show how to achieve complex database development with simple drag-and-drop techniques. Users learn how to access and modify database files, use Form and Report Designers and Experts, program with ObjectPAL and more—all with icons, buttons, graphics and OLE. The companion disk contains sample macros, forms, reports, tables, queries and a ready-to-use database.

Books marked with this logo include a free Internet *Online Companion*™, featuring archives of free utilities plus a software archive and links to other Internet resources.

Internet Resources

The Web Server Book

$49.95, 680 pages, illustrated

The cornerstone of Internet publishing is a set of UNIX tools, which transform a computer into a "server" that can be accessed by networked "clients." This step-by-step guide to the tools also features a look at key issues—including content development, services and security. The companion CD-ROM contains Linux™, Netscape Navigator™, ready-to-run server software and more.

Walking the World Wide Web

$29.95, 360 pages, illustrated

Enough of lengthy listings! This tour features more than 300 memorable Websites, with in-depth descriptions of what's special about each. Includes international sites, exotic exhibits, entertainment, business and more. The companion CD-ROM contains Ventana Mosaic™ and a hyperlinked version of the book providing live links when you log onto the Internet.

Internet Roadside Attractions 🌐

$29.95, 376 pages, illustrated

Why take the word of one when you can get a quorum? Seven experienced Internauts—teachers and bestselling authors—share their favorite Web sites, Gophers, FTP sites, chats, games, newsgroups and mailing lists. In-depth descriptions are organized alphabetically by category for easy browsing. The companion CD-ROM contains the entire text of the book, hyperlinked for off-line browsing and Web hopping.

To Order any Ventana Press title, complete this AND MAIL OR FAX IT TO US, WITH PAYMENT, FOR QUICK S

TITLE	ISBN	QUANTITY	PRICE	TOTAL
HTML Publishing on the Internet for Windows	1-56604-229-1	_____	x $49.95 =	$ _____
Internet Publishing Kit for Macintosh	1-56604-232-1	_____	x $149.00 =	$ _____
Internet Publishing Kit for Windows	1-56604-231-3	_____	x $149.00 =	$ _____
Internet Roadside Attractions	1-56604-193-7	_____	x $29.95 =	$ _____
PGP Companion for Windows	1-56604-304-2	_____	x $29.95 =	$ _____
PowerBuilder 4.0 Power Toolkit	1-56604-224-0	_____	x $49.95 =	$ _____
Visual Basic Power Toolkit	1-56604-190-2	_____	x $39.95 =	$ _____
Visual C++ Power Toolkit	1-56604-191-0	_____	x $49.95 =	$ _____
The Visual Guide to Paradox for Windows	1-56604-150-3	_____	x $29.95 =	$ _____
The Visual Guide to Visual Basic 4.0 for Windows	1-56604-192-9	_____	x $34.95 =	$ _____
The Visual Guide to Visual C++	1-56604-079-5	_____	x $29.95 =	$ _____
The Visual Guide to Visual FoxPro 3.0	1-56604-227-5	_____	x $34.95 =	$ _____
Walking the World Wide Web	1-56604-208-9	_____	x $29.95 =	$ _____
The Web Server Book	1-56604-234-8	_____	x $49.95 =	$ _____
The Windows Internet Tour Guide, 2nd Edition	1-56604-174-0	_____	x $29.95 =	$ _____
			Subtotal =	$ _____
			Shipping =	$ _____
			Total =	$ _____

SHIPPING

For all standard orders, please ADD $4.50/first book, $1.35/each additional.
For *Internet Publishing Kit* orders, ADD $6.50/first kit, $2.00/each additional.
For "two-day air," ADD $8.25/first book/$2.25/each additional.
For "two-day air" on the kits, ADD $10.50/first kit, $4.00/each additional.
For orders to Canada, ADD $6.50/book.
For orders sent C.O.D., ADD $4.50 to your shipping rate.
North Carolina residents must ADD 6% sales tax.
International orders require additional shipping charges.

Name _____ Daytime telephone _____

Company _____

Address (No PO Box) _____

City _____ State _____ Zip _____

Payment enclosed ___VISA ___MC ___ Acc't # _____ Exp. date _____

Signature _____ Exact name on card _____

Mail to: Ventana Press • PO Box 13964 • Research Triangle Park, NC 27709-3964 ☎ 800/743-5369 • Fax 919/544-9472

Check your local bookstore or software retailer for these and other bestselling titles, or call toll free: **800/743-5369**

ORDER FORM
HIPMENT.